W9-BZY-298

Encyclopedia of Feminist Literature

MARY ELLEN SNODGRASS

Facts On File
An imprint of Infobase Publishing

Encyclopedia of Feminist Literature

Facts On File, Inc.
An imprint of Infobase Publishing
132 West 31st Street
New York NY 10001

Library of Congress Cataloging-in-Publication Data

Snodgrass, Mary Ellen.
Encyclopedia of feminist literature / Mary Ellen Snodgrass.
p. cm.
Includes bibliographical references and index.
ISBN 0-8160-6040-1 (acid-free paper)
1. Women authors—Bio-bibliography. 2. Women and literature—
Encyclopedias. 3. Feminist literature—Encyclopedias. 4. Feminism and
literature—Encyclopedias. 5. Feminism in literature—Encyclopedias.
6. Women in literature—Encyclopedias. I. Title.
PN471.S58 2006
809'.89287'03—dc22
2005015204

Facts On File books are available at special discounts when purchased in
bulk quantities for businesses, associations, institutions, or sales promotions.
Please call our Special Sales Department in New York at
(212) 967-8800 or (800) 322-8755.

You can find Facts On File on the World Wide Web at
http://www.factsonfile.com

Text design by Joan M. McEvoy
Cover design by Cathy Rincon

Printed in the United States of America

VB Hermitage 10 9 8 7 6 5 4 3 2 1

This book is printed on acid-free paper.

For a feminist sister, Dr. Carol Blessing

Let Greeks be Greeks, and women what they are.

Anne Bradstreet
"The Prologue" (1650)

Woman is learning for herself that not self-sacrifice, but self-development,
is her first duty in life; and this, not primarily for the sake of others
but that she may become fully herself.

Matilda Joslyn Gage
Woman, Church & State (1893)

CONTENTS

ACKNOWLEDGMENTS

Avis Gachet, Book Buyer
Wonderland Books
5008 Hickory Boulevard
Hickory, North Carolina 28601

Susan Keller, Reference Librarian
Western Piedmont Community College
Morganton, North Carolina

Hannah Owen, Deputy Director
Hickory Public Library
Hickory, North Carolina

Wanda Rozzelle, Reference Librarian
Catawba County Library
Newton, North Carolina

Mark Schumacher, Reference Librarian
Jackson Library, UNC-G
Greensboro, North Carolina

I am grateful to Stephen Rhind-Tutt and Eileen Lawrence, president and vice president, respectively, of Alexander Street Press, Alexandria, Virginia, for providing primary sources by African-American female dramatists of the Harlem Renaissance.

PREFACE

Encyclopedia of Feminist Literature invites the feminist, writer, literary historian, researcher, student, teacher, librarian, and reader to sample a wide range of fiction and nonfiction by feminist authors. The text, arranged alphabetically into more than 500 entries, is an easy-to-use source of information. Discussions of feminist themes and women's rights summarize the evolution of feminism. Entries cover authors, literary works, and other related topics of interest and were included after a close examination of the syllabi of women's studies, literature, and social issues classes, as well as the contents of current textbooks, supplemental reading lists, and notable projects and seminars that have drawn together teachers, students, writers, activists, and authorities on feminist concerns.

Enhancing the reader's understanding of philosophical and literary developments are details of feminist theater, utopias, goddess lore, lesbian authors, and gynocriticism (a term describing the breakthrough in interpretation and evaluation of woman-centered works). Individual details on writers (Tanith Lee, Lady Murasaki), sources (women's magazines, journalism, the Feminist Press), women's history (slavery, witchcraft, women's movements), literary history (ecofeminism, captivity narrative, censorship, gothic fiction), genres (letter writing, diaries and journals), oral tradition (fairy tales, storytelling, talk-story), feminist themes (androgyny, violence, aging, dynasty), titles (*Gone with the Wind, The Woman's Bible,* "The Yellow Wallpaper," *The Story of an African Farm*), characters (Bertha Rochester, Jane Eyre, Catherine Earnshaw, Little Red Riding Hood, Cinderella), legends (Virgin Mary, Spider Woman, Lilith, La Llorona, Eve), motifs (wisewomen, Bluebeard, Beauty and the Beast, courtly love), conventions (confinement, secrecy, rescue motif, madness, duality, dreamscapes), and issues (abortion, temperance, stereotyping, single parenting, education, suffrage) contribute to an understanding of feminist works.

Research materials derive from various sources, beginning with the guidance of feminist scholars and historians: Nina Baym, Barbara Ehrenreich, Susan Faludi, Shulamith Firestone, Matilda Joslyn Gage, Wendy Ho, Diane Hoeveler, Judith Halberstam, Luce Irigaray, Elizabeth Janeway, Harriet Taylor Mill, Kate Millett, and Barbara Tuchman. Of particular merit are the analyses of Margaret Atwood, Simone de Beauvoir, Sandra Gilbert, Susan Gubar, Carolyn Heilbrun, Margaret Oliphant, Adrienne Rich, Elaine Showalter, Naomi Wolf, and Virginia Woolf. In addition to a panoply of rediscovered feminist works and facsimile editions are an array of electronic texts, including works from the University of Pennsylvania, Indiana University, Rutgers University, Duke University, Northern Illinois University, Virginia Commonwealth University, Fordham University, and the University of Virginia libraries; the Massachusetts History Project; the Cooper Union for the Advancement for Science and Art; a compilation of speeches from Sweetbriar College; the Gutenberg Project; Bartleby's Great Books Online; the e-text library from Adelaide, Australia; the Women's History Project; and individual archives of works by Carrie Chapman Catt, Martha Ballard, and Victoria Woodhull. To the researcher beginning a probe of feminist texts, invaluable electronic databases include primary texts from Alexander Street Press, Other Women's Voices, and Academic Search Elite via EBSCOhost.

Rounding out *Encyclopedia of Feminist Literature* are reference guides that list titles and authors alphabetically and by genre and date. Other appendices provide an overview of cinematic versions of such women's classics as *Julia* and *The Dollmaker* and separate bibliographies of primary and secondary sources.

INTRODUCTION

Feminist literature is not a new phenomenon. Evidence of women's ability to write songs, rear children, and grow roses and of their skill at weaving and healing survives from early times in sculpture, ritual, dance, needlework, and written texts. Obvious narrative examples include the timeless fairy tales, fables, oral accounts, and cautionary exempla that women have treasured—the stories of Bluebeard, Cinderella, Spider Woman, Devi, and Beauty and the Beast that elders have told young girls to prepare them against threats to their virginity and safety. The resilience of motifs of terror and rescue is evident in Anne Sexton's "Red Riding Hood" and "Briar Rose" and Sylvia Plath's "Bluebeard." The resurgence of goddess lore sparked Eavan Boland's "The Making of an Irish Goddess," Denise Levertov's "Song for Ishtar" and "Goddess," and Marion Zimmer Bradley's reclamation of Druidic worship in *The Forest House*. Diane Wolkstein mined new understandings of male-female passions in *Inanna* and *The First Love Stories*. Literary resettings resulted in feminist classics—Christina Rossetti's "The Goblin Market," H. D.'s "Helen in Egypt," Angela Carter's *The Magic Toyshop*, Timberlake Wertenbaker's stage play *The Love of the Nightingale*, Paula Gunn Allen's revitalized vision quest in *The Woman Who Owned the Shadows*, and Isak Dinesen's *Seven Gothic Tales* and her redemptive fable *Babette's Feast*.

For recording the spirit and viscera of female life, feminist literature belongs in a world-class collection. As a main branch of the arts, it gathers a range of genres: the novels of Marguerite Yourcenar and Sahar Khalifeh, prison fiction by Nawal El Saadawi and Angela Davis, the young adult fiction of Nancy Springer and Judy Blume, poems by Marianne Moore and Nikki Giovanni, fables of Marie de France and Joyce Carol Oates, the philosophy of Margaret Fuller and Harriet Martineau, biography by Fawn Brodie and Santha Rama Rau, syndicated columns by Fanny Fern and Patricia A. Williams, the dramas of Osonye Tess Onwueme and Wendy Wasserstein, one-woman performances of Anna Deavere Smith and Eve Ensler, historical fiction of Rita Mae Brown and Diana Norman, oratory by Pauline Johnson and Sojourner Truth, critiques of Wendy Ho and Elaine Showalter, diaries of Martha Ballard and Ishbel Ross, and the letters of Mary Antin and Abigail Adams. The influx of recovered texts—Laurel Thatcher Ulrich's *A Midwife's Tale*, new versions of Mary Chesnut's Civil War diary, *The Stories of Fanny Hurst*, Lillian Schlissel's *Women's Diaries of the Westward Journey*, and the court diaries of Izumi Shikibu and Murasaki Shikibu—attests to a vigorous search for forgotten passages of female history. In addition to recovered works are evaluations of early works. Energized by Kate Millett's *Sexual Politics* and Sandra Gilbert and Susan Gubar's *The Madwoman in the Attic*, feminist analysis applies a woman-centered perspective on such titles as *To Kill a Mockingbird, Little Women*, the Little House series, the philosophy of Simone Weil, and the writings of Tillie Olsen and Vita Sackville-West.

Even in androcentric milieus, written history carries wisps of female attitudes and activities. Before Greece's Golden Age, Sappho described the eager minds of the students at her female academy on the island of Lesbos. Aristophanes, the fifth-century-B.C. Athenian dramatist, made light of the folly of war in *Lysistrata,* a droll satire in which the women of Athens, through sexual extortion, win anomalous control of when, how, and how often troops go to war. In 11th-century Japan, when islanders were adapting the cultural influence of China, the court writer Murasaki Shikibu penned a diary and a heroic tale that reveal the strictures on upper-class women. In the late Middle Ages, less than a quarter-century after William the Conqueror overthrew the Saxons and seized England, a collection of stories, *L'Ysopet* by the fabulist Marie de France, glimpsed the wiles and loves of women in the Anglo-Norman world. As the Anglo-Saxon, French, and Latin languages merged, the burst of spirited wordcraft from Geoffrey Chaucer's *Canterbury Tales* produced a lasting female character, the ebullient Alys, Wife of Bath, a traveler and raconteur who broadcast candidly her opinion of marriage. Into the Renaissance, the elaboration of women's needs and yearnings from Christine de Pisan, Hélisenne de Crenne, and Margery Kempe, England's first autobiographer, assured the literate world that one-half of the population was not going to stand aside during the growing liberalization of European culture and art that lit up Western culture.

The colonization of the Americas required vigorous women. Among the spokespersons for the female point of view from the New World were the poet Anne Bradstreet and the memoirist Mary Rowlandson, originator of the captivity narrative. In Mexico a bold Hieronymite nun, Sor Juana Inès de la Cruz, evaluated the importance of the Virgin Mary in Catholic dogma and ritual and demanded that women receive education equal to that of men. As North America began to shape itself into a world power, Phillis Wheatley recorded in verse the religious and moral implications of womanhood, while the playwright Mercy Otis Warren teased and satirized men in plays and other works written for the *Massachusetts Spy.* In a more sober vein, Warren produced the first colonial history written by a woman. As the republic assumed international importance, Judith Sargent Murray championed women's rights in essays printed in *Gentleman and Lady's Town and Country Magazine.* Closer to the seat of power was Abigail Adams, a friend of the first U.S. president and the wife of the second. With Yankee pragmatism, she reminded John Adams that women deserved a share of the freedoms guaranteed in the U.S. Constitution.

Contemporaneous with incipient colonial feminism was the establishment by women of careers in writing, pioneered by the English playwright Aphra Behn, a spy for King Charles II and an early abolitionist. Her sympathy for the plight of slaves, as expressed in *Oroonoko,* influenced Gertrudis de Avellaneda's *Sab,* a feminist antislavery melodrama set in Cuba. Early in the 18th century, the English poet and playwright Anne Finch, countess of Winchilsea, wrote letters and poems on the importance of contentment in the lives of women. Focusing on the domestic aspect of womanhood, *The Household Book of Lady Griselle Baillie* ordered the myriad commonalities of kitchen and scullery into a revealing whole. The emergence of the female novel as a unique tool of feminism owes much to Susanna Rowson and Fanny Burney, important purveyors of novels of manners that deplored arranged engagements that omitted the input of prospective brides. Such writers of Gothic fiction as Charlotte Smith, Sophia Lee, and Ann Yearsley presaged groundbreaking shifts in horror literature from cheap titillation—the female as prey—to paeans to the logic and ingenuity of the self-rescuing maiden. At the forefront of the distaff branch of Gothic fiction stood Ann Radcliffe's *The Mysteries of Udolpho* and *The Italian,* both of which set the style and tone for legions of imitators. Contributing psychological studies of male and female emotions were the plays of Joanna Baillie. The pinnacle of female speculative Gothic, *Frankenstein,* revealed the complex views of Mary Shelley, a 19-year-old wife and mother. Shelley recast a dream she had into a classic fable of the obsessive laboratory scientist whose forbidden knowledge costs him his bride. Gertrude Atherton, a Pacific Coast writer, examined an otherworldly dimension in *What Dreams May Come* and turned perpetual youth into nightmare in *Black Oxen.* Catherine Louisa Pirkis created the female detective protagonist Lovelady Brooke, P.I. Holding to Gothic conventions of the previous century, Daphne du Maurier's *Rebecca,* Shirley Jackson's "The Lottery," Isabel Allende's *The House of the Spirits,* and the short stories of Joyce Carol Oates revealed new insights on the psychological terrors of the insecure wife.

Three years before the French Revolution, Mary Wollstonecraft, a famous exponent of feminist literature and author of *A Vindication of the Rights of Women*, began publishing polemics intended to free women from patriarchy and offer them choices in lifestyles and education. Compounding Wollstonecraft's demands were those of the educator and textbook author Maria Edgeworth and the novelist and playwright Mary Robinson, who disclosed the woman's view of seduction and abandonment in *Vancenza; or, The Dangers of Credulity* and *The False Friend, a Domestic Story*. Contributing insights from the intelligentsia, the salon hostess Germaine de Staël found reasons to pity the martyrdom of Marie Antoinette and to honor her motherhood in "Reflections on the Trial of a Queen." De Staël also wrote *The Influence of the Passions on the Happiness of Individuals and Nations*, which targets misogyny as a factor contributing to global distress. Anna Seward injected a distinct note of humanism in *Llangollen Vale*, a verse novel that sympathizes with lesbian lovers trying to survive in a welter of innuendo and public disfavor. Mary Elizabeth Braddon, the queen of Victorian pulp fiction, transfixed readers with *Lady Audley's Secret*, a gripping trickster tale of female deceit and disguise. For the scandalous *East Lynne*, Ellen Wood chose a popular outlet for women's fiction, serialization in *New Monthly Magazine*. Caroline Lamb pursued semiautobiographical fiction to extremes in *Glenarvon* and *Ada Reis*, revealing her passion for Lord Byron, infamous for his cavalier pursuit of the opposite sex. For her daring, Lamb survives in literary history as a scorned woman.

The feminist novel reached its apogee in the works of Jane Austen, Charlotte and Emily Brontë, and George Eliot. In an era when few women could support themselves, Austen's *Pride and Prejudice*, *Emma*, and *Persuasion* assessed with humor and wit the lot of marriageable young women who had no choice but to angle for a likely provider. Female fiction in the 19th century peaked in 1847 with Charlotte Brontë's *Jane Eyre* and Emily Brontë's *Wuthering Heights*. A decade after Queen Victoria ascended to the British throne for an unprecedented 64-year reign, the protagonist Jane Eyre presaged the New Woman by overcoming orphanhood, educating herself, and going to work as a governess and teacher. Jane's triumph over a would-be bigamist contrasts with the sexual liberation of Emily Brontë's heroine, Catherine Earnshaw, a vibrant nature lover who finds in a Gypsy boy a passion that survives even death. More realistic are the works of Mary Ann Evans, who, under the pseudonym George Eliot, scripted masterworks of English village life, including *Silas Marner* and *Middlemarch*, a study of the maturing of Dorothea Casaubon from an idealist to a risk taker who spurns money and marries for love. Moving realism toward the unveiling of the New Woman was the South African feminist Olive Schreiner's *The Story of an African Farm*, a morality tale that exalts a woman of principle for opting for single parenthood over a marriage of convenience. Richmond, Virginia, produced its own New Woman in Ellen Glasgow, an author of novels and stories about uninhibited females.

In the United States feminists wrote classic novels of human quandaries. In New Orleans, Kate Chopin breached the dicta of polite womanhood by publishing *The Awakening*, a quest novella that follows to her death the poet Edna Pontellier, an individualist willing to live and die on her own terms. Sharing market shelf space with E. D. E. N. Southworth's *The Hidden Hand; or, Capitola the Mad-Cap* were two humanistic monuments: Nathaniel Hawthorne's Puritan-era romance *The Scarlet Letter* and Harriet Beecher Stowe's *Uncle Tom's Cabin*. Although dissimilar in historical setting, Hawthorne's story of Hester Prynne, the scorned woman, and her baby, Pearl, and Stowe's novel, which featured plantation overseers chasing Eliza Harris and her son, Harry, onto blocks of ice floating on the Ohio River, both censured society's dehumanization of women and children under the pretense of prosecuting lawbreakers.

As women shrugged off the gendered fetters forged in prehistory, they pitied the lot of slaves, whose bondage paralleled the Western marriage market. The English poet Elizabeth Barrett Browning denounced the sale of humans in "The Runaway Slave at Pilgrim's Point." *The Narrative of Sojourner Truth* told the life story of a brilliant orator who galvanized suffragists with "Women Want

Their Rights" and "Ain't I a Woman?" Abolitionism and feminism infused Frances Ellen Harper's poem "The Slave Mother," Harriet Jacobs's *Incidents in the Life of a Slave Girl,* and the harangues of Frances Wright and Frederick Douglass, author of *Narrative of the Life of Frederick Douglass.* The blend of sympathies for slaves and for beleaguered women energized Anna Laetitia Barbauld, author of "The Rights of Woman," and of the editor Lydia Child, who wrote *An Appeal in Favor of That Class of Americans Called Africans,* "Quadroons," and *Authentic Anecdotes of American Slavery.* The actor and diarist Fanny Kemble hammered more pointedly at the hypocrisy of bondage in the land of the free with *Journal of a Residence in America* and *Journal of a Residence on a Georgian Plantation.* Her charges of white torment of black laborers and wet nurses were undeniable.

Extending the focus of humanitarian concerns, feminist writers traditionally excel at issues of the heart and conscience. Among outstanding early examples are Felicia Heman's poem "The Indian Woman's Death-Song," Helen Hunt Jackson's *Ramona* and *A Century of Dishonor,* and Elizabeth Barrett Browning's *Cry of the Children.* Ruthann Lum McCunn's *Thousand Pieces of Gold* reminded Americans that Chinese women endured their own torments from sexual bondage on the American frontier. Nathaniel Hawthorne's retrospective "Mrs. Hutchinson" summarizes the malice of anti-woman religious fanaticism. Promoting the greater inclusion of Jews in American Life, Grace Aguilar wrote *Women of Israel,* "The Festival of Purim," *Adah, a Simple Story, The Spirit of Judaism,* and a feminist overview of the Old Testament, *The Women of Israel: Character Sketches from the Holy Scriptures and Jewish History.*

The topic of woman's work stressed the issue of fulfillment. The evolution of feminism from domestic texts got a start in the 1830s with Lydia Child's handbook *The Frugal Housewife* and *The Family Nurse.* The mastermind of home-centered texts, Catharine Beecher, turned out *Treatise on Domestic Economy, Letters to Persons Engaged in Domestic Service,* and a best seller, *The American Woman's Home,* published four years after the American Civil War. Susan B. Anthony's "The Homes of Single Women" exemplified the industry and inge-

nuity of women who chose solitary lives. Woman's toil took on new guises as home chores evolved into combat nursing, the subject of Louisa May Alcott's *Hospital Sketches,* and into permanent careers in medicine, described in Sarah Orne Jewett's *A Country Doctor* and Elizabeth Blackwell's "Letter to Young Ladies Desirous of Studying Medicine." Olive Logan offered possibilities for jobs in *The Voice as a Source of Income.* Refusing to overlook residual drudgery that chained women to home and kitchen were the writings of Tillie Olsen, author of the classic "I Stand Here Ironing." Cornelia Otis Skinner found much to admire in *Madame Sarah,* a study of the stagework of Sarah Bernhardt; Beryl Markham explored nontraditional employment for women in *West with the Night,* which recounts adventures as a commercial pilot. As though shining a light over disadvantaged female laborers, Emma Lazarus wrote an ode, "The New Colossus," a tribute to American immigrants that graces the plinth of the Statue of Liberty, a commanding female icon of welcome.

Journalism provided another route to promoting feminism, a topic of Ishbel Ross's celebratory *Ladies of the Press,* the post–World War II reportage of Dorothy Thompson, and Florence King's satiric *Southern Ladies and Gentlemen.* A courageous Parisian, Baronne Dudevant, applauded women who jettisoned domesticity for the sake of personal betterment. Writing under the pseudonym George Sand for *Le Figaro, La République, Revue des Deux Mondes,* and *Revue Indépendante,* she publicized the courage of women. Among these heroines was a coterie of Americans, Harriet Jane Robinson and the Lowell mill girls, who issued the *Lowell Offering,* the world's first magazine produced by women. In England, Harriet Taylor Mill's *Principles of Political Economy* and "The Enfranchisement of Women" pressed those profiteering on the Industrial Revolution to acknowledge the needs of the female labor force. An American, Rebecca Harding Davis, made similar inroads against the inhumane treatment of female workers in the melodrama *Life in the Iron Mills.* To end the frivolous incarceration of women in asylums, the muckraking reporter Nellie Bly had herself committed to a public institution and reported on foul meals and abusive treatment of patients in *Ten Days in a Mad-House.* A longer crusade, Ida Wells-Barnett's exposé of lynchings in the Jim Crow South, resulted in *Southern Horror* and *The Crusade for Justice*, two protests of vigilante-style execution.

Discontent with second-class citizenship emerged in Lydia Child's *The History of the Condition of Women*, Sarah Josepha Hale's *Traits of American Life*, Angelina Grimké's *An Appeal to the Christian Women of the South* and the subsequent "The Rights of Women and Negroes," Elizabeth Blackwell's *Laws of Life with Special Reference to the Physical Education of Girls*, Emily Dickinson's poem "We lose—because we win," and Margaret Fuller's *Woman in the Nineteenth Century*. From individual assaults on misogyny evolved a mass, coordinated "votes for women" campaign in Europe and the Western Hemisphere. In the opinion of the orator and organizer Susan B. Anthony, woman was the "great unpaid laborer." In 1872, Anthony faced the consequences of illegally demanding the vote, the cause of a court record ringing with her outrage at being arrested for performing a citizen's duty. Anthony joined Matilda Joslyn Gage in crafting the "Declaration of Rights of Women," a pivotal document in women's history. Lucy Stone's "Disappointment Is the Lot of Women" clarified for doubters the seriousness of women's complaints; corroborating her views was Carrie Chapman Catt's *The Ballot and the Bullet*. Margaret Oliphant's "Laws Concerning Women," "The Grievances of Women," and "The Condition of Women" challenged the legality of male-mandated statutes. To readers of the *Ladies' Home Journal*, the social activist Jane Addams explained "Why Women Should Vote." The Quaker orator Lucretia Coffin Mott presented a reasoned perspective on social improvements in *Progress of Reforms* and *Discourse on Woman*. A notorious English demonstrator, the suffragist Emmeline Pankhurst, anthologized *Suffrage Speeches from the Dock*. Sarah Orne Jewett subverted the "little woman" paradigm in a satiric short story, "Tom's Husband." Matilda Gage charged organized religion with denigrating womanhood in *Woman, Church, and State*. The temperance advocate Carry Nation fought the saloon and public drunkenness in an autobiography, *The Use and Need of the Life of Carry A. Nation*. *The Subjection of Women* expressed the opinions of the English philosopher John Stuart Mill. From Norway came an unexpected boost to women's issues, Henrik Ibsen's play *A Doll's House*. Summarizing the struggle for women's rights up to the time, Susan B. Anthony, Matilda Gage, Elizabeth Cady Stanton, and Ida Husted compiled *History of Woman Suffrage*, a six-volume testament to the first wave of women's demand for full citizenship.

In the last seven years of the crusade for the vote, female writers presaged a century of women's commitment to stay vocal and active. Emmeline Pankhurst reprised the difficulties of altering sexual politics in *The Suffragette*; the reporter Djuna Barnes covered issues of jailing and torture in "How It Feels to Be Forcibly Fed." The orator Voltairine de Cleyre advocated liberal reforms in "The Woman Question," "The Case of Woman vs. Orthodoxy," and "Sex Slavery." More shocking to conservatives was Elizabeth Cady Stanton's *The Woman's Bible*. In reference to women's functions as noncombatants during World War I, Edith Wharton compiled *Fighting France*. She also wrote *The Buccaneers*, a droll depiction of young American women pursuing rich and prestigious European husbands.

While pragmatic women worked to engineer lasting change on an androcentric world, feminist dreamers imagined fantasy havens. In 1848, Jane Sophia Appleton issued "Sequel to *Vision of Bangor in the Twentieth Century*." Fortifying the vision of feminist utopias was Elizabeth T. Corbett's "My Visit to Utopia" and Eveleen Mason's *Hiero-Salem: The Vision of Peace*. The epitome of the genre, *Herland* and *With Her in Ourland*, presented the all-woman dreamworld conjured by Charlotte Perkins Gilman. She set outlander fiction to practical purposes in "The Waste of Private Housekeeping." Speculative feminist fiction, such as Ursula Le Guin's *The Left Hand of God* and "Sur," Margaret Atwood's *The Handmaid's Tale*, Joanna Russ's *The Female Man*, and Marge Piercy's *Woman on the Edge of Time*, shed light on domestic and civil wrongs. Going back in time allowed Olivia Butler to relive the anguish of her great-grandmother, an enslaved concubine, in *Kindred*.

Postsuffrage writings took on questions of women's new status. Canadian journalist Nellie McClung asked a question posed by many: "Can a Woman Raise a Family and Have a Career?" Of women's influence on world order Kathleen Norris demanded *What Price Peace?* Mary H. Ford proclaimed women's role as vanguard social critics in the essay "The Feminine Iconoclast." Lillian Hellman revealed some women's penchant for cruelty and power in the stage hits *The Children's Hour* and *The Little Foxes.* The short-story author Eudora Welty turned perverse behavior into comedy in *Delta Wedding* and "Why I Live at the P. O." The ethnographer and novelist Zora Neale Hurston danced through scenes of female power and trickery in *Their Eyes Were Watching God* and *Mules and Men.* Flannery O'Connor moved even further from center with two classics of southern Gothic, "Good Country People" and "A Good Man Is Hard to Find."

With the westward expansion of the United States, the unprecedented resilience of women enlivened frontier literature, such as the autobiography of Martha Jane Cannary, alias Calamity Jane. A sobering branch of the literature of journeying westward, captivity narratives, notably *Captivity of the Oatman Girls,* the story of Mary Ann Oatman and Olive Ann Oatman's survival of abduction by Indians, outlined personal triumphs. Elinore Pruitt Stewart revealed epistolary flair in *Letters of a Woman Homesteader.* More engaging is *Down the Santa Fe Trail and into Mexico,* an account of Susan Magoffin's introduction to marriage and overland travel among the native peoples of New Mexico. About the North, Catherine Parr Traill summarized personal experience in *The Backwoods of Canada;* on the West, the adventurer Isabella Bird's *A Lady's Life in the Rocky Mountains* set an example for the hardy. In *Life among the Piutes,* Sarah Winnemucca condemned the seizure of Native homelands and the near-genocide of tribes. Frances Roe viewed the settlement of the West from the opposing perspective in *Army Letters of an Officer's Wife.* The prairie lore of Willa Cather— *O Pioneers!* and *My Ántonia*—honored commitment of agrarian women to the future, a theme also apparent in Jessamyn West's *The Friendly Persuasion* and *Except for Me and Thee.* Edna Ferber spotlighted western movers and shakers in *Cimarron, Show Boat,* and *Giant,* which dramatizes the development of Leslie Lynnton Benedict into a Texas matriarch. For young readers, Laura Ingalls Wilder and her daughter, the journalist Rose Wilder Lane, projected the hope of female settlers

and their daughters in humble beginnings at sod huts and in log cabins.

Twentieth-century fiction witnessed a revolution in depictions of women's confinement within a stifling conservatism, a focus of the carefully plotted stories of Katherine Mansfield and Katherine Anne Porter, the author of the luminous confessional "The Jilting of Granny Weatherall." Leading a revolt against social sequestration was Edith Wharton, herself a member of the New York City elite that she described in *Old New York.* Wharton presented bright but doomed females in *The House of Mirth* and *The Age of Innocence* and a doubly damned male in *Ethan Frome.* Concerning the South, the Atlanta journalist Margaret Mitchell limned the heroic Civil War matriarch in *Gone with the Wind,* a blockbuster novel that contrasts methods of female survival. Tangential to women functioning as detectives and law officers, Mary Roberts Rinehart instituted the female detective novel, a genre further explored by Sue Grafton and Sara Paretsky. Gertrude Stein and Virginia Woolf liberated fiction itself with experiments in syntax and rhetoric in *Tender Buttons* and *To the Lighthouse,* respectively. Djuna Barnes impressed on readers the private hells of lesbian life in *Nightwood,* composed in emulation of Radclyffe Hall's *The Well of Loneliness,* a novel that survived suppression and censorship. Less negative are Mary Renault's *The Friendly Young Ladies* and Rita Mae Brown's *The Rubyfruit Jungle.* Tender views of young girls trying to be women were at the core of Carson McCullers's *The Heart Is a Lonely Hunter* and *The Member of the Wedding.* Both preceded a survey of older women, Mary McCarthy's *The Group,* in which alumnae gather to discuss their achievements and the obstacles to their youthful ideals.

Ecofeminism, a maternal reverence for Earth and its denizens, got its start with *The Land of Little Rain,* Mary Hunter Austin's hymn to desert beauty of the southwestern frontier. She elicited wisdom from Native crafters for *The Basket Woman, The Arrow-Maker, Earth Horizon, The Starry Adventure,* and "Walking Woman" and wrote her own nature verse for an elementary school text, *Children Sing in the Far West.* As pollutants compromised Earth's cycles, Rachel Carson struck the complacent citizen with terrible scenes of a possible near future in

Silent Spring. Developing nonfiction terrors into fiction, the Chickasaw poet Linda Hogan crafted chants and prayers in *Book of Medicines.* Erica Jong's *Witches* revised the legend of the charmer and caster of spells into a more believable nature worshipper who gains power from earthly sources. Barbara Kingsolver complimented female survivalism in *Animal Dreams* and *The Poisonwood Bible* but warned of coming doom in *Last Stand: America's Virgin Lands.*

As did their predecessors, 20th-century feminists excelled at matters of heart and conscience. Patricia MacLachlan and Carol Sobieski reprised the demands on mail-order brides in *Sarah, Plain and Tall* and *The Skylark.* Maxine Kumin's *Our Ground Time Here Will Be Brief* looked to the feminine for insights into the human condition. Gloria Naylor applauded women for brightening ghetto blight in *The Women of Brewster Place;* Jamaica Kincaid's *Annie John* performed a similar service for Caribbean women. Monuments to the era's acknowledgment of human pain, Toni Morrison's *The Bluest Eye* and *Beloved* touched the issues of racial denigration, sexual opportunism at the expense of young girls, and the hurtful residue of slave times.

From other parts of the world, writers echoed the energy and determination of Americans to put an end to patriarchy in the elevation of biblical matriarchs of Anna Akhmatova's *Anno Domini MCMXXI,* Colette's lighthearted coming-of-age novel *Gigi,* the Indian domestic vignettes of Nayantara Sahgal, the quest novels of Bette Bao Lord, and accounts of immigrant travail in Mary Antin's *The Promised Land* and in Anzia Yezierska's *Hungry Hearts and Other Stories* and *Bread Givers.* Emilia Pardo Bazán exposed rot at the core of Spain's aristocracy in *The House of Ulloa.* Sigrid Undset won a Nobel Prize for following the daily compromises and disappointments of a married woman in her trilogy *Kristin Lavransdatter.* The journalist Louise Bryant examined the changes in women's lives under communism in *Six Months in Red Russia.*

The poet and teacher Gabriela Mistral focused on one aspect of Chilean feminism, the role education plays in relieving girls of drudgery, cyclical maternity, and early death. Ama Ata Aidoo wrote about the African New Woman and her confrontation with tribal constraints on females. Pearl Buck, a bicultural American, captured in daily commonalities the humble lives of Chinese peasant women in *The Good Earth* and *The Woman.*

Biography featured the front-line observations of reformers. A respected memoir, *Twenty Years at Hull-House,* depicted the settlement established by Jane Addams. Colleagues Margaret Sanger and Marie Stopes described the uproar caused by women's health care clinics and the distribution of barrier methods of contraception. In *Anarchism and Other Essays,* the socialist agitator and editor Emma Goldman outlined her own struggles in the causes of labor organization and birth control for women. Margaret Mead stirred controversy through her sojourn in the South Seas to gather material for *Coming of Age in Samoa,* a study of adolescent sex. During the Great Depression Meridel Le Sueur looked closer to home for female endurance in *Women on the Breadlines.* Marjorie Kinnan Rawlings observed her own backyard in *Cross Creek.* In similar detail, Anaïs Nin discussed the perversions of her childhood in *The House of Incest.*

Twentieth-century verse explored the unknown in the imagist and modernist writings of Amy Lowell, Mina Loy, and H. D. Refined images and insightful themes buoyed the collections of Elinor Wylie, Marianne Moore, Sara Teasdale, and Edna St. Vincent Millay. The resetting of mythic figures in feminist poems suited the style of Meridel Le Sueur's "Persephone." Less elegant, but no less telling, were the satiric jingles of Dorothy Parker and the lacerating wit of Sylvia Plath's "Daddy" and Stevie Smith's "Papa Love Baby." Gwendolyn Brooks turned feminist eyes toward the gritty truths of the black ghetto in *A Street in Bronzeville,* a forerunner of Rita Dove's *Thomas and Beulah* and of Mari Evans's "I Am a Black Woman." With "Housewife," Anne Sexton set the tone and atmosphere of confessional verse. Less me-driven were the womanly wisdom of Denise Levertov's "Stepping Westward" and the psychological insight of Margaret Atwood's "The Woman Who Could Not Live with Her Faulty Heart." A beacon to the age, the feminism of the poet-critic Adrienne Rich set followers on a solid basis for working toward wholeness. The pivotal poem "Diving into the Wreck" spelled out the perils of the mission as well as its rewards.

Drama examined scenes of domestic and social misery. Susan Glaspell achieved a one-act classic for the Provincetown Players in *Trifles*, a revelation of a housewife driven to murder. Anita Loos made light of male pursuit of the Beauty Myth in *Gentlemen Prefer Blondes* and its sequel, *But Gentlemen Marry Brunettes*. The African-American female playwright Lorraine Hansberry stepped into the limelight in 1959 with *A Raisin in the Sun*, a play that garnered national awards. Eve Ensler introduced women to their genitals through performances of *The Vagina Monologues* and *The Good Body*. In 2004 Elfriede Jelinek earned a Nobel Prize as a result of her feminist dramas, including *We Are Decoys*, *Baby*, *The Piano Teacher*, *Lust*, and the grimly revelatory *Wonderful, Wonderful Times*.

Critical attention to women's right to express their uniqueness directed the world of a host of feminist philosophers and literary historians. Taking its cue from Virginia Woolf's *A Room of One's Own*, gynocriticism, a term invented by Kate Millett and Elaine Showalter, retrieved from neglect insightful feminist works. Introduced to reading lists were Mary Shelley's *Frankenstein*, Zora Neale Hurston's *Their Eyes Were Watching God*, Sarah Grand's New Woman novels, and Charlotte Perkins Gilman's Gothic short story "The Yellow Wallpaper," in addition to the Harlem Renaissance dramas of Rachel Crothers and Marita Bonner. Significant critical texts include Nina Baym's *Woman's Fiction*, Simone de Beauvoir's *The Second Sex*, Shulamith Firestone's *Women's Rights Movement in the U.S.*, Germaine Greer's *The Female Eunuch*, Kate Millett's *Sexual Politics*, Robin Morgan's *Sisterhood Is Powerful*, and Ellen Moers's "Angry Young Women" and *Literary Women*. The pivotal expression of female discontent, Betty Friedan's *The Feminine Mystique*, mapped out "the problem that has no name," a malaise common to women in the 1950s and 1960s. She reprised the defining moment of modern feminism with an overview of responses to it in *It Changed My Life* and looked ahead in *The Second Stage*.

A number of feminists chose their own sphere in which to flourish. Rosalie Maggio's *Talking about People* simplified the selection of language that gives

no offense on the basis of gender or sexual orientation. The Christian philosophy of Simone Weil offered hope for the European factory worker. Harper Lee's caricature of Aunt Alexandra, the corseted matriarch in *To Kill a Mockingbird*, contrasted with the loving surrogacy of Cal in raising Atticus Finch's tomboyish Jean Louise "Scout" Finch. Margaret Edson's Pulitzer Prize–winning play *Wit*, as did Audre Lorde's *The Cancer Journals*, interpreted women's fear of dehumanizing treatments for cancer. Several works—Simone de Beauvoir's *A Very Easy Death*, Jamaica Kincaid's *An Autobiography of My Mother*, and Barbara Kingsolver's "Homeland"—place the independent woman in the unenviable position of parent to an aged parent, a reversal that is both liberating and pitiable.

The past held firm in feminist works. Clarissa Pinkola Estés's *Women Who Run with the Wolves* offered insight into the pack mentality in early human behavior. For the Feminist Press, Barbara Ehrenreich and Deirdre English revisited medical history in *Witches, Midwives, and Nurses*. Leslie Marmon Silko restored the centrality of indigenous female oral tradition in *The Storyteller* and *Ceremony*; Marion Zimmer Bradley applied the same logic to fresh tellings of Arthurian lore in *The Mists of Avalon*. Nonfiction such as Susan Sontag's "The Third World of Women," Susan Brownmiller's *Against Our Will*, Yoko Kawashima Watkins's *So Far from the Bamboo Grove*, and Andrea Dworkin's *Woman Hating* revealed more of the gender-related angst of history in accounts of stalking, rape, and torture. As though reliving misogyny in the skin of a foremother, Margaret Walker pictured a Civil War widow's quandary in *Jubilee*. The Caribbean author Jean Rhys overturned Charlotte Brontë's *Jane Eyre* in *Wide Sargasso Sea*, an exoneration for the madwoman Antoinette/Bertha Cosway Rochester's having burned Thornfield Manor. Maya Angelou reprised the black child's terror of the Ku Klux Klan and urban violence in *I Know Why the Caged Bird Sings*. Jeanne Wakatsuki Houston and her husband, James Houston, explained the dissolution of Japanese-American families in *A Farewell to Manzanar*, a first-person memoir of an American concentration camp. Hélène Cixous's *The Newly Born Woman* gave reasons for hope.

Polemical writings took wing from the formal definition of feminism and feminist literature, giving new life to newspapers in the columns of Ellen Goodman, Katha Pollitt, Anna Quindlen, and Molly Ivins. For *Ms.* magazine, Gloria Steinem promised that "Women's Liberation Aims to Free Men, Too" and mused on possibilities in "If Men Could Menstruate." Angela Davis focused outrage at racism in *If They Come in the Morning;* Kate Millett's *The Prostitution Papers* and Sheila Rowbotham's *Hidden from History* defended sex workers. Elizabeth Janeway's *Man's World, Woman's Place* and *Women: Their Changing Roles, the Great Contemporary* refused to give ground on issues of gender equity. For children, Marlo Thomas filled a need with *Free to Be, You and Me.* From a Mayan's point of view, female rebellion held firm against tyranny in *I, Rigoberto Menchú.* Luce Irigaray's *This Sex Which Is Not One* highlighted new views of gender differences; Elaine Showalter's *Women's Liberation and Literature* and *A Literature of Their Own* summarized the effects of feminist politics on the arts.

Imaginative but hard-edged, late 20th-century fiction held to the tenets of feminism. Jean Auel envisioned the emergence of the prehistoric thinking woman in Ayla, heroine of the Earth's Children series. The short-story writer Toni Cade Bambara demanded dignity for the underclass in "Blues Ain't No Mockin Bird." Ntozake Shange explored self-destructive urges in *for colored girls who have considered suicide when the rainbow is enuf.* The seriocomic playwright Caryl Churchill earned critical regard for probing female sexuality in *Cloud Nine* and *Top Girls;* her contemporary, Wendy Wasserstein, straddled the line between hilarity and rage in *Any Woman Can't* and *The Heidi Chronicles.* Erica Jong's *Fear of Flying,* Diane di Prima's *Loba,* Susan Sontag's *On Photography, The Diary of Anaïs Nin,* Marie-Claire Blais's *Nights in the Underground,* and Marian Engel's *Bear* forced overt eroticism into the feminist arena. The poet Sonia Sanchez's *A Blues Book for Blue Black Magical Women* paid tribute to the blues singers whose lyrics permeate modern novels and verse. Maxine Hong Kingston's *The Woman Warrior* merged self-determination in Chinese-American women with the legends and cautionary tales of

imperial China. Marge Piercy fought the stereotype of the deserving woman in "The Grey Flannel Sexual Harassment Suit."

On behalf of preliberation females, women writers fought with renewed tenacity the denigration and life-shortening assaults of past eras. Setting the pace were works by authors from developing countries, such as Buchi Emecheta's *In the Ditch,* Bharati Mukherjee's *Tiger's Daughter* and *The Wife,* Nawal El Saadawi's *Woman at Point Zero,* and Sahar Khalifeh's *We Are Not Your Slave Girls Anymore.* Angela Carter pressed the case of the first woman in *The Passion of New Eve,* a subject that resonated in Stevie Smith's "How Cruel Is the Story of Eve." Reverence for foremothers was the controlling theme of Ruth Prawer Jhabvala's *Heat and Dust,* Alice Walker's *Possessing the Secret of Joy,* Gayl Jones's *Corregidora,* Cathy Song's *The Picture Bride,* Laurel Thatcher Ulrich's *The Good Wife,* Lillian Schlissel's *Women's Diaries of the Westward Journey,* and Laura Esquivel's *Like Water for Chocolate.* Maryse Condé paid tribute to the black female victim in *I, Tituba, Black Witch of Salem.* Kaye Gibbons's *Ellen Foster* lauded the reclamation of hope and family for a battered child; Terry McMillan's *Mama* unleashed a mother lode of resistance to spousal battery. Beth Henley's play *Crimes of the Heart,* Mari Evans's *Eyes,* Adrienne Rich's retrospective *On Lies, Secrets, and Silence,* Mariama Bâ's *So Long a Letter,* Tatyana Mamonova's *Women and Russia,* Sandra Cisneros's story "Woman Hollering Creek," and Joy Harjo's poem "The Woman Hanging from the Thirteenth Floor Window" reminded readers of the desperation that pressed some women to extremes. Fay Weldon satirized beauty cultists in *The Life and Loves of a She-Devil;* Andrea Dworkin formulated feminist philosophy on pictorial rape in *Pornography: Men Possessing Women.* Contributing a new slogan to feminist cries of "Fight back" and "Take back the night" was Faith McNulty's *The Burning Bed.*

Into the present, feminist literature challenges obstacles to freedom and happiness. Anita Diament pictured women's private rebellions against biblical patriarchs in *The Red Tent.* Velma Wallis wrote the first female epic, *Two Old Women,* on issues of aging and the lethal devaluation of women. Diana Cross imagined female valor in *Pope Joan;* Diana Norman extolled a female businesswoman during the

American Revolution in *A Catch of Consequence*. Betty Mahmoody fought Islamic misogyny in *Not Without My Daughter*. Irina Ratushinskaya's *Grey Is the Colour of Hope* found resilient sisterhood in Russian prison cells. Dorothy Allison's *Trash* and *Bastard Out of Carolina* described the hurt of discounted lower-class southern women; Joyce Carol Oates dramatized the waves of harm from scandal in *We Were the Mulvaneys*. Amy Tan's *The Joy Luck Club* examined a mother's decision to abandon her twin girls in war-torn China. Bessie Head combatted racist standards of beauty in *Maru*. Anna Deavere Smith's *Fires in the Mirror* forced urbanites to search out sources of hatred. Julia Alvarez's *In the Time of the Butterflies* publicized the brash patriotism of a clutch of women who defied a dictator. Looking ahead, Susan Faludi warned in *Backlash* that the gender wars could take unforeseen turns.

Overall, these works reveal the health and breadth of feminist writers, who bolster the spirits of readers through their words and example. For its loyalty to the unvoiced sufferings and longings of females past and present, feminist literature fills a need in the human family for the equitable representation of women.

abolitionism

Women's contributions to dismantling the slave system constitute a valuable segment of feminist literary history. The first feminist abolitionist author, the English playwright Aphra BEHN, exposed SLAVERY for its barbarity in *Oroonoko; or, The Royal Slave* (1688), a classic 17th-century drama. In the early 1770s, decades before a global demand for manumission of slaves, the American letter writer Abigail ADAMS reminded her husband, the future U.S. president John Adams, that he and other founders of the new republic were embarking on a troubled sea if they left unresolved the bondage of black Americans. On March 31, 1776, she remarked that the Virginia delegates were concealing proslavery sentiments behind an egalitarian facade. In England Ann YEARSLEY, a dairymaid and poet, expressed her abolitionist concerns in "Poem on the Inhumanity of the Slave Trade" (1788), a verse frequently cited for its compassion for women separated from their children.

The most incisive of female social reformers—Louisa May ALCOTT, Gertrudis Gómez de AVELLANEDA, Elizabeth Brown BLACKWELL, Elizabeth Barrett BROWNING, Lydia Maria CHILD, Frances HARPER, Harriet JACOBS, Harriet MARTINEAU, E. D. E. N. SOUTHWORTH, Elizabeth Cady STANTON, and Harriet Beecher STOWE—changed the thinking of the Western world. They faced head-on the simpering Old South romances composed by a cadre of plantation novelists—Mary Eastman, Caroline Lee Hentz, Mary Jane Holmes, Maria McIntosh, Augusta Evans Wilson—whose sugared images of an orderly, gladsome plantation utopia promoted an aristocratic code that allegedly offered health, security, Christian salvation, and training to the enslaved. Two eyewitnesses, the sisters Angelina GRIMKÉ and Sarah GRIMKÉ, of Charleston, South Carolina, fled the South to become Quakers and abolitionist agents. In an era when society silenced women and barred them from public forums, the Grimkés addressed audiences on the wrongs that human bondage inflicted on American morals. For their daring, they faced accusations of unladylike behavior and violation of Christian principles. Another female criticized for voicing objections to the mistreatment of blacks was the Scots-American editor and lecturer Frances WRIGHT, author of *A Plan for the Gradual Abolition of Slavery in the United States without Danger of Loss to Citizens of the South* (1825), who, having emigrated from Britain, outraged Southerners by lambasting plantation owners from an outsider's perspective.

In 1837, one of the era's most prominent educators, Catharine Esther BEECHER, directed an essay at women concerning the Christian imperative to end bondage. She says of her gender: "While woman holds a subordinate relation in society to the other sex, it is not because it was designed that her duties or her influence should be any the less important, or all-pervading" (Beecher, 99–100). She explains the value of Christianity as a moral force giving women their true place in society. To ensure women access to the public forum, she urges, "Let every woman become so cultivated and refined in intellect, that her taste and judgment will be respected; so benevolent in feeling and action, that her motives will be reverenced" (*ibid.*, 101). As a model, Beecher suggests that women consider the role of Queen Esther in the Bible in assuring rights to minorities in bondage.

The fractious decade leading up to the Civil War intensified narratives on issues of slavery and states' rights. The most explosive of abolitionist narratives, Harriet Beecher Stowe's melodrama UNCLE TOM'S CABIN; or, *Life among the Lowly* (1852), reportedly earned credit from President Abraham Lincoln for pushing the issue toward its violent conclusion in a war that threatened the Union itself. A prolific novelist, E. D. E. N. Southworth, developed feminist themes in a satiric masterwork, *The Hidden Hand; or, Capitola the Mad-Cap* (1859), serialized three times in the *New York Ledger*. The action follows the orphan Capitola LeNoir, a model of female autonomy, from a Southern plantation. Disguised as a boy, she survives escapades in the South among outlaws and brigands that blast the stereotype of the genteel belle in pantaloons. The author injects hints of the quagmire of enslavement in the heroine's surname—LeNoir, "the black"—and that of her handmaid Pitapat. Both names contain *pit*, a suggestion of the Middle Passage slaving vessel's hold and of the no-win choice that turncoat Southerners faced in denouncing the social and economic systems of their homeland. Similarly informative is the suggestion of self-serving capitalism in "Capitola." In the resolution, Southworth transforms her pubescent heroine into a moral adult who creates joy for others by freeing her slaves.

At the beginning of the Civil War, the editor and humanitarian Lydia Maria Child published *Incidents in the Life of a Slave Girl: Written by Herself* (1861), the AUTOBIOGRAPHY of Harriet Jacobs. A valuable eyewitness account of the slave woman's degradation as breeder of children for sale, the work moves from misery of Jacobs's self-exile in her grandmother's attic to embarkation from Chesapeake Bay to freedom in Philadelphia. Kind strangers, the Reverend and Mrs. Jeremiah Durham, welcome Jacobs. The Anti-Slavery Society offers to pay for transportation to New York. After the Fugitive Slave Law of 1850 threatens Ja-

cobs's safety, an unseen network of abolitionists, including the Quaker rescuer Amy Post, contributes to Jacobs's move to New England and protects her until she is at last free.

A controversial work, the English actor and diarist Fanny KEMBLE's *Journal of a Residence on a Georgian Plantation in 1838–1839* (1863), undermined her marriage to a Georgia slaver with its cutting critiques of Southern segregation and slaveholding clergy. The wealth of indignities suffered by her husband's field hands outraged her sensibilities. Of the plantation cemetery, she remarked on the herding of cattle over all of the graves except those of two whites. She deplored the thought that "parents and children, wives, husbands, brothers and sisters, of the poor slaves, sleeping beside them, might see the graves of those they loved trampled over and browsed over, desecrated and defiled, from morning til night" (Kemble, 308). Kemble characterized the lack of respect as a "disdainful denial of a common humanity [that pursued] these wretches even when they are hid beneath the earth" (*ibid.*). Such indecency caused Kemble to refer to slaves as "human cattle" (*ibid.*, 107).

Long after the drafting of the Emancipation Proclamation in 1862, the legal act of abolishing bondage did not rid people of slavery's wounds. In Elizabeth Blackwell's reflective text *Pioneer Work in Opening the Medical Profession to Women: Autobiographical Sketches* (1895), she describes her dislike of slavery in girlhood. While she enjoyed "hospitality" at a Henderson, Kentucky, home, she perceived that residents wore the mask of gentility as a cover for the brutality of bondage. One hostess placed a small black girl before the fire screen to shield Blackwell from the heat. Blackwell was particularly annoyed by slave owners who congratulated themselves that their slaves lived better than poor whites. She recalls, "I endeavour, in reply, to slide in a little truth through the small apertures of their minds, for were I to come out broadly . . . I should shut them up tight, arm all their prejudices, and do ten times more harm than good" (Blackwell, 21). Her sense of justice was so outraged that she left the area and returned to free territory in New England.

In the wake of freedom, fiction writers produced poignant scenes of slave times. Gwendolyn

Bennetta Bennett, a memorable sonneteer and lyricist of the Harlem Renaissance and administrator of the Works Progress Administration, composed "To a Dark Girl" (1927), an ode to a black child who displays the paradox of the black woman's posture, "something of the shackled slave" and a queenliness derived from Africa's female royalty (Mazer, 4). Pearl BUCK pictured the female enslavement in Asia in THE GOOD EARTH (1931) with Wang Lung's purchase of the servant O-lan for a bride; the Caribbean novelist Jean RHYS described the residual vengeance of black islanders in WIDE SARGASSO SEA (1966), in which resentful former slaves burn Coulibri, the country estate of the Creole Cosway family.

In the last half of the 20th century, slavery remained a viable topic for historical fiction and anticolonial verse, drama, and novels. Gayl JONES's stream-of-consciousness novel *Corregidora* (1975) depicted the sexual atrocities committed in South America to the Brazilian mother of Ursa, a blues singer. In 1981, the biographer Ruthanne Lumm McCunn reminded readers of West Coast slavery in *Thousand Pieces of Gold,* the story of Polly Bemis, who lived the wretchedness of Asian women forced into concubinage in Pacific Coast mining districts before the admission of Oregon, Idaho, and Washington as states. Another biography, the Guadeloupian novelist Maryse CONDE's *Moi, Tituba, Sorcière Noire Salem* (I, Tituba, Black Witch of Salem, 1986), revived the centrality of slavery to the Salem witch trials. Toni MORRISON's BELOVED was one of the greatest recent novels to examine the horrors of slavery. Rita Mae BROWN retraced the debate over slavery in Republican times with *Dolley* (1994), a fictionalized biography of First Lady Dolley Payne Madison, a spokeswoman for liberty for black and white Americans.

Bibliography

Beecher, Catharine E. *Essay on Slavery and Abolitionism, with Reference to the Duty of American Females* (1837). Available online. URL: http://etext.lib.virginia.edu/toc/modeng/public/BeeEssa.html. Accessed on October 17, 2005.

Blackwell, Elizabeth. *Pioneer Work in Opening the Medical Profession to Women.* Delanco, N.J.: privately printed, 2000.

Jacobs, Harriet A. *Incidents in the Life of a Slave Girl: Written by Herself.* New York: Harvest Books, 1983.

Kemble, Fanny. *Journal of a Residence on a Georgian Plantation in 1838–1839.* Athens: University of Georgia Press, 1984.

Mazer, Norma Fox, and Marjorie Lewis, eds. *Waltzing on Water.* New York: Dell, 1989.

Southworth, E. D. E. N. *The Hidden Hand.* New Brunswick, N.J.: Rutger's University Press, 1988.

abortion

The choice to bear or abort a fetus is a persistent theme in women's history and feminist literature. In September 1871, the journalist Victoria WOODHULL and her sister, Tennessee "Tennie" Claflin, publishers of *Woodhull & Claflin's Weekly,* held a spotlight to society's hypocrisy with regard to abortion. They declared the demand for abortion to be an economic and gender issue rather than a religious or moral concern. On September 23, the paper stated: "Some woman has been found coffined in a trunk, her remorseful seducer has committed suicide, an abortionist has been arrested, another case occurs the next day, and, the next, a whole bevy of women are hunted to bay in a doctor's shop of that order. The newspaper men are delighted" (Woodhull & Claflin). The unidentified writer insisted that abortion was a "fixed institution in this country" (*ibid.*) They asserted that the procurer of abortions had to be an upper-class female because laboring women could not afford the fees. The text added, "The shop of the abortionist is a beneficial institution, which protects the *virtue* and heals the heart sore of a thousand otherwise cursed and unfortunate families" (*ibid.*). A century before "reproductive rights" became a feminist rallying cry, Woodhull and Claflin concluded that the need for abortion was evidence of a more serious social plight: "Child-bearing is not a disease. . . . But to our faded-out, sickly, exhausted type of women, it is a fearful ordeal. Nearly every child born is an unwelcome guest. Abortion is the choice of evils for such women" (*ibid.*).

Not all feminists agreed with Woodhull and Claflin on women's health and reproductive issues. In the 1880s and 1890s Olive SCHREINER, a radical

South African novelist and polemicist, filled her writings with references to aborted pregnancies. In *Woman and Labour* (1911), she vilified the parasitism of women's depending on males for economic support as "an abortion of the mind" (Schreiner, 1). Other feminists took a dim view of abortion, especially for its connection with unscrupulous butchers who inflicted their ignorance on the unwary. Elizabeth BLACKWELL, the first female doctor in North America, was so awed by the majesty and wonder of maternity that she recoiled from the very thought of terminating a potential life. In her autobiographical text *Pioneer Work in Opening the Medical Profession to Women* (1895), she challenged "the gross perversion and destruction of motherhood by the abortionist" (Blackwell, 30). Rather than supply clinical justification, she accounted for her indignation and antagonism as visceral feelings against the degradation of women.

Against a head-to-head collision of pro- and antichoice women, cooler heads offered amelioration. In an interview, the French philosopher and women's advocate Simone de BEAUVOIR, author of *Le Deuxième Sexe* (*The Second Sex*, 1949), pointed out that the prochoice element in feminist philosophy does not negate normal maternal feelings or motherhood. She states, "There are feminists who are mothers and, of course, just because one is for abortion—naturally, all feminists are for abortion—but that doesn't mean that there aren't some who have chosen to have children" (Simons, 58). She accounted for the prominence of prochoice fervor among modern women as a reaction to centuries of enslavement to pregnancy, birthing, and parenthood, a three-pronged responsibility that men traditionally place entirely on females.

Women tend to continue the debate on abortion within all-female forums. As the novelist Marge PIERCY indicates in the dystopic novel WOMAN ON THE EDGE OF TIME (1976), the problem of male intervention and the imposition of androcentric opinions on the subject denies women the right to make decisions about their own mental and physical health and about the size and spacing of their families. Dissension over who decides the issue is a major theme in the author Ruth Prawer JHABVALA's colonial novella HEAT AND DUST (1975), which is set in British India in the 1920s. To the surprise of Olivia Rivers, a colonial wife, Maji, a women's health practitioner who is daughter and granddaughter of midwives, offers "assistance" to save Olivia from the scandal of bearing a biracial child. Maji explains that abortion "is a necessary part of an Indian midwife's qualifications because in many cases it is the only way to save people from dishonour and suffering" (Jhabvala, 139). In Olivia's case, the English doctor who provides postabortion treatment recognizes that Olivia has undergone the Indian method of introducing an herbal abortifacient into the uterus with a twig. Out of outrage at her crime, he declares that he "had always known that there was something rotten about Olivia: something weak and rotten," a surmise based on his blanket condemnation of women who choose to end their pregnancies (*ibid.*, 170).

The Chinese-American novelist Amy TAN agrees with Jhabvala's Maji on the importance of a female-controlled system of women's reproductive health. In descriptions of Chinese PATRIARCHY she characterizes abortion rights as crucial to women seeking to control pregnancies that result from rape, employer seduction, or marital abuse. In *The Joy Luck Club* (1989), Ying-ying St. Clair obtains vengeance against a brutal husband, Lin Xiao, by aborting their son. The choice circumvents the ancestral honors that a male child performs for his father. Tan repeats the theme in *The Kitchen God's Wife* (1991), in which the paramours of Wen Fu, a strutting pilot of the Kuomintang air force, terminate the gestation of children they can neither afford nor nurture. Of the two paramours—the vaudeville performer Min and an unnamed 14-year-old servant—the latter dies of the procedure, which she performs with an unsanitary broom straw. Another victim of Wen Fu's violent macho behavior is his wife, Winnie, who complains, "That bad man was using my body . . . as if I were—what?—a machine!" (Tan, 398). Because Wen Fu caused the deaths of his son, Mochou, and his daughter, Yiku, Winnie preserves the life of her son, Danru, but, out of kindness, aborts the next three conceptions to prevent further child abuse by a psychotic father.

Tan connects the theme of unplanned pregnancy to female SILENCING in *The Hundred Secret*

Senses (1995). After Simon Bishop's girlfriend, Elza Marie Vandervort, broaches the subject of the trauma resulting from abortion, he fails to understand the centrality of the topic to their relationship. Overcome by hormonal hysteria, she loses her way on a cross-country skiing trail and suffocates in an avalanche. The heap of snow that stifles her symbolizes the welter of emotion suffered by the female, who is both silenced and unfairly burdened by decision making for their unborn child. Tan returns the scenario to the text in passages on reincarnation, a theological belief that eases Simon's guilt about the deaths of Elza and the fetus.

The gore and dismemberment associated with abortion draw the interest of aberrant characters in feminist fiction. In the cultural epic *Almanac of the Dead* (1991), Leslie Marmon SILKO devotes a chapter to the pervert's fascination with fetal death. She depicts the religious Right's deception in challenging women's control of health issues in the burgeoning trade in abortion films. Beaufrey, a seedy book dealer, specializes in a line of dissection videotapes of sodomy rape, sex change operations, ritual circumcision, and strangulation. Puffing his repulsive breath in the face of a pregnant performer, Beaufrey confides that she will love having her pregnancy terminated under morphine. He muses that, since the U.S. Supreme Court made abortion legal, "The biggest customers for footage was the antiabortionist lobby, which paid top dollar for the footage of the tortured tiny babies" (Silko, 102). In his trade, there is more money in films of late-term procedures than of the early embryonic stage. He enjoys details of crushed skulls and atypical medical situations because collectors prefer them for the "blood and mess" (*ibid.*).

Bibliography

Blackwell, Elizabeth. *Pioneer Work in Opening the Medical Profession to Women.* Delanco, N.J.: privately printed, 2000.

Bradford, Helen. "Olive Schreiner's Hidden Agony: Fact, Fiction, and Teenage Abortion," *Journal of South African Studies* 21, no. 4 (1995): 623–641.

Hamilton, Patricia L. "Feng Shui, Astrology, and the Five Elements: Traditional Chinese Belief in Amy Tan's *The Joy Luck Club*," *MELUS* 24, no. 2 (Summer 1999): 125–145.

Jhabvala, Ruth Prawer. *Heat and Dust.* New York: Touchstone, 1976.

Schreiner, Olive. *Woman and Labour* (1911). Available online. URL: http://etext.library.adelaide.edu.au/s/schreiner_o/woman/woman.html. Accessed on October 13, 2005.

Silko, Leslie Marmon. *Almanac of the Dead.* New York: Simon & Schuster, 1991.

Simons, Margaret A. *Beauvoir and the Second Sex.* Lanham, Md.: Rowman & Littlefield, 2001.

Tan, Amy. *The Kitchen God's Wife.* New York: Putnam, 1991.

Woodhull, Victoria, and Tennessee Claflin. *Woodhull & Claflin's Weekly,* (1871–1872). September 23, 1871. Available online. URL: http://www.victoria-woodhull.com/wcwarchive.htm. Accessed on October 17, 2005.

Adams, Abigail (1744–1818)

Often characterized as the United States' first formal feminist voice, letter writer Abigail Smith Adams envisioned democracy as the first true liberation of women. Born at a Congregationalist parsonage in Weymouth, Massachusetts, she and her two sisters studied at home with their Grandmother Quincy and read what they chose from shelves stocked with French literature, drama and poetry, history, and philosophy. After marrying attorney and future president John Adams, for 54 years Abigail kept house at Braintree, reared their five children, and earned the family's living. While enduring the rumble of cannon, widespread smallpox, inflation, and shortages, she observed the 24-hour battle of Bunker Hill and defended her rural property from Redcoat invaders, whom she described in detail. Her son, John Quincy Adams, later remarked on his mother's courage: "For the space of twelve months my mother with her infant children dwelt, liable every hour of the day and night to be butchered in cold blood, or taken and carried to Boston as hostages" (Roberts, 67). Abigail Adams stressed in her correspondence that women seldom received credit for the everyday challenge of patriotism, which in her case included management of personal finances and weathering of the uncertainty and loneliness of a long separation from John.

During a decade of her husband's attention to the formation of the nation, Adams had to let correspondence replace normal conjugal conversations. Admitting that words on paper freed her tongue and sent her thoughts into taboo subjects, she riposted to his quip about listing her faults that outsiders considered him arrogant, ill bred, and unsociable. On more serious topics, she described the hardships of managing their Weymouth home and farm business in his absence. Her letters named shortages of common household necessities that required imaginative substitutions and excoriated the British general John Burgoyne as a master of wickedness. According to the historian Cokie Roberts, author of *Founding Mother: The Women Who Raised Our Nation* (2004), Adams claimed the title of "Sister Delegate" and asked of her husband, "Why should we not assume your titles when we give up our names?," a spirited rebuke to men who take lightly a woman's abandonment of her surname (*ibid.*, 61).

Abigail Adams's more pointed texts denounced SLAVERY, an economic system she abhorred, and expounded on the paltry education offered to girls. Of the latter she proposed a startling innovation: "If we mean to have heroes, statesmen and philosophers, we should have learned women" (*ibid.*, 76). She also supported the career of the poet and pamphleteer Mercy Otis WARREN and asked John Adams to commission an occasional verse from Warren celebrating the Boston Tea Party. At a difficult pass, John acknowledged the tenuous times and requested that Abigail support him in the struggle for liberty and home rule. When he left up to her whether he should return to Congress, she encouraged him to continue the good fight. After the British capture of New York, she promised him that, even if all males were unavailable to protect residences and families, "You would find a race of Amazons in America" (*ibid.*, 77).

On March 31, 1776, Adams, then the mother of two sons and two daughters, spoke directly to the question of equal representation of and for women in the new nation. She phrased to John her concerns that the Constitution ennoble women as free citizens and accord them legal and property rights that would circumvent the absolute power of husbands, whom she compared to political tyrants. Accompanying her polite but firm statement was her warning that American women were sure to rebel if men excluded them from representation in a free society. On April 5, 1776, she predicted that gender discrimination would hinder the fight for freedom: "If Women are not represented in this new republic there will be another revolution" (Adams, "Correspondence").

After her husband's subdued reply, Abigail Adams enlisted Warren in a women's coalition and remarked, "I ventured to speak a word in behalf of our sex, who are rather hardly dealt with by the laws of England," a direct reference to the denial of property ownership to females or the negotiation of contracts by women (*ibid.*). Abigail chided John on May 7 with a stronger prediction that women would not go meekly into arbitrary enslavement to males. After the issuance of the Declaration of Independence, she left her sickbed in Boston after variolation for smallpox by the Sutton method to cheer for the reading of the text from the state house balcony.

Bibliography

"Correspondence between John and Abigail Adams" (1762–1801). Available online. URL: http://www.masshist.org/digitaladams/aea/letter/. Accessed on June 20, 2004.

Roberts, Cokie. *Founding Mother: The Women Who Raised Our Nation.* New York: William Morrow, 2004.

Adcock, Fleur (1934–)

The editor, translator, librettist, and poet Kareen Fleur Adcock concentrates on relationships jeopardized by betrayal and gender inequities. A native of Papakura, New Zealand, and the daughter and sister of writers, she began composing verse at age five. In the mid-1940s she studied in England for 12 years while her parents were involved in the war effort and postwar refugee settlement. She earned an advanced degree in classics at the Victoria University of Wellington. After marrying the Anglo-Polynesian poet Alistair Campbell, she initiated a career in literature and library work. She left one of her two sons behind in 1963 when she obtained a divorce, settled in Dunedin, and married the adventurer Barry Crump, who became abusive and forced an end to their union within five months.

After a second divorce Adcock emigrated to England and served the British Foreign and Commonwealth Office as librarian. The following year, she published her first poetry collection, *The Eye of the Hurricane* (1964). In the early 1980s, when she began writing full time, she earned critical applause for her translation *The Virgin and the Nightingale: Medieval Latin Poems* (1983). In 1988, she edited *The Faber Book of Twentieth Century Women's Poetry*, a collection of verse by the leading feminist writers, including Margaret ATWOOD, Elizabeth BISHOP, Louise BOGAN, H. D., Louise GLÜCK, Maxine KUMIN, Edna St. Vincent MILLAY, Marianne MOORE, Sylvia PLATH, Adrienne RICH, and Stevie SMITH. Adcock produced lyrics for a song cycle and, with the New Zealand composer Gillian Karawe Whitehead, supplied the libretto for the opera *Alice* (2003), a monodrama on the poet's adventuresome great-aunt, who migrated to New Zealand in 1909. For the authenticity of lyrics Adcock drew phrases from family letters. For her skill at feminist scenarios, she earned an Order of the British Empire medal and nomination as England's first female poet laureate.

Although Adcock writes conversationally about her own observations and experiences, her graceful verse applies drollery and irony as means of avoiding too personal an involvement. One example, "Against Coupling" (1971), expresses a woman's distaste for tongue thrusts in the mouth and sexual intercourse, which she describes as the regular enforcement of an "unpleasure" (Adcock, 49). In lucid, but restrained glimpses of male-female intimacy, she compares the boredom of marital duty to the viewing of *The Sound of Music* multiple times or the school drama coach's staging of *A Midsummer Night's Dream* seven years in a row. The fifth stanza advocates masturbation as a casual, unfussy five minutes of self-service.

Bibliography

Adcock, Fleur. *High Tide in the Garden.* Oxford: Oxford University Press, 1971.

Dart, William. "Something to Sing about in 2003," *New Zealand Herald,* 17 December 2003.

Leithauser, Brad. "The Hard Life of the Lyric," *New Republic* (23 May 1988): 30–34.

McDonough, C. J. "Hugh Primas and the Archpoet," *Review of English Studies* 48, no. 189 (February 1997): 80–81.

Age of Innocence, The Edith Wharton (1920)

A Pulitzer Prize winner, *The Age of Innocence* describes the mannered imprisonment of women in late 19th-century New York. Through Classical allusions, Edith WHARTON contrasts social extremes—the chaste, unapproachable Diana with the scandalous woman, a Venusian siren glimpsed at close range in the glow of passion. Opening at the Metropolitan Opera, where polite attendees live vicariously the untidy loves of daring stage figures, the narrative introduces an attorney, Newland Archer, as a dilettante who savors his pleasures while observing the conventions of his time. His illusions about the innocence of women convince him that his intended, the inoffensive May Welland, studies the scandal of Marguerite, the scorned woman in Charles Gounod's *Faust,* but "doesn't even guess what it's all about" (Wharton, 6). Newland's "tender reverence for [May's] abysmal purity" inspires him to fantasize on his role as educator of a virginal bride (*ibid.*). The tutorial role robs him of intimacy with May, whom he never knows as a lover.

Wharton's decades-long saga follows Newland through a DUALITY that reveals an age-old conflict—what society dictates for women and what women would do if there were no sexual taboos. With a quick shift of his opera glasses he views Ellen, Countess Olenska, a risk taker in the 1870s, an age of moral pretense and social hypocrisy. To the author, who lived both the American and the Continental versions of propriety, Ellen's behavior epitomizes European mores, as she flouts convention and risks approbrium by fleeing an unfaithful husband. Ostensibly discreet, in private, she voices outrageous violations of the New York social code, demanding, "Why not make one's own fashions?" (*ibid.,* 72). Repressing longings for the autonomous countess, Newland remains unfulfilled by his role as parent-husband to May. Unrequited passion generates tides of ambivalence in a man who not only misjudges women but also misreckons his own carnal stirrings.

The author's aptitude for nuance and visual effects enlivens the text with contrasting images. After May fails to develop into a "miracle of fire and ice," Newland pursues Ellen up a path at Skuytercliff, the van der Luydens' Hudson River estate, a symbol of precipitate yearnings (*ibid.*, 5). In contrast to her surroundings, the countess takes on the sparkle of fire and ice by appearing like "a red meteor against the snow" (*ibid.*, 132). A beacon of INDEPENDENCE, she delights in self-reclamation: "When I turn back into myself now I'm like a child going at night into a room where there's always a light" (*ibid.*, 173). Newland, who prefers self-blinding to light, persistently preserves his false view of male-female relations. He dreads scandal but admits the liberation example that Ellen sets: "It was you who made me understand that under the dullness there are things so fine and sensitive and delicate that even those I most cared for in my other life looked cheap in comparison" (*ibid.*, 241). Wharton stresses the irony of Newland's gaining of wisdom—he recognizes that women who are like the countess, a modern version of Helen of Troy, flourish in freedom, but he refuses to shed New York's shallow pretenses to share Ellen's self-liberation.

Bibliography

Hadley, Kathy Miller. "Ironic Structures and Untold Stories in 'The Age of Innocence,'" *Studies in the Novel* 23, no. 2 (Summer 1991): 262–272.

Wharton, Edith. *The Age of Innocence.* New York: Modern Library, 1999.

aging

Feminist literature has made headway against the STEREOTYPING of aged or enfeebled women by validating each stage of female life, particularly that of the seasoned WISEWOMEN. The author Antoinette Brown BLACKWELL spoke directly to the issue of uninteresting activities for older women in "A Plea for the Afternoon" (1868), a short story published in the *Atlantic.* She charged that men retained youth longer because they avoided boredom with stimulating interests. The regional novelist Sarah Orne JEWETT, the author of *A Country Doctor* (1884), honored the spinsters and widows of New England by depicting their work and wisdom as cultural pillars. Nan Prince, the motherless protagonist, recalls the steadying influence of Grandmother Thacher, who saw possibilities in her granddaughter. After Nan decides to become a physician, she remembers how Miss Fraley admired Nan's spirit: "I believe every word you said about a girl's having an independence of her own. . . . I do sometimes envy the women who earn what they spend" (Jewett, 224). In the absence of Nan's mother, these women offer the moral backing that Nan needs to defeat the prejudice that labels female doctors as freaks.

Aged females figure in multigenerational immigration fiction about matriarchs from the old country. In *The Promised Land* (1912), a classic memoir serialized in the *Atlantic Monthly*, the Russian-Jewish author Mary ANTIN enlarges domestic PATRIARCHY to national despotism in the depiction of forced obeisance of peasants to Czar Alexander III. Before her move from Polotsk to Boston, she recalls how imperial soldiers enforced laws requiring the display of the czar's picture and how they kicked in the door of an old woman who did not display the flag on the royal birthday. The men sold her only pillow to pay for a pro-czar banner, which they raised over her tattered roof. Similar morphing of patriarchy into tyranny occurs in the Chilean writer Isabel ALLENDE's historical novel *The HOUSE OF THE SPIRITS* (1982) and the Dominican-American author Julia ALVAREZ's *In the Time of the Butterflies* (1994), both of which picture self-important males who trample lone aged women.

Feminist plays from the era of the Harlem Renaissance feature the hardships of lonely old black women living in penury and ill health, often saddled with raising their grandchildren or orphans. The poet and dramatist Katherine Davis Chapman Tillman describes a 70-year-old seamstress's hardships in the one-act dialect play *Aunt Betsy's Thanksgiving* (1914), an idealistic family scenario set in the early weeks of November. At the depths of despair over a broken leg, Betsy can no longer grow vegetables in the garden to feed herself and her granddaughter. She moans, "Lil Ca'line is a mighty heap of company for me, but I spect I'll hab to let 'em take her to de po' house, long side of me, fore many mo' suns'll rise an' set" (Tillman, 301). In the resolution of Betsy's quandary over the impending sale of the cabin she has lived in for 15 years, she encounters Nellie, Caroline's mother, who fled a cruel husband and abandoned Caroline in infancy to Betsy's care. Tillman turns Nellie into a deus ex machina, the last-minute savior of an elderly woman who has nowhere else to turn. The text implies that Betsy deserves rescue for raising her grandchild in a loving, moral environment and for upholding faith that Nellie will one day return.

In the tradition of feminist FRONTIER LITERATURE, the Texas-born short story writer Katherine Anne PORTER depicted a more substantial pioneer wife and mother in "THE JILTING OF GRANNY WEATHERALL" (1930). A monument to female grit, the 80-year-old matriarch battles her internal demons in private with her last breath. Congratulating herself on fencing 100 acres, "sitting up nights with sick horses and sick negroes and sick children," and "[pulling] through milk-leg and double pneumonia," Ellen Weatherall speaks aloud in a floating DREAMSCAPE the intrusion of death on an active life (Porter, 83, 80). The worst of the bedside scenario are the patronizing of Dr. Harry and the discounting of her daughter, Cornelia, who comments that "Mother was getting a little childish and they'd have to humor her" (ibid., 82). Worse than being patronized and scolded is the burden of humiliation that has haunted her for 60 years, since a fiancé named George diminished her womanhood by abandoning her at the altar. Clinging to shreds of consciousness, she mutters, "I'll never forgive it" (ibid., 89). Porter depicts Granny's spite as an element of her humanity, a grudge that reignites her flagging spirit.

A compelling spokeswoman for female dignity, the French philosopher Simone de BEAUVOIR found in the subject of aging a valuable perspective on the denigration of all women. She personalized the issues of growing old in a memoir, La force des choses (Hard Times: Forces of Circumstances, 1963). More dramatic are the tending and nurturing of the aged and dying in a mother-daughter study, Une mort très douce (A Very Easy Death, 1964), which she wrote after the hospitalization and death of her mother. The gradual detachment from life generates a duality in the mother: "A full-blooded, spirited woman lived on inside her, but a stranger to herself, deformed and mutilated [by cancer]" (Beauvoir, 43). In 1970 Beauvoir published La vieillesse (Old Age), a meditation on the contempt with which capitalistic societies treat unproductive elders. From an existential point of view, the author's texts on aging reflect her belief in the conscious enjoyment of each day.

Feminist literature refutes the denigration of old women as nuisances. A traditional griot role of a strong, wise matriarch empowers Toni Cade BAMBARA's "Blues Ain't No Mockin Bird" (1971), a fast-paced short story. It dramatizes the clash between autonomous black folk of the rural South and the county do-gooders who intrude and try to film their home life for a food stamp campaign. Granny Cora Cain protests their rudeness and reduces the humiliation of her grandchildren by relating a parable about an ignoramus filming the anguish of a wife pleading with her suicidal husband, who wants to leap from a bridge. The name Cora suggests the core values of a loving elderly woman who takes in homeless cousins to support them and to raise their self-esteem. Symbolizing her goodness and the long-range promise of her care are the molasses-smelling Christmas cakes she laces with rum.

With fervor equal to that of Porter and Bambara, the feminist Barbara KINGSOLVER salts her texts with defiant elderly women who refute disparagement and relegation to the rocking chair. She includes Great Mam, matriarch of "Homeland" (1989), who "was like an old pine, whose accumulated years cause one to ponder how long it has stood, and not how soon it will fall" (Kingsolver, 6). As an enduring landmark Great Mam instills in her children and grandchildren the importance of Cherokee creeds of humanism and respect for nature. In Animal Dreams (1990) the author's ecofiction assembles a coterie of Hispanic mothers and grandmothers from Grace, Arizona, who make piñatas out of peacock feathers and sell them on the streets of Tucson to raise money for a legal battle against an industrial polluter. Like the

Cumaean Sibyl in Virgil's *Aeneid* (19 B.C.), Viola Domingos explains to Codi Noline, the lone Anglo, the intent of the Black Mountain mine owners to conceal pollution by diverting the river through Tortoise Canyon, thus depriving Grace, Arizona, of water. Led by Doña Althea, the town matriarch, the group displays considerable experience at peddling goods on an urban street. The women return to Grace to offer nurturing motherhood at the free-form funeral for Codi's sister, Hallie, by gathering stories and memorabilia from Hallie's childhood and by erasing Codi's amnesia with painful memories of the death of her mother, Althea "Alice" Noline, of kidney failure when Codi was three years old. The gifts that elder women offer Codi are the essentials that restock her dwindling supply of self-confidence.

Similarly stout-hearted are housekeeper Mama Tataba and Mama Mwanza, the handicapped matriarch of a Congolese family in Kingsolver's masterwork, *The Poisonwood Bible* (1998). Both reflect the domestic experience of living in a jungle setting on the Kwilu River. Mama Tataba experiences the disdain of the Reverend Nathan Price, an American know-it-all who dismisses her knowledge of planting vegetables against monsoon rains and who loses his crop to subsequent torrents. During drought and famine, Mama Mwanza, the village philanthropist, secretly places chickens and eggs in the Prices' hen yard. Female generosity encourages the flow of good deeds to others. The African women's display of patience and domestic expertise instills in Leah Price Ngemba a willingness to learn from nature. She models her domestic skills in a Kinshasa slum and at an Angolan commune. Another example, Nannie Land Rawley, a shorts-clad 70-something orchardist in *Prodigal Summer* (2000), busies herself with the ongoing task of protecting and renewing her natural surroundings.

The Flemish novelist Anne Provoost expresses the human rewards of nursing a handicapped elderly woman. She captures a unique symbiosis in a solemn epic *In the Shadow of the Ark* (2004), an updated biblical scenario similar in style to Anita DIAMANT's development of the matriarchs Rachel and Leah in *The Red Tent* (1997). Provoost fills in the blanks in a male-centered story from Genesis, a patriarchal work offering little insight into women's thoughts, aims, or actions. She retells the story of Noah's ark from the point of view of Re Jana, a female outsider new to the desert. Crucial to her family's retreat from the overflowing marshlands is the possibility of obtaining jobs building the massive ark several weeks' walk inland. As the father worries about employment, Re Jana devotes her waking hours to her mother, a stroke victim who is limited to a blinking left eye, grunts, and moans for communicating with her father. In the scraggly desert, where the only water is from a pond fouled with mud, Re Jana accepts the task of caregiver, a major motif in feminist literature.

While Noah and Re Jana's father focus on the task of shaping wood into a huge boat to save people from an unlikely drowning in the desert, Re Jana remains committed to domestic needs. To ensure her mother's comfort, Re Jana uses a divining rod to search nearby caves for a trickling spring. The tender cleansing of her mother's skin and the preparation of food and refreshing drink dramatize Re Jana's willingness to relieve her mother of needless suffering. It is not until a second death, that of Re Jana's mother-in-law, that the girl can name the qualities of aged women, whom she honors as conciliators and as founts of "knowledge of motherhood" (Provoost, 323).

Bibliography

Babb, Genie. "Paula Gunn Allen's Grandmothers: Toward a Responsive Feminist-Tribal Reading of *Two Old Women*," *American Indian Quarterly* 21, no. 2 (Spring 1997): 299–320.

Beauvoir, Simone de. *A Very Easy Death*. New York: Pantheon, 1985.

Jewett, Sarah Orne. *A Country Doctor*. New York: Bantam, 1999.

Kingsolver, Barbara. *Homeland and Other Stories*. New York: HarperCollins, 1989.

Porter, Katherine Anne. *The Collected Stories of Katherine Anne Porter*. New York: New American Library, 1965.

Provoost, Anne. *In the Shadow of the Ark*. New York: Arthur A. Levine, 2004.

Tillman, Katherine. *Works of Katherine Davis Chapman Tillman*. New York: Oxford University Press, 1991.

Aguilar, Grace (1816–1847)

The London-born theologian, historian, poet, and fiction writer Grace Aguilar enlightened the early Victorian era on behalf of Jewish women. A major Jewish author of her era, she wrote in multiple genres—journal, historical fiction, sermon, translation, travelogue, and lyric mode—and became the first person to compile *A History of the Jews in England*, which she issued in *Chamber's Miscellany* in 1847. Born of Portuguese-Marrano lineage from the Jews who fled Iberia at the end of the 15th century, she grew up in Hackney, where her mother, Sarah Días-Fernandez, provided home schooling and instruction in harp and piano. At age 12, Aguilar wrote an unpublished historical drama, *Gustavus Vasu* (1828), which she based on the enlightened teaching of her father, the merchant and lay rabbi Emmanuel Aguilar, an expert in Sephardic Jewish history. At age 20 she began a literary career with the novella *The Friends: A Domestic Tale* (1934) and followed with her first verse collection, *The Magic Wreath* (1835), and a second novella, *Adah, a Simple Story* (1838), a fictional introduction to Judaism. She also submitted works to a variety of journals—*Hebrew Review, Jewish Chronicle,* and *Keepsake.*

Aguilar refused to let illness or social barriers impede her work or her activism for WOMEN'S RIGHTS. She compiled *The Spirit of Judaism* (1842) to express her belief in equal education for Jewish girls. At her father's death, she made a living from writing, beginning with *The Women of Israel: Character Sketches from the Holy Scriptures and Jewish History* (1844), a two-volume collection of biographies of Caleb's daughter, Herod's wife Berenice, EVE, Hannah, Naomi, and other figures intended to arouse female pride in culture and heritage. Dipping into the Midrash, a typically male domain, she recovered history of biblical and Talmudic heroines in three segments: wives of patriarchs, women of the Exodus, and women under the Jewish monarchy. As an example of Hebrew female strength, she extolled Deborah for her intellect, logic, and self-control. Overall, the book elevated women from domestic drudges and underlings to conveyors of Jewish oral tradition, which authorities of the Inquisition jeopardized by closing Jewish schools and synagogues. In 1845, Aguilar's poem "Festival of Purim" singled out Queen Esther as

another example of heroism. The poet pictured her as good and beautiful as well as alert: "She sent fleet messengers, that Israel should not die" (Aguilar, 1845).

Two years later, Aguilar turned to didactic domestic themes. She wrote a semiautobiographical novel, *Home Influence, a Tale for Mothers and Daughters* (1847), a moralistic rescue story set in Wales that portrays a daughter's sacrifice for the sake of her brother. The theme expresses the family's androcentrism in valuing him above her. Publication preceded an award from Anglo-Jewish females who admired the author's feminist stance. The book was Aguilar's only work published in her lifetime, which ended at age 31 during a trip to Frankfurt, where the onset of convulsions worsened her lung condition. Issued posthumously, the sequel, *The Mother's Recompense* (1851), appeared the same year as *Woman's Friendship* (1851), a salute to SISTERHOOD among females who value feminine character. Two other late publications remained in print throughout the 19th century: *Days of Bruce* (1852) and *The Vale of Cedars; or, The Martyr—a Story of Spain in the Fifteenth Century* (1874), a popular historical novel on the martyrdom of Doña Marie, a crypto-Jew among Queen Isabella's ladies in waiting. After the Inquisition discloses Marie's faith, torture quickly saps her strength, but not her resolve. In a dramatic conclusion, Isabella chooses sisterhood over orthodoxy by exhorting her female courtiers: "Are ye women? . . . or are we deceived as to the meaning of your words? Pollution! Are we to see a young, unhappy being perish for want of sympathy and succor, because—forsooth—she is a Jewess?" (Aguilar, 1874). Although the queen absolves Marie of concealing her faith, the maiden dies of her wounds.

Bibliography

Aguilar, Grace. "Festival of Purim" (1845). Available online. URL: http://www.jewish-history.com/Occident/volume3/aug1845/stanzas.html. Accessed on October 13, 2005.

———. *The Frankfurt Journal of Grace Aguilar* (1847). Available online. URL: http://www.familyhistory.fsnet.co.uk/aguilar/The%20Frankfurt%20Jornal%20of%20Grace%20Aguilar.htm. Accessed on October 13, 2005.

———. *Grace Aguilar: Selected Writings.* New York: Broadview, 2003.

———. *The Vale of Cedars* (1874). Available online. URL: http://www.abacci.com/books/book.asp?bookID=4233. Accessed on October 13, 2005.

———. *Women of Israel* (1844). Available online. URL: http://aleph.haifa.ac.il/F/?func=find-b&find_code=SYS&request=1015236. Accessed on October 13, 2005.

Kerker, Milton. "Grace Aguilar, a Woman of Israel," *Midstream* 47, no. 1 (February 2001): 35.

Lauter, Devorah. "Out-of-Print Victorian Feminist Worth a Second Read." *Jewish Bulletin of Northern California,* 107, no. 35 (5 September 2003): 34.

Aidoo, Ama Ata (1942–)

The works of the Ghanaian playwright, poet, and teacher Christina Ama Ata Aidoo expose the despotism of Africa's patriarchal roots. Born a chief's daughter in Abeadzi Kyiakor, she had a proud heritage and grew up in a royal compound. During the nation's struggle for freedom, she was educated at the University of Ghana and, under the influence of evolving concepts of freedom, wrote her first short fiction in her undergraduate years. In 1965 she published the whimsical courtship comedy *The Dilemma of a Ghost,* which dramatizes the cultural clash of native customs with competing Western values. At the climax, Eulalie Rush saves the family through her witty patter. In a reworking of the "Whither thou goest" speech from the biblical book of Ruth, the playwright contrasts the humble Jewish heroine to the outspoken Ghanaian mother who demands respect.

Education gave Aidoo the tools to become a force for good. After completing her education at Stanford, she came under the mentorship of Efua Sutherland, founder of the Ghana Drama Studio. As minister of education Aidoo later applied her vision of literacy and knowledge to the elevation of rural Ghanaian women. As she explained in an interview, her motives were nationalistic: "The decay of Africa's social, political, and economic systems is directly related to the complete marginalization of women from developmental discourses" (Needham 123). She asserted that equality in learning and opportunity could save sub-Saharan Africa.

In a period of rapid social and economic change, Aidoo settled in Zimbabwe and began challenging the abasement of African women with vernacular writings that equate the ravages of imperialism with the destructiveness of sexism. Her strongest feminist themes enliven the song play *Anowa* (1970), which depicts a young woman's rebellion against feudal marriage by choosing a man whom she can help to achieve a good life. An opinionated crone honors the spunky Anowa, a representative of Africa's NEW WOMAN, for listening to her own tales, chuckling at her own jokes, and following her own advice. In the last scene Anowa describes traditional female SILENCING under old-style marriage: "In order for her man to be a man, she must not think, she must not talk" (Aidoo, *1987,* 64). Aidoo followed with the semiautobiographical novel *Our Sister Killjoy; or, Reflections from a Black-Eyed Squint* (1977) and verse collected in *Someone Talking to Sometime* (1985). She won the Commonwealth Writers Prize for her second novel, *Changes: A Love Story* (1991), a sympathetic portrait of Esi, a dissatisfied wife who seeks a loving, equitable relationship after a brutal marital rape.

Unlike Western feminist writers who decry inequality in politics and workplace sexism experienced by career women, Aidoo focuses on the grassroots frustrations of rural wives and mothers, the hardships of feeding a family, and the terrors of domestic abuse. In 1995 the FEMINIST PRESS reprinted her collection of 11 stories, *No Sweetness Here* (1970), a survey of African women's lives during a time of a dizzying cultural shift to Western values and behavior. Her style relies heavily on the oral ambience of the Fanti language and a blend of prose with lyric verse. A standout story, "Something to Talk about on the Way to the Funeral," ponders the age-old dilemma of the pregnant woman whose lover is too immature to commit to marriage and family.

Bibliography
Aidoo, Ama Ata. *The Dilemma of a Ghost and Anowa: Two Plays.* Harlow, England: Longman, 1987.

———. "Feminist Furore," *New Internationalist* 336 (July 2001): 5.

———. "The Message." In *Women of the Third World: Twenty Stories Set in Africa, Asia, and Latin America.* London: Victor Gollancz, 1975.

———. *No Sweetness Here and Other Stories.* New York: Feminist Press, 1995.

Elia, Nada. " 'To Be an African Working Woman': Levels of Feminist Consciousness in Ama Ata Aidoo's *Changes,*" *Research in African Literatures* 30, no. 2 (Summer 1999): 136–147.

Needham, Anuradha Dingwa. "An Interview with Ama Ata Aidoo," *Massachusetts Review* 36, no. 1 (Spring 1995): 123–133.

Wilentz, Gay. *Emerging Perspective on Ama Ata Aidoo.* Lawrenceville, N.J.: Africa World Press, 2003.

"Ain't I a Woman?" Sojourner Truth (1851)

A poignant event of the WOMEN'S RIGHTS convention in Akron, Ohio, the testimonial of the former slave Sojourner TRUTH reduced the era's feminist outlook to the basics. The electric moment was her delivery of "Ain't I a Woman?" a five-paragraph presentation reported in the June 21, 1851, issue of the Salem, Ohio, *Anti-Slavery Bugle.* The delegate Frances Dana Gage, who recorded the speech on site, published a more familiar version in her "Reminiscences" (1863), reissued in volume one of *History of Woman Suffrage* (1881–86). In terse I-thou form, the 56-year-old abolitionist Sojourner Truth challenges the gendered traditions for platform oratory to reveal the tribulations of a plantation "breeder." With unself-conscious dialect, she dramatizes an absurdity of mid-19th-century manners, according to which males aid white women into carriages and over puddles but exclude enslaved females from gendered courtesies. Her prowoman advocacy dismantles the specious rationale that white women deserve genteel treatment because they are white and female, but that black women rate no such proprieties.

Distancing herself from the china dolls of the white world, the famed orator examines women's innate strengths through a series of rhetorical questions. She plows, plants, and harvests on a par with male field hands while filling her plate with an equal amount of food and building an appreciably muscular frame. Like a man, she also withstands the overseer's lash, a punishment meted out to male and female slaves. The gendered divide that sets her apart from male slaves are the motherly tears that fall after the sale of most of her 13 children. Her statement implies that enslaved fathers develop less emotional attachment and suffer fewer regrets at seeing their offspring auctioned or traded like livestock.

Although uneducated except in her exposure to pulpit sermons, Sojourner Truth deftly segues to oratorical summation in her choice of Scripture as proof of her thesis. Sweeping aside quibbles about the intelligence of women and blacks, she demands female rights for all women. She concludes her diatribe with a reference to the VIRGIN MARY, who bore Jesus, a child conceived by the almighty without the contribution of human male sperm. Noting the power of EVE to subvert the ideals of Eden, Sojourner Truth rallies her hearers to continue overturning the androcentric world.

Bibliography

Truth, Sojourner. *Narrative of Sojourner Truth: A Bondswoman of Olden Time.* New York: Penguin, 1998.

Zackodnik, Teresa C. " 'I Don't Know How You Will Feel When I Get Through' ": Racial Difference, Women's Rights, and Sojourner Truth," *Feminist Studies* 30, no. 1 (Spring 2004): 49–73.

Akhmatova, Anna (1889–1966)

The Ukrainian poet Anna Akhmatova viewed a complex era of European history through the eyes of dispossessed Russian women. Named Anna Andreyevna Gorenko at birth at Bolshoy Fontan near Odessa, she claimed Russo-Ukrainian lineage. She grew up outside Saint Petersburg, where her mother recited to her children passionate verse about the oppression of women. The poet completed her education at a gymnasium near Kiev. Because preprofessional lectures at the Kiev College for Women bored her, she dismayed her father by choosing to write poetry rather than practice law. At age 22 she adopted her pseudonym, the surname of a family matriarch related to the chieftain Akhmat Khan, the last Tatar leader to defy the Russian czar.

Akhmatova's energies directed her talents in numerous intellectual spheres. She submitted poems to *Sirius*, a journal edited by her husband. After a sojourn in Paris, she established a literary salon in Saint Petersburg. In 1912 she published *Evening*, a verse collection that surveys the stages of love, from infatuation to disillusion. She chose a variety of female characters as points of view, including one whose husband lashes her with a belt. In the double quatrain "It's Strange to Remember" (1911), the poet objects to being treated as a carnal plaything. The poet's interest in female piety and chastity colored *Rosary* (1914), which includes "You Know, I Languish in Captivity" and "We Are All Carousers and Loose Women Here." During World War I, while her husband served in the Russian army, she produced *At the Edge of the Sea* (1915), a long elegy to the passing of girlhood. In 1917, she published *White Flock*, an anthology that reflects her views on world war and on the internal war with herself over her adultery. For *Anno Domini MCMXXI* (1921), she composed poetic portraits of Old Testament women—Lot's wife, Rachel, and Michal, David's first wife.

During the Stalinist regime, Akhmatova survived food shortages, threats, the imprisonment of her son, and the execution of her husband. A private person, she cloaked her emotions in a poetic cycle, *Winds of War* (1946), to hide her anxiety about threats to free speech. On the value of poetry under the oppressive Marxist government, she wrote, "Lyric verse is the best armor, the best cover. You don't give yourself away" (Akhmatova, 2000, 7). In 1946, Communist authorities suppressed Akhmatova's work. When Khrushchev attained power in 1953, her poetry was again available. She earned praise for writing the truth about an era of torture and exile. The poet Yevgeny Yevtushenko wrote a tribute to her: "How could we weep? . . . Alive, / she was beyond belief. / How could she die?" (Brody, 704). Critics honor her as one of the greatest female poets in literary history.

Bibliography

Akhmatova, Anna. *The Complete Poems of Anna Akhmatova.* Brookline, Mass.: Zephyr Press, 1998.
———. *Selected Poems of Anna Akhmatova.* Brookline, Mass.: Zephyr Press, 2000.
Brody, Ervin C. "The Poet in the Trenches: *The Complete Poems of Anna Akhmatova,*" *Literary Review* 37, no. 4 (Summer 1994): 689–704.
Pettingell, Phoebe. "Anna of All Rus." *New Leader* 77 (19 December 1995): 26–27.

Alcott, Louisa May (1832–1888)

A gentle spokeswoman for the rights of women, Louisa May "Lu" Alcott and Harriet Beecher STOWE were the two best-selling female artists to flourish in the literary market alongside the New England giants Nathaniel Hawthorne and Herman Melville. Born in Germantown, Pennsylvania, to a social worker, Abigail "Abba" May, and Amos Bronson Alcott, a transcendentalist, reformer, and commune founder, Louisa grew up at the Wayside Inn and acquired from her father the progressive notion of child-centered education. After training at his school, she gained wisdom from firsthand encounters with the Boston-Concord intelligentsia—Ralph Waldo Emerson, Margaret FULLER, James Russell Lowell, Henry David Thoreau, and Julia Ward. Resettled in Boston at age 17 Alcott welcomed the freedom of spinsterhood and the comfort of creative solitude. She began supporting her family with various jobs—tailor, laundress, housekeeper, tutor, writer, and editor of *Merry's Museum*, which featured submissions by Anna Laetitia BARBAULD, Lydia Maria CHILD, Felicia HEMANS, and Sarah Orne JEWETT.

Alcott admired the writing woman and mentioned in her diary her delight in meeting Rebecca Harding DAVIS, author of *Life in the Iron Mills* (1861). Alcott confided, "I told her I had had lots of troubles, so I write jolly tales; and we wondered why we each did so" (Alcott, 1928, 106). After entering the freelance market with a submission to *Peterson's Magazine*, under a variety of pen names Alcott cranked out melodrama, mysteries, a Faustian plot, and Gothic potboilers for three magazines—*Flag of Our Union*, *American Union*, and *Atlantic Monthly*—and for newspapers and dime novels. At age 25 she returned to her family, who made their first permanent home at Orchard House in Concord. Her writings ventured from commercial romance and horror to ABOLITIONISM, the dignity of domestic work, and WOMEN'S

RIGHTS to full citizenship. She also supplied suffragist and TEMPERANCE essays to Lucy STONE, editor of *Woman's Journal*. A suffragist, she was the first woman to register to vote in Concord. She canvassed neighborhoods encouraging women to take part in the election process and supported Harriet Hanson ROBINSON in the publication of *Massachusetts in the Woman Suffrage Movement* (1881).

Alcott volunteered in Washington, D.C., at the Union Hospital for two months, until the onset of typhoid sent her home. Despite hallucinations and flashbacks of exhausting ward duty, she felt invigorated by personal involvement in the nurse corps. She lauded the courage of Dorothea Dix, the first woman appointed to a major governmental department. Upon recovery, Alcott published the Gothic novel *Pauline's Passion and Punishment* (1862), under the pen name A. M. Barnard. She serialized her letters home in *Commonwealth* and issued them in book form as *Hospital Sketches* (1863), a valuable eyewitness account of female efforts on behalf of the wounded.

Although Alcott never regained robust health, she turned out feminist fiction at a rapid rate, including *Moods* (1865), in which she states women's need for self-cultivation: "The duty we owe ourselves is greater than that we owe others" (Alcott, 1991, 28). In 1873, she wrote a utopian meditation on the failed Fruitlands commune in "Transcendental Wild Oats," issued in the *Independent*, in which she condemned male utopian ideals for demanding unacknowledged female labor. At a climactic moment Alcott states the gendered roles in the grand scheme: "So 'mother's lamp' burned steadily, while the philosophers built a new heaven and earth by moonlight" (Alcott 1873). In the final line, a knowing wife remarks to a dispirited husband on Fruitlands's collapse: "Don't you think Apple Slump would be a better name for it, dear?" (*ibid.*).

For all her polemical efforts Alcott is best known for a realistic overview of teenagers' life in the mid-1800s. Her fortunes improved with the popularity of the autobiographical novels LITTLE WOMEN (1868–69) and *Little Men* (1871), wholesome domestic stories that gave her celebrity and her family substantial royalties. She characterized the growing up years of girls, their schooling, home training in deportment and morals, adolescent psy-

chology, and incipient feminism. Revolutionary concepts crop up in her depiction of girls growing into adulthood, notably gentle reproofs of Victorian prudery and the value of assertiveness and individuality in girls, particularly her protagonist Jo March, Alcott's alter ego, who channels strong passions into composition. Through Jo in *Little Women* and later through Christie Devon in *Work: A Story of Experience* (1871), Alcott promotes the satisfaction of an outside career and financial independence for women. She also validates the need for male-female relationships to prepare a woman for the selection of a worthy mate, for example, Jo's friendship with the fatherly, philosophical Professor Friedrich Bhaer, whom Jo eventually marries. The warmth and optimism of the fictional March family and the bond of SISTERHOOD of the four March girls have served four film versions as well as stage adaptations and audio readings of the classic novel. Alcott's writing has influenced generations of feminists, including the ecofeminist Barbara KINGSOLVER.

Bibliography

Alcott, Louisa May. *Louisa May Alcott, Her Life, Letters, and Journals*. Boston: Little, Brown, 1928.

———. *Moods*. Piscataway, N.J.: Rutgers University Press, 1991.

———. "Transcendental Wild Oats" (1873). Available online. URL: http://www.vcu.edu/engweb/transcendentalism/ideas/wildoats.html. Accessed on October 13, 2005.

Bernstein, Susan Naomi. "Writing and Little Women: Alcott's Rhetoric of Subversion," *ATQ* 7, no. 1 (March 1993): 25–43.

Keyser, Elizabeth Lennox. *Whispers in the Dark: The Fiction of Louisa May Alcott*. Knoxville: University of Tennessee Press, 1993.

Moers, Ellen. *Literary Women*. New York: Oxford University Press, 1977.

Allende, Isabel (1942–)

The expatriate Latina journalist and social critic Isabel Allende is a leading figure in feminist writings protesting elitism, racism, and sexism. Born to Tomás Allende, a Chilean legate, and his upper-class wife in Lima, Peru, Isabel grew up in a Catholic household in Santiago, Chile, from age three; traveled to Bolivia and Lebanon with her mother and stepfather; and studied at a Swiss boarding school. She began a writing career as a television interviewer, translator, magazine columnist, feature writer, and editor for *Paula* and *Mampato*. In rebellion against Christian dogma, she pursued occult knowledge by learning native rituals and by summoning the dead in seances. She achieved global recognition after publishing a best-selling female Gothic novel, *La casa de los espíritus* (The HOUSE OF THE SPIRITS, 1982), which is set in the repressive era of the dictator Augusto Pinochet. Drawn from the STORYTELLING of her grandparents in Santiago, the text condemns a rigid class system that fosters a grim domestic scenario. The fictional conflict derives from male dominance and adultery that escalate into torture-chamber rape and imprisonment of female dissidents.

From her initial success, Allende continued paralleling social and political powerlessness and domestic brutality with *De amor y de sombra* (*Of Love and Shadows*, 1984), which portrays the function of the crusading newspaperwoman Irene Beltrán in revealing Pinochet's graft and political double-dealing. With the aid of a photographer Irene uncovers a Chilean nightmare, the concealment in an abandoned mine of the remains of people kidnapped and murdered as an expedient of the monstrous regime. After settling in California with her second husband, Allende wrote a third narrative, *Eva Luna* (1987), which follows an imaginative orphan who survives on the proceeds of storytelling. The novel spawned *Los cuentos de Eva Luna* (*The Stories of Eva Luna*, 1990), a collection featuring feminist themes. It pictures sadism in the burying of Azucena in mud in "And of Clay Are We Created," a tale made more horrific by a male rescuer's failure to free her. Another story, "Two Words," exalts the itinerant female storyteller as the conveyor of culture. She is so armored by her calling that she risks crossing the desert without water and embraces the wonder of words that elevates a would-be president among voters.

At a tragic turn in her life Allende composed *Paula* (1991), a hymn to memory and a tribute to her firstborn, who was diagnosed with porphyria, a genetic anomaly, at a Madrid hospital. While watching over Paula during the child's 12-month coma, the author charted changes in the girl's condition and interwove anecdotes, one-sided conversations, and events from family history. In 1998, Allende abandoned straight narrative to compose *Aphrodite, A Memoir of the Senses*, an erotic fantasy of mystic visions, love amulets, and sensual memories. That same year, she won a signal honor, the Sara Lee Frontrunner in the Arts Award, which praised her as a pacesetter for Latina writers. The historical fiction in Allende's female quest novel, *Daughter of Fortune* (1999), carries Eliza Sommers, a doorstep foundling and adventurer, and her friend, Tao Chi'en, from Valparaíso, Chile, to San Francisco during the 1849 Gold Rush. In the style of FRONTIER LITERATURE, the rambunctious, decidedly male environment offers independence to self-confident female cooks, healers, merchants, innkeepers, and prostitutes.

Allende returned to memoir with *Mi país inventado* (*My Invented Country: A Nostalgic Journey through Chile*, 2003), which recaps a tempestuous national history and the themes of dictatorship and repressive racism and class structure. Of women's lot, she recalls, "I grew up in a patriarchal family in which my grandfather was like God: infallible, omniscient, and omnipotent" (Allende 2003, 29). Unawed by iconic males, her grandmother trailed the Chilean Nazi Party hurling tomatoes. Allende generalizes that most Chilean women are martyrs to family and home, but she asserts that they are liberated and more interesting than men: "Free and well organized, they keep their maiden names when they marry, they compete head to head in the workforce and not only manage their families but frequently support them" (*ibid.*). She asserts that Chilean women are accustomed to absentee husbands and that they trace their ancestry to the raped and humiliated Indian females seized by the *conquistadores*. This matrilineage accounts in part for the author's staunch feminism and defense of the underclass.

Bibliography

Allende, Isabel. *My Invented Country*. New York: HarperCollins, 2003.

———. "Pinochet's Ghost," *New Perspectives Quarterly* 16, no. 3 (Spring 1999): 22–26.

Foreman, Gabrielle. "Past-on Stories: History and the Magically Real, Morrison and Allende on Call," *Feminist Studies* 18, no. 2 (Summer 1992): 369–388.

Roof, Maria. "Maryse Conde and Isabel Allende: Family Saga Novels," *World Literature Today* 70, no. 2 (Spring 1996): 283–288.

Allen, Paula Gunn (1939–)

A writer, educator, and lecturer, Paula Gunn Allen has set standards for feminist and lesbian literature and for the reclamation of women's preservation and furtherance of the oral tradition. A Laguna-Sioux author from Albuquerque, New Mexico, Allen spent her childhood in a matriarchal society in the hamlet of Cubero and studied at Christian academies. With a background in English literature and creative writing, she earned a doctorate in American studies from the University of New Mexico and taught in California. Key to her success as a spokeswoman for feminism is her reverence for tribal WISEWOMEN and authors of indigenous female narrative: "They were great sorceresses, divine shamans. They brought life to the planet, they became the planet. This is the power of the feminine" (Horrigan, 128).

Allen is a visible spokeswoman for sexual liberty. She championed the Native American tolerance of gay women with the essay "Beloved Women: Lesbians in American Indian Cultures," published in *Conditions* in 1982. That same year, she posed her vision of native rhythms and imagery in *Shadow Country*, a verse anthology that received an honorarium from the Before Columbus Foundation. She challenged the Eurocentrism of the feminist movement with a landmark essay, "Who Is Your Mother: Red Roots of White Feminism," issued in *Sinister Wisdom* in 1984. Her leadership introduced activism to a generation of uninvolved Indian women.

Allen skillfully merged the journey and vision quest with lesbianism in the novel *The Woman Who Owned the Shadows* (1983), which explores the unique social position of the southwestern medicine woman. The protagonist, Ephanie, suffers displacement of gender, race, status, and name. Suitably, her name lacks one syllable to be *epiphany*. The ambiguity of the title image refers to a place of withdrawal and reunion with the dead as well as an occluded atmosphere of fear and sexual misidentity. Allen sympathizes with the outcast female, whose double consciousness as woman and lesbian threatens mental collapse. Ephanie's rescue results from immersion in the mythic past, which heals by granting her balance and full womanhood after decades of self-abandonment.

Allen's achievements have heaped honors on a unique branch of Western feminism. She earned an American Book Award and a Ford Foundation grant for *Spider Woman's Granddaughters: Traditional Tales and Contemporary Writing by Native American Women* (1990), a collection of tales and sketches that honors the voices of Indian wisewomen as culture keepers and storytellers. Deepening her interest in the female point of view is her research in *Grandmother of the Light: A Medicine Woman's Sourcebook* (1991), which reveals mythic knowledge and spirituality among native female mystics. In 2003, Allen became the first Native American scholar to correct romantic notions of the colonial era with a biography, *Pocahontas: Medicine Woman, Spy, Entrepreneur, Diplomat*. In Allen's historical account Pocahontas was a young wisewoman in the making, who sought her "manito—her sacred medicine power, her connection to the Great Spirits" (Allen, 3).

Bibliography

Allen, Paula Gunn. *Pocahontas: Medicine Woman, Spy, Entrepreneur, Diplomat*. New York: HarperCollins, 2003.

Donovan, Kathleen M. *Feminist Readings of Native American Literature: Coming to Voice*. Tucson: University of Arizona Press, 1998.

Horrigan, Bonnie J. *Red Moon Passage: The Power and Wisdom of Menopause*. New York: Harmony Books, 1996.

Allison, Dorothy (1949–)

Dorothy Gibson Allison champions unflinching free speech as an antidote to the hidden pain and dehumanization of the poor. The firstborn of a single 14-year-old mother in Greenville, South Carolina, the author grew up in shame and despair because of the sexual predations of her drunken, abusive stepfather. In retrospect she admitted of the Gibson clan, "We were not noble, not grateful, not even hopeful" (Burton-Hardee, 243). She won a National Merit Scholarship that paid her tuition to Florida Presbyterian College, the beginning of her self-liberation. The women's movement gave her a new view on life and purpose by separating her from a destructive clan environment in which name-proud relatives shunned her as the illegitimate pariah. In renegade style, she expressed her lesbianism in a verse collection, *The Women Who Hate Me* (1983), and through regional short fiction in *Trash* (1988), in which she confronts the Ma and Pa Kettle stereotype of the agrarian South.

A self-proclaimed Zen Baptist redneck, Allison outed the past in a wrenching AUTOBIOGRAPHY. With the publication of *Bastard Out of Carolina* (1992), a fierce overview of the physical and emotional want in her alter ego, Bone Boatwright, the author garnered critical accolades along with the Ferro Grumley and Bay Area Book Reviewers citations and a nomination for a National Book Award. The poignant portrait of Bone's unwed mother arises from images of silent suffering: "Under that biscuit-crust exterior she was all butter grief and hunger, that more than anything else in the world she wanted someone strong to love her like she loved her girls" (Allison, 1993, 10). Countering maternal love is the stepfather's possessive rage. Bone recalls, "I heard the sound of the belt swinging up, a song in the air, a high-pitched terrible sound" (*ibid.*, 106). In 1996, the director Anjelica Houston filmed the novel for Showtime with unblinking revelations of a household ruled by a sadist.

Allison's writings continue to earn popular and critical praise. A slender collection of autobiographical short pieces, *Two or Three Things I Know for Sure* (1995), received a *New York Times Book Review* commendation and additional recognition as a Public Broadcasting System (PBS) documentary. The text studies a peasantry Allison identifies as "the lower orders, the great unwashed, the working class, the poor, proletariat, trash, lowlife and scum" (Allison, 1996, 1). From an initial degradation, she builds on the endurance of poor

southern survivors, the women who run away—"A witch queen, a warrior maiden, a woman with a canvas suitcase, a daughter with broken bones" (*ibid.*, 4). Both raw and elegant, the lyric narrative that follows derives from a womanly oral tradition that preserves the courage of a legendary few who escape.

In the same vein of bold confessional is Allison's second novel, *Cavedweller* (1998), an encomium to redemptive SISTERHOOD and motherhood, which won the Lambda Literary Award and a nomination for the Lillian Smith Prize. The story chronicles the suppressed rage that empowers the protagonist rock singer Delia Byrd "to go back to Cayro and fight those crazy people for her daughters" (Allison, 1999, 6). The epic struggle to reintegrate her family concludes tenderly with Delia's exclamation, "It's time for some new songs" (*ibid.*, 434). Her choice of music to celebrate reunion exemplifies women's needs for artistic outlet.

Bibliography

Allison, Dorothy. *Bastard Out of Carolina.* New York: Plume Books, 1993.

———. *Cavedweller.* New York: Plume Books, 1999.

———. *Two or Three Things I Know for Sure.* New York: Plume Books, 1996.

Bouson, J. Brooks. " 'You Nothing But Trash': White Trash Shame in Dorothy Allison's *Bastard Out of Carolina,*" *Southern Literary Journal* 34, no. 1 (Fall 2001): 101–123.

Burton-Hardee, C. "Red Dirt Girl as Hero: Dorothy Allison's *Cavedweller* as Southern White Trash Hero," *Journal of American and Comparative Cultures* 25, no. 3/4 (Fall 2002): 243–245.

Alvarez, Julia (1950–)

The Dominican-American poet and novelist Julia Alvarez captures the integrity and inner strengths of women who fight back. Born in New York City and reared in the Dominican Republic during Generalissimo Rafael Trujillo's despotic rule, she remained aliterate in an overwhelmingly oral Caribbean culture. Her parents, members of a lost generation that tried to oust the dictator, had to flee for their lives in August 1960. A U.S. immigrant at age 10, she wandered an English-speaking world that overwhelmed her. Her favorite retreat from the wearying translation of New York City's babble was the world of imagination.

After earning an M.A. in literature from Syracuse University, Alvarez wrote while earning a living on staff at her alma mater, Middlebury College. In 1991, she made a splash in the American fiction market with her first novel, *How the García Girls Lost Their Accent,* winner of the PEN Oakland/ Josephine Miles Award. Glimmers of Hispanic feminism add gravity to the lighthearted story of a widow and her four daughters. A dominant motif is the unfaithfulness of Dominican husbands. In a structured time frame, women prepare dinner for husbands who enjoy late afternoon Happy Hour, which extends into "Whore Hour . . . the hour during which a Dominican male of a certain class stops in on his mistress on his way home to his wife" (Alvarez, 1992, 7). Because of the long tradition of husbandly philandering, islanders accept it as a standard of male behavior.

After settling in Champlain Valley, Vermont, Alvarez devoted herself to writing and to a new type of teaching at Alta Gracía, a Dominican farm center that offers literacy training. In subsequent publications, journal style invigorates the verisimilitude of two works of historical fiction, *In the Time of the Butterflies* (1994) and *In the Name of Salomé* (2002), paired histories of the author's Caribbean home. The author based the protagonists of the first work on real heroines—the martyr Dr. Minerva Mirabal de Tavarez and her sisters, Patria Mercedes Mirabal de Gonzalez and Maria Teresa Mirabal de Guzman, who died grotesquely after Trujillo's thugs gunned them down on the roadside as they drove to a distant prison to visit their jailed husbands. The second title features the poet Salomé Ureña de Henriquez, a late 19th-century crusader for women's education during a period of blatant government corruption.

Often compared to themes in Isabel ALLENDE's historical novel *THE HOUSE OF THE SPIRITS* (1982), Alvarez's prospectus on courage and SISTERHOOD melds into a sustaining force against social and political SILENCING. She pictures a brash patriotism in Minerva Mirabal, the lead *mariposa* (butterfly), who defies her parents by plotting against the dictatorship. She retorts to

her father's slap that she no longer respects him. After he sags with a sigh, she experiences a feminist epiphany: "I was much stronger than Papá, Mamá was much stronger. He was the weakest one of all" (Alvarez, 1994, 89). In a journal entry to the Organization of American States (OAS) Committee Investigating Human Rights Abuses, a nameless prisoner reports torture by a man she called Bug Eye, who wields a cattle prod: "When he touched me with it, my whole body jumped with exquisite pain. I felt my spirit snapping loose" (*ibid.,* 255). In honor of the Mirabal sisters' courage in forming underground cells against the Trujillo government, the United Nations declared November 25 the International Day against Violence against Women.

Bibliography

Alvarez, Julia. *How the Garcia Girls Lost Their Accents.* New York: Plume, 1992.
———. *In the Time of the Butterflies.* Chapel Hill, N.C.: Algonquin, 1994.
Pulio, Gus. "Remembering and Reconstructing the Mirabal Sisters in Julia Alvarez's *In the Time of the Butterflies,*" *Bilingual Review* 23, no. 1 (January–April 1998): 11–20.

American Woman's Home, The Catharine Beecher (1869)

Catharine Beecher, the initiator of domestic science, expressed the nobility of home arrangement, care, and management in *The American Woman's Home, or Principles of Domestic Science,* the nation's first best-selling handbook on household arts. As an expression of her upbringing by the Reverend Lyman Beecher, one of the great pulpit ministers of the 19th century, she added a pious subtitle: "Being a Guide to the Formation and Maintenance of Economical, Healthful, Beautiful, and Christian Homes." Brimming with progressive ideals and respect for women's intelligence and creativity, the text honors those who concentrated their energies on bettering the life of their family. She stressed that women were not born knowing how to set up and run a home. The work required ingenuity, devotion, and a measure of sacrifice, but not at the cost of health and longevity.

With the aid and advice of her sister, Harriet Beecher STOWE, Catharine Beecher promoted efficiency by comparing kitchen management to the operation of a ship's galley. By reducing the unwieldy size and waste of the average farm or boardinghouse kitchen and pantry, she lightened a day's cookery, food preservation and service, and cleanup. Her vision of a work-saving house plan placed the dumbwaiter near the woodbox, coal scuttle, and furnace and recommended a mechanical self-emptying grate. The laundry tubs she situated near the water supply to limit unnecessary steps and lifting. She appended warnings about grease fires, flues, and carbon monoxide. Although the Beecher sisters wrote a century and a quarter before the women's movement, their advice ennobled home skills as valuable to the health and safety of Americans. Simultaneously, the sisters suggested alternative careers for women in hotel and hospital kitchen management, appliance and housewares demonstration, and the compilation of recipe books and home economics textbooks.

Bibliography

Hoy, Suellen. *Chasing Dirt: The American Pursuit of Cleanliness.* New York: Oxford University Press, 1995.

Hymowitz, Carol, and Michael E. Weissman. *A History of Women in America.* New York: Bantam Books, 1978.

Weisman, Leslie Kanes. *Discrimination by Design: A Feminist Critique of the Man-Made Environment.* Urbana: University of Illinois Press, 1994.

"Ancient Airs and Dances"   Denise Levertov (1992)

A selection from *Evening Train* (1992), Denise LEVERTOV's 20th poetry anthology, "Ancient Airs and Dances" is one of 84 collected poems describing the writer amid an era of external pressures and internal change. In a two-stage internal monologue, the poem speaks in first person a mature woman's handling of unbefitting physical desire. In the first stave, she admits to being too old for naiveté, yet too willful to halt a romantic gesture, the kissing of a man's wineglass. The self betrays her by splitting into wrangling voices, the

youth versus its admonishing parent. As a teenager experiences passion for the first time, she gives in to the impulse, yet smiles at herself for the déjà vu of past romances. When the unnamed male takes her to visit friends, she sleeps apart on a rainy night and watches the dying fire. Levertov relives the experience through sense impressions of the drumming rain and glowing embers, reminders that a beating heart and impulsive libido render her sleepless and questing.

Levertov's dialogue between mind and body reprises a time-honored motif, the courtship dance. The speaker rouses from sexual complacency to rein in impulses that advancing age fails to quell. She experiences an epiphany—that gray hair does not prohibit the active mind and body from violating good sense. Lacking ascetic restraint, she admonishes a heart that learns nothing from the upright heron, whose stance implies a power in nature to resist temptation. Unlike the quiet mist cloaking a waterfall and the remote hill country, the sexual self sidesteps self-control to clamor for gratification. She regrets that sensual impulse overrules wisdom, but the ongoing colloquy between id and ego refuses placation. Resembling the disruptive child "demanding attention, / interrupting study and contemplation," her inner forces drag her away from late-in-life serenity toward the satisfaction of an intense carnal urge (Levertov, 1992, 31).

Bibliography

Janssen, Ronald R. "Evening Train: Preview and Excursus," *Twentieth Century Literature* 38, no. 3 (Fall 1992): 353–359.

Levertov, Denise. *Evening Train.* New York: New Directions, 1992.

androgyny

The blending of strengths and traits of male and female is a social transfiguration favored by feminist writers. The concept of unisex character influences the authors Margaret ATWOOD, Charlotte Perkins GILMAN, Marge PIERCY, Louise ERDRICH, and Joanna RUSS, whose novels view human resilience as a given in both genders. As Carolyn G. Heilbrun explains in *Toward a Recognition of An-*

drogyny (1982), unisex traits transcend social customs and taboos: "Androgyny seeks to liberate the individual from the confines of the appropriate" (Heilbrun, x). The concept of merged gender qualities inspired the philosopher Margaret FULLER's *Woman in the Nineteenth Century* (1845), North America's first feminist manifesto. In the preface, which she published in the *Dial* in July 1843, she referred to the two genders as "two halves of one thought" (Fuller, 3). The text warns that neither half can come to fruition without the other, a humanistic axiom that invigorates the feminist cause.

During the Harlem Renaissance, Jessie Redmon FAUSET, a progressive editor and novelist, pictured androgyny in the emerging NEW WOMAN of the 1920s. Replacing the fussy domestic of the Victorian Age, the post–World War I do-all female valued self by cultivating home, education, and career. In Fauset's *Plum Bun: A Novel without a Moral* (1929), the artist Pauline seizes on androgyny as a pragmatic solution to her difficulty in balancing dual social roles. To achieve creative and personal fulfillment, she embodies both male and female assets. In self-defense, she declares her masculinity as an antidote to sexism: "I see what I want; I use my wiles as a woman to get it, and I employ the qualities of men, tenacity and ruthlessness, to keep it. And when I'm through with it, I throw it away just as [men] do" (Fauset, 1990, 105). With admirable spunk, she adds, "I have no regrets and no encumbrances" (*ibid.*).

In England, the experimental novelist Virginia WOOLF considered the role of merged gender traits in creative writing. She blended fantasy and history in the novel *Orlando* (1928), which features an androgynous protagonist who advances over centuries through a variety of roles. In *A Room of One's Own* (1929), Woolf used chapter 6 as an opportunity to laud the harmony of masculine and feminine perspectives in one spiritual cooperative. Citing Samuel Taylor Coleridge's definition of the androgyny of great minds, Woolf described the fusion of gender traits as a magic moment when "the mind is fully fertilised and uses all its faculties" (Woolf, 102). She chooses the descriptives "resonant and porous" to explain the incandescence of pure creativity, an intellectual form of critical mass that "explodes and gives birth to all kinds of other ideas" (*ibid.*, 105).

In the heyday of feminist confessional poetry Adrienne RICH redirected attention to androgynous strengths in the title poem of *Diving into the Wreck: Poems 1971–1972* (1973), a frequently cited image of the female explorer. Picturing a competent skin diver whose face is concealed by mask and breathing tube, the poet implies that no observer can guess her gender by interpreting her deft movements as either masculine or feminine. Without the stereotypical behavior associated with femininity, the female diver becomes an anonymous seeker, the iconic pilgrim who has dominated world literature from its inception. Skillfully, she retrieves from past generations the traditions that undergird modern feminism. The pictorial quality of Rich's poem validates the move of American femininity away from a frilly, weak-willed otherness to reclamation of a more muscular, self-reliant humanity.

The androgyny of 20th-century feminism faced down critics with a bold self-acceptance. In her first story, "Rose-Johnny," published in the *Virginia Quarterly* in 1988, the novelist Barbara KINGSOLVER broached the subject of ridicule of androgynous females. Her main character, like the tomboys in Carson MCCULLERS's novels *The Heart Is a Lonely Hunter* (1940) and *The Member of the Wedding* (1946), is a 10-year-old naive narrator who is puzzled why her mountain community ostracizes Rose-Johnny, a lesbian store clerk who dresses as a man. Unkind remarks from hillbillies vilify Rose-Johnny as "half man and half woman, a freak akin to the pagan creatures whose naked torsos are inserted in various shocking ways into parts of animal bodies" (Kingsolver, 1989, 204). By turning the protagonist into a metaphoric beast, her detractors exonerate their inhumane behavior.

Kingsolver's representation of ambiguous gender distinctions recurs in Taylor Greer in *The Bean Trees* (1988), Leah Price Ngemba in *The Poisonwood Bible* (1998), and 47-year-old Deanna Wolfe, the armed game warden for the Forest Service and the National Park Service and a late-in-life mother in *Prodigal Summer* (2000). In *Prodigal Summer*, the author suggests a fusion of opposites in the character's name, which allies a feral canid with the Greek Diana, goddess of virginity and of wild things. Deanna addresses her own uniqueness in her admiration for the coyote: "He's nobody's pet; he doesn't belong to anybody but himself" (Kingsolver, 2000, 176). To a macho game hunter eager to shoot a coyote, she has the authority and self-possession to order him: "*Leave* it . . . the *hell* . . . *alone*" (ibid., 323). In all three of Kingsolver's novels, the uninhibited protagonists function admirably as wives/lovers, mothers, and libertarians. Kingsolver's depictions defy scorners who fear that mannish women lose their humanity.

Bibliography

Fauset, Jessie Redmon. *Plum Bun*. Boston: Beacon Press, 1990.

Fuller, Margaret. *Woman in the Nineteenth Century*. New York: Norton, 1971.

Heilbrun, Carolyn G. *Toward a Recognition of Androgyny*. New York: W. W. Norton, 1982.

Kingsolver, Barbara. *Homeland and Other Stories*. New York: HarperCollins, 1989.

———. *Prodigal Summer*. New York: HarperCollins, 2000.

Trotman, Nat. "The Burning Between: Androgyny/Photography/Desire," *Women's Studies* 28, no. 4 (September 1999): 379–402.

Woolf, Virginia. *A Room of One's Own*. New York: Harbinger, 1957.

Angela Davis: An Autobiography Angela Davis (1974)

The social theorist Angela DAVIS's political AUTOBIOGRAPHY puts a face on the civil rights activism of the 1960s and 1970s. Dramatic rather than theoretical, the narrative characterizes her girlhood amid a supportive network of friends and colleagues at Dynamite Hill in Birmingham, her studies on a Quaker exchange program at Elizabeth Irwin High School in New York City, her membership in the Community Party, and her work to raise support for three black convicts known as the Soledad Brothers. She became the third woman to be listed among the Federal Bureau of Investigation's (FBI's) Top 10 Most Wanted Criminals. After 16 months in prison for abetting the kidnapping, conspiracy, and murder of a prison guard in California, a vigorous international "Free Angela"

campaign rebutted the charges of Governor Ronald Reagan that Davis was a dangerous leftist. In her book, dynamic involvement in picketing, protest, and interstate flight from the FBI progress to the next stage, the lives of women in New York's Women's House of Detention in the hands of sadistic matrons. An unflinching glimpse of sexual release among inmates, the text also exposes the sexism of male authority figures, black and white, who relegate black women to the role of social and economic drones.

Davis extols individual action on Marxist ideals as the root of social change. Although depicted in the media as a radical hard-liner, she is adept at passion and humor. One anecdote pictures her joining a female friend in deceiving a shoe store clerk in the South. By addressing him in French, the two women pretend to be exotic islanders from the Caribbean rather than ordinary American blacks. The shift in nationality strips them of the STEREOTYPING of black women as ignorant and socially inept. With a return to their true personae, Davis and friend reveal to the befuddled salesman his faulty perceptions. For the author's sympathy with the struggles of black women in a white-dominated world, during Davis's flight from arrest, homeowners placed in windows signs reading, "Angela, Sister, You Are Welcome in This House."

Davis's reflection on her political awakening introduces a stream of concepts that infuse her later works. In addition to police and prison guard abuse of women, she denounces control of prisoners with psychotropic drugs, racism in the criminal justice system, domestic VIOLENCE, and the social abandonment of poor women and their children. At the heart of her personal creed is the empowerment of the laboring class, the most undervalued stratum of American society, through solidarity movements and workers' cooperatives. As a result of her successful autobiography, Davis led the National and International Alliance against Racism and Political Repression, a multiracial coalition that began examining the inhumanity of American prisons. With her contributions to liberal issues Davis developed into a key proponent of prison reform, anticapitalism, and civil and WOMEN'S RIGHTS.

Bibliography

Carey-Webb, Allen. "Teaching to the Contemporary Crisis," *College Literature* 22, no. 3 (October 1995): 1–16.

Davis, Angela. *Angela Davis: An Autobiography.* London: Hutchinson, 1974.

Langer, Elinor. "Autobiography as an Act of Political Communication," *New York Times,* 27 October 1972.

Perkins, Margo V. *Autobiography as Activism: Three Black Women of the Sixties.* Jackson: University Press of Mississippi, 2001.

Angelou, Maya (1928–)

The women's advocate and freedom fighter Marguerite Johnson "Maya" Angelou stirs readers with her bold, witty fiction, AUTOBIOGRAPHY, and poems. Her childhood embraced two environments—the Deep South maternalism of Grandmother Annie Henderson at her grocery store in Stamps, Arkansas, and the flashy good times of Saint Louis, Missouri, her birthplace and the home of her divorced parents, Bailey Henderson and Vivian Baxter Jackson. A best-selling childhood memoir, I KNOW WHY THE CAGED BIRD SINGS (1969), describes the loving camaraderie Angelou shared with brother, Bailey Junior, and the terror of a pedophile, Mr. Freeman, Vivian's lover, who silenced seven-year-old Maya with brutal trauma. Shipped back south to Momma Henderson, Maya recovered through recitations of literature, which became a healing refuge.

While enrolled at the California Labor School in San Francisco, Angelou demanded that the city hire her as streetcar conductor. After giving birth to her son, Guy, she pursued a number of jobs—clerk, cook, dancer, singer, actor—before allying with the Harlem Writers Guild. While living in Johannesburg, South Africa, during the early 1960s, she reported news for the *Arab Observer.* She returned to California during the civil rights movement, played the grandmother of Kunta Kinte in the television production of Alex Haley's *Roots,* and published drama, memoirs, and verse. She read one of her poems, "On the Pulse of the Morning," aloud during the 1993 inauguration of President Bill Clinton.

Accolades and honorary degrees have accumulated in testimony to Angelou's feminist writings as well as to her teaching career, public appearances, and activism. The most honored work, *I Know Why the Caged Bird Sings,* presents Maya as an impressionable girl who internalizes two views of womanhood—the proud rural matriarch from Stamps and the silky-smooth urban mother who can jitterbug or shoot a pistol with equal aplomb. Angelou caricatures her preteen features as those of "a too-big Negro girl, with nappy black hair, broad feet and a space between her teeth that would hold a number-two pencil" (Angelou, 1970, 2). At an Easter church service, she appears skinny in a cut-down dress above legs "greased with Blue Seal Vaseline and powdered with the Arkansas red clay" (*ibid.,* 2). She saves for the 34th chapter her summation of the hard-pressed black female, who "is assaulted in her tender years by all those common forces of nature at the same time that she is caught in the tripartite crossfire of masculine prejudice, white illogical hate and Black lack of power" (*ibid.,* 231). The made-for-TV version, which depicts her emergence as a survivor and artist, boasts a cast of Esther Rolle, Ruby Dee, Diahann Carroll, and Constance Good as Maya.

An overlooked Angelou tour de force, the illustrated womanist verse cycle *Now Sheba Sings the Song* (1994), allies poetry with the sepia sketches of artist Tom Feelings. Celebrating the mysticism and resilience of black women, the poem speaks the sassy egotism of Angelou, who delights in the woman's tight, teasing buttocks, which "introduce frenzy into the hearts of small men" (Angelou, 1994, 33). The stanzas overflow with a variety of female wiles—"Lip smacking, finger snapping, toe tapping, / Shoulder bouncing, hip throwing, breast thrusting, eye flashing" (*ibid.,* 48). With bold insouciance, the speaker claims to be "mate to Kilimanjaro" (*ibid.,* 54), hyperbole that typifies Angelou's self-confidence both as black poet and as female. In 2004 she redirected her creative entries to the African diaspora and the Afro-American kitchen in *Halleluia! The Welcome Table: A Lifetime of Memories with Recipes.* Like Marjorie Kinnan RAWLINGS's *Cross Creek Cookery* (1942) and Ntozake SHANGE's anecdotal *If I Can Cook / You Know God*

Can (1998), Angelou's guide to 73 recipes strays from the stereotypical hoppin' john and gumbo to spoonbread, cassoulet, and smothered pork chops, the specialities of ethnic cooks that date to their West African foremothers.

Bibliography

Angelou, Maya. *I Know Why the Caged Bird Sings.* New York: Bantam Books, 1970.

———. *Maya Angelou: Poems.* New York: Bantam Books, 1986.

———. *Now Sheba Sings the Song.* New York: Plume Books, 1994.

Burr, Zofia. *Of Women, Poetry, and Power: Strategies of Address in Dickinson, Miles, Brooks, Lorde, and Angelou.* Chicago: University of Illinois Press, 2002.

Anne (Ann) of Swansea (1764–1838)

A protofeminist of the early Gothic groundswell, the dramatist and fiction writer Anne (Ann) of Swansea fought the DOUBLE STANDARD that held female authors to more stringent criteria than males. Born Anne (Ann) Julia Kemble Curtis Hatton, she grew up in London with her sister, the actor Sarah Kemble Siddons. Because of a physical handicap, Anne settled in a bordello and made her living by writing song lyrics, poems, plays, romances, and Gothic potboilers for Minerva Press, a promoter of women's works. After her husband's death, at age 36, she retired to the Welsh port of Swansea and cranked out *Conviction; or, She Is Innocent!* (1814); *Chronicles of an Illustrious House; or, The Peer, the Lawyer, and the Hunchback* (1816); *Gonzalo de Baldivia; or, A Widow's Vow* (1817); *Cesario Rosalba; or, The Oath of Vengeance* (1819); and *Guilty or Not Guilty; or, A Lesson for Husbands: A Tale* (1822). She gentled her later fiction with less forbidding material in *Deeds of the Olden Time* (1826) and *Gerald Fitzgerald: An Irish Tale* (1831).

While appealing to public tastes to make her living, Anne of Swansea kept at the forefront of her writings the perils common to the lives of the unfortunate poor, widows, and deceived heiresses. She characterizes the pride of working women in Mrs. Greville, widow of Alfred Greville in the five-volume novel *Lovers and Friends* (1821), whose lost finances force her to earn a living by managing a boarding school. In volume 1, the author champions the headmistress, whose "seminary for young ladies became the most fashionable establishment for the daughters of bilious nabobs and gouty persons of distinction" (Anne of Swansea, 1821). Nonetheless, critics accused the author of preferring sexually audacious heroines, heinous villains, compromising scenarios, and themes and motifs too indelicate for a gentlewoman's pen. Despite unfair critiques by male colleagues Anne of Swansea continued to supply bookshops and circulating libraries with popular fiction. Feminists reclaimed her canon as a monument to the self-supporting female artist.

Bibliography

Anne of Swansea. *Lovers and Friends* (1821). Available online. URL: http://www.chawton.org/novels/Lovers/Lovers1.html. Accessed on October 13, 2005.

"Ann Julia Hatton." *Sheffield Hallam University: Corvey Women Writers* (2000). Available online. URL: http://www2.shu.ac.uk/corvey/CW3/AuthorPage.cfm?Author=AJKH. Accessed on October 13, 2005.

Haining, Peter, ed. *Gothic Tales of Terror.* New York: Taplinger, 1972.

"Anniad, The" Gwendolyn Brooks (1949)

In urbanized mock-epic style, the 43 stanzas of Gwendolyn BROOKS's "The Anniad," published in *Annie Allen* (1949), muse in satiric rhymed couplets on society's false assumptions about romance and femininity. Just as the jingoistic doctrines of democracy and opportunity ring false during World War II, the ideal of deathless love proves a mirage, which the poet dramatizes as outdated musical strains "Fairy-sweet of old guitars" (Brooks, 38). The DUALITY of the prodigal husband and the racist nation takes palpable shape in a metaphor of a wind-shredded red and blue, which suggests both a worn housedress and a tattered flag. Rejecting submission to a dominant male and to a macho society, the heroine Annie Allen, "sweet and chocolate," retreats from union with a womanizer who prefers lighter-skinned honeys (Brooks, 38). The insult requires shoring up of her damaged psyche. In place of wedlock, she commits herself to motherhood, her compensation for marital betrayal by a tan man, who fades in color and substance from battlefield trauma and the unfulfilled postwar promises of the mid-1940s.

Choosing the African-American concepts of female strength and physical beauty, Annie abandons her dreamworld "featherbeds" and nurtures a viable consciousness as the survivor of both racism and sexual constraints that limit her from infancy (*ibid.*). Growing insightful with the passing seasons, she develops a sophistication that Brooks depicts in Homeric lyric diction intermeshed with black dialect. Ironically, for form and allusions, the poet adopts familiar strains from the Harlem Renaissance by the male writers Countee Cullen and Langston Hughes, notably Annie's abandonment by the higher and lower gods and the rebellious posturing that extends upward to her "black and boisterous hair" (*ibid.*, 39). From Emily DICKINSON and from Zora Neale HURSTON's *THEIR EYES WERE WATCHING GOD* (1937), Brooks adapts the conceit of woman as queen, an innate royalty that confers dignity, even in Annie's sorrow at tan man's funeral after he succumbs to alcoholic debauchery and venereal disease.

Brooks's inspired choice of a feminized version of Homer's *Iliad* and Virgil's *Aeneid* supplants the androcentric ideal of the woman-rescuing paladin with a feminist defiance of SEXUAL POLITICS. As gendered myth crumbles, both husband and wife do battle with chimeras—tan man with the tarnished glamour of soldiery and Annie with her Eurocentric dreams of the dashing cavalier. As does Janie Crawford Woods, Hurston's protagonist, Annie outlives her man and falls back on memories. To reestablish autonomy, she works at overcoming tan man's "intimidating teeth" that chew at her green tips and "[nibble] at the roots beneath" (*ibid.*, 39). In taffeta and fur, she first pirouettes into the sexual marketplace with a frenetic "flirting bijouterie" (*ibid.*, 45). Failure at coquetry proves therapeutic by stripping her of illusions. In the appendix to "The Anniad," the bulwark of MATRIARCHY appeals to Annie. As the naif, she whimpers, "Oh Mother Mother where is happiness?" (*ibid.*, 51).

Bibliography

Brooks, Gwendolyn. *Selected Poems.* New York: Harper-Perennial, 1999.

Jimoh, A. Yemisi. "Double Consciousness, Modernism, and Womanist Themes in Gwendolyn Brooks's 'The Anniad,'" *MELUS* 23, no. 3 (Fall 1998): 167–186.

Stanford, Ann Folwell. "An Epic with a Difference: Sexual Politics in Gwendolyn Brooks's 'The Anniad,'" *American Literature* 67, no. 2 (June 1995): 283–301.

Annie John Jamaica Kincaid (1985)

From an Antiguan point of view, Jamaica KINCAID's semiautobiographical novel *Annie John* (1985) depicts the approach-avoidance tensions of the MOTHER-DAUGHTER RELATIONSHIP within the lush setting of a Caribbean isle. In early girlhood, the title character experiences the gendered treatment common to females, including bathing with her mother in warm scented water by candlelight rather than in the night-chilled basin that her father uses to strengthen his back. Triggered by Annie's terror of death and a growing fear of her mother's mortality, the story allies the phobias that form in childhood with paradoxes of teen liberation. Subtextually competing with the beautiful mother who sews, cooks, and swims, Annie begins the process of self-actualization by setting her own behavioral standards. At the height of resultant family dissonance, she admits, "I couldn't bear to have anyone see how deep in disfavor I was with my mother" (Kincaid, 45).

Complicating the mother-daughter angst is the onset of menarche, which causes Annie to mutter, "What a serpent!" in scorn of her mother, the implied cause of menstruation (*ibid.*, 52). At school, Annie faints after envisioning herself soaked in blood, a scenario implying that the arrival of womanhood is a serious bodily loss caused by the snake of Eden that lured EVE into disobeying God. The image morphs into a crocodile after Annie's white-toothed mother tricks her into eating breadfruit for lunch. As Annie progresses to age 15, Kincaid vivifies the text with more graphic metaphors, which picture the girl's mounting discontent as a black ball "no bigger than a thimble, even though it weighed worlds" (*ibid.*, 85). The power struggle reaches a climax after her mother calls Annie a slut for lying about afternoon jaunts in the cemetery with foul-mouthed schoolmates. By retorting tit for tat, Annie severely weakens the psychological umbilical cord.

In a full-fledged psychological study, Kincaid tethers the warring females in numerous respects, including Annie's memories of swimming like a papoose on her mother's back, dresses cut from the same bolt, and the same given name. After "Little Miss" Annie equals the elder Annie in height, the two stare eye to eye and avoid the simmering differences that dispel the family's former serenity (*ibid.,* 105). The three-months' illness that overwhelms Annie requires a surrogate mother, Ma Jolie, an obeah practitioner from Dominica who oversees Annie's recuperation. In the final separation from home and parents, Annie expresses her experiences and desires in terms of a lifelong dependence on her mother. Kincaid indicates that the formation of the individual begins with a necessary severance of child from mother, a postbirth trauma that replicates the cutting of the cord. The parting from an adoring family leaves Annie feeling "that someone was tearing me up into little pieces" (*ibid.,* 144).

Bibliography

Caton, Louis F. "Romantic Struggles: The Bildungsroman and Mother-Daughter Bonding in Jamaica Kincaid's 'Annie John,'" *MELUS* 21, no. 3 (Fall 1996): 125–143.

Kincaid, Jamaica. *Annie John.* New York: Farrar, Straus & Giroux, 1997.

Anthony, Susan B. (1820–1906)

Late in joining the campaign for gender equality, Susan Brownell Anthony, a native of Adams, Massachusetts, earned world renown as the spearhead of American WOMEN'S RIGHTS. Born to a Quaker family in 1820, she grew up in a household pledged to independence. At the Quaker meetinghouse she saw women achieve equality in worship far beyond their participation in everyday society. At age 19, she pursued teaching, the only profession open to a woman of her talents, and joined the staff at a New York seminary in New Rochelle.

Nine years later, Anthony began carving a niche for herself as one of America's most revered female orators. She delivered a speech, "Woman: The Great Unpaid Laborer" (1848), in which she charged that females are deliberately weakened: "Taught that a low voice is an excellent thing in woman, she has been trained to a subjugation of the vocal organs, and thus lost the benefit of loud tones and their well-known invigoration of the system" (Anthony, 1848). She had withering remarks to deliver about outdoor play and physical education for girls: "Forbidden to run, climb, or jump, her muscles have been weakened, and her strength deteriorated" (*ibid.*). An interest in personal and public morality earned her friends among abolitionists, including the former slave Frederick DOUGLASS, publisher of *The North Star,* and the Boston activist William Lloyd Garrison. As an agent and organizer of the American Anti-Slavery Society, in 1856, she served as chief of New York operations and founded the Women's Loyal National League, a patriotic foundation supporting Union efforts during the Civil War.

Anthony set the tone for the SUFFRAGE movement with sobriety and unshakable determination. An unmarried activist, she warded off sexist criticism by dressing primly in dark-colored bonnet and dress trimmed with white collars and cuffs. In 1851, she formed a professional partnership with her friend and colleague Elizabeth Cady STANTON that lasted over a half-century. The following year, their dynamism invigorated an assembly of suffragists in Syracuse, New York. Across the nation, Anthony delivered speeches written by Stanton at assemblies, in meeting halls, and on street corners. While Anthony risked ridicule and social ostracism in traveling alone by stagecoach, riverboat, and carriage, Stanton, the mother of seven children, remained in the background. Over time the two campaigners evolved complementary philosophies.

Anthony's profound belief in human rights led her away from the TEMPERANCE movement into a single-minded crusade for women's empowerment, which she believed was the only path to social betterment. A fiery speaker and tireless organizer of rallies and seminars, she was a charismatic apostle who bombarded officials with demands that women control their wealth, property, and children and that they participate fully in national events by voting in elections. In December 1866 at the New York City equal rights convention at the Cooper Institute, she demanded equality: "If men will talk in Congress . . . of impartial suffrage, universal suffrage, we mean to have them understand that women are to be included in its impartiality and universality" (Anthony, 2000, 2). Two years later, she issued a newspaper, the *Revolution,* in which she broached tough issues, including management's exploitation of female laborers, church misogyny, divorce, and PROSTITUTION. The paper incurred a debt of $10,000, which Anthony retired in six years of speaking tours. One of her most impassioned orations was "Woman Wants Bread, Not the Ballot!," which she delivered in 1879 in Terre Haute, Indiana. Justifying her theme was the fact that 3 million American women were self-supporting. She castigated the teaching profession for keeping women in low-paying classroom positions and for denying them access to jobs as principals, supervisors, superintendents, and school board members.

Anthony's victories for women were often piecemeal. The success in the key state of New York preceded a dormant period during the four years of the Civil War, when she and Stanton joined the Grimké sisters, Angelina and Sarah, and the freedom fighter Harriet Tubman in antislavery campaigning while temporarily diverting attention from gender equity. The efforts were not wasted, for, by organizing the Women's Loyal National League and collecting 300,000 supporters demanding the freeing of slaves, Stanton and Anthony honed their talents at initiating grassroots efforts. Anthony concentrated on Kansas in 1867 to gain passage of state enfranchisement. She also saw an opportunity to lobby for women's rights during the drafting of the Fourteenth Amendment, which granted the vote to nonwhite males. On visiting Salt Lake City in Utah Territory in 1871, she regretted that Mormon women tolerated polygamous marriages and cited the absurdity of a dozen women or more and their brood's relying on one husband for financial support. During her second journey to address Mormon women, she was pleased to discover that they supported the addition of women's voting rights to the Utah state constitution.

Anthony's lecture tours generated name recognition. A U.S. marshal arrested her and a dozen followers in Rochester, New York, in November 1872 for casting a vote for the presidency. According to a dramatic court record, *The Trial of Susan B. Anthony* (1872), at a presentencing hearing on June 17, 1873, she used the moment as a public platform and, for the good of her listeners and the press, launched into a tirade against outrages suffered by women. She accused the judge of denying her rights: "Robbed of the fundamental privilege of citizenship, I am degraded from the status of a citizen to that of a subject" (Anthony, 1873). The verdict, issued at a Canandaigua courthouse, amounted to nothing, leaving her unencumbered by jail time or the court fine of $100, which she had no money to pay. She continued packing her alligator satchel for more campaigns for women's suffrage in California, Colorado, the Dakotas, Michigan, and Wyoming. In subsequent addresses, she complained that the Preamble to the Constitution promised the blessings of liberty yet denied them to women.

At the height of Anthony's activism, real progress buoyed spirits of suffragists and their supporters. She coauthored the "Declaration of Rights of Women" (1876) with Matilda Joslyn GAGE and joined Stanton and Gage in compiling the first three volumes of the six-volume *History of Woman Suffrage* (1881–86). In 1877 Anthony delivered a speech, "Homes of Single Women," in which she bluntly stated the choice for unsatisfied women: "If women will not accept marriage *with subjection,* nor men proffer it *without,* there is, there can be, no alternative. The women who *will not be ruled* must live without marriage" (Stanton & Anthony, 148). She added that single women conveyed by their comfortable, efficient homes and stable lives an ability to flourish on their own.

At the merger of the suffrage initiatives into the National American Woman Suffrage Association (NAWSA) in 1892, Anthony, then age 72, accepted the presidency of the new organization, another demand on her life. In an interview with the investigative reporter Nellie BLY, Anthony admitted that she had been in love many times. She shied away from matrimony lest she become a poor man's drudge or a wealthy man's trophy wife. To a question about prayer, she declared that she communicated with God by uplifting women from degradation. The journalist Charlotte Perkins GILMAN reported on the 1899 Woman's Congress in London, where Anthony met Queen Victoria. Of the event, Gilman remarked that Anthony "[stood] waiting in the hot sun till the royal carriage appeared. . . . She wanted to see the woman whose reign has meant so much to England; and it is to be hoped that that much-honored lady felt how much these uncrowned heads and noble hearts were doing for the world" (Gilman, 350). At Stanton's death on October 28, 1902, Anthony wrote a letter to the journalist Ida Husted HARPER, Anthony's official biographer, expressing grief: "Well, it is an awful hush—it seems impossible—that the voice is hushed" (Anthony, "Letter"). Without her researcher and speechwriter, Anthony spent the majority of her time in transit to new territory, making public appearances until only months before her final illness and death on March 13, 1906. She left her supporters a motto, "Failure is impossible" (Sherr and Kazickas, 330).

It is difficult to imagine the attainment of voting rights without Susan B. Anthony. She submitted an essay to the *North American Review*, "Woman's Half Century of Evolution" (1902), in the style of the Declaration of Independence. It retains a crisp, unsentimental logic: "The effect upon women themselves of these enlarged opportunities in every direction has been a development which is almost a regeneration. The capability they have shown in the realm of higher education, their achievements in the business world, their capacity for organization, their executive power, have been a revelation" (Anthony, 1902, 810). In the decades following her spirited oratory, her honors have grown, including the novelist Gertrude STEIN's tribute opera *The Mother of Us All* (1947). At the passage of the Nineteenth Amendment to the Constitution, the media referred to it as the "Anthony amendment." Late 20th-century feminists elevated her for selflessness and dedication to complete liberty for all. In 1979, the U.S. government acknowledged her heroism with a new dollar coin, making her the first female depicted on the nation's currency.

Bibliography

Anthony, Susan B. *"Letter Written by Susan B. Anthony to Ida Husted Harper the Day Before Elizabeth Cady Stanton's Funeral"* (1902). Available online. URL: http://ecssba.rutgers.edu/docs/sbatoharp.html. Accessed on October 13, 2005.

———. *"Remarks by Susan B. Anthony at Her Trial for Illegal Voting"* (1873). Available online. URL: http://ecssba.rutgers.edu/docs/sbatrial.html. Accessed on October 13, 2005.

———. *The Selected Papers of Elizabeth Cady Stanton and Susan B. Anthony: Against an Aristocracy of Sex, 1866–1873*. Piscataway, N.J.: Rutgers University Press, 2000.

———. *"Woman's Half Century of Evolution"* (1902). Available online. URL: http://etext.lib.virginia.edu/toc/modeng/public/AntWoma.html. Accessed on October 13, 2005.

———. *"Woman: The Great Unpaid Laborer"* (1848). Available online. URL: http://etext.lib.virginia.edu/railton/uncletom/womanmov.html#g. Accessed on October 13, 2005.

Gilman, Charlotte Perkins. "The Woman's Congress of 1899" (1899). Available online. URL: http://wyllie.lib.virginia.edu:8086/perl/toccer-new?id=SteWoma.sgm&images=images/modeng&data=/texts/english/modeng/parsed&tag=public&part=1&division=div1. Accessed on October 13, 2005.

Sherr, Lynn, and Jurate Kazickas. *Susan B. Anthony Slept Here: A Guide to American Women's Landmarks*. New York: Times Books, 1976.

Stanton, Elizabeth Cady, and Susan B. Anthony. *Elizabeth Cady Stanton/Susan B. Anthony: Correspondence, Writings, Speeches*. New York: Schocken, 1981.

Antin, Mary (1881–1949)

A prominent Jewish lecturer and chronicler of the immigrant experience in the United States, Maryashe "Mary" Antin Grabau published first-person accounts based on her radical individualism. Antin's protofeminism was a personal struggle against a repressively patriarchal religion and the example of family life in which the father's beliefs and dictates were law. Born to Russian Jews in Polotsk, she spent her first 13 years in the Pale, a strip of ghettos on the Polish border patrolled by the czarist government and regularly assailed by pogroms. The terrors inspired her crusade for the rights of silenced minorities.

Early in her life, in addition to the struggle of her Jewish family for equality in a prejudiced land, Antin fought traditional preferential treatment of males. She resented her spoiled only brother, Pinchus, whom she called the family hero for his gender. His grandmother pawned candlesticks, shawl, and sabbath cap for his upkeep and carried him on her back through the snow to classes in the ghetto boys' school. Because of the limited expectations for girls, Antin did not attend a formal institution. Rather, the family paid for secular home tutoring for Mary and her older sister, Frieda, in arithmetic, Russian, and Yiddish.

Antin considered herself reborn at age 13 when her mother escorted her children to America. After the family immigrated to the Chelsea section of Boston, her father, the Talmudic scholar Israel Antin, insisted that his beloved "Mashinke" take advantage of free education (Antin, 1912, 67). He increased her eligibility by listing her age as 11. She studied French and Latin at Boston Girls' Latin School, where she completed five grades in one semester. As classwork and a free library improved her competence in the new language, she quickly learned English and published her first English article, "Snow" (1894). In 1913, she turned her father's age-shaving fib into an article for *Atlantic Monthly* entitled "The Lie."

Antin's career derived from her adoption of a new land and a new language. In her midteens, she published Yiddish letters in *The American Hebrew* and English verse in the *Boston Herald.* Hindering her progress were hospital stays to treat neurasthenia. While living in New York City, in 1901, she married a German Lutheran, Amadeus William Grabau, a famed geologist and paleontologist on staff at Columbia University. She extended her education at Barnard College and at Teachers' College. Grabau's loss of patriotism during World War I as a result of sympathy with the German kaiser cost Grabau his job and his wife, who neared nervous collapse as her marriage disintegrated. In 1919, Grabau left the United States to join the China Geological Survey.

Antin was prepared for living on her own. After honing her skills with articles submitted to popular journals, from October 1911 to March 1912, she serialized in *Atlantic Monthly* a personal view of assimilation in *The Promised Land* (1912), a valuable feminist memoir. The work is a classic of American immigrant AUTOBIOGRAPHY and the first best seller in the nation written by and about a Jew. At the core of the text she denounced a patriarchal culture that ignores the talents of its female members. She recalls life in Russia under Orthodox Jewry: "It was not much to be a girl you see. Girls could not be scholars or rabbonim [rabbis]" (*ibid.*, 33). Angered at the limitation of most girls' education to cooking and sewing, she grumbled, "There was nothing in what the boys did in [religious school] that I could not have done—if I had not been a girl" (*ibid.*, 34).

Boston gave Antin a new perspective on womanhood. In delight at the equal treatment of American women, she exulted, "A long girlhood, a free choice in marriage, and a brimful womanhood are the precious rights of an American woman" (*ibid.*, 45). Even her mother, Esther Weltman Antin, shed the domestic strictures of Orthodox Judaism—multiple sets of dishes for meat and dairy items, stringent cleaning procedures, ritual bathing, and head covering—and embraced a liberal American faith enough to abandon kosher shopping and to buy meats from a Christian butcher. In looking forward to the next generation, Antin promised to support the choice of career of her own daughter, Josephine Esther Grabau, even if she wanted to be a grocer. Because of Antin's public abandonment of Judaic faith and custom and her breach of gender boundaries, male Jewish critics lambasted her as a turncoat against her cultural heritage.

Antin pursued the same themes in a manifesto to new citizens, *They Who Knock at Our Gates: A Complete Gospel of Immigration* (1914). Her thesis was optimistic that both immigrant and adopted native land profited from the infusion of energy and self-betterment brought about by free education of male and female alike. To critics who charged her with turning against the traditional Jewish upbringing, she refuted accusations with letters collected in *From Plotzk to Boston* (1899) that she had written to her uncle, Moshe Hayyim Weltman; the *Atlantic* editor Ellery Sedgwick; the scholar Israel Zangwill; President Theodore Roosevelt; and others. Her activism on behalf of newcomers to America included congressional opposition to restricted immigration. On behalf of the newcomers, she stated, "They were going to the foreign world in hopes only of earning their bread and worshiping their God in peace" (Antin, 1899, 11).

Bibliography

Antin, Mary. *From Plotzk to Boston.* Boston: W. B. Clarke, 1899.

———. *The Promised Land.* Boston: Houghton Mifflin, 1912.

———. *Selected Letters of Mary Antin.* New York: Syracuse University Press, 2000.

McGinity, Keren R. "The Real Mary Antin: Woman on a Mission in the Promised Land," *American Jewish History* 86, no. 3 (September 1998): 285.

Proefriedt, William A. "The Immigrant or 'Outsider' Experience as Metaphor for Becoming an Educated Person in the Modern World: Mary Antin, Richard Wright, and Eva Hoffman," *MELUS* 16, no. 2 (Spring 1989/1990): 77–89.

Shavelson, Susanne A. "Anxieties of Authorship in the Autobiographies of Mary Antin and Aliza Greenblatt," *Prooftexts* 18, no. 2 (May 1998): 161–186.

Anzaldúa, Gloria (1942–2004)

The Chicana poet, children's writer, and editor Gloria Evangelina Anzaldúa introduced synthesized views of womanhood in bilingual verse and memoir. A Texan from Jesus Maria of the Valley, she was born to Mexican immigrants who nourished her mind with Native American myth. The STORYTELLING of her grandmother, Mamagrande Ramona, related accounts of the iconic LA LLORONA, the weeping woman, as well as the spiritual IDEAL WOMAN in the VIRGIN MARY. Anzaldúa ended days of arduous ranch chores in Hargill, Texas, with secret reading under the covers by flashlight. She internalized the femininity of La Llorona, whom she later described as "my muse, my dark angel" (Anzaldúa, 2000, 180). After earning a teacher's degree from Pan Ameri-

can University and an M.A. from Texas Women's University, she worked among the children of migrant laborers and taught at the University of California at Santa Cruz, Georgetown University, and Colorado University.

With submissions to *Ikon* and *Third Woman,* Anzaldúa established herself as a writer and supporter of an inclusive humanism. Her goals were the revival of Native American GODDESS LORE and the revamping of male-centered mythos with modern versions that exalt and empower women rather than shackle them to an ascetic, unempowered Virgin Mary. After coediting *This Bridge Called My Back: Writings by Radical Women of Color* (1981) with Cherríe MORAGA, published by KITCHEN TABLE/WOMEN OF COLOR PRESS, Anzaldúa received the Before Columbus Foundation American Book Award for broadening the feminist movement to welcome nonwhite and lesbian women. At age 45, Anzaldúa published the award-winning *Borderlands/La Frontera: The New Mestiza* (1987), a multilayered study in tutorials and verse of psychological, spiritual, racial, and gendered boundaries throughout Central American history. Of particular value to world mythology is her explanation of how Spaniards and the Catholic hierarchy syncretized ancient Earth deities with Christian faith. The newcomers first demonized Indian religion and Nahua Aztec ritual as pagan and reworked the myths of female deities to desex the Virgin of Guadalupe by dissociating her from the serpent, a symbol of sexuality and evil. By 1660, Guadalupe had become God's mother and the patron saint of all Mexicans. Anzaldúa makes a plausible explanation of the political and psychological origins of a trinity of mother goddesses—the Virgin of Guadalupe, LA LLORONA (the weeping woman), and *Cihuacoatl* (Snake Woman). For the author's summation of the gender split among Aztecs that fostered the rise of males over females, *Hungry Mind Review* and *Utne Reader* chose *Borderlands* as one of the top 100 books of the 20th century. After completing *Making Face, Making Soul/Haciendo Caras: Creative and Critical Perspectives by Feminists of Color* (1989), she also garnered a Lesbian Rights Award, Lambda Literary Best Small Book, National Endowment for the Arts citation, American Book Award, *Library Journal* Best Book, and a Sappho Award of Distinction.

The author, aided by the editor AnaLouise Keating, more recently published *Interviews/Entrevistas* (2000) and reprised the style of *This Bridge Called My Back* in *This Bridge We Call Home: Radical Visions for Transformation* (2002), a feminist anthology of 80 original works. Anzaldúa prefaced the collection with an essay, "(Un)natural Bridges, (Un)safe Places." The foreword of the second edition expresses her respect for women and her sympathy for their trials: "Haven't we always borne jugs of water, children, poverty? Why not learn to bear baskets of hope, love, self-nourishment and to step lightly?" (Anzaldúa & Keating, 19). The value of her "bridge" to collectivism lies in its ability to unite the hungry with the privileged, the underrepresented with the politically savvy, and the undereducated with the elite women of academe.

Bibliography

Anzaldúa, Gloria. *Borderlands/La Frontera: The New Mestiza.* San Francisco: Spinsters/Aunt Lute, 1987.

———. *Interviews/Entrevistas.* New York: Routledge, 2000.

———, and AnaLouise Keating, eds. *This Bridge We Call Home: Radical Visions for Transformation.* New York: Routledge, 2002.

Love, Heather. "The Second Time Around," *Women's Review of Books* 20, no. 4 (January 2003): 1–2.

Reuman, Ann. "Coming into Play: An Interview with Gloria Anzaldúa," *MELUS* 25, no. 2 (Summer 2000): 3–45.

Are You There God? It's Me, Margaret
Judy Blume (1970)

A preteen feminist classic and perennial addition to banned books lists, Judy BLUME's tender coming-of-age novella follows 11-year-old Margaret Ann Simon through an unsettling time in her life. After moving from a New York City apartment to a home in Farbrook, New Jersey, she joins a new clutch of friends in forming a secret club to discuss the female topics of the day—bras, menstruation, and boys. In scorn of a superior schoolmate, Laura Danker, envious girls reduce her to physical assets—"The big blonde with the big *you know whats!*" (Blume, 30). Out of anxiety about being undersized, Margaret petitions God, "Please help me grow God. You know where" (*ibid.*, 37). To be on the safe side, she joins the club in bust-developing exercises, a droll touch with which sensitive girls identify.

The intergenerational relations of daughter, mother, and two grandmothers disclose universal assurances and misgivings. As in the mother-daughter tiffs in Jessamyn WEST's Cress Delanty series and those of the title figure in Jamaica KINCAID's *ANNIE JOHN* (1985), Margaret squabbles with her mother, but she also muses to herself, "Why are mothers always right?" (*ibid.*, 25). Parallel to the physical concerns of growing up are pressing spiritual qualms, which Margaret shares with Grandma Sylvia Simon. Blume stresses the need for a sturdy maternal figure. On a hunch, Grandma returns to Margaret's life during a family crisis concerning religious EDUCATION from a Christian mother and Jewish father. The wisdom of an elder female prompts Grandma to promise Margaret, "We'll still be as close always" (*ibid.*, 22).

Classed with the realist authors S. E. Hinton and Harper Lee, Blume earned a place in the lead of frank, readable writing for curious and troubled youngsters. She won critical acclaim for establishing the logic of a child entering womanhood at a time that she questions the existence of a deity, the source of human growth potential. Isolation and self-doubt point Margaret to God as the omnipresent solace and confidante. The narrative alternates childish and mature behavior, juxtaposing leaping in the lawn sprinklers with fear of peer rejection for deodorant fade-out or flat-chestedness. Blume builds these common tensions of puberty to a reassuring catharsis, the arrival of menarche and a release of Margaret's apprehensions about femininity.

Bibliography

Blume, Judy. *Are You There God? It's Me, Margaret.* New York: Dell, 1970.

Oppenheimer, Mark. "Judy Blume and the Embarrassment Factor." *Lilith* (30 September 1999): 32.

Arnow, Harriette (1908–1986)

The novelist and short story writer Harriette Louisa Simpson Arnow captured in fiction the self-confidence and resilience of the mountain women of Appalachia. A native of Wayne County, Kentucky, she was born in a log house and grew up among moonshiners, ridge-running outlaws, and female survivors who traced their lineage to the colonial era. With two years' training from Berea College she taught in a one-room school before finishing a degree at the University of Louisville. At age 26 she settled in Cincinnati, Ohio, and published short fiction in *Southern Review* before writing a first novel, *Mountain Path* (1936). She married and lived in Detroit, where she added a second work, *Hunter's Horn* (1949), to her developing mountaineer trilogy.

Arnow is best known for the cyclic tragedies of *The Dollmaker* (1954), the third of her country life dialect novels and a nominee for a National Book Award. Featuring the stout-willed Gertie Nevels, the story describes her family's migration from the hill country north to factory workers' shanties in Detroit, a city awash in the sound, soot, and smell of heavy industry. The high-rise walls morph into a monstrosity of tenements, back alleys, and random crime. On her first view of steam pipes and smokestacks and her first hearing of trains and trucks, she describes the urban wasteland as hostile to human life: "Here there seemed to be no people, even the cars with their rolled-up windows, frosted over like those of the cab, seemed empty of people, driving themselves through a world not meant for people" (Arnow, 168). Arnow's protoECOFEMINISM presages more stringent late 20th-century activism by Rachel CARSON, Barbara KINGSOLVER, and Leslie Marmon SILKO.

In the unwelcoming cityscape Arnow stresses feminist survival tactics in Gertie's search inward for a quiet haven. Her respite from pollution, noise, and a nagging, antiwoman fundamentalist upbringing is woodcarving, a mannish outlet common to hill people. Working in fragrant wood restores her dignity and self-assurance. The materials, which mountaineers derive from nature, require search and study in a treeless city. Once Gertie has the appropriate wood in hand, she follows its contours and retrieves from within the spirit of the grain. Artistry is therapeutic to hands and spirit, reuniting her with the commonalities of mountain life and her unique creativity.

Key to the novel's importance is the urban exploitation of Gertie, an awkward, ambivalent frontierswoman who wants only to be wife and mother but is too cowed to insist on her dream of owning a farm. The clangor of wartime factory bustle and the influx of too-large immigrant families confuse and uproot her from the agrarian values that sustained her clan for two centuries. Like women migrating from foreign lands to ugly housing developments in the industrial North, she is overwhelmed by new and puzzling demands of forced acculturation. She recoils from the crude, crass lifestyle that turns daily existence into a scramble for just enough cash to cover expenses. At a low point in her recovery from her daughter, Cassie's, death under the wheels of a train, Gertie declares the need to make do: "Everybody had holes, but a body had to live with holes, fill them" (*ibid.*, 436). Lacking the vocabulary to express her despair and sorrow, she regrets her passivity in allowing her husband to move to the Detroit project bearing the ludicrous name of Merry Hill: "I stood still fer it—I kept shut—I could ha spoke up" (*ibid.*, 584). Her regret enhances her humanity as struggling wife, mother, and neighbor whose Christlike love for others elevates her above callous city folk. The 1984 made-for-TV film version by Fox Entertainment featured Jane Fonda in the title role. In a postscript to the Avon edition of *The Dollmaker*, the author-critic Joyce Carol OATES remarked on the simple beauty of Gertie's artistry, calling Arnow's novel "our most unpretentious American masterpiece" (*ibid.*, 601).

Bibliography

Arnow, Harriette. *The Dollmaker.* New York: Avon, 1954.

Chung, Haeja K. "Harriette Simpson Arnow's Authorial Testimony: Toward a Reading of *The Dollmaker,*" *Critique* 36, no. 2 (Spring 1995): 211–223.

Atherton, Gertrude (1857–1948)

A champion of women's political, economic, and sexual rights, Gertrude Franklin Horn Atherton was a popular West Coast author of eccentric, sometimes shockingly erotic fiction. A native of San Francisco, she defied social conventions for the genteel class by becoming a novelist and short story writer. Her in-laws were outraged at the serialization in the *San Francisco Argonaut* of *The Randolphs of Redwoods* (1882), a story of alcoholism and social scandal among the city's elite. Widowed at age 29, Atherton began publishing in earnest two years later under the whimsical pseudonym Frank Lin and continued writing for six decades. Her canon includes 50 novels and scores of Gothic tales and periodical articles as well as screenwriting for Goldwyn Studios.

Atherton's first Gothic novel, *What Dreams May Come* (1888), takes its title from William Shakespeare's *Hamlet.* The love story tells of Harold Dartmouth's passion for the Welsh noblewoman Weir Penrhyn and for the revenant spirit of Lady Sionèd Penrhyn, Weir's deceased grandmother. When Dartmouth and Weir meet, her sensual shape overwhelms him into a swoon. She recalls her own lapse of consciousness, a cataleptic state that terrified her with claustrophobia. The story progresses to a dark night when Dartmouth encounters the cause of their unusual mental states—the appearance of Lady Penrhyn, his grandfather's lover, who floated millions of miles to locate Dartmouth. When day dawns, the spirit merges with the body of Weir. As an explanation of the power of love to trigger metempsychosis, Atherton muses, "Their souls must be the same as when the great ocean of Force had tossed them up, and evolution worked no essential change" (Atherton, 1888, 150).

As late 19th-century GOTHIC FICTION reshaped sensibility from positive emotions toward a realistic complexity, Atherton established a strand of American Gothic. She merged a lethal terror with grief in a short allegory, "Death and the Woman" (1892). As the female protagonist watches the personified Death overtake her husband, she pictures herself in widowhood. The sound of footsteps on the stairs and a knock at the door of the chamber freeze her hands in the act of comforting the dying. After terror overwhelms her, she joins her mate in death. Atherton's original style won an extensive readership. For *Godey's Magazine,* she wrote *The Christmas Witch* (1893). She returned to the subject of transported souls in "The Bell in the Fog" (1905), a popular tale of

reincarnation that stresses the theme of male dominance.

Atherton gradually emerged as a feminist author. In the novel *Julia France and Her Times* (1912), published in *Hearst's Magazine,* she pursued the issue of women's earning a living wage nearly two decades before the Great Depression reshuffled America's economic order. After issuing the novel *The White Morning* (1918), she completed a provocative work, *The Foghorn* (1934), basing it on period attitudes toward female insanity. For her best-selling sensational novel, *Black Oxen* (1923), she reprised the BEAUTY MYTH as glimpsed in the extended life span of the youth-obsessed Mary Ogden, who destroys her life by seeking injections of ox hormones that shave off the years by half. The rejuvenation and sexual reawakening of the 60-year-old socialite illustrate Atherton's willingness to shock the staid upper middle class with issues that deserved attention. In 1938, she broached gender inequities with an essay collection, *Can Women Be Gentlemen?* The text presages Betty FRIEDAN's *The Feminine Mystique* (1963) by pondering the female mask that shrouds rage and frustration with polite, but brittle demeanor. For *The House of Lee* (1940), Atherton studied the responses of three generations of aristocratic women to fearful shifts in the American economy that forced them to seek jobs.

Bibliography
Atherton, Gertrude. *Black Oxen.* New York: Boni & Liveright, 1923.
———. *What Dreams May Come* (1888). Available online. URL: http://www.gutenberg.org/etext/12833. Accessed on October 13, 2005.
Bradley, Jennifer. "Woman at the Golden Gate: The Last Works of Gertrude Atherton," *Women's Studies* 12, no. 1 (1986): 17–30.
Prebel, Julie. "Engineering Womanhood: The Politics of Rejuvenation in Gertrude Atherton's *Black Oxen,*" *American Literature* 76, no. 2 (June 2004): 307–337.

"At the Bay" Katherine Mansfield (1922)
Prefatory to the impressionism of Virginia WOOLF's *To the Lighthouse* (1927), Katherine MANSFIELD's innovative story from *The Garden Party and Other*

Stories (1922) layers glimpses of domesticity on a disarmingly lovely day by the New Zealand shore. The pounding breakers mirror the restlessness that dominates the seaside idyll. The discontinuity of attitudes toward femininity and fulfillment results in a kaleidoscope of women's interwoven lives. Composed of Mrs. Fairfield; her daughters, Beryl Fairfield and Linda Burnell; and Linda's children, the MATRIARCHY crystallizes yearnings and misgivings through sense impressions. Representative tableaus take on the impact of art—the impersonal parade of waves striking the shore, the shower of dew that beglitters flowers, and Linda Burnell's staring at the smile of her unloved infant son. Underlying the disquiet in Linda and her unmarried sister are passionless lives. In a letter to her husband, the editor Jack Murry, composed May 6, 1913, the author described her view of the well-ordered home that lacks passion: "The house fell fast asleep, and it refuses to wake up or so much as smile in a dream" (Hankin, 13). As in a South Pacific version of Rip Van Winkle, Beryl and Linda lapse into a troubled repose as life passes them by.

The author tinges "At the Bay" in a similar drowsiness, an out-of-focus drape that parts to reveal scenes that sparkle like the gold dust that bare feet churn up from the ocean floor. She creates humorous irony in the sea change that turns the cottage into a female haven. The women delight that the peevish, self-absorbed Stanley Burnell has left them alone for the day: "Oh, the relief, the difference it made to have the man out of the house. Their very voices were changed as they called to one another; they sounded warm and loving and as if they shared a secret" (Mansfield). Even Alice the maid relaxes.

The subtext of "At the Bay" juxtaposes complex relationships that range from love and affection to suspicion, disrespect, and self-blame. Without the tension created by Stanley's infantile demands, the females retreat into private domains freed of male intrusion. Grandma Fairfield expresses her maternalism by guarding two rings and a gold chain while the children swim. Lottie Burnell needs the help of her older sister, Kezia, in crossing a stile, a symbol of the compromises and struggles that precede advancing maturity. Mrs. Harry Kember, a slovenly neighbor, admires Beryl for refusing to wear stays. Mrs. Kember remarks, "I believe in pretty girls having a good time. . . . Why not? Don't you make a mistake, my dear. Enjoy yourself" (*ibid.*). An anonymous note tacked at the waterside seeks the return of a lost gold brooch. As though surveying all stages of womanhood, Mansfield comments on the passing of youth with a rhetorical question: "Who takes the trouble—or the joy—to make all these things that are wasted, wasted?," a suggestion of François Villon's enigmatic query, "Where are the snows of yesteryear?" (*ibid.*)

Through abstract examinations of women's isolation and alienation from total commitment to family, Mansfield anticipates modern FEMINISM and its emphasis on the individual's commitment to a secret self. Her venture beyond tight 19th-century story construction to an expanded consciousness introduces a host of little crises in female characters seeking control of circumstances. For Kezia, the thought of Grandma Fairfield's death terrorizes. To hang on to the older generation, Kezia demands of mortality, "Promise me! Say never!" (*ibid.*). To Alice, a photo of Mrs. Stubbs's dead husband elicits a widow's warning to the unwed, "Freedom's best!" (*ibid.*). For Beryl, private fantasies of a dashing male rescuer lighten the solitude of her room by night. At story's end, Harry Kember's attempt to seduce her by moonlight overwashes the narrative with more passion than Beryl is prepared for. As though withdrawing the camera lens from the fictional household, Mansfield retreats into nature's serenity, the backdrop for ongoing human discontent.

Bibliography

Banfield, Ann. "Time Passes: Virginia Woolf, Post-Impressionism, and Cambridge Time," *Poetics Today* 24, no. 3 (Fall 2003): 471–516.

Hankin, Sherry, ed. *Letters between Katherine Mansfield and John Middleton Murry.* New York: New Amsterdam Books, 1990.

Mansfield, Katherine. *The Garden Party and Other Stories* (1992). Available online. URL: http://digital.library.upenn.edu/women/mansfield/garden/garden.html. Accessed on October 13, 2005.

Smith, Angela. *Katherine Mansfield: A Literary Life.* New York: Palgrave, 2000.

Atwood, Margaret (1939–)

The Ottawa-born feminist Margaret Atwood has achieved global stardom with criticism, verse, children's books, essays, and well-plotted fiction that surveys the suppression and persecution of women. In childhood, she followed her father, an entomologist, into the Canadian outback. On her own, she read at will from adventure lore by James Fenimore Cooper and Robert Louis Stevenson, Sir Arthur Conan Doyle's Sherlock Holmes detective stories, and utopian novels. After a thorough grounding in Canadian literature at the University of Toronto, Radcliffe College, and Harvard University, she lectured and submitted clever verse to *Acta Victoriana*, *Alphabet*, *Blew Ointment*, and the *Strand*. She anthologized her poetry in *Double Persephone* (1961), winner of a Pratt Medal, and in *The Circle Game* (1966), which reaped both Centennial Poetry Competition and Governor General's awards. Her first critical volume, *Survival: A Thematic Guide to Canadian Literature* (1972), established her reputation as scholar and proponent of North American authors, including Tillie OLSEN.

Atwood is famous for restructuring FAIRY TALES into prowoman scenarios of sexual politics. She told a *New York Times* interviewer about being marked by *Grimm's Fairy Tales*, in which "every blood-stained ax, wicked witch and dead horse is right there, where the Brothers Grimm set them down, ready to be discovered by us" (Tatar, 2.1). For the semiautobiographic *Cat's Eye* (1988), she blends strands of Rapunzel with the Snow Queen in a survey of girlish bullying. For a fool tale, *The Robber Bride* (1993), a modern version of the Grimm brothers' "Der Räuberbräutigam" (The robber bridegroom, 1857), she turns thievery by a male seducer into a slick woman-centered mystery. Zenia, a sociopathic bandit, tricks three classmates into believing that she is dead. In a sexual romp through the classmates' love lives, Zenia displays the guile of a 19th-century femme fatale. As sparks fly, Atwood remarks with deadpan resignation, "A disaster is a disaster; those hurt by it remain hurt, those killed remain killed, the rubble remains rubble" (Atwood, 1998, 3). With a more promising tone, the dystopian classic *The HANDMAID'S TALE* (1985) pictures a lost-in-the-woods heroine, Offred, as an updated LITTLE RED RIDING HOOD living in the fundamentalist hell of Gilead. Offred must extricate herself from ruin by guile, seduction, and bargaining. Atwood expresses through Gilead's female hierarchy the dangers of surrogate motherhood, which she foresees as another form of bondage that values women such as Offred only as drones and breeders.

Atwood returned to the hurts of real women with a 10th novel, *The Blind Assassin* (2001), a Booker Prize–winning metafiction that portrays sisters who live a family nightmare during the Great Depression. As in the claustrophobic anti-woman milieu of Edith WHARTON's *The Age of Innocence* (1920), Atwood's story within a story replicates female Gothic conventions to portray the self-rescue of the sisters Laura and Iris Griffen Chase. Atwood relies on surrogate mothering, family secrets, an attic hideout, and mystery to comment on the girls' powerlessness to relieve patriarchal misery. In a description of Laura, who kills herself by driving Iris's car off a bridge, the text pictures the dead woman in the pose of a nun: "Penitential colours—less like something she'd chosen to put on than like something she'd been locked up in" (Atwood, 2001, 2). In a brief memory of childhood pain, Iris concludes, "Some people can't tell where it hurts. They can't calm down. They can't ever stop howling" (*ibid.*). In 2003, Atwood extended her dark vision of human demise with another dystopian fantasy, *Oryx and Crake*, an absorbing sci-fi thriller that projects humanity's doom through genetic misengineering. In all her works, she champions women as their own saviors.

Bibliography

Atwood, Margaret. *The Blind Assassin*. New York: Anchor Books, 2001.

———. *The Robber Bride*. New York: Anchor Books, 1998.

Tatar, Maria. "It's Time for Fairy Tales with the Bite of Reality," *New York Times*, 29 November 1998, sec. 2, p. 1.

Weisser, Susan Ostrov, and Jennifer Fleischner. *Feminist Nightmares: Women at Odds: Feminism and the Problems of Sisterhood*. New York: New York University Press, 1995.

Wilson, Sharon Rose. *Margaret Atwood's Fairy-Tale Sexual Politics*. Jackson: University Press of Mississippi, 1993.

Auel, Jean (1936–)

Jean Marie Untinen Auel imagines through popular romance the role of women in the Middle Paleolithic age. A native Chicagoan, she studied physics and calculus briefly at Portland State University. Although she lacked a college diploma, she earned an M.B.A. from the University of Portland and obtained a job designing circuit boards and managing credit for Tektronics, an electronics firm in Beaverton, Oregon. At age 44, she altered her lifestyle by researching prehistoric human life and by writing *The Clan of the Cave Bear* (1980), the first of a massive five-part series called Earth's Children. The phenomenally successful novel earned a Friends of Literature citation and nomination for an American Book Award.

Auel surprised paleoanthropologists with her factual depiction of Europe during the Ice Age and the appearance of the first modern humans. To understand how a clan survived 27,000 years ago, she relived their saga by studying the cave drawings of bison and reindeer in Dordogne and by camping in the remains of prehistoric residences in Austria, Czechoslovakia, Germany, Hungary, Kenya, Russia, and the Ukraine. Vital to her project was mastery of the spear and atlatl (spear thrower), identification of edible and healing herbs and plants, surveying the Danube, tanning hides and weaving rushes, knapping flint, and constructing a snow cave with only a crude obsidian knife as a tool.

Auel's disciplined focus on Ayla, the Cro-Magnon protagonist orphaned by an earthquake in the Crimea, corrects false beliefs that prehistoric women were ignorant drones and sex slaves. Her innate pragmatism appears in early girlhood as she faces the elements with only a mirage of her mother to guide her: "[Ayla] lived only for the moment, getting past the next obstacle. . . . It was the only thing that gave her any direction, any purpose, any course of action. It was better than doing nothing" (Auel, 1984, 6). Through Ayla's study of fire making and weaponry and her domestication of a wolf, she illustrates intellectual curiosity and ingenuity while living among patriarchal Neanderthals, the taboo-ridden hunter-gatherers who preceded Cro-Magnons. Auel resumed Ayla's story in *The Valley of Horses* (1982) and *The Mammoth Hunters* (1985), both major best sellers. After researching *The Plains of Passage* (1990) and *The Shelters of Stone* (2002), she mapped out a fifth sequel. Even in the sixth stage of Auel's saga, Ayla faces the assembled Zelandonii with the same question, "Would they accept her? What if they didn't?" (Auel, 2003, 4). With feminist determination, she averred, "She couldn't go back" (*ibid.*). Her mate, Jondalar, a model of the liberated male, introduces her with a string of titles: "Ayla of the Mamutoi, Member of the Lion Camp, Daughter of the Mammoth Hearth, Chosen by the Spirit of the Cave Lion, and Protected by the Cave Bear" (*ibid.*, 6).

Auel's contribution to women's history is unusual. By studying anthropology from an amateur's point of view, the author validated shrewd guesses of how a talented female, a prehistoric version of the NEW WOMAN, thrived in a sexist migrant clan. The author surmised how tribe members evolved female fertility rites and supplanted cartoon images of the Flintstones with her own assumptions about the role of women in decision making and technology. Ayla's rejection of male belligerence, her conciliatory response to squabbles, and her formation of a SISTERHOOD elevate prehistoric females to shrewd, intuitive clan builders and worthy contributors to civilization. For their accuracy, Auel's books serve anthropology students as classroom texts. A film version of *The Clan of the Cave Bear*, starring Darryl Hannah as Ayla, displeased Auel, who sued Warner Brothers for releasing the film without her approval.

Bibliography

Auel, Jean. *The Clan of the Cave Bear*. New York: Bantam, 1984.

———. *The Shelters of Stone*. New York: Bantam, 2003.

Edgar, Blake. "Chronicler of Ice Age Life," *Archaeology* 55, no. 6 (November 2002): 36–41.

Wilcox, Clyde. "The Not-So-Failed Feminism of Jean Auel," *Journal of Popular Culture* 28, no. 3 (Winter 1994): 63–70.

Austen, Jane (1775–1817)

A British feminist of the Regency period, Jane Austen was a homebody who developed into an accomplished domestic satirist. She was born at Steventon and lived for seven years amid the sparkling social life at Bath. Well read in the essayists, romanticists, and novelists of her day, including the feminist works of Lady Mary WALKER, Austen received guidance and homeschooling from her father, the Reverend George Austen. Privately, she flourished at observing female deportment and decorum among Georgian England's gentry. In the estimation of the feminist critic Carolyn G. Heilbrun, author of *Toward a Recognition of Androgyny* (1982), "[Austen's] quiet miracle was to be able to represent the lineaments of society by an art in which men and women move in ambience of equality" (Heilbrun, 74). Significant to Austen's writings is the era that countenanced a young woman's mercenary scouting of a beau who promised a comfortable living.

In an era that denied equal educational and career opportunities to women, Austen was conversant with a woman's need to look out for her own welfare. To ease financial shortfalls in her family, at age 36, she elected to write for profit, a profession she pursued in her remaining six years, though she had already been writing for several years. She published the first of back-to-back English classics, *Sense and Sensibility* (1811) and *Pride and Prejudice* (1813), and followed with *Mansfield Park* (1814) and *Emma* (1815). Her Gothic spoof *Northanger Abbey* (1818), a parody on the silly extremes of the era's fantasists, mocks Ann RADCLIFFE's classic *The Mysteries of Udolpho* (1794) with a new version of the BLUEBEARD myth. The central character, Catherine Morland, is so taken by escapist fiction that, while vacationing at Bath, she schedules recreational reading of Eliza Parsons's *The Castle of Wolfenbach* (1793) and *Mysterious Warnings* (1796), Peter Teuthold's *The Necromancer of the Black Forest* (1794), Eleanor Sleath's *Orphan of the Rhine* (1796), Peter Will's *Horrid Mysteries* (1796), Francis Lathom's *The Midnight Bell* (1798), and Regina Maria Roche's *Clermont* (1798). Catherine, who greatly enjoys reading fright novels, tries to track down evidence of mystery, secrets, and coercion at Northanger

Abbey, which fails to live up to her standards of sensationalism. After Austen's death at age 42 of Addison's disease and rheumatoid arthritis, she left unfinished *Sanditon* and *The Watsons*. Posthumously, the Austen family published *Persuasion* (1818), perhaps her most autobiographical work.

Through understatement, social farce, caricature, irony, and restrained humor, Austen excelled at parent-daughter and sisterly relationships and at the quandaries arising from harmful tittle-tattle and unexpected turns in male-female socializing, matchmaking, and marriage proposals. Her themes emphasize faulty education of female children, limited expectations for girls and women, the perils of the MARRIAGE MARKET, and a society that forces women like the fictional Eliza and Jane Bennet, Jane Fairfax, Anne Elliot, and Emma Woodhouse to depend on their menfolk—Fitzwilliam Darcy, Charles Bingley, Frank Churchill, Captain Frederick Wentworth, and Mr. Knightley—for approval, social prestige, and financial support. The author does not hesitate to censure such characters as the immature Marianne Dashwood for chasing the unworthy Willoughby, the forward Louisa Musgrove for nearly breaking her skull while throwing herself at a sea captain, and the immodest Lydia Bennet for eloping to London with Wickham, a charming womanizer in uniform. In the tone of a prim governess, Austen also disapproves of the judgmental Emma for sneering at the tedious Miss Bates and sets up for ridicule the ditzy Catherine Morland for expecting Northanger Abbey to conform to the romantic excesses of fictional gothic settings.

For their conservatism, Austen's dispassionate novels of manners have stumped literary historians and critics who struggle to define her personal concept of feminism. The subtext of her droll and, at times, melodramatic didacticism implies a sympathy with young women who are immobilized by PATRIARCHY and a consternation at social settings in which deliberate slights and trivial errors in judgment threaten the future of heretofore marriageable young women. In reference to the future of the five Bennet daughters, Austen comments that Longbourn, the family home, "was entailed, in default of heirs male, on a distant relation; and their mother's fortune, though ample for her situation in life, could but ill supply the deficiency of his" (Austen, 1980, 22). For pragmatic reasons, the author's conclusions favor marriage as the ultimate solution on a series of personal issues, but her pairings predict happiness, even for Marianne's choice of the middle-aged Colonel Brandon, Anne Elliot's marriage to Frederick, and Emma's union with the paternal Mr. Knightley.

Austen's fine opinion of her gender reached a height of candor in chapter 8 of *Persuasion,* in which Sophia Musgrove retorts to a sexist remark from her brother: "I hate to hear you talking so, like a fine gentleman, and as if women were all fine ladies, instead of rational creatures. We none of us expect to be in smooth water all our days" (Austen, 1995, 52–53). In chapter 23 Austen summarizes one view of the narrow realm of womanhood. In contrast to the active world of men at business and the professions, the Cinderella-like protagonist Anne Elliot describes to Captain Harville the typical environs of gentlewomen: "We live at home, quiet, confined, and our feelings prey upon us" (*ibid.,* 179). Balancing her overstatement of female limitations is the character herself, a model of good sense, propriety, intellectualism, and constancy. For her ideal qualities and game spirit, the author awards her a fully integrated, yet unconventional life among the gentry and allows her to sail away with a handsome husband. Austen's self-confident females influenced the writings of Sarah Orne JEWETT, Alison LURIE, Anna QUINDLEN, and Sigrid UNDSET.

Bibliography

Austen, Jane. *Persuasion.* Ware, England: Wordsworth Editions, 1995.

———. *Pride and Prejudice.* New York: Signet Classic, 1980.

Heilbrun, Carolyn G. *Toward a Recognition of Androgyny.* New York: W. W. Norton, 1982.

Morrison, Sarah R. "Of Woman Borne: Male Experience and Feminine Truth in Jane Austen's Novels," *Studies in the Novel* 26, no. 4 (Winter 1994): 337–349.

Wallace, Miriam L. "Laughing Feminism," *Women's Studies* 29, no. 5 (September 2000): 695–698.

Warhol, Robyn A. "The Look, the Body, and the Heroine: A Feminist-Narratological Reading of *Persuasion,*" *Novel: A Forum on Fiction,* 26, no. 1 (Fall 1992): 5–19.

Austin, Mary Hunter (1868–1934)

A multitalented author of folklore, drama, vignette, and children's verse, Mary Hunter Austin established a writing career while familiarizing herself with the ecosystem of California's Joaquin Valley. A born rebel from Carlinville, Illinois, she rejected the pose of tidy little mama's girl. Eluding her widowed mother's gloomy Methodism, she sought education at Blackburn College and the State Normal School at Bloomington before homesteading on the West Coast in sight of the Sierra Madre and Mojave Desert. She befriended Native women, Hispanic shepherds, and the grizzled desert rats who made their home in rough terrain. When her ill-advised marriage failed, she supported herself and her mentally-handicapped daughter, Ruth, by working as domestic and cook at a Bakersfield boardinghouse and as a public school teacher in Los Angeles.

A dedicated campaigner for birth control, American Indian rights, the environment, and full citizenship for women, Austin received encouragement from the feminist writers Charlotte Perkins GILMAN, Emma GOLDMAN, Margaret SANGER, and Ida Tarbell. After testing the literary market with submissions to *Harper's, Land of Sunshine, Outwest, Overland Monthly,* and *Young Woman Citizen,* Austin serialized in the *Atlantic Monthly* a frontier classic, *The Land of Little Rain* (1903). Rhapsodic in its immersion in desert beauty, the text extols the crafts and healing remedies of native Comanche, Mojave, Navaho, Paiute, Papago, Shoshone, and Ute women. Of feminine creativity, Austin observed, "Every Indian woman is an artist,—sees, feels, creates, but does not philosophize about her processes" (Austin, 1903, 86). The author continued her perusal of female dwellers on a spare and unforgiving landscape with short fiction in *The Basket Woman* (1904) and the three-act play *The Arrow-Maker* (1910), the story of a healer, which opened on Broadway in 1911. In her story "Walking Woman" (1907), the author admires the unfussy outlook of tribal females and WISEWOMEN. The title character has no need for adornment: "It was the naked thing the Walking Woman grasped, not dressed and tricked out, for instance, by prejudices in favor of certain occupations; and love, man love, taken as it came, not picked over and rejected if it carried no obligation of permanency; and a child; *any* way you get it, a child is good to have" (Austin, 1907, 220).

Austin's ECOFEMINISM reflects a love of land and of indigenous peoples that materialistic Americans had abandoned and banished in the rush to urbanize and profit from industry. For her pupils, she composed a witty quatrain on the ladybug and the ravenous scale bug, a symbolic male. The last line urges, "Ladybug, ladybug, go and eat him!" (Austin, 1928, 214). The poem joined "Firedrill Songs," "Furryhide," and "Rain Song of the Rio Grande Pueblos" in the collection *Children Sing in the Far West* (1928), an anthology intended to instill the same love of place and aboriginal lore that European children felt for Grimms' fairy tales and Arthurian romance. During her years in Santa Fe, Austin composed a tender novel, *Starry Adventure* (1931), and an AUTOBIOGRAPHY, *Earth Horizon* (1932), which advances personal theories on conventionality and its harm to women's creativity. In the 1970s, feminists revived the popularity of Austin's spare, informative nature writing and her regard for First Nations.

Bibliography

Alaimo, Stacy. "The Undomesticated Nature of Feminism: Mary Austin and the Progressive Women Conservationists," *Studies in American Fiction* 26, no. 1 (Spring 1998): 73–96.

Austin, Mary Hunter. *Children Sing in the Far West.* Boston: Houghton Mifflin, 1928.

———. *The Land of Little Rain* (1903). Available online. URL: http://etext.lib.virginia.edu/toc/modeng/public/AusRain.html. Accessed on October 13, 2005.

———. *Walking Woman* (1907). Available online. URL: http://etext.lib.virginia.edu/toc/modeng/public/AusWalk.html. Accessed on October 13, 2005.

Stout, Janis P. "Mary Austin's Feminism: A Reassessment," *Studies in the Novel* 30, no. 1 (Spring 1998): 77–101.

autobiography

Women's life stories reveal the gendered mores that belittle or degrade females and detail survival techniques that free them from VIOLENCE and sexism. Early in the 11th century, the world's first novelist, MURASAKI Shikibu, filled a diary with details of her life in the royal court of Japan. During the spiritual stirring that preceded the Renaissance, MARGERY KEMPE, a peripatetic mystic, produced *The BOOK OF MARGERY KEMPE* (1436), an emotion-charged examination of the conflict between life as wife and mother and the mission of the soul-hungry pilgrim. In colonial America, the poet Anne BRADSTREET permeated a collection of verse, *The Tenth Muse Lately Sprung Up in America* (1650), with concerns related to breast-feeding, a house fire, the death of her grandson, and her dislike of sour-faced Puritans. In *The SOVEREIGNTY AND GOODNESS OF GOD* (1682), Mary ROWLANDSON summarized a terrifying episode in her adult life, a kidnap by Wampanoag Indians. They also murdered members of her family, including her daughter, Sarah, whom a warrior slays in Mary's arms. From her forthright recall of sewing and bartering to earn her keep emerged a separate strand of memoir, CAPTIVITY NARRATIVE. The unique subgenre of frontier autobiography ingathered impressions of seizure, forced march, and confinement in Elizabeth Meader Hanson's abduction memoir *God's Mercy Surmounting Man's Cruelty* (1728) and a similar episode during the French and Indian War in *The Life and Times of Mrs. Mary Jemison* (1827). These intricate tellings of racial violence helped to set the tone for later autobiography and fiction picturing the lives of female settlers of North America.

A steady outpouring of autobiography chronicles the varied ways in which the authors retrieve their past and reclaim autonomy and direction, the purpose of *The Household Book of Lady Griselle Baillie* (1733), Anna Laetitia BARBAULD's self-revelatory poem "To a Little Invisible Being Who Is Expected Soon to Become Visible" (ca. 1795), the author Mary ROBINSON's *Memoirs of the Late Mrs. Robinson* (1801), and Anna Howard Shaw's *The Story of a Pioneer* (1915). The altruist Elizabeth BLACKWELL surveyed the squalor and starvation of immigrant German women and children in *Pioneer Work in Opening the Medical Profession to Women: Autobiographical Sketches* (1895). Less ladylike is Cary Nation's blend of religious fervor with violence during the TEMPERANCE crusade, which fills the pages of *The Use and Need of the*

Life of Carry A. Nation (1905), a fiery self-defense from the woman who amused and amazed Americans by swinging an ax into the bars and tables of seamy saloons.

Some glimpses arose from the innocence of girlhood, before society jaded the spirit and hardened the heart. In 1910, the progressive social worker Jane Addams reported on the sufferings of the poor in *Twenty Years at Hull-House*, a memoir of her battle against poverty and ignorance. She recalled viewing the shabby streets of rowhouses and asking her father "why people lived in such horrid little houses so close together" (Addams, 5). With another child's point of view, the frontierswoman Laura Ingalls WILDER captured on paper the solitude and daily chores common to female homesteaders in *Little House in the Big Woods* (1932) and *Little House on the Prairie* (1935), two classic children's memoirs. From the point of view of a naif in the wild, Marjorie Kinnan RAWLINGS preserved in *Cross Creek* (1942) the change of outlook that followed her move from the city to the Florida outback, where she developed into a writer, cook, orchard keeper, and neighbor. In each instance, the drive to succeed and overcome barriers fortified the autobiographer to face challenge.

Autobiography supplies readers with unique solutions to recurrent antiwoman motifs. The editor Gloria STEINEM exposed the sexism of waitressing in men's bars and nightclubs in a personal essay, "I Was a Playboy Bunny" (1963), the impetus for her filmscript for the droll ABC-TV film *A Bunny's Tale* (1985), which starred Kirstie Alley as Steinem. Similarly inspired by degradation, Lorraine Hansberry's posthumous autobiography *To Be Young, Gifted, and Black* (1969) pinpoints the events that turned her into a successful playwright and compassionate activist for the ghetto poor. Of the female scientist's difficulties, Margaret MEAD reported in *Blackberry Winter: My Earlier Years* (1972) on her methods of earning collegial respect through dogged field work. In *The Hidden Face of Eve: Women in the Arab World* (1980) and *Walking through Fire* (2002), the Egyptian writer Nawal EL SAADAWI speaks of the bitter choices that confront an Islamic female intellectual. In a lengthy retrospective of career achievements and social progress, the sisters Bessie Delany and Sadie Delany fill *Having Our Say: The Delany Sisters' First 100 Years* (1991) with character struggles they manage through their early home training in industry and dignity. Through the mask of Bone Boatwright in *Bastard Out of Carolina* (1992), the author Dorothy ALLISON expresses the terrors of pedophilia and child rape she recalls from her past.

The composition of the author's own experience is a valuable statement of minority life. Sojourner TRUTH's as told to *The Narrative of Sojourner Truth: A Bondswoman of Olden Time* (1850) and Harriet Jacobs's *Incidents in the Life of a Slave Girl, Written by Herself* (1861) picture for white readers the hardships of slave life, particularly the mother's fear of losing her children to the auction block. In *Mourning Dove: A Salishan Autobiography* (1990), the author, born in Idaho in 1888, accounts for her dread of marriage by describing Salishan polygamy and the power of males to abuse their wives. She explains, "Next to the dog, the native woman had no equal in taking abuse from 'her man'" (Mourning Dove, 56). Abandoned women could wreak revenge through a dramatic suicide—hanging, drowning, or stabbing. The male-centered Salishan society required death for the female adulterer, who could either kill herself or be shot with an arrow by a male relative. Mourning Dove remarks, "Her feelings were never considered, only the lawful resentment of her community" (*ibid.*, 57).

The Native author Beatrice Culleton applied feminist themes to a specific Amerindian crisis, the white-controlled social system that steals Metís girls from their homes. Displacement from Native surroundings strips them of Native female traits through residence in a series of foster families. In the autobiographical novel *In Search of April Raintree* (1983), which draws on Culleton's sisters, who took their own lives, the story of April and Cheryl, one light and one dark, describes their alcoholic parents trapped in the demoralizing Winnipeg welfare system. The replacement of tribal pride and unity by poverty, promiscuity, and brawling predisposes the girls to faulty judgment and seduction by exploitive Euro-Canadian males. Worsening the situation for April and Cheryl is the absence of a strong female community to provide wisdom and counsel.

Culleton's themes pervade other first-person accounts of life as an indigenous female. The disappearance of Native community triggers the despair of the autobiographer Maria Campbell in *Halfbreed* (1973), in which she tries to retrace the diaspora but finds no home to which she can return. The worst of the loss is the absence of Cheechum, the grandmother and storyteller who once affirmed pride and dignity in the clan's girls. In Lee Maracle's autobiography, *Bobbi Lee, Indian Rebel: Struggles of a Native Canadian Woman* (1975), the issue of the feminism of elitist white colonizers forces Maracle into a tribal corner. Courageously, she calls for a race-free, woman-to-woman cooperative that will name the real enemy, the patriarchal male.

Bibliography

Addams, Jane. *Twenty Years at Hull House.* New York: Signet, 1999.

Davis, Allen F. *American Heroine: The Life and Legend of Jane Addams.* Chicago: Ivan R. Dee, 1973.

Donovan, Kathleen M. *Feminist Readings of Native American Literature: Coming to Voice.* Tucson: University of Arizona Press, 1998.

Ehrenreich, Barbara. *Nickel and Dimed: On (Not) Getting By in America.* New York: Owl Books, 2002.

Morgan, Janice, and Colette T. Hall, eds. *Redefining Autobiography in Twentieth-Century Women's Fiction.* New York: Garland, 1991.

Mourning Dove. *Mourning Dove: A Salishan Autobiography.* Lincoln: University of Nebraska Press, 1990.

Avellaneda, Gertrudis Gómez de
(1814–1873)

The unconventional Hispano-Cuban sonneteer and playwright Gertrudis Gómez de Avellaneda denounced racism and slavery in her fiction 11 years before Harriet Beecher STOWE wrote UNCLE TOM'S CABIN (1852). A native of Puerto Principe, Cuba, she was the daughter of an island beauty and an aristocratic Spanish naval officer, who had his bright daughter tutored in poetry and literature rather than the usual classes in needlework. Because of racial unrest in Cuba, in 1836, she resettled in La Coruña, Spain, and published her first poetry anthology five years later. She witnessed the staging of her first play, *Leoncia* (1840), and of a romantic tragedy, *Alfonso Munio* (1844), a vehicle for her melancholy perspective. Married and widowed in 1846, she continued writing for the theater, producing a biblical play, *Said* (1849), and a classical drama, *Baltasar* (1858). On return to Cuba the next year, she established a women's journal, *Album Cubano de lo bueno y lo bello* (The Cuban album of the good and the beautiful).

Avellaneda's masterwork is *Sab* (1841), a feminist antislavery melodrama that captures the misery and powerlessness of a mulatto Cuban. Influenced by a French translation of Aphra BEHN's *Oroonoko; or, The Royal Slave* (1688), the anticolonial story depicts taboo subjects—the humiliation of bondage, biracial love, miscegenation, and the black Cuban's right to freedom. The author's feminism emerges in candid depictions of aristocratic women as silent adornments to their husbands. Avellaneda condemns arranged marriage, which she considers a form of female social enslavement that denies women their hearts' desires. As abolitionism encroached on the island in the 1870s, *Sab* enjoyed a new burst of popularity as well as serialization in a rebel journal.

Bibliography

Davies, Catherine. "Founding-Fathers and Domestic Genealogies: Situating Gertrudis Gómez de Avellaneda," *Bulletin of Latin American Research* 22, no. 4 (October 2003): 423–444.

Gómez de Avellaneda, Gertrudis. *Sab and Autobiography.* Austin: University of Texas Press, 1993.

Pastor, Brigida. "Cuba's Covert Cultural Critics: The Feminist Writings of Gertrudis Gómez de Avellaneda," *Romance Quarterly* 42, no. 3 (Summer 1995): 178–189.

Awakening, The Kate Chopin (1899)

A landmark psychological novella criticizing the gender roles assigned to women by a prudish Louisiana society, Kate Chopin's controversial novella *The Awakening* depicts a sensitive 28-year-old woman's embrace of passion and free expression. Based in the elitist strictures of the New Orleans gentry, the text characterizes social customs and faults that confine middle-class women to a predetermined "woman's sphere" as wives, hostesses, and mothers. Through interior landscapes that the protagonist conceals from outsiders, Chopin illustrates Edna Pontellier's willingness to risk social approbation by achieving total fulfillment as a woman, artist, and human being. Her joy of complete freedom actualizes the theme of Chopin's early beast fable, "Emancipation" (1869), in which a cage-born animal is more willing to drink from a dirty pool than to return to the comforts and shelter of its cell.

Contrast explains the angst of the imprisoning Pontellier union. Chopin pictures Edna as engaging and witty, but restless. In the opening lines, a caged parrot, a symbol of Edna's unease, shrieks gibberish blended from English, French, and Spanish. He clearly orders in French, "Allez vous-en! Allez vous-en!" (Go on! Go on!), a cry that recurs a few weeks later in the plot (Chopin, 43). The author portrays Edna's predictable Creole husband, Léonce, as a stodgy stockbroker set on currying favor among the upper middle class. For the sake of social standing, he insists, "Why, my dear, I should think you'd understand by this time . . . we've got to observe *les convenances* if we ever expect to get on and keep up with the procession" (*ibid.,* 101). Weeping without knowing why, Edna senses that she cannot accept her part as corporate wife or the motherly role in which her friend Adèle thrives.

A change of setting from urban constraints offers the protagonist an opportunity to explore a new self. Primed for romance, Edna enjoys the female refuge on Grand Isle, a pension that Madame Lebrun operates for the women and children who vacation apart from the men of the family. On the weekend, Léonce joins Edna. While she refreshes herself at the beach, she gives him her rings to hold, an act heavy with implication. At one evening musicale, she begins to drop her reserve. She finds a model for her emerging self in the fervid piano performance of Mademoiselle Reisz, a daring woman who is unashamed of her inner drive. Although Edna is still tentative about rebelling against propriety, she exhibits daring by going for a moonlight swim, slipping outdoors in peignoir and mules to sleep in a hammock, and sailing in a boat with Robert Lebrun, a handsome young flirt. Her choices seem to ease "an indescribable oppression"

that she feels "in some unfamiliar part of her consciousness" and to vent her agitation in an unforeseen bout of weeping (*ibid.,* 49).

The epiphany that changes Edna is the realization that individuality is more important to her than marriage or motherhood. She differentiates between her own personality and that of the mother-women "who idolized their children, worshiped their husbands, and esteemed it a holy privilege to efface themselves as individuals" (*ibid.,* 51). In contrast, her controlling husband strolls about his fashionable home on Esplanade Street and admires his possessions "chiefly because they were his," a suggestion of his arrogant ownership of Edna as well (*ibid.,* 99). To free herself from confining bourgeois traditions, she gives up weekly visiting hours and the friendships her husband cultivates for the sake of business. She flings her wedding band on the carpet and stamps on it, then indulges mood swings and caprices. The sudden venting of frustration perplexes her husband, her father, and the unsympathetic family doctor, who retreats from Edna's problems because "he did not want the secrets of other lives thrust upon him" (*ibid.,* 124). Chopin stresses not only the male exasperation with contrariness in women but also the men's unwillingness to examine Edna's restive behavior sympathetically.

Through Edna's fights with both husband and father, Chopin pictures the protagonist's break with unbearable patriarchal standards. Her move from the imposing family residence to a small house and the peace that results from activities of her own choosing precede a final act, a swim as far out into the Gulf of Mexico as she is able. In her last moments, she reverses the mythic emergence of Aphrodite from the sea with an escape from Louisiana-style gentrification. Edna "[feels] like some new-born creature, opening its eyes in a familiar world that it had never known" (*ibid.,* 175). She realizes that loving a mate and children should not require her to surrender "body and soul" (*ibid.,* 176). Critics have debated the ambiguous image of Edna's forcing her body to swim away from the shore to the limit of her strength. The bark of an old dog chained to a tree and the clang of a cavalry officer's spurs suggest the male-dominated life that Edna abandons through suicide.

Bibliography

Chopin, Kate. *The Awakening and Selected Stories.* New York: Penguin, 1983.

Elz, A. Elizabeth. "*The Awakening* and *A Lost Lady:* Flying with Broken Wings and Raked Feathers," *Southern Literary Journal* 35, no. 2 (Spring 2003): 13–27.

Hackett, Joyce. "The Reawakening," *Harper's* 307, no. 1,841 (October 2003): 82–86.

B

Backlash Susan Faludi (1991)

The Pulitzer Prize winner Susan FALUDI surveys gender issues in *Backlash: The Undeclared War against American Women* (1991), a best seller and winner of a National Book Critics Circle Award for nonfiction and a *Progressive* Best Reading of 1992. Through aggressive reportage, she defends the life choices of unmarried, career-minded, or divorced women, a beleaguered female subset during the Reagan-Bush era. Against conservative propaganda about a spinster boom, a "marriage crunch" from a shortage of single men, workplace burnout, pervasive depression, and an infertility epidemic, Faludi asserts that these myths "have one thing in common: they aren't true" (Faludi, 10, 4). She emphasizes that such fallacies demean female achievements since the rise of the WOMEN'S MOVEMENT in the 1960s. To prove her point, she analyzes popular catch phrases—"the biological clock," "birth dearth," "Breck girl," "cocooning," "fetal rights," "Iron John," "New Traditionalism," "no-fault divorce," and "trophy wife." She characterizes "masculinist" motivation as a male fear of losing power to females, a source of toxic political rhetoric. Against psychological brainwashing based on frivolities, Faludi concentrates on serious matters of unequal pay, mistreatment in the workplace, relegation to pink-collar jobs, unfair layoffs, sexual harassment, and limited promotions of qualified women.

Dedicated to her mother, Faludi's comprehensive study of popular culture revisits the first backlash of the 1850s, the second in the 1920s after passage of the Nineteenth Amendment, and the third, the return of Rosie the Riveter to the hearth in the late 1940s. The author's summation of the fourth backlash takes in the unsubtle put-downs of films such as *Fatal Attraction* (1987), fluffy "mommy" TV series, antifeminists such as Camille PAGLIA, pop psychology urging women to "get over it," baby doll fashions and neo-Victorian underwear, and advertisements from the beauty industry that extol the temptress. In part 3 Faludi blames the New Right for strategies that restore to prominence the silent-but-happy good wife of the post–World War II era. Antiwoman tactics range in menace from demoralizing women whose children are in day care and ridiculing legitimate protesters as "strident" or "hysterical" to the religious Right's demonizing of those who choose ABORTION over unwanted maternity. Faludi stresses that the legal power behind the antichoice drive is overwhelmingly male.

Backlash had a palliative effective on the antifeminism of the 1990s by outlining the "budget cuts that helped impoverish millions of women, fought pay equity proposals, and undermined equal opportunity laws" (ibid., ix). Faludi uplifted female spirits by demanding that "women not be forced to choose between public justice and private happiness" (ibid.). Elaine SHOWALTER, in a critique for the *Los Angeles Times Book Review,* praised the work's passion for facts over myths generated by entrenched neoconservatives. The author Barbara EHRENREICH admired the author's ethical clarity and effective logic. Although some critics charged Faludi with pessimism, readers gleaned from her arguments an admiration for women who refuse to be restrained or reduced to less than whole human beings.

Bibliography

Faludi, Susan. *Backlash: The Undeclared War against American Women.* New York: Anchor Books, 1992.

Fink, Virginia S. "Review: *Backlash: The Undeclared War against American Women,*" *American Journal of Sociology* 99, no. 3 (November 1993): 824–825.

Shore, Paul. "Review: *Backlash: The Undeclared War against American Women,*" *Humanist* 52, no. 5 (September/October 1992): 47–48.

Bâ, Mariama (1929–1981)

The Senegalese journalist and novelist Mariama Bâ, a proponent of international feminism, wrote about the political, social, and personal rebellion of West African women against feudal PATRIARCHY. The child of a prominent Dakar family, she lived with her mother's parents, who raised her according to Islamic standards that discouraged extensive schooling for girls. She studied the Koran at home and was formally educated in Rufisque at L'Ecole Normal for girls, where she wrote her first essays. In adulthood, while teaching school and serving the district as educational inspector, she was the wife of Member of Parliament Obèye Diop, father of her nine children.

After a divorce, Bâ led other West African women toward liberation from an oppressive patriarchy and toward the solidarity of SISTERHOOD. As a writer of feminist articles for newspapers, she took on as a sacred vocation the mission of rooting out "archaic practices, traditions, and customs that are not a real part of our precious cultural heritage" (Bâ, 1989, i). She persevered in her crusade until a fatal illness ended her life shortly before the publication of *Scarlet Song* (1981), her second novel, the story of a bicultural marriage that ends in the wife's abandonment and insanity. The text rings with the author's challenge to the duplicitous colonial authority: "Noble sentiments have forsaken the African soul. Look how many of our African leaders, who were in the vanguard of the movements for national liberation, are unrecognisable now that they have their feet in the stirrups of power. Now they censure the very things they used to preach" (Bâ, 1995, 45–46).

Bâ attracted critical attention of the Western world with the publication of an epistolary novella, *So Long a Letter* (1979), which received the Noma Award for Publishing in Africa for its expression of the healing grace of friendship. She dedicated the text to "all women and to men of good will" and intended it to enlighten other Senegalese women about their rights as human beings (Bâ, 1989, i). Originally composed in French, the novel was translated into English in 1981 and published in 16 languages. The first-person story takes place in modern Dakar, where the schoolteacher Ramatoulaye Fall is newly widowed from Modou Fall, formerly a technical adviser in the Ministry of Public Works. She calls on her confidante Aissatou in ritual style— "My friend, my friend, my friend"—as though invoking a deity before revealing a humiliating turn of events (*ibid.,* 1). To stabilize turbulent emotions after her husband's ritual burial, Ramatoulaye clings to faith in her friend and in experience: "If over the years . . . dreams die, I still keep intact my memories, the salt of remembrance" (*ibid.,* 1).

Bâ's account of an African Islamic funeral and a 40-day mourning period focuses on the bonding of female friends and family with the widow. Bitterly, Ramatoulaye relates her husband's disloyalty in marrying Binetou, a young woman the age of his daughter, Daba. Ramatoulaya scorns his lame excuse that Allah intended him to marry a second wife. In her own defense, Ramatoulaye cites a 30-year marriage and her 12 pregnancies. During a brief respite, she details the womanly care that her sisters-in-law offer in loosening her hair and escorting her to the red mourning tent, which they rid of evil spirits with a handful of coins cast onto its canopy. In addition to surrendering her possessions to Modou's family, Ramatoulaye regrets having to give up "her personality, her dignity, becoming a thing in the service of the man who has married her, his grandfather, his grandmother, his father, his mother, his brother, his sister, his uncle, his aunt, his male and female cousins, his friends" (*ibid.,* 4). The text won international fame for its depiction of a strong woman who rises above disappointment to nurture her grown children through their own hardships.

Bibliography

Bâ, Mariama. *The Scarlet Song*. London: Longman, 1995.

———. *So Long a Letter*. Portsmouth, N.H.: Heinemann, 1989.

Dubek, Laura. "Lessons in Solidarity: Buchi Emecheta and Mariama Bâ on Female Victim(izer)s," *Women's Studies* 30, no. 3 (June 2001): 199–223.

Baillie, Joanna (1762–1851)

The populist Scots bard and playwright Joanna Baillie infused late 18th- and early-19th-century British psychological drama with a feminist perspective. The daughter of a rural minister, she was born in Bothwell, Scotland, and attended boarding school in Glasgow, where she began learning stagecraft in girlhood by writing original theatricals. She had as mentor Sir Walter Scott, whom she loved and revered as if he were a member of her family. Ruled by severe Scots Presbyterian values, she tackled the issue of public morals with *A Series of Plays on the Passions*, a 14-year project of emotion-revealing drama she initiated in 1798. She astounded critics, who marveled at the range of neuroses and psychoses that the author dramatized in vivid cautionary scenarios. Her psychological tragedy of hate, *De Montfort* (1800), a popular stage thriller, succeeded at Drury Lane Theatre by involving the audience in terror. Contributing to the staging were its atmosphere, setting, sound effects, and the combined efforts of the actors John Kemble, who played the lead, and Sarah Siddons, who portrayed the magnetic, but distant beauty Jane de Montfort. Unlike the characters of the Gothic conventions of the period, Baillie's Jane was a multidimensional match for the male lead.

Baillie remained single by choice while populating her stage works, closet plays, and dialect verse with independent women. She recognized the paralyzing strictures of marriage, which she alludes to in the winsome wedding day ballad "Song: Woo'd and Married and a'" (1822). An outstanding example of a courageous rebel in the author's poem *The Legend of Lady Griseld* [sic] *Baillie* (1821) relieved Scottish history of its all-male bastion of heroes by asserting a woman's ability to think logically and act with valor in perilous times. The real Lady Grisell [sic] Baillie, an early 18th-century Scots heroine and author of *The Household Book of Lady Griselle* [sic] *Baillie* (1692–1733), slipped into an Edinburgh dungeon at age 12 to deliver a message to a prisoner, Robert Baillie. After the family fled by sea to safety in Utrecht, she rescued her sister, Julian, from possible hanging for defying the anti-Calvinist regent Charles II by carrying Julian piggyback out of danger. The poem extols a full range of Lady Baillie's qualities and "[gives] to fame / A generous helpful Maid,—a good and noble Dame" (Baillie, 1821, 259).

Late in her career, Baillie wrote *Ahalya Baee* (1849), a verse romance about a legendary queen whose 30-year reign in central India was one of peace. The poem, as does Baillie's well-rounded image of Lady Baillie, presents Queen Ahalya as both authority figure and mother, a blend of rule and domesticity. Of her devotion to duty, the poet writes: "But ne'er a Brahmin of them all / Could win her for his blinded thrall, / Could e'er her noble mind persuade / To do what inward rectitude forbade" (Baillie, 1849, 18). An Asian version of the upright Queen Victoria, Ahalya becomes the defender of the national family, a champion of the poor, and a defier of warlords. For contrast, Baillie inserts reference to Muchta Baee, the queen's widowed daughter, who accepts the patriarchal horror of suttee as her only honorable choice. As a nun takes the veil, the queen grieves in private and lives out her 60 years in prim, understated duty to the realm, another element drawn from the model of Queen Victoria. Baillie encouraged the writing of the poet Felicia HEMANS. One of Baillie's admirers, the sociologist Harriet MARTINEAU, lauded the poet's works as the writing of an able female.

Bibliography

Baillie, Joanna. *Ahalya Baee: A Poem*. London: Spottiswoodes & Shaw, 1849.

———. *Metrical Legends of Exalted Characters*. London: Longman, 1821.

Burroughs, Catherine B. "A Reasonable Woman's Desire": The Private Theatrical and Joanna Baillie's 'The Tryal,'" *Texas Studies in Literature and Language* 38, no. 3/4 (Fall–Winter 1996): 265–284.

Carney, Sean. "The Passion of Joanna Baillie: Playwright as Martyr," *Theatre Journal* 52, no. 2 (May 2000): 227–252.

Bambara, Toni Cade (1939–1995)

Like Rumpelstiltskin, black activist, educator, and writer Toni Cade Bambara spun observations and experiences into gold in masterful short fiction about working-class black life. A native New Yorker, she was named Milton Mirkin Cade at birth. She grew up in Harlem and Bedford-Stuyvesant in a feminist household in which her single mother taught her children black history and encouraged their dreams of success. Bambara became the community scribe for illiterate and semiliterate neighbors and friends and adopted her pseudonymous surname from the name of the Bambara, an ethnolinguistic group of Niger. After earning a degree in English and drama from Queens College and a graduate degree from City College of New York, she amassed human stories from working in a variety of jobs in social work, family programs, youth guidance; directing a psychiatric ward; and managing the Theatre of the Black Experience.

After initial success submitting feminist essays to *The Black Woman: An Anthology* (1970) and folklore to *Tales and Stories for Black Folks* (1971), Bambara created 15 dazzling vernacular narratives in *Gorilla, My Love* (1972), a story collection rife with comic exchanges and intense emotion. In the description of bell HOOKS, Bambara's friend and colleague, the author "dished out a kinda down-home basic black humor converging sometimes with a wicked wit" (hooks, 15). The anthology features female survivors such as Hazel, the child-protecting protagonist of the title story who refuses adult manipulation. One of the most popular stories, "The Lesson," depicts Miss Moore, the black-as-night tribal instructor and knowledgeable adult who spares children from having to learn by trial and error.

In Bambara's second anthology, *The Sea Birds Are Still Alive: Collected Stories* (1977), her breezy, energetic writing profits from first-person interviews with women in Cuba and Vietnam as part of her work for the North American Academic Marxist-Leninist Anti-imperialist Feminist Women. Her female protagonists, such as the provocative Granny Cora Cain in "Blues Ain't No Mockin Bird" (1971), reject despair and counter loss with keen-edged wit, controlled rage, and everyday pragmatism. In 1980 Bambara produced an American Book Award–winning novel, *The Salt Eaters*, the story of Velma Henry, a female activist who expends too much of self in trying to uplift her community. To revitalize her spirit, she submits to the faith healing of the wisewoman Minnie Ransom, a community authority figure and wielder of mystic powers.

Bambara uses STORYTELLING as the bulwark to save Velma, describing the process in physiological terms: "Retinal images, bogus images, traveling to the brain. The pupils trying to tell the truth to the inner eye. The eye of the heart. The eye of the head. The eye of the mind. All seeing differently" (Bambara, 1980, 6–7). Minnie consults Old Wife, her mystic fount, to ask about the disempowerment of "the daughters of the yam" (*ibid.*, 44). Minnie fears that her generation "don't know how to draw up the powers from the deep like before. Not full sunned and sweet anymore" (*ibid.*). Through the spirit guide, Minnie revives "tales nobody much wants to hear anymore except this humble servant of a swamphag" (*ibid.*, 43). The seriocomic woman-to-woman therapy reintegrates Velma's perceptions by reconnecting her with ancestral ties and turning her into a fighter, a "burst cocoon" (*ibid.*, 295).

The author expressed her devotion to oral tellings in the essay "Salvation Is the Issue," her contribution to the anthology *Black Women Writers (1950–1980)* (1984). She proclaimed that heirloom narratives "keep us alive. In the ships, in the camps, in the quarters, fields, prisons, on the road, on the run, underground, under siege, in the throes, on the verse—the storyteller snatches us back from the edge to hear the next chapter" (Bambara, 1984, 41). In a single sentence, she reprises elements of women's history that have tested valor and stamina. The voice of the narrator infuses new sources of strength by reminding women of the complex MATRIARCHY from which they sprang. With examples of courage in their ears, listeners find new reasons not to give up or give in.

In other projects, Bambara beamed to her readers her faith in "matriarchal currency" (Bambara, 1980, 36). She embraced film; scripted and narrated *The Bombing of Osage Avenue* (1985), a documentary on an attack on black families in urban Philadelphia; and wrote the introduction to *Daughters of the Dust: The Making of an African American Woman's Film* (1992). Bambara extolled the feminist filmmaker Julie Dash for "[fulfilling] the promise of Afrafemcentrists who choose film as their instrument for self-expression" (Bambara, 1996, 97). After the author's death of intestinal cancer at age 56, the editor Toni MORRISON completed *Those Bones Are Not My Child* (2000), Bambara's fictional speculation on the Atlanta child assaults and murders of 1979–81.

Bibliography

Bambara, Toni Cade. *Deep Sightings and Rescue Missions: Fiction, Essays, and Conversations.* New York: Pantheon, 1996.

———. *The Salt Eaters.* New York: Vintage, 1980.

———. "Salvation Is the Issue." In *Black Women Writers (1950–1980), A Critical Evaluation.* Edited by Mari Evans. New York: Doubleday, 1984.

Harrison, Elizabeth. "Intolerable Human Suffering and the Role of the Ancestor: Literary Criticism as a Means of Analysis," *Journal of Advanced Nursing* 32, no. 3 (September 2000): 689–694.

Heller, Janet Ruth. "Toni Cade Bambara's Use of African American Vernacular English in 'The Lesson,'" *Style* 37, no. 3 (Fall 2003): 279–293.

hooks, bell. "Uniquely Toni Cade Bambara," *Black Issues Book Review* 2, no. 1 (January–February 2000): 14–16.

Muther, Elizabeth. "Bambara's Feisty Girls: Resistance Narratives in *Gorilla, My Love,*" *African American Review* 36, no. 3 (Fall 2002): 447–459.

Barbauld, Anna Laetitia (1743–1825)

The poet, critic, and essayist Anna Laetitia Aikin Barbauld directed Gothic romanticism toward the real anguish of women's lives. She studied at home with her minister father, who validated her interest in verse and languages. Out of sympathy for the less fortunate, she expressed humanistic concern for slaves in the "Epistle to William Wilberforce" (1790). She also voiced anger at the entrapment and torment of small animals in the prose poem "Epitaph on a Goldfinch" (1774) and "The Mouse's Petition, Found in the Trap Where He Had Been Confined All Night" (1771), a poem she left for the chemist Joseph Priestley within the wire lattice of the mouse's cage. The latter poem comments on the victims of his experiments with lethal gas; the subtext questions the values of the male-controlled scientific realm. When *Critical Review* assessed her poems, the anonymous reviewer applauded her sensitivity to the needless death of harmless creatures in laboratory gadgetry.

As romanticism took hold of the literary world, Barbauld wrote "On the Pleasure Derived from Objects of Terror, with Sir Bertrand" (1773), a treatise that legitimizes Gothic literature as a form of intellectual stimulus at the same time that it models the conventions of suspenseful literature. After her marriage to the Reverend Rochemont Barbauld, she superintended their private school and wrote text material collected in *Evenings at Home; or, The Juvenile Budget Opened* (1794), which pictures young female characters studying earth science, morality, and animal advocacy. She followed with two more anthologies, *Hymns in Prose for Children* (1808) and *Farm-Yard Journal* (1834), and then turned to editing and writing as a means of supporting the family after her husband became an invalid as a result of his schizophrenia. Of the intensity of her writing Harriet MARTINEAU, the first female sociologist, reported that Barbauld's hymns made her quake in awe.

In widowhood, Barbauld gave full rein to the scholarship she prized in girlhood. In her early 50s, she composed "The Rights of Woman" (ca. 1792), a call to end degradation, scorn, and oppression of women by dethroning boastful male dominators. In eight stanzas, she lauds the sacred mysticism of females as the true means of ridding men of destructive pride and coldheartedness and of transforming them into suitable mates. In this same era, she described the joys of late pregnancy in "To a Little Invisible Being Who Is Expected Soon to Become Visible" (ca. 1795). In 1797 she revealed the creativity of housewives' unspoken thoughts in "Washing-Day," which describes quiet musings as soap bubbles that escape the laundress's humble toils and vanish into the sky. In her critical masterwork, *The British Novelists* (1810–20), she not only defended the novel as a molder of civilization but also equated the works of Ann RADCLIFFE, Maria EDGEWORTH, Fanny BURNEY, and Jane AUSTEN with the writings of Henry Fielding, Samuel Richardson, and Tobias Smollett.

Bibliography

Bellanca, Mary Ellen. "Science, Animal Sympathy, and Anna Barbauld's 'The Mouse's Petition,'" *Eighteenth-Century Studies* 37, no. 1 (2003): 47–67.

Johnson, Claudia L. " 'Let Me Make the Novels of a Country': Barbauld's *The British Novelists (1810–1820),*" *Novel: A Forum on Fiction* 34, no. 2 (Spring 2001): 163.

Watson, Mary Sidney. "When Flattery Kills: The Silencing of Anna Laetitia Barbauld," *Women's Studies* 28, no. 6 (December 1999): 617–643.

Barnes, Djuna (1892–1982)

The journalist, fiction writer, dramatist, and graphic artist Djuna Chappell Barnes explored experimental novel construction through the development of free-spirited examples of the NEW WOMAN. Born in Cornwall-on-Hudson, New York, she lived a bucolic childhood and received homeschooling from her father and her grandmother, the feminist reporter Zadel Barnes. After settling among like thinkers in Greenwich Village, Djuna submitted fiction to *Vanity Fair*, interviewed celebrities, and wrote sensational, exhibitionist pieces for the *Brooklyn Eagle* and *New York Press*. For "My Adventures Being Rescued" (1914), she posed in the arms of a firefighter carrying her down a rope. In "How It Feels to Be Forcibly Fed" (1914), an illustrated study for *New York World Magazine* of the fight for woman suffrage, she exposed the cruelty of the force feeding of the British suffragists Christabel Pankhurst and her ebullient mother, Emmeline PANKHURST. Barnes volunteered to undergo the process herself; mummied in a sheet, she lay as if she were a corpse and relived the hysteria and feminist anger of "a hundred women in grim prison hospitals, bound and shrouded on tables, . . . held in the rough grip of callous warders while white-robed doctors thrust rubber tubing into the delicate interstices of their nostrils" (Barnes, 1914, 3).

Barnes joined the creative feminists Susan GLASPELL and Edna St. Vincent MILLAY in cofounding and writing for the Provincetown Players.

At age 23 Barnes again captured the panic of powerlessness by anthologizing eerie verse profiles of eight female New Yorkers in *The Book of Repulsive Women* (1915), a text illustrated by five of her disarming graphics. In "To a Cabaret Dancer" Barnes enlarges on a no-win situation. The last entry is the ultimate SILENCING—a female suicide whom patriarchal society has minimized and deflated "like some small mug / Of beer gone flat" (*ibid.*, 36). The accumulated hopelessness parallels Barnes's personal and professional dead end in New York City.

After her dispatch to Europe for *McCall's* in 1919, Barnes blossomed during her expatriate days among the literary elite in Paris. Under the influence of European liberal-mindedness, she wrote an Elizabethan parody, *Ladies Almanack* (1928), and imagined a female Tom Jones character for *Ryder* (1928), which the U.S. Post Office censored for its ribaldry. She created lesbian and sexually ambivalent characters, the major strength of *Nightwood* (1930), a semi-autobiographical classic of gay psychological fiction much admired by the Welsh poet Dylan Thomas. Based on the Gothic conventions of desire, alienation, corruption, and otherness, the story portrays the prowling lesbian femme fatale. In a gloomy, mystic atmosphere, the protagonist, Nora Flood, wavers before committing herself to Robin, her mate. Their match threatens the patriarchal Flood family, who attempt to "cure" lesbianism through psychoanalysis. Upon the author's return to New York City in the early 1940s, she wrote in seclusion for the remainder of her life. Her works were favorites of the feminist scholar Susan SONTAG.

Bibliography

Allen, Carolyn. *Following Djuna: Women Lovers and the Erotics of Loss.* Bloomington: Indiana University Press, 1996.

Barnes, Djuna. *The Book of Repulsive Women.* Los Angeles: Sun & Moon, 1994.

———. "How It Feels to Be Forcibly Fed." *New York World Magazine,* 4 September 1914, pp. 3, 17.

Green, Barbara. "Spectacular Confessions: 'How It Feels to Be Forcibly Fed,' " *Review of Contemporary Fiction* 13, no. 3 (Fall 1993): 70–88.

Martyniuk, Irene. "Troubling the 'Master's Voice': Djuna Barnes's Pictorial Strategies," *Mosaic* 31, no. 3 (September 1998): 61–81.

Wilson, Deborah S. "Dora, Nora, and Their Professor: The 'Talking Cure,' 'Nightwood,' and Feminist Pedagogy," *Literature and Psychology* 42, no. 3 (Summer 1996): 48–71.

Bastard Out of Carolina Dorothy Allison (1992)

An edgy, painfully graphic first novel, Dorothy Allison's *Bastard Out of Carolina* surveys the bleak childhood of Ruth Anne "Bone" Boatwright, the illegitimate daughter of Anney, a proud, dirt-poor southern woman. The author bore similar shame and male contempt from girlhood in Greenville, South Carolina. Still reeling from General Sherman's destruction at the end of the Civil War, Allison's South remained underfed, undereducated, and overly violent. With noble purpose, she set out to tell Bone's story in verse, then segued into a flinty narrative related with the grace of gospel music and the heartache of a country ballad.

Beset by the stereotypical behavior of backwoodsmen, the fictional Boatwright household suffers the rages of Bone's grandmother, who drives the child's father out of town, and the sexual libertinism and viciousness of "Daddy Glen" Waddell, Anney's second husband. Bone recalls the first whipping: "I heard the sound of the belt swinging up, a song in the air, a high-pitched terrible sound. . . . I screamed at its passage through the air, screamed before it hit me. I screamed for Mama" (Allison, 106). To lighten her mother's tenuous position as submissive mate to a sadist, the child, like the protagonist in Kaye GIBBONS's *Ellen Foster* (1987), shoulders an unthinkable load of sexual innuendo, psychological terrorism, and shame that make her feel unlovable. She at first concludes that she is innately evil because she requires so much physical discipline. As she nears puberty, she grows more sophisticated in her assessment of male dominance and is able to realize, "It wasn't sex . . . but then, it was something like sex" (*ibid.*, 109).

Through redneck dialect and measured understatement, Allison pictures Bone and other rural white women not unlike her own family as survivors clawing at their milieu for sustenance, shelter, and self-respect. Against a sorry coterie of brawling, drunk-driving, hate-mongering males, the family matriarchs—Alma, Carr, Raylene, and Aunt Ruth—establish a semblance of civility and rescue for harried wives and children. Before Bone can reclaim herself, she must develop the indomitability of her Aunt Raylene and throw off Glen's psyche-rending accusations: "Everything felt hopeless. He looked at me and I was ashamed of myself. It was like sliding down an endless hole, seeing myself at the bottom, dirty, ragged, poor, stupid" (*ibid.*, 209). A crisis in the home forces Anney to stop shielding Glen after he twice rapes Bone and breaks her clavicle. Fortunately for the child, he feeds her anger and will to claim truth and to move on to a safer residence.

Allison's tragic coming-of-age tale was nominated for a National Book Award and was selected as one of *Library Journal's* best books of 1992. The film version, scripted by Anne Meredith and directed by Anjelica Houston, paired Jennifer Jason Leigh and 12-year-old Jenna Malone as mother and daughter. The resulting gritty resilience of poor Carolina women and the grotesquerie of southern Gothic so shocked Ted Turner that he refused to run the film on Turner Network Television (TNT). Showtime picked up the option for a December 14, 1996, airing. Critics raised a second wave of accolades to Allison for her honesty and daring.

Bibliography

Allison, Dorothy. *Bastard Out of Carolina.* New York: Plume Books, 1993.

Bouson, J. Brooks. " 'You Nothing but Trash': White Trash Shame in Dorothy Allison's *Bastard Out of Carolina*," *Southern Literary Journal* 34, no. 1 (Fall 2001): 101–123.

Bazán, Emilia Pardo (1851–1921)

A dynamic literary critic, naturalist, and idealist, Contessa Emilia Pardo Bazán introduced a nontraditional perspective in 19th–century Spanish fiction. A native of La Coruña in Galicia, Spain, she was born to a court official, a member of the privileged class. From girlhood, she chose from a variety of books, including the works of Dante Alighieri, Alexandre Dumas, and Johann Wolfgang von Goethe; recited whole chapters of *Don Quixote*; and gained for herself a broad understanding of many subjects. Wed in 1866 to a law student, José

Quiroga Pérez, she felt unfulfilled from "a sense of emptiness in my soul, an inexplicable sense of anguish" (Bazán, 9). She gave up on marriage and turned to a life of literature. Her favorite works, the novels of Nikolai Tolstoy and Émile Zola, helped shape her style. She began writing some 580 short stories, many published in *El Cuento Semanal, El Libro Popular, La Novela Corta,* and *Los Contemporáneos.* In 1879, she published her first novel, *Pascual López: The Autobiography of a Medical Student.*

Bazán's skill at depicting the motivation of female characters earned comparison to the Gothic verse of the French poet Charles-Pierre Baudelaire and the short and long Gothic fiction of the American novelists Eudora WELTY and Edith WHARTON. In the 1890s Bazán began writing on feminist topics for the *Nuevo Teatro Critico.* She stated publicly that women in elitist Spanish society fell into two huge categories—beasts of burden and sex objects, both silenced by males. In restatement of the extremes of women's lives, she reported that the Spanish offered their girls the choice of wedlock, a convent, PROSTITUTION, or beggary.

Bazán's fiction explores the female perspective on decadent morals, antifemale clergy, illicit sexual relations, incest, and illegitimacy, especially as these topics impacted the middle class. Among her 21 novellas, *Mujer* (Woman, 1895) received critical attention for its sophisticated examination of gender roles. She won international recognition for the naturalistic dynasty novel *The House of Ulloa* (1886), a recovered feminist classic that portrays the decline of the Galician aristocracy. The story depicts the classism, sexism, and religious hypocrisy of Don Pedro Moscoso, the so-called marquis of Ulloa, through the disparate struggles of his wife, Doña Marcelina, and his mistress, the earthy peasant Sabel. To educate Spanish women, Bazán edited the Women's Library, a book collection geared to feminist issues. At age 65, she chaired the literature department of Madrid University. Despite her brilliance, patriotism, and activism, the all-male Royal Academy refused her admission as a member.

Bibliography

Amago, Samuel. "The Form and Function of Homosocial Desire in *La Madre Naturaleza,*" *Romance Quarterly* 48, no. 1 (Winter 2001): 54–63.

Bazán, Emilia Pardo. *The House of Ulloa.* London: Penguin, 1990.

DeCoster, Cyrus. "Pardo Bazán and Ideological Literature," *Romance Quarterly* 40, no. 4 (Fall 1993): 226–234.

Santana, Mario. "An Essay in Feminist Rhetoric: Emilia Pardo Bazán's 'El Indulto,'" *MLN* 116, no. 2 (March 2001): 250.

"Beauty and the Beast"

Beauty and the Beast is a beloved FAIRY TALE and Walt Disney film staple as well as a pervasive Gothic motif of the cowering, well-meaning young ingenue who fears to wed an ogreish groom. Originally issued in the fablist Charles Perrault's *Contes de Ma Mère l'Oye (Mother Goose Tales,* 1698), the myth resets the Greek abduction story of PERSEPHONE, the flower-picking naif whom the underworld god Hades seizes in a meadow, spirits away in his chariot, and installs on his throne as queen of the dead. The story, tense with unexplored sexuality and murderous threat, symbolizes the terrors faced by a timorous virgin in a male-dominated world, a scenario exploited in vampire novels and King Kong movies. That same year, the Norman raconteur Marie-Catherine le Jumelle de Barneville, comtesse d'Aulnoy, wrote the story "La chatte blanche" (The white cat, 1698), the reverse of "Beauty and the Beast," picturing a bewitched princess covered with a beast pelt.

The paradigm of the bestially handsome male and quaking female suited the Gothic fiction of numerous writers. Their view of the structured male-female relationship is a Victorian belief that a woman's goal in marriage is to tame the beast in her husband. The magical cure of his fundamental faults, according to the psychologist Bruno Bettelheim, is the metamorphosis of filial love for father into heterosexual love and coital union with a mate. The female power to stabilize a chancy union is a motivation for the governess's reclamation of the surly Edward Rochester in Charlotte BRONTË's novel *JANE EYRE* (1847), the explosive pairing of the Gypsy boy Heathcliff with the civilizer Catherine EARNSHAW in Emily BRONTË's *WUTHERING HEIGHTS* (1847), and Dorothea Brooke's idealistic marriage to the gruff elderly scholar Edward Casaubon in George ELIOT's MID-DLEMARCH (1872). In both of the Brontës' novels, the gentling of semibarbaric males demands a price from the heroines—Jane Eyre must wander far from her lover to find inner strength and financial INDEPENDENCE before marrying Edward; Catherine must breach the gates of the netherworld to return in ghostly form to make amends for abandoning Heathcliff.

The Greco-American poet Olga BROUMAS turned the paradoxical attraction of beauty for the beast into psychological drama. She reset the brutal rape of beauty in the verse anthology *Beginning with O* (1977). The gaining of knowledge of the beauty and beastliness of intercourse resonate in the last lines of "Beauty and the Beast." After an impromptu coupling with a drunken boy on the linoleum floor of a kitchen, the speaker laughs the "beast" out of the room, then turns to her own flesh to caress her genitals. In amazement at her own sexual hunger, she "touched you, mesmerized, woman, stunned / by the tangible pleasure that gripped my ribs" (Broumas, 56). Beauty realizes that the beast is actually the caged passion within, which she labels "this essential heat" (*ibid.*).

In an updated myth, the children's writer Robin McKinley applied Gothic convention to a coming-of-age novel, *Beauty* (1978), which retains the fundamental outlines of the original. Based on themes of honor, truth, and loyalty, the story retreats to FAIRY TALE for a domestic contretemps in which the father is too poor to afford his daughter's dream wedding. After the family moves from town to an enchanted forest, Beauty encounters the Beast, a humanoid monster whose refined manners contrast with his hirsute body, rumbling voice, and ungainly snout and paws. Contrasting the Beast is Beauty's trusty mount Greatheart, which carries her safely to and from a wild habitat protected by unseen supernatural watchers. Contributing to the magical atmosphere are mystic DREAMSCAPES through which Beauty can view Beast in his castle. The story ends with a child-pleasing display of goodness and compassion, a reversal of the Sleeping Beauty myth, after Beauty's innate goodness retrieves the Beast from near-death. A double transformation dispels the curse

that turned a prince into a beast and, in the end, decks Beauty like a queen.

In *The Bloody Chamber and Other Stories* (1979), an anthology of subversive short fiction, the English feminist Angela CARTER liberates powerless girl victims from fairy tales. Her original plots invert "Nursery fears made flesh and sinew; earliest and most archaic of fears, fear of devourment" (Carter, 67). In "The Tiger's Bride," source of the Neil Jordan film *The Company of Wolves* (1984), Beauty faces the challenging male with an unusual form of armament. Feral beneath his mask of Italian gentleman, he purrs, then crawls forward to lick off the false layer of femininity. His rough tongue reveals her instinctive sexuality that is as fierce and unrelenting as male desire. In *Women Who Run with the Wolves: Myths and Stories about the Wild Woman Archetype* (1992), the Jungian theorist Clarissa Pinkola ESTÉS repositions the female from crouching victim into the pose of advancing beast. To explain her upending of myth, she erases the stereotype of submissive, maternal female and replaces her with *la loba,* the feral wolf bitch whose gut instinct controls sensuality, vision, and the risky impulses of the female in heat.

In a second late 20th-century revision, the Canadian author Marian Searle Engel chose Beauty and the Beast as the background of a revelation of women's innate sexual desire. The erotic novel *Bear* (1977), winner of a Governor General's Award, reprises the familiar girl-meets-beast plot in an unsettling love story that develops between woman and animal. Engel chooses a plausible wilderness, a deserted island in northern Ontario, where Lou, the female cataloger of a 19th-century library, lives in solitude for five years much as the cloistered single women of the 1800s did. The microcosm furthers Engel's allegorical study of the barbaric and civilized sides of the human personality. Because of Lou's complete privacy, curiosity motivates her to explore her feelings and yearnings in unconventional methods. To relieve the tedium imposed by her employer, a historical society, she befriends a bear. Their offbeat pairing escalates from hugs, prances, swims, and rests by the fireside to sensual sniffing of animal musk, ecstatic sexual foreplay, and attempted coitus. In a rhapsodic surrender, Lou begs, "Bear, take me to the bottom of the ocean with you, bear, swim with me, bear, put your arms around me, enclose me, swim, down, down, down with me" (Engel, 112). Enshrouded in a feral scent that permeates her skin and hair, she ignores social taboos and acknowledges the mythic side of female nature.

Bibliography

Broumas, Olga. *Beginning with O.* New Haven, Conn.: Yale University Press, 1977.

Carter, Angela. *The Bloody Chamber and Other Stories.* London: Penguin, 1987.

David, Kathy S., "Beauty and the Beast: The 'Feminization' of Weyland in the Vampire Tapestry," *Extrapolation* 43, no. 1 (Spring 2002): 62–80.

Engel, Marian. *Bear.* New York: Atheneum, 1976.

Glyn-Jones, William, "Beauty and the Beast: The Hellenic Culture Model as a Tool for Recovering the Original Human Blueprint," *Kindred Spirit* (Winter 2002): 45–47.

beauty myth

A blight on young women's coming of age, the beauty myth trains all eyes on an unachievable goal, the idyllic grace and perfection that crown a dewy virginal state. Discontent with feminine beauty dates to medieval myths and folklore. In the FAIRY TALE "Snow White," the magic mirror becomes the judgmental voice that refuses to assuage the misgivings of the wicked stepmother, a cunning narcissist who assesses her own worth in terms of facial loveliness. The early European versions of the tale carry the quest for eternal youth and beauty to cannibalistic extremes as the stepmother orders the woodsman to kill the sweet-natured Snow White and retrieve her lungs and liver. By boiling the parts and eating them, the stepmother intends to incorporate in her body the innate strengths of her rival.

Marina Warner, author of *From the Beast to the Blonde: On Fairy Tales and Their Tellers* (1994), notes that the blonde fairy-tale heroine is a dominant symbol in folklore. The subject undergirds a wide range of feminist literature, in particular, Toni MORRISON's psychological novel *THE BLUEST EYE* (1970), which characterizes white America's love affair with innocent blue-eyed blondes during the mania over Shirley Temple films, posters, dolls, and clothing. In explanation of the role of ugly women in a beauty-obsessed culture, Morrison's white character states, "All of us—all who knew [Pecola]—felt so wholesome after we cleaned ourselves on her. We were so beautiful when we stood astride her ugliness" (Morrison, 205). The author ventures further into the beauty theme by exposing the unachievable standards of beauty and lighter black–against–darker black bias among black women. She expands the result of rejection of unlovely females to a dissociation from all creation—"The Thing to fear was the Thing that made [another girl] beautiful, and not us" (*ibid.*, 74).

Suffragists took a strong stand against the empty-headed female clotheshorse. In 1854 Elizabeth Cady STANTON addressed the New York legislature about the solidarity of women except "a small class of the fashionable butterflies" (Schneir, 116). She predicted that the onset of winter, a symbol of sexism, would soon cause the frail beauties to "demand in their turn justice and equity at your hands" (*ibid.*). In 1915, Charlotte Perkins GILMAN serialized 12 articles in *Forerunner* magazine on the conventions and consequences of female costume, a paradigm of the DOUBLE STANDARD. She noted that women made little attempt to please themselves with safe, comfortable, low-care costumes. Rather, they served vanity, competition, and public dictum by selecting clothes and finery intended to make them beautiful—neck-wearying plumes and hats, steel and whalebone corsets, petticoats and trains that trailed the ground, and stylish, ill-fitting shoes. Their models were advertisements and works of art that depicted females as too delicate for adventure or exercise and too feminine for anything but decoration. That same year, she designed her own perfect world in *HERLAND*, a female utopia in which women dress to suit health and comfort and ridicule feathered hats as absurd personal trumpery. Their choice of short hair, tunics over knee pants, straw hats or warm hoods and capes, and numerous pockets enhances their work in an agricultural haven planted in fruit and nut trees. For aesthetic purposes, graceful, tasteful lines mirror the dignity of females who have no reason to compete with other women in ever-changing hair-dos and faddish clothing.

The playwright, novelist, and folklorist Zora Neale HURSTON attacked a race-based beauty code that valued lighter-skinned Negroes over darker. In the bitter four-act play *Color Struck,* featured in the magazine *Fire!* in November 1926, she dramatized a mental vortex in Emma, a protagonist who looks into the mirror with loathing. A tragic romance, the play describes how self-hatred denies Emma peace and the ability to love others. Her rabid jealousy costs her John, a loving mate who retreats for two decades to Philadelphia, ironically the City of Brotherly Love. On his return, his tender ministrations to their light-skinned daughter revive Emma's two-pronged enmity. Hurston concludes the play with John's departure, the daughter's death, and Emma's maintaining of her belief that she is unlovable because of her dark skin and African features.

In "Old Mortality" (1930), the short-story writer Katherine Anne PORTER captures the socially constructed IDEAL WOMAN in the mind of Miranda. A motherless neophyte, she has no female guide to differentiate between the dream woman and the real. Further obstruction arises from the fact that her saintly mother died in childbirth, a separate myth that preserves unsullied by reality the glory of sacrificial motherhood. As a bookend to the story Porter composed a masterwork, "The JILTING OF GRANNY WEATHERALL" (1930), highlighting the regrets of a dying matriarch long separated from the myth of Venusian beauty by failed romantic anticipations spawned in girlhood. By looking at mortality from both extremes, young and old, Porter captures the pitfalls of womanhood that must shed temporal elements to look deeper into the qualities of being.

Racial pride complicates the issue of who has beauty and who does not. For black women the achievement of a romantic ideal is particularly unlikely in a milieu that awards white or exotic traits the highest praise. In Gwendolyn BROOKS's feminist epic "The Anniad" (1949) the poet commiserates with Annie Allen, a "sweet and chocolate" protagonist who struggles toward self-definition. She is "emotionally aware / Of the black and boisterous hair, / Taming all that anger down" (Brooks,

105, 100). Thwarting Annie's efforts at glamour is the preference of her "tan man" for gold- and maple-colored beauties (*ibid.,* 103). The sad truth of her life is the abandonment of self-esteem in favor of alcohol and "minutes of memory," which are all her fragile self can tolerate (*ibid.,* 109). In a war-torn setting in the Chinese-American novelist Amy TAN's *The Bonesetter's Daughter* (2001), a nun, Sister Yu, counters the pride of both Amerasian and Eurasian orphan girls with a stern warning about "arrogance in what you were born with" (Tan, 200). The admonition serves all races by replacing pride in looks with Christian humility.

In commentary on criteria for judging female beauty, Tan attacks Asian misogyny, particularly foot binding. In the imperial era males developed perverted sexist notions of the physical qualities that made women appealing. To keep upper-class females delicate and birdlike, society valued tiny feet that forced them to toddle as if they were birds. A system of slenderizing the foot with bindings turned into the grotesque custom of halting the normal lengthening of bones. Small girls lived the daily torment of confining foot wrappings that left them virtually crippled. As the bones turned inward, foul odors and hideous pain resulted from decaying tissue and feet that doubled back rather than extending forward. By the end of the growth cycle, the adult women of aristocratic households were incapable of heavy work and could only pad along with a limited tread. In times of danger, like pigeons with clipped wings, they were powerless to flee or stand up to pursuers.

Tan explains in *The Hundred Secret Senses* (1995) that the Hakkanese visionary Hung Hsiuch-uan tried to end the mutilation of women's feet as well as the misogyny of Confucianism by launching the Taiping Rebellion of 1864, which died out as a result of internal squabbling and defections of converts. Unlike other women, Precious Auntie, a key figure in *The Bonesetter's Daughter,* grows up privileged under the protection of a father who not only leaves her feet unbound, but also teaches her the healer's trade. Freedom from social custom is achieved at a price, the reduction of her marriageability. In *The Kitchen God's Wife* (1991), Tan characterized the modernity of the unnamed second wife of Jiang Sao-yen as an example of the Westernization of China after the fall of the Ching dynasty in 1912. Tan's ironic depiction of the coddled daughter Peanut mimics the crippling of foot binding in the fashions of the 1920s. To look up-to-date, Peanut chooses a hobble coat and totters unsteadily about the marketplace much as her foremothers did.

A Western enemy of female content is the desire for a voluptuous, head-turning form. In a grotesque novel, *The Life and Loves of a She-Devil* (1983), the British satirist Fay WELDON pokes fun at the character Ruth Patchett, who does just what her name indicates by hiring a plastic surgeon to patch up her old body as an enticement to a straying husband. By emulating her man's new love interest, Ruth becomes her own rival. In the collection *In Mad Love and War* (1990), the poem "The Book of Myths" by the Native American poet Joy HARJO sees the rebirth of Helen of Troy "in every language," in particular, Marilyn Monroe, a victim of the beauty myth who was "dark earth and round and full of names / dressed in bodies of women, / who enter and leave the knife wounds of this terrifyingly / beautiful land" (Harjo, 55). By depicting the film goddess as a national sacrifice, Harjo bestows both female grandeur and feminist sympathy on the actor's suicide.

In *Pigs in Heaven* (1993), the novelist Barbara KINGSOLVER reaps both pathos and humor out of Barbie, a bulimic counterfeiter and brigand who models her life and wardrobe on the Barbie doll. Shallow and neurotic to the extreme, Barbie is the stereotypical decorative woman. She accepts without question the pop culture definition of beauty based on impossible body measurements and ludicrous get-ups. With airheaded rationalizations she explains away her makeup fetish and conceals a cache of stolen silver dollars clutched tight to her body in a black purse. Pondering Barbie's role as the overdressed outsider, Taylor Greer, a no-frills hillbilly from Kentucky, "wonders what it must have taken to turn someone's regular daughter into such a desperate, picture-perfect loner" (Kingsolver, 204).

Feminist theater strikes back at mutilations of the body and self-image in service to the beauty myth. The humorist and playwright Eve ENSLER commented on the impetus in her play *The Good Body* (2003), a Broadway production about self-acceptance. The text encourages women to ignore the media barrage urging them to "fix something" via fat camps, Weight Watchers, tofu recipes, and plastic surgery (Tolin, 8H). Reprising sources of 21st-century female guilt, Ensler chuckled: "Between the combination of Judeo-Christian religious 'be good be good be good' and Capitalist 'something's wrong with you, buy this' and the parental upbringing, which is 'you're wrong, you're not thin enough, you're not smart enough' I mean, hello! We don't have a shot" (*ibid.*). In place of the beauty myth, her play promotes celebration of all forms of the female physique. Her upbeat tone echoes Marlo Thomas's classic children's work *Free to Be, You and Me* (1974), a title that developed into a feminist slogan.

Bibliography

Brooks, Gwendolyn. *Blacks.* Chicago: Third World Press, 1987.

DiCicco, Lorraine. "The Dis-Ease of Katherine Anne Porter's Greensick Girls in 'Old Mortality,' " *Southern Literary Journal* 33, no. 2 (Spring 2001): 80–98.

Harjo, Joy. *In Mad Love and War.* Middletown, Conn.: Wesleyan University Press, 1990.

Hurston, Zora Neale. *Color Struck* in *Black Female Playwrights: An Anthology of Plays before 1950,* edited by Kathy A. Perkins. Bloomington: Indiana University Press, 1989.

Jimoh, A. Yemisi. "Double Consciousness, Modernism, and Womanist Themes in Gwendolyn Brooks's 'The Anniad,' " *MELUS* 23, no. 3 (Fall 1998): 167–186.

Kingsolver, Barbara. *Pigs in Heaven.* New York: HarperCollins, 1993.

Krasner, David. "Migration, Fragmentation, and Identity: Zora Neale Hurston's *Color Struck* and the Geography of the Harlem Renaissance," *Theatre Journal* 53, no. 4 (December 2001): 533–550.

Morrison, Toni. *The Bluest Eye.* New York: Plume Books, 1993.

Schneir, Miriam, ed. *Feminism: The Essential Historical Writings.* New York: Vintage, 1972.

Tan, Amy. *The Bonesetter's Daughter.* New York: Putnam, 2001.

Tolin, Lisa. " 'Monologues' Author Expands Scope," *Charlotte Observer,* 28 November 2004, p. 8H.

Warner, Marina. *From the Beast to the Blonde: On Fairy Tales and Their Tellers.* New York: Noonday Press, 1994.

Beauvoir, Simone de (1908–1986)

The Parisian feminist, activist, and intellectual Simone de Beauvoir issued a formal manifesto of women's liberation. Her philosophy of total gender equity undergirds the feminist activism of the mid to late 20th century. From childhood, which she described in *Mémoires d'une jeune fille rangée* (Memoirs of a dutiful young girl, 1958), she rejected her mother's strict Catholic dogma and believed that women were the equals of males, a concept she gained from reading the speeches of the Quaker suffragist Lucretia MOTT. After Beauvoir's father lost his fortune during World War I, she and her sister, Poupette, had no dowries to ensure them noble husbands. The sisters had to abandon bourgeois restrictions and educate themselves to become self-supporting.

The intellectual life suited Beauvoir. While studying philosophy at the Sorbonne in 1929, she met the existentialist Jean-Paul Sartre, her mentor and longtime lover. She taught social studies at schools in Marseilles, Rouen, and Paris for 12 years. After World War II, she internalized Sartre's philosophical text *Being and Nothingness* (1943). The couple cofounded and coedited a monthly literary review, *Le Temps Modernes* (Modern Times), and traveled widely in China, Italy, Portugal, Switzerland, Tunis, and the United States to gather material for articles and lectures.

Beauvoir began writing novels and AUTOBIOGRAPHY, both geared to her crusade for gender neutrality in all areas of society. Starting with the metaphysical novel *L'Invitée* (She Came to Stay, 1943), based on Sartre's affair with another woman, Beauvoir quickly staked out original territory for her feminist concepts. In keeping with existentialism, she stressed her belief in isolation, a painful solitude in which each person must work out a way of coping with a disappointment as hurtful as a philandering lover. She issued *Tous les hommes sont mortels* (All Men Are Mortal, 1946) and analyzed the parameters of existentialism in *Pour une morale de l'ambiguité* (The Ethics of Ambiguity,

1947). In 1954 she received the Prix Goncourt for *Les Mandarins* (*The Mandarins*), which presents the postwar era in historical, philosophical, and political perspective. In *La femme rompue* (*Woman Destroyed*, 1968) she pictures the cruelties of poverty for the aged in the scrounging of an old woman for butcher scraps and the leavings of produce stalls.

In the compilation of *Le deuxième sexe* (*The SECOND SEX*, 1949), Beauvoir made her greatest contribution to women and to subsequent feminists, particularly Marilyn FRENCH, the American author of *Beyond Power: On Women, Men, and Morals* (1985). Beauvoir breaks down the nature of sexism under the headings of destiny, history, and myths followed by formative years, situation, justification, and liberation. The encyclopedic text promotes a revolutionary reevaluation of the place of women in society. For its radical view of human history, the book raised an outcry from both genders. After reading the book, Adrienne RICH noted in the essay "Blood, Bread, and Poetry: The Location of the Poet" (1984) that she identified with Beauvoir's debunking of European Gothic STEREOTYPING, which pictured woman as other and kept her "entrapped in myths which robbed her of independent being and value" (Rich, 245). Beauvoir also inspired feminist revolt in the author Robin MORGAN, a former editor in chief of Ms. magazine; the Mexican journalist Rosario Castellanos; and the British social critic Sheila ROWBOTHAM.

Bibliography

Levy, Bronwen. "Agony and Ecstasy: Feminists among Feminists," *Hecate*, 26, no. 1 (May 2000): 107.

Rich, Adrienne. *Adrienne Rich's Poetry and Prose.* New York: W. W. Norton, 1975.

Simons, Margaret A. *Beauvoir and the Second Sex.* Lanham, Md.: Rowman & Littlefield, 2001.

Beecher, Catharine (1800–1878)

The teacher and reformer Catharine Esther Beecher elevated homemaking from drudgery to an honorable science. Choosing her profession over wedlock, she campaigned for the relief of the homemaker from incessant and life-threatening toil. Her method of improving woman's lot, especially that of the downtrodden immigrant, lay through classroom training and through boosting the self-esteem of wives and mothers. A native of East Hampton, New York, she gained practical experience as the eldest of the factory worker Roxanna Foote and the Congregationalist pastor Lyman Beecher's brood of eight. She studied art, literature, math, and science at Sarah Pierce's Litchfield Female Academy in Litchfield, Connecticut. After her mother's death in 1816, she was able to care for the Beecher family.

An advocate of equality in learning, Beecher established the Hartford Female Seminary in 1823 and augmented basic EDUCATION for girls with classes in language and philosophy. She agreed with the educator Bronson Alcott on the value of hands-on training and organized labs in chemistry, astronomy, and home economics. Eight years later she initiated teacher education course work and promoted careers for women in domestic science and home demonstration. She not only lectured on practical matters along the Eastern Seaboard and in frontier towns, but also offered more choice in life to females who preferred professions similar to hers rather than marriage and childrearing. Her forthright counseling prompted jeers and criticism from conservatives, but it proved prophetic of the changes in women's lives by the beginning of the 20th century.

In an age when the home became a symbolic bulwark and sanctuary during national expansion, Beecher issued classic texts available to readers of all ages. One of her most forceful commentaries, *A Treatise on Domestic Economy for the Use of Young Ladies at Home and at School* (1841), decried the waste of female lives in exhausting home regimens. Her proposals for cleanliness, kitchen organization, home nursing of invalids and sickly children, care for the elderly, and hygiene, diet, and exercise for homemakers reached an appreciative audience. She followed with *Letters to Persons Engaged in Domestic Service* (1842), a handbook that encouraged the careers of professional housekeepers, dormitory and hospital matrons, and innkeepers. Her most enduring work, *The AMERICAN WOMAN'S HOME; or, Principles of Domestic Science* (1869), reconfigured the residence by moving outdoor kitchens indoors and adjacent to the dining room for ease of service. The shift helped to ennoble domestic skill and to honor women's contribution to family living. Her fast-selling books provided a glimpse of the simplification of household tasks that freed 20th-century women of heavy lifting and enslavement to wood stoves.

Bibliography
Aresty, Esther B. *The Delectable Past*. New York: Simon & Schuster, 1964.

Cowan, Ruth Schwartz. *More Work for Mother*. New York: Basic Books, 1983.

Kaplan, Amy. "Manifest Domesticity," *American Literature* 70, no. 3 (September 1998): 581–606.

Behn, Aphra (1640–1689)
A feminist marvel during the English Restoration era, Aphra Behn initiated the role of female freelancer. Born to pioneer stock in Wye or Harbledown, Kent, she traveled to Surinam with her parents but arrived fatherless after her father, John Amis, an innkeeper, died en route. Her mother reared Aphra and her brother at St. John's Hill and encouraged diary keeping and free reading as sources of self-education. The West Indian setting provided Behn with material for her classic stage romance *Oroonoko; or, The Royal Slave* (1688), which features the African woman warrior Imoinda and the grisly death of Caesar by quartering. The play earned the Gothic novelist Clara Reeve's regard and Algernon Swinburne's praise as the work of the first literary abolitionist. The themes influenced *Sab* (1841), an abolitionist play by the Hispano-Cuban writer Gertrudis Gómez de AVELLANEDA.

In her early 20s, the author returned to London, married a Dutch merchant named Behn, and assumed the pen name Astrea, a name derived from the Latin for "star." Widowed at age 25 in 1665 during the Great Plague of London, she hired on as a spy in Antwerp for Charles II, who neglected to issue her salary. She briefly entered debtors' prison in 1667 and turned to drama as a much-needed source of income in a penal system that required inmates to pay for their meals and upkeep. At a time when women were playing female roles in public theater, she produced 18 plays, including a domestic tragicomedy, *The Forc'd Marriage; or, The Jealous Bridegroom* (1670); an espionage plot for *The Amorous Prince; or, The Curious Husband* (1671); a romance, *The Dutch Lover* (1673); and *Abdelazar; or, The Moor's Revenge* (1676), a tragedy that reveals women's sexual desire. A stage success, *The Rover; or, The Banish't Cavaliers* (1677), which satirizes the libidinous man of action, established the playwright's celebrity. In act 1, Hellena, a convent novice, trivializes married love to an uninspiring mate: "The Giant stretches it self, yawns and sighs a Belch or two as loud as a Musket, throws himself into Bed, and expects you in his foul Sheets, and e'er you can get your self undrest, calls you with a Snore or two" (Behn, 1677). Whigs called for her arrest after the success of *The Roundheads; or, The Good-Old Cause* (1682) and *The City Heiress; or, Sir Timothy Treat-all* (1682), both scathingly political, but no more so than the stage outrages of John Dryden. In an epilogue, Mrs. Botler smirks: "In other things the Men are Rulers made; / But catching Woodcocks is our proper Trade. / If by Stage-Fops they a poor Living get, / We can grow rich, thanks to our Mother-Wit" (Behn, 1862, 299).

Behn's career concluded with multiple hardships—poverty, gout, crippling caused by an accident, and the DOUBLE STANDARD by which critics castigated female authors for writing with the same level of scandal and eroticism men employed. She laced an epistolary romance, *Love Letters between a Nobleman and His Sister* (1684–87), with semiautobiographical consternation at a corrupt world that forces women into incest, humiliating wedlock, and crime as means of survival. At a height of outrage, Sylvia explodes in a letter to Philander, "I cannot forget I am daughter to the great *Beralti*, and sister to *Myrtilla*, a yet unspotted maid, fit to produce a race of glorious heroes! And can *Philander's* love set no higher value on me than base poor prostitution? Is that the price of his heart?—Oh how I hate thee now!" (Behn, 1687). That same year, the playwright further denounced sexism and arranged marriage in *The Luckey Chance; or, An Alderman's Bargain*. After publishing a series of novels into her last days, she was interred in Westminster Abbey and lauded as the English SAPPHO.

With the rise of feminist literature, the biographer Vita SACKVILLE-WEST and the novelist Virginia WOOLF revived interest in Behn's plays, verse, and novels, which grant fictional women multidimensional lives and express their difficulties in a male-dominated society.

Bibliography

Behn, Aphra. *The City Heiress* (1862). Available online. URL: http://etext.lib.virginia.edu/toc/modeng/public/BehCity.html. Accessed on October 13, 2005.

———. *Love Letters between a Nobleman and His Sister* (1687). Available online. URL: http://www.gutenberg.org/dirs/etext05/8lvlr10h.htm. Accessed on October 13, 2005.

———. *The Rover, or The Banish't Cavaliers* (1677). Available online. URL: http://etext.library.adelaide.edu.au/b/behn/aphra/b42r/. Accessed on October 13, 2005.

Conway, Alison. "The Protestant Cause and a Protestant Whore: Aphra Behn's Love-Letters," *Eighteenth-Century Life* 25, no. 3 (Fall 2001): 1–19.

Spencer, Jane. *Aphra Behn's Afterlife*. Oxford: Oxford University Press, 2001.

Todd, Janet M. *The Secret Life of Aphra Behn*. Piscataway, N.J.: Rutgers University Press, 1997.

Bell Jar, The Sylvia Plath (1963)

Published under the pen name Victoria Lucas, the novel *The Bell Jar* is an intense first-person narrative of the neurosis and mental instability of Esther Greenwood, an introspective young writer. The alter ego of PLATH, Esther is an admirer of the Irish novelist James Joyce, whose labyrinthine novel *Finnegans Wake* parallels Esther's search for wholeness. She undergoes a terrifying treatment with insulin shock therapy and suffers additional grief for a fellow mental patient. Set during the Eisenhower years, the slangy study of self-absorption and depression reveals Plath's distaste for traditional female roles of wife, mother, and housekeeper. Often compared to Holden Caulfield, J. D. Salinger's famed protagonist in *The Catcher in the Rye* (1951), Esther models the teen angst and cynicism of the post–World War II generation, when the First Lady Mamie Eisenhower, television's *I Love Lucy*, and the Hollywood wife Doris Day were the proposed models for women's lives. As does Holden, Esther longs to escape the lockstep social pattern of the upper middle class that prods her unstintingly from prep school to a fashion-conscious college. She flees a life sentence of housewifery relieved at intervals by fatuous cocktail parties.

Revolted by the era's materialism and vacuous domesticity, Esther faces a mounting malaise that reaches its climax in an episode of food poisoning, a symbol of the creeping toxicity that undermines her sanity. To save the tone from total gloom, Plath inserts sardonic humor in the philosophy of Nelly Willard, who instructs her son, Buddy, "What a man wants is a mate and what a woman wants is infinite security" (Plath, 58). Plath turns Nelly into a deliverer of comic relief from her unintentional phallic imagery in the rigidly gendered truism "What a man is is an arrow into the future and what a woman is is the place the arrow shoots off from" (*ibid.*). Esther's foil, the shallow clotheshorse Hilda, sets Esther on a caroming course of madness that redeems her from the "long, dead walk from the frosted glass doors of the Amazon [Hotel] to the strawberry-marble slab of our entry on Madison Avenue" (*ibid.*, 81). Her first sexual adventure involves a gulp of "Nuits-St. Georges," a liqueur she chooses for its heraldic significance. The alcohol braces her for the loss of "virginity [that] weighed like a millstone around my neck," a humorous physical impossibility (*ibid.*, 186). The evening concludes with her disillusion with sexual intercourse and her anticlimactic transportation by taxi to the emergency room of a hospital to stop a hemorrhage that soaks her clothes and fills her shoes with black blood.

Forays against sanity gradually reduce Esther from confident scholar to aberrant fashion editor, jaded loner, and bare-bones survivor. She foresees as the disembodied cat in Lewis Carroll's *Alice in Wonderland* (1865) the hanging death of her friend Joan. Esther gazes into the gravesite and clings to her shrinking self with an existential mantra: "The old brag of my heart. I am, I am, I am" (*ibid.*, 199). She regrets that female social customs lack "a ritual for being born twice—patched, retreaded and approved for the road" (*ibid.*). Plath, consumed by doubts that medical science can reclaim the bright women of the 1950s, ends the story on an ambiguous step forward with no indication of Esther's success. The resolution captures the mind-set of Plath herself, who killed herself two weeks after the novel's publication.

Bibliography

Becker, Jillian. *Giving Up: The Last Days of Sylvia Plath.* New York: St. Martin's, 2003.

Plath, Sylvia. *The Bell Jar.* New York: Bantam, 1972.

Wagner, Linda W. "Plath's *The Bell Jar* as Female Bildungsroman," *Women's Studies* 12, no. 1 (1986): 55–68.

Beloved **Toni Morrison** (1987)

Toni MORRISON's *Beloved* is a complex neogothic fiction of conscience that investigates the pathology of American slavery. In the style of a classical epic, the landmark novel opens in medias res to flood the reader with confusion and fragmented memories, the legacy that slaves carried with them as they looked back on Africa from the holds of slave ships and ahead at the bitter Middle Passage. Even after emancipation, freed slaves were confused as they traversed free territory without the literacy skills to decipher letters, messages, maps, or road signs. The only source of learning for the unschooled was a makeshift system of dame schools, like that of Lady Jones, a maternal lover of black children who teaches the alphabet from her only textbook, a Bible.

Morrison pictures evil as an insidious stalker. Replacing plantation terror is "the Klan. Desperately thirsty for black blood, without which it could not live, the dragon swam the Ohio at will" (Morrison, 66). In a welter of opposites, Sethe, the home-bound woman, and Paul D, the roving man, unite to recapture some of the sweetness of youth in mutual sexual pleasures. Event by event, they recall and restructure an oral story of bondage and flight—Sethe from enslavement in Kentucky and Paul D from torture and near drowning while serving on a chain gang. By filling in gaps for each other, they relive the terror of a violent night that cost Paul A and Sixo their lives, sent Paul D on the run, and separated Sethe from her daughter, sons, and husband.

Sex and procreation revive for former slaves such as Ella and Sethe sexual nightmares of the cyclical bearing of slave children, whether sired by black males or by white overseers or owners for dogged labor or the auction block. Luckier than the rest in being able to choose her mate, Sethe bears emotional scars from sending her toddler ahead with slave stealers and from remaining behind at Sweet Home, the Kentucky plantation that morphs from a Southern model of benevolence to a den of monsters. In her last month of pregnancy, Sethe undergoes the horrors of lashing and mammary rape from the sucking of her breast milk by the new owner's mossy-toothed nephews. In a dash through dense forest to the Ohio border, Sethe survives lacerated feet and childbirth in a half-sunk canoe, which bears in its framework the oval outline of female labia. Upon reunion with her mother-in-law, two sons, and first baby girl, Sethe and her infant daughter relish cleansing, massage, and a 28-day respite that appears to promise more free days to come. Superintending her family's recuperation is Baby Suggs, Halle's mother, the expert preacher-psychotherapist who gathers the frayed souls tramping north within a hedged clearing, where she coaxes them limb by limb to sing, cry, dance, and accept and love bodies tainted by slavery.

Creating tension with conflicting images of dismemberment and reunion, Morrison reveals the details of a ghost story about the return of Beloved, the wanderer who eats, speaks, and behaves as a toddler and seeks redress from Sethe, the single parent who nearly beheaded her girlchild. The quick murder required a slice of a handsaw to spare Beloved the misery of a female exploitation peculiar to the American plantation system. Like a demon, "Beloved ate up her [mother's] life, took it, swelled up with it, grew taller on it" (*ibid.*, 250). The corroborating images of severance—Baby Suggs's memories of seven children sold from the Whitlows' Carolina plantation, chicken parts that Sethe throws from Sawyer's restaurant kitchen, a pair of girls skimming the ice on three skates, black prostitutes servicing clients in the slaughterhouse pen, and a wobbly table held upright on three legs—impress the reader with the raw impermanence of the former slave's life, even in the free state of Ohio. Contrasting Sethe's experience with

a trial for murder is Paul D's term on the chain gang, during which fellow road laborers communicate by twitches and jerks on the links of their leg irons. Through a shared bed and shared meals of soul food, Sethe and Paul D begin the reclamation of self.

In *Beloved*, household items anchor the story to the domestic realm of wife, mother, and slave counselor. A recurrent image, worn-out shoes, is a mainstay of the questing journeyman and a suitable chore for Baby Suggs, the salver of hurts who also cobbles worn brogans. Another dominant image, the patchwork quilt, is a universal female symbol of fractious times and fractured kinships joined into a utilitarian source of warmth and comfort. Embodying fragments and leftovers from constant slave migrations through Baby Suggs's way station on Bluestone Road is a quilt joyous with a sprinkling of orange squares amid blues, grays, and browns as though celebrating the African American's pell-mell rush to freedom. In the compelling falling action a community of black women converge on the haunted way station to exorcise the offending ghost-child and to free Sethe from despair at reminders of infanticide. The sybaritic riot of ribbons and gay-colored clothing with which Sethe placates Beloved retreats in the novel's resolution to a single plane—the "quilt of merry colors" under which Sethe, hopeless and "not a bit all right," withdraws from her struggle (*ibid.*, 271). Reminded of Patsy's spiritual repair of the slave Sixo's tattered self, Paul D soothes Sethe and longs to make his own quilt by putting "his story next to hers" (*ibid.*, 273).

Bibliography

Daniel, Janice Barnes. "Function or Frill: The Quilt as Storyteller in Toni Morrison's *Beloved,*" *Midwest Quarterly* 41, no. 3 (spring 2000): 321–329.

Hamilton, Cynthia S., "Revisions, Rememories, and Exorcisms: Toni Morrison and the Slave Narrative," *Journal of American Studies* 30, no. 3 (1996): 30–32.

Morrison, Toni. *Beloved.* New York: Plume, 1987.

"Big Blonde"   Dorothy Parker (1929)

The winner of an O. Henry Award, Dorothy PARKER's poignant cautionary tale "Big Blonde," published in the February 1929 issue of *Bookman*, pictures a vulnerable protagonist confined to stereotypes of womanhood, particularly that of the overripe, promiscuous blonde. Stressing the restraint of social codes is the choice of the character Hazel's marital surname, Morse, a reference to the dot-and-dash code of Samuel Morse. The narrative pictures her as a "type," the eroticized image of the "dumb blonde" who "incites some men when they use the word 'blonde' to click their tongues and wag their heads roguishly" (Parker, 275). In anticipation of society's expectations, Hazel degrades herself with "inexpert dabblings with peroxide" and squashes her feet into small "champagne-colored slippers," which echo her washed-out hair color (*ibid.*, 277, 292). Her sexual self-image, further limited by macho expectations, fosters the sequential love affairs that reduce her to a passed-around rag doll. Parker's commentary on self-destruction through complicity with sexism denounces women who waste opportunities to rescue themselves by rejecting stereotypical behavior.

Parker focuses on the insubstantial life of a sex object such as Hazel, who retreats from reality into "romantic uselessness" (*ibid.*, 288). As a kept woman, she survives on day-to-day handouts; as a wife, she assumes that bedroom delights will secure her marriage. When her loneliness advances to clinical depression, one good-timer at Jimmy's place complains that a cheerless flapper "[spoils] everybody's evening" (*ibid.*, 290). Her only escape from self-devaluation is sleep induced by alcohol, the antidote that numbs her emotions until the next evening of 1920s-style carousing. Because booze fails to cure spiritual emptiness and advancing flab, she attempts total negation through suicide via scotch and Veronal tablets. Her literary foil, the maid Nettie, becomes the safety "net" who halts the slide into coma and advancing death by summoning a doctor and by watching over Hazel for two nights. In contrast to men who use and discard Hazel, Nettie symbolizes a feminist lifeline woven of the survivor's instincts.

Parker dramatizes the bittersweet irony of woman helping woman. The pairing of discounted white female with black servant replicates the role assignments for both Hazel and Nettie, who subsist in a male-controlled world. The concept of the white woman functioning on a level with the black female handmaiden of the slave era dates to pre–Civil War suffragist philosophy. The most prominent, Elizabeth Cady STANTON, recognized that control from any source facilitated a SISTERHOOD of diminished, emotionally needy women. In 2003, the actor-playwright Shirley Anderson adapted the story as a one-woman drama, which premiered on January 28 at Sacred Fools Theater in Hollywood, California, to critical acclaim.

Bibliography

Eliason, J. A. "Big Blonde at Sacred Fools Theater." *Back Stage West*, 13 February 2003, p. 15.

Parker, Dorothy. *Dorothy Parker*. New York: Viking, 1944.

Simpson, Amelia. "Black on Blonde. The Africanist Presence in Dorothy Parker's 'Big Blonde,' " *College Literature* 23, no. 3 (October 1996): 105–116.

biography

Honest biographies of women have done much to reclaim lost acts of feminism. Worthy examples include preservation of the life of an illiterate agent of the Underground Railroad in Sarah Elizabeth Hopkins Bradford's *Scenes in the Life of Harriet Tubman* (1869). In 1902, the journalist and biographer Ida Husted Harper captured the spirit of the TEMPERANCE and SUFFRAGE movements in the article "Elizabeth Cady Stanton," a brief overview of one of the most powerful feminist researchers and speech writers of the 19th century. A Scots-Canadian biographer, Ishbel ROSS, made a career of lauding the overlooked strengths of women, including brief life stories of newspaperwomen in *Ladies of the Press: The Story of Women in Journalism by an Insider* (1936) and a collection of lives in *Charmers and Cranks: Twelve Famous American Women Who Defied Conventions* (1965), which covers the muckraking journalist Nellie BLY, the dancer Isadora Duncan, the temperance crusader Carry Nation, and the rambunctious suffragist Victoria WOODHULL. Ross's individual biographies identify the achievements of the nurse and Red Cross proponent Clara Barton, the Civil War physician Elizabeth BLACKWELL, the frontier stage performer Lola Montez, the Confederate spy "Rebel Rose" O'Neal, and the first ladies Varina Howell Davis, Mary Todd Lincoln, and Edith Wilson. The social critic Sheila ROWBOTHAM exposed the lower-middle-class strength of an English suffragist in a prison play, *The Friends of Alice Wheeldon* (1986). A more intimate telling are mother-daughter efforts, such as Alice Stone Blackwell's *Lucy Stone: Pioneer of Women's Rights* (1930) and Mary Catherine Bateson Kassarjian's life story of the anthropologist Margaret MEAD in *With a Daughter's Eye: Letters from the Field, 1925–1975* (1984). To account for the death of a Hollywood superstar, Gloria STEINEM wrote *Marilyn: Norma Jeane* (1986), a reflection of the BEAUTY MYTH that drove Marilyn Monroe to suicide.

According to biographers, the midwife, herbalist, reformer, and feminist philosopher Anne Hutchinson enjoyed a career in colonial New England that paralleled the fictional life of Hester PRYNNE. In Nathaniel Hawthorne's description, "Mrs. Hutchinson" (1830), the historical figure, spread revolutionary heresies and opinions that proved to be "a burthen too grievous for our fathers" (Hawthorne). In Hawthorne's estimation, Anne, too, "bore trouble in her own bosom, and could find no peace in this chosen land" (*ibid.*). In kitchen homilies to local women, she overturned the male contention that God grants grace solely to those who perform good works. Her outspoken tenets alarmed Cotton Mather, spokesman for Massachusetts Bay ministers, who considered her a radical troublemaker. The subtext of their clash was the temerity of a female to speak her own mind while ignoring male convictions. Such a dissident, by word and gender, disordered their self-serving theocracy.

Biography has been a successful venue for feminist history, for example, the solitude of the female artist in Genevieve Taggart's *The Life and Mind of Emily Dickinson* (1930), the role of the actor Sarah Bernhardt in liberalizing the entertainment world's male control in Cornelia Otis SKINNER's *Madame Sarah* (1967), and Fawn Brodie's depiction of the third U.S. president's seduction of his slave, Sally Hemings, in a controversial life story, *Thomas Jefferson: An Intimate Biography* (1974). In *Dolley* (1994), a fictionalized account of First Lady Dolley Payne Madison, the novelist Rita

Mae BROWN examines through feminist eyes the subject's views and history. Madison's early scrapes as young widow and single parent prepare her for the rigors of Washington politics. An alert, spirited equal of her husband, she maintains the duties of wife and White House hostess while retaining the spunky personality that sets her apart from other 18th-century women in public roles. In addition to carefully managing a tiny budget and to welcoming hordes of dignitaries to receptions and dinners, she finds time to teach a friend to shoot craps. When finances cramp the Madisons' personal budget, Dolley quietly sells a necklace to pay for a new team of horses.

For an early 19th-century woman reared as a Quaker, Dolley is surprisingly flexible in matters of male-female relations. She investigates the amours of her husband's slave Sukey with André Daschkov, a Russian ambassador and flagrant rake. Dolley is open-minded about Sukey's after-hours liaisons and ponders how the relationship might prove beneficial to the president. In comparing her own powerlessness, the first lady states her aversion to flesh marketing, but she must admit, "I can't vote any more than you can" (Brown, 160). The comment characterizes the affinity between the era's disenfranchised women and slaves and the merged issues of abolitionism and suffrage.

Brown's version of Dolley Madison creates feminist dialogue that suits the era. Of the obstacles the first lady's Creole friend Lisel Serurier encounters in slogging through state protocol, Dolley summarizes the hurdles succinctly as "All male" (*ibid.*, 20). Of Lisel's Caribbean beauty and her presence in a racist environment, Dolley comments in her diary entry, "It would put the pedigree worshipers in a curious position, having to accept on equal terms a person who might carry a drop of African blood" (*ibid.*, 21). At a telling point in Dolley's service as first lady, she refuses to be cowed by the advance of the British on the White House and wishes only for pants rather than "these damned skirts" (*ibid.*, 295). Of her service to family and country, she erroneously assumes that she will be forgotten, "except as a notation: wife of James Madison, fourth President of the United States" (*ibid.*, 223).

In 2000, the biographer and critic Elizabeth Hardwick produced the life story of a revered male author, *Herman Melville*, a volume of the Penguin Lives series that earned a respectable assessment from reviewers and literary historians. A feminist stance enabled her to evaluate the classic author's unacknowledged love of Nathaniel Hawthorne and ambivalence toward women. Of his avoidance of his wife, Elizabeth, and his resultant burst of creative energy Hardwick remarked that "marriage was more prudent for Melville than for his wife. He might long for male companionship, even for love, but marriage changed him from an unanchored wanderer into an obsessive writer" (Hardwick, 51). Hardwick's male perspective on mid-19th-century SEXUAL POLITICS evidences the value of female writers as biographers.

Bibliography

Brown, Rita Mae. *Dolley.* New York: Bantam Books, 1995.

Hardwick, Elizabeth. *Herman Melville.* New York: Penguin, 2000.

Hawthorne, Nathaniel. "Mrs. Hutchinson" (1830) Available online. URL: http://www.eldritchpress.org/nh/mrsh.html. Accessed on October 13, 2005.

Kalfopoulou, Adrianne. *A Discussion of the Ideology of the American Dream in the Culture's Female Discourses.* Lewiston, N.Y.: Edwin Mellen Press, 2000.

Bishop, Elizabeth (1911–1979)

The poet Elizabeth Bishop composed restrained lyric miniatures in demanding verse forms, including erotic hymns to her passions. The losses of childhood marred her chances for a normal family. Only months after her birth in Worcester, Massachusetts, her father died. Less than five years later, her mother's mental instability required permanent care in a sanitarium. Left with her maternal grandparents in modest circumstances in Great Village, Nova Scotia, she grew up in a tender Baptist atmosphere. She fought chronic bronchitis and asthma that kept her home from school, but not out of the family library. In "Sestina" (1956), the poet pictures herself as a child drawing a flower-fronted house while a singing grandmother envelopes her in the welcoming milieu of women. A prose vignette, "Gwendolyn" (1953), honors the dignity and artistry of WOMAN'S WORK.

The wealthy Bishop clan reclaimed 16-year-old Elizabeth and took her back to Massachusetts. In 1976, the poet relived the tenuous times of early girlhood in the poem "In the Waiting Room," which captures the little girl terror of "falling off / the round, turning world / into cold, blue-black space" (Bishop, 1979, 159). Resettled with Aunt Maud outside Boston, Bishop enrolled in North Shore Country Day School and Walnut Hill School in Nantick, where she excelled at impromptu verse and classroom skits. At Vassar, she abandoned thoughts of studying medicine or of earning a fine arts degree in piano and chose to write poetry. She published early works in the *Vassar Review* and in a campus miscellany, *Con Spirito,* which she cofounded with her classmates Muriel RUKEYSER and Mary MCCARTHY.

Guided by her mentor, Marianne MOORE, Bishop initiated her own poetry career. She invigorated her verse with impressions of her travels to the Mediterranean, Mexico, Haiti, and Key West, Florida. Having made a splash with poems in *Partisan Review,* in 1949, she accepted a one-year term as poetry consultant to the Library of Congress. In a second home in Pètropolis, Brazil, she found rejuvenation with her friend, Lota de Macedo Soares. Their blissful sexual union nursed Bishop back to health and relieved her allergies. She translated from Portuguese Alice Brant's *The Diary of Helena Morley* (1957), the late 19th-century journal of a Brazilian girl in the mining town of Diamantina, where strict gendered codes rule behavior.

Bishop received acclaim for two anthologies, *North and South* (1946), winner of a Houghton Mifflin Poetry Award, and *A Cold Spring* (1955), which generated her first Pulitzer Prize. After introducing English readers to Brazilian verse, Bishop completed *Questions of Travel* (1965), winner of the National Book Award. In her 50s, she began a classroom career that took her first to the University of Washington, then to Harvard. In 1976, she was honored as the first female and first American recipient of the Books Abroad/Neustadt International Prize for Literature. The following year, the verse anthology *Geography III* (1976) earned her a second Pulitzer Prize.

Bishop was loath to express her sexual orientation. She recoiled from such blatant carnal verse as Adrienne RICH's classic anthology *Diving into the Wreck: Poems 1971–1972* (1973). Late 20th-century reevaluations of Bishop's reticent feminism disclosed that she spoke in impersonal geographic terms her appreciation of the female and her disdain for imperialism and androcentrism. Rich praised Bishop for "her powers of observation, her carefully articulated descriptive language, her wit, her intelligence, the individuality of her voice . . . the marvelous flexibility and sturdity of her writing, her lack of self-indulgence" (Rich, 126). In 2000 the posthumous issuance of Bishop's "Vague Poem" revealed a joy in the beauty of the female breasts and genitals, which the poet extols with repetitions of the word *rose*, a stereotyped symbol of perfection dating to the art and poetry of the Middle Ages. In "Crusoe in England," she confessed the loss of a beloved companion some 17 years after the death.

Bibliography

Bishop, Elizabeth. *The Collected Prose of Elizabeth Bishop.* New York: Farrar, Straus & Giroux, 1984.

———. *The Complete Poems of Elizabeth Bishop, 1927–1979.* New York: Farrar, Straus & Giroux, 1979.

Paton, Elizabeth M. "Landscape and Female Desire: Elizabeth Bishop's 'Closet' Tactics," *Mosaic* 31, no. 3 (September 1998): 133–151.

Rich, Adrienne. *Blood, Bread, and Poetry: Selected Prose, 1979–1985.* New York: W. W. Norton, 1986.

Blackwell, Antoinette Brown (1815–1921)

The famed lecturer, writer, and Congregational and Unitarian minister Antoinette Louisa "Nettie" Brown Blackwell formulated a Christian philosophy based on gender equality. Born in Henrietta, New York, she was a convert to the era's evangelistic movement and an early proponent of equal schooling for women. With diplomas from Monroe County Academy and Oberlin College, she readied herself for the pulpit at age 35. Although she found no churches willing to hire her, in 1853, after a formal ritual at the First Congregational Church in Wayne County, New York, she became the first U.S. female ordained for the ministry. She devoted her speaking talents to social issues—ABOLITIONISM, prison reform, SUFFRAGE, TEMPERANCE, WOMEN'S RIGHTS—as well as to religious causes.

After marrying Samuel Blackwell, the brother of Elizabeth BLACKWELL, the nation's first female doctor, Antoinette Blackwell wrote novels, verse, and essays while rearing five daughters. She issued a collection of progressive articles from the *Women's Journal* in *Shadows of Our Social System* (1856) and compiled numerous textbooks, beginning with *Studies in General Science* (1869). In *The Sexes Throughout Nature* (1875) she expressed her support of women for demanding their rights: "Many women have grievously felt the burden of laws or customs interfering unwarrantably with their property, their children, or their political and personal rights" (Blackwell, 1976, 6). She denounced "that most subtle outlawry of the feminine intellect which warns it off from the highest fields of human research" (*ibid.*). In 1868, she published in *Atlantic Monthly* a short story, "A Plea for the Afternoon." The story condemns social constraints on women that make them old before their time: "Men have more variety, more change, more stimulus in their lives, and they refuse to give up this rightful heritage to any one" (Blackwell, 1868, 396). In contrast, Blackwell pictures elderly women relegated to knitting stockings in chimney corners.

In a summation of women's history in 1855, the orator Lucy STONE extolled Antoinette Blackwell's example in the speech "Disappointment Is the Lot of Women." Stone noted that "when [Blackwell] applied for ordination they acted as though they had rather the whole world should go to hell than that Antoinette Brown should be allowed to tell them how to keep out of it" (Schneir, 109). In 1893, Stone stood before the women's pavilion at the World's Columbian Exposition to deliver "The Progress of Fifty Years." She noted, "The first woman minister, Antoinette Brown, had to meet ridicule and opposition that can hardly be conceived to-day. Now there are women ministers, east and west, all over the country" (Stone).

Bibliography

Blackwell, Antoinette. "A Plea for the Afternoon" (1868). Available online. URL: http://cdl.library.cornell.edu/cgi-bin/moa/sgml/moa-idx?notisid=ABK2934-0021-61. Accessed on October 13, 2005.

———. *The Sexes throughout Nature.* New York: Hyperion, 1976.

Schneir, Miriam, ed. *Feminism: The Essential Historical Writings.* New York: Vintage, 1972.

Stone, Lucy. "The Progress of Fifty Years" (1893). Available online. URL: http://womenshistory.about.com/library/etext/bl_1893_lucy_stone.htm. Accessed on October 13, 2005.

Blackwell, Elizabeth (1821–1910)

America's first female medical doctor, Elizabeth Blackwell also lectured and wrote AUTOBIOGRAPHY, textbooks, and essays on venereal disease, sex education, women's health and hygiene, obstetrics, and WOMEN'S RIGHTS to EDUCATION and a career in the professions. Born in Counterslip, England, she was reared a Quaker and became an enthusiastic reader. After a fire destroyed her father's sugar refinery in 1832, the Blackwells emigrated to Long Island, New York, and became active abolitionists. She entered private school and received tutoring in modern foreign languages as well as introductions to libraries, museums, art, theater, and ballet in New York City.

After her father died, Blackwell at age 27 joined her sisters, Anna and Marianne, in establishing a girls' boarding school. When her friend Mary Donaldson was diagnosed with terminal cancer, Blackwell decided to study medicine and to dedicate herself to women's health. Supported in her career choice by the fiction writer Sarah Josepha HALE, editor of *Godey's Lady's Book,* Blackwell apprenticed with Dr. Samuel H. Dickson of Charleston, South Carolina. On a one-time dispensation to a female, she enrolled in Geneva Medical School in Geneva, New York, the only school that agreed to admit a woman to premed courses. Mocked as "the doctress," she resided alone and studied contagious diseases privately in Philadelphia's Blockley Almshouse while involving herself in Susan B. ANTHONY's growing battle for the ballot. In 1849, Blackwell graduated first in her class.

Blackwell sought postgraduate training at the Collège de France and La Maternité in Paris. Her career required redirection after a surgical accident forced the removal of one eye, which was blinded by ophthalmia. After working as a colleague of Florence Nightingale at Saint Bartholomew's Hospital in London, Blackwell settled near her family in Cincinnati to lecture on women's need for exercise, cleanliness, and simple diet, the subject of her first medical text, *The Laws of Life with Special Reference to the Physical Education of Girls* (1852). She found no staff that welcomed female doctors. In her memoirs, she recalled "ill-natured gossip, as well as insolent anonymous letters" and "unpleasant annoyances from unprincipled men" (Blackwell, 2000, 197). She set up the New York Dispensary, a clinic for ghetto women and the nation's first hospital run by an all-female staff. Aided by her sister, Dr. Emily Blackwell, an anesthetist specializing in childbirth, and a German midwife, Marie "Dr. Zak" Zakrzewska, Blackwell founded the Women's Medical College of the New York Infirmary, forerunner of a medical department at Cornell University.

Shortly before the outbreak of the Civil War, Elizabeth Blackwell pushed for the modernization of medicine. She produced clinical texts that offered an equal concentration on male and female needs. In January 1859, she submitted "Letter to Young Ladies Desirous of Studying Medicine" to the *English Woman's Journal.* The text asserted, "A lady can enter in such a capacity as I here recommend, without injury to health, and, with a little womanly tact and real earnestness in the work, this residence may be made a most valuable time of study" (Lacey, 458). To sweep aside the superstition and misinformation from the past, particularly about conception and childbirth, she advised first-year doctors to learn modern obstetrics by avoiding "many old midwife prejudices and practices clinging to that institution" (*ibid.,* 459).

As an aid to the Union medical corps, Elizabeth Blackwell readied the Women's Central Association of Relief by teaching nursing superintendents the Nightingale method of nurse care and by preparing battlefield nurses for the rigors and privations of combat. In 1893 the orator Lucy STONE stood before the women's pavilion at the World's Columbian

Exposition to deliver a speech, "The Progress of Fifty Years." In her overview of great moments in women's history, she praised Blackwell, who "was regarded as fair game, and was called a 'she doctor.' The college that had admitted her closed its doors afterward against other women; and supposed they were shut out forever" (Stone).

Into her 80s, Elizabeth Blackwell trained surgeons and midwives and crusaded for improvements to urban sanitation. In 1885, she issued *The Decay of Municipal Representative Government*, a scathing denunciation of civic machinery guarding clean water and sanitation. A decade later, she completed *Pioneer Work in Opening the Medical Profession to Women: Autobiographical Sketches* (1895), which describes her first consultation with a fidgety male doctor. To direct female scientists toward total objectivity, she urges them to question erring medical opinions of male scientists. In retrospect on her clinical experience, she summarizes treatment of poor immigrant German women and children, who needed money for food more than medical care. In her memoir, she justifies her adoration of mothers: "I had always felt a great reverence for maternity—the mighty creative power which more than any other human faculty seemed to bring womanhood nearer the Divine" (Blackwell, 2000, 30).

At age 81, Blackwell compiled *Essays on Medical Sociology* (1902), a two-volume overview of her contention that women's moral instincts are the foundation of a civilized society. The text asserts that mothers express their value to the family through "the subordination of self to the welfare of others; . . . the joy of creation and bestowal of life; the pity and sympathy which tend to make every woman the born foe of cruelty and injustice" (Blackwell, 1902, 10). She stressed the faulty logic of relying on the male half of the population for medical methodology and scientific conclusions. At the same time, she warned male scientists that they must adjust their thinking on human issues as females began contributing thought and practical knowledge to medical advancement.

Bibliography

Blackwell, Elizabeth. *Essays on Medical Sociology*. London: Ernest Bell, 1902.
———. *The Laws of Life with Special Reference to the Physical Education of Girls*. Colville, Wash.: Reprint Service, 1989.
———. *Pioneer Work in Opening the Medical Profession to Women*. Delanco, N.J.: privately printed, 2000.
Lacey, Candida Ann, ed. *Barbara Leigh Smith and the Langham Place Group*. New York: Routledge & Kegan Paul, 1987.
Morantz-Sanchez, Regina. "Feminist Theory and Historical Practice: Rereading Elizabeth Blackwell," *History and Theory* 31, no. 4 (December 1992): 51–69.
Stone, Lucy. "The Progress of Fifty Years" (1893). Available online. URL: http://womenshistory.about.com/library/etext/bl_1893_lucy_stone.htm. Accessed on October 13, 2005.

Blais, Marie-Claire (1939–)

An influential Canadian feminist, Marie-Claire Blais explores through drama and fiction the dangers of free choice. A native of Quebec, she exited the oppressive Catholicism of a convent school to enter the workforce, then continued her education at Laval University. She began her fiction career at age 20 with the novel *La belle bête* (1959), published in English as *Mad Shadows* (1960), a somber psychological study of a toxic three-member family that replicates the mythos of BEAUTY AND THE BEAST. The mother's preference for a mentally handicapped son and her rejection of her daughter, Isabelle-Marie, foreshadow the Blais family's denunciation of Marie-Claire when she declared her homosexuality.

Blais contributes to gay literature a frank neogothic eroticism and respect for PROSTITUTION. She earned the Prix France-Quebec and Prix Médicis for *Une saison dans la vie d'Emmanuel* (*A Season in the Life of Emmanuel*, 1965), a grim assessment of rural Quebec farm life and the hypocrisies of Catholic parochial schools. In a clash between the incensed Abbé Moisan and Madame Octavie, keeper of a brothel, she defends the dignity of women relegated to the sex trade: "They are orphans, bastards, cripples, and I rescued them from the garbage heap, Monsieur l'Abbé. My charge is as great as yours" (Blais, 128). Late in her career Blais spoke candidly of female identity, intimacy, and lesbian clannishness in four novels—*Les nuits de l'underground* (*Nights in the Underground*, 1978), *Un sourd dans la ville* (*Deaf to the City*, 1979), *Visions d'Anna ou le vertige* (*Anna's World*, 1982), and *L'ange de la solitude* (*The Angel of Loneliness*, 1989). In pervasive motifs of women's SEXUALITY, threats to straight and gay females from VIOLENCE, marginalizing, and disease override glimpses of satisfying love and camaraderie.

To honor the dispossessed female pariah, Blais develops the interior monologue as a window on women's hidden conflicts. In the stream-of-consciousness novel *Anna's World* the author examines the hidden fear and distancing between mother and daughter as a young girl begins molding her individuality. By fragmenting narrative into brain impulses, Blais navigates the loose thoughts and feelings that impinge on choices. The author increases the interweaving of emotion and memory in *Soifs* (*Thirsts*, 1995), winner of the Governor General's Literary Award, which illuminates mother-daughter clashes, homophobia, and subtle forms of PATRIARCHY and misogyny.

Bibliography

Blais, Marie-Claire. *A Season in the Life of Emmanuel*. New York: Farrar, Straus & Giroux, 1966.

Tremblay, Victor-Laurent. "L'Inversion Mythique dans 'La Belle Bete' de Marie-Claire Blais," *Studies in Canadian Literature* 25, no. 2 (Summer 2000): 74–95.

Zabus, Chantal. "Review: Soifs," *World Literature Today* 71, no. 4 (Autumn 1997): 745–746.

Bloody Chamber and Other Stories, The
Angela Carter (1979)

A feminist Gothic classic, Angela CARTER's slim collection *The Bloody Chamber and Other Stories* (1979) updates 10 fantasies of beauty and VIOLENCE that derive validity from oral folklore and FAIRY TALES. By reworking subtextual motifs and gendered attitudes, she turns universal stereotypes into dark meditations on male lechery, sadism, and voyeurism versus female coping and cunning. With a skill similar to that of Margaret ATWOOD and Joyce Carol OATES, Carter turns vampirism and lycanthropy into coded models of sensuality that illuminate images of desire and death. As a

detailed miniature, each revisionary story peruses the erotic for truth and metaphysical nuance, the themes of "The Werewolf" and "The Lady of the House of Love."

Carter's version of Gothic convention highlights the ambiguities of aggression and victimization. In the suspenseful title story, she recasts the BLUEBEARD legend with a bestial, paternal husband who wears the mask of the incestuous wooer. The protagonist, a 17-year-old bride beset by doubts of her sexual appeal, sits on his knee in a good-little-girl pose and tolerates his irritating dalliance. In private, she snoops into the marquis's past three marriages and identifies with the corpses of previous victims. Cowed by the opal ring of a matriarchal line and by the housekeeper's sway over the groom, the bride fights back by summoning her mother through "maternal telepathy," a call for help that elicits a powerful matriarchal support system as old as time (Carter, 40).

The author's intent to strip past literary modes of sexism is pleasingly successful. In "The Courtship of Mr. Lyon," she subverts the sacrifice of another dewy virgin with repetitive ironies that undercut the sentimentality of wedding night clichés. The narrator interjects a fresh take on the predatory male: "[Lions] belong to a different order of beauty and, besides, they have no respect for us: why should they?" (*ibid.*, 45). Set in czarist Russia, the next story, "The Tiger's Bride," pictures discounted Beauty as an avenger. She finds the inner strength to retaliate against her father's gambling and whoring, the vices that killed her aristocratic mother. Beauty concludes, "It was not my flesh, but, truly, my father's soul that was in peril" (*ibid.*, 54). Through feral shape-shifting into a feline carnality equal to that of the pacing, tail-twitching beast, Beauty domesticates him into a feisty male.

By connecting misogyny to specific historical eras, Carter displaces the once-upon-a-time mirage with actual times and social shifts. A reduction of "Snow White" to "The Snow Child" enhances incestuous tensions between the count and the dream daughter, the countess's rival for affection and title. The three-sided power struggle reveals female complicity in exploitation of the girlchild. Left voiceless and naked in the forest, the child represents the situation of premodern woman, who succumbs to the machinations of feudal female bondage. The author's unflinching gaze at the bartering and menacing of womanflesh revives the universality of fairy tales with lethal charges against late 20th-century misogyny. In the final charge against the child-turned-rose, the countess must admit, "It bites!," a comeuppance to a titled woman who makes no effort to spare her peasant alter ego (*ibid.*, 92). For their richly layered metaphor, Carter's stories are without equal in feminist revisionary lore.

Bibliography

Brooke, Patricia. "Lyons and Tigers and Wolves—Oh My! Revisionary Fairy Tales in the Work of Angela Carter," *Critical Survey* 16, no. 1 (2004): 67–88.

Carter, Angela. *The Bloody Chamber and Other Stories.* London: Penguin, 1987.

Kaiser, Mary. "Fairy Tale as Sexual Allegory: Intertextuality in Angela Carter's 'The Bloody Chamber,' *Review of Contemporary Fiction* 14, no. 3 (Fall 1994): 30–36.

McLaughlin, Becky. "Perverse Pleasure and Fetishized Text: The Deathly Erotics of Carter's 'The Bloody Chamber,' " *Style* 29, no. 3 (Fall 1995): 404–422.

Bluebeard

The archetypal figure of Bluebeard, the wife destroyer of FAIRY TALES, embodies the terrors of the imprisoner and serial killer of women. As the Jungian psychoanalyst Clarissa Pinkola ESTÉS explains in *Women Who Run with the Wolves* (1992), Bluebeard is a monolithic predator, a recurring figure in women's thoughts and dreams. His assault "severs the woman from her intuitive nature, . . . [leaving her] deadened in feeling, feeling too frail to advance her life" (Estés, 39). In the wreckage left behind lie women's dreams and thoughts, "drained of animation," like the bloodless victims of vampires in Gothic fiction (*ibid.*). Estés substantiates her conclusions with a Hungarian story she heard in childhood, a story spread by Slavic farmwomen. The plot depicts the victim's turning from prayers to SISTERHOOD by calling on her sisters for aid. The arrival of the victim's brothers ends Bluebeard's predations with slashing and whipping. In the end, triumph over a killer of women leaves behind "for the buzzards his blood and gristle" (*ibid.*, 43). Estés interprets the long-lived tale as an atavistic war on "young feminine forces of the psyche" (*ibid.*, 45).

The history of Bluebeard points to a human source of myth. The journalist Susan BROWN-MILLER stresses in *Against Our Will: Men, Women, and Rape* (1975) that the original Bluebeard, Gilles de Rais, kidnapped, sodomized, and slew 140 small boys in the privacy of his castle in Brittany before his execution in 1440. When the story recurred in Charles Perrault's "La Barbe Bleue" in *Contes de Ma Mère l'Oye* (Tales of Mother Goose, 1697), Bluebeard morphed from pederast and child killer to roué and despoiler of seven wives, whom he dispatched for indulging their curiosity. In this guise, the literary Bluebeard is the worst of PATRIARCHY, the foul Breton womanizer in search of new sources of nubile womanhood. On the pretense of marriage, he contracts unnatural unions that conclude with the bride's deflowering and murder. The female role in the story requires a curiosity equal to that of the Greek Pandora and Psyche and to the biblical Eve, three women who refused to accept their place in a gendered pecking order and who suffered for their rebellion.

The sexual allegory of the Bluebeard motif has gripped the imaginations of feminist authors. Charlotte BRONTË's novel *JANE EYRE* (1847) incorporates the glowering male suitor and timorous wife to be in the love match of Edward Rochester and his unsuspecting hireling Jane Eyre. As does Bluebeard's bride, Jane stumbles on the closeted evil at Thornfield manor when she first hears the demented yowls of Bertha Mason ROCHESTER, Edward's insane wife. Angela CARTER updated the tale in the anthology *The Bloody Chamber and Other Stories* (1979) with the story of a snooping bride who pays dearly for intruding in a room her husband declares off limits. The poet Sylvia PLATH revisited the myth in the poem "Bluebeard" (1981), which resets the timeless story with modern technology: "I can see / my X-rayed heart, dissected body" (Plath, 305). The gothic short fiction maven Shirley JACKSON fine-tuned the Bluebeard tale in "The Honeymoon of Mrs. Smith," collected in *Just an Ordinary Day* (1996). The version pictures an old maid so desperate for a husband that she abets a serial killer who knifes each of his six brides in the bathtub.

Bibliography

Brownmiller, Susan. *Against Our Will: Men, Women and Rape.* New York: Bantam Books, 1975.

D'Eramso, Stacey, "Just an Ordinary Day." *Nation,* 23 December 1996, pp. 25–26.

Estés, Clarissa Pinkola. *Women Who Run with the Wolves: Myths and Stories about the Wild Woman Archetype.* New York: Ballantine, 1997.

Lovell-Smith, Rose, "Anti-housewives and Ogres' House-keepers: The Roles of Bluebeard's Female Helper," *Folklore* 113, no. 2 (October 2002): 197–214.

Plath, Sylvia. *The Collected Poems of Sylvia Plath.* New York: HarperCollins, 1981.

Weinert, Laurent, "Angela Carter's 'The Bloody Chamber' at the Metal Shed at the Toy Factory." *Back Stage West,* 23 January 2003, p. 19.

Wolf, Leonard. *Bluebeard: The Life and Crimes of Gilles de Rais.* New York: Clarkson N. Potter, 1980.

Bluest Eye, The **Toni Morrison** (1970)

A literary monument ennobling the emotional hurts of young black girls, Toni Morrison's polyphonic novel *The Bluest Eye* dramatizes the brief mother-hood and madness of an unattractive incest victim. Set in Lorain, Ohio, the novel denounces both the white-conceived BEAUTY MYTH and domestic violence in a surreal mockery of an elementary school Dick and Jane reader. The vulnerable, passive protagonist is the epitome of unlovely female looks— "hair uncombed, dresses falling apart, shoes untied and caked with dirt" (Morrison, 92) She bears the ironic name of Pecola Breedlove, a combination of the Latin for "little sins" and an anglicized surname that is the antithesis of her experience. Pecola suffers from racial self-loathing and prays to Jesus for blue eyes so people will love and value her. Reared in the era of Shirley Temple films and posters, she grasps a cup picturing the white child star and gulps down three quarts of milk, which symbolize her need for nurturing and love from Pauline "Polly" Williams Breedlove, her mother.

Gradually unfolding Pecola's tragedy, Morrison's elegy describes her as a waste of human beauty.

The author parallels the 11-year-old's silent forbearance with shunning and erasure with the squalor and shame of a fractious, alcoholic father, Cholly Breedlove. A scrapper, batterer, and arsonist, he is in jail when his daughter experiences menarche. Contributing to irony are the dismissal Pecola receives from a lighter-skinned black girl, the welcome a trio of prostitutes offers the outcast, and the chastisement that Polly dumps on Pecola for dropping a blueberry cobbler. Similar to the spreading blue stain on the kitchen floor of a white family, Pecola herself devolves into a blot on a piercingly judgmental community by babbling like a madwoman and rummaging in alleyway garbage cans.

Morrison's even-handed view of cyclic family uproar, child molestation, and debasement moves back in time to the roots of dysfunction. She surveys the humiliation in Cholly's coming of age story and accounts for Polly's marriage to a shiftless rascal who has served time on a chain gang and been shot by a woman. Still naive, Polly absorbs the movie romance of Clark Gable and Jean Harlow at the Dreamland Theatre but bumps up against the white-centered culture when the instructor at a teaching hospital informs young residents that black women such as Polly give birth as painlessly as horses. The misguided mother fails to protect Pecola and passes on to her the gendered expectation of misery and unstinting labor. In Morrison's words, "Into her daughter [Polly] beat a fear of growing up, fear of other people, fear of life" (*ibid.,* 128). Round-shouldered with head drooping, Pecola bends to her legacy as a mule to harness, causing her guilty father to want "to break her neck—but tenderly" (*ibid.,* 161). Crawling like a beast toward his unsuspecting child as she washes a frying pan, Cholly enjoys her shock, rigidity, and swoon at the seizure of her body and the rupture of her hymen.

The author lodges a far-reaching charge against pedophiles as well as those who dehumanize Pecola Breedlove and rob her of potential because her black African face refuses to assimilate into genteel white society. As are the doomed marigold seeds of the MacTeer girls' garden, Pecola is unable to germinate. Her subsequent breakdown triggers psychotic episodes of talking to her mirrored reflection and of rationalizing a second rape by Cholly. Of her ego's inability to restore order, Morrison remarks on the pathetic loss of self-esteem: "She is not *seen* by herself until she hallucinates a self" (*ibid.*, 215). The premature birth of an infant and its immediate death tip Pecola into full-blown insanity. Morrison's 1993 afterword accounts for the story's source and the beginnings of the fictional version, which she outlined in 1962. The author regrets that readers and critics initially "dismissed, trivialized, misread" the novel, just as neighbors, family, and schoolmates discounted Pecola's short life (*ibid.*, 216).

Bibliography

Cormier-Hamilton, Patrice. "Black Naturalism and Toni Morrison: The Journey Away from Self-Love in *The Bluest Eye*," *MELUS* 19, no. 4 (Winter 1994): 109–127.

Malmgren, Carl D. "Texts, Primers, and Voices in Toni Morrison's *The Bluest Eye*," *Critique* 41, no. 3 (Spring 2000): 251–262.

Morrison, Toni. *The Bluest Eye*. New York: Plume Books, 1993.

Blume, Judy (1938–)

A pacesetter for writers of juvenile fiction, Judy Blume introduced candor in young adult short stories and novels by incorporating taboo topics. A native of Elizabeth, New Jersey, she earned a degree in education from New York University. In 1970, she published a groundbreaking girl's story, *Are You There God? It's Me, Margaret*. The popular work precipitated a lengthy onslaught of conservative criticism and censorship of Blume's books, making her one of the nation's most suppressed authors. The protagonist Margaret Simon's eagerness for secondary gender characteristics and kissing and her prayers for menarche reveal the 12-year-old's readiness to become an adult. The poignant humor of her one-to-one relationship with God attests to her sincerity: "Have you thought about it God? About my growing, I mean. I've got a bra now. It would be nice if I had something to put in it" (Blume, 50). Impatient for results, she later reminds the almighty: "I mean, I know you're busy. But it's already December and I'm not growing" (*ibid.*, 81). The warmth of Blume's portrayal of pu-

berty in Margaret eased qualms in young female readers that they might not be reaching womanhood on schedule.

In *Places I Never Meant to Be* (1999), Blume reflected on three decades of censorship. School principals and public librarians removed from their shelves *Then Again, Maybe I Won't* (1971) for its depiction of nocturnal emissions. A similar attack on *Deenie* (1973) forced the suppression of a story in which the title character masturbates. In *Blubber* (1974), Blume set the BEAUTY MYTH at grade-school level to express the agony of an overweight girl. In *Forever: A Novel of Good and Evil, Love and Hope* (1975), the author creates as a focus Kathy, a sexually active teen.

Blume is vocal about the need for honesty in children's books. In an interview, she outlined Kathy's motivation and the gender-based allotment of guilt and suffering: "Girls had sex because there was something terribly wrong in their lives. . . . And when they inevitably got pregnant, the pregnancy was linked with punishment. Always. If you had sex you were going to be punished. Now the guys, they were never punished, only the girls" (Sutton, 26). To rescue *Tiger Eyes* (1981) from unstinting barrages from the religious Right, Blume allowed her editor to remove even a hint of masturbation from the story. For her courageous stand against book banning in 2004 Blume became the first children's book author to receive a National Book Award for lifetime achievement and literary courage.

Bibliography

Blume, Judy. *Are You There God? It's Me, Margaret*. New York: Dell, 1970.

Sutton, Roger. "An Interview with Judy Blume Forever . . . Yours," *School Library Journal* 42, no. 6 (June 1996): 24–27.

Bly, Nellie (Elizabeth Jane Cochrane) (1864–1922)

Through investigative reporting, the newswoman Nellie Bly, a born detective and grandstander, pioneered passionate humanitarianism and media defense of women and children. Named Elizabeth Jane "Pink" Cochran in infancy (she later added an *e* to her surname), she grew up in Cochran's Mills, Pennsylvania. The death of her father, Judge Michael Cochran, left the family virtually penniless. Her mother, Mary Jane Kennedy Cochran, had to remarry to support her 13 children, but she inadvertently placed them under the abusive control of John Jackson Ford, a cruel stepfather. From the powerlessness of childhood grew Nellie's love of writing stories and her fearless feminism. In 1885, after family finances provided one semester at the Indiana State Normal School, she landed a reporter's beat on the *Pittsburgh Dispatch* by penning an anonymous reply to a sexist editorial that elevated homemakers by belittling working women. She issued a retort that all women are deserving, regardless of their physical beauty, skills, or social and economic background.

Under the pseudonym Nellie Bly, the title of a Stephen Foster ballad, she concealed her identity while writing a daring form of crusader journalism. She championed the rights of women and immigrants and spotlighted the miseries caused by drunken husbands, miserly landlords, corrupt ward heelers, and exploiters of low-paid female employees. To understand the privations of maids and cooks, she applied to a domestic service, the Germania Servants' Agency, and divulged the name and address of a client who snubbed an Irish applicant for hire. Thinking back over the girls clogging the office anteroom at Mrs. L. Seely's agency, Bly recalled in her report, "Trying to Be a Servant" (1890): "Some girls laughed, some were sad, some slept, some ate, and others read, while all sat from morning till night waiting a chance to earn a living" (Bly, 1890, 109). While investigating sweatshop sexism, she labored as a box girl at $1.50 per week as background for the article "Nellie Bly as a White Slave" (1890). Prominent in her report were the numerous occasions when dissolute men attempted to take advantage of the girls. In their defense, Bly concluded, "I have seen many worse girls in much higher positions than the white slaves of New York" (*ibid.*, 120).

Bly's undercover muckraking during a sojourn in Mexico in 1886 earned her ouster from the country for revealing government corruption and poverty. She turned the series into a book,

Six Months in Mexico (1888). Of women and children living on the street, she said, "They merely exist. Thousands of them are born and raised on the streets. They have no home and were never in a bed" (Bly, 1888, 19). One small boy tending a tiny sibling stood on the street in dismay as the infant died in his serape. Bly concluded that the poor of Mexico City "are worse off by thousands of times than were the slaves of the United States" (*ibid.*, 25).

Reassignment to the society page caused Bly to quit her first job in disgust at tea parties and frivolous fashions. On staff of the *New York World*, she took her riskiest assignment to observe in person the treatment of the 1,600 inmates at the Women's Lunatic Asylum on Blackwell's Island in Manhattan. Committed as an hysteric, she fooled police, a judge, and four doctors at Bellevue into believing her insane. She noted that their most frequent questions were about her morals. For the next 10 days, she observed high doses of morphine and chloral, unsanitary towels and bathtubs, stench and flies, repulsive meals doctored with vinegar and mustard, and discipline of unruly patients with showers of icy water, taunting, throttlings, and beatings. Of Tillie Mayard's sufferings from cold, nurses replied, "Let her fall on the floor and it will teach her a lesson" (Bly, 1890, 75). On Bly's discharge, she felt selfish to leave the inmates in torment: "I felt a Quixotic desire to help them by sympathy and presence" (*ibid.*, 94).

Bly's report charged that a punitive atmosphere and verbal and physical abuse of patients were more likely to cause derangement than to curb it. Most pathetic were immigrants who spoke only German and Yiddish and who were unable to plead for release. From Bly's experiences resulted her first-person testimony, *Ten Days in a Madhouse* (1888), which states in the introduction, "The City of New York has appropriated $1,000,000 more per annum than ever before for the care of the insane. So I have at least the satisfaction of knowing that the poor unfortunates will be the better cared for because of my work" (*ibid.*, introduction).

Bly continued her detective work on behalf of women, especially indigent and unwed mothers. She took notes on women's shelters and reported on the abysmal life of downtrodden, homeless females, some of whom were pregnant. At age 25, she expanded her reputation for audacity by beating Jules Verne's fictional around-the-world voyage by eight days. From Hoboken, New Jersey, she set sail aboard the *Augusta Victoria* on November 14, 1889, and returned in 72 days. Along the way she met Verne in France. The stunt sold 300,000 papers. Because her employers failed to offer a bonus for her chutzpah, she abandoned the *New York World,* joined the lecture circuit, and wrote *Nelly Bly's Book: Around the World in 72 Days* (1890). On her sojourn in England, she expressed admiration for Queen Victoria and commented on her value to the realm: "I could not help but think how devoted that woman, for she is only a woman after all, should be to the interests of such faithful subjects" (Bly, 1998, 64). In contrast to royalty, Bly mused on the status of Japanese women, who "carry everything in their sleeves, even their hearts" (*ibid.,* 100). She concluded that they were guileless and sweet, qualities that even geishas displayed.

Returned to the *New York World* in 1893, Bly limited her outspoken writings to gender and class issues and exposés of public corruption and mistreatment of striking workers. At age 31 she retired to marry the industrial mogul Robert Livingston Seaman, owner of Iron Clad Manufacturing in Brooklyn. In widowhood at 40 she upgraded medical and workplace benefits for the 1,500 employees at the company's metal barrel factory. The business eventually foundered after the pre–World War I severance from German and Austrian clients. In 1914, as the first female combat reporter, she observed the eruption of war on the Russian and Serbian fronts, warned General John J. Pershing and President Woodrow Wilson about Bolshevism, and pled the cause of war widows and orphans through a series of newspaper columns. Covering exhaustion and cholera outbreaks in soldiers, she remained in Austria until 1919, when she took a post as columnist at the *New York Evening Journal.* In her last three years, she concentrated on slum life and on orphaned and abandoned children. After her death from pneumonia, the *New York Evening Journal* obituary described her as the nation's best reporter.

Bibliography

Bly, Nellie. *Around the World in 72 Days.* Brookfield, Conn.: Twenty-First Century Books, 1998.

———. *Six Months in Mexico.* New York: American Publishers, 1888.

———. *Ten Days in a Mad-House and Miscellaneous Sketches: "Trying to Be a Servant," and "Nellie Bly as a White Slave."* New York: Ian L. Munro, 1890.

Kroeger, Brooke. "Nellie Bly: She Did It All," *Quarterly of the National Archives* 28, no. 1 (Spring 1996): 7–15.

Bogan, Louise (1897–1970)

The prolific poet and critic Louise Bogan produced a dense, epigrammatic style of psychologically intense verse based on intuitive truths. A native of Livermore Falls, Maine, she escaped from a grimly embattled Catholic home and from boredom at Mount Saint Mary's Academy and Girls' Latin School in Boston by composing verse imitating late 19th-century British style. She published her first efforts in school papers, the Boston *Evening Transcript,* and the campus journal of Boston University. At age 20, she rejected a scholarship to Radcliffe to marry Curt Alexander and rear Mathilda, their daughter, who was born during the father's military assignment to Panama. When the marriage failed, she left her husband and settled in Greenwich Village, New York. After his death, at age 23, she studied piano in Vienna.

Bogan worked at Brentano's bookstore and a public library while perfecting the compaction and sleek lines of her poetry, which she submitted to *Atlantic Monthly, New York Evening Post, Measure, Nation, New Republic, New Yorker, Others, Poetry, Scribner's,* and *Vanity Fair.* Among her favorite literary models were the writings of SAPPHO and Virginia WOOLF. Bogan's first two collections were *Body of This Death* (1923) and *Dark Summer* (1929). She established her faith in female liberation and in equality in relationships by such poems as the compassionate "The Crows" (1923) and "Women" (1923), a muted praise for benevolence in women and an advisory on being less servile and seeking adventures that broaden and uplift. At age 33, she received the John Reed Memorial Prize from *Poetry* magazine.

In 1931, after three months of treatment for depression, Bogan began critiquing verse for the *New Yorker* in a stable job she retained to age 72. Her mature anthologies—*The Sleeping Fury* (1937) and *Poems and New Poems* (1941)—preceded a year as poetry consultant to the Library of Congress, from 1945 to 1946. From this era arose a pictorial glimpse of an asylum ward for insane women, "Evening in the Sanitarium" (1941). The poet offers a sympathetic evaluation of the ennui and despair that immobilize women, wasting their promise and crushing them into human wreckage. She followed with *Collected Poems* (1954) and translations of Ernest Juenger's *The Glass Bees* (1961), Johann von Goethe's *Elective Affinities* (1963), and *The Journal of Jules Renard* (1964). Her scholarly commentary in *Selected Criticism: Poetry and Prose* (1955) secured her place in American letters. In *Achievement in American Poetry, 1900–1950* (1951), Bogan judged the best in a half-century of verse. Of female writers, she admired those of an era when "rejection of moral passivity, economic dependence, and intellectual listlessness" preceded full involvement in life and art (Bogan, 1951, 23). She singled out for praise Gertrude STEIN's experimental novel *Tender Buttons* (1914).

Bogan maintained high literary standards for verse and denounced the breast-beating confessional poems of the 1960s. Her straightforward style influenced the poets May SARTON and Sonia SANCHEZ, both of whom enrolled in Bogan's class at New York University. Numerous citations for Bogan's verse include the Bollingen Prize, Helen Haire Levinson Prize, Harriet Monroe Award, a $10,000 National Endowment for the Arts award, and two Guggenheim fellowships. Her final volume, *The Blue Estuaries: Poems 1923–1968* (1968), preceded her death from coronary disease. A posthumous work, *A Poet's Alphabet* (1970); a translation of Goethe's *The Sorrows of Young Werther, and Novella* (1971); personal letters in *What the Woman Lived* (1973); and a memoir of her troubled childhood, *Journey around My Room* (1980), kept her writing and criticism in circulation beyond the 20th century.

Bibliography

Bogan, Louise. *Achievement in American Poetry.* Los Angeles: Gateway, 1951.

———. *The Blue Estuaries: Poems 1923–1968.* New York: Farrar, Straus & Giroux, 1995.

Frank, Elizabeth. *Louise Bogan: A Portrait.* New York: Columbia University Press, 1985.

Kerr, Frances. " 'Nearer the Bone': Louise Bogan, Anorexia, and the Political Unconscious of Modernism," *Literature Interpretation Theory* 8, no. 3/4 (June 1998): 305–330.

Boland, Eavan (1944–)

The Dubliner Eavan Aisling Boland staked out Irish womanhood as the focus of her art. After education in convent schools, she cowrote a verse collection while studying English at Trinity College, Dublin. At age 23 she solidified her basic themes by balancing the broad, encompassing masculinity of Celtic history and lore with a humanistic view of women's lives and sacrifices at the far edge of the bardic tradition. Influenced by the American confessional poets Sylvia PLATH and Adrienne RICH, Boland submitted verse to the *Atlantic, New Yorker, Northwest Review, Ontario Review, Partisan Review, Seneca Review,* and *Ontario Review.* Her poems, collected in *New Territory* (1967), earned the Irish Arts Council Macauley Fellowship for their stark glimpses of women's longings and frustrations and the intersection of individual lives with history. Her next anthology, *The War Horse* (1975), presented mature reflection on the somber themes of want and family sufferings in the poems "The Famine Road," "Sisters," "Suburban Woman," and "Child of Our Time."

In 1980, Boland's *In Her Own Image* turned more specifically to feminist concerns with a collection widely honored for its moral authority. Her taut, unflinching poems speak directly of spousal abuse, eating disorders, menstruation, breast cancer, and depression. In the verse suite *Domestic Interior* (1982), the poet describes the trivializing of WOMAN'S WORK in "Degas's Laundresses," in which the artist looks for physical beauty without validating their domestic skills. The canto "Night Feed" pictures the dawn bottle feeding of a daughter, whose innocence conjures up mythic glimpses of humanity's frailty as the day grows light. In the sixth canto, "The Muse Mother," Boland puzzles over an image of a parent wiping stickiness from her son's mouth. The poet seeks to move step by step back into human history to be "able to speak at last / my mother tongue" (Boland 1997, 143).

The author delved further into mother-daughter relations in *The Journey* (1986). In 1987, she crafted one of her finest poems, "Mise Eire" (I am Ireland), a personal credo that pictures the starving immigrant and her babe traveling west by steamer from an Irish wharf. The mother abandons the nation's brutal past for a life of homesickness and hope for better times. More graphic is "Fever" (1987), an elegy to the poet's grandmother, dead at age 31 in a fever ward of Dublin's National Maternity Hospital. The dense litany ties the lyric Irish past Boland learned in childhood to the traditional female sufferings of gendered punishments, witch-hunts, and domestic neglect.

Bibliography

Boland, Eavan. *In a Time of Violence.* New York: W. W. Norton, 1995.

———. *An Origin Like Water: Collected Poems 1957–1987.* New York: W. W. Norton, 1997.

———. *Outside History: Selected Poems, 1980–1990.* New York: W. W. Norton, 2001.

Burns, Christy. "Beautiful Labors: Lyricism and Feminist Revisions in Eavan Boland's Poetry," *Tulsa Studies in Women's Literature* 20, no. 2 (Fall 2001): 217–236.

Bone Black: Memories of Girlhood
bell hooks (1996)

A vital AUTOBIOGRAPHY rich in elegiac lyricism, bell HOOKS's *Bone Black: Memories of Girlhood* connects events and themes from family mythos. Like Dorothy ALLISON's BASTARD OUT OF CAROLINA (1992), hooks's impressions on rural southern poverty focus on toxic home life and a tender girlchild's burden of rejection by five sisters. Through innovative metafiction the author aligns 61 candid shots that shift perspectives on the growing-up years of "she," the partially identified protagonist. Juxtaposition contrasts the child's rewards from her clairvoyant grandmother, Saru; from wise Daddy Gus; and from Miss Erma for reading scripture aloud with the estrangement generated by a disapproving paternal grandmother named Sister Ray, a conflicted father, and a mother

and older sister who mock the child's introduction to menstruation. The image of a jettisoned Christmas tree left naked in the snow suggests both the personal and the racial seclusion of the spirit.

Sensitivity both guides and confounds the protagonist, whose gravity is a target of family contempt. She asserts, "Only grown-ups think that the things children say come out of nowhere. We know they come from the deepest parts of ourselves" (hooks, 24). She opens her memoir on the ritual of mother's gifts from her chest of treasures and the stories that replace heirlooms lost in a fire. Unlike her sisters, who have nuptial hope chests, the protagonist collects perceptions rather than bride goods for later use because she "[does] not want to be given away" (*ibid.*, 2). Confronting the stranger she calls father as he holds her mother at gunpoint, in stave 50 the protagonist imagines a shooting and a fall that destroy not the mother's body but the ideal of love. The scene echoes a universal truth—that the father's threats pump abstract bullets into the succeeding generation. In reverie, the child recalls, "I am remembering how much I want that woman to fight back" (*ibid.*, 152). The child's reward for loyalty stings in captured memories of her mother's choosing the out-of-control husband over their neediest child.

Introspection provides the writer's haven, a home within the "bone black inner cave" of words (*ibid.*, 183). The protagonist is a dreamer who identifies with "boxes of unwanted, unloved brown dolls, covered with dust" on store shelves (*ibid.*, 24). She retreats into internal discourse to ponder the pathetic strategies of integration. A minority among whites, she views the administration's intent to change blacks without requiring any adaptation from the white majority. In sight of uniformed national guardsmen she relives the safety of Crispus Attucks School, the source of self-acceptance and celebration of blackness in an institution named for a black rebel. Driven to revisit a youngster's hardening to a callous, racist world, hooks validates girlhood fantasy as a necessary escape from untenable domestic and social conditions.

Bibliography

hooks, bell. *Bone Black: Memories of Girlhood.* New York: Henry Holt, 1996.

Shockley, Evelyn E. "Review: *Bone Black: Memories of Girlhood*," *African American Review* 31, no. 3 (Fall 1997): 552–554.

Vega-González, Susana. "The Dialectics of Belonging in bell hooks's *Bone Black: Memories of Girlhood*," *Journal of English Studies*, 3 (2001–2002): 237–243.

Bonner, Marita (1899–1971)

The dramatist, essayist, and short-story writer Marita Odette Bonner Occomy used realism and cynicism to shed light on women's issues of economic and social INDEPENDENCE. A Bostonian and the oldest of three surviving children, she enjoyed a middle-class childhood outside Brookline, Massachusetts. Although banned from white women's dormitories, she studied English and comparative literature at Radcliffe and thrived intellectually and socially. She taught high school in West Virginia and Washington, D.C., before joining the Krigwa Players and becoming a leading intellectual of the Harlem Renaissance. During the salon maven Georgia Douglas JOHNSON's Saturday Nighters, Bonner gained the confidence to submit short pieces to *Crisis*, the *Journal of Negro Life*, and *Opportunity*.

Bonner resisted the trend toward writing about Harlem by picturing poorly educated protagonists in the multicultural environs of Chicago. In 1928, she revealed a sophisticated understanding of psychological theater with the writing of *The Purple Flower*, a prize-winning allegorical play more fully realized than *Exit* (1923), more daring than *The Pot Maker* (1927). In the characterization of red-horned White Devils challenging nonwhites of a range of skin tones, the tone and atmosphere reflect the moral determinism of medieval morality plays. Surreal in its setting, *The Purple Flower* predicts the chaotic looting and bloodletting of racial clashes during the 1960s and 1970s. The theme of society's arbitrary treatment based on shades of pigment expresses Bonner's jaundiced outlook. At age 42, she abandoned her literary career and devoted her energies to educating her three children.

Retrieved by feminist writers in 1987, Bonner's short stories and plays began filling slots in women's studies texts. One essay, "On Being Young—A Woman—and Colored" (1925), became a cogent model of feminist polemics against gendered and racial glass ceilings. She pictures the patient female seated like a smiling Buddha and awaiting the arrival of opportunity. A complex view of womanhood in the story "Light in Dark Places" (1941) characterizes the reluctance of Tina, a working-class female teen, to value her high school years for more than chasing boys. The motif of girls' marrying young and depending on male financial support often concludes in disillusion and single parenthood bereft of a living wage because the working mother lacks marketable skills. More pathetic is Nora, the housemaid in "One True Love" (1941), who observes the homes and lifestyles of white career women. She longs to "get beyond a stove, a sink, a broom and a dust-mop and some one else's kitchen" (Bonner, 223). In the struggle for career training, she fails to complete law school in night courses at City College because of limited reading comprehension, a lack of counseling, and low expectations for black females.

Bibliography

Berg, Allison, and Meridith Taylor. "Enacting Difference: Marita Bonner's 'Purple Flower' and the Ambiguities of Race," *African American Review* 32, no. 3 (Fall 1998): 469–480.

Bonner, Marita. *Frye Street and Environs: A Collection of Works of Marita Bonner*. Boston: Beacon Press, 1987.

Musser, Judith. "African American Women and Education: Marita Bonner's Response to the 'Talented Tenth,'" *Studies in Short Fiction* 23, no. 1 (Winter 1997): 73–85.

Book of Margery Kempe, The Margery Kempe (1436)

An enigmatic medieval classic, Margery KEMPE's AUTOBIOGRAPHY reveals the torments of discontent that precipitate mental and emotional regrouping. *The Book of Margery Kempe* (1436) is a mystic memoir that she dictated over a four-year period into her early 70s during a reign of Henry V. The narrative glimpses the emergence of unconventional zealotry in a seriously disturbed wife, mother, business owner, and religious traveler whom historians dub "God's madwoman." An undiagnosed psychosis causes her to spout slander, scold, covet, delight in evil, bite and maim her flesh, and plot suicide. Physical restraints prevent her from doing more harm to herself as she brokers peace between Christian tenets and bourgeois values.

As does Nathaniel Hawthorne's Hester PRYNNE, Kempe scrutinizes pride and secret sin from a rebel's perspective. Narcissism and infantile outbursts at table and in church limit her attempts at a socially acceptable Christian demeanor. Repetitive strands of discourse suggest a mind controlled by raging emotions, arrogance, and unresolved guilt about sexual pleasures. In loose chronology, she confesses that "her enemy—the devil" misled her into self-directed penance of "fasting on bread and water," prayer, and alms (Kempe, 1). In chapter 2, she implies that a flair for fashionable hair dressings, hoods, and cloaks draws attention and gossip from the envious. Reverberating through the text are proofs of her own greed and envy, sources of her manic clutching after a change of heart and behavior.

Economically diminished from the mayor's daughter to the beleaguered wife of a "worshipful burgess," Kempe makes a career of a doomed brewery and horse-powered mill. Her neighbors charge that God has cursed her when the businesses fail. Unlike Chaucer's secular WIFE OF BATH, Kempe invests her hopes in Christ, whose appearance precedes a peripatetic life of adventures to holy shrines (ibid.). Significantly, he appears to her "sitting upon her bedside" and gazing at her with a serene and amiable countenance, a nonthreatening pose that is the antithesis of a lover's glance (ibid., 42). After the encounter she chooses "to enter the way of everlasting life," her description of the holy pilgrimage (ibid., 45). Heavenly music lures her from her bed and ends her enjoyment of coitus, which she compares to "the ooze and muck in the gutter" (ibid., 46). After she gives birth to a 14th child, probably during the layover in Venice, her joy in travel reaches fruition at the approach to Jerusalem, where religious ecstasy overtakes her with a physical reenactment of Christ's passion on Calvary. The epiphany releases emotions that cause her penitential grief whenever she witnesses suffering and bloodshed in beast or humankind. Critics suggest that the sight of blood allows Kempe

to mourn female suffering in menstruation, childbirth, and sexual obligation to a husband and to anticipate redemption in death.

Bibliography

Ashley, Kathleen. "Historicizing Margery: *The Book of Margery Kempe* as Social Text," *Journal of Medieval and Early Modern Studies* 28, no. 2 (Spring 1998): 371–389.

Howes, Laura L. "On the Birth of Margery Kempe's Last Child," *Modern Philology* 90, no. 2 (November 1992): 220–225.

Kempe, Margery. *The Book of Margery Kempe.* London: Penguin, 2000.

Bowen, Elizabeth (1899–1973)

The Welsh-Irish Gothic novelist and short story writer Elizabeth Dorothea Cole Bowen spoke openly about feminism and lesbianism. Although she avoided turning her fiction into a platform for WOMEN'S RIGHTS, she posed female characters in each fictional milieu as viable, contributing figures. The Dublin-born daughter of Irish gentry from County Cork, she inherited Bowen's Court at Kildorrey but lived in England under unsettled conditions with her mother and nanny. After her mother's death of cancer in 1909, Bowen floundered as the outsider while studying at Harpenden Hall, Hertfordshire, and at Down House School in Kent. By the age of 19, she had acquired enough poise and self-control to work among shell-shocked officers invalided to Dublin.

After relocating to London and attending art school, Bowen lived the next 29 years with her husband, Alan Charles Cameron, a schoolteacher for the British Broadcasting Corporation's (BBC's) radio classes. She published her first story in 1921 in the *Saturday Westminster*. At age 24, she completed *Encounters* (1923), the first collection of her well-wrought stories. Her contributions to the female bildungsroman include two fine examples, *The Last September* (1929), a comedy of manners set in Dublin during the Irish troubles, and *The Death of the Heart* (1938), a novel about Portia, a teenage orphan despoiled by a womanizer. In midcareer Bowen chronicled her family's history in *Bowen Court* (1942). To the lesbian canon, she added *Friends and Relations* (1930). She described the blitz of World War II in *The Demon Lover* (1945), a short fiction collection. In a wartime love story, *The Heat of the Day* (1949), she realigned gender relationships to reflect the phasing-out of notions of women's weaknesses and dependence on strong males. Her kindness to a young interviewer, the poet Sylvia PLATH, influenced a budding genius.

Bibliography

Hoogland, Rene C. *Elizabeth Bowen: A Reputation in Writing.* New York: New York University Press, 1994.

Hopkins, Chris. "Elizabeth Bowen," *Review of Contemporary Fiction,* 21, no. 2 (Summer 2001): 114–151.

Bowles, Jane (1917–1973)

A Jewish-American writer of inventive, unpredictable fiction, Jane Auer Bowles earned a select audience for glimpses of whims and relationships of complex, intriguing women. A native Long Islander, she was the daughter of Sidney Majer Auer, a domineering parent who urged her to outgrow dramatizing. Bowles grew up bilingual and studied under tutors and at elite schools in Manhattan, Massachusetts, and Switzerland, where she simultaneously received treatment for tuberculosis. During her travels and residence in Tangier with her husband, the composer and writer Paul Bowles, she developed a lesbian relationship with a Moroccan peasant and added fluency in Arabic to her accomplishments.

Bowles earned a select readership for her avant-garde use of interior monologues revealing hysteria and neurosis. In addition to the autobiographical novel *Two Serious Ladies* (1943) and the musical drama *In the Summer House* (1953), she wrote short fiction published in *Cross Section, Harper's, Mademoiselle, Paris Review,* and *Vogue.* She is best known for the stories "Camp Cataract" (1949) and "A Stick of Green Candy" (1957). The latter is an austere tale of a young girl's betrayal of her feminist values and imagination for the love of a boy. Bowles's career virtually ended in 1957 after blindness and paralysis from strokes.

Bibliography

Bassett, Mark T. "Imagination, Control, and Betrayal in Jane Bowles' 'A Stick of Green Candy,' " *Studies in Short Fiction* 24, no. 1 (Winter 1987): 25–29.

Bowles, Jane. *The Collected Works of Jane Bowles.* New York: Noonday Press, 1966.

Kanfer, Stefan. "Odd Couples." *New Leader,* 9 August 1993, pp. 22–23.

Braddon, Mary Elizabeth (1835–1915)

One of the female freelancers who thrived at writing blood-and-thunder novels, gaslight thrillers, and detective fiction, the author and actor Mary Elizabeth Braddon Maxwell turned out popular fiction that stocked the shelves of circulating libraries. Her father, the Cornishman Henry Braddon, was a layabout and bounder who deserted the family. Her Irish mother, Fanny White Braddon, earned a pittance writing for *Sporting Magazine.* She home-schooled her daughter, who was well read in French and English classics, including Mary SHELLEY's *Frankenstein* (1818), the sci-fi thriller of the era. On the sly, Braddon got a taste of Gothic plots from the family cook's collection of pulp serials. When Braddon initiated her own writing career in her late teens, she produced melodrama, poems, and plays for popular magazines published under the ambiguous name M. E. Braddon.

Braddon gained recognition for a stage comedy, *The Loves of Arcadia* (1860), and acted for two years under the name Mary Seaton. Her first long work, *Three Times Dead; or, The Secret of the Heath* (1860), preceded a sensational novel, *The Octoroon; or, The Lily of Louisiana* (1861–62), serialized in *Halfpenny Journal.* The author continued in formulaic Gothic style with *The Black Band; or, The Mysteries of Midnight* (1861–62), published under a pseudonym, Lady Caroline Lascelles. The thriller pictures Austrian anarchists menacing a fragile dancer, Clara Melville. For Clara's ability to avoid rape, the author awards her a suitable husband, the standard conclusion to Victorian Gothic.

Braddon altered her style after *The Black Band* and portrayed women as more than nubile pawns within an orderly Victorian PATRIARCHY. She laced *John Marchmont's Legacy* (1863) with a train accident, suicide, secret marriage, and a missing wife presumed dead. The novelist reset Gustave Flaubert's *Madame Bovary* (1857) as *The Doctor's Wife* (1864), a story of the adultery, scandal, and suicide of a woman who ventures out of a stifling marriage. Braddon introduced original girl detectives with Eleanor Vane in *Eleanor's Victory* (1863) and *Thou Art the Man* (1864) and Margaret Dunbar in *Henry Dunbar* (1864). While rearing 11 children, Braddon issued stories and sketches in major magazines, published more than 90 novels, and started her own fiction journals, *Belgravia* and *The Mistletoe Bough*. By the time her earnings reached £2,000 per title, she was boldly covering slow poisoning, insanity, illicit passion, secret marriage, bigamy, blackmail, bastardy, missing persons, arson, ghosts, delirium tremens, and hints of homoeroticism and incest. Feminist readings of Braddon's daring prose note the frequency with which power is in the hands of a female, for example, the lady vampire in "Good Lady Ducayne" (1896) and the protagonist of *Aurora Floyd* (1862), who brandishes a whip over a male stablehand who kicked her dog.

To her lasting fame, Braddon freed her lover, John Maxwell, publisher of the periodical *Robin Goodfellow,* from bankruptcy by writing the classic Victorian domestic crime novel *Lady Audley's Secret* (1862), a best-selling sensational novel reprised in *Sixpenny Magazine*. Literally overnight Braddon launched the 150,000-word tale of the chameleon-like Lucy Audley, whose inability to support herself forces her to seek marriage. She adopts numerous names and poses as her tickets to free movement in a milieu that confined women to a limited range. Her exasperated nephew by marriage, Robert Audley, exclaims, "Good heaven! what an actress this woman is. What an arch trickster—what an all-accomplished deceiver" (Braddon, 169). In a subsequent confrontation, he compares her thinking processes to the diseased mind of LADY MACBETH. Braddon expresses her own respect for the aggressive female in Lucy's decline: "The game had been played and lost. I do not think that my lady had thrown away a card, or missed the making of a trick which she might by any possibility have made; but her opponent's hand had been too powerful for her, and he had won" (*ibid.,*

245). Thus, it is circumstance rather than audacity or brilliance that enables Robert to outsmart Lady Audley.

A smash hit in serialized form and in nine bound editions, *Lady Audley's Secret* won readers to Braddon's cool, unhurried unpeeling of layers of mystery and secrecy. The novel served the dramatist Cohn Henry Hazlewood for a stage adaptation that popularized red hair as the mark of the female criminal. More English and American stage adaptations, a musical, and a five-reel film in 1915 milked the convoluted plot for its thrills and mystery. Over more than a half-century, Braddon, the darling of upscale pulp, was widely read and admired by, among others, Henry James, Sir Arthur Quiller-Couch, William Makepeace Thackeray, Oscar Wilde, and Queen Victoria.

Bibliography

Braddon, Mary Elizabeth. *Lady Audley's Secret.* New York: Dover, 1974.

Carnell, Jennifer. *The Literary Lives of Mary Elizabeth Braddon.* Hastings, England: Sensation Press, 2000.

Nemesvari, Richard. "Robert Audley's Secret: Male Homosocial Desire in *Lady Audley's Secret,*" *Studies in the Novel* 27, no. 4 (Winter 1995): 515–528.

Pearl, Nancy. "Gaslight Thrillers: The Original Victorians," *Library Journal* 126, no. 3 (15 February 2001): 228.

Willis, Chris. "Mary Elizabeth Braddon and the Literary Marketplace: A Study in Commercial Authorship" (1998). Available online. URL: http://www.chriswillis. freeserve.co.uk/meb2.html. Accessed on October 13, 2005.

Bradley, Marion Zimmer (1930–1999)

The popular sci-fi writer Marion Zimmer Bradley expanded the burgeoning branch of feminist utopian and fantasy literature with mythic strands of Arthurian lore. She set herself apart from other recreators of Camelot by portraying women's rationality and their affinity for mystic power. A farm girl born in Albany, New York, she spent her free time reading romances about Arthur and Guinevere. In 1944, she began a juvenile novel and continued testing fantasy modes and motifs during her years at the New York State College for Teachers.

These early efforts prepared her for a successful career as a feminist mythographer and epicist.

At age 19, Bradley saw her first work on the pages of *Fantastic/Amazing Stories* and followed with a submission to *Vortex Science Fiction.* Influenced by the experimental ANDROGYNY in Ursula LE GUIN's *The Left Hand of Darkness* (1969), Bradley moved beyond stale thrillers into more cerebral inventions based on classic legends and myths. Over a lengthy career, she published occult fantasy, science fiction, and lesbian novels under a variety of male and female pen names. She used the proceeds to pay tuition to Hardin-Simmons University and the University of California at Berkeley, where she completed a graduate degree at age 37.

Bradley had no difficulty picturing women in masterful roles. In *The Shattered Chain* (1976) and *Thendara House* (1983), a pair of utopian novels featuring strong female characters, she establishes an all-woman Eden. Free of male interference, the characters enjoy personal INDEPENDENCE and a SISTERHOOD based on the medieval guild system. Bradley extended the application of DREAMSCAPES as psychological insight into women's subconscious thoughts, a trait she emulated from the Gothic writers Clara Reeve and Mary Wollstonecraft SHELLEY. At her best, Bradley depicted women as wielders of power in *The Ruins of Isis* (1978) and, over a 15-year period, applied medieval mysticism to a suite of arcane feminist novels set in the Arthurian era—*The Mists of Avalon* (1982), *The Forest House* (1994), *Return to Avalon* (1996), and *The Lady of Avalon* (1997).

Bradley is best known for her version of Round Table lore. A salute to matriarchal STORYTELLING, *The Mists of Avalon,* her masterwork, portrays Arthur's sister, mother, aunts, and wife retelling familiar events of Celtic legend from the female perspective. Bradley overturns the androcentric Arthurian cycle into a survey of the rise and fall of Camelot through the experiences of Morgaine and Gwenhwyfar, two females possessing opposite types of womanly dynamism to control the chaos engendered by King Arthur. The priestesses of the Holy Isle, a Celtic academy for future rulers reminiscent of SAPPHO's Greek girls' school, receive novices who show promise of understanding abstract concepts. The Lady of the Lake promotes only those capable of learning the humility and patience required of priestesses of the Old Ways, the foundation of modern Wicca. In 2001, Warner compressed Bradley's epic into a three-hour film, in which Anjelica Huston played Viviane, the Lady of the Lake.

Bradley earned regard from feminist critics for depicting the conflicted role of woman as a three-dimensional being and as a revered conduit of nature-based religion and mysticism. One heroic work, *The Firebrand* (1987), surveys the clash of Greeks with Trojans from the perspective of Kassandra, the Trojan priestess of Apollo who is cursed to see the truth but doomed to convince no one of the accuracy of her prophecies. Bradley stressed that in a period of cultural turmoil such as the Trojan War, the powers of the female visionary undergo a fearful test. In the Avalon series, the Old Ways give place to patriarchal Christianity by suffusing Mariology with a weakened form of the powers of the WISEWOMEN who protect the Holy Grail. At the author's death in Berkeley, California, in 1999, she left unfinished *Priestess of Avalon* (2002), a third-century quest novel. The posthumous text glimpses the early Christian era when the British princess Helena, mother of the Roman emperor Constantine, learned goddess lore from the Old Ways. She lost her cultic consciousness after falling in love with a warrior. The text dramatizes the task of the female pilgrim in refining a relationship with God and with mystic powers.

Bibliography

Bradley, Marion Zimmer. *The Forest House.* New York: Roc, 1995.

———. *The Mists of Avalon.* New York: Del Rey, 1987.

———. *Priestess of Avalon.* New York: Roc, 2002.

Dole, Pat. "Review: *Priestess of Avalon,*" *Kliatt* 36, no. 1 (January 2002): 46.

Bradstreet, Anne (1612–1672)

A touchstone of American thought, the poet Anne Dudley Bradstreet earned a unique place in literary history for intimate glimpses of colonial womanhood. A native of Northampton, England, she was reared in genteel comfort in a cultivated home. She gained a grounding in Puritanism and scripture and a thorough familiarity with English literature, which she read in the library of the earl of Lincoln, the employer of her father, Thomas Dudley. In 1630, three years after surviving smallpox, she emigrated to Boston. While living in Ipswich, she joined a faction that supported EDUCATION for women. Among enlightened colonists, she began writing poetry.

At age 30, Bradstreet completed a sheaf of pious, modest poems, which she displayed to her father, the governor of Massachusetts Bay Colony. Eight years later her brother-in-law, the Reverend John Woodbridge, published the work of his "dear sister" in England as *The Tenth Muse Lately Sprung Up in America* (1650) (Bradstreet, 4). His preface urged the reader to "believe it from a woman when thou seest it" (*ibid.*, unpaginated). The edition constituted the New World's first verse anthology, but the poet remained largely unrecognized. An expanded version, *Severall Poems, Compiled with Great Variety of Wit and Learning, Full of Delight* (1678), written after her death from tuberculosis, incorporated more accomplished verse, notably, "Contemplations," a summation of the role of the arts in creation. To her spouse, Simon Bradstreet, she declared in "To My Dear and Loving Husband" (1678) his value as a well-matched and loving mate.

Bradstreet's canon reveals more of the Tenth Muse's human hand in prose. She composed a letter to her eight children, a meditation on surviving fever, references to weaning a breast-fed child, a memoir of the burning of her house, and epitaphs for her parents. In 1643, an original elegy, "In Honour of That High and Mighty Princess Queen Elizabeth of Happy Memory" (1650), exalted Elizabeth I as a female monarch blessed with enough reason and mercy to set the standard for future kings. The poem "The Author to Her Book" (1650) discloses a sense of humor at odds with dour Puritanism; in grief, she struggles to control her doubts of God's mercy in "On My Dear Grandson Simon Bradstreet" (1678), a farewell to a boy dead in infancy. Diverting from the patriarchal dogmas of Puritanism, "The Prologue" (1650) rejects the gendered role of woman as needleworker and defends the female place in the literary arts

against those who might accuse her of succeeding as a result of luck or plagiarism.

Bibliography

Bradstreet, Anne. *The Works of Anne Bradstreet.* Cambridge, Mass.: Belknap Press, 1981.

Fischer, Avery R. "Bradstreet's 'On My Dear Grandchild Simon Bradstreet' and 'Before the Birth of One of Her Children,'" *Explicator* 59, no. 1 (Fall 2000): 11–14.

Harvey, Tamara. " 'Now Sisters . . . Impart Your Usefulnesse, and Force,' " *Early American Literature* 35, no. 1 (March 2000): 5–28.

Brand, Dionne (1953–)

The Trinidadian-Canadian teacher, poet, film director, and activist Dionne Brand glimpses a somber future for poor women of color. She was born in Guayguayare, Trinidad, and graduated from Naparima Girls' High School. An immigrant to Toronto at age 17, she completed degrees in English, philosophy, and women's history at the University of Toronto. She taught literature and writing at Canadian universities before returning to her alma mater as poet in residence. In addition to outreaches to immigrant peoples, in 1986, she facilitated union activities, aided battered women, and established a newsletter, *Our Lives*. Her screen documentaries—*Older, Stronger, Wiser* (1989), *Long Time Comin'* (1993), *Listening for Something—Adrienne Rich and Dionne Brand in Conversation* (1996), and *Sisters in the Struggle* (2000)—cover various aspects of women's lives and art. Brand won a Governor-General's Award in Poetry and the Trillium Book Award for *Land to Light On* (1997).

Influenced by the feminism of the novelists Toni MORRISON and Jean RHYS, Brand's stories, novel, and poems focus on the realities of a black woman living in a white milieu. She has published essays and verse in *Canada Review, Fuse, Network, Poetry,* and *Spear* and earned the praise of the poet Adrienne RICH for *In Another Place, Not Here* (1996), a dialect novel contrasting the lives of women in Canada and Trinidad. The island protagonist Elizete represents the self-deflating drudge: "I never wanted nothing big from the world. Who is me to want anything big or small. . . . I born to clean Isaiah' house and work cane" (Brand, 1996, 3). Her literary foil and lover Verlia flees urban Canada to find a new life in the West Indies as a revolutionary firebrand. Ironically, Verlia dies in the Granadian uprising. Brand's Caribbean saga novel, *At the Full and Change of the Moon* (1999), retreats to a Trinidadian black MATRIARCHY that features Bola, daughter of Marie-Ursule, a leader of militant slaves who harbors self-hatred for her sufferings under the whip and in leg irons. She orders mass suicide of black islanders by ingestion of woorara, a form of strychnine derived from Carib plants. Marie-Ursule leaves Bola alive to bear the matrilineage far into the future.

Bibliography

Brand, Dionne. *At the Full and Change of the Moon.* New York: Grove, 1999.

———. *In Another Place, Not Here.* New York: Grove, 1996.

Saul, Joanna. "In the Middle of Becoming: Dionne Brand's Historical Vision," *Canadian Woman Studies* 23, no. 2 (Winter 2004): 59–63.

Brontë, Charlotte (1816–1855)

A fount of women's fiction, Charlotte Brontë created a female protagonist for mid-Victorian Gothic lore who is capable of directing her own destiny. In the estimation of the critic Carolyn G. Heilbrun, Brontë wrote "in absolute and passionate awareness of the disabilities under which women, and particularly gifted women, struggle for a place to put their lives" (Heilbrun, 78). The daughter of the Reverend Patrick Brontë, Charlotte grew up in a pious Anglican household in rural Haworth, Yorkshire, where she read the *Arabian Nights*, works of the romantic poets, the tales of Sir Walter Scott, and the novels of Jane AUSTEN. The six Brontë children enjoyed free access to Gothic articles and serials in *Blackwood's Edinburgh Magazine* and the *Methodist Magazine*, which inspired their juvenile imitations. After the death of their mother, Maria Branwell Brontë, of cancer, the father tended Charlotte and her siblings and aided the four survivors in overcoming grief for their older sisters, Maria and Elizabeth, who died of consumption. From a loyal nursemaid named Tabby, Brontë adapted maternal

characters in her fiction, including the servant Bessie, the teacher Maria Temple, the housekeeper Mrs. Fairfax, and Mary and Diana Rivers, all mother figures in *JANE EYRE* (1847).

Homeschooled at the parsonage, Charlotte and her siblings, Anne and Emily Jane Brontë, studied under their Calvinist aunt, Elizabeth "Bess" Branwell. As was typical for the times, their brother, Patrick Branwell, pursued a more thorough education in the classics. In 1835 Charlotte held two jobs—teaching classes at Roe Head and working as a governess, a post that gave her background material for the character Jane Eyre. When Charlotte's health declined, she and Emily studied French, German, and music in Brussels, where Charlotte cultivated a fantasy romance with a school principal, Constantin Héger.

On their return to Haworth Charlotte and Emily joined Anne in launching serious writing projects. To conceal their gender from the critical world, they published under a set of pseudonyms—Acton (Anne), Currer (Charlotte), and Ellis (Emily) Bell. Charlotte set her Belgian romance as a novel, *The Professor,* but gave up the story in favor of less self-revealing material. The opening chapter discloses the author's terror of arranged marriage: "Oh, how like a nightmare is the thought of being bound for life to one of my cousins!" (Brontë, 1985, 2). For *Jane Eyre,* the author chose a pilgrimage motif about an orphan who turns adversity into a challenge, a quest theme derived from Sophia LEE's classic novel *The Recess; or, A Tale of Other Times* (1783–85). By overcoming educational, class, and career barriers, Jane is able to transform a tawdry marriage proposal by a would-be bigamist into a legal union. Informing her choices along the way to the altar are DREAMSCAPES and clairvoyant episodes that offer glimpses of her lover, Edward Rochester. Upon their reunion, she rescues him from depression after the horrific death of his wife, Bertha Mason ROCHESTER, and the burning of Thornfield, his patrimonial estate. The name of the manse symbolizes the struggles of Rochester and Jane in their search for a lasting love.

Through the metamorphosis in Rochester, Charlotte Brontë illustrates the rise of the middle-class female, symbolized by the humble, self-effacing governess he prefers to Blanche Ingram, a beautiful heiress. Jane's influence over her aristocratic employer generates sexual tension as Rochester abandons his insane wife and reputation to betroth himself to Jane. At a climactic point in their courtship when Rochester reveals the secret wife in a locked upstairs chamber, Jane refuses to be his mistress and flees his virile presence to assure her virtue. Jane's authority reaches its height in the reunion scene, in which Rochester, humbled by blindness and depression, accepts from Jane a tray bearing candles and water, domestic symbols of the home that Jane later superintends for her husband and child.

The successful balance of Jane's love for her employer and her observance of social and moral proprieties suited the Victorian public, whom Charlotte Brontë rewarded with a blissful domestic scenario of Jane, Edward, and their son at Ferndean, their unassuming home. In the wake of pursy critiques in *Spectator, Quarterly Review,* and *Guardian,* the author was gratified by the overwhelmingly positive response of critics at the *Berkshire and Buckinghamshire Gazette, Critic, Morning Post,* and *Oxford Chronicle.* Even more gratifying was the praise of the reading public, which included Queen Victoria, who read the novel aloud to her husband, Prince Albert. One of Brontë's strongest feminist allies was the critic and novelist Margaret OLIPHANT, who valued *Jane Eyre* as a model of high standards in domestic and Gothic literature. The split between male reviewers and female readers suggests an increasing number of women hungry for fiction about a no-nonsense heroine who is willing to take risks to satisfy her passion, yet unwilling to compromise her principles by settling for less than marriage.

Left alone to care for her father after the deaths of Anne, Emily, and Patrick Brontë, Charlotte published *Shirley: A Tale* (1849) and drew on the Belgian phase of her education to write *Villette* (1853). A nested story-within-a-story, the latter novel portrays the Protestant outsider Lucy Snowe, an apathetic, listless protagonist, in a Catholic convent in Belgium. Worsening her mental strain is the onset of melancholia complicated by anger and bitterness, negative emotions that Brontë dramatizes to justify Lucy's unhappiness. As Lucy abandons naiveté for maturity, she tames

a runaway imagination with logic and self-control. Like Jane Eyre, she becomes a full-fledged professional after opening a school, an attainable post for an ambitious woman in Victorian England. Marian Evans, who later wrote as George ELIOT, extolled the novel for Lucy's enterprise and her refusal to be cowed by PATRIARCHY.

In a scene of males' humiliating Lucy in *Villette,* Brontë pictures her heroine's poise. To demonstrate her capabilities, she composes an essay on human justice while two professors watch to see that the words she writes are her own. Lucy depicts justice as a female sitting at her hearthside to judge a clamor of beggars and peevish children. When the uproar rose too high, "My jolly dame seized the poker or the hearth-brush; if the offender was weak, wronged, and sickly, she effectually settled him; if he was strong, lively, and violent, she only menaced" (Brontë, 1997, 386). Lucy's skillful use of imagery and diction convinces the suspicious men that women are capable of verbal excellence.

In her last 10 months, Charlotte Brontë was married to an Irish curate, Arthur Bell Nicholls, who lived with her and the Reverend Brontë at the Haworth parsonage. Shortly before her death at age 39 from exhaustion, consumption, and a fall from a horse, she began a fourth novel, *Emma* (1860), which made little impact on her literary reputation. In 1893, fans formed the Brontë Society to honor Charlotte and Emily and to preserve Haworth as a museum and shrine. Both the novelist Elizabeth GASKELL and the sociologist Harriet MARTINEAU wrote stirring accounts of Brontë's life. The dramatist Adrienne KENNEDY and the writers Jamaica KINCAID and Grace PALEY named *Jane Eyre* as a significant influence on their lives and art. Jean RHYS wrote a famous reimagining of the life of Bertha Rochester called *THE WIDE SARGASSO SEA (1966).*

Feminist critics seized on Jane Eyre as one of the most fully developed working-class heroines in literature. Because her intellect and cool self-possession level social and economic differences between the governess and her employer, the novel offers stirring proof that such ephemeral obstacles as social rank and money are not insurmountable. *Jane Eyre* influenced Adrienne RICH's verse and

Daphne Du Maurier's plotting of the murder romance *Rebecca* (1938). Brontë's novel served stage adaptations and four films of the Brontë original. The last, made by Miramax in 1996, features Charlotte Gainsbourg and William Hurt in the lead roles as the governess Jane Eyre and her employer Edward Rochester with Anna Paquin and Joan Plowright in supporting parts as Jane's pupil Adèle and Mrs. Fairfax, Edward's housekeeper. The feminist poet Eleanor Wilner honored the steadfast sister Charlotte in "Emigration" (1980), a poem published in *Ms.* magazine that characterizes the novelist as the one "who stayed in the rectory and helped her sisters die in England" (Mazer & Lewis, 1989, 20).

Bibliography

Brontë, Charlotte. *Jane Eyre*. New York: Bantam Books, 1981.

———. *The Letters of Charlotte Brontë: With a Selection of Letters by Family and Friends*. Vol. 2. 1848–1851. New York: Oxford University Press, 2000.

———. *The Professor and Emma*. London: J. M. Dent, 1985.

———. *Villette*. New York: Modern Library, 1997.

Forsyth, Beverly. "The Two Faces of Lucy Snowe: A Study in Deviant Behavior," *Studies in the Novel 29*, no. 1 (Spring 1997): 17–25.

Gilbert, Sandra M., and Susan Gubar. *The Madwoman in the Attic*. 2nd ed. New Haven, Conn.: Yale University Press, 2000.

Heilbrun, Carolyn G. *Toward a Recognition of Androgyny*. New York: W. W. Norton, 1982.

Mazer, Norma Fox, and Marjorie Lewis, eds. *Waltzing on Water*. New York: Dell, 1989.

Brontë, Emily (1818–1848)

A prize producer of sensational feminist fiction, Emily Jane Brontë attained instant celebrity for creating the love story of Heathcliff and Catherine Earnshaw, protagonists of *Wuthering Heights* (1847). Of the author's greatness, the critic Carolyn G. Heilbrun declared: "[Her] passion for freedom and her confined destiny as a woman fired her imagination, and placed her great gifts under the pressure necessary to creation" (Heilbrun, 80). A sister of the authors Anne and Charlotte

Brontë, Emily was the daughter of Maria Branwell and the Reverend Patrick Brontë, an Anglican minister. Born at the parsonage at Haworth, Yorkshire, Emily grew up in the rural countryside, where the wilds of nature observed in solitude provided the backdrop for her classic Gothic novel. After her mother died of cancer, Emily suffered the loss of two older sisters, Maria and Elizabeth, of consumption and depended on her father and the nursemaid Tabby for parental love.

While studying under the Reverend Brontë at the parsonage, Emily received tutoring in music and drawing. She read freely from popular journals and borrowed books from the neighborhood circulating library, including Gothic novels and the feminist writings of Mary Wollstonecraft. In 1835, Emily boarded at Miss Wooler's school at Roe Head near Halifax until weak lungs signaled the onset of consumption. At age 19, she recuperated and taught a six-month term at Law Hill school. Seven years later, she accompanied Charlotte to Brussels for an eight-month study of music, French, and German.

In 1845, Emily Brontë joined her two sisters in professional writing endeavors. The trio chose the pen names Acton (Anne), Currer (Charlotte), and Ellis (Emily) Bell to fend off prejudice against female writers. In the months preceding her death from tuberculosis, Emily wowed the literary world with *Wuthering Heights* (1847), a vigorous romantic melodrama. Out of shyness she remained behind when her sisters negotiated for the publications of Anne Brontë's *Agnes Grey* (1847) and Charlotte's *Jane Eyre* (1847). Shortly after their brother, Branwell's, death from tuberculosis complicated by addiction to alcohol and opium, Emily died at home.

Emily Brontë's genius left critics wondering how she might have developed if she had continued writing. Her passionate rebel, Catherine Earnshaw, presages the emergence of female rebellion against patriarchal society. The sensational novel springs to life with shifting fortunes, shocking scenarios, and revelations of character through alternating points of view. Emily transforms Heathcliff from Gypsy brat from Liverpool to a powerful male protagonist crazed by sexual desire for his foster sister. Although critics charged the author with godless vice, impropriety, and perverted notions of love, she thrilled readers with Catherine and Heathcliff's visceral hunger for each other, a carnal yearning that survives the grave. Among admirers of the novelist's emotional scenes are the columnist Anna QUINDLEN and the Danish epicist Sigrid UNDSET. Subsequent authors have imitated wild scenes in extremes of weather, notably Adrienne RICH in "Storm Warnings" (1951) and Daphne DU MAURIER in her romantic murder mystery *Rebecca* (1938).

Bibliography

Armstrong, Nancy. *Desire and Domestic Fiction: A Political History of the Novel.* Oxford: Oxford University Press, 1995.

Brontë, Emily. *Wuthering Heights.* New York: New American Library, 1959.

Heilbrun, Carolyn G. *Toward a Recognition of Androgyny.* New York: W. W. Norton, 1982.

Hoeveler, Diane Long. *Gothic Feminism.* University Park: Pennsylvania State University Press, 1998.

Brooks, Gwendolyn (1917–2000)

A poet, novelist, and autobiographer, Gwendolyn Elizabeth Brooks expressed an abiding faith in womanhood. Born to loving, literate parents in Topeka, Kansas, she read essays and poems from her father's Harvard Classics and seemed destined to become a writer. While growing up in Chicago's South Side, she kept a journal that noted her rejection by others of her strong African traits that violated the white world's BEAUTY MYTH. Lacking distractions from a vigorous social life, she read the poets of her day and mastered versification. By her early teens, she was composing original poems. For theme and subject, she avoided the exoticism of the Harlem Renaissance and culled characters and actions from common street events. After her mother took her to recitations by James Weldon Johnson and Langston Hughes, she pursued her dream with a flurry of works submitted to *American Childhood, Chicago Defender,* and *Hyde Parker.* At age 18 she married the poet Henry Lowington Blakely Jr. and bore a son and daughter. She wrote for the *Women's National Magazine* and taught at Chicago Teacher's College.

Brooks's readiness for professional writing was obvious in *A Street in Bronzeville* (1945), a series of poetic profiles of urbanites dedicated to her parents, David and Keziah Corinne Wims Brooks. The text pictures idiosyncratic characters in "The Ballad of Pearl May Lee," "Queen of the Blues," and Hattie Scott." An elegaic confessional, "The Mother" (1945) tackles the issue of grief and regret for aborted "children you got that you did not get" (Brooks, 1999, 4). A feistier portrait, "When Mrs. Martin's Booker T" (1947), voices the shame and anger of a conservative mother whose son has impregnated a girl. The mother sides with the soiled girlfriend and refuses to cede her moral fortress until Booker T chooses marriage over abandonment of the mother-to-be.

With two Guggenheim fellowships, grants from the National Institute of Arts and Letters and the American Academy of Arts and Letters, and an award from *Mademoiselle* as one of the 10 outstanding women of 1945, Brooks turned to feminist verse. She is best known for "The Anniad," a modern mock heroic in 43 stanzas, which she published in *Annie Allen* (1949). In rhymed couplets, the suite questions the insubstantiality of cinematic, featherbed notions of romantic love. Envisioning Annie Allen as a deliberate role player rather than a pampered amour, the poet defines her unforeseen coming to knowledge about love as a "soft aesthetic . . . looted lean" (Brooks, 1987, 108). The poet legitimizes Annie's rejection of passivity and powerlessness. After comparing herself to her husband's mistress, Annie redirects her life with womanist resolve and aggressive motherhood, a sublimation of desires "when the desert terrifies" (*ibid.,* 107). For its forthright survey of the intermeshed barriers of married women's lives and the emotional wasteland they call home, the book won the Eunice Tietjens Prize. As a result of critical acclaim, Brooks succeeded Carl Sandburg as Illinois's poet laureate and, in 1940, became the first black to receive a Pulitzer Prize.

Brooks further probed the female's toying with the taunting otherness of the bad woman. In "A Song in the Front Yard" (1971), the poet studies a young girl's approach-avoidance of the weedy, untended backyard of femininity, a metaphor for PROSTITUTION. With only a glimmer of understanding, the speaker imagines herself tricked out in splendor and gives herself permission to wear black lace and makeup. The humor of the little-girl daydream is her clinging to the safety of the front yard, where she remains chaste and only partially apprised of sexual adventurism in society's unkempt backyard.

After publishing the semiautobiographical novel *Maud Martha* (1953) and a children's collection, *Bronzeville Boys and Girls* (1956), Brooks completed the critically successful *The Bean Eaters* (1960), an outpouring of militant verse anthologies, and a memoir, *Report from Part One: The Autobiography of Gwendolyn Brooks* (1972). Rewards flooded in from varied sources, notably the National Endowment for the Arts and, in 1973, the honor of being the first black woman appointed as poetry consultant to the Library of Congress. Late in her career, the poet continued to examine the many roles that life hands women. In *Winnie* (1991), a reflection on the South African freedom fighter Winnie Mandela, Brooks pictures the redoubtable leader as founder and mother. Cloaked in the dignity of a hero's wife and helpmeet, Winnie tolerates the persecutions of President Pieter Willem Botha's thugs. She admits that their torments rob her of dignity. Still buoyed by her mission, Winnie proclaims, "I Prop, I Proclaim my people" (*ibid.*, 16).

Brooks was more familiar with ordinary women than with celebrities such as Winnie Mandela. The poet envisioned the struggle of the title character in "An Old Black Woman, Homeless and Indistinct" (1993). For a woman once filled with artistic promise and admired for beauty, "Your every day is a pilgrimage" (Brooks, 1992/1993, 120). Brooks's encouragement to women on survival's edge recurs in the poem in "To Black Women" (1998), in which she tells them to ignore the lack of reward in their lives and simply prevail. Her feminism inspired the novelist Margaret WALKER and the radical poet Sonia SANCHEZ.

Bibliography

Brooks, Gwendolyn. *Blacks*. Chicago: Third World Press, 1987.

———. "An Old Black Woman, Homeless and Indistinct," *Drum Voices Revue* (Fall–Winter 1992/1993): 120.

———. *Selected Poems*. New York: HarperPerennial, 1999.

———. *Winnie*. Chicago: Third World Press, 1991.

———. *The World of Gwendolyn Brooks*. New York: Harper, 1971.

Gayles, Gloria Wade. *Conversations with Gwendolyn Brooks*. Jackson: University Press of Mississippi, 2003.

Giles, Ron. "Brooks's 'A Song in the Front Yard,'" *Explicator* 57, no. 3 (Spring 1999): 169–171.

Broumas, Olga (1949–)

A Greco-American lesbian writer, Olga Broumas derives from myth and FAIRY TALES a deep dedication to FEMALE VICTIMS. Her interest in feminist themes began in childhood in her native Syros, an island in the Cyclades. In the poem "Eye of Heart," she reveals that frequent punishments by a mother confused by her emotion caused Broumas to long for consummation. She wrote poetry in Greek and pored over Greek mythology and Charlotte BRONTË's JANE EYRE (1847), which mirrors the motifs of BEAUTY AND THE BEAST. At age 19, while absorbing the poetic genius of Louise BOGAN, Sylvia PLATH, Adrienne RICH, and Anne SEXTON, Broumas studied architecture at the University of Pennsylvania and the University of Oregon. Her initial poems spoke the hunger, passion, and misgivings of women. In a challenge to patriarchal silencing, she says to other female authors, "We must find words or burn" (Kalfopoulou, iv).

Broumas earned critical attention for a first collection, *Caritas* (1976), and became the first non–Native American to win a Yale Younger Poets citation. The award honored *Beginning with O* (1977), a postmodern study of mythic females and goddesses—the Amazons, Aphrodite, Artemis, Calypso, Demeter, Io, and Leda. Composed in the Hellenic tradition, her verses feature an urgency, ecstasy, and dynamism of Classical Greek authors. Of Circe's man-hating spells, Broumas exults in the ability to turn men into grunting boars. In "Thetis," the poet depicts a trusting MOTHER-DAUGHTER RELATIONSHIP as the older woman demonstrates to the younger how to insert kelp into the vagina as a barrier method of contraception. In "Maenad" the mother's hellish fury extends to her daughters, who display their navels as proof of birth. The matriarchal link accounts for the female worshiper's DUALITY in that her rapture can be both loving and lethal.

The poet delved more openly into lesbian relationships in *Pastoral Jazz* (1983) and *Black Holes, Black Stockings* (1985). In 1999, Broumas issued *Rave: Poems 1975–1999*, which recaps her mythic scenarios and resettings of CINDERELLA, LITTLE RED RIDING HOOD, Rapunzel, Sleeping Beauty, and Snow White. Broumas's most recent verse returns to classic forms—the aubade, elegy, love plaint, ode—and honors SAPPHO, a touchstone of feminist poetry. In "Amazon Twins," she pictures the female's sexual release in swelling genitals. The insistent physicality sets Broumas apart from more timorous poets, yet recalls a similar woman worship in the biblical Song of Solomon. In the opening suite of *Rave* she creates metaphors for pubic hair and labial love that link lesbian sex with the ecstatic female cults of Classical Greece.

Bibliography

Broumas, Olga. *Beginning with O.* New Haven, Conn.: Yale University Press, 1977.

———. *Rave: Poems 1975–1999.* Townsend, Wash.: Copper Canyon Press, 1999.

Kalfopoulou, Adrianne. *A Discussion of the Ideology of the American Dream in the Culture's Female Discourses.* Lewiston, N.Y.: Edwin Mellen Press, 2000.

Reid, Jo-Ann. "Inside Our Secrets," *Lesbian Review of Books* 7, no.1 (Fall 2000): 24.

Browning, Elizabeth Barrett (1806–1861)

The writer and reformer Elizabeth Moulton Barrett Browning, England's most famous female poet, created images of the IDEAL WOMAN, female SEXUALITY, maternity, and childhood innocence. The first of 12 children, Browning was the great-grandchild of a West Indian slaver who established the family fortune with his sugar mills. She was born at Coxhoe Hall in Durham to Mary Graham Clarke and Edward Moulton Barrett, an investor in colonial Jamaica. She grew up at Hope End, Herefordshire, where she read history and philosophy. While her brothers received preferential educa-

tion, she taught herself Greek, Hebrew, and Latin with the aid of her brother Edward's tutor. With the encouragement of her mother, she read Greek mythology and began writing verse while recovering from a spinal weakness.

Because of her semi-invalidism, Browning imagined herself the damsel locked in the tower. Because she "had lived / A sort of cage-bird life, born in a cage, / Accounting that to leap from perch to perch / Was act and joy enough for any bird," she learned feminist ideals from reading Mary WOLLSTONECRAFT (Browning, 1996, 305). The poet's father grew more possessive after his wife's death in 1828 and forced on Elizabeth a belief that she was helpless. Complicating her self-image was an addiction to morphia that quelled excruciating muscle spasms. She used her time in a darkened bedroom–sitting room writing letters, epic verse, romantic ballads, and dramatic monologues. At age 15, she published her first work, a poem on Greece; she later translated Aeschylus's *Prometheus Unbound*, a foretokening of her eventual escape from obsessions with illness. Three decades later, her maturation into a leading writer earned her nominations as England's poet laureate.

Despite an upbringing in genteel behavior for young ladies, Browning developed into a radical. She protested the censorship of women's reading that confined them in a state of ignorance of sexuality and human vice, which she called "the common, ugly human dust" (*ibid.*, 163). In the essay "Blood, Bread, and Poetry: The Location of the Poet" (1984), Adrienne RICH countered denigration of women's poetry by recalling Elizabeth Browning's ardent abolitionist and feminist verse. Browning involved herself in humanitarian causes and wrote *The Cry of the Children* (1843), a protest of the employment of small children in coal mines and sweatshops. The image of helpless mothers hearing their children weep pictures the family as birds chirping from the nest, a piteous sound drowned out by the grinding of iron factory wheels. In 1844, she met Robert Browning, an acclaimed poet, who also had ties to Caribbean slavery. That same year, Elizabeth praised the rebel novelist George SAND in two sonnets and upended John Milton's depiction of EVE in *A Drama of Exile* (1844), which portrays the first woman as a delightful, lyrical individual rather than the temptress who caused the human downfall.

After the Brownings eloped to Italy, Elizabeth's friend the sociologist Harriet MARTINEAU noted in her *Autobiography* (1855): "They are a remarkable pair, whom society may well honour and cherish" (Martineau, 315). Even though the secret marriage enraged her father, 39-year-old Elizabeth enjoyed her first taste of INDEPENDENCE and the birth of a son, Robert Wiedemann "Pen" Browning. At her home at Casa Guidi, Florence, she wrote her most mature works, which rejected the sequestering of women like her from full involvement in the world. In 1846, she rebelled against her family's role in slavery by publishing a graphic abolitionist poem, "The Runaway Slave at Pilgrim's Point," which she wrote on behalf of Boston's Anti-Slavery Bazaar. Set at Plymouth Rock, in Massachusetts, the dramatic narrative pictures a female slave who despairs after whites have killed her mate and raped her. In a frenzy, she sees in her infant's face a resemblance to white masters and strangles him with her shawl. Browning reset the pose of the male sonneteer writing to his mistress in the autobiographical *Sonnets from the Portuguese* (1850), a 44-verse cycle showcasing the female's adoration of her lover. A less sanguine view of male-female relationships generates the baleful tone of "A Year's Spinning" (1850), in which she pities the plight of outcast mothers and unwanted babies that result from seduction and entrapment of females. The melodic ballad depicts the female spinner as a ruined woman who receives her mother's scorn for falling in love with a seducer and for giving birth to an illegitimate child.

In 1847, Browning addressed the issue of the woman artist's freedom in a popular melodrama, *Aurora Leigh,* a nine-book verse novel that pictures females as carriers of "the burning lava of a song / The full-veined, heaving, double-breasted Age" (Browning, 1996, 216). Browning sets the opening canto in the chilly social and personal atmosphere common to Victorian households. The young poet-protagonist speaks a melancholy line reminiscent of the poet's troubled life: "I, Aurora Leigh, was born / To make my father sadder and myself / Not overjoyous, truly" (*ibid.*, 6). Aurora rejects marriage to Romney, a man who discounts

her intelligence and trivializes her composition of ballads on everyday experience. Aurora confronts gendered issues by rescuing a ruined female, Marian Erie, from social exclusion. After escorting her to Italy, Aurora feels that her altruistic act relieves Marian of social, class, and economic oppression of women.

Browning's social consciousness drove much of her late canon toward realism. In 1854, she championed urban street urchins in "A Song for the Ragged Schools of London," which pleads on behalf of the poor for more money to feed and educate children. A posthumous poem, "Lord Walter's Wife" (1861), was so unapologetically feminist that the editor, William Makepeace Thackeray, refused to publish it in *Cornhill* magazine. The theme remains true to Browning's contention that women pay the price for male adventuring and violation of moral codes. In "Mother and Poet" (1861), Browning's last work, she dramatizes the anguish of Italian women whose sons die in war during the nationalist movement. The poet's ability to sympathize with women of any race or caste earned the regard of the feminist authors Susan B. ANTHONY, Emily DICKINSON, Margaret FULLER, Elizabeth Stuart PHELPS, Christina ROSSETTI, and Harriet Beecher STOWE.

Bibliography

Browning, Elizabeth Barrett. *Aurora Leigh*. New York: W. W. Norton, 1996.

———. *Elizabeth Barrett Browning: Selected Poems*. London: Gramercy, 2000.

Markus, Julia. *Dared and Done: The Marriage of Elizabeth Barrett and Robert Browning*. Athens: Ohio University Press, 1998.

Martineau, Harriet. *Harriet Martineau's Autobiography* (1877). Available online. URL: http://www.indiana.edu/~letrs/vwwp/martineau/martineau1.html. Accessed on October 13, 2005.

Mermin, Dorothy. *Elizabeth Barrett Browning: The Origin of a New Poetry*. Chicago: University of Chicago Press, 1989.

Rich, Adrienne. *Adrienne Rich's Poetry and Prose*. New York: W. W. Norton, 1975.

Schatz, Sueann. "*Aurora Leigh* as Paradigm of Domestic-Professional Fiction," *Philological Quarterly* 79, no. 1 (Winter 2000): 91.

Brownmiller, Susan (1935–   )

In an incisive study of male-on-female violence, the journalist and novelist Susan Brownmiller shattered the stereotype of the helpless FEMALE VICTIM. Born in Brooklyn, New York, to a working-class family, she grew up amid the gendered restructuring of World War II, when women replaced men in home, factory, office, and community. On scholarship, she attended Cornell University for two years and then left school to work at odd jobs while studying acting. She got her start in polemical writing while reporting for the *Village Voice* and researching and composing items for ABC News. Her peripatetic career took her to *Book Review, Esquire, Mademoiselle, Nation, Newsday, Newsweek,* the *New York Times, Rolling Stone,* and *Vogue.* She became so involved in newscasts of the Vietnam War that in 1994 she compiled *Seeing Vietnam: Encounters of the Road and Heart,* a travelogue that takes her to the same territory in peacetime.

Energized during the era of lunch counter sit-ins, Brownmiller got her first taste of WOMEN'S RIGHTS issues in Betty FRIEDAN's *The Feminine Mystique* (1963). At age 33, Brownmiller was able to confide her experiences with abortion at a consciousness-raising session, her introduction to face-to-face feminism. Increasing activism placed her at protests of civil rights infractions, draft boards, the Miss America pageant, porn shops, and the frilly worldview of *Ladies' Home Journal.* She attracted critical attention for an essay, "Let's Put Pornography Back in the Closet" (1969), which tackles one of the most divisive issues of the women's liberation movement. Although she gave no testimonials for writers of salacious literature, Brownmiller did not hesitate to come down on the side of First Amendment rights to free speech.

In 1971, Brownmiller helped to redirect American attitudes toward violence against women with a radical research project on various motivations and historical settings for sexual assault. In a provocative social document, *Against Our Will: Men, Women, and Rape* (1975), she explores how the FAIRY TALE prepares little girls for a vague martyrdom. Just as the parable of LITTLE RED RIDING HOOD teaches that the forests are hiding places for lascivious, sometimes murderous wolves, other archetypal stories indicate a similar social order that stacks the odds in favor of male brawn over female ingenuity. Brownmiller develops the sources of menace in chapters on world wars, pogroms, revolutions, Mormonism, the Ku Klux Klan, slavery, gangs, prison rape, and pedophilia. The book, published in 16 languages, stresses women's terror of male genitals used as weapons. She accounts for the long history of barbarity against women as the result of male codification of law: "Written law evolved from a rudimentary system of retaliatory force, a system to which women were not particularly well adapted to begin with, and from which women were deliberately excluded, ostensibly for their own protection" (Brownmiller, 1975, 452). She concludes the text with some hope that concerted efforts to teach women to fight back will reduce the incidence of sexual assault on females.

Because of a male backlash against Brownmiller's implication of all men in violence against women, *Against Our Will* resonated through editorial columns and reviews for two decades. In January 1993 Brownmiller returned to the subject of females as sexual pawns in "Making Female Bodies the Battlefield," an essay for *Newsweek.* Of the combat and genocide in the Balkans, she lamented: "The plight of raped women as casualties of war is given credence only at the emotional moment when the side in danger of annihilation cries out for world attention" (Brownmiller, 1993, 37). Of the compilation of formal histories, she complains that male bravado turns lurid criminal acts into sources of heroism: "When the glorious battles for independence become legend, [women's] stories are glossed over, discounted as exaggerations, deemed not serious enough for inclusion in scholarly works. And the women are left with their shame" (*ibid.*).

The author published a retrospective, *In Our Time: Memoir of a Revolution* (1999), an overview of the American feminist movement from the inside. From her own involvement, she followed the first wave of feminism to the early 1980s. Her chapter headings indicate the themes of the text: "The Founders," "Abortion Is a Woman's Right," "Rape Is a Political Crime against Women," and "No Man Is Worth Dying For." The text recognizes feminists for giving a formal name to the issues of reproductive rights, sexual harassment, and domestic abuse. In 2004, Brownmiller wrote the script for *Chisholm '72: Unbought and Unbossed,* a documentary film on the political career of Shirley Chisholm, the first black female to run for U.S. president.

Bibliography

Brownmiller, Susan. *Against Our Will: Men, Women, and Rape.* New York: Bantam Books, 1975.

———. *In Our Time: Memoir of a Revolution.* New York: Delta, 2000.

———. "Making Female Bodies the Battlefield," *Newsweek,* January 1993, p. 37.

Pitono, Stephen P. "Susan Brownmiller and the History of Rape," *Women's Studies* 14, no. 3 (1988): 265–276.

Brown, Rita Mae (1944–)

A bisexual wit, radical individualist, and spokeswoman for equality, Rita Mae Brown extols the female social rebel. Born illegitimate and abandoned in early childhood in Hanover, Pennsylvania, she grew up in a loving foster home filled with strong, emotionally volatile women. As she explains in a mellow memoir, *Rita Will: Memoir of a Literary Rabble-Rouser* (1997), she displayed genius to her adoptive parents, Julia Ellen and Ralph Brown, by reading at age three and by teaching herself enough Latin to translate the sophisticated odes of the Roman poet Horace. To encourage more writing, Ralph Brown bought a typewriter for his eight-year-old prodigy.

Brown recognized her attraction to women at age 15, but she refused to think of herself as a warped person or an outsider. She thrived at tennis and enjoyed a brief enrollment on scholarship at the University of Florida. A false accusation of illegal civil rights demonstration on behalf of integration halted her college training. A member of the Student Homophile League, the nation's first campus gay group, she spearheaded a gay rights platform for the neophyte women's movement. After resuming her education at Broward Community College, at age 20, she hitchhiked north and, while living in poverty, completed a B.A. in Classical literature and English from New York University.

Brown's writing career moved rapidly from rollicking verse in *The Hand That Cradles the Rock*

(1971) and *Songs to a Handsome Women* (1973) to essays in *A Plain Brown Rapper* (1973), screenplays for film and ABC-TV, and translations of medieval Latin drama as novels. At age 29, she designed a feminist adventurer, Molly Bolt, as the sassy protagonist of the lesbian crossover novel *Rubyfruit Jungle* (1973), a semiautobiographical coming-out story that describes the social obstacles to a female bastard. The book became a cult hit among feminist and gay readers. Subsequent female protagonists, such as First Lady Dolley Payne Madison in the fictionalized BIOGRAPHY *Dolley* (1994), the uncloseted gay gallery owner Mary Frazier Armstrong in *Venus Envy* (1996), rival sisters in *Loose Lips* (1999), and the fox hunter "Sister" Jane Arnold in *Hotspur* (2002) and in *Full Cry* (2003), furthered Brown's retort to a judgmental world that women have no reason to conceal their true selves.

Bibliography

Brown, Rita Mae. *Full Cry.* New York: Ballantine, 2003.

———. *Rita Will: Memoir of a Literary Rabble-Rouser.* New York: Bantam, 1999.

———. *Rubyfruit Jungle.* New York: Bantam, 1983.

Levy, Barbara. "Southern Rebel," *Women's Review of Books* 15, no. 10/11 (July 1998): 36–37.

Bryant, Louise (1885–1936)

The radical journalist and foreign correspondent Louise Bryant was skilled at humanizing the face of revolutionaries and noncombatants. Born of Irish-American lineage in San Francisco to the orator and newspaper reporter Hugh Moran, she later adopted the surname of Sheridan Bryant, her stepfather. She grew up in the horse culture of Reno, Nevada, where she learned to ride and tend livestock. While enrolled at the University of Oregon, she adopted the suffragist cause. After teaching school in Portland, she drew illustrations and wrote a column for the *Spectator,* a weekly social newspaper, and published essays in Emma GOLDMAN's anarchist journal *Mother Earth.* Bryant married and joined the staffs of the *Blast* and the *Masses,* a Communist journal for which she wrote pacifist diatribes against Woodrow Wilson. Pulled further toward socialism, she deserted her too-conservative husband and joined a radical commune in New York City.

After marrying John "Jack" Reed, an unconventional journalist and labor activist, Bryant lived with him near the Massachusetts shore. The couple joined the Provincetown Players, cofounded by the dramatist Susan GLASPELL, in what has been called the birth of modern American drama. In addition to writing the one-act play *The Game* (1916) for the opening season, Bryant participated in stage productions. After separating from Reed and journeying to Europe to cover World War I for William Randolph Hearst's media syndicate, Bryant reunited with Reed in Saint Petersburg to observe and report on the Russian Revolution of 1917. The couple, who favored Bolshevism, observed turmoil, shifting loyalties, and the death of adults and street waifs of combat, disease, exposure, and starvation. Reed gathered political data for *Ten Days That Shook the World* (1919). After his death from typhus in Moscow in 1920, she returned to New York.

Bryant is best known for on-the-scene reporting in *Six Months in Red Russia: An Observer's Account of Russia before and during the Proletarian Dictatorship* (1918), a summary of evolving equality between the sexes that resulted from the revolt. She based her text on observations of soldiers, laborers, and peasants. Crucial to the first book is her survey of women standing in line in freezing weather to buy staples to feed their families. She observed wives screaming their grief for dead husbands and throwing themselves into fresh graves. Chapter 21 features the camaraderie of the females composing the Death Soldiers, who fought in the final offensive. Of their all-woman battalion, she noted, "Women in Russia have always fought in the army. In my opinion the principal reason for the failure of the woman's regiment was segregation. There will always be fighting women in Russia, but they will fight side by side with men and not as a sex" (Bryant, 1918). A subsequent chapter reminds readers in England and North America that more children died during World War I in Russia than in all the other European countries together.

Bryant continued writing articles in New York and Paris. She followed her first volume with the essay "Fables for Proletarian Children" (1919), issued in the *Revolutionary Age,* and *Mirrors of Moscow* (1923). In the preface of the latter, her high hopes for Bolshevism are obvious: "Here, then, they are: the Russians of today: Close to the Tartar and the Cossack of the plain, children of serfs and Norsemen and Mongols—close to the earth and striving for the stars" (Bryant, 1923). A biographical film, *Reds* (1981), featured an all-star cast: Diane Keaton and Warren Beatty as Bryant and Reed, Maureen Stapleton as Emma GOLD-MAN, Richard Herrmann as Max Eastman, and Jack Nicholson as Eugene O'Neill.

Bibliography

Bryant, Louise. "Fables for Proletarian Children" (1919). Available online. URL: http://www.marxists.org/archive/bryant/works/fables.htm. Accessed on October 13, 2005.

———. *Mirrors of Moscow* (1923). Available online. URL: http://www.marxists.org/archive/bryant/works/1923-mom/index.htm. Accessed on October 13, 2005.

———. *Six Months in Red Russia* (1918). Available online. URL: http://digital.library.upenn.edu/women/bryant/russia/russia.html. Accessed on October 13, 2005.

Dearborn, Mary V. *Queen of Bohemia: The Life of Louise Bryant.* Boston: Houghton Mifflin, 1995.

Buck, Pearl (1892–1973)

The first female Nobel Prize winner in literature, the novelist and humanitarian Pearl Comfort Sydenstriker Buck honored the unheralded female by placing peasant protagonists in positions of domestic and economic importance. The daughter of Absalom and Caroline Sydenstriker, Southern Presbyterian evangelists in China, she was born in Hillsboro, West Virginia, but came of age in Kiangsu. Influencing her views on the trials of womanhood were her father's fanatic religion and his abasement of his faithful wife. Buck attended local theater performances with Alma, her beloved Chinese nanny, and studied Confucianism under a native tutor before entering a private school in Shanghai. One of the horrors of her childhood occurred during the Boxer Rebellion of 1900, when a secret society of assassins dispatched by the empress dowager Tz'u-hsi targeted whites.

After earning degrees from Randolph Macon and Cornell, Buck settled in China and taught English literature at Chung Yang and Nanking. At age 31, she submitted short fiction to magazines and completed a first novel, *East Wind: West Wind* (1925). After a second trauma during the Chinese Nationalist assault on Nanking in March 1927, she began work on her masterpiece, THE GOOD EARTH (1931), a classic of peasant life that won a Pulitzer Prize. The text moves impersonally over the hardships of Chinese farm and servant women in the early 20th century. Buck remarked candidly on the issue of children born of military men during wartime: "It is one of the benefits of the soldier's life—his seed springs up behind him and others must tend it!" (Buck, 1975, 240). Contributing to the American public's awareness of her novel was the promotion of Dorothy Canfield FISHER, a personal friend and the director of the Book-of-the-Month Club. With the publication of *Sons* (1932) and *A House Divided* (1935), Buck expanded the characters and setting into the House of Earth trilogy. She retired to Pennsylvania and supported national efforts during World War II to ensure a decent life for orphans fathered by American GIs.

Buck was an influential voice for gender equality, birth control, and multiculturalism a half-century before the terms had worldwide regard. She thought of herself as a perpetual minority, whether in Asia or in her homeland. She refused to espouse government-approved views of Asia and its struggles under imperialism and communism. A bestselling author and most admired female, she was one of the first 20 people named to the Women's Hall of Fame. She earned the regard of a number of other authors, including John Hersey, Maxine Hong KINGSTON, James Michener, and Toni MORRISON. In 1988, the actor Valerie Harper coauthored a one-woman play, *All under Heaven*, set in the office of Buck's home in Danby, Vermont, a year before her death. The action captures the sincerity and commitment that Buck gave to beleaguered women and unwanted children.

Although revered as an altruist and goodwill ambassador to Asia, Buck is seldom recognized for feminism. However, in testimony to her radical views on gender equality is the famed farm wife O-lan of *The Good Earth*, who survives a series of misfortunes common to China's laboring class.

In 1934 Buck delved more deeply into the Chinese peasant woman's hard life with *The Mother*, a moral study of agrarian life. The nameless protagonist, a figure of biblical sobriety and understated majesty, simplifies her life by aborting a pregnancy after her husband abandons her. She continues to labor at farm chores and care for her blind daughter and elderly mother-in-law. The mother's durability helps her survive the rigors expected of a farm beast. Buck pictures the woman reflecting in old age on life and losses and concluding "how little there had been of any good to lay hold on in her years" (Buck, 1971, 300). With a defiant gesture at heaven, she asks the faceless God whether she has not suffered enough. Relieving her despair is the birth of a grandson.

Bibliography

Buck, Pearl. *The Good Earth*. New York: Pocket Books, 1975.

———. *The Mother*. New York: HarperCollins, 1971.

Conn, Peter. *Pearl S. Buck: A Cultural Biography*. Cambridge: Cambridge University Press, 1996.

Wales, Ruth Johnstone. "Pearl Buck Shines in a New Biography," *Christian Science Monitor*, 9 June 1997, p. 13.

Burney, Fanny (1752–1840)

Frances "Fanny" Burney D'Arblay, a revered letter writer, playwright, diarist, and fiction writer, excelled at subversive, antipatriarchal fiction. She earned a place in literary history as the first English female fiction writer to speak from a woman's point of view. Born in King's Lynn, Norfolk, and reared in London, she began writing poems, tales, and plays in girlhood. At the urging of her stepmother, who believed that women writers made poor wives, at age 15, Burney cast her juvenilia into the fire. A year later she initiated a secret diary that covered two decades of her life and the impact of personal, social, and political events.

As did Jane AUSTEN, Burney concerned herself with the economic stresses on young female protagonists who need to make wise matches to ensure themselves an adequate living. She became the most famous of the female writers who freelanced for Minerva Press, a pulp publisher that supplied a chain of circulating libraries with domestic and Gothic fiction. Of the publication of a best-selling novel of manners, *Evelina; or, A Young Lady's Entrance into the World* (1778), the essayist Mary K. Ford commented in "Woman's Progress: A Comparison of Centuries" on the "veritable sensation" it generated: "The book was published anonymously, for in those days 'female delicacy' was such that it was supposed to shrink at the bare idea of publicity" (Ford, 621). Burney earned instant celebrity for the story, which features a young woman of exceptional character and good sense.

The author ventured into more radical feminism in her next work, *Cecilia; or, Memoirs of an Heiress* (1782), a domestic novel about a woman who chooses to retain autonomy and her patronym after marriage. The advice that her suitor, Edgar Mandlebert, receives from his adviser indicates the mercenary nature of wife selection in Georgian England: "Whatever she does, you must ask yourself . . .: 'Should I like such behaviour in my wife?' . . . the interrogatory, Were she mine? must be present at every look, every word, every motion; . . . justice is insufficient" (Burney, 1983, 160). The adviser's view of marital stability is clearly lopsided in favor of male rights. He suggests to Mandlebert that "instead of inquiring, 'Is this right in her?' you must simply ask, 'Would it be pleasing to me?'" (*ibid.*, 160). Because of Burney's didactic tone in describing the economic quandaries faced by Englishwomen, *Cecilia* was less popular than *Evelina.*

Burney, who considered herself a dramatist rather than a novelist, composed nine plays. Only one, the tragedy *Edwy and Elgiva* (1795), was performed. Although the cast featured Sarah Siddons and John Kemble, the show closed after only one night at Drury Lane. Burney's most famous, *The Witlings* (1779), a satire on a bluestocking, Lady Smatter, and on the Esprit Society, a women's literary club, begins in a millinery shop, one of the few professions open to women. A second comedy, *Love and Fashion* (1799), surveys the protagonist Hilaria's dilemma in choosing a husband and the folly of a father's attempt to control his daughter. After completing a lighthearted satire of manners,

A Busy Day (1801), Burney wrote a melodrama, *The Woman-Hater* (1801), which describes the pretentious Lady Smatter and gender conflicts in Georgian England. The playwright's stamina in fighting repression of women's humor suggests her resolve to confront male fears of female artists who pose a threat to the androcentric social order.

At age 34 Burney accepted an appointment from Queen Charlotte as royal wardrobe keeper and dresser at the court of George III. Because trivial work bored her, she resigned; married a French nobleman, General Alexandre D'Arblay; and reared a son. In 1796 she issued a third novel, *Camilla; or, Female Difficulties*, the five-volume story of Camilla Tyrold, a decent woman beset by petty accusations of wrongdoing. Burney champions her heroine for surviving the pitfalls of social and moral criticism. After internment outside Paris during the Napoleonic Wars, the author published *The Wanderer* (1814) and wrote a famous letter series, the first commentary by the survivor of a mastectomy. Burney died at age 84. In 1843 a niece published *Diary and Letters*, which preceded *The Diary and Letters of Madame d'Arblay* (1889), a seven-volume survey of Burney's intimate thoughts and lively observations on the foibles of genteel society.

Bibliography

Bilger, Audrey. *Laughing Feminism: Subversive Comedy in Frances Burney, Maria Edgeworth, and Jane Austen.* Detroit, Mich.: Wayne State University Press, 1998.

Burgess, Miranda J. "Courting Ruin: The Economic Romances of Frances Burney," *Novel: A Forum on Fiction* 28, no. 2 (Winter 1995): 131–153.

Burney, Fanny. *Camilla.* Oxford: Oxford University Press, 1983.

———. *Evelina; or, A Young Lady's Entrance into the World.* New York: Modern Library, 2001.

———. *The Witlings and the Woman-Hater.* New York: Broadview, 2002.

Copeland, Edward. *Women Writing about Money: Women's Fiction in England, 1790–1820.* Cambridge: Cambridge University Press, 1995.

Ford, Mary K. "Woman's Progress: A Comparison of Centuries" (1909). Available online. URL: http://etext.lib.virginia.edu/toc/modeng/public/ForWoma.html. Accessed on October 13, 2005.

Burning Bed, The Faith McNulty (1980)

The feminist slogan "the burning bed" has a unique beginning. It was popularized by a 1984 NBC-television film, Rose Leiman Goldemberg's adaptation of the book *The Burning Bed: The True Story of Francine Hughes, a Beaten Wife Who Rebels* (1980). The book was the work of Faith McNulty, a children's author and reviewer and staff writer for the *New Yorker*. The true story, set in Dansville, a small town near East Lansing, Michigan, captures the desperation of Francine, a 29-year-old wife and mother who endured 13 years of psychological and physical abuse from her former husband, James "Mickey" Hughes. Examples of his volatile nature erupted after she gave birth to their first child. Hughes refused medical care to their dog, Lady, and left her outdoors to freeze while she was giving birth to pups. Hughes also killed their pet cat. In one round of punches to the face, he vowed, "I'm gonna keep it up . . . until you're sorry you were born" (McNulty, 130). Although he threatened to kill Francine if she tried to leave him, the police took no action.

For Francine, victimization reached a desperate point. On March 9, 1977, while 31-year-old Hughes lay passed out in bed, she doused the mattress with gasoline and set the bed on fire. As the residence burned, she fled by car with her children to turn herself in for arson and murder. Her attorney, Aryon Greydanus, successfully defended the vicious murder as an act of temporary insanity resulting from recurrent bullying and brutalizing and from fear for her life. One of the high points of his case was Francine's account of their cat's death: "Mickey had warned [the child] that if he found the cat on the porch he'd wring its neck. When he caught her with it the second time he took it out of her arms and just broke its neck in his two hands" (*ibid.*, 165). The precedent-setting exoneration was a triumph for women, especially female prisoners seeking clemency for similar crimes against cruel mates.

A surprisingly graphic true crime movie, *The Burning Bed* first aired on October 8, 1984, drawing 75 million viewers, one of the largest audiences for a made-for-TV drama. It features Farrah Fawcett, who earned an Emmy nomination for the role of Francine, a Mississippi-born mother of four and vic-tim of battered wife syndrome. After the couple meet in 1963, Mickey, a hard drinker and carouser played by Paul Le Mat, persuades her to quit high school and marry him. When he belittles and controls her, her mother offers no sympathy. A crisis occurs after he loses his job and forces Francine to destroy books that promise her an education and relief from poverty. To end the daily trauma of spousal assault and fear of harm to her or the children, she burns Hughes alive and turns herself in at the police station. The image of a burning mattress soaked in gasoline incited feminist demand for civic response to marital assault and death threats. To rescue women from the domestic hell of alienation and shame, grassroots efforts like Take Back the Night and Fight Back! put conjugal violence under serious scrutiny by psychologists, educators, ministers, attorneys, judges, and law enforcement officers.

Bibliography

Lootens, Tricia. "Women Who Kill: The Burning Bed." *Off Our Backs*, 31 December 1983, p. 16.

McNulty, Faith. *The Burning Bed*. New York: Harcourt Brace Jovanovich, 1980.

Zoglin, Richard. "The Burning Bed." *Time*, 8 October 1984, p. 85.

Butler, Octavia (1947–2006)

Octavia Estelle Butler was best known for female Gothic, utopian, and speculative fiction on the subjects of hierarchy, power, male-on-female violence, and gender disparity. Born in Pasadena and educated in creative writing through the University of California-Los Angeles's (UCLA's) night school, she began publishing short stories in *Clarion, Chrysalis 4, Isaac Asimov's Science Fiction Magazine, Future Life,* and *Transmission*. The winner of Hugo and Nebula Awards and a MacArthur Foundation "genius" Fellowship, Butler built her career slowly and methodically. In defiance of rescue motifs, she excelled at female characters who think their way out of complex dilemmas. One of her paragons of self-reliance is Lauren Olamina, protagonist of the dystopian novel *Parable of the Sower* (1993) and its sequel, *Parable of the Talents* (1998). A visionary teen, Lauren intends to save humankind by introducing the new religion of Earthseed, which encourages people to think independently.

Butler's most famous fantasy novel, *Kindred* (1979), allows her literary license with issues of miscegenation and mulatto genealogy dating to slave times. She pictures a Californian, Dana Franklin, in a time warp that sweeps her and her husband, Kevin, to a Maryland plantation outside Eaton before the Civil War. In the grip of slavery, Dana applies her knowledge of subsequent black history to a predicament that temporarily robs her of liberty. As she awaits the birth of her grandmother, Hagar, Dana observes slave whipping and torture, rape, and sexual enslavement to the white master, Tom Weylin, a series of atrocities that threatens the speaker's matrilineage. Butler poses the paradox of the proud African American who must acknowledge that the strength and endurance of the family tree are owed in part to the rapacious white slaver, Dana's great-grandfather.

Through Dana's "what if" reconnections with the past, Butler reconstructs the sexual plight of black slave women. Her command of motivation stirs suspense as Dana, an independent woman of the late 1970s, protects Weylin's emotionally battered son, Rufus, and solaces Alice Greenwood, her alter ego. Lacking Dana's education and energy, Alice is doomed to become her owner's bed servant and breeder of mixed-race children. The author breaches the barriers for black Americans by warding off white night riders and by reading, a crime for blacks under laws forbidding literacy training for slaves. Gradually, Dana recognizes the slow dulling of her will as bondage drains her of the power to fight back. Escape from her lustful master in 1831 costs Dana an arm as she attempts to slip back into her own time, ironically on July 4, 1976, the nation's 200th birthday.

Bibliography

Allison, Dorothy. "The Future of Females: Octavia Butler's Mother Lode." In *Reading Black, Reading Feminist.* Edited by Henry Louis Gates, Jr. New York: Meridian, 1990.

Barnes, Steven. "Octavia E. Butler," *American Visions* 15, no. 5 (October–November 2000): 24–28.

Govan, Sovan Y. "Homage to Tradition: Octavia Butler Renovates the Historical Novel," *MELUS* 13, no. 1–2 (1986): 79–96.

Reed, Brian K. "Behold the Woman: The Imaginary Wife in Octavia Butler's *Kindred*," *CLA Journal* 47, no. 1 (September 2003): 66–74.

Yaszek, Lisa. "A Grim Fantasy: Remaking American History in Butler's *Kindred*," *Signs: Journal of Women in Culture and Society* 28, no. 4 (Summer 2003): 1,053–1,066.

captivity narrative

Female captivity narrative is a New World adaptation of a popular motif from Barbary pirate and Crusade era memoirs and fiction. Unlike male-centered exploration and battle lore, captivity histories express the fortitude and quick thinking of girls and women seized from home amid horrendous bloodshed, looting, and burning. Readers of frontier literature turned such wilderness escape stories into best sellers. Setting the tone and atmosphere of the new genre was the writing of the Puritan settler Mary White ROWLANDSON, who endured nearly three months of captivity after her kidnap by Wampanoags during King Philip's War. The seizure, which began in Massachusetts, preceded a forced march of Rowlandson and her children over rough woodland trails and through swamps. The ordeal concluded with her sale to white rescuers in New Hampshire for £20. She published *The Sovereignty and Goodness of God: The True Story of the Captivity of Mrs. Mary Rowlandson among the Indians* (1682), a literary fount to later writers of captivity lore. Fiction writers combed her text for eyewitness stories of white girls and women in the custody of Indian males. In an era when stories and drama about women stereotyped them as frail and dependent on males for support and survival, captivity narrative attested to stamina and a will to endure brutality, forced labor, and tribal marriage.

Readers in the colonies and the British Isles clamored for works about kidnapped women and children, perhaps expecting lurid details of rape, sexual enslavement, torture, infanticide, and scalping. In 1728, four years after her capture, Elizabeth Meader Hanson, a Quaker pacifist, composed *God's Mercy Surmounting Man's Cruelty*, a tempered narrative of her abduction from Dover, New Hampshire, and her ransom six months later. By making friends with Native women, she learned how to compound infant gruel from corn meal and walnuts. Her restraint in omitting Puritan conventions of divine providence gave rise to pulp romances that embroidered abductees' sufferings with graphic hyperbole and sentimentality. Two additions to the genre were *An Account of the Captivity of Elizabeth Hanson, Now or Late of Kachecky, in New-England: Who with Four of Her Children and Servant-Maid Was Taken Captive by the Indians and Carried into Canada* (1796), a subsequent version of Hanson's oral narrative, and Susannah Willard Johnson's *A Narrative of the Captivity of Mrs. Johnson: Containing an Account of Her Suffering during Four Years with the Indians and French* (1796). The latter, a realistic first-person retelling of Johnson's capture by Abenaki, went through 50 editions over a half-century. She demonstrated grit during the last two days of pregnancy and childbirth in the wilderness on the tramp north from Charlestown, New Hampshire, to Lake Champlain. Interpolations in later editions added spurious details, but her claims of humane treatment by Indians and her sale into slavery in Montreal are true.

Captivity narrative exhibits the gendered expectations of Native Americans. In 1824, James Seaver published interviews with Mary Jemison as

The Life and Times of Mrs. Mary Jemison. The as-told-to text describes the captivity of the 15-year-old on April 5, 1758, during the French and Indian War, when female slaves were a valuable trade item. Six Shawnee warriors and four French abductors traded her to the Seneca, who moved west into Ohio. She lived as a tribe member under the name Dehgewanus. After her first marriage, she wed a second Indian husband and resided in western New York, where Natives called her the Old White Woman of the Genesee. Less sanguine is the account of Rachel Plummer's two years among Comanche with her infant son in *Narrative of the Capture and Subsequent Sufferings of Mrs. Rachel Plummer* (1839). After Indians seized her from Fort Parker, Texas, in 1836, she described a mother's torment in seeing her child brutalized: "They tied a platted rope round the child's neck, and threw its naked body into the large ledges of prickly pears . . . until my little innocent was not only dead, but literally torn to pieces" (Plummer, 1839). The emphasis on duress that only a parent could undergo elevated her account to a serious feminist memoir.

One popular addition to the genre, *Captivity of the Oatman Girls: Being an Interesting Narrative of Life among the Apache and Mohave Indians* (1859), is a ghost-written account by the Reverend Royal B. Stratton of the sufferings of Mary Ann and Olive Ann Oatman. Caught by Yavapai or Apache raiders in winter 1851 as their family joined Mormon pioneers moving west over Mexican territory toward the Gila River, the girls witnessed the slaying of others and then trudged 350 miles to the Mohave Valley. Of hardship along the way, Olive recalls, "When I could not be driven, I was pushed and hauled along. Stubs, rocks, and gravel-strewn mountain sides hedged up and embittered the travel of the whole day" (Stratton, 127). Captors stripped the girls to the waist and tattooed their chins with blue dots. Olive survived and, in 1856, returned to Fort Yuma to be claimed by her relatives. Simultaneous with the Oatman ordeal was the capture of a homesteader, depicted in a straightforward text, *The Thrilling Narrative of the Sufferings of Mrs. Jane Adeline Wilson during Her Captivity among the Comanche Indians* (1853). As did the Oatman girls and other women seized by Indians, Wilson worked hard to stay alive and save herself from beatings until she could escape.

In 1903, the serialization of seven-year-old Minnie Bruce Carrigan's captivity among the Sioux increased the readership of the *Buffalo Lake News.* Her narrative, *Captured by the Indians* (1862), describes how the Sioux spirited her away from Renville County, Minnesota, on August 18, 1862. Her release in November through army negotiations with the Sioux ended a 10-week sojourn in an Indian camp. The sexual tension and swift action of such captivity narratives influenced James Fenimore Cooper's Leatherstocking series and inspired the Kentucky writer Caroline GORDON's *The Forest of the South* (1945), which contains the frequently anthologized story "The Captive." FEMINIST CRITICISM values captivity narrative for allowing women to document true models of courage as they are forced out of the domestic domain into the wilderness. Autobiographical tales validate unorthodox survival methods, which include sexual barter and transformation into female outsiders as methods of staying alive.

Bibliography

Carrigan, Minnie Bruce. *Captured by the Indians* (1862). Available online. URL: http://womenshistory.about.com/library/weekly/aa020920c.htm. Accessed on October 13, 2005.

Hartman, James D. "Providence Tales and the Indian Captivity Narrative: Some Transatlantic Influence on Colonial Puritan Discourse," *Early American Literature* 32, no. 1 (January 1997): 66–81.

Johnson, Susannah. *A Narrative of the Captivity of Mrs. Johnson* (1796). Available online. URL: http://womenshistory.about.com/library/weekly/aa020920c.htm. Accessed on October 13, 2005.

Kelly, Fanny Wiggins. *Narrative of My Captivity among the Sioux Indians, 1845* (1871). Available online. URL: http://womenshistory.about.com/library/weekly/aa020920c.htm. Accessed on October 13, 2005.

Plummer, Rachel. *Narrative of the Capture and Subsequent Sufferings of Mrs. Rachel Plummer* (1839). Available online. URL: http://womenshistory.about.com/library/weekly/aa020920c.htm. Accessed on October 13, 2005.

Rowlandson, Mary White. *The Sovereignty and Goodness of God: The True Story of the Captivity of Mrs. Mary*

Rowlandson among the Indians. Tucson, Ariz.: American Eagle Publications, 1966.

Seaver, James. *The Life and Times of Mrs. Mary Jemison* (1824). Available online. URL: http://womenshistory. about.com/library/etext/bl_nlmj00.htm. Accessed on October 13, 2005.

Stratton, R. B. *Captivity of the Oatman Girls: Being an Interesting Narrative of Life among the Apache and Mohave Indians.* Lincoln: University of Nebraska Press, 1983.

Cardinal, Marie (1929–   )

A talented French-Canadian writer of the personal, Marie Cardinal appears frequently in the media and at seminars as a spokeswoman for feminism. She flourishes at the autobiographical self-examination that Hélène Cixous named *l'écriture féminine* (feminist literature). A native Algerian, Cardinal grew up in a colonial situation greatly influenced by Catholic tyranny, sexism, elitism, and PATRIARCHY. After completing a degree in philosophy from the Université d'Alger in 1953, she resettled in France and later moved to Québec. As a professional writer and speaker, she promotes women's right to words that express their unique experiences and points of view.

Cardinal violates social and religious taboos by voicing WOMEN'S RIGHTS to enjoy their female bodies and carnal urges. She earned devoted fans in Europe and North America for *Les mots pour Le dire* (*The Words to Say It*, 1975), a landmark autobiographical study of Freudian psychoanalysis. The text features mother-daughter dissonance and the daughter's recovery from stultifying psychotropic drug treatment for anxiety attacks. The novel, which won the Prix Littré and was adapted for film, not only frees the daughter from bourgeois repression but also generates sympathy for her mother, a victim of those same strictures. Cardinal followed with examination of her own motherhood in *La clé sur la porte* (The key in the door, 1972) and *Les grands désordres* (Disorderly conduct, 1987), of marital stress in *Une vie pour deux* (A life for two, 1979), and of father-daughter angst in *Le passé empiété* (The past encroached, 1983). In the latter novel, the speaker in late middle age identifies herself as Clytemnestra, the wife and murderer of the Greek king Agamemnon. She blames herself for earning money from embroidery, a common feminist metaphor for female careers in writing. She admits to "having disobeyed people, their rules, their laws, the culture, the morals, what they call 'the feminine mystique' " (Cardinal, 1984, 47). Her hesitance to demand autonomy illustrates the great leap for women from male control to INDEPENDENCE.

Bibliography
Cardinal, Marie. *The Past Encroached.* New York: French & European, 1984.

———. *The Words to Say It.* Cambridge: Van Vactor & Goodheart, 1983.

Ha, Marie-Paule. "The (M)otherland in Marie Cardinal," *Romance Quarterly* 43, no. 4 (Fall 1996): 206–216.

Carson, Anne (1950–   )

The prize-winning Canadian poet, translator, and classicist Anne Carson anchors her verse and poetic essays to retellings of female stories from Greek myth. Born in Montreal and reared Catholic, she and her brother, Michael, grew up in Stoney Creek, Port Hope, and Timmins, Ontario, small towns where their father worked in banks. Intrigued by ancient Mediterranean civilization, in the mid-1960s she studied classical Greek with a high school teacher. In fits and starts Carson completed a B.A. and M.A. along with courses in art, which competed with literature as her first love. With additional study at the University of Scotland, she completed a doctorate in Greek and Latin at the University of Toronto. Her Canadian teaching career, begun at McGill University, ended after curriculum planners reduced classical studies to a task for history teachers. Carson delivered a harsh salvo against the diminution of the liberal arts and began teaching classics, comparative literature, and English at the University of Michigan.

Early on, readers admired Carson's elegance and her ability to juxtapose past and present. *Eros the Bittersweet* (1986), her first perusal of the Greek concept of passion, explores the impossibility of love without hurt, a conundrum she describes as "sweetbitter" (Carson, 1998, 3). In 1987 she received critical attention for "Kinds of Water," which she published in the American literary journal *Grand Street*. Her stock of awards includes a nomination for the Forward Prize for *Glass, Irony, and God* (1995), which opens on a lyric survey of a lover's abandonment and a mother's assuaging the grief of her bereft daughter. Carson won nominations for the National Book Critics Circle Award and a T. S. Eliot Prize for *Autobiography of Red: A Novel in Verse* (1998), a contemporary setting of Herakles's 10th labor as a homosexual encounter accompanied by a scholarly inquiry into *Geryoneis*, the work of the seventh-century B.C. poet Stesichorus.

Carson is adept at hybridizing prose with verse, a process that developed from her interest in collage. In *The Beauty of the Husband: A Fictional Essay in 29 Tangos* (2001), she characterizes the one-sided marriage of a woman who tolerates an adulterous mate. She frames for the dumped wife the question that arises from sexual despair: "Why did I love him from early girlhood to middle age and the divorce decree came in the mail?" (Carson, 2002, 9). Carson turned her dissertation on the writings of the Greek poet SAPPHO into *If Not, Winter: Fragments of Sappho* (2002), a brilliant study that treats Sappho's love for women as just another complexity of human passion. At the core of the work is an assessment of desire as an echoing emotion—both an impetus to and the result of passion. Carson pictures the famed poet beseeching Aphrodite to be an ally.

Bibliography

Altman, Meryl. "Looking for Sappho," *Women's Review of Books* 21, no. 4 (January 2004): 8–10.

Carson, Anne. *The Beauty of the Husband: A Fictional Essay in 29 Tangos*. New York: Vintage, 2002.

———. *Eros the Bittersweet*. Normal, Ill.: Dalkey Archive Press, 1998.

———. *If Not, Winter: Fragments of Sappho*. New York: Vintage, 2003.

Scroggins, Mark. "Truth, Beauty, and the Remote Control," *Parnassus: Poetry in Review* 26, no. 2 (2002): 127–147.

Carson, Rachel (1907–1964)

A prominent environmentalist and nature writer, Rachel Louise Carson earned worldwide fame for riveting global attention to threats to the survival of life on Earth. Born in the Allegheny mountains at Springdale, Pennsylvania, she grew up in the rhythms and demands of farm life. On her own, she read about wildlife and the sea and, by age 10, began publishing original essays. After majoring in zoology at Pennsylvania College for Women and postgraduate study at Johns Hopkins University, she devoted summers to sea life at Woods Hole, Massachusetts. Far removed from the agrarian setting of childhood, she reveled in the biota of dunes and marsh pools. Financial responsibilities resulting from her father's death in 1935 ended her hopes of completing a Ph.D.

While working as an aquatic specialist for the U.S. Bureau of Fisheries, Carson was overwhelmed by proof that life on Earth is finite. She developed into an activist against the polluting of waterways with agricultural biocides and chemical fertilizers. She enlarged an essay, "Undersea" (1937), published in *Atlantic Monthly*, into *Under the Sea-Wind* (1941), an imaginative work geared to average readers rather than scientists. A decade later she serialized a best seller, *The Sea around Us* (1951), in the *New Yorker* and followed with *The Edge of the Sea* (1955). In 1956 as advice to parents, she wrote "Help Your Child to Wonder" for *Woman's Home Companion*, an ecotheological article that drew on her belief that a strong relationship with nature equips the human spirit with courage and a oneness with the universe. She reached a height of influence on conservation with *Silent Spring* (1962), a lyric, scholarly work that galvanized a generation of readers into action against industrial greed and human indifference to plant and animal life. In a fablelike rendering she introduces a dying town: "On the mornings that had once throbbed with the dawn chorus of robins, catbirds, doves, jays, wrens, and scores of other bird voices there was now no sound" (Carson, 2). As a result of her urgent admonition, President John F. Kennedy empaneled an investigatory group that led to banning of the use of DDT.

A recipient of the Audubon Medal and the Presidential Medal of Freedom, Carson became the fount of ECOFEMINISM, a movement that allies female sensibilities with radical solutions to pollution. She ignored threats of lawsuits by chemical corporations, which attempted to reduce her impact to female hysteria and to debase her objective reportage. Refusing to be dismissed because of gender, she continued to lecture on the importance of sustainable ecology and to denounce the plunder of natural resources. She championed the holistic concept of the interrelation of all living things. As a result of her efforts in the final months before her death from breast cancer she assured the growth of a collective wisdom and a global effort to rescue Earth from human exploitation and waste. One of the 100 most important figures of the 20th century, according to *Time Magazine*, Carson inspired Earth Day, a celebration of nature and a reminder of ongoing commitment to protect all forms of life.

Bibliography

Carson, Rachel. *Silent Spring.* Boston: Houghton Mifflin, 1962.

Lear, Linda. *Rachel Carson: Witness for Nature.* New York: Henry Holt, 1997.

Seager, Joni. "Rachel Carson Died of Breast Cancer: The Coming Age of Feminist Environmentalism," *Signs: Journal of Women in Culture and Society* 28, no. 3 (Spring 2003): 945–973.

Carter, Angela (1940–1992)

A master of magical realism and female gothic, the cult queen Angela Olive Stalker Carter produced her own imaginative revisions of cruel tales, plays, and children's and adult fiction. A native of Eastbourne, Sussex, she was the daughter of a newspaperman. While separated from home during the Blitz, she lived in Yorkshire with her grandmother and cultivated fantasies from girlhood based on her readings of stock British children's lore. In addition to studies in psychology and sociology at Bristol University, she gained the requisite writing experience as reviewer for the *Croyden Advertiser* to launch a career in fantasy, beginning with *Shadow Dance* (1966) and the Rhys Prize winner *The Magic Toyshop* (1967). She filled her works with a variety of changelings, detective investigations, disguises, utopian settings, and tender rescues.

Carter commented that the targeting of females—Mother Goose, old wives' tales, gossips—as spreaders of fantasy denigrates the stories as worthless woman talk. In her first collection of FAIRY TALES the author describes a poor Kenyan who feeds his wife's spirit on folklore, a nourishment of the tongue that banishes female SILENCING. Carter probed the male and female roles in sadomasochistic relationships in *The Sadeian Woman* (1979) and found reason to admire a prostitute: "At least the girl who sells herself with her eyes open is not a hypocrite and, in a world with a cash-sale ideology, that is a positive, even a heroic virtue" (Carter, 1979, 55). She advanced to less fettered females in the gaslight novel *Nights at the Circus* (1984), a flight of fancy that dramatizes the allure of Sophia Fevvers, the swan-girl who bedazzles men with aerial wizardry. The text satirizes media hype with lines from circus posters: "Up she goes in a steatopygous perspective, shaking out about her those tremendous red and purple pinions" (Carter, 1986, 7). As does the unattainable IDEAL WOMAN, Sophia satisfies a male fantasy.

To balance antique tales that stereotype women as prattling, witless victims, Carter creates in *The Bloody Chamber and Other Stories* (1979) female fiends every bit as lethal as male villains. In the title story, she implies torments to come in a postnuptial train ride from Paris. The 17-year-old bride recalls, "His kiss, his kiss with tongue and teeth in it and a rasp of beard, had hinted to me, though with the same exquisite tact as this nightdress he had given me, of the wedding night" (Carter, 1987, 8). The author's version of LITTLE RED RIDING HOOD, named Rosalee, matches the wolf's lust with her own considerable libido, a proof that women are men's erotic equals. The cost of Rosalee's surrender to carnality is the death of the grandmother, a killing off of prefeminist mores to make way for the liberated woman. Carter's skill at fantasy, magic, and shape shifting influenced the costuming and action of Neil Jordan's film version, *The Company of Wolves* (1984).

In 1995, a posthumous collection of mythic tales in *Burning Your Boats: Collected Stories* plucked the best of Carter's works over a 30-year period. The anthology reprises Hansel and Gretel in "Penetrating to the Heart of the Forest" and depicts a quirky objectification of women in "The Man Who Loved a Double Bass." With exquisite satire, Carter ridicules the musician Johnny Jameson's lust for

Lola, a stringed instrument that becomes "his great, gleaming, voluptuous bass . . . a full-breasted, full-hipped woman, recalling certain primitive effigies of the Mother Goddess" (Carter, 1997, 3). At her death at age 51, Carter left a cadre of fans mourning the cessation of delightfully quirky stories and novels.

Bibliography

Boehm, Beth A. "Feminist Metafiction and Androcentric Reading Strategies: Angela Carter's Reconstructed Reader in *Nights at the Circus*," *Critique* 37, no. 1 (Fall 1995): 35–49.

Carter, Angela. *The Bloody Chamber and Other Stories.* London: Penguin, 1987.

———. *Burning Your Boats: Collected Stories.* London: Penguin, 1997.

———. *Nights at the Circus.* London: Penguin, 1986.

———. *The Sadeian Woman and the Ideology of Pornography.* New York: Pantheon, 1979.

Orenstein, Catherine. *Little Red Riding Hood Uncloaked: Sex, Morality, and the Evolution of a Fairy Tale.* New York: Basic Books, 2002.

Warner, Marina. *From the Beast to the Blonde: On Fairy Tales and Their Tellers.* New York: Noonday Press, 1994.

Cather, Willa (1873–1947)

Wilella Sibert Cather produced a body of plaintive fiction filled with female characters who accept diminished lives without losing their creativity and zeal. A southerner from Back Creek Valley, Virginia, she loved the outdoors as well as her grandmother's readings from the Bible. At age seven Cather acclimated to the midwestern frontier after her family moved to Nebraska. Home schooled and allowed the freedom of the town of Red Cloud, she acquired a rare education in Classics and drama as well as the language and culture of neighboring Bohemians, French Catholics, Poles, Russians, Scandinavians, and Slavs. By age 15 she felt a compelling DUALITY, as though an internal male persona was trapped in her female body.

Literature helped to quell Cather's youthful restlessness and conflicted self-identity as Willa/William. At 17 she abandoned hopes of becoming a surgeon and enrolled in courses in Classics and literature at the University of Nebraska, the beginning of a career in journalism and fiction. She settled in Pittsburgh, where she reviewed books, edited the domestic journal *Home Monthly,* critiqued drama for the *Daily Leader,* and taught high school English and Latin. Still attuned to the prairie, she maintained sympathy with heartland farmers by sending money to drought-plagued agrarian families during the disastrous Dust Bowl period.

While on the editorial staff of *McClure's,* Cather took the advice of the feminist fiction writer Sarah Orne JEWETT and began writing prairie novels. With *O PIONEERS!* (1913), Cather developed a pervasive female persona, the farm owner and manager Alexandra Bergson. The story imbues her with the gritty resolve of energetic midwestern women and the instinct of an agricultural visionary. Without losing the tenderness or yearnings of an isolated woman on the midwestern frontier, she manages to teach other farmers by example to introduce alfalfa to their year's plantings and to create more sanitary conditions for raising hogs. Cather pursued her interest in strong women in *The Song of the Lark* (1915), MY ÁNTONIA (1918), *A Lost Lady* (1923), and *Sapphira and the Slave Girl* (1940). For a World War I novel, *One of Ours* (1922), Cather won a Pulitzer Prize.

As the women's movement gained steam, feminist critics reevaluated Cather's canon, particularly the female protagonists of *O Pioneers!* and *My Ántonia.* Cather's images of industrious, stout-spirited women emerge in cooking and food preserving, birthing and death rituals, church socials, waltzing and dancing the schottische, dialect STORYTELLING, and home and agrarian labors. Among her achievers are the individualists who earn a living as cooks, seamstresses, dance instructors, and domestics. Other of Cather's females display variations of the female ability to turn a profit—Tiny Soderball, an innkeeper in the Klondike; Lena Lingard and Bohemian girls who hire out as farm laborers but spend free time dancing on the public square; and Ántonia Shmerda, who wears her father's boots and shocks wheat like a man. The admirable trait of Cather's women is their willingness to accept hardships and loss while making the most of economic opportunity.

Bibliography

Acocella, Joan. "Cather and the Academy." *New Yorker,* 27 November 1995, pp. 56–70.

———. *Willa Cather and the Politics of Criticism.* New York: Vintage, 2002.

Wussow, Helen. "Language, Gender, and Ethnicity in Three Fictions by Willa Cather," *Women and Language* 18, no. 1 (Spring 1995): 52–55.

Catt, Carrie Chapman (1859–1947)

The pacifist and WOMEN'S RIGHTS campaigner Carrie Chapman Catt composed essays, history, and platform oratory that boosted the spirits of second-wave suffragists. Born Carrie Clinton Lane to a pioneer family in Ripon, Wisconsin, and educated in Iowa, she introduced to East Coast feminism the viewpoints of rural women. At age 13 she realized that her mother could not vote, as her father and their hired male help could. Because her father believed that a college degree was wasted on a woman, Catt taught school in Iowa to earn tuition to Iowa State Agricultural College, from which she was the only female graduate in her class. After studying law and serving as a school principal, in her mid-20s, she took up the fight for the vote by writing a feminist column for the *Mason City Republican.*

With the blessing of her second husband, the engineer George Catt, "C. C." Catt established a career on the West Coast as a feminist orator and TEMPERANCE leader. She joined Mary Garrett Hay and Susan B. ANTHONY in empowering the National American Woman Suffrage Association (NAWSA) with strategies to secure full citizenship for women. In a speech delivered in Washington, D.C., in 1902, Catt observed that the world denied education and opportunity to women, then charged them with illogic and ignorance. In global travels, she gathered information on women's status in Africa, China, England, India, Japan, Korea, the Philippines, Sumatra, and Sweden. With these sources, she composed leaflets and polemical articles in *Harper's, Ladies' Home Journal,* and the *New York Times.* She issued a compelling essay, "Do You Know?" (1918), outlining the success of suffrage campaigns worldwide. She declared: "Woman suffrage is just a part of the eternal forward march of the human race toward a complete democracy" (Catt, 1918, 10). Filled with data organized in simple parallel statements, the text urged voters to ponder their citizenship in the Western world and to wonder why U.S. women lagged so far behind their global sisters. Catt's strategy gathered experienced campaigners into the national crusade, increasing NAWSA membership to 2 million. She issued persuasive arguments in *The Ballot and the Bullet* (1897), in which she deflated the historian Francis Parkman's assertion that women are too weak to fight for their country.

When dissension caused liberal women's rights campaigners to falter, leaders of NAWSA adopted Catt's "Winning Plan" to lobby state and national leaders of both political parties. In an atmosphere sullied by name calling, character assassination, rumors of scandal, and flagrant vote buying, she led the group in the final push and involved President Woodrow Wilson, whom she had supported during World War I. To sway fence sitters, Catt addressed Congress in 1917, giving fair warning to "woman haters" who stubbornly blocked the inevitable that they were antagonizing women: "When the party or parties which have so delayed woman suffrage finally let it come, their sincerity will be doubted and their appeal to the new voters will be met with suspicion. This is the psychology of the situation. Can you afford the risk? Think it over" (Catt, 1917). In retrospect, of the growth of American democracy she posed a pointed question to Congress: "With such a history behind it, how can our nation escape the logic it has never failed to follow, when its last unenfranchised class calls for the vote?" (*ibid.*). In 1920 she followed up on victory for suffrage by organizing the League of Women Voters, a nonpartisan organization that encouraged women to assume responsibility for their vote by informing themselves on issues, registering to vote, and participating at all levels of government with their support. In 1923 Catt coauthored with Nettie Rogers Shuler *Woman Suffrage and Politics: The Inner Story of the Suffrage Movement,* a history that preserves the names and deeds of gallant suffragists.

Bibliography

Catt, Carrie Chapman. *The Ballot and the Bullet* (1867). Available online. URL: http://www.catt.org/ccread3.html. Accessed on October 13, 2005.

———. "Do You Know" (1918). Available online. URL: http://memory.loc.gov/cgi-bin/query/S?ammem/ nawbib:@field(TITLE+@od1(Do+you+know? ++)). Accessed on October 13, 2005.

———. "Speech before Congress" (1917). Available online. URL: http://womenshistory.about.com/library/etext/bl_1917_catt_congress.htm. Accessed on October 13, 2005.

———. *Woman Suffrage by Federal Constitutional Amendment* (1917). Available online. URL: http://www.catt.org/ccread3.html. Accessed on October 13, 2005.

———, and Nettie Rogers Shuler. *Woman Suffrage and Politics: The Inner Story of the Suffrage Movement.* New York: William S. Hein, 2004.

censorship

Censorship of feminist writings is as unpredictable as the whims of politics, social conservatism, and religious zealotry. The examples vary in literary style and purpose. Censors have suppressed the works of the children's fantasist Nancy SPRINGER, the exotic novels of Marie CORELLI, Marian Engel's bestial BEAUTY AND THE BEAST love story *Bear* (1977), Marilynne ROBINSON's *Mother Country: Britain, the Welfare State, and Nuclear Pollution* (1989), and Dr. Marie STOPES's marriage manual *Married Love: A New Contribution to the Solution of Sex Difficulties* (1918). In the essay "Blood, Bread, and Poetry: The Location of the Poet" (1984), Adrienne RICH mentions the FBI harassment of Tillie OLSEN and the federal stalking of the writer Meridel LE SUEUR, whose books were banned and employment terminated. For political reasons, book banners silenced the Ukrainian poet Anna AKHMATOVA under communism and the novelist Nadine GORDIMER under apartheid. In the Middle East, censors seized the anti-Israeli fiction of Sahar KHALIFEH and denounced Oriana FALLACI's anti-Islamic *The Rage and the Pride* (2002). The Hispano-Cuban feminist Gertrudis Gómez de AVELLANEDA experienced the suppression in Cuba of *Sab* (1841), an anticolonial, antislavery novel that equates patriarchal marriage with island bondage.

Censorship frequently backfires by creating a demand for books, such as Anne RICE's erotic Sleeping Beauty trilogy. The most severe repression sparks under-the-counter business in smuggled and pirated editions. The most studied model, Radclyffe HALL's *The Well of Loneliness* (1928), a feminist classic, generated a cult following among libertarian and gay readers and civil rights advocates for its depiction of lesbian love. Although suppressed in England and excoriated at the author's trial for obscenity, at which E. M. Forster and Virginia WOOLF testified for the defense, the novel had a reverse effect on the American publishing industry, which issued the work to a ready audience.

In addition to sullying the reputation of major female writers, book proscription manages to remove from public and school library shelves and from reader experience a number of feminist works, including the novels of Nayantara SAHGAL and George SAND. A puzzling choice for ouster is the anthropologist Margaret MEAD's *Coming of Age in Samoa: A Psychological Study of Primitive Youth for Western Civilisation* (1928), an ethnographic study of teenage women in the South Seas. The famed sociological text earned her the sobriquet of "dirty old lady" for suggesting that American parents should be less intolerant about youthful sexual experimentation. The annual listing of censored titles from the American Library Association names among its top contenders Isabel ALLENDE's *The House of the Spirits* (1982), Maya ANGELOU's AUTOBIOGRAPHY *I Know Why the Caged Bird Sings* (1969), Judy BLUME's *Blubber* (1974) and *Forever* (1975), Jean AUEL's Earth's Children series, Margaret ATWOOD's dystopic *The Handmaid's Tale* (1985), Toni MORRISON's *The BLUEST EYE* (1970), and all of Flannery O'CONNOR's works. Complainants list as objectionable vivid portrayals of homosexuality, rape, adultery, sexual abuse, and incest, as well as mundane mention of menstruation, intercourse, childbirth, and breasts.

Challenges to free speech have increased incidents of publishers' self-bowdlerizing. The expatriate journalist and graphic artist Djuna BARNES created a stir with the radical feminism of *Ryder* (1928), a Joycean novel rejected by the Post Office as morally offensive, both in text and in illustration. To the expurgated version issued by the publisher Horace Liveright, she appended a disclaimer: "This book, owing to censorship, which has a vogue in America . . . has been expurgated. Where such measures have been thought necessary, asterisks have been employed, thus making it matter for no speculation where sense, continuity, and beauty have been damaged" (Barnes, vii). Lillian HELLMAN met with the same response to *The Children's Hour* (1934), a play about the undercurrent of disapproval of lesbianism at a girls' academy. Ironically, the gossip generated by a malicious student at the Wright-Dobie School forces a teacher, Martha Dobie, to admit to herself that she is a lesbian.

Homosexuality is a common target of book prohibition. In 1965 May SARTON published *The Education of Harriet Hatfield*, the second of her self-outing lesbian novels. The conciliatory story of a 60-year-old Bostonian whose lover dies after 30 years of a harmonious life together turns female anguish into energy and vision. The protagonist opens a feminist bookshop in a working-class neighborhood, a neutral zone in which straight and gay customers meet. Hatfield idealizes her stores as "a meeting place, a welcoming refuge where people could browse and talk" (Sarton, 10). She takes a stand for humanism by refusing to define people by their sexual orientation. In 1995 the banning and seizure of classroom copies of Sarton's relatively inoffensive novel and two other books in New Ipswich, New Hampshire, caused the firing of a high school teacher, Penny Culliton. She earned public censure and the admiration of free speech advocates for introducing junior and senior students to gay and lesbian literature and for organizing a professional workshop on homophobia.

Interdictions took a frightening form in 1981 for the Egyptian author Nawal EL SAADAWI, a socialist physician and freedom fighter. She suffered arrest by a military task force armed with rifles and bayonets. Her writings, which outraged Arab rulers and fundamentalist Muslims, fell under the ban of President Anwar Sadat and provoked death threats and outrageous charges of impiety against the author. She revived her career by moving publishing operations to Beirut, Lebanon. In 2004, the Islamic Research Academy of Al Azhar University lashed out at El Saadawi's *The Fall of the Imam* (1987), the story of Bint Allah, the illegitimate daughter of an imam. To save face, he levels a false charge of adultery and sentences her to death by stoning. Because El Saadawi dared to expose hypocrisy in the male-dominated religious state, some 17 years after the book's debut and its translation into 14 languages, fundamentalists launched a new campaign to convict the author of apostasy.

Community standards often defy the most humanistic works. Alice WALKER stirred virulent anger for *The COLOR PURPLE* (1982), the story of a jazz singer who teaches a repressed wife about sexual pleasure. In public schools the novel stirred more heated debate than other works in classroom curricula. In Hayward and Oakland, California, school boards debated the appropriateness of explicit sex and sexual language for high school readers. For some 12 years censors continued to muzzle Walker, even after the filming of *The Color Purple* in 1985. The uproar spread across the country to Connecticut, Florida, Michigan, North Carolina, Oregon, Pennsylvania, Tennessee, Virginia, and Wyoming before dying out.

Feminists continue to face down injunctions against their works. On March 30, 1996, the Chinese-American author Amy TAN incurred a last-minute denial of her right to address 450 international guests at a fund-raiser for orphans and crippled children. Without stating specific objections, the Chinese government limited subsequent appearances, and allowed readings by Tan only at the American embassy. On a more humorous note, Erica JONG, author of *Witches* (1981), received from a young reader a Polaroid shot of the book's cover scorched crisp at the edges and a request for a replacement of the copy her father burned. Jong chortled, "So much for the efficacy of censorship" (Jong, 36). Both instances suggest that feminist words regularly net reactions from the politically powerful, even if the denier of First Amendment rights is only a father.

Bibliography

Barnes, Djuna. *Ryder.* Elmwood Park, Ill.: Dalkey Archive, 1990.

Bottum, J. "Flannery O'Connor Banned," *Crisis* 18, no. 9 (October, 2000): 48–49.

Durantine, Peter. "For Pa, Author, Censors Weave Scariest Tales," *Philadelphia Inquirer,* 10 October 1993, p. B1.

Jong, Erica. *What Do Women Want?* New York: Harper-Collins, 1998.

Martyniuk, Irene. "Troubling the 'Master's Voice': Djuna Barnes's Pictorial Strategies," *Mosaic* 31, no. 3 (September 1998): 61–81.

Rich, Adrienne. *Adrienne Rich's Poetry and Prose.* New York: W. W. Norton, 1975.

Sarton, May. *The Education of Harriet Hatfield.* New York: W. W. Norton, 1993.

Weir, Jonh. "The 10 Most Hated Books," *Advocate* no. 736 (24 June 1997): pp. 91–96.

Chesnut, Mary Boykin (1823–1886)

The famed Civil War diarist Mary Boykin Miller Chesnut balanced fear and incipient panic with savvy and courage as she noted the progress of a war that tore her country apart. The daughter of South Carolina's governor, she was born in Camden to southern aristocracy. She learned reading from her paternal grandmother and studied foreign languages, history, science, rhetoric, and literature at Madame Talvande's French School for Young Ladies. Late in Chesnut's life she put language skills to work and earned a pittance from translating French into English. At age 17 she married a state senator, James C. Chesnut, and eventually settled in Charleston.

At age 37 Chesnut was in the perfect spot to observe Southern secession and the onset of hostilities with the firing on Fort Sumter on April 12, 1861. Her entry remarks on the chiming of 4:00 A.M. by Saint Michael's bells: "I began to hope. At half-past four, the heavy booming of a cannon. I sprang out of bed. And on my knees—prostrate—I prayed as I never prayed before" (Chesnut, 1981, 46). Bolstered by a cool objectivity, she filled a dozen volumes with 400,000 words comprising eyewitness accounts of the war years that put an end to slavery. A keen observer of morals and manners, she despised the DOUBLE STANDARD of miscegenation that allowed male slave owners to breed mixed-blood children by their black servants. Her knowledge of states' rights and lengthy encounters with debate on slavery issues made her almost eager for settlement of the argument, even if chaos ensued. At one point, she climbed to the roof to bay at the Moon in dismay at a disintegrating society, devalued currency, and the decline of the mon-

eyed class. To remain solvent, she partnered with a freedwoman in selling butter and eggs, the standard merchandise of enterprising peasant women.

Chesnut's frequent moves to safer locales gave her a good view of events. She witnessed the formation of the Confederacy in Montgomery, Alabama, and the war's progress in North Carolina. In Richmond, Virginia, she entertained the presidential staff and Confederate hierarchy, including President Jefferson Davis and First Lady Varina Davis, Mary's old friend and confidante. Chesnut observed hiring strictures on prospective combat nurses, which valued practical women over socialites. She smirked when the nursing supervisor "saw them coming in angel sleeves displaying all of their white arms, and in their muslin, showing all of their beautiful white shoulders and throats" (ibid., 414). The head nurse so disdained decorative women that she "felt disposed to order them off the premises" (ibid.). As danger increased, Chesnut fled military invasion and kept her trunks packed for sojourns at hotels.

Chesnut maintained an ambivalent protofeminist stance. She refused to excoriate the English novelist George ELIOT for living with a married man but denigrated the author Harriet Beecher STOWE as a Yankee agitator. Although abolitionist in intent, Chesnut perpetuated an outlook grounded in Old South ethics, which included a dependence on chivalrous men and on black females who served as cooks, nursemaids, housekeepers, and women-of-all-work. Nonetheless, she believed that white women and slaves had much in common. Comparing the auction block with the MARRIAGE MARKET, she denounced a woman's being "sold into marriage" and lamented, "You know what the Bible says about slavery—and marriage. Poor women. Poor slaves" (ibid., 15).

Chesnut's diary took a circuitous route to its present state. In 1881 she began a four-year reorganization of her war memoir, which filled 460 notebooks. For brevity and coherence she reduced the original text to three-eighths its original length and bequeathed it to a friend, who published it as *A Diary from Dixie* in 1905. The issuance of the complete diary, *Mary Chestnut's Civil War*, in 1981 earned its editor, C. Vann Woodward, the Pulitzer Prize in history. Additional revelations in *The Private Mary Chesnut: The Unpublished Civil War Di-*

aries (1984) offer an intimate interiority that divulges her private thoughts. Concerning slavery, she mused, "I wonder if it be a sin to think slavery a curse on any land" (Chesnut, 1984, 42–43). The dramatist and actor Chris Weatherhead adapted the diary to stage as a one-woman play, *Mary Chesnut's War for Independence!* (1997).

Bibliography

Chesnut, Mary Boykin. *Mary Chesnut's Civil War.* New Haven, Conn.: Yale University Press, 1981.

———. *The Private Mary Chesnut: The Unpublished Civil War Diaries.* Oxford: Oxford University Press, 1984.

Strout, Cushing. "Border Crossing: History, Fiction, and Dead Certainties," *History and Theory* 31, no. 2 (May 1992): 153–162.

Child, Lydia Maria (1802–1880)

A staunch defender of women, children, and beleaguered slaves and Indians, the writer and editor Lydia Maria Francis Child advanced the cause of the underdog. Born in Medford, Massachusetts, she grew up among legends of white settlers' predations on the Abenaki and Penobscot. She envied the freedom of Native women, who were unencumbered by European notions that females are delicate and useless for serious work. She absorbed the liberal vision of her Unitarian brother, Convers Francis, a theologian at Harvard University, and the reform spirit of her friend the transcendentalist writer and philosopher Margaret FULLER. At age 22 Child inaugurated her writing career with the nation's first historical novel, *Hobomok: A Tale of Early Times* (1824), a romance about a happy interracial marriage of a Native American to Mary Conant, a rebellious white Puritan whom he saves from deep depression.

After founding *Juvenile Miscellany*, the nation's first periodical for children, Child supported her family and their involvement in the Underground Railroad on the proceeds of the magazine and the royalties from *The Frugal Housewife: Dedicated to Those Who Are Not Ashamed of Economy* (1829), a popular domestic handbook. Snippets of advice spool out, forming a verbal quilt, a patchwork image unique to female writing. In her view of frugality, "The true economy of housekeeping is sim-

ply the art of gathering up all the fragments, so that nothing be lost" (Child, 1989, 3). The subtext advances a vision of woman's work as a cornerstone of citizen welfare, capitalism, and the national economy. In the domestic mode, she followed with *The Mother's Book* (1831), an early text on child psychology and rearing that advocates sex education for girls; first-aid training in *The Family Nurse* (1838); and a long-lived domestic Thanksgiving verse, "Over the river and thro' the woods" in *Flowers to Children* (1844), which advocates children's alliance with the elder WISE-WOMEN of their families.

A recruit of the polemicist William Lloyd Garrison, Child stirred controversy with a jeremiad, *An Appeal in Favor of That Class of Americans Called Africans* (1833), the first American abolitionist treatise in book form and one of the most crucial libertarian manifestos of the era. The text is a brave statement of her abolitionist sentiments that cost her close friends and subscriptions to her magazine. In chapter 7 she stressed the salutary influence of black women on their race and their tendency to welcome, nourish, and comfort visitors and people in trouble. Her image of black women breast-feeding infants while awaiting their sale at the slave market anticipates Harriet Beecher STOWE's outrage at the dehumanizing effects of commercialism on the slave family. As a result of Child's vehement denunciation of slavery, the board of the Boston Athenaeum revoked her library privileges.

Child's feminism took on new genres for expressing pro-woman sentiment. She chronicled women's accomplishments in *History of the Condition of Women, In Various Ages and Nations* (1835). In her late 30s she published a New York reform weekly, the *National Anti-Slavery Standard*, followed by a tract calling for the release of John Brown for his role in the Harper's Ferry raid. She adorned the title page of *Authentic Anecdotes of American Slavery* (1838) with a generous gesture from a white matron to a female slave in chains and the slogan, "Am I Not a Woman, and a Sister?" (Child, 1838, 1). Her election to the board of the American Anti-Slavery Society dismayed boardsmen, who were more committed to the rights of black males than to those of women of any color. In 1860 she encouraged Harriet JACOBS to publish *Incidents in the Life of a Slave Girl: Written by Herself,* an autobiographical exposé of the white male's sexual exploitation of black women. Lacking Jacobs's experience with slavery, Child chose fiction for "The Quadroons," a story anthologized in *The Liberty Bell* (1843) of the mixed-race Rosalie and her child Xarifa, whom Edward, a white exploiter, abandons to advance his political career. In remorse, Edward takes to drink and dies by a roadside. In the epilogue, Child legitimized her story as a faithful re-creation of truth: "Scenes like this are no infrequent occurrence in the South" (Child, 1843, 141).

After the Civil War Child pursued humanitarian and suffragist causes. She founded the Massachusetts Woman Suffrage Association and verbally opposed a constitutional amendment granting citizenship to black males only. She compiled sketches and poems by black authors in *The Freedmen's Book* (1865), which post–Civil War schools for former slaves used as a primer. In her mid-60s Child wrote *An Appeal for the Indians* (1868), a reflection of the army's turn from civil war to pacification of the West by displacing native residents. Feminists honor Child as America's first professional female journalist and the first American woman to make a living by writing.

Bibliography

Child, Lydia Maria. *An Appeal in Favor of That Class of Americans Called Africans.* Boston: Allen & Ticknor, 1833.

———. *Authentic Anecdotes of American Slavery.* Newburyport, Mass.: Charles Whipple, 1838.

———. *The Frugal Housewife: Dedicated to Those Who Are Not Ashamed of Economy.* Boston: Applewood, 1989.

———. *Hobomok: A Tale of Early Times.* Cummings, Hilliard, 1824.

———. *The Liberty Bell.* Boston: Anti-Slavery Fair, 1843.

Hoeller, Hildegard. "A Quilt for Life: Lydia Maria Child's *The American Frugal Housewife,*" ATQ 13, no. 2 (June 1999): 89.

Children's Hour, The Lillian Hellman (1934)

Lillian HELLMAN based the plot and themes of her landmark play on a significant moment in women's history—the Great Drumsheugh Case of 1809 as recorded by the criminologist William Roughead in *Bad Companions* (1931). In an era when women's friendships were coming under suspicion, the scandal erupted into a complex tangle of gender and sexual, class, racial, and colonial issues along with disapproval of women who succeed outside the domestic sphere. A libel charge resulted from false accusations of homosexuality against Jane Pirie and Marianne Woods, two unmarried headmistresses at an Edinburgh boarding school. Spearheading the whisper campaign was a student, Jane Cumming, a Hindu-Scots orphan from India fathered by a prominent British soldier. The school closed two days after Cumming lodged complaints to her grandmother. The House of Lords ruled against the two defendants, who never worked again and who lost their school, reputation, and savings during 12 years of appeals.

Reflecting an era of economic and sexual autonomy for women, the intense feminist drama focuses on gay bashing and the dangers of even a hint of pedophilia against educators. Mary Tilford, a pubescent bully at the Wright-Dobie School, spies on the faculty through a keyhole and accuses a teacher, Martha Dobie, of lesbianism. Martha admits to Karen Wright, "It's there. I don't know how. I don't know why. But I did love you. I do love you. I resented your marriage; maybe because I wanted you; maybe because I wanted you all along" (Hellman, 63). Martha stops short of naming lesbianism as the "something" she feels for Karen.

Censors banned the production of *The Children's Hour* in Chicago and Boston. It received acclaim in Paris, but in London producers managed only a private showing. The play had a smash run of 691 performances on Broadway and a moderately successful revival in 1952, directed by Hellman and starring Kim Hunter and Patricia Neal. Because Hellman showcased the ruin of women by a socially forbidden topic, several actresses turned down roles and the Pulitzer committee snubbed the author's efforts. Hellman adapted the text for a movie, *These Three* (1936), which catered to the Hays Code, a set of government-issued guidelines to moral acceptability of films, by altering the plot motivation from lesbianism to the love of two women for one man. As the Hays Code lost steam after a quarter-century of dictating Hollywood ethics, in 1961 Universal Pictures produced a weak adaptation of the original text, starring Audrey Hepburn, Shirley MacLaine, and Miriam Hopkins.

Bibliography

Hellman, Lillian. *The Collected Plays of Lillian Hellman.* Boston: Little, Brown, 1971.

Chin, Marilyn (1955–)

A vivid and uncompromising spokeswoman for female liberty, Marilyn Chin has earned critical attention for expressing gender, class, and racial issues through terse, finely honed poesy. Born Mei Ling Chin in Hong Kong and reared in Portland, Oregon, she received an American name from her father, who wanted to honor the actor Marilyn Monroe. Chin completed degrees in ancient Chinese literature at the University of Massachusetts and in creative writing at the University of Iowa. After publishing an award-winning anthology, *Dwarf Bamboo* (1987), she taught creative writing at San Diego State University.

The poet creates DUALITY in her many visions of Asian women and the displaced Asian-American citizens they become. Like the two-faced Roman god Janus sits over the doorsill to watch comings and goings, immigrant females look back on the past at the same time that they gaze to the future. In a second collection, *The Phoenix Gone, the Terrace Empty* (1994), she writes poignantly about freedom in "Composed near the Bay Bridge" and memorializes the Chinese girls sold into bondage. Her overlay of the Central American goddess Coatlicue with the mythic gorgon Medusa warns of the fine line that separates self-destruction and regeneration. For guidance, the female speaker in "Turtle Soup" looks to her mother, who warns of the extremes of fortunes that await women in exile.

Critics laud Chin's blend of Asian legend and myth with contemporary feminist issues, particularly the sorrows and regrets of the displaced female. In *Rhapsody in Plain Yellow* (2002), she assuages grief over the loss of her Asian mother with plaintive reminiscence of sitting by her grave. The poet recalls her grandmother with similar elegiac grace in "The Floral Apron" (1987), in which

lessons in endurance and courage from the Old World prove valuable in the new. In "Altar" Chin acknowledges the power of the family matron, who remains in memory cultivated by traditional Chinese ancestor worship. The grandmother's statue is both grand and pathetically passé: "But there she sits / a thousand years, hands folded, in a tattered armchair, / with yesterday's news, 'the Golden Mountain Edition' " (Chin, 1994, 29). The line refers to Chinese dreams of North America, which they perceived as a glittering mountain.

Bibliography

Chin, Marilyn. *The Phoenix Gone, the Terrace Empty.* New York: Milkweed Editions, 1994.

———. *Rhapsody in Plain Yellow.* New York: W. W. Norton, 2002.

Gery, John. " 'Mocking My Own Ripeness': Authenticity, Heritage, and Self-Erasure in the Poetry of Marilyn Chin," *LIT: Literature Interpretation Theory* 2, no. 1 (2001): 25–45.

Slowik, Mary. "Beyond Lot's Wife: The Immigration Poems of Marilyn Chin, Garrett Hongo, Li-Young Lee, and David Mura," *MELUS* 25, no. 3/4 (Fall–Winter 2000): 221–242.

Chopin, Kate (1851–1904)

A revered southern regionalist and leader in the effort to emancipate women's voices, Katherine "Kate" O'Flaherty Chopin revealed the married woman's secret yearnings for personal and creative liberty. In the description of the critic Deborah Barker, author of *Aesthetics and Gender in American Literature* (2000), Chopin was the first woman to write works that are both artistic and feminist. A native of Saint Louis, Missouri, she was reared by her French Creole mother, Eliza Faris O'Flaherty, after the death of Kate's immigrant father, Thomas O'Flaherty, in a train accident. Restrained under Catholic dogma at home and at the Academy of the Sacred Heart, she learned deportment, French, and music from her great-grandmother, Madame Victoria Charleville, a model of primness and rectitude and a source of the author's midlife revolt against the DOUBLE STANDARD.

Chopin lived in high-bourgeois style after marrying a French financier, Oscar Chopin, and settling in the American district of New Orleans. When the family wealth dried up, the Chopins moved to Natchitoches, where Kate familiarized herself with the passions and social conventions of the Cajuns, Creoles, and blacks of Cloutierville. In widowhood Chopin experienced severe personal and economic stress, which she relieved by reading books by Charles Darwin, Thomas Huxley, and Herbert Spencer and by writing vignettes, the novel *Bayou Folk* (1894), and some 100 stories for *Atlantic Monthly, Harper's,* and *Vogue.*

In her first stories the author anticipates the boldness of her later work. In one of the early pieces, "A Respectable Woman" (1894), sensual urges threaten to topple the protagonist, Mrs. Baroda: "She wanted to reach out her hand in the darkness and touch him with the sensitive tips of her fingers upon the face or the lips. She wanted to draw close to him and whisper against his cheek—she did not care what—as she might have done if she had not been a respectable woman" (Chopin, 1894, 395). Chopin expressed sympathy for the poor women's need for a break from housewifery and penury in "A Pair of Silk Stockings" (1897). The main character, after paying for her purchase, "seemed for the time to be taking a rest from that laborious and fatiguing function and to have abandoned herself. . . . How good was the touch of the raw silk to her flesh! She felt like lying back in the cushioned chair and reveling for a while in the luxury of it" (Chopin, 1897, 191).

Chopin gained critical and popular success with *A Night in Acadie* (1897), a story collection that ventured beyond regionalism to examine social and sexual differences in Louisiana's rich ethnic mix. Her story "The Storm" became a classic of spontaneously released female desire. With "Miss Witherwell's Mistake," Chopin derided the newspaper convention of the woman's page, which limited the female realm to polite social gatherings and domesticity. One of Chopin's most ironic short stories, "The Story of an Hour," earned renown for an ironic scenario of a woman made giddy with joyous liberation at the news of her husband's death. The release proves only temporary, when her husband's appearance at the door plunges her into fatal regret for her short-lived freedom.

In 1899 Chopin's writing abandoned romance and turned to more overt feminism. She faced public charges of immorality and pornography for publishing THE AWAKENING (1899), an anti-Victorian novel about the psychological suffocation of a spirited, creative woman longing for validation. Reviewers declared the work unwholesome and dismissed its protagonist, Edna Pontellier, as a narcissistic Emma Bovary. Edmund Wilson was the only major American critic to defend Chopin's frank delineation of male-female relationships, which he compared to the writings of D. H. Lawrence. By the 1930s a shift from the sentimental novel to realism generated praise for Chopin's command of psychological fiction. During the women's movement *The Awakening* won new respect for its fluid style and the existential vision of Edna, an unfulfilled wife and mother, who chooses to strip naked and drown herself in the sea to free herself from society's negation.

Bibliography

Barker, Deborah. *Aesthetics and Gender in American Literature.* Cranbury, N.J.: Associated University Presses, 2000.

Chopin, Kate. "A Pair of Silk Stockings" (1897). Available online. URL: http://etext.lib.virginia.edu/toc/modeng/public/ChoSilk.html. Accessed on October 13, 2005.

———. "A Respectable Woman" (1894). Available online. URL: http://wyllie.lib.virginia.edu:8086/perl/toccer-new?id=ChoResp.sgm&images=images/modeng&data=/texts/english/modeng/parsed&tag=public&part=1&division=div1. Accessed on October 13, 2005.

Christ, Carol P. *Diving Deep and Surfacing: Women Writers on Spiritual Quest.* Boston: Beacon Press, 1980.

Jones, Ann Goodwyn. *Tomorrow Is Another Day: The Woman Writer in the South, 1859–1936.* Baton Rouge: Louisiana State University Press, 1981.

Christine de Pisan (1364–ca. 1431)

The late medieval balladeer, biographer, essayist, and protofeminist Christine de Pisan (or de Pizan) anticipated the artistic awakening of the Renaissance, the writings of Machiavelli, and the liberalization of woman's position in society. A native of Venice, she lived in Paris from early childhood after her father, the physician and astrologer Tomasso di Benvenuto da Pizzano of Bologna, obtained a court position serving Charles V. In a learned environment, she became fluent in French, Italian, and Latin and read history, science, and literature from well-stocked shelves. Wed in her midteens to the scholarly court secretary Étienne du Castel, she enjoyed a balanced marriage and flourished in intellectual pursuits until the king's death ended her family's security.

After her husband's death from bubonic plague, in her mid-30s, Christine de Pisan supported their surviving son and daughter, Jean and Marie, and Christine's mother and niece by writing rondeaux, songs, allegory, and incisive nonfiction. Under the patronage of the duc de Berry, Louis I, Isabella of Bavaria, and Philip II of Burgundy, Christine issued saintly exempla and polemics on chivalry, the military, and women's moral and intellectual EDUCATION, in particular, *Le livre des trois vertus* (*The Book of Three Virtues*, 1406). The first salvo in defense of the merits of women occurred around 1399 with *Epistre au dieu d'amours* (Letter to the god of love), which condemns the misogyny that pervaded the Middle Ages, especially Jean de Meung's virulent antifemale diatribe in part two of *Le Roman de la rose* (1277). In *Epistres du débat sur le roman de la Rose* (Letters on the debate of "The Romance of the Rose," 1402), she denounced the abuse of females as the butt of Classical literary humor and satire. She stressed the tolerance of Catholic prelates for works maligning women and reminded churchmen that such antifemale invective extended to the VIRGIN MARY, the era's icon of the IDEAL WOMAN.

Christine de Pisan's survey of famous women, *Livre de la cité des dames* (*Book of the City of Ladies*, ca. 1405), a rewrite of Giovanni Boccaccio's *De claris mulieribus* (On famous women, 1375), justifies the place of women in history, including Saint Catherine of Alexandria and the warriors Hippolyta and Semiramis. As does Geoffrey Chaucer's audacious WIFE OF BATH, the coarse feminist storyteller in *The Canterbury Tales* (1387), Christine de Pisan defies Bible-based castigation of women as causes of the fall. She rewrites theological and Classical misogyny, including the story of Saint Barbara, the prototype for the FAIRY TALE of

Rapunzel. Barbara's father seals her in a tower for rejecting marriage proposals. In retreat at the Dominican abbey of Poissy in 1418, Christine de Pisan composed *Le dittie de Jeanne d'Arc* (Hymn to Joan of Arc, 1429), a pro-Valois treatise in the French language opposing the English occupation of Paris. For her courage and brilliance, she was called the nation's first female intellectual and the first feminist to challenge misogyny in formal pro-woman literature.

Bibliography

Blumenfeld-Kosinski, Renate. "'Femme de Corps et Femme par Sens': Christine de Pizan's Saintly Women," *Romanic Review* 87, no. 2 (March 1996): 157–175.

McRae, Laura Kathryn. "Interpretation and the Acts of Reading and Writing in Christine de Pisan's 'Livre de la Cité des Dames,' " *Romanic Review* 82, no. 4 (November 1991): 412–433.

Rigby, S. H. "The Wife of Bath, Christine de Pizan, and the Medieval Case for Women," *Chaucer Review* 32, no. 2 (Fall 2000): 133–165.

Willard, Charity Cannon. *Christine de Pizan: Her Life and Works*. New York: Persea Books, 1984.

Churchill, Caryl (1938–)

The playwright Caryl Churchill, a bright and daring stage innovator, batters the unfairness of SEXUAL POLITICS. A Londoner educated in Montreal, she completed an English degree at Lady Margaret Hall, Oxford, at the same time that she introduced *Downstairs* (1958), her first play. She began exploring the possibilities of drama on radio and television and on the stage with blunt, provocative scenarios laced with wry humor. In her early 30s, when she juggled creativity with the duties of mothering her three sons, she challenged England's best dramatists with a strong feminism, beginning with the teleplay *The Judge's Wife* (1972), which extends sympathy to a widow. She wrote *Owners* (1972) to expose the successful male's fear of a competitive wife through the butcher Clegg's intent to murder his wife, Marion, a thriving realtor. With overt hostility toward sexism, Churchill composed *Objections to Sex and Violence* (1975), an experiment in head-on feminism. She produced a more refined pro-woman statement in *Vinegar Tom*

(1976), a musical reexamination of the male-led witch burnings of women. The victims are the social misfits and creators who violate Christian dogma that forces women into unquestioning obedience to church and husband.

More popular on both sides of the Atlantic is Churchill's *Cloud Nine* (1979), a seriocomic experimental drama probing the changes in social expectations for expression of female SEXUALITY. The character Betty, an adoring housewife often played by a male, speaks in robotic verse. Betty declares herself a creation of men who abandons innate volition to be "what men want" (Churchill, 1995, p. 1). Her mechanized behavior suggests Nora Helmer's childish comebacks and ethnic dancing for her husband, Torvald, in Henrik Ibsen's A DOLL'S HOUSE (1879).

Churchill followed with *Top Girls* (1982), a topical Obie-winning drama about the social and personal ramifications of a competitive woman's rise to wealth and power. The play opens with a fantasy banquet scene, a satire of Plato's all-male symposia. The conflict results from the choices that domesticity foists on the protagonist, Marlene, who has just been named the head of an employment agency. For stability, she surrounds herself with voices from the past. Seated at the table are the legendary Pope Joan, the Japanese courtesan Nijo, Geoffrey Chaucer's patient Griselda, and Dulle Gret, a figure from a Breughel painting. Gret pictures the medieval paintings of Hellmouth, a setting that summarizes the inescapable outlook universal to womanhood: "We come into Hell through a big mouth" (Churchill, 1982, 67). Churchill noted that the play is a commentary on the methods and outlook of Margaret Thatcher, Europe's first female prime minister, who furthered the male-dominated power structure by ignoring women's needs and obstructing the woman-engineered collectivism advocated by the women's movement.

Bibliography

Churchill, Caryl. *Cloud Nine*. New York: Theatre Communications Group, 1995.

———. *Top Girls*. London: Methuen, 1982.

Fletcher, Andrew. "Top Girls or Iron Ladies?" *English Review* 12, no. 2 (November 2001): 32–33.

Cinderella

The resilient Cinderella FAIRY TALE permeates world lore as a delightful tutorial of the dynamics of wooing and an acknowledgment of the ostracism of working-class women out of favor among their family and peers. Madonna Kolbenschlag, author of *Kiss Sleeping Beauty Good-bye* (1979), describes the Cinderella paradigm as the female striver "deliberately and systematically excluded from meaningful achievement" (Kolbenschlag, 63). The critic concludes that there is a paradox at work by which "this acceptance of a condition of worthlessness in the self, along with a conviction of the ultimate worthiness and heroism of one's role, is part of the terrible appeal of the fairy tale" (*ibid.*, 64). Her commentary accurately pictures the quandary of June May Woo, a lackluster first-generation American in Amy TAN's *The Joy Luck Club* (1989). With her hair formed into Shirley Temple sausage curls, she daydreams her transformation into the typical American girl. The end to mental escapism results from June's mother's boasting and her "[hope] for something so large that failure was inevitable" (Tan, 154). In affirmation of self, June retorts, "I won't let her change me . . . I won't be what I'm not" (*ibid.*, 134).

Feminist versions of Cinderella combat the notion that women are powerless against the status quo until some magic fairy godmother or well-meaning male rescues them. A hard-working drudge by the hearth, Anne Elliot, protagonist of Jane AUSTEN's *Persuasion* (1818), is an unfashionable woman of the Regency era. She bides her time, remains useful and dependable, and claims her prize prince in the form of a sea captain, Frederick Wentworth. He relieves her tedium and devaluation by carrying her away in his ship from England's narrow social roles. The Cinderella stereotype of rescue permeates a range of feminist fiction, stage musicals, ballet, and film, including the movies *Working Girl* (1988), *Pretty Woman* (1990), *Ever After* (1998), and *Maid in Manhattan* (2002), a wish-come-true vehicle for the pop star Jennifer Lopez.

Late 20th-century versions of Cinderella reveal the feminist themes of the orphan's mother hunger. In the poet Anne SEXTON's resetting in *Transformations* (1971), the ash girl is desperate for female guidance. She retreats to her mother's grave and wails to her mother to send her to the royal ball. Drawing on Sexton's feminist themes, an admirer, the Greco-American writer Olga BROUMAS, describes in *Beginning with O* (1977) the loneliness of the woman estranged from others in the house. Cinderella, the handy receptacle of princes who fumble with her in the dark, knows the anguish of life in a strange castle, a symbol of the male-dominated realm. She pictures herself as the one item of laundry, blowing on a long clothesline and regrets being deceived by false promises. She characterizes the fate of women in an androcentric society as victims of erroneous or superficial judgements.

In the 21st century self-rescue adds zing to the tired image of Cinderella awaiting a prince. Margaret Peterson Haddix's *Just Ella* (2001) opens with a feminist jolt, the discontent of the soon-to-be-married princess, 15-year-old Cynthiana Eleanora, for whom "the fire had gone out" (Haddix, 1). The author rejects the notion that marriage to a prince is the answer to female discontent. In a cloying scenario in which Ella—minus the cinders—paints and does needlework under the tutelage of her decorum coach, Madame Bisset, Ella acknowledges the imprisonment of boredom. She grows to value the keen mind of her friend Jed and digs her way out of politically arranged wedlock to embrace a soulmate rather than the wooden-headed prince. Her evasion of stultifying matrimony embodies the feminist belief that women should avoid the altar if they long to satisfy their intellect.

Bibliography

Haddix, Margaret Peterson. *Just Ella*. New York: Aladdin, 2001.

Kolbenschlag, Madonna. *Kiss Sleeping Beauty Good-Bye: Breaking the Spell of Feminine Myths and Models*. Toronto: Bantam, 1981.

Sexton, Anne. *Transformations*. Boston: Houghton Mifflin, 1971.

Tan, Amy. *The Joy Luck Club*, New York: Putnam, 1989.

Tatar, Maria, ed. *The Annotated Classic Fairy Tales*. New York: W. W. Norton, 2002.

Cisneros, Sandra (1954–   )

The author Sandra Cisneros has made the Chicana experience a source for feminist verse, essays, and short fiction. Shy and introspective from childhood, she was born in Chicago to a working-class Mexican father, Alfredo Cisneros, and Elvira Cordero Anguinao, a Mexican–American Indian mother of eight. During the family's financial struggles they moved often among slum apartments and traveled annually to Mexico City to visit relatives, who dredged up stories about a family fortune lost on the roll of dice. Bicultural rootlessness deprived Sandra of a sense of home and of long-term friends. The death of an infant sister left her the lone girl among six brothers. In 1966 the family settled permanently in a Puerto Rican barrio, where Sandra gathered memories of a sexist Catholic milieu for the autobiographical works *The House on Mango Street* (1983), winner of a Before Columbus American Book Award, and *Caramelo* (2003), a complex multigenerational fiction that critics compared to Isabel ALLENDE's Chilean saga *The HOUSE OF THE SPIRITS* (1982).

Ever the outsider, Cisneros took refuge in the city library at age six and, with her mother's help, began writing. While earning a B.A. in English at Loyola University, she discovered Latino literature and began composing feminist verse. In 1978 she completed a master's degree in creative writing from the University of Iowa Writers Workshop and began examining through poetry her deep feelings of otherness. Because of her skill at first-generation Latina-American speech and thought, she found jobs in Mexico, Europe, and the United States reading, teaching, and contributing vignettes and poems to *Contact II*, *Imagine*, *Nuestro*, and *Revista Chicano-Riqueña*.

Central to Cisneros's intent are the empowerment of silent women and the filling of a void in devalued ghetto women such as her mother. For the cheery, intuitive vignettes in *The House on Mango Street*, a female quest suite, the author creates an observant child narrator called Esperanza [hope] Cordero. She explains that she was named for a great-grandmother, "born like me in the Chinese year of the horse—which is supposed to be bad luck if you're born female—but I think this is a Chinese lie because the Chinese, like the Mexicans, don't like their women strong" (Cisneros, 1983, 10). She misunderstands Sally, a literary foil who is sexually mature. After her elopement, Sally discovers that her husband, the equal of a patriarchal father, confines her at home and limits her to domestic chores. From experience with barrio morality, Esperanza resolves not to depend on a male rescuer.

The impetus to Cisneros's first book matures in subsequent depictions of risqué women. In a story collection, *Woman Hollering Creek and Other Stories* (1991), the first work by a Chicana writer issued by a major American publisher, the author pictures the jubilation of female liberation. She spotlights the stark reality of alcohol-triggered marital abuse in the life of Cleófilas Enriqueta DeLeon Hernandez, a Mexican immigrant newlywed living in Texas. An unmarried friend named Felice is the only outsider to recognize domestic misery and to offer an escape route. More moving vignettes of vigorous, sexually ripe women fill the poems in the anthology *Loose Woman* (1994), which pictures women who flirt, sorrow, and swear. Among the revealing titles are "Old Maids," "Black Lace Bra Kind of Woman," "Waiting for a Lover," "Pumpkin Eater," and "I Am So In Love I Grow a New Hymen." Typical of the poet's daredevil exuberance is the close of "Little Clown, My Heart," which depicts her leap into an ocean of fire.

Bibliography

Cisneros, Sandra. *The House on Mango Street.* Houston: Arte Público, 1983.

———. *Loose Woman.* New York: Vintage, 1995.

———. *Woman Hollering Creek and Other Stories.* New York: Random House, 1991.

Ganz, Robin. "Sandra Cisneros: Border Crossings and Beyond," *MELUS* 19, no. 1 (Spring 1994): 19–29.

Saldivar-Hull, Sonia. "Women Hollering Transfronteriza Feminisms," *Cultural Studies* 13, no. 2 (April 1999): 251–262.

Wheatwind, Marie-Elise. "Breaking Boundaries," *Women's Review of Books* 15, no. 12 (September 1998): 18–20.

Cixous, Hélène (1937–)

A prolific writer, critic, and activist, Hélène Cixous turns the resentment of the displaced person into energetic, transforming verse, drama, and fiction. A native of Oran, Algeria, she was born to Georges Cixous, a Sephardic Spanish army doctor, and Eva Klein Cixous, an Ashkenazic German-Austrian-Czech midwife. The author first encountered anti-Jewish sentiment at age three from other children at the Officers' Club. She mastered Arabic, English, French, German, and Hebrew but felt that no single language linked her to a mother country, culture, or history. She holds a doctorate in English literature with emphasis on the works of James Joyce and directs the Centre de Recherches en Études Féminines (Center for Research in Women's Studies) in Saint-Denis, France. She has taught at major universities in England and the United States and has issued feminist classics through the French publisher Des Femmes.

Brought up during world cataclysm, Cixous learned early that in a land legend-rich in heroic fighters no male warrior fought to improve the lot of woman. Through experience, she surmised that most males demanded uncomplaining passivity. To liberate women from incapacitating iconery, she pursued *écriture féminine* (feminine writing), a style recognized through its economy of words and its ability to express women's thoughts and perceptions with energy and direction. The intent is to relieve the sexism of society and politics. In 1968 she launched *Poétique*, a literary review; the following year she earned the Prix Médicis for a first novel, *Dedans* (Inside), an autobiographical response to her father's death in 1948 from tuberculosis.

Cixous's plunge into a frank, joyous feminism began in 1975, when she issued a visceral, sensual, body-freeing imagery in *Le rire de la Meduse* (The laugh of the Medusa) and *La jeune née* (The Newly Born Woman), coauthored by Catherine Clément. The latter work turned an unprejudiced eye on the confluence of female myth and history—the mythic Ariadne, Sphinx, Phoenix, Cassandra, and the Greek Helen of Troy blended with the Roman Lucretia, Nordic Brunhild, and the biblical Delilah and Mary Magdalene. For Théâtre du Soleil (Sun Theater) she wrote the stage play *Portrait of Dora* (1976), a delightful flip-flop of Sigmund Freud's male-centered study of lesbianism and female desire. With *Le livre de Promethea* (The book of Promethea, 1983), Cixous examines the complexities of woman-to-woman love and rejoices in the inexhaustibility of female imagination and ardor.

By blurring gender differences, her seductive, lyrical fiction validates the experience of womanhood while avoiding unnecessary denigration of men.

Cixous frees herself from a tangle of gender, religious, national, and linguistic boundaries to generate sociopolitical change for women. She finds release through the poet's magic—an all-out manipulation of language in its myriad meanings and implications. She remarks in *Coming to Writing* (1986) on the way that composition grips and seizes her torso, literally halting her breath. She links the flow of women's words from ink with the maternal image of the full and nourishing breast. In "We Who Are Free," the author describes the oneness of poet and reader as a sharing of unhappiness that allows them to be aliens together. In "Sorties" (Exits), anthologized in *The Newly Born Woman*, she sums up a dark, forbidding female history as "Bridebed, childbed, bed of death" and, without rancor, exults in freedom from phallocentrism, the dominance of maleness (Cixous & Clément, 66).

Bibliography

Blyth, Ian. "An Interview with Hélène Cixous," *Paragraph* 23, no. 3 (November 2000): 338–343.

Cixous, Hélène. *The Hélène Cixous Reader.* New York: Routledge, 1994.

———, and Catherine Clément. *The Newly Born Woman.* Minneapolis: University of Minnesota Press, 1986.

Rye, Gill. "Agony or Ecstasy? Reading Cixous's Recent Fiction," *Paragraph* 23, no. 3 (November 2000): 298–312.

Savona, Jeanelle Laillou. "Hélène Cixous and Utopian Thought: From 'Tancredi Continues' to 'The Book of Promethea,' " *University of Toronto Quarterly* 72, no. 2 (Spring 2003): 615–630.

Clifton, Lucille (1936–   )

The prominent children's author, educator, and feminist poet Thelma Lucille Sayles Clifton finds elements of women's lives to celebrate. A native of Depew, a steelmill village near Buffalo, New York, she was the child of manual laborers whom she described as a verbal people. She grew up in poverty and suffered sexual abuse from her father but found the grace to forgive. Of bitter memories, she said, "He hurt us all a lot and we hurt him a lot, the way people who love each other do" (Clifton, 1989, 273). An early and fervent reader, Clifton learned the nuances of STORYTELLING from her father and memorized the sonnets of Edna St. Vincent MILLAY.

Clifton took an interest in oral Bible readings and in recitations of the Sale/Sayles family tree. She traced her lineage to the birth of a family matriarch, her great-great-grandmother, Caroline "Mammy Ca'line" Sale Donald, in Dahomey in 1822. The author pursued the woman-to-woman thread to Caroline's daughter, her great-grandmother, Lucille Sale, whom the state of Virginia hanged after she killed the white exploiter who sired her children. The poet later honored her "dazzling" foremothers in the poem "Daughters" (1993). On scholarship to study drama at Howard University and at Fredonia State Teachers' College, she developed confidence in her own style, a musical rhythm, polished elegance, and an idiom that leans heavily on the black oral tradition.

Opportunities to develop her art arose late for Clifton. After bearing six children within 10 years, she won a Discovery Award with the aid of the poet Carolyn KIZER. Clifton took the advice of the poet Maxine KUMIN and wrote children's books. In 1969 the *New York Times* lauded Clifton's first poetry collection, *Good Times*, an anthology of spare free verse featuring urban motifs. In one of the poems, "Miss Rosie," Clifton elevates the discounted bag lady, who used to be the prettiest gal in Georgia. To a fellow female confronting hard times, the poet pictures herself standing as a gesture of honor. "I stand up / through your destruction / I stand up" (*ibid.*). Additional poems on female strength and promise find similarities between ordinary women and historic heroines such as Naomi from the Bible, the abolitionists Harriet Tubman and Sojourner TRUTH, and the "wereladies" of Salem.

To honor her parents, Clifton completed a genealogy, *Generations: A Memoir* (1976). A year after she was named Maryland's poet laureate, she wrote *Two Headed Woman* (1980), a collection paying homage to SISTERHOOD. One of her most unusual verse cycles is a mystic dialect cycle she dedicated to the VIRGIN MARY. In "The Astrologer Predicts at Mary's Birth" the annunciation overwhelms the young girl's senses, striking ear and eye with the wonder of divine conception. That of a black woman accustomed to scrubbing, the older woman's voice in "Anna Speaks of the Childhood of Mary Her Daughter" urges her child to keep working as an antidote to outsized visions. Clifton recognizes in Mary's dreams a terrifying element that is beyond Anna's understanding. In "Holy Night," Mary undergoes an epiphany and discloses to Joseph her fear of stars. A sublime light illuminates her breasts, an image that allies a heavenly grace with sources of human sustenance for the Christ Child.

In 1991 Clifton focused on women's strengths and artistry. She returned to the patchwork of past generations in *Quilting: Poems 1987–1990*, which names and describes traditional quilt patterns as a female inheritance from centuries of foremothers. For *The Book of Light* (1993), she imagines a feminist version of *Roots*. In "Climbing," she looks upward to a woman leading the ascent up a single strand of MATRIARCHY that directs the poet's ambitions. In 2000 she introduced contemporary issues in *Blessing the Boats: New and Selected Poems, 1988–2000*. Lamenting catastrophic illness, incest, and children shooting children, she reprised recurrent light images. With mystic fervor, she speaks of the revelations of darkness by the secretive moon. Clifton's gynocentric verse influenced the poet Sharon OLDS.

Bibliography

Clifton, Lucille. *Blessing the Boats: New and Selected Poems, 1988–2000*. New York: Boa, 2000.
———. *The Book of Light*. Townsend, Wash.: Copper Canyon Press, 1993.
———. *Good Woman: Poems and a Memoir, 1969–1980*. New York: Boa, 1989.
Holladay, Hilary. *Wild Blessings: The Poetry of Lucille Clifton*. Baton Rouge: Louisiana State University Press, 2004.

Clive, Caroline (1801–1873)

The English writer Caroline Meysey-Wigley Clive questioned Victorian morality through psychological fiction. Born to affluence in Brompton Grove, London, she was handicapped from age three and left to solitude, home schooling, and reading. She began her writing career with a collection of religious meditations, *Essays of the Human Intellect* (1828), published anonymously under the male pen name Paul Ferrol, which she altered 27 years later to Ferroll for her most memorable character, an unrepentant wife killer. At age 39 she married the Reverend Archer Clive, rector of Solihull. They kept a joint journal, in which she recorded her tribulations during pregnancy and childbirth. Under the pseudonym V, she published verse, *IX Poems by V* (1840), the first of five volumes of poetry. She was unsuccessful in persuading *Blackwood's Edinburgh Magazine* to accept *Saint Oldooman: A Myth of the Nineteenth Century*, which satirized the Oxford Movement. In 1847 she published "The Queen's Ball," a ghost narrative lamenting the shortness of life.

At age 54 Clive inflicted doubt about the middle-class Victorian husband's capacity for VIOLENCE. She published a Gothic classic, *Paul Ferroll* (1855), a thrust in the direction of sensational urban fiction that she serialized the next year in *Putnam's Magazine*. The tale of a wife slayer, the novel follows him from the act of shoving a probe into the cranium of his sleeping wife, Anne Gordon Ferroll, to the prosecution of an elderly woman for the crime. Rather than face punishment, he flees to Boston with his daughter, Janet. To his unsuspecting lover, he hints at his duplicitous nature: "Could you not bear it, my Elinor; would it change me for you though I had even done that deed?" (Clive, 1855, 118). The moral ambiguity of Ferroll's barbaric crime and his public pose of community leader exhibits the author's outrage at male-on-female violence. The novel produced such notoriety that Clive was ever afterward known as "the author of *Paul Ferroll*."

To account for Ferroll's escape and his yearning for Elinor, the author issued a moralistic prequel, *Why Paul Ferroll Killed His Wife* (1860), serialized in the *Continental Monthly* in 1862. The motivation for murder is the stymying of male autonomy: Ferroll feels "fast bound in the meshes, which a woman, a mere woman, had found the means to twine around him, and fiercely did he resent the injury, and gaze sternly at her falsehood and successful deceit" (Clive, 1860, 332). By overturning action featuring the standard powerless female, Clive unleashes fury in the frustrated husband who resorts to murder as his way out of a suffocating marriage. She pictures him still haunted by his deed after 18 happy years of marriage to his beloved. Felled by paralytic stroke at age 64, Clive continued writing at a desk in her boudoir and died of severe burns after her dress caught fire.

Bibliography

Clive, Caroline. *Paul Ferroll* (1855). Available online. URL: http://www.indiana.edu/~letrs/vwwp/clive/ferroll.html. Accessed on October 13, 2005.

———. *Why Paul Ferrol Killed His Wife* (1860). Available online. URL: http://www.indiana.edu/~letrs/ vwwp/ clive/why.html. Accessed on October 13, 2005.

Timleck, Sarah Lorraine. "Volumes of Silence: The Non-Narratability of Middle-Class Wife-Assault in the Victorian Novel." (Master's thesis, University of Guelph, 1998).

"Closing Door, The"   Angelina Weld Grimké (1919)

Published in Margaret SANGER's journal *Birth Control Review* in September 1919, Angelina Weld GRIMKE's melodramatic story "The Closing Door" epitomizes the Jim Crow era's rejection of the black child. Tinged with autobiographical mother hunger, the narrative pictures the loneliness and rejection that Lucy, a 15-year-old orphan, experiences in a series of foster homes. Rootlessness produces a self-image of "a yellow, scrawny, unbeautiful girl" (Grimké, 124). Grimké builds cruel irony out of the protagonist's attachment to 25-year-old Agnes "Ag" Milton, a loving mother blessed with a "wonder-quality of her soul" (*ibid.*). Agnes bonds with Lucy at the time that Agnes and her husband, Jim, conceive a son. At Agnes's lapse into severe depression, the disappointment resulting from a failed refuge and from thwarted maternity accounts for the title image. The author's purpose in picturing a new generation of devalued black women was the promotion of birth control as a source of sexual and personal emancipation.

An emotional testimony, the first-person narrative attests to the mothering qualities in Agnes, Lucy's distant relative. Lucy remarks on Agnes's yearning for a daughter and her gift for happiness, openhandedness, and compassion. Set in May, the story suggests a tender hope for the future in Agnes's first pregnancy. Her brother, Joe's, arrival from the South with news of their brother Bob's lynching, burning, and dismemberment by a white mob overwhelms Agnes with the futility of bearing children. She envisions herself as a black breeder "doomed! cursed!—put here! For what?" (*ibid.*, 140). To Agnes, the early 20th century is a time when "no colored child . . . will be safe—in this country" (*ibid.*, 141). The great sorrow at seeing Agnes decline into a vacant-eyed recluse leaves Lucy with a longing to trade places. In Grimké's opinion, the loss of a consoling parent is worse than the perpetual darkness and lovelessness of death.

Grimké's fiction portrays the disenfranchisement of the black mother in her choice of the unthinkable, maternal infanticide. Reminiscent of Toni MORRISON's *BELOVED* (1987), the bizarre conclusion of Grimké's story contrasts the ebullience of Lucy's first impressions of Agnes with MADNESS generated by the historical milieu. Crushed by family catastrophe, Agnes denies God's pity and retreats behind closed doors to tend her infant son in joyless silence. By supplanting the ailing mother, Lucy briefly delights in fostering an endearing baby. In a graphic chiaroscuro, Grimké rushes to a chilling conclusion. Across external darkness, a shaft of moonlight discloses the stilled child, smothered by Agnes. The author characterizes Agnes's renunciation of VIOLENCE through a deliverance of her innocent babe from future brutality. Lucy bitterly acknowledges Agnes's demise as another form of deliverance: "God, I think, may be pitiful, after all" (*ibid.*, 145).

Bibliography

Dawkins, Laura. "From Madonna to Medea: Maternal Infanticide in African American Women's Literature of the Harlem Renaissance," *LIT: Literature Interpretation Theory* 15, no. 3 (July 2004): 223–240.

Grimké, Angelina Weld. "The Closing Door." In *The Sleeper Wakes: Harlem Renaissance Stories by Women*, 124–125. Piscataway, N.J.: Rutgers University Press, 1993.

Hirsch, David A. Hedrich. "Speaking Silences in Angelina Weld Grimké's 'The Closing Door' and

'Blackness,'" *African American Review* 26, no. 3 (1992): 459–474.

Cloud Nine Caryl Churchill (1979)

Caryl CHURCHILL's darkly cartoonish satire *Cloud Nine* (1979) characterizes a female suppression of will that reduces women into mechanical drones and subservient harlots. Set over a swathe of time frames beginning in colonial South Africa and progressing to Victorian England and then late 20th-century London, the innovative play tinkers with gender reversals and audience perceptions to re-vamp standard views on gender, love, and social judgments. In the style of Bertolt Brecht, Churchill juggles the cast, choosing male to play female, adult to represent child, and white to pose as black. Glimmers of sexual adventurism break the monotony of a life overwhelmed with sameness and social hypocrisy. In the background, the horrors of imperialism range from floggings to shoot-ing and immolation of natives and the East India Company's rape of natural resources.

The Gilbert-and-Sullivan style of the opening song skewers the duty and fierce optimism of En-glish colonials. At the head of the family is Clive, a morally smug paterfamilias named for Robert Clive, India's first English powermonger. As though extolling himself as family dominator, Fa-ther Clive sings his loyalty to Queen Victoria. Echoing the male supremacy of the times, he as-serts that he is father of his family and of Indians, a blunt expansion of home role to global imperial-ism. Betty's antiphonal echo parodies the ever-faithful wife who lives for her husband by living his ideal. Continuing the round are more unappealing characters—the black servant Joshua, a sly subver-sive ostensibly devoted to his master as "boy," and Edward called Ned, the infantile gay son of Betty and Clive who lives the mock respectability of a gardener while carrying on a two-year affair with the dissolute Gerry (*ibid.*, 4). Compounding the in-termeshing of characters are the governess Ellen's attraction to Betty and the "explorer" Harry Bagley's buggery of Joshua and molestation of Ned.

Churchill's provocative romp over a century of British history airs a panoply of social ills. She breaks the social colonization of individuals into

family roles with droll sexual innuendo, such as Clive's fatigue after a "long ride in the bush" and Edward's propensity for playing with his sister's doll (*ibid.*, 2). Put-downs of English dash and dar-ing compare dying on the frontier with venturing out at night without a shawl and dying of poisoned arrows with missing a picnic. Joshua's creation myth of the great goddess vilifies Africa's despoil-ers as a hundred-eyed, green-tongued monster that befouls the edenic land with greed and exploita-tion. The wooden conversations that reveal wom-anizing, adultery, bisexuality, and marriage of convenience impress on viewers the social con-straints that allow Victorian rigidity to infect the British raj until the rise of FEMINISM in the next century. Churchill's text suggests that Betty's over-throw of her androcentric husband is a model for the salvation of Western civilization.

Bibliography

Amoko, Apollo. "Casting Aside Colonial Occupation: Intersections of Race, Sex, and Gender in *Cloud Nine* and *Cloud Nine* Criticism," *Modern Drama* 42, no. 1 (Spring 1999): 45.

Churchill, Caryl. *Cloud Nine*. New York: Theatre Com-munications Group, 1995.

Nightingale, Benedict. "An Imagination That Pulls Ev-eryone Else Along," *New York Times*, 10 November 2002, sec. 2, p. 7.

Cogewea, the Half-Blood Mourning Dove (1927)

MOURNING DOVE's social romance, *Cogewea, the Half-Blood: A Depiction of the Great Montana Cattle Range* (1927), portrays the Métis (or "mixed race") people and the author's concern for their welfare. Opening in June in the shadow of the Montana Rockies along the Pend d'Oreille River in the early 1900s, the narrative explores the sexism of two white males, the father and the husband of 21-year-old Cogewea McDonald. She remains true to her mother's Okanogan ways despite being "regarded with suspicion by the Indian; shunned by the Cau-casian" (Mourning Dove, 17). Reared along with two sisters in a nurturing MATRIARCHY, she prizes her grandmother's lodge and sweat lodge and splashes in the cold river as rudiments of Native health. The author pictures Cogewea as "own-headed" as well as athletic, adventuresome, and loath to "scorn that which was sacred to the generations past" (ibid., 15, 242). Convent training and the Carlisle Indian School in Pennsylvania introduce her to the white mind-set. She acknowledges the dangers of white EDUCATION, as Indians "had suffered as much from the pen as from the bayonet of conquest" (ibid., 91–92). A sturdy constitution and the absence of eastern fakery earn Cogewea the respect of half-breed cowboys.

From the outset Cogewea accepts the likelihood that her life as an educated half-blood will be difficult, perhaps tragic. She comments, "Life is a gamble, a chance, a mere guess. Cast a line and reel in a splendid rainbow trout or a slippery eel" (ibid., 21). Ruining her first marriage is the deception of Alfred Densmore, a smooth seducer who enriches himself on her federal allotment. Detractors consider him a white cannibal—"Shoyahpee . . . one who eats up everything he sights" (ibid., 289). The author suggests that the invasion of whites into Native lands has reached a saturation point that threatens the survival of indigenous traditions. Living on the cusp, Cogewea eludes assimilation by posing in a teepee in "the custom among the tribes snows ago" and by entering the Fourth of July horse races for ladies and for squaws (ibid., 97–98). She emulates the rebellion of willful half-breeds who "break from the corral erected about us" (ibid., 283).

In a subversion of the androcentric Western romance Cogewea represents both the modern American Indian and the NEW WOMAN. She does penance for her ill-advised marriage to Densmore and revises her expectations in response to Stemteema's wise adage, "The wind changes its course and the hunter must regulate his steps accordingly" (ibid., 249). By rejecting both the white world and the anomalies of reservation life, Cogewea establishes an individualism that is neither squaw nor lady. She finds happiness on the H-B ranch with Jim LaGrinder, the "best rider of the Flathead" and a symbol of enduring Native traditions (ibid., 284). Mourning Dove concludes the plot with a positive omen from a buffalo skull and from the Moon, which appears to bless a more suitable union. The novel extols Cogewea as a heroine for her loyalty to authentic Okanogan values and for her humanity as a survivor refuting the myth of the vanishing Indian.

Bibliography

Cannata, Susan M. "Generic Power Plays in Mourning Dove's Co-ge-we-a," American Indian Quarterly 21, no. 4 (Fall 1997): 703.

Mourning Dove. Cogewea, the Half-Blood: A Depiction of the Great Montana Cattle Range. Lincoln: University of Nebraska Press, 1981.

Coleridge, Mary Elizabeth (1861–1907)

The London-born poet, educator, essayist, and fiction writer Mary Elizabeth Coleridge energized her writings with feminist views on artistry and freedom from restraint. The daughter of musicians, she longed from girlhood to be a member of the School of Pre-Raphaelite painters. She enjoyed the company of two artists, Holman Hunt and John Millais, and of England's Victorian literati, including Robert Bridges, Robert Browning, Fanny KEMBLE, John Ruskin, and Alfred, Lord Tennyson. After thorough tutoring by William Johnson Corey in philosophy, literature, Greek, Hebrew, French, Italian, and German, Coleridge taught grammar and English literature at the Working Women's College for the rest of her life.

Coleridge was content with her classroom teaching and art. She cultivated the Quintette, a network of female students of the Classics. She extolled the single life in "Marriage" (1908), a poem that depicts the wedded woman as the killer of maidenly freedom and joy. In "A Clever Woman" (1907), Coleridge championed women's right to an EDUCATION. Her artistic stimuli were the social elan of Elizabeth GASKELL and the luminosity of Christina ROSSETTI, but Coleridge lacked the enthusiasm for society of the first and the religious fervor of the second. From her writings, she allowed the publication of stories, reviews, and essays in Charlotte Yonge's Monthly Packet, Cornhill Magazine, the Guardian, Monthly Review, Reflector, and Times Literary Supplement. She published novels and historical romances, including a fictionalized biography of Madame de STAËL. However, perhaps out of fear of comparison to Samuel Taylor

Coleridge, a distant relative, Mary Coleridge kept most of her poems hidden or else issued them anonymously under the Greek name *Anados* (the wanderer).

Much of Coleridge's renown derives from posthumously published verse that reflects her receptivity to the great writers of the romantic and Victorian eras and to her vision of the NEW WOMAN. "The Witch" (1907) dramatizes the mature female who responds at last to the creative spirit. The poem directs the threat of the pleading witch to the Victorian woman's insularity. As Emily BRONTË's *WUTHERING HEIGHTS* (1847) through the boldly sensual Catherine EARNSHAW, Coleridge's poem "The White Women" (1908) conjures up wild, Medusa-like divinities, belligerent femmes fatales who slake their sexual passions. In *The Madwoman in the Attic* (1981), the feminist critics Sandra GILBERT and Susan GUBAR seized on one of the author's most intensely dualist images, "The Other Side of the Mirror" (1908), a portrait of normality facing simmering discontent. The fierce tone unmasks the speaker's rage at the imprisonment of self, "wild / With more than womanly despair" (Gilbert & Guber, 15). Like the unnamed victim in Charlotte Perkins GILMAN's short story "THE YELLOW WALLPAPER" (1892), Coleridge's prisoner is disheveled, speechless, and suffering in secret. The poet's life ended abruptly at age 46 as a result of a burst appendix, leaving her unedited work to be anthologized in 1910 as *Gathered Leaves*.

Bibliography

Coleridge, Mary Elizabeth. *Poems* (1910). Available online. URL: http://www.poemhunter.com/mary-elizabeth-coleridge/poet-3048/. Accessed on October 17, 2005.

Gilbert, Sandra M., and Susan Gubar. *The Madwoman in the Attic.* 2nd ed. New Haven, Conn.: Yale University Press, 2000.

"The Other Side of a Mirror," *Victorian Poetry*, 35, no. 4 (Winter 1997): 508.

Colette (1873–1954)

The urbane columnist, playwright, and literary critic Sidonie Gabrielle Claudine "Gabri" Colette surveyed the relationships of men and women with wit, satire, and realism. A native of Saint-Sauveur-en-Puisaye in Bourgogne, France, she was a liberated female and author before the formal evolution of feminism. From her freethinking mother, she learned contempt for purity, marriage, parenthood, and devotion to only one male. She looked back on the repressed bourgeois womanhood of 1880 and pitied women's shackles. To her they were "idle and cloistered young girls . . . sweet-tempered cattle ruled by men [given to] incurable feminine solitude, ignoble resignation" (Thurman, xiv). Despite her refusal to be enslaved by a husband, she loathed the political side of feminism and ridiculed suffragists, on whom she wished "the whip and the harem" (*ibid.*, xv).

After marrying the music critic Henri "Willy" Gauthier-Villars, Colette settled in Paris at age 20. She involved herself with gay and heterosexual writers, artists, and musicians and began writing the four capricious Claudine novels, which her husband published. She invigorated the texts with her delight in female freedom, amorality, and the cult of hedonism. In *Claudine at School* (1900), the author symbolized the end of 19th-century hypocrisy by razing the double-walled building that attempted to contain a gaggle of lusty schoolgirls. The popular novel sold 40,000 copies in eight weeks.

After a divorce in 1910 Colette danced and mimed at the Moulin Rouge, provided fashion commentary for *Le Matin* and *Vogue*, remarried, and in 1913 gave birth to a daughter, Bel-Gazou. The author's major works were the products of the 1920s and 1930s, a period in which she campaigned for WOMEN'S RIGHTS to "public health, the physical and moral protection of childhood, and with the goal of improving their own condition" (*ibid.*, 417). Despite invalidism caused by degenerative arthritis, Colette campaigned to end the exploitation of the female worker. As did the like actor Sarah Bernhardt, she modeled the bravado of the venturesome female artist who defied the sexism of the stage. She maintained her celebrity after receiving a Royal Belgian Academy citation and the Legion of Honor for volunteer work during World War I. She also became the first woman elected member and subsequent president of the Académie Goncourt. Although the Catholic Church refused her sacramental rites, thousands mourned her at a military funeral and at her interment in Père Lachaise Cemetery.

Colette's writing enlarged the scope of female AUTOBIOGRAPHY by merging the boundaries between memoir and imagination. By remaining upbeat and purposeful, she defied the Gallic male hierarchy with 50 titles exposing moral decadence, jaded social intercourse, and tarnished aesthetics tinged with her own brand of delightful, but mercenary feminism. Her stories and novellas, filled with innuendo and double-entendre, play innocent, experienced, and idealistic females against gigolos, roués, philanderers, bisexuals, and madams. As France returned to normal after World War II, she published *Gigi* (1944), a droll account of the molding of a coquette, Gilberte, for success and INDEPENDENCE in the demimonde. Tutoring her is a seasoned Grandmama, who insists, "Drawers are one thing, decorum is another. . . . Everything depends on the attitude" (Colette, 1952, 4) Aunt Alicia, a pragmatist, warns the charming Gilberte that girls of her class marry "after" rather than "before." Two pervasive themes in this and other of Colette's works are the joys of sensuality and the self-knowledge and self-regard that women earn by reserving the inner female for themselves. Her charming insouciance offered material for two screen adaptations by the scenarist Anita LOOS, *Gigi* (1952) and *Cheri* (1959), and influenced the feminist writings of Erica JONG, who provided an introduction for *The Colette Omnibus* (1974).

Bibliography

Brunazzi, Elizabeth. "The Question of Colette and Collaboration," *Tulsa Studies in Women's Literature* 13, no. 2 (Fall 1994): 281–291.

Colette. *The Colette Omnibus.* Garden City, N.Y.: Nelson Doubleday, 1974.

———. *Gigi, Julie de Corneilha, and Chance Acquaintances: Three Short Novels.* New York: Farrar, Straus & Giroux, 1952.

Southworth, Helen. "Rooms of Their Own: How Colette Uses Physical and Textual Space to Question a Gendered Literary Tradition," *Tulsa Studies in Women's Literature* 20, no. 2 (Fall 2001): 253–278.

Thurman, Judith. *Secrets of the Flesh: A Life of Colette.* New York: Ballantine, 1999.

Color Purple, The **Alice Walker** (1982)

Based on the experiences of a family matriarch, the author's great-grandmother, who was raped at age 12, *The Color Purple* set the standard for truth-telling feminist fiction. Its author, Alice WALKER, chose epistolary form for its intimate glimpse of the inner pain of Celie, the betrayed daughter and wife living on a rural Georgia farm early in the 1900s. The author subverts both villains by erasing Alphonso as Celie's birth father and by calling her callous husband Mr. _____, conferring no surname to dignify his malice. He ignores her inner needs while exploiting her body as a bearer of domestic burdens and a source of unilateral sexual release. At a pivotal moment in the text, he sneers at Celie that she is black, poor, unattractive, and female. Mr. _____, among his crimes against Celie, hides letters from her sister, Nettie, the family safety "net," the one source of joy in Celie's life.

A victim of incest, infanticide, father murder, and mother madness, Celie depersonalizes herself as a means of enduring cyclical wretchedness. She explains, "I make myself wood. I say to myself, Celie, you a tree" (*ibid.,* 23). When she writes painfully naive letters to God, she asks for nothing, expects nothing. The author indicates that SISTERHOOD is a more viable source of aid than piety by supplying Celie with earthly models of courage and self-assertion. From her daughter-in-law, Sofia, Celie witnesses a woman willing to demand respect from a man; from the hard-charging soul singer Lilly "Shug" Avery and her pulsing jazz performances, Celie learns to answer her own needs, both carnal and emotional, and to stop writing letters to God. At Shug's manipulation of her clitoris, Celie acknowledges the rightness of sexual expression: "A little shiver go through me . . . just enough to tell me this the right button" (*ibid.,* 82). Shug accuses Celie of bowing under mule's work: "It's scandless [*stet*], the way you look out there plowing in a dress" (*ibid.,* 153). The grand makeover occurs appropriately at Easter. By reclaiming SEXUALITY, autonomy, and voice, Celie is able to look her master in the eye and undermine his self-esteem as he had once robbed her of worth: Walker further demeans Mr. _____ with his startled reply, "ButButButBut-But" (*ibid.*).

Celie's reclamation by the women in her life raised a stir among censorious conservatives and male readers, who charged Walker with exalting lesbianism over heterosexual love, blaspheming against God, and maligning all black men as daughter rapists and wife exploiters. Nonetheless, from a feminist perspective, Celie's rise to urban entrepreneur and landowner is a life-affirming triumph. Improvising a career much as Shug improvises songs, Celie turns inborn talent into a source of income after making a gift for Shug, "the perfect pair of pants," a symbol of liberating ANDROGYNY (*ibid.*, 219). Swamped with orders, Celie opens Folkspants, Unlimited, in Memphis. Like a small child, she sums up the change in her outlook: "I am so happy. I got love, I got work, I got money, friends and time" (*ibid.*, 222). As though ending a FAIRY TALE, Walker cancels the privations of Celie's childhood with an inheritance of her family's house and land and a reunion with her two children and her sister, Nettie.

Bibliography

Marvin, Thomas F. " 'Preachin' the Blues': Bessie Smith's Secular Religion and Alice Walker's *The Color Purple*," *African American Review* 28, no. 3 (Fall 1994): 411–421.

Selzer, Linda. "Race and Domesticity in *The Color Purple*," *African American Review* 29, no. 1 (Spring 1995): 67–82.

Walker, Alice. *The Color Purple*. New York: Washington Square Press, 1983.

Coming of Age in Samoa Margaret Mead (1928)

One of the acknowledged female intellectuals of the early 20th century, 23-year-old Margaret MEAD produced a classic study of tribal life in *Coming of Age in Samoa: A Psychological Study of Primitive Youth for Western Civilisation* (1928). In an examination of the relatively carefree life passages of girls on the island of T'au, the author showed to a generation of social scientists that gendered behaviors are not innate. Influenced by the philoso-

phy of the anthropologist Franz Boas, she took advantage of her gender to enlighten a consortium of mostly male ethnographers on the behavior of girls, whom field workers tended to ignore. At the outset, she attempted to explain an American phenomenon, "the omnipresent and obvious symptoms of an unrest" known as the "awkward age" (Mead, 4, 5). Over a period of five months she scrutinized cultural constraints in American Samoa and the more arbitrary standards of the United States that both helped and hindered the young in acclimating to adulthood.

Mead's forthright examination of island morality in the chapter "Formal Sex Relations" shocked the puritanical Christian reader. She describes the formal acceptance of wedlock, fornication, and adultery as the major patterns of adult sexual behavior. Of relations between unmarried heterosexuals, she lists clandestine amours, elopements, polite boy-girl wooing, and the "surreptitious rape, called *moetotolo*, sleep crawling, resorted to by youths who find favor in no maiden's eyes" (*ibid.*, 89). In the style of a travelogue, she summarizes her adaptation to island culture to glimpse teen girls within their peer group and to observe an adult SISTERHOOD at birthings and rituals. She observes the women's feast, dances, and sexual partnering and draws conclusions about women's attitudes toward virginity, birth control, infant and child care, monogamy and straying husbands, and barrenness.

In a comparison to the Western romantic ideals of her own time, Mead draws inferences from Samoans concerning the illogic of Western sexual mores. Among island children reared on a relaxed attitude toward free love, she discloses a lack of jealousy, suicide, and crimes of passion. She reports no frigidity, sexual dysfunction, or neurosis based on the suppression of masturbation. She concludes that Samoan society maintains control of overt SEXUALITY by admonishing displays of affection and promiscuity. She adds that having "many lovers as long as possible . . . [was a] uniform and satisfying ambition" yet dims any misreading of enforced debauchery by stressing that "sex activity is never urged upon the young" (*ibid.*, 156, 157, 232). One of her most significant observations is the atmosphere in which the islanders are "urged to learn, urged to behave, urged to work, but . . . not urged to hasten in choices which they make themselves" (*ibid.*, 231). Her treatise encouraged decades of child-rearing theories on natural development and a focus on individual happiness as a life goal.

Bibliography

Cote, James E. "The Implausibility of Freeman's Hoaxing Theory: An Update," *Journal of Youth and Adolescence* 29, no. 5 (October 2000): 575.

Mead, Margaret. *Coming of Age in Samoa: A Psychological Study of Primitive Youth for Western Civilisation.* New York: Perennial, 2001.

Rappaport, Roy A. "Desecrating the Holy Woman," *American Scholar* 55, no. 3 (Spring 1986): 313–347.

Condé, Maryse (1937–)

The dramatist, critic, folklorist, and historical novelist Maryse Boucolon Condé, dubbed the Grande Dame of French Caribbean literature, is skilled at the hypnotic telling of female lives. Literary historians credit her with being the first author to connect the French Caribbean with the New England colonies and the first to create an introspective narrative on what it means to be West Indian. A native of Pointe-à-Pitre, Guadeloupe, and daughter of a business executive and a schoolteacher, Condé grew up in a strict middle-class, Francophile environment that allowed no island customs or Creole speech from the eight children. When at age 16 Maryse left the Caribbean for Paris to study English at Lycée Fénélon and the Sorbonne, she deliberately sought fellow expatriates from the French Antilles as friends. She taught language arts in Ghana, the Ivory Coast, and Senegal before settling in London in 1968 to produce media programs for the British Broadcasting Corporation (BBC). In her 30s and 40s she returned to the classroom in Jussieu and Nanterre and at the Sorbonne, the University of California at Berkeley, and Columbia University.

Simultaneously with her teaching career, Condé began writing. She supplied dramas for the stage in the 1970s and produced two novels, *Hérémakhonon* (1976) and *Une saison à Rihata* (A Season in Rihata, 1981), both of which place female

protagonists in the grip of colonial corruption. She earned critical acclaim for *Ségou: Les murailles de Terre* (*The Children of Segu*, 1984) and *Ségou: La Terre en miettes* (Segu: The earth in pieces, 1985), a two-part saga of the Traore DYNASTY at the height of the slave trade. After considerable research at Occidental College in Los Angeles on a Fulbright scholarship, she won a Grand Prix Littéraire de la Femme for *Moi, Tituba, sorcière noire Salem* (*I, Tituba, Black Witch of Salem*, 1986), a fictional *marronisme*, a literary portrayal of renegade blacks in flight from slavery. The author grew so enamored of her subject that she described in the dedication the close relationship between female author and female protagonist: "Tituba and I lived for a year on the closest of terms. During our endless conversations she told me things she had confided to nobody else" (Condé, 1994, xii).

The story describes the historical Anglo-Ashanti slave Tituba, who was born as the result of an English sailor's rape of her mother on the *Christ the King*, a slave ship that carried her over the Middle Passage from Africa. Tituba served a prison sentence for allegedly introducing the girls of Salem, Massachusetts, to fortune-telling and WITCHCRAFT. Unlike Nathaniel Hawthorne's Hester PRYNNE, who chooses silence over confession of her child's parentage in *The SCARLET LETTER* (1860), Condé's Tituba returns to Barbados and goes to the gallows before she can give birth. Her brutal SILENCING illustrates the lack of choices open to people in bondage. In the novel's introduction, the freedom fighter Angela Y. DAVIS admired the black slave for her persistence: "In the final analysis, Tituba's revenge consists in reminding us all that the doors of our suppressed cultural histories are still ajar" (*ibid.*, xiii).

In the novel's introduction, Davis lauds Condé for defeating the exoticized stereotypes of black females by identifying Tituba as the unloved child of her rape. As a historic practitioner of the African oral tradition Tituba internalizes the misogyny of the times, which teaches her that "Men do not love. They possess. They subjugate" (*ibid.*, 14). After her relocation from the Caribbean to the Massachusetts Colony, she voices her rejection of the racism, oppression, and religious superiority of New England Puritans: "Oh no, they won't get me to be the same as they are! I will not give in" (*ibid.*, 69). Her firm self-possession helps her survive the insanity of witch hunting.

Condé specializes in tracing sources of alienation and otherness in females. The interrelated themes invigorate the three-generational matrilineage in the novel *Désirada* (2000) and in *Célanire Cou-coupé* (2001), the story of Marie-No'lle, an infant left to die in a trash heap after her attacker jaggedly sliced her throat. Having identified with Emily BRONTË's gothic novel WUTHERING HEIGHTS (1847) in her teens, Condé reset the story in the Caribbean under the title *La Migration des Coeurs* (*Windward Heights*, 1995), a tale of passion told in Faulknerian stream of consciousness through such peripheral female voices as Mabo Sandrine and Sanjita the Housekeeper. In addition to the multigenerational melodrama of Razye's fascination with Cathy, the author details postemancipation issues of racism and elitism in Cuba and Guadeloupe and stresses the emergence of Creole culture from its various roots, including voodoo. Of the residual strength of island slavery, Mabo Julie predicts, "Oh no, slavery isn't over for someone like me. I suppose I'll always remain a slave to white folks" (Condé, 1998, 111). More hopeful, but less realistic is Etiennise, Sanjita's daughter, who eludes colonialism in dreams of a male rescuer who will take her far away.

Bibliography

Condé, Maryse. *I, Tituba, Black Witch of Salem.* New York: Ballantine, 1994.
———. *Windward Heights.* New York: Soho, 1998.
Nuñez, Elizabeth. "Talking to Maryse Condé: Grand Dame of Caribbean Literature," *UNESCO Courier* 53, no. 11 (November 2000): 46–51.
Pascale, De Souza. "Demystifying Female Marooning: Oppositional Strategies and the Writing of Testimonies in the French Caribbean," *International Journal of Francophone Studies* 3, no. 3 (2000): 141–150.
Singh, Christine. "Review: Windward Heights," *Canadian Woman Studies* 20, no. 1 (Spring 2000): 110.

confinement

The subject of cloistering women or locking them in prison cells, tower rooms, or asylums besets much of feminist literature. The concept is as old as the imprisonment of PERSEPHONE in hell in Greek mythology, the nursery rhyme "Peter, Peter Pumpkin Eater," and the FAIRY TALES of Rapunzel and Snow White. An integral plot device in gothic convention, imprisonment takes place in nunneries, oubliettes, tower rooms, trapdoors, caves, and dungeon cells, all of which afflict the victim with a living death such as that faced by the heroine Emily St. Aubert in Ann RADCLIFFE's *The Mysteries of Udolpho* (1794). In 1783, the historical novelist Sophia LEE used the metaphor of confining spaces as a commentary on the lives of suppressed females, the heroines of her three-volume domestic novel *The Recess; or, A Tale of Other Times* (1783–85). Lack of liberty derives from the long-lived DOUBLE STANDARD, which blesses men with freedom of expression and exploration of SEXUALITY while restricting women to more stringent social, educational, moral, and religious codes. The physical shackling in distressed damsel fiction is an overt twin of covert patriarchal decision making that chooses for women whom they will see, where they will go, what they will read, and which men they will marry.

The concerted attack on confinement caused literary critics, the clergy, and male traditionalists to shame and ostracize feminist writers such as Aphra BEHN, the BRONTËs, George ELIOT, and Mary WOLLSTONECRAFT. Despite the outcry from conservatives, in 1832, the rebellious French novelist George SAND published *Indiana*, a novel that replicates the terrors of BEAUTY AND THE BEAST. The action follows a wife from unhappy submission to Colonel Delmare, her husband, to full revolt against the institution of marriage. In part 3 at the height of their confrontation of wills, she declares, "You used violence in keeping me in my chamber. I escaped by my window to show you, that reigning over a woman's will is exercising an imaginary sway. . . . I depend upon myself alone on this earth" (Sand, 1900). Indiana's self-rescue expresses a feminist belief that women should abandon the fantasy rescue motif of Gothic fiction and look to themselves for succor. Male writers such as the American novelist Charles Brockden Brown also entered the fray by depicting stout-hearted women who were capable of deciding their own destiny. In

Nathaniel Hawthorne's moral romance *The SCAR-LET LETTER* (1850), the adulteress Hester PRYNNE sits out part of her pregnancy, childbirth, and early motherhood in a New World lockup gated in oak beams and iron bands. When she gains her freedom, Hawthorne describes Hester's daily confrontations with a judgmental citizenry, male and female, that extends her imprisonment through gossip, taunts, and social marginalizing of mother and child. A small symbolic gesture, a wild rose blossoming by the prison door, suggests the author's tribute to a character who receives little comfort or relief from a lifetime of boundaries.

The novelist and ghostwriter Santha Rama RAU offered an Asian example of confinement that affected only upper-class women and royalty. She expounded on the stultifying existence of refined Indian women under traditional purdah, which required shielding from the public eye and constant chaperonage for brief ventures outdoors. In *A Princess Remembers: The Memoirs of the Maharani of Jaipur* (1976), the author pictures variations in the degree of seclusion that Indian women experienced. At home, Princess Gayatri Devi, one of the last of Jaipur's queens, rode in cars with darkened window glass. When she traveled to Udaipur, she was forced into a medieval form of seclusion— "to go about in a car with heavy wooden shutters, enclosing us in a blind, airless box" (Rau, 203). Even worse is lake travel in a boat veiled in curtains, which limits Devi's picturetaking and enjoyment of scenery and cooling breezes. Ironically, the queen has less personal freedom than does the lowest female servant.

In *The BURNING BED: The True Story of Francine Hughes, a Beaten Wife Who Rebels* (1980), Faith McNulty's famed book, confinement is more emotional, more lethal than the draped cells of Indian purdah. The story, based on a true crime, depicts the continual terrorizing of a wife and mother of three. Francine's drunken husband, Mickey, batters her about the face and trunk and tyrannizes her three children by making them stay in their rooms. Francine's thoughts roil with the urgency of a situation that may kill her, the children, or all four. Her state of mind at the time she burns Mickey alive becomes crucial to her attorney's defense. McNulty records, "Get in the car and go.

Drive all night. Drive all tomorrow. Don't think about what happens after that! Don't think of anything except going! Go! And never turn back!" (McNulty, 193). The mystic impetus to flee stems from an adrenaline rush that leaves Francine "thrilled; scared; elated; the way you feel just before the roller coaster begins to roll" (*ibid.*).

Alice WALKER produced a layered study of marital and racial confinement in *The COLOR PURPLE* (1982), a feminist work that earned the Pulitzer Prize. She contrasts multiple forms of shackling beginning with the sexual abuse of the protagonist Celie when she enters puberty. The mental chains desensitize her through a series of agonies—her stepfather's siring of her daughter and son, the reported deaths of her children, a brokered marriage to Mr. _____, and domestic toil on behalf of messy, demanding stepchildren. After her stepson Harpo marries, the decline of Celie's daughter-in-law, Sofia, broadens the author's survey of confinement with the injustice of Sofia's undeserved prison sentence. In Celie's description to Nettie, "Polices [sic] lock her up for sassing the mayor's wife and hitting the mayor back. First she was in prison working in the laundry and dying fast" (Walker, 205). Sofia summarizes the effects: "They won't let me see my children. They won't let me see no mens. Well, after five years they let me see [my oldest boy] once a year. I'm a slave" (*ibid.*, 108). When she gains an early release and sits like a sphinx at an Easter feast with her family, she surprises all with her first words, "like a voice speaking from the grave" (*ibid.*, 207).

In a gesture of respect for China's emergence from the imperial era, the Chinese-American novelist Amy TAN pictures women who outsmart the closeting of feudal marriage. In *The Joy Luck Club* (1989), she portrays the child bride Lindo Jong confined to her bed until she can produce a son by her immature husband Tyan-yu. With nothing to do but reflect on her confinement, Lindo plots the perfect escape by pretending to have a dream that requires Tyan-yu to marry a servant girl. Lindo's mother-in-law is so pleased with the propitious dream that she frees Lindo from the marriage contract and gives her money to make a new life. In Tan's second novel, *The Kitchen God's Wife* (1991), the protagonist, Winnie Louie, makes a symbolic gesture of escape by choosing a jail sentence over a return to her psychopathic husband, Wen Fu. Although the women's prison is foul, she uses the time to teach other women how to fend for themselves in the outside world through personal grooming, good manners, and manufacturing skills. As do the tough women in Jeanne Wakatsuki HOUSTON and James Houston's *A Farewell to Manzanar* (1973), Isabel ALLENDE's *The HOUSE OF THE SPIRITS* (1982), and Margaret DRABBLE's *The Red Queen* (2004), Winnie maintains a positive attitude during her incarceration and uplifts other women. She triumphs over the trumped-up sentence and returns to freedom much stronger for the experience.

Bibliography

Lee, Sophia. *The Recess; or, A Tale of Other Times.* Louisville: University Press of Kentucky, 2000.

McNulty, Faith. *The Burning Bed.* New York: Harcourt Brace Jovanovich, 1980.

Rau, Santha Rama. *A Princess Remembers: The Memoirs of the Maharani of Jaipur.* Philadelphia: J. B. Lippincott, 1976.

Sand, George. *Indiana* (1900). Available online. URL: http://digital.library.upenn.edu/women/sand/indiana/indiana.html. Accessed on October 13, 2005.

Walker, Alice. *The Color Purple.* New York: Washington Square Press, 1983.

Cooper, Anna Julia (1856–1964)

A fount of black American feminism, Anna Julia Hayward Cooper exposed the interwoven tyranny of colonialism, sexism, elitism, and racism. A North Carolinian from Raleigh, she was conceived from the sexual bondage of Hannah Stanley to a white master, George Washington Haywood. While working as a nanny in the white lawyer's home, Cooper educated herself with books from Haywood's library. Well schooled in history, math, and classical and Romance languages at Oberlin, the Sorbonne, and Columbia University, she developed radical notions of liberty and equality that required the crushing of the powerful white male and a simultaneous elevation of the black female. While teaching at Saint Augustine's Normal and Collegiate Insti-

tute in her hometown, she campaigned for educational opportunities for women. She promoted learning experiences for blacks in Camp Fire Girls and the Young Women's Christian Association (YWCA) and lauded support for working mothers at a settlement house in Washington, D.C., and at the nontraditional Frelinghuysen University, a night school that offered adult literacy, religious, and vocational programs.

Cooper produced a landmark collection of essays, *A Voice from the South by a Black Woman of the South* (1892). Without reserve, she charges men for a deceptive courtesy toward females: "Respect for women, the much lauded chivalry of the Middle Ages, meant what I fear it still means to some men in our own day—respect for the elect few among whom they expect to consort" (Cooper, 55). The text expresses the frustration of black female writers that their EDUCATION is limited and their voices remain suppressed after nearly four decades of emancipation. In Cooper's view, educated women temper the male search for truth with the female gift for mercy. She exalts the necessity of educating children and urges humanity to "resolve to make the most of it—not the boys less, but the girls more" (*ibid.*, 87).

Bibliography

Cooper, Anna Julia. *The Voice of Anna Julia Cooper.* Lanham, Md.: Rowman & Littlefield, 1998.

Gates, Henry Louis, ed. *Reading Black, Reading Feminist: A Critical Anthology.* New York: Meridian, 1990.

Smith, Margaret Supplee, and Emily Herring Wilson. *North Carolina Women Making History.* Chapel Hill: University of North Carolina Press, 1999.

Corelli, Marie (1855–1924)

A lesbian author of occult and exotic verse and fiction, Marie Corelli chose ambiguous diction and muted images to veil her portrayals of women in their rightful expression of SEXUALITY. Born Mary "Minnie" Mills Mackay in Perth, Scotland, she was the illegitimate child of a musician and his serving woman. For the rest of her life, questions concerning Corelli's birth fueled her mistrust of the highborn and privileged. She loved books and music in childhood and developed diverse interests in concert piano, astral projection, and spiritualism. She studied at home under governesses and attended a convent academy. As she developed literary skills, she chose as a pseudonym the Italian surname *Corelli*, meaning "little heart." At Mason Croft, Stratford, she resided with Bertha Vyver, her lover and biographer, and developed a reputation for public oratory and for exhibitionism by rowing up the Avon River in a gondola. At the peak of her popularity, Corelli outsold her classic contemporaries Sir Arthur Conan Doyle, Rudyard Kipling, Robert Louis Stevenson, H. G. Wells, and Oscar Wilde and provided plots for 15 silent films.

Corelli mastered the Gothic conventions of blood oaths, secrets and disguises, live burials, and sensual glamour. Her daring scenarios resulted in suppression of her works by some circulating libraries. After *Blackwood's Edinburgh Magazine* refused to publish her stories, she seized a large share of the Gothic market with a first novel, *The Romance of Two Worlds* (1886), a study of faith and skepticism. She followed with a horror romance of Europe's black plague epidemic, *Vendetta!; or, The Story of One Forgotten* (1886). As an introit to despair and doom Corelli depicts Fabio, the Italian misogynist, bedazzled by the IDEAL WOMAN, an unspoiled young woman named Nina: "One face beaming out like a star . . . a loveliness absolutely perfect, lighted up by two luminous eyes, large and black as night—one face in which the small, curved mouth smiled half provokingly, half sweetly!" (Corelli, 1886). The grandiose imagery prepares the reader for the downfall of a man already primed for disillusion and betrayal.

Corelli experimented with dominant female characters. She applied the overpowering female to supernatural fiction in *Ardath: The Story of a Dead Self* (1889), one of her most popular titles. In a lascivious moment, the author pictures the angel Edris mastering the male protagonist: "Fear nothing, my beloved! . . . Thou hast slept ONE night on the Field of Ardath, in the Valley of Vision!—but lo! the Night is past! . . . Rise! and behold the dawning of thy new Day!" (Corelli 1889). In the final paragraph, Corelli sweeps away the gauzy fantasy and identifies Edris as "Nothing but a woman, most pure womanly; a woman whose influence on all is strangely sweet and last-

ing" (*ibid.*). The author implies that ordinary women are capable of the same powers as fantasy women if given a chance to develop their amiability and sensual allure.

Corelli was an experimenter. She chose a Faustian mystique for *The Soul of Lilith* (1892), a depiction of clairvoyance. Still testing the market, Corelli completed a historical melodrama, *Barabbas: A Dream of the World's Tragedy* (1893), which she packed with satanism, decadence, and religious ambiguities. The sequel, *The Sorrows of Satan; or, The Strange Experience of One Geoffrey Tempest, Millionaire* (1895), portrayed urban vice and the emergence of the NEW WOMAN in the writer Mavis Claire. For its delineation of male vanity, the novel became the nation's first overnight sensation, selling 100,000 copies in one year. It was adapted to the screen in 1911, 1916, 1917, 1920, and 1926.

Corelli claimed as fans the stage elite—the actors Lily Langtry and Ellen Terry—and royalty—Czarina Alexandra of Russia and her mother, Queen Victoria. The writer's ability to meet reader demand soon earned her advances of 10,000 pounds per book. In a decade that yielded celebrity, she learned the price exacted from a talented female. In the introduction to *The Murder of Delicia* (1896), Corelli stated her feminist creed: "The woman who paints a great picture is 'unsexed'; the woman who writes a great book is 'unsexed'; in fact, whatever woman does that is higher and more ambitious than the mere act of flinging herself down at the feet of man and allowing him to walk over her" (Corelli, 1997, 1). In 1905, she summarized her opinions on the advancement of women and feminist art in *Free Opinions Freely Expressed on Certain Phases of Modern Social Life and Conduct*. Her next immediate best seller, *The Treasures of Heaven: A Romance of Riches* (1906), burdened bookshops with reader demand for 100,000 copies the first day.

Bibliography

Corelli, Maria. *Ardath* (1889). Available online. URL: http://www.gutenberg.org/etext/5114. Accessed on October 13, 2005.

———. *The Murder of Delicia.* Whitefish, Mont.: Kessinger, 1997.

————. *Vendetta* (1886). Available online. URL: http://www.gutenberg.org/dirs/etext03/vndtt10.txt. Accessed on October 13, 2005.

Forward, Stephanie. "Idol of Suburbia: Marie Corelli and Late-Victorian Culture," *Critical Survey* 13, no. 2 (May 2001): 141–144.

Jones, Susan. " 'Creatures of Our Light Literature': The Problem of Genre in *The Inheritors* and Marie Corelli's *A Romance of Two Worlds*," *Conradiana* (Spring–Summer 2002): 107–122.

Moers, Ellen. *Literary Women*. New York: Oxford University Press, 1977.

Corinne, or Italy Madame de Staël (1807)

The semiautobiographical novel *Corinne, ou l'Italie* (*Corinne, or Italy*) presents Madame de STAËL's progressive vision of the NEW WOMAN as intellectual and artist. The title figure, an independent poet compared to the Greek SAPPHO, dies of the repressive nature of her relationship with a 25-year-old Scotsman, Oswald, Lord Nevil. Echoing the constraints of the Napoleonic era, the novel depicts the influence of the historical period on the romantic ideal. Amid the pageantry of Holy Week in 1794–95 Italian architecture and statuary, traditions, music, festivals, and countryside, the tragic romance plays out, beginning with Oswald's expatriation to cure weak lungs and emotional ennui. His invigorating encounter with the brilliant, ambitious Corinne introduces him to a populist spirit dedicated to pure art, which the author describes as the voice of God rendered in lyric verse and improvisational drama.

During Corinne's affair with Oswald, the author depicts her as the sybil leading the uninitiated through Italy's physically ingratiating milieu. The threat of malaria in Rome, a symbol of Europe's destabilization in the years after the French Revolution, forces the couple to recuperate out of season in Venice for six weeks, from early September to mid-November. Their arrival coincides with cannonfire that signals a young novice's acceptance into a convent, a subtextual comment on female oppression. The metaphor foretokens Corinne's willing retreat from metropolitan Rome to a confining atmosphere. Oswald's increasing PATRIARCHY presages the SILENCING of women, a symbolic overlayering of feminine perspective that the couple had viewed in the lava burial of ancient Romans in Pompeii. Like a walled medieval city that sequesters its citizens, his authority over Corinne suppresses her creativity, rewarding her with letters in decreasing number.

In the end, Corinne is unable to turn her ideal of self-determination into reality. After concealing her birth to an Englishman, Corinne suffers betrayal after Oswald follows his father's dictates to marry Lucile, Corinne's home-centered half sister. Suitably, he recedes into dull home life with doubts about his treatment of his lover and his devaluation of her genius. The falling action shifts from literary attainment to disillusion and emotional vulnerability, the weaknesses that precede her retreat from celebrity and her eventual death of isolation and a broken heart. At the demise of her frail body, her spirit remains alive in the influence of her art and in the genetic inheritance of her niece Juliette. Corinne's poetry becomes the legacy to all women who seek inspiration from art. The immortality of Corinne's republican zeal and her female productivity defied stodgy gendered conventions of the early 1800s and influenced a host of readers, including the major Victorian feminists—Jane AUSTEN, Elizabeth Barrett BROWNING, George ELIOT, Felicia HEMANS, Mary SHELLEY, and Harriet Beecher STOWE.

Bibliography

Levy, Gayle A. "A Genius for the Modern Era: Madame de Staël's *Corinne*," *Nineteenth-Century French Studies* (Spring–Summer 2002): 242–254.

Schlick, Yael. "Beyond the Boundaries: Staël, Genlis, and the Impossible 'Femme Celebre,' " *Symposium* 50, no. 1 (Spring 1996): 50–63.

Staël, Germaine de. *Corinne; or, Italy*. Piscataway, N.J.: Rutgers University Press, 1987.

Corregidora Gayl Jones (1975)

A tribute to matrilineal memory, Gayl JONES's multilayered novella *Corregidora* salutes the passing of wisdom from elders to succeeding generations. In the 1930s, the protagonist, Ursa Corregidora, learns from her great grandmother, Great Gram, the family's history of bondage, concubinage, rape, and incest that targeted Usa's mother and grand-mother. The STORYTELLING that begins when Usa is five years old impresses on her the task of the family witness "to burn out what they put in our minds, like you burn out a wound" (Jones, 72). Like a laboratory animal, Ursa grows up imprinted by the 19th century as though "Their past in my blood. . . . My veins are centuries meeting" (*ibid.*, 45–46). Stream-of-consciousness images nurture female rage. Disturbing scenes illuminate the Por-tuguese slaver Corregidora as the sadist who fa-thered Ursa's mother and grandmother and as the focus of Ursa's loathing and mistrust of white males. She suffers his feral cruelty "howling" within and demands, "How many generations had to bow to his genital fantasies?" (*ibid.*, 46, 59).

Complicating Ursa's survival is the loss of her womb, a truncation of the genetic line that threat-ens the transmission of the Corregidora saga. Her weapon against despair is a career in singing the blues at the Happy Café, an ironic name for the destructive atmosphere that dooms her love life. Her creative "new world song" becomes both catharsis and solace (*ibid.*, 59). She explains, "I sang because it was something I had to do" (*ibid.*, 3). Her lyrics speak the traumas of the silenced and oppressed, "as if their memory, the memory of all the Corregidora women, was her memory too, as strong with her as her own private memory, or almost as strong" (*ibid.*, 129). Jones builds to Ursa's confrontation with the past when Mutt, her pos-sessive first husband, returns after a 20-year ab-sence, bearing the threat that the Corregidora women had known from slave days. Ursa's epiphany results during fellatio, an act meant to placate Mutt. Ursa realizes that her Great Gram also avoided penetration by taking the penis of "the Portuguese slave breeder and whoremonger" in her mouth and becoming temporarily the recep-tacle of his semen and the controller of his genera-tive powers (*ibid.*, 8).

Jones uses naming as an indicator of her pro-tagonist's legacy from colonial times to the future. Ursa's mother identifies her before birth as "one of us" (*ibid.*, 117). Ursa's strength shines through the given name meaning "bear woman," but the trans-lation also implies a pun on "bearing" children, the obligation to "make generations" that the loss of

her uterus thwarts (*ibid.*, 10). Through two mar-riages, she retains her birth surname, which once identified the Portuguese tormentor as the "disci-plinarian" of slaves. "Corregidora" brands her an il-legitimate offspring and simultaneously exalts her as the "corrector" of the evils inflicted on black women, a quest that she accomplishes by replacing burned records of SLAVERY with oral tradition. Tadpole McCormick, her employer and second husband, contributes to the naming trend by nick-naming her "U.C.," pronounced, "You see," a shorthand reference to her value as witness of the crimes that undergirded Brazil's plantation econ-omy (*ibid.*, 4).

Bibliography

Hochberg, Gil Zehava. "Mother, Memory, History: Ma-ternal Genealogies in Gayl Jones's *Corregidora* and Simone Schwarz-Bart's *Pluie et Vent sur Télumée Miracle*," *Research in African Literatures* 34, no. 2 (Summer 2003): 1–12.

Jones, Gayl. *Corregidora.* New York: Random House, 1975.

Yukins, Elizabeth. "Bastard Daughters and the Posses-sion of History in *Corregidora* and *Paradise*," *Signs: Journal of Women in Culture and Society* 28, no. 1 (Autumn 2002): 221–247.

Country of the Pointed Firs, The Sarah Orne Jewett (1896)

A gemlike novella, Sarah Orne JEWETT's *The Country of the Pointed Firs* (1896) exemplifies the tourist allegory. Surrounded by "the rocky shore and dark woods," the seaboard in the story is a haven of cottages that nest among ledges like bird sanctuaries among rocks (Jewett, 1). The repetitive nature of tides and seasons rejuvenates and liber-ates local people from the unremarkable tragedies of disappointment, illness, and death. Even women who have died remain vivid in memory. The wid-ower Elijah Tilley remarks of his companionable wife, Sarah, eight years after her death, "I miss her just the same every day" (*ibid.*, 121). The herbalist Almira Todd, the widowed healer of the ailing neighbors of Dunnet Landing, Maine, becomes the region's story keeper. The antithesis of the brutal-ized females of the New England witch hunts,

Almira bears the name of the wonder worker, a doer of good akin to the Hispanic *curandera.*

Lauded by the novelist Willa Cather as an American classic equal in importance to Nathaniel HAWTHORNE's *The SCARLET LETTER* (1850) and Mark Twain's *Huckleberry Finn* (1884), Jewett's meditative summer idyll celebrates the female realm for its serenity and cyclical perspective. The female cycle dominates a cheery herb bed, where Almira grows pennyroyal, an abortifacient essential to folk gynecology of both New England Indian women and white pioneers (*ibid.,* 5). Character miniatures dramatize the intimacy and quiet grace of rural folk—a "wisdom-giving stroll" with Almira, Mrs. Blackett's consensus building, Mrs. Fosdick's farewell to Calvinist guilt, the nobility of bakers of apple pies, and the thrift of braiders of rag rugs. The latter handicraft is a familiar project of women of limited means, who place frayed materials in a new context, a form of pulling the past into the present to form new patterns of design and texture.

Jewett's focus on creative solitude, conversational visits, the social fluidity of the rare "high days and holidays," and the sharing of anecdotes centers women in the oral tradition that builds community (*ibid.,* 76). The subtle dynamics of friendship and spiritual uplift capture the soul of FEMINISM—the bonding and sharing that hearten individuals and validate their ambitions. In crises, female endurance prevails, as delineated by Joanna Todd after her jilting and self-isolation on Shell-heap Island: "I have come to know what it is to have patience, but I have lost my hope" (*ibid.,* 76). Jewett confers immortality on Joanna with a message from nature—the song of the wild sparrow that lights on Joanna's coffin and chirrups to mourners.

By beginning with a funeral and concluding with a wedding, Jewett points toward the legacy of anticipation that one hearty generation passes to another. The soft, comforting dialect of coast dwellers welcomes the protagonist, an unnamed outsider who sails into the harbor in June as an explorer of a new world. At first, she denigrates the countryside for its "childish certainty of being the centre of civilization" (*ibid.,* 5). Within inclusive female territory, she becomes enwebbed in the his-tories of women. At the Bowden family reunion, she witnesses the "transfiguring powers" of an "altar to patriotism, to friendship, to the ties of kindred" (*ibid.,* 76). In retrospect the narrator observes of her welcome, "We were rich with the treasure of a new remembrance" (*ibid.,* 98).

Bibliography

Graham, Margaret Baker. "Visions of Time in *The Country of the Pointed Firs," Studies in Short Fiction* 32, no. 1 (Winter 1995): 29–37.

Jewett, Sarah Orne. *The Country of the Pointed Firs and Other Stories.* New York: Signet, 2000.

Welburn, Ron. "The Braided Rug, Pennyroyal, and the Pathos of Almira Todd: A Cultural Reading of *The Country of the Pointed Firs," Journal of American Culture* 17, no. 4 (Winter 1994): 73–78.

courtly love

Like the concept of the IDEAL WOMAN, *l'amour courtois* (courtly love) is an outgrowth of the romanticism of 12th-century Provence and a testimony to the power of female SEXUALITY. Troubadours sang of a man's adoration of his lady love. The attraction began with a distant view of a high-born female who was unattainable for a variety of marital, class, economic, geographic, or religious reasons. Intended to refine militarism and curtail the murderous nature of men, the courtly code was formulated as a deterrent to soldiers' uncleanliness, coarse language and manners, and arrogant, brutish behavior. The courtly relationship developed into infatuation, formal wooing, and a pledge of love bound up in obedience and loyalty, two themes of Arthurian lore and of *Monna Innominata* (1881), a Petrarchan sonnet sequence by the English poet Christina ROSSETTI.

In place of patriarchal domination of women, in courtly love the female controlled the male, whom she forced into submission by channeling the man's desire into a permissible equivalent of goddess worship. To win the lady's favor, the male performed acts of athletic prowess and courageous deeds that ennobled the love match with their sportsmanship, selflessness, and honor. More virtuous acts exhibited devotion to God or the veneration of a saint or of the VIRGIN MARY, the height of idealized womanhood. Unlike actual wedlock or sexual liaisons, these platonic relationships survived primarily on parchment and arras and in song and story as models for behavior. They overlooked reality in ignoring the humanity and erotic potential of real women and in glossing over the pervasive misogyny described by the late medieval balladeer CHRISTINE DE PISAN in *Epistre au dieu d'amours* (Letter to the god of love, 1399) and *Epistres du Débat sur le Roman de la Rose* (Letters on the debate of "The Romance of the Rose," 1402).

In the journalist Susan BROWNMILLER's social criticism *Against Our Will: Men, Women and Rape* (1975), a condemnation of sexual VIOLENCE against women, she returned to the era of courtly love for some implications of aggression against women along with admiration from afar. She cites a passage on chivalry from Chrétien de Troyes, who warned that the wandering knight would lose his reputation by "dishonoring" a lone damsel. However, if the knight confronted another male with a female, "If it pleased him to give combat to that knight and win the lady by arms, then he might do his will with her just as he pleased, and no shame or blame whatsoever would be held to attach to him" (Brownmiller, 322). Brownmiller backs up the text with substantiation from Sir Thomas Malory's *Le Morte d'Arthur* (1450), which describes the king's gratitude when a knight dragged a shrieking woman from the dining hall. The knight's courtesy toward male diners spared them her sobs and pleas for rescue.

In 1978, the historian Barbara Tuchman cited in *A Distant Mirror* additional evidence that sexual barbarity was more the rule of real life than courtly love, for example, Edward III's rape of the countess of Salisbury in 1341. The chronicler Jean le Bel reports that the king "left her lying in a swoon bleeding from the nose and mouth and other parts" (Tuchman, 71). Tuchman clarifies the shortfall between courtly relationships and actual male-female pairings: "Married love, despite the formula of courtly romance, was still a desired goal to be achieved after, rather than before, the tying of the knot" (ibid., 227). The establishment of mutually satisfying wedlock fell to the woman, who had to earn love by being biddable, pleasant, patient, and docile, much like a trusty steed or hunting dog.

When the ideal love match failed to materialize, the result looked much more like contemporary wife battery. Tuchman names as an example the count of Armagnac, who "was accused of breaking his wife's bones and keeping her locked up in an effort to extort property" (ibid., 229).

Bibliography

Brownmiller, Susan. *Against Our Will: Men, Women and Rape.* New York: Bantam Books, 1975.

Tuchman, Barbara. *A Distant Mirror.* New York: Alfred A. Knopf, 1978.

Cross Creek Marjorie Kinnan Rawlings (1942)

The regional AUTOBIOGRAPHY *Cross Creek* and its homey sequel, *Cross Creek Cookery* (1942), characterize an urban writer's hunger for respite and self-sustenance. In the tropical wilds south of Gainesville, Florida, Marjorie Kinnan RAWLINGS arrives in 1928. She spends a quarter-century smoking Lucky Strikes and sipping whiskey on the screened-in porch of a shabby farm cottage, tapping out stories and novels on her typewriter and tending 72 acres of pecan, grapefruit, orange, and tangerine trees. Nature invites her to enjoy the Big Scrub, a landscape teeming with waxy magnolia blooms, fragrant night winds, and morning birdcalls; solitude allows her to shuck off the ghosts of a failed marriage and stalled career in fiction. In the privacy of her bedroom hearth, she flavors coffee with a dollop of thick country cream, enjoys an aromatic woodfire, and muses, "What have I done to deserve such munificence?" (Rawlings, 260). Echoing aboriginal philosophy, she concludes that no one can horde such blessings.

The network of female neighbors introduces the homesteader to a variety of new experiences. The arrival of 'Geechee, a volunteer housekeeper, initiates a friendship between city woman and black country "lioness" (ibid., 65). The author respects 'Geechee for an African ancestry with slaves who were "very black; strong, with a long stride; their bodies straight as palm trunks; violent, often, and as violently loyal" (ibid.). From a black matriarch, the tenant farmer Martha Mickens, Rawlings learns the high cost of maternity to women who, lacking three dollars for contraception, revert to hazardous home remedies for "throwing away" a developing fetus (*ibid.*, 274). From local gossip, the author learns about a love triangle that winds down to feuding males' deserting a female, who dies in Martha's care. Even the author's pointer dog Mandy pays the price of worldly evils by convulsing to death from strychnine administered by an unknown assailant. The author refutes human treachery by placing her finger on "the pulse of the great secret and the great answer," her metaphor for the harmony of community life and respect for the land and its denizens (*ibid.*, 277).

In tone and pacing, Rawlings's reflections anticipate the ecological fervor of Marjorie Stoneman Douglas's nature tribute *The Everglades: River of Grass* (1947) and the community involvement of Frances Mayes's memoir *Under a Tuscan Sun: At Home in Italy* (1996). At a low point in Rawlings's spirits, she and her friend Dessie defy male protests and motor from Fort Christmas hundreds of miles down the Saint John's River. Enfolded in March freshets, the questers steer through false channels in acres of water hyacinths past Puzzle Lake's shoals toward clear water. A symbol of Rawlings's search for wholeness and an authentic literary voice, the jaunt engenders gratitude: "If I could have, to hold forever, one brief place and time of beauty, I think I might choose the night on that high lonely bank above the St. John's River" (*ibid.*, 267). Without direct reference to World War II, the text contrasts the terrors ravaging Europe with the understated grace of the tropical swamps. Returned to dry land, Rawlings relishes a pervasive beauty, "a forgotten loveliness" that she contrasts to "the only nightmare . . . the masochistic human mind" (*ibid.*, 272). In 1992, the author's real housekeeper and companion, Idella Parker, revisited their life together in a bittersweet memoir, *Marjorie Rawlings' "Perfect Maid,"* which honors the author for reaching beyond segregation to a humane appreciation of blacks.

Bibliography

Jones, Carolyn M. "Race and the Rural in Marjorie Kinnan Rawlings's *Cross Creek*," *Mississippi Quarterly* 57, no. 2 (Spring 2004): 215–230.

Parker, Idella. *Idella: Marjorie Rawlings' "Perfect Maid."* Gainesville: University Press of Florida, 1992.

Rawlings, Marjorie Kinnan. *Cross Creek.* Atlanta: Mockingbird Books, 1974.

Cross, Donna (1947–)

The educator and historical fiction writer Donna Woolfolk Cross blends shrewd surmise with sound research to fill in the blanks of women's history. A native New Yorker, she is the child of two writers. A graduate of the University of Pennsylvania and the University of California at Los Angeles with degrees in English literature and creative writing, she is well read in hagiography and feminist history, particularly the writing of Mary WOLLSTONECRAFT. Cross lived in London in her 20s to edit manuscripts for the publisher W. H. Allen. After returning to the United States, she wrote copy for a Madison Avenue ad agency, Young and Rubicam. In 1973, she settled in Syracuse, New York, and taught English at Onandaga Community College. She has published two books on the use and abuse of language, *Word Abuse: How the Words We Use Use Us* (1979) and *Mediaspeak: How Television Makes Up Your Mind* (1982), and coauthored with the comic book writer William Woolfolk, her father, *Daddy's Little Girl: The Unspoken Bargain between Fathers and Their Daughters* (1982), a feminist study of girls' relationships with male parents. The latter text exposes the dark strand of father-daughter love that precipitates delinquency, incest, lesbianism, and alcoholism. In the summation, the authors admit that "a daughter's symbiotic attachment to her father does not eliminate conflict" (Cross and Woolfolk, 201).

With the publication of a historical novel, *Pope Joan* (1996), which sold out in the first three weeks, Cross earned feminist recognition for speculative fiction based on seven years' research on a ninth-century legend. She began tracing the story of a female pope after locating the name Jeanne (Joan) in a French text. The idea of a woman disguised as a male prelate received no substantiation from the Vatican, yet recurred with frequency in 500 manuscripts, including works by Boccaccio, Petrarch, and Platina. Over a period of seven years, Cross fleshed out scraps from the past with a plausible life story based on extreme DUALITY. She bolstered her argument for the woman pope's existence by pointing out the popularity of Joan's story, which exceeded that of King Arthur. Her intent was to reclaim lost feminist heritage from the Middle Ages, which includes chronicles of Joan's existence by Catholic authors and a statue of the female pope alongside those of her predecessors. Cross charged Catholic authorities with a cleansing of history to expunge all record of a female on the throne of Saint Peter.

The novel *Pope Joan*, which Doubleday and Literary Guild selected for readers, dramatizes ninth-century misogyny in Ingelheim, Germany, where the protagonist was born in A.D. 814. Superstitions about women's menses and patriarchal control of women's life and personal wealth relegated women to perpetual suspicion. The text cites the absurd belief of Joan's father that "a woman's hair . . . is the net wherein Satan catches a man's soul" (Cross, 11). Laws stripped wives of property rights and control of their children and rendered them powerless against marital battery. Without the freedom to study, travel, or act on their creative urges, females were veritable prisoners. Contributing terror to their perpetual house arrest were Viking raids and the savaging of females as blood sport. Joan's survival of a Norse attack and her progress at Fulda illustrate courage and empowerment through self-education, a constant in feminist success stories. Cross emphasizes Joan's skill at herbalism, which earns her entrée to the papal hierarchy. Defeated by passion for Gerold, a married soldier, and by her pregnancy and a sudden birthing, Joan ends a brilliant two-year term in the highest ecclesiastic office. Her story was popular among English, French, and German readers. Cross sold the rights to Constantine Films, which engaged her to write a screenplay to be produced in 2006.

Bibliography

Cross, Donna. *Pope Joan*. New York: Ballantine, 1997.

———, and William Woolfolk. *Daddy's Little Girl: The Unspoken Bargain between Fathers and Their Daughters*. Englewood Cliffs, N.J.: Prentice-Hall, 1982.

Mitchell, Penni. "Pope Joan," *Herizons* 12, no. 1 (Spring 1998): 39.

Walker, Gina Luria. "Learning History's Lessons," *Women's Review of Books* 14, no. 8 (May 1997): 22–23.

Cruz, Sor Juana Inés de la (ca. 1648–1695)

Proclaimed America's 10th muse, Sister Juana Inés de la Cruz, a Hieronimite nun, defied the male church hierarchy by demanding that women's souls be valued and their minds educated. Born Juana Inés Ramírez de Asbaje in San Miguel Nepantla southeast of Mexico City, she overcame the shame of illegitimacy by living at her maternal grandfather's hacienda, educating herself, and learning the subtleties of scholarly debate. She went to court at age 13 as a lady in waiting to the marquise de Mancera. Juana refused to marry and, in 1669, took the veil to assure the freedom to read, study, and write erotic verse, songs, sacramental drama, and Christian allegory without male intrusion. Some of the emotionally complex love sonnets, dedicated to the countess de Paredes, the poet addresses to women, calling them by name—Inez, Laura, Lysi, Phyllis, Portia, Sophia. Sister Juana also analyzes the problematic role of the VIRGIN MARY within church doctrine.

While assigned to Mexico, Sister Juana taught drama and music and distinguished herself as playwright, poet, and polemicist. She outraged the church establishment by denouncing the use of the Bible as a justification for dehumanizing, demonizing, and enslaving women. In 1691, she challenged a sexist archbishop who thought her arrogant and her works frivolous and threatened her scholarly freedom. Her formal retort, *La Respuesta a Sor Filotea* (The reply to Sister Filotea, 1691), has been called the world's first feminist demand for educational and intellectual freedom. In self-defense, she posed a rhetorical question about gender equity: "Is a woman's soul not as receptive to God's grace and glory as a man's? Then why is she not allowed to receive learning and knowledge?" (Cruz, xlii–xliii). She persisted with blunt accusations of sexism against the church PATRIARCHY: "What divine revelation, what regulation of the Church, what rule of reason framed for us such a severe law?" (*ibid.*, xliii). The text concludes with a hymn to scholarship, which she intended to honor until death. Although she signed in blood a vow to discontinue literary pursuits in 1694, when she died at the Convent of Santa Paula the next year in April during an epidemic, she left behind letters, 100 books, and 185 manuscripts. In 1952, the Chilean poet

Gabriela MISTRAL honored the sister with an elegy, "Profile of Sor Juana Ines de la Cruz."

Bibliography

Cruz, Sor Juana Inés de la. *Poems, Protest and a Dream.* London: Penguin, 1997.

Kirk, Pamela. *Sor Juana Inés de la Cruz: Religion, Art, and Feminism.* New York: Continuum, 1999.

Valis, Noël, and Carol Maier, eds. *In the Feminine Mode: Essays on Hispanic Women Writers.* Lewisburg, Pa.: Bucknell University Press, 1990.

Cushman, Karen (1941–   )

The award-winning children's author Karen Lipski Cushman directs female characters toward a realistic number of choices that liberate and satisfy. A Chicago native, she grew up in Tarzana, California, where she read a variety of books and wrote original essays, vignettes, and plays. With degrees in English, Latin, and Greek from Stanford University and postgraduate work in counseling and psychology from the United States International University, she added another master's degree in museum studies from John F. Kennedy University. While teaching part time, Cushman worked in customer service for Pacific Bell and edited the *Museum Studies Journal.* At age 48, she began writing fiction.

Cushman relies on primary research and readings in women's letters, diaries, and personal papers as authoritative sources of female thought. After studying the life of young girls in the Middle Ages, she wrote in journal form *Catherine, Called Bird* (1994), winner of a Newbery honorarium and best book awards from American Booksellers, *Parent's Choice,* and *School Library Journal.* The historical fiction introduces the daughter of Aislinn and Lord Rollo, 13-year-old Catherine of Stonebridge, at the time of her feudal betrothal. In rebellion, she rejects the ladylike tasks of embroidery and spinning and dreams of studying herbalism or becoming a professional illuminator of manuscripts. When her imagination takes hold, she considers "crusading, swinging my sword at heathens and sleeping under starry skies on the other end of the world" (Cushman, 1994, 8). Amid a wealth of seasonal activity and amusement from a puppet show,

mumming, and the Lord of Misrule, she spends time locked in her room as punishment for scaring off suitors. She ponders expectations that ladies must conceal anger and dark moods and must avoid overdrinking, overeating, and swearing. As she approaches age 14, she eases her mother through a difficult birthing and accepts the inevitable by accustoming herself to the idea of marrying Stephen, a youth of her father's choosing.

A year later, the same data on the Middle Ages grounded Cushman's feminist classic *The Midwife's Apprentice* (1995), winner of a Newbery Medal and an American Library Association Best Book for Young Adults Award. The story follows the fortunes of Alyce, a homeless English waif who shelters with a midwife, Jane Sharp, a sour-tempered scold who offers little encouragement. With a touch of wry humor, Cushman demonstrates that the only way that Alyce can learn midwifery is to spy, "creeping behind trees and under fences, careful to keep out of sight, and the cat stalked along behind her, so they looked like a Corpus Christi Day procession on its way to the churchyard" (Cushman, 1995, 18). By applying what she learned from spying on birthings, Alyce saves a woman and her newborn. Alyce receives a compliment for "her two strong hands and her good common sense" (*ibid.,* 60). In return, she dickers over a choice of futures, an unheard-of opportunity for orphaned peasant girls. Instead of traveling to two possible destinations, she elects to remain with Jane and to continue training as a birthing coach. Cushman researched family life during the California Gold Rush for *The Ballad of Lucy Whipple* (1996) and returned to medieval childhood for *Matilda Bone* (2000), the story of a girl who apprentices in bonesetting under Red Peg, a pragmatic healer. The motif of the healing arts as a career for women supports Cushman's presentation of historic periods in which other professions are open only to males.

Bibliography

Cushman, Karen. *Catherine, Called Birdy.* New York: HarperTrophy, 1994.

———. *The Midwife's Apprentice.* New York: HarperTrophy, 1995.

Elliot, Ian. "Karen Cushman: Pursuing the Past," *Teaching PreK–8* 28, no. 5 (February 1998): 42–44.

D

Danticat, Edwidge (1969–)

The Haitian-American novelist Edwidge Danticat writes of a beleaguered nation where artists sometimes die for their boldness. She speaks gently, powerfully of Caribbean women whose painful stories never make the front page. She was born in Port-au-Prince to ambitious working-class islanders who immigrated to Brooklyn in search of work, leaving her with an aunt. After joining her parents in New York at age 12, Edwidge honored their wish that she earn a college degree. Instead of seeking a nursing certificate, she dismayed the family by abandoning medicine to study fine arts at Brown University and to become a fiction writer and creative writing teacher at New York University and the University of Miami.

Danticat's career got off to a strong start. In addition to earning the Pushcart Short Story Prize, a James Michener Fellowship, and awards for stories in *Caribbean Writer, Essence, Granta, Harper's Bazaar, Jane Magazine, New York Times Magazine,* and *Seventeen,* she published a first novel, *Breath, Eyes, Memory* (1994), which reveals systematic sexual abuse of girls and women by a corrupt military. Dedicated to female relatives and friends, the introduction promises, "We have stumbled but we will not fall" (Danticat, 1994, i). Of women's terrors, she speaks of intense nightmares as the victim "curled up in a ball in the middle of the night, sweating and shaking as she hollered for the images of the past to leave her alone" (*ibid.,* 193). Danticat followed with *Krik? Krak!* (1995), an anthology of nine stories nomi-nated for a National Book Award. The collection affirms the strength of female kitchen poets as story keepers and oral narrators, particularly the female prison story "Nineteen Thirty-Seven" and the Gothic tale of thwarted motherhood "Between the Pool and the Gardenias."

Danticat writes knowledgeably of female terror in Haiti—the rape of island women by the Tontons Makouts, a corrupt police agency of the former Haitian government of the Duvaliers, and of a skilled torturer in *The Dew Breaker* (2004), historical fiction about brutality under the regime of François "Papa Doc" Duvalier. She set her novel *The Farming of Bones* (1998), winner of the American Book Award, during the violent upheaval of 1937 wrought by the massacre of Haitian guest workers authorized by Rafael Trujillo, president of the Dominican Republic, when sudden conflict erupts from the unforeseen ethnic cleansing of Haitians from his domain. While exploring the violations of the human rights of a Haitian laborer, the author avoids overt American feminism by describing without cant or subtextual messages the plight of Amabelle Désir, a native protagonist beset by panic at the disappearance of her lover Sébastien. Central to Danticat's view of female protagonists is the kind of courage that renews itself daily, allowing survivors to reach for hope one day at a time.

Bibliography

Danticat, Edwidge. *Breath, Eyes, Memory.* New York: Soho Press, 1994.

———. *Farming of Bones.* New York: Soho Press, 1999.

Francis, Donette A. " 'Silences Too Horrific to Disturb':
    Writing Sexual Histories in Edwidge Danticat's
    Breath, Eyes, Memory," *Research in African Litera-
    tures* 35, no. 2 (Summer 2004): 75–90.

Wucker, Michele. "Edwidge Danticat: A Voice for the
    Voiceless," *Americas* 52, no. 3 (May–June 2000):
    40–48.

Davis, Angela (1944–)

The famed rebel, orator, and author Angela
Yvonne Davis contributes her scholarship and perceptions to women's literature, memoir, prison literature, and black and feminist history. Born in
Birmingham, Alabama, a crucible of racism and Ku
Klux Klan activism, she learned from her mother
the possibilities for peaceful coexistence of whites
and nonwhites. While attending Elisabeth Irwin
High School in New York City, Davis pledged herself to Marxism. With degrees in French literature
from Brandeis University and the Sorbonne and
postgraduate work in philosophy from the University of Frankfurt and the University of California at
San Diego, she began teaching. Her denunciation
of democracy ended her brief tenure at the University of California at Los Angeles. She involved
herself in liberal causes—prisoner rights, amnesty
for political prisoners, black liberation, women's
health, and an end to the Vietnam War. Her tough
stance resulted in jailing in Marin County in 1970
on charges of murder, kidnapping, and conspiracy.
A "Free Angela" campaign ended her incarceration after 16 months.

In 1971, Davis issued *If They Come in the Morning,* a collection of prison writings. She published an
AUTOBIOGRAPHY, *Angela Davis: An Autobiography*
(1974), which details her formulation of black
power strategy. In her late 30s, after the first of two
failed candidacies for the U.S. vice presidency, she
surveyed abolitionist and woman's suffrage campaigns in *Women, Race and Class* (1981). The text
charges Susan B. ANTHONY and Elizabeth Cady
STANTON with excluding black women from the
fight for the vote. Davis provides data on black
women's contributions to the workforce, beginning
with field labor for the Southern "slaveocracy"
(Davis, 1981, 5). Of the plantation role of breeders

and sucklers, Davis observes that they were "animals, whose monetary value could be precisely calculated in terms of their ability to multiply their
numbers" (*ibid.,* 7). With articles in *Critical Inquiry,
Essence, Nation,* and *Social Justice,* she continued
championing oppressed women and denouncing the
undermining of female lives by acquired immunodeficiency syndrome (AIDS) and the drug culture.
Lauding her early works was KITCHEN TABLE/
WOMEN OF COLOR PRESS, which publishes out-of-
print works by feminist and lesbian authors.

Davis turned to the history of black artists with
*Blues Legacy and Black Feminism: Gertrude "Ma"
Rainey, Bessie Smith, and Billie Holiday* (1998), a
chronicle of the black female singer's contribution to
autonomy and prefeminist rhetoric. By creating the
musical genre of women's blues, the stars of that field
modeled the independence and financial rewards of
a singer's life. Their celebrity made a dent in the exclusion of black entertainers from whites-only
restaurants, clubs, and hotels and gave fans hope for
an end to lynching and segregation. The lesbian
singer Ma Rainey addressed the love of women for
women. Blues lyrics exposed the battery that women
endured from sadistic black males and launched subtextual opposition to degrading drudgery and the
rapid aging and physical decline of black women
through cold, heavy loads, and unremitting toil.

Bibliography

Davis, Angela Y. *The Angela Y. Davis Reader.* Malden,
    Mass.: Blackwell, 1998.

———. *Blues Legacy and Black Feminism: Gertrude "Ma"
    Rainey, Bessie Smith, and Billie Holiday.* New York:
    Vintage, 1999.

———. "Women in Prison," *Essence* 31, no. 5 (Septem-
    ber 2000): 150–151.

———. *Women, Race and Class.* New York: Random
    House, 1981.

Purnell, Kim L. "Blues Legacies and Black Feminism:
    Gertrude 'Ma' Rainey, Bessie Smith, and Billie Hol-
    iday," *Women's Studies in Communication* 24, no. 2
    (Fall 2001): 262–265.

Davis, Rebecca Harding (1831–1910)

The journalist and realist fiction writer Rebecca
Harding Davis denounced industrial white slavery

and championed the cause of female laborers whose lives lacked meaningful work, relaxation, and cultural and creative outlets. A native of Washington, Pennsylvania, she grew up in Florence, Alabama, and in Wheeling, West Virginia, in a middle-class industrial town. She showed intellectual promise in girlhood and was valedictorian of her class from the Washington Female Seminary. She engaged in the ordinary activities of an unmarried woman and wrote for the Wheeling *Intelligencer,* for which she interviewed the Quaker SUFFRAGE orator Lucretia MOTT.

In April 1861, Davis made her mark on feminist history by publishing in the *Atlantic Monthly* America's first proletarian novella, *Life in the Iron Mills; or, The Korl Woman,* an instant sensation among readers. Her sympathy for the weary, soul-starved immigrant factory worker derived from friendships with employees of the iron foundries and factories of Wheeling, which provided creature comforts for the American middle class. Of the appearance of Deborah, an example of a washed-out female face on a cotton mill picker, Davis remarks, "There was no warmth, no brilliancy, no summer for this woman; so the stupor and vacancy had time to gnaw into her face perpetually" (Davis, 1997, 22).

Davis was astounded at reader response. A year later, she completed *Margret Howth: A Story of Today* (1861), which she serialized in the *Atlantic* for $200. A first novel, it exposed the degenerative effects of capitalism on the powerless female laborer. With particular interest in hard labor, Margret pities Lois Yare, called "Lo," a former loom girl reduced to peddling after being crippled by a cotton mill mishap. After the author married one of her admirers, the newspaperman Lemuel Clarke Davis, in 1863, she joined the staff of the *New York Tribune* and, to supplement her husband's income, contributed to *Lippincott's* and *Youth's Companion.* She published in the *Atlantic* "The Wife's Story" (1864), a revealing fiction about the overwhelmed wife who has no time for creative outlets. In the utopian story "The Harmonists" (1866), the author contrasts the ease enjoyed by poets and prophets and the withering of women from drudgery that leaves them faded and vacant-eyed. Davis continued writing social com-

mentary, short and long fiction, and children's stories and encouraged historians to compile accomplishments of admirable female citizens. Her labor themes and style influenced the writer Elizabeth Stuart PHELPS to examine the life of female mill workers.

Davis's issues-oriented works include an assessment of Reconstruction era racism toward blacks and mixed race people in *Waiting for the Verdict* (1868) and of the emancipation of the female worker in *Earthen Pitchers* (1873–74), serialized in seven parts in *Scribner's.* In the latter the author chooses as protagonist the fictional Audrey, a lover of the sea who never attained her aim of becoming a violinist, composer, and singer. She paces like a caged beast in misery at the burden of housework and in longing for her dead mother. Without the nurturing and love her spirit needs to thrive, she expends herself on family. In 1972, at the urging of the Nebraska writer Tillie OLSEN, the Feminist Press recovered *Life in the Iron Mills,* a classic of social protest, the pinnacle of a half-century career that produced 500 works.

Bibliography

Davis, Rebecca Harding. *Life in the Iron Mills.* 1862. Reprint, Houndmills, England: Palgrave Macmillan, 1997.

———. *Margaret Howth: A Story of To-Day* (1862). Available online. URL: http://etext.lib.virginia.edu/ toc/modeng/public/DavMarg.html. Accessed on October 13, 2005.

Henwood, Dawn. "Slaveries 'in the Borders': Rebecca Harding Davis's 'Life in the Iron Mills' in Its Southern Context," *Mississippi Quarterly* 52, no. 4 (Fall 1999): 567–592.

Hood, Richard A. "Framing a 'Life in the Iron Mills,'" *Studies in American Fiction* 23, no. 1 (Spring 1995): 73–84.

de Cleyre, Voltairine (1866–1912)

A shrewd logician, essayist, poet, and orator, Voltairine de Cleyre lived an ascetic life devoted to ending social hypocrisy and men's enslavement of women. Of French-American lineage, she was born in Leslie, Michigan, to abolitionists who aided the Underground Railroad. She suffered neurological disease from childhood and was frequently bedridden in severe pain. At age 13, she underwent forced religious training after her father placed her in the Convent of Our Lady of Lake Huron in Sarnia, Ontario. She recalled four years of misery in a memoir, "The Making of an Anarchist" (1914), which describes the authoritarian penances that destroyed her health and forced her toward atheism. After committing herself to free thought and libertarianism, she read the feminist works of Mary WOLLSTONECRAFT and learned about socialism from the attorney Clarence Darrow. After the hanging of the Haymarket rioters in 1887 turned her toward anarchism, she lectured for the Woman's National Liberal Union.

While writing pacifist and feminist essays for the *Alarm, Liberty, Mother Earth,* the *Progressive Age,* and the *Rebel,* De Cleyre earned a meager living teaching English to Jewish immigrants at slum schools in Chicago, New York, and Philadelphia. Her pro-female essays focused on threats to liberty: "Sex Slavery" (1890), "The Gates of Freedom" (1891), "The Case of Woman vs. Orthodoxy" (1896), "Those Who Marry Do Ill" (1908), and "The Woman Question" (1913). In "Sex Slavery," she exhorted, "Yes, our masters! The earth is a prison, the marriage-bed is a cell, women are the prisoners, and you are the keepers!" (de Cleyre, 1890). She charged Christianity with complicity in female bondage: "From the birth of the Church, out of the womb of Fear and the fatherhood of Ignorance, it has taught the inferiority of woman" (*ibid.*). During the socialist orator Emma GOLDMAN's jailing at Blackwell's Island Penitentiary, de Cleyre delivered an apologia, "In Defense of Emma Goldman and Free Speech" (1893). On behalf of female laborers and SUFFRAGE, in 1897, she lectured in England, Norway, and Scotland. In 1902, a crazed gunman thought she was an anti-Semite and shot her. She recuperated in Norway, but pain and suicidal urges stalked her consciousness. In *Anarchism and American Traditions* (1914), she fought the contradictions between the promise of democracy and the reality of American life for nonwhites, Jews, immigrants, and women. She died at age 45 of brain inflammation but has retained her reputation for bold feminism into the 21st century.

Bibliography

Avrich, Paul. *An American Anarchist: The Life of Voltairine de Cleyre.* Princeton, N.J.: Princeton University Press, 1978.

de Cleyre, Voltairine. *Anarchism and American Traditions* (1914). Available online. URL: http://www.infoshop.org/texts/voltairine_traditions.html. Accessed on October 13, 2005.

———. *The Selected Works of Voltairine de Cleyre, Pioneer of Women's Liberation.* New York: Revisionist Press, 1972.

———. "Sex Slavery" (1890). Available online. URL: http://dwardmac.pitzer.edu/Anarchist_Archives/bright/cleyre/sexslavery.html. Accessed on October 13, 2005.

———. "Those Who Marry Do Ill" (1908). Available online. URL: http://praxeology.net/VC-MDI.htm. Accessed on October 13, 2005.

Goldman, Emma. "Voltairine de Cleyre" (1932). Available online. URL: http://sunsite.berkeley.edu/Goldman/Writings/Essays/voltairine.html. Accessed on October 13, 2005.

Delany, Annie Elizabeth (1891–1995) and Delany, Sarah Louise (1889–1999)

A unique pair, Annie Elizabeth "Bessie" and Sarah Louise "Sadie" Delany collaborated on an AUTOBIOGRAPHY. Inseparable from childhood, the two were granddaughters of former slaves and daughters of administrators at the Saint Augustine School in Raleigh, North Carolina, where the girls were born. They learned in childhood the importance of setting an example for Saint Augustine students with displays of cleanliness, morality, and hard work, which included scrubbing laundry outdoors in a washtub. At Saint Athanasius School, Pratt Institute, and Columbia, Sadie studied home economics, a developing career for women. Because of a lack of money and the public's disdain of female physicians, Bessie gave up her aim to study medicine and entered the dentistry program at Columbia as the only black in her class. To earn their way through school, the Delanys worked in a needle factory and ushered at a movie theater. When they began working in the North during the Harlem Renaissance, they were among the first black professional women in New York City. In

1989, they undertook a two-year project of narrating their life stories to Amy Hill Hearth, a journalist with the *New York Times*, as the beginning of a best-selling autobiography, *Having Our Say: The Delany Sisters' First 100 Years* (1991).

While recounting their early lives with wit and humor, the Delanys vivified from their own experience the hardships that women faced before the feminist movement extended equality in civic and business affairs. The sisters' survey of Reconstruction, churches with balconies reserved for blacks and communion for whites only, Jim Crow railway cars, and the screening of the racist film *Birth of a Nation* (1915) singles out VIOLENCE against females at a Ku Klux Klan lynching of a black woman, whose fetus dangled from her uterus. The text tempers the horrors of the nation's heritage of racism with the triumphs of the inventor Sarah Walker, Eleanor Roosevelt's campaign for civil rights, and Rosa Parks's refusal to sit in the back of the bus. Bessie's disgruntlement at the plutocratic rule of the affluent emerged in April 1912, when she recalled thinking, "Too bad the *Titanic* didn't take more rich white people down with it, to its watery grave!" (Delany and Delany, 1993, 127).

The sisters joined the wave of black women who demanded rights for African Americans of both genders. Bessie took pride in being the second black woman to gain certification in dentistry in both New York and North Carolina. Her testimony reveals the chutzpah of females who refused second-class citizenship: "You got the message that some of the colored *men* thought the colored *women* should not be involved. Too bad, I was there whether they liked it or not! You couldn't keep me at home" (*ibid.*, 202). Just as they influenced students at Saint Augustine School, the duo set an example of civic duty in Harlem by registering and voting as well as by voicing their opinions about candidates and issues.

The Delanys' autobiography proved so pleasing to readers that, at ages 103 and 106, the duo published *The Delany Sisters' Book of Everyday Wisdom* (1914), a miscellany of Delanyana that ranges from advice on health and happiness to recipes. After Bessie's death at 104, Sadie published *On My Own at 107: Reflections on Life without Bessie* (1998), a meditation on grief and the afterlife. In 1995, the feminist dramatist Emily MANN adapted a stage play from the Delanys' lives for McCarter Theatre in Princeton, New Jersey. It completed a nine-month run on Broadway that spawned a successful tour. In April 1999, the memoir reached a wider audience as a CBS-TV movie adapted by Mann and starring Diahann Carroll and Ruby Dee as the Delany sisters. One tart line from the text— "We never had husbands to worry us to death"— implies that being single was one reason for their longevity (Istel, 6).

Bibliography

Delany, Sarah L. *On My Own at 107: Reflections on Life without Bessie.* San Francisco: HarperSanFrancisco, 1998.

———, and A. Elizabeth Delany. *The Delany Sisters' Book of Everyday Wisdom.* New York: Kodansha America, 1996.

———, and A. Elizabeth Delaney. *Having Our Say: The Delany Sisters' First 100 Years.* New York: Dell, 1993.

Hearth, Amy Hill. "The American Century of Bessie and Sadie Delany," *American Heritage* 44, no. 6 (October 1993): 68–79.

Istel, John. "Say It, Sisters," *American Theatre* 12, no. 5 (May–June 1995): 6–7.

Mann, Emily. *Having Our Say: The Delany Sisters' First 100 Years.* New York: Dramatists Play Service, 1998.

Deloria, Ella (ca. 1888–1971)

The ethnographer, educator, and linguist Ella Cara Deloria preserved for women's history the roles of pre-reservation Sioux women. From a French-Irish-Yankton Sioux lineage, she was born on the Yankton Dakota Reservation at White Swan, South Dakota, and grew up speaking three Sioux dialects—Dakota, Lakota, and Nakota. Her father, Black Lodge, an Episcopalian missionary, named her *Anpetu Wastewin,* meaning "Beautiful Day Woman." After learning English at Saint Elizabeth Mission School at Wakpala and All Saints' Episcopal High School at Standing Rock, she completed her education at the University of Chicago, Oberlin College, and Columbia University. She taught physical education, hygiene, and dance at the Young Women's Christian Association (YWCA) and at Haskell Indian School in Lawrence, Kansas.

Influencing Deloria's career as a teacher, story collector and storyteller, and lecturer were years spent at Pine Ridge, Rosebud, and Standing Rock Reservations among the Hunkpapa and Sihasapa Lakota. At the urging of the anthropologists Ruth Benedict and Franz Boas, Deloria taught Siouxan dialect and translated 1,000 pages of the folklore of George Bushotter for the Smithsonian Institution. In 1929, she published in the *Journal of American Folk-Lore* a description of the Sun Dance. She and her sister, Susan Mable Deloria, composed a pageant, "The Life Story of a People" (1940). In 1941, Ella Deloria compiled a Sioux grammar textbook and a Sioux-English dictionary. For her work as a consultant to schools, missions, and museums as an authority on native traditions, such as the origin of the courting flute and the importance of kinship responsibilities, at age 55 she received from the Indian Council Fire of Chicago the annual Indian Achievement Medal.

In addition to translating documents for the Bureau of Indian Affairs, Deloria interviewed elderly Sioux women in the United States and Canada to learn their stories, dances, and jokes and facts about marital sex, polygyny, and religious ritual. She respected the oldest females as bone carriers, the Sioux term for culture keepers and interpreters. She stated in a letter in 1940, "If every Dakota woman disappeared today, and all the men took white wives, then the language and customs would die" (Gardner, 2000, 481). With the largest compilation of data on the culture and language of any Plains tribe, she shaped native folklore into *Dakota Texts* (1932) and wrote *Speaking of Indians* (1944), a history featuring character traits of the Dakota.

Deloria's novel *Waterlily* (1947) made a lasting impact on feminist literature with images of womanhood from the point of view of Plains Indians living at the time of the Sun Dance ritual. She described a MATRIARCHY dating to Grandmother Gloku and the submissive role of the Sioux wife Blue Bird and her fatherless daughter, Waterlily, who was married twice and widowed before the age of 20. Set in the mid-19th century, the story interprets for white readers the tribal expectations for Sioux women as integral members of the community. Most important to young women were their husband's relatives, who exercised control over the bride. Waterlily remarks, "A relentless watchfulness was needed, especially at first," but a communal SISTERHOOD relieves her of fears of mistakes in a complicated family composed of men with numerous wives and many children (Deloria, 162). The book remained unpublished until 1988, when the University of Nebraska Press issued an abridged version.

Bibliography

Deloria, Ella. *Waterlily.* Lincoln: University of Nebraska Press, 1988.

Gardner, Susan. "Speaking of Ella Deloria," *American Indian Quarterly* 24, no. 3 (Summer 2000): 456–481.

———. " 'Though It Broke My Heart to Cut Some Bits I Fancied': Ella Deloria's Original Design for *Waterlily,*" *American Indian Quarterly* 27, no. 3/4 (Summer 2003): 667–696.

Desai, Anita (1937–)

The Indian educator and fiction writer Anita Mazumdar Desai interweaves feminist nuances in her views of the rapid changes in Asian women's lives. Born of German-Bengali parentage in Mussoorie, she was reared bilingual in Hindi and German and acquired English when she learned to write. By being a good listener, she mastered the female oral tradition of transmitting fables, god lore, and family genealogies. At age nine, she had an epiphany after reading Emily BRONTË's gothic novel *WUTHERING HEIGHTS* (1847), which opened Desai's mind to female power. Educated in English at Queen Mary's Higher Secondary School and at Miranda House, Delhi University, she earned a degree in English literature and began publishing in her late teens. To pursue a broad range of literary experiences, she emigrated to Cambridge, Massachusetts, and taught at Smith College and Mount Holyoke College. She now divides her time between India and the United States, where she teaches at the Massachusetts Institute of Technology.

In children's and adult fiction, Desai stresses postcolonial, urban, and feminist themes. In *Cry, the Peacock* (1963), Maya, the childlike, superstitious protagonist, attempts to maintain an orderly household. After suffering in silence, she goes mad. The text implies that she obliterates both obligation and need for self by pushing her husband, Gautama, off the roof to his death and leaping after him. Similarly stunted by a lack of privacy and self-development is Monisha, the bookish, melancholy protagonist of *Voices in the City* (1965). To grasp sanity, she learns from the Bhagavad Gita how to detach from the world. She retreats into a Gothic madness: "They have indoor minds, starless and darkless. Mine is all dark now. The blessing it is" (Desai, 1965, 139). When solitude forces her toward mania, she rushes to her room to set herself aflame. Desai dramatizes in *Fire on the Mountain* (1977) the oppression of rural Indian women at a Kasuli hill station and the importance of female chastity among English colonials.

Desai varies viewpoints to present a range of female lives. She won the Winifred Holtby Prize for a story collection, *Games at Twilight and Other Stories* (1978). In one of the entries, "The Farewell Party," she takes a compassionate view of 35-year-old Bina Raman, who has devoted herself for 15 years to Nono, her spastic child, and to hospital protocols. At a tender moment at a farewell gathering, she sits on the verandah near the Queen of the Night, a scented flowering shrub that symbolizes the stability and sweetness of her role as wife and mother. In an anthology, *Diamond Dust: Stories* (1999), Desai employs wit and subtle cameos to expose middle-class hypocrisy and the circumscribed life of females within family expectations. In the first story, "Royalty," Sarla is a dutiful, but unfulfilled wife who orders her days around the demands of her husband, Raja, a name suggesting male tyranny. In *Journey to Ithaca* (1996), Desai satirizes the misguided sincerity of Matteo in going to the Mother's ashram, which rapidly depletes his commitment to his wife, Sophie. With a single toss of the head, Matteo communicates to Sophie his devaluation of home and family under the influence of the charismatic guru: "They did not count. They were what he had left behind" (Desai, 1996, 4).

Bibliography

Desai, Anita. *Diamond Dust: Stories.* New York: Mariner Books, 2000.

———. *Fasting, Feasting.* New York: Mariner Books, 2000.

———. *Journey to Ithaca.* New York: Penguin, 1996.

———. *Voices in the City.* New Delhi: Orient Paperbacks, 1965.

Rege, Josna. "Codes in Conflict: Post-Independence Alienation in Anita Desai's Early Novels," *Journal of Gender Studies* 5, no. 3 (November 1996): 317–328.

DeSalvo, Louise (1943–)

The author, scholar, and teacher Louise A. DeSalvo has devoted her career to self-expression as well as to the nurturance of other people's writing. The daughter of a hero of the Pacific theater during World War II, she grew up among working-class Italian-Americans in Hoboken and Ridgefield, New Jersey. Conflicting messages of two cultures disturbed her girlhood, when she identified with the female imposter who falls to her death in the Alfred Hitchcock film *Vertigo* (1958). In 1984, while she was teaching English at Hunter College, her sister, Jill, hanged herself, the first event DeSalvo mentions in *Vertigo: A Memoir* (1996). The author revealed more of the beauty and pain of her ethnic background in *Crazy in the Kitchen: Food, Feuds and Forgiveness in the Italian-American Family* (2004), which describes immigrant strength in women from Puglia and Campania, Sicily, and the Abruzzi, Italy.

From a self-help point of view, DeSalvo restated the importance of personal composition in *Writing as a Way of Healing: How Telling Our Stories Transforms Our Lives* (2000). Meticulously outlined stages of perception and performance express ways of examining survival from "dislocation, violence, racism, homophobia, anti-Semitism, rape, political persecution, incest, loss, illness" (DeSalvo, *Writing*, 4). As a restorative, writing frees the spirit of hostility and hurt while stabilizing in the mind the nature and direction of trauma. She took her own advice in surviving chronic asthma and in weathering her husband's infidelity by writing *Breathless: An Asthma Journal* (1998) and *Adultery* (1999), a study of COLETTE, Sylvia PLATH, Edith WHARTON, Virginia WOOLF, and other authors who wrote on marital betrayal.

DeSalvo's chief contributions to feminism are her formatting of Virginia Woolf's unpublished *Melymbrosia* (2002), a novel of sexual awakening. DeSalvo contributed more to Woolf's canon with

The Letters of Vita Sackville West to Virginia Woolf (2002) and a feminist biography, *Virginia Woolf: The Impact of Childhood Sexual Abuse on Her Life and Work* (1989). In the latter, DeSalvo describes the male-centered Victorian home in which Woolf grew up. The biographer validates Woolf's sufferings from sexual abuse by her brother, Gerald Duckworth, and excoriates the adults in the family for allowing incest to continue. Central to DeSalvo's text is a frontal assault on blaming the victim, one of the psychosocial themes of feminist literature. Critics and literary historians accept DeSalvo's feminist point of view as a sound introduction to Woolf's fiction.

Bibliography

Cook, B. W. "Books: The Womanly Art of Biography," *Ms.*, January–February 1991, pp. 60–62.

DeSalvo, Louise. *Adultery.* Boston: Beacon Press, 2000.

———. *Vertigo: A Memoir.* New York: Plume, 1997.

———. *Writing as a Way of Healing: How Telling Our Stories Transforms Our Lives.* Boston: Beacon Press, 2000.

Pearce, R. "To the Light," *Novel: A Forum on Fiction* 24, no. 2 (Winter 1991): 222–225.

Diamant, Anita (1951–)

The Jewish-American journalist and novelist Anita Diamant specializes in faith fiction that builds the dependence of females on each other into an unshakable community. A native New Yorker, she is the child of Holocaust survivors, a typesetter and a worker in the needle trade. A writer of verse in her early years, she grew up in two different environments—Newark, New Jersey, and Denver, Colorado. Influenced by the writings of Tillie OLSEN and Virginia WOOLF, she studied literature at the University of Colorado. She completed a degree in comparative literature at Washington University and graduate work in American studies at the State University of New York at Binghamton. In 1975, she worked in Boston as a freelance radio commentator for WBUR and National Public Radio and became a feature writer and columnist for the *Boston Globe*, *Boston Magazine*, *Boston Phoenix*, *Equal Times*, *McCalls*, *Ms.*, *New England Monthly*, *Parenting*, *Parents*, *Self*, and *Yankee*. A decade later, she focused on contemporary Jewish culture and ritual in submissions to *Hadassah* and *Reform Judaism*, the webzine *Jewish-family.com*, and in handbooks on ritual, community, and family practice. When nonfiction palled, she turned to fictionalized Bible stories as a part of what she terms "a larger cultural shift in which women have reappropriated the Bible and other texts" (Rosen, 31).

Over 30 months, a steady reader groundswell transformed *The Red Tent* (1997), Diamant's first novel, into a best seller and the Booksense Book of the Year. She founded her fictional plot on solid research completed with a fellowship at Radcliffe. Set in 1500 B.C., in an engaging kitchen-table-style feminism, the story fleshes out Dinah and other women in Genesis whom Old Testament writers reduced to two-dimensional handmaidens. The author sequesters male-dominated Hebrew women in a liberating atmosphere, a "room of their own" that houses girls and women after they birth and during their menstrual cycles, both natural physical conditions involving the male-feared taint of blood. Through woman-to-woman STORY-TELLING and instruction in tribal history and social issues, the females cope with scoldings, polygyny, jealousy and petty grudges, birth trauma, and bride capture.

Diamant structures the novel around the theme of matriarchal relationships nurtured in a private community setting. Through conversation and stories, girls learn from the experiences of Leah, Rachel, Bilhah, and Zilpah, the four mates of the patriarch Jacob. Diamant energizes the heart of the text with womanly beauty, wisdom, and skill. Of Rachel, Diamant begins, "[Her] presence was powerful as the moon, and just as beautiful . . . rare and arresting," an image of dynamic femininity enriched by connection to the Moon, regulator of ovulation, conception, and birth (Diamant, 1998, 8). Dinah connects her aunt Rachel's earthy scent to fresh water, a symbol that recalls the fateful meeting between Rachel and Jacob at Laban's well.

In an insightful second novel, *Good Harbor* (2002), Diamant moves the SISTERHOOD and camaraderie of *The Red Tent* to present-day Gloucester, Massachusetts, where Kathleen, a librarian facing breast cancer, finds support and friendship in a visit from Joyce, a writer seeking to advance her career. The author stokes the womanly motifs with additional females—a masseuse, a rabbi, the daughter Nina, Fiona the gym teacher, Cleo the parakeet, and Magnolia Dukes, heroine of a romance novel. Diamant followed with *Pitching My Tent: On Marriage, Motherhood, and Other Leaps of Faith* (2003), a trove of the Jewish author's award-winning observations published in the *Boston Globe Sunday Magazine* and *Parenting*. The universal feminist themes consist of love, marriage, children, friendship, middle age, and religion.

Bibliography

Diamant, Anita. *Good Harbor.* New York: Scribner, 2002.
———. *Pitching My Tent: On Marriage, Motherhood, and Other Leaps of Faith.* New York: Scribner, 2003.
———. *The Red Tent.* New York: Picador, 1998.
Rosen, Judith. "Anita Diamant's *Red Tent* Turns to Gold," *Writer* 114, no. 4 (April 2001): 30–33.

diaries and journals

The keeping of a daybook is a signal part of feminist literature. In times and places where women have no access to publishing, a private journal, such as the one the children's author Jennifer HOLM acquired from her great-aunt, is the equivalent of a lump of modeling clay or a blank canvas—a clean, impersonal starting place on which to record longings, sensibilities, events, sketches, imaginary letters, or loose thoughts left for development at a more convenient time. Beginning with the earliest EDUCATION of women, the opportunity to compose in a diary offered a window on the self, for example, Lady MURASAKI's court diary, the sister books that recorded thoughts of women in the private female-created Nushu script in the Hunan province of China, Japanese "pillow books," the novelist Fanny BURNEY's reflections on the Napoleonic era, the challenges of living in the wild in Catherine Parr Traill's *The Backwoods of Canada* (1871), and commentaries on women, art, and love by COLETTE, Anaïs NIN, and Sylvia PLATH.

Social dissension and peril increase the value of an emotional outlet to the writer. A historic model is the diarist Sarah KEMBLE's dismay at the Southern attitude toward SLAVERY. Examples from Mary Boykin CHESNUT's reportage on the Civil War from a Southern female abolitionist perspective and Anne Frank's diary during her family's concealment in Nazi-occupied Holland provide readers and historians with eyewitness narratives that evaluate the place of the individual at a moment in women's history. Although limited in scope, these front-line observations give some perspective on cause and effect. One diarist, Etty Hillesum, a Dutch contemporary of Anne Frank, exhorted herself to value her daily entries: "You must continue to take yourself seriously, you must remain your own witness, marking well everything that happens in this world, never shutting your eyes to reality. You must come to grips with these terrible times" (Schiwy, 18). Her chronicle became a way to impose order and coherence on chaos.

Whatever its shortcomings as a literary genre, the diary offers self-validation and catharsis, a simple scribble on paper that sets the record straight for the silenced or discounted woman who refuses to be squelched. In 1920, the poet and translator Amy LOWELL published *Diaries of Court Ladies of Old Japan,* an illustrated edition featuring three journals—Izumi Shikibu's lyrical account of a love affair that began after A.D. 1002; Murasaki Shikibu's precise daybook, begun in A.D. 1007; and the *Sarashina Diary,* which opens on a woman's journey begun in 1021. Izumi Shikibu's overly poetic courtship story contains a surprisingly modern admission by an unmarried woman of the early 11th century: "I wish to yield to your mind, whatever it may be, yet my thoughts are troubled when I anticipate my fate and see myself neglected by you afterwards" (*Diaries,* 181). Murasaki Shikibu's commentary on strict protocol in the queen's birthing chamber reports that "certain older women wept secretly," a suggestion of the danger to female courtiers of displaying normal emotion in the presence of male dignitaries (*ibid.,* 80). The Sarashina diary validates TALK-STORY as the writer's introduction to male-female relations: "Somehow I came to know that there are such things as romances in the world and wished to read them. When there was nothing to do by day or at night, one tale or another was told me by my elder sister or stepmother" (*ibid.*, 5). In each text, the idiosyncratic style of the diarist affirms a woman's life, her observations and opinions, and her role in a stilted environment.

Twentieth-century feminists treasured recovered journals, such as the Civil War meditations in Georgia Eliza Frances "Fanny" Andrews's *The Wartime Journal of a Georgia Girl, 1864–1865* (1908); Elinore Pruitt Stewart's *Letters of a Woman Homesteader* (1914); Lillian Schlissel's *Women's Diaries of the Westward Journey* (1982); the historian Laurel Thatcher ULRICH's Pulitzer Prize-winning *A Midwife's Tale: The Life of Martha Ballard, Based on Her Diary, 1785–1812* (1990); and a Mormon pioneer's meditations on a religious pilgrimage in *Winter Quarters: The 1846–1848 Life Writings of Mary Haskin Parker Richards* (1996). Ulrich's commentary on the work of the midwife Martha Ballard sets in perspective the lives of colonial New England women, who depended on the respected birthing coach to assure a healthy start for their young. Richards's, Stewart's, and Schlissel's additions to FRONTIER LITERATURE reveal the valor of women intent on crossing the frontier to make trans-Mississippi homes and farms or to build churches, mount missions among Indians, or open schools. Glimpses of woman's work on the move emerge from the stoic accounting of stillbirths, babies lost to wild animals or scarlet fever, bacon half cooked in rainy weather over a sputtery fire, and blankets washed wherever there was adequate water. In all these works, the cost of transporting a family into the outback is both heart-rending experiences and a cause for pride.

Journaling also serves as a faux form for imaginative writing, such as the Jazz Age confessional of Lorelei Lee, the stereotypical dumb blonde in *Gentlemen Prefer Blondes: The Illuminating Diary of a Professional Lady* (1925), by Anita LOOS. The multicultural author Ruth Prawer JHABVALA used the recovered journal as a structural source of information for the novel *HEAT AND DUST* (1975). An unnamed female relative, intrigued by the unconventional life of her aunt, Olivia Rivers, retrieves information from colonial India of the 1920s and applies the wisdom of her relative to the 1970s. The setting of parallel lives a half-century apart produces humor in the similarities of two women's

foolish decisions to love men who have no intention of committing themselves to a relationship. The sudden halt to Olivia's portion of the novel gives the author a means to leave to the reader's imagination how Olivia coped with ending a dull marriage in the British sector, seeking an abortion from an Indian women's clinic, and retreating into the hills to cultivate self rather than the attentions of either husband or lover. Another proponent of daybooks is the novelist Isabel ALLENDE, who establishes in *La casa de los espíritus* (*The HOUSE OF THE SPIRITS*) (1982) the value of the journals of the wisewoman Clara del Valle. Her daughter, Blanca, survives imprisonment and torture by holding fast to her mother's advice and example. The author Laura ESQUIVEL applies the same form of matriarchal history in *Like Water for Chocolate* (1989), which records the damage to women by a family tradition requiring the daughter, Tita de la Garza, to abjure marriage and personal happiness by remaining with her mother as cook and caretaker. Matriarchal strength survives from Tita's recipes and commentary on sexual satisfaction and a cosmic love that overcomes death.

Bibliography

Diaries of Court Ladies of Old Japan (1920). Available online. URL: http://digital.library.upenn.edu/women/omori/court/court.html. Accessed on October 13, 2005.

Richards, Mary Haskin. *Winter Quarters: The 1846–1848 Life Writings of Mary Haskin Parker Richards*. Logan: Utah State University Press, 1996.

Schiwy, Marlene A. *Voice of Her Own: Women and the Journal Writing Journey*. New York: Fireside, 1996.

Dickinson, Emily (1830–1886)

A favorite of feminists, the poet Emily Elizabeth Dickinson continues to gain popularity for her incisive images of a woman's life and art. Known as the "Belle of Amherst" and the "New England mystic," she spent most of her life in her Massachusetts hometown within the brick walls of her grandfather's manse, the Dickinson Homestead. In a domicile controlled by a pompous father, the U.S. legislator Edward Dickinson, the introverted daughter produced sparks of brilliance in early childhood but remained on the outskirts of his attention and approval. She explained much later, "They put me in the Closet— / Because they liked me 'still' " (ca. 1862) (Dickinson, 302). Feminist critics have mused on the implications of the poet's SILENCING, whether it resulted from the father's disdain for female voices or his intimidation by his middle-child's genius.

While studying at Amherst Academy, where her father was treasurer, and at Mount Holyoke Female Seminary, Dickinson recognized the DOUBLE STANDARD and expressed her distaste for bias against intellectual women in the poem "We lose—because we win" (ca. 1858). She demonstrated a ladylike revolt against her father's Calvinist dogma and quietly turned to witty, subtle letters and poetry as outlets for rebellion against a domineering male parent and his insistence on orthodox Christianity. She modeled the timidity expected of women in "Why—do they shut Me out of Heaven?" (ca. 1861) and produced a quietly subversive jab at the refined gentlewomen of her day, whose "Dimity Convictions" supplanted their true glory (ibid., 191). She was also capable of militance toward the exclusion of women from political conventions. Her verse counters society's demand that the unmarried female refrain from an unseemly passion, the theme of "Wild Night" (ca. 1861), in which the speaker longs to "moor— Tonight— / In Thee!" (ibid., 114). A year before her death, she stated the importance of passion to her life in "Take all away from me, but leave me Ecstasy" (ca. 1885).

Dickinson is best remembered for domestic hermetism, a willful retreat from the loneliness of New England she describes in "What Is Paradise" (ca. 1860) and from the mental anguish she mentions around 1864 as "a Cleaving in my Mind" (ibid., 439). In her silent upstairs room, she turned private epiphanies and personal losses into elegant lyrics and sedate elegies. In "Vesuvius at Home: The Power of Emily Dickinson" (1975), a lecture delivered at Brandeis University, the poet Adrienne RICH declared that "Dickinson chose her seclusion, knowing she was exceptional and knowing what she needed" (Rich, 179) The result was a full-fledged womanhood, a cultivated intelligence, and an idiosyncratic style allowed to flower outside the usual constraints of wifedom and parenthood. As Rich described the result of Dickinson's bold incubation of ideas, "Wherever you take hold of her, she proliferates" (ibid., 194).

After the 1853 death from tuberculosis of a freethinking friend, the law clerk Benjamin Franklin Newton, mortality and the afterlife dominated Dickinson's poetic themes. Her industry took wings in her early 30s, when she produced hundreds of spare, provocative verse miniatures, some edged in personal commentary and implied confession. Her influences were often religious sources. In *Achievement in American Poetry* (1951), the poet Louise BOGAN summarized the unique fount: "Behind the Dickinson stanza stands the hymn, and the hymn alone" (Bogan, 23). One of Dickinson's early efforts, "Hope Is the Thing with Feathers" (ca. 1861), written near the beginning of the Civil War, pictures the birdlike nature of her optimism, a buoyant antidote to her fears. A decade later, as her health declined as a result of eyestrain, Bright's disease, and the emotional trauma of tending her invalid mother, she withdrew to an upstairs bedroom, where books by the BRONTËS, George ELIOT, and Elizabeth Barrett BROWNING substituted for human companionship.

A self-shielding individualist, Dickinson was adamant about defying literary conventions as well as standard punctuation and capitalization to evolve a sophisticated form of versification. Partly because editors dared to alter the lines of seven poems she submitted for publication, she refused to issue more of her work for public scrutiny. In strict sequestering in her room, she composed an astonishing canon of verse. Her ties to the outer world included a literary friendship with the author of *Ramona* (1881), Helen Hunt JACKSON, a bold reformer and champion of prairie Indians, whom Dickinson revered as another Helen of Troy. At Dickinson's death at age 55, her younger sister, Lavinia, disobeyed her orders to burn a sizable cache of letters, a majority written to her sister-in-law, Susan Huntington Dickinson, and 1,775 poems, some bound into collections with needle and embroidery floss. It was not until 1955 that Dickinson's writings appeared in their original form and established her reputation as one of the great lyric poets of all time.

Content in solitude, Dickinson enjoyed a privacy that nourished her radical, self-defining interiority. She commiserated with the lot of woman, for example, the bereft lover in "Where Thou art—that—is Home" (ca. 1863) and the mother of the hanged felon in "Upon the gallows hung a wretch" (unknown date). About 1859, she spoke openly about love for a female in "Her Breast Is Fit for Pearls." Glints of suppressed rage emerged in 1863 with "My Life had stood—a Loaded Gun," an acknowledgment of the power of her verse. Around 1876 she composed a bold quatrain, "Forbidden Fruit," which refers metaphorically to female masturbation. With an oblique allusion to EVE in the Garden of Eden the poet depicts the social constraints against women who manipulate "The Pea that Duty locks" (Dickinson, 592). A year later she crafted a double quatrain, "Crisis Is Sweet," in which the speaker pursues the private joys of self-manipulation on "the hither side" of the "rescinded Bud" rather than accept sexual intercourse as an outlet to passion (*ibid.*, 604).

Feminist analysis reads these occluded intimacies as evidence of Dickinson's INDEPENDENCE of the gendered mores of the mid-19th century. However, their readings of such images as "Within that little Hive / Such Hints of Honey lay" (ca. 1884) and the phallic worm and snake she dreams of in "In Winter in my Room" (unknown date) refuse simple interpretation. One category of criticism declares the nature images such as the visions of sea and desert in "To lose thee—sweeter than to gain" (unknown date) as erotic code concealing the normal sexual yearnings of a self-cloistered spinster. She expressed apparently erotic views of woman's love for woman, the subject of "Her sweet Weight on my Heart" (ca. 1862) and "Her face was in a bed of hair" (unknown date), in which the speaker remarks on the subject's tender tongue. The outrage of the silenced female, is a subtext of Dickinson's "Tell All the Truth but Tell It Slant" (ca. 1868). Whatever the impetus to Dickinson's views on passion and WOMEN'S RIGHTS, she makes clear in "Who Is It Seeks My Pillow Nights" (ca. 1884) that conscience gives her no respite from seeking sexual pleasure through a burst of physical release she terms "The Phosphorus of God" (*ibid.*, 661).

Dickinson's influence took a variety of shapes in the lives of the poets Amy LOWELL, Adrienne RICH, and May SARTON and the authors Anna QUINDLEN and Jean RHYS. The feminist playwright Susan GLASPELL won a Pulitzer Prize for reprising the poet's life in *Alison's House* (1930). Set after the death of the hermetic title figure, the play describes her niece, Elsa's, gradual realization that her aunt was able to satisfy desires by abandoning any hope of romantic love. The play opened in New York City at Eva Le Gallienne's Civic Repertory Theatre a century after Dickinson's birth. In 1987, the dramatist Micheline Wandor won an International Emmy Award for her adaptation of the teleplay *The Belle of Amherst*, which starred Claire Bloom in the role of Emily Dickinson.

Bibliography

Bennett, Paula. "Critical Clitoridectomy: Female Sexual Imagery and Feminist Psychoanalytic Theory," *Signs: Journal of Women in Culture and Society* 18, no. 2 (Winter 1993): 235–259.

Bogan, Louise. *Achievement in American Poetry.* Los Angeles: Gateway, 1951.

Dickinson, Emily. *The Complete Poems of Emily Dickinson.* Boston: Little, Brown, 1957.

Farr, Judith. *The Passion of Emily Dickinson.* Cambridge, Mass.: Harvard University Press, 1994.

Fuss, Diana. "Interior Chambers: The Emily Dickinson Homestead," *Differences: A Journal of Feminist Cultural Studies* 20, no. 3 (Fall 1998): 1–46.

Juhasz, Suzanne, and Christanne Miller, eds. *Emily Dickinson: A Celebration for Readers.* New York: Gordon & Breach, 1989.

Rich, Adrienne. *Adrienne Rich's Poetry and Prose.* New York: W. W. Norton, 1975.

Dinesen, Isak (Karen Christence Dinesen, baroness Blixen) (1885–1962)

A wartime journalist and successful producer of horror tales, fantasy, and fables, Isak Dinesen used feminist fiction as a means of liberating women from the DOUBLE STANDARD. Born Karen Christence Dinesen in Rungsted, Denmark, she was homeschooled by a feminist grandmother and aunt who involved themselves in the second wave of the WOMEN'S RIGHTS movement. She studied at Miss Sode's Art School and the Royal Academy of Art in Copenhagen. In 1914 she married Baron Bror Blixen and bought a coffee plantation outside Nairobi, Kenya.

Multiple crises shaped Dinesen's writing. After a disastrous fire, a serious bout with syphilis, and the collapse of the coffee market, she divorced Blixen. She repatriated to her native Rungstedlund to recuperate and turned to short fiction, beginning with *Seven Gothic Tales* (1934), and to memoir in *Out of Africa* (1937) and *Shadows on the Grass* (1961). As did Gertrude ATHERTON, the BRONTËS, George ELIOT, and George SAND, Dinesen wrote under a male pen name to obscure her gender from critics and readers. From the Old Testament, she chose *Isak,* which is Hebrew for "laughter." Aided by the author Dorothy Canfield FISHER, Dinesen finally published her first text in the United States.

A teller in the traditional style, Dinesen succeeded both critically and financially by mastering the hypnotic power of oral fiction and by according female characters their own mastery of individual talents as ammunition against SILENCING. Her clever use of conventional Gothic buildings and gendered social settings, such as convents, boardinghouses, and kitchens, showcases a number of female characters who reject Victorian standards and define their own identity. In one example, the metamorphosis of Pellegrina Leoni in "The Dreamers" (1934) portrays a determined female who evolves from suppressed grand diva to courtesan, rebel, and saint. In her 70s, Dinesen composed a feminist fable, *Babette's Feast* (1959), which pictures one of the author's own dream careers in the actions of a famed cook, Babette Hersant, a humble mother figure fleeing revolution in France. In one grand display of culinary expertise and of generosity with foodstuffs bought with 10,000 francs, all her winnings from the French lottery, she contrasts the pettiness and unloving behavior of Norwegian pietists. As though advancing Christian communion into a love feast, she serves an exquisite menu to open their hearts to affection, passion, and forgiveness.

Bibliography

Dinesen, Isak. *On Modern Marriage and Other Observations.* New York: St. Martin's, 1986.

Kanaganayakam, Chelva. "Isak Dinesen and Narrativity: Reassessments for the 1990s," *University of Toronto Quarterly* 66, no. 1 (Winter 1996–1997): 7.

Mullins, Maire. "Home, Community, and the Gift That Gives in Isak Dinesen's 'Babette's Feast,'" *Women's Studies* 23, no. 3 (July 1994): 217–228.

Stambaugh, Sara. "Isak Dinesen in America." (1998). Available online. URL: http://www.ualberta.ca/%7Ecins/lectures/isak_dinesen.htm. Accessed on April 28, 2004.

Di Prima, Diane (1934–)

The Italian-American memoirist and feminist poet Diane Di Prima crystallizes archetypal views of women and their innate strengths. Reared in her native Brooklyn, she grew up among strong women, particularly her immigrant grandmother, Antoinette Mallozzi. After attending college-preparatory courses at Hunter High School for gifted girls, Di Prima was dissatisfied with her conventional education at Swarthmore College, which she abandoned in 1953. She allied with the avant-garde beat poets and lived the unfettered bohemian lifestyle of a bisexual artist, disciple of Zen Buddhism, lover of Le Roi Jones, and single parent of five, all of which she describes in the autobiographical novel *Memoirs of a Beatnik* (1969) and in *Recollections of My Life as a Woman: The New York Years* (2001). During her personal liberation, she worked as cofounder of Poet's Press and Poet's Theatre and editor of *The Floating Bear,* an influential beat newsletter.

Di Prima's prolific writings in 300 periodicals and 70 anthologies challenge the records of the top male beatniks. Her canon breaches the overriding taboo among Italian-American females against revealing the secrets of the ethnic community by picturing women in novel settings. In the first canto of her eight-part epic cycle *Loba* (1978) she introduces the primacy of the self-worshiping she-wolf: "Even field mice knew she called the shots" (Di Prima, 1998, 1). Sinuous and graceful, the speaker gathers bones as material for reconfiguring the past, a motif that suggests the patchwork of quilting. She enjoys her feral body and the feminine qualities of her instincts, which emerge in the mythic figures of Ariadne, Iseult, the Babylonian goddess Ishtar, the seductress LILITH, the mythic captive PERSEPHONE, the Indian deities Siva and Kali, and the VIRGIN MARY.

As in Jean AUEL's *Clan of the Cave Bear* (1985), the zest of the verse cycle arises from animal GODDESS LORE and the bestial power that the primal female releases in herself. Segments glimpse shape shifting, visions., and dreamy rituals that touch on ecstatic forms of worship of the world's native cultures. In more caustic sections, Di Prima presses a fundamental feminist question: How did so strong a creative force surrender to subjugation and discounting by males?

Bibliography

Di Prima, Diane. *Loba.* New York: Penguin, 1998.
———. *Recollections of My Life as a Woman: The New York Years.* New York: Viking, 2001.
Warshall, Peter. "The Tapestry of Possibility," *Whole Earth* 98 (Fall 1999): 20–22.

"Diving into the Wreck" Adrienne Rich (1973)

The American master poet Adrienne RICH anchored her collection *Diving into the Wreck: Poems 1971–1972* (1973) to the title allegory. A model of the controlling metaphor, the poem describes the quest of the lone female adventurer who demands more of life than what floats on the surface. Topside, Rich pictures the savvy diver as a reader of myth who chooses to explore obscure relics with camera and knife, emblems of realism and self-protection. Down the innocent-looking ladder, she ventures into the black depths with the empowerment of an oxygen mask, a suggestion of the feminine persona that shields her in a tricky undersea environment. With her go the patience and self-confidence of the unaided woman, who, unlike the legendary naturalist Jacques Cousteau, chooses to maneuver within the watery element in awkward flippers, but without the aid of a power sled.

The goal of the dive is an eyewitness survey of the wreck, which faulty words and maps have scarred and eroded. For all the years of damage, the speaker anticipates finding the remains of a treasure "more permanent / than fish or weed" (Rich, 54). Encased in water, a symbol of infinity,

the exposed ribs testify to endurance. A metaphor for women's history, the hulk suffers salt damage, a suggestion of tears, as well as the hauntings of centuries of ghostly visitors. The androgynous mermaid/merman takes the plunge into the hold, a dramatic moment at the climactic confrontation with the corpse that female seekers from ancient times "once held to a course" (*ibid.*, 55). Rich implies that women have lost their way, leaving their instruments, log, and compass to ruin. To retrieve the truth about women's role in civilization, she encourages them to grasp the true eye of the camera, the protective blade of the knife, and healthy skepticism about "myths / in which / our names do not appear" (*ibid.*)

Redemptive in its rigors, the dive to the wreck penetrates political and gender barriers that silence and dismiss females. The effort reacquaints the lone explorer with a beauty grown more appealing after centuries of neglect and patriarchal corrosion. The colors of green and blue connect the sunken remains with blue skies and verdant nature. Remarkable in its resilience, the shell of a past era rewards the diver with a touch of female achievement concealed by layers of time. The boundaries that require careful navigation give way to narrative, the inscription of female names that refute androcentric lore. As gender salvage, the rewriting of the past is worth the dive.

Bibliography

Gilbert, Roger. "Framing Water: Historical Knowledge in Elizabeth Bishop and Adrienne Rich," *Twentieth Century Literature* 43, no. 2 (Summer 1997): 144–161.
Rich, Adrienne. *Adrienne Rich's Poetry and Prose.* New York: W. W. Norton, 1975.
Stansell, Christine. "Diving into the Wreck." *Off Our Backs,* 28 February 1974, p. 15.

Doll's House, A Henrik Ibsen (1879)

The radical Norwegian dramatist Henrik Ibsen, the father of modern realistic drama, earned ridicule and reproof for revealing women's need for validation and for INDEPENDENCE from male authority. In 1879, he displaced the standard pattern of domestic playwriting in his landmark social drama *A Doll's House.* Critics and moralists assailed him for publishing a decadent and subversive play that lionizes a woman guilty of fraud and of deserting her husband, home, and children. Ibsen's depiction of Nora Helmer as a sensible family financier helped to direct the course of feminist stage drama and to establish themes of middle-class hypocrisy and the emotional and financial strangulation of women by patriarchal marriage. Neither comic nor tragic in structure, the play depicts the daily tides in domestic lives that erode accepted social and religious codes.

By stripping the dialogue of the amusing husband-wife badinage common to domestic drama, the playwright relieves the atmosphere of sentimentality. He reveals the growing discontent that prefaces Nora's lengthy statement of unhappiness and that sends her on a yet-to-be discovered path to a new life. Of his perspective, he remarked, "There are two kinds of spiritual law . . . one in man and one in woman . . . but the woman is judged in practical matters by man's law" (Ferguson, 230). He stressed that Europe "is exclusively a male society with laws written by men and with prosecutors and judges who judge women's behavior from the male standpoint" (ibid.). He was successful with his experimental drama of ideas, which flourished in productions in Copenhagen, Munich, Oslo, and Stockholm. His publisher reprinted the play twice within 12 weeks and ordered translations in English, Finnish, German, Italian, Polish, and Russian. One of the strongest performers of the role of Nora Helmer was the Italian actress Eleanora Duse.

Ibsen's focus on the theme of miseducation and subjugation of women derives clout from the title, which suggests the gingerbread dollhouses in which little girls set make-believe families in structured domestic scenarios. Torvald miniaturizes his wife with his choice of demeaning epithets—"my little lark," "my little squirrel," "my little spendthrift," and "little featherhead" (Ibsen, 3, 4). From his self-ennobling perspective as bank manager, he further devalues her for thinking "like a woman" by borrowing money against his wishes (ibid., 4). The pet names dot the dialogue of act 1—"odd little soul," "Miss Sweet-Tooth," "poor little girl" (ibid., 6, 7). Echoing the father-daughter charade, Nora cajoles, connives, and lies like a

child as her only means of negotiating with a husband who confuses his conjugal role with fatherhood. As an automaton, she performs the appointed tasks of mother, hostess, and nurse during his illness. In breaking out of the harness of the well-disciplined mate, she violates his dictates by negotiating a loan with a forged signature to pay for his year's recuperation in Italy.

The revelation of Nora's violation of the male banking hegemony forces viewers to examine the absurdity of treating women as senseless children. After eight years as husband and wife, they react differently to blackmail by Nils Krogstad, a disgruntled bank clerk. To Torvald, the clerk's coercion threatens scandal and an end to Torvald's reputation for refinement and business acumen. He sees Nora as "a hypocrite, a liar—worse, worse—a criminal!" (ibid., 59). To Nora, Torvald's superficial response and his removal of their three children from Nora's care produce a climax to mounting disenchantment that sends her over the edge. No longer willing to dress, dance, and recite like a wind-up toy, she denounces the patriarchal system that transfers women from their fathers' hands into those of paternal husbands. She rejects Torvald's offer to retrain her and takes responsibility for her own rehabilitation.

Bibliography

Ferguson, Robert. *Henrik Ibsen: A New Biography*. London: Cohen, 1996.

Hardwick, Elizabeth. *Seduction and Betrayal*. New York: Vintage, 1975.

Ibsen, Henrik. *A Doll's House*. In *Four Great Plays by Ibsen*. New York: Bantam, 1984.

Mitchell, Hayley R., ed. *Readings on* A Doll's House. Westport, Conn.: Greenhaven, 1999.

Templeton, Joan. *Ibsen's Women*. Cambridge: Cambridge University Press, 2001.

domestic abuse

Feminist writers capture the dramatic context of marital battery, a central theme in drama, screenplay, verse, stories, and novels as well as memoir and AUTOBIOGRAPHY. In 1926, the folklorist Zora Neale HURSTON spoke through a washwoman's experience in "Sweat" the ongoing nightmare of the overbearing husband: "Delia's work-worn knees crawled over the earth in Gethsemane and up the rocks of Calvary many, many times" (Hurston, 79). The ramifications of flight from abuse dominate the novelist Amy TAN's *The Kitchen God's Wife* (1991), the story of Winnie Louie's domestic nightmare set during the bombings and ravages of the Sino-Japanese War (1937–45), which amplify her inner horror. To escape sadistic sex and the abuse of her son, Danru, she plots a way out of feudal marriage but lacks direction. In terror of making her own way, she admits, "If I had known I was running away to something better, that would have been different. But I had no such hope to run to" (Tan, 273).

The tone of abuse literature ranges from black humor about wife battery in Beth HENLEY's three-act comedy *Crimes of the Heart* (1979) and thoughtful speculation in Joanna RUSS's feminist utopian fiction to the American Indian poet Joy HARJO's poem of desperation, "The Woman Hanging from the Thirteenth Floor Window" (1983). At the far end of revenge literature, Faith McNulty's true-crime account *The BURNING BED: The True Story of Francine Hughes, a Beaten Wife Who Rebels* (1980) describes a spouse murderer pushed beyond her limit of endurance. In McNulty's terrifying narrative, the husband's pummeling and death threats spill over from wife to children and house pets. Francine recognizes the pattern of drinking and television watching that prefaces sexual assault. To herself, she ponders her wifely duty: "I've got to do this and I've got to do that, and Mickey is going to want sex. After I clean house, mow the lawn, and do the laundry, Mickey will want sex; then I can do something else" (McNulty, 137). The lack of affection and tenderness generates self-abusive feelings: "I felt dirty. I'd hate myself for letting it happen" (*ibid.*). She sinks into hopelessness relieved at intervals by a desire to spirit her children away from cyclical terror.

A comic examination of spousal abuse after the fact occurs in Lynn Nottage's one-act surreal comedy *Poof* (1993), which debuted at Actors Theatre of Louisville on March 20, 1993. After causing her husband, Samuel, to vanish in a cloud of ash by damning him to hell, Loureen stands in her kitchen amazed at her instant liberation. She declares that the power to liquidate a hard-handed mate will change her life forever: "All that needs to happen now is for my palms to bleed and I'll be eternally remembered as St. Loureen, the patron of battered wives. . . . Women from across the country will make pilgrimages to me, laying pies and pot roast at my feet and asking the good saint to make their husbands turn to dust" (Nottage, 7). Rejoicing in her freedom, she marvels, "All these years and just words," a comic reminder of the SILENCING of women through menacing words and gestures and domestic battery against wives and children (*ibid.*, 11). Lightening the mood is Loureen's suggestion that she mail the ashes to Samuel's mother.

In *Breath, Eyes, Memory* (1994), the Haitian novelist Edwidge DANTICAT describes the after-effects of sexual abuse. Sophie, the daughter of a wife batterer, visualizes the male as "the large shadow of a man [who] mounted her [mother]" (Danticat, 210). Sophie receives advice from a psychologist, who notes, "Your mother never gave him a face. That's why he's a shadow. That's why he can control her. I'm not surprised she's having nightmares" (*ibid.*, 209). The novel concludes with the mother's vengeful suicide by stabbing her womb 17 times with a rusted knife to end a pregnancy. Honoring a woman haunted by terrors are handfuls of dirt thrown on her coffin by mother, sister, and daughter. Another clump is tossed by the daughter to represent her own female child, the last addition to a loving matrilineage. The grandmother calls to the deceased's spirit, "Ou libéré!" (Are you free?) (*ibid.*, 233).

Bibliography

Danticat, Edwidge. *Breath, Eyes, Memory.* New York: Soho Press, 1994.

Hurston, Zora Neale. *The Complete Stories.* New York: HarperCollins, 1995.

McNulty, Faith. *The Burning Bed.* New York: Harcourt, Brace Jovanovich, 1980.

Nottage, Lynn. *Poof in Plays for Actresses.* Edited by Eric Lane and Nina Shengold. New York: Vintage, 1997.

Tan, Amy. *The Kitchen God's Wife,* New York: Putnam, 1991.

Doolittle, Hilda (H. D.) (1886–1961)

Hilda Doolittle, the imagist poet and Sapphic spiritualist known by the initials H. D., feminized views of literary tradition by resetting male-centered aesthetics and by extolling the goddess cult. Born in Bethlehem, Pennsylvania, and reared in Philadelphia, Hilda was the daughter of the university professor, mathematician, and astronomer Charles Leander Doolittle and of Helen Eugenia Wolle, a patron of the arts and mystic religion. At Miss Gordon's School and the Friends' Central School in Philadelphia, Hilda excelled at classical and modern language but felt out of place because of her defiance of Edwardian prissiness. After a year and a half at Bryn Mawr, she wearied of educational and social regimentation and abandoned heterosexual monogamy through tentative amours with men and women.

A permanent expatriate quartered in London, H. D. married the writer Richard Aldington, editor of the *Egoist*, and shared a translation project with him that produced Classic Greek lyrics in English, including the verse of SAPPHO. During World War I, H. D. read Virginia WOOLF and James Joyce and studied free verse under the coaching of the poet Ezra Pound. After issuing her finely honed minimalist poems in Pound's compilation *Des Imagistes* (Some Imagists, 1914), H. D. began writing for *English Review, Poetry,* and the *Transatlantic Review.* She coedited the *Egoist* and compiled a first anthology, *Sea Garden* (1916). The collection, encouraged by the poet Amy LOWELL, contains "Sea Rose," a meditation on idealized female beauty and the vulva shapes revealed in flowers, an erotic symbolism that later energized the paintings of Georgia O'Keeffe. A series of personal tragedies and an emotional collapse preceded H. D.'s union with her lifelong lover, Annie Winnifred "Bryher" Ellerman, with whom the poet traveled Europe, America, and the Mediterranean. After World War II they shared a home at Lake Geneva overlooking the Alps.

H. D. pursued a feminist career by publishing woman-centered verse in *Hymen* (1921) and *Heliodora and Other Poems* (1924). The latter work contains an apologia on the sins of Helen of Troy and a feminist form of Hellenism dominated by the mother creator. The poet moved into the international spotlight with *The Collected Poems of H. D.* (1925), which contains a defense of Eurydice, the wife of Orpheus, whom he dooms to the Underworld by disobeying a divine command. In retort to the husband who violates the terms of her reclamation, Eurydice calls him ruthless and arrogant. In "Orchard," the poet creates a disjunctive vision of freedom from feminine restrictions. H. D. followed with *HERmione* (1927), a roman à clef that explores her ambivalence about bisexuality. During World War II, she examined themes of MATRIARCHY and antimilitarism in *The Walls Do Not Fall* (1944), *Tribute to the Angels* (1945), and *Flowering of the Rod* (1946).

After an upturn in her health and outlook, H. D. produced *Tribute to Freud* (1954), a statement of gratitude for two years of psychoanalytic treatment for depression. More settled in her last decade, she made a home for her daughter, Perdita, until her own death of a paralytic stroke and influenza. One of the many feminist authors recovered in the 1980s, H. D. earned the regard of the poets Adrienne RICH and May SARTON and an extensive reevaluation as writer and feminist. Among the poet's contributions to female emancipation are the defeat of gendered STEREOTYPING, respect for women as artists, and the transformation of androcentric myth, particularly in *Hymen,* which she devoted to females from ancient Greek lore.

Chief among H. D.'s innovative retellings are revisions to depictions of Helen of Troy, scapegoat of the Trojan War, particularly in Euripides' play *The Trojan Women* (415 B.C.), which relegates her to the trash heap of sirens and strumpets. In 1924 H. D.'s "Helen" pictured the wan queen as the child of a god and as the female sacrifice that Greeks could love only in death. To retrieve a resplendent female figure, H. D.'s epic *Helen in Egypt* (1961) introduces Helen as "hated of all Greece" and pictures the warring heroes "cursing Helen through eternity" (Doolittle, 1974, 1, 4). The poet reconfigures Helen as an illusion of the real woman, a version that Stesichorus of Sicily introduced in the sixth century B.C. H. D. strips Helen of idealized traits and supplies her a voice to defy critical distortions. The poet's feminist ideals influenced the verse of Rita DOVE and Denise LEVERTOV.

Bibliography

Collecott, Diana. "Remembering Oneself: The Reputation and Later Poetry of H. D.," *Critical Quarterly* 27, no. 1 (Spring 1985): 7–22.

Doolittle, Hilda. *Helen in Egypt.* New York: New Directions Publishing, 1974.

———. *Hymen* (1921). Available online. URL: http://digital.library.upenn.edu/women/doolittle/hymen/hymen.html. Accessed on October 13, 2005.

Friedman, Susan Stanford. *Penelope's Web: Gender, Modernity, H. D.'s Fiction.* Cambridge: Cambridge University Press, 1991.

Keeling, Bret L. "H. D. and 'The Contest': Archaeology of a Sapphic Gaze," *Twentieth Century Literature* 44, no. 2 (Summer 1998): 176–203.

Rainey, Lawrence S. "Canon, Gender, and Text: The Case of H. D.," *College Literature* 18, no. 3 (October 1991): 106–125.

double standard

The codification of laws, rules, and social expectations for women forces on half the world's population a more stringent regulation based solely on gender. The feminist essayist and orator Voltairine DE CLEYRE insisted that such unfair and unwarranted supervision of girls and women was both life-altering and life-threatening. In the essay "Sex Slavery" (1890), she charged males with perpetuating "pestiferous ideas": "To preserve your cruel, vicious, indecent standard of purity, you drive your daughters insane, while your wives are killed with excess. Such is marriage. Don't take my word for it; go through the report of any asylum or the annals of any graveyard" (de Cleyre). She described the restraints on little girls, who could not swim, go barefoot, or climb trees without risking a scolding for improper behavior. Her remedy for the double standard was complete liberty for both genders.

The famed feminist intellectual and writer Charlotte Perkins GILMAN dramatized society's double standard of domestic expectations in HERLAND (1915), a landmark utopian novel. After three conventional males, Jeff, Terry, and Van, visit the all-woman society, they express gender-based expectations that their own society forces on women. The men admire the corseted, hobbled figures of American fashion plates but choose for themselves more comfortable, practical garments than feathered hats, laced corsets, trains, and pointed-toed shoes. Gilman gently ridicules conventional homes that pamper men while heaping women with drudgery. In planning a home for their new wives, the men project a welcoming place where their mates anticipate the men's needs, serve their favorite foods, and tend to laundry and cleaning without male involvement. More dismaying to the female citizens of Herland is the prevalent male attitude toward child rearing, which society thrusts upon women and demands that they enjoy despite the martyrdom and isolation of day-to-day responsibility for socializing, disciplining, and educating each new addition to the family.

The sexual double standard evokes more heated attacks on PATRIARCHY. The Chilean novelist Isabel ALLENDE's female gothic novel *The HOUSE OF THE SPIRITS* (1982) describes the social climbing of Esteban Trueba, a brutalizer of his native labor force, particularly its females. After building up Tres Marias into a respectable hacienda, he discovers his daughter, Blanca's, love for a teenager, Pedro Tercero García, and lashes her with a whip. His wife, Clara, appropriately named for the clarity of her moral vision, reminds him that Pedro "hasn't done a thing you haven't done yourself! . . . You also slept with unmarried women not of your own class" (Allende, 200). She adds for good measure, "The only difference is that he did it for love. And so did Blanca" (*ibid.*). The logic of her argument so stuns Esteban that he beats his wife senseless. The end of the double standard in their household also puts an end to their marriage. To enforce her accusations against Esteban, Clara removes her wedding band, forgoes her married name, and takes Blanca to live at Clara's family home. Allende hyperbolizes Esteban's hypocrisy by blaming his illegitimate son, Esteban García, for the arrest, torture, and rape of Blanca during a military coup. Thus, Esteban's clandestine womanizing in the outback evolves into vicious incest by his son against Blanca.

Bibliography

Allende, Isabel. *The House of the Spirits.* New York: Bantam, 1986.

de Cleyre, Voltairine. "Sex Slavery" (1890). Available online. URL: http://dwardmac.pitzer.edu/Anarchist_Archives/bright/cleyre/sexslavery.html. Accessed on October 13, 2005.

De La Motte, Eugenia. "Refashioning the Mind: The Revolutionary Rhetoric of Voltairine de Cleyre." *Legacy,* 30 April 2003, p. 153.

Douglass, Frederick (ca. 1817–1895)

A social reformer and author of a compelling slave narrative, the orator and polemicist Frederick Douglass furthered ABOLITIONISM and eased the Civil War years and their aftermath with advice on how to involve former slaves in American life. Born into bondage in Talbot County, Maryland, he taught himself to read and write, learned the caulking trade, and fled his owner in 1838 for the free North. At age 24, he settled in Lynn, Massachusetts, and aided the freedom fighter William Lloyd Garrison by giving eyewitness accounts of the inhumanity of bondage and promoting abolitionist journals, the *Anti-Slavery Standard* and the *Liberator.* At antislavery meetings Douglass recounted experiences under cruel masters and overseers. In 1845 he published his best-selling AUTOBIOGRAPHY, *Narrative of the Life of Frederick Douglass, an American Slave,* an account of his bondage that could have resulted in his recapture under the Fugitive Slave Law. He traveled England before relocating his family to Rochester, New York, where he published the *North Star* and aided blacks fleeing over the Underground Railroad. As his philosophy extended from slaves to all subject peoples, he assisted Elizabeth Cady STANTON in the fight for WOMEN'S RIGHTS. In July 1848 he was the only male supporting woman suffrage at the Seneca Falls women's rights convention in New York. He expressed his admiration for the delegates and declared that women should enjoy the same rights that men claim. In the *North Star* the following August 10, he asserted that women are "entitled to an equal participancy in all the designs and accomplishments allotted to man during his career on earth" (Douglass, 48).

During the Civil War, Douglass encouraged blacks to rely on themselves. According to the reporter Harriet Beecher STOWE, summarizing an eyewitness meeting with the orator for *Atlantic Monthly,* at a public meeting in Faneuil Hall in Boston, Douglass allowed emotion to dramatize his discourse. He "grew more and more excited, and finally ended by saying that they had no hope of justice from the whites, no possible hope except in their own right arms. It must come to blood; they must fight for themselves, and redeem themselves, or it would never be done" (Stowe, 480). He canvassed for votes for Abraham Lincoln and championed the Union army's addition of the 54th and 55th Massachusetts Colored Regiments, which allowed black males to fight for their own freedom.

Douglass did not stint on activism after the war. During Reconstruction, he demanded EDUCATION and prison reform for blacks, an end to white supremacy groups, TEMPERANCE, and sexual and racial equality in employment, polling places, and public office. In 1867, he thundered from the pages of *Atlantic Monthly* a rebuke against partial SUFFRAGE: "Disfranchisement in a republican government based upon the idea of human equality and universal suffrage, is a very different thing from disfranchisement in governments based upon the idea of the divine right of kings, or the entire subjugation of the masses" (Douglass, 115). While living in Washington, D.C., in the 1870s, he presided over the Freemen's Bank and accepted posts as U.S. marshal under Rutherford B. Hayes and, in James A. Garfield's administration, as the recorder of deeds for the District of Columbia. After the death of his wife, Anna Murray Douglass, in 1884, he toured Europe and served as consul general of Haiti. In his mid-70s, he supported the journalist Ida B. WELLS's antilynching campaign at the World's Columbian Exhibition in Chicago. While waiting to speak at a woman suffrage rally on February 20, 1895, he collapsed at the podium and died of cardiac arrest.

Feminists revere Douglass for championing the powerless and voiceless in orations delivered at the rate of more than 300 per year and in print almost daily. Eyewitness accounts of his dignified stance, rich voice, and noble features account for his ability to sway hostile audiences with the motto "Right Is of No Sex." Speaking with scriptural gravity, he challenged hearers to take seriously the injustices suffered by blacks and women. In 1848, he declared women's rights a universal concern: "This cause is not altogether and exclusively woman's cause. It is the cause of human brotherhood as well as human sisterhood, and both must rise and fall together. Woman cannot be elevated without elevating man, and man cannot be depressed without depressing woman also" (Kimmel, 30).

In admiration for women, Douglass predicted that the history of American abolitionism would feature females who refused to accept enslavement and disenfranchisement of any citizen. His vision of the future materialized during the Harlem Renaissance with the work of the playwright Georgia Douglas JOHNSON, who in 1935 added historical drama to her domestic plays with *Frederick Douglass*, a one-act melodrama set in a kitchen, her standard placement of characters and action. Sniffing gingerbread fresh from the oven, Fred remarks, "This here little bit of kitchen of yours is the nearest I ever been to heaven since I been born" (Johnson, 5). He recalls at age six his one meeting with his mother, who walked 40 miles to embrace him. Engaged to Ann, who fosters her orphaned brother, Bud, and coengineers her sweetheart's escape to the North, Douglass anticipates the mother love he missed in boyhood.

Bibliography

Douglass, Frederick. *Frederick Douglass on Women's Rights*. Westport, Conn.: Greenwood, 1976.

Johnson, Georgia Douglas. *Frederick Douglass* in *Negro History in Thirteen Plays*. Edited by May Miller and Willis Richardson. Washington, D.C.: Associated Publishers, 1935.

Kimmel, Michael S. "Men Supporting Women," *UNESCO Courier* 48, no. 9 (September 1995): 30–31.

Schneir, Miriam, ed. *Feminism: The Essential Historical Writings*. New York: Vintage, 1972.

Stowe, Harriet Beecher. "Sojourner Truth, the Libyan Sibyl" (1863). Available online. URL: http://wyllie. lib.virginia.edu:8086/perl/toccer-new?id= StoSojo.sgm&images=images/modeng&data=/ texts/english/modeng/parsed&tag=public& part=1&division=div1. Accessed on October 13, 2005.

Dove, Rita (1952–)

A groundbreaking playwright and poet in service for two terms to the Library of Congress, Rita Frances Dove explores home-centered roles of women as wives, housekeepers, and mothers. The daughter of Elvira Elizabeth Hord and Ray A. Dove, a lab chemist for Goodyear, she was born in Akron, Ohio, and grew up amid upper-middle-class standards. Her family filled her life with art, opera, drama, and plenty of books. As an exercise in translation, she rendered a poem by the German author Friedrich von Schiller into English. Miss Oechsner, a high school English teacher, introduced Dove to live poetry at a reading by John Ciardi. A chance discovery of Toni MORRISON's novel *The BLUEST EYE* (1970) in the school library relieved Dove's isolation in the predominantly white Midwest. At her graduation in 1970 she received a National Merit Scholarship and the Presidential Scholarship, which placed her among the top 100 college applicants nationwide.

A Phi Beta Kappan and graduate of Miami University, Dove chose poetry over law as her life's work. After analyzing the work of Paul Celan and Rainer Maria Rilke at the University of Tübingen on a Fulbright/Hays scholarship, she edited *Callaloo*, *Gettysburg Review*, and *TriQuarterly*. She earned an M.F.A. from the University of Iowa, where she studied the works of H. D. under the supervision of the poet Louise GLÜCK. In earnest Dove began composing impressionistic poems with an economy of words that required intense rewriting. At her cabin near Charlottesville, Virginia, her thoughts branched out from remembered sounds and everyday feelings into spare imagery, the source of "Crab-Boil" and "My Mother Enters the Work Force." Her first collection, *Ten Poems* (1977), preceded her marriage to her translator, Fred Viebahn.

At age 28, Dove published *The Only Dark Spot in the Sky* (1980) and *The Yellow House on the Corner* (1980). The latter is a verse imitation of historic slave narratives filled with the terrors of sexual abuse. "The House Slave" depicts "Massa" as a man obsessed by "asses, rum and slave-funk" (Dove, 28). In "Belinda's Petition," Dove crafts a pathetic memoir of a black girl pursued by men who "ride toward me steadily for twelve Years" (*ibid.*). Dove followed with *Museum* (1983) and her masterwork, *Thomas and Beulah* (1986), an ode to her mother's parents, Georgiana and Thomas. The domestic setting pictures the era of black migration from South to North, which Dove details with meals of hambone and greens and the blues lyrics of Billie Holliday and Lightnin' Hopkins. Covering four decades of love and devotion, the verse novel gives individuality to husband and wife. In a sharp flashback, "Taking in Wash" depicts a mother as enraged as an Old Testament matriarch over threats of incest in her home. She threatens mayhem to her drunken husband if he lays hands on their daughter. In 1991, notoriety from *Thomas and Beulah* gained Dove two additional boosts in prestige as juror for the National Book Award and recipient of the Pulitzer Prize in poetry. In 1993 she became the first black poet and second female to serve U.S. legislators as poetry consultant to the Library of Congress.

A year after composing the melodrama *The Darker Face of the Earth* (1994), the story of a white mother's reunion with her biracial son, Dove examined the mother-daughter relationship in the verse suite *Mother Love* (1995), which she modeled on Rilke's "The Sonnets to Orpheus" (1922). From Greek examples, she chose female mythic figures for "Persephone, Falling" and "Demeter Mourning." The first poem reprises the terror of Hades's outdoor rape of the maiden PERSEPHONE as she picks flowers. Too late, like LITTLE RED RIDING HOOD, she recalls the mother's warnings about encounters with strange men. The second poem shares the grief of the tenacious mother Demeter, who can never know happiness so long as her daughter, Persephone, resides with a pedophile. A lighter poem, "Used," chuckles with a wife who returns to the marital bed after giving birth. As an inducement to passion, she buys silk sheets. The boost to lovemaking leaves husband and wife grasping at slick surfaces as they slide to the floor.

The reading public lauds Dove for satisfying black female soul hunger for sensuality and recognition. "Cameos" in *On the Bus with Rosa Parks* (1999) positions Lucille, the pregnant wife, in garden rows between lush feminine tomato shapes and phallic pole beans. As EVE does in Eden, she gains a snake's-eye view of creation and bases her hopes for happiness on conjugal bliss. At the high point of the collection, an image of the historic bus rider in "Rosa" notes fire in her eyes and an unflinching posture. Dove concludes with "inside gertrude stein," a confessional tour de force that credits a feminist forerunner with directing Dove's inner thoughts on womanhood.

Bibliography

Dove, Rita. *The Yellow House on the Corner.* Pittsburgh: Carnegie Mellon University, 1980.

Hogue, Cynthia. "Poetry, Politics and Postmodernism," *Women's Review of Books* 17, no. 9 (June 2000): 20–21.

Pereira, Malin. "An Interview with Rita Dove," *Contemporary Literature* 40, no. 2 (Summer 1999): 182–213.

Drabble, Margaret (1939–   )

Margaret Drabble is a multitalented writer, lecturer, and editor with a keen vision of women's trials. A native of Sheffield in England and student of Mount School and Newnham College, she won double honors while earning a degree in English. She dabbled in theater in 1960 with the Royal Shakespeare Company. Her marriage to the actor Clive Swift lasted 15 years, during which she reviewed for the *Daily Mail* and wrote *The Millstone* (1965), winner of the John Llewelyn Rhys Prize for its depiction of the trials of the intellectual woman. After a period of writing BIOGRAPHY and AUTOBIOGRAPHY, she published four works on the theme of male dominance: *The Waterfall* (1967), *The Needle's Eye* (1972), *The Realms of Gold* (1975), and *The Ice Age* (1977). In her 40s, she devoted her literary expertise to editing *The Oxford Companion to English Literature* (1985), *Twentieth Century Literature* (1987), and *Studies in the Novel* (1988).

While denying her ties to feminism, the author exhibits the influence of the novelist and theorist Virginia WOOLF. Drabble veered toward feminist fiction with *The Witch of Exmoor* (1996), a study of an AGING woman's revenge on her malignant family, and *The Seven Sisters* (2002), a metafictional quest novel describing the resurgence of a 59-year-old divorcée suitably named

Candida Wilton. Drabble's most recent fiction, *The Red Queen* (2004), incorporates Gothic convention as a means of linking 18th-century Korea with the Western world of the 21st century. The first half of the novel depicts the title character in an imprisoning microcosm, where feudal marriage and royal expectations limit her choices as severely as a prison cell. The text debunks romantic notions of court life, costumes, and pageantry and reduces all to an endless set of protocols for every word and gesture. Like lower-class women, the queen has little choice but to devote her life to rearing children and soothing the ego of a husband who descends into madness. Ironically, he dies in disgrace after his father shuts him into a wicker chest, an appropriate fate for a confiner of women. The most pathetic aspect of so delineated a life is the queen's inability to capitalize on her talents and intellect and the waste of her natural gifts for love and nurturance on a primitive, male-centered Asian culture.

Bibliography

Bromberg, P. S. "Margaret Drabble's *The Radiant Way:* Feminist Metafiction," *Novel: A Forum on Fiction* 24, no. 1 (Fall 1990): 5–25.

Dickson, E. Jane. "Somerset Mourn: What's Eating Novelist Margaret Drabble," *The Australian,* 21 September 2002.

Drabble, Margaret. *The Seven Sisters.* Orlando, Fla.: HarcourtBooks, 2002.

dreamscapes

Through flights of fantasy, feminist authors envision a more just world. In 19th-century Gothic narratives, dreamscapes reflect the psychological needs and drives of inhibited characters. In Emily BRONTË's novel *WUTHERING HEIGHTS* (1847) Catherine EARNSHAW experiences prenuptial jitters through a dream that she confides to Nelly Dean, a family servant. At the sight of heaven in her night vision Catherine's sobs cause the angels to toss her back to Wuthering Heights, where she weeps with joy. Catherine interprets the dreamscape as a warning: "I've no more business to marry Edgar Linton than I have to be in heaven" (Brontë, 82). To her sorrow, the capricious Cather-

ine allows a love of luxury and gentility to persuade her to violate her inner nature and to marry a mild-mannered, overrefined mate.

In Charlotte BRONTË's novel *JANE EYRE* (1847), dreams similar to those of Catherine Earnshaw alert the title figure to possible disaster in her love life. The forewarning allows Jane Eyre to penetrate a festering secret, the imprisonment of a madwoman on the third floor of Thornfield. During the four weeks preceding her marriage to Edward Rochester Jane experiences precognition of the stately hall in ruins. A mirage of Jane carries a child and anticipates a lengthy parting from Edward. The filmy night phantasm predicts her flight from Edward and his intended bigamy. On the night before Jane departs, a benign dream pictures her dead mother haloed in light. As a result of the series of dreams, Jane makes informed choices and saves herself from the grief a degraded relationship as Edward's mistress would have caused.

In the novel *What Dreams May Come* (1888), the American Gothic writer Gertrude ATHERTON uses night visions to bestow justice on a couple separated for three generations. She depicts reveries in which a contemporary romance between Harold Dartmouth and Weir Penrhyn replicates the passions of their grandparents, who shared an illicit affair. After lapsing into sleep, Dartmouth hovers on the rim of the past: "Why was he falling—falling?—What was that terror-stricken cry? that wild, white face of an old man above him? Where had this water come from that was boiling and thundering in his ears? What was that tossed aloft by the wave beyond?" (Atherton, 192). The illusion spurs him to action: "If he could but reach her!—She had gone!" (*ibid.*). He feels himself pulled toward the spirit of Weir's grandmother, Lady Sionèd Penrhyn, the lover of Dartmouth's grandfather. The magnetism of blunted passion from a past generation allows Dartmouth to intercede and, by reliving his grandfather's amour, to express unrequited love for Weir, the incarnation of Lady Sionèd. Atherton's use of revenant dreams suggests grief for past generations, who lived under the tyranny of stricter codes of sexual behavior.

Maya ANGELOU's version of race and gender politics generates a dramatic and droll dream episode in her classic AUTOBIOGRAPHY, *I Know Why the Caged Bird Sings* (1969). After her grandmother, Annie Henderson, receives a turn-down from Dentist Lincoln, whose "policy is I don't treat colored people," the Maya character forgets her aching jaw while imagining a woman-to-man showdown (Angelou, 160). As a feminist challenger at a High Noon–style walkdown, Maya daydreams the furious figure of Momma Henderson stalking into the white dentist's office, yanking him to attention, and tongue lashing him for his incivility, witnessed by her granddaughter. In reply to his stuttered apology, the dream grandmother snorts, "Sorry is as sorry does, and you're about the sorriest dentist I ever laid my eyes on. . . . I wouldn't waste a killing on the likes of you" (*ibid.*, 161, 162). Through fantasy Angelou is able to counter the white man's revulsion toward black women. Returned to reality, she reports Momma's mad-to-the-bone outrage: "He gonna be that kind of nasty, he gonna have to pay for it" (*ibid.*, 164). The author concludes that Momma possesses an "African-bush secretiveness and suspiciousness . . . compounded by slavery and confirmed by centuries of promises made and promises broken" (*ibid.*).

Through dreamscape other female characters elude persecution and potential death. In Ann PETRY's historical novel *Tituba of Salem Village* (1964), the title character finds release from the mob VIOLENCE of Massachusetts's colonial theocracy only in dreaming herself free once more under the palms that line the shores of Barbados. Connie Ramos, the heroine of Marge PIERCY's dystopic novel *Woman on the Edge of Time* (1976), projects herself far into the future in a utopia that liberates her from incarceration in a women's mental institution. The dreamscape fails to protect Connie from evil technology that threatens her autonomy with wires implanted in her brain and activated at a distance as remote controls maneuvering a robot. The Asian-American novelist Amy TAN uses a dreamscape to dramatize a father-daughter relationship in *The Kitchen God's Wife* (1991). Pearl Louie Brandt lessens the distance between herself and her deceased father by picturing them both as patients in a terminal ward. The designation becomes a leveling device that allows Pearl to admit that she is mortal.

In less fearful form the Chickasaw author Linda HOGAN sculpts a mystic dreamscape out of bird lore and the invisible currents of air on which eagle feathers waft to Earth. Voicing the ecofeminist oneness of soul with nature in *Dwellings: A Spiritual History of the Living World* (1996), she admits, "This event rubs the wrong way against logic. How do I explain the feather, the bird at my window, my own voice waking me, as if another person lived in me, wiser and more alert" (Hogan, 17). Taking a domestic perspective, she revives the importance of tribal WISEWOMEN and story keepers by comparing the magic of the feather with the protection of her granddaughter, Vivian's, umbilicus, which the mother dried and enclosed in a beaded medicine bag as a traditional guardian of life and wellness. To Hogan the potency of these life elements dates "all the way back to the creation of the universe and the small quickenings of earth, the first stirrings of human beings at the beginning of time" (*ibid.*, 19).

Bibliography

Angelou, Maya. *I Know Why the Caged Bird Sings.* New York: Bantam Books, 1970.

Atherton, Gertrude. *What Dreams May Come* (1888). Available online. URL: http://www.gutenberg.org/etext/12833. Accessed on October 13, 2005.

Brontë, Emily. *Wuthering Heights.* New York: New American Library, 1959.

Hogan, Linda. *Dwellings: A Spiritual History of the Living World.* New York: Touchstone, 1996.

duality

Dual personae in feminist literature echo the complex duality in women's lives. The novelist Emily BRONTË contrasts the overt and hidden selves in *Wuthering Heights* (1847), in which marriage ends Catherine EARNSHAW's enjoyment of freedom of movement. The latticework on Edgar Linton's windows at Thrushcross Grange implies that gentrification offers her affluence and prestige at the same time that it bars her access to the moors. Without freedom to enjoy nature with her beloved companion Heathcliff, she must wear the mask of contented domesticity, a deceit that results in her cries of despair from her deathbed and the wanderings of her restless ghost. In Charlotte Perkins GILMAN's short story "The YELLOW WALLPAPER" (1892), a more menacing confinement squeezes the life from a restless wife whose husband/doctor seeks to rid her of ambition. Like Catherine Earnshaw, the unnamed protagonist tries to please, but the extremes of her husband's "rest cure" push her to a surreal battle with an arabesque decor. Her arguments with the wall covering reduce her to MADNESS, which sends her crawling about the room in search of an outlet for her true self.

An uplifting dimension of feminist utopian literature is ANDROGYNY created from the merger of male and female traits. Eveleen Laura Knaggs Mason's speculative novel *Hiero-Salem: The Vision of Peace* (1889) pictures a midwestern couple rearing their children, Robert and Ethel. The parents' appreciation of duality precipitates a holistic adult outlook in brother and sister that directs them toward gender equality and self-fulfillment. No longer missing the characteristics of the opposite gender, they experience an end to fragmentation and a joy in completeness of soul and intellect. Robert predicts to Ethel that the utopian marriages of the future will join two whole people who are capable of achieving their aims.

Margaret ATWOOD chooses duality for her study of women's inner torments. In the poem "The Woman Who Could Not Live with Her Faulty Heart" (1976), she pictures a childish series of desires in a fist pounding a bedspring: "I want, I don't want. / How can one live with such a heart?" (Atwood, 1987, 6). The author found humor in duality by envisioning the female artist as celebrity. She invented comic Gothic for *Lady Oracle* (1976), her third novel, which describes in flashback the two lives of Joan Foster, author of Gothic romances under the pen name L. Delacourt. Atwood inserts the BEAUTY MYTH in a legacy from a dead aunt that stipulates that Joan lose 100 pounds. After weight loss and sudden fame turn Joan into a celebrity, she attracts a blackmailing former CBC newspaperman and develops a chameleonlike personality, a subtextual commentary on women's adaptability to the demands of androcentric society. She faces the sadism, stalking, and alienation of gothic convention and survives with wit and spunk by fleeing to Terremoto,

Italy, and faking her own death. In retrospect, she complains, "They should have been mourning but instead they seemed quite cheerful. It wasn't fair" (Atwood, 1998, 5).

A familiar burden in feminist verse is the duality of woman and poet. The Irish writer Eavan BOLAND's *In a Time of Violence* (1994) wrestles with the author's complex life as mother and poet in the chauvinistic milieu of Ireland. Her task mounts from concern to struggle as she carves out a place for the female muse in a land where myth and lore have traditionally limited woman's role to passive icons of the good mother and farm wife, to healers such as Saint Attracta, and to sanctified females such as Saint Bridget. In the autobiographical *Object Lesson: The Life of the Woman and Poet in Our Time* (1995), Boland addresses the problem of the "ancient world of customs and permissions" that bases history of the pacification of Irish women (Boland, 1996, 27).

Bibliography

Atwood, Margaret. *Lady Oracle*. New York: Anchor Books, 1998.
———. *Selected Poems II: 1976–1986*. New York: Mariner Books, 1987.
Boland, Eavan. *In a Time of Violence*. New York: W. W. Norton, 1995.
———. *Object Lesson: The Life of the Woman and Poet in Our Time*. New York: W. W. Norton, 1996.
Maguire, Sarah. "Dilemmas and Developments: Eavan Boland Re-Examined," *Feminist Review* 62 (Summer 1999): 58–66.

Dudevant, Amandine Aurore Lucie Dupin, baronne

See SAND, GEORGE.

du Maurier, Daphne (1907–1989)

A popular writer of mysteries and adventure lore, Daphne du Maurier turned the rudiments of psychological fiction into a feminist classic. A native Londoner, she was a member of a literary family. To escape domestic pressures, in 1928 she initiated a career in fiction by writing short stories and by completing a period romance, *The Loving Spirit*

(1931). Within the next decade, she produced Gothic skullduggery in her most famous works, *Jamaica Inn* (1936), *Rebecca* (1938), and *Frenchman's Creek* (1941). For material she collected tales from the windy Cornwall peninsula about ghosts, smugglers, and pirates and studied the buildings and seaside estates that contributed to the fictional de Winter ancestral estate, her most fully realized setting. The location suits the diminution of the unnamed heroine, whose self-doubt, lonely walks, and secret longings reflect her unease in a grand country home.

While du Maurier's husband was billeted with the Grenadier Guards in Alexandria, Egypt, she worked at the atmosphere and tone of *Rebecca,* a thriller based on the undetected murder of a cruel, mocking femme fatale. The story opens with a phantasm, "Last night I dreamt I went to Manderley again," the main character's retreat to the scene of her uneasy marriage and near destruction (du Maurier, 1971, 1). Her suave husband, Maxim de Winter, registers an indecipherable expression that worsens the protagonist's diffidence and heightens the threat from his first marriage to a paragon of beauty and grace. At a telling moment early in Maxim's second marriage, the protagonist admits that she sees Rebecca as the official Mrs. de Winter. The second wife is so lacking in domestic authority that she does not answer the telephone: "My faux-pas was so palpably obvious, so idiotic and unpardonable that to ignore it would show me to be an even greater fool if possible, than I was already" (*ibid.,* 84). The cutting self-criticism suggests that she is unable to settle into the marriage and the demanding social position as hostess at Manderley.

By orchestrating flashback, memories, and evocative reports from secondary characters, du Maurier advances the psychological probe into the new wife's inferiority. Through the taunts and undermining of the housekeeper, the sinister Mrs. Danvers, du Maurier resets the BLUEBEARD myth. The housekeeper becomes an obsessive villain whose love for Rebecca suggests repressed lesbianism. The new Mrs. de Winter must struggle for a hold on Manderley and on self-esteem. She deflates herself with a bestial comparison to the family dog: "I'm being like Jasper now, leaning against

[Maxim]. He pats me now and again, when he remembers, and I'm pleased, I get close to him for a moment. He likes me in the way I like Jasper" (*ibid.,* 101). The narrative requires tragic memories of Rebecca's death to exorcise the ghost that pulls unceasingly on the protagonist's self-identity.

The novel diminishes the potency of the ghostly first wife by contrasting Rebecca's breezy self-centeredness with her successor's sincerity and innocence. In the plot resolution du Maurier jolts the reader with Maxim's unforeseen admission of hostility toward Rebecca: "I hated her, I tell you, our marriage was a farce from the very first. She was vicious, damnable, rotten through and through. We never loved each other, never had one moment of happiness together" (*ibid.,* 271). As arson levels the country home, the flames cleanse the de Winter marriage of the residue of Rebecca's tenancy. No longer Maxim's handmaiden, his second wife, like Charlotte BRONTË's Jane EYRE, rescues her husband from depression by asserting herself to the full state of wife and helpmeet. The story became a world favorite, including with Anna QUINDLEN.

In *The Rebecca Notebook* (1980), du Maurier described the suspenseful project as the pinnacle of her career and a surprising triumph for the book world with the sale of 45,000 copies in the first month. It connected instantly with North American readers and dominated best seller lists. Du Maurier adapted the novel as a play. An influence on Victoria Holt and Shirley JACKSON's contemporary Gothic fiction, *Rebecca* succeeded through skilled narration and the characterization of a downhearted young wife who judges herself by faulty standards. Du Maurier won a National Book Award and a citation from the American Literary Society. In 1940 Alfred Hitchcock's screenplay won two Academy Awards and eight additional nominations. The film's appeal lay in the casting of Laurence Olivier as Max, Joan Fontaine as his self-effacing wife, George Sanders as the cad Favell, and Judith Anderson as the sinister Mrs. Danvers.

Bibliography

du Maurier, Daphne. *Rebecca.* New York: Avon Books, 1971.
———. *The Rebecca Notebook and Other Memories.* Garden City, N.Y.: Doubleday, 1980.

Fleenor, Juliann E., ed. *The Female Gothic.* Montreal: Eden Press, 1983.

Forster, Margaret. *Daphne du Maurier.* New York: Doubleday, 1993.

Dunbar-Nelson, Alice (1875–1935)

The journalist, dramatist, and suffragist Alice Ruth Moore Dunbar-Nelson expressed sympathy for single and nonwhite women. Born in New Orleans and reared in a woman-centered home, she felt at ease in the caste system of southern Louisiana. She was educated at Cornell University, the University of Pennsylvania, and Dillard University. At age 23 she married the poet Paul Laurence Dunbar and began composing essays, verse, and dialect stories issued in *Modern Language Notes* and *Monthly Review* and collected in *Violets and Other Tales* (1895) and *The Goodness of St. Rocque and Other Stories* (1899).

In the story "Sister Josepha" (1899) Dunbar-Nelson pictures a Creole child trapped by a social system that fosters extremes for female sexuality—either promiscuity or celibacy. The author remarks on Josepha's experience with a lustful male adult: "Untutored in worldly knowledge, she could not divine the meaning of the pronounced leers and admiration of her physical charms which gleamed in the man's face, but she knew it made her feel creepy, and stoutly refused to go" (Dunbar-Nelson, 1994, 159). The author herself experienced gendered crises after her marriage broke down as a result of Dunbar's womanizing and spousal abuse. After a divorce in 1902 she taught English at Howard High School in Wilmington, Delaware, and coordinated mid-Atlantic women's efforts to acquire voting rights.

In maturity Dunbar-Nelson contributed more tangibly to the intellectual ferment of the Harlem Renaissance with a column in the Pittsburgh *Courier* and submissions to *Crisis, Ebony and Topaz, Messenger,* and *Opportunity.* She empowered *Gone White,* an undated work, with the difficulties of women who nurse the young, elderly, and handicapped and who sacrifice love to marry men who offer a stable future. A racist note pictures the quandary of a dark-skinned girl, whom a relative warns, "A girl of your complexion and class would be only a hindrance" (*ibid.,* 10). In the drawing room comedy *The Author's Evening at Home* (1900), Dunbar-Nelson makes light of a woman's attempt to engage her author husband in conversation. To win his affection and interest, she questions him about the Boer War and the Orange Free State. The subtext indicates a marriage based on a superior husband who diminishes his wife's intellect and her influence on his career.

The only play by Dunbar-Nelson to reach the stage was *Mine Eyes Have Seen* (1919), a kitchen-table drama that opened before publication at Howard High School in Wilmington, Delaware, in April 1918. As in the domestic stage works of her contemporary Georgia Douglas JOHNSON, Dunbar-Nelson sets her didactic drama in the urban home of three black siblings. After their father's lynching in the South, they regret displacement to a northern industrial center, where their mother died of pneumonia and heartbreak. The dialogue introduces a potential rescuer, Mrs. O'Neill, a war widow with five children, who offers respite from hardship. In a thick Irish brogue, she announces: "Down by the chain stores they be a raid on the potatoes, an' ef ye're wantin' some, ye'd better be after gittin' into yer things an' comin' wid me" (Dunbar-Nelson, 1919, 7). The subtext discloses the sufferings of girls, old women, and babies in war-torn Europe and the calm that women instill in draftees who fear leaving their families unprotected. Before Chris departs to the army, the Irishwoman's words boost his pride: "Ye'll make the sacrifice, me boy, an' ye'll be the happier" (*ibid.,* 14).

Bibliography

Brooks, Kristina. "Alice Dunbar-Nelson's Local Colors of Ethnicity, Class, and Place," *MELUS* 23, no. 2 (Summer 1998): 3–26.

Dunbar-Nelson, Alice. "The Author's Evening at Home," *Smart Set,* September 1900, pp. 105–106.

———. "Mine Eyes Have Seen," *Crisis* (April 1919): 271–275.

———. *The Works of Alice Dunbar-Nelson.* Oxford: Oxford University Press, 1994.

Hull, Gloria T., Patricia Bell Scott, and Barbara Smith, eds. *But Some of Us Are Brave: Black Women's Studies.* New York: Feminist Press, 1982.

Duras, Marguerite (1914–1996)

A major literary presence in France, the Anglo-French author Marguerite Duras wrote erotic novels and screenplays that depict the importance of love to female characters. Born Marguerite Donnadieu in Gia Dinh, Vietnam, she was the daughter of Henri Donnadieu, who taught mathematics in Vietnam and Cambodia and died of dysentery when Marguerite was four years old. Reared by her mother, Marie Legrand, a neurotic, dictatorial English widow, Duras and her younger brother, Paul, grew up racially and linguistically isolated in Sadec's French Quarter. On money her mother earned by teaching French and playing piano to accompany silent movies, Marguerite attended a girls' boarding academy in Saigon while her older brother, Pierre, the family favorite, entered technical training in France.

In the autobiographical novel *L'Amant* (*The Lover,* 1984), an international best seller and winner of the Prix Goncourt, Duras describes an early maturity at age 15 and a realization of the allure of female beauty. As a result, the protagonist concludes, "I grew old at eighteen" (Duras, 1998, 4). Her first affair, an escape from poverty and colonial alienation, begins after she meets an older man, a Chinese millionaire's son from Cholon, on the ferry ride home from school over the Mekong River. She reprises the story in *Amant de la Chine du Nord* (*The North China Lover,* 1990), which she unfolds in inventive cinema-style scenarios as though filming a documentary of her life. She alternates precise scenes with opaque glimpses that require the reflection and analysis of her mature years. Central to the domestic situation is the mother's abdication of control.

At 17 Duras escaped the misery and poverty of the family home and went to France to study math and law at the Sorbonne, leaving her mother to develop a Cambodian rice plantation. At a pivotal time in European politics Marguerite found a secretarial post at the colonial ministry. She married the poet Robert Antelme, who was deported to Dachau during World War II and who returned in fragile health. A diminutive but gutsy political radical and a feminist a quarter-century before the term was popular, Duras joined the French Resistance and allied with the Communist Party. To her

dismay she could do nothing for her brother Paul, who died of pneumonia while living in poverty in Saigon. The powerlessness of females as well as the losses and sufferings of the old, handicapped, imprisoned, sick, and insane informed her early writings, which she published under the pseudonym *Duras,* the name of a French village.

The author marked out historical parameters for feminist writing. In 1959 she was nominated for an Academy Award for the Cannes Film Festival award-winning screenplay *Hiroshima, Mon Amour,* the director Alain Resnais's innovative telling of a love affair between a French actor, Emmanuelle Riva, and a Japanese architect, Eiji Okada. The story takes place in Hiroshima 15 years after an atomic bomb leveled the city. The resulting novel, which Duras extrapolated from the film in 1961, pictures beauty amid destruction and captures the author's dominant themes of pain, struggle, passion, and memory. She describes the disintegration of female beauty: "Anonymous heads of hair that the women of Hiroshima, when they awoke in the morning, discovered had fallen out" (Duras, 1987, 17). The combined sufferings and rewards enable her female characters to escape the no-win retreats into insanity or substance abuse, a vice that she considered an abomination in women.

Bibliography

Duras, Marguerite. *Hiroshima, Mon Amour.* New York: Grove, 1987.

———. *The Lover.* New York: Pantheon, 1998.

———. *The North China Lover.* New York: New Press, 1992.

Kovac, Ita. "Marguerite Duras: From Silent Writing to a Film without Pictures," *Bread and Roses* 12 (Fall 1999).

Lennon, Peter. "The Brutal Realist of Romance," *Manchester Guardian,* 13 June 1992, p. 28.

Winston, Jane. "Marguerite Duras: Marxism, Feminism, Writing," *Theatre Journal* 47, no. 3 (October 1995): 345–365.

Dworkin, Andrea (1946–2005)

A radical lesbian leader among first-wave American feminists, Andrea Dworkin directs unflinching fury at the perpetrators of sexism, VIOLENCE against females, and the DOUBLE STANDARD. Born to Jewish parents in Camden, New Jersey, she was the grandchild of Holocaust victims. She grew up in a liberal household that was pro-labor and pro-choice, but experienced exclusion and anti-Semitism in grade school when her teacher urged her to sing "Silent Night" along with Christian students. Part of her childhood she spent caring for her brother and mother and part unsupervised on the streets in defiance of the conformity expected of girls. From her gentle father she learned self-respect and a humanistic attitude toward others. From frequent readings of the revolutionary Che Guevara, she learned to fight back.

Before becoming a writer, Dworkin won a scholarship and majored in literature and philosophy at Bennington College. Her three-year marriage ended in Amsterdam after her husband's spousal abuse. Relocated to New York City, she directed altruism and energy to civil rights demonstrations and protests of the Vietnam War. She submitted contemporary feminist essays and stories to the *American Voice, Michigan Quarterly Review, Ms.,* and the *New York Times.* As did the strident mother-daughter suffragists Emmeline and Christabel PANKHURST of the 19th century and the platform mavens Voltairine DE CLEYRE and Emma GOLDMAN, Dworkin makes no apology for rage. She exposed the brutality of police after her arraignment for rioting, when a matron's rough internal examination caused Dworkin heavy vaginal bleeding.

To verbalize her experience with gender hostility, Dworkin published *Woman Hating* (1974), which covers savagery that ranges from foot binding in China and witch burning around the world to modern images of marital battery. Of the sufferings in FAIRY TALES she echoes Simone de BEAUVOIR's classic manifesto *The SECOND SEX* (1949), insisting, "We have not formed that ancient world—it has formed us. We ingest it as children whole, have its values and consciousness imprinted on our minds as cultural absolutes" (Dworkin, 1974, 32). She followed with a collection of speeches in *Our Blood* (1976) and in *Pornography: Men Possessing Women* (1981), in which she sides with sex workers against their parasitic pimps, johns, and vice squads. She cred-

its the misogyny of children's folklore and erotic fiction for perpetuating male-on-female battery. Her later works—*Right-Wing Women: The Politics of Domesticated Women* (1983), *Intercourse* (1987), and *Letters from a War Zone, 1976–1987* (1988)—address the dangers of GENDER BIAS and expose the causes of carnage against women. In the latter work she describes the feminist war on pornographers, whom she describes as a form of sexual mafia, "the organized trafficking in women and girls" (Dworkin, 1993, 99). Of sexual abusers she blasts the male-dominated professional world, where police, judges, and psychologists ask insinuating questions: "Did you provoke it? did you like it? is this what you really wanted all along?" (*ibid.,* 10).

Dworkin directs her autobiographical fiction to the same issues. *Ice and Fire* (1988) features a heroine who writes feminist fiction as an antidote to sexual abuse. More horrific is the protagonist of *Mercy* (1991), the story of a nine-year-old victim who tries to report fondling by a stranger who sat next to her at a movie theater. The narrative reports the violation of personal space through a stream-of-consciousness reportage bristling with indignant repetition: "my legs; *my legs;* me; my; my legs; my; my; my legs" (Dworkin, 1992, 7). At the height of frustration with sympathetic adults, she states, "I wanted God to see me crying so He would know and it would count" (*ibid.,* 9–10). The child fights sexual assault by becoming a murderer. In *Heartbreak: The Political Memoir of a Feminist Militant* (2002), Dworkin returns to the issues of pedophilia and damns the adults who take advantage of the very young.

Bibliography

Altman, Meryl. "Lives on the Line," *Women's Review of Books* 19, no. 7 (April 2002): 6–7.

Dworkin, Andrea. *Heartbreak: The Political Memoir of a Feminist Militant.* New York: Basic Books, 2002.

———. *Letters from a War Zone.* Brooklyn, N.Y.: Lawrence Hill Books, 1993.

———. *Mercy: A Novel.* New York: Four Walls Eight Windows, 1992.

———. *Woman Hating.* New York: Dutton, 1974.

Thom, Mary. *Inside Ms.: 24 Years of the Magazine and the Feminist Movement.* New York: Henry Holt, 1997.

dynasty

Dynasty is a dehumanizing motive for proposing marriage and establishing a family. The plotting of a patriarchal lineage in literature often takes on the outlines of breeding a thoroughbred stable for running and racing rather than giving birth to beloved children and valuing both sexes. The domestic relationship of Abraham and Sarah in Genesis suggests the father's willingness to accept Hagar as makeshift mate to actuate God's promise that Abraham would not die childless. The self-glorification through children, specifically male offspring, generates a splintering of family, with Sarah pushing her husband to banish Hagar and Hagar's son, Ishmael, into the desert to preserve for Isaac the plum position of oldest son. More terrifying is the novelist Maxine Hong KINGSTON's description in *The WOMAN WARRIOR* (1976) of smothering of baby girls, a practice common in Imperial China. The concept of vengeance through ABORTION colors *The Kitchen God's Wife* (1991), in which the novelist Amy TAN describes a tormented wife's decision to end her husband's opportunities to torment more of their children.

Following the tradition of dynastic yearnings, authors characterized the psychological rot at the heart of male-centered families. Emily BRONTË features pride in family as the root cause of tragedy in *WUTHERING HEIGHTS* (1847). Her hero-villain Heathcliff avenges himself on classism by marrying well and by acquiring both his foster father's estate and Thrushcross Grange, the family home of Catherine EARNSHAW, Heathcliff's childhood love. The Spanish novelist Emilia Pardo BARZÁN's naturalistic saga *The House of Ulloa* (1886) places women more fully in the development of lineage in the overt sizing up of potential wives as bearers of a dynasty. Don Pedro's examination of Rita delights him with her possibilities as a healthy mother. As though choosing prize fruit trees, he dreams of a self-ennobling future: "A magnificent stock on which to graft his heir and namesake! . . . The marquis imagined not the pleasures of the flesh, but the numerous and masculine offspring she was capable of producing" (Bazán, 97). The author stresses that Don Pedro not only envisions excellent children but specifi-

cally the birth of males to bear his surname and extend his family line.

A perversion of human genetics tends to place potential mothers under scrutiny as the sole contributors to the next generation of offspring. In "Désirée's Baby" (1893), one of Kate CHOPIN's most frequently anthologized stories, the responsibility for dynasty falls on the wife of Armand Aubigny, a Parisian planter who is careless about falling in love with a Louisiana foundling of obscure origin. Chopin creates multiple ironies in the fact that the birth of their son, paralleling the biblical Abraham's contentment with Ishmael and Isaac, "had softened Armand Aubigny's imperious and exacting nature greatly" (Chopin, 191). The sudden change in Armand, exacerbated by the intrusion of Désirée's foster mother, results from the gradual development of the baby's negroid features. Chopin resorts to melodrama in Désirée's disappearance into the bayou and Armand's later discovery that his mother was an African slave. The blame for the birth of a biracial child thus boomerangs back to the planter himself, who destroys an otherwise happy nuclear family.

As feminism began to take shape in the late era of SUFFRAGE, dynasty became a polarizing subject in already tense male-female relations. In Charlotte Perkins GILMAN's novel *With Her in Ourland* (1916), the sequel to the feminist utopian classic *Herland* (1915), the author expresses outrage at a male-dominated world similar to the one that Kate Chopin portrays. As the heroine Ellador Jennings travels the globe with her husband Van, she makes notes, asks pointed questions, and comments on the disparities of the lives of males and females. She challenges the dominance of the father figure: "The egoism of him! 'My name! . . . My house—my line—my family'" (Gilman, 132). More ominous is Margaret ATWOOD's dystopian fable *The HANDMAID'S TALE* (1985), a speculative novel that envisions a time in which men are so threatened by loss to sexual potency that they subvert women into quasi-religious concubines.

Bibliography

Bazán, Emilia Pardo. *The House of Ulloa.* London: Penguin, 1990.

Chopin, Kate. *The Awakening and Selected Stories.* New York: Penguin, 1983.

Foy, R. R. "Chopin's 'Désirée's Baby,' " *Explicator* 49, no. 4 (Summer 1991): 222–223.

Gilman, Charlotte Perkins. *With Her in Ourland.* Westport, Conn.: Praeger, 1997.

Sexton, Anne. *Transformations.* Boston: Houghton Mifflin, 1971.

E

Earnshaw, Catherine

A gripping characterization for its time, Emily BRONTË's Catherine Earnshaw, the female protagonist of *WUTHERING HEIGHTS* (1847), shocked readers by exhibiting rapacious sexual desire. In an era that lauded the domesticity of Queen Victoria and her rapidly growing family, Catherine displays an unswerving love of horses and freedom on the English moors, a subtextual rejection of the homeyness and sedate behavior demanded of a genteel landowner's daughter. From early girlhood she is the "wild, wicked slip" (Brontë, 45). She demands adventure by pairing with Heathcliff, a Gypsy boy her father rescues and rears. She bonds with Heathcliff, embracing him as her "all in all" (*ibid.,* 124). In her diary she confesses, "H. and I are going to rebel—we took our initiatory step this evening," the preface to their "scamper on the moor" (*ibid.,* 25, 27). She expresses a gendered DUALITY by adopting Heathcliff's persona; as though seeing herself as a male child, she declares, "He's more myself than I am" (*ibid.,* 82). Her need for liberty parallels his misery at Wuthering Heights, where Catherine's brother, Hindley, browbeats and demeans the boy as an unfitting addition to the Earnshaw DYNASTY.

In a subtextual expression of the many sides to the female personality, Catherine's ambivalence flickers between two extremes—the gentrified daughter and the headstrong hoyden. Her inability to settle on a single personality type dooms her to a conflicted adulthood as first one, then the other side of her nature takes control. After one of her rovings with Heathcliff near Thrushcross Grange, she suddenly drops the pagan side of her nature to develop courtesies suited to the Lintons' stable lifestyle. After a five-week stay while her foot heals after a bite by the dog Skulker, she discovers that sparkling chandeliers, gilt edgings on the ceiling, and deep red carpets are elements of the good life that gratify and elevate her. To make herself worthy of the neighbors' hospitality, she abandons her Gypsy near-brother, abjures the wanderings that have bound them, and wears the ill-fitting mask of a lady. For the time being suppression of the natural woman affords her a happiness and belonging that she has never known at Wuthering Heights.

Brontë dramatizes the way self-deception takes its toll. The change in Catherine bodes ill for her and for Heathcliff by forcing him into the role of hostile aggressor. Having sold out her real self for the position of self-centered, spoiled wife of Edgar Linton, Catherine tries to maintain a private love for Heathcliff, her male alter ego. Failing to convince herself that marriage to Edgar gives her a chance to refine Heathcliff, Catherine discovers that a passive husband has no chance of satisfying her sexual longings. Brontë punishes her heroine for betrayal by picturing Heathcliff wooing Isabella Linton and by causing Catherine to die young in the days after childbirth. As she slips away, Heathcliff charges her with self-deceit: "Why did you betray your own heart, Cathy. . . . You have killed yourself" (*ibid.,* 158).

The author uses Catherine's sickroom ravings to exhibit the error of suppressing the sexual side of human nature for the sake of wealth and prestige. Despairing in a predelivery fever, Catherine lashes out at the housekeeper, Nelly Dean, her surrogate mother, and dies two hours after giving birth to a seventh-month baby. Catherine's soul, still vital with unrequited passion, refuses Christian burial. Wandering the moor in a downpour of sleet and snow, like an Irish banshee or the mythic LA LLORONA, after 20 years of solitude, she scratches at the window and wails for her childhood love.

Bibliography

Brontë, Emily. *Wuthering Heights.* New York: New American Library, 1959.

Hoeveler, Diane Long. *Gothic Feminism.* University Park: Pennsylvania State University Press, 1998.

Thormahlen, Marianne, "The Lunatic and the Devil's Disciple: The Lovers' in 'Wuthering Heights,' " *Review of English Studies* 48, no. 190 (May 1997): 183–197.

ecofeminism

A gynocentric connection with the environment, ecofeminism results in a motherly nurturance of Earth's fragile life-forms and the steward's reclamation of areas that have suffered harm. The concept of an Earth mother permeates world mythology in the figures of Ceres/Demeter and PERSEPHONE/Proserpina and in the Amerindian lore of SPIDER WOMAN. Under the eye of the deified mother in Eavan BOLAND's "The Making of an Irish Goddess" (1990), the divine female looks out on silver arteries in rock, evenly spaced wheat stalks, and "a seasonless, unscarred earth" (Boland, 39). According to the Jungian psychoanalyst Clarissa Pinkola ESTÉS, author of *Women Who Run with the Wolves* (1992), females are born with a divine sense of ecology. The mutual nurturing of woman and Earth is beneficial to both: "It is through the love for and the caring for our natural seasons that we protect our lives from being dragged into someone else's rhythm, someone else's dance, someone else's hunger" (Estés, 320). In the late 18th century the poet and letter writer Anna SEWARD voiced her dismay with the sludge and smoke of the Industrial Revolution, an economic shift that

primarily earned the regard of men. Because she and other women lived outside the realm of engineering, she vented fury at the destruction of Coalbrookdale Gardens by pollutants.

Nineteenth-century FEMINIST UTOPIAS lost hold as reality eroded hopes of a self-sustaining paradise. An early utopian fantasy, Charlotte Perkins GILMAN's *HERLAND* (1915), anticipates the need for female stewardship by designing an all-female agricultural eden in which three million EVEs plant and tend fruit and nut trees and recycle wastes as fertilizer. The prototype of a self-nourishing haven made little headway in convincing Earthlings that their planet is finite. In 1998 the spokeswoman Marilynne ROBINSON, essayist and novelist, warned in an essay for *Wilson Quarterly* of the dangers of profligacy: "What have we done for the whale, if we lose the sea? If we lose the sea, how do we mend the atmosphere? What can we rescue out of this accelerating desperation to sell—forests and weapons, even children—and the profound deterioration of community all this indicates?" (Robinson, 63).

Forerunners of the conservation movement were animal advocates such as Anna Laetitia BARBAULD; lyric regionalists such as the novelist Willa CATHER, a lover of the American heartland; and the homesteader and orchard keeper Marjorie Kinnan RAWLINGS, who settled in central Florida and grew to love the interconnectedness of flora and fauna. Another, Sarah Orne JEWETT, expressed the value of mountains, rivers, and austere New England shores to human contentment in *A White Heron and Other Stories* (1886) and *THE COUNTRY OF THE POINTED FIRS* (1896). The growth of late 20th-century utopian fiction and fantasy sparked a renewed respect for the planet in the Earthsea series of the sci-fi master Ursula LE GUIN and in the apocalyptic writings of Kate Wilhelm. Le Guin describes the Raft Folk as wanderers of the Earthsea archipelago who revere fresh water and thrive on fish and seaweed stews. They cling to a tradition of the Long Dance, a barefoot performance without music to a traditional chant honoring the albatross, dolphin, and whale. Similarly reverent of nature are dwellers of Lorbanery, the Isle of Silk far to the south of the Earthsea cluster. All citizens support a silkworm culture by tending orchards until apathy causes them to abandon their traditions and squander their natural resources. Wilhelm's ecofeminist romance *Where Late the Sweet Birds Sang* (1977) looks to a future when only one family survives polluted landscapes and radiation poisoning. Relocated to a mountain glade, they are forced to rely on cloning rather than natural conception to provide new population. The value placed on females elevates them and their children as saviors of Earth.

Verse is a potent strand of ecofeminism in the hands of such authors as Maxine KUMIN, Marge PIERCY, and the Laguna-Latina poet Leslie Marmon SILKO. With limited fanfare Kumin captured late 20th-century angst in the gradual loss of songbirds and field animals to technological progress. She honors the country woman's joy in "The First Rain of Spring" (1961). In "Hark, Hark" (2001), the poet muses on the demise of the Carolina parakeet. Her contemporary, the speculative novelist Piercy, introduced fears for Earth in *WOMAN ON THE EDGE OF TIME* (1976), in which Luciente, a Massachusetts resident in A.D. 2137, looks back on the 20th century as a world-destroying era dependent on pesticides and given to polluting water sources with petrochemicals and sewage. He turns to black humor with jokes about the Manhattan Project, America's manufacture of the first atomic bomb.

The Chickasaw poet Linda HOGAN and Brenda Peterson recognized the link between feminism and Earth guardianship. They collected the cream of ecofeminist writings in *The Sweet Breathing of Plants: Women Writing on the Green World* (2002), which features the sentiments of Rachel CARSON, the godmother of ecofeminism, and of the writers Paula Gunn ALLEN, Isabel ALLENDE, Mary Crow Dog, Marjory Stoneman Douglas, Zora Neale HURSTON, Rigoberto MENCHÚ, and Alice WALKER. The opening piece, "Orchid Fever," by Susan Orlean, links the horticultural importance of orchids with flowered headdresses of Elizabethan women, who treasured a touch of nature on their unnaturally starched costumes. The feeling of female reverence for beauty permeates the collection, establishing a mystic alliance between women and the natural world.

Authors from the American West delineate the gender specifics of ecofeminism. In the Native American poet Joy HARJO's beautyway prayer "Eagle Poem" (1990), she speaks the ecofeminist's reverence for living things. As her commitment implies, the female-driven crusade against wasteful materialism, corporate greed, technology's arrogance, and pollution relies on intuition and networking to revive aboriginal reverence for nature and to preserve for future generations a planetary home. In a classic desert hymn *The Land of Little Rain* (1903), Mary Hunter AUSTIN expressed a uniquely female awe of Southwest desertscapes. A central voice of the progressive Earth First movement, she spoke of the horizon in *Stories from the Country of Lost Borders* (1909) as "stretching interminably whity-brown, dim and shadowy blue hills" (Austin, 106). In a metaphor that feminizes the plains she mused on terrain "deep-breasted, broad in the hips, tawny, with tawny hair, a great mass of it lying smooth along her perfect curves, full lipped like a sphinx, but not heavy-lidded like one, eyes sane and steady as the polished jewel of her skies" (*ibid.*). As an artist, she valued the spare beauty of the wild for its impetus to native female crafters, who turned vistas and found materials into baskets, pottery, sand art, and fiber work. The alliance of women with an expansive, naked land disavowed domestic stereotypes by freeing desert dwellers to follow their imagination.

The doyenne of ecofeminism into the 21st century, the novelist and essayist Barbara KINGSOLVER has amassed a faithful following for concerns for the planet and its denizens. In *Last Stand: America's Virgin Lands* (2002), she genders the Earth with a feminine pronoun that refers to the southwestern desert, the land on which her family settled. For her characterization of conservationist themes, she received the Earth Day Award from the Kentucky Environmental Quality Commission and was a four-time nominee for the Sierra Club's Edward Abbey Award for Ecofiction and a nominee for the Pulitzer Prize. To Diana Pabst Parsell, an interviewer for *National Geographic*, Kingsolver expressed the urgency of conservation efforts. She charged Americans with profligacy: "We've behaved for two hundred years as if the resource base is unlimited" (Parsell). The accusation restates the words of Codi Noline, a biology teacher in the ecofeminist romance *Animal Dreams* (1990): "People can forget, and forget, and forget, but the land has a memory. The lakes and the rivers are still hanging on to the DDT and every other insult we ever gave them" (Kingsolver, 1990, 255).

Kingsolver reached a height of authority with the best-selling political allegory *The Poisonwood Bible* (1998), an ecofeminist masterwork set in the Congo during the downfall of colonialism. The mother figure, Orleanna Price, sees the exploited nation as the "barefoot bride of men who took her jewels and promised the kingdom" (Kingsolver, 1998, 201). With wifely pragmatism she challenges her missionary husband's belief in biblical inerrancy. Her choices refute the order to Adam in the book of Genesis to "have dominion over every creature that moved upon the earth" (*ibid.*, 9). Rather than denigrate black Africans, she admires Congolese women and their "hours of labor spent procuring the simplest elements: water, heat, anything that might pass for disinfectant" to ward off malaria, *kakakaka* (enteritis), ants, and poisonous snakes (*ibid.*, 29). In step with their mother's reverence for human life, the twins Adah and Leah take seriously their roles—Adah as a specialist in the contagious diseases of Africa and Leah as an agronomist and teacher of hygiene and nutrition in Angola.

In an erotic vein Kingsolver published a fifth novel, *Prodigal Summer* (2000), a satisfying dramatization of rural female lives, SEXUALITY, procreation and mothering, and respect for the environment. The author harmonizes the voices and actions of three conservationists—the goat farmer Lusa Maluf Landowski, the orchardist Nannie Land Rawley, and the forest ranger Deanna Wolfe, who works toward ecological balance on Zebulon Mountain by valuing the roles of all plants and animals. Kingsolver pictures the daily concerns of ecofeminists who take seriously nature's needs and the small reforms and revisions that boost the chances of survival. With the $30,000 Kingsolver solicited from donors during a book tour, she supported the Huron River Watershed Council in Michigan, the San Diequito River Project in California, and the Washington State Environmental Learning Center.

Bibliography

Aay, Henry. "Environmental Themes in Ecofiction: *In the Center of the Nation* and *Animal Dreams*," *Journal of Cultural Geography* 14, no. 2, (Spring–Summer 1994): 65–85.

Alaimo, Stacy. "The Undomesticated Nature of Feminism: Mary Austin and the Progressive Women Conservationists," *Studies in American Fiction* 26, no. 1 (Spring 1998): 73–96.

Austin, Mary Hunter. *Stories from the Country of Lost Borders.* New York: Harper & Brothers, 1909.

Boland, Eavan. *Outside History: Selected Poems, 1980–1990.* New York: W. W. Norton, 2001.

Born, Brad S. "Kingsolver's Gospel for Africa: (Western White Female) Heart of Goodness," *Mennonite Life,* 56, no. 1 (March 2001).

Estés, Clarissa Pinkola. *Women Who Run with the Wolves: Myths and Stories about the Wild Woman Archetype.* New York: Ballantine, 1997.

Gray, Paul, "Call of the Eco-feminist," *Time,* 24 September 1990, p. 87.

Harjo, Joy. *In Mad Love and War.* Middletown, Conn.: Wesleyan University Press, 1990.

Hogan, Linda, and Brenda Peterson, eds. *The Sweet Breathing of Plants: Women Writing on the Green World.* New York: Farrar Straus & Giroux, 2002.

Kingsolver, Barbara. *Animal Dreams.* New York: Harper-Collins, 1990.

———. *Last Stand: America's Virgin Lands.* Washington, D.C.: National Geographic Society, 2002.

———. *The Poisonwood Bible.* New York: HarperCollins, 1998.

———. *Prodigal Summer.* New York: HarperCollins, 2000.

Parsell, D. L. "New Photo Book an Homage to Last U.S. Wildlands," *National Geographic News,* 29 October 2002.

Robinson, Marilynne. "Surrendering Wilderness," *Wilson Quarterly* 22, no. 4 (Autumn 1998): 60–64.

Smiley, Jane. "In the Fields of the Lord," *Washington Post,* 11 October 1998.

Edgeworth, Maria (ca. 1767–1849)

The Anglo-Irish children's author, translator, and novelist Maria Edgeworth expressed prefeminist notions on criteria for women's happiness. She was born at her grandparents' home in Black

Bourton, Oxfordshire, but had a primarily Irish lineage and upbringing. Motherless from age five, she shrank from the piety of her first stepmother. At age seven Edgeworth attended boarding school at Derby, where she learned to speak French and Italian and to write. Seven years later her father, an author and educator, sent her to Ireland to superintend his landholdings at Edgeworthstown, where she remained unmarried and actively publishing the rest of her life. In her free time she composed drama, children's morality tales, a translation of a French novel, and letters to her literary friends Jane AUSTEN and Anna Laetitia BARBAULD. Of Edgeworth's meticulous style the sociologist Harriet MARTINEAU remarked in her *Autobiography* (1855) that the novelist, who began with "scribbling first, then submitting her manuscript to her father, and copying and altering many times over till, (if I remember right) no one paragraph of her 'Leonora' stood at last as it did at first,—made me suppose copying and alteration to be indispensable" (Martineau, 93).

Enlightened in her views of feminism, Edgeworth was a proponent of female EDUCATION, the theme of *Letters for Literary Ladies* (1795). The text notes, "From academies, colleges, public libraries, private associations of literary men, women are excluded, if not by law, at least by custom" (Edgeworth, 1798). The author adds that, even when women enter the all-male domain, social strictures on behavior "forbid us to argue or to converse with them as we do with one another:—we see things as they are; but women must always see things through a veil, or cease to be women" (*ibid.*). Equal opportunity for women was also the intent of *The Parent's Assistant* (1795), a six-volume collection of stories for classroom reading. In 1798 she wrote *Practical Education*, followed three years later by *Early Lessons* (1801) and, in 1809, *Essays on Professional Education*, in which she called for equal course offerings for boys and girls. She earned a wide readership for comic regional fiction in *Castle Rackrent, an Hibernian Tale* (1800), called England's first historical novel.

In domestic novels Edgeworth attacked criticism of female INDEPENDENCE. She established gender boundaries in *Belinda* (1801), a drawing-room satire on women entering the MARRIAGE MARKET. As did the novelist Jane AUSTEN, Edgeworth debated the financial and moral values that marriageable women seek in a future mate. The chapter entitled "Rights of Women" exposes the faulty logic of well-intentioned males like Mr. Percivel, who champions women's happiness over their liberty. The line dividing the two outcomes of marriage is more applicable to Belinda than to Percivel, who is oblivious to women's self-definition. In *The Absentee* (1812) Edgeworth titters at women who try too hard to emulate gentility. Lady Langdale, in a harsh criticism of Lady Clonbrony's affectations, notes, "If you knew all she endures to look, speak, move, breathe like an Englishwoman, you would pity her" (Edgeworth, 1812). With the women's movement the accuracy of Edgeworth's characterizations won her a new readership and inclusion on college reading lists.

Bibliography

Bilger, Audrey. *Laughing Feminism: Subversive Comedy in Frances Burney, Maria Edgeworth, and Jane Austen.* Detroit, Mich.: Wayne State University Press, 1998.

Edgeworth, Maria. *The Absentee* (1812). Available online. URL: http://emotional-literacy-education.com/classic-books-online-a/bsnte10.htm. Accessed on October 13, 2005.

———. *Belinda* (1811). Available online. URL: http://digital.library.upenn.edu/women/edgeworth/belinda/belinda.html. Accessed on October 13, 2005.

———. *Letters for Literary Ladies* (1798). Available online. URL: http://digital.library.upenn.edu/women/edgeworth/ladies/ladies.html. Accessed on October 13, 2005.

Martineau, Harriet. *Harriet Martineau's Autobiography* (1877). Available online. URL: http://www.indiana.edu/~letrs/vwwp/martineau/martineau1.html. Accessed on October 13, 2005.

Edson, Margaret (1961–)

Margaret "Maggie" Edson, a kindergarten teacher in Atlanta, Georgia, surprised the literary world by winning a Pulitzer Prize for her philosophic play *Wit* (1999). The child of a newspaperman and a social worker, she was born in Washington, D.C.; grew up near American University; and attended the elite Sidwell Friends School. After earning a degree in Renaissance history from Smith College, she entered a convent in Rome for a year. On return to Washington, she volunteered as a clerk and roving social worker on the acquired immunodeficiency syndrome (AIDS) and cancer wards at the National Institute of Health research hospital. Jobs in bicycle sales and in grant writing for the Saint Francis Center for Loss and Healing preceded her decision at age 30 to write the play. Her day jobs continued—tutoring Kindergarten to sixth-grade (K–6) students in reading in an English-as-a-second-language setting and completing postgraduate work in English at Georgetown University. In 1995 the South Coast Repertory in Costa Mesa, California, staged *Wit*, which Edson had whittled down by an hour. *Wit* went on to become a major work in both women's studies and medical school curricula.

Edson continues to live and work in Atlanta teaching heterogeneous kindergarten students at Centennial Place Elementary.

Bibliography

Martini, Adrienne. "The Playwright in Spite of Herself," *American Theatre* 16, no. 8 (October 1999): 22–25.

education

The fight for learning and career opportunities undergirds feminist demands for gender equity. For centuries China's imperialistic regime forbade education for females. In the 1850s in the Jiang Yong Prefecture of Hunan, China, women so hungered for learning and creative outlets that they invented their own script, Nushu, a shortcut to the complicated Chinese alphabet that made them literate in less than a year. With their private, female-created writing method they were able to record their thoughts, songs, and poems and to correspond with each other. They even decorated fans and embroidered vests and jackets with sayings and slogans in Nushu. A lasting matriarchal heirloom, the San Chao Shu (Third Day Missives), was the prewedding oral instruction passed from mother to daughter or a gift book passed between female friends. In 2004 the death of Yang Huanyi, the last woman proficient in Nushu, ended a female tradition of self-education.

The craving for literacy was not limited to peasant cultures. The Hispano-Cuban sonneteer and playwright Gertrudis Gómez de Avellaneda denounced the Spanish system of education of brothers and exclusion of their sisters. In the essay "Woman" (1860), she satirized "bearded academies" that barred women because "unfortunately the greatest intellectual prowess is unable to make that animal abundance that requires cutting by a razor sprout on a [female] face" (Avellaneda, xvi). In her opinion the growing of whiskers was the only insurmountable distinction between male and female students. She had a personal stake in wanting universities open to women: without a formal education, she could not collect from the Spanish government a writer's stipend.

In the novel *The Beth Book: A Study in the Life of Elizabeth Caldwell McClure, a Woman of Genius* (1897), Sarah Grand, a spirited Anglo-Irish feminist writer, expressed through a fictional alter ego her defiance of a lopsided social order. As Beth, the outspoken heroine, begins sizing up the favoritism toward adolescent males, she draws a number of conclusions. She learns that men consider themselves superior to women, even to those females who match and top male academic accomplishments. The DOUBLE STANDARD explains away the anomaly of a woman adept at Latin declensions and conjugations: "Any evidence of reasoning capacity in a woman [young men] held to be abnormal, and they denied that women were ever logical. They had to allow that women's intuition was often accurate, but it was inferior" (Grand, 274).

The Spanish writer Emilia Pardo BAZÁN, author of *The House of Ulloa* (1886), challenged the sexism of her time in forthright essays. She noted that men "have no idea how difficult it is for a woman to acquire culture and fill in the blanks of her education on her own" (Bazán, 13). She understood why men were familiar with concepts that women never encountered. As did many privileged feminists, she filled in her own blanks by reading and educating herself. From the satisfaction that resulted grew her intent to contribute new points of view to Spanish fiction. When critics found fault with her unique style, she answered their challenges point by point by explaining how she had departed from the literary style of Émile Zola and Victor Hugo, the prominent male novelists of her time.

The Scots-American orator and editor Frances WRIGHT angered Americans with lectures and editorials lambasting the limited opportunities available to bright, ambitious women. One of the examples of U.S. women who refused to be ejected from schooling was Elizabeth BLACKWELL, an English Quaker who became the first female doctor in North America. In her autobiographical *Pioneer Work in Opening the Medical Profession to Women* (1895), she expressed a philosophical drive to become a doctor. She explained, "The idea of winning a doctor's degree gradually assumed the aspect of a great moral struggle, and the moral fight possessed immense attraction for me" (Blackwell, 29). She listed the discouraging arguments foisted on her by outsiders; that education for women was impossible to accomplish, that there was no facility willing to take women, and that the required training was arduous and expensive and entailed too many obstacles to make it practicable.

GENDER BIAS in education encountered its share of satiric humor. In 1892 Anna Julia COOPER published *The Voice of Anna Julia Cooper,* which focuses on the issue of education for women. She denounced the men who kept the biblical Ruth and Naomi ignorant and who prevented PENELOPE, Andromache, Lucretia, Joan of Arc, and Charlemagne's daughter from writing their own names. Cooper recognized that patriarchal males feared that "if women were once permitted to read Sophocles and work with logarithms, or to nibble at any side of the apple of knowledge, there would be an end forever to their sewing on buttons and embroidering slippers" (Cooper, 72).

In an optimistic era in the battle for enfranchisement, speeches by Susan B. ANTHONY and other suffragists on behalf of the National American Woman Suffrage Association (NAWSA) focused on state amendments that would force Congress to accept the grassroots efforts of individual women's groups in building support for voting rights. In 1900 a membership drive called the "society plan" aimed to draw more wealthy and educated women into the campaign. The concept derived in part from a plateau in development from 1896 to 1910, when no new state adopted a suffrage amendment. Joining the slate of platform lecturers to revive action at the state level was a Methodist minister, Dr. Anna Howard Shaw, a graduate of Boston University and recipient of the Distinguished Service Medal for her work in national defense. Another collegian, the dean of Bryn Mawr College, Martha Carey Thomas, author of "Should Higher Education for Women Differ?" (1899), helped form the national College Women's Equal Suffrage League in 1908.

The Russian-Jewish memoirist Mary ANTIN, a proponent of America's free education system, describes in *The Promised Land* (1912) the gendered educational system of her homeland. While her brother, Pinchus, received a shower of family blessings upon entering heder, Jewish education for boys, the Antin girls were less fortunate. Antin explains, "In the mediaeval position of the women of Polotzk education really had no place. A girl was 'finished' when she could read her prayers in Hebrew" (Antin, 111). The only erudition expected of a female was doing sums, signing her name, and composing a letter in Yiddish. Fortunately for Antin her parents adopted liberal notions from outside their shtetl and imported tutors to add arithmetic, German, and Russian to the obligatory Hebrew. Antin added to her lessons with covert study of a Russian primer and the addition of the Cyrillic alphabet and some simple words. After the family's immigration to Boston she abandoned Orthodox Judaism and embraced a thorough American-style education, the basis of her citizenship.

In much feminist literature, such as the English novelist Maria EDGEWORTH's *Letters for Literary Ladies* (1795), the American writer Louisa May ALCOTT's LITTLE WOMEN (1868–69), and Antin's AUTOBIOGRAPHY, the struggle to supplement women's faulty education called for alternatives to public schools and standard curricula. In *My Own Story* (1914) the feminist orator Emmeline PANKHURST puzzled over the female academy's concern with preparing English gentlewomen to serve men: "A girl's education at that time seemed to have for its prime object the art of 'making home attractive'—presumably to migratory male relatives" (Pankhurst, 6). At home Pankhurst discussed the issue with her brothers. She discovered,

"It was never suggested to them as a duty that they make home attractive to me. Why not? Nobody seemed to know" (*ibid.*).

As the fictional NEW WOMAN became a reality, feminist writers pondered the costs in human unhappiness. In 1909 the essayist Mary K. Ford summarized in "Women's Progress: A Comparison of Centuries" the situation in the 1800s, when gender-specific textbooks edited material for girls by reducing pure scientific data and replacing them with popular and entertaining fare. These works came with a warning to girls "to avoid all disputes, to give up their opinions, even if they knew they were in the right, and finally (and in this all authorities, male and female, united as one man) never to allow it to be suspected that they knew anything" (Ford, 621). The punishment for intellectuals was social ostracism, which meant that "their matrimonial chances were gone forever" (*ibid.*). The shadow of retaliation hovered into the late 20th century. In her opening essay in *Dancing at the Edge of the World: Thoughts on Words, Women and Places* (1990), Ursula Le Guin describes the waste of human intelligence: She pictures the average woman as lacking education "to anything like her capacity, and that is a shameful waste and a crime against humanity" (Le Guin, 6). Although blessed with wit, patience, and shrewdness, she hesitates to volunteer ideas. Compounding the sin against her are self-doubts about her usefulness.

In more recent writings, for example, Barbara KINGSOLVER's *Animal Dreams* (1990), the realization of career goals often pits the ambitious female against a host of obstacles. In retort to her inability to match work with education, Codi Noline, a dropout from medical school, describes herself as a "bag lady with an education" and declares to her father, "I know that a woman's ambitions aren't supposed to fall and rise and veer off course this way, like some poor bird caught in a storm" (Kingsolver, 1990, 259, 107). The answer to her quandary is a form of coursework recycling—the application of her training in the biology classroom, where she enlightens teenagers about hygiene, disease, and human reproduction. Similarly liberating in Kingsolver's masterwork, *The Poisonwood Bible* (1998), the evolution of Leah Price Ngemba from introspective teen into agronomist

and teacher hinges on an unrestricted work environment where she can "wear pants if at all possible" (Kingsolver, 1998, 149).

Bibliography

Antin, Mary. *The Promised Land.* Boston: Houghton Mifflin, 1912.

Avellaneda, Gertrudis Gómez de. *Sab and the Autobiography.* Trans. and ed. by Nina M. Scott. Austin: University of Texas Press, 1993.

Barbauld, Anna Laetitia. *A Legacy for Young Ladies.* Boston: David Reed, 1826.

Bazán, Emilia Pardo. *The House of Ulloa.* London: Penguin, 1990.

Blackwell, Elizabeth. *Pioneer Work in Opening the Medical Profession to Women.* Delanco, N.J.: privately printed, 2000.

Cooper, Anna Julia. *The Voice of Anna Julia Cooper.* Lanham, Md.: Rowman & Littlefield, 1998.

Ford, Mary K. "Woman's Progress: A Comparison of Centuries" (1909). Available online. URL: http://etext.lib.virginia.edu/toc/modeng/public/ForWoma.html. Accessed on October 13, 2005.

Grand, Sarah. *The Beth Book.* New York: Dial Press, 1980.

Kingsolver, Barbara. *Animal Dreams.* New York: HarperCollins, 1990.

———. *The Poisonwood Bible.* New York: HarperCollins, 1998.

Le Guin, Ursula. *Dancing at the Edge of the World: Thoughts on Words, Women, and Places.* New York: Grove Press, 1997.

Lin-Liu, Jen. "In China, a Scholar, a Once-Forbidden Script, and Tourism," *Chronicle of Higher Education* 51, no. 11 (5 November 2004): A56.

Pankhurst, Emmeline. *My Own Story* (1914). Available online. URL: http://www.fordham.edu/halsall/mod/1914Pankhurst.htm. Accessed on October 13, 2005.

Ehrenreich, Barbara (1941–)

The political columnist, lecturer, and social analyst Barbara Ehrenreich has made a forceful statement about GENDER BIAS and injustice in the workplace. From undercover investigation she compiled a best-selling social critique, *Nickel and Dimed: On (Not) Getting By in America* (2001). Born in Butte, Montana, she observed working-class lifestyles in childhood and learned from her parents that people who are willing to work are never poor. She studied chemistry and physics at Reed College and earned a doctorate in cell biology at Rockefeller University. In addition to establishing a freelance writing career, she taught journalism at Brandeis University and the University of California at Berkeley.

Ehrenreich's progressivism derives appeal from its empathy with women. One of her first works, *Witches, Midwives and Nurses: A History of Women Healers* (1973), coauthored with Deirdre English, traces some of the antifemale practices of the late 20th century to the misogyny and witch burning of the Middle Ages. The duo followed with *For Her Own Good: 150 Years of the Experts' Advice to Women* (1978). The research testifies to colonial women's subjugation by men at every turn: "At home was the father, in church was the priest or minister, at the top were the 'town fathers,' the local nobility. . . . For women, it was total, inescapable" (Ehrenreich and English, 1978, 7). Those who rebelled could be beaten, tried, and executed for WITCHCRAFT or banished from the colony, the solution of the Massachusetts Colony hierarchy to the troublesome herbalist-midwife and Bible teacher Anne Hutchinson.

Ehrenreich's public persona as champion of the underdog derives from reader response to her essays in *Time* and a column for the Manchester *Guardian*. She has written on war, the court system, health care, sexual relations, and feminism in *Atlantic, Esquire, Mirabella, Ms., Nation, New Republic, New York Times Magazine,* the *Progressive, Social Policy,* and the *Washington Post.* In 1992 she published "Stamping Out a Dread Scourge," a humorous take on the notion that small breasts constitute a disease called micromastia. With a sly poke at sexism, she explains, "In a society so unnurturing that even health care can sadistically be perverted for profit, people are bound to have a desperate, almost pathological need for the breast" (Thames and Gazzaniga, 162). She regularly defends poor women with essays and books denouncing a business climate that lists women under "cheap labor." Her best-selling text *Nickel and Dimed,* which earned the Sydney Hillman Award, began as "Maid to Order: The Politics of Other Women's Work," an article in the April 2000 issue of *Harper's.* The essay denounces the heavy lifting and thankless toil that keep female employees weary, unwell, poorly nourished, and despairing of ever escaping poverty.

Ehrenreich turned the essay into a book to discover what would happen to poor women tossed off social service rolls in 1998 by the Welfare Reform Bill. While conducting covert research, she worked for a month each in Key West, Minneapolis, and Portland, Maine, at minimum-wage jobs— waitress at a chain restaurant, dietician's aide at a nursing home, maid and hotel housekeeper, and clerk at Wal-Mart. Contributing to the decline of finances and welfare of female coworkers were the lack of affordable housing and transportation and the danger of homelessness in crime-ridden urban areas. In the conclusion she called the working poor "philanthropists" for neglecting their own homes and families to tend to the homes and families of the upper-middle class. In accepting onerous management, female blue-collar workers also accept racial, gender, and ethnic bias. They must lose their basic freedoms of privacy, speech, assembly, and freedom from unlawful search and seizure of handbags. The book made such an impact that college curricula added it to reading lists in economics, sociology, urban planning, American history, and women's studies.

Bibliography

"Down and Out in America," *Women's Review of Books* 18, no. 10/11 (July 2001): 6–7.

Ehrenreich, Barbara. *Nickel and Dimed: On (Not) Getting By in America.* New York: Owl Books, 2002.

———, and Deidre English. *For Her Own Good: 150 Years of the Experts' Advice to Women.* Garden City, N.Y.: Anchor Books, 1978.

———. *Witches, Midwives and Nurses: A History of Women Healers.* New York: Feminist Press, 1973.

Thames, Susan, and Marin Gazzaniga. *The Breast: An Anthology.* New York: Global City Press, 1995.

Eliot, George (1819–1880)

Under the pseudonym George Eliot, Mary Ann Evans, a renowned Victorian intellectual, became one of the literary viragos of English and feminist literature. A native of Nuneaton in rural Warwickshire, she was the daughter of Robert Eliot, a carpenter and overseer of an estate. She augmented her limited formal schooling at Miss Latham's evangelical boarding school with independent reading in philosophy and theology and with study of German, Greek, Italian, Latin, and music. Around 1841 she denounced Christian dogma, a stance that temporarily estranged her father, a religious conservative. She refused to join the nation's suffragists in demanding the vote for women but ventured into feminism by honoring the novelist Harriet Beecher STOWE's contributions to human freedom, by extolling the feminine qualities of the writers George SAND and Charlotte BRONTË, and by pledging a charter subscription to Girton College, England's first women's college.

The author published a translation of a BIOGRAPHY of Jesus and began issuing book reviews and articles in *Blackwood's Edinburgh Magazine*. After assuming a post on the editorial staff of the *Westminster Review* in 1849, she formed a long-standing romantic attachment to a married intellectual, George Henry Lewes, who encouraged her work. With a steady income bequeathed by her father's will, she worked steadily at five novels—*Scenes of Clerical Life* (1857), *Adam Bede* (1859), *The Mill on the Floss* (1860), and two moral masterworks, *Silas Marner* (1861) and MIDDLEMARCH: *Life in a Provincial Town* (1872), both of which offer fallible humans a second chance.

Critics and writers, including Sarah Orne JEWETT, Elizabeth Stuart PHELPS, Anna QUINDLEN, Susan SONTAG, and Virginia WOOLF, praised Eliot for perceptive characterization and for a compassionate view of human struggles, particularly those associated with marriage and home life. *Scenes of Clerical Life* features the alcoholism of the battered wife and commiserates with the cheated woman pressed to the limit of self-control. In *Silas Marner* the failure of Nancy Lammeter Cass to establish a family pictures the suffering of a woman who has buried one child and then lost an opportunity to parent a stepchild. The text remarks on Nancy's self-criticism by "asking herself continually whether she had been in any respect blamable" (Eliot, 157). A less amenable character, the rebellious, bookish Maggie Tulliver in *The Mill on the Floss*, exhibits the heart hunger for affection and validation. In Eliot's

last major work, *Daniel Deronda* (1876), Gwendolen Harleth's maturing conscience frees her from youthful self-absorption and shallowness after she marries for money and learns the hard way the difference between specious value and real worth.

Bibliography

Eliot, George. *Silas Marner*. New York: New American Library, 1960.

Moers, Ellen. *Literary Women*. New York: Oxford University Press, 1977.

Sypher, Eileen. "Resisting Gwendolen's Subjection': Daniel Deronda's Proto-Feminism," *Studies in the Novel* 28, no. 4 (Winter 1996): 506–518.

El Saadawi, Nawal (1931–)

Nawal El Saadawi, a psychiatrist, freedom fighter, and writer, contributes to feminist literature her keen observations of women in developing countries and their attempts to unveil Arab minds. Born in Kafr Tahla, Egypt, to a family of nine children sired by educated parents, she grew up on the Nile River north of Cairo. Her father was a government supervisor of education; her mother suffered brunted ambitions after marriage at age 17 and "cursed marriage as a cemetery for women" (El Saadawi, 2002, 1). Nawal was an introspective child who learned the art of STORYTELLING from her grandmother. At age six El Saadawi lost her childhood innocence during an abrupt and brutal circumcision. She witnessed the same folk surgery performed on her four-year-old sister. The secrecy and barbarity of FEMALE GENITAL MUTILATION traumatized El Saadawi, who was shocked to see her mother's complicity with the circumciser.

Sexism was an obvious element of El Saadawi's home life. In the autobiographical *The Hidden Face of Eve: Women in the Arab World* (1980), she grieved at her loss of trust in family. She pondered unlimited love and nurturance for her brother: "Why did they favour my brother as regards food, and the freedom to go out of the house . . . whereas I was not supposed to look into people's eyes directly, but was meant to drop my glance" (El Saadawi, 1980, 9–10). In subsequent rebellions against preferential treatment for boys, the author received no answer from her parents, only the scolding of her grandmother for displaying a "long tongue" (*ibid.*, 10).

El Saadawi's medical practice and writing career emerged from a lifetime of researching the causes and extent of society's disdain for women. Her personal accounts expose high infant and maternal mortality rates among Arab females, who too frequently die of malnutrition, neglect, and murder. In 1971, while teaching medical courses at Ain Shams University in Cairo, she began to feel estranged from her country for her honest evaluations of widespread misogyny and of the abasement of Islamic women, who, like slaves, were forbidden to write. The following year the Ministry of Health revoked her appointment as its director and removed her from the post editing *Health* magazine. To protest the brutalization of peasant women, she composed a novella, *Woman at Point Zero* (1973), and a political allegory, *God Dies by the Nile* (1974), the story of a mayor who sates his lust on young females under his jurisdiction.

After her self-exile to Addis Ababa, Ethiopia, El Saadawi served as a consultant for the United Nations but discovered that the organization was riddled with male-centered thinking that discounted the needs and concerns of poor, disadvantaged women: Under UN supervisors females "slide to the bottom of the heap" (El Saadawi, 1994, p. 3). She resigned her consultancy in 1980 and returned to Egypt. Her candid commentary on Arab women's misery provoked censure and imprisonment in Giza in 1981 under the regime of Anwar Sadat, who banned her books for both national and religious reasons. She produced a classic of women's prison literature, *Memoirs from the Women's Prison* (1983), which describes her day labor in the prison garden and her classes in health measures and calisthenics to help inmates improve both body and spirit.

Among women El Saadawi is a respected proponent of *tahrir al-ma'rah*, the Arab world's women's liberation. She earned international regard for organizing the Arab Women's Solidarity Association; for sponsoring its magazine, *Noon*; and for being the first Arab female to write about the significance of sex to Arab economics, health, and politics. In 2002 she published an AUTOBIOGRAPHY, *Walking through Fire*, a sequel to the memoir *Daughter of Isis* (1999). At odds with the past, she filled her reflections with love and hate for the motherland. She expressed a paradox, the personal and professional liberation of blacklisting and exile from Egypt and of studying at Duke University. While enjoying classroom teaching, she felt the terror of being named on the death list of a fundamentalist group for organizing militant Arab women and for describing Islamic PATRIARCHY in her works, which are widely read from Morocco to Yemen and throughout Europe and the Americas.

Bibliography

Afshar, Haleh, ed. *Women in the Middle East: Perceptions, Realities, and Struggles for Liberation.* London: Macmillan, 1993.

El Saadawi, Nawal. *The Hidden Face of Eve: Women in the Arab World.* London: Zed Books, 1980.

———. *Memoirs from the Women's Prison.* Berkeley: University of California Press, 1994.

———. *Walking through Fire: A Life of Nawal El Saadawi.* London: Zed Books, 2002.

Emecheta, Buchi (1944–   )

Buchi Emecheta produces short and long fiction and children's works that express the African female perspective as tribal woman and as emigrant. An Ibo tribeswoman from Yaba outside Lagos, Nigeria, she was orphaned in childhood and grew up at a missionary compound, where she attended the Methodist Girls' High School. She married at age 16 and lived in London, where she bore five children in six years before completing a sociology degree at the University of London. From a tribal perspective she developed fiction that portrays femininity and womanhood as limited by SEXUALITY and childbearing. Through the character Adah in the autobiographical novel *In the Ditch* (1972), Emecheta describes separation from her husband, working as a librarian at the British Museum, and raising her children in a slum.

In relation to issues of PATRIARCHY in Nigeria the author speaks of Ibo customs in *Second-Class Citizen* (1974), autobiographical fiction that examines a father's sorrow that his child, Adah, is born female. His male-dominant outlook is a painful thrust at his daughter's self-image. Of her wilted spirit Emecheta laments, "Since she was such a disappointment to her parents, to her immediate family, to her tribe, nobody thought of recording her birth. She was so insignificant" (Emecheta, 1983, 7). In a later novel, *The Joys of Motherhood* (1979), Emecheta describes how Nnu Ego survives destitution and the insult of her husband's marriage to a second mate, a privilege accorded only to righteous Islamic men. In a welter of anger and despair Nnu hurries toward a bridge to hurl herself into the river to release her wounded spirit from her body. In the afterlife she intends to ask her *chi* (personal deity) why women are so punished. With a touch of sarcasm, she assumes her *chi* is female because "only a woman would be so thorough in punishing another" (Emecheta, 1980, 9). Single parenting continues to dominate Emecheta's fiction in *Head above Water* (1986), which follows the fictional Adah to college and into professional writing.

Bibliography

Dubek, Laura. "Lessons in Solidarity: Buchi Emecheta and Mariama Bâ on Female Victim(izer)s," *Women's Studies* 30, no. 3 (June 2001): 199–223.

Emecheta, Buchi. *The Joys of Motherhood.* New York: George Braziller, 1980.

———. *Second-Class Citizen.* New York: George Braziller, 1983.

Ensler, Eve (1953–)

The Jewish American actor, scenarist, and Obie-winning dramatist Eve Ensler popularizes frank talk about female genitalia through a powerful form of STORYTELLING. A native of New York City, she grew up in affluent Scarsdale, where her father ran a food distributorship. Her mother failed to protect five-year-old Eve from beatings with a belt and from sexual abuse inflicted by her father over the next five years. In high school she turned to alcohol as a solace for self-loathing. While studying English at Middlebury College, she allied with militant feminists and expressed dark thoughts by writing on the theme of suicide in contemporary verse. Because she could not pay tuition at Yale Drama School, she gravitated toward alternatives to EDUCATION—alcoholism, drug experimentation, and rowdy bar brawls.

In 1977 Ensler gave up drinking, studied drama under the actor Joanne Woodward, and began writing plays on populist themes. An activist for peace and WOMEN'S RIGHTS, Ensler infused her stage works with the FAIRY TALE lore of CINDERELLA and with feminist health issues, the underpinning of the humorous hit play *The Vagina Monologues* (1996). Ensler based the 90-minute monologue on 200 interviews. Through witty narratives she took the roles of a prostitute, a lesbian, an elderly woman, and a late-blooming orgasmic female. The humor and irony remove the embarrassment and unease that women have about viewing and talking about their SEXUALITY and the shape, odor, and function of their pudenda. In the introduction the essayist Gloria STEINEM lauds Ensler's truth telling: "Women's sanity was saved by bringing these hidden experiences into the open, naming them, and turning our rage into positive action to reduce and heal VIOLENCE" (Ensler, 1998, xv).

Ensler's play flourished in the SoHo Theater and gained acceptance as an HBO-TV production. She credited the success to a reprioritizing of female ideals: "I think our preoccupation and the distraction of fixing ourselves is keeping us away from really focusing on the substantial issues at hand" (Tolin, 8H). When female celebrities—Glenn Close, Calista Flockhart, Jane Fonda, Whoopi Goldberg, Winona Ryder, Susan Sarandon, Marisa Tomei, Lily Tomlin, and Kate Winslet—began performing the work, Ensler redirected her renown and profits to women's issues, particularly violence and spousal abuse. Translated into 35 languages, the play has entertained and enlightened audiences in 76 countries. Sponsors further the theme with celebrations of V-Day, an antiviolence cooperative campaign each February 14 to end suffering from battery, incest, rape, FEMALE GENITAL MUTILATION, and sexual slavery.

The response to the first play kept Ensler's momentum humming. In 2002 she produced *Necessary Targets: A Story of Women and War* (2001). Set among female Bosnian refugees, the drama focuses on their refusal to harbor vengeful feelings against their enemies, who abased them through sexual torture. In the introduction she remarks on women who "shake, pace, smoke, choke, weep as they describe the gang rapes, the public rapes, the rapes of mothers, sisters, and grandmothers" (Ensler, 2001, xii). Her campaign against female battery earned a Matrix Award and the 2002 Amnesty International Media Spotlight Award for Leadership.

In 2003 Ensler performed *The Good Body,* a one-woman drama that became her first role on Broadway. The play derives from her insights on midlife crises: "I want women to be free. . . . I want us to get up in the morning and go, 'Oh my God, I've got a body, what a miracle!'" (Tolin, 8H). Based on interviews with women in 14 countries, the play makes hash of the BEAUTY MYTH by satirizing Judeo-Christian guilt complexes, liposuction, vagina tightening, Botox, ab rollers, low-carb diets, tofu salads, and fat camps for obese teens. The play delights audiences by normalizing every woman's physical imperfections and reassuring audiences about the flexibility and variety in beauty standards.

Bibliography

Bartlett, Karen. "When Caprice and Meera Get Together." *New Statesman,* 15 March 2004, pp. 26–27.

Ensler, Eve. *Necessary Targets: A Story of Women and War.* New York: Villard, 2001.

———. *The Vagina Monologues.* New York: Villard, 1998.

Tolin, Lisa. "'Monologues' Author Expands Scope," *Charlotte Observer,* 28 November 2004, p. 8H.

"Envelope, The" Maxine Kumin (1978)

Maxine KUMIN's maternal ode "The Envelope," collected in *The Retrieval System* (1978), packs into 16 lines an impressive trio of conceits. The first stanza furthers a scholarly tone with an allusion to the philosopher Martin Heidegger's existentialist writings on death fears, which the reviewer Rosaly DeMaios Roffman calls the poet's "nagging bad dream" (Roffman, 1978, 1,179). The female speaker acknowledges the fear of nothingness but dispels terror with the knowledge that her "daughters will absorb me," a spiritual form of osmosis that preserves the departed parent in memory and biological imprinting (Kumin, 148). Kumin muses on the next generation's reverse procreation, an incubation that bears the "arrested fetus" much as the speaker harbors her own mother's ghost, an "androgynous person, a miracle / folded in lotus position" (*ibid.*). As an internal bud, the mother-essence becomes both burden and promise for womenfolk, who have no way of eluding the responsibilities and benefits of matrilineage.

The poet chooses a tactile puzzle in stanza 2—nested Russian dolls, the pear-hipped female figurines packed one within the other like toy treasures inside the amnion and chorion of a carved wooden womb. The image admits that the mother within shrinks in size and force to a "pea-sized, irreducible minim," a compact, but potent grain similar in form to the fertilized egg (*ibid.*). For Kumin the endurance of feminine tradition results in an "Envelope of Almost-Infinity," a guarantee of reincarnation shaped by subsequent generations of daughters (*ibid.*). In her final phrase Kumin compares the envelope to the receptacle of a chain letter that allows the mother to survive for another 68-plus years, a virtual lifetime lived out through the outlook and accomplishments of daughters.

Kumin's benediction on the MOTHER-DAUGHTER RELATIONSHIP envisions cyclical solidarity as the reward for parenting and the deliverance from mortality. The paradox of a protective case clings to the notion of a coffin, the inevitable burial of the past generation's physical remains. Unlike a corpse left to rot in the ground, the image of the implanted mother-spirit suggests seeding and rebirth. In the style of myths of insurrection from ancient Isis and Demeter lore, the resilient parent springs from familiar ground to invigorate young women. In 2003 the upbeat ode inspired the poet-collographer Kate Cheney Chappell to assemble a one-woman exhibition, "Envelope," in Damariscotta, Maine. The artistic offshoots of Kumin's mother-salvaging poem aided the artist in overcoming grief for her own mother by recapturing her in word, image, and color.

Bibliography

Kumin, Maxine. *Selected Poems 1960–1990.* New York: W. W. Norton, 1998.

Roffman, Rosaly DeMaios. "Review: *The Retrieval System.*" *Library Journal,* 1 June 1978, pp. 1,178–1,179.

Erdrich, Louise (1954–)

A shamanic storyteller and poet in the Ojibway tradition, Karen Louise Erdrich creates memorable female protagonists from ANDROGYNY and cross-cultural beginnings. Female DUALITY permeated her perspective in childhood. Born in Little Falls, Minnesota, she grew up Catholic and spent her girlhood in North Dakota with Native American grandparents at the Turtle Mountain Chippewa Reservation. With degrees in creative writing from Dartmouth College and Johns Hopkins University, she began publishing award-winning stories and verse in the early 1980s, filling them with complementary strands of Catholicism and Native lore. Her rise to fame culminated in a National Book Critics Circle Award for *Love Medicine* (1984), the first of a tetralogy of story collections that she coauthored with her husband, Michael Dorris.

Erdrich achieved a feminist breakthrough with *Tracks* (1988), a novel that extolls STORYTELLING as a source of authority for Fleur Pillager, a reputed shape shifter and one of Erdrich's intriguing female survivors. To Nanapush, the authoritative male elder, Fleur is a cultural icon, "the funnel of our history" (Erdrich, 178). In the estimation of her foil, Pauline, Fleur breaks through gender and cosmic barriers to grasp forbidden powers: "She messed with evil, laughed at the old women's advice and dressed like a man. She got herself into some half-forgotten medicine, studied ways we shouldn't talk about" (*ibid.*, 12). Pauline's disapproval symbolizes the backwash from women who fail to activate themselves and who fear to abandon female stereotypes to take on an androgynous shift toward liberation.

In her second decade of writing Erdrich turned more pointedly toward feminist themes and issues overlaid with ethnic mythology. In 1996 she summarized in *The Blue Jay's Dance: A Birth Year* the welter of emotion that accompanies the conception, grueling labor, and birth of a child. The author marvels at the body's knowledge of its task, even when pain and frustration intervene. She expressed the acceptance of mutual satisfaction in *Tales of Burning Love* (1997), in which a building contractor, Jack Mauser, overcomes impotence by learning to give rather than demand pleasure from his mate. Set at Easter, the story resurrects Jack's manhood by literally hurling him into a supine position after an icon of the VIRGIN MARY falls on top of him and nearly crushes his penis. She added to her Ojibway saga *The Last Report on the Miracles at Little No Horse* (2001), told by the Native story keeper Nanapush. The communicator of love and redemption is Agnes, who, as Father Damien Modeste, conceals her gender and ministers to North Dakota's rural reservation Indians. The story reveals the duality of a woman who is uniquely talented at hearing confessions and aiding tortured souls.

Bibliography

Erdrich, Louise. *Tracks.* New York: Harper & Row, 1988.

Siegel, Lee. "De Sade's Daughters," *Atlantic Monthly* 279, no. 2 (February 1997): 97–101.

Weisser, Susan Ostrov, and Jennifer Fleischner. *Feminist Nightmares: Women at Odds: Feminism and the Problems of Sisterhood.* New York: New York University Press, 1995.

Esquivel, Laura (1951–)

The Mexican writer and scenarist Laura Esquivel values the feminist traditions of STORYTELLING and kitchen-table conversations, central elements of her famed parody of romance novels. A native of Mexico City, she grew up in a three-generation atmosphere that included her mother, Josephina; her telegrapher father, Julio Caesar Esquivel; three siblings; and a grandmother living across the street. From the blended aromas of chili and garlic, nuts, and herbs, in her grandmother's kitchen and carnations in her home chapel grew the impetus for a best-selling Tex-Mex melodrama on matriarchal traditions *Como agua para chocolate: Novela de entregas mensuales con recetas, amores, y remedios* (*Like Water for Chocolate: A Novel in Monthly Installments, with Recipes, Romances and Home Remedies*, 1989). The author adapted the ABBY-winning border novel for film, which her husband, Alfonso Arau, directed. One of the highest-grossing foreign-language films in the United States, it won 11 Ariel awards from the Mexican Academy of Motion Pictures for lively, fantasy-rich scenes of births, weddings, SISTERHOOD, healings, and reunions.

The folkloric account of the curse, rebellion, and transformation of Tita de la Garza centers on the command of her witchy mother, Mama Elena, that Tita, her youngest, care for Elena by remaining unmarried and superintending the family farm. The mounting sexual tension that fuels Tita's adultery with her brother-in-law, Pedro, leads to open rebellion against her mother. Conflicting wills and emotions clash in a grand orchestration of magical realism. Along the way to Tita's late middle age, she fills the narrative with military invasions; her sister, Gertrudis's, capture from a burning outhouse; Tita's false pregnancy; and exaggerated accounts of 12 special dishes that inspire emotional responses from diners. When frustration threatens her sanity, her mother snorts, "If she is acting crazy, then I'm going to put her in an asylum. There's no place in this house for maniacs!" (Esquivel, 97). Tita retreats to a fetal position in the upper-story dovecote, a symbolic alliance with harmless birds that suggests her gentleness and her desire to break out of her shell and fly away.

The obstacles and rewards to true love confer a FAIRY TALE atmosphere that concludes in an eruption of cosmic passion. As Tita's story passes to her niece, Esperanza, and to Esperanza's daughter, Gothic events mark the narrative with touches of menace by the Mexican Revolution, memories, wooings, ghosts, a spell of madness, and persistent hyperbole. In the kitchen, the center of Tita's life and a reservoir of female creativity, the labor-intensive preparation of chilis, onions, nuts, cilantro, and mint for special dishes absorbs her energies and sublimates her sorrow and hostility against a cruel mother. Tita reaches the breaking point that generates the title, " 'like water for chocolate'—she was on the verge of boiling over" (ibid., 147). The bonding of Tita with her nanny, the wisewoman Nancha, and with Tita's sister Gertrudis attests to the female strengths that dispel hopelessness. Like favorite recipes do, the women's stories express a patience and wisdom similar to the skills necessary for fine cookery and for resilience against adversity. Tita's foil, her haughty older sister, Rosaura, fosters jealousy and cruelty that take the form of halitosis and intestinal gas, the poison and internal pressure that eventually kill her. Magical events, particularly Tita's production of breast milk to feed her hungry niece and Tita's exorcism of Elena's ghost, create a mythic aura that enhances themes of womanly passion and mother love.

Bibliography

Esquivel, Laura. *Like Water for Chocolate.* New York: Bantam, 1992.

Jaffe, Janice. "Hispanic American Women Writers' Novel Recipes and Laura Esquivel's *Como Agua para Chocolate,*" *Women's Studies* 22, no. 2 (March 1993): 217–230.

Estés, Clarissa Pinkola (1949–)

The controversial poet, essayist, lecturer, New Age evangelist, and Latina *cantadora* (story keeper) Clarissa Pinkola Estés gives substance and meaning to feminist philosophy. Born in rural Indiana of Mestizo lineage, she was the adopted child of Holocaust survivors from Hungary who sheltered in refugee camps. At war's end she explains, "My childhood home overflowed with haunted refugees who struggled so hard to come back to life" (Estés, 2003, 16). She grew up in a Catholic environment enriched by family spiritualism and by a grandmother's Slavic myths and FAIRY TALES. She later noted, "We consider story our living relative" (Estés, 1995, 3).

While she and two daughters were subsisting on welfare, Estés majored in intercultural studies and clinical psychology at Loretto Heights College, Union Institute, and the International Association for Analytical Psychology in Zurich, Switzerland. After settling in Denver, in the 1970s, she directed two aid centers, the Women in Transition Safe House and Beyond Divorce. She managed the C. G. Jung Center for Research and Education for a quarter-century and submitted spiritual essays and poems to the *National Catholic Reporter, Publishers Weekly, U.S. Catholic, Washington Post,* and *Women's Sport and Fitness.* In the name of a Latina goddess, the Virgin of Guadeloupe, she established the C. P. Estés Guadaloupe Foundation, a human rights organization in Boulder, Colorado, that beams healing stories by shortwave radio into world trouble spots. Her outreach to homosexuals and acquired immunodeficiency syndrome (AIDS) patients earned her acceptance into an unofficial sorority of women who love women.

Estés began publishing overviews of the female consciousness in multiple forms—storyteller, wisewoman, creator, healer, and seeker of truth. She is best known for *Women Who Run with the Wolves: Myths and Stories of the Wild Woman Archetype* (1992), a seminal work that held a top spot on the *New York Times* best seller list for 68 weeks. The treatise examines the challenges of human life through the eyes of women who have lost their appreciation for innate talents. She characterizes the archetypal flow of female intuition as "the *Río Abajo Río*, the river beneath the river" (Estés, 1997, 322). Her work has been acknowledged by the feminist community, including the authors Dorothy ALLISON, Maya ANGELOU, Carolyn FORCHÉ, Gloria STEINEM, and Alice WALKER.

Estés continued reviving spirit and initiative through subsequent works. In *Warming the Stone Child: Myths and Stories about Abandonment and the Unmothered Child* (1992), she examines issues of neglect, sexual abuse, and child endangerment in such familiar narratives as LITTLE RED RIDING HOOD and explains how cautionary tales provide nurturing, reassuring life scripts for girls. She describes the internalized voice of wisdom as the Inner Mother, the guide who provides a balm and wholeness to the fragmented psyche. In *The Gift of Story: A Wise Tale about What Is Enough* (1993), she strings nested narratives that describe women's ability to turn despair and loss into triumph. Three years later she reprised in *The Faithful Gardener: A Wise Tale about That Which Can Never Die* (1995) stories of birth, pain, destruction, and rebirth, a hope-filled cycle that gives meaning to suffering.

Bibliography

Estés, Clarissa Pinkola. *The Faithful Gardener: A Wise Tale about That Which Can Never Die.* San Francisco: HarperCollins, 1995.

———. "The Rose Warrior," *National Catholic Reporter,* 17 October 2003, p. 16.

———. *Women Who Run with the Wolves: Myths and Stories about the Wild Woman Archetype.* New York: Ballantine, 1997.

King, Patricia. "The Call of the Wild Woman." *Newsweek,* 21 December 1992, p. 59.

Evans, Mari (1923–)

The poet, dramatist, scenarist, and storyteller Mari Evans crystallizes the memories and realities that delight and burden black women. Left motherless at age seven, she grew up in a housing project in her native Toledo, Ohio, under the care of a loving father. He taught her about African-American heritage and preserved her juvenilia as testimony to early literary promise. While rearing her two boys, she held a number of community jobs, including programmer for the Young Man's Christian Association (YMCA), organist and choir director, and activist in prison reform. After study at the University of Toledo, she moved to Indianapolis to become a writer and teacher of creative writing and black literature at Indiana University, Cornell University, Northwestern University, and Purdue University. For five years she pioneered television programming for black audiences by writing, producing, and hosting a series, *The Black Experience,* for WTTV in Indianapolis. Episodes drew on the cultural direction of the black community during the civil rights movement.

Evans's themes range from black female experience with SLAVERY and poverty to colonial oppression and American segregation and injustice. Energized by the black arts movement, she began publishing verse in *Negro Digest* and in the anthologies *Where Is All the Music?* (1968), *I Am a Black Woman* (1970), *Nightstar: 1973–1978* (1981), and *A Dark and Splendid Mass* (1992). She edited *Black Women Writers, 1950–1980: A Critical Evaluation* (1984), featuring the work of Maya ANGELOU, Toni Cade BAMBARA, Alice Childress, Nikki GIOVANNI, Toni MORRISON, and Alice WALKER. In a midlife burst of creativity Evans composed a choric play, *River of My Song* (1977); a children's collection, *Singing Black: Alternative Nursery Rhymes for Children* (1978); and the one-act one-woman show *Boochie* (1979). Evans's musical, *Eyes* (1979), an adaptation of Zora Neale HURSTON's feminist novel *THEIR EYES WERE WATCHING GOD* (1937), captivated Chicago audiences in 2004 with its 20 jazz songs.

Evans specializes in wry humor and kinetic scenes from life, which she orders through shaped lines reflecting the lift and fall of the human voice. She accounts for the centrality of oral tradition in poetry: "We are a tongued folk. A race of singers. Our lips shape words and rhythms which elevate our spirits and quicken our blood. . . . I have spent fifty years listening to my people" (Evans, 1993, 3). In the lyric poem "I Am a Black Woman" (1970) she stresses musical voices that sing through tears and hum into the night. Her auditory visions enfold the Middle Passage along with World War II and the Vietnam War. A companion piece, "Vive Noir!" (1970), pictures the rise of blacks from urban slums and from an enforced obeisance to white masters. No longer dependent on handouts, the proud speaker promises to move up into the tall buildings erected by black labor. Less ebullient is a female text in "Where Have You Gone?" (1970), a plaintive regret that a lover left with the rent money and the speaker's heart.

Bibliography

Evans, Mari. *Black Women Writers, 1950–1980: A Critical Evaluation.* New York: Anchor Books, 1984.

———. *I Am a Black Woman.* New York: Writers and Readers, 1993.

Kensey, Barbara. "Mari Evans' Musical, Eyes, Debuts in Chicago on ETA's Mainstage," *Chicago Defender,* 24 June 2004, p. 19.

Evans, Mary Ann

See ELIOT, GEORGE.

Eve

Feminist literature often returns to the mythic, much-maligned figure of Eve to determine the universal themes that derive from the downfall of the first woman. The feminist critic Marina Warner, author of *From the Beast to the Blonde: On Fairy Tales and Their Tellers* (1994), considers the original myth and ponders the role of female beauty in the condemnation of Eve. In Jerome's Vulgate translation of the Bible into Latin he chooses the word *seducta* to describe her crime, thus picturing her beauty and persuasive words as the cause of Adam's fall. Eve's oral immorality begins with addressing the serpent, then biting the fruit of the tree of knowledge. Her curse is desire for her mate's kisses, the initiation of intimacies that force

her to bear children. Warner comments that female writers of fairy tales, notably Henriette-Julie de Murat and the Norman raconteur Marie-Catherine le Jumelle de Barneville, comtesse d'Aulnoy, denounced the stereotype of the libidinous Eve and fought the social custom of selling young girls into marriage to older men who could afford virgins.

According to the second chapter of Kate MILLETT's *Sexual Politics* (1970), the male framing of Pandora and Eve myths introduced the notion that women initiated SEXUALITY in humankind. In 1709 the English poet Anne FINCH, countess of Winchilsea, mocked Adam as the namer of all Eden's creatures in "Adam Posed." The witty poem pictures his first view of woman as a fashionable 18th-century butterfly, a period Eve who stumps Adam for an appropriate category in which to place her. The novelist Charlotte BRONTË uses Edenic imagery in the proposal scene of *JANE EYRE* (1847), in which Edward Rochester describes his love for Jane as an invisible tie from his rib to hers. In the mid-Victorian era, Christina ROSSETTI describes Adam's wife from a traditional Anglican perspective. The poet sets "Eve" (1865) in the aftermath of disobedience and expulsion from Eden. The rueful first wife regrets tempting her husband and lover with bitter fruit, the foretokening of sins and the first murder, in which Cain slew Abel. Rossetti tempers blame with compassion by portraying birds and animals within earshot of Eve's lamentations commiserating with her. Only the serpent, the embodiment of temptation, grins in the knowledge that he overturned God's earthly paradise. By picturing the gleeful snake, Rossetti implies that Eve, a vulnerable human, was fated to succumb to verbal seduction.

During the rise of Marxist feminism the concept of heaven on Earth permeated utopian dreams of the perfect world peopled by men and women who brought the traditional war of the sexes to a permanent truce. The radical South African novelist and polemicist Olive SCHREINER concluded *Woman and Labour* (1911) with a rejection of biblical guilt assigned to Eve alone. The author looks beyond a perpetual struggle to a golden age: "We dream that woman shall eat of the tree of knowledge together with man, and that side by side and hand close to hand, through ages of much toil and labour, they shall together raise about them an Eden . . . created by their own labour and made beautiful by their own fellowship" (Schreiner 1911). With reference to Revelation, Schreiner, the Bible-reared daughter of a Lutheran missionary, depicts a new heaven and Earth where Eve joins Adam as his coworker.

Angela CARTER, a master of bizarre Gothic fiction, inverts standard male-centered cosmology in the hilarious grotesque novel *The Passion of New Eve* (1977). In a Gothic parody of the United States in the turbulent 1960s, she sets a female mad scientist named Mother over a male captive with the droll name of Zero. Mother, a version of the creation goddess, intends to emasculate her prisoner. Of the mystic surgeon Zero recognizes too late his misjudgment of female guile: "I did not know, then, who it was that waited for me, I did not know . . . the patience of she who'd always been waiting for me, where I'd exiled her, down in the lowest room at the root of my brain" (Carter, 58). Mother transforms Zero into Eve by fitting him with a uterus. She impregnates him with his own sperm to produce Earth's savior. As awareness sinks in, Eve realizes the reduction yet to come as she evolves backward into prehistory: "I have not reached the end of the maze yet. I descend lower, descend lower. I must go further" (*ibid.*, 150). The revision of male sexual identity to serve the perverted notions of a dominatrix satirizes a standard Svengalian motif in which a male manipulator turns a female victim into his IDEAL WOMAN.

Late 20th-century musings on Eve permeate feminist writings. In a complex meeting of Old and New Testament women the English poet Stevie SMITH improvised a dialogue between Eve and the VIRGIN MARY in "A Dream of Comparison" (1957), which extends feminist sympathy to the fallen Eve. The meeting portrays her as the more philosophical and tragic of the two women. In 1966 Smith reprised the myth of Eden in the poem "How Cruel Is the Story of Eve," which describes the first woman's story as the fount of cruelty and misery and a touchstone of male dominion over females. Smith describes women's coping skills as the masking of wisdom to allow men to think that they are in charge. The Irish poet Eavan BOLAND adds her own version of female strategy in "The Serpent in the Garden" (1990), which pictures the first woman leaving her bath to apply makeup. In anticipation of beguiling Adam, she remarks on the flickering of her cold, slick tongue. Such Eve-like trickery assures the continuation of male-female relationships. Moving still further from Eden, Denise LEVERTOV branches out to the myth of the first human family with "Abel's Bride" (1967), a two-stanza contrast of the male's reach outward for self and conquest and the female's inner contentment and sexuality. The poet pictures in an atavistic metaphor of bones at a cave hearth the DUALITY of Eve the fire tender and Eve the devourer.

Food, knowledge, and peril resonate in other Eve poems. In the heavily ironic "Anorexic" (1980), Boland speaks in first person the claustrophobia, torment, and inner blame of the self-starved female. As does the doomed Eve, the self-starver slips toward a forked tongue in the python's mouth. The poet Carolyn KIZER surveys women's history in a seriocomic poem, "Fearful Women" (1996), in which she pictures Adam scapegoating his wife for disobeying God. Kizer describes knowledge as woman's great fault and source of trouble. The poet spreads the alarm that EDUCATION for women ends submission to a mate and leaves them vulnerable to such ends as those suffered by Joan of Arc and Helen of Troy.

Bibliography

Ahearn, Edward J. "The Modern English Visionary: Peter Ackroyd's *Hawksmoor* and Angela Carter's *The Passion of New Eve*," *Twentieth Century Literature* 46, no. 4 (Winter 2000): 453–469.

Boland, Eavan. *Outside History: Selected Poems, 1980–1990.* New York: W. W. Norton, 2001.

Carter, Angela. *The Passion of New Eve.* New York: Gollancz, 1977.

Kizer, Carolyn. *Harping On.* Port Townsend, Wash.: Copper Canyon Press, 1996.

San Souci, Robert D. *The White Cat: An Old French Fairy Tale Retold.* New York: Orchard Books, 2000.

Schreiner, Olive. *Woman and Labour* (1911). Available online. URL: http://etext.library.adelaide.edu.au/s/ schreiner_o/woman/woman.html. Accessed on October 13, 2005.

Warner, Marina. *From the Beast to the Blonde: On Fairy Tales and Their Tellers*. New York: Noonday Press, 1994.

Eyre, Jane

Jane Eyre is the central figure of a feminist literary monolith, Charlotte BRONTË's novel JANE EYRE (1847). An obscure English naif during the economic and social ferment of the Industrial Revolution, she betters herself from orphanhood and the job of governess to teacher at her own school and wife of the man of her choice. Although these are small achievements by current standards, for the early Victorian era, Jane's rise is meteoric. A plain-featured, working-class outsider, at age 10 she survives desultory treatment at Gateshead Hall, the unwelcoming home of her aunt, Sarah Reed, and of her cousins, Augusta, Georgiana, and the spiteful John. When the meddling educator Mr. Brocklehurst questions Jane about charges of deceit, she defeats the illogic of his fundamentalist trick of threatening damnation to hell for trivial misbehavior. To his question about how she should avoid the fiery pit, she replies, "I must keep in good health and not die" (Brontë, 26). Her ability to outmaneuver mean-spirited cousins, aunts, and a cagey pietist bodes well for Jane's future.

EDUCATION is the tool that opens the bars of Jane's imprisoning milieu. Her aunt Sarah wants only that Jane "be brought up in a manner suiting her prospects," but Jane refuses to play the cringing dog to her aunt's condescension (ibid., 29). After a verbal sparring Jane celebrates the bitter triumph of besting an adult. She reflects, "It was the hardest battle I had fought, and the first victory I had gained" (ibid., 31). At Lowood, a pinch-penny girls' school, Jane educates herself beyond expectations with mastery of conversational French and painting in watercolors. Along the way she weathers deprivation and, out of mother hunger, turns hero worship of Miss Temple into friendship. An unjust accusation of lying causes a temporary setback, during which Jane lists her immediate aims: "I had meant to be so good, and to do so much at Lowood, to make so many friends, to earn respect, and win affection" (ibid., 60). She later summarizes a far-reaching goal—"to seek real knowledge of life amidst its perils" (ibid., 77). Aiding Jane's accomplishments are her dedication to work, the enjoyment of art as a stress reliever, and prescience, a foreknowledge that warns her of trials to come.

Brontë describes her heroine as a quick study. Jane's desperation grows for "liberty; for liberty I gasped; for liberty I uttered a prayer," but, at age 18 she settles for "a new servitude," for which she takes out an advertisement in the —shire Herald (ibid., 77). Upon encountering an unidentified man on her walk from Thornfield, Jane risks the pawing hooves of the horse Mesrour and the jaws of the dog Pilot to help the fallen man gain his footing and remount the saddle. Unknown to her, she makes a valuable impression on her moody, willful employer Edward Rochester, who deliberately conceals his identity. Her show of competence and character with a downed stranger eventually leads to his admiration and pledge of love. Edward's unqualified selection of Jane as wife bridges the chasm between their two social levels and the 20-year difference in their ages.

Negating the strictures of a CINDERELLA rescue, Brontë allows Jane to work out her own destiny. The author provides her with caution and pragmatism that suit a character who symbolizes the rise of females in Victorian England. In the presence of the haughty Blanche Ingram, who Jane supposes is Edward's intended, the governess recedes from the parlor as a dowdy church mouse to a hole in the wainscoting. Paternal and sadistic, Edward torments Jane by pretending to find employment for her in Ireland, then makes an impromptu marriage proposal in a melodramatic setting, beneath the horse chestnut tree in the Thornfield orchard. She disclaims connivance in winning him: "I had not intended to love him" (Brontë, 163). She ruefully adds, "I could not unlove him now" (ibid., 174). Her honest tears elicit candor and warmth from him in a preview of their eventual life together as marriage partners.

To the surprise of the reading public, Brontë inverts the standard sentimental novel by ennobling Jane above the gentry who visit Edward. The author indicates that Jane's love is worth more than marriage to the master of Thornfield and warden of a pathetic raving wife locked away on an upper floor. After Jane learns of his deceit, her levelheadedness guides her through temptation and trial, but her love for Edward holds firm. Their eventual pairing demands a rough justice, the loss of Edward's left hand and eye and the wandering of Jane on the moor until hunger and exhaustion threaten her survival. In a moment of anguish for him, she hears "a voice somewhere cry—'Jane! Jane! Jane!'—nothing more" (*ibid.*, 401). As though saving him from drowning, she hurries toward a cry that "spoke in pain and woe, wildly, eerily, urgently" (*ibid.*). In a moment of self-reliance, she exults, "It was *my* time to assume ascendancy. My powers were in play and in force" (*ibid.*). To Edward's questions about her economic and personal status, Jane speaks the feminist's creed, "I am my own mistress" (*ibid.*, 416).

Bibliography

Brontë, Charlotte. *Jane Eyre.* New York: Bantam Books, 1981.

Franklin, J. Jeffrey. "The Merging of Spiritualities: Jane Eyre as Missionary of Love," *Nineteenth-Century Literature* 49, no. 4 (March 1995): 456–482.

Frost, Robert. "The Fable of the Poor Orphan Child," *English Review* 10, no. 2 (November 1999): 10.

F

fairy tales

Fairy tales bear more than entertaining adventure for children. These timeless narratives began as bawdy morality stories until their refinement by such familiar 17th- to 20th-century adapters as Charles Perrault, Jacob and William Grimm, Hans Christian Andersen, and Walt Disney. The settings present structured societies in a one-size-fits-all realm lacking identifiable place or historical era and devoid of the boundaries of science and natural law. Embedded in the collective texts are the universal behavioral and sexual truths needed for the cautioning and socializing of children, particularly nubile females who reach the age of consent. In addition to racy details and stereotypes of female beauty, such as Snow White's pale skin and Rapunzel's golden hair, the stories contain the collective wisdom of hard knocks—the accumulated experiences that humankind treasures as warnings to the naive. The poet Anne SEXTON captured the coded messages to women in *Transformations* (1971), a collection of fairy tales set in verse. The depiction of Snow White as a china doll reminds the reader that the fragile maid is programmed to express her feelings only with her eyes, whether acknowledging Mama or shutting out a sexual aggressor.

According to Catherine Orenstein, author of *Little Red Riding Hood Uncloaked: Sex, Morality and the Evolution of a Fairy Tale* (2002), women have traditionally valued the moral underpinnings of folklore. In intimate kitchen-table and hearth settings, mothers and grandmothers churned, kneaded, spun, and wove while passing oral wives' tales to listening ears. The disguise motif, a feature of Gothic tales, warns the young of DUALITY, trickery, and hasty judgments. By shifting identities in "Snow White," the wicked enchantress conceals evil under the guise of an aged apple vendor and takes her sweet-natured prey by surprise. In "BEAUTY AND THE BEAST," Beauty misjudges the beast until she proves herself worthy of his love. In his true identity he enfolds her in a loving atmosphere, the reward for a woman who learns that passion can be clouded by the BEAUTY MYTH.

In 1994 the feminist critic Marina Warner introduced *From the Beast to the Blonde: On Fairy Tales and Their Tellers* with an acknowledgment of the importance of change through shape shifting and magic. Metamorphosis is appealing to women readers because it offers an opportunity to wonder at marvels and to grasp the possibility of happy endings. Warner resurrects feminist tellers, notably Marie-Catherine le Jumel de Barneville, comtesse d'Aulnoy, a Norman writer of *Tales of the Fairies* (1699), which contains her versions of forced marriages of young girls mated to metaphorically beastly men. D'Aulnoy's Briton friend, Henriette-Julie de Castelnau, comtesse de Murat, compiled *Histoires sublimes et allegoriques* (1699), tales of the hags and beggarwomen whom society discounts because of their ugliness, crippled limbs, age, and penury. Murat languished under house arrest for ridiculing the mistress of King Louis XIV, one of the termagant females who turn against their own gender. Warner characterized the uppity stories of these French writers as "polite and not so polite revolt" against the establishment (Warner, 24).

During the 1600s feminist arguments against the SILENCING of women took a prominent place in folklore. To reveal barbarity deep within society, 17th-century fairy tales divulged a number of male-on-female cruelties. Marie-Jeanne L'Héritier de Villandon, a contemporary of d'Aulnoy and Murat, described the cunning seducer Riche-en-Cautèle in "The Subtle Princess" (1694). His match is Finessa, the motherless girl who lures him to a bedchamber, menaces him with an ax, then rolls him downhill in a barrel spiked inside with nails, the torture he intended for her. One of the bolder stories, "Peau d'Ane" (Donkeyskin), the story of a father's lust for his daughter, was the subject of a film, *The Magic Donkey* (1971), which starred Catherine Deneuve. In *Winter's Tales* (1942) Isak DINESEN reset fairy-tale imagery to her own purposes, for example, the stress on a woman's long, Rapunzel-like hair in "Peter and Rosa." Another reprise of fairy lore, Jane Campion's screenplay *The Piano* (1993), mingles Beauty and the Beast lore with the Little Mermaid to produce the story of a mutilated pianist who escapes a cruel husband and, under the tender care of her lover, learns to speak.

The feminist writer Charlotte BRONTË incorporated the perils of womanhood in *JANE EYRE* (1847), a bildungsroman in which the youthful heroine triumphs over disappointment, temptation, and threat to wander the wild moor in search of a professional and domestic niche suited to her needs. Like Beauty, Jane develops self-assurance that leads her back to Edward Rochester in a new form, a confident adult who is equal to her surly lover and to the challenge of his physical impairment. Without a fairy godmother, Jane achieves the happily-ever-after ending through self-empowerment. Daphne DU MAURIER, a Brontë fan, retains the Beauty and the Beast trappings in a feminist mystery, *REBECCA* (1938). She places the unnamed naif on a quest in the social setting of mistress of a coastal manor, where the gruff, preoccupied husband, Maxim de Winter, appears to stifle her with remembrances of his deceased first wife. The heroine revives the marriage through loyalty and compassion for Max and through the fiery exorcism of the Rebecca presence, a menacing aura stoked in intensity and threat by

the witchlike housekeeper, Mrs. Danvers. The fairy tale ending retreats from happily ever after to a realistic husband-wife intimacy stripped of the palatial trappings of Manderley.

Folkloric SEXUALITY and desire intrigued Olga BROUMAS, a Greco-American poet and author of a verse anthology, *Beginning with O* (1977). Her collection examines a full range of fairy tales for their reflection of female yearning. She uses the Rapunzel story as springboard to compare heterosexual love with lesbian embraces. Broumas warns the too eager maiden of the brief joys of coupling and its punishment—pregnancy that forces them to resort to herbal abortifacients (Broumas, 59). She reaches a fearful poetic climax with the prediction of a shift to "old bitch" from "young darling" (*ibid.*). Eager to "out" a preference for a female lover, the poet promises to "break her silence" (*ibid.*, 60). More fervid is the awakening in Broumas's "Sleeping Beauty," in which Judith's public kiss of her lesbian mate shocks onlookers. In delight at a satisfying lesbian love life, the speaker exults in awakening passion in a female mate (*ibid.*, 62).

In 1981 the medievalist and raconteur Ethel Johnston Phelps, author of *The Maid of the North: Feminist Folk Tales from around the World*, collected a variant of the helpless female lore as a counterbalance to fragile, blue-eyed blondes such as Snow White, Rapunzel, and Cinderella. Phelps's choices, culled from thousands of candidates, stress pluck and heart in winsome heroines, who do not have to be exorbitantly lovely or graceful or well born to rate admiration. Phelps explains in her introduction that commendable rural females from early centuries survived in oral tellings for their self-sufficiency and quick wit. Her selections picture the self-confidence of Mulha, a Southern African girl who hoodwinks an ogre into releasing her captive sisters. Phelps exalts an elderly Japanese woman who engineers an escape from a subterranean troll. She also honors the sturdy enchantress Louhi, one of the Finnish rulers of the epic *Kalevala*.

Bibliography

Broumas, Olga. *Beginning with O.* New Haven, Conn.: Yale University Press, 1977.

Lake, Rosemary. *Once upon a Time When the Princess Rescued the Prince.* Guerneville, Calif.: Dragon Tree Press, 2002.

Phelps, Ethel Johnston. *The Maid of the North: Feminist Folk Tales from around the World.* New York: Holt, Rinehart & Winston, 1981.

Sexton, Anne. *Transformations.* Boston: Houghton Mifflin, 1971.

Tatar, Maria, ed. *The Annotated Classic Fairy Tales.* New York: W. W. Norton, 2002.

Warner, Marina. *From the Beast to the Blonde: On Fairy Tales and Their Tellers.* New York: Noonday Press, 1994.

Fallaci, Oriana (1930–   )

The Florentine journalist, fiction writer, and memoirist Oriana Fallaci takes a personal interest in women's history and the abuse of power. Born to a liberal activist family, she was the daughter of a cabinetmaker, who filled her room with books. Her favorites were the adventure stories of Jack London. As World War II engulfed Europe, she began composing short fiction at age nine. Emulating her father, who fought with the Italian resistance, she joined the Corps of Volunteers for Freedom and earned an honorable discharge from the Italian army. At the height of peril to her hometown, when Allied bombs fell on the city center, her father slapped her for crying. At war's end, she was in her midteens when she got a job at a local newspaper.

Fallaci the writer is a product of Fallaci the resister. The hardships that Italians survived shaped her feminist consciousness. She remembers the poverty and activism of women under the thumb of the fascist dictator Benito Mussolini and his bullying Black Shirts. A brief introduction to premed courses at the University of Florence prepared her for a bicultural career in Europe and New York City. She set the pace for hard-driving interviews with such world figures as Ingrid Bergman, Maria Callas, Indira Gandhi, and Golda Meir. Over 60-plus years, Fallaci's confrontational style suited the demands of *Corriere della Sera, Der Stern, Europeo, La Nouvelle Observateur, Life, Look, New Republic,* the *New York Times Magazine,* and the *Washington Post.* Her writings earned worldwide recognition in translations into Croatian, Dutch, English, French, German, Greek, Spanish, and Swedish. She taught her high-impact style of journalism at Columbia, Harvard, and Yale Universities and the University of Chicago.

Fallaci introduced feminism in her canon with *Penelope alla guerra* (*Penelope at War,* 1962) and *Il sesso inutile: Viaggio intorno all donna* (The useless sex: voyage around the woman, 1964), an overview of women's lives in a variety of Asian and Pacific Rim countries. In a fictional monologue, *Lettera a un bambino mai nato* (*Letter to a Child Never Born,* 1975), based on personal experience, Fallaci became the first feminist writer to survey the tortuous progression from conception to ABORTION. The story probes the psychological and emotional tether between a single mother and the fetus she conceived through casual sex. By battling the pros and cons of abortion from the adult's perspective, she elevates the prochoice debate from a black-and-white issue to a poignant study of priorities.

For Fallaci subjectivity is a mode of climbing inside events and issues. In 1979 she enlarged on personal grief with *Un homo: Romanzo* (*Man,* 1979), a fictional elegy to her dead lover, the Greek freedom fighter Alexandros Panagoulis. After retirement in her Manhattan apartment and a lengthy recuperation from breast cancer, she stirred to fury after the destruction of the World Trade Center on September 11, 2001. In *The Rage and the Pride* (2002) she expressed her disdain for the paganism and filth of Islam, which she claims produces arrogant males who urinate on the streets and gesture lasciviously to young girls. To prove her point, she described the inhuman torture of FEMALE GENITAL MUTILATION and dismissed Arab males as unsuitable mates for women of good taste. Though couched in pro-woman rhetoric, the diatribe generated heated debate and demands in France for the book's suppression.

Bibliography

Aricò, Santo L. *Oriana Fallaci: The Woman and the Myth.* Carbondale: Southern Illinois University Press, 1998.

Douglas, Foster. "Love, Death, and the Written Word: The Lonely Passion of Oriana Fallaci," *Los Angeles Times,* 10 January 1993, p. 20.

Fallaci, Oriana. *The Rage and the Pride.* New York: Rizzoli, 2002.

Faludi, Susan (1959–)

A controversial mediator in the wars between the sexes, the journalist and lecturer Susan Faludi aims for middle ground in her surveys of contemporary gender relations. Born in New York City to a highly literate family, she wrote on emotional topics for her high school newspaper, including the constitutionality of on-campus Christian clubs. While earning a degree in history and literature from Harvard, she stirred animosities with an article on sexual harassment. She found work as a copy girl at the *New York Times,* her entrée to subsequent jobs at the *Atlanta Journal-Constitution, Double Take, Esquire, Miami Herald, Nation, Newsweek, New Yorker, San Jose Mercury News,* and *Tikkun.* In 1991 she won a Pulitzer Prize for "The Reckoning," an article for the *Wall Street Journal* on human fallout from the sale of the Safeway supermarket chain.

To preserve a necessary objectivity, Faludi avoids the label of feminist. She earned acclaim for a best-selling examination of gender issues in *Backlash: The Undeclared War against American Women* (1991), winner of a National Book Critics Circle Award. Reviewers recognized her insightful coverage of a welter of anti-female feeling fostered by Reagan era conservatism. When she issued *Stiffed: The Betrayal of the American Male* (1999), editors pro and con debated her notion that males were in crisis from identity conflicts caused by American feminism. She studied the macho messages from American males in "The Moms' Secret Weapon." The essay sketches an unflattering portrait of the American male: "Whether defending their right to bear arms against government 'jack-booted thugs,' or proclaiming their right to save fetuses from the clutches of 'the abortion mill,' these men are compelled by the same desire: to resurrect their traditional male role as family protector" (Faludi, "Moms'," 30). In another *Newsweek* essay, "Don't Get the Wrong Message" (2001), she analyzed the derailment of women's liberation and the resulting discontent: "The women's movements of the last two centuries sought women's equality and INDE-

PENDENCE not so women could be happy shoppers but so they could be responsible public citizens, so that they could remake social forces instead of surrendering to commercial siren calls" (Faludi, 2001, 56). Her place at the contact point between clashing ideals suits her style of reportage, which is more concerned with result than with process.

Bibliography

Faludi, Susan. *Backlash: The Undeclared War against American Women.* New York: Anchor Books, 1992.
———. "Don't Get the Wrong Message." *Newsweek,* 8 January 2001, p. 56.
———. "The Moms' Secret Weapon." *Newsweek,* 15 May 2000, p. 30.
———. *Stiffed: The Betrayal of the American Male.* New York: Perennial, 2000.
Odessky, Marjory H. "The Feminist as Humanist," *Humanist* 55, no. 1 (January–February 1995): 34–35.

Fauset, Jessie Redmon (1882–1961)

A neglected participant in the Harlem Renaissance who was reclaimed by the feminist movement, Jessie Redmon Fauset viewed the struggle for equality through the eyes of passionate black female protagonists. Born to a sedate family in Snow Hill (now Lawnside), New Jersey, she grew up in a cultured environment in Philadelphia and graduated as valedictorian of her high school class. She achieved scholarly aims by becoming the first black female enrolled at Cornell and the first black female Phi Beta Kappan. After completing degrees in French at the Sorbonne and the University of Pennsylvania, she taught French and Latin for 14 years. From 1919 to 1926 she edited *Crisis,* an outlet for a host of female Harlemites, including Alice DUNBAR-NELSON, Zora Neale HURSTON, and Georgia Douglas JOHNSON.

In addition to channeling the talents of others into the public view, Fauset contributed to the New Negro and NEW WOMAN movements by publishing four woman-centered novels. Her first, *There Is Confusion* (1924), violates black stereotypes of the period by introducing a dominant motif in her feminist works, the self-empowerment of middle-class black females as theater performers and dancers. Through the mind-set of the protagonist Joanna Marshall, the author proves that autonomy emboldens: "She had the variety of honesty which made her hesitate and even dislike to do or adopt anything artificial, no matter how much it might improve her general appearance. No hair straighteners, nor even curling kids for her" (Fauset, 1989, 20). Similarly authentic were her dealings with men and women.

In a second novel, *Plum Bun: A Novel without a Moral* (1929), Fauset captures the feminist yearning of young Angela Murray. As does Joanna Marshall, Angela embraces INDEPENDENCE: "Freedom! That was the note which Angela heard in the melody of living" (Fauset, 1990, 13). To liberate herself from middle class hypocrisy and to grasp at FAIRY TALE happiness, Angela must defeat both PATRIARCHY and the color barrier. In an era of change that preceded the Great Depression, Fauset used Angela as a spokeswoman for two progressive themes—black feminist pride and the Black Arts Movement. To Angela's dismay, after she moves to New York City, she finds the sexist objectification of women a greater burden than racism.

As Fauset described in the short stories "Emmy" (1912) and "The Sleeper Wakes" (1920), the obstacles to opportunity cause Angela to fall victim to romantic dreams. She retrieves herself from penury and lost love by emulating a female role model, the artist Paulette: "She was so alive, so intense, so interested . . . that all her nerves, her emotions even were enlisted to accomplish the end which she might have in view" (*ibid.*, 100). Paulette's liberation permits smoking, drinking, and casual sex. Angela stops short of adopting Paulette's amorality and evolves a unique set of principles that involve her in an artistic milieu in which she thrives.

Fauset reframed the sentimental novel in the writing of *The Chinaberry Tree* (1931), a venue for sociological and gender issues. The resulting feminist narrative examines the illicit biracial love affair of Sarah "Aunt Sal" Strange, a bold matriarch who pursues a sexual relationship with a white man. Rejecting the victimization that black women suffered in the past from such liaisons, Aunt Sal treasures memories of a satisfying love. Fauset focuses on Aunt Sal's illegitimate daughter,

Laurentine, and the girl's cousin, Melissa Paul, an upwardly mobile heroine who is unaware of her own tainted heritage. The subtext of tangled black lineage illuminates the roots of shame and guilt that reach back to slave times. As Asshur, Melissa's suitor, notes, "How many of us can trace his ancestry back more than three generations?" (Fauset, 1995, 73).

Fauset's modernism evolved from her belief that post–Civil War blacks should relieve themselves of outdated mental anguish. Of those who succeed, the author offers congratulations: "He is a dark American who wears his joy and rue very much as does the white American. He may wear it with some differences but it is the same joy and the same rue" (*ibid.*, xxxii). In the resolution to the novel the author groups the three women and Melissa and Laurentine's suitors under the chinaberry tree for a picnic. Aunt Sal allows herself tender memories of her white lover and summarizes the difference between squalid affairs and joyous couplings: "She had always been willing to pay the Piper" (*ibid.*, 340). Her rewards are a clear conscience and "the Piper's tune," which Fauset identifies as "the immanence of God" (*ibid.*, 341).

Bibliography

Fauset, Jessie Redmon. *The Chinaberry Tree and Selected Writings.* Boston: Northeastern University Press, 1995.

———. *Plum Bun.* Boston: Beacon Press, 1990.

———. *There Is Confusion.* Boston: Northeastern University Press, 1989.

Miller, Nina. "Femininity, Publicity, and the Class Division of Cultural Labor: Jessie Redmon Fauset's 'There Is Confusion,' " *African American Review* 30, no. 2 (Summer 1996): 205–220.

Tomlinson, Susan. "Vision to Visionary: The New Negro Woman as Cultural Worker in Jessie Redmon Fauset's 'Plum Bun,' " *Legacy: A Journal of American Women Writers,* 19, no. 1 (January 2002): 90–97.

Fear of Flying Erica Jong (1973)

Erica JONG's innovative first novel, *Fear of Flying,* precedes *How to Save Your Own Life* (1977) and *Parachutes and Kisses* (1984) to form a semiautobiographical trilogy of the female rebel's discovery of sensual pleasure. In a generation inspired by Doris Day's chaste, but coy film roles, the liberated protagonist, 29-year-old Isadora Zelda White Wing, is an updated WIFE OF BATH who seeks validation through a witty quest for orgasm. Maneuvering past insecurities as her avian surname suggests, she reprises the daring of a historical namesake, the dancer Isadora Duncan, who displayed to art lovers the centrality of the female body to stage performance. Through the protagonist's rambunctious examination of the male-female status quo, Jong questions the sexual presumptions of the times.

Decked in fantasy and candid erotica, Jong's novel provided a female voice for the 1970s generation and according to Laura Miller of the *New York Times* introduced the genre of "chick lit" (Miller, 39). The protagonist's recovery of identity derives direction and power from sexual exploits and private stream-of-consciousness liberation. On a Pan American flight with 117 psychoanalysts to Vienna, home of Sigmund Freud, Isadora sheds her sexual inhibitions. The mental constraints that inform and guide her actions pose a bold examination of marriage. In a bedroom scene of honeymooners, Isadora rages over faulty communication with her husband, Bennett: "As if my not being able to read your mind were my greatest sin. I *can't* read your mind. . . . I *can't* intuit your every wish. If that's what you want in a wife, you don't have it in me" (Jong, 2003, 108). Isadora realizes that the monogamy of her second marriage provides her a best friend and lover, but intercourse with one man fails to satisfy her yearnings for random sexual frolics. After years of stifled libido Isadora escapes sexual boredom and cultural taboos through guilt-free coupling with a British therapist named Dr. Goodlove. Her satisfaction from a palpitating clitoris bears out the theme that one bedmate cannot satisfy all needs for carnal exploration and passion. More to the point, Isadora obliterates the CINDERELLA rescue myth by saving herself from stimulus starvation.

Published three years after Germaine GREER's social critique *The FEMALE EUNUCH* (1970), Jong's *Fear of Flying* retains the freshness and flamboyance that made it an international best seller at 19 million copies in 27 languages. Once censored as

pornography by shocked clerics and parents, the lusty narrative is a classic text on the reading lists of women's studies courses for admitting a feminist truth, that wedlock drains marriage of sparkle by smothering intimacy in sameness. Reissued in 2003 in a 30th anniversary volume, *Fear of Flying* appears alongside Eudora WELTY's *The Robber Bridegroom* (1942), Harper LEE's *To Kill a Mockingbird* (1960), Jean AUEL's *The Clan of the Cave Bear* (1980), and Marilynne ROBINSON's *Housekeeping* (1981) in *Booklist*'s selection of the great first novels. In 1998 Jong's novel earned a place on Modern Library's list of the 20th century's 100 best novels.

Bibliography

Jong, Erica. *Fear of Flying.* New York: Signet, 2003.
———. "The Zipless Fallacy," *Newsweek,* 30 June 2003, p. 48.
Lacher, Irene. "Her Banner Yet Waves: Erica Jong Has Made a Career of Asserting Women's Right to Be Sexual Beings," *Los Angeles Times,* 20 June 2003, p. E.1.
Miller, Laura. "Taking Wing," *New York Times Book Review,* 1 June 2003, p. 39.

female detective novels

The liberation of female characters from the passive observation of crime to active crime detection has kept pace with the interest of real women in crime prevention and investigation. During the era of Gothic crime serials, penny dreadfuls, Newgate novels, and gaslight thrillers, the private eye genre became the first literary field to accept the incursion of women such as Mary Elizabeth BRADDON as worthy writers equal in respect and earnings to their male counterparts. A cofounder of the sensational novel, Braddon took her cue from a smash success—Wilkie Collins's melodrama *The Woman in White* (1860). In addition to creating vivid male sleuths and pioneering the sensational novel, in the midst of the Victorian era she broadened the range of sleazy fiction called the "yellowback railway reader" with two intrepid female private investigators—Eleanor Vane in *Eleanor's Victory* (1863) and Margaret "Madge" Wentworth in *Henry Dunbar* (1864). Central to Braddon's depiction of female gumshoes is the obliteration of the mid-Victorian cliché of women as scatterbrained, weepy, and prone to fainting spells at the sight of blood or danger. Second to thrive in the female detective market was Catherine Louisa Pirkis, author of *The Experiences of Loveday Brooke, Lady Detective* (1893). Loveday, devoid of the frivolity and vanity of decorative women, takes her profession seriously. Plain, but brainy, she excels at observation and the style of deductive reasoning that made Sir Arthur Conan Doyle's Sherlock Holmes a staple of the mystery market.

In the 20th century the fictional personae of detective novels became as well known as their creators: Agatha Christie and Miss Marple, Amanda Cross and Kate Fansler, Katherine Forrest and Kate Delafield, Ellen Hart and Jane Lawless, Claire McNab and Carol Ashton, Dorothy Sayers and Miss Climpson, and Barbara Wilson and Pam Nilsen. Mary Roberts Rinehart, a former nurse, padded her family's income on royalties from mysteries and gaslight thrillers and entered the novel market with a serial, *The Man in Lower Ten* (1906). She followed with a classic, *The Circular Staircase* (1907–08), composed in monthly installments for *All-Story* featuring Rachel Innes, a spinster and amateur snoop. After succumbing to midlife madness, Innes rebukes her prissy niece, Liddy, for devaluing a woman with gray hair: "No . . . I'm not going to use bluing at my time of life or starch either" (Rinehart, 1). Fearless in a murky nest of shadows and hidden passages, Innes challenges the know-it-all male detective by embodying a new take on sleuthing stories and on women as logicians—women who act rather than react.

Sue Grafton intrigues readers with her best-selling alphabet mysteries. Drawing on recall of spooky tales from childhood, she introduced the Kinsey Millhone series with *"A" Is for Alibi* (1983), in which the 32-year-old California-based Kinsey tackles a case involving the betrayed wife, a stock figure in detective lore. Grafton's no-nonsense heroine is clever and curious enough to risk VIO-LENCE to solve a case. In her first investigation she has no trouble questioning a male who "[thinks] women are a pain in the ass" (Grafton, 1987, 10). To his diminution of her gender Millhone, a regular at Rosie's Bar, brags that she once belonged to the Brownie Scouts but quit within the week because she had to paint a rose on a Mother's Day hanky. In the fourth of the series, *"D" Is for Deadbeat* (1987), Millhone opens the chapter with a more detailed self-introduction by declaring herself easygoing, but occasionally testy and "tempered (perhaps) by an exaggerated desire for INDEPEN-DENCE" (Grafton, 1988, 1). In 1995 Millhone's redoubtable adventures won the author a Doubleday Mystery Guild Award for *"K" Is for Killer* (1994). Available in paperback, audio books, and etexts and in some 14 languages, the alphabet mysteries occupy a significant niche in feminist literature.

In a union of standard private eye scenarios, historical fiction, and the novel of ideas, the Iowa-born historian Sara PARETSKY, a late 20th-century phenomenon, introduced a tough Chicago attorney turned gumshoe, 37-year-old Victoria Iphigenia "V. I." Warshawski. In addition to crime fighting, Paretsky's heroine sets a brisk pace for female readers while defeating the sexism in American institutions and challenging the conventional masculinity of fictional crime study. In the opening chapter of *Blood Shot* (1988), winner of a Silver Dagger Award, she compliments the growth of athleticism in women with a confessional appraisal, "They looked muscular and trim, much fitter than my friends and I had been at that age" (Paretsky, 3). Both sturdy and smart-talking, V. I. can manage a one-woman agency, belt down Johnnie Walker Black at a respectable pace, leave a lover in his bed and slip out at dawn, and concoct clever escapes from cliff-hangers. In addition to challenging the warren of hospital policies and navigating morgues, in *Tunnel Vision* (1994), she confronts stories of female battery at a women's shelter.

The founder of Sisters in Crime, an international consortium of female mystery and detective writers, Paretsky is herself a model of the genre and a crusader for fair representation of women authors in national book publishing, distribution, and reviewing. In her texts she is a straight shooter who wastes no pity on gangster profiteers, industrial polluters, insurance fraud, red baiting and blacklisting, corrupt Catholic priests, and the masterminds of the Holocaust. A Warner film version of Peretsky's heroine, *V. I. Warshawski* (1991), starred Kathleen Turner in a screen adaptation of *Indemnity Only* (1982). In 1995 Paretsky won a citation from Friends of American Writers for *Deadlock,* a fast-paced Warshawski investigation of the murder of her cousin, Boom Boom, a hockey player, that leads the detective through the Soo Locks of Michigan to uncover corruption in the Chicago shipping industry.

Bibliography

Fleenor, Juliann E., ed. *The Female Gothic.* Montreal: Eden Press, 1983.

Grafton, Sue. *"A" Is for Alibi.* New York: Bantam, 1987.

———. *"D" Is for Deadbeat.* New York: Bantam, 1988.

Green, Michelle. "Sara Paretsky's Cult Heroine Is a Woman's Woman—V. I. Warshawski, the Funky Feminist Private Eye," *People Weekly,* 14 May 1990, pp. 132–134.

Johnson, Patricia E. "Sex and Betrayal in the Detective Fiction of Sue Grafton and Sara Paretsky," *Journal of Popular Culture* 27, no. 4 (Spring 1994): 97–106.

Munt, Sally. *Murder by the Book? Feminism and the Crime Novel.* New York: Routledge, 1994.

Paretsky, Sara. *Blood Shot.* New York: Dell, 1989.

Pearl, Nancy. "Gaslight Thrillers: The Original Victorians," *Library Journal,* 15 February 2001, p. 228.

Reddy, Maureen T. *Sisters in Crime: Feminism and the Crime Novel.* New York: Continuum, 1988.

Rinehart, Mary Roberts. *The Circular Staircase.* New York: Dover, 1997.

Female Eunuch, The Germaine Greer
(1970)

Issued seven years after Betty FRIEDAN's *The FEMININE MYSTIQUE* (1963), Germaine GREER's social critique *The Female Eunuch* (1970) outlines the causes and symptoms of the insidious "problem that has no name," as Friedan called it. With theatrical flair, Greer demonstrates that sexual freedom must precede total selfhood for women. Her text reveals that the rigidity of norms required of females contrasts with the privileges enjoyed by male sexual adventurers. Her insistence on physical and emotional wholeness refutes the male expectation of sweet, submissive women. The title image captures the stunting of female lives by reminding males of a similar barbarity in their own history. Like foot bindings and chastity belts, such emotional cloistering disables girls from birth to death. Bullied, mocked, and degraded, obedient women struggle to attain impossibly high standards of behavior and to swallow their frustrations without complaint.

Greer divides the text into logical segments. Under "Body," she begins with "Gender" and covers the skeleton, shape, hair, sex, and "The Wicked Womb." She stresses the importance of gender to the persona and charges, "To make any assumptions about superiority or inferiority on this basis is to assume what is very far from being proved" (Greer, 29). By using Nazi anthropologists as model falsifiers of scientific inquiry, the commentary establishes Greer's aim—to repudiate faulty logic about women's place in creation. From "Soul" and "Love," she moves deftly to the final division, "Hate," by outlining the abuse and misery that goad women to resent their cages. Greer's solution emulates Karl Marx's summons to the proletariat—a mass revolt against household drudgery and sexual bondage to pompous overlords.

Women recognized their personal crises in Greer's fierce mustering of the amazons. An international best seller translated into 12 languages, it was banned in South Africa alongside the writings of the sex therapist Ruth Westheimer. In the vanguard of second-wave feminist texts, Greer's dazzling prose jump-started a generation of readers by spotlighting the natural bent of possessiveness toward spousal abuse, a topic that was beginning to dominate media response to the gender wars. The London *Times* declared her work one of five must-read classics along with Samuel Pepys's diary, Adam Smith's *The Wealth of Nations,* Edward Gibbons's *Decline and Fall of the Roman Empire,* and Kenneth Clark's *Civilisation.*

Bibliography

Greer, Germaine. *The Female Eunuch.* New York: Farrar, Straus & Giroux, 2002.

Mitchell, Marea. "Ambitious Women and Strange Monsters: Simone de Beauvoir and Germaine Greer," *Hecate* 26, no. 1 (2000), pp. 98–106.

female genital mutilation

Barbaric notions of sexual cleanliness, morality, and wifely duty undergird such feminist works as

Alice WALKER's *Possessing the Secret of Joy* (1992) and the screenplay *Warrior Marks: Female Genital Mutilation and the Sexual Blinding of Women* (1993), political essays by Katha POLLITT, Anaïs NIN's erotica, and Eve ENSLER's one-woman plays *The Vagina Monologues* (1996) and *The Good Body* (2003). Many female infants and children in the Middle East, Asia, and parts of Africa lose some or all of their sexual responsiveness through genital mutilation, a cultural practice of circumcision. After centuries of concealment by silenced women and girls the practice has raised a world outcry against a repellent form of VIOLENCE against females. Clitoridectomy is performed without anesthesia or localized numbing by midwives or community women. The ritual mutilation involves the clipping or removal of tender nerve endings in the clitoris, the sexual organ that gives pleasure from normal sexual contact. A more extreme version is the slicing away of the vulva or external genitalia. In her dedication to *Possessing the Secret of Joy,* Walker offers a gesture of "Tenderness and Respect to the Blameless Vulva" (Walker, intro.).

A more invasive, life-threatening surgery, infibulation or pharaonic circumcision, involves the pinning together of the bloodied labial stumps over the vaginal opening to assure potential mates of female chastity. To encourage a strong bond of scar tissue, perpetrators tie girls' legs together, leaving a sliver of wood in the urethral opening to accommodate urination. In 2001 the World Health Organization estimated that debilitating ritual amputation had damaged the genitals of approximately 140 million females living in the 21st century. As the French author Anaïs NIN describes in short stories collected in *Delta of Venus* (1969) and *Little Birds* (1979), some brutally desexed girls die of pain, shock, infection, and loss of blood. Walker enlarges on the terror and its sexist purpose: "A proper woman must be cut and sewn to fit only her husband, whose pleasure depends on an opening it might take months, even years to enlarge. Men love and enjoy the struggle . . . I am weeping now, myself. For myself" (*ibid.,* 224).

Feminist literature refuses to let the world shrug off the horrific custom of child genital abuse. In 1980 the Cairo-born physician and journalist Nawal EL SAADAWI published *The Hidden Face of Eve: Women in the Arab World,* which demands the female right to a whole body. The text opens on the seizure of the author, who was then a sleepy child, in preparation for folk surgery—the excision of her clitoris to satisfy a primitive demand that females be bereft in childhood of their pudendal pleasure centers. El Saadawi suffers a dual trauma from physical agony and the realization that her mother condones the practice. When the same rough hands grasp her younger sister, the girls exchange a look that says, "Now we know what it is. Now we know where lies our tragedy. We were born of a special sex, the female sex. We are destined in advance to taste of misery, and to have a part of our body torn away by cold, unfeeling cruel hands" (El Saadawi, 1980, 8). Her autobiographical account contrasts the simpler form of female circumcision in Egypt with pharaonic circumcision, the full excision of clitoris and labia among the Sudanese. The terror makes El Saadawi wary of other secrets that family members may conceal. Fear follows her into adulthood and her own medical practice.

In Barbara KINGSOLVER's *The Poisonwood Bible* (2000), genital mutilation is a stipulation for a proposed intercultural betrothal. The fictional Chief Tata Ndu anticipates the procedure as a prenuptial preparation for Rachel Price, his prospective child bride. Men in Ndu's village of Kilanga, Congo, perpetuate the barbarism as an assurance of female purity. The androcentric custom, which is pervasive among Muslims in the Middle East and Africa, is a boost to male egocentrism by enhancing the notion that females are a form of reward to their possessive mates and a domestic treasure to be guarded from intrusion by other males. In the understanding of Ruth May Price, Rachel's five-year-old sister, routine female surgery is "the circus mission where they cut her so she wouldn't run around with people's husbands" (Kingsolver, 271). Kingsolver leaves unspoken the lack of assurance to women that their suitors are equally chaste and blameless of sexual debauchery.

Bibliography

El Saadawi, Nawal. *The Hidden Face of Eve: Women in the Arab World.* London: Zed Books, 1980.

———. "The Rite and the Right," *Feminist Voices* 9, no. 6 (30 September 1996): 1.

George, Olakunle. "Alice Walker's Africa: Globalization and the Province of Fiction," *Comparative Literature* 53, no. 4 (Fall 2001): 354–372.

Kingsolver, Barbara. *The Poisonwood Bible.* New York: HarperCollins, 1998.

Walker, Alice. *Possessing the Secret of Joy.* New York: Pocket Books, 1993.

female victims

The rescue and healing of female victims are common strands in the motifs of feminist literature. The natural harmonics between goodness and appreciation of nature explain the setting of horrific tales of female abuse in uncommon locales, the particularly confining or menacing cells and towers in the Gothic settings of the FAIRY TALE "Rapunzel" and in Ann RADCLIFFE's *A Sicilian Romance* (1790), *The Mysteries of Udolpho* (1794), and *The Italian* (1797). In the folkloric strayings of girls in "Goldilocks," "Hansel and Gretel," and "Little Red Riding Hood," innocent heroines leave themselves open to predators who operate outside the regulatory agency of family, community, church, and state. As a result, Goldilocks awakens in a small bed under the eyes of bears, Gretel and her brother discover the fattening-up cages of the witch, and Little Red Riding Hood shares her mother's bedroom with a wolf in drag.

Examples of traditional female perils energize the classics of feminist literature in an array of genres: the muckraking reporter Nellie BLY's *Ten Days in a Mad-House* (1887), Caroline GORDON's abduction story "The Captive" (1945), Beth HENLEY's three-act comedy *Crimes of the Heart* (1979), Harper LEE's novel *To Kill a Mockingbird* (1960), Sylvia Plath's poem "Daddy" (1962), and Christina ROSSETTI's female rescue story *The Goblin Market* (1862). These models of feminist writings resonate with the pairing of innate wickedness with naiveté and credulity, two female failings imposed by a social order that deprives women of EDUCATION and INDEPENDENCE. In one of the pinnacles of Victorian Gothicism, *JANE EYRE* (1847), the author Charlotte BRONTË applies the motif of male-on-female harrying to the title character, an orphaned governess who takes employment at Thornfield, a country manor that harbors a madwoman. Lacking sophistication at job hunting, Jane assumes that her employer is a decent father figure for his ward Adèle. Jane's faulty idea takes her to the altar to marry a bigamist until his acknowledgment of wrong forces her to flee. Daphne DU MAURIER's *REBECCA* (1938) reprises Brontë's themes and characterizations but creates menace from internal torments and self-abasement. By placing the narration in the charge of an unnamed young woman, the author allows suspense and foreboding to control the psychological atmosphere as the protagonist attempts to settle at Manderley, the woman-haunted coastal estate of Max de Winter. No less Gothic than *Jane Eyre*, the story requires a similar burning of an ancestral estate and the exorcism of a stalker, the housekeeper Mrs. Danvers, to free the protagonist of unfounded suspicions about her womanhood and her marriage.

Female victimization is a pervasive plot element in colonial fiction, which pictures an era of white male authoritarianism. The first paragraph of the French Caribbean author Maryse CONDÉ's biographical novel *Moi, Tituba, sorcière noire de Salem* (*I, Tituba, Black Witch of Salem*, 1986), brandishes VIOLENCE to stress the title character's rage and revenge against colonial slavers for their predations against the Ashanti. Tituba knows little about her mother, Abena, except for the ironic rape "by an English sailor on the deck of *Christ the King* one day in the year 16** while the ship was sailing for Barbados" (Condé, 3). The complex MOTHER-DAUGHTER RELATIONSHIP of the rape victim and the child of rape results in a lifetime of contempt and hatred toward white males. As an adult living far from the Caribbean, Tituba labors under a wretched heritage—memories of the burning of Akwapim, her mother's village, and the stabbing of Mama Yaya, Tituba's maternal grandmother, during the rounding up of blacks for transfer to the hold of a slave ship. Condé stresses the irony of the master's choice of Yao as Abena's black mate and improbable savior. He eases her sadness with the animal fables they both remember from childhood. Reviving Abena's fear of harm is the birth of Tituba, a girl fated to join the next generation of ill-treated females. The mother regrets that, for slaves, "a woman's fate was even more painful than a man's" (*ibid.*, 6).

In urban fiction Barbara KINGSOLVER contrasts a variety of female abuses in *The Bean Trees* (1988). The literary foils Taylor Greer and Lou Ann Ruiz confront two types of child neglect and single parenting: Esperanza's daughter, Ismene, and Taylor's adopted Cherokee child, April Turtle, suffer abuse from different sources, deliberately hurtful adults and a corrupt Central American regime that kidnaps Ismene as political leverage against freedom fighters. When a new form of victimization looms in the play yard at Roosevelt Park, the author elevates an unlikely savior, Edna Poppy, a blind child sitter who swings her white cane in the direction of sounds of struggle between a pedophile and three-year-old April. Although Edna repulses the would-be child molester, April, still obsessed by memories of violence from babyhood, retreats behind two staring eyes that look blankly at an untrustworthy world.

In 1998, Kingsolver altered her vision of victimization through a series of meditations from different points of view on the daily misery of Orleanna Price, the African missionary's wife in *The Poisonwood Bible.* Realizing that her metaphorical wings are clipped, Orleanna reflects on shallow, uninitiated American women who delighted in "a Maytag washer . . . and called it happiness" (Kingsolver, 1998, 186). Her own contentment withers daily from the privations of the Congo and her husband's decline from evangelist to family tyrant and unpredictable abuser of wife and daughters. Upon her escape and resettlement at Sanderling Island, Georgia, Orleanna salves her bruised spirit with gardening, a contact with nonthreatening elements of nature that restore nourishment and color to her life. Training her eyes toward Africa, the mother endures the fallout of living too long with the wrong man. The bitter marriage, long past, refuses to release its hold on her mind and conscience, which charges Orleanna with the death of six-year-old Ruth May from a snakebite. In the estimation of Orleanna's daughter, Adah, "Her [mother's] body was locked up tight, years ago, by the boundaries of her costly liberty" (*ibid.*, 531).

Bibliography

Condé, Maryse. *I, Tituba, Black Witch of Salem.* New York: Ballantine, 1994.

Gilbert, Sandra M., and Susan Gubar. *The Madwoman in the Attic.* 2nd ed. New Haven, Conn.: Yale University Press, 2000.

Hoeveler, Diane Long. *Gothic Feminism.* University Park: Pennsylvania State University Press, 1998.

Kingsolver, Barbara. *The Bean Trees.* New York: Harper & Row, 1988.

———. *The Poisonwood Bible.* New York: HarperCollins, 1998.

Feminine Mystique, The   Betty Friedan (1963)

In midlife the magazine writer Betty FRIEDAN, a former stay-at-home mother from Peoria, Illinois, jolted society with *The Feminine Mystique*, a declaration of war against gendered CONFINEMENT. Her text stresses the infantilization of grown women in suburban playpens. Watching from the bars, housewives observe their husbands achieve career aims. Wreathed in raises and promotions, husbands allocate to their mates a hollow, secondhand success as goodwife and goodmother. Basing her text on personal experience, Friedan castigates a society that allots freedom and opportunity to boys while reserving domestic drudgery and child care for girls. For her exposé of skewed values and wasted talents arose the feminist demand for choice. On the crest of the first feminist wave, Friedan began lobbying for WOMAN'S RIGHTS by mobilizing the National Organization for Women, which she launched in the Johnson White House at a conference on the status of women on June 30, 1966. Her aim was "to take the actions needed to bring women into the mainstream of American society, now . . . in fully equal partnership with men" (Friedan, 2003, 48).

Friedan's interest in "the problem that has no name" emerges from a study of "a strange stirring, a sense of dissatisfaction, a yearning" for existence (Friedan, 2001, 20, 15). Through interviews with a variety of females, she charted somatic complaints—aching heads and joints, straying minds, crying jags and churning stomachs, depression, and chronic fatigue. Shredding the "happy housewife" mask, her book gives shape and dimensions to a pervasive identity crisis. At the top of her list of charges is the misdirection of energies as "housewifery expands to fill the time available" (*ibid.*, 33, 233). Friedan decries the "progressive dehumanization" of females, many of whom comply with their keepers by "[forfeiting] self" (*ibid.*, 282, 310). In chapter 5, she accuses Freudianism of misinterpreting female malaise and for heaping women with "shoulds" (*ibid.*, 103). Contributing to their slide into kitchen-centered conformity is media propaganda featuring vacuous models admiring a waxed floor and glowing at the installation of a state-of-the-art washer-dryer.

Shocking conservative elements was Friedan's antidote to the depersonalization of females—she advocated the "WOMEN'S MOVEMENT and sex-role revolution," which her detractors called gender anarchy (*ibid.*, 392). *The Feminine Mystique* and the personal appearances and lectures that it spawned persuaded women to halt self-sacrifice in favor of a return to college, the opening of businesses, and the reapportionment or cessation of lopsided marital obligations. Domestic egalitarianism encouraged women to demand respect and to shed the illusion that marriage and children were the ends of their being. Self-confident women began invading the male-dominated bastions of Wall Street, the media, surgical suites, legislatures, courtrooms, and the priesthood. An icon in the National Women's Hall of Fame, Friedan convened the Women's Political Caucus, a formal challenge to male complacency. Her audacity and sound leadership generated the characterization "mother of the feminist movement."

Bibliography

Friedan, Betty. "Demanding Full Equality," *Time*, 31 March 2003, p. 48.

———. *The Feminine Mystique.* New York: W. W. Norton, 2001.

Hume, Janice. "Changing Characteristics of Heroic Women in Midcentury Mainstream Media," *Journal of Popular Culture* 34, no. 1 (Summer 2000): 9, 21.

feminism

Feminism is a broad term for an amalgam of positive, pro-woman philosophies. Feminist literature such as Susan B. ANTHONY's SUFFRAGE orations, Margaret SANGER's monthly journal *The Woman Rebel*, Gloria STEINEM's philosophical text *Outra-geous Acts and Everyday Rebellions* (1983), and Betty MAHMOODY's captivity memoir *Not without My Daughter* (1987) dramatizes the impetus to revolt against PATRIARCHY and antifemale religions and bureaucracies. The droll humor of Eve ENSLER's hit play *The Vagina Monologues* (1996) collects in one act a series of women's insights into the possibilities of womanhood and the myths and misconceptions that hold them back. The life stories of fictional characters, such as Celie in Alice WALKER's *The COLOR PURPLE* (1982) and Winnie Louie in Amy TAN's *The Kitchen God's Wife* (1991) reveal the possibility of reformation from obedient drudge to full-fledged human being, the goal of feminism.

Uplifting much of feminism is a pervasive sense of heritage, an enriching theme that soaks into women's verse and prose like wine into bread. The poet Cynthia Huntington exalts the gift of womanly crafts and wisdom in "Patchwork" (1989), a common image drawn from women's dominance in fiber work and their reliance on make-do housewifery through recycling. The speaker wraps herself in a handmade quilt and discovers that woman's work outlasts the woman, while the "day of the making are lost" (Mazer and Lewis, 79). The poet rejoices in the piecing together of oddments of women's humble moments and in the challenge of knowing what to bequeath to the next generation.

After the first wave of feminism female survival developed into a public outcry. In Faith McNulty's *The BURNING BED: The True Story of Francine Hughes, a Beaten Wife Who Rebels* (1980), flight is the only choice of the protagonist, a real person who set her husband's mattress aflame and escaped with their three children. The author characterizes the domestic violence that leads to murder as an outcome of alcoholism and machismo. In the epilogue she explains, "The macho code has to do with maintaining territory—as dogs do. In the human male it is not territory in the literal sense, but self-esteem that is physically defended" (McNulty, 301). Thus, Mickey Hughes becomes an emotional cannibal, feeding off his wife's character strength, then threatening her life out of jealousy and hurt pride. The dichotomy of the possessive male and the maternal, self-preserving female gained momentum in late 20th-century feminist literature, which posed EDUCATION, art, and SIS-TERHOOD as possible solutions to the misery of women like Francine. As summarized by the feminist literary historian Carol Farley Kessler, author of *Daring to Dream* (1984), the traditional immersion in SEXUALITY, marriage, and family expanded after the women's movement of the 1960s, when women broadened their horizons to "freedom for the development and expression of potential, especially within the context of a supportive community, occasionally composed of women only" (Kessler, 7).

A central issue in feminism is the right to one's person. In an example in Barbara KING-SOLVER's masterwork *The Poisonwood Bible* (1998), the Reverend Nathan Price, a fanatic Baptist minister in Kilanga, Congo, rules an all-female household as a petty sheik. When he fails to subdue or coerce his family with smacks, stroppings, and disparagement, he mutters a vague protest against "dull-witted bovine females" (Kingsolver, 73). His repulsive behavior and diatribes prepare the reader for his wife's revolt and flight from their jungle home with her twins, Adah and Leah. In reaction against the insults to their girlhood, the twins develop strong woman- and family-centered careers in medical research and agronomy. In view of Kingsolver's furtherance of female autonomy, it is not surprising that hostile male readers ignore, downgrade, even mock her pro-woman writings. In reference to the appeal of Kingsolver's best-selling novels, the *New York Times* reviewer Sarah Lyall characterizes gendered criticism: "Some men seem puzzled by her appeal, pigeonholing her as a touchy-feely women's author even as their sisters, mothers, girlfriends, and wives read, reread, borrow, lend and discuss her books" (Lyall, 1993).

Bibliography

Kessler, Carol Farley. *Daring to Dream*. Boston: Pandora Press, 1984.

Kingsolver, Barbara. *The Poisonwood Bible*. New York: HarperCollins, 1998.

Lyall, Sarah. "Termites Are Interesting but Books Sell Better," *New York Times*, 1 September 1993.

Mazer, Norma Fox, and Marjorie Lewis, eds. *Waltzing on Water*. New York: Dell, 1989.

McNulty, Faith. *The Burning Bed*. New York: Harcourt Brace Jovanovich, 1980.

feminist criticism

Feminist criticism approaches literature from a woman's perspective. Contributing to a feminist vision are the findings of anthropology, history, theology, psychology, political science, physiology, and sociology on such crucial subjects as the patriarchal home and religious upbringing, limited EDUCATION and physical training, diminished self-esteem, and the absence or diminution of a MOTHER-DAUGHTER RELATIONSHIP, a focus of analysts reviewing the writings of the science-fiction author Mary Wollstonecraft SHELLEY. On the personal level feminist writers express their debt to woman-to-woman networking and SISTERHOOD, reconciliations, fiber work and other creative outlets, healing, and emotional counseling by WISE-WOMEN, a motif in Paula Gunn ALLEN's *Spider Woman's Granddaughters* (1990), Marion Zimmer BRADLEY's *The Mists of Avalon* (1982), and Velma WALLIS's *Two Old Women* (1993). Of major importance to feminist appreciation of the female gender are matriarchal STORYTELLING and TALK-STORY, two forms of tradition passing that keep alive through generations the privations and heroisms of the past, as demonstrated in Leslie Marmon SILKO's prize-winning collection *Storyteller* (1981), the autobiographical novels of Amy TAN and Maxine Hong KINGSTON, Isabel ALLENDE's *The HOUSE OF THE SPIRITS* (1982), and Joy HARJO's poetry anthology *In Mad Love and War* (1990).

Feminist criticism recovers neglected female tradition and literary history from letter writers, diarists, journalists, poets, playwrights, and fiction writers who have received little scholarly recognition, such as the ethnography of Zora Neale HURSTON, the diaries of American pioneer women, the slave narrative of Harriet JACOBS, and the plays of Aphra BEHN, the first Western woman to earn a living by writing. Nina Baym, author of *Woman's Fiction: A Guide to Novels by and about Women in America, 1820–70* (1978), single-handedly recovered creators of self-empowering heroines such as the columnist Augusta Evans, Fanny FERN, E. D. E. N. SOUTHWORTH, and Ann Sophia STEPHENS. Baym persuaded publishers to restore their works to print and launched a groundswell of inclusion of neglected works in literature and women's studies classes. Feminist criticism accounts for the need of women such as Gertrude ATHERTON, George ELIOT, H. D., Ruth Prawer JHABVALA, Ann PETRY, George SAND, and the Brontës to conceal their gender under male or ambiguous pen names. The feminist perspective also enhances the reader's awareness of literature that dramatizes the DOUBLE STANDARD, political enslavement and disenfranchisement, social and economic injustice, female battery, and other examples of wronged womanhood, the controlling themes of Nathaniel Hawthorne's *The SCARLET LETTER* (1850) and Ann PETRY's *TITUBA OF SALEM VILLAGE* (1964). A particularly valuable mode of righting wrongs is the creation of literary utopias and dystopias, such as Charlotte Perkins Gilman's *HERLAND* (1915), Joanna RUSS's *The Female Man* (1975), Marge PIERCY's *WOMAN ON THE EDGE OF TIME* (1976), and Margaret AT-WOOD's *The HANDMAID's TALE* (1985).

Feminist criticism has rediscovered significant aspects of literary history and achievement. Literary historians accentuate women's urge to write in a climate that discounts, belittles, and/or censures their efforts, as is the case with the works of Sor Juana Inés de la CRUZ, a Hieronimite nun, and with Julia ALVAREZ's *IN THE TIME OF THE BUT-TERFLIES* (1994), a description of female silencing and capricious jailing in the Dominican Republic under Rafael Trujillo. From a new perusal of efforts of 19th-century novelists grew a fresh appreciation of George Henry Lewes's evaluation in the essay "The Lady Novelists" (1852) that women's views add a new element to the study and appreciation of literature. He warned that the tasks of the female writer are to avoid the mores and perceptions of male writers and to strike out into unexplored territory, which includes a unique feminine aesthetic based on women's responses to war, civil unrest, and threats to reproductive rights. Another male literary critic, John Stuart MILL, recognized the difficulty of breaking with the past to make up for centuries of denigration and STEREOTYPING. In *The Subjection of Women* (1869), he commented that the job of writing feminist literature is fraught with pressures to conform to the man's point of view and to imitate false and unjust ideologies that perceive woman as the lesser gender, a predictably frail being more suited to domestic duties than to philosophy. Disproving these faulty images of the female gender was the feminist manifesto "The Enfranchisement of Women" (1851), written by Mill's wife and colleague, Harriet Taylor MILL.

Feminist criticism reevaluates characters and works with an eye toward fair representation of women. Feminist critics insist on including in academic world history trivialized legendary characters such as Semiramis, Cleopatra, Joan of Arc, and Pope Joan. A new fairness in gender portrayals encourages fresh readings of the myths of Isis, Cassandra, LA LLORONA, Demeter and PERSEPHONE, Arachne, Lilith, and Medusa; of Geoffrey Chaucer's WIFE OF BATH; of William Shakespeare's Miranda and Portia; and of the FAIRY TALES of CINDERELLA, Goldilocks, Sleeping Beauty, Snow White, LITTLE RED RIDING HOOD, and the heroine of BEAUTY AND THE BEAST. A gynocritical investigation of female writers places new emphasis on the chain of literary advances preceding classics such as Louisa May ALCOTT's *LITTLE WOMEN* (1868–69) and George ELIOT's *MIDDLEMARCH* (1871) as well as on the essays of Margaret FULLER, Germaine GREER, and Susan SONTAG. A crowning achievement, Mary WOLL-STONECRAFT's female advocacy essay *A Vindication of the Rights of Women* (1792), earned the critic Elaine Showalter's acclaim for its "Amazonian spirit" (Showalter, 2001, 11).

Feminist critics revive woman-centered writings, for example, classics from the Harlem Renaissance—Rachel Crothers's *A Man's World* (1910) and her comedies *39 East* (1925) and *Let Us Be Gay* (1929), Alice DUNBAR-NELSON's "I Sit and Sew" (1920), Marita BONNER's one-act play *Exit* (1923), and Jessie Redmon FAUSET's novel *Plum Bun* (1929). New scholarly analysis of other works from this era—Susan GLASPELL's *Trifles* (1916) and of the lesbian subtext of the fiction of Marie CORELLI and the poems of Amy LOWELL—invokes deeper insights into women's function in a male-dominated world. Recovery through female publishing houses and Web sites of women's studies departments has rewarded readers, students, and researchers with copies of unique feminist models, including Rebecca Harding DAVIS's *Life in the Iron Mills* (1861), Mary Wilkins FREEMAN's

The Revolt of Mother and Other Stories (1891), and Tillie OLSEN's *Mother to Daughter/Daughter to Mother: Mothers on Mothering* (1984). Simultaneously, feminist critics foster alternative readings of classic works and fine-tune standards of feminist criticism to rid them of androcentric criteria and modes of judging human behavior, a goal of such ecofeminists as Barbara KINGSOLVER, Clarissa Pinkola ESTÉS, and Rachel CARSON. Proponents of feminist criticism encourage current innovators through publication of women's literary magazines such as *Calyx* and *Lilith* and through feminist consortia that critique new models and suggest ways of reaching appreciative audiences, including lesbian, nonwhite, young adult, disabled, and elderly readers.

The term *gynocriticism*—formalized in the 1970s by the feminist Kate MILLETT, author of *Sexual Politics* (1970), and by Elaine SHOWALTER—differentiates between the female reader's perceptions of male-written and male-centered texts and of those works written by women for women, such as the SUFFRAGE speeches of Elizabeth Cady STANTON and Susan B. ANTHONY, the birth control campaigns of Margaret SANGER and Dr. Marie STOPES, the pacifism of Helen KELLER and Emma GOLDMAN, the protest writing of Voltairine DE CLEYRE and Angela DAVIS, and the ABOLITIONISM of Angelina GRIMKÉ, Harriet Beecher STOWE, and Fanny KEMBLE. Gynocriticism alerts female readers to the assumptions and issues that ignore or distort female ideals, particularly regarding SEXUALITY, women's creativity, economic INDEPENDENCE, marriage, family, SILENCING, personal freedom, empowerment, and CONFINEMENT, all elements of Charlotte BRONTË's *JANE EYRE* (1847) and Emily BRONTË's *WUTHERING HEIGHTS*. At the same time gynocriticism promotes literature written by women from a distinctly female point of view emphasizing self-discovery, for example, Jane AUSTEN's depictions of body image and courtship in early 19th-century novels, Sarah GRAND's commentary on self-determination and professionalism in NEW WOMAN novels, and the condemnation of male-dominated mental institutions and psychiatric treatments in Charlotte Perkins GILMAN's Gothic short story "The YELLOW WALLPAPER" (1892).

Bibliography

Showalter, Elaine. *Inventing Herself: Claiming a Feminist Intellectual Heritage.* New York: Scribner, 2001.
———. *A Literature of Their Own: British Women Novelists from Brontë to Lessing.* Cambridge, Mass.: Princeton University Press, 1998.

Feminist Press

A nonprofit educational publishing house, Feminist Press is the world's oldest women's press. Under the direction of Florence Howe, Feminist Press went into business in 1970 at City University of New York. Its purposes from the outset were to eliminate sexual STEREOTYPING and to rescue from oblivion important feminist titles by such authors as Zora Neale HURSTON, Elizabeth JANEWAY, Meridel LE SUEUR, and Paule MARSHALL. The organization's long-range goal is cultural EDUCATION for the long line of daughters and granddaughters who need grounding in women's history. In addition, the mission supports world peace and human rights and provides schools and public and home libraries with inexpensive race- and gender-neutral works and classroom aids.

In 30 years the effort paid off with a backlist of some 200 titles covering issues of sexual preference, competition, women's contributions to the workforce, and abuse of power. Among the feminist reprints are George SAND's *The Castle of Pictures and Other Stories* (1859), Rebecca Harding DAVIS's *Life in the Iron Mills* (1861), Mary Wilkins FREEMAN's *The Revolt of Mother and Other Stories* (1891), Charlotte Perkins GILMAN's "The YELLOW WALLPAPER" (1892), Kate CHOPIN's *The Storm and Other Stories* (1897), Meridel Le SUEUR's *Ripening: Selected Work, 1927–1980* (1982), and Tillie OLSEN's *Mother to Daughter/Daughter to Mother: Mothers on Mothering* (1984). For juvenile readers the company issues young adult biographies of the significant female activists Aung San Suu Kyi, Ela Bhatt, and Rigoberta MENCHÚ. To aid in the selection of nonsexist works for children and adults, the staff publishes *Women's Studies Newsletter, Women's Studies Quarterly,* and a series of pamphlets, beginning with Barbara EHRENREICH and Deirdre English's *Witches, Midwives and Nurses: A History of Women Healers* (1973). Such fundamental feminist works as *Women Writing in India: 600 B.C. to the Present* (1993), the anthology *Bearing Life: Women's Writings on Childlessness* (2000), Laura Flanders's *The W Effect: Bush's War on Women* (2004), and *The Stories of Fanny Hurst* (2005) bolster college and university teaching and research and influence the compilation of reading lists for book clubs, school curricula, and classroom texts.

Bibliography

Danford, Natalie. "Feminist Publishing for Fun and Profit." *Publishers Weekly*, 6 October 2003, p. 18.

Howe, Florence. "From Race and Class to the Feminist Press," *Massachusetts Review* 44, no. 1/2 (Spring–Summer 2003): 117–135.

feminist theater

Female contributions to theater have been largely underrated and dismissed as regional writings or domestic drama, a term intended as a pejorative. As did many males, girls born into stage families absorbed stagecraft as mother's milk. They involved themselves in the family craft wherever their skills were needed, from managing companies and casting and coaching beginners to ghost-writing and translating foreign plays. However, theater has not returned the favor by rewarding or even acknowledging contributions to drama from women as far back as Hroswitha von Gandersheim of Germany in the 10th century and Henrietta Maria, the wife of Charles I of England, who wrote and staged a pastoral in 1625. The first full-time American female dramatist, Mercy Otis WARREN, declared that those women willing and eager to advance theater should think of their work as more than a passing fancy. The playwright Anna Cora Mowatt, author of *Fashion* (1845), added her own viewpoint that female playwrights and actors are of value to a despised profession as reformers and paragons of purity, nobility, and blamelessness.

The feminist novelist, dramatist, and lecturer Olive Logan, author of the plays *Eveleen* (1864) and *Apropos of Women and Theatre* (1869), proposed a more egalitarian notion. She suggested that independent, ambitious women should look to theater as a creative outlet because serious acting was one of few venues for imaginative females. Her forthright examination of the obstacles in the path of female theatrical professionals included the degrading leg shows and nudity of burlesque houses, uncouth breeches roles, and the condemnation of religious fanatics for any woman involved in stagecraft. In the preface to *The Mimic World and Public Exhibitions: Their History, Their Morals, and Effects* (1871), Logan envisioned "[stripping] off some of the 'gauze and vanity' from the 'show world' " to present a just and fair vision of theater to the "ungenerous and unenlightened eye" (Logan, preface). Her defense of stage parts for women in *The Voice as a Source of Income* (1874) inspired the dancer Isadora Duncan, who wanted to project grace and emotion rather than cheap peep show SEXUALITY. Supporting Logan was the suffragist Mary Shaw, a speaker at the 1899 International Congress of Women in London, who declared women significant influences in the stage arts. She proposed a women's theater project as a venue for distinctly pro-woman views and emotions.

As women began to influence the plays themselves, particularly frequent adaptations of Harriet Beecher STOWE's *Uncle Tom's Cabin* (1852), the female perspective gained ground. The first American feminist to write drama was Rachel Crothers, author of *A Man's World* (1910) and the comedies *39 East* (1925) and *Let Us Be Gay* (1929), presented on Broadway 25 times from 1906 to 1937. By featuring female protagonists overshadowed, coerced, or maligned by males, Crothers achieved notoriety for her fair, but definitely pro-woman views. Corroborating her themes are Marita BONNER's one-act play *Exit* (1923), a complex death scenario from the Harlem Renaissance in which Buddy proclaims his ownership of Dot. In reference to a shadow figure named Exit Mann who stalks Dot, Buddy snorts hostility toward a rival. Another work about the possessive male's stranglehold is Susan GLASPELL's *Trifles* (1916), a one-act classic about the silences and exasperations of a wife who loses control and suffocates her cruel husband in his sleep, a death that parallels the kind of existence she has known in her marriage.

Contemporaries of Crothers and Bonner, Georgia Douglas JOHNSON and Helen Webb Harris, build drama from female action. Johnson pictures the SISTERHOOD of Charity Brown and her friend, Tildy, in a prize-winning folk play, *Plumes* (1927). Like her domestic melodramas *Sunday Morning in the South* (ca. 1925), *Blue Blood* (1926), *Blue-Eyed Black Boy* (ca. 1930), and *The Starting Point* (1931) and the history plays *Frederick Douglass* (1935) and *William and Ellen Craft* (1935), the one-act dilemma scenario, performed by the Harlem Experimental Theatre, takes place in a kitchen and features women as authority figures. *Plumes* expresses the difficult decisions facing a widow as she sits by her dying daughter, Emmerline. The support that Tildy offers counters the dollars-and-cents advice of Dr. Scott, a cold-hearted physician. Symbolizing Emmerline's innocence is the white dress that Tildy hems, then reshapes as a shroud. Another contemporary of Crothers, Harris, contributed to feminist tragedy with *Ganifrede* (1935), which dramatizes the pleas of a daughter to save her father from execution. Set in 1802 during the revolt of Toussaint Louverture on San Domingo, the plot illustrates women's vigorous but doomed attempts to intervene in politico-military conflicts.

A major innovator of the late 1930s and 1940s, Lillian HELLMAN took a holistic approach to depictions of the female psyche. By revealing faults in the NEW WOMAN, she achieved a breakthrough in realism with *The Children's Hour* (1934), a multilayered examination of class, gender, and sexual issues based on a Scottish court case that criminalized two female teachers for alleged lesbianism. The bold topic outraged conservatives who preferred predictable themes and motifs devoid of sensationalism. More damning of ambitious women was Hellman's *The Little Foxes* (1939), a landmark study of middle-class greed in the character of Regina Hubbard Giddens, a choice part that stirred competition among actors.

The rise of the black female dramatist Lorraine HANSBERRY, author of *A RAISIN IN THE SUN* (1959), underscored the value of resilient female characters to playgoers. With greater access to staging, the creativity of feminist playwrights furthered the growth of feminist theater, which came into its own in the last quarter of the 20th century. In England, Caryl CHURCHILL developed a career

in radio, television, and stage works that exposed the DOUBLE STANDARD. *Owners* (1972) reveals a murderous strain in the butcher Clegg, who is being outclassed by the financial rise of his wife, Marion, a successful realtor. Four years later Churchill produced *Vinegar Tom* (1976), a reexploration of the misogyny underlying witch hunts. Geared to domestic issues is *Cloud Nine* (1979), a seriocomic innovative play depicting a woman's deliberate submission to a vapid husband. Churchill won an Obie for *Top Girls* (1982), which reprises the issues of female earning power that the playwright introduced in *Owners*.

During an uptick in popular feminist theater, Marsha NORMAN and Wendy WASSERSTEIN captured the Pulitzer Prize for *'night, Mother* (1983) and *The HEIDI CHRONICLES* (1989), respectively, which assured the literary public that the day of the female dramatist had arrived. In the seriocomic *Mam Phyllis* (1990), a three-act play by Elizabeth Brown-Guillory, the action triangulates the relationships among the aged title character; her headstrong daughter, Helena; and Sister Viola, the town gossip. In the style of *A Raisin in the Sun,* Brown-Guillory stresses the need for forgiveness among family members and a realliance of older authority figures with the younger generation. Mam Phyllis, as a resilient jack-in-the-box, pops up after her alleged drowning in a ditch, silences Viola's talebearing tongue, and reconciles with Helena in time for the birth of the next generation.

Gynocentric drama of more recent times has shed light on some of women's most feared crises, notably Eve ENSLER's one-woman hit show *The Vagina Monologues* (1996) and *The Good Body* (2003) and Robbie McCauley's Obie-winning experimental play *Sally's Rape* (1992), a salute to the silenced women during slave times whose rapes produced the blended colors of subsequent mixed-race people. The Canadian playwrights Maxine Bailey and Sharon Mareeka Lewis coordinate the major feminist themes—narrative, beauty, WOMAN'S WORK, child rearing—in *Sistahs* (1998), a kitchen-table dialogue that allows multiple generations of women to sustain each other. During the peeling and chopping of plantain, mango, and dasheen for a traditional Trinidadian soup, their open-ended conversation introduces comments on lesbianism, oral sex, and female cancer. The coauthors verbalize the modern woman's dilemma in Sandra Grange-Mosaku's outburst about coping with cancer treatment and controlling a truculent female teenager: "Three years of cutting and slicing, and pricking and burning. Cursing myself each day for not being more careful. It didn't feel like *my* body anymore. So many things in my life have been beyond my control" (Bailey, 64).

The private griefs and covert invasions of women's bodies in feminist health drama reflect fears of political and social reduction of females to mere bodies. The Pulitzer Prize–winning dramatist Margaret EDSON focuses on a victim of medical manipulation in *Wit* (1999), which views the steady decline of a scholar's body and spirit as a result of brutal treatment for uterine cancer. A similar melange of women's issues percolates to a climax in Susan Miller's *My Left Breast* (1995). The loss of a breast to cancer generates Susan's urgent cry, "I am a One-breasted, Menopausal, Jewish, Bisexual Mom and I am the topic of our times. I am the hot issue. I am the cover of *Newsweek.* . . . All at once, timely. All at once, chic" (Miller, 219). The characters bear witness to lethal trauma and encourage playgoers to rethink medical politics and the need of women for the caregiving and hope they have traditionally dispensed to others.

Bibliography

Bailey, Maxine, and Sharon M. Lewis. *Sistahs.* Toronto: Playwrights Canada Press, 1998.

Bonner, Marita. *Frye Street and Environs: A Collection of Works of Marita Bonner.* Boston: Beacon Press, 1987.

Brown-Guillory, Elizabeth. *Mam Phyllis.* In *Wines in the Wilderness: Plays by African American Women from the Harlem Renaissance to the Present.* Edited by Elizabeth Brown-Guillory. New York: Greenwood Press, 1990.

Chinoy, Helen Krich, and Linda Walsh Jenkins, eds. *Women in American Theatre.* New York: Theatre Communications Group, 1987.

Deshazer, Mary K. "Fractured Borders: Women's Cancer and Feminist Theatre," *NWSA Journal* 15, no. 2 (Summer 2003): 1–26.

Diamond, Elin. *Unmaking Mimesis: Essays on Feminism and Theater.* New York: Routledge, 1997.

Harris, Helen Webb. *Genifrede.* In *Negro History in Thirteen Plays.* Edited by Willis Richardson and May Miller. Washington, D.C.: Associated Publishers, 1935.

Logan, Olive. *The Mimic World and Public Exhibitions: Their History, Their Morals, and Effects.* Philadelphia: New-World Publishing, 1871.

Martin, Carol, ed. *A Sourcebook of Feminist Theatre and Performance.* New York: Routledge, 1996.

McCauley, Robbie. *Sally's Rape.* In *Black Theatre, U.S.A.: Plays by African Americans: The Recent Period, 1935–Today.* Edited by James V. Hatch and Ted Shine. New York: Free Press, 1996.

Miller, Susan M. *My Left Breast.* In *The Breast: An Anthology.* Edited by Susan Thames and Marin Gazzanniga. New York: Global City Press, 1995.

feminist utopias

Dreamworlds are a natural part of feminist literature. For their open-ended channels of energy and imagination, feminist utopias like those portrayed in Margaret Lucas Cavendish Newcastle's lesbian play *The Convent of Pleasure* (1668), Lady Mary WALKER's *Munster Village* (1778), and Marion Zimmer BRADLEY's Avalon series ease the repression of women with escapes into realms unfettered by the sexism and misogyny of the past and present. As the Princess in *The Convent of Pleasure* comments on entry to Lady Happy's all-woman commune, the Convent of Pleasure, a female lover provides more contentment than life in a convent or the love of a prince. Soon, the Princess is so content with her new life that she admits to full satisfaction in her new life (Newcastle, 33).

Europe's discovery of the New World generated dreams of starting over and building societies that avoided past mistakes. Incubation of North American utopias began with observations of MATRIARCHY among the Iroquois and with the religious leader Mother Ann Lee and the Shaker ideal. Over 83 years, from 1836 to 1919, American female writers made significant forays into the male-dominated genre of utopian literature, paving the way for the giants of the genre in the late 20th century. Varying in mode and style from exotic treks and DREAMSCAPES to romance, dialogue, speculative fiction, and satire, feminist stories and novels offer a unique perspective on the unmet needs of the real world, where women suffer the preponderance of suppression and contempt.

In the first half of the 19th century feminist utopias sought a realignment of the earthly power structure. In 1826 Mary Griffith, a New Jersey native who wrote novels, tales, and horticultural texts, published *Three Hundred Years Hence,* a vision of the United States in 2126 after the passage of WOMEN'S RIGHTS and other laws guaranteeing that they could purchase and inherit property in their own name. The essayist and TEMPERANCE worker Jane Sophia Appleton submitted to *Voices* magazine "Sequel to *The Vision of Bangor in the Twentieth Century*" (1848), a riposte to the misogyny of the author, the Maine governor, Edward Kent. She describes a world free of weaponry or orthodox religions, a realm where women are more than sex slaves fawning for caresses. In her vision of gender equality, "Man is not thought of as the solid masonry of life and woman as the gingerbread-work" (Appleton, 54). Both radical in outlook, Griffith and Appleton chafed at a world that disenfranchised women.

A droll turnabout of responsibilities energized the utopia of an emerging writer, Elizabeth T. Corbett. In 1869 she made sport of gender prejudice through satire. Applying the same philosophy as that of Griffith, she produced "My Visit to Utopia" for the January issue of *Harper's* magazine. Through a series of dreams the female speaker looks down on a great city where men are the Bridgets, cooks, housekeepers, launderers, and baby-sitters. She remarks on the unappealing appearance of males made weak, stoop-shouldered, and whiny by relegation to menial work. As a result of the appropriation of gross labors to males, women grow strong and beautiful and increase their wisdom through EDUCATION. Corbett extends the humor in dream two by describing men as shallow slaves to fashion. She depicts sons as complaining dreamers who want to learn a trade rather than marry and care for a home and children. In dream three males campaign for men's rights and emancipation from kitchen and nursery. In a twist on women's fears, a man remarks that he would attend a men's rights lecture if he had company. He adds, "It would not look well for me to go

alone: besides, I would be afraid to go home so late" (Corbett, 88). Adding to the dry humor is a woman's spurious reasoning that because women have more extensive brain capacity for language, "women as senators and representatives, as lecturers and orators, are where they belong, where Nature intended they should be" (*ibid.,* 94). Her logic diminishes men to silence in important matters, a parody of the reduction of women to wordless observers in the public sphere.

Essential to feminist utopias is a communitarian dimension requiring an end to SEXUAL POLITICS and some degree of cooperation. Early female utopians combatted in fiction the patriarchal control of female labor. Liberation followed SUFFRAGE, education, paid labor, and shared endeavors, the proposal of the radical novelist Olive SCHREINER. With faith in the newness of colonial South Africa, she recorded her visions of an equitable society in two allegories, *Dreams* (1891) and *Dream Life and Real Life: A Little African Story* (1893). Marie Stevens Case Howland of Lebanon, New Hampshire, proposed free love as a means of unyoking women from male-controlled harness. In "Papa's Own Girl" (1874) she plots the perfect world on the basis of cooperative labors. Another dreamer, Elizabeth Stuart PHELPS, composed an unusual trio of religious utopian works, *The Gates Ajar* (1868), *Beyond the Gates* (1883), and *The Gates Between* (1887), all set in paradise, a genderless haven where no one suffers earthly ills.

A variant of earlier utopias is *Mizora: A Prophecy* (1880–81), a groundbreaking woman's world created by the Ohio schoolteacher Mary E. Bradley Lane. Serialized anonymously over three months in the *Cincinnati Commercial,* it anticipates Charlotte Perkins GILMAN's *Herland* (1915) by picturing a realm of blonde beauties elevated to an intellectual oasis by open-minded teaching. Through a hole in the Earth that trails inward from the North Pole, the explorer Vera Zarovitch, a Russian noblewoman educated in Paris, discovers an enlightened society that ignores men. Mizora is a nonviolent municipality that concentrates community efforts on cooperation and scientific research. Children are their mother's delight; illness and physical deformity no longer mar growth and happiness because science ensures the sound health of all. Neither poverty nor social barriers prevent any from cultivating their mind through the arts.

Late 19th-century utopias pondered a wider field of reforms to earthly life. Choosing suffrage as a means of social betterment, Mary Theresa Shelhamer explained in *Life and Labor in the Spirit World* (1885) that women should have a voice in governance and should control both their own lives and those of their children. Eveleen Laura Knaggs Mason, who published *Hiero-Salem: The Vision of Peace* (1889) four years later, envisioned a fusion of gender differences through "dualization." The main characters, a midwestern couple, Althea Eloi and Daniel Heem, rear a daughter and son, Ethel and Robert, by Judeo-Christian values and instruct them in the Bill of Rights and feminist philosophy. The merger of traits results in Elohim, the Hebraic concept of a sexless divinity. The breach of New England's Puritanic values suits the American prairie, where experimental lifestyles are less objectionable to neighbors.

In 1889 Mary H. Ford challenged Edward Bellamy's *Looking Backward* (1888), one of America's most esteemed utopian novels. In "A Feminine Iconoclast," a dialogue for the *Nationalist*, she denounced Bellamy's paternalism and his perpetuation of male control of women's education and choice of career. One of the two speakers, Miss Frances, declares the feminist ideal: "I don't want to have any privileges doled out to me like slices of gingerbread cut thin. I want to feel I can stand up under any star and shine just as independently and vigorously as I choose" (Ford, 151). She proposes educating men to the female's misery at being treated as a china doll on a pedestal. She suggests confining males with gold chains to palace chairs, wafting perfume with a fan, and feeding them candy and ice cream until they sicken of their privileged position.

Space travel distanced fictional womanhood further from the errors of earthly androcentrism. In 1893 the novelist Alice Ilgenfritz Jones and her coauthor Ella Merchant composed *Unveiling a Parallel: A Romance,* set on Earth and Mars. For its classless society free of racial and religious bias, the text proposes the Boston marriage, a female-to-female relationship, as an antidote to unsatisfactory traditional marriages. As a pointed critique of Western society, the authors remark, "Marriage not being an economic necessity . . . [Martians] are released from certain sordid motives which often actuate women in our world in their frantic efforts to avert the appalling catastrophe of missing a husband" (Jones and Merchant, 165). Without the trappings of male-initiated wooing and proposals, the woman is free to choose the right man at the right time—or never, if she prefers.

The concept of a shift in SEXUAL POLITICS furthered the ingenuity of feminist utopias. A year after Jones and Merchant's publication, Adeline Eliza "Lois" Nichols Waisbrooker, a Boston teacher, lecturer, and radical tractarian, completed *A Sex Revolution* (1894), which she based on her belief in female superiority. Her text asserts that women have the right to their own bodies and to their offspring. By extension the novel demands that governments stop drafting women's sons for war. Waisbrooker dramatized her notions of even distribution of property as a solution to PROSTITUTION, alcoholism, and patriarchal religion. At the end of the 19th century Rosa Graul serialized "Hilda's Home: A Story of Women's Emancipation" (1897) in *Lucifer, the Light Bearer,* a radical sex journal. By practicing free love, men and women infuse their community with contentment. Because of total liberty, all residents exist in a perpetual courtship free of shame and guilt.

Sexual liberty meshed well with an era of socialistic experimentation. The journalist, lecturer, and writer Winnifred Harper Cooley ushered in 20th-century feminist utopias with *A Dream of the 21st Century* (1902), published in the November issue of *Arena* magazine. A stilted dialogue, the novel tends toward a Marxist explanation of human ills. Similarly disappointing is Zona GALE's utopian fantasy, *Romance Island* (1906), which she sets at a never-never land in the southern Atlantic Ocean and focuses on a woman's choice of mate. The high point of feminist dreams was Charlotte Perkins Gilman's *Herland* (1915), a pastoral idyll in which women live without males. The author's purpose in designing an all-woman commune was the ouster of contention, combat, and silly wooing traditions, which diminished females to quarry in the MARRIAGE MARKET. By creating a cast of resilient, thoughtful women, Gilman proposed a place of order and industry where no arcane set of gendered behaviors distracted any citizen from committed labors. In the ironic sequel, *With Her in Ourland* (1916), Gilman inverts the telescope to look back on her own society from the point of view of Herlanders. Seen as a honeymoon retreat for the heroine Elladör and her husband, Van, the plot introduces the female outsider to the world's miseries, which include male selfishness, cruelty to women, piracy, colonialism, and warfare.

The Marxist ideal of shared land and labor empowered additional 20th-century utopias. Near the end of World War I Caroline Dale Parke Snedeker of New Harmony, Indiana, published a new wrinkle in visionary dimensions with *Seth Way: A Romance of the New Harmony Community* (1917), a fictionalized biography of a zoologist living in a commune. Snedeker, a great-granddaughter of the commune designer Robert Owen, used family lore as a background for her fantasy history of New Harmony. She wrote a sequel, *The Beckoning Road* (1929), a juvenile utopia accounting for the collapse of New Harmony. A contemporary, Martha S. Bensley Bruère, wrote *Mildred Carver, U.S.A.* (1919), which she based on a belief in shared domestic duties. As did Mary Ford, Bruère revised Edward Bellamy's scheme with a plan for universal public service based on individual tastes and skills rather than gender. Serialized from 1918 to 1919 in *Ladies Home Journal*, the novel depicts a balance of social concern and labor in the title character, who gives up the socialite's round of parties for the challenge of driving a tractor on a Minnesota farm.

In the second half of the 20th century shifts in social philosophy generated by the Women's Movement created new visions of ethnic, gender, and class parameters. To reexamine issues of justice and governance, feminist utopias by Kathleen NORRIS, Ursula LE GUIN, Joanna RUSS, and Marge PIERCY competed more directly with those written by classic male authors. Norris's *Through a Glass Darkly* (1957) balances a perfect world by establishing a management paradigm that allows both genders to select the type of work that satisfies their needs to achieve. The sci-fi maven Le Guin manipulated gender in *The Left Hand of Darkness* (1969), a technothriller based on the creation of androgynous characters who can choose their role in procre-

ation. In an award-winning short story, "Sur" (1982), Le Guin plotted a feminist excursion to the Antarctic that succeeds by applying women's tendency to cooperate rather than grandstand. The next year she published in *Millennial Women* (1983) "The Eye of the Heron," the story of a brave female colonist on planet Victoria who builds a less competitive, violent society in the wilderness.

Biological alterations and threats to procreation produced greater changes in humankind in literature. Russ experimented with a fragmented persona in *The Female Man* (1975), a denunciation of Western sexism through the severance of one person into four distinct character strands. Piercy produced a best seller, WOMAN ON THE EDGE OF TIME (1976), which validates utopian escapism as a mental respite from an insane asylum. By exposing the male-controlled medical hierarchy, she elevates her protagonist, 35-year-old Consuelo "Connie" Camacho Ramos, as a feminist rebel against such coercive treatments as mood-altering drugs, induced shock therapy, and electronic brain implants. More realistic is the sororal networking in Alice WALKER's *The COLOR PURPLE* (1983), a feminist best seller and overnight classic based on emancipation and self-help. Freed from the dystopian misery of patriarchal marriage, survivor Celie relies on her sewing talents to liberate her from husband and marriage. Two years after Walker's freeing of Celie from the evil Mr. _____, Margaret ATWOOD introduced terror in the dystopian novel *The HANDMAID'S TALE* (1985) by orchestrating realistic threats to humanity and the environment. Proposing enough pollution and radiation fallout to endanger normal conception, she pictures Gilead, a New England society overwhelmed by inverted Puritanism that forces fertile women into the role of breeder. Beyond Gilead the protagonist Offred flees to the frontier, an untried territory where humanity can rebuild and recoup its losses.

Bibliography

Appleton, Jane Sophia. "Sequel to *The Vision of Bangor in the Twentieth Century.*" Chapter 2 of *Daring to Dream*, edited by Carol Farley Kessler. Boston: Pandora Press, 1984.

Corbett, Elizabeth T. "My Visit to Utopia." Chapter 3 of *Daring to Dream*, edited by Carol Farley Kessler. Boston: Pandora Press, 1984.

Ford, Mary H. "A Feminine Iconoclast." Chapter 8 of *Daring to Dream*, edited by Carol Farley Kessler. Boston: Pandora Press, 1984.

Griffith, Mary. *Three Hundred Years Hence*. Boston: Gregg Press, 1975.

Johns, Alessa. *Women's Utopias of the Eighteenth Century*. Chicago: University of Illinois Press, 2003.

Jones, Alice Ilgenfritz, and Ella Merchant. *Unveiling a Parallel: A Romance*. In *Daring to Dream*, edited by Carol Farley Kessler. Boston: Pandora Press, 1984.

Kessler, Carol Farley. *Daring to Dream*. Boston: Pandora Press, 1984.

Kitch, Sally L. *Higher Ground: From Utopianism to Realism in American Feminist Thought and Theory*. Chicago: University of Chicago Press, 2000.

Lane, Mary E. Bradley. *Mizora: A Prophecy*. Syracuse, N.Y.: Syracuse University Press, 2000.

Newcastle, Margaret Cavendish. *The Convent of Pleasure and Other Plays*. Baltimore: Johns Hopkins University Press, 1999.

Waisbrooker, Lois. *A Sexual Revolution*. New York: New Society Publishers, 1984.

Ferber, Edna (1887–1968)

The famed Hungarian-American Jewish feminist Edna Ferber composed historical fiction that honors women's place in the settlement and prosperity of the New World frontier. A native of Kalamazoo, Michigan, she grew up in Protestant communities in Wisconsin and Iowa, where the taunting of Jews was the norm. Her father's death ended her aim of studying theater. Upon graduating from high school, she became the first female on staff at the *Daily Crescent* in Appleton, Wisconsin. After reporting for the Chicago *Tribune*, the Milwaukee *Journal*, and the U.S. Army Air Force, she began a career in fiction and produced 30 stories featuring an autonomous divorcée, Emma McChesney, an itinerant drummer of women's fashions and lingerie who achieves wedlock as well as the American dream. At a high point in a public life spent in trains and hotels, Emma's eyes mist over as her fingers stroke the gold lettering on her office door reading "Mrs. McChesney," but sentimentality loses out to commerce when she rushes from her honeymoon trip to conduct business at a station platform. Ferber published three episodic volumes,

Roast Beef Medium: The Business Adventures of Emma McChesney (1913), *Personality Plus: Some Experiences of Emma McChesney and Her Son Jock* (1914), and *Emma McChesney & Co.* (1915), American visions of NEW WOMAN literature.

Woman-centered STORYTELLING suited Ferber. Her semiautobiographical novel *Fanny Herself* (1917) is now regarded as one of her best. In 1924 she won the Pulitzer Prize for *So Big*, the story of Selina Peake DeJong, daughter of a gambler. Selina becomes a successful asparagus farmer and wise matriarch who sets her own standards of dignity and self-respect. A romance, *Show Boat* (1926), was a source for a popular stage musical, a radio series, and a film. Its melodramatic saga of riverboat theatricals and the heart-sick Magnolia, a mulatto actress yoked to a wastrel gambler, Gaylord Ravenel, allows female ambitions to come to fruition in the next generation through her daughter Kim's success on Broadway. The cinema versions, both called *Showboat*, were vehicles for the actresses Irene Dunne and Katharine Grayson and the lyricist Jerome Kern, who wrote "Can't Help Lovin' Dat Man," "Life on the Wicked Stage," and the achingly romantic duet "You Are Love."

To place women in the Oklahoma land rush, Ferber researched the state's history for details. Her frontier adventure novel *Cimarron* (1929) celebrates a "brand-new, two-fisted, rip-snorting country, full of Injuns and rattlesnakes and two-gun toters and gyp water and desper-*ah*-does!" (Ferber, 1998, 322). The story salutes the pioneer protagonist Sabra Venable, who, like Selina DeJong and Magnolia, chooses a second-rate mate. A principled female married to an alcoholic scamp, Yancey Cravat, Sabra bears the tenacity of a go-getter. Echoing her resolve is the pluck of an unnamed young homesteader who rides over open land on the Cherokee Strip to claim her stake: "She leaped from the horse, ripped off her skirt, tied it to her riding whip . . . dug the whip butt into the soil of the prairie—planted her flag—and the land was hers" (*ibid.*, 329). Sensibly, Sabra follows her example. She frees herself of her husband's escapist bent and turns her success as newspaper publisher in Osage, Oklahoma, into the introit to a term as Oklahoma's first U.S. congresswoman. In 1931 RKO developed the novel into the first Western film to win an Oscar as best picture. A 1960 remake featured Maria Schell as the stereotype-smashing Sabra.

In a follow-up to Sabra, Ferber created Leslie Lynnton Benedict, the outspoken Virginia bluestocking of *Giant* (1952), a saga of Western materialism among livestock-and-oil tycoons. Like Sabra Venable, Leslie rejects the outdated sexist, racist notions of her husband, the Texas cattle baron Jordan "Bick" Benedict. She lends her money and prestige to advance the racial equality of Chicano ranch hands, migrant workers, and domestics. (In the role of Leslie, Elizabeth Taylor gave one of her finest film performances.) Three years before her death Ferber earned a place in the Women's Hall of Fame at the New York World's Fair. Her vigorous female characters place her name in the feminist canon and keep her literature in circulation.

Bibliography

Ferber, Edna. *Cimarron*. New York: Amereon Limited, 1998.

———. *Giant*. New York: Perennial Classics, 2000.

———. *Show Boat*. New York: Lightyear Press, 1992.

———. *So Big*. New York: Perennial Classics, 2000.

Hyman, Paula E., and Deborah Dash Moore, eds. *Jewish Women in America: An Historical Encyclopedia*. New York: Routledge, 1997.

Fern, Fanny (1811–1872)

The journalist, satirist, children's writer, and domestic novelist Sara Payson Willis Parton, better known by the pseudonym Fanny Fern, became America's first female to write a weekly newspaper column. A native of Portland, Maine, she grew up in Boston, where her father published *Youth's Companion*. While she studied at Catharine Beecher's Hartford Female Seminary, Fern contributed sketches to the magazine, a preparation for a lifetime of writing short informative pieces. The mother of three daughters, she was widowed and penniless in 1845. When a desperation marriage failed within months, she left her second husband and began supporting the family with needlework, teaching, and freelance journalism.

Fern earned her way writing for the *Mother's Assistant, Olive Branch,* and *True Flag,* for which she produced lighthearted dialect vignettes. They succeeded undeniably for their balance of humor, irony, and drama and earned comparison to the social satires of Charles Dickens and Harriet Beecher STOWE. Fern joined the *New York Musical World and Times* as a columnist. She issued an anthology of essays in *Fern Leaves from Fanny's Portfolio* (1852), one of America's first best sellers, and its sequel the following year. Their content includes ironic scenarios on children's rights, tyrannic husbands, literary women, and bluestockings. She began another column for the *Saturday Evening Post* and delighted young readers with *Little Ferns for Fanny's Little Friends* (1854).

In retrospect about a distressing phase of her adult life, Fern parodied her unsympathetic family and condescending in-laws in an autobiographical novel, *Ruth Hall: A Domestic Tale of the Present Time* (1854), an episodic 90-chapter cliffhanger that sold more than 70,000 copies. A subversive work, it employs the conventions of sentimental fiction to reveal the faults of PATRIARCHY and the strengths of the NEW WOMAN. The night before the heroine's wedding day, Fern queries, "Tears, Ruth? What phantom shapes of terror glided before those gentle prophet eyes?" (Fern, 1997, 8). An ominous rumble issues from the intrusive mother-in-law: "What is the use of all those ruffles on her underclothes, I'd like to know? Who's going to wash and iron them?" (*ibid.*, 26). Counted "bold, for a woman," by her neighbors, Ruth in early widowhood succeeds as a writer under the pen name Floy (*ibid.*, 385). As does Fern, she endures spiteful comments such as "Authoress! Humph! Wonder how the heels of her stockings look?" (*ibid.*, 387). The conclusion showcases female autonomy after Ruth succeeds as a single mother and newspaper reporter and accrues 100 shares of capital stock in the Seton Bank.

Fern established a reputation among journalists for a wide readership and an impressive income. Upon joining the *New York Ledger,* she became the highest-paid columnist of the day at $100 per column. In 1856 she moved on to the *Ledger,* where she published weekly until her death at age 61. Literary historians acknowledge her contribution to understated style and journalistic paragraphing and to feminist themes—divorce, economic dependence on males, limited EDUCATION for girls, exploited domestics and factory laborers, female poverty, PROSTITUTION, single-parent homes, and venereal disease.

Bibliography

Baym, Nina. *Woman's Fiction: A Guide to Novels by and about Women in America, 1820–70.* Chicago: University of Illinois Press, 1993.

Fern, Fanny. *Fern Leaves from Fanny's Portfolio.* (1853). Available online. URL: http://www.merrycoz.org/voices/leaves/LEAVES00.HTM. Accessed on October 14, 2005.

———. *Ruth Hall: A Domestic Tale of the Present Time.* New York: Penguin, 1997.

Firestone, Shulamith (1945–)

The Canadian-American feminist theoretician and social critic Shulamith "Shulie" Firestone lends a keen intellect and philosophical momentum to the Women's Movement. Born to Orthodox Jews in Ottawa, she came of age in Saint Louis. She studied at the Art Institute of Chicago and settled in New York City to paint. In her early 20s she helped to launch the women's liberation movement. She shaped the *Notes from the First Year,* a left-wing journal of the era's essays and speeches. In a radical community she cofounded the Redstockings, intellectual female iconoclasts who met in Greenwich Village apartments to plot strategy for publicizing their mission. They characterized the male-female status quo as an objectification of women as breeders, sex objects, housekeepers, and cheap labor. The Redstockings drew battle lines for the confrontation of the sexes by defying the BEAUTY MYTH as female bondage to male ideals and by summoning women to unite in subverting society's gendered order. In 1968 Firestone published *The Women's Rights Movement in the U.S.: A New View,* a retrospect on women's strivings for the vote and for social and economic equality. The text questions why girls are unfamiliar with activists such as Margaret FULLER, Harriet Tubman, Sojourner TRUTH, and the GRIMKÉ sisters.

At age 25 Firestone published a bold manifesto, GENDER BIAS, *The Dialectics of Sex: The Case for Feminist Revolution* (1970), a best-selling feminist text that was the first formal political theory of the feminist movement. The work, lauded as the missing link between Karl Marx and Sigmund Freud, characterizes women as a separate social caste, which she called a "sex class" (Firestone, 1979, 3). Agreeing with the era's feminist utopists, she held out one hope for women's liberty—a release from biological enslavement. In her opening arguments she confides, "If there were another word more all-embracing than *revolution* we would use it" (*ibid.*). In the style of Karl Marx and Friedrich Engels she called for a formal disavowal of women's low-caste position and the abandonment of their place as child bearers and child socializers. Her ideology includes a startling denunciation of romance and childhood itself and a suggestion that children be treated as adults, with civic rights as well as sexual freedom.

Bibliography

Davy, Jennifer Anne. "The Trace of Desires: Sexuality, Gender and Power," *Journal of Women's History* 12, no. 2 (Summer 2000): 227.

Echols, Alice. *Daring to Be Bad: Radical Feminism in America, 1967–1975.* Minneapolis: University of Minnesota Press, 1990.

Firestone, Shulamith. *The Dialectics of Sex.* New York: Women's Press, 1979.

———. *The Women's Rights Movement in the U.S.: A New View* (1968). Available online: URL: http://scriptorium.lib.duke.edu/wlm/notes/#newview. Accessed on October 14, 2005.

Fisher, Dorothy Canfield (1879–1958)

The best-selling fiction writer, educator, and essayist Dorothea Frances "Dorothy" Canfield Fisher considered breakthroughs in children's EDUCATION as a promising upgrade in the formation of character and learning styles. Educated in her hometown of Lawrence, Kansas, and in Lincoln, Nebraska, with one year's language study in Paris, she grew up with her classmate Willa CATHER, who later critiqued Fisher's novels and gave advice on realistic detail. Despite hearing loss, Fisher mastered both French and Spanish. She prepared for a scholarly career with a degree in modern foreign languages from Ohio State University and the Sorbonne and a Ph.D. from Columbia University with research on the classical French dramas of Pierre Corneille and Jean Racine. When her parents' health demanded care, she rejected an invitation to teach at Western Reserve University. Instead, she moved to the family home in New York City and joined the staff of the Horace Mann School.

At the beginning of her writing career Fisher translated works from Italian to English and submitted verse and short sketches to *American Illustrated Magazine, Atlantic,* the *Los Angeles Examiner, Munsey's Magazine,* and *Scribner's.* She favored controversial subjects—racism, anti-Semitism, fascism, the tyranny of female fashions, single women, and the changing lives of women as wives and mothers. The title piece of *The Bedquilt and Other Stories* (1906) portrays the devaluation of a spinster, Aunt Mehetabel. Concerning the loss of status in elderly single women, Fisher summarizes: "An unmarried woman was an old maid at twenty, at forty was everyone's servant, and at sixty had gone through so much discipline that she could need no more in the next world" (Fisher, 1997, 33). Surviving on "crumbs of comfort," Mehetabel achieves worth and dignity in the family's eyes by winning a prize for quilting (*ibid.,* 34). In the same vein Fisher's novel *The Squirrel Cage* (1912) depicts as a form of social entrapment the maze of responsibilities and strictures that impede women's progress.

From observation of Maria Montessori's teaching methods at the Casa dei Bambini (House of the Children) in Rome in 1911, Fisher published *A Montessori Mother* (1912), a handbook on child learning. In 1916 she introduced *Understood Betsy,* a classic children's reader that features the title character as a sensitive nine-year-old orphan. Under the guidance of a matriarchal family, she develops into an independent learner. Fisher joined a relief effort among French civilians during World War I and refined her experience into *Home Fires in France* (1918) and *The Deepening Stream* (1930). As the only female director of the Book of the Month Club, she influenced the reading habits of the American public. Two of her discoveries

were the gothic stories of Isak DINESEN and Pearl BUCK's *The GOOD EARTH* (1931). Late in the 20th century Fisher herself underwent a rediscovery by feminist editors.

Bibliography

Fisher, Dorothy Canfield. *The Bedquilt and Other Stories.* Columbia: University of Missouri Press, 1997.

———. *Understood Betsy.* New York: Henry Holt, 1999.

Madigan, Mark J. "Willa Cather's Commentary on Three Novels by Dorothy Canfield Fish," *ANQ* 3, no. 1 (January 1990): 13–15.

Forché, Carolyn (1950–)

The feminist poet, translator, journalist, and humanitarian Carolyn Louise Sidlosky Forché turns narrative, folk-wise verse into testimonies to the lives of women and their children. A native of Detroit, she and her six younger siblings were born of Slovak ancestry, grew up in rural Michigan, and attended Catholic parochial schools. The conversations of her grandmother, Anna Bassar Sidlosky, an Uzbek immigrant, taught Forché to appreciate the nuances of English that were foreign to Czechoslovakians. After studying creative writing, English, and French on scholarship at Michigan State University, she mastered Russian, Serbo-Croatian, and Spanish. She married a Vietnam veteran, the combat photographer Harry Mattison, and made a home in the wilds of New Mexico, where she added Tewa to her list of spoken languages. In 1975 she completed postgraduate work at Bowling Green State University.

Through visual imagery Forché became a poet of witness. With her husband, she visited war-torn regions in Guatemala, Israel, Lebanon, and Northern Ireland. In *Gathering the Tribes* (1976), winner of a Yale Series of Younger Poets Award, she honored elderly matriarchs, kitchen work, birthings, and Pueblo ritual. A pun on *morning/mourning* in "The Morning Baking" (1976) describes the mundane chores that revive memories of the poet's Slavic grandmother, Anna. Because of common physical characteristics, Forché looks forward to her transformation by advancing age into the likeness of a gypsy milkmaid. Another home-centered poem, "Burning the Tomato Worms" (1976), pictures Anna's hands "like wheat rolls" as she shells peas (*ibid.*, 4). In "San Onofre, California" (1976), Forché muses on old women in black shawls who continue shelling beans after their loved ones have been kidnapped.

On a Guggenheim fellowship, Forché visited Spain to translate *Flowers from the Volcano* (1982) and *Sorrow* (1999), the work of the poet Claribel Alegría, who lived in exile from El Salvador. For Amnesty International Forché visited Alegría's homeland to write about political and economic chaos. In "Reunion" (1981) she relives the realistic detail of a love affair. With the aid of the Canadian writer Margaret ATWOOD, Forché published *The Country between Us* (1982), a Lamont Selection of the Academy of Poets and nominee for a *Los Angeles Times* Book Award. She translated the poems of Robert Desnos and edited the work of political activists in *Against Forgetting: Twentieth Century Poetry of Witness* (1993), which covers natural cataclysm war by war in poems by Anna AKHMATOVA, Denise LEVERTOV, Irina RATUSHINSKAYA, Muriel RUYKEYSER, and Gertrude STEIN. While teaching at George Mason University, Forché translated from Arabic the poems of Mahmoud Darwish and completed another verse collection, *The Angel of History* (1994), a summary of 20th-century moral disasters.

Bibliography

Forché, Carolyn. *Against Forgetting: Twentieth Century Poetry of Witness.* New York: W. W. Norton, 1993.
———. *The Country between Us.* New York: Perennial, 1982.
———. *Gathering the Tribes.* New Haven, Conn.: Yale University Press, 1976.
Ostriker, Alicia. "Beyond Confession: The Poetics of Postmodern Witness," *American Poetry Review* 30, no. 2 (March–April 2001): 35–39.

for colored girls who have considered suicide / when the rainbow is enuf
Ntozake Shange (1975)

In the dialect feminist drama *for colored girls who have considered suicide / when the rainbow is enuf* (1975), a female consortium raises a unison shout of outrage at exploitation. Structured in hybridized choric verse, the blazing dialogue gives voice to age-old horrors of womanhood—betrayal, sexual VIOLENCE, and the shades of bruising in between. Ntozake SHANGE dedicated the performance piece to "our mothers, from Isis and Marie Laurencin, Zora Neale Hurston to Käthe Kollwitz, Anna May Wong to Calamity Jane" (Shange, x). One by one, seven actresses from Baltimore, Chicago, Detroit, Houston, Manhattan, San Francisco, and Saint Louis tumble on stage to make their pitches for FEMINISM. The first, the beautiful lady in brown, is an informal emcee who looks out on the "spook house" to absorb the "dark phrases of womanhood . . . the melody-less-ness of her dance" (*ibid.*, 3). As an invitation to the six silent players, the speaker charges that female lives are a succession of "interrupted solos / unseen performances" (*ibid.*, 4).

Robust and affectionate, the 20-section choreopoem honors a fierce SISTERHOOD that bolsters and sustains with a visceral joy in feminine beauty and a celebration of possibilities. Intermeshed in speeches are lyricism, song and dance, lip syncing to top 40 tunes, memories, and jump rope rhymes. The delicate, naive lady in yellow testifies to the sultry temptations of graduation night and concludes, "i shd be immune / if i'm still alive" (*ibid.*, 47). The lady in green bewails the theft of self by mr. louisiana, a two-timing user who casually strips her of significance and tosses her symbolically into the sewer. At the climax, "A Nite with Beau Willie" relieves the pent-up memories of female abuse, a cyclical crime that isolates and cows its victim. Fully informed of the miseries of other women, the seven players are ready to acknowledge the emcee's "righteous gospel let her be born let her be born & handled warmly" (*ibid.*, 5).

At its debut at the Booth Theater on Broadway in September 1976, the dance-drama individualized a panoply of females—the righteous lady in purple, the magical lady in blue, the flashy lady in orange, the complicated lady in red, and the musical lady in green. The performance launched a soul search among black women from matrilineage, ritual, and spiritual renewal. A simultaneous snarl arose from black men who charged that Shange with male bashing for the audacity of such subtextual criticism as "my spirit is too ancient to understand the separation of soul and gender" (*ibid.*, 48). In September 1995 Shange directed a 20th anniversary production at the Tribeca Performing Arts Center in New York City to remind playgoers that much remained unchanged in black America. Three decades after its publication, *for colored girls* continues to inspire audiences, players, and drama students who see themselves in the color, vibrance, and pain of Shange's text.

Bibliography

Lewis, Barbara. "Back over the Rainbow," *American Theatre* 12, no. 7 (September 1995): 6.

Shange, Ntozake. *for colored girls who have considered suicide when the rainbow is enuf.* New York: Scribner, 1975.

Splawn, P. Jane. " 'Change the Joke[r] and Slip the Yoke': Boal's 'Joker' System in Ntozake Shange's 'for colored girls . . . ,' " *Modern Drama* 41, no. 34 (Fall 1998): 386.

Frame, Janet (1924–2004)

A shy, introverted poet and fiction writer, Janet Paterson Frame detailed the cultural background and daily lives of female storytellers in her native Dunedin, New Zealand. Reared in a working-class home near a swamp in Oamaru, she knew sorrow in childhood through her brother, Gordon's, epilepsy and the accidental drowning of her younger sisters, Myrtle and Isabel. From their gifted mother Frame learned stories of shipwrecks and Maori life; from her paternal grandmother she heard Scots brogue and American songs from the antebellum South. The author took an interest in slavery and female oppression as a result of early readings in Harriet Beecher STOWE's UNCLE TOM'S CABIN (1852). Frame displayed language gifts at public schools in Southland and South Otago and at Dunedin Teachers College, where she majored in English, French, and psychology.

Questions about Frame's sanity dogged her life and career. After ending her first teaching job abruptly, she voluntarily entered Seacliff Mental Hospital under a diagnosis of schizophrenia and remained in psychiatric care until age 30. She retreated to the women's ward in her autobiography to mourn the brain surgery that crippled her friend: "Nola died a few years ago in her sleep. The legacy of her dehumanizing change remains no doubt with all those who knew her; I have it with me always" (Frame, 1991, 223). During treatment for depression, the author published her first short fiction collection, *The Lagoon and Other Stories* (1951), which received the Herbert Church Memorial Award. In 1954 she toured Iberia, spending time in Andorra, Barcelona, and Ibiza. While residing in London, she learned that her mental illness had been grossly misdiagnosed.

Frame's canon includes 11 novels and three more story collections plus a volume of verse, a children's story, and three memoirs. In *Owls Do Cry* (1957) she spools out a verse cycle that depicts obstacles to female happiness, including her mother's loss of identity after marriage. Of the effects of electroshock on women, the author pictures patients' expectations of repeat treatments: "And the gabbling jibbering forest-quiet women wait in crocodile for the switch that abandons them from seeing and fear" (Frame, 1960, 56). In 1961 she characterized the relationships of nurses with female mental patients in *Faces in the Water*, in which the staff of an asylum tries to convince the protagonist, Estina, that she can live normally if she agrees to be lobotomized. Frame developed self-confidence in the 1970s through experiences at the McDowell Colony and the Yaddo Foundation. At age 65 she earned national recognition with her receipt of the Commonwealth Prize. The next year Jane Campion directed a film version of *An Angel at My Table*, a made-for-TV series that depicts Frame's survival of 200 electroshock treatments and her escape from debilitating brain surgery. In 1991 the author issued her three-stage memoir as *Janet Frame: An Autobiography*. Still focused on her mother's deterioration from the burdens of marriage and family, the narrative pictures her in "an immersion so deep that it achieved the opposite effect of making her seem to be seldom at home, in the present tense, or like an unreal person with her real self washed away" (Frame, 1991, 8). For its honesty and imaginative imagery, the autobiography earned critical respect as Frame's masterwork.

Bibliography

Frame, Janet. *Janet Frame: An Autobiography.* New York: George Braziller, 1991.

———. *Owls Do Cry*. New York: George Braziller, 1960.
Tinkler, Alan. "Janet Frame," *Review of Contemporary Fiction* 24, no. 2 (Summer 2004): 89–122.

Frankenstein Mary Shelley (1818)

An unusual feminist fable for its time, *Frankenstein; or, the Modern Prometheus*, became one of classic English literature's most analyzed works. Overturning the typical traits of the swooning female, the novelist Mary Wollstonecraft Godwin SHELLEY infects her protagonist, the brash young scholar Victor Frankenstein, with an effete neurasthenia. In his obsessive pursuit of medieval alchemy, he displays a tendency toward peevishness and brooding in solitude. Worsening his career is his refusal to accept the wisdom of his elders, respected members of the scientific community who recognize recklessness and self-aggrandizement in his ambition. He suffers episodes of agitation and fainting and a heightened sensitivity to light, sound, taste, smell, and touch. For all his interest in corpses and crypts, he seems particularly vulnerable to thoughts of death. Heightening the irony of his behavior is his given name, a reference to triumph that lies beyond his grasp.

Self-CONFINEMENT exacerbates Victor's bizarre tendencies. Like the house bound heroine of domestic fiction, he retreats into an emotion-free state while dabbling in forbidden secrets in "a cell, at the top of the house, and separated from all the other apartments by a gallery and staircase" (Shelley, 1984, 53). Giving no indication of sexual impetuosity, he neglects Elizabeth Lavenza, his foster sister, whom his mother, Caroline Beaufort, has selected and groomed to be his future wife. The droll reversal of patriarchal betrothal liberates Victor from mature endeavors to indulge his hobby, the perusal of necrotic tissue in the isolation of his lab. For rare moments of relaxation he goes on jaunts with Clavel, a male friend. The choice of Clavel rather than Elizabeth as a companion suggests that Victor has made little progress in psychosexual development from youth to manhood.

Shelley's foray into science fiction won accolades for so skillful a venture by an inexperienced teenaged female. The only Gothic work of its kind to survive to the 21st century, the plot subverts motherhood through Victor's self-ennobling structuring of a male offspring, a parody of God's creation of Adam. In place of the scriptural fall and expulsion from Eden, the repulsive eight-foot ghoul takes charge of his destiny by bolting from the lab to run amok through central Europe. As does his progenitor, the monster withdraws from warmth to wander the forests and to wreak vengeance on Victor in the frigid wasteland of the Arctic Circle. Victor's punishment for rejecting normal life and for violating professional scientific ethics is the deprivation of sexual consummation of his marriage. On Victor and Elizabeth's wedding night, the unnamed humanoid exacts revenge by making Elizabeth pay for Victor's inhumane lab project. The strangulation of the innocent fiancée parallels the SILENCING of women as well as the social price exacted from the Victorian wife for the shortcomings of her husband. By living vicariously through the accomplishments and/or faults of the male, the woman who accepted patriarchal marriage lost her surname, wealth, and identity. In Elizabeth's case she also loses her life.

Bibliography

Mellor, Anne K. *Mary Shelley: Her Life, Her Fiction, Her Monsters*. New York: Routledge, 1989.
Shelley, Mary. *Frankenstein*. New York: Bantam, 1984.

Freeman, Mary Wilkins (1852–1930)

As did Nathaniel Hawthorne, the Massachusetts-born regionalist Mary Eleanor Wilkins Freeman blamed the hardscrabble life of New England women on the rigorous Puritanism that mandated social behavior. Educated for one year each at Mount Holyoke Female Seminary and Mrs. Hosford's Glenwood Seminary, Freeman established a home with a friend, Mary Wales, with whom she lived for two decades. She overcame poverty and cyclical nightmares by submitting short fiction to local newspapers and magazines, including "Two Friends" (1887), a tale published in *Harper's Bazaar* about females who hope to remain together until they die. Similar in motivation is "The Long Arm" (1895), a Gothic murder mystery with a lesbian subtext serialized in *Chapman's Magazine* that describes the lengths to which Phoebe Dole will go to preserve her relationship with Maria Woods. Based on the Lizzie Borden trial involving the ax murdering of her family, the text features psychological DUALITY in a female defendant. The author collected her earliest stories in *A Humble Romance and Other Stories* (1887) and *A New England Nun and Other Stories* (1891). At the end of a prolific career in psychological, Gothic, and satiric modes, she won the William Dean Howells Medal of the American Academy of Arts and Letters in fiction.

A recurrent figure in Freeman's 238 dilemma stories is the resilient rural female who supports herself despite isolation and the limited opportunities offered to the female underclass, especially the aged and unmarried. In "A Moral Exigency" (1891) the author speaks through Eunice Fairweather a pragmatism that overrides religious truisms. Lacking beauty and fortune, she faces wedlock to the widowed minister Wilson and motherhood to his four children in a male-arranged deal that provides Wilson with a capable housekeeper who requires no salary. To her father's insistence that God would provide for her, Eunice retorts in the New Englander's dry humor: "I don't know whether he would or not. I don't think he would be under any obligation to if his servant deliberately encumbered himself with more of a family than he had brains to support" (Freeman, 5).

Freeman's own middle age as wife of Dr. Charles Manning Freeman, an alcoholic and mentally unstable physician, attested to her ability to survive the degrading scenarios that her heroines faced. She confronted gender discrimination in "A Church Mouse" (1891), which opens with the discussion of Hetty Fitfield's role as meetinghouse sexton. With the support of Mrs. Gale, on December 23, Hetty stands off male complaints about her hiring and wins respect for initiating the ringing of Christmas bells. A second work from this era, "A New England Nun" (1891), reprises the patience of women abandoned by men seeking their fortunes on new frontiers. The source of thematic substance is the high morality of Louisa Ellis, who refuses her intended, Joe Dagget, after he seduces a local woman. Freeman's most anthologized story, "The Revolt of 'Mother'" (1891), is a feminist parable that turns the disgruntled Sarah Penn into

a rebel. Triggering her revolt is a husband who ignores the ramshackle state of their home and who turns his attention to building a new barn. To dramatize her anger, she moves the household into the new barn, which is cleaner and more commodious than her home. The act shames her husband at the same time that she acquires better quarters for herself and her two children.

Bibliography

Cutter, Martha J. "Beyond Stereotypes: Mary Wilkins Freeman's Radical Critique of Nineteenth-Century Cults of Femininity," *Women's Studies*, 21, no. 4 (September 1992): 383–395.

Freeman, Mary Wilkins. *The New England Nun and Other Stories*. New York: Penguin, 2000.

Gardner, Kate. "The Subversion of Genre in the Short Stories of Mary Wilkins Freeman," *New England Quarterly* 65, no. 3 (September 1992): 447–468.

Shaw, S. Bradley, "New England Gothic by the Light of Common Day: Lizzie Bordon and Mary E. Wilkins Freeman's 'The Long Arm,'" *New England Quarterly* 70, no. 2 (1997): 211–236.

French, Marilyn (1929–)

Through prickly, uncompromising narratives, Marilyn Edwards French, a prominent scholar, philosopher, lecturer, and author, speaks truths about women's sufferings from millennia of betrayal and injustice. A native New Yorker of Polish lineage, she grew up poor and earned two English degrees from Hofstra College. She began writing professionally at age 28 while absorbing the feminist works of Simone de BEAUVOIR. French taught at Hofstra and College of the Holy Cross while completing a doctorate at Harvard with research on James Joyce, which she later published.

In 1977 French joined the upper echelons of theorists with publication of a controversial best seller, *The Women's Room*, which portrays a tangible feminism. The plot describes the growth of Mira Adams toward autonomy during the boom years of the Eisenhower administration. Following the motifs of Mary McCarthy's sociological novel *The Group* (1963), French's plot obliterates the euphemistic word *ladies* and all the fake gentility it implies. The 1980 made-for-TV film version of *The Women's Room* for *ABC Theatre* featured a cast of top-ranking actors: Lee Remick, Colleen Dewhurst, Patty Duke, Tovah Feldshuh, and Tyne Daly. French extended her original study of female intellectuals in *The Bleeding Heart* (1980) and in *Shakespeare's Division of Experience* (1981), a critique of the playwright's depiction of SEXUALITY in female characters.

French's subsequent works remained focused on the social expectations that cripple and demoralize women. After analyzing the defeat of gynocentric societies by male aggressors in *Beyond Power: On Women, Men, and Morals* (1985), she developed a subjective view of a Polish-American MATRIARCHY in *Her Mother's Daughter* (1987), a tribute to women's stories and memories through four generations. In a reprise of her earlier assertions about gender bias, she divided *The War against Women* (1992) into four sections, covering systemic, institutional, cultural, and personal vendettas that males hold against women. The global reduction of women to wives, mothers, domestic workers, and cheap labor takes on more force in light of total earnings, which split 10 percent–90 percent, with women getting the lesser amount. In 1998 she took the medical profession to task in *A Season in Hell: A Memoir,* which chronicles her treatment for esophageal cancer.

Bibliography

French, Marilyn. *A Season in Hell: A Memoir.* New York: Ballantine, 2000.
———. *The War against Women.* New York: Ballantine, 1993.
———. *The Women's Room.* New York: Ballantine, 1988.
Woodward, Kathleen. "In Sickness and Health," *Women's Review of Books* 16, no. 4 (January 1999): 1–3.

Friedan, Betty (1921–2006)

Dubbed the godmother of the feminist movement, the journalist and lecturer Bettye Naomi Goldstein Friedan spearheaded a shift in thought about fair treatment of the female half of the world's population. She grew up in her native Peoria, Illinois, amid family discussions of anti-Semitism, unionism, fascism, and socialism. She studied social psychology at Smith College and edited the campus newspaper. In New York City she worked as a news reporter for the Federated Press and United Electrical (UE) News before completing her studies at the University of California at Berkeley and the Esalen Institute. At age 42 she capitalized on research and her marriage and rearing of three children as ample background for *The Feminine Mystique* (1963), which uncorked a national pressure point. The social theorist Alvin Toffler lauded it as "the book that pulled the trigger on history" ("Betty," 29). Boosting morale among women, the best seller described the imprisonment of women in motherhood and housework as involuntary servitude and a form of live burial. In addition to hoisting red flags, Friedan proposed an equalizing of life ambitions and responsibilities to the benefit of both genders and their children. The work inspired a generation of budding feminists, including the journalist Susan BROWNMILLER and the ecofeminist Barbara KINGSOLVER.

Friedan turned women's overwhelming response to the book into human capital. In 1966 she helped to found the National Organization for Women (NOW), a militant women's-rights lobby demanding true equality through the crushing of gender prejudice and discrimination in government, labor and industry, religion, education, and the professions. As the first president, she lobbied from NOW's Washington, D.C., headquarters for laws that ended discrimination in such areas as housing, insurance, Social Security, employment, EDUCATION, and women's health and ABORTION rights. The organization pressed court suits on behalf of women and called for a nationwide women's strike to protest the lack of equal rights.

Friedan's admirer Anna QUINDLEN, a columnist for *Newsweek,* knew from her growing-up years the importance of Friedan to incipient feminism: "Friedan's [*The Feminist Mystique*] lobbed a hand grenade into the homes of pseudohappy housewives who couldn't understand the malaise that accompanied sparkling Formica and good-looking kids" (Quindlen, 74). Friedan's portrayal of the "problem that has no name" is a knowing description of women's unease—"a strange stirring, a sense of dissatisfaction, a yearning that women suffered in the middle of the twentieth century in the United States" (Friedan, 2001, 15). The "problem" recurs in literature as the diminution of women as children in Henrik Ibsen's play *A DOLL'S HOUSE* (1879) and the postpartum depression that felled Charlotte Perkins GILMAN and precipitated the solitary confinement of an unnamed wife in Gilman's short story "The YELLOW WALLPAPER" (1892). Friedan continued turning out thought-provoking feminist writings, including *"It Changed My Life": Writings on the Women's Movement* (1976), *The Second Stage* (1981), *Beyond Gender: The New Politics of Work and Family* (1997), and "The Feminist Papers," four articles for the *Nation*. In *The Fountain of Age* (1994), which she issued at age 73, she quashed stereotypes about little-old-ladyhood with redefinitions of advancing age as the onset of wisdom and new enthusiasms. Of particular interest is her exposure of slanted media coverage, which tends to ignore or abase older people, especially females. She died of congestive heart failure on her 85th birthday.

Bibliography

"Betty Friedan," *Workforce* 81, no. 1 (January 2002): 29.

Friedan, Betty. *The Feminine Mystique.* New York: W. W. Norton, 2001.

———. *The Fountain of Age.* New York: Simon & Schuster, 1994.

Quindlen, Anna. "Still Needing the F Word." *Newsweek*, 20 December 2003, p. 74.

Thom, Mary. *Inside Ms.: 24 Years of the Magazine and the Feminist Movement.* New York: Henry Holt, 1997.

Weir, Robert E. "Betty Friedan and the Making of the Feminine Mystique: The American Left, the Cold War, and Modern Feminism," *Journal of American and Comparative Cultures* 23, no. 3 (Fall 2000): 133–134.

frontier literature

Frontier writings—fiction, poems, diaries, journals, essays, letters, and news articles—preserve a defining era in women's history that brought venturesome females face to face with lands, peoples, and cultures unknown to European whites. Lillian Schlissel's *Women's Diaries of the Westward Journey* (1982) reports from a letter by Helen M. Carpenter about her honeymoon spent squatting by a campfire to cook, wash dishes, and set out food for breakfast. When the wagon halts, "then there is washing to be done and light bread to make and all kinds of odd jobs" (Schlissel, 78). Another Westerner, Esther Hanna, hated the piercing winds. While she tended the fire for cooking and baking, she complained of "the smoke blowing in your eyes so as to blind you, and shivering with cold so as to make the teeth chatter" (*ibid.*, 80). Charlotte Stearns Pengra lamented her rest ruined by a pelting rain that soaked through her tent and dripped into her face. Exposure to cold and damp cost many lives, including those of children, whom mothers dressed for burial along the trail.

Despite constant toil, discomfort, and personal loss, the women who migrated to colonies in the New World managed to earn greater autonomy because new settlements demanded the contributions of male and female for survival, a theme in the journalist Isabella Bird's pro-Indian dispatches to a British weekly, *Leisure Hour*, and in her memoir, *A Lady's Life in the Rocky Mountains* (1888). The concept of females' sharing their husband's ambitious plans recurs in Susan Magoffin's *Down the Santa Fe Trail and into Mexico* (1926), in which Susan travels where most women fear to go and ventures among Indian women to trade goods. European newcomers to North America, who looked down on Native tribes as primitive and pagan, discovered that Indians respected WOMEN'S RIGHTS, a topic that Helen Hunt JACKSON disclosed in nonfiction, *A Century of Dishonor: The Early Crusade for Indian Reforms* (1881), and in a best-selling melodrama, *Ramona* (1894), a kernel story reprised in outdoor spectacle and film. Similar themes direct Jessamyn WEST's historical novel *The Massacre at Fall Creek* (1975), which characterizes a confrontation between the Seneca and whites.

From early North American narrative arose folklore and fables about LA LLORONA and SPIDER WOMAN, two examples of female icons who impacted people's lives through cautionary stories and poems and through creation myth. These Earth-focused oral compositions were the basis for the Laguna fiction writer Leslie Marmon SILKO's *Ceremony* (1977) and the Laguna Sioux editor Paula Gunn ALLEN's collection *Spider Woman's Granddaughters: Traditional Tales and Contemporary Writing by Native American Women* (1990). The latter anthology includes the Crow author Pretty Shield's self-determination in the story "A Woman's

Fight." Another eyewitness author, the naturalist Mary Hunter AUSTIN, enhanced the white world's appreciation for Native women with the publication of *The Basket Woman* (1904), a view of women's art in a dry desert environment. For the classroom Austin compiled a poetry anthology, *Children Sing in the Far West* (1928), which expresses the *ecofeminism* inherent among southwestern nations.

The impetus for women migrating west to make individual contributions grew from the beginning. An archaic androcentrism did not suit the strong libertarian values of the North American colonists, who worked together—male and female—at house building, farming, fishing, hunting, and trapping. In the absence of their husbands, professionals such as the herbalist Anne Hutchinson of Boston, the midwife and diarist Martha Moore Ballard of Maine, and the memoirist Sophie Trupin of the Dakota Territory maintained families while operating printshops, bakeries, laundries, farms, stockyards, dairies, inns and stagecoach stops, and plantations. Without equal legal rights, they lacked powers to sign contracts and engage fully in financial and real estate settlements. Treated more as children than adults, American women were legally barred from pressing lawsuits, profiting from their work, and writing their own wills. Willa CATHER extended the East Coast's awareness of Plains business- and professional women and their frontier ideals with the creation of the farm owner Alexandra Bergson, protagonist of the novel *O PIONEERS!* (1913), and the farm laborer Ántonia Shmerda, the title figure in the classic prairie novel *MY ÁNTONIA* (1918). The autobiographer Mary Ellen Canaga Rowland, a physician in Kansas and Oregon, expressed in *As Long as Life: The Memoirs of a Frontier Woman Doctor* (1995) her concern for women's health needs, particularly those of battered wives. Patricia MacLachlan and Carol Sobieski, children's authors, pictured another type of frontier laborer, the mail-order bride Sarah Wheaten, protagonist of *Sarah, Plain and Tall* (1985) and its sequel, *The Skylark* (1994). The two books were a vehicle for the actor Glenn Close, who played the stalwart farm bride in a pair of Hallmark made-for-TV movies.

Feminist issues accompany a majority of female travels to the trans-Mississippi West. In 1874 the Mormon writer Fannie Stenhouse, a pro-woman writer among fundamentalist immigrants to Utah, composed some somber observations about her faith in a domestic exposé, *Tell It All, the Story of a Life's Experience in Mormonism*. In chapter 17 she regrets, "Polygamy, the knowledge that before long I should be brought personally within its degrading influence,—had now for years been the curse of my life" (Stenhouse, 223). Of a patriarchal religion and male-dictated Scripture, she pointed out that the dictates of God and the fiat of Brigham Young were not synonymous. In the Envoi that follows a lengthy and passionate text, Stenhouse avowed, "Not a day passed but what more and more evidence of the wickedness of the system, and its cruel debasement of woman's nature, was brought beneath my observation" (*ibid.*, 600). At issue was the question of male powers: "The husband became the lord, and frequently the tyrant and the despot; and the wife was either the toy of the hour, or the drudge who looked after the children" (*ibid.*). She looked forward to the day that federal law overturned the Mormon hegemony.

Mormon women were not the only settlers who questioned male authority. The memoirist Nannie Tiffany Alderson expressed ambivalence about her commitment to male-initiated homesteading in *A Bride Goes West* (1942): "I said Yes, of course, I would. But when I did go out and sit down to table in the dirt-floored kitchen, with those grizzled coatless men in their grimy-looking flannel work shirts they had worn all day, a wave of homesickness came over me" (Alderson, 29). The absence of birth control concerned Alice Kirk Grierson, a military wife and mother of six whose letters form the text of *The Colonel's Lady on the Western Frontier: The Correspondence of Alice Kirk Grierson* (1989). A piteous plaint derives from Ruthanne Lum McCunn's *Thousand Pieces of Gold* (1981), a biographical novel about an Asian slave. The protagonist, Lalu Nathoy, obeys her parents and learns the four virtues expected of Chinese women. Submissive to a fault, she accepts the fact that she has to "be sold so the family could live" (McCunn, 25). When Chen, her owner, drops her off at the House of Heavenly Pleasure, he describes her as "a new pullet ready for plucking" (*ibid.*, 78). Upon her transport up the Pacific Coast to a northern mining camp, she discovers a left-handed compliment to female newcomers: "Women in the Gold Mountains are scarcer than hen's teeth and even a plain or ugly girl has value" (*ibid.*, 101).

Women's frontier literature exposes the horrific struggles of those migrating west and of Native Americans. A prurient interest in kidnapped women precipitated the subgenre of CAPTIVITY NARRATIVE, initiated by the publication of Mary White ROW-LANDSON's *The Sovereignty and Goodness of God: The True Story of the Captivity of Mrs. Mary Rowlandson among the Indians and God's Faithfulness to Her in Her Time of Trial* (1682) and followed by similar works by Elizabeth Meader Hanson, Susannah Willard Johnson, Mary Jemison, Rachel Plummer, and Mary Ann and Olive Ann Oatman. Concerning suffering among Native women, the English poet Felicia HEMANS composed a graphic narrative, "Indian Woman's Death-Song," anthologized in *Records of Woman and Other Poems* (1828), a lament for Ampota Sapa, a suicidal mother who drowns herself and her newborn in the Mississippi River after the father deserts them. Indian women also told their own stories, notably in Sarah WINNEMUCCA's *Life among the Piutes: Their Wrongs and Claims* (1883), the first autobiography of a female Indian. In *Mourning Dove: A Salishan Autobiography*, published posthumously in 1990, the author, born in Idaho in 1888, describes the shame of a woman compromised by a man who wants to elope with her but is unwilling to marry her. Censured on the MARRIAGE MARKET as soiled goods, the woman remains out of the family circle until her rescue by another suitor, who, in FAIRY TALE fashion, relieves her dilemma by marrying her. Refuting the happily-ever-after tradition, Mollie Sanford thought otherwise about the outcome of her move to the prairie. In *Mollie: The Journal of Mollie Dorsey Sanford in Nebraska and Colorado Territories, 1857–1866* (1959), she labors at enduring solitude, particularly her husband's absence when their newborn son lies dead in a crude coffin like "one pet lamb" (Sanford, 157).

Personal observations enhance the vision of many women involved in individual ways in the settlement of the West. In 1896 the published autobiography of Calamity Jane, the alias of Martha Jane Cannary Burk, discloses the West's version of the NEW WOMAN, the female who competes for jobs in the male arena. She explains the importance of equestrian skills and a sure aim: "I acted as a pony express rider carrying the U.S. mail between Deadwood and Custer. . . . It was considered the most dangerous route in the Hills, but as my reputation as a rider and quick shot was well known, I was molested very little" (Calamity Jane, 4). Less dramatic is the Little House series of Laura Ingalls WILDER, whose *Little House in the Big Woods* (1932) and *Little House on the Prairie* (1935) detail the western migration's loneliness, night terrors, and daily toil, much of it WOMAN'S WORK. Parallel dangers shape the encounters of the children's writer and memoirist Catherine Parr Strickland Traill, author of *The Backwoods of Canada* (1871), who describes rearing seven children in the Ontario outback and increasing the family's income with freelance writing. Recovered diaries, journals, and letters such as Schlissel's *Women's Diaries*; the historian Laurel Thatcher ULRICH's Pulitzer Prize–winning *A Midwife's Tale: The Life of Martha Ballard, Based on Her Diary, 1785–1812* (1990); a Mormon pilgrim's *Winter Quarters: The 1846–1848 Life Writings of Mary Haskin Parker Richards* (1996); and the children's author Jennifer HOLM's *Our May Amelia* (1999) perpetuate the traditions and themes of feminist frontier literature.

Bibliography

Alderson, Nannie T. *A Bride Goes West*. Lincoln: University of Nebraska Press, 1942.

Calamity Jane. *The Life and Adventures of Calamity Jane* (1896). Available online. URL: http://etext.lib.virginia.edu/toc/modeng/public/CalLife.html. Accessed on October 14, 2005.

McCunn, Ruthanne Lum. *Thousand Pieces of Gold*. San Francisco: Design Enterprises, 1981.

Moodie, Susannah. *Roughing It in the Bush* (1852). Available online. URL: http://digital.library.upenn.:edu/women/wr-mine.html. Accessed on October 14, 2005.

Murphy, Emily. *Janey Canuck in the West* (1910). Available online. URL: http://digital.library.upenn.edu/women/murphy/west/west.html. Accessed on October 14, 2005.

Sanford, Mollie. *Mollie: The Journal of Mollie Dorsey Sanford in Nebraska and Colorado Territories, 1857–1866.* Lincoln: University of Nebraska Press, 1959.

Schlissel, Lillian. *Women's Diaries of the Westward Journey.* New York: Schocken, 1982.

Stenhouse, Fannie. *Tell It All, the Story of a Life's Experience in Mormonism* (1874). Available online. URL: http://www.antimormon.8m.com/fstenhouseindex.html. Accessed on October 14, 2005.

Fuller, Margaret (1810–1850)

The transcendental philosopher, journalist, editor, and letter writer Sarah Margaret Fuller issued a call to her peers to initiate the Women's Movement. A native of Cambridgeport, Massachusetts, she was home schooled in philosophy, history, the Classics, and German language and literature. Her teacher, her father, the attorney Timothy Fuller, demanded the same excellence from her that he would have asked of a son. As a young girl, she dazzled adults with brilliance and held her own in conversation with Ralph Waldo Emerson, Horace Greeley, and Henry David Thoreau, the leading intellectuals of the day. After spending her mid-teens at Miss Prescott's Young Ladies' Seminary, she abandoned institutional education for private reading and the teaching of her eight siblings. To satisfy her considerable intellectual curiosity, she translated texts of Johann von Goethe and conducted research at Harvard, becoming the university's first female student. While writing for Greeley's newspaper, the *Tribune*, she became the first American correspondent assigned to Europe.

After her father's sudden death from cholera in 1836, Fuller recognized the financial dependence of women. She sought employment as a teacher in Bronson Alcott's Temple School in Boston; the next year she taught at Green Street School, a liberal girl's academy in Providence, Rhode Island. She offered a private feminist course, "Conversations with Women," and at age 30 began editing the *Dial*, America's first literary journal. Among her innovations was a demand for original American thought and observation devoid of mimicry of European writing. In 1843 she published "The Great Lawsuit," an essay on social criticism that demon-

strates the need for balanced relations between male and female for the sake of social harmony. Praised by the feminist historian Harriet Jane ROBINSON in *Massachusetts in the Woman Suffrage Movement* (1883), the essay encourages women to give up looking to men for EDUCATION and for a smattering of privileges that males enjoy, particularly the right to address public assemblies.

Fuller criticized woman's lowly position within society as wife, housekeeper, and mother and her expectations of nothing more. In Fuller's estimation society treated women as children. She shocked some readers by discussing the marital relationships between men and women as a basis for her arguments for equality. Graphically she charged that white men thought nothing of keeping white women out of the fray of public affairs, yet forced black slave women into the fields, even pregnant and lactating workers. She echoed Mary WOLLSTONECRAFT's demands for offering equal education for boys and girls and for challenging young women to make use of all their talents and to enjoy rich, satisfying lives.

In *Summer on the Lakes in 1843* (1843), Fuller described her tour of the northern prairie states by rail, stage, and steamer to view the lifestyles of immigrant laborers, settlers, and Native Americans. Of her fact-finding mission she concluded, "The great drawback upon the lives of these settlers, at present, is the unfitness of the women for their new lot. . . . [Domestic labor] must often be performed, sick or well, by the mother and daughters, to whom a city education has imparted neither the strength nor skill now demanded" (Fuller, 1991, 38). She departed from travelogue to cite specific instances of an unjust burden that overwhelmed and dismayed westering women. As a result of her visit to the West, Fuller dedicated her life and work to reform. She challenged the incarceration of the poor in workhouses and prisons. She sought a just place in society for the Ojibwa and for undervalued and undereducated women.

In a revolutionary treatise, *Woman in the Nineteenth Century* (1845), the first work of feminist philosophy in North America, Fuller anticipates the NEW WOMAN. She predicts that the late 19th century will see women shake off Puritanism and the traditional subordination that patriarchal society dictates. Drawing on Greek mythology, she states, "The time is come when Eurydice is to call for an Orpheus" (Fuller, 1971, 12). At the crux of her writings is the single initiative to convince women of their worth. In a discussion of past faults in gender equity, she characterizes the dilemma of the era's concept of wedlock. Her philosophy charges that women had to accept the full onus of matrimony and its responsibilities for training children in morality and spirituality. To accomplish so serious a task, she urges the INDEPENDENT woman to escape society's intent to keep her ever the docile child—too intellectually limited to take part in the public forum, vote for the best candidates, or run for public office. The text presents a sink-or-swim choice to the pacesetter. It declares that autonomy is the only choice for women seeking full adulthood: "That her hand may be given with dignity, she must be able to stand alone" (ibid., 176).

Among the readers agreeing with Fuller's demand for a well-rounded education and unlimited opportunity were Susan B. ANTHONY and Elizabeth Cady STANTON, the pillars of the SUFFRAGE groundswell. As partners in reform, they churned out letters, articles, and pamphlets and essays to the *New York Tribune,* an influential and liberal newspaper that employed Fuller as literary editor. Out of respect for Fuller's wisdom and belief in full citizenship for women, more than four decades after she and her family drowned off Fire Island, New York, on a voyage from Italy, Anthony and Stanton dedicated to the feminist philosopher their *History of Woman Suffrage* (1881).

Bibliography

Fuller, Margaret. *My Heart Is a Large Kingdom: Selected Letters of Margaret Fuller.* Ithaca, N.Y.: Cornell University Press, 2001.

———. *Summer on the Lakes in 1843.* Urbana: University of Illinois Press, 1991.

———. *Woman in the Nineteenth Century.* New York: W. W. Norton, 1971.

Kornfeld, Eve. *Margaret Fuller: A Brief Biography with Documents.* New York: Bedford/St. Martin's, 1997.

Martineau, Harriet. *Harriet Martineau's Autobiography* (1877). Available online: URL: http://www.indiana.edu/~letrs/vwwp/martineau/martineau1.html. Accessed on October 14, 2005.

Showalter, Elaine. "Feminist Foremother," *Wilson Quarterly* 25, no. 1 (Winter 2001): 129–131.

Warren, James Perrin. *Culture of Eloquence: Oratory and Reform in Antebellum America.* University Park: Pennsylvania State University Press, 1999.

G

Gage, Matilda Joslyn (1826–1898)

The journalist, editor, and feminist historian Matilda Joslyn Gage compiled impeccable scholarship attesting to the plight of women, particularly since the advance of Christianity. A native of Cicero, New York, she heard reform philosophy from her father, a physician and abolitionist who operated a station of the Underground Railroad. She performed abolitionist songs and handed out antislavery leaflets on the street. At home her father directed her study in anatomy and physiology and her mastery of multiple languages in preparation for training at the Geneva Medical College. After completing her education at the Clinton Liberal Institute, at age 19, she disappointed her father by marrying a dry goods merchant and bearing five children.

In pursuit of equality for women, Gage became an officer of the New York Woman Suffrage Association and a first-time platform orator at the 1852 National Woman's Rights Convention. After cofounding the National Woman Suffrage Association, which based its radical program on civil disobedience, she wrote polemics for the organization's newspaper, the *Revolution*. At Susan B. ANTHONY's trial for illegal voting in 1873 Gage reported to the Kansas *Leavenworth Times* the famed suffragist's self-defense. Into the 1870s Gage wrote tracts on SUFFRAGE and the genocide of the American Indian. She edited her own journal, the *National Citizen and Ballot Box*, in which she noted the equality of genders among the Iroquois. When women received the right to vote in school board elections in 1880, she was the first female citizen of Fayetteville, New York, to cast a ballot.

With the activists Anthony and Elizabeth Cady STANTON, Gage formed the third of the triumvirate and coauthored the "Declaration of Rights of Women" (1876) and the first three volumes of the six-volume *History of Woman Suffrage* (1881–86), which pictured the fiery Scots-American orator Frances WRIGHT on the cover. Key to the trio's demands were ownership of their own wages, which appealed to lower-class women, and the right to act as free agents without relying on husbands, fathers, or other male relatives to speak for them, a concept designed to enlist aristocratic women. Of domestic lives a line in volume 1 regrets that women receive no pay for their labors. Gage followed Anthony on a campaign through California, Michigan, Wyoming, the Dakotas, and Colorado. Gage spoke in 16 towns in defense of Anthony's efforts and rang doorbells to establish a consensus on WOMEN'S RIGHTS.

Gage drew blood with a feminist chronicle, *Woman, Church and State* (1893), a controversial scholarly work that named Christianity as a major source of misogyny and as a stumbling block to female emancipation. Under Christianity, she stated, women gradually lost not only the control of the home, but also possession of property and the fruit of their industry. She charged male churchdom with reducing women to a status much lower than the prestige they enjoyed as priestesses to goddess cults in ancient civilizations, for example, among the Ishtar worshipers of Babylonia, the Isis sect in Egypt, and the Vestal Virgins of ancient Rome. She justified her assertion with an abbreviated history of "a form of society . . . known as the Matriarchate or Mother-rule . . . [where] woman ruled; she was first in the family, the state, religion" (Gage, 12, 14). Gage declared that the women of her own time, like slaves, possessed liberty only if they fell into the hands of a just master.

Bibliography

Brammer, Leila R. *Excluded from Suffrage History: Matilda Joslyn Gage, Nineteenth-Century American Feminist.* Westport, Conn.: Greenwood, 2000.

Gage, Matilda Joslyn. *Woman, Church and State* (1895). Available online: URL: http://www.sacred-texts.com/wmn/wcs/. Accessed October 14, 2005.

Gale, Zona (1874–1938)

The suffragist, newspaperwoman, and regional fiction writer Zona Gale revealed the dark side of women's lives on the America Plains. She lived her era's ideal of the progressive NEW WOMAN. The only child of solid midwesterners, she was born of English-Scotch-Irish parentage in Portage, Wisconsin, the setting of her writings. After graduating from Wayland Academy and the University of Wisconsin with two degrees in literature, she coedited Milwaukee's *Evening Wisconsin* and the Milwaukee *Journal*. At age 27 she reported for the New York *Evening World.* In 1906 she published a utopian fantasy, *Romance Island,* set in the southern Atlantic Ocean where temples preserve goddess worship on a par with the Greek reverence for Aphrodite. In chapter 10 as attendees enter the glistening Hall of Kings, the outsider, Saint George, is amazed at the difference between women in this haven and those at home: "And they were all—alive—, fully and mysteriously alive, alive to their finger-tips. It was as if in comparison all other women acted and moved in a kind of half-consciousness" (Gale, 1906).

Gale produced midwestern fare in a story cycle, *The Loves of Pelleas and Etarre* (1907), and in *Friendship Village* (1908), a chronicle of small-town life in the prairie states that spawned a sequel, *Peace in Friendship Village* (1919). In 1914 while submitting stories and poems to *Aegis, Century,* and *Success,* she advanced the cause of community the-

ater with a one-act play, *The Neighbors,* which she composed for the Wisconsin Players. She ventured into liberal causes by involving herself in public school reform, WOMEN'S RIGHTS, and social justice. Under the influence of the settlement worker and memoirist Jane Addams, Gale wrote a pacifist novel, *Heart's Kindred* (1915), and a feminist denunciation of workplace conditions for women in *Daughter of the Morning* (1917). Abandoning idyllic writing was her realistic novel *Birth* (1918), which she adapted for stage in 1925 as *Mister Pitt.* She made a popular breakthrough with *Miss Lulu Bett* (1920), a sharp-edged feminist novella depicting a single woman's disillusion with and revolt against family constraints and parochial hypocrisy.

In 1921 Gale became the first woman to receive a Pulitzer Prize in drama for the stage version of *Miss Lulu Bett,* a terse, intense domestic play that she adapted from her novella in a span of eight days. The action follows the metamorphosis of the title figure, a repressed 34-year-old sister-in-law who becomes the "family beast of burden" in a stodgy midwestern town appropriately named Marbleton (Gale, 1994, 18). Often compared to Sinclair Lewis's *Main Street* (1920), Lulu's story discloses psychological disorder at the core of family unity after Lulu chooses self-affirmation over marriage. Because of critical protestations of the controversial theme of bigamy, a week after her play debuted on Broadway Gale rewrote the ending by killing off the extra wife to provide Lulu with a happy marriage to a suitable eligible male.

Gale's lengthy career extended into her 60s. At age 49 she achieved popular fame for *Faint Perfume* (1923), a novel adapted to the silent screen in 1925 and to play form in 1934. She continued writing realistic scenarios in the story collections *Yellow Gentians and Blue* (1927) and *Bridal Pond* (1930). She chose the Gothic mode for *Preface to a Life* (1926), *Borgia* (1929), and *Papa La Fleur* (1933). Her mastery of literary modes includes a biography of Frank Miller, short pieces in *Portage, Wisconsin, and Other Essays* (1928), and radio plays based on her short fiction.

Bibliography

Gale, Zona. *Miss Lulu Bett: Birth.* Oregon, Wis.: Badger Books, 1994.

————. *Romance Island* (1906). Available online: URL: http://www.gutenberg.org/newsletter/gutenbergglobe/newsletters/PGWeekly_2004_10_13_Part_2.txt. Accessed October 14, 2005.

Simonson, Harold P. *Zona Gale.* New York: Twayne, 1962.

Williams, Deborah Lindsay. *Not in Sisterhood: Edith Wharton, Willa Cather, Zona Gale, and the Politics of Female Authorship.* New York: Palgrave Macmillan, 2001.

Gaskell, Elizabeth (1810–1865)

Across the spectrum of class differences, the novelist Elizabeth Cleghorn Stevenson Gaskell reproduced the lives of women in Victorian England. A native Londoner, she was born in Chelsea and survived seven siblings to become her parents' only child. Left motherless in toddlerhood, she lived in Knutsford, Cheshire, with Hannah Lumb, a maternal aunt, who educated her niece at home. At age 12 Gaskell advanced to the Byerley sisters' boarding academy in Warwickshire. In 1832 she married William Gaskell, who, like her father, was a Unitarian minister in Manchester. Elizabeth and William Gaskell were coauthors of *Sketches among the Poor* (1837), a sentimental verse suite. Her marriage and the births of five children did not change her intent to refer to herself as "Elizabeth Gaskell" rather than the domesticated "Mrs. Gaskell." Her feminist activism included a proposal for the Establishment for Invalid Gentlewomen, relief work during famine, and support for female emigration to North America.

At the core of Gaskell's feminist themes was her concern for the DUALITY of women as individuals and as wives and mothers. She began submitting tales to Charles Dickens's weekly journal *Household Words* and to *Howitt's Journal* before venturing to write long fiction. In 1857 at the request of the Reverend Patrick Brontë she compiled *Life of Charlotte Brontë*, a concise biography of his daughter, Gaskell's dear friend. At the height of the Industrial Revolution woman's work absorbed the author. In four short stories—"Lizzie Leigh," "The Manchester Marriage," "The Three Eras of Libbie Marsh," and "The Well of Pen-Morfa"—Gaskell describes the lives of laboring-class women in 19th-century Victorian England. Vignettes of cotton mill workers contrast with the polite women's fiction of the day in their gritty details and the differences in male and female values. As an antidote to managerial tyranny of laborers, Gaskell proposed female intervention in *Mary Barton: A Tale of Manchester Life* (1848) and in *North and South* (1855), a comparison of social classes and the difference between genteel country life and the dangerous, unhealthful climates for girls and women working in mills.

Gaskell moved amiably from class to class and among a variety of dramatic social situations. In 1853 she pondered the outcast ruined female in *Ruth*, the story of an unwed mother in an era when the DOUBLE STANDARD condoned male sexual ventures but castigated their female partners as irredeemable sluts. At the core of the action is the subjugation of laboring-class girls, who at two in the morning are "stitching away as if for very life," an indication of how willing they are to knuckle under to cruel management (Gaskell, *Ruth*, 7). Lacking leverage, the seamstresses demonstrate obedience and industry in hopes of continued employment. Their task resumes the next morning at eight in preparation for a dress ball for local aristocrats. More upbeat is *Cranford* (1855), a mildly satiric novel published in *Household Words* from 1851 to 1853, in which Gaskell tells about a clutch of unmarried countrywomen who enjoy freedom from male domination. In the opening chapter one woman confides, "A man . . . is *so* in the way in the house!" (Gaskell, *Cranford*, 1). A more serious examination of women's unhappiness in matrimony followed in *Sylvia's Lovers* (1863). The next year Gaskell pictured sexual stirrings in *Cousin Phillis* (1864), in which the protagonist suffers more than her share of grief from the double standard.

Anticipating retirement, Gaskell died suddenly while writing her last novel, *Wives and Daughters: An Every-Day Story* (1866), a witty two-volume work that she serialized in *Cornhill's Magazine* from August 1864 to January 1866. The text subtly penetrates women's psyches by studying the maturation of the stepsisters Molly and Cynthia Gibson under the scrutiny of the gossips of Hollingford. Working against the girls' choice of husbands are class and gender prejudices, especially against the bluestocking, the era's term for an intellectual female. The author explains in the opening chapter that changes are astir in the pro-Tory countryside: "It was just before the passing of the Reform Bill, but a good deal of liberal talk took place occasionally between two or three of the more enlightened freeholders" (Gaskell, 2001, 6). Gaskell perceived changes in the economy that foretold more liberal treatment of women. Her feminism influenced the writing of Grace PALEY.

Bibliography

Gaskell, Elizabeth. *Cranford*. Oxford: Oxford University Press, 1998.

———. *Lizzie Leigh and Other Tales* (1896). Available online: URL: http://www.bookrags.com/ebooks/2547/1. html#1. Accessed on October 14, 2005.

———. *Ruth*. London: Penguin, 1998.

———. *Wives and Daughters*. London: Penguin, 2001.

Starr, Elizabeth. " 'A Great Engine for Good': The Industry of Fiction in Elizabeth Gaskell's *Mary Barton and North and South*," *Studies in the Novel* 34, no. 4 (Winter 2002): 386–404.

gender bias

Feminist literature voices the outrage of women at one-sided gender politics. The first American feminist author to cry foul at the betrayal of women was Hannah Webster Foster, the Massachusetts native who wrote a best-selling roman á clef, *The Coquette; or, The History of Eliza Wharton, a Novel Founded on Fact* (1797), one of North America's first novels. Foster based the story on a scandal that arose from the seduction, betrayal, and death of the 37-year-old poet Elizabeth Whitman and her stillborn child alone at an inn in Danvers, Massachusetts, on July 25, 1788. Foster's epistolary format channels her protest against gendered social codes. Through fiction she demands that society address the sexual plight of women seeking upward mobility. In outrage at the DOUBLE STANDARD, she insists that the authorities impose more stringent punishments on men who trifle with women and then abandon them and their illegitimate children to shame and penury.

Foster makes good use of the protagonist, Eliza Wharton, and her aphoristic letters. In reference to society's expectations for bereaved women, Eliza, whose fiancé has died, declares an intolerable impertinence "the absurdity of a custom, authorising people at a first interview to revive the idea of griefs, which time has lulled, perhaps obliterated" (Foster, 9). As advice to the unwary survivor and her response to male blandishments, Eliza is blunt: "[Reputation] is an inestimable jewel, the loss of which can never be repaired" (*ibid.*, 133). Foster details the scapegoating of women through Eliza's candid observations to her friend Julia Granby, Major Sanford's cavalier pose as libertine and despoiler of women, and Eliza's eventual self-silencing because of her remorse for sexual misconduct. Turning the text into a cautionary tale, Foster denounces the overselling of virtue and matrimony to powerless young women who deserve the truth about premarital sex, docility, ruination, and the economic, social, and political shackles on female citizens of the new republic.

In 1890 the anarchist orator Voltairine DE CLEYRE addressed the pervasiveness of gender bias in institutions. In the essay "Sex and Slavery," she charged Christianity and the state with conspiracy to control the soul and body of women: "We are tired of promises, God is deaf, and his church is our worst enemy. Against it we bring the charge of being the moral (or immoral) force which lies behind the tyranny of the State" (de Cleyre). With a deft turn of phrase gained from her four years of forced residence in an Ontarian convent, she created a biblical image of collusion: "The State has divided the loaves and fishes with the Church; the magistrates, like the priests, take marriage fees; the two fetters of Authority have gone into partnership" (*ibid.*). She contrasted the plight of the fleeing wife with that of the escaping slave or runaway dog: There were agencies in her day to aid the slave and the dog, but none to succor the despairing woman.

As did de Cleyre, Mary Wilkins FREEMAN, a New England regionalist, wrote about the extremes of desperation. She expresses the civic-mindedness and empathy of women in "Old Woman Magoun" (1909). At Barry's Ford, a community overburdened with lazy men, the protagonist prods them to build a new bridge. She is stymied by a demand from her granddaughter, Lily's father, the degenerate Nelson Barry, who wants custody of the 13-year-old to betroth to Jim Willis, to whom Nelson owes gambling debts. Lacking the authority to refuse, the grandmother helps Lily to eat poisonous nightshade berries and die rather than be a commodity in a male-to-male financial deal. Freeman confers honor on Mrs. Magoun, an example of a female who combats male power the only way she can.

Into the 20th century the motif of gender bias in feminist fiction reflected the greater sophistication and INDEPENDENCE in women. In the 1930s through the 1950s COLETTE, a world-wise journalist and fiction writer, published a flurry of realistic novels on the gender politics of her time. The most famous, *Gigi* (1952), is a resilient comedy about old-fashioned aunts' training their young niece for serious coquetry. Unlike Eliza Wharton, who is too late smart, Gigi traps a wily roué by wielding her charms as inducements to marriage. The popularity of Colette's book paled beside the immense reception of two adaptations. The stage version, cowritten by the playwright Anita LOOS in 1954, preceded the 1958 cinema musical, a multiple Oscar winner for the performances of Leslie Caron, Louis Jourdan, Hermione Gingold, and Maurice Chevalier.

As is implied by the contrast between Mary Wilkins Freeman and Hannah Foster's tragic fiction and Colette's jolly tone and comedic falling action, fictional versions of female oppression vary from instance to instance. Unlike the amiable French, Marxist states appear to excel at gender-based intimidation. In 1979 Tatyana Mamonova, a feminist short fiction writer, editor, and reviewer for *Aurora* magazine, compiled *Women and Russia: Feminist Writings from the Soviet Union.* This underground essay collection forced five female Soviet dissidents into exile and may have sparked a KGB assassination of a sixth rebel in a staged car collision in Leningrad. Editor Mamonova introduced the work with bold charges of patriarchal threats and grievous data on the lack of sex EDUCATION and contraceptives and the inhumanity of state-run ABORTION clinics. Contributor Ekaterina Miranova alleged that society demanded that women be sex toys: "Both the soul and body of women were transformed into the shape of a vessel that was pleasing to men, much as the Chinese did

when they deliberately bred grotesque people for the amusement of the emperor" (Mamonova, 127). Natasha Maltseva accused the government of deliberately demeaning unwed mothers and blamed state physicians for conducting cruel gynecological examinations intended to inflict pain. A more pathetic national difference describes the plight of the Chinese-American slave Lalu Nathoy, protagonist of Ruthanne Lum McCunn's *Thousand Pieces of Gold* (1942). Before her father sold Lalu to a bicoastal slaving operation, he "was fed first, before his wife and children, and with the better food" (McCunn, 33). To Lalu's questions about the unfairness, her overworked mother replied as though by rote, "Men are the pillars of the family" (*ibid.*).

The theme of gender bias has been the impetus for one of the most incisive feminist's works. In the essay "Blood, Bread, and Poetry: The Location of the Poet" (1984), Adrienne RICH states the centrality of gender politics to her work. She determines to change the status quo after perceiving that "the myths and obsessions of gender, the myths and obsessions of race, the violent exercise of power in these relationships could be identified, their territories could be mapped." (Rich, 245) The epiphany set her on a course to right the wrongs of historical misogyny through poetry, notably, through the controlling metaphor of "Diving into the Wreck" (1973). By picturing the female diver penetrating dark waters in search of matriarchal lore, Rich symbolizes the liberated woman as doing the difficult and sometimes perilous work necessary to freeing women from anti-woman traditions that date to prehistory.

Bibliography

Baker, Dorothy Z. "'Detested Be the Epithet!': Definition, Maxim, and the Language of Social Dicta in Hannah Webster Foster's 'The Coquette,'" *Essays in Literature* 23, no. 1 (Spring 1996): 58–68.

de Cleyre, Voltairine. "Sex Slavery" (1890). Available online: URL: http://dwardmac.pitzer.edu/Anarchist_Archives/bright/cleyre/sexslavery.html. Accessed on October 13, 2005.

Finseth, Ian. "'A Melancholy Tale': Rhetoric, Fiction, and Passion in *The Coquette,*" *Studies in the Novel* 33, no. 2 (Summer 2001): 125–159.

Foster, Hannah Webster. *The Coquette*. Oxford: Oxford University Press, 1987.

Mamonova, Tatyana, ed. *Women and Russia: Feminist Writings from the Soviet Union*. Boston: Beacon Press, 1984.

McCunn, Ruthanne Lum. *Thousand Pieces of Gold*. San Francisco: Design Enterprises, 1981.

Norton, Caroline. *English Laws for Women* (1854). Available online: URL: http://digital.library.upenn.edu/women/norton/elfw/elfw.html. Accessed on October 14, 2005.

Rich, Adrienne. *Adrienne Rich's Poetry and Prose*. New York: W. W. Norton, 1975.

Gibbons, Kaye (1960–)

A master of feminist stories about autonomy and courage, the novelist Kaye Gibbons specializes in humble settings and characters who establish order in their lives. A North Carolinian from a farm on Bend of the River Road, she was the child of semiliterate parents. She later drew on their locutions and idioms for authentic southern dialect. She began reading newspapers at age four; two years later she was memorizing from *Child Craft Encyclopedia* the poems of William Shakespeare and Emily DICKINSON. After Gibbons's mother, a manic-depressive, died of suicide and her father drank himself to death, the author lived with aunts in Rocky Mount until she graduated from high school. At the University of North Carolina at Chapel Hill on a governor's scholarship, she majored in creative writing and planned to teach at the college level.

At age 25 Gibbons completed a best-selling semiautobiographical novella, *Ellen Foster* (1987), a story of child neglect, pedophilia, and self-rescue. The novel, which earned a Sue Kaufman Prize and Ernest Hemingway Foundation citation, features a Dickensian waif whom critics compare to Carson MCCULLERS's Frankie Addams and Mick Kelly. Self-willed and determined, 11-year-old Ellen flees her predatory father. At his death her overtaxed brain scrambles for safety: "They put . . . him in a box oh shut the lid down hard on this one and nail it nail it with the strongest nails. Do all you can to keep it shut and him in it always" (Gibbons, 1990, 70). Ellen turns the title into a pun by locating a family that shelters foster children. On her way to creating her own ideal household, she rejects the pap assigned to elementary school readers and opts for novels by Charlotte and Emily BRONTË and for "the laughing Middle Ages lady that wore red boots," Ellen's identification of Geoffrey Chaucer's WIFE OF BATH (*ibid.*, 10).

Touches of grace in Gibbons's novels elevate woman-centered rescues from melodrama and didacticism. In 1989 she earned a National Endowment for the Arts grant, her financial means of completing *A Cure for Dreams* (1991). She followed with *Charms for the Easy Life* (1993), her most feminist undertaking, which details the influence of an autocratic midwife and herbalist on her daughter and granddaughter. In the 2002 Showtime made-for-TV film adaptation Gena Rowlands plays the part of the grandmother, Miss Charlie Kate Birch, who enjoys complete autonomy in a joyously manless household. In her ministrations to poor women, she admonishes a drunk physician for blinding a newborn baby girl with silver nitrate drops. Gibbons turned to more Gothic feminism in *Divining Women* (2004), a novel about male coercion in the home of Troop, who subdues his wife, Maureen, with treatments for her "hysteria." The birth of Maureen's first child and her redemption from a daily hell are the work of Troop's niece, a confident young humanist who recognizes Troop's potential for female destruction.

Bibliography

"*Ellen Foster* and *A Virtuous Woman*," *Wilson Quarterly* 14, no. 1 (Winter 1990): 95.

Gibbons, Kaye. *Charms for the Easy Life*. New York: Avon, 1994.

———. *Divining Women*. New York: Grosset & Dunlap, 2004.

———. *Ellen Foster*. New York: Vintage Books, 1990.

Gigi Colette (1944)

In the falling action of World War II COLETTE issued *Gigi* (1944), a satiric tutorial on the ingenue's embrace of freedom. Trained by old hands at sexual connivance—Mamma Andrée Alvar and grandmamma Inez Alvarez—16-year-old Gilberte "Gigi" Alvar literally sits at the feet of WISEWOMEN to learn the joys of materialism and the dangers of foolish expenditures of youth and charm. The witty tone, freed of coarseness, relies on sophistication to delineate the choices and decisions that await the naive Gigi, a tall, ash-blonde beauty with the scampish look of Robin Hood. In an atmosphere heavy with decadence and euphemism, she accepts admonition about keeping her knees together but despises having to worry about public interest in her "you-know-what" (Colette, 5).

Colette's miniature female melodrama sets its sights on values. Against the antibourgeois sentiments of the household, Gigi holds to an innate faith in love and decency, yet manages to snare an aristocratic womanizer. The narrative sets up literary foils to Gigi in Gaston "Tonton" Lachaille, an aging roué and bored voluptuary, and in Baron Ephraim, who woos 15-year-old Lydia Poret with a diamond solitaire. Complicit in Gigi's rigorous preparation for deflowering are lessons from Grandmamma on avoiding face powder and corsets and from Mamma on eating lobster, a worthy symbol of the grasping belle-Époque. From the example of Liane d'Exelmans, Gigi observes the dramatics of pretending to overdose on laudanum to lessen the shame of a lapsed love affair. From Great-Aunt Alicia, Gigi learns that sex is a better basis for a relationship than love because physical involvement leaves the mind free of entanglements. Hanging in the balance is the family's income, which they obtain from Lachaille's generous gifts. Fortunately none of these models and pressures diminishes Gigi's preference for truth over deception.

In chronicling the young woman's introduction to corrupt French society, *Gigi* exhibits the candor indigenous to women's fiction written by women about women. In the novella's introduction, Erica JONG exalts Colette as "the most authentic feminist heroine of all women writers' (*ibid.*, vii). Reviewing for *Atlantic*, the critic C. J. Rolo admires Colette's ability to "[convey] with economy no end of subtle nuances" (Rolo, 84). In response to Lachaille's profession of love the heroine spews out her distaste for the sordid affairs in his past and for gossip that embroiders his knavery. Rather than measure her worth in ropes of pearls from lovers or in trysts on romantic beaches, Gigi values herself as a lovable woman. The relevance

of her position in a cynical family speaks to 21st-century youths who face their own dilemmas of love versus material comforts.

Bibliography

Colette. *Gigi, Julie de Corneilha, and Chance Acquaintances: Three Short Novels.* New York: Farrar, Straus & Giroux, 1952.

Rolo, C. J. "Review: *Gigi,*" *Atlantic*, January 1953, p. 84.

Gilbert, Sandra (1936–) and Gubar, Susan (1944–)

The authors of a landmark feminist text, Sandra Mortola Gilbert and Susan D. Gubar combined teaching experience with pro-woman vision to disclose the restrictive nature of androcentrism. Gilbert, a professor of English at the University of California at Davis, and Gubar, a professor of English and women's studies at Indiana University, generated a historic synergy in the writing of a literary best seller, *The Madwoman in the Attic: The Woman Writer and the Nineteenth-Century Literary Imagination* (1979), a nominee for a National Book Award and a Pulitzer Prize. Their feminist criticism of major women's works from Gothic and Victorian literature replaced standard analyses of familiar works, particularly Charlotte BRONTË's JANE EYRE (1847), the touchstone of their study. Gilbert and Gubar's research shook up curricula with new approaches to women's studies and to such classic literature as Jane AUSTEN's Gothic parody *Northanger Abbey* (1818), Emily BRONTË's WUTHERING HEIGHTS (1847), Emily DICKINSON's verse, George ELIOT's novels, and Mary SHELLEY's sci-fi fable *Frankenstein* (1818). A 20th-anniversary edition of *Madwoman in the Attic* marked two decades of influence for Gilbert and Gubar's insights. Additional collaborations produced *Shakespeare's Sisters: Feminist Essays on Women Poets* (1979), *The War of the Words* (1987), *No Man's Land: Sexchanges: The Place of the Woman Writer in the Twentieth Century* (1989), *Letters from the Front* (1994), and *Masterpiece Theatre: An Academic Melodrama* (1995). With Diana O'Hehir, the duo compiled *Mothersongs: Poems for, by, and about Mothers* (1995), which features an outpouring of works of the feminist poets Fleur ADCOCK, Elizabeth Barrett BROWNING, Emily DICKINSON, Louise GLÜCK, Maxine KUMIN, Audre LORDE, Adrienne RICH, Anne SEXTON, Stevie SMITH, and Mitsuye YAMADA. The anthology covers the phases of mothering as well as reverence for the GODDESS LORE of Earthwoman, Maia, and the VIRGIN MARY. Of the mother's physical death Erica JONG muses in "The Buddha in the Womb" that "the experience of being mortal is a lesson to pass on to the upcoming generation.

In their provocative ideology of the literary past Gilbert and Gubar discredit male-generated theories for their superior, authoritarian perspective. The editors reflected an ongoing gender war: They perceived woman's lot in the 1800s and 1900s to be perceived by men as aliens. In the same period, women viewed men as defenders of an outworn gender creed. The revelations of *Madwoman in the Attic* expose the root of faulty logic in the male hierarchy—that women were created for the glorification of men. For the sake of clarity the two scholars abandoned male-devised critiques and conventions and set new parameters for women's literary traditions. In the basic model the motivation in *Jane Eyre*, the contrast of Edward Rochester's wives, becomes the central issue. Picturing Jane EYRE and Bertha Mason ROCHESTER, his crazed Creole wife, as two halves of the female persona, Gilbert and Gubar's study characterizes Jane as a creative woman in an era that suppressed female artistry. As a subconscious outcry against patriarchal control Bertha burns Thornfield, a manse bearing a name emblematic of the terrain covered by women on their way to fulfillment. By novel's end Jane's rejuvenation from a pilgrimage into the wild and her establishment of a school level the differences between the former governess and her employer. As a female rescuer she inverts the order of standard Gothic melodrama to establish an equal partnership with Edward.

In the summation of Gilbert and Gubar, the creation of women's true stories ends the subordination of female art: "The old silent dance of death became a dance of triumph, a dance into speech, a dance of authority" (*ibid.*, 44). The theorists expanded on their original model to find female indebtedness to the precursors and iconoclasts of feminist literature, including the novelists

Jane AUSTEN, George ELIOT, and Elizabeth GASKELL. The originality of Gilbert and Gubar's logic exposed the fallacies of Freudian interpretation, which ties the perspectives of women of letters to fathers and father figures and ignores matriarchal legacies. As feminist criticism evolved, the duo compiled a landmark textbook, *The Norton Anthology of Literature by Women: The Traditions in English* (1985, 1996). In the preface to the second edition the editors celebrate the exuberance and variety of works that exemplify diversity of race, nationality, sexual preference, religion, class, and cultural heritage.

Bibliography

Donaldson, Elizabeth J., "The Corpus of the Madwoman: Toward a Feminist Disability Studies Theory of Embodiment and Mental Illness," *NWSA Journal* 14, no. 3 (Fall 2002): 99–119.

Gilbert, Sandra M., and Susan Gubar. *The Madwoman in the Attic.* 2nd ed. New Haven, Conn.: Yale University Press, 2000.

———. *No Man's Land: Sexchanges: The Place of the Woman Writer in the Twentieth Century: The War of the Words.* New Haven, Conn.: Yale University Press, 1989.

———, and Diana O'Hehir, eds. *Mothersongs: Poems for, by, and about Mothers.* New York: W. W. Norton, 1995.

Heller, Scott, "The Book That Created a Canon: 'Madwoman in the Attic' Turns 20." *Chronicle of Higher Education,* 17 December 1999, pp. 20–21.

" 'The Madwoman in the Attic': The Woman Writer and the 19th Century Literary Imagination," *Women and Language* 24, no. 1 (Spring 2001): 39.

Peters, John G., "Inside and Outside 'Jane Eyre' and Marginalization through Labeling," *Studies in the Novel* 28, no. 1 (Spring 1996): 57–75.

Gilchrist, Ellen (1935–)

A southern writer of essays, short stories, and novels, Ellen Louise Gilchrist creates accessible female characters whose hilarious interactions have the ring of true SISTERHOOD. Her identity as a writer derives from her birth in Vicksburg, Mississippi, where matriarchal traditions dating to a great-great-grandmother provided her first name. She

developed a love of rural life at Hopedale Plantation outside Greenville and learned in childhood
of the undercurrents and character assassination in
adult relations. In *Falling through Space: The Journals of Ellen Gilchrist* (1987) she records autobiographical glimpses of family quirks and loyalties. At
age 14 she produced a column for a Kentucky daily
and advanced to editing for her high school paper.

Well read in philosophy, verse, and science,
Gilchrist completed a degree in philosophy from
Millsaps College. At age 40 she edited the *New
Orleans Vieux Carré Courier* while dabbling in verse
and short sketches. In 1976 she entered the University of Arkansas and began publishing short fiction collections—*In the Land of Dreamy Dreamas*
(1981), *Victory over Japan* (1984)—and novels—
The Annunciation (1983) and *The Anna Papers*
(1988). She turned down a lucrative offer to write
filmscripts and in 1984 joined the staff of National
Public Radio's *Morning Edition* as creator of a series
of whimsical meditations.

Gilchrist excels at stories about the social
classes of the Mississippi Delta and its ruling-class
female rebel. She earned popular and critical acclaim for the friendship of Miss Crystal and her
maid, Traceleen. Crystal's flights from constrictive
gender roles widen the eyes of Traceleen, who
gawks in silence at the amorality of the southern
aristocracy. For regional womanhood Gilchrist
patterns her characters in the style of Carson
MCCULLERS, Katherine Anne PORTER, and Eudora
WELTY and sets her themes on humanistic foundations. In 1995 Gilchrist won a National Book
Award for *Rhoda: A Life in Stories,* a collection of
character studies from past books that portray
Rhoda Manning gaining in wisdom through a lifetime of wildness and selfishness. A subsequent
anthology, *Flights of Angels* (1998), explores the relationship of women to blueblood patriarchs, the big
daddies who frequent Gilchrist's writings as the
progenitors of rambunctious, unpredictable women.

Bibliography

Bauer, Margaret Donovan. *The Fiction of Ellen Gilchrist.*
    Gainesville, Fla.: University Press of Florida, 1999.
Gilchrist, Ellen. *Falling through Space.* Boston: Little,
    Brown, 1987.
———. *Flights of Angels.* Boston: Little, Brown, 1998.
———. *Rhoda: A Life in Stories.* New York: Back Bay
    Books, 1995.
Monteith, Sharon. *Advancing Sisterhood? Interracial
    Friendships in Contemporary Southern Fiction.* Athens:
    University of Georgia Press, 2001.

Gilman, Charlotte Perkins (1860–1935)

A social scientist and author of landmark feminist
fiction and nonfiction, Charlotte Anna Perkins
Gilman is one of the revered 19th-century artists
recovered in the 20th century by the Women's
Movement. With a lineage of abolitionists and suffragists, she attained literary authority in the era of
the NEW WOMAN. A less naive, more politically
astute generation of women swelled the national
labor force and acquired more spending power
after finding employment in publishing, hospitals,
food service, and factory work. Among them were
motivated women who refused to accept what the
writer Charlotte Perkins Gilman called a smothering negative.

The niece of Catharine BEECHER and Harriet
Beecher STOWE, Gilman grew up in Hartford,
Connecticut, under tenuous financial circumstances after her father, Frederick Beecher Perkins,
deserted the family. While studying at the Rhode
Island School of Design, she chose public betterment as her goal. She reprised her decision in the
fictional conflicts resolved by her heroine Delia
Morrison in the story "Three Thanksgivings"
(1909) and by Mrs. Joyce in "Martha's Mother"
(1910). Gilman achieved greatness by ignoring
Theodore Dreiser's instruction that she produce
only what editors want to publish. Instead she
wrote realistic sketches and submitted feminist essays to Emma GOLDMAN's subversive periodical
Mother Earth. In Gilman's autobiography she described her writings as social invention, the creation of human happiness.

An unhappy marriage to the painter Charles
Walter Stetson suffocated Gilman's talents and
ambitions. In 1887 her postpartum nervous breakdown required aggressive treatment. The Philadelphia neurologist Silas Weir Mitchell counseled her
on the dangers of intellectualism and recommended that she give up her career and content
herself with husband and child. The advice re-

sulted in more depression and her divorce from Stetson. She resettled with her daughter, Katherine, and her friend, Grace Ellery Channing, in Pasadena, California, and supported her family by lecturing, teaching, and writing. The author remained unmarried until correspondence with her cousin, the attorney George Houghton Gilman, produced a satisfactory pairing in 1900. They remained a couple until her self-euthanasia by chloroform during the last stages of breast cancer.

Much of Gilman's prolific canon—*The Dress of Women* (1886), *Concerning Children* (1900), *The Home: Its Work and Influence* (1903), and *The Crux* (1910)—illuminates the core of feminist concerns. In 1892 she published the short story "The YELLOW WALLPAPER," a terrifying first-person account of a woman forced into a gendered rest cure that drives her irrevocably into delusion and insanity. Six years later Gilman issued *Woman and Economics: A Study of the Economic Relation between Men and Women as a Factor in Social Evolution* (1898), an incisive survey of society's repression of women by denying them a full range of life options and meaningful outlets. The scholarly survey asserts that women are not capable of "threading of earth and sea in our vast systems of transportations, the handling of our elaborate machinery of economic development" (Gilman, 1998, 137). The reason for female ineptness is not an absence of intellect or a physical weakness in the female frame. Rather, Gilman blames "the present condition of woman, forbidding the development of this degree of economic ability" (*ibid.*, 137). She found consensus among the women of the world at the week-long International Woman's Congress of 1899, held in London, where "just plain women from anywhere, by virtue of doing something, and by reason of organization, become the guests of countesses and duchesses—if they wish; and meet with their own peers from all across the world" (Gilman, 1899, 344). In an article describing the event, she delighted in the "mobilization of women" for free speech and in the demand for coeducation of youth as well as "for peace, for abolition, for TEMPERANCE, and the international union of press clubs, of the Friends of Young Girls, the world's Y.W.C.A. [Young Woman's Christian Association], the International Order of King's Daughters, and the General Federation of Women's Clubs" (*ibid.*, 347, 349).

Gilman was adamant that a fair division of labor was the answer to women's inequitable role. In *What Diantha Did* (1910) and later in the article "The Waste of Private Housekeeping" for the July 1913 issue of *Annals of the American Academy of Political and Social Science*, she offers an alternative to individual housekeeping. In a utopian novel, *Moving the Mountain* (1911), she proposes an equitable arrangement by which cooperative labor frees women from full responsibility for infants and children. To dramatize her theory, she expounds on the hobbling of women in *The Man-Made World; or, Our Androcentric Culture* (1911), a treatise on human enterprise. Gilman expresses her dismay "that one sex should have monopolized all human activities; called them 'man's work'" (Gilman, 1970, 206). She declares that women became chattel to be traded and merchandised as property. As is that of a domestic, "the duty of the wife is held to involve man-service as well as child-service" (*ibid.*, 210). As a result of degraded domestic labor, women suffered arrested development beneath the thumb of dominant males. In 1915 Gilman became the rare female to contribute to classic utopian literature with HERLAND (1915), a female haven that generates no gender expectations. Without the coercion of androcentric government and laws or the patriarchal church, the female characters flourish in a society invigorated by equality and total freedom.

Bibliography

Gilman, Charlotte Perkins. *The Man-Made World; or, Our Androcentric Culture.* Rochester, N.Y.: Source Book Press, 1970.

———. "The Woman's Congress of 1899" (1899). Available online: URL: http://wyllie.lib.virginia.edu:8086/perl/toccer-new?id=SteWoma.sgm&images=images/modeng&data=/texts/english/modeng/parsed&tag=public&part=1&division=div. Accessed on October 13, 2005.

———. *Women and Economics.* New York: Dover, 1998.

———. *The Yellow Wallpaper and Other Writings.* New York: Bantam, 1989.

Lane, Ann J. *To Herland and Beyond: The Life and Works of Charlotte Perkins Gilman.* New York: Penguin, 1991.

Wilson, Christopher P. "Charlotte Perkins Gilman's Steady Burghers: The Terrain of Herland," *Women's Studies* 12, no. 3 (1986): 271–292.

Giovanni, Nikki (1943–)

The poet, children's writer, essayist, and teacher Yolande Cornelia "Nikki" Giovanni incorporates in her works an assertive feminism drawn from the struggles of the 1960s for black and WOMEN'S RIGHTS. Native to Knoxville, Tennessee, she grew up in the black Lincoln Heights district of Cincinnati, Ohio, and majored in fine arts, history, and literature at Fisk University, the University of Pennsylvania, and Columbia University. While teaching, she joined the civil rights movement, the beginning of her submissions of flowing, self-referencing verse to *Black Collegian, Black Dialogue, Ebony, Essence, Journal of Black Poetry,* and *Negro Digest.*

The jog and jolt of Giovanni's early verse expressed an uncompromising defiance of a white-controlled America. She self-published militant poems in *Black Feeling / Black Talk* (1968) and *Black Judgement* (1970) and honored feminist foremothers in an essay on Phillis WHEATLEY for *Gemini: An Extended Autobiographical Statement on My First Twenty-five Years of Being a Black Poet* (1971). Giovanni moved into the feminist realm with *The Women and the Men* (1975), *Cotton Candy on a Rainy Day* (1978), and *Those Who Ride the Night Wind* (1983). To interviewers she explained her concept of domestic feminism by describing how she let her son, Tommy, learn to cook eggs by wasting a few in the process. To establish a credible position on womanhood, she jettisoned the fluff that critics expected of female poets. In *Racism 101* (1994), she commanded the dreamer to commit words to paper (Giovanni, 1994, 177).

A proponent of the Black Arts Movement and of matriarchal STORYTELLING, Giovanni extends to the beleaguered female artist a manifesto of self-determination. Through personal verse in "For Saundra" (1996) and "My Poem" (1970) and debate in *A Dialogue: James Baldwin and Nikki Giovanni* (1975), she aired the frustration of trying to follow a poetic muse during an unsettled time for black Americans. In a reflective mood she wrote a personal essay, "Griots" (1994), which recalls family strands of narrative in tandem with post–World War II political dissent. The constant stream of talk in her three-generation household caused her to conclude that language is a gift and that heeding the words is a responsibility. In "Light the Candles" (1995), she expresses a mature vision of the woman as bearer of culture. The wrapping of traditions in love illustrates Giovanni's belief that affection for future generations is the prime motivation of the seasoned female artist.

Bibliography

Giovanni, Nikki. "Light the Candles," *Essence* 26, no. 1 (May 1995): 109–111.
———. *Racism 101.* New York: HarperCollins, 1994.
Lund, Elizabeth. "Poet's Challenge: Speaking in a Distinctive Voice That Elevates," *Christian Science Monitor,* 20 March 1996, p. 13.

Glasgow, Ellen (1873–1945)

The Virginia-born poet, essayist, and fiction writer Ellen Anderson Gholson Glasgow produced regional works with a strong regard for female satisfaction. Reared as a post–Civil War patrician belle in Richmond, the former capital of the Confederacy, she grew up in a male-centered Calvinist environment dominated by her father, Francis Glasgow, a pillar of the Old South. As she explains in a memoir, *The Woman Within: An Autobiography* (1954), she studied at home because of mental depression and delicate health, conditions foisted on her by overly solicitous parents. After entering genteel society at the Saint Cecilia Ball, she soon rebelled against the cloying Tidewater traditions she termed the "expiring gestures of chivalry" and launched the Equal Suffrage League of Virginia (Glasgow, 1929, ix).

Defying her iron-willed father, despite increasing deafness, the author moved to New York City and began submitting verse and short stories to *Atlantic, Harper's,* and *Scribner's* magazines. Her attempt at publishing a novel earned a sexist quip from a male editor to the "unchilded" spinster: "Go back to the South and have some babies. . . . The greatest woman is not the woman who has written the finest book, but the woman who has had the finest babies" (Glasgow, 1980, 108). Her offspring took shape in print. Beginning with a first novel, *The Descendant* (1897), she exposed the weakened condition of the only part of the United States to lose a war. From a feminist perspective she depicted male authorities in the story "A Point of Morals" (1899) as victims of their own STEREO-TYPING of the weakling female. One unenlightened male asks with complete candor, "Can a woman ever consider the ethical side of a question when the sympathetic one is visible?" (Glasgow, 1899, 982). In *The Deliverance: A Romance of the Virginia Tobacco Fields* (1904), Glasgow portrayed a more disturbing delusion—an infantile woman who dreams of restoration of the plantation South long after the Emancipation Proclamation rendered that economy impossible.

Glasgow sculpted a cast of durable, realistic characters who choose republican ideals over the exploded puffballs of the past. Her subversive novels—*Virginia* (1913), *Life and Gabriella: The Story of a Woman's Courage* (1916), and *Barren Ground* (1925)—attack the IDEAL WOMAN as a mirage created solely by and for males. In place of submissive trophy wives, Glasgow modeled intelligent, self-motivated women who take responsibility for their own happiness and who live the single, celibate life that the author enjoyed. She examined the moral and mental decline of southern manhood in "Jordan's End," an eerie tale anthologized in *The Shadowy Third and Other Stories* (1923). Told from a postsuffrage point of view, the story pictures the NEW WOMAN in the person of Mrs. Jordan, an energetic, self-defined female who suffers no qualms about murdering her spouse. In *The Battle-Ground* (1925), Glasgow exalts the assertive Betty, a precursor of Margaret MITCHELL's Scarlett O'Hara. In the closing line, Betty lends spine and valor to Dandridge "Dan" Montjoy, a shilly-shallying male: "We will begin again . . . and this time, my dear, we will begin together" (Glasgow, 1929, 444).

In the ironic style of Jane AUSTEN, Glasgow defied a male-dominated society and the DOUBLE STANDARD, the themes of feminist satire in her urban Queensborough cycle—*The Romantic Comedian* (1926), *They Stooped to Folly* (1929), and *The Sheltered Life* (1932). In the latter novel Glasgow

introduces a nine-year-old's celebr[ation of her] unique self: "I'm alive, alive, alive a[nd I'm] Blair Archibald," a chant she had su[ng] since age five (Glasgow, 1994, 4). As [the au]thor herself, the unconventional fema[le protago]nists rely on self-contentment and SISTERHOOD rather than the chancy rewards of marriage. Three years before her death of heart disease, Glasgow was awarded a Pulitzer Prize, an appropriate validation for a writer whose works outsold those of her contemporaries Willa CATHER and Edith WHARTON. After a period of neglect Glasgow's canon came into fashion again with the rise of feminism in the late 20th century.

Bibliography

Davies, Kathleen. "Spinster's Revenge: Creating a Child of One's Own," *Mississippi Quarterly* 49, no. 2 (Spring 1996): 227–239.

Glasgow, Ellen. *The Battle-Ground.* Garden City, N.Y.: Doubleday, 1929.

———. *The Deliverance: A Romance of the Virginia Tobacco Fields* (1904). Available online. URL: http://www.readbookonline.net/title/238/. Accessed on October 14, 2005.

———. "A Point of Morals" (1899). Available online: URL: http://etext.lib.virginia.edu/subjects/Women-Writers.html. Accessed on October 14, 2005.

———. *The Sheltered Life.* Charlottesville: University Press of Virginia, 1994.

———. *A Woman Within.* New York: Hill & Wang, 1980.

Goodman, Susan. *Ellen Glasgow: A Biography.* Baltimore: Johns Hopkins University Press, 1998.

Glaspell, Susan (1876–1948)

The Pulitzer Prize–winning fiction writer and playwright Susan Keating Glaspell voiced women's need to be true to their inner yearnings. The scion of Iowa pioneers, she grew up among pious evangelicals of the Davenport Christian Church. From the stories of westerners related in her youth, she drew the characteristics of Grandmother Morton, a settler in *The Inheritors* (1921), which pictures her offering a plate of cookies to a dark-eyed Indian who reciprocates with a string of fresh fish. Glaspell studied French and Greek at Drake University before reporting for and contributing stories to newspapers in Davenport and Des Moines. At age 26 she began freelancing fiction by submitting short works to *The American, Booklovers, Harper's, Leslie's,* and *Youth's Companion.* In 1903 she initiated work on a postgraduate degree in English at the University of Chicago. Six years later she completed *The Glory of the Conquered: The Story of a Great Love* (1909), her first romance.

After marrying the editor and critic George Cram Cook and settling in New York City, Glaspell summered at Cape Cod and staged her first play, *Suppressed Desires* (1915), a satiric jab at Freudian psychoanalysis through the confused patient Henrietta Brewster. A year later Glaspell wrote a masterwork, the one-act feminist play *Trifles* (1916), a melodrama of spousal abuse that results in the strangulation of the husband in his bed. Ironically, the killer bears the name of Mrs. Minnie Foster Wright, the author's bold exoneration of wives whom domestic misery diminished and drove to desperation. As a doughty neighbor, Mrs. Hale, observes to the sheriff and county attorney, "How—she—did—change" (Glaspell, 1987, 74). A string of clues suggests that after John Wright throttled his wife's canary, she halted the sifting of flour and channeled her terror and confusion into a quilt piece. Symbolically she could not decide whether to quilt it or knot it, a pun on *not it,* a subtextual reference to her dysfunctional life.

Trifles catapulted Glaspell to lasting fame. On August 8 the play premiered at the Wharf Theatre as a vehicle for the Provincetown Players, which Glaspell cofounded as a venue for such famed writers as Djuna BARNES, Louise BRYANT, Edna FERBER, Edna St. Vincent MILLAY, and Eugene O'Neill. Glaspell's concern for female coercion recurred in "Jury of Her Peers" (1917), the short story version of *Trifles* published in *Every Week.* The narrative form allowed Glaspell to comment directly on female thinking. At a significant moment in the investigation of the murder, Martha Hale notes an unusual deviation from Minnie Wright's fastidious housewifery, a poorly sewn quilt block. The item becomes a woman-to-woman message: "Holding this block made her feel queer, as if the distracted thoughts of the woman who had perhaps turned to it to try and quiet herself

were communicating themselves to her" (Glaspell, 1917, 272–273). The author ventured into a similarly troubled mind in *The Verge* (1921), an experimental psychological study of Claire Archer, an innovative amateur botanist who lapses into insanity after embracing radicalism.

After settling in Delphi, Greece, Glaspell married the poet Norman Häghem Matson. She produced *Brooke Evans* (1928), the basis for the film *The Right to Love* (1930), and chronicled the collapse of her second union in *Fugitive's Return* (1929). She earned the Pulitzer Prize at age 55 for *Alison's House* (1930), a dramatization of Genevieve Taggart's biography *The Life and Mind of Emily Dickinson* (1930). Glaspell's writing slowed considerably in 1936, when she moved to Chicago to superintend the Works Projects Administration Federal Theater Project. In 1942 she looked to the past in the novel *Norma Ashe,* in which the protagonist recognizes in young college women an ignorance of the suffragist strivings to ensure full citizenship and EDUCATION for women. The reprinting of the novel *Fidelity* (1915) by feminist fans reprised Glaspell's view of the cost of gender liberation on the first generation of New Women.

Bibliography

Glaspell, Susan. *Every Week.* New York: Crowell, 1918.

———. "A Jury of Her Peers" (1917). Available online. URL: http://etext.lib.virginia.edu/toc/modeng/public/GlaJury.html. Accessed on October 14, 2005.

———. *Plays by Susan Glaspell.* New Haven, Conn.: Cambridge University Press, 1987.

Makowsky, Veronica. *Susan Glaspell's Century of American Women: A Critical Interpretation of Her Work.* Oxford: Oxford University Press, 1993.

Rajkowska, Barbara Ozieblo. *Susan Glaspell: A Critical Biography.* Chapel Hill: University of North Carolina Press, 2000.

Glück, Louise (1943–)

The Pulitzer Prize–winning poet and essayist Louise Elisabeth Glück focuses on the essence of womanhood as revealed by disturbing, urgent glimpses of domestic life and mothering. A native of New York City, she grew up on Long Island in a literate family who encouraged reading of Greek mythology and spirited conversation. Although she cut her high school years short to treat anorexia with sessions of psychoanalysis, she completed her EDUCATION at Sarah Lawrence College and Columbia University before becoming a professional writer. As did other late 20th-century writers, she devised innovative styles and poetic techniques to escape the male-dominated field of poetry.

Under the mentorship of the literary historian Stanley Kunitz, Glück completed *Firstborn* (1968), a fledgling verse collection. Entries introduce austere, lush visions, which reveal the influence of Sylvia PLATH and Anne SEXTON. One reflective poem, "Thanksgiving," pictures Glück's mother skewering the turkey shut as the act of a mother who misses her children. Other female images fill the lines of "Nurse's Song," "The Lady in the Single," "Portrait of the Queen in Tears," "Grandmother in the Garden," and "Abishag," a lyric reverie on the young concubine who solaced the Hebrew king David in his last months. In "Bridal Piece" and "The Wound," waves of feminine imagery characterize the cost of deflowering and pregnancy. Glück followed with *The House on Marshland* (1975), which contains "All Hallows," an ambiguous image of the matriarchal figure in a FAIRY TALE setting and the cost of sowing her golden seed. Other poems in the collection—"Poem," "Japonica," "Nativity Poem," and "For My Mother"—echo the concept of female sacrifice.

Glück turned to Hebrew mythology for two series of poems. In 1976 she ended a long silence to issue *The Garden*, a pentad based on EVE, the first matriarch of the Old Testament. The familiar story advances into a human anticipation of loss and death, a controlling metaphor in her mothering scenarios. The motif returned in *The Wild Iris* (1992), in which the poet pictures Eve and her mate planting a garden that they will never see to fruition. Eve predicts that death will be a SILENCING, an end to her productivity, a concept that Glück probes in *Descending Figure* (1980).

The poet joined the faculty of Williams College in 1985. Returning to mythic figures in *Meadowlands* (1996), she pities the solitude and sadness of Penelope, wife of the Greek wanderer Odysseus.

In 2002 she reprised the form and demise of the World Trade Center's Twin Towers in "October," an introspective poem published in the *New Yorker*. She returned to the theme of the child's reliance on woman in *The Seven Ages* (2002) with "Fable," an autobiographical glimpse of her childhood, when her mother attended her sickbed. On August 29, 2003, Glück accepted the post of 12th U.S. poet laureate. The next year she won the Barnard Medal of Distinction for her contributions to poetry and classroom instruction. Among her protégés is the poet Rita DOVE, another writer and consultant to the Library of Congress.

Bibliography

Dodd, Elizabeth. *The Veiled Mirror and the Woman Poet: H. D., Louise Bogan, Elizabeth Bishop, and Louise Glück.* Columbia: University of Missouri Press, 1992.

Glück, Louise. *First Four Books of Poems.* New York: Ecco, 1990.

———. *The Seven Ages.* New York: Ecco, 2002.

———. *The Wild Iris.* New York: Ecco, 1994.

Rudnitzky, Lesi. "Darkness Visible." *Nation*, 31 May 2004, pp. 29–30.

"Goblin Market" Christina Rossetti (1862)

The Italian-English devotional poet Christina ROSSETTI's fame rests primarily on an enigmatic rescue narrative, the poem "Goblin Market," a dark, rhythmic text redolent with female sin and expiation, which was published in the book *Goblin Market and Other Poems*. Her brother, the artist and poet Dante Gabriel Rossetti, illustrated the book with grotesque, ratlike goblins and his familiar full-bodied female figures clasped in each other's arms, an indication of the themes of menace and SISTERHOOD. The cautionary tale recreates the fall of the biblical EVE in Laura's enrapturing by a cooing, purring "fruit call" that sounds "morning and evening" (Rossetti, 1994, 4). The story overthrows the male RESCUE THEME by dramatizing Lizzie's retrieval of her sister, Laura, from sinister entrapment by bestial goblins. Critics value the quest poem as an allegory on Victorian restrictions on female artists and the flesh peddling of nubile young women on the MARRIAGE MARKET.

In Keatsian profusion Rossetti draws out the seduction myth. The enticement of berries, plums, dates, grapes, and citrus fruit produces two responses from sisters who are as dissimilar as the biblical Mary and Martha. While Laura halts by a brook to listen to the goblins, Lizzie blushes and commands her sister to resist the evil charms. The two crouch close to each other, clasped sister to sister out of sight of passersby. The watery setting re-creates in imagery similar to poses that Dante painted on his woman-centered canvases. In lieu of money, Laura severs a gold tress from her head, a suggestion of the price women pay to satisfy their curiosity about forbidden trysts. Quickly she rasps her lips raw by sucking fruit juice and tosses aside empty rinds, a symbol of the evanescence of hasty sexual affairs. The price of illicit love is Laura's loss of consciousness to night and day. Even worse is the solitude that requites her sin, a metaphor suited to the ascetic Christianity that pervades Rossetti's poems.

The change in Laura is dramatic—a loss of body heat and a cessation of sweeping, tending livestock, and baking honeyed cakes. At her bedside Lizzie contemplates "Life out of death," which threatens the enchanted Laura with fever, malaise, and suppressed pulse and respiration from poisoned blood (*ibid.*, 14). Lizzie braves the fruit merchants' lair, where misshapen humanoids pelt her with juicy globes. On her return to Laura, she urges her ailing sister to lick the sweet nectar from her skin, a complex image of the eucharist and a suggestion of indulgence in oral sex and sensuality. On balance the ballad honors Lizzie, the female rescuer, for her devotion to the wayward Laura, a target of male wickedness. Critics read into the text the damning of two forms of forbidden fruit, sybaritic delights and lesbianism. In the resolution the poet consoles young women that their urge to venture into uncharted territory will decline with maturity, marriage, and motherhood.

Bibliography

Arseneau, Mary, Anthony H. Harrison, and Lorraine Jansen Kooistra, eds. *The Culture of Christina Rossetti: Female Poetics and Victorian Contexts.* Athens: Ohio University Press, 1999.

Rossetti, Christina. *The Goblin Market.* New York: Dover, 1994.

Scheinberg, Cynthia, and Gillian Beer, eds. *Women's Poetry and Religion in Victorian England: Jewish Identity and Christian Culture.* Cambridge: Cambridge University Press, 2002.

goddess lore

The advance of the female mortal to godhood is an indigenous effort to further procreation and the survival of humankind on planet Earth. The emergence of a deity from history anchors Eavan BOLAND's poem "The Making of an Irish Goddess" (1990). She examines a normal mother's flesh that carries into old age the stretch marks of child bearing. From there the female figure, as does the classic Demeter / Ceres, undergoes its transformation to the divine. The concept of goddess worship is a motif in Charlotte Perkins GILMAN's feminist utopian fantasy HERLAND (1915), in which Gilman describes it as a mother cult characterized by a maternal pantheism akin to ECOFEMINISM. The 3 million inhabitants of the mythic Herland extol Maaia, goddess of motherhood, as the progenitor of a land of women. In her honor female residents produce offspring without male assistance via parthenogenesis or virgin birth. Gilman's speculative fiction presaged more militant anti-male proposals for the human family, such as those of the social critics Andrea DWORKIN, Shulamith FIRESTONE, and Marilyn FRENCH.

The American imagist H. D. advanced goddess lore with optimistic gynocentric imagery in *Trilogy: The Walls Do Not Fall* (1944), *Tribute to the Angels* (1945), and *The Flowering of the Rod* (1946). Interweaving Babylonian, Christian, Egyptian, Greek, and Roman symbols, she summons the various faces of female godhood in Aset (another name for Isis), Astarte, the Cumaean Sibyl, Psyche, Mary Magdalene, Sancta Sophia, and the VIRGIN MARY. In 1952 the poet undertook in a three-year project the study of female heroism and divinity in an epic, *Helen in Egypt* (1955). In retort to the harpers of the ancient Mediterranean world, the poet rids Helen of blame for the Trojan War. In a lyric reverie H. D. promises peace to Helen, whom Greeks reviled. "Here there is peace / For Helena, Helen hated of all Greece" (Doolittle, 2). The poet predicts that the curse of sexual allure will eradicate the past. H. D.'s intent was to cancel the soulless view of the divine phantom female from ancient times and replace outworn images with a vigorous modernist goddess freed from womanhate.

The fantasist and mythographer Marion Zimmer BRADLEY reverences the female as fount of the regeneration of human life through conception, birth, and breast-feeding. She provides lyric passages linking all women with the powers of the universe. In introducing Druidic lore in *The Forest House* (1994), she apprentices to a priestess protagonist Eilan, who hovers at the threshold of womanhood. Breathing in the night scents of the forest, "her body moved with a rhythm both unfamiliar and completely natural, as if she had been trained to do this in some ancient past" (Bradley, 1). The instinctive communion with nature derives from her "moonblood," the monthly cycle that confers fertility much as a spring awakens the creative power of the land (*ibid.*). In a pre-Beltane ritual that is both acknowledgment of menarche and obeisance to Mother Earth, Eilan prays, "Sacred spring, you are the womb of the Goddess. As your waters cradle all life, may I bear new life into the world" (*ibid.*, 2). Bradley's unforced juncture of puberty with cosmic dynamism illustrates the feminist celebration of goddess lore for empowering womanhood.

Erica Jong shares with Bradley a reverence for the divine female that phallocentric religions have suppressed and ignored. In *Witches* (1981), Jong remarks on the Mother Goddess archetype: "She cannot be eradicated as long as man (and woman, too) is born of woman" (Jong, 17). Jong notes that all that remains of the Ishtar-Diana-Demeter triad from the eastern Mediterranean world are three disparate figures—Mother Nature, the Wicked Witch, and the VIRGIN MARY. Jong explains that women have no model for their own SEXUALITY: Mother Nature is an all-powerful spirit, the Wicked Witch is a wizened crone drawn to spells and poisons, and the Virgin Mary is a sanitized IDEAL WOMAN stripped of passion and sexuality because she conceived a god-child without sexual intercourse or knowledge of coition with the Almighty. In contrast, the ordinary female "is damned for doing the very thing that keeps the race alive" (*ibid.*, 20). Jong's text educates readers of the need for a new appraisal of womanspirit based on the criteria of prehistory.

Bibliography

Boland, Eavan. *Outside History: Selected Poems, 1980–1990.* New York: W. W. Norton, 2001.

Bradley, Marion Zimmer. *The Forest House.* New York: Roc, 1995.

Doolittle, Hilda. *Helen in Egypt.* New York: New Directions, 1974.

Jong, Erica. *Witches.* New York: Harry N. Abrams, 1999.

Golden Notebook, The Doris Lessing (1962)

Doris LESSING's autobiographical novel *The Golden Notebook* (1962) captures the post–World War II angst in the emotional swirl engulfing the writer and single parent Anna Wulf. A brilliant metafiction set in London in 1957, the five-strand narrative moves from a DIARY to a novel called *Free Women*, a notebook on Leftist politics, another on the writer's psychoanalysis, and a third containing stories derived from Wulf's coming of age in Africa and her canvassing for the Communist Party. Emotional baggage from her marriage to the unfaithful Richard inserts festering hostility toward a bourgeois adulterer. When love and sexual release return to her life in the form of an American writer in his 20s, her salvation is the golden notebook in which she collects fragments of identity and art to retrieve her mind from breakdown.

Lessing's multifaceted psychological probings connect the demise of Marxist radicalism to a time when formal feminism was in its infancy. Early on Anna states a complaint that impacted the feminist movement: "They still define us in terms of relationships with men," a subtle self-accusation for her despair about vapid male-female relationships (Lessing, 4). The hard-won candor leads the text into blind alleys and embarrassing, masochistic confessions: "I don't care a damn about politics or philosophy or anything else; all I care about is that Michael should turn in the dark and put his face against my breasts" (*ibid.*, 299). As Anna and her actor friend, Molly Jacobs, reassess their needs and priorities, the author indicates through Anna's daughter, Janet, that forward leaps in one generation often result in recoil from the next toward a safe, shallow conservatism.

The author took readers by surprise with her frank commentary on female undercurrents. She litters the dialogue with a range of intimate details—tampons, penis worries, and women's bed games to please their mates. An epiphany justifies *Free Women* as an internal title: "Every woman believes in her heart that if her man does not satisfy her she has a right to go to another" (*ibid.,* 143). Anna accepts the pathfinder's role and acknowledges that her courageous efforts at self-unification demand suffering. Her resolve takes on the stoicism of Sisyphus relentlessly shoving his boulder uphill. On a philosophical level she abandons cynicism to seek the ideal: "Humanism stands for the whole person, the whole individual" (*ibid.,* 360). Compared to James Joyce's *Ulysses* (1922), Lessing's ambitious text recognizes in Anna a voice for the discontent of the times, a posttraumatic shock that sets off waves of self-discovery as the Western world retreated from world chaos to new visions of wholeness.

Bibliography

Franko, Carol. "Authority, Truthtelling, and Parody: Doris Lessing and 'the Book,'" *Papers on Language and Literature* 31, no. 3 (Summer 1995): 255–285.

Lessing, Doris. *The Golden Notebook.* London: Michael Joseph, 1972.

Mort, Jo-Ann. Review of *The Golden Notebook, Dissent* 51, no. 3 (Summer 2004): 87–90.

Goldman, Emma (1869–1940)

A fiery socialist agitator, orator, editor, and memoirist, Emma Goldman commended women's liberation from Puritanic moral standards and from sexual and procreative enslavement. A Lithuanian Jew from Kovno, she was the unwanted female child of an antagonistic father whose authority aped that of the Russian czar. During a period of pogroms, persecution, and forced conscription of the peasantry, she studied French, literature, and music in Königsberg, Prussia, and Saint Petersburg, Russia. While living with her grandmother, Goldman took pity on women despoiled by the elite military hierarchy and by government officials. She immigrated to America with her parents at age 16, when she worked as a garment seamstress in a Rochester, New York, sweatshop. After the hanging of perpetrators of the Chicago Haymarket strike and riot in 1887, she became an anarchist. The Federal Bureau of Investigation (FBI) named her Red Emma, America's most dangerous woman. At age 23 she aided her lover, Alexander Berkman, in a foiled assassination plot against Henry Clay Frick, a strikebreaker. She was later falsely accused of assisting the Polish gunman who shot President William McKinley.

While serving a year at Blackwell's Island Penitentiary for inciting a riot, Goldman studied nursing and trained in midwifery to aid immigrant women. She traveled England and Scotland to promote birth control and free love. With earnest rhetoric in Russian, German, Yiddish, and English, she denounced marriage as an exploitation of wives. In 1906 she established *Mother Earth,* a radical periodical issued from her Harlem office. It contained literary essays by Louise BRYANT, Voltairine DE CLEYRE, Charlotte Perkins GILMAN, Margaret SANGER, and Mary WOLLSTONECRAFT. Goldman's most perceptive articles were "The Traffic in Women" and "Marriage and Love," both published in 1910. The former accounts for the sexual solicitation of factory girls, who had no entertainment but the street. The second essay charges the church and state with curtailing women's access to birth control information and with offering no other outlet for female love than the corrupt institution of marriage. She kept the subversive magazine in circulation for 11 years despite the condemnation of the postmaster general, who found its content treasonous. In 1918 federal agents subpoenaed Goldman's subscription list of 8,000 readers and began an investigation of their ties to Bolshevism.

Despite support for WOMEN'S RIGHTS, mothers, and family planning, Goldman's active publication of anarchism helped to revile her name as the era's most feared and hated iconoclast. She compiled her lectures from the early 20th century in *Anarchism and Other Essays* (1911), in which she supports woman SUFFRAGE and exonerates women who turn to PROSTITUTION as their only source of income. In *The Social Significance of the Modern Drama* (1914), she expressed her regard for the Norwegian playwright Henrik Ibsen, author of *A DOLL'S HOUSE* (1879), the first work of feminist theater. In 1919 federal authorities deported Goldman to Russia for violation of anti–birth control laws and for support of draft dodgers during World War I. She wrote an autobiography, *Living My Life* (1931), which reflects her pacifism, disillusion with Bolshevism, and loyalty to women's issues. During the Spanish civil war she and her fellow feminist, Rebecca WEST, joined the Committee to Aid Homeless Spanish Women and Children. Goldman's forthright values influenced the writings of the socialist Meridel LE SUEUR.

Bibliography

Chalberg, John. *Emma Goldman: American Individualist.* Harlow, England: Pearson Education, 1997.

Goldman, Emma. *Anarchism and Other Essays* (1911). Available online. URL: http://arthursclassicnovels. com/arthurs/women/nrcsm10.html. Accessed on October 14, 2005.

———. *Living My Life.* New York: Dover, 1930.

———. "Victims of Morality." (1913). Available online. URL: http://www.positiveatheism.org/hist/goldman-mor.htm. Accessed on October 14, 2005.

Greenland, Cyril. "Dangerous Women—Dangerous Ideas," *Canadian Journal of Human Sexuality* 11, no. 3/4 (2002): 179–186.

Gone with the Wind Margaret Mitchell (1936)

The journalist Margaret Mitchell earned phenomenal popularity after her publication of *Gone with the Wind,* the world's top-selling romance. Although fastidious literary critics dismissed the work as sentimental melodrama, it presented to a receptive public the author's view of Negro womanhood and Southern class differences before, during, and after the Civil War. During the rise of gynocriticism discussion of Mitchell's skill at creating fictional female archetypes began reversing the trend begun by academic snobs. New readings negated criticism that discounted the ordinary female fans near the end of the Great Depression who thrived on a hopeful message. A contribution to women's history,

Mitchell's wartime set pieces, drawn on the wartime model of William Makepeace Thackeray's *Vanity Fair* (1848), delineate the female boundaries of Old Guard Atlanta. At the peak of social prominence are the pampered beauties sired by landowners such as Gerald O'Hara and John Wilkes. Superintending youthful social events are the obligatory female dragons—Dolly Meade, Fanny Elsing, Maybelle Meriwether, and Aunt Pittypat Hamilton, the scatterbrained elitist who recites a family DYNASTY that extends its tentacles over Georgia society.

In a tightly controlled milieu the uninhibited Scarlett O'Hara, somewhat like Thackeray's selfish parvenu Becky Sharp, becomes a social pariah for anticipating the war era's dissolution of patriarchal regulations. With unladylike daring Scarlett displays her decolletage in midafternoon and eats barbecue with a perky appetite rather than nibbling like a bird. As war advances on Georgia, she nurses the sick and wounded soldiers housed in Atlanta's makeshift military hospital. Before delivering the baby of her sister-in-law, Melanie Wilkes, her rival and a mirror image of Thackeray's Amelia Sedley, Scarlett hears the dictum of Dr. Mead, a wise observer of women, "You seem to be a young woman of common sense, so spare me your blushes. . . . I don't want to hear of you going home, either" (Mitchell, 321). Mead's astute summation of Scarlett's courage precedes a string of audacious acts, including her assumption of control over Tara and the shooting of a Union straggler and would-be rapist. Mitchell approves her heroine's spunk for "blowing a man's face to a pulp and then burying him in a hastily scratched-out hole!" (*ibid.,* 438). At a telling moment with her second husband, merchant Frank Kennedy, Scarlett depends on her vivid imagination to cover for an ungenteel visit to the makeshift jail: "Mary, Mother of God, let me think of a real good lie" (*ibid.,* 586). Beyond Mitchell's humor is the author's intent to design an admirable female capable of venturing forth, then retreating to the safe zone of decent womanhood. Scarlett's chutzpah extends to marrying for money to save the plantation, a coup she manages by deceiving and snagging Kennedy, who is already betrothed to her sister, Suellen.

Mitchell's main strength as a feminist author lies in her portrayal of the tense relationship of

Scarlett with her upper-crust mother, Ellen Robillard O'Hara, the Catholic moralist and supervisor of labor at Tara, and with Mammy, the human bulwark who stabilizes the family after Scarlett's parents die. A manipulative minx, Scarlett allows narcissism to run amok in the ruins of postwar Atlanta, but she never escapes memories of her mother's high-toned discipline or the disapproving snorts and rolling eyes of Mammy, her former nursemaid and duenna. Contributing to Scarlett's break with antebellum decorum is her emergence as a NEW WOMAN capable of financial dealings with carpetbaggers and Yankee oppressors. Paralleling Scarlett's moneymaking scheme to operate a sawmill with contract prison labor and to sell lumber to despised interlopers is the business acumen of another New Woman, Belle Watling, Atlanta's prize madam, who is equally disdainful of overly mannered relations between ladies and gentlemen. Melanie, a softer touch, surprises the assembled ladies of Atlanta with a winsome lie to save the menfolk from arrest for rousting out former slaves, the postwar homeless living in shanties outside polite society.

For its vivid portrayal of racial and class divisions, Mitchell's resilient novel continues to spark controversy. In 1992 the estate of Margaret Mitchell sanctioned the publication of *Scarlett*, a poorly plotted melodrama written by Alexandra Ripley that expands the story with gun-running, Fenian plots in Ireland and Boston, Scarlett's fornication with the perverse Lord Fenton, and her trial in London for stabbing him to death in her bed. Two years after the sequel's publication, Joanne Whalley and Timothy Dalton starred in the roles of Scarlett and Rhett in a colorful television miniseries with Esther Rolle in a brief deathbed appearance as Mammy.

In retort to Mitchell's racism in picturing Georgia slaves as simple-witted darkies and the Ku Klux Klan as gentlemen defending their womenfolk, the Detroit-born author Alice Randall parodied *Gone with the Wind* through the eyes of the mulatto slave Cynara, the protagonist of *The Wind Done Gone* (2001). As the black alter ego of Scarlett, Cynara presents a less genteel version of the New Woman. She describes her sale in the Charleston battery followed by a "time of shawl-fetch slavery" (Randall, 4). Justifying Randall's

anger at Mitchell are such racist lines in *Gone with the Wind* as Tony Fontaine's justification of murdering the former Tara overseer, Jonas Wilkerson, for "[having] the gall—the— . . . to say niggers had a right to—to—white women" (Mitchell, 637). Contributing to the humor of Randall's parody is the fact that Cynara, the protagonist, is Mammy's daughter sired by the planter, in a practice that permeated Southern SLAVERY. The ribaldry of Randall's book enraged Mitchell's relatives, who blocked publication of *The Wind Done Gone*. The case concluded in federal court with an overturn of a lower court decision to suppress the parody.

Bibliography

Mitchell, Margaret. *Gone with the Wind*. New York: Time Warner, 1964.

Pyron, Darden Ashbury. *Recasting:* Gone with the Wind *in American Culture*. Miami: Florida International University, 1983.

Randall, Alice. *The Wind Done Gone*. Boston: Houghton Mifflin, 2001.

Good Earth, The Pearl Buck (1931)

Pearl BUCK, an American novelist brought up in China, stressed the fears and superstitions of Chinese peasants in the saga *The Good Earth* (1931), winner of a Pulitzer Prize. To augment the gravity of her story, she tells it in quasi-biblical narrative style. Focused on the life of Wang Lung, a peasant farmer in Anhwei province, and on the example of his greedy father, uncle, and nephew, the novel stresses the selfish regard for male wants and preferences. After Wang rises from smallholder to man of wealth, pride overcomes his judgment. The author notes the importance of females to family status: "Men mentioned with envy the women in his inner court; it was as though men spoke of a rare jewel or an expensive toy that was useless except that it was sign and symbol of a man who . . . could spend his money on joy" (Buck, 154).

Buck stresses the role of women in the pervasive discontent that prevents Wang from attaining happiness. At the heart of the conflict is his exclusion of his wife from an equal share in marriage and family. In hard times couples who had unwanted girls turned them into profit by selling them as household servants or concubines to the rich. At the House of Hwang, Wang easily locates one of these unfortunates, O-lan, a potential bride in his price range. He heeds the admonition of his aged father, who warns against buying a pretty female: "She will be forever thinking about clothes to go with her face! . . . Moreover, who has heard of a pretty slave who was virgin in a wealthy house?" (*ibid.*, 6). Wang's matter-of-fact transaction dramatizes the lowly place of women in imperial China. As though discussing a purchase of livestock, the two men ready the house for the addition of a woman as household menial, field laborer, and bearer of sons. The author enhances O-lan's lowliness by viewing her, silent and submissive, as she walks behind Wang on the way to her new home.

Buck, a crusader for orphans, stresses the gendered nature of China's regard for small children. Men who blame the mothers for producing only girl babies can avenge their frustration by beating, scalding, banishing, or even murdering a woman who bears no sons. The action emphasizes that married couples who conceive too many females resort to routine strangulation or suffocation of unwanted newborns or to the sale of girls into bondage. Such sales or selective infanticides limit the family's financial burdens of rearing girls and of pledging dowries to their future husbands. When Wang locates of O-lan, he learns from the great lady who owns her that the girl's parents sold her in Shantung in a year of famine. Because of Wang's lack of interest in his wife's past, Buck withholds until late in the novel O-lan's personal account of a pitiful girlhood. The disclosure suggests that O-lan has much to tell, but no opportunity to put her story into words.

The novel applies a bald contrast between Wang's wife and his mistress, whom he purchases from a teahouse. O-lan makes savvy commentary on finances and farm matters, locates a cache of jewels in a rich man's house during a riot, and gives birth without fuss, causing her husband to remark, "She was a woman such as is not commonly found" (*ibid.*, 26). Buck speaks impersonally about the difference between his healthy desire for his wife "as a beast for its mate" and the gnawing ache that drives him to Lotus, a sly courtesan with tiny

hands and feet and no skill other than pleasuring him in bed (*ibid.*, 131). The only tears O-lan sheds are the result of Wang's theft of two pearls, her only personal possessions, which he gives to Lotus. After a cancer weakens O-lan, he experiences his own bout of weeping in the darkened kitchen, an appropriate spot that had been her main domicile, even during her wedding reception, when she slept in the straw by the family ox. In delirium during protracted illness she mutters, "Well I know I am ugly and cannot be loved" (*ibid.*, 186). After her death Wang vacates their marriage bed to avoid thoughts of her purple-lipped corpse, but his mind clasps images of her loyalty. Buck implies that his conscience is late to form, but no less insistent in its punishment of his disregard for females.

Contributing to the absence of peace in Wang's life are his obsession with Lotus and his lack of concern for his female dependents. After he beats his mistress to end her perpetual whining and demands, he retreats to his old farmhouse and adds Pear Blossom, a young bed warmer, to his household. Buck depicts his love for his retarded daughter, his "poor little fool," as a fondness similar to love for a pet (*ibid.*, 114). As his own life approaches its end, he purchases poison to save her from neglect: "And well I know that no one will trouble when I am gone to feed her or to bring her out of the rain and the cold of winter or to set her in the summer sun" (*ibid.*, 254). The late-in-life sentiment partially redeems a man whose patriarchal line has traditionally disparaged women as sex objects and adjuncts to the good life. At his decline his sons smile wantonly over his head as they plot their own self-centered future. Buck gets ironic mileage from the fact that Wang's sons desert him, but Pear Blossom remains faithful.

Bibliography

Buck, Pearl. *The Good Earth.* New York: Pocket Books, 1975.

Conn, Peter. *Pearl S. Buck: A Cultural Biography.* Cambridge: Cambridge University Press, 1996.

Goodman, Ellen (1941–)

A Pulitzer Prize–winning columnist in more than 400 newspapers, Ellen Holtz Goodman provides thought-provoking updates on feminist issues. The daughter of a politically active family in Newton, Massachusetts, she grew up in affluence. After earning a degree in European history from Radcliffe College, she joined the staff of *Newsweek*. She recalled, "In those days, women were hired as researchers and men were hired as writers . . . and that was that" (Goodman, "Women Still," 9A). She quickly moved on to report for the *Detroit Free Press*. By age 26 she found a comfortable long-term post at the *Boston Globe*. She later remarked on the impetus to her writing: "What I write about— values, relationships, women's issues, families, change—[had not] been taken 'seriously' by the newspaper world" (Goodman, 1981, vii). To brush up on the dynamics of social change, she enrolled at Harvard for postgraduate study as a Nieman Fellow.

Goodman won readers to her syndicated op-ed pieces by stating earnest convictions about world events and by relating her opinions on the common ground where public and private lives meet. In her first book, *Turning Points* (1979), she commented on late 20th-century demands on women. She issued collections of columns in *Close to Home* (1979), *At Large* (1981), *Keeping in Touch* (1985), *Making Sense* (1989), and *Value Judgments* (1993). With Patricia O'Brien she coauthored a best seller, *I Know Just What You Mean: The Power of Friendship in Women's Lives* (2000), and followed with *Paper Trail: Common Sense in Uncommon Times* (2004), which ranges over such issues as threats against ABORTION clinics, child abduction, Afghani women's sufferings under the Taliban, and domestic violence. Goodman's fresh approach to issues such as WOMEN'S RIGHTS keep her columns relevant, especially during the war in Afghanistan when she wrote about Lt. Col. Martha McSally, who had to wear a long black *abaya* in public, forgo driving a car, and venture out only in the company of males. During the brouhahas preceding George W. Bush's reelection, Goodman commiserated with political wives. She declared that it is "easier to be judged for yourself than to have every move you make, every breath you take, calibrated for its effect on your husband" (Goodman, "Life of," 3P). Her constructive commentary has earned the American Society of Newspaper Edi-

tors Distinguished Writing Award, a Hubert H. Humphrey Civil Rights Award from the Leadership Conference on Civil Rights, a Lyndhurst Prize, an American Woman Award, and the International Matrix Award from the Association for Women in Communications.

Bibliography

Goodman, Ellen. *At Large*. New York: Fawcett Crest, 1981.

———. "The Life of a Political Wife: Who Wants It?" *Charlotte Observer*, 25 July 2004, p. 3P.

———. "Women Still Fight for Rights," *Charlotte Observer*, 26 June 2004, p. 9A.

Hetter, Katia, and Dorian Friedman. "The Animating Role of Women's Pundits." *U.S. News and World Report*, 7 August 1995, pp. 33–34.

Gordimer, Nadine (1923–)

The South African fiction writer, scenarist, and human rights activist Nadine Gordimer views political and social shifts through the disrupted lives of women. She was born to Anglo-Lithuanian Jewish immigrants escaping pogroms. In early childhood she left her native town of Springs in Transvaal to attend school at the all-white Convent of Our Lady of Mercy. A rapid heart rate forced her to study at home with tutors and to read at the whites-only library rather than to enjoy dancing, which she preferred. At age 15 she published a short piece and continued submitting stories about colonial South Africa and the rigors of apartheid to *Atlantic*, *Critical Arts Journal*, *Harper's*, the *New Yorker*, and *Yale Review*. Of her submission to a racist father she later mused, "I cannot understand why I did not free myself in the most obvious way, leave home and small town and get a job somewhere" (Temple-Thurston, 3).

Saving Gordimer from her parents' racism were numerous friendships among activists and artists in Sophiatown. It was her own emergence as a writer that stripped her of white superiority and sent her "falling, falling through the surface of the South African way of life" (*ibid.*). After a year's study at the University of Witwatersrand she wrote a semiautobiographical novel, *The Lying Days* (1953), and for the next half-century, she created collections of short fiction—*Face to Face: Short Stories* (1949), *Friday's Footprint* (1960), *Something Out There* (1985), *Selected Stories* (1975), *Crimes of Conscience* (1991), and *Loot and Other Stories* (2003). Because of her election to remain in black Africa, she championed WOMEN'S RIGHTS, but felt out of place in the American Women's Movement because of its dominance by the white middle class.

While the issue of apartheid dominated South African literature, Gordimer portrayed the harsh separation of races and its impact on pregnant teens, interracial love and miscegenation, and the relationships of mothers with daughters. Her earnest depiction of human lives won her a Booker Prize for *The Conservationist* (1974) and triggered the banning of *Burger's Daughter* (1979). The latter is the compelling story of a naif, 14-year-old Rosemarie Burger, an Afrikaner who takes an adult place in the family after her father's death in prison and her mother's detainment by the authorities. In 1990 Gordimer validated the black woman's centrality to issues of gender and race in *My Son's Story*. When bigotry pushes Johannesburg blacks into action, the heroine, Aila, claims her space with the cry "My turn, now" (Gordimer, 1990, 233). The following year Gordimer earned the Nobel Prize for being what some critics term the literary conscience of South Africa.

Bibliography

Gordimer, Nadine. *Burger's Daughter.* London: Penguin, 1980.

———. *My Son's Story.* London: Penguin, 1990.

Head, Dominic. *Nadine Gordimer.* Cambridge: Cambridge University Press, 1991.

Knox, Alice. "No Place Like Utopia: Cross-Racial Couples in Nadine Gordimer's Later Novels," *Ariel* 27, no. 1 (January 1996): 63–80.

Temple-Thurston, Barbara. *Nadine Gordimer Revisited.* New York: Twayne, 1999.

Gordon, Caroline (1895–1981)

The Kentucky-born critic and fiction writer Caroline Ferguson Gordon expressed low-key feminism in her stories and novels about female survivors. Educated in the Classics at Merry Mont in the Todd County farmhouse where she was born, she learned regional STORYTELLING from informal porch sessions. She studied at her father's Classical School for Boys in Clarksville, Tennessee, and earned a teaching degree from Bethany College. From high school teaching she moved on to reporting society events for the *Chattanooga News*. Although always an outsider, she was influenced by the Fugitive Agrarian critical school, led by Allen Tate, whom she married. While she lived in Paris, she published her first short sketch, wrote for the *Transatlantic Review*, and began a genealogical romance, *Penhally* (1931). She later taught in the English Department of Women's College of the University of North Carolina and wrote textbooks on the analysis of verse and fiction.

As did her contemporaries, the authors Ellen GLASGOW and Katherine Anne PORTER, Gordon stressed themes of moral and material deterioration in the South. In some of her works, particularly the novels *The Women on the Porch* (1944), a southern version of Eurydice's departure from Orpheus, and *The Malefactors* (1956), which she based on the life of the Catholic activist Dorothy Day, she chose as protagonists tough women. Patterning her fiction on the CAPTIVITY NARRATIVE of Mary White ROWLANDSON and subsequent kidnap victims, Gordon composed a frontier tale, "The Captive," anthologized in *The Forest of the South* (1945). The plight of Jinny Wiley begins with the seizure and bashing of her children with tomahawks as the elder Crowmocker and Mad Dog force the mother and her suckling babe onto the trail toward a Shawnee hideout. Surviving grief, exhaustion, and raw feet, Jinny follows a brave from whose belt swings the blonde-haired scalp of her daughter, Sadie. Gordon implies that Jinny is in danger of rape by Mad Dog, who leers at her along the way. Gordon demonizes him by describing the black and red paint on his face and calls him "A devil. A devil come straight from hell to burn and murder" (Gordon, *Collected Stories*, 176). At a huge cave phallic rattlesnake images arise from a peeled elm, symbols of the male domination and sexual menacing of captive white women.

Gordon expresses the value of women to Indians on the frontier as trade items. Validating her work is Crowmocker's snatch of a buckskin sack of brooches in exchange for Jinny. Without sympathy he turns away and leaves her to the younger man. Feminism overtakes the plot at the point when Jinny accepts responsibility for her own survival. Following flowing streams downhill to the settlement, she arrives on the opposite shore from the blockhouse. The suspenseful rafting across to the fort within sight of pursuers contributes to the heroism of Jinny, who achieves her own reclamation. The story has earned frequent anthologizing for its recreation of her frontier vigor and determination.

Bibliography

Gordon, Caroline. *The Collected Stories of Caroline Gordon*. Nashville, Tenn.: J. S. Sanders, 2000.
———. *The Women on the Porch*. Nashville, Tenn.: J. S. Sanders, 2000.
Jonza, Nancylee Novell. *The Underground Stream: The Life and Art of Caroline Gordon*. Athens: University of Georgia Press, 1995.

Gothic fiction

The alliance of Gothic conventions with female characters originally derived from prurient interest in women as captives or victims of overpowering evil. Unlike realistic human beings, female characters tended to be swooners and hand wringers or wailing wraiths such as LA LLORONA. The market for late 18th-century Gothic pulp fiction and bestselling novels welcomed female freelancers, who were quick studies of the female-littered landscapes in vampire and horror scenarios. Two of the most prominent, Charlotte SMITH, author of *Emmeline, the Orphan of the Castle* (1788), and Ann RADCLIFFE, creator of *The Mysteries of Udolpho* (1794) and *The Italian; or, the Confessional of the Black Penitents* (1797), were the most successful of the many women who wrote blood-and-thunder tales to earn quick cash to support their family. Centuries after the emergence of Gothic sensationalism, the atmosphere of secrecy and the possibility of lurid disclosures kept the genre afloat as short story, horror novel, murder and detective play, and slasher film. The critic Judith Halberstam, author of *Skin Shows: Gothic Horror and the Technology of Monsters* (1995), typified the Gothic mode as cloaking the sins of promiscuity, female

madness, and illegitimacy, three themes that Maxine Hong KINGSTON's *The Woman Warrior* (1976) conjoins as the causes of an unnamed aunt's plunge down a well with her base-born babe. To the family the woman's death became a cautionary tale to young girls about the price of fornication.

A literary development in the Gothic mode, domestic Gothic is the gynocentric terror fiction that crossbreeds sensationalism and the refined horrors of Radcliffean novels with the epistolary novel, the novel of manners, and sentimental fiction. The intent of domestic Gothic is an exploration of the ways women search for identity and liberate themselves from social and marital containment. One of the classic female Gothic heroines, Emily BRONTË's Catherine EARNSHAW, protagonist of *WUTHERING HEIGHTS* (1847), shocked the Victorian reader with her preference for Heathcliff, her Gypsy lover, over the effete Edgar Linton, her lawful husband. Because Catherine rejects Edgar's paternal control of her life, she sets the example for rebellion against the stifling 19th-century marriage model, a paradigm established by Queen Victoria. Catherine's punishment lends cachet to the Gothic action after she takes her outsized passion to the grave. The novel turns into a haunting of the moors by a female spirit whose desires give her no peace in the afterlife.

By the 1860s domestic Gothic burgeoned with violent cityscapes during the shift to gaslight fiction, which abandoned haunted castles in favor of such urban crime and domestic chaos topics as murdered wives, blackmail, adultery, and bigamy. At the forefront of the new Gothic subgenre were the works of the novelist Mary Elizabeth BRADDON, who described the trickery of the MARRIAGE MARKET, an abstract form of incarceration in *The Lady's Mile* (1866). An American proponent, Louisa May ALCOTT, depicted in "A Whisper in the Dark" (1863) the loveless wedlock of the heiress Sybil, whose husband confines her to a madhouse. From her cell she hears the soothing voice of her mother, who redirects her daughter's frantic thoughts from rescue to self-reclamation. In 1879 the Norwegian dramatist Henrik Ibsen carried domestic Gothic toward realism with his play *A DOLL'S HOUSE*, a story of forgery and blackmail that ends the marriage of Torvald Helmer, the obsessive banker who drives his wife, Nora, to desperation and flight from home and children.

A more positive depiction of women is the theme of female Gothic, a subset of the Gothic genre that relieves women of cringing, cowering stereotypes and frees them to use logic and guile to extricate themselves from patriarchal control or endangerment by stalkers or villains. In *Literary Women* (1977) the feminist critic Ellen MOERS coined the term *female Gothic* as a label for woman-liberating Gothic literature in which female writers redirect claustrophobic elements as symbols of women's circumscribed lives. In *The True Story of the Novel* (1996), the critic Margaret Anne Doody explained the use of female Gothic as a podium from which to "[accuse] the 'real world' of falsehood and deep disorder" (Fleenor, 13). From this inversion of men's voyeuristic Gothicism arose the feminist works of Radcliffe, Gertrude ATHERTON, the Brontës, Harriet Beecher STOWE, and Daphne DU MAURIER. These authors illustrate by tone their denunciation of voyeuristic images of scantily clad heroines in distress. Instead female Gothic writers commiserate with the fettered female or the heroine suppressed by the misogyny of church or state. The motif elevates Eliza, the escaping slave of Stowe's abolitionist melodrama *UNCLE TOM'S CABIN* (1851–52), and ends the diffidence of the unnamed second Mrs. de Winter, heroine of Du Maurier's *REBECCA* (1938).

The struggle for domestic control tends to set female Gothic on home turf, as at Thornfield, Edward Rochester's mansion in Charlotte BRONTË's *JANE EYRE* (1847), and at Manderley, the seaside estate in *Rebecca*. The critic Kate Ferguson Ellis, author of *The Contested Castle* (1989), describes how male Gothic imprisons female characters in home territory, usurps property from the female inheritor, or exiles the rebellious wife or daughter from the household. In contrast female Gothic restores the female to the misappropriated home. The historical and critical parameters of female Gothic engird the work of the authors Christina ROSSETTI, Mary Wollstonecraft SHELLEY, Charlotte SMITH, and Mary WOLLSTONECRAFT. Under the criteria of female Gothic, protagonists such as the wife in Charlotte Perkins GILMAN's "The YEL-LOW WALLPAPER" (1892) feel trapped in confining social roles and seek as outlets SISTERHOOD, adventure, satisfaction of intellectual curiosity, or artistic expression. These involvements that follow the bursting of cells retain their significance in 20th-century works, notably in flight from house arrest in Margaret ATWOOD's dystopic novel *The HANDMAID'S TALE* (1985) and in the recovered slave lore in Toni MORRISON's *BELOVED* (1987), a "rememory" of the tight-packed slave hold during the Middle Passage and the servitude of female breeders on Southern plantations.

Additional masters of female Gothic include the Caribbean and Latin American authors Isabel ALLENDE, Maryse CONDÉ, Laura ESQUIVEL, and Jean RHYS, all producers of best-selling female-centered fiction. Allende explored the Hispanic conquest of mestizo females in *La casa de los espíritus* (*The HOUSE OF THE SPIRITS*, 1981). Condemning Esteban Trueba to a life of loneliness and despair is his rape of Pancha García, who recognizes the long tradition of interracial sexual violation—that "before her, her mother—and before her, her grandmother—had suffered the same animal fate" (Allende, 57). Esquivel's fablelike novel *Like Water for Chocolate* (1989) enacts the restriction of Tita de la Garza to the kitchen in service to her mother, Mama Elena, a Mexican dominatrix who demands that Tita remain unmarried. Cursed by lovelessness and the longing for sexual fulfillment and motherhood, Tita compensates with inspired recipes that feed her family, guests, and her infant niece and nephew. When the home scene grows too callous for Tita to endure, she retreats to a dovecote "naked, her nose broken, her whole body covered with pigeon droppings . . . and curled up in a fetal position," the beginning of her rebirth as a whole woman (Esquivel, 97). Rhys portrays male coercion and crazy making in the psychological novel *WIDE SARGASSO SEA* (1966), a similar setting of confinement and enforced behavior that triggers the insanity of Antoinette Cosway Rochester, an island beauty. As a prequel to *Jane Eyre*, Rhys's novel accounts for the renaming of Antoinette as Bertha Rochester and for her mad cries from an upstairs room at Thornfield hall, where she dreams of the warm Sun and uninhibited passion of Jamaica. Into the late 20th and early 21st centuries women's search for INDEPEN-DENCE and artistic recognition pervaded female Gothic writings, as in parental and marital restraint in Atwood's *The Blind Assassin* (2001), the BEAUTY AND THE BEAST retellings of Angela CARTER, the reliving of slave women's nightmares in Octavia BUTLER's time-tripping novel *Kindred* (1979), and the dramatist Marsha NORMAN's *'night, Mother* (1982), a two-actor psychodrama that pits daughter against spiteful mother in a conversation that concludes with the daughter's freeing herself from domestic misery with one shot of a pistol.

Bibliography

Allende, Isabel. *The House of the Spirits.* New York: Bantam, 1986.

Atwood, Margaret. *Strange Things: The Malevolent North in Canadian Literature.* Oxford: Clarendon Press, 1995.

Carnell, Jennifer. *The Literary Lives of Mary Elizabeth Braddon.* Hastings, England: Sensation Press, 2000.

Ellis, Kate Ferguson. *The Contested Castle: Gothic Novels and the Subversion of Domestic Ideology.* Urbana: University of Illinois Press, 1989.

Esquivel, Laura. *Like Water for Chocolate.* New York: Anchor Books, 1992.

Fleenor, Juliann E., ed. *The Female Gothic.* Montreal: Eden Press, 1983.

Halberstam, Judith. *Skin Shows: Gothic Horror and the Technology of Monsters.* Durham, N.C.: Duke University Press, 1995.

Keyser, Elizabeth Lennox. *Whispers in the Dark: The Fiction of Louisa May Alcott.* Knoxville: University of Tennessee Press, 1993.

Moers, Ellen. *Literary Women.* New York: Oxford University Press, 1977.

Grand, Sarah (1854–1943)

Sarah Grand, England's matriarch of feminist fiction writers, encouraged the evolving NEW WOMAN to revolt against the confinement of patriarchal marriage. Born Frances Elizabeth Bellenden Clarke in Donaghadee, Ireland, she was the daughter of English parents, Margaret Bell Sherwood and Edward John Bellenden Clarke, a coast guard lieutenant who died in 1861. After his wife and five children moved to Yorkshire, in 1868 Sarah produced mediocre grades in two English boarding schools, one that locked up women as inmates and the other teaching only charm and husband hunting. Two years later she wed Surgeon-Major David Chambers McFall, a 39-year-old officer of the Royal Irish Fusiliers, a widower and father of two.

The author regretted that science and factories offered no purposeful work for the unmarried woman, who at one time baked and spun, wove and sewed, pickled and preserved, and concocted kitchen pharmaceuticals and cosmetics. Grand hoped that her fiction would help idle, unchallenged women improve by "[throwing] off all the silliness and hysterical feebleness of her sex" (Richardson, 228). From submitting articles and short stories to the *Woman at Home* she advanced to writing novels. She began with *Ideala* (1888), a New Woman fiction praised by the feminist critic Margaret OLIPHANT for describing a hapless girl who contracts syphilis and becomes insane. As a result of public reception of Grand's work, she altered her identity to Madame Sarah Grand. With the proceeds of early publications she abandoned her family, resettled in London, and completed a study of adultery in *A Domestic Experiment* (1891). She wrote a second best seller, *The Heavenly Twins* (1893), an early polemic on the DOUBLE STANDARD, venereal disease, character formation, and the need for women's liberation from dysfunctional Victorian wedlock. Of the stagnation of married women in chapter 1, Grand observes of Mrs. Caudle's lack of initiative: "Had she gone out and amused herself with other wives similarly situated, and had tobacco and beer, if she liked them, every evening, it would have been better for herself and her husband" (Grand, 1893). Grand's willingness to blame women for their own boredom exhibits a late Victorian reevaluation of women's need to advance feminist causes.

Grand's experiences with a pub-hopping father and a husband who treated streetwalkers for syphilis form the core of *The Beth Book: A Study in the Life of Elizabeth Caldwell McClure, a Woman of Genius* (1897), a best-selling denunciation of male dominance of social and political debate and a call for women's right to education, independence, and meaningful work. The story champions the female's need of a profitable trade, privacy in the management of her personal funds and correspondence, and control of her love life. Beth, the redoubtable protagonist, protests the inequities of female life. In reference to the Bible she rejects the cruelty, servitude, and gendered social order of the Old Testament and explains, "I do not say there is no God; I only say this is not God—this blood-lover, this son-slayer, this blind omniscience, this impotent omnipotence, this merciful cruelty, this meek arrogance, this peaceful combatant" (Grand, 1980, 500). After marrying the smug, deceitful Dr. Dan McClure, Beth wearies of their marital rut and ponders "a sad majority of wives whose attitude towards their husbands must be one of contemptuous toleration" (*ibid.*, 353). In addition to writing novels and serving the city of Bath as a six-term mayor, Grand supported radical females through membership in the Women Writer's Suffrage League and the National Council of Women.

Bibliography

Bogiatzis, Demetris. "Sexuality and Gender: 'The Interlude' of Sarah Grand's 'The Heavenly Twins,'" *English Literature in Transition 1880–1920* 44, no. 1 (Winter 2001): 46–63.

Grand, Sarah. *The Beth Book.* New York: Dial Press, 1980.

———. *The Heavenly Twins* (1893). Available online. URL: http://www.gutenberg.org/etext/8676. Accessed on October 14, 2005.

Jusova, Iveta. "Imperialist Feminism: Colonial Issues in Sarah Grand's 'The Heavenly Twins' and 'The Beth Book,'" *English Literature in Transition 1880–1920* 43, no. 3 (Summer 2000): 298–315.

Richardson, Angelique. "The Eugenization of Love: Sarah Grand and the Morality of Genealogy," *Victorian Studies* 42, no. 2 (Winter 1999): 227–255.

Greer, Germaine (1939–)

A powerful provocateur for feminist thought, the Australian critic, orator, and journalist Germaine Greer remains on top of cultural and economic issues that affect women's lives and choices. Born in Melbourne, she detested her lowbrow family and twice ran away from home, a fact she dramatizes in the autobiographical novel *Daddy We Hardly Knew You* (1989). She studied at Star of the Sea Convent and majored in British drama and French at the University of Melbourne and at the University of Sydney. On scholarship to Newnham College, Cambridge, she completed a doctoral thesis, "The Ethics of Love and Marriage in Shakespeare's Early Comedies." In addition to lecturing on Elizabethan and Jacobean drama, she wrote articles for *Esquire, Harper's, Lancet, Listener, Oz, Rolling Stone, Spectator,* and the *London Sunday Times,* some of which she collected in *The Madwoman's Underclothes: Essays and Occasional Writings* (1986). The topics range from GENDER POLITICS to female desire, seduction, ABORTION, contraception, and the treatment of women by the medical profession.

After departing her homeland, Greer taught in Oklahoma and lectured in England and Italy. At age 31 she wrote a landmark social document, *The Female Eunuch* (1970), which chronicles women's devitalization by STEREOTYPING. Authorized as a handbook of the second wave by leaders of the women's movement, the text advocates sexual and personal liberation as the energizer that 20th-century women needed to rid them of ennui, anger, and depression. Her subsequent feminist works include *The Obstacle Race: The Fortunes of Women Painters and Their Works* (1979), an examination of patriarchal treatment of female painters. Greer comments in the opening chapter on the failure of women to explore their talents: "The great number of male painters who were not members of painting dynasties could have been equalled by as great a number of women who actually never painted a stroke" (Greer, 1982, 12).

In 1999 Greer returned to the forefront of feminist thought with the publication of *The Whole Woman,* an anecdotal sequel to *The Female Eunuch.* Her concerns include the male management of female health and cosmetic surgeries and the choice of the "hipless, wombless, hard-titted" Barbie dolls and pop culture icons such as Madonna and Princess Di as models for the IDEAL WOMAN (Greer, 2000, 10). The author redirects women's attention to more pressing needs than liposuction and tooth whitening by reminding them of unfair divorce settlements, their paltry earnings, workplace harassment, and perpetual household and child care duties, which still rely primarily on women's labors. In a lecture in Toronto she warned listeners that for what liberation women have won, they have paid dearly in solitude, lowered income in menial jobs, media-led denigration, and additional responsibility for children and elderly parents.

Bibliography

Greer, Germaine. *The Female Eunuch.* New York: Farrar, Straus & Giroux, 2002.
———. *The Madwoman's Underclothes: Essays and Occasional Writings.* London: Picador, 1986.
———. *The Obstacle Race: The Fortunes of Women Painters and Their Works.* New York: Farrar, Straus & Giroux, 1982.
———. *The Whole Woman.* New York: Anchor, 2000.
Mitchell, Marea. "Ambitious Women and Strange Monsters: Simone de Beauvoir and Germaine Greer," *Hecate* 26, no. 1 (2000): 98–106.

Grimké, Angelina Weld (1880–1958)

Angelina Emily Weld Grimké, an imagist poet, biographer, and playwright during the Harlem Renaissance, used race propaganda as a weapon against lynching. The child of a white attorney and a Boston slave, she was the great-niece of an abolitionist duo Sarah and Angelina GRIMKÉ. She wrote poetry in her youth and studied at Carleton Academy, Boston Normal School of Gymnastics, and Harvard before her employment in the public school system in Washington, D.C., to teach English. At age 19 she submitted her first verse to the Norfolk County *Gazette,* and she later published poems in *Crisis.* In 1923 she issued her most anthologized poem, "The Black Finger," in *Opportunity;* two years later she completed a biography of her father.

Grimké focused on white-on-black atrocities targeting pregnant women and mothers and their children. At age 36 she made her mark on the Harlem Renaissance by writing *Rachel* (1916), a three-act antilynching tragedy sponsored by the National Association for the Advancement of Colored People (NAACP) as a riposte to D. W. Griffiths's racist film *Birth of a Nation* (1915). The play's domestic setting features a widowed seamstress, Mrs. Loving, and her son, Tom, and daughter, Rachel, whom she tells about the mob murder of her oldest child, George, and of her husband, a newspaper publisher. Contributing to the horror is her description of the perpetrators: "Yes—by Christian people—in a Christian land. We found out afterwards they were all church members in good standing—the best people" (Grimké, 30). Mrs. Loving's words enlighten Rachel about racism and its impact on the family. Rachel pictures the rest of the South, where "hundreds of dark mothers . . . live in fear, terrible, suffocating fear" (*ibid.,* 33). She concludes, "Why—it—makes—you doubt—God!" (*ibid.*).

Grimké's motif of residual VIOLENCE motivates a change in Rachel over the next four years. As a jumpy, overprotective foster mother she perpetuates her mother's example through idealistic allegory of a land of laughter, which she narrates to her son, Jimmy. By age 22 Rachel loses hope of rearing her family, experiencing a depression that manifests itself in visions; "I am afraid—to go—to sleep, for every time I do—my children come—and beg me—weeping—not to—bring them here—to suffer" (*ibid.,* 94). Ultimately she descends into antimaternal neurosis. A success in Georgia, Massachusetts, New York, Pennsylvania, and Washington, D.C., the play was the first full-length drama composed by a black female American and the first staged with an all-black cast. The author reprised the motif of female mourners of male lynching victims in a story, "The Closing Door" (1919), about the smothering of an infant.

Bibliography

Gourdine, Angeletta K. M., "The Drama of Lynching in Two Blackwomen's Drama, or Relating Grimké's *Rachel* to Hansberry's *A Raisin in the Sun,*" *Modern Drama* 41, no. 4 (Winter 1998): 533.
Grimké, Angelina Emily Weld. *Rachel: A Play in Three Acts.* Boston: Cornhill, 1920.
Hester, Michelle. "An Examination of the Relationship between Race and Gender in an Early Twentieth Century Drama: A Study of Angelina Weld Grimké's Play 'Rachel,'" *Journal of Negro History* 79, no. 2 (Spring 1994): 248–256.

Grimké, Sarah (1792–1873) and Grimké, Angelina (1805–1879)

In spite of strictures against public appearances by genteel women, Sarah Moore Grimké and her younger sister, Angelina Emily Grimké Weld, supported ABOLITIONISM and WOMEN'S RIGHTS through letters, essays, demonstrations, and public oratory. Natives of Charleston, South Carolina, they and their 11 siblings grew up amid the evils and miseries of plantation slavery. Their wealthy father, Judge John Faucheraud Grimké, refused to educate them, but the girls taught themselves with the family's sizable library. Sarah specialized in Latin and law but knew she could never open her own law office. After the sisters moved to Pennsylvania, they battled their private feelings about bondage and determined that there was no logic that justified one person's ownership of another. Received by Quakers, Angelina became the first woman to address a mixed audience and, on behalf of the Female Anti-Slavery Society, gave eyewitness details of the anguish of black laborers on Southern plantations. Despite condemnation from the Council of Congregationalist Ministers of Massachusetts of the impropriety of women's delivering polemical addresses, both sisters began making platform appearances across the state.

In reply to their critics the two women published their philosophies of women's place in the fight against human bondage. Sarah Grimké exposed the un-Christian behavior of the ministry toward slaves and slave owners in *Epistle to the Clergy of the Southern States* (1836). That same year Angelina Grimké wrote *An Appeal to the Christian Women of the South* (1836), calling on other female abolitionists to voice the unpopular belief that the slave trade should be banned. She enlarged on her original document with *An Appeal to the Women of the Nominally Free States* (1837) and with *Letters to Catharine Beecher in Reply to an Essay on Slavery and Abolitionism Addressed to A. E. Grimké* (1837). Strong in courage and well grounded in biblical theology, Angelina compared the position of the silenced white woman to that of a black slave, a concept that accounts for close ties between suffragists and abolitionists. While still on her New England tour Sarah Grimké composed *Letters on the Equality of the Sexes and the Condition of Women* (1838), the nation's first feminist tract. Its logical defense of women's rights influenced the first wave of feminist leaders—the orator Lucretia MOTT, the speechwriter Elizabeth Cady STANTON,

and the activist Lucy STONE—and earned the admiration of the feminist historian Harriet Jane ROBINSON in *Massachusetts in the Woman Suffrage Movement* (1883).

Sarah refused suitors and chose to live with Angelina, who married her fellow antislavery crusader Theodore Dwight Weld and settled on a farm in Belleville, New Jersey. The trio withdrew from oratory, but the sisters continued writing essays and letters on women's rights to newspapers and journals and to notable individuals, including correspondence to Queen Victoria in 1837 in which they appealed to her womanhood on behalf of other women. They begged her "on behalf of the down trodden millions in our own country, and the hundreds of thousands in thy dominions to abolish the system of apprenticeship which is fraught with so much suffering" (Lerner, 51). While running a boarding school, the sisters completed *American Society As It Is* (1859), which delineates weaknesses in the national fiber resulting from slavery.

In New York in 1863 Angelina Grimké Weld delivered "The Rights of Women and Negroes," an oration that compared the lot of two identifiable groups of subjugated people. While deploring the state of women's EDUCATION, she declared, "I feel that we have been with [the Negro], that the iron has entered into our souls. True, we have not felt the slave-holder's lash, true, we have not had our hands manacled but our hearts have been crushed" (Weld, 1863). She denounced the relegation of women to trivialities such as needlework and social dance: "I was not made for embroidery and dancing, I was made a woman; but I can not be a true woman, a full-grown woman, in America" (*ibid.*). Three years before her death in the midst of a winter snowstorm Sarah joined Angelina in organizing a demonstration of 58 female marchers for SUFFRAGE. Literary historians note that the unpublished writings of the Grimké sisters, which Theodore Weld kept in a scrapbook, are typical of the neglected works of intellectual women of the early 19th century.

Bibliography

Lerner, Gerda. *The Feminist Thought of Sarah Grimké.* Oxford: Oxford University Press, 1998.

Schneir, Miriam, ed. *Feminism: The Essential Historical Writings*. New York: Vintage, 1972.

Weld, Angelina Grimké. *An Appeal to the Christian Women of the South*. Whitefish, Mont.: Kessinger, 2004.

———. "The Rights of Women and Negroes" (1863). Available online. URL: http://etext.lib.virginia.edu/railton/uncletom/womanmov.html#g. Accessed on October 14, 2005.

H

Hagedorn, Jessica (1949–)

The European-Filipina dramatist, poet, and novelist Jessica Tarahata Hagedorn probes the problems of multicultural identity through experimental impressionism. A native of Manila, she learned narrative technique from her Filipina grandmother, American tastes from movies, horror themes from radio, and the rhythms of rock and roll from broadcasts of Chuck Berry and Fats Domino. In 1963 her family immigrated to San Francisco, where she absorbed the extremes of beat poetry and studied acting and mime at the American Conservatory Theater. In the ferment of the 1970s ethnic renaissance Hagedorn published a feminist poetry collection, *Four Young Women* (1973), edited by Kenneth Rexroth. She followed with a verse anthology, *Dangerous Music* (1975), and a play, *Mango Tango* (1977).

While residing in New York, Hagedorn expressed her sympathy with the underdog in the award-winning novella *Pet Food and Tropical Apparitions* (1981). She earned a National Book Award nomination and Before Columbus Foundation American Book Award for *Dogeaters* (1990), a kaleidoscopic urban novel depicting government-ordered VIOLENCE against citizens and women's sufferings under the regime of Ferdinand Marcos. Scenes depicting young Rio Gonzaga and her family stress the powerlessness of Filipinas, who play their gender-specific roles and channel their rage through Catholic ritual, fanatic movie attendance, and daily weep sessions before televised soap operas. Hagedorn ends the novel with a prayer to a pagan female deity, the icon of power and redemption for the nation's demoralized women. Developed with the aid of three fellowships to the MacDowell art colony, her stage adaptation of *Dogeaters* opened at the Joseph Papp Public Theater in New York City in 2001. Hagedorn also edited *Charlie Chan Is Dead: An Anthology of Contemporary Asian American Fiction* (1993) and composed an autobiographical novel, *The Gangster of Love* (1996), which describes her decade as lead singer of the Gangster Choir rock band.

Bibliography

Evangelista, Susan. "Jessica Hagedorn and Manila Magic," *MELUS* 18, no. 4 (Winter 1993–1994): 41–52.

Hagedorn, Jessica. *Dogeaters.* New York: Penguin, 1991.

Mendible, Myra. "Desiring Images: Representation and Spectacle in *Dogeaters*," *CRITIQUE: Studies in Contemporary Fiction* 43, no. 3 (Spring 2002): 289–305.

Hale, Sarah Josepha (1788–1879)

The first female magazine editor in the United States, Sarah Josepha Buell Hale was a prominent conservative feminist who encouraged female authors, including Madame de STAËL, Lady Mary Wortley Montagu, George SAND, and Madame de Sévigné. A native of Newport, New Hampshire, after she was widowed at age 34 she initiated a literary career to support her five children. She quickly staked out peace, patriotism, and humanitarianism as her major themes and led women in fund–raising for the Bunker Hill Monument and the preservation of Mount Vernon, the home of George and Martha Washington. Hale published a first novel, *Northwood, a Tale of New England* (1827), the beginning of the slave genre in American fiction that preceded Harriet Beecher STOWE's UNCLE TOM'S CABIN (1852). Hale featured the cloistering of young women in repressive religious orders in a Gothic story, "The Catholic Convert," collected in *Traits of American Life* (1835) and characterized the marginalization of females in a husband's SILENCING of Marian Gayland, protagonist of *The Lecturess; or, Woman's Sphere* (1839), a novel that influenced the writing of Henry James's *The Bostonians* (1886).

At age 40, Hale edited *Ladies' Magazine* in Boston; through it she championed the creation of Thanksgiving as a national holiday. In 1837 she progressed to significant influence over women's reading as editor of *Godey's Lady's Book*, a post she held in Philadelphia for four decades. She continued crusading for a national day of thanks until 1863, when President Abraham Lincoln accepted her idea. Hale lauded female roles in industry and introduced American readers to women's lives in China, Japan, and Turkey. She shied away from raucous bluestockings, but in her editorial commentary in February 1850 she asserted woman's modeling of American morals for the sake of their children. The following month she called for equality in EDUCATION. In the July 1855 edition, she raged, "A grossly ignorant woman is unfit to be the mother of an American citizen" (Hale, 1857, 82).

Hale believed that genius and public service have no gender. For the public good she participated in the Boston Ladies Peace Society. She supported calisthenics for women, female property rights, and the founding of Vassar College and promoted careers for women in the classroom, religious missions, and medicine. She prompted young women to develop writing skills through diary keeping. Her magazine favored such American feminist authors and book reviewers as Nathaniel Hawthorne, Harriet Beecher Stowe, and her sister, Catharine BEECHER. Hale pursued a policy of identifying women's submissions under their own names rather than under initials or masculine pen names.

In an era of massive national expansion Hale described the domestic sphere as woman's empire. Her dialect novel *Liberia; or, Mr. Peyton's Experiment* (1852) depicts the plantation mistress, symbolically named Virginia, as the salvation of home and family when rumors warn of a slave insurrection. Her black parallel, Keziah, the plantation nurse who returns to Africa, applies Christian principles to resettlement and strengthens her husband, Polydore, who fears repatriation in the motherland. A model of wise womanhood, Keziah succeeds by cultivating arrowroot and African fruits, raising poultry and sheep, adopting children, and opening a school to teach reading and sewing. By stabilizing the family, she introduces peace and productivity in Africa. The following year Hale completed *Woman's Record, or Sketches of Distinguished Women, from the Creation to A.D. 1868* (1853, 1855, 1872), a women's history that claims the female role in furthering domestic order, morality, and civilization.

Bibliography

Hale, Sarah Josepha. "Editor's Table," *Godey's Lady's Book* 51, no. 1 (July 1857): 82.

———. *Liberia; or, Mr. Peyton's Experiments.* New York: Harper & Brothers, 1853.

Kaplan, Amy. "Manifest Domesticity," *American Literature* 70, no. 3 (September 1998): 581–606.

Levander, Caroline Field. *Voices of the Nation: Women and Public Speech in Nineteenth-Century American Literature and Culture.* Cambridge: Cambridge University Press, 1998.

Mather, Anne. "A History of Feminist Periodicals, Part 1," *Journalism History* 1, no. 3 (Autumn 1974): 82–85.

———. "A History of Feminist Periodicals, Part 2," *Journalism History* 2, no. 1 (Spring 1975): 19–23, 31.

Hall, Radclyffe (1880–1943)

The English novelist and poet Marguerite Radclyffe-Hall legitimized lesbian relationships as valid outlets for female passion. A native of Bournemouth, Dorset, and child of Anglo-American parents, she was born into an unhappy home in which abuse was common. In early childhood she received home tutoring and enjoyed setting original verse to music.

After inheriting her father's fortune at age 18, she attended King's College and studied in Germany. Freed of monetary dependence, she emigrated to the United States to live with her maternal grandmother, who privately published Hall's first lesbian poetry anthology, *'Twixt Earth and Stars* (1906). It was in America that Hall dropped her Christian name and started calling herself "Radclyffe." In a stable love life with the singer Mabel Veronica "Ladye" Batten, Hall also called herself John and began dressing as a man and smoking a pipe. She composed woman-to-woman love verse and issued *The Unlit Lamp* (1925), the story of Joan Ogden's thwarted longing to study medicine. For *Adam's Breed* (1926), a story of the frustrated female artist, Hall won the Prix Femina and the James Tait Black Memorial Prize.

Batten died in 1915, and Hall moved in with her lover's cousin, Una Troubridge. They lived together in London for most of the 1920s. During this time Hall wrote the first overtly lesbian novel, The WELL OF LONELINESS (1928). The novel precipitated an obscenity trial for Hall, and in 1928, the book was banned throughout England. However, Hall's publisher, Jonathan Cape, sent the type molds of the novel to the Pegasus Press in Paris, and the book was published and distributed widely throughout Europe and the United States. During the course of Hall's lifetime the book was translated into 11 languages and sold more than 1 million copies. Two years after the ban Hall won the prestigious Eichelberger Humane Award.

Hall's later fiction dramatized less controversial hardships of female lives, including short stories in *Miss Ogilvy Finds Herself* (1934) and *The Sixth Beatitude* (1936), which lauds as heroine a working-class woman. Hall died October 7, 1943, in London.

Bibliography

Hall, Radclyffe. *The Well of Loneliness.* New York: Pocket Books, 1950.
———. *Your John: The Love Letters of Radclyffe Hall.* Albany: New York University Press, 1997.
South Bank University. "Radclyffe Hall." Lesbian and Gay Staff Association. Available online. URL: http://myweb.lsbu.ac.uk/~stafflag/johnhall.html. Accessed on April 14, 2004.
Virago Press. "Radclyffe Hall." Available online. URL: http://www.virago.co.uk/virago/meet/hall_profile.asp?TAG=BVNT7X5X6X6XX5186RG2NM&CID=virago. Accessed on April 14, 2004.

Handmaid's Tale, The Margaret Atwood (1985)

The Canadian novelist Margaret ATWOOD's contribution to dystopian fiction sheds light on conservative religious fanatics and their dehumanization of women. Set outside Boston, Massachusetts, in the mid-1980s, *The Handmaid's Tale* looks toward a future nuclear calamity that spews radioactivity and toxic chemicals that suppress human procreation. As did the Gothic nightmares of the 19th century, the novel places under benign house arrest Offred, a breeder living in the house of Commander Frederick Waterford and his wife, Serena, in Gilead, a town in a fascist police state. Compared to Nathaniel Hawthorne's *The SCARLET LETTER* (1850) and to George Orwell's *1984* (1949), Atwood's thriller portrays women as the target of a perverted technocracy and of a state-mandated concubinage intended to save humankind from extinction. To rescue the protagonist from sexual bondage, the author draws on abolitionist history for the Underground Frailroad, a women's recovery system that spirits concubines such as Offred away from their keepers and rescues from a death threat those who bear "shredders" rather than healthy children.

In a form that hybridizes fable and terror motif, *The Handmaid's Tale* retreats to gothic CONFINEMENT conventions to picture Offred in the tentacles of a gender-polarized totalitarian state. Regimentation assigns uniforms that reflect women's roles: whores tricked out in slit skirts and garish makeup, subservient Marthas in veils and demure blue, and handmaids, robed as anti-nuns in red habits and capped with white winged wimples that obscure the face. Bearing the traditional color of the prostitute and of menstrual discharge, the handmaids become walking billboards advertising the scarlet woman. An overzealous spy network, the Eyes, patrol streets to enforce stringent rules. The pervasive paranoia subdues Offred, who admits, "My hands are shaking. Why am I frightened? I've crossed no boundaries, I've given no trust, taken no risk, all is safe. It's the choice that terrifies me. A way out, a salvation" (Atwood, 80).

Atwood maximizes gender treachery with antiwomen called the aunts, a subset of torturers and indoctrinators. At the Rachel and Leah Re-education Center, a female concentration camp, Aunt Lydia and her henchwomen supervise barracks, punish rebels with cattle prods, and conduct public hangings. Silenced in an ominous atmosphere that could spell the noose, the boldest inmates rely on SISTERHOOD by "[whispering] almost without sound. In the semidarkness we could stretch out our arms, when the aunts weren't looking, and touch each other's hands across space. We learned to lip-read, our heads flat on the beds" (*ibid.*, 4). Under threat for minor infractions the handmaids reclaim identity by introducing themselves by their former names. Moira, a survivor of structured torture, reports: "It was the feet they'd do, for a first offense. They used steel cables, frayed at the ends. After that the hands. They didn't care what they did to your feet or your hands, even if it was permanent" (*Ibid.*, 91). Atwood acknowledges the street smarts of supportive prostitutes in Moira's engineering of escapes at the risk of more torture.

A modernist twist on female regimentation, the naming of Offred—"of Fred," a snide alternate reading of *off red*—portrays female identity subsumed by sexual service to a single male. In the company of his childless wife, Serena, Offred and Fred perform a threeway intercourse that parodies modern monogamy. Fred forces the handmaid into a DUALITY that requires pious sex acts sanctified by the reading of scripture, but that frees her to dress in a tart's attire for covert forays to Jezebel's, an institutionalized bordello where Fred acts out the fantasy of sporty womanizer. Offred recognizes the psychological posturing that confers a risqué manhood on an otherwise dull set of middle-aged men: "It's like a masquerade party; they are like oversize children, dressed up in togs they've rummaged from trunks" (*Ibid.*, 235). The episodes of nightclub revelry force on Offred an enhanced version of the 1980s social behavior that Atwood satirizes. Offred's reward for posing as Fred's female trophy date is the promise of information about Offred's daughter. Thus, the handmaid's yearning for her

kidnapped child becomes the tool by which Fred manipulates her obedience to his bizarre fantasies.

With satire, irony, and dark humor, Atwood guides the reader through a woman-obsessed future. Through a carefully worded pun, Ofglen can greet Offred with a warning in the subversive doublespeak, "It's a beautiful May day," a "Mayday" alert from a fellow handmaid that implies the activity of an underground resistance group called Mayday (*ibid.*, 58). The text teases with ambiguous fragments of data from June 25, 2195, that prove Offred's escape from Gilead. By nighttime visits to the quarters of Nick, the Commander's chauffeur, Offred enhances the likelihood of conception with sperm from a second male. With Nick's complicity she plots a daring breakout acted out by an unidentified goon squad that arrests her and hauls her away in a KGB-style police van. Atwood indicates that Offred's flight to Bangor, Maine, frees her from possible assignment to the radioactive outlands for failure to produce a child for Fred. The subtext bears more complex freight—a warning to complacent women that the illusion of freedom and social order can mask a lethal intent to subjugate women at the whim of males who seek to replicate themselves through enforced female childbearing.

Bibliography

Atwood, Margaret. *The Handmaid's Tale*. New York: Anchor Books, 1998.

Cavalcanti, Ildney. "Utopias of/f Language in Contemporary Feminist Literary Dystopias," *Utopian Studies* 11, no. 2 (Spring 2000): 152.

Wagner-Lawlor, Jennifer A. "From Irony to Affiliation in Margaret Atwood's *The Handmaid's Tale*," *Critique* 45, no. 1 (Fall 2003): 83–96.

Hansberry, Lorraine (1930–1965)

In the era of male theatrical giants—Eugene O'Neill, Thornton Wilder, and Tennessee Williams—the radical dramatist Lorraine Vivian Hansberry ended the dearth of black female authors represented on Broadway. Reared in Chicago by recent immigrants from Tennessee, she enjoyed a level of prosperity that contrasted with the Southside ghetto's squalor. In 1938 her father, the realtor and financier Carl A. Hansberry, sued the city to overturn laws blocking his family's move to a white, middle-class neighborhood. After their move Lorraine was standing beside a window when an unknown assailant tossed a hunk of concrete through it. The family's struggle to live well impressed her with images that recur in her first drama, *A RAISIN IN THE SUN* (1959), an American stage classic.

Hansberry's divergent creativity required street knowledge and realistic writing. After abandoning her education at the University of Wisconsin, she began studying drama on her own terms at Roosevelt College and the Jefferson School for Social Research in New York City. For the publisher Paul Robeson in 1953 she cowrote and edited *Freedom* magazine, which she also supplied with line drawings. In 1957 she submitted a letter to *The Ladder,* a lesbian magazine, protesting the antifemale hatred at the core of antigay persecution. It wasn't until the 1980s that the gay culture claimed her as one of its own. That same year in an essay on Simone de BEAUVOIR, Hansberry lamented the life of the female: "Woman like the Negro, like the Jew, like colonial peoples, even in ignorance *is incapable of accepting the role with harmony.* This is because it is an unnatural role" (Rich, 21). She rejected the constant "ferment and agitation" of the female condition, which constantly struggled against oppression (*ibid.*).

At age 20 Hansberry settled in Greenwich Village and composed satire for *Black Scholar* and the *Village Voice.* With the backing of her ex-husband, Robert Nemiroff, at age 29 she launched *A Raisin in the Sun,* the first Broadway play directed by a black, Lloyd Richards. The cast featured Ruby Dee in the lead role of a gentle, stouthearted family matriarch seeking to better her family's pride and living conditions. The author was the first black and youngest playwright to receive the New York Drama Critics Circle award for the year's best play. The public's response to 530 performances was so positive that blacks picketed the block to demand tickets to the segregated Ethel Barrymore Theater.

Hansberry's posthumous autobiography, *To Be Young, Gifted, and Black* (1969), expressed her humanism in simple terms: "One cannot live with sighted eyes and feeling heart and not know and react to the miseries which afflict this world"

(Hansberry, 1995, 11). Her activism during the civil rights era led to her friendship with Robert Kennedy and Martin Luther King Jr. and the enmity of J. Edgar Hoover and the House Un-American Activities Committee. The filming of her landmark play with the same cast renewed adulation of her work with an Oscar nomination as best screenplay, a Cannes Film Festival Special Award, and the Screen Writers Guild Nomination as best American drama. In 1973 Nemiroff and Charlotte Zaltzberg's musical adaptation of the text ran for 847 Broadway performances and earned a Tony. At her death of intestinal cancer at age 34 Hansberry left incomplete a biography of Mary WOLLSTONECRAFT as well as a novel, three plays, and an opera on the Caribbean freedom fighter Toussaint L'Ouverture. In 1987 Danny Glover starred in a televised version of *A Raisin in the Sun;* three years later a revival opened at the Kennedy Center, with Esther Rolle and Glover as mother and son. Hansberry's unflinching libertarianism influenced the one-woman stage performances of Anna Deavere SMITH.

Bibliography

Gourdine, Angeletta K. M. "The Drama of Lynching in Two Blackwomen's Drama, or Relating Grimke's *Rachel* to Hansberry's *A Raisin in the Sun," Modern Drama* 41, no. 4 (Winter 1998): 533.

Hansberry, Lorraine. *A Raisin in the Sun.* New York: Penguin, 1988.

———. *To Be Young, Gifted, and Black.* New York: Vintage, 1995.

Rich, Adrienne. *Blood, Bread, and Poetry: Selected Prose, 1979–1985.* New York: W. W. Norton, 1986.

Harjo, Joy (1951–)

A Native American teacher and creator of verse history, Joy Harjo Foster preserves in poetry her American Indian views on racism and sexism. Her works picture the cultural rape perpetrated by racist European conquerors such as Hernan de Soto and the subsequent displacement of modern Indians in the white world. She energizes her poems with glimpses of Native journey lore, shape shifting, ghost dancers, and the geographic displacement that fractures clans and tribes. Born in Tulsa, Oklahoma, of Cherokee, Muscogee Creek, French, and Irish lineage, Harjo took comfort in her mother's Native American stories, which instilled pride in self and culture. Because Joy's background was bicultural, she was able to enjoy the rhythms of the Native stomp dance as well as jazz, but music alone could not relieve her from cultural estrangement. In poetry she followed the example of Gandhi by channeling bitterness and anger into action. After completing degrees in creative writing at the University of New Mexico and the University of Iowa, she advised Native American Public Broadcasting and the National Indian Youth Council on First Nations culture and directed the National Association of Third World Writers.

An admirer of the writings of Flannery O'CONNOR and Leslie Marmon SILKO, Harjo published her woman-centered verse in *The Last Song* (1975), *What Moon Drove Me to This?* (1980), and *She Had Some Horses* (1983). She also issued poems in *Conditions* magazine, *The Third Woman* (1980), and *That's What She Said* (1984). Among this era's poems featuring internal conflicts was a masterwork, "The Woman Hanging from the Thirteenth Floor Window" (1983), a dramatic emergency scenario picturing a female tormented by conflicting roles as a mother and the spouse of a tyrant. The woman's chipped teeth attest to the hard job of chewing and swallowing the sorrows that alienate and depress her.

Harjo's subsequent work, invigorated by feminism, focuses on all women's responses to displacement and rejection. In 1989 she mourned the Native loss of place in the preface to *Secrets from the Center of the World*. The text of *In Mad Love and War* (1990) surveys the poet's emotions that enrage the spurned lover, justify the belligerance of the female activist, and energize the nude go-go entertainer in "Deer Dancer." In "Resurrection" she lauds the oral tradition as an antidote to VIOLENCE: "The songs here speak tenderly of honor and love / sweet melody is the undercurrent of gunfire" (Harjo, 17). "Rainy Dawn" identifies the sources of Acoma stories as "the sound of our grandmothers' voices," an affirmation of aging WISEWOMEN (*ibid.*, 32). "Javelina" delves more deeply into nature by exalting a mythic female animal that is capable of redeeming the world.

Poems in *The Woman Who Fell from the Sky* (1996) turn from self-assessment to the image of woman as the universal creator. In "A Postcolonial Tale" Harjo pictures the poet as the truth bearer, the tribe member who must voice social and historical fact. To increase the public's awareness of female Native American poets and thinkers, she edited a collection, *Reinventing Ourselves in the Enemy's Language: Contemporary Native Women's Writing of North America* (1997); as editor of *Contact II*, *High Plains Literary Review*, and *Tyuonyi*, she continues to offer opportunities to Native authors.

Bibliography

Alexie, Sherman. "She Had Some Horses: The Education of a Poet," *Teachers and Writers* (March–April 1995): 1–3.

Donovan, Kathleen M. *Feminist Readings of Native American Literature: Coming to Voice.* Tucson: University of Arizona Press, 1998.

Harjo, Joy. *In Mad Love and War.* Middletown, Conn.: Wesleyan University Press, 1990.

Leen, Mary. "An Art of Saying: Joy Harjo's Poetry and the Survival of Storytelling," *American Indian Quarterly* 19, no. 1 (Winter 1995): 1–16.

Ruppert, Jim. "Paula Gunn Allen and Joy Harjo: Closing the Distance between Personal and Mythic Space," *American Indian Quarterly* 7, no. 1 (1983) 27–40.

Harper, Frances (1825–1911)

The abolitionist reformer and suffragist poet Frances Ellen Watkins Harper was the rare black female who succeeded financially as a writer. She was a native of Baltimore adopted by an uncle, the educator William Watkins, and his wife, Henrietta, after Harper's parents' deaths in 1828. After working as a nanny in a Quaker household and later as a teacher of embroidery at Union Seminary in Wilberforce, Ohio, she aided the Underground Railroad and joined the antislavery movement in Maine as lecturer and reader of original verse. At age 29 while writing for the *Provincial Freeman*, she anthologized *Poems on Miscellaneous Subjects* (1854), a brisk seller that expressed antislavery and feminist views and earned funds for the abolitionist cause. A dramatic favorite of the collection, "The Slave Mother," evolves from her own mother hunger by picturing the terror of a female in the slave market as she is separated from her son. In 1858 Harper published in the *Anti-Slavery Bugle* the poem "Bury Me in a Free Land," which became her rallying cry at public gatherings. Her platform performance was so moving that hearers suspected she was neither black nor female.

Harper advanced from sympathy for black slave women to promotion of nonviolence and of equality for all women, whom she saluted for supporting EDUCATION for black children. She became the first black American to publish a work of short fiction, the story "The Two Offers," featured in the 1859 issue of *Anglo-African Magazine*. The feminist text describes the coming to knowledge of a woman who expects more out of life than wedlock. Widowed after four years of marriage, Harper continued in her oratorical career and pressed for universal education, TEMPERANCE, and women's SUFFRAGE. From 1868 over the next two decades she serialized three works—*Minnie's Sacrifice, Sowing and Reaping,* and *Trial and Triumph*—in the *Christian Recorder.* Feminists reclaimed the neglected pieces late in the 20th century. She settled in Philadelphia with her daughter, Mary, and became a Unitarian. For her issuing of polemics against lynching, arranged marriage, child and spousal abuse, drunkenness, and racial discrimination, Harper earned the titles of the Bronze Muse and the matriarch of African-American journalism.

In the first period fiction featuring Reconstruction, Harper created a survivor's persona in Aunt Chloe, the focus of *Sketches of Southern Life* (1872). After achieving freedom from slavery at age 60, Chloe rejoices in learning to read, a liberating experience that begins with hymns and sections of the New Testament. Harper produced an inclusive glimpse of mixed-race people after the Civil War and the motif of the white male's sexual dominance of white women in a feminist novel, *Iola Leroy; or, Shadows Uplifted* (1892). Speaking for the author, Iola, a Civil War nurse, believes that women should shuck off helplessness and learn marketable skills. In a speech to the 1893 World's Congress of Representative Women Harper visualized a feminist era in which women could use intellect and energies for good. Two years later in *The Martyr of Alabama and Other*

Poems (1895), the title selection, a dramatic monologue on the street murder of Tim Thompson, expressed her outrage that cruel whites waylaid, trampled, and shot a small black boy. Another poem from the period, "A Double Standard" (1895), challenges the victimization of fallen women while their despoilers receive no blame or punishment.

Bibliography

Boyd, Melba Joyce. *Discarded Legacy: Politics and Poetics in the Life of Frances E. W. Harper, 1825–1911.* Detroit: Wayne State University Press, 1994.

Harper, Frances. *Iola Leroy or Shadows Uplifted.* Boston: Beacon Press, 1999.

Harper, Ida Husted (1851–1931)

The newswoman, historian, pamphleteer, and poet Ida A. Husted Harper, the official biographer of Susan B. ANTHONY, documented the spirit and organization of the American SUFFRAGE movement. The daughter of an educator Harper was born to a political family at Fairfield outside Brooksville, Indiana. After a year as principal of a high school in Peru, Indiana, she began writing for the Terre Haute *Saturday Evening Mail* and later for the Indianapolis *News,* the *Brotherhood of Locomotive Fireman's Magazine,* the *Los Angeles Examiner,* and the *New York Sunday Sun.* She produced a feminist column, "A Woman's Opinions," and, for *Harper's,* the regular feature "Votes for Women." Her topics ranged from keeping informed and supporting suffrage to controlling family size, promoting local libraries and EDUCATION for women, and choosing to remain single.

At age 33 Harper published her first work, *Poems on Miscellaneous Subjects* (1884). In 1887 she cofounded the Indiana Woman Suffrage Society to press for women's voting rights. After two years at Stanford University she became press secretary for the National American Woman Suffrage Association, on behalf of whom she wrote 8,000 letters. For the December 1902 issue of the *American Monthly Review of Reviews* she produced brief biographies of Anthony and her researcher and speechwriter, Elizabeth Cady STANTON. In a summary of the synergy of Stanton and Anthony,

Harper declared: "That First Woman's Rights Convention, and those which followed in the early '50's, did not obtain emancipation for woman, but they attracted the attention of the whole country to the injustice under which she struggled, and set people to thinking" (Harper, 718).

For the three-volume *Life and Work of Susan B. Anthony* (1898, 1908) Harper resided at Anthony's home in Rochester, New York, the command center where volunteers wrote letters, leaflets, and pamphlets. Harper covered the gist of the organized suffrage drive and preserved facts from frail clippings and correspondence. She collaborated with Anthony and others on volume 4 of the *History of Woman Suffrage* (1886–88) and completed the next two volumes without help. Late in Harper's career she wrote feminist articles for papers in Boston, Chicago, New York, Philadelphia, and Washington, D.C., and edited the women's section of *Harper's Bazaar.*

Bibliography

Anthony, Susan B., and Ida Husted Harper, eds. *History of Woman Suffrage*, vol. 4 (1902). Available online. URL: http://www.alexanderstreet6.com/wasm/wasmrestricted/doctext/S10010057-D0076.001.htm. Accessed on October 13, 2005.

Harper, Ida Husted. "Elizabeth Cady Stanton" (1902). Available online. URL: http://etext.lib.virginia.edu/toc/modeng/public/HarStan.html. Accessed on October 14, 2005.

Head, Bessie (1937–1986)

The South African fiction writer and journalist Bessie Amelia Emery Head focused intense libertarian writings on women's identity, patriarchy, social inferiority, and insanity. Her birth challenged the strictures of apartheid. A native of Pietermaritzburg, she was born of Scots-African heritage in an asylum infirmary, where her mother, Bessie Amelia "Toby" Emory, was incarcerated by her family after they disowned her for having an affair with a black stableboy. In "Notes from a Quiet Backwater I" (1982), Head ponders bicultural people: "There must be many people like me in South Africa whose birth or beginnings are filled with calamity and disaster, the sort of person who is a skeleton in the cupboard or the dark and fearful secret swept under the carpet" (Head, 1990, 3). After Head's mother committed suicide, the author grew up in a white foster home until the physical features of her unknown black father appeared. South African law forced social workers to place her with black parents.

Trained for the classroom, Head completed her education in Durban at Saint Monica's Mission School, an Anglican facility where treatment was so un-Christian that she ended her allegiance to organized religion. In 1955 she acquired a Natal Teachers' Senior Certificate, but she did not take to classroom work. After separating from her husband, she wrote a column for newspapers in Capetown and Johannesburg, where her biracial features resulting from her parents' miscegenation were an invitation to slurs and to exclusion. Fleeing north, she declared, "I found the South African situation so evil that it was impossible for me to deal with, in creative terms" (Abrahams, back cover). She reared her son, Howard, in Serowe, Botswana; wrote for *Drum* magazine and the *Golden City Post*; and aided political refugees. Of her shared experiences with others in flight from apartheid, she explained, "Here, the shattered bits began to grow together. There is a sense of wovenness, a wholeness in life here; a feeling of how strange and beautiful people can be—just living" (Head, 1977, x).

Critics acclaim Head's first novel, *When Rain Clouds Gather* (1969), a story of refugee activism and suicide. The story validates her decision to write about the personal and sexual difficulties of mixed-blood women. In *Maru* (1971), she explodes the BEAUTY MYTH by finding loveliness in Elizabeth, a woman whose heritage blended her mother's English traits with those of her Bushman father. Of the terrors of seeking identity and finding madness, she laments, "Journeys into the soul are not for women with children, not all the dark heaving turmoil. They are for men, and the toughest of them took off into the solitude of the forests and fought out their battles with hell in deep seclusion" (Head, 1997, 50). Her empathy for the hunted pariahs of South Africa produces a psychological survey of the outsider. She muses, "No wonder they hid from view. The inner life is ugly" (*ibid.*). The prevailing melancholy replicates the author's lifetime experiences and her doubts about human kindness.

On recovery from nervous collapse, Head returned to writing about social and political situations that compromise women's happiness. She produced an autobiographical novel, *A Question of Power* (1973), which describes female alienation. She reprised early themes in "The Deep River: A Story of Ancient Tribal Migration," one of a series of parablelike stories anthologized in *The Collector of Treasures and Other Botswana Village Tales* (1977). The story accounts for blame placed on women for human losses during apartheid and postcolonial exile. Another story in the collection, "Snapshots of a Wedding," depicts the haughtiness of a betrothed girl who lords her education over peasant relatives until marriage returns her to patriarchal control. After Head's death of hepatitis at age 49 editions of her sketches and essays appeared as *A Woman Alone* (1990), in which she outlined the sources of her feminism.

Bibliography

Abrahams, Cecil. *The Tragic Life: Bessie Head and Literature in South Africa.* Trenton, N.J.: African World Press, 1990.

Head, Bessie. *The Collector of Treasures and Other Botswana Village Tales.* London: Heinemann, 1977.

———. *Maru.* London: Heinemann, 1997.

———. *A Woman Alone.* London: Heinemann, 1990.

Mackenzie, Craig. *Bessie Head.* New York: Twayne, 1999.

Heat and Dust   Ruth Prawer Jhabvala   (1975)

Ruth Prawer Jhabvala expresses intense feminism in *Heat and Dust*, a bicultural epistolary novella that builds irony out of contrast. Developed with understated satire, the story teems with the types of females the author observed in her wide experience of world cultures. In the fictional setting of Satipur, she pictures a hippie roaming the region in search of data on her maternal aunt, Olivia. Tinged with melancholy, the story develops from self-revelatory letters describing how an unfulfilled colonial wife, the rebellious Olivia Rivers, violates British gender and race restrictions by satisfying her curiosity about Indian men. Scandalous in the tense atmosphere of the British Raj is her affair with the suave, rakish Nawab of Khatm, a robber prince and married bisexual with numerous male lovers. Offsetting British women in the colonies and their proprieties and snobbery are the icy, manipulative Begum, confined in palace purdah; the unfulfilled Ritu, a victim of emotional seizures; the promiscuous bohemian Marcia; the *hijra* female impersonators; Maji, a generous wisewoman and midwife of female untouchables; and Leelavati, a street beggar who dies in Maji's arms. Jhabvala indicates the authority that each female wields in her limited milieu, from the Begum's poisoning of a deceiver to the love and acceptance that Maji bestows on the lowly.

The author's unassuming title evolves a number of themes from the Indian subcontinent—colonialism, passion, immolation of Indian widows, and meaningless affairs. The beginning of an unthinkable relationship occurs with the flirtation of eyes at the dinner table, where Olivia realizes that "here at last was one person in India to be interested in her the way she was used to" (Jhabvala, 17). Immaturity and vanity prevent her from registering a deeper analysis of the Nawab, a man far more cunning and more sophisticated in male-female relations than Olivia. The stimulus of his masculinity and exotic charm cause Olivia to look and feel feverish, a foreshadowing of a dangerous passionate alliance. In the presence of Douglas Rivers, Olivia retreats from his pipe and snaps, "I hate you with that thing" (*ibid.*, 39). The oppositional forms of heat quickly end her love for Douglas as she transfers her thoughts and desires to the Nawab.

Jhabvala emphasizes a cross-cultural dilemma—that Olivia is unable to abort her possibly biracial child in a British hospital. A normalization of ABORTION as women's business originates in the East, where "It is a necessary part of an Indian midwife's qualification because in many cases it is the only way to save people from dishonour and suffering" (*ibid.*, 139). Ironically Olivia crosses from a less humane British culture to a welcoming Indian clinic run by women. In her passage she conceals herself in native guise—a burka, the Muslim female's walking tent, a mummying costume that often dismays Western women for its negation of female characteristics. As anonymous as other swathed females, Olivia enters a primitive Indian women's clinic and yields to an unsanitary procedure that native practitioners perform with a twig. The event bears subtextual commentary on British women's faulty notions of superiority over Indian women, who have long controlled their own health needs without intervention of men or of state or religious laws. Establishing the difference between a romance and a feminist novel is Olivia's choice. She opts for neither husband nor lover, but chooses to remain true to herself by following the dictates of her conscience and emotional needs.

Bibliography

Jhabvala, Ruth Prawer. *Heat and Dust.* New York: Touchstone, 1976.

Merchant, Ismail. "Ismail Merchant, Britain's Foremost Maker of Indian Films, Reflects on a Subcontinent's Change as Seen through His Lens." *New Statesman,* 15 August 1997, p. 29.

Heidi Chronicles, The Wendy Wasserstein (1989)

Wendy WASSERSTEIN's *The Heidi Chronicles* reprises through episodic drama the cultural transitions in feminist ideals, morals, and intellectual and personal aims. Representing everywoman, the art historian Dr. Heidi Holland relives the first quarter-century of the feminist movement in two monologues and 11 scenes that carry her back to a high school dance. In her 40s she challenges the presentation of art as the achievement of great men by introducing students at Columbia University to works by Sofonisba Anguissola, Clara Peeters, Artemisia Gentileschi, Lilla Cabot Perry, and Georgia O'Keeffe. In an offhand remark Holland observes that such female pioneers "watch closely and ease the way for the others to join in" (Wasserstein, 206). The personal perspective attests to her closeness to students and to the creators of the past, whose art she hopes to revive.

Through measured ironies, the comedy settles into a familiar urban intellectualism that is alternately hollow and affirming to the earnest protagonist, a university professor educated at Vassar and Yale and in England on a Fulbright scholarship. To help viewers visualize the historical milieu, Wasser-stein salts the social odyssey with handholds—acquired immunodeficiency syndrome (AIDS), anti–Vietnam War demonstrations, bell-bottoms, encounter sessions, go-go clubs, Bobby Kennedy, John Lennon, Eugene McCarthy, the power lunch, rap groups, and talk shows. While delivering the speech "Women, Where Are We Going?" at an alumnae luncheon, Holland's heart interrupts her brain, causing her to lose her grasp on perky self-confidence. To achieve satisfaction from middle age, Holland remains true to key humanistic tenets. For personal warmth she adopts a Panamanian daughter, a seedling for the future who becomes the professor's antidote to disenchantment.

Wasserstein makes a salient point about the difference between historical feminism and realism. Holland happily immerses herself in the creative fireworks of centuries past. Replicating them in her own life becomes downright scary. She confesses to feeling stranded. On October 15, 1995, a TNT broadcast of *The Heidi Chronicles* introduced television audiences to Dr. Holland, played by Jamie Lee Curtis, and to two failed loves, Tom Hulce as Dr. Peter Patrone, the gay high school sweetie, and Peter Friedman as Scoop Rosenbaum. The latter is an undependable lover who edits *Boomer* magazine and miffs Holland by marrying someone less competitive than she. The edgy verbal sparring suggests that Holland was better off unmarried. For the antiyuppie revelations that Wasserstein foists on Holland, the critic Robert Brustein called the play "*The Big Chill* of feminism" (Brustein, 33).

Bibliography

Brustein, Robert. "Review: *The Heidi Chronicles.*" *New Republic,* 17 April 1989, pp. 32–33.

Nelson, Robert S. "The Slide Lecture, of the Work of Art History in the Age of Mechanical Reproduction," *Critical Inquiry* 26, no. 3 (Spring 2000): 414–434.

Wasserstein, Wendy. *The Heidi Chronicles and Other Plays.* New York: Vintage, 1991.

"He Is Like the Gods" Sappho (ca. 590 B.C.)

In one of her most complete surviving lyrics from sixth-century Lesbos, the Greek poet SAPPHO of

Mytilene produces a sense impression of the besotted lover convulsed in anguish by the beloved's possession by another. The brief drama, which one translator entitled "Seizure," shudders with passion as the first-person speaker compares the male rival to the divine. Lifting him above mortals is the privilege of sitting with his mate, looking into her eyes, and hearing the soft nuances of her words and laughter. The stave ends with the sorrow-filled reminder that love is a winner-take-all competition. Projecting universality is the ambiguity of gender in the speaker. Because the poet is female, feminist literature claims the poem as a fundamental statement of frustrated lesbianism.

Strict adherence to the speaker's perspective on a magnetic moment leaves many questions unanswered. In decline at loss of the beloved to the unnamed man, the speaker feels broken, damaged, with a heart traumatized by envy. Omitted from the poem is the beloved's awareness of the watcher or any indication that the beloved deliberately baits the speaker by playacting at flirtation with the man. Whatever the motivation on either side, the speaker continues visually stalking the prize. The masochism of the voyeur presses on from genital arousal into erotic misery with glances at the beloved and failed attempts to make polite conversation. As the lacy heat of desire permeates the speaker's skin, eyesight darkens; tinnitus overwhelms hearing. The limbs quake with ague that drains sweat from the body. Pale and queasy, the speaker compares lovesickness to death, a mortal demise of sensual torment.

Bibliography

Altman, Meryl. "Looking for Sappho," *Women's Review of Books* 21, no. 4 (January 2004): 8–10.

Green, Peter. "On Fire with Longing." *New Republic*, 7 October 2002, pp. 34–40.

Sappho. *The Poems of Sappho.* New York: Prometheus, 1999.

Hélisenne de Crenne (fl. 1530–1552)

A Renaissance humanist and spokeswoman for the merits of women, Hélisenne de Crenne, the pen name of the author Marguerite de Briet of Picardy, championed silenced women. She refuted late-me-

dieval biblical arguments relegating women to a shameful place in creation and in human history. Ignoring the charge that vocal women are immoral, she fought the DOUBLE STANDARD with passion and erudition by debunking stereotypes drawn from the Bible depiction of Abigail, Judith, and Susannah. Hélisenne also crafted facile pro-woman arguments based on examples from the classics—the learned Deborah and Zenobia, the martyrs Iphigenia and Lucretia, the virtuous Cornelia and prophetess Cassandra, the chaste amazon Atalanta and the Vestal Claudia, the courageous Camilla, and the rejected females Medea, Oenone, Queen Dido, and Thisbe.

A native of Abbeville, Picardy, Marguerite de Briet left hints, but few details of her life. In reference to her life, she spoke of the atmosphere of Paris, where she lived among cultivated, refined people who appreciated her intellectual gifts. Around 1530 she made an unfortunate match with Philippe Fournel, seigneur de Crenne, a dominating husband who overruled his wife's intent to publish feminist works. Eight years later she initiated a writing career with the first of three works, *Les angoysses douloureuses qui procedent d'amours* (The painful torments that proceed from love, 1538), an immensely popular first-person confession of a young wife's affair and her retreat from a vengeful husband. Speaking candidly to female readers, Hélisenne remarks on intimate moments in bed with her husband, whom she loves as a friend. She outlines her internal debate with reason concerning the advisability of yielding to illicit love. Although she warns women of the peril of luxuriating in adultery, she chooses sensuality because it answers a need that marriage leaves unfulfilled.

Within a year the author wrote 18 highly personal letters in *Les epistres familières et invectives* (Personal and invective letters, 1539) in defense of the brutalized wife. Derived from her personal experience, the letters take on the tone of a heart-to-heart talk between female friends on the subject of keeping love alive as a necessary part of a well-rounded life. The author admits her intent to love whom she will. In the 10th letter, addressed to her friend, Galazia, she states, "No task will wear me down, no peril will put me off; no accident will retain me nor prison hold me" (Hélisenne, 64). She followed with *Le songe de Madame Hélisenne* (The dream of Madame Hélisenne, 1540), an allegorical reenactment of the Venus and Pallas amour and a defense of the human need to satisfy erotic desires. Composing at a furious pace, in 1541, Hélisenne translated into prose the first four books of Virgil's *Aeneid*.

Bibliography

Hélisenne de Crenne. A *Renaissance Woman: Hélisenne's Personal and Invective Letters*. Syracuse, N.Y.: Syracuse University Press, 1986.

Nash, Jerry C. "Renaissance Misogyny, Biblical Feminism, and Hélisenne de Crenne's 'Epistres Familieres et Invectives,' " *Renaissance Quarterly* 50, no. 2 (Summer 1997): 379–410.

O'Brien, John. "Vox Faucibus Haesit," *Symposium* 49, no. 4 (Winter 1996): 297–306.

Hellman, Lillian (1905–1984)

A liberator of female characters in drama, screenplays, and memoir, the author Lillian Florence Hellman focused on the amorality and darker ambitions of human nature. She lived part time in Manhattan and New Orleans, her childhood home, where Sophronia, her black wet nurse and nanny, cared for her and instilled the plight of the underdog. Hellman was well read on her own and through study at New York University and Columbia. As a writer she applied shrewd critical skills to book reviews for the *New York Herald-Tribune*. While living in Europe with her first husband, Arthur Kober, she observed the rise of fascism, a menace that also informed her liberal political opinions and her writing of *Watch on the Rhine* (1941), a play that warned Americans of the encroachment of European politics.

A lifelong companion of the mystery writer Dashiell Hammett, Hellman developed into a writer of feminist short fiction, articles, and plays. Under his mentorship she developed gossip about lesbianism into her first play, *The CHILDREN'S HOUR* (1934), a Broadway landmark.

Hellman's next major play was *The Little Foxes* (1939), an anticapitalism drama of viciousness and greed in a southern merchant-class family. The schemer Regina Hubbard Giddens is a multiple sinner—a seeker of controlling interest in a family-owned cotton mill, a manipulator of cheap labor, and a blackmailer of her two inept brothers, Ben and Oscar. She gloats, "I don't want to hear any more from any of you. *You'll do no more bargaining in this house*" (Hellman, 1971, 197). Regina's predations force to maturity her daughter, Alexandra, a daddy's girl who recognizes her mother's excesses, including the murder of her invalid husband, Horace. Hellman contrasts Regina's willful spite with the spineless whimpering of Birdie Hubbard, a perpetual victim who deserves to be ignored. When the play opened on Broadway, it generated acclaim for Tallulah Bankhead, the actor who played the evil Regina. An operatic version, *Regina* (1949), composed by Marc Blitzstein, opened on Broadway in 1949. In addition to revealing the myriad cruelties in Regina's villainy, the libretto accentuated her sibling rivalries and Birdie's retreat into silence and alcoholism. For the 1991 film adaptation, completed by Hellman and the satirist Dorothy PARKER, Bette Davis won an Oscar nomination for her sex-charged version of Regina.

Hellman stayed in the public eye with successful productions of *Watch on the Rhine, Another Part of the Forest* (1947), and *Toys in the Attic* (1960). Two late autobiographical works endeared her to feminists. Her National Book Award–winning memoir, *An Unfinished Woman* (1969), pictures her activism during the Spanish civil war and her retort to anti-Semites who had dismissed her as an uneffectual Jewish Leftist playwright. A second memoir, *Pentimento: A Book of Portraits* (1973), features a spy episode, "Julia," the source of another successful film, which starred Jane Fonda and Vanessa Redgrave. The screen version earned Oscars for Jason Robards and for Redgrave, who plays Julia, a brave amputee who risks her life to overthrow Hitler. Additional accolades swept in nominations for best picture, direction, photography, music, and the performances of Fonda and Maximilian Schell. After blacklisting in Hollywood in 1948 for expressing Leftist sentiments, in 1952 Hellman earned a reputation for tough talk during the McCarthy era, when she testified before the House Un-American Activities Committee, an event she recapped in a memoir, *Scoundrel Time* (1976).

Bibliography

Anderlini-D'Onofrio, Serena. *The "Weak" Subject: Modernity, Eros, and Women's Playwriting.* Cranbury, N.J.: Associated University Press, 1998.

Case, Sue-Ellen, ed. *Performing Feminisms: Feminist Critical Theory and Theatre.* Baltimore: Johns Hopkins University Press, 1990.

Faderman, Lillian. *Scotch Verdict: Miss Pirie and Miss Woods v. Dame Cumming Gordon.* New York: Columbia University Press, 1994.

Hellman, Lillian. *The Collected Plays of Lillian Hellman.* Boston: Little, Brown, 1971.

———. *Pentimento.* Boston: Little, Brown, 1973.

Martin, Robert K. "*The Children's Hour:* A Postcolonial Turn of the Screw," *Canadian Review of American Studies* 31, no. 1 (2001): 101–107.

Hemans, Felicia (1793–1835)

The popular English narrative poet, hymnographer, translator, historical fiction writer, and dramatist Felicia Dorothea Browne Hemans championed the humble female cottager as well as the sword-waving virago as examples of women's self-affirmation. Born to a merchant-class family of Irish, Italian, and German heritage, she spent early childhood in Liverpool. After her father left for Canada, her mother home schooled Hemans at Gwyrch on the northern coast of Wales in modern foreign languages, Latin, music, and sketching. She began publishing verse in her midteens and corresponded with the feminist playwright Joanna BAILLIE. Before marriage Hemans completed *The Domestic Affections and Other Poems* (1812), the first of a quarter-century's work that critics compared to the verse of William Wordsworth and Lord Byron.

In her most feminist writings Hemans warned girls that their freedom ends at the altar. After her husband, Captain Alfred Hemans, abandoned her during her last pregnancy, she supported their five sons, all younger than age six, on freelance reviewing for the *Edinburgh Review.* She also issued verse in *New Monthly Magazine* and translated fiction from French, German, Italian, Latin, Portuguese, and Spanish. She became the highest-paid staff member at *Blackwood's Literary Magazine* and rivaled Sir Walter Scott and Byron in book sales in Europe and North America for *Modern Greece* (1817), *Translations from Camoëns and Other Poets* (1818), *Tales and Historic Scenes in Verse* (1819), and *Wallace's Invocation to Bruce* (1819). She witnessed the staging of her tragedy, *The Vespers of Palermo* (1823), which opened at Covent Garden on December 12 and featured Fanny Kemble in the main role. At the more successful Edinburgh debut in 1824, Harriet Siddons played the lead. A popular work, *Records of Woman and Other Poems* (1828), recovered for history heroic figures, including the Renaissance Italian sculptor Properzia di' Rossi, Joan of Arc, and Native Americans. To the mother abandoned soon after giving birth, she wrote a suicide poem, "Indian Woman's Death-Song" (1828). After the issuance of *National lyrics and Songs for Music* (1834) and *Scenes and Hymns of Life* (1834), she died at age 41 in Dublin of a rheumatic heart condition worsened by scarlet fever.

Hemans had reason to depict men as traitors and child deserters. She left a number of works that have earned a second glance for their departure from romanticism's idealization of wives and marriage, notably her sensitive treatment of royalty in "Stanzas on the Death of the Princess Charlotte" (1818). In *The Widow of Crescentius* (1819) the strength of the Roman widow Stephania in poisoning the emperor Otho is noteworthy, as is the stabbing of two sons performed publicly by a mother shamed by a traitor husband in *The Wife of Asdrubal* (1819). In *Forget Me Not* (1826) she anthologized a popular narrative, "Evening Prayer, at a Girls' School," a wistful look at the innocence of childhood. Another memorable work, *The Bride of the Greek Isle* (1828), tells of a victim of pirates who burns them to death in a fire at sea for murdering her husband.

Bibliography

Hemans, Felicia. *Records of Women: With Other Poems* (1828). Available online: URL: http://digital.library.upenn.edu/women/hemans/records/records.html. Accessed on October 14, 2005.

Lundeen, Kathleen. "Who Has the Right to Feel? The Ethics of Literary Empathy," *Style* 32, no. 2 (Summer 1998): 261–271.

Sweet, Nanora, and Julie Melnyk. *Felicia Hemans: Reimagining Poetry in the Nineteenth Century.* New York: St. Martin's Press, 2001.

Henley, Beth (1952–)

A master of black humor and unpretentious southern Gothic stage works, the dramatist and screenwriter Elizabeth "Beth" Becker Henley expresses through oddball situations and hilarious dialogue a regard for women's strengths. While growing up in Jackson, Mississippi, she suffered chronic asthma and read plays as entertainment. The precocious stagehound learned the rudiments of drama from community performances at the New Stage Theater, where set builders hoisted flats that she fantasized were three-sided dollhouses. Her mother, Elizabeth "Lydy" Josephine Henley, played a variety of stage parts. When the writer's father, the attorney Charles Henley, ran for the Mississippi senate, she made platform appearances to advance his campaign. Despite dyslexia, she earned a B.F.A. in acting at Southern Methodist University, where she absorbed the southern Gothicism of Tennessee Williams, Eudora WELTY, and Flannery O'CONNOR. By age 20 Henley saw the production of a preliminary one-act work, *Am I Blue* (1973), an assignment for a playwriting class that features the compassion and sexual honesty of 16-year-old Ashbe Williams.

After a year of postgraduate coursework at the University of Illinois and an apprenticeship in acting and drama instruction Henley gravitated to the high-energy milieu of Los Angeles and pursued writing rather than acting. She earned critical acclaim for two woman-centered works, which she mapped out in longhand in a spiral-bound notebook. The first, the three-act comedy *Crimes of the Heart* (1979), features a reunion in Hazelhurst, Mississippi, of the raffish Magrath sisters, Meg and Lenny. The two celebrate the release from jail of their impetuous younger sister, Babe Botrelle, for shooting her husband, Zackary, a self-important politician and wife beater who threatens to have her committed to an asylum. After explaining that she made lemonade while the victim bled, Babe exults in breaking silence about her husband's marital abuse and enjoys the freedom to play her saxophone. A Broadway hit in 1981 at 535 performances, *Crimes* earned Henley a Pulitzer Prize, a New York Drama Critics Circle Award, a Tony, and an Oscar nomination for the screen adaptation. The second play, *The Miss Firecracker Contest*

(1980), depicts a Brookhaven, Mississippi, hopeful, Carnelle Scott, as a dupe of the beauty title cult. Her name suggests the focus of Henley's satire— the carnal roles that men create for their ideal playmates. Both works flourished in screen versions, the first with an all-star cast—Jessica Lange, Diane Keaton, Sissy Spacek, and Sam Shepard— and the second starring Holly Hunter as the desperate, fanatical outcast Carnelle, whom London playgoers applauded.

Henley's next works had mixed results for a distinct blend of empathy and off-center humor, which the theater critic Pamela Renner typifies as "girl-powered lunacy" (Renner, 18). *The Wake of Jamey Foster* (1982), an autobiographical depiction of a woman's rejuvenation at her husband's funeral, failed with readers and audiences; the two-act *The Debutante Ball* (1985) returned to issues of arbitrary devaluation of female worth from formulaic definitions of beauty. With the antiheroic *Abundance* (1990) Henley followed the traditions of FRONTIER LITERATURE by portraying the bonding of two mail-order brides, Macon Hill and Bess Johnson. Over a quarter-century the two friends survive boredom, their husbands' bad table manners, a prairie fire, and abduction by Indians in the Wyoming outback.

In reference to her focus on women's problems, Henley declared them human problems deserving of universal concern. Out of regard for her humanism, in 1993 Blackfriars Theatre of San Diego performed *Abundance* in Khabarovsk and Vladivostok, Russia. Henley reprised the female BEAUTY MYTH in *Impossible Marriage* (1998), an eccentric comedy about Pandora Kingsley, a southern bride, and her panic that she will lose the spotlight after her one big day. Worsening her qualms is the cynicism of her sister, Floral, a lackluster wife in the last stage of pregnancy. Another quirky alliance fuels *Family Week* (2000), a female-centered play that joins a mother, sister, and niece at a rehab clinic. The repartee is a minefield of character assassination and murder that draws to a warm, snuggly conclusion.

Stripped of frivolities, Henley's stage romps bear comparison to Anton Chekhov's works. Her flaky females, often silenced by dark family secrets, share fragility and loneliness along with far-fetched solutions to their problems. An example of bizarre behavior is that of Mother Magrath, who hanged her cat, then herself so she would not have to die alone. Beneath gales of audience mirth lie the rumbles of domestic rage, VIOLENCE, battered wives, alienated daughters, soiled reputations, and death wishes. Henley tends to contrast those bearing heartache, such as Lenny Magrath and her malformed ovary, with the powderpuffs and clotheshorses, such as Cousin Chick the Stick and Pandora Kingsley, who take comfort in self-absorption. The literary foils to Hensley's vapid kewpie dolls are fiercely loyal women such as best friends Bess Johnson and Macon Hill and Carnelle Scott, who gives earrings to the seamstress Popeye Jackson as a token of SISTERHOOD.

Bibliography

Hargrove, Nancy D. "The Tragicomic Vision of Beth Henley's Drama," *Southern Quarterly* 22, no. 4 (Summer 1984): 54–70.

Laughlin, Karen L. "Criminality, Desire, and Community: A Feminist Approach to Beth Henley's *Crimes of the Heart*," *Women and Performance* (1986): 35–51.

Renner, Pamela. "The Mellowing of Miss Firecracker," *American Theatre* 15, no. 9 (November 1998): 18–19.

Shepard, Alan Clarke. "Aborted Rage in Beth Henley's Women," *Modern Drama* 36, no. 1 (March 1993): 96–108.

Herbst, Josephine (1892–1969)

A committed political writer and social and political chronicler, Josephine Frey Herbst repudiated the SILENCING and denigration of women, children, and ethnic minorities. In a memoir, *Nothing Is Sacred* (1928), and a posthumous autobiography, *The Starched Blue Sky of Spain and Other Memoirs* (1991), she describes her childhood with three sisters in Sioux City, Iowa, where their father eked out a living selling farm implements. After working her way through school and completing a degree in English at the University of California at Berkeley at age 27, she moved to Greenwich Village in New York City and published short stories in *The Smart Set*.

While living in Berlin and Paris, Herbst began her career as a novelist. In the late 1920s she and her husband, John Herrmann, relocated to Erwinna, Pennsylvania, where she involved herself in social issues and completed *Money for Love* (1929), a wacky comedy about failed romance and the dependence of females on men for money. At her height in the 1930s she embraced socialism. She traveled to Cuba and Russia and wrote on labor protests and strikes for the *New Masses* and the *Nation*. As Hitler gained power, she covered political shifts in Germany and toured Spain to report on civil war.

In a Marxist trilogy of the fictional Trexler-Wendel family Herbst chronicled eight decisive decades from the 1860s to the 1930s. The realistic saga—*Pity Is Not Enough* (1933), *The Executioner Waits* (1934), and *Rope of Gold* (1939)—incorporates historic events that motivate society, especially the rise of capitalism, threats to traditional masculinity, and the subjugation of women and the laboring class. From a feminist perspective the trilogy challenges the CONFINEMENT of women to the home, women's banishment from the male sphere of politics, and the dangers of illegal ABORTION. Herbst turned to polemical writing in her last decade by lauding civil rights and denouncing the Vietnam War. Although she died in poverty and neglect by readers, feminist literary historians restored her to fame in the 1990s.

Bibliography

Herbst, Josephine. *Pity Is Not Enough*. Urbana: University of Illinois Press, 1998.

———. *The Starched Blue Sky of Spain and Other Memoirs*. Boston: Northeastern University Press, 1999.

Hubler, Angela E. "Josephine Herbst's 'The Starched Blue Sky of Spain and Other Memoirs': Literary History 'In the Wide Margin of the Century,'" *Papers on Language and Literature* 33, no. 1 (Winter 1997): 71–98.

Roberts, Nora. *Three Radical Women Writers: Class and Gender in Meridel Le Sueur, Tillie Olsen, and Josephine Herbst*. New York: Taylor & Francis, 1996.

Herland Charlotte Perkins Gilman (1915)

The novelist and lecturer Charlotte Perkins GILMAN devoted her life to WOMEN'S RIGHTS and radical social reform. Choosing a utopian vehicle, five years before the passage of women's right to vote she produced *Herland,* the rare classic edenic fantasy written by a woman. In a 2,000-year-old pastoral setting surrounded by jungle, 3 million women live in ecofeministic harmony in an Eden planted in nut and fruit trees and mulched with recycled organic wastes. They remove stress and misery from their haven by ousting male citizens, VIOLENCE and war, sentimentality, flirtation and courtship, the social constraints of female virginity, seduction, and romantic love. Gilman's protagonists are agile, capable women whose ancestors drove out belligerent males and abolished SLAVERY. Left without men, Herlanders occupy a vice-free, shame-free ecofeminist realm: "Everything was beauty, order, perfect cleanness, and the pleasantest sense of home over it all" (Gilman, 1992, 21).

As contrast Gilman introduces three randy male outsiders, the sociologist Vandyke Jennings, Terry O. "Old Nick" Nicholson, and Jeff Margrave, who view Herland through conventional gendered perspectives. The trio observes that Gilman's parthenogenetic race of Herlanders survives contentedly with woman-centered customs and attitudes. They prefer short, unfussy hairstyles and wear sun hats and comfortable jerkins that suit an athletic lifestyle: "Each was in the full bloom of rosy health, erect, serene, standing sure-footed and light as any pugilist" (*ibid.,* 22). They rid themselves of stress and exhaustion by keeping no labor-making horses or cattle or vicious dogs that might bite children. For worship they revive Maaia, the goddess of motherhood, whom they revere in a temple. In her honor Herlanders exalt childbearing as a personal fulfillment. They breastfeed infants for two years and rear each in a child-safe environment. Rational policies make plausible a number of variations from the outside world— living in a cooperative SISTERHOOD without kings or priests and ridding themselves of surnames and DYNASTY. For the sake of subsequent generations, they limit the number of births, rear children communally and teach them through interactive games, and educate their daughters to enjoy wholesome, unfettered lives.

As humor Gilman inserts the comments of the male visitors, who are loath to give up stereotypes of the female simpleton, the blushing damsel, the trendsetter, the clinging vine, and the oversexed voluptuary. Terry blurts out, "We all know women can't organize—that they [squabble] like anything—are frightfully jealous" (*ibid.,* 59). Van diagnoses Terry's limited vision as the result of nine months in "Ma-land," where he lives as a monk "with neither Love, Combat, nor Danger to employ his superabundant energies," Gilman's polite term for libido (*ibid.,* 145, 60). With greater insight than Terry, Van deduces that the American notion of femininity has a false basis, a "mere reflected masculinity—developed to please us because they had to please us, and in no way essential" (*ibid.,* 60).

Testosterone is the visitors' undoing. Terry's failure at marriage results from another stereotype, the belief that his new wife must be mastered and sexually subdued. In Van's view Terry, like the egotistical husband in Robert Browning's dramatic monologue "My Last Duchess" (1844), thinks of his bride as "some quarry he was pursuing, something to catch and conquer" (*ibid.,* 131). The men quickly change their predatory views. They discern that Herlanders "were not servants, they were not timid, inexperienced, weak" (*ibid.,* 141). Because Van can abandon male superiority and other forms of sexism, he becomes the most contented man of the trio and the most likely escort for his wife, Ellador Jennings.

In a sequel, *With Her in Ourland* (1916), set at the beginning of World War I, Gilman denounces global chaos by introducing Ellador to the rest of the world. She rapidly connects the brutal, violent world of men with the advance of navigation and the spread of piracy, colonialism, and warfare. More puzzling are the denigration of motherhood and the complicity of Chinese women in binding the feet of tiny girls. In chapter 11, which Gilman devotes to feminism, Van learns that over centuries males shaped the female gender through law, religion, and EDUCATION to suit their selfish desires.

The couple's return to Herland is inevitable. Ellador rejoices in her first glimpse from the airplane that carries them back: "No smoke! . . . no brutal noise, no wickedness, no disease" (Gilman, 1997, 192). Gilman rounds out the sequel with the best of civilization's skills and science, which Ellador introduces to Herland. By winnowing out only the bad, she looks forward to a progressive era in which the next generation will usher in a two-gender society that is even more prosperous than the original Herland. Her contribution is precedent setting, the birth of a son.

Bibliography

Deegan, Mary Jo, and Christopher W. Podeschi. "The Ecofeminist Pragmatism of Charlotte Perkins Gilman," *Environmental Ethics* 23, no. 1 (Spring 2001): 19–36.

Gilman, Charlotte Perkins. *Herland and Selected Stories.* New York: Signet Classics, 1992.

———. *With Her in Ourland.* Westport, Conn.: Praeger, 1997.

Greene, Carol Hurd. "This Land Is Her Land," *Nation,* 11 February 1991, pp. 172–174.

Hudak, Jennifer. "The Social Inventor: Charlotte Perkins Gilman and the (Re) Production of Perfection," *Women's Studies* 32, no. 4 (June 2003): 455–477.

Hogan, Linda (1947–   )

The dramatist, essayist, and ecofeminist poet Linda Henderson Hogan speaks with incantatory power the frustration of the dispossessed and the peace of living at one with nature. Born to a Chickasaw army sergeant and a silenced Anglo mother in Denver, Colorado, she grew up at midwestern military camps and used alcohol and preteen sex as escapes from an unhappy home. After completing an M.A. at the University of Colorado, she taught creative writing in Colorado and Minnesota. At age 32 she published a verse anthology, *Calling Myself Home* (1979), the beginning of an outpouring of poems, dramas, and short and long fiction. Her play *A Piece of Moon* (1980) earned a Five Civilized Tribes Museum award. She pursued the link of mother to daughter in *Daughters, I Love You* (1981) and *Seeing through the Sun* (1985), which pictures in "Daughters Sleeping" the mystic umbilicus that binds mother to child.

Hogan's female protagonists wield their authority unself-consciously, gently, as though ruled by a spirit of hospitality. In the verse collection *Savings* (1988), her depictions of women move beyond victim to savior and savant, the image in the poem "The Avalanche," in which a woman clings to Earth cycles as she lets go of the cliff face and gives way to emotional collapse. In the same volume

Hogan honors female elders as WISEWOMEN in "Germinal" and as storytellers in "The Hands." Her novel *Mean Spirit* (1990), a finalist for the Pulitzer Prize and winner of the Oklahoma Book Award, earned Hogan a fellowship from the National Endowment for the Arts. Amid an atmosphere of doom for indigenous lifestyles, Belle Graycloud clings to a fallen meteor and to the knowledge of healing with herbs from her cutting bed, where she sleeps in hot weather. Faith in Earth wisdom sets Belle and other Natives apart from grasping whites who care only for profit from oil derricks.

The author stresses positive forms of feminism. She expresses an intense belief in ECOFEMINISM in *Book of Medicines* (1993), a verse and prayer anthology that urges women to seek spirituality through oneness with the universe. In the healing motifs of *Solar Storms* (1995) she creates a matrilineage through which the protagonist, Angela Jensen, investigates two generations of mother-on-daughter abuse. The text opens on a meal of welcoming, down-home foods and a give-away ceremony expressing feminine generosity. In *Power* (1999) Hogan bestows on the character Omishto, a Taiga woman, an innate ability to observe nature and to embody the prophecies and interpretations of two female oracles, her mother and her grandmother. Guided by matriarchal wisdom, Omishto believes that her physical makeup is uniquely observant: "I watch everything and see deep into what's around me. I have a strong wind inside me. A wind with eyes" (Hogan, 1999, 4).

Bibliography

Brice, Jennifer. "Earth as Mother, Earth as Other in Novels by Silko and Hogan," *Critique* 39, no. 2 (Winter 1998): 127–138.

Hogan, Linda. *Dwellings: A Spiritual History of the Living World.* New York: Touchstone, 1996.

———. *Power.* New York: W. W. Norton, 1999.

———. *Solar Storms.* New York: Scribner, 1997.

———. *The Woman Who Watches Over the World: A Native Memoir.* New York: W. W. Norton, 2002.

Holm, Jennifer L. (1968–   )

The Finnish-American children's author and historian Jennifer L. Holm presents a realistic world of female choice and action. Reared in Audubon, Pennsylvania, she enjoyed the company of four brothers, the impetus for her most popular children's historical novel. Their parents encouraged an appreciation of American history by introducing the children to colonial Williamsburg. By age 12, she was writing fiction. After graduating from Dickinson College, she began producing television ads for a New York agency, Ogilvy & Mather. Central to her production of children's stories was her interest in genealogy, American history, and family STORYTELLING about the settlement of the Pacific Northwest. She gradually reconstructed the role of the Holm clan in pioneer history. During a boom in Scandinavian immigration, the patriarch of the family, Great-Grandfather Charles Holm, arrived from Finland in the 1870s and established a clan home place in Little Finland in the Nasel River valley of Washington Territory, one of the last stands of valuable undeveloped timberland in North America.

Holm earned a Newbery Honor Book honorarium for *Our Only May Amelia* (1999). To create 12-year-old May Amelia, Holm's most lauded heroine, she took events from the diary of her great-aunt, Alice Amelia Holm, a teenaged Finn born in 1888 who helped settle Washington State's Nasel River Valley. Found in an old suitcase at the author's grandmother's home in 1993, the text required translation by the author's bilingual aunt Elizabeth Holm. In the style of FRONTIER LITERATURE May Amelia, the first female born in the territory, tackles WOMAN'S WORK as her daily chore, but she has the freedom to wear overalls as her seven brothers do, explore a logging camp, and weave fishnets. Holm impresses on her protagonist the hard realities of married women's lives during May Amelia's mother's pregnancy and after the death of a newborn baby sister.

Holm pursued more unfettered female daring in a trio of historical novels, *Boston Jane: An Adventure* (2001), *Boston Jane: Wilderness Days* (2002), and *Boston Jane: The Claim* (2004). The ongoing story features Jane Peck's journey to Washington, D.C., and her reaction to the disappearance of her fiancé in the wilderness. With good humor she summarizes the threats to a lone female as "the company of rough men and Chi-nook Indians, not to mention a flea-ridden hound" (Holm, 2002, 1). As the manager of an oyster business she feels outclassed by the posturing of Sally Biddle, a model of the ladylike decorum Jane should have learned at finishing school. In the final installment Jane faces the legal prohibition of female ownership of land in Shoalwater Bay, Washington Territory.

Bibliography

Holm, Jennifer. *Boston Jane: The Claim.* New York: HarperCollins, 2004.

———. *Boston Jane: Wilderness Days.* New York: HarperCollins, 2002.

———. *Our Only Amelia May.* New York: HarperCollins, 1999.

Roper, Ingrid. "Jennifer Holm," *Publishers Weekly,* 28 June 1999, pp. 28–29.

hooks, bell (1952–)

Renowned for intellect and vision, the feminist theoretician and culture critic bell hooks speaks knowledgeably about SEXUALITY and sexism that permeate postmodern textbooks, literature, the media, and film. Called Gloria Jean Watkins at birth in Hopkinsville, Kentucky, she grew up in the rural tradition of black southern STORYTELLING. She abandoned her birth name for a matriarchal link to her great-grandmother, Bell Hooks. Influenced by the personal mythography of the poet Audre LORDE, in 1996 hooks produced an autobiography, *Bone Black: Memories of Girlhood.* She opened the work with a matriarchal motif, a glimpse at her mother's hope chest and the gift of a quilt, a standard symbol of the scraps and ends of life passages that women unite into a functional domestic object. She recalls, "I feel I am witnessing yet another opening of Pandora's box, that the secrets of her youth, the bittersweet memories, will come rushing out like a waterfall and push us back in time" (hooks, 1996, 1–2).

As a columnist for the *Shambhala Sun* hooks warned female readers that solutions to racism tend to offer PATRIARCHY as the answer to the black woman's place in society and art. Growing up under the hand of a strong father, hooks weathered her own rebellion against limitations on females. She repeatedly heard a common threat to female divergent thinkers—"that I am crazy, that I will end up in a mental institution. This is my punishment for wanting to finish reading before doing my work" (hooks, 1996, 101). During her EDUCATION in newly integrated schools she enjoyed the freedom from family criticism that let her fantasize and choose her own identity. She completed studies in English literature at Stanford University, the University of Wisconsin, and the University of California at Santa Cruz while defining a unique vision of feminism and its impact on the classroom experience.

Hooks maintained her focus on the female sphere. In her first work, *Ain't I a Woman: Black Women and Feminism* (1981), she confronted the devaluation of black females and extolled their unique qualities within the feminist movement. She addressed the black segment of the feminist movement in *Feminist Theory: From Margin to Center* (1984). With a broad sweep the preface to the second edition defines feminism as the struggle that "takes place anytime anywhere any female or male resists sexism, sexist exploitation and oppression" (hooks, 2000, xi). Her position as professor of literature, black studies, and women's studies at City College of New York gives her opportunities to fine-tune feminist curricula, her outreach to the next generation. In *Teaching to Transgress* (1994) she urges teachers to instruct young feminists in clear, jargon-free terms about the importance of class prejudice in discrimination against women.

Bibliography

Bartlet, Alison. "A Passionate Subject: Representations of Desire in Feminist Pedagogy," *Gender and Education* 10, no. 1 (March 1998): 85–92.

hooks, bel. *Bone Black: Memories of Girlhood.* New York: Henry Holt, 1996.

———. *Feminist Theory: From Margin to Center.* Cambridge, Mass.: South End Press, 2000.

———. *Killing Rage-Ending Racism.* New York: Henry Holt, 1995.

———. "Postmodern Blackness" (1990). Available online: URL: http://jefferson.village.virginia.edu/pmc/text-only/issue.990/hooks.990. Accessed on October 14, 2005.

———. *Teaching to Transgress.* New York: Routledge, 1994.

Housekeeping Marilynne Robinson (1981)

A dreamy saga of catastrophe and salvation, Marilynne ROBINSON's *Housekeeping* (1981) elevates the importance of female ties in the life of an orphan. Growing up in the Western town of Fingerbone, the protagonist, Ruth Stone, and her younger sister, Lucille, suffer mother longing, even under the care of Grandmother Sylvia Foster and two great-aunts, Lily and Nona Foster. Leftovers of family tragedy, the girls wither into "small, unnoticed, unvalued clutter," the detritus of a ruined family (Robinson, 116). After Lucille moves in with Miss Royce, a home economics teacher, Ruth becomes her sister's alter ego in avoiding the conventionality and order that shelter Lucille. Ruth remains anchored in her grandmother's house, a stable image that appears to counter the watery death of Sylvia's husband, Edmund, who died on a train that plunged into a deep blackwater lake. The sudden gobbling of the train disturbs nature more seriously than the death of Ruth's mother, Helen, who plunges a borrowed Ford over Whiskey Rock. Although Grandmother Sylvia promises, "So long as you look after your health, and own the roof above your head, you're as safe as anyone can be," the prophecy holds truer than the love of Ruth's father, who abandons the family (*ibid.,* 27). Symbolically, Edmund's homestead, a paternal house, does not contain and satisfy Ruth, who yearns for a mother house.

Much as Mark Twain's *Huckleberry Finn* (1884) does, Robinson's allegorical novel uses water imagery both as threat and as gateway to freedom. Ruth grows to love Aunt Sylvia "Sylvie" Fisher, an asocial migrant laborer and surrogate mother who tends her niece after the house floods four inches deep in lake water. Significantly Ruth undergoes a metaphoric rebirth in a boat, where she "lay like a seed in a husk . . . and I swelled and swelled until I burst Sylvie's coat" (*ibid.,* 162). As does the canoe birthing in Toni MORRISON's *BELOVED* (1987), the boat shape mimics not only a husk, but also the vulva, the passage through which the fetus passes from water animal into a land existence. Ruth and Sylvie nurture each other—the lost child and the rootless, suicidal elder. Gradually the exterior of the house merges with the interior, giving new meaning to *Sylvie,* from the Latin for "woods." The unconventionality of her domestic style advances to full-time vagrancy, a life on the fly like that of "marooned survivors of some lost pleasure craft" (*ibid.,* 96). By eluding the securities of the past that failed Ruth and Lucille, Sylvie and Ruth find their own assurance in a shared life.

Set free from obligatory householding, the duo constructs a lakeside lean-to of stone and driftwood that is "to all appearances random and accidental" (*ibid.,* 114). The construction mimics the duality of Ruth's early years—built on stone, then freed to drift as a tree limb on the current. In her dream, Ruth learns from Sylvie how to walk under water, a fantasy of their alternate lifestyle out of kilter with society. Until the sheriff of Fingerbone imposes the outside world's constraints, Ruth is content: "I was hungry enough to begin to learn that hunger has its pleasures, and I was happily at ease in the dark, and in general, I could feel that I was breaking the tethers of need" (*ibid.,* 204). After attempting to burn the homestead, Ruth and Sylvia abandon androcentric tradition and embrace transience as their true home.

Bibliography

King, Kristin. "Resurfacings of The Deeps: Semiotic Balance in Marilynne Robinson's *Housekeeping,*" *Studies in the Novel* 28, no. 4 (Winter 1996): 565–580.

Robinson, Marilynne. *Housekeeping.* New York: Bantam, 1982.

Smyth, Jacqui. "Sheltered Vagrancy in Marilynne Robinson's *Housekeeping,*" *Critique* 40, no. 3 (Spring 1999): 281–291.

The House of the Spirits   Isabel Allende
(1981)

A roman à clef and international best seller translated into 27 languages *La casa de los espíritus (The House of the Spirits),* the expatriate writer Isabel Allende's first novel, contrasts the male domains of politics, finance, landownership, and the military with the domestic skills, affection, and extrasensory powers of women. The plot grew out of a fearful period of exile that followed the assassination of her uncle and godfather Salvador Allende and the overthrowing of the dictator Augusto Pinochet. The text captures the author's rage when she; her husband, Miguel Frias; and their children fled Chile in 1974 for safety in Caracas, Venezuela. She later relocated to the United States, where she admired the feminist movement, especially the American regard for female authors. To preserve her grandfather's memory, she initiated the historical saga as a long letter to him in which she outlines family events. Proclaimed Allende's masterwork—a Latin American *Gone with the Wind*—and nominated for the Paperback Book Club New Voice Award, *The House of the Spirits* earned tributes for denouncing male self-aggrandizement, greed, and corruption as the cause of national chaos.

The saga covers the resilient matrilineage of Nívea, Clara, Blanca, and Alba, four generations linked by names expressing whiteness as a symbol of clear vision as well as political innocence. The dominant voice, Clara del Valle, is "the soul of the big house" (Allende, 1986, 283). She relates her terror and grief at age 10 when she witnesses the autopsy of her sister, Rosa, by a crass technician. Illogically blaming herself for Rosa's poisoning, Clara falls mute until age 19, when she breaks the silence to announce her intention to marry Rosa's former fiancé, Esteban Trueba, master of the Trés Marias hacienda. A colonial tyrannizer, he has already manhandled an Indian servant, Pancha García, and sired a demonic namesake, Esteban García. Clara, who brandishes the domestic power of plantation mistress, attempts to civilize Esteban with the affection she offers him and their children. The subject of speech returns at the decline of their intimacy, when she thrusts him out of her bedroom in punishment of his belligerence. Her reasoning expresses the importance of communication to their union: "If we had nothing to say to each other, we would also be unable to share a bed" (*ibid.,* 179).

A token of female authority in the novel is the issue of naming. Seizing the moment at her children's conception, Clara foresees the birth of male twins and overrules her husband's paternal prerogative by naming the fetuses Jaime and Nicolás rather than Esteban. Countering her husband's wounded pride, she pleads pragmatism—by introducing new names, she avoids confusion in the Trueba DYNASTY. During the couple's ongoing power struggle, the author builds the irony of Clara's maternal might. Her husband, who is given to tantrums and selfish demands, struts and flatters himself: "His house would be the reflection of himself, his family, and the prestige he planned to give the surname that his father had stained" (*ibid.*, 93). Clara expresses her hatred for Esteban's outbursts and VIOLENCE by reverting to her maiden name of del Valle, a proof of her self-worth. His many Indian-Hispanic bastards inherit no rights to the Trueba surname, and his legitimate sons maintain the matronym del Valle as a political gesture denouncing his furtherance of conservative, sexist, and racist traditions. The exception to a string of del Valles is Alba, a rebel who annoys her self-important grandfather, Esteban, by flaunting the maiden patronym of Trueba and by glorying in her illegitimate siring by a working-class revolutionary, Pedro Tercero García, Esteban's sworn enemy.

Allende expresses the shift in Chilean history by changes in the del Valle matrilineage. In contrast to Clara's home-centered life is the emergence of her granddaughter, Alba, as a liberated woman and socialist who survives a sexual assault in childhood and rape and torture during political imprisonment by her father's bastard, Esteban García. The support and nursing by her fellow inmate Ana Díaz, the singing of Beethoven's "Ode to Joy" by other female prisoners, and a visit from Clara's ghost reaffirm Alba's optimism. After her release she exalts the strength of women: "I understood that the days of Colonel García and all those like him are numbered, because they have not been able to destroy the spirit of these women" (*ibid.*, 429). In an interview the author acknowledged the need for Chile to expunge the memory of these atrocities: "It will be impossible for the new (Chilean) government to punish all those who should be punished: the torturers won't be tortured; the rapists won't be raped; the murderers won't be killed. And people will have to understand that it is not out of revenge that we will rebuild our country but out of love and forgiveness" (Allende, 1999, p. 24).

Bibliography

Allende, Isabel. *The House of the Spirits.* New York: Bantam, 1986.

———. "Pinochet's Ghost," *New Perspectives Quarterly* 16, no. 3 (Spring 1999): 22–26.

Foreman, Gabrielle. "Past-on Stories: History and the Magically Real, Morrison and Allende on Call," *Feminist Studies* 18, no. 2 (Summer 1992): 369–388.

Rodden, John. "The Responsibility to Tell You: An Interview with Isabel Allende," *Kenyon Review* 13, no. 1 (Winter 1991): 113–123.

The House on Mango Street
Sandra Cisneros (1983)

Through 44 vignettes Sandra CISNEROS's *The House on Mango Street* looks through the eyes of a 12-year-old naif, Esperanza Cordero, at the limited choices of displaced Chicanas. At the threshold of womanhood she is aptly named the Spanish for "hope." She enjoys barrio games of "tee-tottering" in high heels with Lucy, dreams of having red lipstick, and admires her little sister, Nenny's, gold earrings, a life-passage marker of a female's first communion (Cisneros, 40). Esperanza's mother fears her older daughter's inquisitive nature, which violates the stereotypical passivity of la Virgen de Guadalupe. Esperanza confides, "My mother says I was born on an evil day and prays for me" (*ibid.*, 58). The comment suggests an impasse that dominates the parent-child writings of her writer contemporaries Gish JEN, Maxine Hong KINGSTON, and Amy TAN—a daughter's failure to live up to impossible mythic standards and the fears of immigrant mothers for first-generation American daughters.

Jump-rope rhymes about the fat-hipped waitress "[paying] the rent with taxi tips" presage Esperanza's introduction to seamy adult realism (*ibid.*, 51). She witnesses the disconnect between Rose Vargas and a brood of fatherless children. A perplexing series of events begins with the hermitism of Sally, who hides bruises made by her father's belt buckle. She compensates for child abuse by sexual experiments with Tito and his friends in the monkey garden. Other forms of female escapism take a hit-and-miss approach to limited horizons. Marin sells Avon fragrances and dreams of rescue by a well-dressed man on the subway; to ease loneliness, Minerva scribbles poems on paper scraps. A Mexican friend from Guadalajara named Alicia fantasizes about escaping her widower father by enrolling at a university. Mamacita, a recent immigrant, retreats into television to ease boredom and isolation. Rafaela drinks coconut and papaya juice after her husband locks her in their upstairs flat. The image of juice as a substitute for intimacy reflects Cisneros's choice of a title that names a plump, curvaceous fruit that entices as does lush femininity.

With strobe-light intensity, Esperanza tempers voyeurism with introspection. She imagines the physical intimacies of Sire and his gang, swarthy punks who romance Lois in the alley. By contemplating Great-Grandmother Esperanza's marriage to a tyrannic husband, the young namesake acknowledges that "Mexicans don't like their women strong" (*ibid.*, 10). She fantasizes a form of womanly power by renaming herself "Zeze the X" (*ibid.*, 11). A part-time job at the Peter Pan Photo Finishers is more alienating than liberating after a customer unexpectedly fondles and kisses Esperanza. A more workable empowerment is that given by Aunt Lupe, a blind lover of children who suggests that Esperanza can liberate herself through writing. Contributing to Esperanza's ambitions are three elderly sisters, who predict that she will retain the female lives of Mango Street as sources of her adult identity. In preparation Esperanza employs STORY-TELLING both as an escape and as a literary rescue of Latinas trapped in poverty and PATRIARCHY.

Bibliography

Cisneros, Sandra. *The House on Mango Street.* Houston: Arte Público, 1983.

Petty, Leslie. "The 'Dual'-ing Images of la Malinche and la Virgen de Guadalupe in Cisneros's *The House on Mango Street*," *MELUS* 25, no. 2 (Summer 2000): 119–132.

Houston, Jeanne Wakatsuki (1934–)

A gentle feminist voice for humanity and inclusion, Jeanne Toyo Wakatsuki Houston recaptures from a woman's point of view the cruelties of American history. The youngest of the 10 children of a Japanese-American fishing family, she was born in Inglewood, California, and came of age in Ocean Park. In early childhood she witnessed her father's departure for incarceration in a North Dakota prison and her mother and siblings' internment at Manzanar, a desert camp that segregated citizens of Japanese ancestry for the duration of World War II. After studying sociology at the University of San Jose and completing her education at the Sorbonne, she suppressed bad memories for three decades as she reared her family.

As did the poet Mitsuye YAMADA and the short-story writer Hisaye YAMAMOTO, Houston suffered internal grief over her family's imprisonment and loss of home and income. In 1973 she and her husband, the writer James Houston, issued *Farewell to Manzanar,* a memoir and source of a 1976 teleplay dramatizing the multiple losses of Japanese families as a result of racist paranoia in the 1940s. Broad themes of civil rights violations and the costs of freedom cap a pervasive subtext of women's ability to withstand humiliation and CON-FINEMENT. The rigidity of Ko, Jeanne's exhibitionist father, a scion of the samurai class, contrasts with the flexibility and pragmatism of her Hawaiian-born mother, Riku Sugai Wakatsuki. In recognition of the assault on manhood Jeanne says that internment "brought [Ko] face to face with his own vulnerability, his own powerlessness. He had no rights, no home, no control over his own life" (Houston & Houston, 52). In crowded, dust-choked shacks, Jeanne turns to the Maryknoll nuns as models of solace and goodness while her mother networks with other women, who restore privacy in the latrine by holding up a cardboard Oxydol box to divide the space between toilets.

Upon Ko's reunion with the family at Manzanar, Jeanne Houston pictures him as spiritually whipped by imprisonment and devaluation. Explosive in self-defense, he restores his manhood through threats of assaulting his mother-in-law and of murdering his wife. The melodramatic scenes force Jeanne to hide under a bed or leave the house rather than watch Ko brutalizing Riku. As the traditional pecking order disintegrates, Ko withdraws into swaggering, solitude, and homemade rice wine while his wife pads the flimsy barracks walls and finds work as a hospital dietician.

Jeanne studies ballet, odori dance, and baton. The falling action pictures a gendered differentiation—the male parent slips into fantasies of building a government-subsidized housing project while the stoic mother of the family returns to labor in a fish cannery and faces marital difficulties through passive aggression.

Contrasting responses of male and female internees guide the memoir to its resolution. In maturity Jeanne Houston returns to Manzanar to lay to rest the ghosts of her early girlhood behind barbed wire. She looks back on her father's failure to adapt to social cataclysm as a failure of masculine traditions in times of crisis. She recognizes in Riku a yang-over-yin ability to value changing female roles in American society and a pride in her daughter's liberation from Japanese PATRIARCHY. In Jeanne's words, "Acceptance, in her eyes, was simply another means for survival" (*ibid.*, 128).

Memory continues to fuel Houston's writings, which include two expanded editions of *Farewell to Manzanar*. In *The Legend of Fire Horse Woman* (2003) the author exalts the pride, power, and cunning of 64-year-old Sayo Matsubara, a picture bride who emigrates from Japan to California in 1902 to enter a disappointing arranged marriage. Upon presentation to her father-in-law Sayo is unable to conceal her independence: "Matsubara felt his hara [gut] suck in involuntarily. For one moment he felt panic. Unmistakable power gleamed from those eyes" (Houston, 260). Like Houston's mother, Riku, the fictional matriarch is stoic and strong-willed in the face of humiliation at the immigrant reception center. She recommends endurance and dignity to her daughter, Hana, and granddaughter, Terri, during their term at Manzanar. The suppression of Japanese patriarchy allows Hana to grow up assertive and strong, encourages Terri's intellectualism, and accords Sayo a suitable lover.

Bibliography

Goto, Hiromi. "Manzanar as Metaphor," *Women's Review of Books* 21, no. 10/11 (July 2004): 22.

Houston, Jeanne Wakatsuki. *The Legend of Fire Horse Woman*. New York: Kensington, 2003.

———, and James Houston. *Farewell to Manzanar*. New York: Bantam, 1973.

Hurst, Fannie (ca. 1885–1968)

A writer of popular feminist fiction and screenplays, Fannie Hurst created realistic situations that found favor among Hollywood filmmakers and with readers in a dozen countries. The daughter of German Jews, she was born in rural Ohio near Hamilton and grew up in Saint Louis. While studying literature and history at Washington University and Columbia University, she began submitting short fiction to periodicals and scored a sale of "Ain't Life Wonderful" (1909) to *Reedy's Weekly*. She lived in New York City under her own name happily separate from her beloved husband, the Russian-Jewish pianist and music teacher Jacques S. "Jack" Danielson. Over 55 years the author established a prolific and profitable canon of novels and stories featuring the hardships of working women, single mothers, prostitutes, and immigrants. In an exclusive contract with Hurst *Saturday Evening Post* negotiated for subsequent works.

Hurst's first successes were the story collection *Gaslight Sonatas* (1918), an anthology of six stories about human crises, and the novels *Star-Dust: The Story of an American Girl* (1921) and *Lummox* (1923), a sentimental commentary on the diminished self-esteem of a Scandinavian domestic. The key to Hurst's appeal are spunky, slangy dialogue and authentic details provided by her research assistant, Zora Neale HURSTON. Hurst's quick action acknowledges the small cataclysms that result in domestic and social chaos in homes, boardinghouses, sweatshops, and the counters of cafés and lingerie shops, workplaces the author knew firsthand. She made light fare of a popular story, "Hattie Turner versus Hattie Turner," a feature in *Cosmopolitan* in 1935 that pictures the remorse of a wife whose wish that her cruel husband die comes true.

At the depths of the Great Depression Hurst wrote *Back Street* (1932) and *Imitation of Life* (1933), two smash hits, on the topics of parental sacrifice, adultery, racism, working women, and denial of culture. *Back Street*, the story of a Jewish male's three-decade affair with Ray Schmidt, a Gentile woman, discloses Ray's tragic waste of passion and loyalty. The novel was the source of three films, the 1932 Universal screenplay, starring Irene Dunne; the 1942 remake, which allied Margaret

Sullavan and Charles Boyer as secret lovers; and Universal's 1961 revision, starring Susan Hayward opposite John Gavin. Two film versions of *Imitation of Life* pictured the rise of a white cook and her black maid in the pancake business. In 1934 Universal Pictures featured Claudette Colbert and Louise Beavers as the business partners Bea Pullman and Delilah Johnston in a two-hanky screenplay that earned an Oscar nomination. The Universal-International remake in 1959 paired Lana Turner and Juanita Moore as the heroines and reaped an Oscar nomination for Moore's depiction of Delilah.

Bibliography

Hurst, Fannie. *Anatomy of Me*. New York: Arno Press, 1958.

———. *Gaslight Sonatas*. New York: Harper's, 1918.

———. *Imitation of Life*. Durham, N.C.: Duke University Press, 2004.

———. *Lummox*. London: Howard Baker, 1970.

Koppelman, Susan. "Fannie: The Talent for Success of Writer Fannie Hurst," *Women's Review of Books* 17, no. 1 (October 1999): 20.

Swindell, Larry. "There's Nothing Funny about Fannie Hurst's Literary Legacy," *Fort Worth Star-Telegram*, 19 January 2000, p. K3.

Hurston, Zora Neale (1891–1960)

The most prominent black female author of the early 20th century, Zora Neale Hurston mastered essay, griot lore and folk arcana, domestic novel, drama, short story, and autobiography, but she died broke and virtually forgotten. She was born in Notasulga, Alabama, 10 years earlier than her claim to friends and the press. Reared in Eatonville, Florida, the nation's first incorporated black town, she came of age observing the exuberant southern folk wit that is the backbone of her work. In a memoir, *Dust Tracks on a Road: An Autobiography* (1942), she soaked up southern black dialect and idiom of the region's people—both "kinfolks and skin folks"—and extolled local women for their interminable labors, "squatting around St. John's Hole on their haunches, primitive style, washing clothes and fishing" (Hurston, 1996, xviii, 8). The most important to the author's life was Lucy Ann

Potts Hurston, her 90-pound mother, who assured her children that "all good traits and leanings come from the mother's side" (*ibid.*, 20).

After the sudden death of her mother in 1904, Hurston could not accept a stepmother or reconcile with her philandering father. Impelled by her mother's dying words to "Jump at de sun," like the protagonist in her first story, "John Redding Goes to Sea" (1921), at age 13 Hurston left home, the "sorrow's kitchen" she recalled in *Dust Tracks* (*ibid.*, 13). Two years later she began traveling with a stage troupe as wardrobe mistress. In 1917 she earned a high school diploma at Morgan Academy in Baltimore while supporting herself as a barbershop manicurist and cabaret waitress. Literary historians surmise that she began shaving 10 years from her age to lessen the difference between her and other students. During the next six years at Howard University she submitted short pieces to *Forum, Messenger, The New Negro, Opportunity,* and *Stylus*, a campus literary journal. Her first critically successful story, "Drenched in Light" (1924), offers glimpses of her creative exhibitionism in the person of Isis, the prancing child who eludes poverty through imagination by wrapping herself in a self-glorifying red tablecloth.

Hurston's interest in the arts steered her toward Harlem, where she served the novelist Fannie HURST as research aide. Hurston collaborated with the poet Langston Hughes on publishing the magazine *Fire!* and writing the three-act play *Mule Bone: A Comedy of Negro Life* (1930). Early on she echoed the vivid emotions of rural black speech, such as the cry of Mrs. Tony Roberts in "The Eatonville Anthology" (1926), who "sing-songs in a high keening voice . . . 'Lawd knows me an' mah chillen is SO hongry! Hits uh SHAME! Tony don't fee-ee-eee-ed me!'" (Hurston, 1995, 59). The first black to enroll in and graduate from Barnard College, Hurston majored in anthropology. She researched the *Clothilde*, the slave ship that delivered the last load of captured Africans to American auction blocks. Under the guidance of the anthropologist Franz Boas, she traveled the South, Central America, and the Caribbean as the first female to conduct field work in black folklore. She unearthed forgotten elements of conjuring and herbalism, sermons and aphorism, work songs, children's rhymes, gendered behavior, and her specialty, front-porch humor, fool tales, and teasing. Easing her passage were her disdain for pedantic intellectuals and a great-heartedness toward the poor.

Beyond the belly laughs of her characters, in much of her writing Hurston acknowledged female bondage, particularly the novel *Jonah's Gourd Vine* (1934). In the domestic squabble that opens the work, Amy Crittenden refuses to be cowed and expresses the author's liberated womanhood by protecting her son from her husband's slander: "Dat's uh big ole resurrection lie, Ned. Uh slew-foot, drag-leg lie at dat. . . . Hit me if you dare! Ah'll wash yo' tub uh 'gator guts and dat quick" (Hurston, *Jonah,* 3). Hurston's landmark contribution to feminism, THEIR EYES WERE WATCHING GOD (1937), is the product of a seven-week sojourn in Haiti to recover from a failed amour. The story carries the defense of women to one of literature's most satisfying resolutions. Throughout the 1930s and 1940s she worked steadily at vernacular folklore for *Mules and Men* (1935) and *Tell My Horse* (1938); the novel *Moses, Man of the Mountain* (1939); and submissions to *American Mercury, Negro Digest, Saturday Evening Post,* and the *Southern Literary Messenger.* While living in Honduras, she completed a novel, *Seraph on the Suwanee* (1948), the story of Arvay Henson, one of Hurston's female seekers.

As do Marjorie Kinnan RAWLINGS's stories and memoirs, Hurston's re-creation of regional mores and speech rhythms legitimizes a neglected strand of southern lore. Dogged by ulcers, heart disease, and poverty in her last years, Hurston taught drama in North Carolina and Florida, reviewed for the *New York Herald Tribune,* and freelanced for the *Pittsburgh Courier.* In 1973 the novelist Alice WALKER located Hurston's remains in an unmarked pauper's grave; five years later *Their Eyes Were Watching God* returned to print as another monument to feminist recovery of lapsed titles. Ruby Dee dramatized the author's zippy repartee in a PBS teleplay, *Zora Is My Name* (1990). Six decades after the composition of *Mule Bone,* it opened at Lincoln Center in New York City in February 1991. Subsequent reevaluation elevated Hurston not only for her sympathetic depiction of peasant culture but also for her infectious jests and bawdy tall tales chock full of insight into female yearnings. Her honest portrayals of WOMAN'S WORK and female ambition influenced the feminism of the novelist Terry McMILLAN.

Bibliography

Hemenway, Robert. *Zora Neale Hurston: A Literary Biography.* Champaign: University of Illinois Press, 1977.

Hurston, Zora Neale. *The Complete Stories.* New York: HarperCollins, 1995.

———. *Dust Tracks on a Road.* New York: Harper Perennial, 1996.

———. *Jonah's Gourd Vine.* New York: Harper Perennial, 1990.

———. *Mules and Men.* New York: Harper Perennial, 1990.

———. *Their Eyes Were Watching God.* New York: Harper Perennial, 1990.

Kaplan, Carla. *Zora Neale Hurston: A Life in Letters.* New York: Anchor, 2003.

West, Genevieve. "Feminist Subversion in Zora Neale Hurston's 'Jonah Gourd Vine,' " *Women's Studies* 31, no. 4 (July–August 2002): 499–515.

I

ideal woman

The idealized female is a product of history and human fantasy. The fall of the Roman Empire in the fifth century A.D. cost much of the Western world's female population even the small gains they had made in obtaining basic EDUCATION, authority over their children, and civic and religious self-empowerment. During the early Middle Ages as Donna CROSS describes in her historical novel *Pope Joan* (1996), many wives and mothers functioned no more successfully than those of prehistory. Their foibles and errors of judgment directed myths, fables, nursery rhymes, and FAIRY TALES toward the disobedience of Goldilocks; the curiosity of Snow White, Gretel, LITTLE RED RIDING HOOD, and the victim of BEAUTY AND THE BEAST lore; and the sexual yearnings of CINDERELLA and Rapunzel. The solution to achieving their place in society was the touch of a magic wand or the intervention of some masculine force: rescue of Bluebeard's wife from a serial killer, the awakening of Sleeping Beauty, and the transformative power that turns Cinderella into a fairy princess and alters the Beast into a proper husband for Beauty.

Instead of proclaiming women's innate qualities, in European art, songs, and verse, the concept of COURTLY LOVE, a romantic notion that lacked verisimilitude, pictured the adoration of the ideal female. The cherished woman, such as the VIRGIN MARY and the English poet Geoffrey Chaucer's legendary obedient and patient wife Griselda, fit a male-oriented pattern of perfection—loyal, meek, gracious, and unflawed in face, figure, and behavior. Fiction described these rare and treasured fantasy women from a distance, never close up, talking, expressing opinions, deciding important matters, or being fully involved in home and community life. In Chaucer's "The Clerk's Tale" (1387), the comely spiritual Griselda wins hearts by an innate goodness extended to all: "She had increased to such an excellence / Of grace she was as bounty on a throne, / Wise, and so lovely in her eloquence, / So grave and so benign, she charmed the sense / And gathered every heart in her embrace" (Chaucer, 203). For her qualities people loved her on sight.

Like sparkling jewels, Griselda and her idealized sisters were valuable only for external grace, poise, and submission to men. As the feminist essayist Gloria STEINEM explained in her speculative biography *Marilyn: Norma Jeane* (1986), life on so high a pedestal is destructive to real people. Steinem characterizes Marilyn Monroe as a childlike sex idol who has no opportunity to discover her worth in normal human relations. Steinem concludes that a retreat to the real girl would have dispelled the illusion: "Clearly, the public Marilyn could never have survived the game without revealing the lost Norma Jeane" (Steinem, 202). Tragically male fantasy triumphed as "the shy girl began to disappear inside a created image" (*ibid.*, 204). Ironically, in death Marilyn was further dehumanized as the serene martyr, the ageless, ever alluring sex siren flash-frozen in time by a mouthful of barbiturates.

The critic Marina Warner's *Alone of All Her Sex: The Myth and Cult of the Virgin Mary* (1976) relates the harm of exalting the unique, faultless female and forcing girls to aspire to her uniqueness. In real-life situations women like those pictured by the Greek poet SAPPHO and in the verse of MARIE DE FRANCE battled for the right to be human. In Judeo-Christian societies women suffered the castigation of EVE and LILITH through male scapegoating and accusations of WITCHCRAFT. At the far end of idealization the degraded female bore blame for the world's ills. Each suffered accusations and persecutions for causing original sin, the sole reason that God forced Adam and Eve to vacate the Garden of Eden. Guinevere, the most prominent example of medieval womanhood, married Arthur, a Celtic king who built the fabled realm of Camelot. According to royal tradition, their engagement was a father-to-suitor political arrangement based on the good of the nation rather than on Guinevere's love for her betrothed. The wedding was a state occasion, a public display to the king's subjects of his wealth, power, and statecraft. Surrounded by her ladies in waiting, she lived as a caged bird that never tried its wings in solitary flight. Because Sir Lancelot, Arthur's faithful knight, wooed her for her humanity, she bore much of the blame for the fall of Camelot and spent the remainder of her life in a convent seeking forgiveness for illicit love. The mythographer Marion Zimmer BRADLEY dispelled the false accusations of Guinevere in *The Mists of Avalon* (1982), in which the cause of the queen's undermining of Arthur's ideal state was a new ideal. The suppression of goddess worship and Druidism by a new player, Christianity, demanded a new conquest of land and people, especially females. Sorrowing in memories of the last battle, Guinevere testifies to the horrors of crushed ideals in the heaped remains of "bodies, bones, blood" (Bradley, 486).

With full knowledge of the skewed logic of the perfect women, feminist authors apply the concept of idealized womanhood to suit insightful literature. The English poet Elizabeth Barrett BROWNING revived the Edenic Eve in *A Drama of Exile* (1844), a narrative that retrieves the first woman from ignominy by praising her virtues and exonerating her of evil. Similarly the lesbian author Marie CORELLI created a lovely ingenue for *Vendetta!; or, The Story of One Forgotten* (1886), a tale that

names female perfection as the cause of male self-delusion. The Caribbean novelist Jean RHYS pictures in *WIDE SARGASSO SEA* (1966) the insanity of Antoinette Cosway Mason, whose girlhood introduction to saints precipitates an unattainable image of womanhood in a Jamaican setting that prefers passion and pleasure to wooden idols. For *The Woman Warrior: Memoirs of a Girlhood among Ghosts* (1976), Maxine Hong KINGSTON retrieves from eons of male militarism the legendary Chinese warrior Fa Mu Lan as a testimony to the prowess of a superwoman who can be lover and mother as well as protector and soldier. In a satiric utopian fable the English Gothicist Angela CARTER describes a sex-change operation in *The Passion of New Eve* (1977) to express a reverse evolution from the flawed male Zero to the faultlessness of Eve. Carter's model implies that the depletion of human virtues increased through time as society lost contact with the GODDESS LORE and accepted androcentrism in its stead.

Far from lost on society is the role of the feminine ideal in advertising and politics. In a retrospect of the Madison Avenue ideal, the columnist Anna QUINDLEN asserts the feminist concerns of the late 20th century, when "hanging over the lives of every little girl born in the second half of the 20th century was the impossibly curvy shadow (40-18-32 in life-size terms) of Barbie" (Quindlen, F4). Quindlen demands accountability from the standard bearers for their sexist, racist mania: "Whose ideal? The perfect girl projected by the white world simply didn't apply to [black women] or their community, which set beauty standards from within" (*ibid.*). For polemical purpose, the Australian philosopher Germaine GREER's *The Whole Woman* (1999) alerts women to the insidious nature of such pop icons as Barbie, Jackie O, Madonna, and Princess Di whose media-generated perfection skimps on truth. A more practical examination of perfection is Tracy Chevalier's novel *The Girl with a Pearl Earring* (1999), a fictional explanation of a real-life Cinderella's rise from Dutch pot girl to elegant, enigmatic face on a canvas painted by Jan Vermeer. Along the way to fame as the classic look of innocence, Griet encounters the cruelty of a higher-class contemporary, the gropings of a self-important art patron, and the jealousy of Vermeer's wife. Couching her text in Griet's re-grets and dashed hopes, Chevalier stresses the illusion of effortless perfection crafted from humble beginnings.

Bibliography

Bradley, Marion Zimmer. *The Mists of Avalon*. New York: Del Rey, 1987.

Chaucer, Geoffrey. *The Canterbury Tales*. Translated by Nevill Coghill. London: Cressed Press, 1992.

Chevalier, Tracy. *The Girl with a Pearl Earring*. New York: Plume Books, 2001.

Lawrence, Kelli-an, David Taylor, and E. Sandra Byers. "Differences in Men's and Women's Global, Sexual, and Ideal-Sexual Expressiveness and Instrumentality," *Sex Roles: A Journal of Research* 34, no. 5–6 (March 1996): 337–357.

Quindlen, Anna. "What Damage Has Barbie Wrought? Barbie at 35: She Isn't Just a Toy," *Greensboro News Record*, 18 September 1994, p. F4.

Steinem, Gloria. *Marilyn: Norma Jeane*. New York: New American Library, 1986.

I Know Why the Caged Bird Sings Maya Angelou (1969)

Through gritty detail, hyperbole, and winsome humor, Maya ANGELOU describes the coming of age of the Maya character, an examination of her child-self as Marguerite "Maya" Johnson, the focus of the AUTOBIOGRAPHY *I Know Why the Caged Bird Sings*. Maya learns the basics of southern womanhood from her grandmother, Annie Henderson, owner of the Wm. Johnson General Merchandise Store in Stamps, Arkansas. The womanly side of life requires rolling out biscuit circles, attending Sunday services, and dressing as a lady for an eighth-grade graduation ceremony at Toussaint L'Ouverture Grammar School. During household chores Maya regrets one of the tests of domesticity—having to "iron seven stiff starched shirts and not leave a cat's face anywhere" (Angelou, 14). When the family situation shifts, Maya lives in Saint Louis with the strutting, amoral Vivian "Bibbi" Baxter Bailey, Maya's mother, and under the supervision of Grandmother Baxter, a female political force for whom there is no analogy in the South. The differences in the matriarchal line pose

new thoughts about womanhood that Maya takes time to ponder.

The cyclical banning of *I Know Why the Caged Bird Sings* from school and public libraries stems from the brutality of chapter 12, Maya's rape by Bibbi's lover, Mr. Freeman. Delicately, Maya recalls, "The act of rape on an eight-year-old body is a matter of the needle giving because the camel can't" (*ibid.*, 65). Angelou accounts for the muting of Maya during a rapid retribution against the pedophile, who dies near a slaughterhouse of the pummeling of Bibbi's three brothers. The family accepts the child's self-SILENCING as "a post-rape, post-hospital affliction" (*ibid.*, 73). Bibbi's flamboyant femininity does little to revive Maya's self-confidence. Returned by train to Momma Henderson, Maya forces herself to serve a five-year penance for causing Freeman's murder. A gentle tutor, Mrs. Flowers, helps Maya to memorize verse to restore her voice and self-esteem. Maya pictures her mentor as the IDEAL WOMAN, who "made me proud to be Negro, just by being herself" (*ibid.*, 79).

The onset of womanhood increases internal conflict. Adolescence arouses both rebellion and vulnerability in Maya, whose "need for change bulldozed a road down the center of my mind" (*ibid.*, 224). While living in Los Angeles and San Francisco, she observes her mother's self-empowerment as a casino owner and learns from a teacher, Miss Kirwin, that EDUCATION is the right of all students. After running away from Daddy Bailey's girlfriend, who stabs Maya in the side, Maya grasps at autonomy by living in a teen community in a junkyard and by wearing down prejudice to become the first black female streetcar conductor in San Francisco. Among other teenaged girls she finds belonging in SISTERHOOD: "I was never again to sense myself so solidly outside the pale of the human race. The lack of criticism evidence by our ad hoc community influenced me, and set a tone of tolerance for my life" (*ibid.*, 254).

Maya's final obstacle is an understanding and acceptance of her sexuality. Still confused after she reads Radclyffe HALL's *The Well of Loneliness* (1928), Maya tests her sexual preference by coupling impersonally with a male neighbor. While explaining her dilemma to her mother, Maya uses euphemisms for anatomical terms. The worldly,

uninhibited Bibbi retorts, "Don't use those Southern terms. There's nothing wrong with the word
'vagina' " (*ibid., 234*). The strength of mothering
comes, ironically, from Bibbi, who convinces Maya
that instinct will provide caution during her
daughter's care of her newborn son. As the raw
edges of self coalesce into the future writer and
celebrity, Angelou indicates the multiple strands of
womanly autonomy that nudge Maya toward
wholeness. She reprised the themes of *Caged Bird*
in a film on female friendships and artistry, *How to
Make an American Quilt* (1995), a feminist tour de
force featuring actors Winona Ryder, Ann Bancroft, Ellen Burstyn, Jean Simmons, Lois Smith,
Alfre Woodard, and Kate Capshaw.

Bibliography

Angelou, Maya. *I Know Why the Caged Bird Sings.* New
    York: Bantam Books, 1970.
Lupton, Mary Jane. *Maya Angelou.* Westport, Conn.:
    Greenwood Press, 1998.
Walker, Pierre A. "Radical Protest, Identity, Words, and
    Form in Maya Angelou's *I Know Why the Caged
    Bird Sings,*" *College Literature* 22, no. 3 (October
    1995): 91–108.

Incidents in the Life of a Slave Girl, Written by Herself Harriet Jacobs (1861)

The former slave Harriet JACOBS wrote an account
of her life with the aid of Lydia Maria CHILD, editor of the *National Anti-Slavery Standard,* and of
Amy Kirby Post, founder of the Western New York
Anti-Slavery Society. Doubters charged that the
autobiography was fictional, but feminist authenti-
cation of events and sources attests to its truth.

Written under the pseudonym Linda Brent,
the text conceals identities but exposes the sexual
exploitation of female slaves and the threats to
slave children by which white owners manipulate
black women. Essential to the text are the gender
dilemmas that force Jacobs to forgo virginity. As
she describes puberty, "the war of my life had
begun" (Jacobs, 31), a reference to the common
practice of "breaking in" young girls to concubinage. She mentions "licentiousness and fear" as
well as lashings, bloodhounds, the master's indecent talk, and the smothering of unwanted new-

borns (*ibid.,* 45). Even though she knows the perils
of reaching above her station for a freedman, she
grasps the romantic ideal: "Youth will be youth. I
loved, and I indulged the hope that the dark
clouds around me would turn out a bright lining"
(*ibid.,* 34). When her master hears that she prefers
another man, he contemplates murdering her on
the spot and, for the first time, strikes Harriet. Ultimately, she has no choice but to initiate an affair
with a white man of her choice. She rationalizes,
"There is something akin to freedom in having a
lover who has no control over you" (*ibid.,* 48).

In escape from the horror of relations with
males and the retribution of the master's jealous
wife, Jacobs seeks refuge in her family's matrilineage. She retreats to her mother's twin sister and
finds a maternal haven in her saintly grandmother.
Of the grandmother's charity and piety Jacobs offers high praise: "We longed for a home like hers.
There we always found sweet balsam for our troubles. She was so loving, so sympathizing!" (*ibid.,*
18). The years in the attic crawlspace torment Jacobs by providing through a peephole glimpses of
her children and the sounds of their voices, but no
contact or even an indication of that she still lives.
These events from her years of bondage, sexual
torment, and frustrated parenthood have made
Harriet Jacobs one of the most familiar former
slave woman in feminist history.

Bibliography

Blackford, Holly. "Figures of Orality: The Master, the
    Mistress, the Slave Mother in Harriet Jacobs's *Inci-
    dents in the Life of a Slave Girl: Written by Herself,*"
    Papers on Language and Literature 37, no. 3 (Sum-
    mer 2001): 314–336.
Jacobs, Harriet A. *Incidents in the Life of a Slave Girl:
    Written by Herself.* New York: Harvest Books, 1983.
Randle, Gloria T. "Between the Rock and the Hard
    Place: Mediating Spaces in Harriet Jacobs's *Inci-
    dents in the Life of a Slave Girl,*" *African American
    Review* 33, no. 1 (Spring 1999): 43–56.

independence

Independence is a resounding theme in feminist
literature for its acknowledgment of all sides of
womanly character and ambition. As the novelist

George ELIOT explained, "We women are always in danger of living too exclusively in the affections . . . we ought also to have our share of the more independent life—some joy in things for their own sake" (Heilbrun, 76). In the abstract MOURNING DOVE, the author of *Mourning Dove: A Salishan Autobiography,* published posthumously in 1990, chose a bird pseudonym as a symbol of freedom and escape from tribal disapproval of her writing career. Similarly Barbara KINGSOLVER populates her novels with resilient women who need no male rescuers. Beginning with the single parents Lou Ann Ruiz and Taylor Greer, the adoptive mother of April Turtle, a Cherokee foundling, in *The Bean Trees* (1988), the author progressed to Lusa Maluf Landowski, the entomologist turned livestock manager in *Prodigal Summer* (2000). Lusa saves her farm from bankruptcy with a novel approach to moneymaking—raising goats to sell in New York City during Easter, Passover, and Muslim high holy days. Although her rejection of tobacco as a crop alienates her from local male farmers, her success brings them around to admiration of female ingenuity.

Breaking away from androcentric thinking can cast doubts about feminine virtue and adherence to community and religious mores. The feminist critic Carol Gilligan, author of *In a Different Voice: Psychological Theory and Women's Development* (1982), characterizes ambivalence toward liberation as the dilemma between being a nice girl and becoming a full-fledged, self-directed woman. It is the difference between virtue and power that "the feminine voice struggles to resolve in its effort to reclaim the self and to solve the moral problem in such a way that no one is hurt" (Gilligan, 71). The dilemma of sexual desire versus morality is a source of tension in Charlotte BRONTË's *JANE EYRE* (1847). The governess in the title longs for the love of her married employer, but she chooses to allow sexual union only as his legal wife. Jean RHYS, who redirected Brontë's text with a prequel, *WIDE SARGASSO SEA* (1966), speaks the wisdom of the autonomous woman through the character of Christophine, a celibate nanny from Martinique. She considers dependent women fools and mutters, "No husband, I thank my God. I keep my money. I don't give it to no worthless man" (Rhys,

110). Thus Christophine takes a shortcut to independence by denying sexual needs and avoiding intimate contact with males.

Celibacy is an issue in FRONTIER LITERATURE, in which the needs of lone farm women are second to a plentiful harvest. In framing the family argument about female ownership of farmland in *O PIONEERS!* (1913), Willa CATHER allows a sour brother, Lou Bergson, to deride his industrious sister's autonomous womanhood: "Alexandra ain't much like other women-folks" (Cather, 129). What her brothers misinterpret is that Alexandra willingly pays the price of success in male-centered agrarianism. She lives with hired help on her acreage; cultivates friendship with her neighbor, Marie; and raises the hackles of conservative males whom she outclasses by the application of modern seed culture and experimental methods of raising pigs and of interplanting alfalfa with corn. By postponing sexual satisfaction until midlife, she aches for her old friend, Carl Linstrum, who returns long after their youth has passed. Out of respect for her accomplishments and reputation among local farmers and bankers, Carl offers a suitable compliment to her persistence: "You belong to the land" (*ibid.,* 229).

In this same era independence resonated through suffragist writings in which getting the vote promised a range of opportunities for women who chose to live alone, rear children, get an EDUCATION, and function in business or the professions. In addition to supporting full citizenship rights, the writer and intellectual Charlotte Perkins GILMAN sought a soul-satisfying life for all women, especially older women, widows, single parents, and divorcées. She described autonomy for fictional females in the short stories "My Poor Aunt" (1891), "Three Thanksgivings" (1909), "Her Housekeeper" (1910), and "Martha's Mother" (1910), examples in which ungendered options set the parameters for behavior. In each instance characters find ways of achieving their heart's desire by ignoring social pressures and by following individual paths. To prevent fictional women from needing pity or rescue, Gilman ends their stories with triumphs.

Near the end of the 20th century the Asian-American novelist Amy TAN turned to historical fiction to mark the divide between women's Old

World submissiveness and New World liberation. From TALK-STORY, she mined a wealth of information about the life of her grandmother, Gu Jingmei, life under imperial Chinese PATRIARCHY and about Tan's mother, Daisy Du Ching Tan, who fled the motherland to enjoy the gender liberation of North America. As the author demonstrates, autonomy of self and finances is the only reliable escape from feudal marriage, which was the domestic model in China from prehistory until the rise of communism. In *The Joy Luck Club* (1989) she pictures the unnamed concubine of the womanizer Wu Tsing as too confined by a dominating husband to flee. Her only choice is a suicide that she carries out by ingesting an overdose of opium, which she ironically bakes into New Year's pastries. Illustrating the sacrifices of the first wave of Chinese wives to liberate themselves from coercive patriarchs such as Wu Tsing is Lindo Jong, who is too enterprising to kill herself. She gladly trades wealth from a traditional Chinese marriage to a boy groom for gender freedom in California. Stepping over the divide, she promises her inner self that she will never abandon independence in exchange for security through wedlock. As a symbolic reward to the liberated self, she regularly treats herself: "Every few years, when I have a little extra money, I buy another bracelet. I know what I'm worth" (Tan, 63).

Feminist writings by authors in the developing world express some of the hesitance of women to confront the divide between Old and New World ideals. A witty, cynical look at female independence is that of West African feminist theater. Flora Nwapa, a Nigerian playwright, debates the possibilities of marriage, adultery, and polygyny in *Two Women in Conversation* (1993). Set in a chaotic period after the attempted military coup of April 22, 1990, the domestic scene pictures a relaxed and candid exchange between Niki and Juma, two disgruntled wives. Juma alarms her friend by commenting on a handgun she acquired after she fought with the militia and by reliving the dismemberment of a schoolmate, Onyeze, after an air raid. Worsening Juma's despair at the futility of housewifery are her husband's attitude and his miserliness: "I had the children. I ministered to my husband. I cooked, washed and ironed his clothes.

I took care of the children. He never lifted a finger to help" (Nwapa, 20). To assure his control, he opened a checking account in his name alone. Niki validates Juma's recall of marital misery: "You are in a kind of bondage if you have an unclean heart" (*ibid.*, 24). Exulting in political and marital freedom, Juma summarizes her independent status, "I don't want anyone to restrict my movement or begin to preside over my life as if I were his property" (*ibid.*, 55).

Bibliography

Cather, Willa. *O Pioneers!* New York: New American Library, 1989.

Gilligan, Carol. *In a Different Voice: Psychological Theory and Women's Development.* Cambridge, Mass.: Harvard University Press, 1982.

Heilbrun, Carolyn G. *Toward a Recognition of Androgyny.* New York: W. W. Norton, 1982.

Kingsolver, Barbara. *The Bean Trees.* New York: Harper & Row, 1988.

———. *Prodigal Summer.* New York: HarperCollins, 2000.

Motley, Warren. "The Unfinished Self: Willa Cather's *O Pioneers!* and the Psychic Cost of a Woman's Success," *Women's Studies* 12, no. 2 (1986): 149–165.

Nwapa, Flora. *Plays: Conversations.* Enugu, Nigeria: Tana Press, 1993.

Rhys, Jean. *Wide Sargasso Sea.* New York: W. W. Norton, 1982.

Tan, Amy. *The Joy Luck Club.* New York: Putnam, 1989.

Indiana George Sand (1832)

Written by George SAND, the cautionary novel *Indiana* prefigures the motifs and themes of feminist and anticolonial realism. The melodrama of 19-year-old Indiana Delmare sets a standard for women who denounce the bondage of loveless wedlock and the coercion of manipulative seducers. As the wife of the tyrannic Colonel Delmare, a rich manufacturer and retired army officer, Indiana hovers on the edge of despair and physical collapse at the couple's country manse in Brie. Sand introduces her heroine, shy and red-eyed, in the corner of a cold marble mantel and pictures her as a "newly-opened flower in an antiquated vase," a foreshadowing of the woman who frees herself from outdated PATRIARCHY (Sand, 16).

Significantly, Indiana names her pointer dog Ophelia, the name of Hamlet's suicidal lover, and shudders at the cruel commands of the colonel, who killed her previous spaniel in a fit of pique. Sand indicates that the colonel confuses the roles of husband and father, a marital fault that George ELIOT sets at the heart of the May-December union in MIDDLEMARCH (1872).

Sand's depiction of female misery flirts with the intensity of the realistic novel. Born on an island in the Indian Ocean to a brutish father, Indiana serves the dual role of repressed daughter and wife and the colonial outsider. After her three years of marriage to the colonel, an affair with the womanizer Raymon de Ramière worsens Indiana's perception of herself as a trophy wife and kept woman. Duplicating the model of the outsider victimized by the European adventurer is the ruination of Indiana's Creole maid, Noun, from Ile Bourbon, a second victim of de Ramière's indiscriminate self-gratification. After Indiana displaces Noun in his affections, the maid uses her mistress's notepaper to communicate her terror at being pregnant and abandoned. In contrast to the disenfranchised woman, Indiana fends for herself. In a hunting episode she dresses in the attire of the amazon, a visual semblance of self-assertion. Sand elevates her heroine as a social model of women who refuse to be confined.

Bibliography

Murdoch, H. Adlai. "Ghost in the Mirror: Colonialism and Creole Indeterminacy in Brontë and Sand," *College Literature* 29, no. 2 (Winter 2002): 1–31.

Sand, George. *Indiana* (1900). Available online: URL: http://digital.library.upenn.edu/women/sand/indiana/indiana.html. Accessed on October 13, 2005.

Irigaray, Luce (1939–)

The Belgian philosopher and psycholinguistic clinician Luce Irigaray suggests ways for women to decentralize the male perspective in human relations, philosophy, and literature. To ensure objectivity, she guards personal data about her family. She earned a degree from the University of Louvain and taught at a Brussels high school. After completing advanced certification in linguistics and in psychology from the University of Paris, she began intense language analysis in Belgium. She directed scholarship at the Centre National de la Recherche Scientifique and promoted WOMEN'S RIGHTS to ABORTION and contraception.

In 1973 after a study of language erosion in senile patients at l'Ecole Freudienne de Paris (the Freudian School of Paris), Irigaray applied her findings to aspects of female hysteria. She advanced concepts of patriarchal intrusions on female language in *Speculum de l'autre femme* (*Speculum of the Other Woman*, 1985). Her thesis exposes coded speech patterns that reduce females to their reproductive function, thus marginalizing them as mother figures and castigating them with otherness and negativity. Her insights, which ended her professional ties to Freudianism, posited pro-female interpretations of gendered language, female writing, and "woman-speak," the themes of *Ce sexe qui n'en est pas un* (*This Sex Which Is Not One*, 1977). A branch of her philosophy repudiates Sigmund Freud's androcentric positions on mother-daughter relations, which Irigaray considers crucial to female emotional health. In 1982 she delved further into women's language in *Passions élémentaires* (Basic passions), a survey of feminist metaphor in Greek mythology, particularly the Demeter-PERSEPHONE relationship.

Irigaray's language paradigms propose rehabilitation of gender communications to compensate for the erasure of women's history. A groundbreaking shift in her interdisciplinary probes preceded *L'ethique de la différence sexuelle* (*An Ethics of Sexual Difference*, 1984), which assesses the way that people of opposite genders communicate. Another advancement of her basic philosophy, *Je, tu, nous: Pour une culture de difference* (I, you, we: toward a culture of difference, 1990), attests to the tendency of language to validate men's concerns and opinions while suppressing those of women and trivializing their place in human history. Her provocative study of female identity in *Essere due* (*To Be Two*, 1994) introduces new views of loving relationships and of barriers to women's self-definition and autonomy. She asserts that "all of the great spiritual masters . . . have testified to the necessity of having a woman close to them, better still if she is a virgin or spiritual mother, to act as a living memory of the common sense of everyday life" (Irigaray, 2001, 22). She lists as examples the pivotal social roles of the VIRGIN MARY and of Aphrodite and Athena, Greek goddesses of passion and wisdom.

Bibliography

Dellamora, Richard. "Apocalyptic Irigaray," *Twentieth Century Literature* 46, no. 4 (Winter 2000): 492–512.

Irigaray, Luce. *Speculum of the Other Woman.* Ithaca, N.Y.: Cornell University Press, 1985.

———. *To Be Two.* New York: Routledge, 2001.

In the Time of the Butterflies Julia Alvarez (1994)

The polyphonic *In the Time of the Butterflies* reprises the BIOGRAPHY of the Mirabal sisters— *Las Mariposas* (The butterflies)—and accounts for the shaping of feminist activism into legend. The Dominican-American author Julia ALVAREZ justifies her method as a humanistic effort: "A novel is not, after all, a historical document, but a way to travel through the human heart" (Alvarez, 324). As the four protagonists grow from obedient daughters of a rural cacao planter into shapers of Caribbean history, they pass through stages of defiance. By manipulating Papá Mirabal, they gain convent school educations that precede Minerva's law degree. Mate's study of architecture, Patria's marriage and Dedé's rise to business success in life insurance. Along the way to self-determination, the girls make their peace with macho traditions of wedlock and maternity by shedding the submission of the past and achieving full partnership in marriage. At a significant moment Minerva, the boldest sister, faces off against Papá by ramming her Jeep into his Ford in punishment for his secret love nest and his four illegitimate daughters. The complete emergence from metaphoric cocoons plunges the adult Butterflies into the peasant fight for sexual freedom and civil rights.

To parallel private and public challenge of PATRIARCHY, Alvarez links episodes of the SISTERHOOD's collective memory. The narrative creates individualized heroism in the four Dominican Butterflies, who help to oust Generalissimo Rafael Leandro Trujillo from power. At the head of the clan

the text pictures Minerva, a resolute conspirator who slaps Trujillo for pelvic thrusts during their dance on Discovery Day. Of his menace she admits, "Everytime I'd hear one more secret about Trujillo I could feel the tightening in my chest," yet she rebels against public SILENCING (*ibid.*, 23). A later eyeball-to-eyeball confrontation results in the roll of dice to determine whether Minerva will attend law school. Such risk taking sets her apart from her compliant sisters, who avoid provoking the dictator. A surprising pairing is Minerva with Mate, the youngest Mirabal. Mate lives with her older sister at Monte Cristi and learns the SECRECY and cunning necessary to outwit Trujillo's secret police. Her naive dairy entries echo the emerging maturity of Anne Frank. At a dramatic meeting with investigators for the Organization of American States, Mate symbolically binds innocence with savvy by braiding into her hair a written disclosure of the torture of female prisoners with an electric charge.

Alvarez salutes women who overcome fear and hesitation to commit themselves to activism. Late to join the cabal is Patria, the would-be nun, who seeks strength from prayers to the VIRGIN MARY. Patria's metamorphosis into an amazon results from the jailing of her risk-taking son, Nelson. She explains her slow development into a rebel: "I got braver like a crab going sideways. I inched towards courage the best way I could, helping out with the little things" (*ibid.*, 154). After witnessing the shooting death of a young boy at the Maryknoll motherhouse in Constanza, Patria experiences an epiphany that zeal for husband and children must expand to the "human family" (*ibid.*, 162). Her new perspective coincides with the realization among island priests that Christian service to parishioners demands defiance of tyranny.

Alvarez enhances poignance in the role of Dedé, the enigmatic sister who survives the other family members and becomes the Mirabal story keeper. Her testimonial reflects the imminent danger in a country where "people who opened their mouths didn't live very long" (*ibid.*, 18). The narrative pictures her as brave enough to hurl challenges into the face of the secret police and to divorce Jaimito Fernandez, her controlling husband. The days that follow the assassinations present eyewitness material that leaves her "composing in my head how that last afternoon went" (*ibid.*, 301). In the 32 years that follow the shooting and bludgeoning of Minerva, Patria, and Mate, Dedé dreads the influx of reporters each November 25 to pry loose more details of the famed sisters' revolutionary cell and their wayside murder. Dedé concurs with the demand for a legend: "We had lost hope, and we needed a story to understand what had happened to us" (*ibid.*, 313). Sequential tellings produce a national identity shaped by female wisdom and martyrdom.

Bibliography

Alvarez, Julia. *In the Time of the Butterflies.* Chapel Hill, N.C.: Algonquin, 1994.

Johnson, Kelli Lyon. "Both Sides of the Massacre: Collective Memory and Narrative on Hispaniola," *Mosaic* 36, no. 2 (June 2003): 75–91.

Pulio, Gus. "Remembering and Reconstructing the Mirabal Sisters in Julia Alvarez's *In the Time of the Butterflies*," *Bilingual Review* 23, no. 1 (January–April 1998): 11–20.

Rich, Charlotte. "Talking Back to El Jefe: Genre, Polyphony, and Dialogic Resistance in Julia Alvarez's *In the Time of the Butterflies*," *MELUS* 27, no. 4 (Winter 2002): 165–183.

"I Stand Here Ironing" Tillie Olsen (1956)

Tillie OLSEN's classic story of the Great Depression and World War II, "I Stand Here Ironing," parallels two generations—a 38-year-old mother and her 19-year-old daughter, Emily. Published in a collection, *Tell Me a Riddle* (1956), and the following year in *The Best American Short Stories of 1957*, the brief piece gained feminist fame in the 1960s for its commentary on the hard choices that confront the single working parent. The firstborn of three, the child is beautiful at birth but loses her bloom. The mother regrets that she has to apply for jobs and to seek day care for eight-month-old Emily. Deserted by her husband, the mother sends Emily to her paternal grandparents for care for 16 months, then enrolls her in "nurseries that are only parking places for children" (Olsen, 265). After Emily is grown, the mother regrets, "We were poor and could not afford for her the soil of easy growth" (*ibid.*, 271). Although the circumstances reflect hard times for all Americans, the mother is unable to forgive herself for being a poor provider.

The physical act of smoothing wrinkles with an iron echoes the mental realignment of memories of the mother's actions and emotions. Without self-pity she stresses the hardships of the 1930s and 1940s, particularly conditions while her second husband serves in the military. The intrusion of social services indicates that government intervention in cases of child neglect offers little more than institutional caging. Through her shuffling to various environments, Emily responds to alienation and terror with loss of appetite and dwindling concentration, crucial factors in a child's ability to learn. Furthering her diffidence is the fad of the era, dimpled blonde beauties like actor Shirley Temple, a period mania that Toni MORRISON mentions in *The BLUEST EYE* (1970). The sudden appearance of a stage persona, Emily the comedian, surprises her mother and stepfather. Although Emily seems on the right path toward adulthood, nagging regrets disturb the mother's peace of mind that she did the right things to help family flourish and mature.

Olsen's sympathy for mothers covers an array of obstacles to worthy parenting. The fictional mother regrets being a teenager when she gives birth and rues the failure of a marriage that leaves few options. A surprising criticism from an elderly male neighbor reminds her to smile at Emily to relieve the tension of their spare subsistence. A dramatic revolt during one of the mother's nights out with her new husband, Bill, results in Emily's tossing the clock on the floor and leaving the front door open, a child's methods of circumventing a lengthy separation and lessening time alone in the house. With reverence for a mother's growing wisdom, Olsen concludes the story with a prayer that Emily will realize that a woman's life need not be a constant yielding to fate, like the wrinkled dress before the iron.

Bibliography

Cullum, Linda. "Lost and Found in Space: Using Tillie Olsen's 'I Stand Here Ironing' to Encourage Resistance and Identification in the Introductory Literature Classroom," *WILLA* 4 (Fall 1995): 10–12, 27.

Olsen, Tillie. "I Stand Here Ironing," *The Best American Short Stories of 1957*. Boston: Houghton Mifflin, 1957.

Ivins, Molly (1944–   )

The political satirist, lecturer, and nationally syndicated columnist Mary Tyler "Molly" Ivins confronts society's confusion and dismay with a sensible and humane feminism. A tall Texan by adoption, she was born in Monterey, California, but honed an authentic southern style and identity in Houston, where she grew up. She completed a degree in French at Smith College and postgraduate work in journalism at Columbia University and the Institute of Political Sciences in Paris. From a lowly post at the *Houston Chronicle* to the position of first woman on the police beat at the *Minneapolis Tribune*, she began covering the women's movement in her mid-20s. She settled into political coverage as coeditor of the *Texas Observer*, a post that satisfied her love of social justice for the deserving.

After a stint as Rocky Mountain bureau chief for the *New York Times*, Ivins initiated a populist column for the *Dallas Times-Herald* and the Fort Worth *Star-Telegram*, a position that won her the William Allen White Award, the Ivan Allen Jr. Prize for Progress and Service, the Pringle Prize for Washington Journalism, and the Eugene V. Debs Award. At the same time she freelanced for the *Atlantic*, *Esquire*, *Harper's*, *Mother Jones*, the *Nation*, National Public Radio, the *Progressive*, and CBS's *Sixty Minutes*. Her irreverent quips enlivened *Molly Ivins Can't Say That, Can She?* (1991), *Nothin' but Good Times Ahead* (1993), and *You Got to Dance with Them What Brung You: Politics in the Clinton Years* (1998). The career of George W. Bush fueled hilarious commentary in *Shrub: The Short but Happy Political Life of George W. Bush* (2000), which mixes contempt with anger at his lackluster oratory and his anti-woman, anti-child policies, which he classifies as compassionate conservatism. While reducing the following for male dema-

gogues, Ivins introduced readers to achieving women, notably the former Texas governor Ann Richards, U.S. Senator Kay Bailey Hutchison, and the attorney and orator Barbara Jordan, the first black woman elected to the Texas Senate and the U.S. Congress.

On the subject of feminism Ivins tends toward cheering the underdog while deflating self-promoters. She enjoyed pillorying the self-appointed social critic Camille PAGLIA as "Big cheese in New York intellectual circles. The latest rage. Hot stuff. Controversial" (Ivins, 1991, 8). Identifying herself as "both a country-music fan and a feminist for years," Ivins felt qualified to dismiss Paglia as "a crassly egocentric, raving twit" (*ibid.*, 9, 10). In a speech to Floridians Ivins ribbed Texas for its backwardness: "where earlier this century idiots, imbeciles, aliens, the insane, and women were legally forbidden to vote, raising the age of consent for girls from seven to ten was a major change, and men were allowed to kill unfaithful wives and their lovers" (Youngman, 1999). Ivins took part in the pro-choice march on Washington, D.C., in 2003 and rejoiced, "This time, almost everyone came as family, ranging from Gloria STEINEM, now 70, to Ann Richards' granddaughters. Pregnant women for choice flecked the crowd, marching for their unborn sons and daughters" (Ivins, 2003). In support of choice Ivins applauded courage: "Abortion providers who have been subject to acts of terrorism for years were there to speak—the bombed, the shot, the maimed, the widows. Still strong, still working" (*ibid.*). On the vital issues of hungry families and limited opportunity for EDUCATION or jobs, Ivins is a wholehearted humanist, using as examples the immigrant working mothers and their children living along the Rio Grande. With prickly drollery she declares, "There is no evidence that motherhood makes a woman less adept at adding figures or making airplanes" (Ivins, 2004).

Bibliography

Ivins, Molly. "Class Warfare and the Decline of Feminism" (January 2, 2004). Available online. URL: http://progressivetrail.org/articles/040101Ivins.shtml. Accessed on October 14, 2005.

———. "I Am the Cosmos," *Mother Jones*, September/October 1991, pp. 8–10.

———. "One Million Women Strong" (April 27, 2004). Available online. URL: http://www.funnytimes.com/notfunny/20040427Ml.html. Accessed on October 14, 2005.

Youngman, Nicole. "Molly Ivins Spoke in Honor of Women's History Month in Pensacola" (1999). Available online. URL: http://www.theharbinger.org/xvii/990330/youngman.html. Accessed on October 14, 2005.

J

Jackson, Helen Hunt (1830–1885)

The crusading author Helen Maria Fiske Hunt Jackson turned to feminist fiction to express her views on Native American rights. A native of Amherst, Massachusetts, and literary friend of the poet Emily DICKINSON, Jackson was orphaned in childhood and educated at Ipswich Female Seminary and Abbott Institute. She recovered from widowhood at age 35 and from the deaths of her sons, Murray and Rennie, by writing verse, children's stories, travelogues, novels, book reviews for the New York *Independent,* and short fiction for *Harper's* and *Scribner's* and for *Atlantic,* often under the pseudonym Jane Silsbee. To recuperate from a lung ailment, she moved to Colorado; in 1875 she married a Quaker, William Sharpless Jackson, president of the Denver, Rio Grande Western Railroad.

In the West near the end of the 37 Indian wars, Jackson joined the pro-Indian activists of California and issued *A Century of Dishonor: The Early Crusade for Indian Reforms* (1881), one of North America's first critiques of federal policy regarding the displacement of Native tribes. To substantiate her accusations of near-genocide, she quotes Native authorities—Black Kettle, Chief Joseph, Red Iron, Sitting Bull, Standing Bear, and Sarah WINNEMUCCA. Jackson praised the bravery of Northern Cheyenne women of Nebraska during the army's attempt to starve and freeze them out of hiding: "Not a woman would come out" (Jackson, 1965, 98). She further extolled the acts of Red Cloud, chief of the Ogalalla Sioux, who in-vited female Cheyenne survivors and their children to live with his people. The book, distributed to every U.S. legislator, preceded the Dawes Severalty Act of 1887, which restored land on reservations to individual families.

In 1894 Jackson emulated her friend Harriet Beecher STOWE, author of *UNCLE TOM'S CABIN; or, Life among the Lowly* (1852), by producing pro-Indian propaganda. Jackson researched mission archives and published a fictionalized biography, *Ramona* (1884), the first novel set in Southern California. The plot supports Jackson's pro-Native vision through the tragic love of historic figures, Victoria Bartolomea and Hugo Reid. To expose whites' mistreatment of California's Mission Indians, the author describes Ramona Ortegna, a blue-eyed Cahuilla-Scots orphan adopted by Señora Gonzago Moreno, an overbearing martinet. In travail after the señora locks her in a bedroom, Ramona receives the sympathy of Margarita, a fellow peon in the house, who resolves, "She shan't starve her to death, anyhow. I'll never stand by and see that" (Jackson, 2002, 112).

Jackson pictures Ramona as a strong female survivor who embraces liberty and her own SEXUALITY. She chooses to leave an easy life in a Spanish hacienda and unites with her Indian husband, Alessandro, by reiterating the vow from the biblical book of Ruth, "Your people are my people" (*ibid.,* 179). The newlyweds reside in a Native enclave in the San Jacinto Mountains. At Ramona's decline with fever after Alessandro's death, Jackson pictures a female healer, Aunt Ri, who rides into the desert to pick a curative plant and to spoon a tea from its leaves into Ramona's mouth. Jackson concludes with a standard romantic device, marriage to Felipe Moreno, Ramona's old friend, and the prosperity and beauty of young Ramona, Alessandro's daughter.

Initially the novel sold well over 600,000 copies and went through 300 reprints, but the author died of stomach cancer at age 55 without realizing the success of her fictional polemic. The popular novel and the song "Ramona" (1927) drew thousands to visit Southern California. Adapted three times to screen and once to outdoor drama, the story survives in an opera, in Loretta Young's title role in the 1936 film, and in a Ramona pageant performed by 400 actors each spring at a 6,600-seat amphitheater in Hemet, California. In 1959 the pageant, American's longest-running outdoor drama, featured Raquel Welch as Ramona.

Bibliography

Jackson, Helen Hunt. *A Century of Dishonor.* New York: Harper Torchbook, 1965.

———. *Ramona: A Story.* New York: Signet Classics, 2002.

Kirsch, Jonathan. "Westwords: The Woman behind 'Ramona,'" *Los Angeles Times,* 30 March 2003, p. R2.

Jackson, Shirley (1919–1965)

A respected author of domestic Gothic fiction, Shirley Hardie Jackson was a master of the complex story blended of humor, satire, and shudders. In her native San Francisco she enjoyed solitude and reading. After graduating from Syracuse University, she married the critic and teacher Stanley Edgar Hyman and settled in North Bennington, Vermont. Uninspired by housewifery, she satisfied her intellectual curiosity with books on voodoo and the occult, the sources of *Come Along With Me,* a novel left unfinished at her death. A bored stay-at-home faculty wife, she began submitting stories to *Charm, Fantasy and Science Fiction, Good Housekeeping, Harper's Bazaar, Redbook, Saturday Evening Post,* and *Woman's Home Companion.* In 1953 she described the chaos of the Hyman/Jackson home in *Life among the Savages,* a jovial work that exposes the stress of small crises in the homemaker's day.

Jackson based her depictions of women's lives on their psychological reactions to coercion and menace. She employed an insidious terror in atmospheric stories of lone females as a commentary on women's struggle against male-dominated society, particularly in *Hangsaman* (1951), a novel that indicts chummy campus life. Contributing to existential scenarios are ambivalent relations between mothers and daughters. She achieved lasting fame in 1948 with a story for the *New Yorker,* "The LOTTERY," a disturbingly misogynistic tale of traditional human sacrifice in a New England burg. In 1959 the author chose a mousy, underloved loner, 32-year-old Eleanor Vance, as the central character of *The Haunting of Hill House,* a novel recast twice in film as *The Haunting.* In the original description Eleanor, at age 21, began caring for her dying mother while warding off "small guilts and small reproaches, constant weariness, and unending despair" (Jackson, 6). The inexplicable shower of stones that strikes Hill House suggests the lifetime of "malicious backbiting" that damages her beyond repair (*ibid.,* 7). Distraught with loneliness, she gladly accepts any invitation, even one to a pseudo-scientific probe of personal hauntings.

Jackson turned her quirky humor to profit with a witty Gothic novel, *We Have Always Lived in the Castle* (1962), a satiric jab at vitriolic family relations. Again drawing on female protagonists, the author pictures two neurotic sisters, Constance Blackwood and Mary Katherine "Merricat" Blackwood, who incur ostracism because of local suspicion that they poisoned their other relatives. To characterize the explosive pressures of quiet anger, Jackson carries the tale to a tragic conclusion. After the author's unexpected death of coronary disease, her daughter and son, Laurence Jackson and Sarah Jackson, compiled *Just an Ordinary Day* (1996), a collection of unpublished stories featuring WITCHCRAFT, claustrophobia, the macabre, and victimization of females.

Bibliography

Bellman, Samuel Irving, "Shirley Jackson: A Study of the Short Fiction," *Studies in Short Fiction* 31, no. 2 (Spring 1994): 282–293.

Hall, Joan Wylie. *Shirley Jackson: A Study of the Short Fiction.* New York: Twayne, 1993.

Jackson, Shirley. *The Haunting of Hill House.* New York: Penguin, 1984.

Siegel, Kristi. *Women's Autobiographies, Culture, Feminism.* New York: Peter Lang, 2001.

Jacobs, Harriet (1813–1897)

A major contributor to the female perspective on SLAVERY, Harriet Ann Jacobs expressed the sexual entrapment common to slave women that worsened the misery of bondage. Born to the carpenter Daniel Jacobs and the slave breeder Delilah Horniblow and orphaned at age six, Jacobs and her little brother, William, remained on the plantation in Edenton, North Carolina, where their parents had been slaves. She learned domestic tasks from her owner, Margaret Horniblow, a kind woman who taught her needlework, reading, and spelling. At age 12 Jacobs passed to the family of Dr. James and Mary Matilda Norcom as the caretaker of their small daughter. Advancing womanhood, light skin, and the clothing Jacobs sewed for herself increased her appeal to Norcom, a sexual predator. Of his bestial lust Jacobs wrote, "No animal ever watched its prey more narrowly" (Jacobs, 40). Because he denied her request to marry a free black carpenter, at age 15 she chose the lesser evil by becoming the mistress of Congressman Samuel Tedwell Sawyer, a white attorney.

Jacobs bore a son and daughter, Joseph and Louisa Matilda, who looked for livelihood to their great-grandmother, a freedwoman named Molly Horniblow, who had been cook and seamstress on a South Carolina plantation. When the children were aged six and two, Sawyer refused to free them as he had promised. To save Joseph and Louisa from the auction block, Jacobs escaped into the eastern Carolina swamps, then hid in a cubbyhole in her grandmother's attic. Jacobs fled across the Chesapeake Bay to Philadelphia in 1842 and sent for her children. At age 37 she gained emancipation with the help and funding of the abolitionist Cornelia Grinnell Willis, who bought Jacobs and set her free.

With the aid of Lydia Maria CHILD, editor of the *National Anti-Slavery Standard,* and of Amy Kirby Post, founder of the Western New York Anti-Slavery Society, Jacobs recounted her early years in INCIDENTS IN THE LIFE OF A SLAVE GIRL, WRITTEN BY HERSELF (1861) under the pen name Linda Brent. During the Civil War Jacobs worked as a nurse. Afterward, while living in Alexandria, Virginia, she served as a nurse and teacher to former slaves, then retired to Louisa's home in Washington, D.C. She died in Washington, D.C., on March 7, 1897.

Bibliography

Africans in America. "People and Events: Harriet Jacobs." WGBH/PBS Online. Available online. URL: http://www.pbs.org/wgbh/aia/part4/4p2923.html. Accessed on April 15, 2005.

Jacobs, Harriet A. *Incidents in the Life of a Slave Girl: Written by Herself.* New York: Harvest Books, 1983.

Levander, Caroline Field. *Voices of the Nation: Women and Public Speech in Nineteenth-Century American Literature and Culture.* Cambridge: Cambridge University Press, 1998.

Jane Eyre Charlotte Brontë (1847)

Jane Eyre, Charlotte BRONTË's standard-setting feminist novel, focuses on the breakout of the title character from obscurity and orphanhood to fully realized adulthood. As such, Jane EYRE becomes the yardstick by which critics and literary historians measure other liberated female characters. Influenced by the quest theme of Sophia LEE's Gothic classic *The Recess; or, A Tale of Other Times* (1783–85), the plot puts Jane through a series of allegorical character tests that prove her worth. In the Red Room at Gateshead Hall, her aunt, Sarah Reed's, manse, 10-year-old Jane collapses in the presence of a hovering spirit but faces down the pious Mr. Brocklehurst, who implies that Jane is doomed to hell. While studying over the next eight years at Lowood school to ready herself for employment, she survives hunger, cold, epidemic typhus, and the death of a friend, Helen Burns. Proof of Jane's preparation for self-support are her graduation and her acceptance of a teaching post among the faculty who taught her.

Brontë, who was physically unable to hold down a job for more than a few months at a time, knew the value of financial INDEPENDENCE for women. At age 18 Jane, her alter ego, moves on to the world of work. Upon her arrival at Thornfield, the country manor of Edward Rochester, she makes friends with the housekeeper, Mrs. Fairfax, who bolsters Jane's confidence in the same way that Bessie comforted her at Gateshead Hall and that Helen and Miss Temple received her at Lowood. In a self-study on her first official day as governess, Jane describes herself as plain, but neat: "It was not my habit to be disregardful of appearance, or careless of the impression I made" (Brontë, 90). She proves industrious and equal to responsibility as the bilingual teacher to Adèle Varens and as companion to her employer. The author stresses Edward's lack of interest in rearing a young female and Jane's competence in handling the challenge. More surprising is Jane's ability to draw Edward into conversation. He remarks on how unusual it is "for a man like me to tell stories of his opera-mistresses to a quaint, inexperienced girl" (ibid., 134). His admission compliments Jane for her humanity in listening to his youthful indiscretions without judging him.

Because of class differences the love that develops between Edward and Jane presents a seemingly insurmountable obstacle. When his proposal of marriage proves to be bigamous, he rationalizes the disastrous arranged marriage to his mad wife, Bertha Mason ROCHESTER. He calls Jane "my better self—my good angel," a contrast that demonizes Bertha (ibid., 300). In a moral quandary Jane swoons and prays, "Be not far from me, for trouble is near: there is none to help" (ibid., 282). Not waiting for divine intervention, she flees a sexually compromising role as mistress and Edward's offer of her own residence at a Mediterranean villa. She escapes emotional battery by journeying into the moorlands with no thought to self-preservation. Like Christ's soul-testing 40 days in the desert, the retreat indicates that she is being true to herself rather than kowtowing to society.

Brontë uses the lovers' separation as an opportunity for Jane to reflect on her ideals. With virtue intact, she accepts rescue by cousins she has never met and receives an unforeseen inheritance from her uncle in Madeira. A sixth sense warns her to reject the pompous St. John Rivers's offer of marriage and his plan for mutual service in the mission fields of India. The author's skillful ordering of details begins

the equalizing of the former governess and Edward, who Jane fears has died in the fire that destroyed Thornfield. At his new residence, Ferndean, she accepts the pared-down fortunes of a sadly depleted man and tends his physical hurts with affection. She declares her willingness to be his helpmeet and presents him a tray bearing half a glass of water and candles, symbols of domesticity and of a dramatic tension between opposites. He rewards her with a watch, the emblem of the lady of the house. Without hesitation she announces her new-found confidence: "I am an independent woman now" (ibid., 416).

Bibliography

Brontë, Charlotte. *Jane Eyre*. New York: Bantam Books, 1981.

Deiter, Kristen. "Cultural Expressions of the Victorian Age: The New Woman, *Jane Eyre*, and Interior Design," *Lamar Journal of the Humanities* 25, no. 2 (2000): 27–42.

Gilbert, Sandra M., and Susan Gubar. *The Madwoman in the Attic*. 2nd ed. New Haven, Conn.: Yale University Press, 2000.

Janeway, Elizabeth (1913–   )

A provocative social critic, reviewer, lecturer, folklorist, and novelist, Elizabeth Hall Janeway examines the rewards and compromises of women's lives. A native of Brooklyn, New York, she mastered the short story at Swarthmore College. After halting her studies during the Great Depression to earn tuition by writing advertising copy for a department store, she completed a bachelor's degree from Barnard College. At age 30 she wrote a novel, *The Walsh Girls* (1943), which contrasts the choices of two sisters, one to marry and one to remain single. *Daisy Kenyon: A Historical Novel, 1940–1942* (1945), the author's perusal of a woman's choices during World War II, served Otto Preminger as a screen subject, starring Joan Crawford as a career woman among New York's smart set. A deeper analysis of women's lifestyle options in *The Third Choice* (1959) broadened the scope of Janeway's feminist works.

The women's movement influenced Janeway's shift to social commentary and support of the all-woman FEMINIST PRESS, which reissued her novel

Leaving Home (1953). Her pronouncements on gender roles in *Man's World, Woman's Place: A Study in Social Mythology* (1971) tend toward an equitable arrangement that gives both genders opportunities to develop their talents. The treatise won the regard of the anthropologist Margaret MEAD for reassessing the importance of the homemaker to the social order. In 1973 Janeway compiled a feminist history, *Women: Their Changing Roles*, which chronicles rapid social shifts during the two world wars. She followed with *Between Myth and Morning: Women's Awakening* (1974) and *Women on Campus: The Unfinished Liberation* (1975), which earned her a Matrix Hall of Fame award.

Critics warmed to the feminist concepts that Janeway posited in her later works. Both *Powers of the Weak* (1980) and *Cross Sections from a Decade of Change* (1982) won regard for analyzing the needs of vulnerable women and the dynamics of PROSTITUTION and the causes of incest. In *Improper Behavior: When and How Misconduct Can Be Healthy for Society* (1987), her most incisive text, she discusses the authority of society to define and limit human choices and actions. Of major concern is the intrusiveness into family life of soap operas and VIOLENCE on television, especially harm done to women and children. Her essays for *Architectural Digest, Christian Science Monitor,* the *Los Angeles Times, Modern Maturity, Monthly Labor Review, MS.,* the *New York Times Book Review, U.S. News and World Report,* and *World Monitor* treat the place of older women in such life-altering activities as volunteerism, political campaigns, and job changes. Among model feminists is Eleanor Roosevelt, whom Janeway called the first lady of the United Nations.

Bibliography

Astrachan, Anthony. "Rebellion and the Rules We Live By," *Washington Post,* 12 July 1987, p. O3.

Janeway, Elizabeth. *Improper Behavior: When and How Misconduct Can Be Healthy for Society.* New York: William Morrow, 1987.

Jelinek, Elfriede (1946–   )

The controversial Austrian dramatist, fiction writer, and social critic Elfriede Jelinek defines the mutually destructive differences between the genders in a competitive, violent world. A native of Mürzzuschlag, Styria, she grew up in a Catholic household in Vienna, where she took lessons in piano, ballet, and French from age four. She entered the Vienna Conservatory in her midteens and majored in art history and theater at Vienna University. With submissions to literary journals and radio she began publishing verse and prose at age 21. Over a period of 18 years she won Bochum's Peter Weiss Prize, Aachen's Walter Hasenclever Literary Prize, Bremen's Literary Prize, the Georg Büchner Prize, the Berlin Theatre Prize, the Heinrich Heine Prize, the Mülheim Dramatists Prize, and the Else Lasker Schüler Prize. In 2004 Jelinek received the Doris Lessing Prize in criticism and became the 10th women to win the Nobel Prize in literature for plays and novels that counter gender cliches.

Radicalized by student revolts in the 1970s, Jelinek produced a satire, *Wir sind lockvögel, Baby* (We are decoys, Baby, 1970), which attracted serious critical attention. She got a start in drama with *Was geschah, nachdem Nora ihren mann verlassen datte oder stützen der gesellschaften* (What happened after Nora left her husband; or, pillars of societies, 1979), source of a Federal German Ministry of the Interior Screenplay Prize. She followed with *Lust* (1989), the dramatization of the cyclical marital rape that the protagonist Gerti endures from her drunken husband Hermann. The domestic scene expresses the author's disdain for romantic illusion and her denunciation of marriage as legalized concubinage. In her words, "[Hermann] is as puffed up as a pig's bladder, he sings, plays, yells, fucks" (*ibid.,* 10). In contrast, "[Gerti] is a receptacle into which Hermann pours his juices, nastily, briefly, brutally" (Jelinek, cover).

To universalize actions, Jelinek conceals place and character names and pursues plots through disjointed action. Her pessimism extends from gross imagery, disaffected lives, and shocking caricatures of human clashes to suicide and murder. One example of excessive rage in nihilistic youth is the attack of a teen gang on an innocent pedestrian in *Die ausgesperrten* (Wonderful, Wonderful Times, 1980). The play depicts the dramatist's belief that Austria committed criminal acts under the grotesque powers of the Third Reich that turned survivors into war invalids. The story describes 18-year-old Anna Witkowski and her twin brother, Rainer Maria, and their disdain for their mismatched parents, the kowtowing mother and her hulking husband, Otto, a former officer of the German SS who brutalized Polish peasants. The playwright comments, "Father often thinks of the dark skeletons of people he killed. The white and immaculate snow of Poland turned bloody and maculate. But snow goes on falling, again and again, and by now it bears no trace of those who disappeared there" (Jelinek, 1990, 32). To recover the thrills of fascism, the father poses his battered wife in the kitchen for pornographic snapshots that rid him of impotence. With this image Jelinek links the exploitation of women to the male-initiated war crimes of World War II.

Jelinek creates character malaise in her masterpiece *Die klavierspielerin* (*The Piano Teacher*, 1983), winner of the Heinrich Böll Prize. The action depicts a toxic MOTHER-DAUGHTER RELATIONSHIP between a conniving stage mother and her unmarried 38-year-old daughter, Erika Kohut, a piano teacher at the Vienna Conservatory. The dramatist begins, "Mother worries a lot, for the first thing a proprietor learns, and painfully at that, is: Trust is fine, but control is better" (Jelinek, 1989, 5). Because the mother monitors Erika's activities and shares her bed to prevent her daughter from masturbating, Erika advances from committing petty furtive acts against home bullying to cutting herself with a razor and viewing seamy peep shows and sadomasochistic films in Vienna's underworld. Late at night she is almost caught in a voyeuristic pose as she spies on couples engaged in coitus. She turns her self-destructive sexual perversions against a student, 17-year-old Walter Klemmer, who agrees to beat and degrade her. In 1995 Jelinek applied the same themes of out-of-control SEXUALITY to *Services*, a modernization of Wolfgang Amadeus Mozart's opera *Così fan Tutte* (1790), that depicts two bored wives who pay for sex from anonymous male prostitutes. Her jaundiced view of human sexuality has produced a demand for her plays and fiction, which is available in most European languages.

Bibliography

Hanssen, Beatrice. "Elfriede Jelinek's Language of Violence," *New German Critique* 96, no. 68 (Spring–Summer 1996): 79–112.

Jelinek, Elfriede. *Lust*. London: Serpent's Tale, 1993.

———. *The Piano Teacher*. London: Serpent's Tale, 1989.

———. *Wonderful, Wonderful Times*. London: Serpent's Tale, 1990.

Jen, Gish (1955–   )

A first-generation Chinese-American writer and teacher, Lillian "Gish" Jen molds a buoyant writing career from the connections and dissonances of biculturalism. The daughter of immigrants from Shanghai after World War II, she was born in Yonkers, New York, in a tense era when the U.S. government prohibited her engineer father from returning home. During her girlhood in Scarsdale neighbors hurled rocks at family members to express distaste for anyone who might bear the taint of Communist China. After studying at Harvard under the poet Robert Fitzgerald, Jen changed her major from premed and earned a degree in English. Although her choice of writing as a career alienated her parents, she worked for a year at Doubleday, dabbled in business administration at Stanford University, and completed a graduate degree at the Iowa Writer's Workshop. After publication of "Bellying Up" in the *Iowa Review* in 1983, she turned wholeheartedly to freelance writing.

In addition to short stories in the *Atlantic*, *New Republic*, *New Yorker*, *Southern Review*, and *Yale Review*, Jen published a novel, *Typical American* (1991), which reveals the unease of the Chang family as ancient gendered codes weaken in the presence of more liberal American behavior. Jen wrings humor out of the Chinese mother, a traditional Confucian, who views Theresa, her American convent-trained daughter, as she is playing baseball and swaggering as the pros do with hands in pockets. The splicing of gender roles generates initial discomforts in the girl, but New World ANDROGYNY lays the foundation of a smooth assimilation into Westernization. The novel's sequel, *Mona in the Promised Land* (1996), offers a comic take on new-found female liberation in the title character's conversion to Judaism and the morphing of her surname from Chang to Changovitz. Jen's anthology, *Who's Irish?* (1999), a collection of eight short stories, replots a Chinese family's gender map with unsettling arrangements. The author ventures into domestic issues, including spousal battery, and features in the title story the displacement of a Chinese matriarch from her daughter's home.

Bibliography

DelRosso, Jeanna. "The Convent as Colonist: Catholicism in the Works of Contemporary Women Writers of the Americas," *MELUS* 26, no. 3 (Fall 2001): 183–201.

Friedman, Susan Stanford. *Mappings: Feminism and the Cultural Geographies of Encounter.* Princeton, N.J.: Princeton University Press, 2001.

Lee, Rachel. "Who's Chinese?" *Women's Review of Books* 19, no. 5 (February 2002): 13–14.

Jewett, Sarah Orne (1849–1909)

The fiction writer Sarah Orne Jewett established through realism the alternate lifestyles of women who choose self-direction rather than subjugation to a husband. After her birth in South Berwick, Maine, she lived a confident, easy life and roamed the New England woods and Atlantic shores. Her father, Theodore Jewett, a rural physician, encouraged her reading, notably the novels of Jane AUSTEN and George ELIOT and Harriet Beecher STOWE's melodrama UNCLE TOM'S CABIN (1852). Jewett acknowledged her love of women and honed her narrative skills by maintaining a lively correspondence with female friends, some of whom she met on trips to Boston, Cincinnati, New York, and Washington, D.C. By age 14 she had published her first sketches and verses.

Writing suited Jewett, who was often homebound during debilitating bouts of rheumatoid arthritis. After graduation from Miss Raynes School and the Berwick Academy she began compiling impressionistic vignettes and poems about her region and its inhabitants and submitting them to the *Atlantic Monthly* and *Merry's Museum,* a children's miscellany edited by Louisa May ALCOTT. The first collection appeared under the title

Deephaven (1877), a suggestion of the contentment and security she derived from mother love in girlhood. An anonymous reviewer for the *Atlantic* remarked: "The truthfulness, the fidelity to nature, and the frank, winning manner of the narrative easily persuaded readers that this young writer was innocently recording personal experience, and varying but slightly from actual fact" ("Review," 131). Jewett validated the lives of single, poor, elderly, and rural New England women in *Old Friends and New* (1879). Key to her characters' vigor was the choice to relish life as nurses, shopkeepers, and farmers rather than to crumble under the denigration of spinsterhood or suffocating pity as aging, loveless widows.

Jewett gravitated toward the intellectual milieu of Boston and formed a domestic partnership with a publisher's widow, Annie Adams Fields. After their tour of the British Isles Jewett began surveying the fortunes of Irish immigrants for *McClure's* and *Scribner's.* For the February 1882 issue of the *Atlantic Monthly* she wrote a wryly titled short story, "Tom's Husband," a commentary on a married couple with unusual aptitudes—the wife for commerce and the husband for domestic duties. The author comments, "Most men like best the women whose natures cling and appeal to theirs for protection," but Tom Wilson's wife, Mary, prefers to head a large business rather than keep house (Jewett, 1882, 206).

In the same vein Jewett contributed to feminist fiction *A Country Doctor* (1884), the story of the protagonist, Nan Prince, and her dedication to the medical profession despite self-doubt, social disapproval, and public ridicule. A dominant theme in the novel is the need of outlets for independent women who are unwilling or unfit to marry or be mothers. At the climactic point when Nan begins to adopt a professional demeanor, she develops "a capacity for hard study and patient continuance" (Jewett, 1999, 138). In the examining room she wears the impassive facial expression that sets the patient's mind at ease. When Aunt Nancy contributes to Nan's disquiet, Nan follows an internal compass, the "something which always tells me I am right" (*ibid.,* 239). Jewett describes the "something" as a religious calling. She compares Nan's choice of profession to that of Christ, who "came to his, not to be ministered unto but to minister" (*ibid.* 253).

Jewett's career maintained its feminist course. For "In Dark New England Days" (1890), published in *Century* magazine, she examined adversarial roles between a miserly old sea captain and his motherless daughters, Betsey and Hannah Knowles. A dire tale of feminine fury, the story replicates the motif of cursed wealth that Nathaniel Hawthorne applied to *The House of the Seven Gables* (1851). A decade after the publication of a successful anthology, *A White Heron and Other Stories* (1886), Jewett completed THE COUNTRY OF THE POINTED FIRS (1896), a regional novel about the healing friendship of Almira Todd, an elderly herbalist who aids isolated and poor residents of Dunnet Landing, Maine, while preserving their stories. Jewett issued a historical novel, *The Troy Lover* (1901), and became the first woman to receive an honorary degree from Bowdoin College. Before her death of cerebral hemorrhage she spent her last seven years in semi-invalidism after a carriage mishap injured her spine. Her uncluttered style and vivid glimpses of nature and women's friendships influenced the feminist authors Willa CATHER, Kate CHOPIN, and Mary Wilkins FREEMAN.

Bibliography

Hobbs, Michael. "World beyond the Ice: Narrative Structure in *The Country of the Pointed Firs*," *Studies in Short Fiction* 29, no. 1 (Winter 1992): 27–34.

Jewett, Sarah Orne. *A Country Doctor.* New York: Bantam, 1999.

———. "Tom's Husband," *Atlantic Monthly* 49, no. 292 (February 1882): 205–213.

"Review: Sarah Orne Jewett" (1894). Available online. URL: http://etext.lib.virginia.edu/toc/modeng/public/AnoJewe.html. Accessed on October 14, 2005.

Jhabvala, Ruth Prawer (1927–   )

The screenwriter and novelist Ruth Prawer Jhabvala presents the outsider's view of women's passions and perils as victims of male charlatans, posers, users, and fakes. From age six in her native Cologne, Germany, she composed stories. In 1938 the growing menace of Nazi-led anti-Semitism revealed in Kristallnacht, the "Night of Broken Glass," forced her parents to relocate the family to Coventry, England. At nights during air raids Jhabvala carried with her to the community shelter a copy of Margaret MITCHELL's period novel GONE WITH THE WIND (1936). Well schooled in English literature at London University and Queen Mary College, Jhabvala married the architect Cyrus S. H. Jhabvala and settled in New Delhi, the source of social and cultural situations for her fiction. In 1951 she began publishing under a gender-neutral name, R. Prawer Jhabvala, and submitted stories to *Encounter, Kenyon Review, Ladies' Home Journal, London Magazine, New Statesman, New Yorker, Redbook,* and *Yale Review.*

In 1975 Jhabvala moved to New York City, living apart from her husband and three daughters. Although she had no intention to write for film, she adapted the 1983 screen version of her Booker Prize–winning epistolary novel HEAT AND DUST (1975), a slim feminist period piece about a British woman who abandons her culture for the complex gender restrictions and stereotypes of colonial India. Jhabvala's collaboration with the director Ismael Merchant and the screenwriter James Ivory resulted in a series of admirable films: an adaptation of Jean RHYS's novel *Quartet* (1981), a version of Henry James's *The Bostonians* (1983), the Oscar-winning *A Room with a View* (1986), *Madame Sousatzka* (1988), and *Howard's End* (1992), the source of the writer's second Oscar. She earned an Academy Award nomination for *The Remains of the Day* (1993) and followed with an original script, *Jefferson in Paris* (1995), and an adaptation of James's novel *The Golden Bowl* (2000). In 2004 she separated her persona into nine directions she might have taken in *My Nine Lives: Chapters of a Possible Past,* a metafictional compilation of invented memories.

Bibliography

Campbell, Elizabeth. "Re-visions, Re-flections, Re-creations: Epistolarity in Novels by Contemporary Women," *Twentieth Century Literature* 41, no. 3 (Fall 1995): 332–348.

Gooneratne, Yasmine. *Silence, Exile, and Cunning: The Fiction of Ruth Prawer Jhabvala.* New Delihi: Orient Longman, 1983.

Jhabvala, Ruth Prawer. *My Nine Lives: Chapters of a Possible Past.* Washington, D.C.: Shoemaker & Hoard, 2004.

"Jilting of Granny Weatherall The"
Katherine Anne Porter (1930)

A classic of feminist reflection, Katherine Anne PORTER's oft-anthologized story "The Jilting of Granny Weatherall," collected in *Flowering Judas and Other Stories*, applies stream-of-consciousness and symbolic realism to the last days of an 80-year-old all-weathering matriarch. In a comfortable prone position in her own bed the protagonist welcomes the uncertainties of sleep and, beset by ghosts of the past, misidentifies the living hoverers around her. Through DREAMSCAPE she revisits unsettled issues and seeks redress for nagging resentments. As memory flickers on and off like a candle flame, she awaits death and tolerates the patronizing of Doctor Harry, a young country doctor who urges her to "be a good girl" (Porter, 80). The cinematic frames of her youth halt distressingly on the day she was left at the altar. Replacing her anticipated love match was a frontier marriage that offered a dependable mate, unending chores, and nursing of children, slaves, and livestock, a full schedule of WOMAN'S WORK replicated in the stories "María Concepción" (1922) and "He" (1930).

Porter depicts recall as a two-edged weapon that can redeem as well as lacerate. As a good housekeeper, Granny Ellen Weatherall, although "taken by surprise," is pleased "to have everything clean and folded away" (*ibid.*, 88, 81). She has difficulty relinquishing her authority, calling witlessly to her children, "I hear thunder. There's going to be a storm. Close all the windows. Call the children in" (*ibid.*, 88). Porter suggests a falling away from piety in the rosary that falls from Granny's fingers. As her body curls and retreats into a "mass of shadow," she prefers a firm handhold on "something alive" to religious abstractions (*ibid.*).

As the end approaches like fog over the orchard, Granny enjoys the mixed blessing of reclaimed joys as well as of things done poorly or left undone, particularly the love letters left in the attic in plain sight of her snooping adult children. The faintness that distorts her perceptions reminds her of collapsing on that would-be wedding day, "blind and sweating with nothing under her feet and the walls falling away," an image of gravitational pull that foreshadows a final descent into the grave (*ibid.*, 87). In the last moments of life she summons the womanly strength that has supported her during a long marriage. With her last breath she puffs out the imaginary candle flame. Porter maintained the strength and outrage of Ellen Weatherall through the semiautobiographical Miranda, protagonist of "Old Mortality" (1930).

Bibliography

Hoefel, Roseanne L. "The Jilting of (Hetero)sexist Criticism: Porter's Ellen Weatherall and Hapsy," *Studies in Short Fiction* 28, no. 1 (Winter 1991): 9–20.

Porter, Katherine Anne. *The Collected Stories of Katherine Anne Porter*. New York: New American Library, 1965.

Johnson, Georgia Douglas (1886–1966)

Georgia Blanche Douglas Camp Johnson, the famed feminist poet, songwriter, and author of domestic and historical dramas, pictured the gendered differences in racial suffering. Reared in her native Atlanta, Georgia, she graduated from Atlanta University Normal School and took postgraduate courses in organ and violin at Oberlin Conservatory and Cleveland College of Music. At age 19 she published her first verse in *Voice of the Negro* and submitted writings to *Challenge, Crisis,* and *Opportunity*. After marrying Henry Lincoln Jackson, a prominent attorney and registrar of deeds for Washington, D.C., she hosted the Saturday Nighters at the S Street Salon, a convivial gathering open to the literati and musical greats of the Harlem Renaissance.

Under the mentorship of Jessie Redmond FAUSET, the editor of *Crisis*, at age 41 Johnson compiled *The Heart of a Woman and Other Poems* (1918), her first verse anthology. Central to feminist images are metaphors of soft feathers and fluttering wings, a compromise between femininity and INDEPENDENCE. Four years later she turned more pointedly to racial themes in *Bronze: A Book of Verse* (1922). In widowhood she supported two sons with teaching, secretarial work for the Office of Immigration, and freelance writing. Contemporaneously with her poetry she composed radical drama for the Federal Theatre Project of the Works Projects Administration, notably *Sunday Morning in the South* (ca. 1925), a kitchen-table drama that protests the execution of a black teenager accused of raping a white girl, the familiar gendered clash at the core of many of the nation's racial uprisings. Set in Sue Jones's kitchen, the play features the familiar family arrangement of a pious, hymn-singing grandmother rearing two grandsons. Sue is a model of WOMAN'S WORK—wetnursing, cooking, and raising the boys with Christian values. Beloved by the black community, she is nonetheless discounted and silenced by the police, who consider her too old and ignorant to testify on behalf of Tom Griggs, her 17-year-old grandson, whom they lynch.

Johnson's later plays were fraught with human misery. With *Blue Blood* (1926), a Reconstruction Era drama set in Georgia, she creates consternation in the discovery by May and John that they are siblings. Their mothers were rape victims of the same white male, Captain Winfield McCallister. Easing the heart sickness of the bride-to-be is the arrival of Randolph, a second beau, who elopes with her, ending the contretemps over potential incest. In 1927 Johnson returned to feminist themes with a prize-winning folk play, *Plumes*, a one-act dilemma scenario dramatizing female employment as nurses, cooks, and seamstresses. The conflict hinges on Charity Brown's decision to save money spent on undependable doctors and to put her last $50 into plumes to adorn her daughter, Emmerline's, funeral cortege. Johnson embraced love verse in *An Autumn Love Cycle* (1928), featuring "Autumn," in which she expressed the paradox of love for a famous male with an image of the female prisoner gazing through bars at a brilliant Sun. Most frequently anthologized is the rhapsodic apostrophe "I Want to Die While You Love Me," which a mourner read at her funeral.

In later works Johnson enlarged on her original themes. Piety, guile, and SISTERHOOD permeate her history play *William and Ellen Craft* (1935) and resonate in two recovered lynching plays, *And Yet They Paused* and *A Bill to Be Passed*, which the researcher Judith Stephens relocated in the National Association for the Advancement of Colored People (NAACP) papers at the Library of Congress in 1999. In the same vein the dramatist produced *Safe* (ca. 1929) and *Blue-Eyed Black Boy* (ca. 1930), the latter a wise mother's last-minute

message to Governor Tinkham to save Tom Waters, his mulatto son, from lynching. The ironic title of *Safe* derives from Liza's postpartum strangulation of her male infant. In trauma after seeing a lynching outside her home, she proclaims, "Now he's safe—safe from the lynchers! Safe!" (Johnson, *Safe*, 15). Also ironic is the description in *Blue-Eyed Black Boy*, a reference to the blue eyes that the governor recognizes as proof of Tom's siring.

Johnson interspersed dialogue with group prayer, individual pleas to God, and the singing of gospel hymns and of "Sisters, Don't Get Weary," a stanza of the spiritual "This Work Is 'Most Done" (1909). In musical counterpoint to brutality her female characters are verbally aggressive, lobbing back talk against a PATRIARCHY that is both socially superior and sexually threatening. The vocal support system, like Janey's conversation with Pheoby in Zora Neale HURSTON's feminist novel *THEIR EYES WERE WATCHING GOD* (1937) and in Toni MORRISON's supportive network of women in the falling action of *BELOVED* (1987), typifies females' employing oral weapons against social, marital, and biological bondage.

Bibliography

Hull, Gloria T. *Color, Sex, and Poetry: Three Women Writers of the Harlem Renaissance.* Bloomington: Indiana University Press, 1987.

Johnson, Georgia Douglas. *Blue Blood.* In *Wines in the Wilderness: Plays by African American Women from the Harlem Renaissance to the Present.* Edited by Elizabeth Brown-Guillory. New York: Greenwood Press, 1990.

———. *Blue-Eyed Black Boy.* In *Wines in the Wilderness: Plays by African American Women from the Harlem Renaissance to the Present.* Edited by Elizabeth Brown-Guillory. New York: Greenwood Press, 1990.

———. *Plumes.* In *Plays by American Women, 1900–1930.* Edited by Judith E. Barlow. New York: Applause, 2001.

———. *Safe.* In *Wines in the Wilderness: Plays by African American Women from the Harlem Renaissance to the Present.* Edited by Elizabeth Brown-Guillory. New York: Greenwood Press, 1990.

———. *The Selected Works of Georgia Douglas Johnson.* New York: G. K. Hall, 1997.

———. *A Sunday Morning in the South.* In *Black Theatre, U.S.A.: Plays By African Americans: The Early Pe-*

riod, 1847–1938. Edited by James V. Hatch and Ted Shine. New York: Free Press, 1996.

———. *William and Ellen Craft.* In *Negro History in Thirteen Plays.* Edited by May Miller and Willis Richardson. Washington, D.C.: Associated Publishers, 1935.

Stephens, Judith. " 'And Yet They Paused' and 'A Bill to Be Passed': Newly Recovered Lynching Dramas by Georgia Douglas Johnson," *African American Review* 33, no. 3 (Fall 1999): 519–522.

Johnson, Pauline (1861–1913)

A North American voice for the mixed-race female caught between two worldviews, the balladeer and nature poet Emily Pauline Johnson respected the woman's place in the white-Indian society of Ontario. Named Tekahionwake (Double Life) in honor of her great-grandfather, she was the biracial daughter of an English mother and Canadian Mohawk father. At Chiefswood in the Six Nations Reserve outside Brantford, Ontario, she received home schooling in Native lore and classic literature from her paternal grandfather and mother. Johnson produced original verse in her late 20s and published in *Boy's World,* the *Brantford Expositor, Gems of Poetry, Mother's Magazine and Family Journal, Saturday Night,* and an anthology, *The White Wampum* (1895).

Johnson had a lengthy career as a lecturer and stage performer in North America and England, where she performed a dramatic monologue, "Cry from an Indian Wife," and other audience favorites. In retirement she dedicated herself to poetry with a second anthology, *Canadian Born* (1903), in which she resets the Greek myth of Echo's reverse SILENCING in "The Legend of Au'Appelle Valley." Johnson intrigued white readers with *Legends of Vancouver* (1911), which features "The Two Sisters," the story of the peacemaking daughters of Chief Tyee. Her next collection, *Flint and Feather* (1912), is the source of the ghost poem "Dawendine," the nostalgic "Wave-Won," and "The Quill Worker," a pictorial image of WOMAN'S WORK as Neyka demonstrates native quilling. As ill health sapped the author's strength and ended her work, the Canadian Woman's Club of Vancouver provided a stipend.

In the year of Johnson's death from cancer in Vancouver, sympathetic semiautobiographical stories appeared in a posthumous anthology, *The Moccasin Maker* (1913), which opens on a BIOGRAPHY of the author's mother. The collection epitomizes the bicultural Métis, who can be neither wholly white nor completely claimed by First Nations. Because of the dominance of Caucasians in Canada, Johnson's protagonists try to make peace with internal conflicts by choosing Amerindian values and lifestyle. Her most favored story, "A Red Girl's Reasoning," pictures the revolt of Christie McDonald, a liberated woman who scorns her white husband's preference for white ritual to Native custom. She tosses her wedding band across the room before leaving him.

Bibliography

Brant, Beth. *Writing as Witness: Essays and Talk.* Toronto: Women's Press, 1994.

Donovan, Kathleen M. *Feminist Readings of Native American Literature: Coming to Voice.* Tucson: University of Arizona Press, 1998.

Johnson, Pauline. *Flint and Feathers.* Toronto: Musson Books, 1913.

Jones, Gayl (1949–)

The novelist Gayl Amanda Jones is a spokeswoman for women's pain caused by male treachery, social oppression, and trauma to female bodies. Born in Lexington, Kentucky, she came from a long line of female storytellers and began writing at age eight. She studied English at Connecticut College and Brown University before beginning a classroom career in creative writing at Wellesley and the University of Michigan. In her mid-20s, with the aid of the editor Toni MORRISON, Jones began illuminating the hidden past of fictional characters whose lives are filled with domestic warfare: Their psyche wilts under the stress of concealed hurt that requires the healing of layered STORYTELLING through black dialect and stream-of-consciousness narration.

In *Corregidora* (1975) Jones speaks through a Brazilian-American protagonist, Ursa Corregidora, of a need in the nonwhite female to rejoice in and explore positive, life-enhancing experiences. From childhood she learns from her great-grandmother, Great Gram, that Ursa must bear witness to a cruel family history. She remarks, "Their past in my blood. . . . . My veins are centuries meeting" (Jones, 1975, 45–46). Through blues singing Ursa, a symbolic bear-woman, transcends the pain of inherited matrilineal sufferings from enslavement, incest, forced PROSTITUTION, and rape of both her mother and her grandmother. Her own barrenness—caused by Mutt, her first husband, who tosses her down a flight of stairs, causing a miscarriage—is a lesson in male tyranny. To maintain INDEPENDENCE and fight SILENCING, Ursa declares, "I have tears for eyes. I was made to touch my past at an early age. . . . Let no one pollute my music" (*ibid.*, 77). Her own tears express grief that she is the last of her line. She questions the basis of sexism: "What is it a woman can do to a man that make him hate her so bad he wont to kill her one minute and keep thinking about her and can't get her out of his mind the next?" (*ibid.*, 184).

Jones followed with more riveting views of wronged womanhood. In *Eva's Man* (1976), a prison novel about Eva Medina Canada, a damaged woman tells of childhood sexual assaults and CONFINEMENT by Davis, a possessive sadist who treats her as a cheap commodity. Stoic and self-silenced, Eva refuses to satisfy the legal hierarchy with the facts of her murder of Davis, whom she castrates with her teeth, an image of aggression emerging from a silenced mouth. In *Song for Anninho* (1981), a novel-length poem told in free verse, Jones reprises the hardships of late 17th-century Brazilian maroons of Palmares. Almeyda, the protagonist, describes the sexism of a Portuguese soldier, who slices off her breasts, leaving scars that Anninho graces with oil massage. After a lengthy hiatus Jones returned to feminist fiction with *The Healing* (1998), the story of Harlan Jane Eagleton, an itinerant faith healer who bears burdens of past treacheries and physical pain. Haunting her memory is an image of the Middle Passage and of "Africans coming to the New World in them slave ships like sardines in a can" (Jones, 1998, 4). The evocative novel was a National Book Award finalist and a *New York Times* Notable Book of the Year.

Bibliography

Horvitz, Deborah. " 'Sadism Demands a Story': Oedipus, Feminism, and Sexuality in Gayl Jones's 'Corregidora' and Dorothy Allison's 'Bastard Out of Carolina,' " *Contemporary Literature* 39, no. 2 (Summer 1998): 238–261.

Jones, Gayl. *Corregidora.* New York: Random House, 1975.

———. *The Healing.* Boston: Beacon Press, 1998.

Wilcox, Janelle. "Resistant Silence, Resistant Subject: (Re)reading Gayl Jones's 'Eva's Man,' " *Genders* 23 (Spring 1996): 72–96.

Jong, Erica (1942–)

The poet, memoirist, and fiction writer Erica Mann Jong dramatizes the various stages of liberated womanhood. A daughter of New York City's Jewish intelligentsia, she grew up free-spirited and earned degrees in literature from Barnard College and Columbia University. After beginning her career with well-crafted verse, in 1973 she published one of the pillars of feminism, FEAR OF FLYING, the first of a witty, comic, sexually graphic trilogy that also comprises *How to Save Your Own Life* (1977) and *Parachutes and Kisses* (1984), all loosely based on her own marriages and carnal caprices. Jong jolted the feminist reading public with titillating talk about serious issues of the day—date rape, workplace sex, female vanity, erotic fantasies, guilt resulting from masturbation, disillusion with marriage, and recognition of female oppression at all levels. Her heroine, Isadora Wing, reaches a significant conclusion—that liberation, like CINDERELLA's fairy godmother, does not promise to fulfill every wish.

Jong's later works proved to feminist skeptics that the writer can be both fantacist and scholar. In the introduction to *The Colette Omnibus* (1974) Jong pays tribute to the French author—a frank, natural female who made her living by writing about women's lives and loves. Jong castigates the negative reception of COLETTE's overtly sexual writings with a keen observation: "It is a sad paradox that when male authors impersonate women . . . they are said to be dealing with 'cosmic, major concerns'—but when we impersonate *ourselves* we are said to be writing 'women's fiction' " (Jong, 1974, xiii). For additional examinations of historic eras and literature Jong chose Fanny Hackabout-Jones, a picara of the 1700s; the novelist Henry Miller; SAPPHO, the Greek lyric poet; and Serenissima, a fictional daughter of Shylock whom Jong drew from William Shakespeare's *The Merchant of Venice* (1596).

At age 57 Jong abandoned young women's sexual escapades and perused the horrors of male religiopolitical fascism. In *Witches* (1981) she surveys misconceptions about GODDESS LORE and outsized fears of the unknown that targeted medieval women for trial, torment, and gruesome execution. In the introduction she lists the results of persecution: "If you exclude women from churchrites, they will practice their magic in the fields, in forests, in their own kitchens. The point is, female power cannot be suppressed; it can only be driven underground" (Jong, 1999, intro). The text depicts sorcerers as the progeny of "Ishtar-Diana-Demeter," mother goddesses who flourished in the ancient world in the human domain of procreation, birth, and death (*ibid.*, 12). In sexist societies women follow the pattern of female godhood by reaching for magic, a substitute for power. According to Jong, when macho behavior becomes grotesquely anti-woman, men blame women for human boundaries, as demonstrated by Polynesian sacrifice of virgins in a volcano's cauldron to secure predictable weather and good crops. In place of faulty notions of authoritative women, Jong presents witches as benign healers and Earth mothers, wonder workers who soothe and bless humanity.

Bibliography

Altman, Meryl. "Beyond Trashiness: The Sexual Language of 1970s Feminist Fiction," *Journal of International Women's Studies* 4, no. 2 (April 2003): 1–25.

Dederer, Claire. "She's Gotta Have It." *Nation*, 6 October 2003, p. 23.

Jong, Erica. Introduction to *The Colette Omnibus*. Garden City, N.Y.: Nelson Doubleday, 1974.

———. *Fear of Flying*. New York: Signet, 2003.

———. *What Do Women Want?* New York: HarperCollins, 1998.

———. *Witches*. New York: Harry N. Abrams, 1999.

Jordan, June (1936–2002)

A revered populist, teacher, and freedom fighter, June Jordan expressed an inclusive humanism that gave hope to women. A native of Harlem and the daughter of Jamaican immigrants—a postal employee and a nurse—she grew up in the Bedford-Stuyvesant ghetto. According to her memoir *Soldier: A Poet's Childhood* (1999), she endured a miserable home environment rocked by her father's abuse of her and her mother. From Milwood High School Jordan went to Massachusetts to complete her education at Northfield School for Girls, where she began writing verse that tended toward the abrupt, chantlike beginnings of rap. She extended her scholarly and humanitarian interests in literature at Barnard College and the University of Chicago, where she plunged into civil rights activism on a freedom bus ride to Baltimore.

At age 33 Jordan, then a divorced single mother, published her first poetry collection, *Who Look at Me* (1969), and *His Own Where* (1971), a novel nominated for the National Book Award, followed by two plays, eight children's works, and five collections of essays. In the 1990s her activism moved in the direction of feminism. In "A New Politics of Sexuality," published in the July 1991 issue of the *Progressive*, she widened the scope of her concerns with a bold denunciation of sexism—"all of the different ways in which some of us seek to dictate to others of us what we should do, what we should desire, what we should dream about, and how we should behave ourselves" (Jordan, 2001, 131). At her death at age 65 of breast cancer she had been a spiritual mentor to women fighting the disease. Critics laud Jordan's most recent works: *Civil Wars, Selected Essays 1963–1980* (1981), the essay "Report from the Bahamas" (1982), a 22-song libretto for John Adams's opera *I Was Looking at the Ceiling and Then I Saw the Sky* (1995), *Kissing God Goodbye: Poems 1991–1997* (1997), and *Some of Us Did Not Die: New and Selected Essays* (2002), which contains the feminist essay "Where Is the Love?" The text emphasizes a female focus by looking for positive emotions in all human endeavors.

Bibliography

Bashir, Samiya A. "Who Do You Love?" *Lambda Book Report* 11, no. 3 (October 2002): 28–30.

Jordan, June. *Soldier: A Poet's Childhood.* New York: BasicCivitas Books, 2001.

———. *Some of Us Did Not Die: New and Selected Essays.* New York: BasicCivitas Books, 2003.

Scott, Ellen K. "Creating Partnerships for Change: Alliances and Betrayal in the Racial Politics of Two Feminist Organizations," *Gender and Society* 12, no. 4 (August 1998): 400–423.

journalism

Media reporting has offered women an unusually unbiased stance from which to express their observations and concerns. As early as the American Revolution readers depended on the patriotic writings of Mercy Otis WARREN and the postwar Universalist zeal of the feminist poet Judith Sargent MURRAY, a contributor to the *Boston Weekly Magazine* and the *Massachusetts Magazine.* In England in the 1830s Harriet Taylor MILL broached serious feminist topics for the *Monthly Repository,* a Unitarian periodical that carried articles by Harriet MARTINEAU; George SAND performed a similar service in France for *Le Figaro, La République, Revue des Deux Mondes,* and *Revue Indépendante.* In the United States the abolitionist writer Frances HARPER of Maine denounced SLAVERY in the *Provincial Freeman* while Harriet Beecher STOWE submitted principled essays to the *Atlantic, Christian Union, Godey's Ladies' Book,* the *Independent,* and the *New York Evangelist.*

Women's journalism offered a break from economic polemics that dominated newspapers before, during, and after the American Civil War. In the 1850s the author Fanny FERN, America's first female columnist, produced weekly domestic essays for the *Saturday Evening Post* and the *New York Ledger.* Rebecca Harding DAVIS collected material on Reconstruction for the *New York Tribune.* In the late 1860s Susan B. ANTHONY and Elizabeth Cady STANTON coedited the *Revolution,* a radical periodical denouncing the Fifteenth Amendment for excluding women from full citizenship. Providing articles about the National Woman Suffrage Association's campaign was the historian Matilda Joslyn GAGE. In this same period Victoria WOODHULL and her sister, Tennessee Claflin, distributed a reformist journal, *Woodhull & Claflin's Weekly,* which courted New York subscribers and writers bold enough to address feminist issues without the sentimentality and inhibition common in other media. From the perspective of their office on Wall Street they earned a reputation for muckraking by exposing bank fraud and financial malfeasance. They fiercely charged male politicians with denying women rights guaranteed by the Constitution. From the Midwest were Zona GALE's feminist articles for the Milwaukee *Evening Wisconsin,* the Milwaukee *Journal,* and the New York *Evening World;* similarly focused on women's lives were the columns of Ida Husted HARPER for the Terre Haute *Saturday Evening Mail,* Indianapolis *News, Los Angeles Examiner,* and *New York Sunday Sun.* In England Emmeline PANKHURST devoted zeal to supporting the "votes for women" crusade through articles about the Women's Parliament.

Detective work extended the range of feminist journalism from repeating secondhand facts to scoping out cause and effect independently. Beginning in 1885 with the columns of Nellie BLY in the *Pittsburgh Dispatch* investigative journalism and a voice for powerless females and their children arose. Bly's stories enlisted sympathy for immigrants, unwed mothers, inmates of women's asylums, and slum dwellers. Versatile Martha Winifred Sweet Black Bonfils, alias Annie Laurie, the original sob sister journalist, entered the profession in 1890 to gather news for the *San Francisco Examiner.* Working for the publisher William Randolph Hearst during the heyday of undercover reportage and muckraking, she invented "sob sister journalism" by taking the feminist angle. She concealed her identity and pretended to faint on Market Street to evaluate the treatment of women in ambulances and at the city's Emergency Hospital.

As did Bly, Bonfils went directly to the source. She questioned sex workers in a bordello and worked in a fruit cannery and cotton mill to track evidence of male exploitation of female laborers. At age 35 she traveled to Utah for the *Denver Post* to compile an exposé of Mormon polygyny. In 1907 she gave a day-by-day account of the trial of Harry K. Thaw and focused on the spousal abuse that drove his wife, Evelyn, to seek comfort in a lover, the prominent architect Stanford White, whom Harry Thaw shot and killed. At the request of her employer Bonfils wrote a BIOGRAPHY of his mother, a philanthropist who organized the National Congress of Mothers: *The Life and Personality of Phoebe Apperson Hearst* (1928).

According to Emilie Hawkes Peacocke in *Writing for Women* (1936), SUFFRAGE and the growth of reporting by and about women produced the New Journalism, which broadened the scope of media coverage to human interest stories, consumerism, and the concerns of women and families. From soft news—about appliances, cooking, fashions, entertaining, rearing children, EDUCATION—female reporters and columnists branched out to writing hard news about legislation, international relations, investment banking, and the military. In the early 1900s Laura Ingalls WILDER extolled WOMAN'S WORK of the farm economy in the *Christian Science Monitor, Country Gentleman, McCall's, Missouri Ruralist, Missouri State Farmer,* and Saint Louis newspapers. In the 1920s Suzanne LAFOLLETTE reported for the *Nation* and the *Freeman* on the results of suffrage in women's lives; Marjorie Kinnan RAWLINGS developed a following for her woman-centered columns for the *Louisville Courier-Journal* and the *Rochester Journal-American*. In the 1930s Meridel LE SUEUR wrote for the *American Mercury, Daily Worker, Dial, Nation, New Masses,* and *Partisan Review* about women's sufferings during the Great Depression; the Canadian journalist Gabrielle ROY produced articles on female thought and aspirations for *Paris Review* and the *New York Times Book Review.* Caroline GORDON got her start as a social commentator for the *Chattanooga News;* Margaret MITCHELL interviewed celebrities for the *Atlanta Journal Sunday Magazine.* In Paris COLETTE, fashion commentator for *Le Matin* and *Vogue,* ventured into protests on behalf of female workers. Emma GOLDMAN, publisher of *Mother Earth,* supported unions and birth control while denouncing Woodrow Wilson's plans to involve Americans in World War I. One of her contributors, Voltairine DE CLEYRE, supported pacifism and WOMEN'S RIGHTS. Helen KELLER supported socialism and SUFFRAGE during the 1910s with articles published in the *New York Times* and the *New York Call.* During the war Louise BRYANT investigated the enthusiasm of Russian women for the deposing of Czar Nicholas II and the installa-

tion of a Marxist government. In the 1930s Muriel RUKEYSER wrote Marxist articles for the *Masses.*

As males left for the front in World War II, women claimed half the media jobs. In Harlem Ann PETRY reported on Jim Crow era atrocities for the *Negro Digest.* War reporting enticed women writers from other genres, taking Ishbel ROSS, a Canadian writer for the *New York Tribune,* to the Balkan front and, in 1937 during the Spanish Civil War, luring the humorist Dorothy PARKER from satire and light verse to combat analysis for the *Masses.* When Hitler rose to power in Germany, the defiance of his authority by the famed American bureau chief Dorothy THOMPSON caused her expulsion from the country. At the depth of World War II Clare Boothe LUCE interviewed Claire Chennault's Flying Tigers and General "Vinegar Joe" Stilwell as well as Chiang Kai-shek (Jiang Jieshi) and Madame Chiang and Jawaharlal Nehru. She criticized Winston Churchill's lax military preparedness in *Life* magazine features. Luce summarized a survey of battlefields in *Europe in the Spring* (1940). She profiled General Douglas MacArthur in 1941 and was on the scene with camera and notepad the next year after combat in Maymyo, Burma. Her contemporary, Therese Bonney, authored *War Comes to the People* (1940) and *Europe's Children* (1943). For her concern for orphans and displaced persons, she became the focus of the film documentary *The Search* (1948).

Peacetime returned female journalists to women's interests. In the 1950s Paule MARSHALL, a reporter for *Our World,* researched news in the Caribbean islands and Brazil and wrote about immigrant women. By the early 1960s Gloria STEINEM was freelancing protofeminist articles for top American magazines; Letty Cottin POGREBIN exposed sexism and pornography for the *Amsterdam News, Na'amat,* the *New York Times,* and *Tikkun.* The Indian writer Santha Rama RAU traveled Africa, Asia, and Russia and relayed domestic news to *Holiday* magazine and the *New York Times Magazine.* In Italy Oriana FALLACI gathered postwar news for *Corriere della Sera, Der Stern,* and *Europeo;* in London Diana NORMAN summarized financial and political news for the *Daily Herald, Times,* and *Guardian.* In less industrialized nations reportage from Mariama BÂ in Senegal spread to new audiences the value of feminism; in South Africa Bessie HEAD denounced apartheid through news articles and interviews.

In the late 20th century female journalists excelled at syndicated column writing and punditry. Observers of women's advancement—Susan BROWNMILLER, Ellen GOODMAN, Elizabeth JANEWAY, Katha POLLITT, Anna QUINDLEN, and Patricia J. WILLIAMS—introduced to a wide readership the females deserving praise and the obstacles that still inhibited women from top positions in sports, government, the arts, and business, including the media. In the 1970s Carolyn Forché tramped war zones in Guatemala, Israel, Lebanon, and Northern Ireland and turned her journalistic observations into pacifist poems while Florence KING reported her progressive musings for the *Raleigh News and Observer* and the *New York Times*. In the 1980s Barbara KINGSOLVER and her coauthor Jill Barrett Fein teamed up to compile stories about women's bravery during strikes at Arizona mines; Dmae ROBERTS wrote 400 feminist features, audio collages, and documentaries for National Public Radio and Public Radio International. Amy Hill Hearth, a journalist with the *New York Times*, turned interviews with Bessie and Sadie DELANY into a Harlem memoir, *Having Our Say: The Delany Sisters' First 100 Years* (1991). Anita DIAMANT concentrated on females in relation to Judaism for *Hadassah* and *Reform Judaism* and for the Webzine *Jewishfamily.com*; Susan FALUDI surveyed consumer issues for the *Atlanta Journal-Constitution, New York Times*, and *San Jose Mercury News*. In England the Australian journalist Germaine GREER promoted feminist views of ABORTION, gender politics, and medical mistreatment of women for the *London Sunday Time*; in India Nayantara SAHGAL championed civil liberties in global papers.

From the 1990s to the beginning of the 21st century female news staff ranged over as many hard-hitting issues as their male colleagues. Readers and viewers came to accept female reportage as willingly as they read the views of men. Molly IVINS took on the most powerful males, three Republican presidents of the United States, in a series of hilarious revelations about the ineptitude of Ronald Reagan, George Bush, and George W. Bush, the subjects of *Molly Ivins Can't Say That, Can She?* (1991), *Nothin' but Good Times Ahead* (1993), and *Shrub: The Short but Happy Political Life of George W. Bush* (2000). Barbara EHRENREICH undertook an assignment among the laboring class to expose the hazards and disparities faced by housemaids, nursing home staff, waitresses, and K-Mart clerks, the focus of *Nickel and Dimed: On (Not) Getting By in America* (2001).

Bibliography

Beasley, Maurine Hoffman, and Sheila Jean Gibbons. *Taking Their Place: A Documentary History of Women and Journalism.* State College, Pa.: Strata, 2002.

Carter, Cynthia, Gill Branston, and Stuart Allan, eds. *News, Gender, and Power.* New York: Routledge, 1998.

Wagner, Lilya. *Women War Correspondents of World War II.* Westport, Conn.: Greenwood, 1989.

Joy Luck Club, The   Amy Tan (1989)

As does Maxine Hong KINGSTON's *The WOMAN WARRIOR* (1976), Amy TAN's *The Joy Luck Club* (1989) contributes to feminist literature a realistic examination of first-generation Asian-American women. Born to a generation of Chinese women silenced under PATRIARCHY and feudal union, these pathfinders consider the female liberation that their emigrant mothers encounter after the Sino-Japanese War (1937–45). The formation of womanly community in a San Francisco mah jong club that comprised Anmei Hsu, Lindo Jong, Yingying St. Clair, and Suyuan Woo offers subtle strength to their daughters, Rose Hsu Jordan, Waverly Jong, Lena St. Clair Livotny, and June Woo. The interconnected double square requires a realignment of feng shui after the death of Suyuan Woo, who left in China her twin daughters, Chwun Yu and Chwun Hwa Wang. Tan reprises the scenario of Suyuan, seriously depleted by dysentery, as she removes the infants from a shoulder sling and pleads with passersby, "Take my babies, I beg you" (Tan, 325). The last view of her babes haunts her to her grave, leaving for June the completion of unfinished family business.

Tan depicts Americanized daughters who wrestle with language difficulties as they analyze the truncated lives of four mothers who fled national catastrophe. The STORYTELLING and food sharing of the original mah jong club provided respite from the aerial bombardment of Kweilin that countered the terrors of war. Reorganized in California, the new club counters threats to the mothers' notions of femininity, continuity, and parenthood. In the spirited shuttling of mah jong tiles, the oral sharing of wisdom and TALK-STORY sustains the next generation with winnowings from the Chinese motherland. In the style of a bildungsroman Tan pictures June's advancing to her mother's seat at the table and accepting a quest to Shanghai to reclaim her missing half sisters.

A novel of diaspora and longing, the story links females in a universal bond. Fraught with mother-daughter antipathies, the network holds firmly to universal truths. June's reversal of the emigrant pilgrimage enlightens her with a new vision of her mother, who chooses opportunity in an adopted homeland as an antidote to grief for the girls left behind. When the three daughters meet at the air-port, they embrace and murmur, "Mama, Mama," as baby birds stretch their beaks for nourishment (*ibid.,* 331). Through Tan's fictional reunion readers experience the refugee's bereavement and identify with Suyuan as a mother rather than as a war bride escaping the advance of Communism in China. The unprecedented success of the novel by a hyphenated American preceded an outpouring of realistic fiction that baby boomer mothers welcomed for its poignant depiction of mother-daughter schism.

Bibliography

Hamilton, Patricia L. "Feng Shui, Astrology, and the Five Elements: Traditional Chinese Belief in Amy Tan's *The Joy Luck Club*," *MELUS* 24, no. 2 (Summer 1999): 125–145.

Heung, Marina. "Daughter-Text/Mother-Text: Matrilineage in Amy Tan's Joy Luck Club," *Feminist Studies* 19, no. 3 (Fall 1993): pp. 597–616.

Ling, Amy. *Between Worlds: Women Writers of Chinese Ancestry.* New York: Pergamon Press, 1990.

Tan, Amy. *The Joy Luck Club.* New York: Putnam, 1989.

K

"Käthe Kollwitz" Muriel Rukeyser (1968)

Anthologized in *The Speed of Darkness* (1968), Muriel RUKEYSER's "Käthe Kollwitz" is a eulogy for the East Prussian sculptor, portraitist, lithographer, and director of graphic arts at the Berlin Academy who captured the havoc of combat on women and children. A feminist and socialist who defied the CENSORSHIP of the Nazi Party, Kollwitz remained in Berlin until her death in 1945 at age 88. In five first-person staves Rukeyser honors Kollwitz's pacifism with thanks for "[suffering] the gifts and madness of full life, on earth, in our time," a reference to the artist's castigation of the European wars she had witnessed (Rukeyser, 129). Picturing her woodcuts and drawings as an ongoing fugue, the eulogy admires Kollwitz for holding her focus while saturating sketches and statuary with the grace of domestic labor. Her own gnarled hands, like those of refugees, bear a womanly sturdiness from their unstinting grappling with the worst of civilian sufferings.

Rukeyser succeeds at a merger of the historic with the universal. Amid familiar woman-and-child scenarios drawn on "a sheet of the world," the poem pictures graves from World War I and the artist's defiant cry "Nie Wieder Krieg" (No more war) flung at unidentified perpetrators (*ibid.*, 129, 131). The title of her final work, "Seedcorn Must Not Be Ground," accompanies a view of a woman kneeling in a birthing position as death pours from the skies. By linking maternity with the impressment of sons into combat, the poem echoes the demands of two female artists—Kollwitz and Rukeyser—that the fecundity of the female body not be perverted into a soulless device for the production of more killers.

In stave two the poet introduces bisexuality as an artistic given—the ability to view life from male and female perspectives, a motif as old as the Greek myth of the seer Teiresias. Raw, honest, and unsentimental, the black-and-white images reveal Kollwitz's masculine grasp of "one more war" and her introspective maternalism toward the noncombatants starved and terrified by protracted slaughter (*ibid.*, 131). In stave three the poem spools out a face-by-face montage—"patients in waiting-rooms / famine / the street / the corpse with the baby / floating, on the dark river" (*ibid.*, 130). Her prints decry public shame alongside a personal outrage, the twin sorrows of losing her younger son, Peter, and her grandson, Peter, in successive world wars. Rukeyser breaks the lyric flow to pose a rhetorical question—whether a female artist would split the world by divulging her life's truths.

Bibliography

Altman, Meryl. "Beyond Trashiness: The Sexual Language of 1970s Feminist Fiction." *Journal of International Women's Studies*, 1 April 2003, pp. 1–25.

Herzog, Anne F., and Janet E. Kaufman, eds. *"How Shall We Tell Each Other of the Poet": The Life and Writing of Muriel Rukeyser.* New York: Palgrave Macmillan, 1999.

Rukeyser, Muriel. *Out of Silence: Selected Poems.* Evanston, Ill.: Northwestern University Press, 1994.

Kaye/Kantrowitz, Melanie (1945–)

The radical lesbian poet, scholar, and activist Melanie Kaye/Kantrowitz speaks and writes compellingly on the need for women's liberation. Born in Flatbush, a section of Brooklyn, to first-generation Jewish-American shopkeepers from Eastern Europe, she attended the New York City public school system and City College. She internalized Jewish issues of the day—the Holocaust, Zionism, McCarthyism, and the execution of Ethel and Julius Rosenberg for espionage. In her late teens she helped organize rent strikes and an anti-rat campaign in Harlem and began experimenting with verse about social injustice. After a creative writing teacher ridiculed her first-person efforts, Kaye/Kantrowitz ceased composing, but she returned to poetry after the women's movement validated female lives as displayed in letters and DIARIES AND JOURNALS.

While completing a doctorate in comparative literature at the University of California at Berkeley, Kaye/Kantrowitz voiced support for anti–Vietnam War and rape crisis efforts. She initiated women's studies at the university and cofounded *Beyond the Pale: The Progressive Jewish Radio Hour* for WBAI-Pacifica. In addition to cofounding Jews for Economic and Racial Justice and coediting the lesbian journal *Sinister Wisdom*, she directed the Queens College/City University of New York (CUNY) Worker Education Extension Center and served as the Jane Watson Irwin Distinguished Professor of Women's Studies at Hamilton College and the Belle Zeller Professor of Public Policy at Brooklyn College/CUNY. Her published works—*My Jewish Face & Other Stories* (1990); *The Issue Is Power: Essays on Women, Jews, Violence, and Resistance* (1992); and *The Color of Jews* (2004)—are favored titles on religion, sociology, and women's studies reading lists.

Kaye/Kantrowitz filled in a gap in feminist literature by coediting *The Tribe of Dina: A Jewish Women's Anthology* (1989), a collection of essays, vignettes, interviews, verse, fiction, and artwork presenting diverse global views on economic, racial, and gender justice. In 1999 she defended gender scholarship with a broad generalization: "Women's studies . . . is under attack by the same forces which savage affirmative action and public assistance, trash immigrants, defend courses that depict happy slaves, cheerfully bomb Iraq and relentlessly pump out misinformation to keep all of us at each other's throats" (Kaye/Kantrowitz, "Liberation," 16). She espouses a fight-back stance on the issue of male-on-female VIOLENCE and defends "Take Back the Night" campaigns.

Bibliography

Galtz, Liz. "Stories into Words, Words into Attention, Voices into Hearing: The Creative and Political Process of Melanie Kaye/Kantrowitz," *Gay Community News*, 20 January 1991, p. 8.

Kaye/Kantrowitz, Melanie. "How Did 'Correct' Become a Dirty Word? Theory and Practice for a Social Justice." *Transformations*, 30 September 1999, p. 42.

———. "Liberation Studies Now," *Women's Review of Books* 16, no. 5 (February 1999): 15–16.

Keller, Helen (1880–1968)

The pacifist and social reformer Helen Adams Keller overcame physical handicaps and gender barriers to encourage women worldwide. She grew up outside Tuscumbia, Alabama, at Ivy Green, a family estate. At age 19 months she suffered the effects of scarlet fever, which left her blind, deaf, and mute. After the arrival at her home of Anne Mansfield Sullivan, a teacher educated in Boston at the Perkins Institute for the Blind, in 1887, Keller made a dramatic change from unschooled, undisciplined brat to eager independent learner. For communication she mastered finger spelling and understood 625 words within six months. In 1889 she entered the Perkins Institute and learned to speak at the local Horace Mann School for the Deaf. She continued her studies at the Wright-Humason Oral School in New York City.

At age 22 Keller completed her autobiography, *The Story of My Life* (1902), which she serialized in *Ladies' Home Journal*, and she wrote *Optimism* (1903) during her junior year at Radcliffe. Her literary output increased with *The World I Live In* (1908), *The Song of the Stone Wall* (1910), and *Out of the Dark* (1913) and socialist articles for *American Magazine, Atlantic Monthly, Century, Critic, Home, McClures, Metropolitan, New York Times,* and *Youth's Companion.* Fluent in five languages, she developed into a strong voice for the disabled and for women's rights. In 1913 she published in the *New York Call* the essay "Why Men Need Woman Suffrage," which links the vote with women's efforts to assure cleaner food and milk, better schools, and healthier infants and small children. She wrote to presidents and power wielders and championed the birth control crusade of Margaret SANGER to assure each infant a chance for health and affection. Keller's courageous writings influenced the style of Meridel LE SUEUR.

Bibliography
Herrmann, Dorothy. *Helen Keller: A Life.* New York: Alfred A. Knopf, 1998.

Keller, Helen. *Light in My Darkness.* New York: Chrysalis, 2000.

———. *The Story of My Life.* New York: Bantam, 1991.

Kelley, Florence (1859–1932)

A social reformer, lecturer, suffragist, and pamphleteer, Florence Kelley sought humane conditions in the workplace. She was born in Philadelphia to a family respected for its Quaker and Unitarian beliefs. In childhood she and her father, U.S. Congressman William Darrah Kelley, prowled the late-night shifts at factories that employed children. Unsupervised youth endangered their eyes and hands in the manufacture of glass and steel, which required the handling of superheated metals and containers of acid. After studying at Cornell University, the University of Zurich, and Northwestern University Law School, she became a socialist and translated Karl Marx and Friedrich Engels's treatise *The Conditions of the Working Class in England in 1844* (1887).

While living in New York City, Kelley fled a disastrous six-year marriage to a wife beater. Accompanied by her three children, she joined autobiographer Jane Addams in Chicago at Hull House, a pioneering settlement project. Kelley considered charity work among the immigrant poor a nonsectarian religious mission. Her activism supported socialist causes on behalf of women and children, including vocational training and establishment of soup kitchens and health and well baby clinics. She campaigned for protective labor

laws with pamphlets, "Our Toiling Children" (1889) and "The Working Child" (1896), and served Illinois as head factory inspector. At age 40 she directed the National Consumer's League, which lobbied the U.S. Supreme Court for a minimum wage and limited hours of employment for women and for children younger than age 14. For products manufactured under humane working conditions, she designed a white label. She urged buyers to boycott sweatshop goods that did not bear the label.

In addition to lecturing on college campuses against laissez-faire capitalism and coestablishing the National Association for the Advancement of Colored People, Kelley advocated maternal and child health services. Armed with data and graphs, she launched an investigation into high child mortality rates. As World War I began in Europe, she championed peace through involvement in the Woman's Peace Party. Her demands for a standardized birth certificate helped investigators to document illegal child labor practices. She published *Ethical Gains through Legislation* (1905), *Child Labor and Morality* (1911), *The Labor of Women and Children in Tenements* (1912), *Modern Industry in Relation to the Family* (1914), and *The Supreme Court and Minimum Wage Legislation* (1925). At age 68 she wrote *The Autobiography of Florence Kelley* (1927), which summarized a life devoted to the welfare of the less fortunate.

Bibliography
Dublin, Thomas, and Kathryn Kish Sklar. *Women and Power in American History.* Vol. 1. New York: Prentice-Hall, 2001.

Kelley, Florence. *The Autobiography of Florence Kelley.* Chicago: Charles Kerr, 1986.

Kemble, Fanny (1809–1903)

The actor, dramatist, poet, letter writer, and diarist Frances Anne "Fanny" Kemble Butler produced a British female's eyewitness account of the evils of the Southern plantation system. A native Londoner, she was born to the Kemble-Siddons family, one of England's most respected stage lineages. While her parents worked, she lived with an aunt and studied in France. Through extensive reading, she readied herself for a multifaceted career, which included rebellion against outmoded social codes that prevented her from riding horseback astride and in breeches like a man. At age 18 she published *Francis I* (1827), a lyric melodrama. Two years later she rescued her father's acting troupe from bankruptcy with her starring role in *Romeo and Juliet* at Covent Garden, where her mother, Maria Theresa Kemble, played the part of Lady Capulet, and her father, Charles Kemble, played Mercutio.

During Kemble's residence in the United States from 1832 to 1845 she became a celebrity and a pacesetter of fashions and hairstyles. Her performances earned prominent fans, including the poet Walt Whitman and the critic George Henry Lewes. She kept an epistolary diary, which she published as *Journal of a Residence in America* (1835). The entries satirized American social affectations and denounced SLAVERY as a source of affluence for brutalizers of black people. After the failure of her marriage to a slave holder, the Philadelphia attorney Pierce Mease Butler, she issued a sequel, *Journal of a Residence of a Georgian Plantation, 1838–1839* (1863), a frank disclosure of marital coercion and female revolt against a tyrannic and adulterous mate. She described one desperate house slave who tore off her clothing to exhibit evidence of the rawhide whip. Kemble blamed the woman's plight on regional ignorance and barbarity. Interviews with elderly black females introduced Kemble to the shocking overbreeding that kept old women in a state of pregnancy or lactation. With pride, one woman rejoiced in being useful: "Missus, tho' we no able to work, we make little niggers for massa" (Kemble, 1863, 92). Kemble was outraged that unremitting female breeding and labor produced a string of children for farm work or the auction block to keep two lazy white male heirs in luxury.

Kemble's entries recorded family disruptions, poor health, and unsanitary conditions at Butler's Georgia estate on the Altamaha River. As did Harriet Beecher STOWE, Kemble fumed at the slave markets, where auctioneers separated husband from wife and ripped babes from their mothers' arms. She listed slaves by name along with their physical, mental, and nutritional conditions. Of Sarah, the wife of Stephen, Kemble noted that the woman had survived 11 pregnancies, four of which ended in miscarriage. Five of her children had died, and Sarah was again pregnant while suffering a tumor that throbbed during field labor. Against Kemble's in-laws' wishes, she assisted pregnant and breast-feeding slave women whom overseers forced into the cotton fields and rice paddies of Butler Island and Saint Simons Island. To improve conditions for hundreds of blacks, she established a plantation hospital, nursery, vocational center, and dame school. For breaking the law by teaching blacks to read, she risked arrest and imprisonment.

Just as slavery severed black families, Kemble's libertarianism destroyed her marriage. During a formal separation, she described living with her daughters, Sarah and Frances, in Rome, Italy, in *A Year of Consolation* (1847). Divorce cost Kemble a home and the two children, who remained behind with their father when she left for England. At age 39 she returned to the podium to deliver Shakespearean recitations. Publication of translations of the stage works of Friedrich Schiller and Alexandre Dumas and of her memoirs, verse, essays, travelogues, and plays supplied most of her financial support. One of her feminist poems, "A Petition," voices the melancholy of a deserted wife to her rival. Her late works included two memoirs, *Records of a Girlhood* (1878) and *Records of a Later Life* (1882); stage commentary in *Notes upon Some of Shakespeare's Plays* (1882); and a novel, *Far Away and Long Ago* (1889). Still writing stage works at age 80, she also completed a satire, *The Adventures of John Timothy Homespun in Switzerland* (1889). Historians believe that her forthright reportage of lashings and starvation of slaves helped convince British authorities not to side with the Confederacy during the Civil War. In 2000 the British actor Jane Seymour played the part of Fanny Kemble during her early marriage in the CBS-TV film *Enslavement: The True Story of Fanny Kemble*.

Bibliography

Clinton, Catherine. *Fanny Kemble's Civil Wars*. Oxford: Oxford University Press, 2001.

Kemble, Fanny. *Journal of a Residence in America* (1863). Available online. URL: http://etext.lib.virginia.edu/toc/modeng/public/KemPlan.html. Accessed on October 16, 2005.

————. *Journal of a Residence on a Georgian Plantation in 1838–1839.* Athens: University of Georgia Press, 1984.

Kempe, Margery (ca. 1364–ca. 1440)

An energetic ascetic, visionary, and merchant, Margery Kempe (also Margerie or Marjery Kemp) produced England's first autobiography. The daughter of Mayor John Brunham, she was born into the middle class in King's Lynn, Norfolk, but received no formal education. After marrying a city councilman and guildsman, John Kempe, she experienced a vision of Christ at her bedside the night of her first childbirth. She reared their 14 children during bouts of fasting, prayer, and confessing, sometimes wearing a hair shirt. Depression finally drove her to the brink of suicide. After confessing to the parish priest her carnal thoughts and temptations by Satan, she chewed her own arm, ripped her chest with her fingernails, hallucinated, and tried to jump out of a window in fear of damnation. Her husband had her chained to a bed in a locked storage room for eight months. Her poor attempts to work at a brewery and a grist mill caused her hysterics and fits of religious exhibitionism.

When she was about 50 years old, as a result of an emotional or spiritual crisis Kempe abandoned marital sex and asked permission of the bishop of Lincoln to undertake an 11-year pilgrimage to shrines at Canterbury, Leicester, Walsingham, and York. Dressed in white robes, she traveled to holy sites in Aachen, Assisi, Rome, and Palestine and prostrated herself in penance, fits of weeping, and self-abasement at altars in Jerusalem and Santiago de Compostela, Spain's most popular religious site. For multiple eccentricities she earned the title the "madwoman of God." In 1417 she successfully defended herself against a charge of Lollardy, a form of heresy. At age 61 she returned home to the bedside of her dying husband. In widowhood in 1431 she continued seeking holy inspiration at Danzig, Poland, and Bergen, Norway.

Kempe's autobiography earns feminist regard for its vivid portrayal of a wife who dislikes sexual contact with her husband and for a glimpse of the era's mistreatment of insanity in women. Four years before her death she dictated to her son and a priest two stages of *The Book of Margery Kempe* (1436), a mystic memoir in which she describes the onset and course of spiritual and emotional sufferings. When Hope Emily Allen recovered the manuscript from a Lancashire library in 1934, it offered historians and feminists a candid picture of 14th-century married life and motherhood, madness, embryonic theology, and religious ecstasy.

Bibliography
Hard, Wendy. "Medieval Women's Unwritten Discourse on Motherhood: A Reading of Two Fifteenth-Century Texts," *Women's Studies* 21, no. 2 (May 1992): 197–209.

Kempe, Margery. *The Book of Margery Kempe.* London: Penguin, 2000.

Powell, Raymond A. "Margery Kempe: An Exemplar of Late Medieval Piety," *Catholic Historical Review* 89, no. 1 (January 2003): 1–23.

Kennedy, Adrienne (1931–)

The satiric scenarist, fiction writer, and playwright Adrienne Lita Hawkins Kennedy describes women's racial and gender strictures as well as their strengths derived from strong mothers. After her birth in Pittsburgh, Pennsylvania, she grew up in a multiethnic middle-class section of Cleveland, Ohio. Under the influence of the STORYTELLING by her mother, Etta Haugabook Hawkins, the author developed a benevolent Christianity and the stereotypical attributes of a lady. As an introduction to black themes and motifs, her father read aloud the poems and stories of black authors. When enrollment at Ohio State University introduced her to student bigotry, she took refuge in verse by imitating the poems of Edith Sitwell. With creative writing training from Columbia University and study under Edward Albee at the New School of Social Research, Kennedy wrote fiction, beginning with "Because of the King of France" (1960), published in *Black Orpheus.*

A year of travel in Ghana altered Kennedy's approach to drama with the addition of nonlinear surreal scenarios, visions, nightmares, masks, AN-

DROGYNY, and the naked emotions of her own experience to define identity. She won an Obie for the off-Broadway production of *Funnyhouse of a Negro* (1962), a multivoiced internal monologue in which Sarah, the protagonist, tries on the personae of Queen Victoria, the duchess of Hapsburg, Patrice Lumumba, and Jesus. Strands of racism, sexual transgressions, and gender bias account for anxieties and self-examination, which ultimately lead to spiritual healing. A second experimental play, *The Owl Answers* (1963), is an autobiographical effort that combines analysis of self and of the family matriarchs who influenced her. Kennedy described censorship of female words and feelings in *A Lesson in Dead Language* (1964) and attained international fame for *Sun* (1969), a verse play on the martyrdom of Malcolm X.

Kennedy fused childhood memories of movies with a feminist identity quest in *A Movie Star Has to Star in Black and White* (1976). To dramatize the absence of black role models in the American media, the action places Clara Passmore among black family members and the images of white film stars. Kennedy also writes plays for children and has taught drama at Brown, Princeton, and Yale Universities and in Budapest. In 1987 she described her style and methods in a memoir, *People Who Led to My Plays*, which credits Charlotte BRONTË's JANE EYRE (1847), paper dolls, FAIRY TALES, and Bette Davis's movies as contributors to her notions of femininity. In 1996 Kennedy joined her son, the television producer Adam P. Kennedy, in writing *Sleep Deprivation Chamber*, a poignant Obie-winning drama that depicts a mother's support of her son, whom black police officers beat senseless.

Bibliography

Brown, E. Barnsley. "Passover Over: The Tragic Mulatta and (Dis)Integration of Identity in Adrienne Kennedy's Plays," *African American Review* 35, no. 2 (Summer 2001): 281–295.

Kennedy, Adam P., and Adrienne Kennedy. *Sleep Deprivation Chamber.* New York: Theater Communications Group, 1996.

Kennedy, Adrienne. *Adrienne Kennedy in One Act.* Minneapolis: University of Minnesota Press, 1988.

———. *People Who Led to My Plays.* New York: Theatre Communications Group, 1996.

Khalifeh, Sahar (1941–)

The first Palestinian feminist author, Sahar Khalifeh, an activist, scenarist, and editor, writes colonial fiction that captures the details of disrupted domestic life during tense Arab-Israeli conflicts. A native of Nablus on the Israeli-occupied West Bank, she was born seven years before the creation of the state of Israel. The fifth of eight girls, she brought grief to her father, who longed for a son. She completed secondary education at Rosary College in Amman, Jordan. After marrying in her late teens, she despaired of finding happiness in a feudal union arranged by the nuns of Zion.

At the crux of Khalifeh's discontent was the misogyny of her husband, who tore up her writings and drawings. Their marriage ended in divorce in 1972. While mothering two girls, she studied literature and women's issues at Bir Zeit University as preparation for a writing career. After postgraduate work at the University of North Carolina at Chapel Hill and doctoral training in American literature at the University of Iowa, she taught literature at Bir Zeit. To boost women's presence in the intellectual community, she established the Women's Affairs Center in her hometown with branch offices in Amman and Gaza City. She began writing in 1976, the year of the Israeli invasion of the Gaza Strip and the West Bank. Her works depict Islamic women as silent sufferers and as resisters of Israeli dominance.

Khalifeh had difficulty getting her works into readers' hands. Israelis seized her first fiction, *Lam na'ud jawari lakum* (We are not your slave girls anymore, 1974), a novel about WOMEN'S RIGHTS serialized in radio broadcasts and on television in 1977. The text reflects her devaluation in a family that prefers male children and her training in total obedience to men. The second novel, published by an Arab press in Cairo, was *Al-Subar* (*Wild Thorns*, 1976), a landmark eyewitness account of Islamic women's struggles against PATRIARCHY and Israeli insurgents who kill indiscriminately and bulldoze homes. After hearing flute music, Usama, the protagonist, undergoes a moment of doubt in his military mission that discloses his sensitive side. He muses, "Why are we so moved by songs of loss?" Are we a nation of romantics? Well, not anymore"

(Khalifeh, 1984, 163). Khalifeh developed more pro-woman themes in *Abbad ashshams* (The sunflower, 1980) and *Muthakkerat imra'a ghayr waqi'yyah* (Memoirs of an unrealistic woman, 1986), a semiautobiographical study of loveless marriage. Her works, which appear on university reading lists, have been translated into Dutch, English, French, Hebrew, Italian, Malaysian, Russian, Spanish, and Swedish.

Bibliography

Khalifeh, Sahar. "My Life, Myself, and the World," *Aljadid* 8, no. 39 (Spring 2002): 1.

———. *Wild Thorns.* London: Al Saqi, 1984.

Nidal, Nazih Abu. "The Novels of Sahar Khalifeh," *Palestine-Israel Journal of Politics, Economics, and Culture* 10, no. 2 (2003): 113–114.

Kincaid, Jamaica (1949–   )

From contrasting experiences in the Caribbean islands and in New York City, Jamaica Kincaid describes the acceptance of self that eases young girls into adulthood. Born of African-Carib ancestry to Annie Victoria Richardson in St. John's, the capital of the former British colony of Antigua, she was named Elaine Potter Richardson. Happy in a seaside milieu, she learned to read at age three. In the Anglican colonial tradition she studied the Bible and portions of John Milton's *Paradise Lost* and memorized the verse of John Keats and William Wordsworth. The birth of brothers in the household ended her mother's devotion to her. In 1965 Kincaid followed the example of Charlotte Brontë's motherless heroine in *Jane Eyre*, which she read at age 10, by emigrating to Westchester, New York, to work as a nanny. She left her mother's letters unopened and remained the prodigal daughter for the next 19 years.

Kincaid based the novel *Lucy* (1990) on her experiences as well as on the early ferment of the women's movement. Too soon cynical, the protagonist, Lucy Josephine Potter, a 19-year-old from Antigua, is unable to understand the feminism of Mariah, her privileged New York employer, who speaks of "women in society, women in history, women in culture, women everywhere" (Kincaid, 1991, 131). Instead of fulfilling her one-year contract, Lucy quits her au pair position and considers informing Mariah about what to expect from an adulterous husband: "Your situation is an everyday thing. Men behave in this way all the time" (*ibid.*, 141). To herself Lucy muses on male-initiated adultery: "It was expected. Everybody knew that men have no morals" (*ibid.*, 142).

Because she was born female and illegitimate, Kincaid knew in girlhood that she would have to educate herself. After studying at the New School for Social Research, Kincaid mastered photography at Franconia College. Like the fictional Lucy, the author left domestic work to become a writer. Under a pen name she began submitting stories to *Harper's, Ingenue, Paris Review,* and *Rolling Stone,* starting with an expository essay on a West Indian Day parade. She worked on the staffs of *Glamour, Mademoiselle,* and the *New Yorker,* for which she produced columns for "Talk of the Town," later collected in *Talk Stories* (2001). The article "Just Reading" (1993) presages Kincaid's interest in gardening while revealing her disdain for the landscaping style of Gertrude Jekyll, a British horticulturist famed for her naturalistic style. In "Sowers and Reapers" (2001), an essay published in the *New Yorker,* Kincaid reflects on the pride with which Thomas Jefferson spoke of his herb and vegetable garden at Monticello and the footnote in which he indicated that 12 black slaves did the actual cultivating, weeding, and harvesting. Among the dozen laborers mentioned are his paramour, Sally Hemings (or Hemmings), and four of her mixed-race children, including Beverly Hemings, a son sired by Jefferson. To particularize Sally's rewards for sowing and reaping for the master and for bearing his child, Kincaid mentions Sally's pitiful rewards—wool and linen yard goods and a pair of shoes, not manumission.

Currently Kincaid specializes in the metamorphosis of girls into women, particularly those who long to outgrow a love-hate MOTHER-DAUGHTER RELATIONSHIP and to embrace INDEPENDENCE and a mature SEXUALITY. She compiled her first anthology of short fiction in *At the Bottom of the River* (1983), winner of the Morton Dauwen Zabel Award from American Academy. One of the imagistic dreamscapes, "Girl," speaks in a fluid, Faulknerian style of the culinary, domestic, and social lessons that young women learn before entering adulthood. In addition to making home remedies for a cold, the unnamed protagonist develops some sophistication about loving and/or rejecting a man. The story "In the Night" describes a mother's going to her daughter in the dark to explain the mountain lights as a *jablesse*, a shape-shifter that tries to take the form of a beautiful woman. A third story, "My Mother," pictures an autobiographical face-off between parent and child after the daughter wishes her mother dead. Kincaid fantasizes that mother and child transform themselves into slithery reptiles and shape shift in height like the creatures in Lewis Carroll's *Alice in Wonderland* (1865).

Two years later Kincaid published a feminist classic, *Annie John* (1985), the story of a teenager's rocky coexistence with her mother. In the chapter "Columbus in Chains," the girl fantasizes that her mother has developed the body and fierce teeth of a crocodile; during a parable that the mother relates, Annie John envisions herself as the main character, a girl balancing on her head a bunch of figs in which hides a serpent, a symbol of betrayal that alludes to both EVE in Eden and the Egyptian queen Cleopatra. At a fractious moment after the mother calls her daughter a slut, the word seems to "[pour] in through my eyes, my ears, my nostrils, my mouth" (Kincaid, *Annie*, 102). To repel the shame, Annie retorts, "Well, like father like son, like mother like daughter" (*ibid.*). The author's anger at colonial exploitation of Caribbean people erupts full scale in a lengthy treatise, *A Small Place* (1988). She explores the emptiness in 70-year-old Xuela Claudette Richardson in *The Autobiography of My Mother* (1996), the story of a vulnerable girl left motherless at birth. Kincaid returned to her nuclear family with *My Brother* (2000), winner of the Prix Femina Etranger award, and *Mr. Potter* (2002), a wistful reflection on the biological father who never claimed her.

Bibliography

Ferguson, Moira. *Jamaica Kincaid: Where the Land Meets the Body.* Charlottesville: University of Virginia Press, 1994.

Kincaid, Jamaica. *Annie John.* New York: Farrar, Straus & Giroux, 1997.

———. *The Autobiography of My Mother.* New York: Plume, 1997.

———. *Lucy.* New York: Penguin, 1991.

———. *A Small Place.* New York: Farrar, Straus & Giroux, 2000.

Lenz, Brooke. "Postcolonial Fiction and the Outsider Within: Toward a Literary Practice of Feminist Standpoint Theory," *NWSA Journal* 16, no. 2 (Summer 2004): 98–110.

King, Florence (1936–)

A fierce satirist and humorist, Florence King specializes in lampooning the quirks of traditional southern womanhood. She was born on the great divide between South and North—Washington, D.C.—to a British father and an American mother. King acquired her own brand of Virginia feminism from her maternal grandmother, an adamant anti-bluestocking who believed that ladies make their principles known by their priorities—never swearing and never smoking on the street. As King explains in *Confessions of a Failed Southern Lady* (1985), matrilineage dominated her youth: "Granny looked around the family for a malleable girl who would heed her advice, a surrogate daughter cast in the traditional mold, someone delicate and fragile in body and spirit, a true exemplar of Southern womanhood" (King, 1990, 7). The stereotype was nothing approaching a description of Florence.

Early on King set her course in the chapter heading "Spinsterhood Is Nature's Own Feminism" (King, 1989, 49). With degrees in history from American University and the University of Mississippi, she filed documents for a realty firm and briefly taught high school history. She relocated to North Carolina to join the women's page staff of the *Raleigh News and Observer* and to produce a column, "The Misanthrope's Corner." Her freelance career ranged from astute book reviews in *Newsday* and the *New York Times* and essays for *Cosmopolitan, Harper's, Ms., National Review, Playgirl, Penthouse,* and *Southern Magazine* to pious stories for the *Christian* and *St. Joseph's Magazine* and bodice-ripping romances for *Uncensored Confessions.* Her columns blaze away at society's damning of any female out of sync with the expected roles of sedate housewifeliness or genteel hostessing. Her two-edged wit outed her as a lesbian in an AUTOBIOGRAPHY, *Confessions of a Failed Southern Lady,* another droll flaying of the stereotypical frail, sweet-natured girl of the Old South. King ventured into antifeminism with *When Sisterhood Was in Flower* (1982), a novel that pairs a conservative, Isobel Fairfax, with an outspoken feminist, Polly Bradshaw. Shifting from comic irony to her personal philosophy of women's rights, King later clarified her position on women's rise in the workplace: "The ceaseless demands of pseudo-feminists and their arrogant premise that the corporate world exists to provide women with careers regardless of cost and upheaval have caused so much hostility and resentment that sexism and misogyny have been rejuvenated" (King, 1989, 42). She based the underlying idea on her notion of fairness—that women have no right to expect a pro-female stance from male-dominated capitalism.

A sassy, self-proclaimed right-wing feminist, King stresses individualism as woman's redeeming trait and the source of her success and contentment. She blames male propaganda for elevating southern ladies to impossible paragons of modesty, chastity, and high-mindedness. To compile a serio-comic anthology, *Southern Ladies and Gentlemen* (1975), she recycled articles about caricatures from southern fiction—high-strung matrons, club-women, dowagers, egomaniac brides, bosomy cheerleaders, and self-absorbed prom trotters and debutantes. In a chapter on southern womanhood, the author characterizes the conflicting traits of the iconic Dixie female: "She is required to be frigid, passionate, sweet, bitchy, and scatterbrained—all at the same time" (King, 1993, 37). With a journalist's glee, King remarks on the height of feminine pretensions—brides, who "crave their moment of glory" (*ibid.,* 116). With swift undercutting, she adds, "In the South there is a *name* for a woman who dazzles multitudes—a belle," a romanticized figure extolled in art, music, literature, and film, especially in Margaret MITCHELL's iconic Scarlett O'Hara, queen of the county in GONE WITH THE WIND (1936) (*ibid.,* 116).

Although a defender of the basic concepts of the women's movement, King distributes roses and rubbish to the up- and downsides of feminism. She notes that rebellious women defy the BEAUTY MYTH and make an impact on Dixie's traditional racism, classism, sexism, and ageism. As a tutorial on change profiles of the NEW WOMAN appear in the popular press, particularly in advertising and women's magazines. The ebullient liberated female breaks stereotypes at all social levels. As a result, the standard newspaper practice of showcasing girls from prominent families on the bride page gave place to a democratic approach: "There is less difference between the placement, head size, and photo treatment of brides from different walks of life" (*ibid.,* 118).

The satirist turned realist in analyzing the herky-jerky gender shifts that swept America. She stressed that to cope with late 20th-century feminism, southern women compromised. They still bore the yoke of fragile womanhood but began claiming new territory—"the ABORTION debate, the crisis over the dangers of the Pill, the crisis over the dangers of IUDs, the crisis over the dangers of synthetic estrogen, and the crisis over the dangers of silicone breast implants" (*ibid.,* 225–226). According to King the women's movement liberated females, but at a cost. The emergence of unrestricted behavior generated new animosities by making the old-style hausfrau "resentful and jealous of unencumbered women who have never married. . . . It used to be legs and bosoms; now it's careers and lifestyles" (King, 1989, 43).

Bibliography

King, Florence. *Confessions of a Failed Southern Lady.* New York: St. Martin's, 1990.
———. *Reflections in a Jaundiced Eye.* New York: St. Martin's, 1989.
———. *Southern Ladies and Gentlemen.* New York: St. Martin's, 1993.

Kingsolver, Barbara (1955–)

The tireless egalitarian and ecofeminist Barbara Kingsolver applies unflinching principles and a generous dollop of humor to novels and essays. Born in Annapolis, Maryland, she calls home Carlisle, Kentucky, the place where she learned hiking, "snake catching, and paw-paw hunting" (Kingsolver, 2000, xi). While living in the Appalachians and during a two-year sojourn in the Congo, she read female authors—Louisa May ALCOTT, Doris LESSING, Carson MCCULLERS, Margaret MITCHELL, Flannery O'CONNOR, Christina ROSSETTI, Eudora WELTY, and Laura Ingalls WILDER—and developed pacifism and compassion as the bases of empathetic class consciousness. During her undergraduate days studying zoology and English at DePauw University she began shaping her idealism with readings of Betty FRIEDAN and Gloria STEINEM and with internal debates on ABORTION and gender equity. The unusual coupling of science with composition presaged a career writing about nature and ECOFEMINISM.

Through essay and fiction Kingsolver crusades for respect for nature, peace, and fair treatment of all humankind. In explanation of her blend of ethics with fiction she explained to an interviewer: "I devise a very big question whose answer I believe will be amazing, and maybe shift the world a little bit on its axis. Then I figure out how to create a world in which that question can be asked, and answered" (Rubinstein, 254). Her works alert readers to the treachery of polluters and clear cutters of forests, to the waste of materialism, and to profiteering and malfeasance throughout the political structure, from the local mayor to conservative U.S. presidents. She supports "responsibility to our future, the political choices we make, how to begin paying back the debt to rivers and air and oceans and soil we've been borrowing on, cheating on, for decades" (Ross, 289). These ideas she transforms into fictional themes of social justice, freedom, and nature stewardship.

The author's candid portraits extend over an array of female characters who willingly risk their all for a chance at self-fulfillment. In the muckraking style of the early newspaper reporters Nellie BLY and Winifred Bonfils, Kingsolver and her coauthor, Jill Barrett Fein, compiled a feminist documentary, *Holding the Line: Women in the Great Arizona Mine Strike of 1983* (1989), an enlargement of their article for the March 1983 issue of *Progressive* magazine entitled "Women on the Line." Based on the experiences of Anglo and Chicana women during a labor crusade at Ajo and Clifton-Morenci, Arizona, against the Phelps Dodge Copper Corporation, the book cites interviews conducted "in bars, in cars, in their kitchens and back-porch swings, and on the picket line" (*ibid.*, 289). Their working method violated the journalistic tradition of quoting ponderous male commentary by owners, management and union officials, and law enforcement agents. Kingsolver championed the civil liberties of some one thousand female workers and housewives who took to the streets on June 1983 for 18 months of picketing a faceless bureaucracy.

Kingsolver discloses a granite streak in females. In the glare of state troopers armed with automatic weapons and tear gas, the women protested racist hiring practices, a wage freeze, the loss of cost-of-living adjustments, and reduced dental, medical, and retirement benefits. Their courage cost them employment, near starvation, loss of homes, and eviction as a result of jailing and mortgage foreclosures. Justifying her pro-woman chronicle, Kingsolver insisted, "You can't walk into a situation like that and pretend you don't know which side you're on" (*ibid.*). She praised the women's persistence as the source of public speaking and organizational skills developed on the scene.

Early in her career Kingsolver made toughness a standard attribute of female characters. In the short story "Homeland," anthologized in *Homeland and Other Stories* (1989), she pictures Great Mam, a Cherokee matron and WISE-WOMAN, maintaining cultural folkways and reverence for Earth in her family's lives. A second model of strength, Jericha, the young Caribbean hero of "Jump-up Day" (1989), is wise enough to find direction in a pagan Obeah culture that black slaves transferred from West Africa. In Kingsolver's quest novel, *The Bean Trees* (1988), female networking rescues women and children from hunger, pedophilia, and tyranny. Mattie, the widowed owner of the Jesus Is Lord tire dealership, establishes a reception center of a late 20th-century underground railroad to aid Guatemalan and Salvadoran political dissidents and their families from Central America on their way to way stations north of her Arizona business. Taylor Greer, with mountaineer logic, expresses the women's creed: "You can't just sit there, you got to get pissed off" (Kingsolver, 1988, 150). Balancing the women's corps is a sprinkling of altruistic males—Dr. Pelinowsky, Terry the barefoot priest, the magistrate Jonas Wilford Armistead, and Estevan, a Mayan political dissident who gently reminds racists that cooperation can ease the world's worst hurts.

Kingsolver's dedication to the dispossessed increased in intensity in subsequent fictional settings. She creates as a model of selflessness the volunteerism of Hallie Noline, an agronomist in *Animal Dreams* (1990), whom a macho mafia guns down by the roadside in Nicaragua. The range of Kingsolver's empathy with female laborers encompasses Alice Greer, a retired domestic worker, and her minimum-wage-earning daughter, Taylor, a third-shift clerk at the 7-Eleven in *The Bean Trees*; the idealistic Cherokee attorney Annawake Fourkiller in *Pigs in Heaven* (1993); and Orleanna Price, a homemaker and mother of four girls, and her daughter, Leah Price Ngemba, the tutor of West African refugees in *The Poisonwood Bible* (1998). In the latter Kingsolver levels the chasm between Congolese and American women at the funeral of Ruth May Price, who dies of the bite of a green mamba. Women converge at a leafy funereal arbor to keen and mourn in their customary style. To acknowledge the bond that women share, Orleanna, Ruth May's devastated mother, distributes her curtains, pots, and kitchen utensils, domestic gifts that express both thanks and a shared life of PATRIARCHY and housewifely duties. More recently the author interwove motifs of compromise and cooperation in *Prodigal Summer* (2000), a romance that features the idealistic naturalist Deanna Wolfe and the savvy farmer Lusa Maluf Landowski, two mediators in the clash of profit motive versus conservation.

Bibliography

Kingsolver, Barbara. *The Bean Trees*. New York: Harper & Row, 1988.

———. *Holding the Line: Women in the Great Arizona Mine Strike of 1983*. Ithaca, N.Y.: Cornell University Press, 1997.

———. *Prodigal Summer*. New York: HarperCollins, 2000.

Murrey, Loretta Martin. "The Loner and the Matriarchal Community in Barbara Kingsolver's *The Bean Trees* and *Pigs in Heaven*," *Southern Studies* 5, no. 1–2 (Spring–Summer 1994): 155–164.

Ross, Jean W. "Interview." In *Contemporary Authors*. Vol. 134. 284–290. Detroit: Gale Research, 1992.

Rubinstein, Roberta. "The Mark of Africa," *World and I* 14, no. 4 (April 1999): 254.

Tischler, Barbara L. "Holding the Line: Women in the Great Arizona Mine Strike of 1983," *Labor Studies Journal* 17, no. 1 (Spring 1992): 82–83.

Kingston, Maxine Hong (1940–)

A first-generation Chinese American from Stockton, California, Maxine "Ting Ting" Hong Kingston applies inferences from multiple cultures to describe universal female strengths that ward off PATRIARCHY. Like Brave Orchid, the heroine in her autobiographical female Gothic novel *The WOMAN WARRIOR: Memoirs of a Girlhood among Ghosts* (1976), Kingston was born to a family who love peasant oral tradition. She grew up speaking the Say Yup dialect and reading and writing both English and Chinese. With a degree in American literature from the University of California at Berkeley she taught literature and composition in California and Hawaii. Among the feminist authors she promoted was Tillie OLSEN. Using words as a form of social protest, Kingston began a career as a fiction writer and essayist published in *American Girl, American Heritage, English Journal, Mademoiselle, Mother Jones, MS., New Dawn, New West*, the *New Yorker*, the *New York Times, Viva*, and the *Washington Post*. In addition to becoming one of the most studied books on high school and college reading lists, *The Woman Warrior* earned a *Time* Magazine nonfiction books of the decade citation, National Book Critics Circle Award, *Mademoiselle* Magazine Award, and Anisfield-Wolf Race Relations Award.

Kingston crafted *The Woman Warrior* into a feminist touchstone from strands of myth, history, ghost stories, warrior lore, saga, and personal reportage. She employed an Asian staple, intercalary TALK-STORY, a form of cautionary and supportive narrative that girl children receive informally from members of their matrilineage. The most cited of Kingston's characters is "no-name woman," a tragic victim of Confucian PATRIARCHY. In anger at her illegitimate pregnancy, villagers vent their disapproval: "Like a great saw, teeth strung with lights, files of people walked zigzag across our land, tearing the rice" (Kingston, *Woman,* 5). That night she gives birth in a pigsty, then drowns herself and her infant in the family well, taking with her both shame and the name of the child's sire. Not only is the unnamed mother permanently silenced, but even the story of her death, spoken in whispers, becomes a woman-to-woman confession of feudal misogyny that always blames the female. As a feminist antidote to family cautionary figures, the author created Fa Mu Lan, an epic Christ figure who bears her people's crimes carved on her back. A more realistic model is Brave Orchid, a wielder of subversive action against SILENCING, servility, and other forms of male control.

Kingston later explained the unusual blend of legend, myth, memoir, and history in her feminist novel: "It's important for me to show that racial or feminist writing doesn't have to sound like polemics" (Kingston, 1998, 3). Empowered by woman-affirming "[stories] to grow up on," the protagonist acts out female convictions and desires that society had previously suppressed (*ibid.,* 5). For balance Kingston composed a complementary novel, *China Men* (1980), which honors the first Chinese males to immigrate to North America. The text details a humiliating truth—the anti-woman curses of a father to the protagonist that "make me sicken at being female" (Kingston, *China,* 14). For Kingston's candor about Chinese sexism she generated the antipathy in the male Chinese-American authors Jeffery Chan, Frank Chin, and Benjamin Tong and the regard of feminists. In 1998 President Bill Clinton presented Kingston a National Humanities Medal.

Bibliography

Kalfopoulou, Adrianne. *A Discussion of the Ideology of the American Dream in the Culture's Female Discourses.* Lewiston, N.Y.: Edwin Mellen Press, 2000.

Kingston, Maxine Hong. *China Men.* New York: Vintage, 1989.

———. *Conversations with Maxine Hong Kingston.* New York: Jackson, University Press of Mississippi, 1998.

———. *Woman Warrior.* New York: Vintage, 1989.

Yuan Shu. "Cultural Politics and Chinese-American Female Subjectivity: Rethinking Kingston's 'Woman Warrior,'" *MELUS* 26, no. 2 (Summer 2001): 199–224.

Kitchen Table/Women of Color Press

The nation's first all-female literary outlet and the first national advocacy organization operated by nonwhite and lesbian women, Kitchen Table / Women of Color Press expands the outreach of feminist fiction, pamphlets, and art. Discussed in the late 1970s by the black lesbian poet Audre LORDE, the Chicana author Cherríe MORAGA, and the black lesbian activist Barbara Smith, the idea originally focused on a literary journal or another periodical rather than a publishing firm. Smith was a particularly vocal critic of exclusive school curricula that omit or discredit writings other than those of a white, middle-class male Protestant canon. To end exclusionary policies in schools, college curricula, and libraries, the editorial staff met in New York City on Halloween 1980. They decided to form a publishing house and, the next year, went into production.

Shortly before her death from cancer Lorde wrote of the "othered" author's fear of leaving no evidence of thought on important issues. She declared nonwhite and LESBIAN AUTHORS' writings as "part of a continuum of women's work, of reclaiming this earth and our power, and knowing that this work did not begin with my birth nor will it end with my death" (Lockett, 39). Because of the relevance and authenticity of such female writings and scholarship, the consortium, aided by the Laguna Sioux author Paula Gunn ALLEN, turned niche marketing of "othered" writings into a revered vehicle for formerly suppressed or ignored writers. Through the print versions of works by the lesbian poet Cheryl Clarke, the radical philosopher and teacher Angela DAVIS, the Jewish writer Evelyn Torton Beck, the Japanese poet Mitsuye YAMADA, and the lesbian short story author Hisaye YAMAMOTO, Kitchen Table / Women of Color Press issued perspectives and experiences that had previously failed to reach readers, teachers, students, and researchers.

In 1981 the editors Cherríe Moraga and Gloria ANZALDÚA realized a breakthrough in feminist literature with a best-selling anthology/textbook, *This Bridge Called My Back: Writings by Radical Women of Color.* Composed of the prose and verse of third world American authors, the book won an American Book Award from the Before Columbus

Foundation. The firm, which moved to Albany, New York, in 1984, continued meeting the needs of nonwhite feminists with Mariana Romo Camona and Alma Gómez's collection *Cuentos: Stories by Latinas* (1983), Barbara Smith's anthology *Home Girls: A Black Feminist Anthology* (1983), Barbara Omolade's *It's a Family Affair: The Real Lives of Black Single Mothers* (1986), Lorde's *I Am Your Sister: Black Women Organizing Across Sexualities* (1986), Yamamoto's award-winning *Seventeen Syllables and Other Stories* (1988), and Lorde's *Need: A Chorale for Black Women's Voices* (1990). With a list of successes to their company's credit, Smith accounted for strong readership as evidence of the staff's perceptions of reader need: "I believe all the books we have published have made a difference in people's lives" (Giddings, 26). The publisher Andrea Lockett agreed that books by nonwhite and lesbian authors were "so liberating and freeing—there was finally an alternative view of women's lives" (Brownworth, 10). During the staff's 15-year anniversary celebration in 1996, a $40,000 grant from the Nathan Cummings Foundation along with $260,000 from the Union Institute Center for Women, the Sister Fund, and other philanthropic sources helped to keep the Brooklyn office afloat and the press's backlist in print.

Bibliography

Brownworth, Victoria A. "Who Will Publish Our Books? Lesbian and Feminist Presses Imperiled by Industry Crunch," *Lambda Book Report* 5, no. 11 (May 1997): 10.

Giddings, Paula. "Book Marks," *Essence* 19, no. 11 (March 1989): 26.

Lockett, Andrea. "Sister Difference: An Audre Lorde Memorial Conversation," *Belles Lettres* 8, no. 4 (Summer 1993): 39.

Moraga, Cherríe, and Gloria Anzaldúa, eds. *This Bridge Called My Back: Writings by Radical Women of Color.* New York: Kitchen Table / Women of Color Press, 1981.

Kizer, Carolyn (1925–   )

The writer and translator Carolyn Ashley Kizer layers satire and humor to mellow the bite of her pro-woman verse. She was born in Spokane, Washington; grew up in a cultured household; and became the center of her parents' lives. While pursuing comparative literature at Sarah Lawrence College, Columbia University, and the University of Washington, she published verse in the *New Yorker* at age 20, spent a year on Taiwan, traveled Japan, and studied versification privately with the poet Theodore Roethke. She married and bore three children before assembling her first collection, *Poems* (1959). That same year she established *Poetry Northwest*, which, at 46 years, is the nation's longest-lived journal dedicated strictly to verse. Her editorship ended in 1965, when she taught at a women's college in Pakistan for the U.S. Department of State until the bombing of North Vietnam endangered her residence in Asia. The experience fed her enthusiasm for Chinese, Macedonian, and Urdu writings, which she later translated in *Carrying Over* (1988) along with European poems in German, Romanian, and Yiddish.

Kizer's feminism emerges in sympathetic lines that inform readers of women's hardships. She expresses compassion for Maisie, the abused wife in "The Valley of the Fallen" (1984); a feminist victim of mastectomy in "An American Beauty" (1996); and the unappreciated toils of a maid-of-all-work in "Gerda" (1996), a hymn to the surrogate mother. In "For Jan, in Bar Maria" (1964), the poet ennobles SISTERHOOD in two young Italian women who grow up together and who maintain their friendship although people think them "mad as yearling mares in the full moon" (Kizer, *Calm*, 85). In 1965 she published in *Knock upon Silence*, a series of translations of the eighth-century Chinese writer Tu Fu. These austere poems share space with "Pro Femina," a rowdy commentary on feminist literature, in which she characterizes the social and familial brickbats hurled at women who choose to remain unmarried and pursue a career. In 1971 the poem "Bitch" spewed bile-soaked memories of an ex-wife who regrets that she once fawned over an impassive, self-satisfied husband. The controlling image is the inner dog that barks, snarls, and strains against the choke chain in an effort to inflict bodily harm.

In her 20th year publishing verse Kizer compiled *Mermaids in the Basement: Poems for Women* (1984), which speaks her indebtedness to foremothers and WISEWOMEN. That same year she earned a Pulitzer Prize for exploring female consciousness in *Yin: New Poems* (1984), which contains "Fanny," a dramatic monologue to Robert Louis Stevenson's Samoan companion. Kizer reprised submissions to *American Poetry Review, Antaeus, Paris Review,* the *New York Times, Princeton Library Journal, Southern Review,* and *Yale Review* in *Harping On* (1996), containing "Fearful Women," which exults with feminists over white braceleted arms. (Kizer, 22). With a giddy rush at self-mockery, she snickers in "Fin-de-Siecle Blues" at uppity poets as they gaze at their reflection in the mirror (*ibid.*, 63). With a smirk at the old-fashioned macho man, the poem "After Horace" (2002) lauds Licymnia, the scantily clad dancer at Diane's feast who flirts and steals a kiss. Kizer applied her knowledge to editing *100 Great Poems by Women* in 1998. That same year she joined the poet Maxine KUMIN in resigning from the Academy of American Poets for its sexism in mainly naming males as members of the board and winners of awards.

Bibliography

Kizer, Carolyn. "After Horace," *Poetry* 181, no. 1 (October–November 2002): 41.

———. *Calm, Cool and Collected: Poems 1960–2000.* Townsend, Wash.: Copper Canyon Press, 2002.

———. *Carrying Over: Poems from the Chinese, Urdu, Macedonian, Yiddish, and French-African.* Port Townsend, Wash.: Copper Canyon Press, 1989.

———. *Harping On.* Port Townsend, Wash.: Copper Canyon Press, 1996.

———. *The Nearness of You: Poems.* New York: Consortium, 1986.

Pettingell, Phoebe. "Mourners and Harpies," *New Leader,* 24 January 1997, pp. 14–15.

Kogawa, Joy (1935–)

A warrior against denial and SILENCING, Joy Kogawa contributes feminist verse, myth, and fiction to Canada's literary renaissance. A Nisei, or first-generation Japanese Canadian, born in Vancouver, she is the daughter of an Anglican pastor. During wartime internment she was only five years old at the bombing of Pearl Harbor, when the military rounded up ethnic Japanese citizens to serve out the conflict in government-supervised camps. Her autobiographical masterwork, *Obasan* (1981), winner of the Canada First Novel Award, Book of the Year Award, and American Book Award, looks back on the powerlessness of childhood, when Naomi Nakane suffers sexual abuse by Old Man Gower. The emotional isolation worsens after Naomi's mother is detained on a visit to Japan and dies during the atomic bombing of Hiroshima on August 6, 1945. Naomi acknowledges the losses that silence has imposed: "Gentle Mother, we were lost together in our silences. Our wordlessness was our mutual destruction" (Kogawa, 243).

Kogawa's story pinpoints matrilineage as a beacon during dark times. Under the care of a vocal maternal aunt, Emily Kato, Naomi and her little brother, Stephen, accept the makeshift family in place of their father, who spends long stretches in a hospital. Of Emily's moral stature the author sees her in an unusual metaphor: "Whether she's dealing with the Japanese-Canadian issue or WOMEN'S RIGHTS or poverty, she's one of the world's white blood cells, rushing from trouble spot to trouble spot with her medication pouring on wounds seen and not seen" (*ibid.*, 34). Quick to defend the family, she refers to female empowerment as "gluing our tongues back on" (*ibid.*, 36). To ensure that facts pass on to the next story keeper, she ties documents and papers in red string and secures them in her briefcase.

In 1942 the Canadian government uprooted Kogawa's family along with 21,000 others and seized their home in the Marpole district. The Kogawas had to move east to Slocan, then to Coaldale, Alberta, for the duration of World War II. After earning degrees at the University of Toronto followed by studies at the Anglican Women's Training College and the University of Saskatchewan, the author taught school and began writing children's books. After emerging from four decades of recovery from personal and financial loss, Kogawa allied lyricism with memory to produce *Obasan.* The composition gave the author an opportunity to mourn the family dead. In a sylvan setting she pictures the ritual through tactile images of traditional ancestor worship: "Tonight we read the forest braille. See how our stained fingers have read the seasons, and how our serving hands serve you still. My loved ones, rest in your world of stone" (*ibid.*, 246).

In an interview Kogawa reminisced about the yearning "for a primary bond . . . to have an at-homeness" (Clayton, 107). She returned to the fictional persona of Naomi Nakane in *Itsuka* (1993) for the postwar turmoil that left Japanese-Canadians at the mercy of government-sanctioned racism. She drew on the outspoken nature of Aunt Emily to reframe a neglected biblical legend as *A Song of Lilith* (2003), an epic poem based on Talmudic and cabalistic traditions. Her title hero, like Aunt Emily, draws power from within to sprout wings and fly out of the grasp of Adam, the first patriarch and would-be lord over women. The subtext of the book-length poem is the hope of feminists that women's efforts can rescue a greedy, war-ravaged world.

Bibliography

Clayton, Cherry. "Interview with Joy Kogawa," *Canadian Ethnic Studies* 34, no. 2 (2002): 106–116.

Grice, Helena. "Reading the Nonverbal: The Indices of Space, Time, Tactility, and Taciturnity in Joy Kogawa's 'Obasan,' " *MELUS* 24, no. 4 (Winter 1999): 93–105.

Kogawa, Joy. *Obasan*. New York: Anchor, 1993.

Teleky, Richard. "Entering the Silence: Voice, Ethnicity, and the Pedagogy of Creative Writing," *MELUS* 26, no. 1 (Spring 2001): 205–219.

Kumin, Maxine (1925–   )

The elegist, essayist, and fiction writer Maxine Winokur Kumin creates a lyric mesh out of her own and other women's perceptions. Well read in the Old Testament at a Catholic school in the Germantown section of her native Philadelphia, she developed into a career her girlhood love of the outdoors and her knack for verse. While completing a B.A. and M.A. in history and literature at Radcliffe, she and fellow poetry lovers memorized and recited long passages from William Wordsworth's *Intimations of Immortality,* an incantatory hymn to nature. After marrying, she settled on a woodsy hermitage outside Warner, New Hampshire, to raise Arabian horses. In "Letters" (1996), she described the preference of a girlfriend

for privilege, porcelain, and Sheffield silver, while Kumin chose the hard life of a wife, mother, and animal breeder. Her days took on a regularity graced by everyday miracles that she formed into poems. Her focus on female figures took her from the chambermaids at the Marriott Hotel and a mother facing an empty nest after a last child leaves for college to views of Romeo and Juliet as an old married couple and to Helen of Troy taking a morning-after pill.

Parallel to her work in livestock Kumin gravitated toward verse through intense observation and private writing, classroom teaching at Tufts, and friendships with poets. She collaborated with the confessional poet Anne SEXTON on four children's books—*Eggs of Things* (1963), *More Eggs of Things* (1964), *Joey and the Birthday Present* (1971), and *The Wizard's Tears* (1975). In 1961 Kumin collected her verse in *Halfway,* which opens on a reflection of her home birth in Germantown and her growing up years. Her early work balanced snuggly comforts of motherhood against worldly dangers with her images of clean sheets' snapping on the line, breaking kindling into a wood stove, stirring soft beet pulp, and instructing children with the story of "Kaspar the rosy-cheeked" (*ibid.*, 17). She continues to issue incisive lyric views on womanhood in the *Atlantic, Kenyon Review, Literary Review, Ploughshares,* and *Poetry.*

Kumin's ties to nature direct her thoughts toward birth and death cycles. As the elk sheds its annual growth of antlers, she witnesses changes in herself and mourns the ebbing of her femininity. In one pictorial poem, "Making the Jam without You" (1970), the steamy stovetop chore seems safer than the bullet-shaped rain falling outside the window. In the title poem of *The Retrieval System* (1978) she muses on the inevitability of death and the comfort of memory by recalling the females in her life—a piano teacher, elderly aunts, and a sister who died in toddlerhood. For her intuitive free verse, sonnets and pantoums, and Virgilian essays on country life at age 56 Kumin received a consultancy to the Library of Congress, followed in 1989 by the poet laureate's post in New Hampshire and, in 1995, a chancellorship of the Academy of American Poets. Her *Selected Poems 1960–1990* (1997) won a *New York Times* Notable Book of the Year award.

Kumin's writing achieved critical acclaim with *Up Country: Poems of New England* (1972), winner of the Pulitzer Prize. With restrained touches of AUTOBIOGRAPHY she chose the persona of hermit to survey berry picking, bird calls, and an encounter with a skunk. She maintained feminist themes into the late 1970s, as in "The Envelope" (1978), an ode on the matrilineage that lives on in future generations of daughters and granddaughters, as tiny Russian dolls nest into each other. More soul centered is "In the Absence of Bliss" (1985), which reveals her Jewish upbringing and the agnosticism that, in adulthood, beset her with misgivings.

Now in her fifth decade of writing Kumin believes that "the poet cannot escape his or her obligation to bear witness to the times" (Kumin, 2000, cover). In *Our Ground Time Here Will Be Brief* (1982) she presents compelling views of women at crucial moments in their lives. "Birthday Poem" describes from a child's perspective her own conception and birth; "History Lesson" applies a warm nostalgia to the birth and childhood of her son, Steven. "The Fairest One of All," a plaintive FAIRY TALE lyric of motherly regret, fears that "too soon the huntsman will come," a mythic figure who robs the mother of "my darling, my fair first born" (Kumin, 1982, 176). She contributed to ECOFEMINISM the poem "Noted in the *New York Times*" (1989), a lament for the seaside sparrow. She lobs anger at the hubris of technology that cares more for space exploration than for the dwindling populations of mice and birds.

Bibliography

Kumin, Maxine. *Always Beginning.* Port Townsend, Wash.: Copper Canyon Press, 2000.

———. *The Long Marriage: Poems.* New York: W. W. Norton, 2001.

———. *Our Ground Time Here Will Be Brief.* New York: Viking, 1982.

———. *Selected Poems 1960–1990.* New York: W. W. Norton, 1998.

McNair, Wesley. "Taking the World for Granite: Four Poets in New Hampshire," *Sewanee Review* 104, no. 1 (Winter 1996): 70–81.

L

Lady Macbeth

Because of his ability to move audiences to admire, love, or hate his complex stage women, William Shakespeare fueled centuries of curiosity and speculation about unknown or implied elements of his female characters. Of major interest is his masterful Lady Macbeth, the murderous thane's wife turned queen in the tragedy *Macbeth* (ca. 1603). The heat and vigor of her speeches have drawn such actors as Judith Anderson, Mary ROBINSON, Sarah Siddons, and Ellen Terry to the chiaroscuro of her personality, from glamorous hostess to plotter, from articulate politician to savvy assassin. The murky morality, linked by imagery to Hecate and three witch-prophets, characterizes a wife—Macbeth's beloved "dearest chuck"—who on her darker side welcomes night to cloak Medusan deeds (3.1. p. 44). Unable to seize Scotland's throne for herself, she must operate secondhand through a suggestible husband. She dispatches him to stab King Duncan, a meek, beloved house guest who had just complimented the sweet air that welcomes the martin to nest at her castle and who had presented her a diamond as proof of his admiration.

One view of Lady Macbeth is that of a woman who turns SEXUALITY to monstrosity by stripping away femininity and motherhood to enfold herself in a witchy guile more typical of masculine motives and behavior. So willing is she to trade honor for a crown that she speaks of the irrelevance of her children. She is capable of unwomanly metaphors—of transforming breast milk into gall and of plucking a boy babe from her nipple to hurl him to a precipi-

tate death. Her intent is to grasp the promise of the moment rather than waste her hopes on DYNASTY. Upon hearing of Duncan's murder, she feigns a swoon that mocks her true nature. During a sparkling dinner scene she retreats to the woman behind the throne once more by playing the chameleon—the domesticated queen at the royal table before welcome guests only minutes away from the dark doings by the roadside that end Banquo's threat to Scotland's throne. Her sleepwalking scene views the limits of that power. Attesting to women's internal stress, dread, or evil are her unconscious night strolls. The DUALITY of a woman who inspires extremes of love and loathing leaves unanswered the source of her control over Macbeth, a gallant soldier in the field who acquiesces to her rabid plotting.

As do the phantom scorpions that skitter across Macbeth's anxious mind and rob him of sleep, the jarring rhythms of Lady Macbeth's pacing and raking at imaginary bloodstains on her hands charge the falling action with pitiable mental disintegration. Unlike her husband, who dies at a thrust of Macduff's sword, Lady Macbeth bears the inner poignards of guilt and regret. Shakespeare places in the mouth of an anonymous gentlewoman words of pity for a tumultuous spirit: "I would not have such a heart in my bosom, for the dignity of the whole body" (5.1. 47–48, p. 174). The doctor, realizing the import of the patient's ramblings, intends to prevent the queen from committing suicide and to stop himself and the gentlewoman from revealing the privileged information the queen divulges about the king's crimes. The playwright's compassion for the queen's downfall contributes to the feminist literary motif of the plaintive, conscience-plagued madwoman, a staple in such feminist works as *The Book of Margery Kempe* (1436), Charlotte BRONTË's novel *JANE EYRE* (1847), and Jean RHYS's prequel *WIDE SARGASSO SEA* (1966). Relegated to off-stage action is Lady Macbeth's solitary demise, which male action eclipses with its urgency and immediacy and the manly protocols of dueling. Malcolm returns to the issue of Lady Macbeth's guile in the final scene, in which he refers to the king as a butcher and to the queen as a fiend.

Bibliography

Lenz, Carolyn Ruth Swift. *The Woman's Part: Feminist Criticism of Shakespeare.* Chicago: University of Illinois Press, 1983.

Moi, Toril. *Sexual, Textual Politics: Feminist Literary Theory.* New York: Routledge, 1984.

Shakespeare, William. *Macbeth.* New York: Folger Library, 1959.

LaFollette, Suzanne (1894–1983)

The egalitarian journalist, editor, and poet Suzanne LaFollette expressed profound concerns for the quality of life for women and children. Born on the Pacific coast of Washington State, she and her brother, Chester, grew up on a ranch. The family moved to Washington, D.C., after their father's election to the U.S. House of Representatives. After graduation from college in 1915, LaFollette joined the staff of the *Nation* and, in 1920, edited the *Freeman*. She marched in SUFFRAGE parades and in 1921 joined women who pressured President Woodrow Wilson to keep the United States out of world war. In 1925 she freelanced for the *American Mercury*, the *Nation*, *New Republic*, and *Scribner's*. She compiled a classic work on aesthetics, *Art in America from Colonial Times to the Present Day* (1929). At age 36 she established the *New Freeman*, a successful intellectual vehicle for libertarian and pro-choice ideals.

Often compared to the polemicists Louise BRYANT, Voltairine DE CLEYRE, Emma GOLDMAN, and Margaret SANGER, LaFollette expressed an antipathy toward government control of human life. She stated that until revolutionaries dismantled the state, women would remain in a capitalistic form of serfdom caused by the regulation of birth control and the rigor of laws governing divorce, alimony, illegitimate children, and PROSTITUTION. Among LaFollette's most famous works is *Concerning Women* (1926), the first book on libertarian feminism. It expresses a radical belief that women should have complete control of their life choices. The text blames the state, the church, and all men for centuries of failure to provide equality for women. She wrote *Not Guilty* (1937), the summation of the Dewey Commission, which exonerated Leon Trotsky of charges of treason and conspiracy.

At age 61 LaFollette established the *National Review*, a journal that carries incisive articles on human freedom. Her commitment to liberation extended her outreach to females, slaves, and workers in industrial bondage. Her works fought the American plutocracy by recognizing a distribution of land and wealth that placed natural resources and political power in the hands of propertied males. She was skeptical of the value of the vote, marriage ordinances, and protective labor laws to improve women's lives. In 1972 interest in feminism spurred the reissuance of LaFollette's *Concerning Women*.

Bibliography

Buckley, William F. "Suzanne La Follette, RIP," *National Review,* 13 May 1983, p. 541.

LaFollette, Suzanne. *Concerning Women.* New York: Arno, 1972.

McElroy, Wendy. *Sexual Correctness: The Gender-Feminist Attack on Women.* Jefferson, N.C.: McFarland, 2001.

La Llorona

The conflicted apparition of the troubled female, La Llorona is a combination of penitent, alluring siren, and death omen. In *Women Who Run with the Wolves* (1992), the Jungian psychoanalyst Clarissa Pinkola Estés describes the enigmatic figure as "a haunting river woman who is fertile and generous, creating out of her own body. She is poor, breathtakingly beautiful, but rich in soul and spirit" (Estés, 325). As a transcultural symbol of revenge—whether Mayan, Mexican, or Nigerian—La Llorona, the progeny of Cihuacoatl or Snake Woman and the Virgin of Guadalupe, is a grotesque, estranged being doomed to tragic outcomes. Derived from Central American folklore and shaped by Catholic shame and guilt, she is a Mesoamerican version of the Greek myth of Medea and the Shakespearean murderess LADY MACBETH. La Llorona absorbs the strength denied to powerless women and becomes their champion. She permeates the arts and advertising with a grief amassed from female sorrows and betrayals.

Enraged at being devalued and frenzied that she cannot shield her children from neglect or sexual exploitation, La Llorona leaves them or drowns them in a river. The water becomes a metaphor for a timeless memorial that sustains hopelessness entangled with mother love. The maternal archetype of the nightly wailer, the revenant who refuses to be buried, resets in legend, art, dance, Gothic fiction, and folk song the mythic Cihuacoatl, a pre-Columbian fertility goddess and protector of midwives and of parturient women facing death. In some versions La Llorona is a child killer; in others she is the victim of insanity or abandonment. In all settings and modes the result is the same—her ghost keens for her babes.

The root of the La Llorona cautionary tale derives from the Spanish colonization of Mexico, a racial hierarchy under which *conquistadores* ravished, then tossed aside their Azteca-Mexica concubines. Accounts of the Spanish conquest of Tenochtitlan in 1521 support the pro-woman tale in two sources, the Nahuatl histories of the mestizo chronicler Diego Muñoz Camargo and biographies of Hernán Cortés, which picture him as the aristocratic despoiler of a married Indian, Doña Marina, a bilingual guide called La Malinche (the captain's woman). Permeated with racism, classism, and sexism, the story describes her hysteria and the stabbing of their biracial son. In multiple tellings she symbolizes the rape of women by their social betters as well as the seizure of North America by male explorers, who legitimize genocide. Her victimization recurs under subsequent militarists, who tyrannize, imprison, and execute the *desaparecidos* (the disappeared), a motif of Isabel ALLENDE's Chilean saga *The HOUSE OF THE SPIR-*

ITS (1982) and *Of Love and Shadows* (1984). In the latter Evangelina Ranquileo Sánchez, whom Lieutenant Juan de Dios Ramírez drags to a military jeep, leaves haunting evidence of kidnap: "The last her parents saw of her was the flash of a white petticoat in the darkness as the men forced her into the vehicle. For a while, the parents could hear her cries, calling to them" (Allende, 112). The silence that follows creates irony in her name, which means "the good news."

The itinerant figure, like a monster or stalker, morphs into an array of shapes varying from tattered young mother clothed in white to the ragged crone who is too old to conceive again. In all forms she presages death to women and their unborn or to crib babies. In more recent times Antonia Quintan Pigno's poem "La Llorona" pictures the terrified mother facing a nuclear holocaust. Yxta Maya Murray turned the resilient legend into the short story "La Llorona" (1996). The tender lines stress the children's trust in their mother even as she dips them into the fast current. In verse form Mary McArthur's "La Llorona" (2000) focuses on the faceless ghoul who has cried and searched riverbanks for centuries, forgetting the zigzag path that once pointed her toward vengeance. Even God offers no sympathy. From a lesbian point of view the Chicana writer Gloria ANZALDÚA imagines the weeping woman as deliverer of retribution to hard-drinking, wife-beating husbands.

Updating the image of the sobbing fiend into victim of spousal abuse and economic dependence, the title entry in Sandra CISNEROS's *Woman Hollering Creek and Other Stories* (1991) relieves the wanderer of vicious intent and ill omen by picturing her as Cléofilas, the passion-bereft wife saved by oral tradition. In Seguin, Texas, she lives between symbolic neighbors, Soledad (solitude) and Dolores (sorrow). Trapped in a disappointing marriage, she wonders whether her boring existence "drives a woman to the darkness under the trees" (Cisneros, 51). From reading news of brutalized wives and lovers and from experiencing a blow to the face from Juan Pedro, she recognizes the perils of angry batterers, who beat women blue and leave their corpse by the roadside. Graciela (grace) begins the woman-to-woman rescue by advising Cléofilas to leave town with Felice (happiness). In

Felice's macho truck Cléofilas laughs with joy at her escape from "this man, this father, this rival, this keeper, this lord, this master, this husband till kingdom come" (*ibid.*, 49). The raucous departure toward San Antonio and freedom pictures Cléofilas not only escaping the abuser but leaving behind belief in romantic love.

Bibliography

Allende, Isabel. *Of Love and Shadows.* New York: Bantam, 1987.

Anzaldúa, Gloria. *Interviews/Entrevistas.* New York: Routledge, 2000.

———. *Prietita and the Ghost Woman/Prietita y La Llorona.* New York: Children's Book Press, 2001.

Carbonell, Ana Maria. "From Llorona to Gritona: Coatlicue in Feminist Tales by Viramontes and Cisneros," *MELUS* 24, no. 2 (Summer 1999): 53.

Cisneros, Sandra. *Woman Hollering Creek and Other Stories.* New York: Random House, 1991.

Domecq, Alcina Lubitch. "La Llorona," *Literary Review* 43, no. 1 (Fall 1999): 17.

Estés, Clarissa Pinkola. *Women Who Run with the Wolves: Myths and Stories about the Wild Woman Archetype.* New York: Ballantine, 1997.

McArthur, Mary. "La Llorona," *Midwest Quarterly* 42, no. 1 (Autumn 2000): 42.

Murray, Yxta Maya. "La Llorona," *North American Review* 281, no. 6 (November–December 1996): 24–27.

Lamb, Lady Caroline (1785–1828)

The witty feminist novelist, letter writer, and poet Lady Caroline "Caro" Ponsonby Lamb suffered the accusations of madness and nymphomania that the Regency era hurled at independent, passionate female artists. Because she was nervous and erratic from birth, her parents sent her to an aunt for homeschooling and discipline. Lamb learned to love Bible stories read aloud by her grandmother and became adept at speaking French and Italian and at playing the harpsichord. After marrying the statesman William Lamb, the author shared his rise as Lord Melbourne, member of Parliament and prime minister of England. Neurosis dogged her early marriage after she gave birth to Augustus, an epileptic and mentally retarded child. During her husband's frequent absences she resorted to drugs and alcohol and wrote poems, novels, and letters.

Lamb's literary outlets allowed her to enlarge on the subject of the scorned woman with imaginative solutions to failed passion. At age 27 she had a passionate alliance with the romantic poet George Gordon, Lord Byron. She became caught up in the Byromania that devoured rumors and details of the famed poet's life. Four years later she wrote a satiric melodrama, *Glenarvon* (1816), a roman á clef that she published anonymously. Sophisticated readers enjoyed it as commentary on Byron's life as a scapegrace whose crimes against females doomed him to an unquiet death as a rake and despoiler of women. Because of public scandal and ridicule, Lamb's in-laws sought to have the author committed to an asylum. She followed with the realistic crime novel *Graham Hamilton* (1822) and a pirate tale, *Ada Reis* (1823), an Oriental romance about a brigand's abuse and murder of his mistress. When Lamb grieved openly at the death of Byron in 1824, her marriage ended. She died at age 42 of diabetes.

Bibliography

Douglass, Paul. *Lady Caroline Lamb, a Biography.* London: Palgrave Macmillan, 2004.

Lamb, Caroline. *Glenarvon.* London: Everymans Library, 1995.

"Review: Caroline Lamb, This Infernal Woman," *Contemporary Review* 279, no. 1,627 (August 2001): 126.

Larsen, Nella (1891–1964)

Nella Marian Larsen Imes's feminism focused on one issue, the rejection of the light-skinned mulatto woman by both black and white culture. The daughter of an Afro-Caribbean father, Larsen was probably born in New York City. She grew up under the influence of her Danish mother and stepfather in a white section of Chicago and attended a private school. After a year at all-black Fisk University Normal School, she studied at the University of Copenhagen and completed her education with three years of nursing training at Lincoln Hospital in New York City. During the Harlem Renaissance she interrupted her medical career for a brief time to write short stories, the autobiographical novel *Quicksand* (1928), and the melodramatic *Passing* (1929), a tragic tale of Clare Kendry, a mulatto whose white husband hounds her to her death for her biracial heritage. For insightful feminist fiction Larsen became the first black woman to win a Guggenheim fellowship.

Larsen's titles—"The Wrong Man," "Freedom," "Sanctuary," and *Quicksand*—indicate a desperation in her characters. In the latter fiction a tragic DUALITY weighs heavily on the Afro-Scandinavian protagonist, Helga Crane, particularly in regard to SEXUALITY. Images of restlessness and closeting illuminate the mental burden of a biracial life on the fringe. Hindering her ability to fit in are the inflexible roles that white and black culture assign to females. As the wife of a black preacher, Pleasant Green, she embraces passion as a temporary relief of social frustrations. Ultimately she finds herself in the humiliating position of gratifying a sex partner rather than expressing and receiving love. As a gesture of defiance toward Christian hypocrisy the text vilifies marriage as "this sacred thing of which parsons and other Christian folk ranted so sanctimoniously" (Larsen, *Quicksand*, 220). Larsen describes the pull of Helga's five children, which negates thoughts of deserting home and family.

Bibliography

Lackey, Michael. "Larsen's *Quicksand*," *Explicator* 59, no. 2 (Winter 2001): 103–106.

Larsen, Nella. *Passing*. New York: Collier, 1971.

———. *Quicksand*. New York: Collier, 1971.

Williams, Bettye J. "Nella Larsen: Early Twentieth-Century Novelist of Afrocentric Feminist Thought," *CLA Journal* 39, no. 2 (December 1995): 165–178.

Lazarus, Emma (1849–1887)

The poet Emma Lazarus, one of the prominent female writers of her day, helped to launch the Statue of Liberty, one of America's most important feminist achievements. Born to German-Sephardic Jews, she claimed as ancestors Portuguese refugees of the Spanish Inquisition and subsequent colonial American patriots. She grew up among the privileged and affluent in her native Manhattan and in Newport, Rhode Island. Cultivating her mind and sensibilities from childhood were private teachers of the arts and European languages and noted literary figures who frequented her home. From the verses, letters, essays, and translations of Johann von Goethe, Heinrich Heine, and Richard Reinhard that she produced, her father, the sugar refiner Moses Lazarus, published privately his 17-year-old daughter's best work in a miscellany, *Poems and Translations: Written between the Ages of Fourteen and Sixteen* (1866).

Lazarus corresponded with the noted writers of her day, some of whom she visited during lengthy stays in Europe and the British Isles. She contributed poems to *Century, Critic, Index, Lippincott's,* and the *New York Times* and enlarged her poetic range under the mentorship of Ralph Waldo Emerson, a literary father figure to whom she dedicated *Admetus and Other Poems* (1871). She submitted to the *American Hebrew* a stream of original verse and Hebrew-to-English translations from the classic Jewish authors Moses ben Ezra, Solomon ibn Gabirol, and Judah Halevi. From Goethe's biography she drew the elements of a romance, *Alide: An Episode of Goethe's Life* (1874), her sole novel. She completed a closet verse tragedy set in the Italian Renaissance, *The Spagnoletto* (1876), the Gothic tale of Maria, an apprentice artist who abandons Ribera, her jealous and controlling father, to make her way independently toward a love match with Prince John. In the same vein Lazarus published in *Scribner's* "The Eleventh Hour" (1878), a story about the artist's development.

At age 32 Lazarus rekindled her fervor for Judaism in response to the harsh anti-Semitism of Russia. She combatted the snobbery of upper-class Jews by volunteering to aid the newly arrived illiterate, suffering Eastern Europeans. Her contributions included food and clothing distribution, treatment of the sick, purchase of land for agricultural communes, and training for factory work, an outreach that was the start of the Hebrew Technical Institute. She rallied those who hesitated by reminding them that no Jew could feel free so long as the underclass suffered pogroms, poverty, and despair. A forerunner of Theodore Herzl, campaigner for a Jewish homeland in Palestine, the author channeled her writing into *Songs of a Semite: The Dance to Death and Other Poems* (1882), an anthology of Zionist articles, scenarios, and poems. To allow for the budgets of poor readers, she insisted on an affordable edition of her work.

Although her inclinations favored patriotism, humanism, and Zionism, Lazarus turned to feminism for the poem "Echoes" (ca. 1880), a subdued acknowledgment of the barriers that prevent female artists from expressing their talents. To raise money at an auction for the Bartholdi Pedestal Fund to support the Statue of Liberty, in company with the authors Mark Twain and Walt Whitman she wrote "The NEW COLOSSUS" (1883), which charity organizers printed in the *Catalogue of the Pedestal Fund Art Loan Exhibition at the National Academy of Design* as an enticement to potential donors. The text pairs the likeness of Auguste-Charlotte Bartholdi with motherhood and hospitality. The sale of the poem alone netted $1,500 for the cause. At the insistence of her friend, Georgina Schuyler, two decades after Lazarus's death of Hodgkin's disease at age 38 "The New Colossus" appeared in script on a bronze plaque at the statue's base. The theme of the sonnet justifies immigrants' belief in democracy and their rooting of their hopes and ambitions in New World egalitarianism.

Bibliography

Giffen, Allison. "Savage Daughters: Emma Lazarus, Ralph Waldo Emerson, and *The Spagnoletto*," ATQ 15, no. 2 (June 2001): 89–107.

Lazarus, Emma. *Emma Lazarus: Selected Poems and Other Writings.* Peterborough, Canada: Broadview, 2002.

Merriam, Eve, and Morris U. Schappes. *Emma Lazarus Rediscovered.* New York: Holmes & Meier, 1999.

Lee, Harper (1926–   )

A classic author from the publication of her first and only novel, Nelle Harper Lee intertwines in domestic realism the quandary of growing up genteel in the racist South. Lee is a product of Monroeville, Alabama, a small southern town that provided the fictional Maycomb, the setting of *To Kill a Mockingbird* (1960), her Pulitzer Prize–winning novel. After completing a degree at Hunting-ton College and subsequent study of law at the University of Alabama and Oxford University, she moved to New York City to sell tickets for Eastern Airlines and British Overseas Airways while writing stories and sketches in her free time. In 1957 she began developing a short story into *To Kill a Mockingbird,* the story of one man's confrontation with southern VIOLENCE. In 1962 the actor Kim Stanley narrated the 1962 film version, which won Gregory Peck an Oscar for his role as Atticus Finch.

Literary analysts tend to praise Lee's depiction of the relationship of morality to law and justice, but criticism usually overlooks the novel's view of the coming-of-age years of a tender girl, eight-year-old Jean Louise "Scout" Finch. Bright and impressionable, she has been motherless since age two and lives under the rule of opposites, the black housekeeper, Cal, and Aunt Alexandra, a caricature of the bossy, self-important snob. With an eye for hypocrisy Scout allows thorough latherings with Octagon soap from Cal but rejects the fussy femininity that Aunt Alexandra champions as "What Is Best For The Family" (Lee, 131). Cal is a bulwark against racist slurs and irreverence in church; Aunt Alexandra, arriving "enarmored, upright, uncompromising" on the front porch, sets out a curriculum in ladyhood that begins with external behavior and a proper wardrobe (*ibid.*, 129). Already molded in character and outlook, Scout is attentive and obedient but in no way altered by the trappings of stereotypical southern womanhood.

Lee turns Scout's private conclusions into humor. In general Scout steers clear of "ladies in bunches" (*ibid.*, 232). She observes hat-wearing and tea-pouring decorum and, on Sundays, the obligatory corset, which "drew up [Alexandra's] bosom to giddy heights, pinched in her waist, flared out her rear" (*ibid.*, 130). More difficult to overlook are "river-boat, boarding-school manners" and Alexandra's intent to "arrange, advise, caution, and warn" (*ibid.*, 131). When the regimen of the intrusive aunt pushes Scout to tears, she takes refuge in Atticus's version of proper upbringing, but she admits, "It takes a woman to do that kind of work" (*ibid.*, 137). At a climactic moment Lee places in the father's sphere a clarification of ladyhood and the shielding of women from harsh realities. In reference to Scout's knowing about a taboo subject, the Ku Klux Klan, he declares he's "in favor of Southern womanhood as much as anybody, but not for preserving polite fiction at the expense of human life" (*ibid.*, 149).

Bibliography

Lee, Harper. *To Kill a Mockingbird.* New York: Warner, 1982.

Lee, Harriet (1757–1851) and
Lee, Sophia (1750–1824)

Famed English authors of historical fiction and drama, the sisters Harriet and Sophia Lee wrote about the suppression and SILENCING of women who fight back against PATRIARCHY by involving themselves in political intrigue. Born in London to actors, they were left to their own browsing in the French writers of the day and in the English Gothicists. Sophia earned a stable living from publication of a three-act opera, *The Chapter of Accidents* (1780), which won audiences at its debut at the Haymarket Theatre. On the proceeds she tended their younger siblings and established a girls' school at Belvidere House, the most respected female academy at Bath. When the sisters launched a career in drama and fiction and in the transcription of French works for *Ladies' Magazine*, Sophia outstripped in quality and number the works of her sister. Harriet published the three-act stage play *The Mysterious Marriage; or The Heirship of Roselva* (1798) and a Gothic short story, "Kruitzner, the German's Tale" (1797), one of the entries in Sophia's collection *The Canterbury Tales* (1797–1805).

A fount of historical Gothic novels, Sophia Lee earned instant success for an epistolary romance, *The Recess; or, A Tale of Other Times* (1783–85), a three-volume domestic novel picturing the strength of females in the 1500s networking against male domination. During the rule of Elizabeth I the fictional protagonists, the twins Ellinor and Matilda, survive a suspenseful web of family SECRECY about their illegitimate birth and their shadow roles in British royal history of the Stuart DYNASTY. Feminist themes of CONFINEMENT, DREAMSCAPES, and lunacy contribute to

the value of the novel as commentary on women's lives. Living in a warren of concealed rooms at a ruined abbey, the girls occupy a space that is commodious, yet imprisoning: "Every room was distinct, and divided from the rest of a vaulted passage with many stairs," a physical representation of the labyrinth of social codes and laws inhibiting women from leading a full life (Lee, 8). For consolation the sisters turn to their mother: "*She* was our world, and all the tender affections, of which I have since proved my heart so full, centred in her and my sister" (*ibid.*, 9). After parting from their mother, the sisters spend their time questing for an exit from boredom. The motif of coercion of females and retreat into mothering may have influenced the plotting of Ann RADCLIFFE's novels and of Charlotte BRONTË's Gothic classic *JANE EYRE* (1847).

Bibliography

Isaac, Megan Lynn. "Sophia Lee and the Gothic of Female Community," *Studies in the Novel* 28, no. 2 (Summer 1996): 200–217.

Lee, Sophia. *The Recess; or, A Tale of Other Times.* Lexington: University Press of Kentucky, 2000.

Nordius, Janina. "A Tale of Other Places: Sophia Lee's 'The Recess' and Colonial Gothic," *Studies in the Novel* 34, no. 2 (Summer 2002): 162–176.

Lee, Tanith (1947–)

The Anglo-Irish Gothic fantasist, children's author, television scenarist, and poet Tanith Lee Kaiine recaps the constrictive roles of women as prisoners and pawns of males. She pictures women of the future as warriors against sexism. A North Londoner and the daughter of ballroom dancers, she heard the oral FAIRY TALES of her mother, Hylda Lee, and received homeschooling in reading at age eight to overcome dyslexia. The following year she became fascinated with Celtic and Christian mythology and with writing. After a string of low-paying clerical jobs and a year of art college, at age 21 she chose fiction as her future and began publishing short stories and revisionist fairy tales and writing plays for radio and television. She earned critical attention for a first novel, *Birthgrave* (1975), the beginning of a freelance career for *Fan-*

tasy and Science Fiction. She also published under the pseudonym Esther Garber the anthology *Fatal Women* (1998), a collection of lesbian short fiction on themes of lesbian love, moody romance, and Gothic obsessions.

Lee's focus on women invigorates the staid romantic conventions of such predictable genres as horror stories and detective novels. A speculative novel, *The Silver Metal Lover* (1985), sets the theme of sexual awakening in a society that replaces human mates with robotic facsimiles. The MOTHER-DAUGHTER RELATIONSHIP, modeled after the mythic love of Demeter for PERSEPHONE, satirizes technological manipulation of physical features in an effort to create the IDEAL WOMAN. Sixteen-year-old Jane confides, "When I was seven, my mother had a Phy-Excellence chart done for me, to see what was the ideal weight and muscle tone. . . . My mother also had a coloressence chart made up" (Lee, 1985, 4). In a witty anti-CINDERELLA tale, "The Reason for Not Going to the Ball" (1996), Lee describes a child sold to pay her mother's gambling debts and pictures a despicable husband "riding down other slender things with his whip and that sack of poison in him called by some his heart" (Lee, 1996, 91). In 1998 Lee published *Faces under Water*, which reevaluates the stock figure of the silenced woman as a victim masked by facial paralysis. In the semiautobiographical romance *Piratica, Being a Tale of a Singular Girl's Adventure upon the High Seas* (2001), Lee resets standard swashbuckling lore by placing a girl at the helm. She pictures Artemesia "Art Blastside" Fitz-Willoughby as a young boarding-school student eager for a more vigorous, self-determined life than that of gentility.

Bibliography

Lee, Tanith. *Piratica, Being a Tale of a Singular Girl's Adventure upon the High Seas.* New York: Dutton, 2004.
———. "The Reason for Not Going to the Ball," *Fantasy and Science Fiction* 91, no. 4/5 (October–November 1996): 83–91.
———. *The Silver Metal Lover.* New York: Random House, 1985.
———. *White as Snow.* New York: Tor Books, 2001.

"Review: *Piratica: Being a Daring Tale of a Singular Girl's Adventure upon the High Seas.*" *Kirkus Reviews,* 1 September 2004, p. 869.

Le Guin, Ursula (1929–)

The feminist author of utopian and science fiction Ursula Kroeber Le Guin writes of fantasy worlds in which being female is not an obstacle. The daughter of the anthropologist Alfred L. Kroeber and the author Theodora Covel Kroeber, Le Guin was born in Berkeley, California, where she came of age reading the intellectual texts of her parents. Most influential during that time was a copy of the Tao Te Ching, Chinese scripture that directed her toward a philosophy of wholeness and nonVIOLENCE. She studied French and Italian Renaissance literature at Radcliffe and Columbia University and in Paris on a Fulbright scholarship. At her home in Portland, Oregon, she compartmentalized her life into meeting the demands on the wife and mother and creating time for the writer.

Through offbeat novels and short fiction Le Guin challenged the male-dominated realm of science fiction by approaching fantasy and futurism from a woman's point of view. An imaginative stylist, she has published volumes of stories that defy categorization but assure readers of her beliefs in gender equity and ECOFEMINISM, concepts she introduced in the Earthsea series, which she sets in an archipelago. In the third and fourth volumes, *The Farthest Shore* (1972) and *Tehanu* (1990), she gives free rein to her developing feminism by examining the tendency of PATRIARCHY to marginalize women and children. On the island of Gont, northeast of the central isle of Havnor, a culture of wizardry makes light of women's magic as weak and wicked. Area ambivalence toward WISEWOMEN both discounts them as wonder workers and charges them with endangering others via evil spells and potions.

As do her fellow utopists Margaret ATWOOD, Charlotte Perkins GILMAN, Marge PIERCY, and Joanna RUSS, Le Guin predicates the perfect world on gender equality and quality child rearing rather than the military or economic strengths that dominate the utopias of male writers. In a masterwork, *The Left Hand of Darkness* (1969), Le Guin transforms technology from woman endangering to woman assisting and tosses out fixed gender as a deterrent to full humanity. She offers a full range of life experiences to androgynous characters who remain asexual much of the time. In her futuristic nation of Gethen all people can reproduce children. Estraven, the author's spokesperson, muses on Earth's complex single-gender beings, who suffer "a strange sort of low-grade desire . . . spread out over every day of the year (Le Guin, 1969, 232). A subsequent fantasy novel, *The Word for World Is Forest* (1976), balances ecology by setting a MATRIARCHY over Altshe, a pastoral Eden. The all-female culture survives until males, bent on conquest, murder its women and destroy the society.

In the Hugo Award–winning short story "Sur," anthologized in *Compass Rose* (1982), Le Guin speaks directly to two female strengths, collaboration and power sharing. She teams nine female Argentinian, Chilean, and Peruvian explorers of the *Yelcho* Expedition of August 1909. They prosper at sailing by steamer and sledge hauling over Antarctica to the South Pole, following Ernest Shackleton's failed undertaking by a year and beating Roald Amundsen's expedition by two years. Her text explains, "The nine of us worked things out amongst us from the beginning to the end without any orders being given by anybody" (Le Guin, 1983, 257). Keeping the women's secret from the outside world is Luis Pardo, captain of the *Yelcho*.

The theme of multitasking and nonhierarchical organization rather than every-man-for-himself competition lauds the nine women for applying the basic training they learned in housewifery. The author observes: "The backside of heroism is often rather sad; women and servants know that. They know also that the heroism may be no less real for that" (*ibid.*, 261). Speaking as a feminist, Le Guin asserts that "achievement is smaller than men think. What is large is the sky, the earth, the sea, the soul" (*ibid.*). To get the job done, the nine explorers abandon heroic posturing and risk taking for the more productive paradigm of cooperative achievement. Five days before the return rendezvous with the *Yelcho* Teresa reveals a pregnancy she thought was weight gain from the cold. On February 14 she goes into labor with eight birthing coaches helping to welcome a baby girl named Rosa del Sur (Rose of the South) in honor of the expedition.

Bibliography

Bartkowski, Frances. *Feminist Utopias*. Lincoln: University of Nebraska Press, 1991.

Glasberg, Elena. "Refusing History at the End of the Earth: Ursula Le Guin's 'Sur,'" *Tulsa Studies in Women's Literature* 21, no. 1 (Spring 2002): 99–121.

Le Guin, Ursula. *The Compass Rose*. New York: Bantam, 1983.

———. *The Left Hand of Darkness*. New York: Ace Books, 1969.

Zorach, Cecile Cazort, and Charlotte Ann Melin. "Collaborative Expeditions in the Academy: Housekeeping and the Art of the Infinite," *NWSA Journal* 13, no. 1 (Spring 2001): 126.

lesbian authors

Lesbian feminism, an outgrowth of the 1970s women's liberation movement, emancipates female homosexuals and bisexuals from cant and suppression to a full consciousness of self. To honor the gay and bisexual females who had no network or support system for their practice of woman-to-woman love, feminists catalogued writings that form a shadow history of the lesbian in world literature, beginning with the Greek poet SAPPHO. In 1949 the heterosexual French philosopher Simone de BEAUVOIR stated in *Le deuxième sex* (The SECOND SEX) her sympathies for two 17th-century lesbian authors, Anne Finch, Lady WINCHILSEA, author of *Miscellany Poems on Several Occasions* (1713), and the playwright Margaret Lucas Cavendish, the duchess of Newcastle, author of *The Convent of Pleasure* (1668), which depicts women living in an all-female commune. The ambiguity of relations with men is obvious in the confusion of Angelo, the convent deputy, who asks of Isabella, "What's this, what's this? / Is this her fault or mine? / The tempter or the tempted, who sins most, ha? / Not she, nor doth she tempt" (Newcastle, 175). In both cases the lesbian authors suffered anger, hatred, and fear from their attempts to write about honest female feelings for other women. In the case of the duchess of Newcastle an onslaught of ridicule and spite forced her into seclusion, where she retreated into fantasy and MADNESS.

The past 150 years have seen the acceptance of lesbian feminist literature as a bold, insightful wing of women's literature. The growth industry of female Gothic during the 19th century presented new opportunities for expression in a genre that tended to group all women under the heading of "other." A leader of the era, the novelist Marie CORELLI produced vigorous, passionate woman-centered works—*Ardath: The Story of a Dead Self* (1889) and *The Soul of Lilith* (1892). She carefully coded plots and dialogue to conceal lesbian emotions under ambiguous images and implications. The 20th century released lesbian writers from centuries of such veiling. The opening salvo against mental corseting came from Radclyffe HALL, author of the semiautobiographical *The Well of Loneliness* (1928), the first explicitly lesbian novel. Two years later Djuna BARNES issued *Nightwood* (1930), a semiautobiographical classic of gay psychological fiction that features lesbian and sexually ambivalent characters.

As the reading public began exploring less timorous depictions of lesbian relationships, lesbian authors took liberties with established female motifs and themes of CONFINEMENT, SILENCING, and PATRIARCHY. In *Beginning with O* (1977) the Greco-American poet Olga BROUMAS reset in Sapphic style the quandary of Leda, the rape victim of Greek mythology, and of the FAIRY TALE heroes BEAUTY AND THE BEAST, CINDERELLA, Little Red Riding Hood, Rapunzel, and Snow White. Parallel to the publication of works by Gloria ANZALDÚA, June Arnold, COLETTE, Clemence Dane, Audre LORDE, Anaïs NIN, and Gertrude STEIN and to the public embrace of the unabashedly gay writer Rita Mae BROWN was a reclamation of ambiguous, heavily closeted gay and bisexual figures from the classics—Aphra BEHN, Elizabeth BISHOP, Willa CATHER, H. D., Mary Wilkins FREEMAN, Angelina Weld GRIMKÉ, Sarah Orne JEWETT, Amy LOWELL, Katherine MANSFIELD, Carson MCCULLERS, Edna St. Vincent MILLAY, Muriel RUKEYSER, Vita SACKVILLE-WEST, and Virginia WOOLF. By outing lesbianism in familiar places, literary historians disclosed the lesbian themes that critics overlooked or ignored in renowned works, including Christina ROSSETTI's female rescue poem *Goblin Market* (1862) and Emily DICKINSON's poems "Why—do they shut Me out of Heaven?" (ca. 1861) and "Tell All the Truth but Tell It Slant" (ca. 1868). By 1981

KITCHEN TABLE / WOMEN OF COLOR PRESS was distributing a broad span of women's writings that championed the lesbian point of view as a valid perspective on women's issues, including SINGLE PARENTING, MOTHER-DAUGHTER RELATIONSHIPS, AGING, SEXUAL POLITICS, and VIOLENCE.

A spokeswoman for late 20th-century lesbian feminism, the poet Adrienne RICH, wrote critical essays spelling out barriers to women writers. In "Split at the Root: An Essay on Jewish Identity" (1975), she notes her own coming to knowledge, when "the passion of debating ideas with women was an erotic passion for me" (Rich, 1975, 237). She describes the coalescing of a lesbian sensibility, a feeling she had identified in her teens, which caused her "to stretch her limbs, and her first full-fledged act was to fall in love with a Jewish woman" (*ibid.*, 237). Early on, Rich's feminist explorations identified the connection between misogyny and patriarchy and Judaism, a reality she recalled from her father's domination in girlhood. Over a decade later she characterized "compulsory heterosexuality . . . as a political institution which disempowers women" (Rich, 1986, 34–35). She lauded lesbianism as a creative force and a vital revolt within society against the extremes of androcentrism.

Bibliography

Newcastle, Margaret Cavendish. *The Convent of Pleasure and Other Plays.* Baltimore, Md.: Johns Hopkins University Press, 1999.

Pela, Robert L. "Our Lesbian Roots." *Advocate*, 15 August 2000, p. 94–95.

Rich, Adrienne. *Adrienne Rich's Poetry and Prose.* New York: W. W. Norton, 1975.

———. *Blood, Bread, and Poetry: Selected Prose, 1979–1985.* New York: W. W. Norton, 1986.

Simons, Margaret A. *Beauvoir and the Second Sex.* Lanham, Md.: Rowman & Littlefield, 2001.

Lessing, Doris (1919–)

A consummate novelist, dramatist, autobiographer, and essayist, Doris May Taylor Lessing writes of an abyss between male and female that limits the success of feminism, particularly in preindustrial nations. A native of Kermanshah, Persia, she was born of British parentage and from age five grew up on a maize farm in Southern Rhodesia. Alienated by nationality and race, she turned to reading while studying at a convent school in Salisbury. In rebellion against her parents she dropped out without earning a diploma. In 1933 she ended her schooling to work as a nanny, telephone operator, and secretary.

After two divorces at age 30 Lessing moved to London, became a Marxist, and began writing for a living, producing a view of the life of a farm wife in *The Grass Is Singing* (1950). Like her contemporary, the novelist Mary MCCARTHY, Lessing never considered herself a feminist writer, but her characters and ideas influenced the women's movement. In addition to the Somerset Maugham Award, the W. H. Smith Award, and a nomination for the Nobel Prize, at age 85 she received the Prince of Asturias Prize in Literature for defending freedom and developing world causes. Her writing has inspired numerous feminists, notably the ecofeminist Barbara KINGSOLVER.

Lessing is a multitalented author of works about gender roles, race, social upheaval, and the possibilities of the future. She validated the female observer with the autobiographical novels *The Golden Notebook* (1962), a layered story of the conflicted writer Anna Wulf's reclamation from MADNESS, and *The Diaries of Jane Somers* (1984), in which the fictional Janna, a stressed mother and career woman, embraces women's liberation. Influenced by the NEW WOMAN fiction of the South African novelist Olive SCHREINER, Lessing deliberately smashes assumptions about self-fulfillment to reveal the emotional solitude that encases the self-actualized woman. In the second of the Canopus in Argos series Lessing took another look at the balance of power between the genders in *The Marriages between Zones Three, Four, and Five* (1994), an allegorical fable of sexual love and wholeness. In 1997 Thomas Kalb premiered the operatic setting, which dramatizes Lessing's survey of male-female animus and the promise of mutual dependence and acceptance.

Bibliography

Altman, Meryl. "Beyond Trashiness: The Sexual Language of 1970s Feminist Fiction," *Journal of International Women's Studies* 4, no. 2 (April 2003): 1–25.

Klein, Carole. *Doris Lessing, a Biography.* New York: Carroll & Graf, 2000.

Lessing, Doris. *The Diaries of Jane Sommers.* New York: Vintage, 1984.

———. *The Golden Notebook.* London: Michael Joseph, 1972.

———. *The Marriages between Zones Three, Four, and Five.* London: Acacia Press, 1994.

Le Sueur, Meridel (1900–1996)

The populist essayist, poet, and adult and children's fiction writer Meridel Le Sueur concentrated her truth-telling writings on the invisiblity and economic disempowerment of frontier and rural women, immigrants, and the working poor. Born in Murray, Iowa, to Marion Wharton, a mother who agitated for women's right to birth control, the author profited from a strong female role model. She later dramatized the social thrust of her foremothers in *Crusaders* (1955), which honors her grandmother's westering and TEMPERANCE work and ennobles Wharton's prolabor and proeducation stances. At age 12 Le Sueur rejected the American dream as an androcentric illusion and left high school to educate herself in theater at the American Academy of Dramatic Arts and to work on stage and in film as a stuntwoman.

In place of male-generated success stories Le Sueur championed the loyalty and urgency of female networking and of all-woman communes, especially the STORYTELLING sessions among Indian women. Her idealism derived from the speeches and polemics of Emma GOLDMAN, Mother Jones, Helen KELLER, and Margaret SANGER. A pivotal moment in Le Sueur's evolution as an artist occurred with the publication of "Persephone" (1927), a short story that depicts her separation from strong female relatives to become a Depression Era single parent to her own two daughters. The author's connection to famed socialists caused McCarthyites to blacklist her economic treatises *Women on the Breadlines* (1932) and *Women Are Hungry* (1934) and to ban from libraries the children's frontier biography *Nancy Hanks of Wilderness Road: A Story of Abraham Lincoln's Mother* (1949).

To enlighten male readers on the issues of birth control, ABORTION, domestic drudgery, and marital battery, Le Sueur published feminist essays in the *American Mercury, Daily Worker, Dial, Nation, New Masses,* and *Partisan Review.* In 1932 she wrote a first novel, *The Girl,* published in 1978, a pro-female depiction of working-class laborers written in factory argot. The scenarios dramatize the lives of residents of the Saint Paul, Minnesota, Worker's Alliance. One of the suppressed feminists revived by the women's movement, Le Sueur continued writing in old age, publishing *Rites of Ancient Ripening* (1975) in praise of Native American women's traditions. She earned the regard of the Minnesota Center for Book Arts for the beauties of WOMAN'S WORK and for the validation of elderly women in *Winter Prairie Woman* (1990), an anthem to community and sharing. Le Sueur's socialist principles won the admiration of the poet Adrienne RICH, who defended the author against implications of wrongdoing spread by the Federal Bureau of Investigation (FBI).

Bibliography

Coiner, Constance. *Better Red: The Writing and Resistance of Tillie Olsen and Meridel Le Sueur.* Chicago: University of Illinois Press, 1998.

Le Sueur, Meridel. *Ripening: Selected Work, 1927–1980.* New York: Feminist Press, 1982.

———. *Winter Prairie Woman.* Minneapolis: Minnesota Center for Book Arts, 1990.

Roberts, Nora. *Three Radical Women Writers: Class and Gender in Meridel Le Sueur, Tillie Olsen, and Josephine Herbst.* New York: Taylor & Francis, 1996.

"Let No Charitable Hope"   Elinor Wylie (1923)

Anthologized in *Black Amour* (1923), "Let No Charitable Hope" reveals a strand of existentialism in the verse of Elinor WYLIE. The first stanza of the compact tripartite poem reflects the dark tone of the collection's title and alludes to chaotic elements in Wylie's unconventional life. In four lines the speaker rids herself of the romantic notion of being one with mammals and birds. Unlike the antelope and eagle, she claims a kinship with humankind that sets her apart from fleeting hooves and high-soaring wings. Not only does her humanity anchor her to Earth, it necessitates a spiritual

solitude from birth onward. Furthermore, her gender leaves her "hard beset," a tight-lipped summation that offers no details (Wylie, 35). Augmenting social difficulties is the economic task of "squeezing from a stone" her livelihood, an allusion to the poet's small monetary rewards (*ibid.*).

In the style of the 17th-century metaphysical poet John Donne, Wylie ends with an upsurge—a resilient feminist credo. The third stanza lifts the gloom of the opening eight lines by mitigating the harsh dictates of the speaker's condition. Through paradox she surveys a human past that fits no single description. Her life cycle—some 38 years ranging from "outrageous" to "austere"—assures that she is equal to facing her worst fears and capable of finding humor throughout, a dependable source of solace in feminist literature.

Anticipating the female toughness of the feminist movement by nearly a half-century, Wylie extends no possibility of pity or rescue for the beleaguered female. Through the speaker's anti-idealist summation the poet reminds women that survival is an ongoing struggle. From her own observations she affirms that each year's rigors prove that she is equal to the challenge. Frequently anthologized and set to music by the American composer Ned Rorem in the song cycle "Women's Voices" (1979), the poem eases womanly anxieties with the small comforts that life permits.

Bibliography

Hively, Evelyn Helmick. *A Private Madness: The Genius of Elinor Wylie.* Kent, Ohio: Kent State University Press, 2003.

Wylie, Elinor. *Black Amour.* New York: George H. Doran, 1923.

letter writing

The expression of feminist thought and concerns in letters has a long tradition. From FRONTIER LITERATURE during the Indian Wars are the writings of two military wives, Frances M. A. Roe's *Army Letters of an Officer's Wife* (1909) and *The Colonel's Lady on the Western Frontier: The Correspondence of Alice Kirk Grierson* (1989). Compilers of feminist history claim Judith Sargent MURRAY, First Lady Abigail ADAMS, the Civil War nurse Louisa May

ALCOTT, the suffragist Susan B. ANTHONY, the Russian-Jewish author Mary ANTIN, the Scots traveler Frances WRIGHT, and the Colonial poet Anne BRADSTREET as writers of self-revelatory letters to their families and to the media and journals. The correspondence between feminists retains from women's history the glint of the moment, when issues hung in the balance of intellectual exchange, as found in the love letters of Anaïs NIN. In 1837 Sarah Moore GRIMKÉ wrote to her sister, Angelina Emily Grimké, about a change of heart that separated Sarah from decorative women: "My lot was cast among the butterflies of the *fashionable* world, and of this class of women, I am constrained to say, both from experience and observation, that their EDUCATION is miserably deficient" (Lerner, 43–44). Sarah regrets that women summarize their worth in terms of the number of men they can flirt with, dance with, and impress as "mere instruments of pleasure" (*ibid.*). From another point of reference in 1853 Elizabeth Cady STANTON, the mastermind of the early SUFFRAGE movement, summarizes issues of citizenship in prophetic terms. In a letter to Susan B. Anthony, Stanton says, "I feel this whole question of WOMEN'S RIGHTS turns on the point of the marriage relation, and sooner or later it will be the question for discussion" (Stanton & Anthony, 56). The letter declares that rearing of children in negative environments abets the proliferation of hate and VIOLENCE.

Letters have an elastic quality of fitting a wide range of intent. For feminist polemics such as Mary Darby ROBINSON's *Letter to the Women of England, on the Cruelties of Mental Subordination* (1799), the epistle built consensus by speaking directly to the issues that women have in common. The actor and diarist Fanny KEMBLE turned individual letters into two epistolary diaries, *Journal of a Residence in America* (1835) and *Journal of a Residence of a Georgian Plantation, 1838–1839* (1863), which voiced her outrage at the degrading toil and mistreatment of slaves. The English poet Christina ROSSETTI directed her letters to a campaign against vivisection. For the crusading Native American reformer Sarah WINNEMUCCA letters to newspapers informed President Rutherford B. Hayes and other influential easterners of the hunger and displacement of trans-Mississippi Indian tribes, who stood on the brink of extermination. Letters are also a source of AUTOBIOGRAPHY, such as that found in *The Letters of Vita Sackville West to Virginia Woolf* (2002) and in the recovered correspondence of the poet Emily DICKINSON and Margaret FULLER. After the suicide of the confessional poet Sylvia PLATH, the publication of *Letters Home: Correspondence, 1950–1963* (1975) explained to her fans and to literary historians her grievances, sources of domestic unrest, and motivations for killing herself. For Catharine BEECHER, a disseminator of advice to young homemakers, letter form gave the impression of the experienced housekeeper speaking directly to the neophyte.

In addition to personal correspondence, authors use the fictional missive as a personalized form of history and as a tutorial format, as did CHRISTINE DE PISAN in *Le livre des trois vertus* (*The Book of the Three Virtues*, 1406) and HÉLISENNE DE CRENNE in *Les epistres familieres et invectives* (Personal and Invective Letters, 1539). Another example, Hannah Webster Foster's best-selling roman à clef *The Coquette: or, The History of Eliza Wharton, a Novel Founded on Fact* (1797), reveals intimate truths about a real fallen woman killed by hunger, disease, and abandonment during her pregnancy. Fictional letters are a vehicle of the novel, a cathartic convention found in the German-American writer Ruth Prawer JHABVALA's *Heat and Dust* (1975) and Elizabeth Forsythe Hailey's *A Woman of Independent Means* (1978), as well as the German-Australian author Elizabeth Jolley's *Miss Peabody's Inheritance* (1983), the Brazilian writer Helena Parente Cunha's *Woman Between Mirrors* (1983), and the Argentinian author Sylvia Molloy's *Certificate of Absence* (1981). The device, when applied to stream of consciousness and interior monologue, creates an aura of revelation, subjectivity, rebellion, and candor that lends credence to confessional and contemplative novels, as with the woman-to-woman missives passed down to a granddaughter in the Chilean-American writer Isabel ALLENDE's *The HOUSE OF THE SPIRITS* (1982). To bridge a long distance, letters carry the human response to personal issues, for example, the outpouring of hopelessness from Celie to her sister, Nettie, in Alice WALKER's *The Color Purple*

(1982) and the mail-order bride's introduction to the frontier groom in Patricia MacLachlan's young adult novels *Sarah Plain and Tall* (1985) and its sequel, *Skylark* (1994), both vehicles for Hallmark Hall of Fame films starring Glenn Close. In motifs of patriarchal CONFINEMENT and the stifling of female thought women overcome barriers in the abstract by describing their situations, clarifying confusion, and proposing methods of escape, a controlling metaphor in the Canadian author Margaret ATWOOD's dystopian classic *The HANDMAID'S TALE* (1986).

The Senegalese novelist Mariama BÂ chose epistolary form for *So Long a Letter* (1979), winner of the Noma Award for Publishing in Africa. Set in modern Dakar, her hometown, the first-person narrative of the schoolteacher Ramatoulaye Fall contests the fascination of her husband, Modou, for Binetou, his second wife, a patriarchal privilege under Islam. Ramatoulaye recognizes the female need for letter writing as an outlet for the unspoken and the taboo of defying Islamic custom. She tells her friend, Aissatou, "Our grandmothers in their compounds were separated by a fence and would exchange messages daily" (Bâ, 1). The statement reveals the secondary themes of SILENCING and isolation, two obstacles to female friendship in a male-controlled milieu.

Because the two friends live apart, Bâ depicts Ramatoulaye as a contemplative victim relying on memory. She chooses to continue the female form of communication for her own solace: "Our long association has taught me that confiding in others allays pain" (*ibid.*). Immediately she cries out, "My friend, my friend, my friend," a suggestion of the heartache of new widowhood she shares in letter form during the traditional 40 days of mourning (*ibid.*). On paper Ramatoulaye is able to release pent-up rage: "My voice has known thirty years of silence, thirty years of harassment. It bursts out, violent, sometimes sarcastic, sometimes contemptuous" (*ibid.*, 58). Through a process that feminists call autogenesis, Ramatoulaye re-creates herself to fill the void left by a disloyal mate.

Bibliography

Bâ, Mariama. *So Long a Letter.* Portsmouth, N.H.: Heinemann, 1989.

Campbell, Elizabeth. "Re-Visions, Re-flections, Re-creations: Epistolarity in Novels by Contemporary Women," *Twentieth Century Literature* 41, no. 3 (Fall 1995): 332–348.

Dubek, Laura. "Lessons in Soldarity: Buchi Emecheta and Mariama Bâ on Female Victim(izer)s," *Women's Studies* 30, no. 3 (June 2001): 199–223.

Lerner, Gerda. *The Feminist Thought of Sarah Grimké.* Oxford: Oxford University Press, 1998.

Stanton, Elizabeth Cady, and Susan B. Anthony. *Elizabeth Cady Stanton/Susan B. Anthony: Correspondence, Writings, Speeches.* New York: Schocken, 1981.

Stewart, Elinore Pruitt. *Letters of a Woman Homesteader.* New York: Mariner Books, 1998.

Levertov, Denise (1923–1997)

A political activist and perceptive poet, Denise Levertov attuned her senses to the universe at large to intercept its mystic song. Born in Ilfod, Essex, in England, she claimed Welsh and White Russian heritage, which she honored in two poems, "Illustrious Ancestors" (1958) and "Angel Jones of Mold" (1958), which names a Welsh seer as one of her forebears. The descendant of Rabbi Schneour Zalmon, a practitioner of cabala occultism, she learned British folklore from her Welsh mother, Beatrice Adelaide Spooner-Jones; verse from her older sister, Olga; and ballet from a Russian instructor. Denise was homeschooled through British Broadcasting Corporation (BBC) radio lessons and by her father, the Reverend Paul Philip Levertoff, a Talmud scholar and convert from Hasidism to Anglicanism. As Hitler's powers began to threaten eastern Europe, she lauded the resolve of her anti-Nazi parents for providing solace for the terror in refugees staying at her house. In the 1940, she applied a year of nurse's training at hospitals housing victims of the Blitz.

At age 23, while earning a living selling antiques and rare books, Levertov published *The Double Image* (1946), from which Kenneth Rexroth drew poems for the anthology *New British Poets* (1949). She left England to live in Provence with her husband, Mitchell Goodman, an American writer. The couple spent some of their first years together in Genoa, Mexico, and New York City. Influenced by the imagism of Hilda Doolittle

(H. D.), Wallace Stevens, and William Carlos Williams and the dynamism of the Black Mountain school, Levertov entered a fertile period of clean-edged poetry. She collected her verse in *Here and Now* (1957), *Overland to the Islands* (1958), and *With Eyes at the Back of Our Heads* (1959). The latter includes "The Goddess," a song to nature that resounds with Celtic paganism. As poetry editor for the *Nation* she critiqued contemporary verse, and she issued her own work in *The Jacob's Ladder* (1961) and *O Taste and See: New Poems* (1964). In the latter she anthologized "Song for Ishtar," a witty salute to female desire and creativity, and "Hypocrite Women," a poetic commentary on women's dislike of their genitals. A view of wedlock in "The Ache of Marriage" uses biblical images of Jonah in the whale and the paired animals in Noah's ark as examples of CONFINEMENT and limitation, two secret hurts that lie hidden like the core of the atom.

The poet did not shy away from contemporary issues. Public revolt against the Vietnam War informed the pacifism, antiracism, and radicalism of Levertov's *Out of the War Shadow* (1967), *The Sorrow Dance* (1967), *Relearning the Alphabet* (1970), and *To Stay Alive* (1971). In 1967 she coauthored a volume of *Penguin Modern Poets* and contributed to the translation of *In Praise of Krishna: Songs from the Bengali* (1967) and poems by Eugene Guillevic and Jules Spervielle. Prefiguring her feminist period, one of the poems from this era, "The Mutes" (1967), ponders the rude male grunt in acknowledgment of any attractive woman passing by. Another, "Stepping Westward" (1967), probes a midlife satisfaction with female ripeness, a steady, invigorating fecundity. She pictures the abstract gender consciousness as a heavy panier of bread that she lightens by eating as she walks. To justify her trip to North Vietnam with Muriel RUKEYSER, Levertov published the essay "On the Edge of Darkness: What Is Political Poetry?" in *The Poet in the World* (1973). In her view it is the work of a poet to involve the self totally in humanity.

While Levertov taught creative writing at Tufts, Brandeis, and Stanford, the groundswell of feminism energized her female consciousness. She fleshed out *Footprints* (1972), *The Freeing of the Dust* (1975), *Life in the Forest* (1978), and *Candles*

in Babylon (1982) with such woman-centered topics as MOTHER-DAUGHTER RELATIONSHIPS, GODDESS LORE, the necessary unyoking of couples after a divorce, and AGING. In "Canción" (1975), she rejoices in the female's freedom to rend offensive documents and weep as evidence of sensitivity; another, "A Woman Alone" (1978), relates the serenity of an elderly risk taker who is free to sleep alone and read whenever and whatever she wants. An artful, incantatory image, "The Dragonfly-Mother" (1982), seesaws between the everyday life and the mental escape to write poetry. "Pig Dreams" (1982) probes the mystic oneness of women with the divine, a dominant theme of her late verse.

Levertov remained actively writing into her 70s. At a steady clip she completed works with imaginative titles—*Oblique Prayers: New Poems with Fourteen Translations* (1984), *Breathing the Water* (1987), *A Door in the Hive* (1989), *Evening Train* (1993), and *Tesserae: Memories and Suppositions* (1995), a reference to the tiles that form mosaics. She also completed two essay collections, *The Poet in the World* (1973) and *Light Up the Cave* (1981). Her honors were moderate in proportion to a regular output of insightful, energetic verse. The poet's death from lymphoma grieved her worldwide readers and admirers, who had followed her work for some 50 years. A posthumous reorganization of her verse, *The Stream & the Sapphire: Selected Poems on Religious Themes* (1997), posits a spiritual and emotional growth toward mysticism and Christian belief.

Bibliography

"Denise Levertov," *Chicago Review* 45, no. 2 (1999): 107–110.

Levertov, Denise. *The Stream and the Sapphire: Selected Poems on Religious Themes.* New York: New Directions, 1997.

Stone, Carole. "Elegy as Political Expression in Women's Poetry: Akhmatova, Levertov, Forche," *College Literature* 18, no. 1 (February 1991): 84–91.

Life in the Iron Mills Rebecca Harding Davis (1861)

Published in the April 1861 edition of the *Atlantic Monthly*, Rebecca Harding DAVIS's *Life in the*

Iron Mills; or, The Korl Woman, the nation's first working-class novella, shocked refined readers with its powerful exposé of conditions in laborers' lives. Set in Wheeling, West Virginia, the narrative offers laborers a sympathy lacking in the self-indulgent middle-class mill owners, who equate muscle power with dollars. The focus is Deborah, a Welsh immigrant drone who picks cotton in a factory while enduring smoke from the iron works, basement quarters, unsubstantial meals, consumption, and living conditions unfit for humankind. Davis introduces "Deb," a hunchback who has a ghastly complexion, while she enjoys her only meal of the day from a saucepan of cold boiled potatoes and readies a pail of supper to carry to Hugh Wolfe, her man.

Revived in 1972 by FEMINIST PRESS, the melodrama provided women's studies classes with a class-conscious text set in a "scene of hopeless discomfort and veiled crime" (Davis, 9). The narrative bluntly demands redress for exhausted women such as Deb, who weakens from "standing twelve hours at the spools" (*ibid.,* 19). Readers commiserated with the female proletariat who rendered up body and soul to the demands of a factory system that Deb describes as "t' Devil's place" (*ibid.,* 20). Davis describes the withering of the female worker as "soul-starvation," a "living death" common to the underclass (*ibid.,* 23). In Hugh's sculpting of korl, an industrial waste, the figure of Deb takes on the terrible majesty of "horses dying under the lash," an image of bondage to the Industrial Revolution little removed from plantation SLAVERY (*ibid.,* 34).

Bibliography

Davis, Rebecca Harding. *Life in the Iron Mills.* Houndmills, England: Palgrave Macmillan, 1997.

Morrison, Lucy. "The Search for the Artist in Man and Fulfillment in Life—Rebecca Harding Davis's *Life in the Iron Mills,*" *Studies in Short Fiction* 96, no. 2 (Spring 1996): 245–253.

Lilith

A legendary alternate first wife and mother to the biblical Eve, Lilith is a conflicted archetype of the fully sexual female, the original liberated woman.

Less submissive and less gullible than EVE, Lilith judges for herself how to acquire forbidden knowledge. After she rejects Adam's control and abandons Eden, she becomes an earthly pariah for living independently of a husband's powers and for allegedly threatening to kill future babies of Adam and Eve. In meditation Lilith, a patron of babies, withdraws to the Red Sea to think and to express her vibrant SEXUALITY with centaurs, minotaurs, and satyrs, the libidinous males of Greek mythology. Like LA LLORONA, Lilith adapts alienation into a source of strength, a trait that earned her a matriarchal cult, a cache of lore, and inclusion in an 11th-century Bible commentary, *The Alphabet of Ben Sira.* The acknowledgment in print follows centuries of Jewish denial that Orthodox beliefs contained strands of Canaanite goddess worship. Lilith's survival over time suggests that patriarchal editors inverted the original creation myth of Adam's stolen rib to support male dominance over females. To assure Lilith's rejection, rabbinic authorities stereotyped her as an abstract of evil, the sorceress and temptress who leads men to their doom.

A measure of the vigor of women's oral lore are the long life and many metamorphoses of the Lilith character in fiction, poetry, drama, art, dance, and opera. During the Middle Ages she appeared in English folklore as a witch; in the 19th century she reappeared as a DUALITY—the scorned woman and the coaxing, devilish femme fatale of Gothic poetry and art. To extend the boundaries of women's role in Judaism, 20th-century feminism reevaluated the traditional first feminist as a neopagan rebel, whose story appears in the writings of the poet Enid Dame and of the feminist critic Alicia Ostriker. In 1976 the launching of *Lilith,* a feminist magazine for independent Jewish women, offered an outlet for verse and fiction by such established feminist writers as Cynthia OZICK, Grace PALEY, Marge PIERCY, and Letty Cottin POGREBIN. Diane DI PRIMA's epic suite *Loba* (1998) pictures Lilith as a being formed of vapor, a nebulous female formed from starlight. In the novel *Lilith* (1999) Alina Reyes reverts to Victorian Gothic to turn the protagonist's symbolic duality into a vampirism that expresses the female's oral eroticism.

In 2000 the Canadian-Japanese writer Joy KOGAWA published *The Song of Lilith,* a feminist *Paradise Lost* and melodic legend about the loss of God's gifts and about the squandering and destruction of gender equality. The focus is Lilith, "earth's first and elemental woman" born from "earth's volcanic womb," a pictorial birthing captured in illustrations by Lilian Broca (Kogawa, 5). From Lilith's years as an outlaw she returns to the children of Adam and Eve as a female sage offering the wisdom, autonomy, love, and daring that kept her alive. She urges women worldwide to take strength from Lilith griefs. By rejuvenating the forgotten and repressed myth of Lilith, Kogawa foresees a suitable banner for a new age.

Bibliography

Dame, Enid, Lilly Rivlin, and Henny Wenkart, eds. *Which Lilith? Feminist Writers Recreate the World's First Woman.* Lanham, Md.: Jason Aronson, 1998.

Di Prima, Diane. *Loba.* New York: Penguin, 1998.

Kogawa, Joy. *A Song of Lilith.* New York: Laurel Glen, 2001.

Rae, Ian. "Reconsidering Lilith," *Canadian Literature* no. 174 (Autumn 2002): 162–163.

Little House series   Laura Ingalls Wilder
(1932–1962)

The memoirist and journalist Laura Ingalls WILDER's enduring feminist saga replenishes American frontier lore with 20th-century reflections on women's lives on the prairie. Written in collaboration with her daughter, Rose Wilder Lane, the Little House series made Laura the Grandma Moses of children's literature. Begun in her 65th year, the series provides a classic overview of WOMAN'S WORK in a covered wagon, log cabin, sod dugout, homesteader's shanty, and town cottage. Recalling each setting from the perspective of a girl in training to be a wife and mother, the narratives capture the work ethic that undergirded the settlement of unforgiving wilderness. The original eight volumes— *Little House in the Big Woods* (1932), *Farmer Boy* (1933), *Little House on the Prairie* (1935), *On the Banks of Plum Creek* (1937), *By the Shores of Silver Lake* (1939), *The Long Winter* (1940), *Little Town on the Prairie* (1941), and *These Happy Golden Years*

(1943)—preceded three posthumous works, *On the Way Home: The Diary of a Trip from South Dakota to Mansfield, Missouri, in 1874* (1962), *The First Four Years* (1971), and *West from Home* (1974). Laura; her mother, Caroline; and Laura's sisters, Mary and Carrie, display persistence and courage that affirm the role of woman as active pioneer rather than passive observer of male westerers. On the way to her first teaching post at age 15 in *These Happy Golden Years* Pa asserts his faith in her by remarking, "You've never failed yet at anything you tried to do" (Wilder, 1994, 3). After Laura's marriage to Almanzo "Manly" Wilder, she retains the lessons in womanhood that sustain her to age 90.

Key to Laura's maturity are models of humor, self-education, and family bonding that assure her self-worth and competence. Deeply ingrained by loving parents, these tenets enable her to support the family through freelance writing after her husband's stroke. In the second volume, which takes the Ingalls from Wisconsin through Indian Territory in Kansas, she discovers through her involvement that family life demands commitment and input from all members. In *The Long Winter* she accepts the early frost as the death of wheat fields and fresh garden vegetables, yet she finds in crystallized water a unique beauty that sparkles with rainbows. By the final volume, coauthored by Rose Wilder Lane, Laura has developed into an accomplished author, a nature lover, and the matriarch of a new generation on a par with Alexandra Bergson in Willa CATHER's *O PIONEERS!* (1913).

Repackaged as chapter books and samplers, readers, illustrated collectors' editions, paper dolls, cookbooks and song collections, recovered writings, a television series, and audiotapes, the Little House phenomenon added authentic historical views to national culture. The series remains a staple in children's reading experience as the most detailed study of a girl growing up in the American West. The texts, which reflect the mores of the period, met opposition in Thibodeaux, Louisiana, and Sturgis, South Dakota, in 1994, when elementary school librarians banned *Little House on the Prairie* for its racial and cultural offenses to Native Americans. Combating the image of Laura as a racist, the Ojibway author Louise ERDRICH reaffirmed the benefit of cherished pioneer writing for its images of hard work, generosity, and female unity.

Bibliography

Petry, Alice Hall. "Constructing the Little House: Gender, Culture, and Laura Ingalls Wilder," *College Literature* 27, no. 2 (Spring 2000): 213.

Wilder, Laura Ingalls. *These Happy Golden Years.* New York: HarperCollins, 1994.

Little Red Riding Hood

A fundamental cautionary scenario from the late Middle Ages, "Little Red Riding Hood" depicts the wide-eyed girlchild in red as a symbol of menarche, the threshold of womanhood and sexual desire. The action alerts tender young females to beware of wolves, an animal euphemism for lustful male stalkers, ravishers, and date rapists. In French versions, such as Madame Gabrielle-Suzanne Barbot de Gallon de Villeneuve's *La jeune ameriquaine, et les contes marins* (The young American and the sea stories, 1740), the wolf is a *bzou* or a *loup-garou* (werewolf), a woman-devouring demon tailored from Gothic conventions. At the crossroads he meets his prey in daylight, another indication of warning to prepubescent girls. The subtext clarifies the perils of sweet words and dalliances that preface seduction, the theft of virginity, and possibly a loss of life ending in cannibalism, the extreme of oral aggression toward women.

Feminists tend to interpret the devouring of child and grandmother as the symbolic double rape of hapless women, one elderly and one underage. In modern settings of Red Riding Hood's dilemma, including the film *Freeway* (1996), she saves herself without the aid of a woodsman. Her sylvan quandary retains its rakish charm in Anne SEXTON's poem "Red Riding Hood" (1971), which makes short work of the devious wolf in drag by slitting open his belly, a parallel to cesarean birth in which a woman takes the androcentric role of surgeon. The wolf's demise is a deft reversal of impregnation by a rapist—the filling of his abdomen with stones. The poet smirks that his own evil overtaxes him. Similarly Sexton also reset in modern times "Briar Rose" (1981), a cynical first-person examination of the rescue of Sleeping Beauty.

Feminist revisions of Riding Hood and her troubles cover a range of human interactions. To Anne Sharpe, author of "Not So Little Red Riding Hood" (1985), a sweet young hero named Scarlet is so versed in survival tactics that she quickly dispatches the wolf with karate chops and a crotch kick that end his interference in her pleasant afternoon with Grandma. Lois Lowry revisited the scenario of the young girl facing threats in the woods with *Number the Stars* (1989), a hero tale that pits a 10-year-old Danish girl, Annemarie Johansen, against Nazi wolves. They demand to know what she carries in her backpack and stroke the hair of her little sister, Kirsti, by implication threatening the child. In another young adult version, *Briar Rose* (1993), the writer Jane Yolen puts the hero to novel purpose as a survivor of the Holocaust. The British Gothicist Angela CARTER builds Red Riding Hood's story into a demonic feast in "The Werewolf" (1995), a tale of Satan's guidance of witches on a raid intended to procure additional flesh for a picnic. In Rosemary Lake's "Delian Little Red Riding Hood" in *Once Upon a Time When the Princess Rescued the Prince* (2003), the grandmother and granddaughter reverse a perilous swallowing into the wolf's gullet by means of a symbolic implement—sewing scissors from Red's basket, the ever-present emblem of domesticity and womanly ingenuity.

Bibliography

Orenstein, Catherine. *Little Red Riding Hood Uncloaked: Sex, Morality and the Evolution of a Fairy Tale.* New York: Basic Books, 2002.

Sexton, Anne. *Transformations.* Boston: Houghton Mifflin, 1971.

Tatar, Maria, ed. *The Annotated Classic Fairy Tales.* New York: W. W. Norton, 2002.

Little Women Louisa May Alcott (1868–1869)

Issued in two volumes, Louisa May ALCOTT's American domestic classic *Little Women* suited the nation's growing demand for girls' books. The action segues easily from the growing-up years of the fictional March girls into the author's concerns for INDEPENDENCE and self-actualization as they develop into women. At the end of chapter 9 Marmee states her plans for her four daughters in idealistic terms: "to be beautiful, accomplished, and good; to be admired, loved, and respected; to have a happy youth, to be well and wisely married, and to lead useful, pleasant lives" (Alcott, 92). Unlike her foil, Mrs. Moffat, a social climber who develops shallow qualities in her silk-clad, husband-hunting daughters, Marmee prefers that her little women enjoy the love of liberated men who value their wives for their character and spirit.

The utopian bliss and buoyancy of the March home life derive from the work ethic, which Alcott demonstrated in her own busy life. Jo, the voice for Alcott's feminist beliefs, chooses a work-centered spinsterhood over the stalking of likely bachelors. After her first sale of two stories she formalizes her plans "to be independent and earn the praise of those she loved," a fair summation of Alcott's adult life as autonomous author and the supporter of her parents (*ibid.*, 147). In a subsequent gesture of intent Jo has her hair shorn for sale to a wigmaker and applies her earnings of $25 to a family emergency, which requires Marmee to attend Father at a Washington hospital. With her usual insouciance Jo claims, "I never snivel over trifles like that" (*ibid.*, 154). Hannah, the family housekeeper, asserts of Jo's courage: "Jo doos beat all for goin ahead . . . and you never know where she's like to bring up" (*ibid.*, 162). Such half-joking complaints dot the text as the March family realizes that Jo carries into adulthood the verve and energy of a pioneering feminist.

Alcott champions the literary life for women through Jo's complete immersion in writing to the detriment of more frivolous pleasures such as dancing and flirting. The text pictures her scribbling away with a contentment she knows from no other endeavor: "When the writing fit came on, she gave herself up to it with entire abandon, and led a blissful life, unconscious of want, care, or bad weather, while she sat safe and happy in an imaginary world" (*ibid.*, 250). Over a few weeks of intense work the joy she derives "made these hours worth living" (*ibid.*). Alcott expresses Jo's dedication to her career in her refusal of Laurie's proposal: "You'd hate my scribbling, and I couldn't get on without it" (*ibid.*, 342). When her submission to

the *Spread Eagle* wins a $100 prize, she exults in the satisfaction of earning money from writing: "It was *so* pleasant to find that she had learned to do something" (*ibid.*, 253). With the proceeds she is able to relieve the family's penury and to send her weary mother and sickly sister, Beth, to the coast. The pride is exhilarating as Jo "began to feel herself a power in the house" (*ibid.*, 253). Gynocritics find in Jo and her sisters a balance of pride in accomplishment, warm MOTHER-DAUGHTER RELATIONSHIPS, and a SISTERHOOD that bolsters them during the Civil War and after Beth's death and two marriages break up the foursome. In the Columbia pictures version of *Little Women* (1995) Susan Sarandon plays a firm, yet loving and forgiving mother to the rambunctious Jo, the role played by Winona Ryder.

Bibliography

Alcott, Louisa May. *Little Women.* New York: Bantam, 1983.

Bernstein, Susan Naomi. "Writing and Little Women: Alcott's Rhetoric of Subversion," *ATQ* 7, no. 1 (March 1993): 25–43.

Keyser, Elizabeth Lennox. *Whispers in the Dark: The Fiction of Louisa May Alcott.* Knoxville: University of Tennessee Press, 1993.

Lives of Girls and Women Alice Munro (1971)

Alice MUNRO's autobiographical *Lives of Girls and Women* pictures a girl's growing-up years through self-revelatory episodes. Its protagonist, Adele "Del" Jordan, introduces her youth in a description of juicy adolescent frogs, "slim young green ones," on the banks of the Wawanash River, where a "quicksand hole" endangers the adventuresome wader (Munro, 3, 4). The understated vignette introduces Del's forays from her mother's protective wisdom to the outer edges of socially acceptable behavior. Voraciously curious, Del is sweetly erotic and enthralled by books. She reads "all I could hold" and secretly admires her depressed mother, Addie, who travels from farm to farm in rural Ontario selling encyclopedia sets (*ibid.*, 8). In the town of Jubilee, Del, like Jane AUSTEN's Emma, surveys the social web that pits the protagonist against the snobs of Jubilee who demean Addie.

Through Del Jordan's choices and errors in judgment Munro reprises the emergent self-reliance of a 1940s girl. From Addie, Del learns to focus on ambition rather than on sexual fantasies and the stalking of a husband. In the fashion typical of post–World War II teens Del rebels by defying female authority: "I did not want to be like my mother, with her virginal brusqueness, her innocence. I wanted men to love me" (*ibid.*, 178). The core of Del's yearning is physical, spasming "underground, like a canny toothache" (*ibid.* 205). She allows herself to fall for Garnet French, a feed mill employee who satisfies and scares her with his overt SEXUALITY. From caressing her fingers in church, he builds to a love affair that transforms Del, "baptizing" her into female wholeness (*ibid.*, 218). Carnal pleasures distract her from pursuing the scholarship that will rescue her from conventionality, the "deep caves paved with kitchen linoleum" (*ibid.*, 249). For its truth-telling narrative, the novel earned selection to *Booklist's* salute to overshadowed first novels.

Bibliography

Munro, Alice. *Lives of Girls and Women: A Novel.* New York: Vintage, 2001.

Thomas, Sue. "Reading Female Sexual Desire in Alice Munro's *Lives of Girls and Women,*" *Critique* 36, no. 2 (Winter 1995): 107–120.

Loos, Anita (1893–1981)

A 20th-century icon of feminist wit, the journalist and screenwriter Corinne Anita Loos pioneered the entrance of women writers in the entertainment industry. Born in Sissons, California, she debuted on stage at age five in San Francisco, toured in summer stock, and began submitting humorous essays to magazines in her early teens. In New York City, where she reported for the *Morning Telegraph,* she turned to writing for film with *The Road to Plaindale* (1911) and *The New York Hat* (1912), the beginning of a prolific career for Biograph and MGM as scripter and subtitler of comedy and melodrama for silent movies. The films featured such Hollywood stars as Lionel Barrymore, Douglas Fairbanks, Lillian Gish, Mary Pickford, and Constance Talmadge.

Loos made a popular splash with her first novel, *Gentlemen Prefer Blondes: The Illuminating Diary of a Professional Lady* (1925), a Jazz Age satire of female stereotyping that she serialized in *Harper's Bazaar.* Composed in American slang, the satire follows the affairs of Lorelei Lee, a cynical, not-so-dumb blonde sexpot who takes what she can get—dinner at the Ritz, a diamond bracelet—from the womanizer Gus Eisman, the Button King. The subtext skewers men who squander money and reputation on the tawdry conquest of beautiful, but mercenary women. The resilient plot went through numerous adaptations—as a Broadway play in 1926, as a stage musical and vehicle for Carol Channing in 1949, and in 1953 as a hit film starring Jane Russell and Marilyn Monroe. A sequel, *But Gentlemen Marry Brunettes* (1929), also flourished as a *Harper's Bazaar* serial, stage play, musical, and 1955 film, which paired Russell with Jeanne Crain.

When Loos's fortunes ebbed with the Great Depression, she remained solvent by freelancing her familiar witty, lighthearted plots. She returned to scriptwriting for *Red-Headed Woman* (1932), *San Francisco* (1936), *Saratoga* (1937), and two adaptations, the all-woman movie *The Women* (1939), cowritten with Jane Murfin from Clare Boothe LUCE's novel, and *Susan and God* (1940), a resetting of a play by Rachel Crothers. Loos increased realism in stage plays in the 1940s and 1950s with *Happy Birthday* (1946), a boozy hit comedy written for Helen Hayes, and two light romances by the French novelist COLETTE, *Gigi* (1952) and *Cheri* (1959), both frolics based on the sexual allure of coquettes. Two satires, the epistolary novel *A Mouse Is Born* (1951) and *No Mother to Guide Her* (1961), explored Loos's interest in stereotypes of women who want to be Hollywood stars.

Bibliography

Loos, Anita. *Gentlemen Prefer Blondes.* New York: Liveright, 1998.

———. *No Mother to Guide Her.* New York: Prion, 2000.

Yardley, Jonathan. "Anita Loos and the Spell of Lorelei Lee," *Washington Post,* 23 October 1988, p. 3.

Lord, Bette Bao (1938–   )

The Chinese-American writer and human rights activist Bette Bao Lord mediates between East and West to express to American readers the tradition-burdened lives of coastal Chinese women. A native of Shanghai, she was born to an aristocratic family who traveled to Brooklyn, New York, in 1946. When they found their return blocked by Mao Zedong's communist takeover of China, the Bao family acclimated to life in New Jersey. Reared by a strict mother, Lord first opted for a sensible chemistry major but changed her mind and completed a degree in political science from Tufts University. At the Fletcher School of Law and Diplomacy for postgraduate study she met her husband, Winston Lord, later appointed as the U.S. legate to China. She began writing at age 26 with a survey of family history in *Eighth Moon* (1964), the story of the abandonment of her sister, Sansan, when the family left China.

After visiting her homeland in 1973, Lord witnessed firsthand the subjugation of women, many of whom had joined the underground as freedom fighters. Her aunt, the teacher Goo Ma, identified a man who had beaten her and shoved her into a closet in her classroom. From these anecdotes Lord published a best seller, *Spring Moon: A Novel of China* (1981), a sweeping saga of Chinese family life during the postimperial turmoil and civil war. Often compared to the writings of the Chinese-American author Amy TAN, the novel illustrates the powerlessness of women. Lord's epic describes Spring Moon's childhood agonies of foot binding and her subsequent struggles against PATRIARCHY, which Chinese custom disguised as honor and duty. More autobiographical is *Legacies: A Chinese Mosaic* (1990), which depicts Lord's impressions of the Cultural Revolution. She returned to the issues of civil revolt and torture with accounts of the fears of Summer Wishes, a chaste sing-song girl in *Middle Heart* (1996).

Bibliography

Baum, Geraldine. "An Activist in Control of Her Outrage; Diplomacy: Bette Bao Lord Brings a Cool Civility to Her Cause," *Los Angeles Times*, 31 October, 1997, p. 1.

Lord, Bette Bao. *Spring Moon: A Novel of China*. New York: HarperTorch, 1994.

Lorde, Audre (1934–1992)

A forceful lesbian poet, orator, and essayist, Audre Geraldine Lorde tackled perpetrators of misogyny and sang the joys of sexual love and motherhood. Born the last of five girls to Grenadan immigrants to New York City, she later recalled Harlem's fervid beauty and eroticism, two elements that anchor her verse. Educated at parochial schools along with her sister Phyllis, Lorde overcame severe myopia as well as faculty comments about a "black smell" and the principal's insistence that she stop braiding her hair in an Afro-American style. In her early teens she began writing and reciting verse already pulsing with rebellion and hatred of racism. She abandoned a post as children's librarian for the New York Public Library System to attend college. After studying English and philosophy at Hunter College, she worked her way with low-paying pink-collar jobs toward a degree in library science from Columbia University.

During civil rights battles Lorde earned a reputation as a feminist freedom fighter and a composer of allegorical free verse with a bite. At age 34 she ended her job as head librarian at City University of New York to publish a first anthology, *The First Cities* (1968). The poems seek a world that accepts and celebrates human differences. In 1970 she composed "Poem for a Poet," a eulogy for the scholar, teacher, and writer Randall Jarrell. The collection *From a Land Where Other People Live* (1973) contains "The Winds of Orisha," a tribute to long-suffering womanhood that honors the endurance of black females under oppression. The anthology won the respect of Adrienne RICH, who shared a National Book Award with Lorde and Alice WALKER.

Lorde spoke powerfully and eloquently in her last years. She demonstrated the inner splendor of the African female in *The Black Unicorn* (1978), a collection based on GODDESS LORE and women's oral traditions. In "125th Street and Abomey," she introduces the white world to Seboulisa, a West African spirit and muse that she learned to love while living in Dahomey. The text observes a maimed African amazon who loses one breast to gnawing sorrows. Lorde supported women through essay by reprising her terrifying sense of mortality and extended trials with medical treatment in *The Cancer Journals* (1980), winner of an American Library Association Gay Caucus Book of the Year Award. With the poem "Afterimages" (1978) she reprobed the murder of Emmett Till in 1955 in Jackson, Mississippi, for the significance of his martyrdom after allegedly touching a white woman. The poet accepts the burden of Till's death and its aftermath as her inheritance from racial history. In "Poetry Is Not a Luxury," collected in *Sister Outsider: Essays and Speeches* (1984), Lorde defines the inner core of the female as a dark place that nurtures the true self until it can emerge in a touch of beauty that resembles the chestnut. A second essay, "Uses of the Erotic: The Erotic as Power," explores the place of female sensuality in defining self and engendering self-respect.

At the height of her industry Lorde's creativity found expression in a number of guises. Her metaphors cling to her girlhood in Harlem and to black ancestors and story keepers living in Africa and the Caribbean. One of her most compelling metaphors pictures black lignite turning to diamond in "Coal" (1968), an image that parallels the black experience. After a mastectomy she continued to husband her strength for teaching at Hunter College and for serving her home state as poet laureate. She cofounded KITCHEN TABLE / WOMEN OF COLOR PRESS, a vehicle for silenced and ignored nonwhite female writers. The company published Lorde's feminist treatise *I Am Your Sister: Black Women Organizing Across Sexualities* (1986) and *Need: A Chorale for Black Women's Voices* (1990).

The courage Lorde exhibited during her last decade earned admiration. The return of disease prompted her toward universality. She pushed past traditional literary boundaries with *Zami: A New Spelling of My Name: A Biomythography* (1982), a blend of AUTOBIOGRAPHY, myth, and lyric fiction. The text pictures the poet as journeywoman reordering the pieces of self and racial identity. In the poem "October" she begs for strength from Seboulisa, a powerful Earth mother. Feminists recog-

nize the lyric memoir as the first expression of a black female's treatment for breast cancer. She wrote two critically acclaimed poetry collections—*A Burst of Light* (1988), winner of the American Book Award, and *The Marvelous Arithmetics of Distance: Poems 1987–1992* (1993), published the year after her death in Saint Croix of liver cancer. Her activism and writing style influenced the writer bell HOOKS.

Bibliography

Carr, Brenda. " 'A Woman Speaks . . . I Am Woman and Not White': Politics of Voice, Tactical Essentialism, and Cultural Intervention in Audre Lorde's Activist Poetics and Practice," *College Literature* 20, no. 2 (June 1993): 133–153.

Donovan, Kathleen M. *Feminist Readings of Native American Literature: Coming to Voice.* Tucson: University of Arizona Press, 1998.

Lorde, Audre. *The Black Unicorn.* New York: W. W. Norton, 1978.

———. *The Cancer Journals.* New York: Aunt Lute Books, 1980.

———. *The Collected Poems of Audre Lorde.* New York: W. W. Norton, 2000.

———. *Sister Outsider: Essays and Speeches.* New York: Crossing Press, 1984.

———. *Zami: A New Spelling of My Name: A Biomythography.* New York: Crossing Press, 1983.

"Lottery, The"   Shirley Jackson (1948)

An American classic, Shirley JACKSON's short fable "The Lottery" resulted in an outpouring of admiration, curiosity, and rage from readers. Issued in the *New Yorker* on June 28, 1948, the story characterizes ritual murder in the mundane scapegoating of a local citizen chosen at random. As tension mounts among villagers, they anticipate the yearly ritual stoning, an execution method dating to prehistory. The on-the-spot death of the unlikely victim symbolizes the social murder of the outsider, who, for economic, cultural, racial, or religious infractions of the status quo, quickly advances to dispossessed pariah. The selection of a hapless woman parallels Jackson's other losers, who are usually lonely women, crones, outsiders, and young women facing unexpected pregnancies.

Jackson enhances horror with a methodical selection process that mimics the fairness of democracy. The two-stage ritual first names the family, then orders the drawing among parents and children that rapidly alienates the loser, Tessie Hutchinson, from her mate and offspring. The second stage turns to atavism as the nuclear family singles out one of its own, in this case, the mother, for a grisly public death. Jackson enlarges the irony of misogyny with the struggle of Mrs. Delacroix to heave a huge stone and end Tessie's life as a sop to the gods for a needed corn harvest. Frequently anthologized, the story implies a male-engineered barbarity that echoes the sexism and ageism that permeate world history.

Bibliography

Griffin, Amy A., "Jackson's 'The Lottery,' " *Explicator* 58, no. 1 (Fall 1999) p. 44.

Jackson, Shirley. *The Lottery; or, The Adventures of James Harris.* New York: Farrar, Straus & Giroux, 1949.

Lowell, Amy (1874–1925)

A precise poet, essayist, and lecturer, Amy Lawrence Lowell led American peers toward a formal break with traditional poetry. Born at the family estate in Brookline into an illustrious Massachusetts clan, she grew up among Boston patricians and was home schooled before her enrollment in private girls' academies. In her early teens she revealed a remarkable talent in a first publication, *Dream Drops, or Stories from Fairyland* (1887), which she marketed at a charity bazaar. Instead of having a life of New England gentility, after a stellar evening at a stage play starring Eleanora Duse, Lowell chose to write, edit, and translate professionally. By age 40 she completed a poetic apprenticeship and, under the influence of the imagist H. D. and Japanese haiku, introduced an original version of *vers libre* (free verse). She published her breakthrough form in *Sword Blades and Poppy Seeds* (1914) and in submissions to the *Egoist* and *Poetry* magazines, two outlets for modernist literature.

Lowell's considerable literary energies branched out in a number of directions. She satisfied her intellectual curiosity by translating *Six French Poets: Studies in Contemporary Literature* (1915), with literary theoretics in *Tendencies in Modern American Poetry* (1917), and through the editing of *Some Imagist Poets, 1915–1917* (1917), which defined the imagist movement. In 1919 her profuse flower imagery—the parted leaves in "The Weather-Cock Points South," bright crocuses in "Summer Rain," and the crimson amaryllis in "Opal—openly celebrated female genitals and the lover's appetite for woman-to-woman intimacy. She also produced a series of Japanese court DIARIES in 1920; wrote a satire, *A Critical Fable* (1922); and collected translations of Chinese verse in *Fir-Flower Tablets* (1921), cowritten by Florence Ayscough. In her last months Lowell completed a poetic life, *John Keats* (1925), a rigorous study of her first poet hero. That same year she received a Pulitzer Prize for *What's O'Clock* (1925).

Contributing some 600 poems to American literature, the poet created startling, imaginative images of love. For "The Letter" (1919) she pictures the lover wearying of correspondence and "scalding" alone in moonlight. In "Venus Transiens" (1919) she compares her mate to the mythic figure in Sandro Botticelli's painting *The Birth of Venus.* Her frequently anthologized melodrama "Patterns" (1916) is a tense, rhythmic miniature of female grief. A dramatic monologue by a woman who wards off hysteria, the narrative pictures her pacing up and down and coming to terms with her lover's death on the battlefield. Restraining her behavior is the unyielding formal dress of 18th-century women, who lacked free movement in ribboned shoes, filmy trains, whalebone corsets, and brocaded gowns. She blames the world of men for requiring wartime bravado as a test of manhood. Her one release is a fantasy of a seductive chase in the formal garden, a form of rebellion against the era's staid manners.

To feminist literature Lowell contributed one of the first thorough records of a lesbian relationship along with a salute to fellow female writers. "The Sisters" (1925) celebrates women's place in the arts and, by implication, words the poet's gratitude for the contentment gained from a stable lesbian relationship. The poem pictures such female writers as Elizabeth Barrett BROWNING and Emily DICKINSON as seizers of a male prerogative and as imitators of SAPPHO, the Greek lyric poet. The poem rigorously rejects the Victorian prudery and inhibitions in Browning's verse in favor of Dickinson's abrupt, jarring metaphors and rhythms. In a felicitous close Lowell enfolds all female writers into a single family, to which she is privileged to belong. Among the poets she influenced was May SARTON.

Bibliography

Lowell, Amy. *Selected Poems of Amy Lowell.* Piscataway, N.J.: Rutgers University Press, 2002.

Munich, Adrienne, and Melissa Bradshaw. *Amy Lowell, an American Modern.* Piscataway, N.J.: Rutgers University Press, 2004.

Loy, Mina (1882–1966)

The expatriate modern artist, dramatist, poet, and satirist Mina Gertrude Löwy experimented with cubism and verbal, metric, and visual fragmentation for her allusive verse. One of the avant-garde *nouvelles femmes* (new women) of the 1910s and 1920s, the London-born artist at large was the daughter of a prim English mother and a Hungarian-Jewish father, whose surname she shortened to Loy. Schooled in the arts in Munich and Paris at her father's urging, she later abandoned her husband and three children to pursue feminism in Florence, Italy, and the United States. She published sporadically in *Accent, Contact, Dial, Little Review, Others: A Magazine of the New Verse, Pagany: A Native Quarterly, Partisan Review, Rogue, Transatlantic Review,* and *Trend.* The combination of multicultural heritage and exhibitionist temperament earned her a reputation as an exotic show stopper dedicated to a transatlantic quasi career in art, drama, and verse.

Loy was a proponent of women's right to choose their lifestyles and sex partners. In 1909 she composed a radical feminist manifesto in oversized type that opens with an alarm: "**Women** if you want to realise yourselves—you are on the eve of a devastating psychological upheaval—all your pet illusions must be unmasked—the lies of centuries have got to go—are you prepared for the **Wrench**—?" (Loy, 153). In boldface lettering equal to her voice, she condenses the options for her generation of women into a forbidding triad: "you have the choice between **Parasitism, & Prostitution—or Negation**" (*ibid.,* 154). The text upends centuries-old traditions of virginity by demanding that teen women destroy their hymen surgically to end the marketing of nubile females to the highest bidder. To develop themselves fully, she proposes that females rid themselves of fragility and the need to be pampered as lapdogs. To Loy virtue was a specious value that reduced women to lifeless icons of purity and that discouraged them from seeking more concrete values such as courage, introspection, and clear vision.

Influenced by the work of Gertrude STEIN, Loy honored her contemporary in an ode, "Gertrude Stein" (1914), which extols the Lost Generation maven as another Madame Marie Curie for discovering words as rare as radium. In 1916 Loy gravitated to Greenwich Village, befriended the cubist painter Marcel Duchamp, and joined Djuna BARNES, Susan GLASPELL, and Edna St. Vincent MILLAY in productions by the Provincetown Players. After Loy's retreat to the Continent, she resided in Paris to make lamp shades and to hobnob with the literati who gathered at intellectual salons and art exhibitions. Assembling her scattered, gap-ridden verse is a posthumous collection, *The Lost Lunar Baedeker* (1982), which takes its name from the Baedeker, the most popular travel handbook of her day.

An energetic rebel and nonconformist, Loy subverted Victorian diction and violated moral standards as well as grammatical and syntactic conventions. She combatted sentimentality with a lyric exposé of sexual discontent by issuing in *Others* magazine her iconoclastic "Love Songs" (1915). In *Songs to Joannes* (1917), Loy refers with less acid metaphors to the mating of human bodies and voices disappointment that sexual union, for all its physical pyrotechnics, lapses into "Tear drops / Little lusts and lucidities / And prayerful lies" (*ibid.,* 62). In 1920 she published in *Futurism X Feminism: The Circle Squared* the poem "Virgins Plus Curtains Minus Dots." She comments on male-female differences:

> Men's eyes   look into things
> Our eyes   look out. (*ibid.,* 21)

The couplet reveals the poet's ability to size up in standard English the gendered idiosyncrasies that set women apart as the more perceptive half of the population.

The most treasured of Loy's canon is a philosophical work, "Anglo-Mongrels and the Rose" (1923), which found favor with feminist critics a half-century later. The core of the long mythological work is the poet's rebellion against her pious, prudish mother. Loy celebrates orgasm with verbal charges that erupt amid frequent ellipses, profane diction, and sardonic put-downs. After the death of her second husband, the Dada artist Arthur Craven, she composed "The Widow's Jazz" (1931), in which she grieves for him with images of suttee, a barbaric Indian custom of immolating a living wife alongside her husband's corpse. The poem suggests that, for all Loy's salty wisecracks about human love, she missed the camaraderie of a mate.

Bibliography

Burke, Carolyn. *Becoming Modern: The Life of Mina Loy.* Berkeley: University of California Press, 1997.

Kinnahan, Linda A. *Poetics of the Feminine.* Cambridge: Cambridge University Press, 1994.

Loy, Mina. *The Lost Lunar Baedeker: Poems of Mina Loy.* New York: Farrar, Straus & Giroux, 1997.

Luce, Clare Boothe (1903–1987)

Ann Clare Boothe Luce, a noted dramatist, satirist, lecturer, and journalist as well as politician, focused on women's lives, both wasted and exemplary. Reared by a demanding mother and educated at Saint Mary's School and at Castle School for Girls, she developed a longing for wealth and privilege. When her parents parted, she lived with her mother in Paris. In adulthood she settled into the role of wife to George Tuttle Brokaw, a New York millionaire 20 years her senior, and mother to their daughter, Ann Clare. Because of her husband's alcoholic binges and marital abuse at age 26 Luce ended her first marriage.

The author took staff positions first as a writer for *Vogue* and then as managing editor of *Vanity Fair.* She issued witty sketches in a collection, *Stuffed Shirts* (1933), a source of rumor and scandal for its revelations about real notables. After marrying the publishing mogul Henry R. Luce, she turned to writing for the stage with

Abide with Me (1935) and a satiric comedy of manners, *The Women* (1936). The latter, featuring one of the largest all-female casts ever assembled on Broadway, exposed the urban wasteland of bored, spoiled socialites who relied on men for their wealth and social clout. Anita LOOS and Jane Murfin adapted the play three years later for a mordant all-female movie. Starring as idle, back-stabbing female competitors were Norma Shearer, Joan Crawford, Rosalind Russell, Paulette Goddard, and Joan Fontaine, the cream of Hollywood. The play returned to screen in 1956 as the musical *The Opposite Sex,* featuring June Allyson, Joan Collins, and Ann Sheridan, and to the Broadway stage in 1973 and again in 2001. In 1975 Wendy WASSERSTEIN used *The Women* as the springboard for her own all-woman play, *Uncommon Women and Others.*

Luce maintained a vivid presence in American arts and politics. She won acclaim for *Kiss the Boys Goodbye* (1938), an allegory on fascism, and continued her winning streak with *Margin of Error* (1939), a two-act satiric melodrama. After a sojourn in Europe and Asia reporting war news for *Life* magazine, Luce compiled writings on holy figures in *Saints for Now* (1951), which garnered the talents of the writers Kathleen Norris, Barbara Ward, and Rebecca WEST. Luce earned an Oscar nomination for *Come to the Stable* (1949), which opened on Broadway with Loretta Young starring as a nun intent on building a hospital. In the 1950s President Dwight D. Eisenhower posted Luce to Italy as the first female U.S. ambassador. She revisited feminist writing in 1970 with a one-act, two-person domestic play, *Slam the Door Softly* (1971), a resetting of Henrik Ibsen's A DOLL'S HOUSE (1879) that appeared in *Life* magazine on October 16, 1970, as *A Doll's House 1970.*

Bibliography

Luce, Clare Boothe, ed. *Saints for Now.* Fort Collins, Colo.: Ignatius Press, 1993.

———. *Slam the Door Softly.* New York: Dramatists Play Service, 1971.

———. *The Women.* New York: Dramatists Play Service, 1998.

Morris, Sylvia Jukes. *Rage for Fame: The Ascent of Clare Boothe Luce.* New York: Modern Library, 1997.

Lurie, Alison (1926–)

An author of scholarly essays and humorous social novels for more than four decades, Alison Lurie abandons standard fictional convention to satirize courtship, SEXUALITY, and the debased housewife. While growing up in Chicago, her hometown, and in White Plains, New Jersey, she received parental encouragement to write. For style she chose the writing of Jane AUSTEN. With a degree from Radcliffe College Lurie began her career with *Love and Friendship* (1962). While teaching children's literature at Cornell University, she began writing children's FAIRY TALES about sturdy heroines. In the article "Fairy Tale Liberation" (1970) she applied feminist philosophy to refute traditional analysis of children's lore. Her most successful feminist satire, *The War between the Tates* (1974), describes Erica's discontent with GENDER BIAS, which awards her husband, Brian, better jobs and more money while freeing him of domestic duties. The novel was the subject of a 1976 made-for-TV film starring Elizabeth Ashley and Richard Crenna as mates in a disintegrating marriage. Lurie debunked the BEAUTY MYTH in *Only Children* (1979) and wrote a treatise on the conscious intent of fashion, *The Language of Clothes* (1981).

Lurie's feminist plots offer women choices that, on first appearance, lack appeal. In an overview of late-in-life sex in the novel *Foreign Affairs* (1984), winner of a Pulitzer Prize, she builds character in 54-year-old Virginia "Vinnie" Miner, a professor at an Ivy League school. While on sabbatical in London Miner falls in love with a sanitation worker. The story was a vehicle for a 1993 Turner Classic Movie, starring Joanne Woodward and Brian Denehy. Lurie compiled modern fairy stories in *The Oxford Book of Modern Fairy Tales* (1993), which anthologizes the writings of Angela CARTER, Louise ERDRICH, Tanith LEE, and Ursula LE GUIN. Lurie followed with a gynocentric Gothic anthology, *Women and Ghosts* (1994), and another scholarly examination of gendered behavior in *Boys and Girls Forever: Classics from Cinderella to Harry Potter* (2004).

Bibliography

Craig, Amanda. "A Jane for Our Age." *New Statesman,* 22 May 1998, pp. 56–57.

Lurie, Alison. *Foreign Affairs.* New York: Quill, 1995.

———. *The Oxford Book of Modern Fairy Tales.* Oxford: Oxford University Press, 2003.

Lysistrata Aristophanes (411 B.C.)

A classic model of ribaldry, *Lysistrata* is one of the most controversial and most revived plays from the ancient Greek canon. Written by the satirist Aristophanes of Athens, the text is an ebullient feminist farce punctuated by belly laughs at the expense of the battling sexes. To dramatize women's pacifism, the playwright extols their ability to form an antiwar political action group. He chose the title character's name, "disbander of armies," as an introit to his feminist themes, which lionize demonstrative, principled wives as forces for peace and order. Less polite are the names Myrrinhe, a vulgar reference to female genitals, and Kinesias, a slang term for sexual intercourse. By redirecting SEXUALITY from the conjugal bed to a militaristic government, Lysistrata and her women friends turn male lust against their enthusiasm for the Peloponnesian War. The subversion of sexual desire ends warfare, an extreme manifestation of social disorder and a threat to the family.

Aristophanes satirizes male behavior by showing women in comedic soldierly stance. The buildup of drollery begins with the female skill at personal adornment—the draping of see-through gowns and the selection of fragrance—which precedes the group's usurpation of masculine postures and combat savvy. Although Lysistratra dislikes hearing her sex dismissed as sly tricksters, she loses sleep over solving the problem of males' leaving for combat zones in Pylos and Thrace. For patriotic reasons she manipulates assembled female dissidents by turning a shield into a wine bowl and inviting all to drink, a manly gesture that identifies the heroine as great-hearted leader of women and creator of camaraderie. The first to agree is Lampito, whom Lysistrata praises as the only female deserving the name of woman. The assembly pledges an oath to the goddess Persuasion. In army slang, Lysistrata gives orders as a general. Her followers break into two battalions—the younger to return home and the elder to seize the Acropolis and shut down monetary transfers from Athena's treasury.

The playwright uses bawdy repartee to prove the classic aphorism "Laughter tells the truth." Verbal battles tend toward carnal remarks to intimidate the city magistrate and his Scythian henchmen. Lysistrata proposes a radical turnabout—the administration of public funds by females to stop the waste of money and the lives of young male recruits. For metaphors Aristophanes turns to the domestic skills of women, who pick wool tufts free of briars and spin the fibers into spools of yarn for weaving into blankets and garments. Echoing brief set-tos between male and female opponents are comic choruses mocking gender STEREOTYPING. Before the coital boycott by Athenian woman ends city-state warfare, both sides compromise and restore order in the form of personal and sexual harmony.

Bibliography

Aristophanes. *The Birds, Lysistrata, Assembly-Women, Wealth.* Oxford: Oxford University Press, 1997.

Forrest, W. G. "Aristophanes *Lysistrata* 231," *Classical Quarterly* 45, no. 1 (January–June 1995): 240–241.

M

madness

In feminist literature madness is both a life sentence and an escape. In 1436 the religious traveler Margery KEMPE dictated the first AUTOBIOGRAPHY of a woman in English, *The Book of Margery Kempe*, in which she explains her hysteria, hallucinations, and self-mutilation as the result of religious ecstasy. Loosening her grasp on sanity was a vision of Christ she had while she was giving birth to her first child. For women who seized selfhood and lived up to their dreams, as did Kempe and the French warrior Joan of Arc, societies created fearful punishments. Discontented husbands could lock up unhappy wives with the mentally ill, the punishment that awaited Kempe for falling into despair and weeping uncontrollably and for Maria Venables, protagonist of Mary WOLLSTONECRAFT's landmark psychological novel *MARIA; OR, THE WRONGS OF WOMAN* (1798). Those wives whom families spurned and turned out of their home were socially disgraced, the punishment of Molly Farren in George ELIOT's *Silas Marner* (1861). Female unfortunates often found themselves unwelcome if they tried to return to their parents. Shamed and rejected by society, some lived in misery as wandering beggars or fell into PROSTITUTION and crime. The English poet Elizabeth Barrett BROWNING pictures the mother's retreat into hysteria in "The Runaway Slave at Pilgrim's Point" (1846), a poem about a slave who strangles her own infant son because of his resemblance to the white male who impregnated her. In Maxine Hong KINGSTON's best-selling epic *The Woman Warrior: Memoirs of a Girlhood among Ghosts*

(1976) a disgraced family member lapses into lunacy at the birth of an illegitimate child and drowns herself and the baby in a well. The more daring and inventive madwomen, such as the hermit Athanasia of Jerusalem and the actress Pelagia of Antioch, disguised themselves as men and lived out their years acting the roles of males.

While recording in letters and diary entries her perceptions of the Southern plantation system in *Journal of a Residence on a Georgian Plantation in 1838–1839*, the English actor Fanny KEMBLE saw evidence that slavery and constant breeding drove females to insanity. To project realism into her observations, she speaks of the treatment of Sarah, the slave of Kemble's husband. After 12 pregnancies and severe misery in her back, she fled, raving, to the woods "but was at last tracked and brought back, when she was tied up by the arms, and heavy logs fastened to her feet, and was severely flogged" (Kemble, 230). A similar case, that of Judy, resulted in apprehension in the woods and condemnation to the stocks, which worsened her chronic rheumatism. When she went to Kemble for intervention, she "could hardly crawl, and cried bitterly all the time she spoke" (*ibid.*, 238). Judy's madness resulted from resisting her owner's son, who raped her and had her flogged and exiled to a swamp. The symptoms of derangement, according to Kemble, were the predictable outcome of inhumanity.

Mary Elizabeth BRADDON, the queen of Victorian sensational fiction, portrayed the incarceration of aristocratic women for a variety of sins, primarily the tricking of men and the breaching of restraints on female ambition and intellect. In confinement the title character of the best-selling *Lady Audley's Secret* (1862) sees herself as "a species of state prisoner, who would have to be taken good care of. A second Iron Mask, who must be provided for in some comfortable place of confinement" (Braddon, 245). The attending physician, Dr. Alwyn Mosgrave, refuses to back Robert Audley's plan to have his murderous aunt declared insane. He speaks for Braddon an appraisal of the woman who refuses to be a victim of the anti-woman social order: She ran away from a miserable home life and committed bigamy: "She employed intelligent means, and she carried out a conspiracy which required coolness and deliberation in its execution. There is no madness in that" (*ibid.*, 238). Nonetheless, after a 20-minute consultation Mosgrave conspires with Robert against Lady Audley. Mosgrave agrees to spare the family scandal by shuttling her off to a *maison de santé* (madhouse) in Belgium. He describes the move as final: "If you were to dig a grave for her in the nearest churchyard and bury her alive in it, you could not more safely shut her from the world" (*ibid.*, 250). The subsequent death notice arrives in polite French explaining that Lady Audley died of "a *maladie de langueur*" (depression) (*ibid.*, 286).

In Louisa May ALCOTT's Gothic short story "A Whisper in the Dark" (1863) the complicity of the male medical establishment in torture turns the attending physician, Doctor Karnac, into a model of the mad scientist. The heroine, Sybil, encounters her mother in the asylum to which both are committed. Sybil later learns that Karnac intended to experiment on her until she was driven insane. The elder inmate speaks a terrifying truth of madwoman scenarios, particularly those of sane women confined for rebelling against PATRIARCHY: "If you are not already mad, you will be; I suspect you were sent here to be made so; for the air is poison, the solitude is fatal . . . leave this accursed house while you have power to do it" (Alcott, 57). As the names suggest, Karnac, a symbol of the dark doings of ancient Egypt, faces Sybil, a harbinger of a future time when women reject the age-old strictures that leave them helpless in the hands of evil powers.

In 1944 the novelist Jean STAFFORD reflected on the privations of immigrant Russians in *Boston Adventure*. Through the eyes of the teenage daughter, Sonie Marburg, the retreat of her mother into madness seems an appropriate response to a drunken husband, abandonment, poverty, and the drowning of her son, Ivan. Wracked by nightmares and hallucinations, she grows apart from the daily struggle for food and warmth. Sonie recalls, "Her whole life was a fantasy, whether she was awake or asleep. If by chance her mind cleared and the objects about her righted themselves, it was not because she had recovered her senses, but that pain had driven the delusions away" (Stafford, 135). The mental fog progresses into glazed eyes and unintelligible gibberish about birds, a symbol of escape unavailable to a human female. Because 12-year-old Sonie cannot manage her home care, she gives up her only parent to "the vast, labyrinthine asylum where she was known by number and species" (*ibid.*, 173).

Jean RHYS wove a complex pattern of madness in *WIDE SARGASSO SEA* (1966), a prequel to Charlotte BRONTË's *JANE EYRE* (1847). It reinterprets the renaming and incarceration of Bertha Mason ROCHESTER, who destroys Thornfield, home of her husband, Edward Rochester. Rhys attributes Antoinette Cosway Mason's insanity to mistreatment after her mentally retarded brother dies as a result of an attack of hostile black Jamaicans on the family home. Her mother, Annette, gradually loses touch with reality and dies as a result of protracted isolation and estrangement. After Antoinette's husband leaves her: "They tell her she is mad, they act like she is mad. Question, question. But no kind word, no friends, and her husban' he go off, he leave her. . . . She give up, she care for nothing" (Rhys, 157). Just as her mother withered away, Antoinette, renamed a more British "Bertha," suffers a similar loss of personhood. Upon being locked away in England, she asks, "What am I doing in this place and who am I?" (Rhys, 180). Without the familiar smells, sounds, and soft breezes of Jamaica the islander has no proof of identity.

The dystopian novelist Marge Piercy creates a gripping case for the female mental patient in *WOMAN ON THE EDGE OF TIME* (1976), a tale of female battery and incarceration that equates lunacy with flight. Family betrayal and institutional care force the protagonist, 35-year-old Consuelo "Connie" Ramos, into fantasy escapes from what she perceives as a discarded self. In a blistering diatribe against urbanism the author charges builders of skyscrapers and oil refineries of replacing human life with grandiose schemes: "They took and took and left their garbage, choking the air, the river, the sea itself. Choking her. A life of garbage. Human garbage" (Piercy, 280). In Connie's feeble attempts to fight back against dehumanization, she complains that trying to rear a daughter in an unendurable habitat is futile. She visualizes a gradual, but irrevocable demise: "All her life it felt to her she had been dying a cell at a time, a cell of hope, of joy, of love, little lights going out one by one" (*ibid.*). She characterizes her insanity as a form of internal poisoning, just as pollutants destroy the outside world.

The playwright Emily MANN equates the monstrous attempt at genocide during World War II with the extinction of human will. She pictures posttraumatic stress disorder in her Holocaust kitchen drama *Annulla Allen: The Autobiography of a Survivor* (1977). The title figure describes Nazi murder schemes as an out-of-control male-generated mania for conquest. After Annulla's family exits the death camp at Dachau, she suffers anxiety neurosis, a nebulous fear that impedes the victim from eating and sleeping. Flashbacks generate delusions and fearful dreams and inhibit Annula from reading or thinking rationally. The doctor who examines her explains, "No, she is not mad. . . . It is a delayed reaction" (Mann, 28).

From the domestic point of view the theme of institutionalization as a means of oppressing women empowers Beth HENLEY's three-act comedy *Crimes of the Heart* (1979). The protagonist, Babe Botrelle, must act to save herself after her husband, the politician Zackery Botrelle, threatens to commit her to Whitfield psychiatric hospital. Babe first ponders suicide, the escape method of her mother, then chooses to save herself and shoot Zackery. Her action overturns a social DOUBLE STANDARD that condones retaliation in husbands but not in wives. Henley wrings wry comedy from Babe's sweetening of the attempted murder with a

glass of lemonade laced with extra sugar. After her reunion with her sisters, Lenny and Meg Magrath, female companionship restores Babe to a hopeful life that allows time for practicing on her saxophone. Henley's exaltation of SISTERHOOD and creative outlets suggests that normality in the female psyche is the product of acceptance, love, and freedom to explore nonthreatening fantasies.

Bibliography

Alcott, Louisa May. *The Portable Louisa May Alcott*. New York: Penguin, 2000.

Braddon, Mary Elizabeth. *Lady Audley's Secret*. New York: Dover, 1974.

Kemble, Fanny. *Journal of a Residence on a Georgian Plantation in 1838–1839*. Athens: University of Georgia Press, 1984.

Mann, Emily. *Testimonies: Four Plays*. New York: Theatre Communications Group, 1997.

Piercy, Marge. *Woman on the Edge of Time*. New York: Fawcett, 1976.

Rhys, Jean. *Wide Sargasso Sea*. New York: W. W. Norton, 1966.

Shepard, Alan Clarke. "Aborted Rage in Beth Henley's Women," *Modern Drama* 36, no. 1 (March 1993): 96–108.

Stafford, Jean. *Boston Adventure*. Garden City, N.Y.: Sun Dial Press, 1944.

Mahmoody, Betty (1945–   )

A feminist author and a Pulitzer Prize nominee, Betty Mahmoody chose to expose Muslim misogyny to protest abduction and mistreatment of American citizens by Irani religious fanatics. A resident of Detroit and mother of two sons by a previous marriage, she wed an Iranian physician, Sayyed Bozorg Mahmoody, in 1977 and three years later bore a daughter, Mahtob. On August 3, 1984, only weeks before Mahtob was scheduled to enter a Montessori kindergarten, the family journeyed to Teheran to stay with Sayyed's family over a two-week vacation. The visit transformed into a terrifying house arrest. Because Mahmoody eluded attempts to keep her a virtual hostage in an international situation, she earned numerous awards for bravery, including a woman of the year citation from Germany. In the style of frontier

CAPTIVITY NARRATIVE and of Harriet JACOBS's memoir *Incidents in the Life of a Slave Girl, Written by Herself* (1861), Mahmoody wrote an account of her ordeal.

In her best-selling work *Not without My Daughter* (1987), a Literary Guild/Doubleday Book Club selection, and its sequel, *For Love of a Child* (1992), Mahmoody characterizes an unforeseen imprisonment that extends over the next 18 months. Triggering the incident were her husband's firing from a Detroit hospital and resultant changes in his behavior. Against inner forebodings and warnings from friends, Mahmoody donned black stockings, matronly suit, and headscarf in keeping with Islamic veiling customs. On arrival at Teheran airport she watched women in chadors trying to carry luggage with one hand and clutch a facial covering with the other: "The effect is reminiscent of a nun's habit in times past. The more devout Iranian women allowed only a single eye to poke through. . . . I marveled at the power their society and their religion held over them" (Mahmoody, 5). Innocently she pities native women without suspecting that her own freedom is about to end.

Mahmoody provided eyewitness accounts of women's lives as chattel to men under the virulent regime of the Ayatollah Khomeini and its religion-based anti-woman laws. In mid-August her husband refused to return the family to Detroit in favor of remaining in Iran and rearing Mahtob as a Shi'ite, a rigid fundamentalist sect ruled by authoritarian males. Mahmoody's book describes how hostilities against Americans and family prejudices reduce her to CONFINEMENT to squalid quarters. She endured beatings and interrogations, death threats, and long separations from Mahtob, Sayyed's weapon for subduing his wife. The Swiss embassy offered no quarter against a law that made Betty a citizen of Iran once she married an Iranian male. Her only legal choice was to abandon Mahtob and return home alone.

Mahmoody's first-person story of the ordeal won immediate acclaim for her clever escape and for the straightforward account of an American female hostage seeking release. In 1986 on her 500-mile flight into Turkey, she and six-year-old Mahtob traveled on foot, by car, and on horseback through a snowstorm over icy mountaintops. When exhaus-

tion caused Mahmoody to collapse, guides dragged her the remaining yards to freedom. Because of her husband's threats she and her daughter settled in Oswego, Michigan, and lived in terror under assumed names.

Mahmoody dedicated herself to warning others of the perils of marrying into an alien culture and to aiding other women and children threatened by international kidnap. In addition to compiling other cases of intercultural abduction in *For Love of a Child*, she appeared on radio and television talk shows and founded One World: For Children, an altruistic outreach to the offspring of bicultural marriages. Because of her experience she began serving the U.S. State Department as a consultant on thorny issues of WOMEN'S RIGHTS versus androcentric religious custom. Accompanying her to lectures is Mahtob Mahmoody, now a graduate of Michigan State University. In 1991 Universal International filmed *Not without My Daughter* as a docudrama with Sally Field playing the part of Betty. A Hindi film version of the story, *Shakti* (2002), resets the family's move as Canada to India and alters Shiism to fundamentalist Hinduism.

Bibliography

Mahmoody, Betty. *Not without My Daughter.* New York: St. Martin's, 1993.

Steindorf, Sara. "Betty and Mahtob Mahmoody," *Christian Science Monitor,* 6 June 2000, p. 23.

Mann, Emily (1952–)

A translator and creator of provocative historical dramas for nonprofit community theaters, Emily Mann earns popular and critical regard for feminist playwriting that showcases the lives of WISE-WOMEN. A Bostonian reared in Chicago, she is the daughter of Arthur Mann, a history professor and biographer who furthered her interest in research and docudrama. He taught her to respect the zeitgeist, the spirit of the times, of significant eras that infused real people with courage and direction. After graduation from the Chicago Laboratory High School she completed degrees in English and drama at Harvard University and the University of Minnesota. To revitalize community theater, she focused on theatrical testimonials to the moral issues undergirding urgent moments in the history of women, blacks, Jews, and homosexuals. Despite weakening by multiple sclerosis, she became a force in the dynamic, people-centered productions that she writes and directs.

Mann has a knack for adapting for actors the works and stories of real people. She extended an aunt's oral narrative of the Holocaust into play form with *Annulla Allen: The Autobiography of a Survivor* (1977), a kitchen drama that describes female memories as an insistent burden relieved through STORYTELLING. The title character links the barbarity of genocide to the male drive for conquest: "I can tell you what it is like to live always in the shadow of tyrants. . . . If there were a global matriarchy, you know, there would be no more of this evil" (Mann, 1997, 9). The realistic drama settled for Mann disturbing issues she had first heard about upon her introduction to anti-Semitism in the second grade. In 1980 Mann pursued living testimony with *Still Life,* a wrenching drama performed by three players, Mark, a Vietnam veteran and wife beater; his wife, Cheryl; and Nadine, his middle-aged mistress. Of the chaotic feelings generated by combat Mark admits that his emotions are typically male. He adds, "I don't know what it would be for women. What war is for men. I've thought about it. A lot" (*ibid.,* 45). In response to Mark's obsession with reliving the war, Cheryl acknowledges a male need: "Doesn't it kill you when they get into this men-talk?" (*ibid.,* 61). For its depth and candor the play garnered six Obies.

Mann dedicates her writings to humanistic concerns. She turned to American court scenarios for *Execution of Justice* (1984), a bold denunciation of the trial that exonerated the homophobe Dan White for murdering two gay officials, the city supervisor, Harvey Milk, and the San Francisco mayor, George Moscone. The public shooting that erupted in 1978 killed Milk, then aged 48. With the play's opening in New York City, Mann became the first woman to direct her own work on Broadway. The play won a Women's Committee of the Dramatists Guild award, a Drama Desk nomination, and a Burns Mantle Yearbook Best Plays citation.

Near the end of the 20th century Mann focused on women's liberation. She documented black feminism for a rhythm and blues opera based on Ntozake SHANGE's *Betsey Brown* (1989) with music by Baikida Carroll. Mann crafted a retrospective two-woman dialogue from Annie Elizabeth "Bessie" DELANY and Sarah Louise Delany's *Having Our Say: The Delany Sisters' First 100 Years* (1994), which won the Hull-Warriner Award, two Joseph Jefferson Awards, and a Tony Award for Outstanding Regional Theater. The play ran successfully in 1998 at the Market Theatre in Johannesburg, South Africa. For the CBS-TV version, which aired in April 1999, Mann won a Peabody Award for the teleplay.

Mann extended her range with additions to a canon already admired for its denunciation of racism and sexism. In 1996 she interviewed a Ku Klux Klansman and anti-Klan activists in preparation for the writing of *Greensboro: A Requiem* (1996), a retrospect on a massacre that occurred in the downtown area on November 3, 1979. The clash pitted Ku Klux Klansmen and American Nazis against members of an anti-Klan demonstration. Her play, originally titled *To Know a Monster,* recreates the chaos that followed a Ku Klux Klan rally, resulting in the murders of five antiracism demonstrators and wounding of 11 others. The text features a lengthy monologue by the white supremicist David Duke. In 1999 she translated Federico García Lorca's *The House of Bernarda Alba: A Drama about Women in Villages of Spain,* which echoes female wisdom about sexism in the aphorism "Needle and thread for the woman, whip and mule for the man. That's how it is for people born to certain obligations" (Mann, *House,* 10).

Bibliography

Brustein, Robert. "Women in the Theater," *New Republic,* 15 May 2000, pp. 32–34.

Istel, John. "Emily Mann," *American Theatre* 13, no. 2 (February 1996): 44–45.

Mann, Emily. *Having Our Say: The Delany Sisters' First 100 Years.* New York: Dramatists Play Service, 1998.

———, trans. *The House of Bernarda Alba* by Federico García Lorca. New York: Dramatist's Play Service, 1998.

———. *Testimonies: Four Plays.* New York: Theatre Communications Group, 1997.

Mansfield, Katherine (1888–1923)

The New Zealand fiction writer, diarist, letter writer, and essayist Kathleen "Katherine" Mansfield Beauchamp created epiphanies that revealed to innocent female characters the confines and perils of the gendered social order. Born to affluence in Wellington, she learned in girlhood how to withdraw from social interaction and to observe its nuances in words, gestures, and facial expressions. She was educated at Wellington Girls' High School and at Miss Swainson's School, an elite private academy. In 1903 Mansfield and her two sisters studied music at Queens College in London. After a short stint at Wellington Technical College to learn typing and shorthand she moved permanently to London at age 20, to absorb the bohemian freedom of the NEW WOMAN. Her mother took charge after Mansfield's failed marriage by escorting her to a German resort for cold water treatments to rid her of lesbian love for Ida Baker. The brusque plunges caused Mansfield to miscarry her only child.

The author initiated a career in freelance short fiction and critical essay writing for *Athenaeum*, *Blue Review*, *New Age*, *Rhythm*, and *Signature*. Although not a declared suffragist, she displayed feminist sensibilities in a bus altercation, as a result of which she was ejected for rebuking a woman who stated that she wished that all female activists could be trampled by horses. At age 23 Mansfield published her first collected short stories, *In a German Pension: 13 Stories* (1911), a defiantly feminist anthology. The opening narrative, "Germans at Meat," contrasts the ideals of family life in a naive young British wife with the truth according to a German widow with nine children. The pushy German ridicules the vegetarian Englishwoman as being too wrapped up in feminism to tolerate pregnancy and childbirth: "You never have large families in England now; I suppose you are too busy with your suffragetting" (Mansfield, 1941, 38). Filling Mansfield with unease was the reality of war that caused her brother, Leslie's, death in an explosion in France. She incubated her antiwar hostility and later expressed it in a dialect story, "The Fly" (1922), a depiction of the lingering grief of losing a child to battle. At the close of World War I she resided in Cornwall and France to ease hemorrhaging from tuberculosis that killed her at age 35.

Critics credit Mansfield with modernizing the short story. After publishing vital, arresting vignettes in *Bliss and Other Stories* (1920), she anthologized an English classic, *The Garden Party and Other Stories* (1922), an autobiographical collection containing her signature characters, young and untried girls. The author's feminist themes explore women's use of SEXUALITY and their biological dependence on men, as she exposes in the weak mother in "At the Bay." In "The Singing Lesson" mood swings in a fragile music teacher cast her into despair until her lover relieves her anxiety with a new pledge of devotion. More chilling is "Miss Brill," a character study of a lonely single woman who realizes that a pair of young lovers are mocking her solitude. The title story satirizes the compassionless upper class through the sensitivity of Laura Sheridan, a young girl drawn from the family lawn party to the death of a worker and to the need for his widow to support five children.

Bibliography

Mansfield, Katherine. *Bliss and Other Stories* (1920). Available online: URL: http://digital.library.upenn.edu/women/mansfield/bliss/bliss.html. Accessed on October 16, 2005.

———. *The Garden Party and Other Stories* (1922). Available online: URL: http://digital.library.upenn.edu/women/mansfield/garden/garden.html. Accessed on October 13, 2005.

———. *The Short Stories of Katherine Mansfield*. New York: Knopf, 1941.

Moran, Patricia. "Unholy Meanings: Maternity, Creativity, and Orality in Katherine Mansfield," *Feminist Studies* 17, no. 1 (Spring 1991): 105–125.

Smith, Angela. *Katherine Mansfield: A Literary Life*. London: Macmillan, 2000.

Maria, or The Wrongs of Woman
Mary Wollstonecraft (1798)

At the time of Mary WOLLSTONECRAFT's death she left incomplete a psychological novel, *Maria; or, The Wrongs of Woman* (1798), which her husband, the author William Godwin, published posthumously. A milestone of feminist literature, the melodrama is the first to replace hackneyed castles and dungeons as Gothic settings with a mental institution. By nesting stories about distressed and confined women, the work explodes fictional STEREOTYPING and supplants false impressions of women with believable human figures. The plot features the gloom of Maria Venables after her alcoholic husband, George, drugs her and abandons her to solitary CONFINEMENT in a madhouse. Grieved by false information about her child's death, Maria faces a charge of adultery before a judge who surmises that "if women were allowed to plead their feelings, as an excuse or palliation of infidelity, it was opening a flood-gate for immorality" (Wollstonecraft, II, 155). She survives an overdose of laudanum, her escape from "this hell of disappointment" (*ibid.*). Her mind retreats from suffering to delusions of an all-female society.

Wollstonecraft's text focuses on the androcentric control of a traumatized woman. In the preface she explains her purpose "of exhibiting the misery and oppression, peculiar to women, that arise out of the partial laws and customs of society" (*ibid.*, 1). Manacled and secluded from visitors, Maria sees only her physician and the matron, Jemima, a patient, understanding attendant who urges Maria to eat and who smuggles her messages to another inmate. Jemima confides the seduction of her own mother and her father's abandonment of Jemima to a poor wet nurse. Although supportive, Jemima's experiences convince Maria that male-dominated society jeopardizes women's sanity and lives. Sense impressions from the decaying hospital turrets and a small grated window and from the songs and shrieks of madwomen drive Maria further toward lunacy.

Wollstonecraft's intense fiction protests barbarism toward women through accounts of ABORTION, abusive foster care, entrapment, forced labor, homelessness, kidnap, PROSTITUTION, and rape. Maria's story expands on the miseries that Jemima endured with details of the unspeakable cruelties of a carousing, womanizing husband. Maria justifies her loss of interest in personal grooming and her revulsion toward marital sex with a man reeking of alcohol: "The squeamishness of stomach alone, produced by the last night's intemperance, which he took no pains to conceal, destroyed my appetite" (*ibid.*, II, 13–14). Of flight

from his stalking Maria describes herself as "hunted out like a felon" and ultimately buried alive in a cell (*ibid.*, II, 84). She turns to readings of John Dryden's *Guiscard and Sigismunda*, John Milton's *Paradise Lost*, and Jean-Jacques Rousseau's *La nouvelle Heloise* (1761), an epistolary novel based on two lovers' tender correspondence, which contrasts with the reality of marriage that Maria has known. The theme of matrilineage depicts the mother, freighted with the mistakes of her youth, as transmitter of culture and of woman-to-woman warnings to daughters about misery and tyranny. Similarly linked are the women who attest to Wollstonecraft's value to future writers, notably Elizabeth Barrett BROWNING, Donna CROSS, Voltairine DE CLEYRE, Margaret FULLER, Emma GOLDMAN, Lorraine HANSBERRY, Anne RICE, Elaine SHOWALTER, Elizabeth Cady STANTON, and Wollstonecraft's daughter, Mary SHELLEY.

Bibliography

Cosslett, Tess, "Maria, or the Wrongs of Woman," *Notes and Queries* 42, no. 4 (December 1995): 502.

Hoeveler, Diane Long. "Reading the Wound: Wollstonecraft's 'Wrongs of Women; or, Maria' and Trauma Theory," *Studies in the Novel* 31, no. 4 (Winter 1999): 387.

Wollstonecraft, Mary. *Maria; or, The Wrongs of Woman* (1797). Available online: URL: http://etext.lib.virginia.edu/etcbin/browse-mixed-new?id=WolMari&images=images/modeng&data=/lv1/Archive/eng-parsed&tag=public. Accessed on October 16, 2005.

Marie de France (fl. ca. 1160–1190)

A mid-medieval fabulist, Marie de France proposed alternative views to the feudal stereotype of women. Unique in her time, she was an educated writer who pioneered subtle, psychologically ambiguous verse suited to the era. In a collection of 12 *lais* dedicated to an unidentified noble monarch around the mid-1160s she combined Breton tales with singable verse romances probably suited to the tastes of an English court. Unlike the sunny folk songs of the period, she enhanced courtly romance with the emotional conflicts of dissatisfied characters and produced an anomaly, Le Fraisne, a woman who knows what she wants and is willing to defy society by demanding a loving husband. Her name is a pun on *le frein,* the French term for bridle or halter. Late in her poetic career Marie de France issued a translation, *L'Espurgatoire de Seint Patriz* (*St. Patrick's Purgatory,* ca. 1189), a Latin narrative poem picturing Owein, the Irish adventurer, broaching the pit of hell in search of redemption. Some critics also add to her canon a biography of Seinte Audrée (Saint Audrey), a seventh-century paragon who maintained her virginity throughout her marriage.

A biographical enigma, Marie was a multilingual Norman residing at the court of Henry II, where she enjoyed the company of Gascon adventurers and the entertainment of itinerant gleemen. Her writings attest to her knowledge of Aesop, Ovid's *Metamorphoses,* the Roman fables of Phaedrus and Romulus, the *Panchatantra,* Old French romance, and Anglo-Norman poetry. Although she was well known and was befriended by the epicist Chrétien de Troyes, she successfully hid her true name under a pseudonym. By way of introduction her 102 verse fables, *L'Ysopet* (The Aesop collection), completed around 1189, name the author only as Marie from France, a pen name destined to survive to modern times. She remained unmarried by choice and claimed to work late into the night at scholarly tasks usually denied to females. Literary biographers surmise that she retired, perhaps to a convent, around 1190.

The poet fulfilled a didactic purpose in resetting standard lore to suit her outlook on the feudal period. She satirizes knights and clerics as fools and charlatans. In contrast her women are assertive and crafty, for example, the pregnant pig who protects her unborn brood in "The Wolf and the Sow." One of Marie's WISEWOMEN, the pragmatic widow in "The Widow Who Hanged Her Husband," values a live lover over a dead mate. In the fable "The Mouse and the Frog" Marie gives strength to the propertied mouse mother, who takes pride in controlling her own store of grain; "The Fox and the Bear" stresses sympathy for a rape victim. Marie portrays a mother as capable of defending her young in "The Wolf and the Sow" and lauds a self-assured female squabbler in "The

Peasant and His Contrary Wife" as the intellectual equal of her mate.

The poet's feisty females manage their own love affairs in a matched pair of fabliaux, "The Peasant Who Saw Another with His Wife" and "The Peasant Who Saw His Wife with Her Lover," which ridicule husbands as dolts. In defiance of church misogyny Marie produced "The Hermit and the Peasant," which charges the male for sin while exonerating EVE of causing the fall of humankind. Rather than glorify the classic deities, Marie makes a stronger pro-woman statement by replacing male gods with the feminine abstracts of Creativity, Fate, Wisdom, and *la deuesse* [the goddess], the All-Mother.

Bibliography

Barban, Judith. "Lai Ester: Acceptance of the Status Quo in the Fables of Marie de France," *Romance Quarterly* 49, no. 1 (Winter 2002): 3–11.

Cowell, Andrew. "Deadly Letters: 'Deus Amanz,' Marie's 'Prologue' to the Lais and the Dangerous Nature of the Gloss," *Romanic Review* 88, no. 3 (May 1997): 337–363.

Hurtig, Dolliann Margaret. " 'I Do, I Do': Medieval Models of Marriage and Choice of Partners in Marie de France's 'Le Fraisne,' " *Romanic Review* 92, no. 4 (November 2001): 363–379.

McCash, June Hall. "La Vie Seinte Audrée: A Fourth Text by Marie de France?" *Speculum* 77, no. 3 (July 2002): 744–777.

Markham, Beryl (1902–1986)

The English autobiographer, essayist, horse trainer, and aviator Beryl Clutterbuck Markham set an example of the self-assured female achiever. Born in Leicester, she grew up among Boer settlers in the British colony of Kenya on Ndimu Farm. At Njoro, 70 miles from white culture in Nairobi, she learned from Maruni children to speak Masai, Nandi, and Swahili. Through her intimacy with natives, she discovered a tribal society that refused young women the gender freedoms and privileges that she enjoyed. Unlike Kenyan girls confined to domestic chores, she was adept at riding horseback, tracking zebra and water buffalo, spear hunting barefoot for warthogs and lions, and skinning the kill. In 1915 she boarded for five semesters at Miss Seccombe's School in Nairobi. By age 17 she lived on her own while her father made a new start in Peru. Of INDEPENDENCE she exulted, "I learned to wander. I learned what every dreaming child should know—that no horizon is so far that you cannot get above it or beyond it" (Markham, 1983, 185).

Markham established a series of firsts. In 1920 she became the first female to hold an English Jockey Club license in horse training. As did her father, she managed a horse-breeding farm and advised buyers on animal strength and agility. After becoming the first female commercial pilot, she flew short commercial hops into the bush in her Gypsy Moth to deliver mail, gold-mining supplies, and passengers. Headquartered at the Muthaiga Country Club, she also aided safaris by scanning the region for elephants. At age 34 she made history by soloing a single-engine plane in a nonstop east-west crossing of the Atlantic Ocean. The risky flight in her Vega Gull called *The Messenger* took her against the prevailing wind from London to Cape Breton, Nova Scotia. She nosedived into a peat bog and was briefly unconscious after knocking her forehead against the steering mechanism. After a ticker tape parade in New York City she accepted an offer from Paramount Pictures to advise producers on the filming of stunt flying.

Markham surprised her detractors by publishing autobiographical stories on horse racing and aviation in *Argosy*, *Collier's*, *Ladies Home Journal*, and *Saturday Evening Post*. A posthumous collection, *The Splendid Outcast: Beryl Markham's African Stories* (1988), features eight tales about her life in Kenya. One first-person story, "The Splendid Outcast" (1944), describes the author's untamed spirit and her acceptance of life beyond the pale of genteel society. The joy of a cockpit suggests her delight in rising above social boundaries to look down on East Africa. She later exulted, "I fly high—south-southwest, over the Ngong Hills. I am relaxed. My right hand rests upon the stick in easy communication with the will and the way of the plane" (*ibid.*, 16). Out of reach in the clouds she felt the bonds of Earth loosened and her spirit free of the delimiting customs that burdened other European women.

Markham's best-selling memoir, *West with the Night* (1942), edited by her scenarist husband, Raoul Schumacher, earned popular fame. Reviewers for the *Nation* and the *Washington Post Book World* praised the narration for its depiction of an active, pacesetting woman. Of the continent she declared, "Africa is mystic. It is wild; it is a sweltering inferno. . . . It is all of these things but one thing—it is never dull" (*ibid.*, 8). One of her serial adventures involved the rescue of a seriously ill flier whose plane crashed on the Serengeti Plain. With a mature point of view she described an insider's experience with the dwindling colonial empire during a famine, when whites drank champagne while Kikuyu starved. Her autobiography regained its earlier popularity after its rediscovery in 1982. Two films document Markham's place in women's history: *World without Walls: Beryl Markham's African Memoir* (1986) for PBS-TV and *Shadow on the Sun* (1988), an ETV biopic starring Stephanie Powers.

Bibliography

Markham, Beryl. *The Splendid Outcast: Beryl Markham's African Stories*. San Francisco: North Point, 1987.

———. *West with the Night*. San Francisco: North Point, 1983.

Trzebinski, Errol. *The Lives of Beryl Markham*. New York: W. W. Norton, 1993.

Yiannopoulou, Effie. "Autistic Adventures: Love, Auto-Portraiture, and White Women's Colonial Disease," *European Journal of English Studies* 2, no. 3 (December 1998): 324–342.

marriage market

A common theme in feminist literature is the "marketing" of young girls and women into wedlock, a jarring concept implying no escape. Men shop for women as enhancements to male wealth, DYNASTY, political aspirations, or prestige, an arrangement that Chief Tata Ndu, a polygynist and wife beater, proposes to the Price family for their blonde teenager, Rachel, in Barbara KINGSOLVER's *The Poisonwood Bible* (2000). The offer carries a customary stipulation, that Rachel undergo FEMALE GENITAL MUTILATION, a folk surgery to reduce her to a female eunuch. With similar clarity

Mary CHESNUT, the South's most prominent diarist of the 1860s, expressed the similarity between white wives and black slaves, neither of whom were empowered to decide their own destiny. She commiserated with black women on Charleston's famed auction block: "You know how women sell themselves and are sold in marriage from queens downward. . . . Poor women, poor slaves" (Chesnut, 10–11).

The motif of the pawning and trading of women has earned some of feminist literature's most passionate revolts against PATRIARCHY. A sharp rebuttal of a father's right to auction his daughter as he would a prize race horse is that of Sybil, Louisa May ALCOTT's rebel in "A Whisper in the Dark" (1863), one of her most woman-centered narratives. The unwilling bride charges her uncle with trickery and proclaims: "What right had my father to mate me in the cradle?. . . . No! I'll not be bargained away like a piece of merchandise, but love and marry when I please!" (Alcott, 40). For her refusal, her uncle consigns her to an asylum, the stereotypical punishment for headstrong women in GOTHIC FICTION.

As forerunners of the NEW WOMAN, characters created by female writers refused to go meekly and quietly to the altar. The abolitionist and novelist E. D. E. N. SOUTHWORTH condemned 19th-century America for its cavalier attitude toward women's right to a loving union. In the preface to a domestic novel, *The Deserted Wife* (1850), the author laments: "In no other civilized country in the world is marriage contracted, or dissolved, with such culpable levity as in our own. In no other civilized country can divorce be obtained with such facility, and upon such slight grounds" (Southworth, 23). Less critical is the polite observation about women's false assumptions about wedlock by the English novelist Elizabeth GASKELL in her witty novel *Wives and Daughters* (1866). During the fervid preparation for a marriage she notes, "So apt are people to look forward to a different kind of life from that to which they have been accustomed as being free from care and trial" (Gaskell, 175). The subtext alerts the unwary bride-to-be to troubles that single women avoid.

The Caribbean novelist Jean RHYS describes the souring of an arranged marriage in *WIDE SAR-* *GASSO SEA* (1966), in which the Englishman Edward Rochester arranges with male family members to wed an island heiress, Antoinette Cosway. In reference to her fortune he misinterprets the eyes of the house staff and chortles to himself, "Why should they pity me. I who have done so well for myself?" (Rhys, 77). To him the bargain is a male-to-male transaction; Antoinette's future is a casual afterthought. As though completing the purchase of livestock, he admits: "The thirty thousand pounds have been paid to me without question or condition. No provision made for her (that must be seen to)" (ibid., 70). It is the elderly Aunt Cora who goes to the bride's defense and accuses Richard Mason, the woman's half brother, of "handing over everything the child owns to a perfect stranger" (ibid., 114). Cora charges, "You are trusting him with her life, not yours" (ibid., 115).

A classic work, the Venezuelan feminist Teresa de la Parra's *Iphigenia: The Diary of a Young Girl Who Wrote Because She Was Bored* (1924) denounces the humiliating brokerage of a girl made penniless by her uncle's theft of her inheritance. She describes the protagonist, Maria Eugenia Alonso's, shock after she travels from her home in Paris to Caracas, Venezuela, where an Old World grandmother works out a suitable marriage. The grandmother moves quickly to barter the dewy loveliness of her granddaughter to a man who can offer financial INDEPENDENCE. The subtext pictures the degrading social convention of posing marriageable girls in the front window as luxury goods are displayed to advantage before shoppers. Ultimately Parra's protagonist falls prey to forced wedlock to an egotistical male who commercializes a Catholic sacrament as though it were a business deal. The uproar that followed the publication of *Iphigenia* charged the author with undermining the morals of young women throughout the Hispanic world and with encouraging unbridled passion and bohemianism.

According to feminist writers, women who live for marriage and preen themselves for a proposal may realize that they have bartered away self. Susan Fromberg Schaeffer's "Wedding Ring Poem" (1984) sees the hidden discontent in eyelashes cloaking an angry gaze. In Kathleen Norris's poem "The Bride" (1989) the unwed girl resembles a piñata swung at by men until her belly spews wedding finery and the inner bounty to feed guests, husband, and children. Toi Derricotte's "Doll Poem" (1989) imagines the doll-perfect newlywed reduced to housewifely list making and to an existence that is immaculate. For the sake of marriage and appearances the female abandons her humanity to become a paragon.

Bibliography

Alcott, Louisa May. *The Portable Louisa May Alcott.* New York: Penguin, 2000.

Chesnut, Mary Boykin. *A Diary from Dixie.* Boston: Houghton Mifflin, 1949.

Gaskell, Elizabeth. *Wives and Daughters.* London: Penguin, 2001.

Mazer, Norma Fox, and Marjorie Lewis, eds. *Waltzing on Water.* New York: Dell, 1989.

Rhys, Jean. *Wide Sargasso Sea.* New York: W. W. Norton, 1982.

Schaeffer, Susan Fromberg. *Granite Lady.* New York: Colllier Books, 1984.

Southworth, E. D. E. N. *The Deserted Wife.* Philadelphia: T. B. Peterson, 1875.

Valis, Noël, and Carol Maier, eds. *In the Feminine Mode: Essays on Hispanic Women Writers.* Lewisburg, Pa.: Bucknell University Press, 1990.

Marshall, Paule (1929–)

An innovator of Caribbean immigrant fiction, Valenza Pauline "Paule" Burke Marshall is a spokeswoman for biculturalism and female empowerment. The daughter of Barbadian immigrants, Ada and Samuel Burke, Marshall lived in a tight-knit Caribbean community in her native Brooklyn. She read classic authors at the public library and profited from the STORYTELLING of devalued maids and janitors who bore the oral traditions of the West Indies, Africa, and the American South; she remarked in an article for *Writer* that these working-class immigrant women "used language to assert that sense of self. Language for them was not only an artistic expression, but it was also a kind of weapon" (Marshall, 2002, 66). As the author developed her own narrative skills, she viewed the oral tradition as a form of empowerment, a refuge, and an outlet for creative drive.

With a degree from Brooklyn College in 1953 Marshall became the first female researcher-writer for *Our World,* for which she accepted assignments to Grenada, Carriacou, and Brazil. She completed candid autobiographical fiction, *Brown Girl, Brownstones* (1959), her entrée into teaching jobs at Columbia University, Yale University, and the University of Iowa. The dialect story of Selina Boyce epitomizes the woman's ability to compromise by ignoring her mother's materialism. She rebels with a shout, "I'm me. Selina. And there's nothing wrong with my heart" (Marshall, 1981, 47). She discloses her uniqueness while enjoying sensual dance and the passions of a developing body. The theme of female rejuvenation resurges in *Soul Clap Hands and Sing* (1961), four short novels about soulless males who look to female passion and love of life as a new start.

The overriding theme of Marshall's writings is the value of reclaiming family roots and past loves. After publishing *The Chosen Place, the Timeless People* (1969), an overview of racism among Afro-Caribbean islanders, she turned to matrilineage, the focus of *Praisesong for the Widow* (1983). The text gains tension from the restlessness and spiritual aridity of Avey Johnson, a well-off black American traveler. As the female culture bearer, at age 65 she retraces the Afro-American diaspora by journeying to the Caribbean isles of her girlhood to restore communion with patois, songs, juba dances, jests, foodways, and memories that African slaves took with them over the Middle Passage to the New World. With *Daughters* (1991) Marshall invests more character development in dramatizing the ambivalence and shifting loyalties of Ursa Beatrice MacKenzie, an Afro-Caribbean parvenu with one foot in New York City and another in the islands. The bicultural paradigm reflects women's ability to take the best of both worlds without sacrificing integrity. Marshall's great-hearted prose inspired the novelist Gloria NAYLOR.

Bibliography

Dingledine, Donald. "Woman Can Walk on Water: Island, Myth, and Community in Kate Chopin's *The Awakening* and Paule Marshall's *Praisesong for the Widow,*" *Women's Studies* 22, no. 2 (March 1993): 197–216.

Ferguson, Moira. "Of Bears and Bearings: Paule Marshall's Diverse Daughters," *MELUS* 24, no. 1 (Spring 1999): 177–195.

Marshall, Paule. *Brown Girl, Brownstones*. New York: Feminist Press, 1981.

———. *Daughters*. New York: Athenaeum, 1991.

———. "Paule Marshall," *Writer* 115, no. 9 (September 2002): 66.

———. *Praisesong for the Widow*. New York: E. P. Dutton, 1983.

Martineau, Harriet (1802–1876)

Through astute essays, lectures, travelogues, and fiction the English writer Harriet Martineau, the first female sociologist, hammered at injustice in America, a land that boasted of its democracy. Born of Huguenot ancestry in Norwich, she suffered deafness in childhood that worsened as she aged. She was homeschooled in Greek, Latin, French, German, Italian, mathematics, and religion before studying at a boarding academy in Bristol. At age 19 she submitted an essay, "Female Writers of Practical Divinity" (1821), to the Unitarian *Monthly Repository*, but she restricted her writing from family view by working at her desk only in the morning. After her father died and the family cloth factory failed in 1829, she gave up primness and earned a living with subsequent publications, including the essay "On Female Education" (1823) and the 25-volume *Illustrations of Political Economy* (1832–33). Undismayed by the family calamity, she relished an economic and professional freedom that was uncommon among Englishwomen in a patriarchal society. She enjoyed the notoriety of a best-selling author of 50 volumes published over a half-century.

After a two-year sojourn in the United States to bolster her health, Martineau wrote *Society in America: Observations Made during a Stay in 1837* (1837), a major feminist and abolitionist treatise, which influenced the feminist philosophy of Margaret FULLER. Martineau commented on the denigration of female citizens: "While woman's intellect is confined, her morals crusted, her health ruined, her weaknesses encouraged, and her strength punished, she is told that her lot is cast in the paradise of women" (Martineau, 1837). In the author's estimation, women's lot compared to that of slaves, unfortunates she saw firsthand in Baltimore, Charleston, Charlottesville, and New Orleans. She described their pitiable state as "inconsistent with the law of God" and as a "national disgrace" (Martineau, 1877, 351, 357). Because of her outspoken charges against slavers she received death threats and traveled under surveillance by the Southern press and Northern abolitionists. A year after publication her book provoked the Charleston-born poet and historian William Gilmore Simms to write *Slavery in America: Being a Brief Review of Miss Martineau on That Subject* (1838), which not only vilified Martineau's ideas but also derided her deafness and her unmarried status.

The text of *Society in America* develops some of the ideas proposed in Mary WOLLSTONECRAFT's social prospectus *A Vindication of the Rights of Women* (1792). Some 45 years later Martineau launched a reasoned argument against sexism based on the writings of Thomas Jefferson and the framers of U.S. freedoms: "One of the fundamental principles announced in the Declaration of Independence is that governments derive their just powers from the consent of the governed. How can the political condition of women be reconciled with this?" (*ibid.*). Her pointed question summarized an undercurrent of discontent about the inequities forced on female citizens: They could be fined, imprisoned, and executed but could make no impact on unfair legislation. In her estimation American women were politically nonexistent. In part because of the reaction to Martineau's criticisms, shift from coverture—the body of laws governing married women—began in Mississippi in 1839, when legislators relaxed male powers over wives to give them control of their wages and property and to allow them to execute contracts, lawsuits, and wills.

Later in her career Martineau wrote in a variety of modes, including a research manual, *How to Observe Manners and Morals* (1838), and children's stories in *The Playfellow* (1841), the first children's works to feature social problems in fictional scenarios. She published a popular travelogue, *A Retrospect of Western Travel* (1838), in which she commented on American universities, prisons and asylums, disabled people, the plantation system, ABOLITIONISM, and SLAVERY. She turned to domestic fiction for two novels, *Deerbrook* (1839) and *The Hour and the Man* (1841), and to journalism with feminist articles favoring women's EDUCATION and SUFFRAGE for the London *Daily News*, *Edinburgh Review*, *Household Words*, *Tait's Edinburgh Magazine*, and the *Westminster Review*. After five years as an invalid as a result of an ovarian cyst she wrote *Life in the Sickroom* (1844) and praised a mind cure in "Letter on Mesmerism" (1845), published in the *Athenaeum*. After considerable work on *History of England during the Thirty Years' Peace 1816–1846* (1849–50) and on translations of the philosophy of Auguste Comte, she composed a three-volume *Autobiography* (1855), which itemizes her confrontations with American slave holders. She reprised her arguments against slavery in *A History of American Compromises* (1856), a collection of her writings for the *Daily News*, which extended from 1851 to 1866. Issued posthumously was a series of 46 portraits of personal acquaintances in *Biographical Sketches* (1877), including sketches of the novelist Charlotte BRONTË and Queen Victoria. After the women's liberation movement Martineau's works returned to academic favor, particularly among women's studies scholars, sociologists, and Unitarians.

Bibliography

Hill, Michael R., Susan Hoecker-Drysdale, and Helena Z. Lopata. *Harriet Martineau: Theoretical and Methodological Perspectives*. New York: Routledge, 2001.

Martineau, Harriet. *Harriet Martineau's Autobiography* (1877). Available online: URL: http://www.indiana.edu/~letrs/vwwp/martineau/martineau1.html. Accessed on October 13, 2005.

———. *Retrospect of Western Travel*. Armonk, N.Y.: M. E. Sharpe, 2000.

———. *Society in America: Observations Made during a Stay in 1837* (1837). Available online: URL: http://xroads.virginia.edu/~HYPER/DETOC/fem/martineau.htm. Accessed on October 16, 2005.

Marxist feminism

One branch of feminist literature derives from writers who integrate class and gender issues along with worker's rights, unionism, and social reform. Feminists influenced by the leftist philosophies of Harriet Taylor MILL and her husband, John Stuart MILL; by the Scots-American reformist orator and editor Frances WRIGHT; and by Marx's doctrine and Frederick Engels's *The Origin of Family, Private Property, and the State* (1884) include a number of American socialists. They foresaw the destruction of capitalism and the dismantling of discriminatory EDUCATION policies as the beginnings of revolutionary change in women's lives. The social theorist Charlotte Perkins GILMAN supported equitable remuneration for labor in *Woman and Economics: A Study of the Economic Relation between Men and Women as a Factor in Social Evolution* (1898). In *The Man-Made World; or, Our Androcentric Culture* (1911), she branched out to imaginative methods of relieving women who did more than a fair share of drudgery.

Women energized Marxism by directing its assumptions toward more of the population. The famed socialist orator "Red Emma" Goldman founded the subversive periodical *Mother Earth* in 1906 as an outlet for radical essays on WOMEN'S RIGHTS, birth control, and PROSTITUTION. Another speaker, Voltairine DE CLEYRE, described in "The Making of an Anarchist" (1914) the corrupt religious training that turned her from Catholicism to socialism. She also defended Goldman's right to challenge capitalism and religious hypocrisy in regard to the sex trade, a bone of contention that the male clergy and legislators used as a wedge against women's demand for full citizenship.

In other parts of the world Marxism was a welcome partner to feminism. De Cleyre's British colleague, the radical activist Sylvia Pankhurst, edited *Women's Dreadnought*, a journal demanding fair treatment of female factory workers. In South Africa the socialist journalist and fiction writer Olive SCHREINER campaigned against capitalism and produced *Woman and Labour* (1911). In the opening salvo she dramatizes the need for economic INDEPENDENCE as "the choice between finding new forms of labour or sinking slowly into a condition of more or less complete and passive *sexparasitism*" (Schreiner, 1). For models she compares needy females to ticks and termites. Her depiction of the female termite is particularly grotesque— "she has entirely lost the power of locomotion; she can no longer provide herself or her offspring with nourishment, or defend or even clean herself, she has become a mere passive, distended, bag of eggs" (*ibid.*).

In the 1920s and 1930s Marxist-feminist ideas focused on the destabilization of the home and nuclear family caused by sexism. Margaret SANGER issued two monthly journals, *The Woman Rebel*, and in 1921 the *Birth Control Review*. Simultaneously she published the 10-cent pamphlet *What Every Girl Should Know* and *The Pivot of Civilization* (1922), a formal manifesto aimed at liberating women from male control for the good of humankind. Suzanne LAFOLLETTE, creator of the journal *New Freeman*, published a liberatarian text, *Concerning Women* (1926), that demanded that women take charge of their lives, children, and careers. The journalist Meridel LE SUEUR, a follower of Goldman, Mother Jones, Helen KELLER, and Sanger, published socialist-feminist essays in the *Daily Worker, Dial, Nation*, and *New Masses*. Josephine HERBST, a political writer for the *New Masses* and the *Nation*, examined similar territory in a three-part saga, *Pity Is Not Enough* (1933), *The Executioner Waits* (1934), and *Rope of Gold* (1939), which describes the androcentrism of capitalism and the resultant diminution of women. In 1932 Herbst's contemporary, Tillie OLSEN, began work on the autobiographical socialist text *Yonnondio: From the Thirties* (1974), which influenced a number of late 20th-century feminists. Among them, Angela DAVIS aroused major controversy with her strident speeches and writings championing nonwhite women and ghetto dwellers, including prison memoirs in *If They Come in the Morning* (1971), Black Power strategies in *Angela Davis: An Autobiography* (1974), and socialist articles for *Critical Inquiry, Essence, Nation*, and *Social Justice*.

Marxism helped define the gap between democratic ideals and the politics of exclusion. The Parisian writer and activist Simone WEIL exemplified the Marxist purist in her reform efforts and in *Oppression et liberté* (*Oppression and Liberty*, 1955), a discussion of her reformist philosophy published posthumously. The French feminist Simone DE BEAUVOIR merged socialism with existential philosophy in *The SECOND SEX* (1949), a thorough breakdown of factors contributing to the devaluation of women. The Canadian-American feminist theoretician and social critic Shulamith FIRESTONE compiled *Notes from the First Year*, a left-wing journal of essays and speeches from the women's liberation movement. Her first political manifesto on women's rights, *The Dialectics of Sex: The Case for Feminist Revolution* (1970), urged women to shake off the romantic notions that began in the Middle Ages and to demolish a government that withholds full citizenship.

While university departments of economics, history, literature, philosophy, social science, and religion wrangled over a clear definition of feminism, scholars struggled to identify a political consciousness that offered a fair vision of the future for women. Central to the ongoing plight of women worldwide were curricula that reflected the GENDER BIAS of the past and the obligation of societies to acknowledge female equality. Endangering this ongoing discussion was the degree of disruption and anarchy that Marxist feminists demanded as an antidote to sexism. Contributing to the ferment were the writings of the English scholar Sheila ROWBOTHAM, particularly *Women's Liberation and New Politics* (1971), *Women's Consciousness, Man's World* (1973), and *Hidden from History: 300 Years of Women's Oppression and the Fight against It* (1973), a condemnation of centuries of female enslavement and inequitable division of property. Left unsettled at the end of the 20th century were issues pitting the suppression of pornography against First Amendment rights to free speech and the arrest and fining or jailing of sex workers versus their right to sell their favors without hindrance or government regulation. A broader issue, the sanctioning of gay marriage and families through the adoption or fostering of children, paired gay men and lesbians in a crusade for an equal role in communities.

Bibliography

Bryson, Valerie. "Marxism and Feminism: Can the 'Unhappy Marriage' Be Saved," *Journal of Political Ideologies* 9, no. 1 (February 2004): 13–30.

Hennessy, Rosemary. *Materialist Feminism and the Politics of Discourse*. New York: Routledge, 1993.

Schreiner, Olive. *Woman and Labour* (1911). Available online: URL: http://etext.library.adelaide.edu.au/s/schreiner_o/woman/woman.html. Accessed on October 13, 2005.

Mason, Bobbie Ann (1940–)

The southern fiction writer and feminist critic Bobbie Ann Mason characterizes the impact of the media and of social change on women's self-definition. Raised on a dairy farm in western Kentucky near Mayfield, she recognized early the connection between freedom and home base: "We've been free to roam, because we've always known where home is" (Mason, 2000, 13). Of her readings of the Bobbsey twins, Honey Bunch, and Nancy Drew novels, she later composed *The Girl Sleuth: A Feminist Guide to the Bobbsey Twins, Nancy Drew, and Their Sisters* (1975), a survey of young adult detection fiction that influences girls to venture beyond safe, but demeaning boundaries. Mason fled a rural upbringing to study journalism at the University of Kentucky. While working in New York City on the staffs of movie magazines, she interviewed teen stars of the era of Fabian and Annette Funicello. Mason suffered regrets for laboring in a shallow field and admitted, "I knew I wanted sanity and clarity, and I knew I didn't want to waste my life" (ibid., 138). She completed a doctorate in literature at the University of Connecticut. While writing a dissertation, she composed *Nabokov's Garden: A Nature Guide to Ada* (1974).

Mason dedicated her career to short and long fiction, beginning with submissions to the *Atlantic, Double Take, New Yorker, Ploughshares, Redbook, Southern Review,* and *Story*. She collected her first fiction in *Shiloh and Other Stories* (1982), winner of the PEN/Hemingway Award. The title story showcases her most common theme of working-class women seeking stability in a rapidly changing world. After publishing the novels *In Country* (1985) and *Spence and Lila* (1988), she returned to short works in *Love Life: Stories* (1989). That same year Warner produced a film version of *In Country,* which pictures a fatherless girl's struggle to establish identity in the aftermath of the Vietnam War.

Mason's sympathy for unschooled backwoods women dominates her fiction. In *Feather Crowns* (1993), the story of Christianna "Christie" Wheeler's motherhood to quintuplet boys, memories of erotic thoughts load her with guilt as, one by one, the infants die after excessive media attention. Typical of rural beliefs is Aunt Alma's charge that Christie's "crazy idies" may mean that "we'll have to carry you off to the asylum," a standard warning in feminist literature to females who think beyond set limits (Mason, 1994, 3). More ominous is an aphorism from Aunt Sophie, who warns Christie, "It's nine months from the marriage bed to the death bed," an image that stirs terrifying thoughts of lethal motherhood (*ibid,* 7).

Mason's memoir, *Clear Springs: A Family Story* (1999), presents a deeply personal account of southern MATRIARCHY, which tends to confine itself within a distinctive domestic culture to the exclusion of everything else. After living in the North, she tapped into the voices of female storytellers who taught her to value love and belonging. Of her own flight from country life Mason charges herself with "[betraying] my heritage as a farmer's daughter by leaving the land and going off to see the world" (Mason, 2000, 3). The author approaches her mother's life with a sympathy for women who never stray far from their roots and never know self-expression or the satisfaction of intellectual curiosity. With affection for a mother who never got beyond fishing in the pond at Kess Creek and selling blackberries at a dollar a gallon, Mason states her wistful memories of female lives defined by the perimeter of their yards: "I can see my mother holding the weight of her life. It is too much to sum up or dispense with or bury (*ibid.,* 275). Mason ventured through similar emotional territory in her next anthology, *Zigzagging down a Wild Trail: Stories* (2001), which follows women to careers in pottery and corporate spying and on jaunts that take them from Kentucky to Alaska, Texas, London, and Arabia. The opening line captures the pervasive theme of immersion in domesticity: "I never paid much attention to current events, all the trouble in the world you hear about. I was too busy raising a family" (Mason, 2002, 3).

Bibliography

Champion, Laurie. " 'I Keep Looking Back to See Where I've Been': Bobbie Ann Mason's *Clear Springs* and Henry David Thoreau's *Walden,*" *Southern Literary Journal* 36, no. 2 (Spring 2004): 47–58.

Mason, Bobbie Mason. *Clear Springs: A Family Story.* New York: Perennial, 2000.

———. *Feather Crowns.* New York: Perennial, 1994.

———. *The Girl Sleuth: A Feminist Guide to the Bobbsey Twins, Nancy Drew, and Their Sisters.* Athens: University of Georgia Press, 1975.

———. *Zigzagging Down a Wild Trail: Stories.* New York: Modern Library, 2002.

matriarchy

The centrality of matrilineage to feminist literature points to woman-to-woman support and wisdom as pillars of female strength. The concept of the female as story keeper and indoctrinator of the young undergirds the feminist Arthurian lore of Marion Zimmer BRADLEY, the author of *The Mists of Avalon* (1982). In short story, drama, novel, and memoir the ethnologist Zora Neale HURSTON surveyed a range of matriarchal elements. In "Mother Catherine" (1934) the author lauds tolerance and forgiveness as the mother figure's crowning virtues. Of her array of jailbirds, convicts, and prostitutes within her own lineage, the revered hoodoo woman chooses to accept them as her own: "I got all kinds of children, but I am they mother. . . . God got all kinds, how come I cain't love all of mine? So says the beautiful spirit" (Hurston, 104). To young girls, Mother Catherine's Manger becomes a fount of welcome "dedicated to the birth of children in or out of wedlock" (*ibid.*). She exonerates the unwed mother by claiming that no human birth is illicit.

The strength of matriarchy undergirds many of the feminist works that focus on fatherless or parentless families. The poet Jeanne Murray Walker renews the female tie with matrilineage in "The Shawl" (1985), a plaintive memory of an immigrant grandmother reduced to a single palpable keepsake, the mauve and purple crocheted shawl, a symbol of womanly regrets carried from the old country through Ellis Island, and on the train to Minnesota. The French Caribbean author Maryse CONDÉ enlarged on the loss of two levels of matriarchy in *Moi, Tituba, sorcière noire de Salem* (*I, Tituba, Black Witch of Salem*, 1986). A New England slave, Tituba no longer has her Caribbean mother and grandmother, Abena and Mama Yaya, for support. Tituba relies on scents—honeysuckle and spice— to invigorate memories of maternal tenderness and hope. As charges of witchcraft in Salem village begin to narrow down to "a slave originating from the West Indies and probably practicing 'hoodoo,'" Tituba regrets that there are no strong women to defend her (Condé, 110). The silence left by death causes Tituba to mourn that "sometimes nothing can replace words" (*ibid.*, 84).

In 1988 Barbara KINGSOLVER introduced in *The Bean Trees* the matrilineage of the Greer family as the bedrock of family trust. Alice Jean Stamper Greer, deserted wife and single mother of Taylor Greer, guides and empowers her daughter through example and faith, values that Taylor learned in childhood to strengthen her during resettlement and single motherhood. A retired domestic and laundress, Alice relies on love and candor, including her ability to detect sadness and hesitance in her daughter's telephone voice. Equally forthright about life's vicissitudes, Alice confesses to Taylor that she intends to end her loneliness by marrying Harland Elleston. In her mother's absence Taylor continues to obey family adages that dot her memory bank. Far from mother and Kentucky she selects Mattie, a Tucson tire dealer, as a surrogate parent, a makeshift strand in the novel's womanly network who offers crackers, juice, and grandmotherly advice on the care of Taylor's daughter, April Turtle Greer, in the arid Southwest.

Failure is not a death knell in Kingsolver's matriarchies. When the Ellestons' union proves moribund as a result of Harland's daily retreat to his recliner to watch television, Alice quips that the Greers are "doomed to be a family with no men in it" (Kingsolver, 1988, 321). In the nonsequel, *Pigs in Heaven* (1993), she flees to Taylor and creates a bond with April Turtle, her adopted granddaughter. When Taylor divulges the kinks in her plan to keep Turtle, Alice reaches out with the comforting words "You go ahead and fall apart. That's what I'm here for" (Kingsolver, 1993, 128). The resilience and promise of the Greer females remain steady as a beacon as Taylor ponders separation from her lover, Jax Thibodeaux, and Alice once more risks her all by marrying Cash Stillwater, Turtle's real grandfather.

In 1992 the Cuban-American novelist Cristina García was nominated for a National Book Award for *Dreaming in Cuban,* a partly epistolary chronicle of a three-stage matriarchy that survives political chaos. The text is a model of woman-centered history that focuses on tolerance and enduring MOTHER-DAUGHTER RELATIONSHIPS rather than the VIOLENCE and political rhetoric of androcentric history. The family anchor is Celia del Pino, grandmother of Pilar, an artist who joins her mother, Lourdes, in fleeing the pro-Castro island for the freedoms of New York City. Upon the breakup of Abuela Celia's clan she wonders, "Which is worse, separation or death?" (García, 6). She reflects on the nation's losses: "What happens to their languages? The warm burial grounds they leave behind? What of their passions lying stiff and untranslated in their breasts?" (ibid., 73). Despite the intrusion of a Communist-backed revolution on Cuban families, the female ties remain strong and the old lessons indelible through reconciliation and stories of the past.

Bibliography

Condé, Maryse. *I, Tituba, Black Witch of Salem.* New York: Ballantine, 1994.

García, Cristina. *Dreaming in Cuban.* New York: Knopf, 1992.

Hurston, Zora Neale. *The Complete Stories.* New York: HarperCollins, 1995.

Kingsolver, Barbara. *The Bean Trees.* New York: Harper & Row, 1988.

———. *Pigs in Heaven.* New York: HarperCollins, 1993.

Payant, Katherine B. "From Alienation to Reconciliation in the Novels of Cristina García," *MELUS* 26, no. 3 (Fall 2001): 163–182.

Walker, Jeanne Murray. "The Shawl," *Poetry* 147 (November 1985): 76–77.

McCaffrey, Anne (1926–)

One of the late 20th century's dreamers of a feminist perfect world, Anne Inez McCaffrey, the first female to win the Hugo Award, assured the place of women in fantasy and science fiction. A native of Cambridge, Massachusetts, she studied at Stuart Hall and majored in Slavonic language and literature at Radcliffe. After writing fiction in girlhood and working in copywriting in New York City, she became an actor in summer stock in Lambertsville, New Jersey, and studied voice with the intent of becoming an opera singer and staging director. In 1953 she submitted her first story to *Science Fiction Plus Magazine* and followed with a barrage of short works for *Amazing Stories, Analog, Fantasy and Science Fiction, Galaxy, Gateway,* and *Worlds of If.* To improve on the depiction of women in fantasy and science fiction, she created the heroine, Sara, for a first novel, *Restoree* (1967), an ugly-duckling-to-swan reclamation depicting female rootlessness on a distant planet. To lend credence to the technocentric works, McCaffrey studied physics and consulted experts on rocketry and space travel. Crowning her achievements of a half-century of writing was the 2004 L. Ron Hubbard Writers of the Future Lifetime Achievement Award.

In *Dragonsong* (1977), the first of a trilogy, McCaffrey situates Benden Weyr, a matriarchal colony, on planet Pern, her most famous fictional setting. In a type of freedom unknown on Earth, women develop leadership and healing skills. They welcome Menolly, the ingenue in flight from a repressive father who refuses to allow his daughter to become the tribal harper. In conversation with Petiron the Harper, the former culture keeper, Menolly hears the familiar botched logic that negated female ambitions: "One in ten thousand can build an acceptable melody with meaningful words. Were you only a lad" (McCaffrey, 2003, 4). Contributing to Menolly's frustration is her mother's complicity with PATRIARCHY: "Behave yourself while you stand in a man's place. No tuning" (ibid., 11). Only in an all-female environment does the heroine make peace with her ambitions, but McCaffrey stresses that such aspirations exact a steep price. In Menolly's case becoming the colony's harper robs her of home and family.

McCaffrey stuck to her feminist leanings, which bear a resemblance to the passions of youth. Her next book, *The White Dragon* (1978), winner of the Ditmar Award and a Gandalf citation, was the first young adult science fiction work to be named a *New York Times* best seller. In *The Girl Who Heard Dragons* (1994) McCaffrey frees a homeless child from anonymity with the gift of communication with fantastic beings. Typical of McCaffrey's liberation of young heroines from sexist strictures is the title character in *Acorna's Quest: The Adventures of the Unicorn Girl* (1998), a five-book saga coauthored by Margaret Ball. The depiction of brave females in quest literature models for young readers the shared need of boys and girls for adventures that encourage vision and personal growth. The choice of Acorna's name connects her with small beginnings that yield great and majestic results, which take shape in the sequels *Acorna's World* (2000), *Acorna's Search: The Further Adventures of the Unicorn Girl* (2001), *Acorna's Rebels* (2003), and *Acorna's Triumph* (2004). As with Menolly in *Dragonsong*, Acorna's aspirations require a sacrifice, the loss of her true love.

Bibliography

Capozzella, Michele. "Anne McCaffrey: Science Fiction Storyteller," *School Library Journal* 47, no. 9 (September 2001): 257.

Didicher, Nicole E. "Adolescence, Imperialism, and Identity in Kim and Pegasus in Flight," *Mosaic* 34, no. 2 (June 2001): 149.

McCaffrey, Anne. *Acorna's Quest.* New York: Eos, 1998.

———. *Acorna's Triumph.* New York: HarperTorch, 2004.

———. *Dragonsong.* New York: Aladdin, 2003.

McCarthy, Mary (1912–1989)

A feminist icon of the 1960s, Mary Therese McCarthy observed the traditions and trends that altered the lives of the first wave of liberated American women. She lived a happy childhood with three brothers in her native Seattle, Washington. In *How I Grew* (1987), a late memoir, she describes herself as "enamored of the dark principle, fond of frightening herself and her brothers with the stories she made up" (McCarthy, 2004, 6). The 1918 influenza epidemic that left them orphans introduced her to religious tyranny. She summarized in *Memories of a Catholic Girlhood* (1957) the misery of living in Minneapolis for five years with her cruel Uncle Myers. Her grandfather arranged her return at age 11 to Seattle and a loving home and enrolled her at Mesdames of the Sacred Heart convent and Annie Wright Seminary, where she read Latin classics. Known as an intellectual at Vassar, she married and settled in New York City, where she wrote stage reviews, sketches, and articles for *Harper's Bazaar, New Republic, New Yorker, Southern Review,* and *Partisan Review,* which she served as an assistant editor.

With the encouragement of the critic Edmund Wilson, her second husband, McCarthy flourished at writing contemporary novels, essays, travelogue, memoirs, and slick urban stories. In an autobiographical novel, *The Company She Keeps* (1942), she satirized women who allow tawdry sexual affairs to force them into layered deceits and to rob them of integrity and self-respect. Two decades after her choice of a writing career she completed a feminist classic, *The Group* (1963), a sociological novel that emerged from 11 years of writing. It unfolds the interwoven lives of eight upper-crust New England coeds who graduate from Vassar and remain friends during the Second World War. In neatly clipped satire, the author accommodates the individual voices as foremothers of modernity, a literary triumph she referred to as ventriloquism. She labeled her novel a mock chronicle about "progress seen in the female sphere, the feminine sphere . . . the history of the loss of faith in progress, the idea of progress" (Gelderman, 5).

Through the maturation and sexual experiences of her characters McCarthy reveals the hesitation with which a generation of promising youth reached for INDEPENDENCE and self-expression. She surveys their reliance on each other for approval by describing how they "rearranged their fur pieces and smiled at each other, noddlingly, like mature little martens and sables" (McCarthy, 1991, 5). The ironically named Kay Strong, the first of the eight to marry, finds herself cheated of her dreams after Harald, her husband, loses his job, retreats into alcohol, and beats her. McCarthy draws on a strand of Gothic fiction as well as her own experience as an abused wife by following Kay to an asylum, to which Harald commits her for brandishing a butter knife to ward off one of his assaults. Tricked at a vulnerable moment, she struggles to unravel her status: "A terrible doubt possessed her. They were using psychology on her: it was not her own choice, and she was not free" (*ibid.,* 349). The downward spiral of her life ends ambiguously at age 29 with a fall or leap from the Vassar Club to her death while spotting planes for Civil Defense.

The author uses the drama and pathos of Kay's death as a baleful commentary on the changes that await intellectual women and the institution of marriage after World War II. The plot introduces Lakey's lesbianism and her love for Kay as the snake lurking in Eden, an indication of the feminist challenges posed by birth control, psychoanalysis, loosened sexual mores, lapsed religious beliefs, and social disapproval of sexual adventurism. In 1966 United Artists profited from the controversy over McCarthy's best seller in a film adaptation starring Candice Bergen, Joan Hackett, Jessica Walker, and Joanna Pettet.

Bibliography

Gelderman, Carol. *Conversations with Mary McCarthy.* Jackson: University Press of Mississippi, 1991.

McCarthy, Mary. *The Company She Keeps.* New York: Harvest, 2003.

———. *The Group.* New York: Harvest, 1991.

———. *How I Grew.* New York: Harvest, 2004.

———. *Memories of a Catholic Girlhood.* New York: Harvest, 1972.

Ryan, Kay. "Falling in Public: Larsen's *Passing,* McCarthy's *The Group,* and Baldwin's *Another Country,*" *Studies in the Novel* 36, no. 1 (Spring 2004): 95–119.

McClung, Nellie (1873–1951)

The Canadian social reformer, orator, journalist, and fiction writer Helen Letitia "Nellie" Mooney McClung turned her stories and essays toward the liberation of Canadian women. The youngest of six, she was born outside Chatsworth, Ontario, and grew up in rural Manitoba in the Souris Valley. She remained unschooled until age 10, when the family relocated to Winnipeg. With only six years of education she began teaching in Manitou, Manitoba. The Women's Christian Temperance Movement was her introit into Canadian women's crusade for the vote as well as for dower rights and government intervention in sweatshop exploitation. At age 35 she penned a sketch that was the kernel of a best-selling novel, *Sowing Seeds in Danny* (1908), the first of a popular series about an independent female teacher.

McClung's feminism emerged in stages. In *The Second Chance* (1910), a best-selling novel about the suffragist Pearl Watson, and a sequel, *Purple Springs* (1921), she created historical fiction based on Canadian women's campaign against whiskey and for full citizenship. At a stirring moment Peter J. Neelands admits to the women of Purple Springs that the law "gives a married woman no rights. She has no claim on her home, nor on her children. A man can sell or will away his property from his wife. A man can will away his unborn child—and it's a hell of a law" (McClung, 1921, 238). In *Painted Fires* (1925) she extended the survey of female Canadians with a story about an exploited immigrant girl from Finland. After cofounding the Political Equality League, McClung issued a collection of speeches and polemics, *In Times Like These* (1915), a position paper on women's demands that urged less masculinity and more humanity. At the height of political and legal turmoil "Calamity Nell" wrote a fiery newspaper column, "Nellie McClung Says"; with the speech "On Personhood" she demanded clarification of the word *person* in Canadian law, a court case fought all the way to England's Privy Council. The triumph for female "persons" affected all women in the British Empire. Partially as a result of her writings and speeches, in 1916 Manitoba became the first province to permit women to vote.

While serving in the Alberta legislature, McClung continued writing short fiction and articles. On February 15, 1928, in "Can a Woman Raise a Family and Have a Career?" she joked about the tired complaint of neglected homes and families. She trained one of her five children to recite to news reporters, "I am a suffragette's child— and never knew a mother's love" (McClung, 1995, 64). To an interviewer for the *Canadian National Journal* in 1931 she described herself in terms of both motherhood and career. In poor health she turned to memoir in the tradition of FRONTIER LITERATURE with *Clearing in the West: My Own Story* (1935) and *The Streams Run Fast* (1945), a woman's view of the pioneer experience, which summarizes the daily toil of making soap, canning, salting pork, making vinegar, and baking.

Bibliography

McClung, Nellie. "Can a Woman Raise a Family and Have a Career?" *Maclean's,* 12 December 1995, p. 64.

———. *The Complete Autobiography: Clearing in the West and The Stream Runs Fast.* Peterborough, Canada: Broadview, 2003.

———. *Purple Springs* (1921). Available online: URL: http://digital.library.upenn.edu/women/mcclung/purple/purple.html. Accessed on October 16, 2005.

McCullers, Carson (1917–1967)

A compassionate observer of young girls' difficulties in breaking with childhood to establish independent selves, Lula Carson Smith McCullers wrote about memorable girl loners contemplating childhood's end. A southerner by birth, she left her home in Columbus, Georgia, to study classical piano at Juilliard in New York City. By night she learned how to write through courses at Columbia University and analysis of Eudora WELTY's southern Gothic fiction. McCullers began submitting pieces to *Decision, Harper's Bazaar, New York, Saturday Review, Story,* and *Vogue,* most filled with her obsession with motherless, misshapen, and emotionally exiled people. In her first unsold effort, "Sucker" (1933), which *Saturday Evening Post* published 30 years later, she describes an isolated child who talks to himself and fantasizes about an exotic life with gangsters and cowboys: "He'd get in the bathroom and stay as long as an hour and sometimes his voice would go up high and excited and you could hear him all over the house. Usually, though, he was very quiet" (McCullers, 1998, 2). As many of McCullers's conflicted innocents do, Sucker looks inward at his private purgatory and poses "sort of like he was afraid of a whack over the head" (*ibid.,* 5).

A common source of poignancy in McCullers's characters is the awkward, unlovely female's yearning for affection and appreciation for her uniqueness. In addition to 20 short stories, she produced classic feminist works—the novel *The Heart Is a Lonely Hunter* (1940) and the novellas *The Member of the Wedding* (1946) and *The Ballad of the Sad Café* (1951), a depiction of an older woman's failed love relationship. In the latter, a southern Gothic milestone that McCullers serialized in *Harper's Bazaar* in 1943, Miss Amelia Evans, a misfit dressed in boots and overalls, lives in a town that misjudges her motivation and behavior. An androgynous freak, she attempts to secure love by launching a physical attack on her husband, Marvin Macy, further complicated by the interference of Cousin Lymon, a conniving dwarf. The final scene, with Miss Amelia prostrate in defeat and sobbing with her remaining breath, counters the stereotypes of the fragile southern belle or the faultless hostess, replacing them with a cameo of failure and betrayal. After Miss Amelia closes her café, McCullers quips, "You might as well go down to the Forks Falls highway and listen to the chain gang," a cruel jest at the expense of a rueful, forlorn soul (McCullers, 1951, 71). In 1990 Merchant-Ivory filmed the novella, starring Vanessa Redgrave as Miss Amelia.

McCullers, herself a victim of a failed marriage, rheumatic fever, and blindness brought on by paralytic stroke, pondered through fictional females her own isolation and bisexuality. In circular narrative *The Heart Is a Lonely Hunter,* winner of a Houghton Mifflin Fiction Fellowship, follows tomboyish Mick Kelly, a restive 12-year-old, on an odyssey of mismanaged friend making. She treasures a tenuous relationship with her disabled father, whose inability to offer a secure home strains their daddy-and-daddy's girl relationship. Her acquaintance with the café owner Biff Brannon, a cross-dressing widower, introduces an androgynous male who longs to befriend freaks and to mother Mick. The author caps the story ironically with Mick's love for John Singer, a deaf-mute jewelry store engraver who displaces her from her room by boarding at her house. He shares her inability to communicate with others. The text laments on the mismatch: "She talked to him more than she had ever talked to a person before. And if he could have talked he would have told her many things" (McCullers, 1967, 207).

As did the author, Mick Kelly eases her disjunction with family and town by retreating into classical music. On her longing for professional training she muses, "Maybe when people long for a thing that bad the longing made them trust in anything that might give it to them" (*ibid.,* 43). Overshadowing her enjoyment of concerts and symphonies is the awareness of "how lonesome a person could be in a crowded house" (*ibid.,* 45). McCullers captures the wordless anticipation of growth: "Nothing much happened that she could describe to herself in thoughts or words—but there was a feeling of change" (*ibid.,* 82). In the end

McCullers maneuvers Mick into familiar spheres for the early teen—a job at Woolworth's and a brief sexual tryst with Harry Minowitz, a schoolmate. The episodes toughen and placate Mick and ease her into womanhood.

More distilled than Mick's protracted coming of age is that of Frankie Addams, the sulky protagonist of *The Member of the Wedding*, a classic of teen angst. In the kitchen with a housekeeper, Berenice Sadie Brown, Frankie muddles toward maturity without the guidance of a mother and retreats into episodes of fantasy and wishful thinking. Alienated by others and by her own self-torment, she complains that she "belonged to no club and was a member of nothing in the world" (McCullers, 1973, 1). She seeks identity in a name change to the exotic F. Jasmine Addams and contemplates the prophecy of Big Mama. Without proper female guidance Frankie buys a too-mature orange evening gown and flirts with a red-haired soldier. Lacking mothering and a sense of belonging to friends and family, she misidentifies her brother Jarvis's, wedding to Janice as a once-in-a-lifetime event that will ensure security and stability, an emotional belonging Frankie envisions as the "we of me" (*ibid.*, 39). When her cockeyed plans collapse, she rides home on the bus in misery wishing that the whole world would die. Attempting solace is Berenice, the black substitute mother who represents the South's love-hate relationship with blacks who cook their meals, tend their children, and tolerate unsubtle racism.

McCullers teamed with Tennessee Williams at his Key West home for mutual writing and creative support while he completed *Summer and Smoke* and she adapted her tender-funny novella for the stage. In 1950 the play version of *The Member of the Wedding*, which ran 501 performances on Broadway, reduced further Frankie's microcosm to a southern kitchen, a womanly milieu in which Berenice does her best to placate a self-tormenting malcontent. The production, starring Julie Harris and Ethel Waters as Frankie and Berenice, earned McCullers a New York Drama Critic's Circle Award. Hallmark Hall of Fame reprised for television the love of Berenice for Frankie in the pairing of Alfre Woodard and Anna Paquin. McCullers's idiosyncratic style has influenced other feminist authors, including the ecofeminist Barbara KING-SOLVER and the Canadian short story writer Alice MUNRO.

Bibliography

Gleeson-White, Sarah. "A Peculiarly Southern Form of Ugliness: Eudora Welty, Carson McCullers, and Flannery O'Connor," *Southern Literary Journal* 36, no. 1 (Fall 2003): 46–57.

McCullers, Carson. *The Ballad of the Sad Café and Other Stories.* New York: Bantam, 1951.

———. *Collected Stories of Carson McCullers.* New York: Mariner, 1998.

———. *The Heart Is a Lonely Hunter.* New York: Bantam, 1967.

———. *The Member of the Wedding.* New York: Bantam, 1973.

McMillan, Terry (1951–   )

The fiction writer and dramatist Terry McMillan characterizes the off-balance lives of black women who are more successful in the office than in their relationships with husbands and lovers. McMillan introduced her bustling style in a seriocomic novel, *Mama* (1987), a mother-centered domestic story. It fictionalizes some of the author's early life in Port Huron, Michigan, with a mother whose guidance left an indelible list of dos an don'ts. Left fatherless at age 14 by her parents' divorce, the author turned to literature for solace and found a cause for black pride in reading Alex Haley's *The Autobiography of Malcolm X* (1965). While studying sociology in her junior year at Los Angeles City College, she increased her knowledge of black literature with reading of the poet Langston Hughes and ethnographer and novelist Zora Neale HURSTON. At the University of California at Berkeley McMillan contributed editorials to a new magazine, *Black Thoughts*, but still had a hard time picturing herself as a professional writer.

With an advanced journalism degree from Columbia University and a job as a legal typist, McMillan made her first efforts. She reread Hurston's THEIR EYES WERE WATCHING GOD (1937) as a model and composed *Mama* and *Disappearing Acts* (1989), the subject of an HBO-TV film. Her style, which tends toward quippy comebacks, braces informal dialogue with candid, often painful insights into women's needs and their decisions to put themselves first in the search for happiness. She opens *Mama* with Mildred Peacock's securing of an ax, lye, three butcher knives, and a cast iron skillet to separate her, permanently if need be, from Crook, her two-timing, quick-fisted husband. In rapid order McMillan spits out Mildred's complaints: "She hated this raggedy house. Hated this deadbeat town. Hated never having enough of anything" (McMillan, 1994, 1). The list becomes a manifesto for Mildred, who resolves to rear her five children on her own.

Usually lighthearted, McMillan's realistic, but funny plots made a breakthrough in ridding black female fiction of ghetto stereotypes, poverty, and working-class dialect. Her next four novels focus on the 30-somethings who make up the top tier of the black middle class. She targets business owners, public relations experts, accountants, insurance executives, and banking analysts—risk takers who find career opportunities outside urban squalor in such predominantly white cities as Denver and Phoenix. In 1992 her third novel, the best seller *Waiting to Exhale,* depicted the kind of women she does best—zesty black professionals who succeed on their own terms with or without the perfect love life. Her stories feature stouthearted survivors such as Savannah Jackson's mother, who "hasn't had a whole man in her life for seventeen years," and Savannah's sister, Sheila, who calls "collect from some cheap motel where she and the kids are hiding out until she can serve the papers" on a lackluster husband (McMillan, 1995, 1). Though McMillan's fast-talking female characters appeal to women readers, black male critics take issue with McMillan for implying that the most success-driven women are doomed to be unevenly matched by black men who cannot appreciate well-rounded mates or commit to monogamy.

McMillan's fourth, an autobiographical novel called *How Stella Got Her Groove Back* (1996), contributed to "girlfriend fiction" or "sistuh novels" by confronting a familiar feminist dilemma—an older woman, Stella Payne, in love with a young man, Winston Shakespeare. A mother figure, a friend who is dying of cancer, provides Stella with sensible advice. At the height of discontent Stella realizes, "I am getting a sudden over-whelming urge to run the vacuum through my mental house" (McMillan, 1997, 18). A brief rest in Jamaica complicates her life with a sexual alliance with Winston, a charming and sincere island lover less than half her age. A popular 1998 film version paired Angela Bassett and Whoopi Goldberg as best pals who thrash out Stella's difficulties with meddlesome family and friends.

The author's fifth novel, *A Day Late and a Dollar Short* (2001), a saga that some consider her finest fiction, layers the older and younger generations in a holistic study of kinship dynamics. She depicts the sprawling family branching out with former mates and stepchildren and the disruption caused by the parting of Viola Price, the clan matriarch, from her husband, Cecil. At a climactic moment Paris and Janelle, two of their three daughters, examine snapshots of their parents when they were young marrieds. The warmth of domestic poses in house and yard strikes home: "Our history, our lives together as a family; and after looking at our mother and father, I think we both realize where we came from and who we are" (McMillan, 2002, 366.)

Bibliography

McMillan, Terry. *A Day Late and a Dollar Short.* New York: Signet, 2002.

———. *How Stella Got Her Groove Back.* New York: Signet, 1997.

———. *Mama.* New York: Pocket, 1994.

———. *Waiting to Exhale.* New York: Pocket, 1995.

Murray, Victoria Christopher. "Everybody Wants to Be Terry McMillan," *Black Issues Book Review* 4, no. 1 (January–February 2002): 36–40.

Mead, Margaret (1901–1978)

A stellar researcher, author, and iconic NEW WOMAN, Margaret Mead turned an anthropological quest into a sourcebook on the popular feminist controversies of the early 20th century. The child of scholarly Philadelphia Quakers, she became the pampered darling of a paternal grandmother who believed that a woman should set her own course. Mead grew up in Hammonton, kept a diary, and at age 15 wrote for the Doylestown, Pennsylvania, *In-*

telligencer. At Barnard College her mentors were two brilliant anthropologists, Ruth Benedict and Franz Boas. After committing herself to a doctoral study of Polynesian culture requiring six months on the Samoan island of T'au, at age 23 Mead established a career in fieldwork among Pacific Islanders. Her detailed inquiry included questions about how they spaced the births of children and what positions they preferred for sexual intercourse. Setting her apart from other Ph. D. candidates was her belief that data from the web of family and clan ties in the South Seas reflected significant aspects of all human relationships, particularly the malleability of gender roles. Her meticulous notes and subsequent articles and books helped to validate the study of adolescence and promote understanding of pubescence and its importance as a basis for a well-rounded adulthood.

From the curator's office at the American Museum of Natural History in Manhattan, Mead published a popular and critical success, COMING OF AGE IN SAMOA: *A Psychological Study of Primitive Youth for Western Civilisation* (1928), which probed the influence of child rearing and family mores in the psychosexual development of teenagers. She warned readers about the disjunctures of the melting pot: "In American civilisation, with its many immigrant strains, its dozens of conflicting standards of conduct, its hundreds of religious sects, its shifting economic conditions, this unsettled, disturbed status of youth was more apparent than in the older, more settled civilisation of Europe" (Mead, *Coming,* 3–4). Jolting modern readers was Mead's conclusion that the Samoan girls of T'au became women with less tension, rebellion, and guilt than American teens because their parents lacked the Puritan influence found in American society.

With a straightforward style free of cant and corroborated by her own photography, Mead enlightened readers of her books and her columns for *Redbook* on the crucial time span separating childhood and marriage. In a period when advertising idealized hausfrau stereotypes and when novelists, poets, and playwrights tackled married sex in fiction, she traveled among the Omaha and in the Admiralty Islands, New Guinea, and Bali. From her field work she produced a string of nonfiction works—*Growing Up in New Guinea* (1930), The

Changing Culture of an Indian Tribe (1932), *Sex and Temperament in Three Primitive Societies* (1935), and *Male and Female: A Study of the Sexes in a Changing World* (1949)—plus pamphlets for the Office of War Information during World War II. All expressed Mead's scientific views on sexual permissiveness, marriage, and connubial relations. In *Male and Female* she acknowledged the move of industrialized societies from MATRIARCHY to a gender-neutral attitude toward home, school, office, and the public sphere. In light of her findings she confronted questions about the modern mother: "Have we cut women off from their natural closeness to their children, taught them to look for a job instead of the touch of a child's hand, for status in a competitive world rather than a unique place by a glowing hearth? In educating women, have we done something disastrous?" (Mead, *Male,* 3). Her succinct summary of the work-or-home-or-both quandary foreshadowed a half-century of feminist debate that carried over into the 21st century. At the heart of Mead's philosophy was a contention that both genders should develop their full human potential.

At age 71 Mead published an AUTOBIOGRAPHY, *Blackberry Winter: My Earlier Years* (1972), which extended her respectful and affectionate commentary on how American families function. In describing her own nature walks on five acres in Hammonton, she remarked, "Today's children have to find new ways of anchoring the changing moments of their lives" (Mead, 1995, 12). In contrast to the clangor and technical complexities of 20th-century American culture, she pictured the Bushmen of the Kalahari, who sculpted a circle in the sand, arched a sapling for a threshold, and "established a dwelling as sacrosanct from invasion as the walled estates of the wealthy" (*ibid.*). She detailed her own quest for a balance between serious scholarship and a normal home for her and her daughter, the anthropologist Mary Catherine Bateson Kassarjian, author of a biography, *With a Daughter's Eye: Letters from the Field, 1925–1975* (1984). At Mead's death critics marveled at the humanistic pattern of her studies and her 40 published titles stressing the interconnectness of human endeavors. Her belief that committed citizens can change the world became a slogan for hopeful reformers. For contributions to literature and social inquiry she earned a posthumous Presidential Medal of Freedom.

Bibliography

Mead, Margaret. *Blackberry Winter: My Earlier Years.* New York: Kodansha America, 1995.

———. *Coming of Age in Samoa: A Psychological Study of Primitive Youth for Western Civilisation.* New York: Perennial, 2001.

———. *Male and Female.* New York: Perennial, 2001.

Newman, Louise M. "Coming of Age, but Not in Samoa: Reflections on Margaret Mead's Legacy for Western Liberal Feminism," *American Quarterly* 48, no. 2 (June 1996): 233–272.

Menchú, Rigoberta (1959–)

The Mayan social reformer and autobiographer Rigoberta Menchú Tum directs her intelligence and energies to aid the Mayan working poor and to educate illiterate Indian women. Born in Chimel in the northland highlands of Guatemala to the Quiche clan, she is the daughter of a nurse-midwife, a welcome healer in a land where Indian women are often banned from public EDUCATION. From age eight Menchú helped her family farm and, with them, migrated to the Pacific coast to harvest crops at coffee and cotton plantations. During the family's struggles her two oldest brothers starved to death. Through Catholic priests in the mid-1970s she involved herself in progressive activities including the WOMEN'S RIGHTS movement. Government agents jailed and tortured Rigoberta's father, the union organizer Vicente Menchú, on charges of aiding guerrillas in murdering a local *ladino* (plantation owner).

At age 20 Menchú joined the Committee of the Peasant Union to fight corruption in government and big business. In this explosive period military authorities burned her brother to death for suspect activities. Another immolation killed her father in a civil uprising at the Spanish embassy. Her mother died after rape, torture, and execution at a military jail. Menchú prepared herself for radical social intervention by learning Spanish and Mayan dialects. During a farm strike in 1980 she led farm workers seeking improved conditions.

On May 1, 1981, she helped organize a peasant demonstration at the capital. By joining the 31st of January Popular Front, she was able to convince Mayan laborers to resist military threats and economic exploitation. Her reputation for sedition forced her into hiding in Mexico City, where she coordinated assistance to the agrarian uprising through the United Representation of the Guatemalan Opposition.

In 1983 over 26 hours Menchú dictated an autobiography, *I, Rigoberta Menchú, an Indian Woman in Guatemala,* to the anthropologist Elisabeth Burgos Debray. The courage and intelligent strategies of Menchú's revolutionary interventions for the poor and dispossessed drew world attention. She narrated a documentary film, *When the Mountains Tremble* (1984). Against multiple death threats in July 1992 she dodged in and out of her homeland to intercede for rebels facing death sentences. At age 33 she received the Nobel Peace Prize for revealing the atrocities suffered by indigenous Guatemalans, who constitute 65 percent of the country's population. She became a roving ambassador for the United Nations Educational, Scientific and Cultural Organization (UNESCO) and for 12 years was a spokeswoman for the world's first peoples. She wrote a second autobiography, *Crossing Borders* (1997), which contains a political manifesto on behalf of Mayans. In 1999 she faced charges of fabricating episodes of her life story. Menchú has suggested that her work is a testimony, not a biography, and a faithful presentation of the plight of her people.

Bibliography

Arias, Arturo. *The Rigoberta Menchú Controversy.* Minneapolis: University of Minnesota Press, 2001.

Menchú, Rigoberta. *I, Rigoberta Menchú, an Indian Woman in Guatemala.* London: Verso, 1987.

Middlemarch George Eliot (1872)

Although feminists generally admire strands of pro-liberation philosophy in George ELIOT's panoramic masterwork *Middlemarch,* the novel's place in the feminist literary spectrum is debated. The central female character is Dorothea Brooke Casaubon, an ardent idealist and antimaterialist humorously nicknamed "Dodo," the author's pointed reminder that intellectuals can be fools. As does the naive heroine in the FAIRY TALE of BEAUTY AND THE BEAST, Dorothea departs from the Victorian woman's immersion in fashions, sentimental novels, and needlework to roam the village of Middlemarch, study housing reform, and promote sanitation measures and justice for the poor. After marrying Edward Casaubon, a musty, self-important cleric, she lives a sexless imitation of wedlock that fails to satisfy her "soul-hunger," which the author describes in the preface as "meanness of opportunity" (Eliot, 23, 1). Casaubon is pleased with his wife-companion because of her youth, beauty, devotion, and virtue, but he regrets that she is "troublesome" and that "she judged him" (*ibid.*, 381). She comments significantly on his lapdog, a Maltese puppy, "It is painful to me to see these creatures that are bred merely as pets," a salient comment on the infantilizing of adult women into nursemaids and diversions for cranky, paternal males (*ibid.*, 24). In depression at his rejection of intimacy she weeps, "What have I done—what am I—that he should treat me so?" (*ibid.*, 389). In a feminist moment Dorothy, unlike the selfless heroines of Victorian romance, shucks off blame and declares, "It is his fault, not mine" (*ibid.*). The manifesto reflects the clarity of the author's life choices, which countered disapproval from a pious father and prim social milieu.

Dorothea's wrenching coming to knowledge forces her to examine her marital position, which has much in common with that of the Maltese puppy. At a painful moment with rival Rosamond Lydgate, Dorothea admits with a vampirish image that "marriage drinks up all our power of giving or getting any blessedness in that sort of love. . . . it murders our marriage—and then the marriage stays with us like a murder" (*ibid.*, 729). An epiphany that follows the reading of Edward Casaubon's coercive will shocks Dorothea into picturing him as a tyrant. She realizes that receiving any money he left behind would not be worth kowtowing to his fatherly stipulation that she reject the winsome Will Ladislaw as a second husband. As though released from a cell, after two years of widow's weeds she liberates herself from conflict and grief by trying out a new bonnet, a

symbol of her retreat from intellectualism to the feminine side of her nature.

In an inclusive picture of a provincial community during the Victorian era's drive for social reform Eliot's sweeping novel treats in miniature one woman's triumph over a marital mistake. Through her devotion to regionalism and to psychological realism, the author records community progress and extols advances in Dorothea's personal growth and her satiation of sexual needs. In becoming Mrs. Ladislaw, Dorothea intends to remedy her first mistake by claiming her heart's joy. The resolution endorses a period principle that marriage is the height of adult achievement and that marriage for love is by far more beneficial to both parties than the hypocrisy of marriage for money or pious ideals. On the other hand, the novel rejects the restrictive imagery of wedlock as an inescapable union. Eliot lifts the text from romance to social novel by focusing on the small increments of happiness experienced by her female characters— Mary's publication of a children's book, Dorothea's baby son, and the renewed SISTERHOOD of Dorothea and Celia. The author's stance is a gesture of defiance against happily-ever-after ideals.

Bibliography

Chase, Karen, and J. P. Stern, eds. *Eliot: Middlemarch.* Cambridge: Cambridge University Press, 1991.

Eliot, George. *Middlemarch.* New York: Bantam, 1985.

Himmelfarb, Gertrude. "George Eliot for Grown-Ups," *American Scholar* 63, no. 4 (Autumn 1994): 577–581.

Thomas, Jeanie G. "An Inconvenient Indefiniteness: George Eliot, Middlemarch, and Feminism," *University of Toronto Quarterly* 56, no. 3 (March 1987): 392–415.

Mill, Harriet Taylor (1807–1858)

The iconoclastic philosopher, journalist, and essayist Harriet Hardy Taylor Mill framed arguments for WOMEN'S RIGHTS from sociological and economic perspectives. A South Londoner born to Unitarian parents, she educated herself in women's history, literature, and philosophy, including the writings of George SAND, and became fluent in Greek, Latin, French, German, and Italian. To escape a tyrannical father, at age 18 Mill accepted an arranged marriage to the pharmacist John Taylor and reared their three children. She developed into a passionate speaker on issues of liberty and an ardent follower of developments in the first stirrings of the American abolitionist, TEMPERANCE, and SUFFRAGE campaigns. Because John Taylor lacked his wife's intellectual gifts, she separated from him in 1833, but she remained faithful to him until his death of cancer in 1849. At age 44 she married the philosopher John Stuart Mill, whom she had met in 1830 and had admired as a friend and colleague. The couple encouraged each other's projects, particularly John's *Autobiography* (1873), which she edited, and Harriet's article for the *Morning Chronicle* on family VIOLENCE.

Until her death of tuberculosis at the family's home in Avignon, France, Harriet Taylor Mill published book reviews, verse, and philosophical essays for the *Monthly Repository*, a Unitarian periodical. A founding member of the Kensington Society, a suffrage pressure group, she focused her writings on WOMEN'S RIGHTS, civil disobedience of sexist laws, SEXUALITY, divorce, PROSTITUTION, and moral training for children and the working class. Among her beliefs was the axiom that male dominance precipitates both injustice in the courts and social deterioration. Her writings ranked women's influence on society as salutary and beneficent toward the poor and needy. She promoted financial INDEPENDENCE and EDUCATION for women as inducements to activism preceding full involvement in legislation.

Harriet Taylor Mill is best known for a formal feminist manifesto, "The Enfranchisement of Women" (1851), which she submitted to the *Westminster Review*. She wrote it in response to the National Woman's Rights Convention in Worcester, Massachusetts, the previous year, which she believed heralded a new age of gender equality. She ably fielded questions about maternity by disburdening antifeminists of the notion that motherhood consumed women's entire energies and thoughts. She pointed out the number of trades in which women flourished while still maintaining a home, including millinery, catering, sewing, weaving, and innkeeping. For examples of female leaders, she declared, "We look in vain for abler or firmer rulers than Elizabeth [I]; than Isabella of Castile; than [the Spanish Infanta] Maria Teresa; than Catherine of Russia; than Blanche, mother of Louis IX of France; than Jeanne d'Albret, mother of Henri Quatre [Henry IV of France]" (Mill, 1851, 11). The text, later issued as a pamphlet, anticipates 20th-century Women's Liberation in its vision of women's progress after gaining the vote and unlimited choice of education and career. Reprints in North America validated the American and English suffrage movements, which both Harriet and John Mill advocated.

Critics tended to reduce Harriet's role in the couple's collaboration to the level of secretary and editorial aide. To literary historians it appears that the couple coauthored *The Principles of Political Economy, with Some of Their Applications to Social Philosophy* (1848), a pre-Marxist socialist work that proposes improvements to the lives of workers through co-ownership of factories and businesses. John Stuart Mill also credited his wife with helping him develop the essay "On Liberty" (1859). Some of her manuscripts lay neglected in the London School of Economics archives until their reclamation by 20th-century feminists. Current criticism degenerates into wrangles over which ideas were Harriet's and which she gained from or shared with John.

Bibliography

Jacobs, Jo Ellen. *The Voice of Harriet Taylor Mill.* Bloomington: Indiana University Press, 2002.

Mill, Harriet Taylor. "The Claim of Englishwomen to the Suffrage Constitutionally Considered" (1867). Available online. URL: http://www.indiana.edu/~letrs/vwwp/:taylor/suffrage.html. Accessed on October 16, 2005.

———. "The Enfranchisement of Women" (1851). Available online. URL: http://www.pinn.net/~sunshine/book-sum/ht_mill3.html. Accessed on October 16, 2005.

Rossi, Alice, ed. *Essays on Sexual Equality.* Chicago: University of Chicago Press, 1970.

Mill, John Stuart (1806–1873)

The English philosopher, logician, essayist, and feminist activist John Stuart Mill spearheaded an intellectual wing of the women's movement of 1850. A brilliant child, he was born in London to the historian James Mill, who taught his three-year-old son classical Greek. John Stuart Mill consumed books on history and philosophy by age eight and read in the original languages classic texts by Aesop, Xenophon, Isocrates, and Herodotus, the father of Western history. Mill submitted essays regularly to the *Westminster Review* and established the Utilitarian Society. After marrying his intellectual and emotional soulmate, Harriet Taylor, whom he met in 1830, he developed their mutual ideas about the ill effects of the subjugation of daughters and wives. He condemned the legal subordination of women to men and lobbied for more liberal laws throughout the United Kingdom.

A year after his wife's death in 1858 Mill changed minds on the issue of women's liberation with the publication of the five-part essay "On Liberty" (1859), which had significant influence on Victorian era attitudes toward personal freedom. His reverence for women extends to a sympathy for coerced females, especially Mormon women forced into polygyny and Chinese girls whose feet are bound, because the maiming of a "Chinese lady's foot" makes it "stand out prominently and tends to make the person markedly dissimilar" to natural females (Mill, 1983, 135). In chapter 5, "Applications," without defending WOMEN'S RIGHTS as a separate issue from all human liberty, he inveighs against drunken idlers and questions the legality of fornication and pimping. His defense of decency in marriage and family matters illustrates his contention that both men and women bear an obligation to tolerate human foibles without losing sight of morality.

In 1867 Mill addressed Parliament on behalf of England's first voting rights committee. He presented 1,550 signatures urging action to extend full citizenship to women. Because the 1867 Reform Bill ignored the plea, men and women in major cities continued to form SUFFRAGE societies throughout England demanding equal citizenship for women. They collected petitions signed by nearly 3 million people, but these pleas failed to alter Queen Victoria's opinion that voting rights were inappropriate for women. In 1869 Englishwomen earned a partial victory after Parliament allowed them to vote in municipal elections and to be members of city and county councils.

The widower's earlier collaboration with his wife continued to impact his visions of equality for women. When Harriet Mill wrote "The Enfranchisement of Women" (1851), she influenced his philosophy in *The Subjection of Women* (1869), a radical social document that Mill published with the aid of his stepdaughter, the activist Helen Taylor. At the outset he declares wrong the "legal subordination of one sex to the other" (Mill, 1997, 1). The text, a pillar of British feminism, attacks political policy that denies women the vote and the rights to property and custody of their children. Because of his fierce advocacy of women's rights, he became the most prominent British thinker of the 19th century. Long after his death his opinions stirred controversy as well as beneficial debate on the reform of laws, traditions, and social customs. His influence on writers such as Sarah GRAND spurred to the creation of bold, self-defining female heroines for NEW WOMAN fiction.

Bibliography

Capaldi, Nicholas. *John Stuart Mill: A Biography.* Cambridge: Cambridge University Press, 2004.

Mill, John Stuart. *Autobiography.* London: Penguin, 1990.

———. *On Liberty.* New York: Penguin, 1983.

———. *The Subjection of Women.* New York: Dover, 1997.

Millay, Edna St. Vincent (1892–1950)

A blaze of brilliance in the Jazz Age, the playwright and poet Edna St. Vincent Millay expressed the free spirit of the 1920s and the female passion and empowerment that lay beyond. A native of Rockland, Maine, she knew the endurance of a strong woman from seeing her mother, the nurse Cora Millay, replace an absent husband in the rearing of three daughters. As did authors Mary Hunter AUSTIN and Sarah Orne JEWETT, Millay included regional strengths in her feminist verse. She commemorated her mother in a posthumous poem, "The Courage That My Mother Had" (1954), which admires the New England woman's granite resilience.

The poet reveled in reading and playing the piano in girlhood but chose writing over music for a career. In her midteens she published "The Land of Romance" (1906) and competed in a poetry contest sponsored by *St. Nicholas* magazine. Six years later she authored "Renascence" (1912), an emotional plea for female INDEPENDENCE that reveals her mature outlook and poetic sensibilities. Supported by a patron, Caroline B. Dow, Millay studied at Vassar and composed and starred in a school play, *The Princess Marries the Page* (1932). In her last months of college she started an Elizabethan and Shakespearean sonnet cycle. Her first collection, *Renascence and Other Poems* (1917), contains her flippant, sybaritic quatrain about enjoying burning her candle at both ends. The lines support a number of interpretations, including women's delight in artistic expression and their willingness to sacrifice acceptance by their conservative contemporaries for the ebullience of the NEW WOMAN's life.

Millay moved to Greenwich Village to become an actor. Supporting herself with clerical work and the returns from satire and short sketches for *Ainslee* and *Metropolitan* magazines, she found time to compose a one-act war protest pastoral, *Aria Da Capo* (1919). She cofounded the Cherry Lane Theater and performed at the Provincetown Playhouse, a creative effort of the dramatists Djuna BARNES and Susan GLASPELL that preceded the regional theater movement throughout the United States. Millay championed WOMEN'S RIGHTS to sexual equality and self-determination in *A Few Figs from Thistles* (1920), which challenges the smug status quo of the patriarchal social order. In defiance of convention, she begins "Second Fig" with a skyward view to where houses stand rock and concludes in delight with the poet's metaphoric mansion built on sand (*ibid*, 19). In *Second April* (1921) she translated Catullus's limpid "Passer mortuus est" ("The Sparrow Is Dead"), the famed sparrow elegy that mourns, "Death devours all lovely things" (*Ibid.*, 31). After completing two plays, *Two Slatterns and a King* (1921) and *The Lamp and the Bell* (1921), and tramping Europe to report for *Vanity Fair*, she published an occasional poem, "To Inez Milholland" (1928), in honor of the presentation of a Washington monument commemorating woman SUFFRAGE.

Millay reached her literary height with a major sonnet sequence, "Sonnets from an Un-

grafted Tree," and the poem "I, Being Born a Woman and Distressed," anthologized in *The Ballad of the Harp Weaver and Other Poems* (1923). The collection won the first Pulitzer Prize bestowed on a female poet. The Massachusetts lyricist and editor Amy LOWELL chose Millay's essays, satires, and short fiction for inclusion in *Distressing Dialogues* (1924). In poor health caused by head and back pain and blurred vision, Millay settled at Austerlitz in rural New York with her husband, the Dutch coffee importer Eugen Jan Boissevain. At age 58 she died in the night of heart failure with editorial galleys clutched in her hand.

The genius of Millay's final years lay in the breadth of her poetic ventures, including composition of a blank verse libretto for the Anglo-Saxon opera *The King's Henchman*, a spectacular stage success that the Metropolitan Opera introduced on February 27, 1927. In the mode of lyric dissidence she issued *The Buck in the Snow and Other Poems* (1928) and penned "Justice Denied in Massachusetts" and "Fear" for *Outlook* magazine in support of the anarchists Nicola Sacco and Bartolomeo Vanzetti. Along with oratory and weekly radio plays, she revealed autobiographical insights in *Fatal Interview* (1931) and *Wine from These Grapes* (1934), translated decadent French verse in Charles Baudelaire's *Les Fleurs du Mal* (*The Flowers of Evil*, 1936), and interwove political opinions in the unpublished verse drama *Conversation at Midnight* (1937), which was destroyed in a hotel fire but resurrected from memory. In *Huntsman, What Quarry?* (1939), she expressed admiration for the poet Elinor WYLIE with six elegies that compare Wylie to a comet in the night sky. Millay's last six anthologies—*Make Bright the Arrows: 1940 Notebook* (1940), *There Are No Islands Any More* (1940), *Collected Sonnets* (1941), *Collected Lyrics* (1943), *Poem and Prayer for an Invading Army* (1944), and the posthumous *Mine the Harvest* (1954)—were an impetus to the confessional works by Sylvia PLATH and Anne SEXTON and the stories of Dorothy PARKER.

Bibliography

Epstein, Daniel Mark. *What Lips My Lips Have Kissed: The Loves and Love Poems of Edna St. Vincent Millay.* New York: John MacRae Books, 2001.

Millay, Edna St. Vincent. *Renaissance and Other Poems* (1917). Available online. URL: http://etext.lib. virginia.edu/subjects/Women-Writers.html. Accessed on October 16, 2005.

———. *Selected Poems.* New York: Perennial, 1999.

Newcomb, Timberman. "The Woman as Political Poet: Edna St. Vincent Millay and the Mid-century Canon," *Criticism* 37, no. 2 (Spring 1995): 261–279.

Millett, Kate (1934–)

The activist, scenarist, lecturer, and autobiographer Katherine Murray "Kate" Millett challenges women to abandon romanticism and to demand personal and political equality. She grew up fatherless in a strict Catholic home in her native Saint Paul, Minnesota. Her mother instilled in her three daughters the tenets of tolerance and egalitarianism. After earning degrees at the University of Minnesota and Saint Hilda's College, Oxford, Millett taught art in New York City while developing her skills at painting and sculpting. She joined the civil rights and anti–Vietnam War movements of the 1960s. For the National Organization of Women she published *Token Learning* (1967), a critique of substandard college training for women.

Millett's first examination of women's EDUCATION introduced concepts that she enlarged to a national controversy. After earning a doctorate from Columbia University, she published her dissertation, *Sexual Politics* (1970), a best seller that shatters patriarchal myths. The book laid the groundwork for gynocriticism and the development of broader criteria for inclusion of literary works in the world canon. Opening on a segment of raw "man talk" in Henry Miller's *Sexus* (1965), she analyzed the antifemale quality of a carnal encounter that depicts the female partner as the wordless bedmaiden of the male protagonist. In the second chapter Millett cites from the sour Greek poet Hesiod's *Theogony* (ca. 850 B.C.) the damning male-generated evidence of Pandora's myth and the EVE lore from Genesis that these mythic females introduced evil to humankind through SEXUALITY. With the proceeds of her book Millett founded the Women's Art Colony Farm in Poughkeepsie, New York.

Millett's use of oral narrative personalized her documentary film *Three Lives* (1970) for Women's Liberation Cinema Production and validated *The Prostitution Papers: A Quartet for Female Voices* (1971), a sociological document. Describing experiences gathered from a variety of sources, the text of *The Prostitution Papers* mediates between conservative and liberal views of the sex trade, which Millett exonerates. With equal passion she discusses attitudes toward politics, mental illness, and bisexuality in a confessional autobiography, *Flying* (1971), and in two painfully candid memoirs, *Sita* (1977) and *The Loony-Bin Trip* (1980). She confronts VIOLENCE against females in *The Basement: Meditations on Human Sacrifice* (1979), a probe of the extensive assaults on and murder of 16-year-old Sylvia Marie Likens. Similar themes permeate *The Politics of Cruelty* (1994), which Millett based on her volunteer work in Iran with Islamic women. The publication of *Mother Millett* (2001) revealed a vulnerable side of the author. She denounced physicians for trivializing the medical symptoms of elderly women such as her mother, Helen, and challenged the institutional infantilizing of patients to suit the demands of nursing home staffs.

Bibliography

Clough, Patricia Ticineto. "The Hybrid Criticism of Patriarchy: Rereading Kate Millett's 'Sexual Politics,' " *Sociological Quarterly* 35, no. 3 (August 1994): 473–486.

Millett, Kate. *The Loony-Bin Trip.* Urbana: University of Illinois Press, 2000.

———. *Mother Millett.* New York: Verso, 2002.

———. *Sexual Politics.* Urbana: University of Illinois Press, 2000.

Mistral, Gabriela (1889–1957)

An influential Chilean feminist, poet, and educator, Gabriela Mistral was a spirited spokeswoman for girls' EDUCATION in a country where females were marginalized. She was named Lucila Godoy y Alcayaga at birth in the Andean village of Vicuña. Her Basque mother reared her and her sister, Emelina, after their Indian-Jewish father, an itinerant poet, abandoned them. Home schooling, which included Portuguese, Spanish, native lore, and Catholic fables and hagiography, advanced

Mistral's affinity for multiculturalism. She taught school in rural areas and published her own verse and parables as classroom texts. In 1909 the suicide of her lover, Romelio Ureta, a railroad employee, precipitated a mournful strand in her writings that wavered between sorrow and a mystic stoicism. Under a pen name adapted from the Italian writer Gabriele D'Annunzio and the French poet Frédéric Mistral, she won her first literary prize at age 25 for *Sonetos de la muerte* (Sonnets of death, 1914). In 1922 Columbia University's Hispanic Institute published a popular collection, *Desolación*, a source of some of her most anthologized verse.

After being named teacher of the nation, at age 33 Mistral worked harder to uplift Latin America's women and children. She and her companion, Laura Rodig, traveled to Mexico to further a curriculum designed to liberate girls from Catholic PATRIARCHY. Mistral collected cradle songs and poems on children and motherhood in *Lecturas para mujeres* (Readings for women, 1923). Central to her feminist writings is the elevation of WOMEN'S RIGHTS as a cornerstone of nationalism and a prelude to excellence in Chilean life and art. She melded the love of children with admiration for the female body in *Ternura* (Tenderness, 1925), which contains "I Am Not Alone" and "Tiny Feet."

In 1930 Mistral began a rise toward global recognition. She taught Spanish literature at Barnard, Middlebury College, and Vassar. In 1932 she began prolonged consular service as ambassador in Italy, Spain, Brazil, France, and the United States. In 1945 she became the first Latin American to receive the Nobel Prize in literature. She retired to Hempstead, New York, and completed "Profile of Sor Juana Ines de la Cruz" (1952), dedicated to a Hieronimite nun. Mistral returned to nationalistic themes in a long work, *Poema de Chile* (Poem of Chile, 1967), published a decade after her death of pancreatic cancer. Feminists have since claimed her poems, letters, and the essays on women that she contributed to journals. In 2003 the author Ursula LE GUIN published in English *Selected Poems of Gabriela Mistral*, a collection of pieces from the poet's most treasured colloquial works.

Bibliography

Gazarian-Gautier, Marie-Lise. "Teacher from the Valley of Elqui," *World and I* 14, no. 10 (October 1999): 286.

Mistral, Gabriela. *Poemas de las Madres: The Mothers' Poems*. Spokane: Eastern Washington University Press, 1996.

————. *Selected Poems of Gabriela Mistral*. Albuquerque: University of New Mexico Press, 2003.

Mitchell, Margaret (1900–1949)

The journalist Margaret Munnerlyn "Peggy" Mitchell created Scarlett O'Hara, one of the most enduring autonomous female personas in the history of American literature. Born to the Atlanta elite, Mitchell, the daughter of the suffragist Maybelle Stephens Mitchell, defied the codes of ladylike behavior from childhood and developed into a much-sought belle. In her youth she contrived from the anecdotes of relatives woman-centered plots and themes for stories, plays, and two novels. From Woodberry School and Washington Seminary she advanced to premed courses at Smith College. After her mother's death during the 1919 flu epidemic Mitchell returned home to care for her father and reentered the whirl of debutante parties. At age 22 she was briefly married to the bootlegger Berrien "Red" Upshaw, an abusive spouse.

Before her writing career Mitchell trained on the job by writing features and interviews for the *Atlanta Journal Sunday Magazine*. Her hero, the editor H. L. Mencken, spurned her submissions to *Smart Set*. She withdrew into housekeeping for a second husband, John Marsh, and recuperated from a horse riding accident that wrenched her ankle. Out of boredom she began framing a plantation romance, GONE WITH THE WIND (1936), from her grandmother's Civil War memories. Mitchell compiled details gathered from archives of period letters, memoirs, and DIARIES AND JOURNALS at the Atlanta Public Library. In the spotlight she placed Scarlett, an independent NEW WOMAN whose gift for survival derives from the ability to overcome cataclysmic loss, grief, and public disapproval. In 1935 Mitchell sold her 1,037-page manuscript to Macmillan. The astounding reception of the first-time novelist began with sale of a half-million copies within three months, selection as a 1936 Book of the Month Club novel, an American Booksellers Book of the Year, a bidding war for international publishing rights, and translation into 27 languages. Capping Mitchell's success was a Pulitzer Prize.

Reviewers turned in mixed commentary that noted structural weaknesses and sentimental dialogue amid the blood and thunder of cavalry musters and hospital amputation scenes. Others discovered within the love story the firm underpinnings of Civil War history and its political and economic aftermath, which generated "unlovely stories of those families who had been driven from mansions to boarding houses and from boarding houses to dingy rooms on back streets" (Mitchell, 650). As the protagonist takes over plantation labor and fine-tunes the mercantilism of the Reconstruction era, she accepts the lost prosperity of her girlhood, which can never return because the emancipation of slaves has eviscerated Southern agribusiness. She ponders that "nothing her mother had taught her was of any value whatsoever now. . . . Ellen could not have foreseen the collapse of the civilization in which she raised her daughters, could not have anticipated the disappearings of the places in society for which she trained them" (*ibid.*, 427). A born survivor, Scarlett mutes mental messages from the past while forging ahead in the urban business world.

Securing the fame of Mitchell's epic romance was the 1939 MGM screen version, which flourished in theaters and on television, video, and DVD. The spectacle of former dilettantes' surviving General William Tecumseh Sherman's defeat of Atlanta and the burning of city residences and warehouses boosted to cinema legend the roles of Vivien Leigh and Clark Gable as Scarlett and Rhett Butler, her third husband. An unexpected landmark was Hattie McDaniel's portrayal of Mammy, the first Hollywood role to earn an Academy Award for a black actress. To protect herself from being swallowed by the media, Mitchell retreated into home duties and volunteered for the Red Cross and war bond sales during the 1940s. She died at age 49 of a head injury after a taxi struck her in downtown Atlanta. The legendary writer who spawned the GWTW industry in Atlanta left grieving fans who had waited 10 years for a sequel reviving Scarlett and Rhett's love match. Mitchell's romantic sweep influenced the ecofeminist Barbara KINGSOLVER, the columnist Anna QUINDLEN, and the novelist and playwright Ruth Prawer JHABVALA, who retreated into *Gone with the Wind* during the Blitz.

Bibliography

Mitchell, Margaret. *Gone with the Wind.* New York: Time Warner, 1964.

Pyron, Darden Ashbury. *Recasting:* Gone with the Wind in American Culture. Miami: Florida International University, 1983.

Moers, Ellen (1928–1979)

One of the pioneers of feminist literary criticism, the educator Ellen Moers single-handedly carved out an equal place for women writers in the world canon. The daughter of a suffragist, she was born in New York City. She studied comparative literature at Vassar College, Radcliffe College, and Columbia University and taught English at Barnard and Hunter Colleges. In 1963 she accepted a commission from *Harper's* for the article "Angry Young Women," an essay accounting for explosive emotions and attitudes that gave rise to the women's movement. The essay was a precursor to one of the pinnacles of feminist literature and to the restructuring of women's studies and literature courses worldwide.

In 1976 Moers introduced significant commentary on FEMINIST CRITICISM with *Literary Women: The Great Writers,* a staple on the shelves of teachers, researchers, and literary historians. At a midpoint of the groundbreaking feminist criticism of the 1970s Moers's text stands between Kate MILLETT's introductory salvo against sexism in curricula, *Sexual Politics* (1970), and Sandra GILBERT and Susan GUBAR's *The Madwoman in the Attic: The Woman Writer and the Nineteenth-Century Literary Imagination* (1979). Moers speaks with authority on the downtime that women enjoy at night for artistic endeavors: "Night is the longest time when a woman's two hands are free to hold pen and paper" (Moers, 12). Her enthusiasm for the subject of women's writing bubbles up in such passages as a comment on female protagonists in chapter 7: "As a massive force for change in literature, heroism was born, like so much else that was revolutionary, in the last decades of the eighteenth century and the first of the nineteenth" (*ibid.*, 125). Moers substantiates her claims about the relevance of women's writing with myriad examples from the work of Jane AUSTEN, Elizabeth Barrett BROWNING, Emily DICKINSON, Margaret DRABBLE, George ELIOT, Elizabeth GASKELL, Tillie OLSEN, and Ann RADCLIFFE.

For the *American Scholar, Commentary,* the *New York Review of Books, Victorian Studies, Virginia Woolf Miscellany,* and *World,* Moers followed *Literary Women* with a definition of female Gothic and with illustrative essays on Willa CATHER, COLETTE, George SAND, Germaine de STAËL, Mary WOLLSTONECRAFT, and Virginia WOOLF. Moers's monograph, *Harriet Beecher Stowe and American Literature* (1978), retrieved from neglect UNCLE TOM'S CABIN (1852), which male critics tend to ignore because of its focus on feminist themes of blunted motherhood and mother-child separation. Two decades after the publication of *Literary Women* the Modern Language Association honored Moers as an audacious feminist and educator.

Bibliography

Moers, Ellen. *Literary Women.* New York: Oxford University Press, 1977.

Nord, Deborah Epstein. "Commemorating Literary Women: Ellen Moers and Feminist Criticism after Twenty Years," *Signs: Journal of Women in Culture and Society* 24, no. 3 (Spring 1999): 733–737.

Showalter, Elaine. "Killing the Angel in the House: The Autonomy of Women Writers," *Antioch Review* 50, no. 1–2 (Winter–Spring 1992): 207–220.

———. "Responsibilities and Realities: Curriculum for the Eighties," *ADE Bulletin* (Winter 1981): 17–21.

Moore, Marianne (1887–1972)

A maven of modernist poetry for 60 years, Marianne Craig Moore held a place in literary circles for deft treatment of uncommon subjects. A native of Kirkland outside Saint Louis, Missouri, she grew up fatherless after age seven in Carlisle, Pennsylvania, where her mother joined the English staff at Metzger Institute. After studying biology, law, and political history at Bryn Mawr the poet roved the art galleries of England and France and returned home to study typing and shorthand at Carlisle Commercial College. Supporting herself as a librarian, secretary, and teacher at the U.S. Industrial Indian School, Moore submitted imagist verse to the *Egoist, Others,* and *Poetry* magazines and to the *Dial,* which she edited for four years. A 289-line poem, "Marriage" (1923), rich with mythic and biblical allusions, incorporates reflections on EVE's union with the snakelike Adam, whom the poet calls a fabled monster. The poet warns the guileless bride to anticipate the groom's rapid metamorphosis into a tyrant through the pro-male marital power structure that dominates society. The virulence of Moore's scenario suggests why she chose to remain unmarried.

While living in Greenwich Village with her mother, Moore established a profitable career. She published *Observations* (1924), an award-winning collection, and followed with *The Pangolin and Other Verse* (1936), *What Are Years* (1941), and *Nevertheless* (1944). After her mother's death Moore at age 60 translated Jean de La Fontaine's French fables and completed *Collected Poems* (1951), winner of the Bollingen Prize, a National Book Award, the National Institute of Arts and Letters Gold Medal, and a Pulitzer Prize. She continued writing collections of prose and verse, concluding with an updating of Charles Perrault's FAIRY TALES, a 1962 four-act comedy adapted from Maria EDGEWORTH's *The Absentee* (1812). Five years before Moore's death she published *The Complete Poems* (1967).

Although she was a reserved, private artist, Moore brandished a masculine diction, keen satiric wit, and a muscular didacticism that was uncommon in female poets of her day. Around 1915 she composed "Sojourn in the Whale," which reflects her frustration with the male-dominated poetic milieu. She dramatizes the struggle of the speaker, sword in hand, trying to pry her way into a closed culture in which male gatekeepers shut out women because of their otherness. With fairy tale logic the poem imagines the adventuress as Rapunzel, whom PATRIARCHY stereotypes as incompetent. Rather than rage against gendered literary criticism, Moore maintains a cool restraint, the hallmark of her canon. In "Roses Only" (1924) she pictures women as whole human beings equipped with both fragrant petals and thorns. In *The Complete Prose of Marianne Moore* (1986) the author declares that women should develop intellect and enjoy choice. She predicted that full liberation would not endanger a firm American base of nuclear families led by wives and mothers willing to sacrifice for the sake of their children.

Bibliography

Martin, Taffy. *Marianne Moore: Subversive Modernist.* Austin: University of Texas Press, 1986.

Miller, Christanne. *Marianne Moore: Questions of Authority.* Cambridge, Mass.: Harvard University Press, 1995.

Moore, Marianne. *The Complete Poems of Marianne Moore.* New York: Viking, 1981.

———. *The Complete Prose of Marianne Moore.* New York: Viking, 1986.

Zona, Kirstin Hotelling. *Marianne Moore, Elizabeth Bishop, and May Swenson: The Feminist Poetics of Self-Restraint.* Chicago: University of Michigan Press, 2002.

Moraga, Cherríe (1952–)

The award-winning Chicana editor, dramatist, and teacher Cherríe Lawrence Moraga merges literary pursuits with prowoman activism. Born to a tightly monocultural Chicano family in Whittier, California, she described herself as *la guera* (a light-skinned woman). She broke family tradition by seeking an education and entry to the professions. She earned a teaching degree at Musician's Institute, a nonsectarian Hollywood college, and taught at a Los Angeles high school. From the exhilaration of composing her first lesbian lyric verse, she pursued creative writing at San Francisco State University and at age 22 announced her lesbianism to her decidedly patriarchal family.

After completing an M.A., Moraga joined Gloria ANZALDÚA in coediting *This Bridge Called My Back: Writings by Radical Women of Color* (1981), a groundbreaking anthology that expanded the mainstream feminist movement with the inclusion of lesbian, laboring-class, and nonwhite women. The book was a publication of KITCHEN TABLE / WOMEN OF COLOR PRESS, America's first publishing house devoted to the dissemination of works by nonwhite and lesbian women, which Moraga cofounded with Barbara Smith and the poet Audre LORDE. The book, which won a Before Columbus Foundation American Book Award, became a feminist touchstone and a standard addition to women's studies curricula worldwide.

For Moraga the 1980s was a fertile period. In addition to teaching Portuguese, Spanish, and drama at Stanford University, she published *Loving in the War Years: Lo que nunca pasó por sus labios* (What you never said, 1983), the first feminist text written by a Chicana lesbian. In the space of five years she wrote four plays: *La extranjera* (The stranger, 1985), *Giving Up the Ghost: Teatro in 2 Acts* (1986), *Shadow of a Man* (1988), and *Heroes and Saints* (1989). The latter spotlights the prophetess Cerezita, a grotesque female who symbolizes the physical deterioration of stoop laborers that results from contact with pesticides and pollutants. For *Heroes and Saints* Moraga received a Pen West Award for Drama, the Critics Circle Award, and the Will Glickman Prize. She took a bold politicized stand in *The Last Generation: Prose and Poetry* (1993), in which she accuses the Chicano culture of condoning rape, incest, female and child battery, and blatant sexism. Her message to female readers is to stop waiting for rescue by taking action against centuries of maltreatment and devaluation.

In her 40s Moraga continued to embrace her mongrel status as a Chicana lesbian feminist writer by melding the personal with the polemical. She wrote two successful plays, *Circle in the Dirt* (1995) and *Watsonville: Some Place Not Here* (1996), both of which probe the founts of strength in California Chicanas. In 1997 she broached unexplored territory with *Waiting in the Wings: Portrait of a Queer Motherhood*, the story of artificial insemination administered by her mate and co-mother, Ella, with sperm donated by their friend Pablo. Moraga expresses complex emotions at maternity and the rearing of Raul, who was born premature to a circle of supportive women.

Bibliography

DeRose, David J. "Cherríe Moraga," *American Theatre* 13, no. 8 (October 1996): 76–78.

Moraga, Cherríe. *Heroes and Saints and Other Plays.* Albuquerque: University of New Mexico Press, 2001.

———. *The Last Generation: Prose and Poetry.* Boston: South End Press, 1993.

———. *Waiting in the Wings.* Ann Arbor, Mich.: Firebrand Books, 1997.

Morejón, Nancy (1944–)

The African-Cuban poet, translator, historian, and critic Nancy Morejón expresses the truths of life for black Caribbean women. Born in Havana to a seamstress and a stevedore, she became the first black islander to graduate from Havana University. She accepted two demanding posts—as director of the Centre for Caribbean Studies at Casa de las Americas and adviser to the Teatro Nacional de Cuba. With a major in French and intense reading and analysis of imagist poets she began a career with her first collection in 1964 and with submissions to *Black Renaissance, Black Scholar, Boundary,* and *World Literature Today.* In 1985 the *San Francisco Chronicle* identified her as a major feminist writer with the publication of *Where the Island Sleeps like a Wing.* In 1998 she joined the Royal Academy of Cuban Language. At age 60 she became the first black female to receive the National Literature Prize.

Because she labors under an inheritance of otherness from slave times, it is significant that Morejón has become Cuba's most beloved and translated female poet. In striving toward a healthy form of women's liberation, she sets parameters for female figures that define and limit them from the male sphere, particularly the Hispano-Latino milieu. Elements freeing her women from the ghosts of bondage begin with a love of nature and extend to a joy in uninhibited dance and SEXUALITY and in the worship of West African gods through Santería. Her frequently anthologized poem "Amo a mi amo" (I love my master, 1982) studies the womanist elements of dark-skinned sexual exoticism and its appeal to the womanizer.

As do other history-minded feminist writers, Morejón recognizes the debt she owes to fore-mothers. With rhetorical questions she expresses in "Persona" (2001) her physical and spiritual ties to the first black female islanders imported from Benin. In the mid-1980s she provided captions for Milton Rogovin's photographs of WOMAN'S WORK, the focus of *With Eyes and Soul: Images of Cuba* (2004), a tribute to the underappreciated working class. In the poem "Elogia de la Dialéctica" (Praise for debate, 1982) she challenges the female poet to break the code of female SILENCING. In place of the passive female she urges the writer to interact with the world and to denounce social dicta by being tomorrow's woman, who is willing to die for social betterment.

Bibliography

DeCosta-Willis, Miriam. "Afra-Hispanic Writers and Feminist Discourse," *NWSA Journal* 5, no. 2 (Summer 1993): 204–217.

Moi, Toril. *Sexual, Textual Politics: Feminist Literary Theory.* New York: Routledge, 1984.

Morejón, Nancy. *Black Woman and Other Poems.* London: Mango, 2004.

———. "Persona," *Black Renaissance* 3, no. 3 (Summer–Fall 2001–2002), 171–172.

Morgan, Robin (1941–)

The polemicist, poet, and editor Robin Morgan balances radical feminism with passionate verse that discloses female vulnerability. Born of Polish-Russian-Jewish heritage in Lake Worth, Florida, she was the child of a bullying stage mother who convinced her children that their absent father died heroically in battle during World War II. According to Morgan's memoir, *Saturday's Child* (2000), she modeled at age two and had her own radio program two years later. In the 1950s she appeared on *I Remember Mama,* a popular television series, as Dagmar Hansen, the pigtailed youngest child of a Norwegian-American family living in San Francisco. Early in her philosophical formation she looked to the ideologue Bella Abzug and the author Simone de BEAUVOIR as feminist models for such actions as civil rights and WOMEN'S RIGHTS activism at Columbia University. In her 20s Morgan protested the Miss America pageant in 1968, glued the locks of the Stock Exchange in defiance of patriarchal businesses, and joined a sit-in against violent pornography at Grove Press in 1970.

Morgan developed a career in editing feminist works, notably *The New Women* (1970), *Sisterhood Is Powerful* (1970), and *Going Too Far: The Personal Chronicles of a Feminist* (1977). Looking back over a procession of small triumphs, the author, coiner of the slogan "The personal is political," exults, "Thirty years ago, such phrases as 'battered woman,' 'date rape,' or 'sexual harassment,' didn't exist; those awful realities were just called 'ordinary life'" (Thom, 4; Jay, 9). In her early verse Morgan created stark images of society's misperception of females in the poem "The Invisible Woman" (1972), which pictures the male medical world as ignorant of its gendered shortcomings.

Morgan focused increasingly on sexual politics in the 1980s. In *The Anatomy of Freedom: Feminism, Physics, and Global Politics* (1982) she looked longingly toward a utopian era of shared labor and responsibility. Of the prophets and planners of the future she anticipated a time when visionaries gain respect. Of that era she cites the English poet Adelaide Ann Proctor, author of *Legends and Lyrics* (2003): "Dreams grow holy when put in action" (Morgan, 1982, 83). A controversial tie between out-of-control PATRIARCHY and terrorism underlies Morgan's *The Demon Lover: The Roots of Terrorism* (1989), a feminist manifesto denouncing global VIOLENCE by deranged hit men. For material she interviewed Palestinian women in prison camps and discussed terrorism with the Arab feminists Farida Allaghi and Fawzia Hassouna. In the introduction to the 2001 edition Morgan describes the lethal position of women in political upheaval with a Vietnamese aphorism—"the grass that gets trampled when elephants fight" (Morgan, *Demon*, 24). She dates the causes of worldwide violence to "an androcentric cultural heritage from biblical times to the present," which she characterizes as a tool of the American religious Right (*ibid.*).

In her third decade of writing Morgan continued to electrify readers with forthright social theory. In 2003 she commissioned the cream of feminist authorship to supply 60 essays for *Sisterhood Is Forever: The Women's Anthology for a New Millennium*. Among essays on biological determin-

ism, GENDER BIAS, and workplace sexism by Andrea DWORKIN, Anita Hill, Grace PALEY, Pat Schroeder, Eleanor Smeal, Gloria STEINEM, and Faye Wattleton are Morgan's thanks to veteran feminists and a welcome to women new to the movement. The key to Morgan's efficacy as an organizer and essayist is her sensitivity to the grassroots issues of individual constituencies, especially lesbian and bisexual women, farm wives, single mothers, students, and developing world women targeted for government-sanctioned sequential rapes and other war crimes.

Bibliography

Echols, Alice. *Daring to Be Bad: Radical Feminism in America, 1967–1975.* Minneapolis: University of Minnesota Press, 1990.

Jay, Karla. "What Ever Happened to Baby Robin?" *Lambda Book Report* 9, no. 11 (June 2001): 8–11.

Morgan, Robin. *The Anatomy of Freedom: Feminism, Physics, and Global Politics.* New York: Anchor, 1982.

———. *The Demon Lover: The Roots of Terrorism.* New York: Washington Square Press, 2001.

———. *A Hot January: Poems 1996–1999.* New York: W. W. Norton, 2001.

———. *Saturday's Child: A Memoir.* New York: W. W. Norton, 2000.

———. *Sisterhood Is Forever: The Women's Anthology for a New Millennium.* New York: Washington Square Press, 2003.

———. *Upstairs in the Garden: Poems Selected Old and New, 1968–1988.* New York: W. W. Norton, 1991.

Thom, Mary. *Inside Ms.: 24 Years of the Magazine and the Feminist Movement.* New York: Henry Holt, 1997.

Morrison, Toni (1931–)

A revered author of feminist literature and the eighth woman to receive the Nobel Prize in literature, Toni Morrison is a model of compassion for the disempowered. Born Chloe Anthony "Toni" Wofford west of Cleveland in Lorain, Ohio, she grew up in a divided household in which her sharecropper father reviled whites while her mother urged tolerance. Morrison's training in dialogue and STORYTELLING came about naturally through daily contact with community women who treasured myths, fables, and stories passed to them as family heirlooms. A scholar in English literature at Howard University and Cornell University, she taught English and humanities and, while rearing two sons, edited the works of Toni Cade BAMBARA and Angela DAVIS for Random House. During quiet time she composed a short story, the beginnings of *The BLUEST EYE* (1970), one of her most moving visions of the blameless black female victim. The novel energized numerous book clubs and inspired the writing of the novelist Gloria NAYLOR.

After the positive public reception of *Sula* (1973), *Song of Solomon* (1977), *Tar Baby* (1981), and the play *Dreaming Emmett* (1986) Morrison produced *BELOVED* (1987), her masterwork, based on the sufferings of Margaret Garner, a runaway slave and child killer who sacrificed her daughter to spare her the cyclical rape of enslaved females. Set in the early years after the Civil War, the circular narrative bears Gothic elements. She characterizes American slavery as the source of a spiritual haunting that hangs on survivors, black and white, into the 20th century. Subsequent works—*Jazz* (1992), *Playing in the Dark: Whiteness and the Literary Imagination* (1992), *Paradise* (1998), and *Love* (2003)—have secured the author's place in the canon of African-American, feminist, and world fiction. She also collaborated with her son, Slade Kevin Morrison, on five children's books, *The Big Box* (1999), *The Book of Mean People* (2002), *Who's Got Game? Poppy or the Snake?* (2002), *Who's Got Game? The Lion or the Mouse* (2004), and *The Mirror or the Glass* (2005).

Central to Morrison's importance in feminist literature is her creation of fictional individuals who cling to unique, often bizarre qualities and behavior while winning the reader's sympathy for their warmth and basic decency. Pilate, the bootlegging virago of *Song of Solomon*, accounts for her love of her brother, Macon: "He's the *only* one. I was cut off from people early. You can't know what that was like" (Morrison, *Song*, 141). A wanderer escaping a pedophile, she joins migrants and collects rocks from each job site. Driven out by people suspicious of a woman born without a navel, Pilate considers that "although men fucked armless women, one-legged women, hunchbacks and blind women, drunken women, razor-toting women,

midgets, small children, convicts, boys, sheep, dogs, goats, liver, each other, and even certain species of plants," they shy away from the navelless freak (*ibid.*, 148). Drawn to fellow outcasts, Pilate rises to the majesty and authority of a matriarch at the funeral of her spurned granddaughter, Hagar. In a call-and-response duo with her daughter, Reba, Pilate demands mercy and retreats into a solo to question, "Who's been botherin my sweet sugar lumpkin?" (*ibid.*, 318). As an elephant lifts its trunk skyward, she ends the trope with a mighty declaration, "And she was *loved!*" (*ibid.*, 319).

Morrison's skill at such textured scenarios derives from a command of controlling metaphors that enfold and enrich feminist themes, such as the moribund flower seeds in *The Bluest Eye*, the quest for ancestors in *Song of Solomon* and *Love*, and breast milk and the worn shoes of runaway slaves in *Beloved*. The first black woman to publish a Book of the Month Club selection, she claims an enviable slate of awards—the National Book Award, the Ohioana Book Award, a presidential appointment to the National Council on the Arts by President Jimmy Carter, and a Pulitzer Prize for *Beloved*. The 1998 film version, starring Oprah Winfrey and Danny Glover as the lovers, Sethe and Paul D, failed to coordinate strong metaphors or to replicate the powerful archetype of the slave breeder whose humane execution of a baby girl stirs enmity in her own people.

Bibliography

Morrison, Toni. *Beloved*. New York: Plume, 1987.

———. *The Bluest Eye*. New York: Plume, 1993.

———. *Song of Solomon*. New York: Plume, 1987.

Plasa, Carl. *Toni Morrison: Beloved*. New York: Columbia University Press, 1998.

Taylor-Guthrie, Danille Kathleen, ed. *Conversations with Toni Morrison*. Jackson: University Press of Mississippi, 1994.

mother-daughter relationships

A dependable motif in feminist literature, communication between mother and daughter demands candor and constant renewal. As the playwright Siddalee Walker, protagonist of Rebecca WELLS's *Divine Secrets of the Ya-Ya Sisterhood* (1996), explains, motherhood is a source as holy as breast milk: "My creativity comes in a direct flow from my mother" (Wells, 2). The uniqueness of individual families produces wide variations in memories borne from childhood. The author Djuna BARNES exposed the confusion and miscommunication of parent and child in *The Antiphon* (1958), a tragedy in blank verse filled with Gothic elements drawn from her own life. In contrast to Barnes's unsettling memories, her fellow lesbian author Rita Mae BROWN honors her own parent-child relationship in the opening lines of *Rubyfruit Jungle* (1973): "Mother and aunts tell us about infancy and early childhood hoping we won't forget the past when they had total control over our lives and secretly praying that because of it, we'll include them in our future" (Brown, 3). Whether they include or shut them out, daughters have little choice but to pigeonhole their recall of moments in the past when the mother was the giants of their life.

In feminist memoir the relationship of the author to a maternal figure often reveals the roots of pride in womanhood and women's history. In 1912 Mary ANTIN, a Russian-Jewish immigrant to Boston, wrote *The Promised Land*, in which she relived the strong ties to her female parent in motherly Jewish lullabies. Antin recalls hearing "lofty themes . . . the names of Rebecca, Rachel, and Leah" (Antin, 40). The noble songs of Palestine, the loss of Zion, and prayers prepared Antin for her own motherhood. Her parents urged that she marry a pious man and bear many sons, one of them the messiah. She implies that the androcentrism of Orthodox Jewry forced her in the opposite direction. She chose a feminist course as she "learned how to strip from [traditions] the prickly husk in which they were passed down to me" (*ibid.*, 41).

The mother-daughter dyad often reduplicates itself into a lineage of women extending back in time over episodes of pain and threat. In Gayl JONES's stream-of-consciousness novel *Corregidora* (1975) the blues singer, Ursa, requires a matrilineal history to explain her family's suffering. Because her mother refuses to divulge the sexual abuses she endured during SLAVERY in Brazil, Ursa wars against silence. Her own story "was easier than what she wouldn't tell me. I knew she had more" (Jones, 103). Dedicated to a singing career that

calls for truthful lyrics, Ursa is stymied by missing information. She mourns, "How could she . . . refuse me what she had lived?" (*ibid.*). The French feminist philosopher Luce IRIGARAY, author of *Sexes and Genres through Languages: Elements of Sexual Communication* (2003), accounts for the vital, life-nurturing link between mother and daughter, a psychological parallel to the umbilical cord. In her poem "Et l'une ne bouge pas sans l'autre" ("And one doesn't stir without the other," 1977) the insistent filial voice demands, "what I wanted from you, Mother . . . that in giving me life, you still remain alive" (Irigaray, 67).

Negative models of mothering overlay feminist recall of childhood as raw-edged shards. The Haitian-born writer Edwidge DANTICAT characterizes an ongoing treachery in the novel *Breath, Eyes, Memory* (1994), which describes a mother's sexual abuse of her daughter, Sophie. The violations are an outgrowth of Martine Caco's rape and the resulting conception of Sophie, a souvenir of Martine's degradation. To shield family honor and to impress on Sophie the value of virginity, Martine regularly tests her daughter's hymen for rupture. Danticat builds the theme of dual violation, the rape of the mother and a vicious series of child penetrations that challenge the daughter's honesty and assault her modesty. At the height of outrage the daughter restores her autonomy by tearing her hymen with a pestle, a self-mutilation that defeats her mother's probing. Sophie's rash solution suggests how much she longs to restore a loving intimacy with Martine.

Complicating the mother-daughter pairing is the inevitable reversal of roles from child to guardian of a senile parent. Published the year after her mother's death, Denise LEVERTOV's poem "Death in Mexico" (1978) traverses the final stages of her parent's life. As a garden returns from the imposed ideal to the wild, the poem moves through a self-revelatory grief that mortals are as temporary as plants. As though depicting in metaphor the irrevocable loss of health and vigor over a five-week decline, the narrative vivifies the destruction of her mother's garden in a month's time after 20 years of tending. Prefiguring a processional to the grave, Levertov pictures the gardener, borne past her flower beds on a stretcher, as too blind to focus on the transformation of her handiwork. Building on the image of blurred vision, the poet-speaker turns to the obdurate masks of stone gods and their victims, whose fixed gaze allows no response to life, even a crawling vine or scorpion over the face. Alienated by death and Mexican exotica, the speaker portrays the flower beds as her mother's hostages released by her death into their natural surroundings.

The issue of mother hunger in motherless girls overlays feminist writings as a gossamer veil that both conceals and enlightens. In Marilynne ROBINSON's *Housekeeping* (1981) Ruth Stone suffers a longing so much a part of her psyche that it blends seamlessly with her daydreams. In a luminous image the novelist states: "To crave and to have are as like as a thing and its shadow. . . . For to wish for a hand on one's hair is all but to feel it" (Robinson, 161). A paradox solaces the speaker with reward: "So whatever we may lose, the very craving gives it back to us again. Though we dream and hardly know it, longing, like an angel, fosters us, smooths our hair, and brings us wild strawberries" (*ibid.*). Preposterous, yet harmlessly romantic, the state of need transforms painful yearnings into harmless visions of nurturance and affection.

Less tortured memories of mothering focus on the creative acts of conception, birthing, and nurturing. In 1997 the novelist and ecofeminist Barbara KINGSOLVER produced a salute to the right thinking of her mother, Virginia Lee Henry "Ginny" Kingsolver. Anthologized in *I've Always Meant to Tell You: Letters to Our Mothers: An Anthology of Contemporary Women Writers* (1997), the author's praise of high-quality mothering cites natural childbirth and breast-feeding as examples of her mother's belief in instinct: "You risked the contempt of your peers, went right ahead, and did what you knew was best for your babies" (Kingsolver, 260). Ginny's defiance of the parenting fads of her day undergirds the resolve of her daughter. Kingsolver champions in fiction the worth of close mother-daughter ties and of matrilineal traditions that defy the whims of fashion.

Bibliography

Antin, Mary. *The Promised Land.* Boston: Houghton Mifflin, 1912.

Brown, Rita Mae. *Rubyfruit Jungle.* New York: Bantam, 1983.

Danticat, Edwidge. *Breath, Eyes, Memory.* New York: Soho Press, 1998.

Irigaray, Luce. *This Sex Which Is Not One.* Ithaca, N.Y.: Cornell University Press, 1985.

Jones, Gayl. *Corregidora.* New York: Random House, 1975.

Kingsolver, Barbara. *I've Always Meant to Tell You: Letters to Our Mothers: An Anthology of Contemporary Women Writers.* New York: Pocket Star, 1997.

Robinson, Marilynne. *Housekeeping.* New York: Bantam, 1982.

Wells, Rebecca. *Divine Secrets of the Ya-Ya Sisterhood.* New York: Perennial, 2004.

Williams, Gary. "Resurrecting Carthage: *Housekeeping* and Cultural History," *English Language Notes* 29, no. 2 (December 1991): 70–78.

Mott, Lucretia (1793–1880)

The Quaker orator and reformer Lucretia Coffin Mott honed her speaking ability and platform presence in defense of ABOLITIONISM and WOMEN'S RIGHTS. Born to a pious household in Nantucket, Massachusetts, she received a parochial education in Boston in the humanitarian concerns of Quakerism. At age 28 she was appointed to the Quaker ministry. As a platform evangelist for the Society of Friends she developed acumen in gently persuasive speech. After marrying James Mott, she reared their six children to maturity before involving herself in social issues.

At age 40 Mott formed the Philadelphia Female Anti-Slavery Society and took her emancipation platform to a convention in London, where authorities barred women from sessions. While championing the rights of slaves to be free individuals, she recognized the powerlessness of female activists, even though they were white and free. In a letter to her husband concerning her public humiliation she stated, "I never failed in our several tea-parties & soirees to avail myself of every offer made for utterance of our cause—& then I shrank not from the whole truth" (Mott, 2002, 4). Guiding her steps was a resoundingly pro-woman document, Sarah GRIMKÉ's *Letters on the Equality of the Sexes and the Condition of Women* (1838), the nation's first feminist tract.

Mott felt destined to achieve at least some of her reform goals. To plan tactics that would win full citizenship for women, in 1848 she and Elizabeth Cady STANTON gathered activists at Jane C. Hunt's house at Waterloo, New York, at what historians call the Waterloo Tea Party. Stanton was so bold in her tactics that she caused the gentle, even-tempered Mott to murmur, "Thou will make us ridiculous" (Schneir, 110). Nineteen planners reconvened at Mary Ann McClintock's house and wrote out their beliefs that all people, male and female, are created equal. More than 300 delegates attended an historic assembly at the Wesleyan Chapel, where Mott's husband presided. At the opening session Mott spoke eloquently on "Progress of Reforms" from TEMPERANCE to peace, nonresistance, abolition of SLAVERY, and attainment of woman SUFFRAGE. Of her powerful delivery the abolitionist and women's rights champion Frederick DOUGLASS admired the glory and serenity of her presence and the positive, loving tone of her words.

Mott's speeches have the ring of authority. On December 17, 1849, she made her most famous speech, "Discourse on Woman," before the Philadelphia assembly building in support of women's enfranchisement. Basing her argument on a Christian belief that God gave women intelligence and equality, Mott demanded "stronger and more profitable food" than the blandishments of courtiers and flatterers to pretty coquettes (Mott, 1849, 4). Her reasoning struck sparks on the issues of the wife's loss of property to her husband upon marriage and the taxing of single women's property to support colleges that refused their applications. With propriety and grace she concluded with a charge "to water the undying bud, and give it healthy culture, and open its beauty to the sun" (ibid., 20). In 1854 she faced hostile ministers and refuted their scriptural claims that God intended women to be inferior to men. Charging priests with the same misogyny that fueled WITCHCRAFT trials, she insisted that ministers prostituted scripture to their own ends. To misogynistic citations from Saint Paul she quoted Peter, who stated, "Upon my servants and my handmaidens I will pour out my spirit and they shall prophesy" (Schneir, 102). Mott concluded, "Now can anything be clearer than that?" (ibid.).

Mott's rhetorical and personal influence extended far beyond her life span of 87 years. The fiction writer and journalist Rebecca Harding DAVIS met the Quaker orator and recorded in *Bits of Gossip* (1906) that the suffragist was remarkable for brain power and eloquence even in old age. In 1949 the French philosopher and gender advocate Simone de BEAUVOIR published a salute to Mott in *Le deuxième sex* (*The* SECOND SEX). To establish worthy models for young girls, she pointed out, Mott "composed a manifesto of Quaker inspiration which set the tone for all American feminism" (Simons, 64).

Bibliography

Mott, Lucretia. "Discourse on Women" (1849). Available online. URL: http://memory.loc.gov/cgi-bin/query/D?nawbib:1:./temp/~ammem_YWLe::. Accessed on October 16, 2005.

———. *Selected Letters of Lucretia Coffin Mott*. Chicago: University of Illinois Press, 2002.

Schneir, Miriam, ed. *Feminism: The Essential Historical Writings*. New York: Vintage, 1972.

Simons, Margaret A. *Beauvoir and the Second Sex*. Lanham, Md.: Rowman & Littlefield, 2001.

Mourning Dove (1888–1936)

A champion of social justice, Mourning Dove was an innovator of First Peoples' literature and a voice for the half-breed Native American female ostracized by whites and Indians. Much of her biography derives from *Mourning Dove: A Salishan Autobiography*, published posthumously in 1990. It names her parents as Lucy Stuikin and Joseph Quintasket, illiterate Natives. She describes her birthplace as a canoe on the Kootenay River near Bonner's Ferry, Idaho, where her maternal grandmother, Maria, delivered her. Named Christine (or Christal) Quintasket, she claimed Okanogon-Nicola-Scottish lineage and grew up on the Colville Reservation in Washington State. After learning English from Jimmy Ryan, a white adopted brother, Mourning Dove received formal education until age 14 at Goodwin Mission School near Kettle Falls, Washington, the Fort Spokane School for Indians, and the Fort Shaw Indian School in Montana.

Mourning Dove learned reverence for women from her mother, who believed that female healers were as valuable to a tribe as warriors. The author looked back on a time when her mother wept from hunger as she fed her two older children. Mourning Dove realized, "Our childish selfishness did not understand that our mother was going without to keep us alive while she yet had to nurse a third" (Mourning Dove, 1990, 161). Traditional training continued under her mother and Teequalt or Long Theresa, a female WISEWOMAN. Among the gender-specific duties of a female tribe member were introduction to religion and spiritual empowerment through dance, apprenticeship in fishing and hunting, training in courtship ritual, instruction in marriage and wifely duties, preparation for birthing and child care, and acceptance of a widow's lot.

In 1913 Mourning Dove studied secretarial skills at Calgary College in Alberta and taught at an Indian school near Oliver, British Columbia. She earned her living harvesting apples and hops, cooking in camp kitchens, and innkeeping. After work in cabin or tent she valued quiet time to compose her thoughts on a portable typewriter. In 1921 she attained some economic stability by acquiring title to her land allotment. She turned to ethnography in 1993 with *Coyote Stories*, a collection of northwestern American animistic lore she collected and translated into English. After a spirited era of public speaking, promotion of Native tradition and crafts, and election to the Colville council, she suffered from stress and died of rheumatoid arthritis and exhaustion.

Dubbed the first Native American novelist, the author wrote under the pen name Hum-ishu-ma or Mourning Dove. She compiled a lively dialect romance, COGEWEA, THE HALF-BLOOD: *A Depiction of the Great Montana Cattle Range* (1927). A white editor, Lucullus Virgil McWhorter, compromised the controversial text with insertions and bowdlerizing. In the narrative Mourning Dove identifies with and honors the Métis who refuse to tolerate humiliation for having mixed blood or dual background. She charges that young Indians are turncoats who "banish the idea of old tribal customs and laugh to scorn that which was sacred to the generations past" (Mourning Dove, 1981, 242). As a boost to self-esteem her protagonist rejects Christian hypocrisy and materialism. In place of Bible teachings she advances the role of woman as story keeper, visionary, and performer of oral episodes from native prehistory.

Set on the Flathead Reservation in Montana in the early 1900s, Mourning Dove's popular melodrama describes the exploitation of Cogewea McDonald by her white father, who bequeaths her a mere $20, and by her white lover, Alfred Densmore, a "dam' robbin', gal-beatin' son-of-a-cuss" (*ibid.*, 279). In anger at Cogewea's grandmother, the storyteller who refuses his marriage proposal, he howls, "I will yet pluck your dear fledgling and return it to you so soiled that your own foul wing will refuse it shelter!" (Donovan, 249). He invokes white PATRIARCHY as justification for seizing Cogewea's pistol and controlling her money. By picturing Jim, "one of her own kind," as Cogewea's rescuer and future mate, Mourning Dove validates Native ways (*ibid.*, 241). Corroborating her decision are Jim's belief in sweathouse purification rites and positive signs from nature—the smiling Moon and the spirit voice emanating from a gray buffalo skull—that ensure that Cogewea will keep Okanogan culture alive within her family.

Bibliography

Donovan, Kathleen M. *Feminist Readings of Native American Literature: Coming to Voice*. Tucson: University of Arizona Press, 1998.

Kent, Alicia. "Mourning Dove's *Cogewea*: Writing Her Way into Modernity," *MELUS* 24, no. 3 (Fall 1999): 39–66.

Mourning Dove. *Cogewea, The Half-Blood: A Depiction of the Great Montana Cattle Range*. Lincoln: University of Nebraska Press, 1981.

———. *Mourning Dove: A Salishan Autobiography*. Lincoln: University of Nebraska Press, 1990.

Ms.

For feminist readers *Ms.* magazine was a breakthrough from decades of women's periodicals featuring makeup tips, weight loss, kitchen makeovers, and brownie recipes. Established by the feminist diva Gloria STEINEM and the editor Catherine O'Haire, it was the world's first magazine written and edited by women for women. It got its start in

1971 with an initial 85,000 subscribers and with support from the *Washington Post* publisher Katharine Graham, the activist Eleanor Smeal, the Feminist Majority Foundation, the Ford Foundation, and the Rockefeller Trust. *Ms.* took shape during heady times for feminist efforts. Before its formal naming planners considered *Everywoman, Lilith, Sisters,* and *Sojourner;* Rochelle Udall, who was on staff at *New Yorker* magazine, came up with *Ms.*, a form of address that Congresswoman Bella Abzug had introduced in the U.S. legislature. Anne Mather reported in her three-part "A History of Feminist Periodicals" for *Journalism History* that from 1968 to 1973 some 560 feminist journals went into publication. None, however, compared in broad appeal with *Ms.*

From the outset the magazine reached out to independent, responsible women who demanded recognition and equality. Of its mission Steinem, a regular columnist, remarked, "It is the hardest thing I've ever done, the cause of the most lost sleep and income. . . . Yet I'm very proud of *Ms.*, especially as I learn what it means in women's lives" (Frank, 77). In its first issue, dated spring 1972, were the essays "The Sexual Revolution Wasn't Our War," "How to Write Your Own Marriage Contract," and "Welfare Is a Women's Issue." The stimulus preceded a steady outpouring of reader letters that were often the most insightful part of the issue.

In some respects the magazine seemed more a movement than a journal. Subsequent issues insisted that health is more important than beauty and posted straightforward information on date rape, plastic surgery, spousal abuse, stalking, and the danger that acquired immunodeficiency syndrome (AIDS) poses to wives who do not suspect their husbands of bisexuality. Sell-out issues included those of November 1976, featuring the article "How's Your Sex Life?" and September 1977, offering "Why Women Don't Like Their Bodies." During a financial shortfall in 1979 backers made the publication a nonprofit effort. In 1990 staff and supporters worked out a system by which the magazine could support itself without advertisements and introduced their new concept with Steinem's essay "Sex, Lies, and Advertising." The new format gave greater emphasis to literature and photojournalism.

In 1992 when circulation in the United States topped 220,000 and readership reached 450,000, sales extended beyond North America to the United Kingdom and 22 other countries. The staff mailed free subscriptions to women in prisons, battered women's shelters, and welfare centers. Although the magazine shrank from a slick monthly to a quarterly, devoted staff maintained outreach to global issues, book and music reviews, and alerts about CENSORSHIP. Among the projects of the Ms. Foundation were all-women businesses, the Breaking Silence effort against incest, black housing developments, and marketing of the work of Native American craftswomen. The magazine incorporated articles, poetry, and stories by top-rated feminist writers and activists—Margaret ATWOOD, Helen Gurley Brown, Edwidge DANTICAT, Anita DIAMANT, Barbara EHRENREICH, Louise ERDRICH, Susan FALUDI, Marcia Gillespie, Nadine GORDIMER, Germaine GREER, Bessie HEAD, bell HOOKS, Florence KING, Doris LESSING, Robin MORGAN, Grace PALEY, Marge PIERCY, Letty Cottin POGREBIN, Katha POLLITT, Alice WALKER, and Naomi WOLF.

The magazine thrived through incisive observations and high-quality feminist writing. For exposing the virulence of antiabortionists in *Bitter Medicine* (1987), the author Sara PARETSKY earned the staff's admiration. In June 2001 Erica Doyle lauded the feminist fiction of Barbara KINGSOLVER, a writer of meaty stories and novels that satisfy the public's need for fulfilling reading material. Late in 2001 Ms. staffers celebrated a 30th anniversary with a Women of the Year edition. Contributing to the peace effort was the activist author Tillie OLSEN's essay, "Why Peace Is (More Than Ever) a Feminist Issue" (2003), a retrospective on where the women's movement began and why it influences world events. The quality and freshness of the magazine's layout keep demand for Ms. high in public and school libraries and women's shelters as well as in homes, dormitories, and offices.

Bibliography

Campbell, Kim. "It's 'Best' Lists Time: Here's Ms. Magazine's," *Christian Science Monitor,* 13 December 2001, p. 17.

Frank, Christina. "Life as a Lightning Rod," *Biography* 6, no. 3 (March 2002): 74–78.

Thom, Mary. *Inside Ms.: 24 Years of the Magazine and the Feminist Movement.* New York: Henry Holt, 1997.

White, Lesley. "Feminism with No Ad-ditives," *London Sunday Times,* 22 November 1992, pp. 5.1–5.2.

Mukherjee, Bharati (1940–)

The pro-woman essayist and fiction writer Bharati Mukherjee surveys the difficulties of unassimilated immigrant Asian women and their makeshift lives in North America. Born in Calcutta to wealthy Brahmins, she grew up in a society bent on forcing women to be obedient. She learned from her two grandmothers Indian-style STORYTELLING along with the duties of wife and parent. The author recalled that her mother, a protofeminist, "quite literally put her body on the line so that we three sisters would be educated" (Ruta, 13). Mukherjee studied in England and Switzerland and under Irish sisters at an Indian convent school before completing a degree in English at the University of Calcutta. At the Maharaja Sayajirao University of Baroda she earned advanced degrees in English literature and early Indian culture, and she concluded her education in comparative literature at the University of Iowa.

Settled in Canada before her immigration to the United States, Mukherjee reared two sons while writing *The Tiger's Daughter* (1972), a cross-cultural novel about a failed Bengali-American marriage and the attempt of the former wife, Tara Banerjee Cartwright, to revive her former life in India. A more passionate survey of the same motif in *Wife* (1975), the story of the mental collapse of Dimple Dasgupta amid New York City VIOLENCE, preceded publication of the author's travel journal, *Days and Nights in Calcutta* (1977), which she and her husband, the Canadian author Clark Blaise, adapted for film. She turned to more positive immigrant experiences in two volumes of short fiction, *Darkness* (1985) and *The Middleman and Other Stories* (1988), winner of a National Book Critics Circle Award. In a move toward feminism she developed a kernel story into a novel of self-discovery, *Jasmine* (1989), an account of the title character's relocation from Hasnapur, India, to Baden, Iowa, a wrenching lingual and social migration that dominates the author's survey of biculturalism.

Mukherjee's subsequent novels, *The Holder of the World* (1993) and *Leave It to Me* (1997), cover similar psychological territory within women living in foreign cultures. The latter, a *New York Times* Notable Book, opens on the myth of the goddess Devi, "the eight-armed, flame-bright, lion-riding Dispenser of Justice" (Mukherjee, 1998, 5). The novelist introduces the identity crisis and birth mother search of Debby DiMartino, an adopted woman living in Schenectady, New York. Unsuited to an Italian-American family, she feels she is "unrecyclable trash" abandoned in infancy to be "sniffed at by wild dogs, like a carcass in the mangy shade" and rescued by the Gray Sisters of Charity (*ibid.*, 10). A paroled shoplifter at age 13, Debby falls victim to Wyatt, a hippie counselor, who despoils and corrupts her with a semblance of loving acceptance. Mukherjee summarizes Debby's lack of a moral compass as "nothing to keep you on the straight and narrow except star bursts of longing" (*ibid.*, 16). Debby finds an outlet, assuaging her fears and regrets in verse her teacher compares to that of the confessional poet Sylvia PLATH.

In a more recent work *Desirable Daughters* (2002), Mukherjee reached a height of critical acclaim. The suspenseful story of Tara Bhattacharjee depicts an Indo-American culture clash. At the core is her family's shame at her divorce from a martinet husband and at her relationship with a Buddhist carpenter, two violations of strict female decorum. Amid gang VIOLENCE Tara breaches the facade of gentility and Hindu orthodoxy to learn unsettling truths about her kin. In meditations on Tara's cultural heritage the novelist retreats to 1879 to re-create the pathos of a bespangled child bride, five-year-old Tara Lata, borne in a veiled litter to an arranged nuptial. The wedding hymn begins with the virgin's question "What do I hope for in worshiping you?" and closes with domestic rewards: "scoured-shiny utensils" and "a rice-filled granary" (Mukherjee, 2003, 4). In an interview the author commented on the source of her female characters, who "were trained vehemently, virulently, violently, to be docile, pliant, never to talk back to elders, never show impatience" (Ruta, 13).

Through fiction she demonstrates the downside of the reduction of nubile girls to obedient automata.

Bibliography

Mukherjee, Bharati. *Desirable Daughters.* New York: Hyperion, 2003.

———. *Leave It to Me.* New York: Ballantine, 1998.

Ruta, Suzanne. "Decoding the Language," *Women's Review of Books* 19, no. 10/11 (July 2002): 13.

Munro, Alice (1931–)

The Canadian fiction writer and teacher Alice Laidlaw Munro allows her intellectual curiosity to range over the lives of female characters. Born in Wingham in rural Ontario, she grew up on a poultry and silver fox farm and began writing during World War II. After selling short works to the Canadian Broadcasting Corporation, she earned a scholarship to the University of Western Ontario. She established a home in Victoria, British Columbia, where she and her husband operated a bookshop. Munro honed her literary style from readings of the southern writers Carson MCCULLERS, Flannery O'CONNOR, Katherine Anne PORTER, and Eudora WELTY and submitted stories to the *Atlantic, New Yorker,* and *Paris Review.* In 1968 Munro published *Dance of the Happy Shades,* which received the Governor-General's Award. Serious critical attention focused on *Lives of Girls and Women* (1971), her survey of rural women's aspirations and compromises. After the publication of *Something I've Been Meaning to Tell You* (1974) she accepted the Canada-Australia Prize. In 1986 *The Progress of Love* won Munro a second Governor General's Award and the Marian Engel Prize. Four years later Munro added the Canada Molson Prize for *Friend of My Youth* (1990). She also won the National Book Critics Circle award for *The Love of Good Woman* (1998) and the Giller Prize for *Runaway* (2004).

Compared to Anton Chekhov for the clarity of her characterization, Munro recognizes the chanciness of women's choices as they search for happiness and outlets for self-expression. In much of her fiction there is no lasting joy in sexual relations. In *Hateship, Friendship, Courtship, Loveship, Marriage* (2001), an Editor's Choice of the *New York Times Book Review,* she dazzles with sharp imagery, as with her description of a woman's teeth that "crowded to the front of her mouth as if they were ready for an argument" (Munro, 3). In 2004 she published *Runaway,* a moody, atmospheric collection set on home territory in Canada. Rich in memory and realistic social ordering the stories build tension between arresting images of the settled life and the search of fugitives and renegades for havens. One character, the teacher Juliet, dominates three stories with her rebellion against parents and the heartbreak of her daughter's disappearance. Overall Munro's characters mature and adapt to uprooting and risk taking as members of professions and wives in long-shot marriages.

Bibliography

Munro, Alice. *Hateship, Friendship, Courtship, Loveship, Marriage.* New York: Vintage, 2002.

Weinhouse, Linda. "Alice Munro: Hard-Luck Stories or There Is No Sexual Tension," *Critique* 36, no. 2 (Winter 1995): 121–129.

Murasaki Shikibu (ca. 973–ca. 1025)

In an era when Japanese men silenced women and denigrated their imaginings as silly fantasy, the world's first novelist, Murasaki Shikibu, composed in vernacular a diary of her personal observations and, in verse, a glittering court saga. Born an upper-class commoner in Japan at the peak of the Heian period (794–1186), she was a member of the learned Fujiwara clan and the daughter of Fujiwara Tametoki, a scholar who became provincial governor of Echizen in 996. The name *Shikibu* is an honorary patronym indicating her father's governmental rank. Because she was quick-witted, her father lamented that she was smarter than her brother, with whom she studied under a tutor. Although women were denied EDUCATION, Murasaki read classical Chinese literature and learned to write Chinese script, the language of choice for educated males. She was married only three years to a relative, Fujiwara no Nobutaka, an older man who had multiple wives. He died of plague in 1001, leaving her with a daughter, Daini no Sammi, who became a poet.

The author attained the title of Lady Murasaki after she joined the cultured imperial court at the Tsuchimikado estate in Kyoto as lady in waiting to the empress Akiko. A master ironist, Murasaki initiated a diary, which she filled until 1003 with anecdotes of gendered behavior, courtship and birthing rituals, decadent amusements, sexual escapades, embarrassing moments, and codes of conduct expected of the highest Japanese social class. She characterizes the male dismissal of women's emotions in the words of a young prince, "Ah, women! Such difficult creatures at times!" (Murasaki, 1999, 5). Of women's need to dissemble and to mask emotions, she describes the empress's receiving startling news from gossips but "[managing] to hide her feelings as if nothing is amiss" (*ibid.*, 3). Because Murasaki herself wore the mask of fashionable court lady, she concealed her intellectual pursuits for fear of being ostracized. As a result her rivals thought her overly modest, conceited, and standoffish, but Murasaki accepted her intellectual side as a normal facet of her personality.

While living the life of the outsider, Lady Murasaki made history with a lyric novel of manners, *Genji-monogatari* (*The Tale of Genji*, 1019), a best-selling saga of class differences and mother hunger in a social-climbing 10th-century male. Comprising 795 stanzas divided among 54 chapters, the narrative features a male-centered era in which men openly pursued women. In sexually explicit episodes the story characterizes Shining Prince Genji, the son of Emperor Kiritsubo no Mikado and a concubine, Lady Kiritsubo, who died when the prince was three. The author reveals the prince's attempts to marry a suitable woman and his failing in conducting an affair with the emperor's wife, Fujitsubo. Murasaki stresses the exploitation of women's SEXUALITY as a male entertainment and validates the need for writers to record their passions and observations of society. She vanished from history between 1025 and 1031, leaving historians to assume that she died between ages 52 and 58. Her novel lives on in translations, film, dance, and an animated cartoon and in feminist commentary such as that of Virginia WOOLF in *A Room of One's Own* (1929) and in Marguerite YOURCENAR's *Oriental Stories* (1938).

Bibliography

Feldman, Gayle. "Laboring for a Living Classic," *Publishers Weekly*, 20 August 2001, pp. 49–50.

Knapp, Bettina. "Lady Murasaki Shikibu's *The Tale of Genji*: Search for the Mother," *Symposium* 46, no. 1 (Spring 1992): 34–48.

Murasaki Shikibu. *The Diary of Lady Murasaki*. New York: Penguin, 1999.

———. *The Tale of Genji*. New York: Penguin, 2002.

Murray, Judith Sargent (1751–1820)

A poet, dramatist, historian, educator, and journalist of the early American republic, Judith Sargent Murray was an outpoken champion of freedom and WOMEN'S RIGHTS to education for their own betterment. A Gloucester native, the firstborn of Judith Saunders Sargent and Winthrop Sargent, a freethinking merchant-politician in Massachusetts Colony, she joined her younger brother, Winthrop Jr., in free reading in a sizable family library, including a book of Indian philosophy by an ancient Brahmin. She later regretted that she could not follow Winthrop to Harvard but must content herself with home tutoring in composition, Greek, Latin, and math. After marrying a sea captain, she devoted her solitude to lyric verse and published her works under the pen names of Constantia, Vergilius, Zephaniah Doubtful, Penelope Airy, Honora Martesia, and the Gleaner. Because of her family's Universalist ideals the Anglican Church barred them from worship and pillaged their home for goods to retire a church debt.

Skilled at deductive logic and satire, Murray flourished under liberal thought, the subject of her essay "Some Deduction from . . . Divine Revelation" (1782). She applied biblical scholarship to the catechism she supplied the Universalist sect. To *Gentleman and Lady's Town and Country Magazine* she submitted "Encouraging a Degree of Self-Complacency in the Female Bosom" (1784), a call for WOMEN'S RIGHTS to delay marriage and to choose an individual lifestyle that was new to women's history. Predating the feminist philosophy of Mary WOLLSTONECRAFT, at age 28 Murray revealed her feminism in "On the Equality of the Sexes" (1779), an essay introduced by a poem composed in iambic pentameter couplets. Later published in the *Massachusetts Magazine,* the poem demands EDUCATION and economic autonomy for women. She complains of women's unhappiness in being bored, uncultivated, and unfulfilled and denounces the apostasy of violating creation. Of the DOUBLE STANDARD she asserts that women are capable of "honest feelings" and charges that men disempower women and accuse them of being trivial.

Widowed at age 37, Murray wed the Reverend John Murray, a controversial English-born theologian known as the father of American Universalism, with whom she had corresponded for 14 years and whom she had aided as secretary. Equals in intellect, the couple left their Salem wedding, honeymooned at the home of John and Abigail ADAMS, and settled in Boston, where they encountered the enmity of small-minded Calvinists. While operating a dame school for 10 children, including her nieces and nephews, Judith Murray continued writing a column, verse, and essays for the *Boston Weekly Magazine* and the *Massachusetts Magazine,* notably "Lines Occasioned by the Death of an Infant" (1790), a poetic record of the stillbirth of her only son. She published articles in the *Federal Orrery,* ventured into long fiction, and composed a satiric play, *The Medium, or Virtue Triumphant* (1795), performed at the Federal Street Theatre as the city's first American stage play. Although she received an unfavorable review, she persevered with a comedy, *The Traveller Returned* (1796), and an abolitionist drama, *The African* (1807).

In 1798 after a paralytic stroke felled John Murray, the author supported her family on the proceeds of *The Gleaner,* an anthology of her works that contained a novella, *The Story of Margaretta.* Murray's compendium, which earned $2,475, received fan mail from the colonial author Mercy Otis WARREN and proved popular with American readers, a third of whom were women. In widowhood a second time she composed the latter portion of *The Life of John Murray* (1816). At age 64 she retired to Natchez, Mississippi, to live with her daughter, Julia Maria Murray Bingaman, and granddaughter, Charlotte Bingaman. Surviving in the Mississippi Department of Archives are letterbook copies of Murray's correspondence, some

2,500 unpublished letters she wrote between the ages of 14 and 67. They contain her vision of Columbia, a national symbol of rationality and women's rights to enlightenment and opportunity.

Bibliography

Kritzer, Amelia Howe. "Playing with Republican Motherhood," *Early American Literature* 31, no. 2 (September 1996): 150–166.

Murray, Judith Sargent. *The Gleaner.* Schenectady, N.Y.: Union College Press, 1992.

———. *Selected Writings of Judith Sargent Murray.* Oxford: Oxford University Press, 1995.

———. *The Traveller Returned* in *Plays by Early American Women, 1775–1850.* Edited by Amelia Kritzer. Ann Arbor: University of Michigan Press, 1995.

My Ántonia Willa Cather (1918)

In her American prairie classic *My Ántonia* the novelist Willa CATHER celebrates an underrated female substratum, the farm women devoted to family and land. For her belief in the dignity of rural life and ambition she is revered as one of the first American authors to create a robust, autonomous fictional female. To contrast the types of women who succeed in the Midwest, Cather identifies Ántonia "Tony" Shimerda, a Bohemian farm woman, and Lena Lingard, a Norwegian hireling, as objects of Jim Burden's affection. Tony thrives at the brutal, unstinting labors of raising grain and tending livestock. To protect the future of the Shimerdas' investment in America, she atones for bearing an illegitimate daughter by marrying a farmer and producing nine more children to help the family survive. Self-limited by her devotion to motherhood and homemaking, she retains a reputation for expertise in Czech cookery and culture. Voicing her preferences, she tells Jim, "I belong on a farm. I'm never lonesome here like I used to be in town" (Cather, 343).

On the other extreme of prairie womanhood Lena is a free agent, both nationally and personally. She creates true INDEPENDENCE by moving to Black Hawk and establishing herself as a seamstress and fashion designer. She avoids the morose, toilsome farm existence that engulfs Tony by flirting with men and joining the local dances under the Vannis's tent, thus balancing work with amusement. Unlike Tony, Lena has no need of marriage to legitimize her career choice, which requires her to dress smartly and keep abreast of trends. She summarizes her intent to remain unfettered: "I prefer to be foolish when I feel like it, and be accountable to nobody" (*ibid.*, 291). In Jim's estimation "If there were no girls like [Lena] in the world, there would be no poetry" (*ibid.*, 270).

The author appears to disagree with Jim. Her descriptions of women who have founded successful businesses are spare and lackluster compared to the homeyness of farm women's biographies. When Jim arrives at Tony's farm after a 20-year separation from her, he finds the opposite—an unselfconscious, fulfilled woman enjoying the demands of home and children. Lacking the cold, self-centered shell of Lena, Tony takes the time to comfort a child crying over a dead dog and to select photos from her collection that summon memories of the distant and recent past. As though opening treasures, she escorts Jim to the new fruit cave, a produce cellar filled with proofs of husbandry. Cather exalts Tony on her way outside with a rush of children, "a veritable explosion of life out of the dark cave into the sunlight" (*ibid.*, 338–339). The cellar, as a productive womb, rewards the title character for her choice of American farm life as a dignified and worthy profession.

Bibliography

Acocella, Joan. *Willa Cather and the Politics of Criticism.* New York: Vintage, 2002.

Cather, Willa. *My Ántonia.* New York: New American Library, 1989.

Lucenti, Lisa Marie. "Willa Cather's My Ántonia: Haunting the Houses of Memory," *Twentieth Century Literature* 46, no. 2 (Summer 2000): 193–213.

O'Brien, Sharon. *Willa Cather: The Emerging Voice.* Cambridge, Mass.: Harvard University Press, 1997.

N

names

The subject of names and naming looms large in feminist literature. In *The Italian* (1797) the Gothic author Ann RADCLIFFE calls her protagonist Ellena Rosalba, a romantic designation for the orphaned naif. Manipulated by Schedoni, an unscrupulous male adversary capable of intimidating, torturing, or killing her, she survives fresh and unsullied. Enhancing the reader's sympathy for Ellena is a surname that means "white rose," a suggestion of purity, natural loveliness, and vulnerability. Offset by Schedoni, a hard-sounding Italian surname, Ellena's last name suggests a fragility that advances the terror of the Gothic melodrama and justifies her rescue in the end. Similarly the English poet Elizabeth Barrett BROWNING chooses *aurora*, dawn, for the title character in her feminist verse melodrama *Aurora Leigh* (1847). The Chicana fiction writer Helena María VIRAMONTES contrasts mother and daughter migrant workers in *Under the Feet of Jesus* (1995). The mother, named Petra (rock), offers a lifetime of experience at survival to Estrella (little star), a 13-year-old who dreams of escaping poverty and day labor to become a geologist. Her choice of career hints at her admiration for a rock-solid mother. Another aesthetically symbolic name is that of Una Spencer, the protagnoist of Sena NASLUND's historical novel *Ahab's Wife: or, The Star-Gazer* (1999). By identifying the heroine with a name meaning "one," Naslund contrasts the single-minded heroine with the fractured personality of Ahab, which labors under a deadly mania.

In other examples of Gothic fiction symbolic names divulge character traits, attitudes, or attributes. In *FRANKENSTEIN* (1818) Mary Wollstonecraft SHELLEY uses the name *Victor* as a pun on the failings of her obsessive mad scientist. Charlotte BRONTË culled from *Blackwood's Edinburgh Magazine* the surname for the protagonist of *JANE EYRE* (1847), a homonym suggesting the surprise legacy from a relative in the West Indies that elevates Jane from governess to heir and principal of her own school. In Edith WHARTON's Gothic novella *Ethan Frome* (1911) Mattie Silver bears the name of a precious metal, which suggests a sparkling personality that increases her value to the title character. Her literary foil, Zeena Pierce Frome, bears a maiden name appropriate to her venomous strikes at a tenderhearted girl who wants only to please. For the murder mystery *Rebecca* (1938) the novelist Daphe DU MAURIER names the widower Maxim de Winter, a surname that foreshadows the heroine's confusion about his frosty exterior. A dramatic representation of the wife's self-abnegation is the lack of a name beyond "the second Mrs. de Winter."

Image creation furthers feminist allegory. Appropriate names identify survivors like the tough-minded title figure in Katherine Anne PORTER's stream-of-consciousness story "The JILTING OF GRANNY WEATHERALL" (1930). Toni MORRISON builds tragic ironies in *The BLUEST EYE* (1970) from the creation of Pecola Breedlove, a pathetic 11-year-old coerced into MADNESS by lovelessness, rejection, incest, and the birth and death of her infant. More pictorial is Barbara KINGSOLVER's selection of Turtle for a child who withdraws into catatonic silence in *The Bean Trees* (1988). The author advances irony in the choice of Valentine for the middle name of Virgie Parsons, a vocal racist who accuses a gentle Mayan raconteur of telling a "South American, wild *Indian* story" (Kingsolver, 107). In 1998 the sci-fi and fantasy author Anne McCAFFREY created a memorable female achiever in a five-book series beginning with *Acorna's Quest: The Adventures of the Unicorn Girl* (1998), coauthored by Margaret Ball, and ending with *Acorna's Triumph* (2004). By picturing the promise of a seed as the embryo of an oak tree, McCaffrey encourages young readers to think of girls as deserving of adventures and challenges that lead to monumental achievements.

The American system of the wife's taking her husband's surname supports PATRIARCHY. The nuptial renaming puzzles the women of *HERLAND* (1915), Charlotte Perkins GILMAN's female utopia. One Herlander, Alima, sees the inequity: "Then she just loses hers and takes a new one—how unpleasant" (Gilman, 119). Gilman's fictional recoil from patriarchal naming reflects the views of the feminist philosopher and orator Voltairine DE CLEYRE, who described the married woman as "a bonded slave, who takes her master's name, her master's bread, and serves her master's passion; [and] who passes through the ordeal of pregnancy and the throes of travail at *his* dictation" (de Cleyre, 344). A later author of speculative fiction, Joanna RUSS, gives as a model of alternate naming systems the choice of Janet Evason, a protagonist in *The Female Man* (1975). Upon the birth of her daughter she names her Yuriko "Yuki" Janetson, thus yoking in two surnames the MATRIARCHY of Eva, Janet, and Yuriko.

In 1948 the Gothic author Shirley JACKSON generated a stir with the publication of "The LOTTERY," a classic short story submitted to the *New Yorker*. The narratives echoes the theocratic VIOLENCE of New Englanders during the American colonial period. The name of the annual sacrifice, Tessie Hutchinson, suggests two victims—Anne Hutchinson, the herbalist and midwife driven from Massachusetts Bay Colony in 1637 for teaching theology to women, and Tess of the D'Urbervilles,

Thomas Hardy's fictional dairymaid who goes to the gallows for slaying a male tormentor. The weight of foremothers' trials subsumes Tessie, who cowers as family members and neighbors stone her to death to assure a good corn crop.

Name shifts bear foretokenings of loss and suffering. In Jean RHYS's *WIDE SARGASSO SEA* (1966), the English suitor Edward Rochester marries Antoinette Cosway, his passionate island wife, a Jamaican heiress who has no control over her life, her property, her inheritance, even her first name. Foreshadowing the blurring of identities is the cry of the family parrot, who demands in French, "Qui est là? Qui est là? [Who is there?]" (Rhys, 25). When Edward calls his bride Bertha, a proper name for an Englishwoman, her personality splits. She recognizes the mystic power of renaming and accuses, "You are trying to make me into someone else, calling me by another name. I know that's obeah (voodoo) too" (*ibid.*, 147). After Edward transports her to England and locks her in an upstairs room, she asserts, "Names matter, like when he wouldn't call me Antoinette, and I saw Antoinette drifting out of the window" (*ibid.*, 180). The critic Ellen Cronan Rose explains the damage done: "Not only is a woman's quest for identity deflected from engagement with the outside world . . . but that inward quest seems doomed itself to frustration, if not failure" (Rose, 210).

The Asian-American novelist Amy TAN takes a more complex view of names. Her novels express the importance of what lies behind a name, particularly for a Chinese relative who left an old name behind when she emigrated from the motherland. Tan stresses that a name is the first gift to an infant, a place mark that establishes residence and belonging, an anchor in uncertain times, and a permanent tether between the present and past. To express a deep tragedy in *The Joy Luck Club* (1989), the author omits the name of a suicide, An-mei Hsu's mother, who killed herself with an overdose of opium to assert her daughter's value to a cold, unloving family. The absence of a name, such as that of the shamed mother who drowns herself in a well in Maxine Hong KINGSTON's *The Woman Warrior: Memoirs of a Girlhood among Ghosts* (1976), foretokens a wisp of recovered family history that is as frail as the woman it once identified.

Bibliography

Cujec, Carol, "Excavating Memory, Reconstructing Legacy," *World and I* 16, no. 7 (July 2001): 215–223.

de Cleyre, Voltairine. *The Selected Works of Voltairine de Cleyre.* New York: Mother Earth, 1914.

Gilman, Charlotte Perkins. *Herland and Selected Stories.* New York: Signet Classics, 1992.

Kingsolver, Barbara. *The Bean Trees.* New York: Harper & Row, 1988.

Rhys, Jean. *Wide Sargasso Sea.* New York: W. W. Norton, 1982.

Rose, Ellen Cronan. "Through the Looking Glass: When Women Tell Fairy Tales" in *The Voyage In: Fiction of Female Development.* Edited by Elizabeth Abel, Marianne Hirsch, and Elizabeth Langland. Hanover, N.H.: University Press of New England, 1983, pp. 209–227.

Naslund, Sena (ca. 1942–   )

The fiction writer and educator Sena Jeter Naslund reset a classic American novel by moving an unnamed female character from the periphery to center stage. Born in Birmingham, Alabama, Naslund read Laura Ingalls WILDER's Little House series in girlhood and produced a cowboy newspaper and a frontier novel. By her early teens she played cello in the Birmingham Youth and Alabama Pops Orchestras and fell in love with Herman Melville's *Moby-Dick* (1851). After turning down a music scholarship to the University of Alabama, she earned degrees in creative writing from Birmingham-Southern College and the University of Iowa Writers' Workshop. She began publishing short stories in *Alaska Quarterly, Georgia Review, Indiana Review, Iowa Review, Michigan Quarterly,* and *Paris Review* while directing creative writing at the University of Louisville. For her accomplishments the faculty named her the school's first distinguished professor. In addition to a rigorous classroom schedule, she established Fleur-de-lis Press and the *Louisville Review,* which she coedits, and published a collection of stories, *Ice Skating at the North Pole* (1989). In addition to the Harper Lee Award for a Distinguished Alabama Writers, she received the Alabama Writer of the Year 2001.

Drawing on one brief reference from *Moby-Dick,* Naslund fleshed out a passionate May–December love affair in *Ahab's Wife; or, The Star-Gazer* (1999) between Una Spenser and the doomed Captain Ahab. A courageous, autonomous, and multifaceted heroine, Una eludes a moody Puritan father by leaving Kentucky on the run to a lighthouse on the New England coast. In one of her risky adventures at age 16 she disguises herself as a boy, a gender switch that Naslund introduced in *Sherlock in Love: A Novel* (1993). Una goes to sea as cabinboy on a whaler, which a black whale rams and sinks, sending survivors to sea in an open boat. Contributing to feminist themes are Una's rebellion against PATRIARCHY, a mother-daughter intimacy during Una's first pregnancy, examples of ABOLITIONISM and pacifism, and her friendship with Susan, a runaway slave with whom Una shares a bed. A familiar motif from women's writings are the soft bedding and colorful homemade quilts that comfort and reassure Una during the panic that precedes childbirth.

Opposing Melville's description of the unnamed wife perched on an eight-by-eight-foot Nantucket widow's walk looking out to sea, Naslund conceived Una as a visionary female who refuses to be bound by domestication. The author gives her domestic grace and sexual allure that complement the masculine obsession of Ahab. Unlike Ahab, whose mania condemns all his crew but one to a watery grave, Una commits herself to a redemptive quest that renews her life and replenishes her energy and drive. Radiant with possibilities, she looks beyond past errors and losses to open horizons. As guides Naslund assigns Una two friends from women's history, the astronomer Maria Mitchell and feminist newspaperwoman and philosopher Margaret FULLER. For the book's dynamic female friendships, valor, and spirituality *Time* Magazine and *Book Sense* named *Ahab's Wife* one of the five best novels of the year.

Bibliography

Johnson, Sarah Anne. "Women of Substance: Author Sena Jeter Naslund Found Few Heroes in Classic Literature, So She Created Some," *Writer* 1 15, no. 11 (November 2002): 26–32.

Matchie, Tom. "*Ahab's Wife, or the Star-Gazer:* A Wider/Deeper View of Melville's Tragic Hero and His Times," *Journal of American and Comparative Cultures* (Spring–Summer 2001): 85–91.

Naslund, Sena. *Ahab's Wife; or, The Star-Gazer.* New York: Perennial, 2000.

Naylor, Gloria (1950–)

The fiction writer and playwright Gloria Naylor finds in black female protagonists strong will, solidarity, and loving SISTERHOOD. A native of Tunica County, Mississippi, she was born to former sharecroppers. She grew up in New York City (which is sometimes named as her birthplace). Her service to the Jehovah's Witnesses in the Carolinas and Florida and to the study of nursing at Medgar Evers College suggests a fundamental altruism. While completing an English degree from Brooklyn College and advanced work in black studies at Yale, she studied Toni MORRISON's prose style in *The* BLUEST EYE (1970) and took courage from the stories of black lives in the works of Ntozake SHANGE and Paule MARSHALL. She later exclaimed, "That gave me the courage to say 'If they can tell these stories, I can, too' " ("Conversation," 70).

Naylor gained fame with publication of a first novel, *The Women of Brewster Place: A Novel in Seven Stories* (1982), winner of an American Book Award. The interwoven events celebrate seven black females who live on a dead-end street within the pungent smells of garbage and drunks vomiting against the brick walls. Naylor pictures Brewster Place women as "hard-edged, soft-centered, brutally demanding, and easily pleased" (Naylor, 1983, 5). Oprah Winfrey's Harpo, Inc., filmed the polyphonic work as a 1989 television miniseries, featuring Winfrey, Robin Givens, Cicely Tyson, and Lynn Whitfield. The screen version, which covers several decades, presents black female residents as preservers of matriarchal lore and as civic warriors against sexism, intolerance, and tenement squalor. Because of heated controversy over male roles in her first novel Naylor composed *The Men of Brewster Place* (1998), an emotionally vivid sequel that pinpoints the neighborhood barbershop as the place where males can unload their troubles.

To study the variables of human folly, Naylor lets her imagination create unusual settings and groupings of characters. While touring Cadiz, Spain, the author typified the cultural loss of the materialistic black middle class in *Linden Hills* (1985), an allegorical novel based in part on the human frailties in Dante's *Inferno* (1321). Set in a microcosm, Willow Springs, a sea island off north Georgia, *Mama Day* (1988), her third novel, combines mysticism and romance with a plot drawn from William Shakespeare's *The Tempest* (ca. 1610). A legend began in 1819 with the sale of Sapphira to Bascombe Wade, a lustful slave owner who "had claim to her body, but not her mind" (Naylor, 1989, 225). The story builds on a form of woman wisdom that Naylor calls "foremothering" (*ibid.*, 1). In place of Shakespeare's conciliatory hero Prospero Naylor exalts Granny Younger, an elderly visionary and folk healer capable of wedding African tradition to her great-niece, Cocoa's, female emancipation. Without fanfare Granny admits, "Sometimes I know the future in my breast. Sometimes I see the future coming out like a picture show, acrost the trail ahead" (*ibid.*, 27).

Like the leader of a jazz combo, Naylor orchestrated the rhythmic interplay of multiple voices in *Bailey's Cafe* (1992) and adapted its stories of alienated characters for the stage; the Hartford Stage Company performed the play in 1994. The cafe's dead-end atmosphere, as does the cul-de-sac at Brewster Place, pervades the thinking of the pilgrims who patronize it: The place is "nothing but a way station, [where] the choices have always been clear: you eventually go back out and resume your life . . . or you head to the back of the cafe and end it" (Naylor, 1993, 221). Disparate voices, each with a distinctive story to tell, relay the events of black history from slavery through the Jim Crow era and the civil rights movement to the 1990s urban experience. At a pivotal moment Bailey states his cafe's philosophy: "I don't believe that life is supposed to make you feel good, or to make you feel miserable either. Life is just supposed to make you feel" (*ibid.*, 219). The summation speaks volumes about the intent of and reader reaction to Naylor's fiction.

Bibliography

"A Conversation with Gloria Naylor," *Essence* 29, no. 2 (June 1998): 70.

Naylor, Gloria. *Bailey's Cafe.* New York: Vintage, 1993.

———. *Linden Hills.* New York: Vintage, 1995.

———. *Mama Day.* New York: Vintage, 1989.

———. *The Women of Brewster Place.* New York: Penguin, 1983.

Wood, Rebecca S. " 'Two Warring Ideals in One Dark Body': Universalism and Nationalism in Gloria Naylor's *Bailey's Cafe,*" *African American Review* 30, no. 3 (Fall 1996): 381–395.

"New Colossus, The" Emma Lazarus (1883)

No poem so captures the American feminist spirit as Emma LAZARUS's sonnet "The New Colossus," an ode to enlightened altruism and mercy. At the base of the Statue of Liberty, a monument originally called "Liberty Enlightens the World," the last five lines of the ode invoke the majesty and promise of Lady Liberty, the mother of exiles, a beloved American symbol that adorns coins and logos. At the dedication ceremony on October 28, 1886, the stern, proud New World heroine sculpted by Frederic-Auguste Bartholdi quelled speculation that he chose as a model a black female as an emblem of the emancipation of SLAVERY. Instead onlookers gazed on a universal female icon, the likeness of his mother, Auguste-Charlotte Bartholdi, a single parent whose resilience and nurturance he admired. At the unveiling suffragists heckling President Grover Cleveland reminded him that if Lady Liberty were flesh and blood, sexism would reduce her to the outskirts of citizenship.

Reflecting the influence of Rachel, the Old Testament matriarch, and of the subject of Percy Bysshe Shelley's antiheroic poem "Ozymandias," the sonnet contrasts a triumphant Lady Liberty with one of the seven wonders of the ancient world, the Colossus at Rhodes, a nude male monolith of the Sun god Helios. In the style of the vainglorious warrior the grand figure lit Mandrákion harbor of the prosperous Greek island state from 282 B.C. until an earthquake destroyed it around 226 B.C. To establish feminine strength, Lazarus asserts the difference in pose between the bronze giant of Rhodes and the silent, sedate amazon with uplifted flambeau and hair wreathed in light. Unlike the masculine posturing of the Rhodian colossus, America's grand lady offers succor to the poor undesirables, cast up as garbage on the North American shore. Without swagger or vaunted selfhood the figure, dignified in classic drapings, towers above broken chains to welcome the oppressed through the golden door of opportunity. The metaphoric consistency of Lazarus's sonnet stresses that America's triumph over the Old World rests upon the feminine side of its character, which wars on human hurts for the sake of mortals rather than on political rivals for the sake of valor and conquest.

Bibliography

Lazarus, Emma. *Emma Lazarus: Selected Poems and Other Writings.* Peterborough, Canada: Broadview, 2002.

Lehman, David. "Colossal Ode," *Smithsonian* 35, no. 1 (April 2004): 120–122.

Marom, Daniel. "Who Is the 'Mother of Exiles'? Jewish Aspects of Emma Lazarus's 'The New Colossus,' " *Prooftexts: A Journal of Jewish Literary History* 20, no. 3 (Autumn 2000): 231–261.

New Woman

A phenomenon born in the mid-19th century, the abstract concept of a New Woman began forcing out of fashion the genteel lady as a paragon of womanhood. Replacing the submissive, apathetic female of sentimental novels was the decisive, career-minded, unchaperoned go-getter, whom the French dubbed a *nouvelle femme*. With no nostalgia for matrilineal tradition the emergent New Woman, the precursor of the liberated woman of the 1970s, educated herself, traveled, explored her SEXUALITY, bicycled and competed in sports, and chose life-enhancing experiences over domesticity. Filling feminist literature were women like Charlotte BRONTË's Jane EYRE, Emily BRONTË's Catherine EARNSHAW, Henrik Ibsen's Nora Helmer, and Margaret MITCHELL's Scarlett O'Hara, a former southern belle who fights her way out of post–Civil War poverty by marrying moneyed males and by running her own lumberyard.

The shift toward feminism got a nudge in the 1880s. A forerunner of the self-defining female was the title character in Margaret OLIPHANT's *Hester: A Story of Contemporary Life* (1883), which depicts a valiant heroine who faces a challenge that risks more than her own hearth. A vigorous forerunner dominates the FRONTIER LITERATURE with pioneers like the journalist Isabella Bird, who published news dispatches in the British weekly *Leisure Hour* and who compiled adventures in a memoir, *A Lady's Life in the Rocky Mountains* (1888). As early as 1893 the Scots editor Annie S. Swan of Edinburgh was salting issues of the *Woman at Home* with new visions of single women and with stories by Sarah GRAND that acknowledged professional women. Grand, a leader of the New Woman movement and popularizer of the term, explored taboo subjects in *The Heavenly Twins* (1893), a denunciation of the DOUBLE STANDARD and the dysfunctional Victorian marriage. The character Evadne dithers at games of logic with her disparaging father, but in private she stores up predictions from John Stuart MILL's *Subjection of Women* (1869), a radical treatise that exploded stereotypes of the witless prom trotter, the self-adorning clotheshorse, and the dizzy housewife. In the same vein Grand's contemporary, the Gothic writer Marie CORELLI, published a best seller, *The Sorrows of Satan; or, The Strange Experience of One Geoffrey Tempest, Millionaire* (1895), a gaslight thriller that showcased the writer Mavis Claire, a woman whom Mill would have applauded as a female self-loosened from Victorian strictures.

At the beginning of the 20th century the New Woman took a firm hold on New Journalism and on feminist literature. The newspaperwoman and regional fiction writer Zona GALE, who lived the ideal of the progressive female, wrote articles for Milwaukee's *Evening Wisconsin*, the Milwaukee *Journal*, and the New York *Evening World*. Her contemporary, the newspaper reporter Edna FERBER, extolled the strengths of the evolving professional woman in a series of short stories featuring the saleswoman Emma McChesney. On the other side of the Atlantic the English short fiction writer Katherine MANSFIELD relocated to London in 1903 to taste the freedom of the Edwardian era. The poet Mary COLERIDGE depicted the self-starter in "The Witch" (1907), a tongue-in-cheek image of the creative spirit, and ventured toward the sexually independent woman in "The White Women" (1908), which invokes visions of females who express their sexual desires.

The cult of the New Woman energized the SUFFRAGE movement, socialism, and venues and outlets unheard of in the previous century, such as the desert interviews of Mary Hunter AUSTIN, the flying career of Beryl MARKHAM, the detective fiction of Mary Roberts Rinehart and Ellen WOOD, and the family planning clinics of Margaret SANGER and Marie STOPES. The activist Emmeline PANKHURST sold her paintings at an art gallery and promoted the socialist agenda of the International Labour Party. The journalist Djuna BARNES relived Pankhurst's experiences in jail for the article "How It Feels to Be Forcibly Fed" (1914), an illustrated study of feminist agitators for *New York World Magazine*. The writer of the first New Woman novel, the South African author Olive SCHREINER, issued a feminist manifesto in *Woman and Labour* (1911), which rejected the PATRIARCHY that stifled women's advancement.

As a stimulus to change, profiles of the New Woman appeared in the popular press and in WOMEN'S MAGAZINES. The radical essayist Rebecca WEST published "A New Woman's Movement: The Need for Riotous Living" (1913) and "The Sheltered Sex: 'Lotus Eating' on Seven-and-Six a Week" (1913), which demanded a living wage for female laborers on a par with the salaries paid to men. The Virginia novelist Ellen GLASGOW injected New Womanism into the story "Jordan's End" (1923), which describes Mrs. Jordan as a self-affirming wife who chooses to murder her husband to clear the way for new ventures. Anzia YEZIERSKA's dialect immigration novel *Bread Givers* (1925) lauds Sara Smolinsky as a first-generation new woman who realizes her Jewish father's dream of riches in a land of opportunity. In her words, "In America, women don't need men to boss them" (Yezierska, 137).

Parallel strands of female empowerment developed in a variety of genres. During the Harlem Renaissance black authors explored similar aspects of the self-made woman. The editor and fiction writer Jessie Redmon FAUSET showcased the post–World War I girl-of-all-work who educated herself for a career without losing hold of domestic and maternal values. In *There Is Confusion* (1924) she outlines women's rise in the arts to full-time careers in singing, dancing, and acting. The anthropologist Margaret MEAD's living among "primitive" peoples boosted her career as writer and analyst of the familial and cultural directives that shape femininity and motherhood, both controversial issues of the early 20th century. As the vision of the New Woman began to fade, the novelist Doris LESSING stressed the price of pioneering efforts in behavior and choices that alienate adventuresome women from the mainstream.

Bibliography

Ardis, Ann L., and Leslie W. Lewis. *Women's Experience of Modernity 1875–1945*. Baltimore: Johns Hopkins University Press, 2003.

Grand, Sarah. *The Heavenly Twins* (1893). Available online. URL: http://www.gutenberg.org/dirs/etext 05/8htwn10.txt. Accessed on October 14, 2005.

Richardson, Angelique, and Chris Willis, eds. *The New Woman in Fiction and in Fact: Fin-de-Siècle Feminisms*. London: Palgrave Macmillan, 2002.

Yezierska, Anzia. *Bread Givers*. New York: Persea Books, 2003.

Ng, Fae Myenne (1957–)

One of the feminist authors to emerge at the end of the 20th century, Fae Myenne Ng writes of the consequences of women's choices. Born in San Francisco to Chinese parents who immigrated to California in 1940, she and one brother grew up in Chinatown in a Cantonese-speaking household. After studying at the Cumberland Presbyterian Chinese School, she aided her mother, a seamstress, in making fad clothes for women. After graduation from the University of California at Berkeley Ng completed an advanced degree at Columbia, married the author Mark Coovelis, and settled in Brooklyn. While working as a waitress, she published stories in *Americana Voice, Bostonia, Crescent Review, Calyx, City Lights Review, Granta, Harper's,* and the *Pushcart Prize Anthology* (1988). A first novel, *Bone* (1993), contributed to diaspora literature an in-depth examination of first-generation Chinese-American lives. The book earned Ng the Pushcart Prize, a National Endowment for the Arts Award, a nomination for a PEN/Faulkner award for fiction, and fellowships from Lila Wallace-Reader's Digest and the American Academy of Arts and Letters, which supported Ng while she began a second novel in Hong Kong. Subsequently she published in *New Republic* "False Gold" (1993), a biographical sketch of California's Chinese bache-

lor culture, and "Bound and Determined" (1994) in *Allure*.

The author worked for a decade at *Bone*, which she named for the nostalgic practice of Chinese immigrants of sending skeletal remains of their dead back to the motherland. Set in San Francisco's Chinatown, the realistic story describes three girls whose family life reflects the author's biography. Because the father, Leong, sires no sons and is frequently jobless, Chinese-Americans living around Salmon Alley deride him. Mah, a strong mother figure who owns and operates a baby clothing business, teaches her daughters to be submissive and to rely on hard work. Without warning Ona, the middle daughter, leaps to her death from the Nam, the tallest building in the community, after her parents refuse to allow her to marry the man of her choosing. PATRIARCHY follows her beyond death as Leong tries to account for her nonconformity and lethal rebellion: "I mean, Ona not that kind of girl. She talk to me first. I'm her father. She tell her father first, if something was wrong. Somebody put idea in her head. She talk to you, eh? Say something maybe?" (Ng, 149). His uncertainty is a measure of the estrangement of his American daughters from Chinese tradition.

The loss of Ona prompts Nina and Leila, the youngest and eldest sisters, to leave home and live independently of Old World customs. As though protecting herself from blame or from her own spiritual crisis, Leila clings to SISTERHOOD and tries to convince herself "that it'd been Ona's choice" (ibid., 15). Leila commits herself to understanding the unspoken family crisis that caused Ona to kill herself. She admits that thinking and speaking in English set her apart from firm parental control: "I have a whole different vocabulary of feeling in English than in Chinese, and not everything can be translated" (ibid., 18). The motivation for Leila's aggressive SEXUALITY, criticism of Leong, verbalizing of emotions, drinking of scotch, and use of heroin suggests an undercurrent of resistance to the chauvinism of her Asian family and community.

Bibliography

Gee, Allen. "Deconstructing a Narrative Hierarchy: Leila Leong's 'I' in Fae Myenne Ng's *Bone*," *MELUS* 29, no. 2 (Summer 2004): 129–140.

Kim, Thomas W. " 'For a Paper Son, Paper Is Blood': Subjectivation and Authenticity in Fae Myenne Ng's *Bone*," *MELUS* 24, no. 4 (Winter 1999): 41–56.

Ng, Fae Myenne. *Bone*. New York: Perennial, 1994.

Nin, Anaïs (1903–1977)

A revered French diarist, lecturer, and author of erotica, Anaïs Nin captured feminist readers by writing candidly on the inner compunctions and desires of modern women. Born in the Neuilly section of Paris of Cuban-French-Danish ancestry, she and her brother, Thorvald, came of age among artists and notables. A posthumous publication of journal entries in *Incest* (1992) revealed her sexual relationship with her father, the composer and pianist Joaquin Nin. She recounted a late-term ABORTION, which freed her of motherhood and allowed her to resume sexual relations with her parent. Her childhood ended in 1913 when her father left home. On the family's migration from Barcelona to New York City Nin began recording her thoughts in a diary that extended over a half-century. Largely self-educated after quitting school in 1919, she modeled for painters, acted, danced, and designed fashions and advertisements.

After her marriage to the financier Hugh Parker Guiler at age 23 Nin repatriated to France. She began experimenting with catalysts to personal and sexual pleasures, which she wrote about in essays, fiction, and a lengthy poem, *The House of Incest* (1936). Simultaneously she wrote streams of letters baring intimate thoughts and insights. In a note dated February 12, 1932, she summarized her view of the male strutter as a man capable of conquest, but not of love. She lived in New York once more during World War II and composed a psychological trilogy, *Winter of Artifice* (1939); experimental surrealistic stories collected in *Under a Glass Bell* (1944); a fiction series entitled *Cities of the Interior* (1959); and passionate letters to the author Henry Miller.

With an intuitive understanding of the sexes, Nin reached a wider audience from 1966 to 1978 with *The Diary of Anaïs Nin*, published in seven volumes. In the first volume she accounts for her carnal tastes: "Ordinary life does not interest me. I seek only the high moments. I am in accord with the surrealists, searching for the marvelous" (Nin, 1969, 5). Her frank discussion of bisexuality and uninhibited will generated a demand for her lectures on female freedom, collected in 1975 in *A Woman Speaks: The Lectures, Seminars, and Interviews of Anaïs Nin*. Two works of erotica published late in her life, *Delta of Venus* (1969) and *Little Birds* (1979), collect stories that speak openly of public genital exposure, group sex, fantasy sex, incest, bisexuality, pedophilia, bestiality, oral sex, and FEMALE GENITAL MUTILATION.

Bibliography

Jellinek, Estelle. "Anaïs Reconsidered." *Off Our Backs* 4, 31 December, 1974, p. 18.

Nin, Anaïs. *Delta of Venus*. New York: Harvest Books, 2004.

———. *The Diary of Anaïs Nin: 1931–1934*. New York: Harvest Books, 1969.

———. *Incest: From "A Journal of Love," The Unexpurgated Diary of Anaïs Nin, 1932–1934*. New York: Harcourt Brace Jovanovich, 1992.

———. *Little Birds*. New York: Harvest Books, 2004.

Norman, Diana (1933–)

A respected political journalist, biographer, and author of historical fiction, Diana Narracott Norman exposes in figures from England's past the roots of the feminist movement. Born in London the year that Adolf Hitler gained power, she grew up during the Blitz and its aftermath and developed a zest for politics. After an apprenticeship writing the news from Devon and East End London her introduction to Fleet Street began in 1953 with assignments for the *Daily Herald*, a left-wing national paper that Rupert Murdoch devolved into the *Sun*. To escape the paper's plunge into seamy reportage, she freelanced for the *Times*, the *Guardian*, and WOMEN'S MAGAZINES and produced a column on women in history for *She* magazine. On the domestic scene in Datchworth, Hertfordshire, where Norman served as the local magistrate, she and her husband, the film critic and British Broadcasting Corporation (BBC) television personality Barry Norman, reared two daughters.

Norman channeled valuable observation and experience as well as considerable reading of penal codes, divorce law, and fashion toward a career in biography and historical novels. One of her lighter works, *The Stately Ghosts of England* (1963), surveys the scandals and superstitions connected with such storied structures as Longleat and Woburn Abbey. Pacing her suspenseful texts at breakneck speed, she specializes in period upheaval that gives rise to the female self-starter, whether volunteer nurse, self-employed barkeep, pirate, or neophyte actor. She earned critical attention with a first novel, *Fitzempress's Law* (1980), a historical novel of the year selection by BBC Radio. In 1987 she surveyed social rebellion in *Terrible Beauty: A Life of Constance Markievicz (1868–1927),* a compilation of the deeds of Constance Georgina Gore-Booth, the countess Markievicz, a traitor to her own class and a martyr to Irish freedom. The work proceeds from her birth to English Protestants through terms of imprisonment for feminist and anti-British activism. In one violent scene the countess is felled by police: "I could not get out of the crowd of police and at last one hit me a backhand blow across the left side of my face with his baton. I fell back against the corner of a shop, when another policeman started to seize me by the throat" (Norman, 1987, 89). Publication of the biography prompted a reception hosted by Ruairi Quinn, the Irish minister of labor. A subsequent novel, *The Vizard Mask* (1994), introduces crisis in the first sentence: "Penitence Hurd and the plague arrived in London on the same day" (Norman, 1995, 1). Critics at the *Sunday Times* lauded Norman for the novel's wit and humor as well as impressive research into the life and times of the 17th-century English dramatist Aphra BEHN, the rise of Restoration theater, and the nation's reception of women in acting companies.

To unearth the privations of women during the American Revolution, Norman researched VIOLENCE in Massachusetts of patriots versus Tories for *A Catch of Consequence* (2003). The novel features Makepeace Burke, an innkeeper in Boston Harbor who runs afoul of local rumblers after rescuing and falling in love with Philip Dapifer, a British aristocrat. Norman detailed the sufferings of colonial prisoners in British political jails in a sequel, *Taking Liberties* (2004), which carries the story forward to the widowhood of Makepeace, the

outsider, and her assistance to a pirate community near Plymouth, England. The paired novels enlarged Norman's fan base in the British Isles, North America, and Germany for her frank admiration for women living on the edge while rearing a family on the proceeds of quasi-legal businesses.

Bibliography

Norman, Diana. *A Catch of Consequence.* London: Berkley, 2003.
———. *Taking Liberties.* London: Berkley, 2004.
———. *Terrible Beauty: A Life of Constance Markievicz (1868–1927).* London: Hodder & Stoughton, 1987.
———. *The Vizard Mask.* London: Penguin, 1995.
Theiss, Nola. "Review: *A Catch of Consequence,*" *Kliatt* 37, no. 5 (September 2003): 20.

Norman, Marsha (1947–)

The journalist, dramatist, and screenwriter Marsha Williams Norman is adept at finding wry humor alongside inadequacy and crisis in ordinary women's lives. Reared in her native Louisville, Kentucky, she grew up in a strict fundamentalist household in which television and movies were forbidden. She filled lonely afternoons with piano lessons, adventures with an imaginary friend, and the STORY-TELLING of her Aunt Bubbie. With degrees in philosophy from Agnes Scott College and the University of Louisville, Norman refined her writing skills while editing and reviewing books, drama, and films for the *Louisville Times.*

After local performances of her early works by the Actors Theatre of Louisville, Norman got a taste of the big time with the production of *Getting Out* (1978). A winner of the Outer Critics Circle Award, John Gassner New Playwright's Medallion, and George Oppenheimer Newsday Award, the play reflects her work with the mentally ill at the Kentucky Central State Hospital. The story, which she later adapted for television, presents a compassionate view of Arlie Holsclaw, a schizophrenic prostitute confined to the Pine Ridge Correctional Institute in her teens for committing second-degree murder and kidnapping. After eight years she leaves prison without a grasp of functioning in the normal world as Arlene, her repentant, law-abiding alter ego. In a surreal dialogue with self, she describes the DUALITY: "Arlie girl landed herself in prison. Arlene is out, okay?" (Norman, 1998, 8). Norman succeeded again with *Third and Oak: The Laundromat and the Pool Hall* (1978), a pair of one-act urban dramas focusing on the alienation and loneliness of Alberta and Deedee, and with *Circus Valentine* (1979), the story of a trapeze artist's sacrifice for the sake of her family, in whose lackluster road show she performs in a shopping mall parking lot.

In 1983 Norman won the Pulitzer Prize for *'night Mother*, a taut two-character psychodrama about female entrapment, emotional aridity, and despair. Set in the kitchen of a rural cottage, the verbal dual of mother and daughter opens on a raspberry-and-marshmallow-filled snowball and concludes with Jessie's suicide with a single shot of her father's old gun. With a sigh Jessie reviews a succession of daily annoyances and small defeats before reaching the conclusion that she must give up living. The disjointed dialogue reveals Thelma Cates, her badgering mother, as failing to come to grips with her daughter's sadness.

> Jessie: I'm through talking, Mama. . . .
> Thelma: You'll miss. You'll just wind up a vegetable. How would you like that? Shoot your ear off?
>
> (Norman, 1983, 17)

A devoted daughter, Jessie collects old towels to spare Thelma a messy cleanup of the offstage death scene.

Norman's skill at offsetting tragedy with gallows humor won audiences at the debut of *'night, Mother* at the American Repertory Theater in Cambridge, Massachusetts, in 1983. At the play's opening off Broadway in 1984, featuring Anne Pitoniak and Kathy Bates, viewers raved about the balance of tension and comedy. In addition to a Pulitzer Prize, Norman received the Hull-Warriner Award from the Dramatists' Guild, four Tonys, the Susan Smith Blackburn Prize, and Kentucky's National Award for a native who achieves national acclaim. In 1986 the novelist scripted a film version that balanced Sissy Spacek's matter-of-fact departure from life with the sizzling anger and sarcasm of Anne Bancroft as Thelma.

Norman's later works retained the dialogue and nonverbal behavior of vulnerable females that reveal their insecurities and their relationships with authority figures. The novel *The Fortune Teller* (1987) packs mystery into another story of a mother-daughter dyad complicated by issues surrounding ABORTION. In 1991 the author won a Tony for adapting Frances Hodgson Burnett's children's novel *The Secret Garden* (1888) as a Broadway musical. Norman's sympathy with laboring-class woman found expression in *Loving Daniel Boone* (1991), a comic fantasy of a female worker cleaning floors in a historical museum. Vicariously she romances Daniel Boone, the frontier he-man who battled Indians and the British, before she discovers the pitfalls of loving a dream.

Bibliography

Coen, Stephanie. "Marsha Norman's Triple Play," *American Theatre* 8, no. 12 (March 1992): 22–26.

Demastes, William W. "Jessie and Thelma Revisited: Marsha Norman's Conceptual Challenge in *'night, Mother*," *Modern Drama* 36, no. 1 (March 1993): 109–119.

Norman, Marsha. *Getting Out*. New York: Dramatists Play Service, 1998.

———. *'night, Mother*. New York: Hill & Wang, 1983.

Norris, Kathleen (1880–1966)

A dynamic, commercially successful journalist, orator, short-story writer, and novelist, Kathleen Thompson Norris tinged with protofeminist themes her stories about the tempests in ordinary lives. A native San Franciscan, she grew up in an Irish Catholic household. When her parents died—her mother at Thanksgiving and her father at Christmas 1899—Norris and her brother, Joseph, tended the four youngest siblings. After a brief period at the University of California and jobs as bookkeeper, hardware clerk, library aide, and teacher, at 26 she moved on to journalism in time to report on the earthquake that destroyed much of the city. After her marriage to the writer Charles Norris and relocation to New York City and a summer place at Saratoga, she reared seven children, four of them adopted, while submitting stories to *Atlantic, Collier's, Cosmopolitan, Delineator, Everybody's,*

Saturday Evening Post, Telegram, and *Woman's Home Companion.* The publisher of *Good Housekeeping,* in which Norris serialized *Sisters* (1919), announced that her name on the cover ensured sales above 50,000.

In 1911 Norris published *Mother: A Story,* a saga about working girls that gave the author name recognition with readers, especially those seeking Christian values for women. By researching period details, she crafted believable settings and scenes from unremarkable lives—a daughter who returns to her mother with a renewed devotion to their simple community. Speaking of the frustration of a dead-end career, the protagonist, Margaret Paget, summarizes her boredom: "Nothing ever happens to us except broken arms and bills and boilers bursting and chicken pox! It's drudge, drudge, drudge from morning until night!" (Norris, 2001, 18). Subtexts of feminism, temperance, pacifism, and opposition to the death penalty infused her fiction with serious thought, to which Norris later added antinuclear propaganda. Her plain-spoken fiction made her one of the highest-paid female authors of her day.

Norris channeled mature interests into varied writing modes. She serialized *The Rich Mrs. Burgoyne* (1913) and wrote of women as altruists in *Saturday's Child* (1914). She pursued historical fiction in a best seller, *Certain People of Importance* (1922), and autobiography, *Control* (1925), which she followed 37 years later with *Family Gathering* (1959). She won a short story prize for "Sinners" (1929), published in *Cosmopolitan.* In 1930 she sold *Passion Flower* to Hollywood for silent filming by William de Mille and surveyed the issues of sexual emancipation, birth control, and divorce in *Margaret Yorke;* five years later she contemplated the BEAUTY MYTH in *Beauty's Daughter* (1935), a study of Magda, an aging former actor. In 1937 Norris anticipated the having-it-all controversy in a novel, *You Can't Have Everything,* serialized in six parts for *Woman's Home Companion.* Between world wars she issued a feminist polemic, *What Price Peace? A Handbook of Peace for American Women* (1928). During the rise of radio soap operas after World War II she scripted *Bright Horizons* with postwar feminist themes.

Norris grew more contemplative in her 70s. In 1957 she probed FEMINIST UTOPIAS in *Through a Glass Darkly,* in which labor and management maintain a healthy respect for each other. The system encourages unskilled laborers and domestics to choose cleaning, cooking, laundry, or chauffeuring as their job by alloting an annual four-month holiday to each worker. The setting features eight-room cottages built in an orchard and equipped with electric kitchens "so constructed as to appeal to the eternal homemaking instinct of womankind, with a vision of summer breakfasts under the thick shade of an apple tree" (Norris, 1957, 27). Norris contrasts the logic of her utopia with the philosophy of the mid-Victorian period, when girls slaved for subsistence wages and children languished in asylums. Into her late 70s she refused to allow rheumatoid arthritis to curtail a half-century of writing. Her works resurfaced in the late 20th century in classic reprints and online etexts.

Bibliography

Ehat, Carla, and Anne Kent. "Interview with Helen Thompson Dreyfus," *Oral History Project of the Marin County Free Library,* San Rafael, California (20 February 1979).

Norris, Kathleen. *Mother.* San Antonio, Tex.: Vision Forum, 2001.

———. *Through a Glass Darkly.* Garden City, N.Y.: Doubleday, 1957.

Nuñez, Elizabeth (ca. 1950–)

The Carib-American scholar and novelist Elizabeth Nuñez updates feminist literature with views of age-old female struggles. She immigrated from Trinidad to the United States in her teens to finish high school and to study English at Marian College and New York University. An English professor at Medgar Evers College, the City University of New York, she dedicated her career to literary pursuits and vowed to include in all her works the harm done by the Middle Passage, the harsh transatlantic crossing made by slaveships to the Americas and the West Indies. As cofounder of the National Black Writers Conference she has coordinated seminars featuring the feminist authors Maya ANGELOU, Gwendolyn BROOKS, Maryse CONDÉ, Mari EVANS,

Paule MARSHALL, Terry MCMILLAN, Ntozake SHANGE, and Alice WALKER. For Nuñez's enthusiasm for black female authors, in 2002 she received the Go On Girl! Author of the Year Award.

The author gained immediate attention for her early works, beginning with the novel *When Rocks Dance* (1986), a story of a woman's longing for a piece of land all her own. The coming-of-age novel *Beyond the Limbo Silence* (1998) won readers for its exploration of the matrilineage of Sara Edgehill, an island girl drawn into oddly opposing involvements—voodoo and the civil rights movement—after she wins a scholarship to a college in Wisconsin. Nuñez turned to Gothic fiction for *Bruised Hibiscus* (2000), an American Book Award–winning depiction of abusive relationships. The story coordinates themes of SISTERHOOD, colonial predations, and two women's secret guilt from childhood after seeing a man rape and murder a woman. Critical acclaim for *Discretion* (2002) focuses on the author's creation of Oufoula, a politician who allows his fantasy of the IDEAL WOMAN to destroy his life. Nuñez again explored the male perspective in *Grace* (2003), an urban novel about a troubled marriage.

Bibliography

Carroll, Denolyn. "Grace," *Black Issues Book Review* 5, no. 2 (March–April 2003): 34–35.

Nuñez, Elizabeth. *Beyond the Limbo Silence.* New York: Seal Press, 1998.

———. *Bruised Hibiscus.* New York: Seal Press, 2000.

———. *Discretion.* New York: One World, 2002.

———. *Grace.* New York: One World, 2003.

O

Oates, Joyce Carol (1938–)

The scholarly essayist, dramatist, fiction writer, and Princeton professor Joyce Carol Oates holds a place of honor in feminist literature for stories of girls and women at pivotal, terrifying moments in their lives. Born on a farm in Lockport outside Erie, New York, she grew up Irish Catholic in the rural milieu that colors her fiction. Like other writers who grew up during the women's movement, she orchestrated complex self-evaluations and motives. With English and philosophy degrees from Syracuse University and the University of Wisconsin, in 1974 she cofounded the *Ontario Review Press* and the *Ontario Review,* a long-lived literary journal, featuring the works of the feminists Margaret ATWOOD, Rita DOVE, Margaret DRABBLE, Nadine GORDIMER, Maxine KUMIN, Doris LESSING, and Gloria NAYLOR. Oates published her own early stories in *Epoch, Kenyon Review,* and *Southern Review* and submitted surreal and Gothic tales to *Twilight Zone, Exile,* and *Omni.* Her stories hold the record for frequency in two series, *Best American Short Stories* and *Prize Stories: The O. Henry Award.* Critics rate her troubled outsiders on a par with the bizarre, off-beat characterizations of Angela CARTER, Carson MCCULLERS, and Flannery O'CONNOR.

For her most disturbing fiction, such as the confession of a child murderer in the satiric novel *Expensive People* (1968) and the National Book Award–winning series *them* (1969), an examination of urban VIOLENCE, Oates situates characters in seemingly safe, ordinary homes. Her intent is to illustrate how perverse obsessions and primal impulses flourish in seemingly normal people. She turned to feminist allegory for "Where Are You Going, Where Have You Been?" a popular selection in *The Wheel of Love* (1970), and updated John Milton's *Paradise Lost* (1667) in *Marriages and Infidelities* (1972), a fable collection surveying male-female relationships. After her family moved to Princeton, New Jersey, Oates produced a best-selling horror tale, *Bellefleur* (1980), a perplexing, nihilistic saga of emotional turmoil in modern family life symbolized by a werewolf and outré otherness—a freakish girl born with her twin brother's lower half growing out of her torso.

Late in the 20th century Oates intensified her concern for women's issues. For "Lethal" (1992) she entered the psyche of a murderer and rapist. In 2002 another story of rape and family dissolution, *We Were the Mulvaneys* (1995), served as the impetus for a film for Lifetime Television, starring Blythe Danner as a divorced woman who survives abandonment and shattering family upheaval. Oates immersed the reader in teen violence and criminality in *Foxfire: Confessions of a Girl Gang* (1993), a chronicle of loyalty to "a true blood-sisterhood, our bond forged in loyalty, fidelity, trust, *love*" (Oates, 1994, 4). The fervor of belonging resounds as in the fealty pledge of the Three Musketeers: "Foxfire Is Your Heart" (IBID., 4). From the point of view of the victim Mary Jo Kopechne, Oates relived in *Black Water* (1993) the young woman's drowning after Senator Edward Kennedy's car skidded into deep water at Chappaquiddick.

At the core of Oates's writing is the uniqueness of each female protagonist, whether beautiful or grotesque, lovable or vicious. For *Blonde* (2000), a fictionalized feminist biography, she examined the decline of the actor and sex symbol Marilyn Monroe. In sympathy for an exploited, emotionally haggard icon Oates pictures the protagonist remembering "not clearly but in fragments, her own lost emotions, the loneliness of her childhood only partly assuaged by the looming screen. . . . But she can't see ahead to the ending" (Oates, 2002, 10–11). A recent young adult novel, *Big Mouth and Ugly Girl* (2003), returns to the BEAUTY MYTH to depict the character growth of Ursula Riggs, a self-castigating teen who allies with Matt Donaghy, a schoolmate wrongly accused of planning to blow up the building. On the outside of popularity, Ursula keeps up a tough front and boasts, "Nobody ever saw Ugly Girl cry" (Oates, 2003, 8). Like Legs, organizer of the outlaw gang in *Foxfire*, Ursula is the author's vision of the uncertain adolescent who, as would the dog in Aesop's fables, would rather be known for something bad than to be ignored.

Bibliography

Daly, Brenda. "Sexual Politics in Two Collections of Joyce Carol Oates's Short Fiction," *Studies in Short Fiction* 32, no. 1 (Winter 1995): 83–93.

Johnson, Greg, "Blonde Ambition: An Interview with Joyce Carol Oates," *Prairie Schooner* 75, no. 3 (Fall 2001): 15.

Oates, Joyce Carol. *Big Mouth and Ugly Girl.* New York: HarperTempest, 2003.

———. *Blonde.* New York: HarperCollins, 2002.

———. *Foxfire: Confessions of a Girl Gang.* New York: Plume Books, 1994.

———. *We Were the Mulvaneys.* New York: Plume, 1996.

O'Connor, Flannery (1925–1964)

A novelist and short-story writer renowned for quirky characters, allegorical narrative, and mordant irony, Mary Flannery O'Connor was a major player in southern Gothic literature. A native of Savannah, she grew up in a Catholic environment. At age 15 she observed her father's death of lupus erythematosus, a hereditary autoimmune disease that confined her to leg braces and a wheelchair a decade later. In addition to raising hens, peafowl, and quail, she entertained herself by writing about events and observations in her diary and reading the southern Gothic fiction of Eudora WELTY. O'Connor composed short fiction and essays that tended toward the weird, deceitful, deranged, violent, and grotesque in human behavior. After completing a degree in sociology from Georgia State College for Women in 1945, she shifted to postgraduate work in creative writing at the University of Iowa. She published "The Geranium" (1946) in *Accent* before her retirement to Andalusia, the family dairy in Milledgeville, Georgia, to complete a first novella, *Wise Blood* (1952). Additional submissions to *American Letters, Mademoiselle, Partisan Review,* and *Sewanee Review* established her skill at short fiction.

Despite her series of indomitable female characters, O'Connor receives little attention for her contribution to feminist literature. Her writing reflects musings on distorted elements in multigenerational family life, religion, and female friendships. A common point of view, that of elderly and widowed women, emerges from the grandmother in "A Good Man Is Hard to Find" (1955). Clinging to the values of an earlier time, the old lady declares, "In my time . . . children were more respectful of their native states and their parents and everything else," a sentiment that provokes smirks by her grandchildren (O'Connor, 1977, 4). The lack of sympathy for mature wisdom is often a source of disparities that the author builds into her own style of comic absurdity.

O'Connor produced offbeat black humor based on human venality, nihilism, obsessions, bigotry, and hurtful vendettas. From medieval morality drama and John Bunyan's *Pilgrim's Progress* (1678) she drew such allegorical female characters as Sabbath Lily, Ruby, June Star, and Mrs. Cope. For a kitchen table story, "Good Country People" (1955), the author devised a pair of mothers: Mrs. Hopewell, mother of Joy/Hulga, whom a Bible salesman seduces, and Mrs. Freeman, whose obsession with physical ailments resonates in her alarmist narratives to her daughters, Carramae and Glynese. In "Revelation," a story collected in *Everything That Rises Must Converge* (1965), O'Connor emphasizes the Gothic qualities in a rural girl and her apathetic mother. For *The Complete Stories*

(1971) the author received a posthumous National Book Award; another collection, *The Habit of Being* (1979), won a National Book Critics Circle Award for her correspondence with such literary pals as Caroline GORDON. O'Connor's flair for off-kilter characters influenced the feminist author Joy HARJO, the playwright Beth HENLEY, the ecofeminist Barbara KINGSOLVER, and the Canadian short story writer Alice MUNRO.

Bibliography

O'Connor, Flannery. *A Good Man Is Hard to Find and Other Stories.* New York: Harvest Books, 1977.

———. *The Habit of Being: Letters of Flannery O'Connor.* New York: Farrar, Straus & Giroux, 1988.

———. *Mystery and Manners: Occasional Prose.* New York: Farrar, Straus & Giroux, 1969.

Prown, Katherine Hemple. *Revising Flannery O'Connor: Southern Literary Culture and the Problem of Female Authorship.* Charlottesville: University of Virginia Press, 2001.

Olds, Sharon (1942–)

The onetime New York State poet laureate and creative writing teacher Sharon Olds applies clever juxtaposition to verse exalting womanhood. A San Francisco native, she was reared under unremitting Episcopalianism and suffered from a family split that took away her father, a steel salesman. His palpable presence looms in her confessional poems in overtly carnal, child-endangering acts, extending to a conceit of the child murdered in the Holocaust in "That Year" (1980). In a domestic example, "The Chute" (1987), she describes how he dangled his three offspring one by one down a laundry chute, "a story with some cruelty in it" (Olds, *Gold*, 37). Educated at Stanford and Columbia, she read aloud from master poets, notably Lucille CLIFTON and Adrienne RICH, and received training in versification from the poet Muriel RUKEYSER. Olds admired the crafting of fine feminist verse, especially the Ukrainian writer Irina RATUSHINSKAYA's incising with a matchstick her prison verse on soap bars. In anatomically precise rhapsodies Olds replicates Ratushinskaya's painstaking lettering. With the skill of a surgeon or pathologist, Olds moves familiarly over the libido, effluvia, and human terrain, whether a hypothetical being or her own family or self.

Olds is a master of bald metaphor decrying the sexual abuse and savagery of the late 20th century. She crafts the shocking image, for example, in "The Language of the Brag" (1980), a gender-probing vision of a thrown knife, "The haft slowly and heavily vibrating like the cock" (Olds, "Language," 8). In *The Gold Cell* (1987) she initiates intense imagery in the table of contents, which lists "The Pope's Penis," "Outside the Operating-Room of the Sex-Change Doctor," and "Now I Lay Me." Her urgent phrasing forces out the sensory extremes of word relationships, particularly in "Liddy's Orange," which describes the squeezing of sour juice from pulp.

Olds generates controversy through coarse autobiographical details. In *The Wellspring* (1996) the poet fantasizes in verse the wedding night of her parents and scenes of her teen and marital sex and motherhood. Of woman's vulnerability she describes her mother as a vulnerable bride—"the loaf laid into the pan/raw and being fed into the bright oven . . . in the smell of champagne and semen and cruor [gore]" (Olds, 1996, 4). Of her own conception she tinges "The Planned Child" (1996) with regret that she resulted from her parents' study of basal temperature rather than from unfettered passion. From early childhood memories she muses on the odor of coitus, which she compares to the scent of hydrogen sulfide from boiled eggs (*ibid.*, 10). Literary critics alternately dismiss her as an exhibitionist or narcissist or extol her as the poetic voice liberated from flinching or female hesitation to name the sources of pain and pleasure.

Bibliography

Dillon, Brian. " 'Never Having Had You, I Cannot Let You Go': Sharon Olds' Poems of a Father-Daughter Relationship," *Literary Review* 1, no. 108 (Fall 1993): 108–118.

Oldfield, Sybil. "The News from the Confessional— Some Reflections on Recent Autobiographical Writing by Women and Its Areas of Taboo," *Critical Survey* 8, no. 3 (September 1996): 296–305.

Olds, Sharon. *Blood, Tin, Straw.* New York: Alfred A. Knopf, 1999.

———. *The Dead and the Living.* New York: Alfred A. Knopf, 1984.

———. *The Gold Cell.* New York: Alfred A. Knopf, 1987.

———. "The Language of the Brag," *Calyx* 10, no. 2–3 (1987): 8–9.

———. *The Wellspring.* New York: Alfred Knopf, 1996.

Oliphant, Margaret (1828–1897)

The Scottish novelist, literary historian, editor, and biographer Margaret Oliphant Wilson Oliphant elevated through history and incipient NEW WOMAN fiction the rigors of WOMAN'S WORK. A native of Wallyford, Musselburgh, outside Edinburgh, she lived in several large towns where her father supervised customs. Although she never attended school, she learned plot and characterization from family storytellers, who immersed the family in Scots lore and in the religious turmoil of the age. Wed to a cousin, Francis Wilson Oliphant, a stained glass artisan, she settled in London, where her husband died of tuberculosis in 1859. Financial straits forced her to support herself and educate her daughter and two sons and her brother's three children with the proceeds from BIOGRAPHY, gaslight novels, pulp fiction, serials, social satire, and travelogues.

A conservative devoted to hard work, Oliphant set an example of the self-reliant female writer who ignored celebrity and disdained grandstanding feminism. For more than four decades she wrote for *Cornhill, Fraser's, London Magazine,* and *Macmillan's* and produced for the editor William Blackwood III critical studies of Dante Alighieri and Miguel de Cervantes as well as hundreds of Gothic tales and novels, beginning with *Passages in the Life of Mrs. Margaret Maitland* (1849). She veered into comedy with the mock-heroic *Miss Marjoribanks* (1866), a satire of the female power structure undergirding the Victorian home. At the death of Lucilla Marjoribanks's mother, the 16-year-old sets about meeting the demands of "dear papa," the head of the household and chief designer of rigid in-house schedules (Oliphant, 1999, 4). In the privacy of the scullery the cook snorts, "Them men would eat and drink if we was all in our graves" (*ibid.,* 7).

On more sober issues Oliphant crafted trenchant pro-woman essays, notably "The Laws Concerning Women" (1856) and "The Condition of Women" (1858). In a critique of John Stuart MILL's *Subjection of Women* (1869) she endorsed the Married Women's Property Bill and championed full citizenship for single women, career women, and widows, particularly the aged and infirm. In "The Grievances of Women" (1880), a position paper for *Frasier's,* she extolled activists for facing vicious detractors in the street and challenges men to acknowledge that women do half the world's work without pay or appreciation. After completing her last heroic history, *Jeanne d'Arc: Her Life and Death* (1896), Oliphant characterized the female writer's trials in *Annals of a Publishing House* (1897) and in the posthumous *Autobiography and Letters* (1899).

Through domestic fiction Oliphant elevated household commonplaces, the womanly responsibilities, unpaid toils, and compromised circumstances that Victorian literature tended to ignore or deny. Blended with the dash and suspense of Gothic convention, works such as *The Secret Chamber* (1876), *A Beleaguered City* (1880), *A Little Pilgrim of the Unseen* (1882), and *Stories of the Seen and Unseen* (1885) made Oliphant a leader of the genre. Rejecting stereotypes of the noble, enduring Victorian woman, she chose as heroines women paired with worthless suitors and shilly-shallying husbands or girls dominated by fathers and brothers. Obstacles to female contentment complicate *The Greatest Heiress in England* (1879), *The Ladies Lindores* (1883), *Kirsteen* (1890), and *Sir Robert's Fortune* (1895). In her hero story, *Hester: A Story of Contemporary Life* (1883), a precursor of the New Woman novel, Oliphant has the title character shrug off the need to marry as just another pitfall hindering her ambition. In response to Lyndall, an impetuous suitor, she envisions the loss of autonomy through wedlock: "If you once have me you would hold me fast. I shall never be free again" (Oliphant, 2000, 45). The author rewards Hester's courage and intelligence by dramatizing her rescue of a bank from scandal and ruin.

In critiques for *Blackwood's Edinburgh Magazine* Oliphant demanded high standards from writers by monitoring the morality of the era's taste in terror and gore. She chastised female authors for currying favor with male readers by producing gratuitous sensuality that diminished women: "It is a shame to women so to write; and it is a shame to the women who read and accept as a true representation of themselves and their ways the equivocal talk and fleshly inclination herein attributed to them" (Carnell, 169). Her essay upbraided authors for pandering to "that mere desire for something startling which the monotony of ordinary life is apt to produce; but it is debasing to everybody concerned" (*ibid.*). Because of her concerns for honest portraits of female characters, she helped to establish Charlotte BRONTË's novel *JANE EYRE* (1847) as a model of feminist literature and promoted Sarah GRAND's *Ideala: A Study from Life* (1888) as a model of New Woman fiction. In the 1980s feminist editors restored Oliphant's works to print.

Bibliography

Carnell, Jennifer. *The Literary Lives of Mary Elizabeth Braddon.* Hastings, England: Sensation Press, 2000.

Jay, Elisabeth. *Mrs. Oliphant, "A Fiction to Herself": A Literary Life.* Oxford: Clarendon Press, 1995.

Oliphant, Margaret. *Hester.* Oxford: Oxford University Press, 2000.

———. *Miss Marjoribanks.* London: Penguin, 1999.

Williams, Merryn. *Margaret Oliphant: A Critical Biography.* London: Macmillan, 1986.

Olsen, Tillie (1913–)

Tillie Lerner Olsen captures the disillusion and despair of bright, creative women whose aims exceed their grasp. One of the six children born to Jewish-Russian immigrants in Wahoo outside Omaha, Nebraska, she emulated the humanism of her father, Samuel Lerner, an officer in the Nebraska Socialist Party. After leaving high school at age 16 to go to work, she educated herself at the local library. Influenced by Rebecca Harding DAVIS's feminist themes and subject in *Life in the Iron Mills* (1861), Olsen rallied support for working women and at age 17 served a prison term for distributing union pamphlets to the meatpackers of Kansas and Nebraska. Two years later during the onset of chronic lung disease, she began a novel, *Yonnondio: From the Thirties* (1974), which became an ongoing project over much of her career. She continued writing in a San Francisco jail after her arrest for organizing dockworkers.

For radical speaking and published polemics in support of the underprivileged, particularly women and children, Olsen gained the regard of the feminist authors Margaret ATWOOD, Maxine Hong KINGSTON, Ellen MOERS, and Katherine Anne PORTER. Saluting Olsen's courage the critic Adrienne RICH cited Olsen's belief that "every woman who writes is a survivor" (Rich, 1979, 123). In the essay "Blood, Bread, and Poetry: The Location of the Poet" (1984) Rich recalls that Olsen feared the backlash of the Federal Bureau of Investigation (FBI) and political conservatives during the McCarthy years. With a campaigner's pragmatism she responded to a rumor that the government would intern leftists in detention camps to the north by purchasing heavy winter clothes from the Salvation Army in anticipation of another arrest.

After marrying the activist Jack Olsen and rearing their four daughters, Olsen revived her literary career with courses in writing at San Francisco State and Stanford Universities. She spoke for the silenced single mother in a classic short piece "I STAND HERE IRONING" (1956), whose protagonist fervidly supports women's needs and convictions. The vignette became one of the most anthologized of feminist works, published in 11 languages. She won the O. Henry Award in 1961 for "Tell Me a Riddle," the story of Jeannie's immersion in the memories of her grandmother, Eva, another frequently reprinted work. Because of the girl's reverence and admiration for the elderly matriarch, Jeannie is able to accept Eva's wretchedness on her deathbed by visualizing a heaven that rewards deserving women.

During an extended work session at the MacDowell Colony Olsen completed *Yonnondio*, a semi-autobiographical socialist study of farm families and miners of Wyoming during the Great Depression. The dialect story describes Mazie Holbrook as a six-year-old abnormally aged by poverty and fear for men working in the mines. Olsen summarizes the child's days in the economic cycle that numbs and fetters the working class: "Day comes and night comes and the whistle blows and payday comes" (Olsen, 1979, 4). Worsening her cramped view of life are the rounds of abuse that her drunken father, Jim Holbrook, lavishes on his family. Mazie is undersized and big-eyed from meals of fatback and cornmeal. She regrets that a suffocating load of fear and want stop up her tears: "All of the world is a-cryen and I don't know for why" (*ibid.*, 8). Worsening her terror are the actions of a deranged miner who tries to throw her down a shaft as a pagan sacrifice to end deaths of miners in the underground crawl spaces.

Olsen is a renowned champion of the female artist. In the essay "One out of Twelve: Women Who Are Writers in Our Century" (1971), she expresses admiration for females who breach the wall of suppression and neglect that society imposes. In *Silences* (1978), an anthology of her orations and essays, she addresses the exclusion and limitations of female authors who lack the time and money to actualize their skills. She compares distinguished writers of both genders and discloses that few females enjoy an uninterrupted work life. She concludes that women's productivity is either "early beginnings, then silence; or clogged late ones (foreground silences); long periods between books (hidden silences)" (Olsen, 1978, 178). Of those women who publish, the proportion of prizewinners is significant commentary on gender favoritism:

Award	Female Winners	Percentage
Academy of American Poets, 1946–1975	5 of 33	15.2%
American Academy/ National Institute of Arts & Letters gold medal, 1922–1973	7 of 39	17.9%
Bollingen Poetry Prize, 1950–1973	4 of 24	16.7%
Guggenheim Fellowships, 1926–1976	91 of 369	24.7%
National Book Award for Fiction, 1950–1973	3 of 26	11.5%
National Book Award for Poetry, 1950–1973	3 of 26	11.5%
Nobel Prize for Literature, 1920–1972	5 of 49	10.2%
O. Henry Award, 1919–1973	20 of 54	37.0%
Pulitzer Prize for Drama, 1920–1973	6 of 56	10.7%
Pulitzer Prize for Fiction, 1920–1973	16 of 47	34.0%
Pulitzer Prize for Poetry, 1920–1973	11 of 51	21.6%

According to Olsen's tabulation of a total of 774 major literary awards before 1973, women won 171, or 22.1 percent.

More personal motifs of female lives enrich Olsen's later works. In her fifth decade of feminist writing she edited *Mother to Daughter / Daughter to Mother: Mothers on Mothering* (1984), a compendium on parenting featuring the words of such famous feminist writers as Alice MUNRO, Gloria NAYLOR, Olive SCHREINER, Eudora WELTY, and Jessamyn WEST. In 1987 Olsen and her daughter, Julie Olsen Edwards, coedited *Mothers and Daughters: An Exploration in Photographs*, which depicts the range of female relationships, from loving to ambivalent, in writings by Denise LEVERTOV, Adrienne Rich, and Alice WALKER. Olsen's verse meditation expresses the mystic tether between successive generations of women: "Mother, I do not know you. Mother, I never knew you. Daughter— without knowing, you knew me" (Olsen, 1987, 1). Filmways produced a cinema version of *Tell Me a Riddle* in 1980; that same year the feminist filmmaker Midge MacKenzie adapted "I Stand Here Ironing" for screen with Olsen serving as narrator.

Bibliography

Kalfopoulou, Adrianne. *A Discussion of the Ideology of the American Dream in the Culture's Female Discourses.* Lewiston, N.Y.: Edwin Mellen Press, 2000.

Olsen, Tillie. *Mothers and Daughters: An Exploration in Photographs.* New York: Aperture, 1987.

———. *Mother to Daughter, Daughter to Mother.* Old Westbury, N.Y.: Feminist Press, 1984.

———. *Silences.* New York: Dell, 1978.

———. *Yonnondio: From the Thirties.* New York: Delta, 1979.

Rich, Adrienne. *Adrienne Rich's Poetry and Prose.* New York: W. W. Norton, 1975.

———. *On Lies, Secrets, and Silence: Selected Prose, 1966–1978.* New York: W. W. Norton, 1979.

Roberts, Nora. *Three Radical Women Writers: Class and Gender in Meridel Le Sueur, Tillie Olsen, and Josephine Herbst.* New York: Taylor & Francis, 1996.

Onwueme, Osonye Tess (1955–)

The award-winning political dramatist, orator, and folklorist Osonye Tess Akaeke Onwueme puts a universal spin on feminist themes and motifs set in her native Nigeria. Born in Ogwashi-Uku, she studied education and English at the University of Ife and earned a doctorate in literature at the University of Benin. She married and bore five children. While teaching English and cultural diversity at the University of Wisconsin, she produced a dozen plays that inspired comparisons to Henrik Ibsen's *A DOLL'S HOUSE* (1879). At the heart of her stage works is the paradox of change as both destroyer of tradition and harbinger of better times for black African women.

Onwueme's humanism derives from her belief that women are the sufferers of a disproportionate amount of the world's pain and that they are also the source of redress and relief. Her 1993 trilogy— *The Broken Calabash, Parables for a Season,* and *The Reign of Wazobia*—proposes ways to equalize opportunity in gendered societies and to end power struggles. Based on long-lived Nigerian cultural strands, the plays rebel against senseless repetition of mistakes made by predecessors. The third play calls for the women of Ilaaa to turn empty hands into talons to seize what male rulers and priests have denied them. The year after the trio appeared, Onwueme took a post as the first Distinguished Professor of Cultural Diversity at the University of Wisconsin. In *The Missing Face* (1997), a musical drama that opened off Broadway at the New Federal Theatre in 2003, she contrasts traditional tribalism with the lifestyles of Africans displaced by the black diaspora. The plot features the visit of the Detroit resident Ida Bee to her son, Amaechi, in Idu, Nigeria, where Ida is able to work out a livable solution to separation from her husband, Momah.

Onwueme blends literary modes into substantive vehicles for feminist sentiment. She wrote a satiric folk novel, *Why the Elephant Has No Butt* (2000), in which the inequalities of tortoise and elephant force the lesser creature to cower to avoid trouble. In her masterwork, the epic drama *Tell It to Women* (1997), winner of the Association of Nigerian Authors Literary Prize for Drama, she politicizes a gathering of female Idu peasants in tribute to the heroine Yemoja through STORYTELLING, mime, wisdom lore, and dance. Their discussion of Western concepts of women's liberation

and self-determination branches out to the snobbery, peasant ignorance, and SEXUAL POLITICS of their West African situation. Yemoja laments, "I turned my back on all else to be here. And now this is what my life has turned into: another Slavery. Slavery . . . Slavery . . . another Slavery. If I am not trapped in a husband's chain or father's chains, I'm trapped in another woman's chain" (Onwueme, 1997, 153). Another speaker, Okei, complains, "You so-called educated women mistake book sense for wisdom or dismiss the common for the ordinary or inferior" (*ibid.*, 183).

Onwueme's control of verbal pyrotechnics increased in subsequent plays. More poignant than *Tell It to Women* is *Shakara: Dance Hall Queen* (2002), a tale of economic hardship among urban women whose daughters battle a pervasive discontent. On a Ford Foundation grant she completed *Then She Said It* (2002), an explosive drama of disempowered women set amid the civil corruption in the fictional African nation of Hungeria. The dramatist pictures brutalized multinational female citizens leading the cry to the rest of the world for succor, safety, and INDEPENDENCE. In 2003 she turned to specifics by connecting the condition of Africa's poor women to the oil industry, the subject of *What Mama Said,* set in the allegorical state of Sufferland.

Bibliography

Onwueme, Osonye Tess. *Tell It to Women: An Epic Drama for Women.* Detroit: Wayne State University Press, 1997.

———. *Three Plays: An Anthology of Three Plays.* Detroit: Wayne State University Press, 1993.

Waters, Harold A. "Tell It to Women: An Epic Drama for Women," *World Literature Today* 72, no. 3 (Summer 1998): 672–673.

O Pioneers! Willa Cather (1913)

The first of Willa CATHER's famed prairie "dirt books," *O Pioneers!* rebels against classical Euro-American fiction by celebrating the triumph of a pragmatic female farmer on the Nebraska highlands. Cather dedicated the novel to Sarah Orne JEWETT, her mentor and supporter. The classically named main character, Alexandra Bergson, immigrates from Sweden after her grandfather squanders the family fortune on a scheming woman, one of Cather's many literary foils for her heroines. Alexandra breaks the pattern of male-to-male inheritance when her father, John Bergson, leaves her the family acreage. He instructs his sons, Lou and Oscar, on the necessity that there be one head of the household. With an unusual openness to his eldest, he remarks, "She will do the best she can. If she makes mistakes, she will not make so many as I have made" (Cather, 20–21). With a similar generosity toward his wife he urges, "Don't grudge your mother a little time for plowing her garden and setting out fruit trees," a pair of aims that ally female characters with EVE and the Garden of Eden (*ibid.*, 21).

Unfortunately a father cannot relay to sons an openminded regard for women. The expected conflict erupts in the Bergson brothers, whose workaday thinking does not compare with their sister's ingenuity and optimism. Methodically she examines the agricultural methods of her neighbors, notes who prospers and who goes under, and surveys likely stretches of tableland to add to the family holdings. Tenacious and patient, she invests in a silo and alfalfa, introduces cleaner pens for pig raising, and expands her acreage when the time is right. Lou, in a lack-logic argument for male control, dismisses her successes by muttering, "This is what comes of letting a woman meddle in business" (*ibid.*, 125). In fear that Alexandra may marry a fortune-hunting outsider, Oscar follows the patriarchal sentiment with a solemn, but wrongheaded truism: "The property of a family really belongs to the men of the family" (*ibid.*, 126).

In the introduction to a 1989 reprint the critic Elizabeth JANEWAY describes the exemplary protagonist as an epic hero, one of the insightful builders of American prosperity, whom Cather compares to the mythic Amazons. Written in the era when male financiers, oil tycoons, and railroad barons dominated entrepreneurial history, the text portrays the upright, courageous plainswoman as a source of the American work ethic. In girlhood Alexandra symbolically steadies the lantern with her feet during the storm to project a single, unwavering point of light into the murky night. With a visionary's perseverance she settles on the Continental Divide, the symbolic separator of winners and losers, and works harmoniously with nature. She accepts the cost of pioneering—the loneliness and malnourished emotions that threaten to wither her spirit. At a low point she struggles with the moral conflict caused by her younger brother's adultery and the murder of Marie, Alexandra's best friend. The double loss costs the protagonist her quasi motherhood of the brother and a supportive SISTERHOOD with her neighbor Marie.

A generous progressive, Cather's Alexandra is a stable leader who, while shaping the land, paces herself evenly and takes the time to uphold family traditions and to exercise an innate humanism. She favors forgiveness and neighborliness over grudges. Out of charity she harbors Ivar, a barefoot Scandinavian elder who fears committal to an asylum for his eccentric behavior and visions. Her fortune secure through self-empowerment, she enjoys a flower bed, vegetable plot, vigorous livestock, and the leisure to participate in church holidays. Her reward for long labors is a delayed love interest, the artist-engraver Carl Linstrum, a friend from childhood. Unlike the conventional CINDERELLA ending, the denouement blesses the mature love match as a reunion of two old friends who deserve each other. In token of his admiration for Alexandra, Carl murmurs reassuringly, "You belong to the land. . . . Now more than ever" (*ibid.*, 229).

Bibliography

Cather, Willa. *O Pioneers!* New York: New American Library, 1989.

Marquis, Margaret. "The Female Body, Work, and Reproduction in Deland, Cather, and Dreiser," *Women's Studies* 32, no. 8 (December 2003): 979–1,000.

Motley, Warren. "The Unfinished Self: Willa Cather's *O Pioneers!* and the Psychic Cost of a Woman's Success," *Women's Studies* 12, no. 2 (1986): 149–165.

Rundstrom, Beth. "Harvesting Willa Cather's Literary Fields," *Geographical Review* 85, no. 2 (April 1995): 217–228.

Out of Africa Isak Dinesen (1937)

Out of Africa, a memoir-travelogue by the Gothic fiction writer Isak DINESEN, reflects on her emotional investment in Kenya. Set from 1914 to 1931 the life story of Baroness Karen Blixen describes a model NEW WOMAN, who sets her own course. Advancing on society's notion of old-maidhood, she escapes the stuffy Danish gentry at age 28 to marry Baron Bror Blixen-Finecke and to grow coffee in the Ngong high country. Her narrative style ventures from chronological reportage of the business known as Karen Coffee to impressionistic memories that exemplify sensitivity and intellectual curiosity about livestock, cookery, Islam, native dance and ritual, and the effects of colonial agrarianism on east central Africa.

Serene and luminous, the narrative spotlights insights that release the female pathfinder from drummed-in lessons of fragility to a sturdiness equal to Kenya's challenge. As "Msabu," she overthrows Nordic suspicions of barbarous animals and of equatorial dark races to flourish among jungle cats and the neighboring Masai and Kikuyu (Dinesen, 36). Her motherhood instincts thwarted by syphilis, she opens a literacy school and tends the physical hurts of local natives. Her compassion endears her to Kamante, the child of a Kikuyu widow, whom she introduces to the VIRGIN MARY at a Christmas mass. An autonomous figure, Dinesen gains the trust and admiration of native women, who admire her daring.

Dinesen measures out feminist impressions through carefully delineated passages. In Lulu, the rescued antelope, the author witnesses the invigoration of total female freedom: "Lulu of the woods was a superior, independent being, a change of heart had come upon her, she was in possession" (ibid., 78). Of the patriarchal Somali, the author admires the mother-in-law of Farah, her majordomo. The elderly woman garners esteem for educating her daughters on the value of modesty. Dinesen describes her as endowed with "the powerful and benevolent placidity of a female elephant, contented in her strength" (ibid., 185). The subservience of Somali women revives the author's memories of Denmark, where "Scandinavian women of the days of my Mothers, and Grandmothers,—the civilized slaves of good-natured barbarians,—do the honours at those tremendous sacred masculine festivals" (ibid., 190). Without fanfare Dinesen's subtle text depicts the author as a paragon of self-directed destiny in the unlikely setting of colonial Kenya. The 1985 film version, starring Meryl Streep as the author, echoes the moral strength and physical vulnerability of a remarkable woman of her day.

Bibliography

Dinesen, Isak. *Out of Africa and Shadows on the Grass.* New York: Vintage, 1985.

Lewis, Simon. "Culture, Cultivation, and Colonialism in *Out of Africa* and Beyond," *Research in African Literatures* 31, no. 1 (Spring 2000): 63.

Ozick, Cynthia (1928–)

The humanist fiction writer, translator, and essayist Cynthia Ozick threads Judaic lore into imaginative phantasms of human need and fear. The daughter of Jewish-Russian immigrants, she was born in the Bronx and grew up in rural Pelham Bay, where her father, a Hebrew scholar, operated a pharmacy. Her grandmother tried to enroll her at the neighborhood *cheder* (Jewish school), but the rabbi refused admission to girls. Among Gentiles Ozick retreated from Christmas carols and stonings for killing Christ and took refuge in books from a mobile library. Enrolled at Hunter College High School, she wrote in imitation of Henry James, her literary hero.

With degrees in English from New York and Ohio State Universities Ozick taught creative writing, worked in advertising, translated Yiddish poems, and wrote verse and fiction for *Judaism* and *Lilith* magazines. In 1966 she completed the novel *Trust*, an examination of a female writer's search for a workable style. Five years later she collected short works in *The Pagan Rabbi and Other Stories* (1971), winner of a Jewish Heritage Award, a citation from B'nai B'rith, and a National Book Award. Another anthology, *Bloodshed and Three Novellas* (1976), evidences her deep concern for Jewish identity through mysticism and the catastrophic Holocaust. In 1977 she validated women's liberation in the essay "Literature and the Politics of Sex: A Dissent," collected in 1996 in *A Cynthia Ozick Reader.*

Frequently anthologized is the author's "The Shawl" (1980), a parable of death camp starvation and infanticide published in the *New Yorker.* She composed the account of Rosa Lubin, the tragic mother of Magda, an infant whom a Nazi guard plucks from Rosa's breast and tosses into an electric fence. The text, featured in *The Best Short Stories 1981,* pictures Magda's concealment in the shawl and her need for suckling on a dry breast. The author developed the surreal story into a novella, *The Shawl* (1989), a survey of panicky motherhood and breast-feeding under extreme privations. The trauma results 38 years later in Rosa's scavenging, dementia, and hallucinations of Magda as though she were still alive. In 1992 the story served as the basis of a play that Ozick adapted for Playwrights Horizons in New York City and, in 1996, as an off-Broadway production for the American Jewish Repertory Theatre directed by Sidney Lumet and starring Dianne Wiest as Rosa.

Ozick's later feminism deviates from predictable themes and modes. In a comic satire, *The Puttermesser Papers* (1997), she features a quirky protagonist, Ruth Puttermesser, a female Don Quixote named from the Yiddish word for "butterknife." In Ozick's description Ruth exemplifies the isolation of the female intellectual: "In law they called her a grind, a competitive-compulsive, an egomaniac out for aggrandizement. But ego was no part of it; she was looking to solve something" (Ozick, 1998, 3). She enlists the aid of Xanthippe, a girl golem, a monster summoned by magic derived from the medieval cabala and named for Socrates' shrewish wife. Puttermesser uses the creature's power to win an election as New York City mayor and sets out to obtain justice for the disempowered. In 2004 Ozick published *Heir to the Glimmering World,* a woman-centered tale of Rose Meadows, a teenage orphan who uplifts the Mitwissers, a family of German-Jewish refugees, by nursing the ailing wife, tending her five children, and aiding the scholarly father as typist and research assistant.

Bibliography

Frumkes, Lewis Burke. "A Conversation with Cynthia Ozick," *Writer* 111, no. 3 (March 1998): 18–20.

Ozick, Cynthia. *Heir to the Glimmering World: A Novel.* Boston: Houghton Mifflin, 2004.

———. *The Puttermesser Papers.* New York: Vintage, 1998.

———. *The Shawl.* New York: Vintage, 1990.

Scrafford, Barbara. "Nature's Silent Scream: A Commentary on Cynthia Ozick's 'The Shawl,'" *Critique* 31, no. 1 (Fall 1989): 11–15.

P

Paglia, Camille (1947–)

A teacher, philosopher, and rogue social critic, Camille Anna Paglia has established a reputation for sharp opinions, often attacking the feminist movement. A native of Endicott, New York, she is the daughter of the Italian immigrant seamstress Lydia Paglia and her husband, Pasquale Paglia, a scholar who taught his daughter to challenge authority with vocal argument. She outgrew tantrums and matured into an outdoorsy type, a rebel, lover of film, and celibate lesbian. Because her caustic personality traits stymied friendships, she developed intellectualism. With degrees from the State University of New York and Yale University, she entered the classroom at Bennington College, where students and colleagues proved as hostile as high school friends had been. At age 32 she migrated to the Humanities Department of the Philadelphia College of Performing Arts.

In potent books and interviews and on television talk shows Paglia poses as the disruptive maverick and iconoclast, a stance that requires bodyguards for her public appearances, book signings, and lectures. She dismisses research in ancient goddess cults as flotsam of advancing civilization and maintains that feminism, in its contemporary revival, has destroyed human relations and robbed children of mothering. Her clash with the social theorist Kate MILLETT revealed a vengefulness toward old-guard feminists. Paglia became a public figure in 1990 with the publication of a neopagan best seller, *Sexual Personae: Art and Decadence from Nefertiti to Emily Dickinson*, a study in biological determinism. Nominated for a National Book Critics Circle award, the treatise negates feminism as a delusion—a simpleminded solution to the inherent differences between male and female. In the first chapter she charges: "Feminists, seeking to drive power relations out of sex, have set themselves against nature. Sex *is* power. Identity is power. In western culture, there are no nonexploitative relationships" (Paglia, 1991, 2). Despite her penchant for unlikely connections of unrelated thoughts, the punch of short sentences free of philosophical jargon wins converts to her point of view.

Paglia's rant turned to specific examples of female cultural icons, such as Jacqueline Kennedy and Elizabeth Taylor. In a second treatise, *Sex, Art, and American Culture* (1992), Paglia declared her personal distaste for assertive females such as Anita Hill. The philosopher outraged feminists by declining to pity rape victims, whose sufferings she diminished as an unavoidable side effect of the male sex drive. From her analyses of pop culture Paglia lauded Madonna for peddling sex and profiting from antipuritanism, thus beating feminists at their own game of rebellion against religious conservatism. A diatribe against Senator Hillary Clinton and the exoneration of pornography followed in *Vamps and Tramps: New Essays* (1994). The collection perpetuates Paglia's dismissal of female victims of poverty, VIOLENCE, and economic and political gender discrimination.

Bibliography

Booth, Alison. "The Mother of All Cultures: Camille Paglia and Feminist Mythologies," *Kenyon Review* 21, no. 1 (Winter 1999): 27–45.

Paglia, Camille. *Sex, Art, and American Culture.* New York: Vintage, 1992.

———. *Sexual Personae: Art and Decadence from Nefertiti to Emily Dickinson.* New York: Vintage, 1991.

———. *Vamps and Tramps: New Essays.* New York: Vintage, 1994.

Paley, Grace (1922–)

The first official New York State writer, Grace Goodside Paley has contributed jewellike stories, essays, and poems to feminist literature. The daughter of Russian Jewish political exiles, she absorbed STORYTELLING in her native New York City. She advanced to college-level verse studies at Hunter College, New York University, and the New School for Social Research, including a class with the poet W. H. Auden. Paley took charge of her own enlightenment with readings of the feminist authors Charlotte BRONTË, Elizabeth GASKELL, Gertrude STEIN, and Virginia WOOLF. While rearing her two children after a divorce from her first husband, Paley gravitated to the literary ferment of Greenwich Village and began a lifelong involvement in pacifist and antihunger demonstrations. Her jail terms and a peace mission to Hanoi earned the regard of antinuclear picketers and of Vietnam War protesters at the Greenwich Village Peace Center, which she cofounded.

At the beginning of her career Paley taught creative writing at Sarah Lawrence College and wrote wise, witty, woman-centered stories that featured the quandaries of divorced women and single mothers. She published in *Atlantic* and the *New Yorker* and later collected her work in *The Little Disturbances of Man: Stories of Men and Women at Love* (1959). The first entry, "Goodbye and Good Luck," features the WISEWOMAN, Aunt Rose Lieber, who smirks to her niece, Lillie, "Change is a fact of God. No one is excused. Only a person like your mama . . . don't notice how big her behind is getting" (Paley, 1994, 9). At age 52 Paley published *Enormous Changes at the Last Minute* (1974), a collection of 15 stories about the com-

monplace chaos of human life. In "A Conversation with My Father" (1974) the daughter overrides gendered SILENCING by contradicting her downcast father with female beliefs and demands for a hopeful outlook on self and motherhood.

Paley's command of fiction remains firm. Already a subject of feminist literature courses at colleges and universities, she won the 1989 Edith Wharton Award, the 1992 Rea Award for Short Stories, and the Vermont Award for Excellence in the Arts. She received the Jewish Cultural Achievement Award for Literary Arts and a nomination for a National Book Award for *The Collected Stories* (1994), an anthology of her first three compendia. Threaded throughout are studies of Faith, a recurrent allegorical character offering intimate glimpses of the author's life, generosity, and originality. In "Two-Part Story" Paley juxtaposes the chubby two-year-old son with Faith, his frazzled mother, who knows the frustration caused by loving a demanding child and leaving no time for herself. In *Begin Again: Collected Poems* (2001) Paley tosses out one of her succinct glimpses of womanhood: "No metaphor reinvents the job of the nurture of children except to muddy or mock" (Paley, 2001, 4).

Bibliography

Arcana, Judith. *Grace Paley's Life Stories: A Literary Biography.* Chicago: University of Illinois Press, 1993.

Goffman, Ethan. "Grace Paley's Faith: The Journey Homeward, the Journey Forward," *MELUS* 25, no. 1 (Spring 2000): 197–208.

Paley, Grace. *Begin Again: Collected Poems.* New York: Farrar, Straus & Giroux, 2001.

———. *Enormous Changes at the Last Minute.* New York: Farrar, Straus & Giroux, 1985.

———. *The Little Disturbances of Man: Stories of Men and Women at Love.* New York: Penguin, 1994.

Pankhurst, Emmeline (1858–1928)

A Manx-English firebrand, pamphleteer, and journalist, Emmeline Goulden Pankhurst led Englishwomen to partial enfranchisement. Born in Manchester the eldest of 10 children, she was reared by a feminist, abolitionist mother who read aloud the slave Eliza's flight over the icy Ohio

River from Harriet Beecher STOWE's UNCLE TOM'S CABIN (1852). In girlhood Pankhurst collected pennies for the American Freedman's Bureau. She attended SUFFRAGE meetings, where she absorbed the anger of repressed female citizens and learned of the rough justice awaiting incest victims. Even at home she mulled over an inconsistency between her parents' beliefs and their behavior: "I began instinctively to feel that there was something lacking, even in my own home, some false conception of family relations, some incomplete ideal" (Pankhurst, 1914, 7).

In her early teens Pankhurst evidenced the character and methods that made her name anathema to conservative males. She took offense when her parents showed interest in educating their sons. She overheard her father's lamenting, "What a pity she wasn't born a lad" (*ibid.*, 7). In silent riposte to her father's sexism, she and her sister, Mary, paraded alongside queues of voters in green dresses lifted to show red petticoats, the colors of the Liberal Party. Pankhurst completed her education at a boarding school and at the Ecole Normale de Neuilly in Paris, where the principal, Mademoiselle Marchef-Girard, stressed the right of girls to an EDUCATION equal to that of boys. On return to England Pankhurst joined the era of the NEW WOMAN by displaying original paintings at an art gallery, a commercial venture that enraged her father. After marriage at age 21 and the birth of five children, she joined her attorney husband in supporting the International Labour Party.

A spellbinding leader, Pankhurst passed along matrilineal concerns for women's rights to her daughters, Christabel and Sylvia. In 1903 the trio founded the National Women's Social and Political Union, a suffrage army. Its effrontery in heckling Winston Churchill's address to the House of Parliament, setting fire to churches and men's clubs, breaking windows and street lamps, etching putting greens with acid, slashing train seats and lopping telegraph wires, chalking "Votes for Women" on sidewalks, spitting on law officers, and libeling the royal family outraged conservatives. Despite chronic migraine in 1907 Pankhurst remained loyal to the cause by launching a Women's Parliament. In a speech in 1908 she described in persuasive terms her objective in seeking the vote: "It is a symbol of freedom, a symbol of citizenship, a symbol of liberty. . . . Such a thing is worth fighting for" (Pankhurst, 1912, 1). In addition to her rowdyism and muscular oratory, Pankhurst overcame grief for the death of her son, Harry, of polio by writing provocative articles for the journal *Votes for Women* and by publishing *The Suffragette: The History of the Militant Women's Suffrage Movement, 1905–1910* (1911), *The Importance of the Vote* (1912), and a collection, *Suffrage Speeches from the Dock* (1913). In *Why We Are Militant* (1913), a distinctive feminist document, she quoted a speech delivered in New York City exonerating suffragists for acts of civil disobedience against the status quo: "In Great Britain there is no other way. We can show intolerable grievances" (Pankhurst, 1913).

Before World War I Pankhurst remained a potent agitator for women's issues, even when addressing a group or inciting supporters meant a nine-months' sentence at Strangeways Prison. She used an interview with the Scots-Canadian journalist Ishbel ROSS, "Women Will Win the War" (1916), as a vehicle for feminism. Under Pankhurst's influence supportive inmates mounted sleep, thirst, and hunger strikes. The latter resulted in force feeding and deaths of choking, lung damage, and pneumonia. Her experiences as a convict and martyr during five sentences radicalized her attitudes toward women's prisons and infirmaries and strengthened her regard for female bravery. When Germany menaced England, she described her shift from suffrage to a truce in a popular autobiography, *My Own Story* (1914). On October 5, 1915, she took the podium at the London Pavilion to demand an end to the suffrage battle: "All the old prejudices must go and all the old rules and regulations must go. In time of war the rules of peace must be set aside. . . . Let the women stand shoulder to shoulder with the men to win the common victory" (Mackenzie, 294). With a patriot's vigor she recruited men for the British army, enlisted female volunteers for the home front, and reared three war babies. In 1920 she aided war orphans in Canada. After withdrawing to the French Riviera to run a tea room and recover her health, at age 68 she returned to England. With the backing of a conservative suffragist, she ran unsuccessfully for Parliament. Her daughter, Sylvia Pankhurst, chronicled her mother's exploits in *The Life of Emmeline Pankhurst* (1935).

Bibliography

Bartley, Paula. *Emmeline Pankhurst*. New York: Routledge, 2003.

MacKenzie, Midge. *Shoulder to Shoulder*. New York: Alfred A. Knopf, 1975.

Pankhurst, Emmeline. *The Importance of the Vote*. London: Women's Press, 1912.

———. *My Own Story* (1914). Available online. URL: http://www.fordham.edu/halsall/mod/1914Pankhurst.htm. Accessed on October 13, 2005.

———. *Why We Are Militant* (1913). Available online. URL: http://www.cooper.edu/humanities/core/hss3/e_pankhurst.html. Accessed on October 17, 2005.

Purvis, June. *Emmeline Pankhurst: A Biography*. New York: Routledge, 2002.

Paretsky, Sara (1947–)

A powerhouse of the FEMALE DETECTIVE NOVEL, Sara N. Paretsky deserves a place among feminist authors for her sympathetic treatment of women in distress as well as for her stand on free speech issues. A native of Ames, Iowa, she grew up in Eudora, Kansas. She earned a political science degree at the University of Kansas and an M.B.A. and Ph.D. in history from the University of Chicago before settling in Chicago with her husband, the physicist Courtney Wright, and their three sons. Aiding Paretsky's start in writing was a course taught by the suspense novelist Stuart Kaminsky at Northwestern University. She managed an insurance office, a dull job that gave her time to dream up Victoria Iphigenia "V. I." Warshawski, a 37-year-old Polish-Italian lawyer who operates a one-woman private investigation office. In 1982 the first of the series, *Indemnity Only*, introduced a woman determined to succeed in a male-dominated profession. Because Paretsky has what the reviewer Michelle Green calls "the guts to go where other doctorates fear to tread," her mysteries have created a cult following in 14 countries (Green, 132). In 1997 during a residency at Oxford University she advised other female writers on crafting mystery and detective lore.

In 1987 Paretsky received *Ms.* magazine Woman of the Year recognition for putting her female detective in the midst of the antiabortion culture in *Bitter Medicine*, the fourth in the V. I. Warshawski series. The story depicts a mother's assistance to her teenaged daughter, Consuelo, who is diabetic, pregnant, and incapable of supporting a child. The mother, Mrs. Alvarado, views the waste of women's lives as preventable: "She didn't want Consuelo to become a slave, to a baby and to a man who wouldn't even try to find a job. . . . Consuelo was not throwing . . . opportunities away for a life of menial, exhausting jobs" (Paretsky, 12). Paretsky creates an opportunity to comment on the plight of poor nonwhite women by involving V. I. in social muckraking. She exposes an upscale hospital for allowing both Consuelo and her infant to die because the staff dismisses the mother as a migrant Hispanic.

A vocal feminist, V. I. speaks for the author, an activist in the National Abortion Rights Action League, by siding with the mother and validating her experience as a discounted female patient. Of waiting times at a gynecologist's office V. I. testifies from personal observation: "Because they treat only women and women's time has inherently no value, it doesn't matter" (*ibid.*, 50). Her investigation pinpoints much more than a long wait—she proves the malpractice of a physician, Peter Burgoyne, a scion of a hero of the American Revolution. Paretsky's revealing connection between male power in the medical profession with racism and malfeasance in the case of a mother and unborn child elevates the significance of this mystery to the feminist canon.

Paretsky expressed the importance of the media to crime fighting and created as backup for V. I. her friend, Murray Ryerson, a newspaper reporter, whom the author featured in *Hard Time* (1999). In 2003 Paretsky published *Blacklist*, a Warshawski mystery written in reaction to Arab terrorist attacks on the World Trade Center and the Pentagon on September 11, 2001. The author uses the story to lambaste invasions of privacy under the Patriot Act, which gives federal investigators freedom to override constitutional protections. The story takes V. I. through multiple generations of Chicagoans involved in political, social, sexual, and financial secrets during the McCarthy era of red baiting, blacklisting, and wiretaps. To ensure Americans' freedom of speech and freedom from unlawful search and seizure, Paretsky also lectures on First Amendment civil liberties as they pertain to readers and writers.

Bibliography

Abbe, Elfrieda. "Risky Business," *Writer* 116, no. 10 (October 2003): 22–26.

Green, Michelle. "Sara Paretsky's Cult Heroine Is a Woman's Woman—V. I. Warshawski, the Funky Feminist Private Eye," *People Weekly*, 14 May 1990, pp. 132–134.

Paretsky, Sara. *Bitter Medicine*. New York: Dell, 1999.

Parker, Dorothy (1893–1967)

One of America's more trenchant satirists and ironists, Dorothy Rothschild Parker critiqued the faults of society with lacerating humor. Born to a Talmudic scholar in West End, New Jersey, she grew up from age five grieving for her dead mother and, at the insistence of her father and stepmother, enrolled in Blessed Sacrament Convent Academy and Miss Dana's Seminary. To combat a home situation she could not alter, from early girlhood she cultivated snide remarks and private asides, the beginnings of her trade in quick wit. By age 20 she was self-supporting as a pianist and teacher at a dance school. She began a literary career as verse and caption writer for *Ainslee's, Saturday Evening Post,* and *Vogue* and as copy editor and eventually as drama critic for *Vanity Fair.* While writing columns for the *New Yorker* for 32 years, she found a more suitable outlet for caustic comebacks. Her personal life was less carefree in the aftermath of a late-term ABORTION that left her suicidal. She won recognition for sparkling repartee at the Oak Room of the Algonquin Hotel, a hangout for the novelist Edna FERBER and mostly male quipsters who called themselves the Algonks.

Parker's acerbic verse, aphorisms, and short stories denounced hypocrisy in love, marriage, and family life. Her first verse collection, *Enough Rope* (1926), was a best seller. Her most anthologized story, "Big Blonde," published in *Bookman* in 1929, won the O. Henry Award for its depiction of a fe-

male alcoholic. In 1933 Parker introduced the stream-of-consciousness mode in the story "The Waltz," a droll piece punctuated at intervals with the female dancer's comments to her inept partner. Outraged at clumsy partnering, she feels pummeled, disarrayed, and reduced to an image of Madeline, the female wraith in Edgar Allan Poe's Gothic story *The Fall of the House of Usher* (1839). Countering the frail ghostly figure is Parker's description of her partner, who waltzes like Mrs. O'Leary's cow, the legendary cause of the Chicago Fire.

Parker's subsequent writings strayed from the one-liners that made her famous. During the Spanish civil war Parker covered the siege of Madrid on November 23, 1937, for the *Masses*, a Communist journal. She stressed the hunger of some 50,000 refugee babies for scarce supplies of milk, eggs, and cereal. The article dramatized the sufferings of urban mothers and their children, who were at the mercy of the Valencia bombardment. At age 40 she wrote screenplays for Hollywood films, notably *A Star Is Born* (1937), for which she won an Oscar nomination for best script, and the cinema adaptation of the dramatist Lillian HELLMAN's *The Little Foxes* (1941). In 1947 Parker won another Academy Award nomination for the screenplay *Smash-up: The Story of a Woman*, a vehicle for Susan Hayward, who plays Angie Evans, a nightclub singer who drifts into idleness and alcoholism after marriage ends her career.

Parker defended the individual female's right to self-expression. As models she admired pacesetting women such as the dancer Isadora Duncan, the actor Lynn Fontanne, the short-fiction writer Katherine MANSFIELD, and the poet Edna St. Vincent MILLAY. In 1949 Parker courted arrest by singing the "Internationale" in protest at the trial of Nicola Sacco and Bartolomeo Vanzetti for robbing and murdering a paymaster and his guard. In 1951 she joined 300 other artists and public figures questioned by the House Un-American Activities Committee in denying anarchist beliefs and in refusing to link others to the Communist Party. She made a comeback in 1953 with the Broadway play *Ladies of the Corridor,* a story of lonely aged women living in a dreary urban hotel, a lifestyle that Parker knew from personal experience. Four years later she began reviewing fiction for *Esquire*. Defeated in retirement by depression, near blindness, and alcoholism, Parker was living alone at the Volney Hotel when she died of a heart attack at age 74. In 1994 the film *Mrs. Parker and the Vicious Circle* featured Jennifer Jason Leigh in the role of "Dorrie," whose grief at the death of her friend Robert Benchley left the satirist permanently saddened.

Among Parker's amusing, sophisticated writings are dour, sometimes tragic re-creations of the tenuous happiness of women, which the author recorded in a variety of modes. In 1922 she queries in the poem "Fragment" the solidarity of her own marriage. The following year she demands in "Triolet" (1923), that her love return her heart and her freedom. In the style of the Cavalier poets she concludes "The Trifler" (1926) with a bitter quatrain about a faithless lover. Often quoted is her sardonic couplet entitled "News Item" (1925), an accusation that men disdain women who wear glasses. Among her feminist stories is "The Lovely Leave" (1943), a semiautobiographical exploration of a lonely woman's willingness to sacrifice self-respect for one more hour with her soldier husband, Lieutenant McVickers. To manage the day of happiness, she follows a set rule: "Never say to him what you want him to say to you," a self-SILENCING that rules out honest admissions of loneliness and regret (Parker, 1996, 5).

Bibliography

Meade, Marion. *Dorothy Parker: What Fresh Hell Is This?* New York: Penguin, 1989.

Parker, Dorothy. *Not Much Fun: The Lost Poems of Dorothy Parker.* New York: Scribner, 1996.

———. *The Poetry and Short Stories of Dorothy Parker.* New York: Modern Library, 1994.

———. *The Portable Dorothy Parker.* New York: Penguin, 1991.

patriarchy

The squelching and overpowering of females through patriarchal control of homes, EDUCATION, marriages, and creative outlets dominate feminist literature. A glimpse of the atavistic father underlies paternal VIOLENCE in the poet Anne SEXTON's resetting of FAIRY TALES in *Trans-*formations (1971). She describes the father in "The Maiden without Hands" as a villain who sacrifices his daughter's hands to protect him from a wizard. The girl's stumps, like a dog's feet, have a perverse appeal to the wizard. Lacking the means to ward off a would-be rapist, she weeps into her ineffectual stumps. Weeping purifies her, setting her apart from humanity by a moat of tears. Sexton's grim view of patriarchy derives from medieval hagiography, which features virgins fleeing the forced marriages arranged by fathers eager for connections to power or sources of a grand DYNASTY. The girls, no longer able to survive in the normal sphere, advance to sainthood through sorrow.

In 1911 the radical South African novelist and polemicist Olive SCHREINER challenged the world to welcome an antipatriarchal warrior, the NEW WOMAN. She warned readers in *Woman and Labour* that reform faced centuries of paternalism toward women's advancement: "There is no door at which the hand of woman has knocked for admission into a new field of toil but there have been found on the other side the hands of strong and generous men eager to turn it for her, almost before she knocks" (Schreiner, 1911). The interference of men prolongs the daddy's-little-girl image of a female achieving only if she accepts patronizing. In an extended metaphor of barriers Schreiner concluded, "Always in our dreams we hear the turn of the key that shall close the door of the last brothel; the clink of the last coin that pays for the body and soul of a woman; the falling of the last wall that encloses artificially the activity of woman" (*ibid.*). Her choice of the knock on the locked door replicates her own upbringing by a pious, controlling father who drove her away to seek autonomy and self-support at age 12.

The inevitable break with the male on the opposite side prefigures an era of strained male-female relationships. As Donna CROSS and her father, William Woolfolk, explain in *Daddy's Little Girl: The Unspoken Bargain between Fathers and Their Daughters* (1982), "A woman who does not preside over her own life, who keeps trying to attain to a standard set for her by someone else—all too often her father—feels a central lack of purpose" (Cross and Woolfolk, 70). She grows up physically into a full-sized, emotionally dependent child who has no grasp of a true self. In *Woman Hating* (1974) the polemicist Andrea DWORKIN blames fairy tales of childhood for instilling in the female mind the polar opposites of gendered behavior—the handsome prince rescuing the innocent Sleeping Beauty from nonbeing. Children who absorb the motifs of folklore subconsciously differentiate between male and female as actuator and recipient of power. Boys and girls learn early to decode and respond to varying human expressions of this paradigm, whether in gesture, word, social or religious mores, or physical violence, the focus of BEAUTY AND THE BEAST and CINDERELLA plots and of Shirley JACKSON's horrific martyrdom story "The LOTTERY" (1948).

For the results of faulty notions of potency and control the Asian-American novelist Amy TAN turns to historical episodes for examples in adult lives. In fictionalizing her mother's memories, Tan skillfully characterized the dead ends that immigrant Chinese women reached in the motherland under centuries of arbitrary androcentric traditions. In *The Joy Luck Club* (1989) the author carries the motif of the despairing, unappreciated woman to a tragic extreme by describing feudal marriage and polygyny, the male-centered social order in imperial China up to the Communist takeover of 1949. The protagonist, An-mei Hsu, explains why her unnamed mother, the concubine of the rapist and womanizer Wu Tsing, chose suicide by opium-poisoned rice cakes over a life of degradation: "That was China. That was what people did back then. They had no choice. They could not speak up. They could not run away" (Tan, 272).

Through the writing of a classic Spanish novel, Emilia Pardo BAZÁN attempted to enlighten the discouraged women of her nation and era about the patriarchy promulgated by entrenched Catholicism. Her masterwork novel, *The House of Ulloa* (1886), discloses the male sins of Galicia by describing the despotism of Dom Pedro. Her naturalistic images of spousal abuse and the sexual DOUBLE STANDARD, both for the aristocratic Doña Marcelina and for the peasant Sabel, expose antiwoman violence and corruption as major feminist issues in the upper and lower classes. At the crux of Bazán's depiction of 19th-century Spain is the failure of the spineless priest, Father Julian Alvarez, to confront out-of-control male ego, the SILENCING of women and exclusion of the female perspective, and the despoliation of women and peons by greedy landowners. By extension Bazán characterizes religion as a root cause of women's misery.

Of religious patriarchy Mary ANTIN, a Russian-Jewish memoirist, recalls in the autobiography *The Promised Land* (1912) that her mother, Esther Antin, was the obedient type, who "had all her life taken her religion on authority" without questioning one-sided philosophies favoring men (Antin, 245). Even though Esther concealed her private thoughts about male control, "the Jewish faith in her was deeply rooted, as in the best of Jews it always is. The law of the father was binding to her, and the outward symbols of obedience inseparable from the spirit" (*ibid.*). Upon immigration to Boston Esther obeyed her husband, Israel Antin, who sought assimilation in the new land. He commanded that the family abandon the ritual and customs that set the family apart from neighborhood Gentiles. Antin notes that although her father was educated, "his line of thinking had not as yet brought him to include women in the intellectual emancipation for which he himself had been so eager even in Russia" (*ibid.*, 246). He rated his wife's IQ a slight degree above that of cattle and insisted that the dutiful mate follow the husband's example, even if compliance forced her to violate centuries-old practices and beliefs.

More grievous examples of patriarchy are standard fare in feminist works. Outside the Western realm the verisimilitude of undervalued Indian females in Anita DESAI's *Fasting, Feasting* (1999) earned the novel nomination for a Booker Prize. The story contrasts the treasured son, Arun, with his unmarriageable 40-year-old sister, Uma. In his shadow she starves for nourishment to intellect and spirit and longs for freedom from her coercive elderly parents. Uma can do little more than rebel as if she is a peevish child—she "[flounces] off, her grey hair frizzled, her myopic eyes glaring behind her spectacles, muttering under her breath" (Desai, 5). Her parents are so united in misogyny that she speaks of them as "MamandPapa" and observes,

"Having fused into one, they had gained so much in substance, in stature, in authority, that they loomed large" (*ibid.*).

The activist Barbara KINGSOLVER fills her writings with the off-kilter gender relationships that place husbands over wives both in the United States and in Africa. In her first novel, *The Bean Trees* (1988), the protagonist, Taylor Greer, a single mother, ponders a truism: "From my earliest memory, times of crisis seemed to end up with women in the kitchen preparing food for men" (Kingsolver, 1988, 132). One of the author's memorable protagonists, Leah Price Ngemba in *The Poisonwood Bible* (1998), lives in a male-dominated family compound in Kilanga, Congo. She spews her disgust at the male hierarchy by "[damning] many men to hell, President Eisenhower, King Léopold, and my own father included" (Kingsolver, 1998, 421). Leah; her disabled twin, Adah; and their mother, Orleanna, escape after Leah's father, the Reverend Nathan Price, reaches a nadir of authority over his maverick fundamentalist mission. In the opinion of the reviewer Julian Markels the three women "have no choice but to break out of their Southern Baptist female subservience" to save themselves from being totally consumed by Nathan's obsessions with the priestly dispensation of salvation and angry demands for female obedience (Markels, 1).

Kingsolver's reputation suffered a blow in 2001 after the Arab terrorist attacks on the World Trade Center and the Pentagon. In reference to world crisis she challenged the logic of the 1991 Gulf War in a controversial essay, "And Our Flag Was Still There" (2001), which appeared in news media nationwide. To counter the glorification of yet another Middle East war, she noted the absurdity of Middle Eastern patriarchy, which remained as entrenched as it had during the Middle Ages. In her view, "We rushed to the aid of Kuwait, a monarchy in which women enjoyed approximately the same rights as a nineteenth-century American slave" (Kingsolver, 2001, 242). Her commentary made a familiar connection between the patriarchal behavior of males in peacetime and the macho behavior of President George W. Bush and the mayhem inflicted by soldiers in the Iraq War.

Bibliography

Antin, Mary. *The Promised Land.* Boston: Houghton Mifflin, 1912.

Cross, Donna, and William Woolfolk. *Daddy's Little Girl: The Unspoken Bargain between Fathers and Their Daughters.* Englewood Cliffs, N.J.: Prentice-Hall, 1982.

Desai, Anita. *Fasting, Feasting.* New York: Mariner Books, 2000.

Kingsolver, Barbara. "And Our Flag Was Still There," *San Francisco Chronicle,* 25 September 2001.

———. *The Bean Trees.* New York: Harper & Row, 1988.

———. *The Poisonwood Bible.* New York: HarperCollins, 1998.

Markels, Julian. "Coda: Imagining History in *The Poisonwood Bible,*" *Monthly Review Press,* September 2003, p. 1.

Schreiner, Olive. *Woman and Labour* (1911). Available online. URL: http://etext.library.adelaide.edu.au/s/schreiner_o/woman/woman.html. Accessed on October 13, 2005.

Sexton, Anne. *Transformations.* Boston: Houghton Mifflin, 1971.

Tan, Amy. *The Joy Luck Club.* New York: Putnam, 1989.

Valis, Noël, and Carol Maier, eds. *In the Feminine Mode: Essays on Hispanic Women Writers.* Lewisburg, Penn.: Bucknell University Press, 1990.

Persephone

The quest myth of Demeter/Ceres and Persephone/Proserpina elucidates the universal tie between female parent and female child. The structured story reflects links of dependency among all living things, humankind, beast, and plant. The basic plot accounts for the cosmic ramifications of plant life cycles and of the mixed blessing of eternal rounds of death followed by resurrection and renewal. At the same time the story reveals the instinctive parental fear that male suitors such as Hades/Pluto are potential violators of young virgins. On the human level the paradox of the benevolent goddess, Demeter, transformed into a raging exterminator of earthly life illustrates a familiar phenomenon in literature and art—the metamorphosis of mother love into savagery when faced with assault on her young. Compounding the crimes of abduction and rape are the complicity of Zeus/Jupiter, Persephone's father, in helping her uncle, Hades/Pluto, carry out his incestuous plot. Numerous feminist works color the universal characteristics of mother love and filial need with refreshing restatements of myths and new applications of their motifs, including the camaraderie between mother and daughter in the semi-autobiographical *Deephaven* (1877), Sarah Orne JEWETT's first compendium; in Meridel LE SUEUR's short story "Persephone" (1927); and in the withering of marigold seeds in Toni MORRISON's *The BLUEST EYE* (1970), the story of Pecola Breedlove's decline after Cholly, her father, rapes and impregnates her.

Central to the Persephone myth is the theme of multiple losses. In *Beginning with O* (1977) the Greco-American poet Olga BROUMAS vivifies in the poem "Demeter" the mother's terror of severance from the child who issued from her body. Of the end of childhood's dependence the mother voices the most fearful of liberations, that her child will predecease her "Will you die before me, my / bundle of flesh?" (Broumas, 21). Demeter knows the answer to her own question, which hinges on mortal weakness. The poet honors sources of the heartrending scene with a gracious gesture to the feminist authors Anne SEXTON, Sylvia PLATH, Virginia WOOLF, and Adrienne RICH, all of whom have pondered the mother's harsh duty to love and let go.

The Irish poet Eavan BOLAND revisited the Persephone myth as an allegory on gendered power struggles. In "The Pomegranate" (1987) the poet describes a fruit that ties Demeter to rule over earthly vegetation and relegates Hades, the Greek god of death and the dead, to power over the gardens of the underworld. One taste of the pomegranate causes Persephone to abandon her mother and to accept a binding obligation to her seducer. Boland's poem is rich with foreboding and the bitterness and fears of a mother. She knows that her teenaged daughter has entered the time of the pomegranate, the twilight of girlhood, when a male will lure her from home. The speaker acknowledges that the transition is inevitable, a progression leading to adulthood and procreation for the good of the race. The mother knows both gift and grief and must keep silent when her untried girlchild ventures forth literally to taste womanhood for the first time.

The British mythographer Tanith LEE corroborates Boland's themes. In *White As Snow* (2001), a feminist revision of the Snow White FAIRY TALE blended with the myth of Persephone, Lee acknowledges the onset of desire, symbolized by the lure of the pomegranate. The savoring of underworld fruit is part of the price of coming of age. When Arpazia, a raven-haired 14-year-old, gazes into the magic mirror, "She longed for change, not knowing the change of all things was almost upon her, nor what it could mean" (Lee, 32). Following the pattern of oral lore, Lee records the natural order of maturation. She stresses that Arpazia is motherless, a condition that contributes to lack of woman-to-woman cautions as menarche approaches. Arpazia's father is old and visually impaired, a handicap that exonerates him for failure to observe the ripening sexual characteristics of his only legitimate child. Changes in the young female connote the birth of a physical and emotional potency. Arpazia's ripening models a human paradox—adult self-actualization that threatens destruction for the unwary.

To illustrate the cyclical nature of female crises, Lee carries her story through the next generation. After Arpazia's daughter, Coira, falls into the hands of Hadz, Lee satirizes the ennui of marital sex through the husband's persistent demands for make-believe rape. Coira submits to Hadz, who likes to "caress her, taste her and, cramming within her, achieve the pinnacle" (*ibid.*, 303). His obsession for perverse sex requires numerous couplings each day and up to seven coarse, unloving sex acts per night. Her spirit hardened, she wills herself to endure their sessions. As Lee describes her, "She was functional. A chair of orgasm" (*ibid.*, 304). To the exclusion of Demeter and the older woman's authority and wisdom, Lee's version emphasizes the helplessness of the young female in the Persephone myth to elude bestial assault by the lord of the dead.

Bibliography

Broumas, Olga. *Beginning with O.* New Haven, Conn.: Yale University Press, 1977.

Carlson, Kathie. *Life's Daughter / Death's Bride.* Boston: Shambhala, 1997.

Lee, Tanith. *White as Snow.* New York: Tor Books, 2001.

Louis, Margot K. "Proserpine and Pessimism: Goddesses of Death, Life, and Language from Swinburne to Wharton," *Modern Philology* 96, no. 3 (February 1999): 312–346.

Petry, Ann (ca. 1908–1997)

A multitalented writer, Ann Lane Petry holds a place in feminist literature for capturing the lives of working-class women. Among her heroines are two famous black slaves, the freedom fighter Harriet Tubman and Tituba, the supposed corrupter of the bewitched girls of colonial Salem. The author came of age in her hometown of Old Saybrook, Connecticut. Although there were few nonwhite companions, Petry was content in a home environment spiced by her uncles' travel anecdotes and family STORYTELLING. As her father had, she studied pharmacy at Connecticut College and joined the staffs of the family drugstore and, later, a pharmacy in Lyme. After marrying at age 30, she relocated to Harlem and worked for the *Amsterdam News* and the *People's Voice* while taking writing courses at Columbia. She followed a self-composed reading regimen of history and the social sciences and composed children's drama for the American Negro Theatre.

At the start of a 40-year career Petry, under the pseudonym Arnold Petri, published a first story, "Marie of the Cabin Club," in the August 1939 issue of the *Baltimore Afro-American.* Using her own name, she followed with "On Saturday the Siren Sounds at Noon" in a 1943 edition of *Crisis,* followed by stories of the Jim Crow era for *Negro Digest.* She gained critical attention for her best-selling first novel, *The Street* (1946), the first literary profile of Harlem and the winner of the Houghton Mifflin Fellowship Award. Through standard coping ploys—masking, signifying, alternative measures, and disguise—black women in Petry's novel survive on their own by operating businesses and carving out fulfilling lives.

The Street is a violent account of the effects of sexism and ghetto poverty on Lutie Johnson, a rebellious single mother who is unable to cope. Educating her to the ways of a racist society is Granny, the traditional WISEWOMAN, who remarks on the male's self-conferred superiority: "Men like him don't get nowhere. . . . Think folks owe 'em a livin. And mebbe they do, but not nowhere near the way he thinks" (Petry, 1961, 55). Lutie independently concludes why white people despise blacks: "It must be hate that made them wrap all Negroes up in a neat package labeled 'colored' " (*ibid.,* 72). She recognizes the gender and racial bias indicated by "certain kinds of jobs and a special kind of treatment" (*ibid.*). She is less adept at repelling the stare of Super, a carnal ogling that terrorizes her with its sensual implications.

Upon the author's return to Old Saybrook she joined Negro Women Incorporated and began composing articles for *Crisis, Holiday,* the *New Yorker,* the *New York Times Book Review, Opportunity,* and *Redbook.* She set New England lore in *Country Place* (1947), a domestic novel about white family values, and in *The Narrows* (1953), a depiction of a biracial marriage. In anticipation of the civil rights movement she revived forgotten and neglected episodes of black history by characterizing valor in female survivors. In this period she wrote *Harriet Tubman: Conductor on the Underground Railroad* (1955), the story of the beloved "Moses" who led 300 slaves to freedom, and *Tituba of Salem Village* (1964) about the scapegoating of a Caribbean slave. In the former, families in the slave quarters view Harriet as worthless at cookery, fiber work, or sewing. For the latter novel Petry gathered island herbal lore from Barbados to explain Tituba's clairvoyance and knowledge of healing roots. The resulting work draws on Nathaniel Hawthorne's allegorical romance *The SCARLET LETTER* (1860) to account for a period of colonial chaos preceding the Salem witch trials of 1692.

Bibliography
Clark, Keith. "A Distaff Dream Deferred? Ann Petry and the Art of Subversion," *African American Review* 26, no. 3 (Fall 1992): 495–505.

Petry, Ann. *Harriet Tubman: Conductor on the Underground Railroad.* New York: HarperTrophy, 1996.

———. *Harriet Tubman: Conductor on the Underground Railroad.* New York: HarperCollins, 1991.

———. *The Street.* New York: Pyramid, 1961.

———. *Tituba of Salem Village.* New York: Thomas Y. Crowell, 1964.

Phelps, Elizabeth Stuart (1844–1911)

The feminist essayist, poet, and utopian writer Elizabeth Stuart Phelps Ward wrote cleverly and passionately about WOMEN'S RIGHTS. She asserted the need to reform the factory system for the sake of overworked, underpaid mill girls. A Bostonian reared in Andover, Massachusetts, she grew up among pious intellectuals on the campus of Andover Theological Seminary, where her grandfather and father taught scripture. Unfortunately her family denied her the opportunity for a college education or even a private room in which she could write undisturbed by her more privileged brothers. Her mother, the tractarian Elizabeth Stuart Phelps, the author of *The Sunny Side; or, The Country Minister's Wife* (1851) and *A Peep at "Number Five"; or, A Chapter in the Life of a City Pastor* (1852), established for the author the importance of women's literature. Another influence, Phelps's maternal aunt, Sarah Stuart Robbins, was also a writer of two novels, *My New Home: A Woman's Diary* (1865) and *One Happy Winter; or, A Visit to Florida* (1878). By age 22 Phelps voiced her own feminist beliefs through the title character in "Jane Gurley's Story" (1866), a serial for *Hours at Home* magazine that dramatizes the satisfaction of a NEW WOMAN, a self-supporting commercial artist.

After her mother's death in 1852 the grieving author abandoned her birth name, Mary Gray, and assumed her mother's name. The shift in identity presaged Phelps's interest in the afterlife and her search for a mystic communion with the dead. Three years after the end of the Civil War and the death of her brother, Roy, in combat, Phelps published the popular utopian novel *The Gates Ajar* (1868), which was translated into French, German, and Italian. Building on the friendship of Mary, the protagonist, and her wise Aunt Winifred, the author used the meditative text to project a feminist paradise. The haven suited an era when war widows were coping with the loss of husbands in combat and military prisons. Prolonging their sorrow was the impact of postwar political and economic turmoil and religious skepticism.

Phelps's vision of a comforting afterlife abandoned the strict Calvinism of her youth. She pursued the subject in two sequels, *Beyond the Gates* (1883) and *The Gates Between* (1887). The trilogy reconciled theological heavens with her own version of a perfect world for women that restored homes, earthly beauty, and deceased babies in an idyllic setting that Adam and Eve once wandered.

Phelps developed feminist themes that set her apart from the sentimental authors of her day. Influenced by Rebecca Harding DAVIS's eye-opening exposé *Life in the Iron Mills* (1861), Phelps attained renown for a short story in *Atlantic Monthly,* "The Tenth of January" (1868), in which she recounts the death of female mill workers in a factory fire. In the melodramatic novel *Hedged In* (1870) she railed against a DOUBLE STANDARD that aimed social disapproval at single mothers. The story features the plight of factory girls in a run-down waterfront where "the old women turned children, and children old women" (Phelps, 1870, 7).

In her best novel, *The Story of Avis* (1877), an ambitious fictionalized BIOGRAPHY of her mother, Phelps characterized an era of change in gendered roles. For themes she recycles feminist concepts of women and marriage from George ELIOT's MIDDLEMARCH (1872). In a letter to Eliot, Phelps analyzed the novel's themes and commented on the undiscovered territory of female identity. For her own fictional model she drew on Elizabeth Barrett BROWNING's *Aurora Leigh* (1857) for the passion and boldness of Avis Dobell, an artist with a magnetic personality who is both career woman and mother. The downfall of Avis, who is named for the Latin for "bird," is her naive intent to maintain her aesthetic principles after marrying her lover, Philip Ostrander.

Serious feminism colors the subtext of Phelps's subsequent works. She wrote polemical essays for the *Independent* and *Woman's Journal* exposing female discontent in a male-dominated society. In a humanitarian novel, *The Silent Partner* (1871), she centers the action on abuses of the factory system and resultant female SILENCING in an industrial world favoring men as thinkers and women as doers. The story lionizes Perley Kelso as the sole female directing a factory that the male owners turn into a symbol of greed and mismanagement. As a result of Phelps's growing literary reputation, in 1876 she became the first female to lecture at Boston University.

Phelps returned to issues of female self-actualization in a number of works. In the poem "Victurae salutamus" (We women who are about to win salute you, 1880), a variant of the Roman gladiatorial salute *Morituri salutamus* (We [men] who are about to die salute you), the poet lauds women's urge to explore and better themselves: "Ideal of ourselves! We dream and dare" (Phelps, 1885, 99). The poem both praises women for determination and derides men for macho posturing and boasting. She followed a comic take on women's rights in *Old Maids* (1879) and *Burglars in Paradise* (1886) with a study on male-female camaraderie, *Friends: A Duet* (1881).

Phelps's most incisive contribution to feminist literature is *Doctor Zay* (1882), a class study and the first American novel to feature a successful woman doctor. The plot opens on an injured male snob, Waldo Yorke, who accepts treatment for a dislocated shoulder from a female physician. A native of rural Maine, the doctor takes pride in her services to poor, aged, and lonely female patients. Yorke holds female doctors in low esteem: "He had thought of them chiefly as a species of higher nurse,—poor women, who wore unbecoming clothes, took the horse-cars, and probably dropped their g's, or said, 'Is that so?' " (Phelps, 1987, 63). He is surprised to find professionalism in a woman: "She had her dangerous and sacred feminine nerve under magnificent training. It was her servant, not her tyrant; her wealth, not her poverty; the source of her power, not the exponent of her weakness" (ibid., 110–111). Because of the numerous confidences of unhappy female patients, Doctor Zay refuses to marry and share their miseries and disillusion. In the end Phelps allows Doctor Zay both medical practice and matrimony by proving that a country physician can be both professional and genteel.

Bibliography

Kessler, Carol Farley. *Elizabeth Stuart Phelps.* Boston: Twayne, 1982.

Phelps, Elizabeth Stuart. *Doctor Zay.* New York: Consortium, 1987.

———. *Hedged In.* Boston: Fields & Osgood, 1870.

———. *The Silent Partner.* New York: Feminist Press, 1983.

———. *Songs of the Silent World.* Boston: Houghton Mifflin, 1885.

———. *The Story of Avis.* Piscataway, N.J.: Rutgers University Press, 1985.

———. *Three Spiritual Novels:* The Gates Ajar, Beyond the Gates, The Gates Between. Chicago: University of Illinois Press, 2000.

Watson, William Lynn. " 'The Facts Which Go to Form This Fiction': Elizabeth Stuart Phelps's *The Silent Partner* and the Massachusetts Bureau of Labor Statistics Reports," *College Literature* 29, no. 4, (Fall 2002): 6–25.

Philomela

As does the myth of PERSEPHONE and Demeter, the tragedy of Philomela posits troubling models of female vulnerability in a savage human family. In Socrates' version of the Mediterranean rape story King Tereus of Thrace receives Procne (literally, the elder) as a gift: The Attic princess is a war trophy, a standard reward for victory in combat. Because of homesickness for her sweet-voiced younger sister, Philomela (literally, sweet melody), Tereus (literally, the watcher) goes to fetch his sister-in-law but alters his plan after raping her and tearing out her tongue to silence her. In place of a voice, Philomela uses an alternative feminist device, the weaving of a cloak or tapestry, a sisterly gift to Procne to warn her of the king's viciousness. Because Procne achieves revenge by cooking her son, Itys, and serving him to his father, King Tereus tries to execute both his wife and his mute sister-in-law with an ax. The gods take pity and turn the trio into birds—Procne into a nightingale, Philomela into a swallow, and Tereus into a hoopoe or hawk, a suitable symbol of the predatory male.

The violent motif of sex crime, patriarchal censorship, and permanent SILENCING permeates a number of feminist works, notably the colonial stilling of African tongues in Angelina Weld GRIMKÉ's posthumous poem "Life" (1958); the self-silencing of Maya Johnson, the terrorized rape victim in Maya ANGELOU's autobiographical *I KNOW WHY THE*

CAGED BIRD SINGS (1969); and Timberlake WERTENBAKER's stage play *The Love of the Nightingale* (1988), which returns the characters Philomela and Procne to their native Athens. In *The Kitchen God's Wife* (1991) the Chinese-American author Amy TAN pictures Wen Fu's brutal cyclical rape of his wife, Winnie, and his despoliation of girl servants and local females, one of whom dies in a car that he wrecks. Similarly bound to hapless struggle is Pecola Breedlove, the violated daughter of Cholly Breedlove in Toni MORRISON's first novel, *The BLUEST EYE* (1970). Because Pecola's mother refuses to believe that Cholly fathered a child on his only daughter, the child runs mad, "flail[ing] her arms like a bird in an eternal, grotesquely futile effort to fly" (Morrison, 158). Just as Procne and Philomela escape as birds, Pecola voids her sanity and adopts bestial identity with a bird. Morrison insists on realism in picturing the ruined child as a wandering eccentric who rummages in garbage cans.

The pairing of rape with silencing dramatizes society's disapproval of the victimization of women as a heinous, life-altering felony. In a graphic scenario in Alice WALKER's *The COLOR PURPLE* (1982) 13-year-old Celie falls victim in early womanhood to Alphonso, a pedophile she erroneously assumes is her father. The shameful episode that results in pregnancy is brutal and bloody: "He never had a kine word to say to me. Just say You gonna do what your mammy wouldn't. . . . When that hurt, I cry. He start to choke me, saying You better shut up and git used to it" (Walker, 11). To silence her, Alphonso disclaims her charges of rape and pits father fear against mother love with a warning: "You better not never tell nobody but God. It'd kill your mammy" (*ibid.*). In a parallel scene Harpo, Celie's stepson, concludes his violation of Mary Agnes with a discounting of the female voice: "Shut up Squeak. . . . It bad luck for women to laugh at men" (*ibid.*, 182). Both violators take refuge in female silencing as a makeshift cover for their crimes against womanhood.

Walker extends Celie's daily misery through a description of marital sex with Mr. _____, who lusts for Celie as well as for her sister, Nettie. In the conjugal bed, he is little more than a rapist: "He git up on you, heist your nightgown round your waist, plunge in. Most times I pretend I ain't

there. He never know the difference. Never ast me how I feel, nothing. Just do his business, get off, go to sleep" (*ibid.*, 79). To free herself of lawful bondage to Mr. _____, Celie, as Philomela does, escapes an unfeeling androcentric society with the help of Shug Avery. Their flight challenges Mr. _____'s diminution of Celie to the status of drone. In retrospect as though referring to a fleeing bird, he remarks, "I should have lock you up" (*ibid.*, 187). The sewing of a jazzy style of leisure clothes at Folkspants Limited serves as Celie's means of self-support as well as a rebellious retort against Mr. _____'s erasure of her being. Like the mythical phoenix, Celie reinvents herself through the combination of bright reds and purples, the colors she equates with happiness.

Bibliography

Cutter, Martha J. "Philomela Speaks: Alice Walker's Revisioning of Rape Archetypes in *The Color Purple*," *MELUS* 25, no. 3–4 (Fall–Winter 2000): 161–180.

Grimké, Angelina Emily Weld. *Selected Works of Angelina Weld Grimké.* New York: Oxford University Press, 1991.

Morrison, Toni. *The Bluest Eye.* New York: Plume, 1993.

Napieralski, Edmund A. "Morrison's 'The Bluest Eye,' " *Explicator* 53, no. 1 (Fall 1994): 59–62.

Walker, Alice. *The Color Purple.* New York: Washington Square Press, 1983.

Weinert, Laura. "The Love of the Nightingale," *Back Stage West*, 31 January 2002, p. 18.

Piercy, Marge (1936–   )

A poet, novelist, and radical feminist, Marge Piercy clarifies the multiple hurts of contemporary women through speculative fiction and verse. Born in a working-class section of Detroit to Welsh-Jewish parents, she learned the nuances of STORYTELLING through hearing legends and tales shared by her mother and grandmother. Piercy clawed her way out of poverty with hard work and with degrees in creative writing from the University of Michigan and Northwestern University. During the turbulent Vietnam War era she published verse in *Lilith* and other literary journals while leading Students for a Democratic Society in agitating for peace.

Piercy expressed her feminism in a variety of literary modes. She advanced tentatively into feminist utopia with *Dance the Eagle to Sleep* (1971), a novel about an American-Indian revolt at a high school where female students grow restive at the lack of choice in their life. She produced an earnest novel, *Small Changes* (1973), which examines the lives of women who toy with emerging egalitarian philosophy but who hesitate to become full-fledged feminists. In the opening scene Beth anticipates marital misery as she examines her bridal image in the mirror: "It isn't me, isn't me. Well, who else would it be, stupid? Isn't anyone except Bride: a dress wearing a girl" (Piercy, 1996, 12). In the poem "Councils" (1971) she urged women to extend their interests and hopes by speaking for themselves. The tentative tone of the speaker suggests hesitation to accept a difficult task.

Piercy advanced as an author by testing the limits of various modes. She created a classic of feminist utopian lore with WOMAN ON THE EDGE OF TIME (1976), a sci-fi view of androcentric treatment of MADNESS in 35-year-old Consuelo "Connie" Camacho Ramos. Clinging to sanity, she time-trips into the future to escape sexism and brutality. Piercy's first verse anythology, *The Moon Is Always Female* (1980), voices outrage at low wages and limited citizenship for women. She pursued the issue of the pink-collar work in historical fiction, *Gone to Soldiers* (1987), a survey of women's roles as plant workers, supporters of food rationing, and behind-the-lines agents during World War II. She conducted the same study of women's wartime roles in a second historical novel, *City of Darkness City of Light* (1997), which takes place in France during the French Revolution. In the preface she defines broad feminist themes: "Women have fought again and again in causes that, when won, have not given us the freedom, the benefits we expected. I thought looking at a society in crisis so very strange in some ways and so familiar in others might illuminate our situation" (Piercy, 1997, x). In *Three Women* (2001) Piercy moves the battlefield to the contemporary career woman's domain. The action interweaves the lives of a successful laywer, Suzanne Blume; her older daughter, Elena; and the lawyer's ailing mother, a dynamo felled by old age and disease. No less intense than Piercy's war novels, *Three Women* credits the current generation of women with its own brand of valor for facing no-win situations of disrupted families, decline, and death.

Piercy progressed into the realm of autobiographical verse for personal views of womanhood. In a tender collection, *The Art of Blessing the Day: Poems with a Jewish Theme* (2000), the versatile writer organized poems with titles evoking folklore: "The Wicked Stepmother," "The Rabbi's Granddaughter and the Christmas Tree," and "Apple Sauce for Eve." "Woman in a Shoe" alludes to the ominous nursery rhyme in which a mother copes with violent urges while trying to tend to too many children in too small a space. In "Snowflakes, My Mother Called Them," the poet recollects childhood entertainment by her mother and grandmother in snipping shapes from folded newsprint or butcher wrap. One figure is absent from the older woman's papercut animals—the horses that once carried the perpetrators of pogroms. Similar in style and tone to an earlier collection of verse, *My Mother's Body* (1985) reveals memories of faded, unloved women who go to their graves unfulfilled. Of Piercy's coming of age the poem "Putting the Good Things Away" recalls the toughening she gained from MATRIARCHY.

Bibliography

Altman, Meryl. "Beyond Trashiness: The Sexual Language of 1970s Feminist Fiction," *Journal of International Women's Studies* 4, no. 2 (April 2003): 1–25.

Piercy, Marge. *The Art of Blessing the Day*. New York: Knopf, 2000.

———. *Circles on the Water*. New York: Knopf, 1982.

———. *City of Darkness City of Light*. New York: Ballantine, 1997.

———. *Small Changes*. New York: Ballantine, 1996.

Plath, Sylvia (1932–1963)

Sylvia Plath displayed sparkle and genius in her domestic war against gender STEREOTYPING. A native Bostonian of Austrian-Polish heritage, she was the daughter of two teachers. After her father's death in 1940 of diabetic gangrene she mentally "sealed" her little-girl years "like a ship in a bottle—beautiful, inaccessible, obsolete, a fine, white flying myth" (Plath, 1979, 26). Venting frustration and sorrow, at age eight, she saw her first poem in print in the *Boston Traveller*. She studied at Smith College at the same time that she published stories and poems in *Seventeen, Christian Science Monitor,* and *Harper's*. On a scholarship from *Mademoiselle* for her story "Sunday at the Mintons" (1951) she settled in New York City and interviewed the poets Elizabeth BOWEN and Marianne MOORE. In periodic self-evaluation in her journal she observed at age 18 the impossibility of capturing life experiences on paper: "After something happens to you . . . you never write it quite the way you want to" (Plath, 2000, 10). Despite qualms about change, she described her ripening into vibrant female sensuality.

When she was 21, Plath's slumbering demons erupted into manic-depression and attempted suicide. After treatment at McGrath Hospital in Belmont, Massachusetts, she completed a degree in English with highest honors and studied English literature on a Fulbright scholarship to Newnham College, Cambridge. In 1956 she married the British poet Ted Hughes and settled in Eastham, Massachusetts, to a domesticity that gave her no relief from declining self-worth. The feminist critic Phyllis Chesler, author of *Women and Madness* (1972), defined the forces that tormented Plath as the inability to live as a mere woman and an excruciating frustration that she lacked validity as a writer: "Such madness is essentially an intense experience of female biological, sexual, and cultural castration" (Chesler, 76). The result was a slow bleed from death hunger.

While teaching at Smith, Plath spewed out in her diary the burden of depression and a paralyzing ambivalence toward marriage. On advice from the poet Anne SEXTON, Plath published *The Colossus and Other Poems* (1962) and the British Broadcasting Corporation (BBC) radio play *Three Women: A Monologue for Three Voices* (1962), a tone poem on the importance of choice in women's lives. She attained critical stature with an autobiographical psychological novel, *The BELL JAR* (1963), a seriocomic feminist work on women, intellectualism, and insanity. Still battling mental torments, she lost ground after the birth of a son and daughter and her husband's rapid rise to fame. Because of his infidelities and abandonment of the family she moved to Chalk Farm in Devon.

Her death, by gas inhalation, at age 30, gained Plath the public acknowledgment she had yearned for. Her works, managed by her executor, Ted Hughes, became feminist cult favorites. Posthumously published were *Ariel* (1965), *Crossing the Water: Transitional Poems* (1971), *Winter Trees* (1972), *Letters Home: Correspondence, 1950–1963* (1975), and *The Collected Poems* (1981) and *The Unabridged Journals of Sylvia Plath, 1950–1963* (1982), winner of the 1982 Pulitzer Prize in poetry. Feminists internalize the vulnerability of both mother and newborn in "Morning Song" (1961) and the naughty-girl jingle that cloaks "Daddy" (1962), an explosive postmortem accusation of a vampirish father. The singsong voice blames him for confining her in male-conceived strictures, which she compares to the gas ovens of the Holocaust.

In her final weeks Plath crafted "Lady Lazarus" (1963), a surreal exaltation of the self-annihilation tactics that dominate her actions and a celebration affirming INDEPENDENCE from PATRIARCHY. From this same mind-set arose "Fever 103°" (1963), a metaphoric glimpse of death and cremation that spirals into an outcry against destruction of innocent life-forms. The speaker seeks redemption as flame burns away sin. Her posthumously published works disclose the irresolute self still wrestling with trauma from her childhood. In the closing lines of "Electra on Azalea Path" (1981) she pleads, "O pardon the one who knocks for pardon at / Your gate, father—your hound-bitch, daughter, friend" (Plath, 1981, 117). Of Plath's success the critic Adrienne RICH remarked, "Her death is an arrest: in its moment we have all been held, momentarily, in the grip of a policeman who tells us we are guilty of being female" (Rich, 123).

Bibliography

Chesler, Phyllis. *Women and Madness.* New York: Doubleday, 1972.

Plath, Sylvia. *The Collected Poems of Sylvia Plath.* New York: HarperCollins, 1981.

————. *Johnny Panic and the Bible of Dreams: Short Stories, Prose, and Diary Extracts.* New York: Harper & Row, 1979.

————. *The Unabridged Journal of Sylvia Plath, 1950–1963.* New York: Anchor, 2000.

Rich, Adrienne. *On Lies, Secrets, and Silence: Selected Prose, 1966–1978.* New York: W. W. Norton, 1979.

Pogrebin, Letty Cottin (1939–)

A moral polemicist, orator, fiction writer, and co-founding editor of *Ms.* magazine, Letty Cottin Pogrebin writes about the inequalities that confine women to second-class citizenship. Born in Queens, New York, she studied the Torah and Talmud at home. After her mother's death of cancer in 1955 Pogrebin rebelled against Conservative Judaism for denying her the opportunity to be the 10th member of a minyan, the standard quorum of males. Firm in feminist beliefs, she supported the ordination of the first female rabbi, headed the Author's Guild, and coformed the Women's Political Caucus. In the *Amsterdam News, Chatelaine, Lilith, Moment, Na'amat*, the *New York Times*, and *Tikkun* she issued a stream of pertinent essays on the objectification of the female body in the Barbie doll, the racist foundations of Zionism, and the loss to the feminist movement of the beloved U.S. representative Bella Abzug.

Pogrebin approached the feminist market prematurely with *How to Make It in a Man's World* (1970). Advice to ambitious businesswomen appears under a series of witty chapter headings—"How to Succeed in Business without Really Typing," "Executive Sweets," and "If You Can't Stand the Heat, Get Back to the Kitchen." After she agreed to supply a column on working women for *Ladies Home Journal* in 1971, she realized the extent of demand for a feminist magazine. In spring 1973 her name appeared on the cover of the first issue of *Ms.* along with the title of her essay "On Raising Kids without Sex Roles." With the publication of *Deborah, Golda, and Me: Being Female and Jewish in America* (1992) Pogrebin reconciled her Jewish heritage with feminist philosophy. Among her explorations were chapters on ritual, female leadership, and stereotypes of female Jews in the media.

Pogrebin continues to examine women's lives from varying perspectives. She blended humor with wisdom in *Getting Over Getting Older* (1997), a reflection on "what has been happening to my body, mind, health, psyche and spirit since I turned fifty" (Pogrebin, 1997, 3). For moral support she collaborated with her feminist colleagues Betty FRIEDAN, Carolyn Heilbrun, and Gloria STEINEM on ways to reveal "the nobility and power in the elder female" (*ibid.*, 4). In 2000 Pogrebin joined Wilma Mankiller, Byllye Avery, and Carol Gilligan in editing *Woman*, subtitled *A Celebration to Benefit the Ms. Foundation for Women.* Pogrebin contributed to the miscellany a tribute to mature women and to the wisdom gained from experience. Two years later she published a novel, *Three Daughters* (2002), which allies three girls—Shoshanna, Leah, and Rachel Wasserman—from the same Jewish family with varying styles of self-expression, each of which passes under the watchful eye of their father, Rabbi Sam Wasserman. For a lifetime of activism for equality, tolerance, and liberty, in 2003 Pogrebin received the Patricia Barr Peace Award at the Americans for Peace Now Annual Benefit.

Bibliography

Cornfield, Jill. " 'A Prism of Personal Experience': Letty Cottin Pogrebin Will Speak about Being Jewish and a Feminist," *Baltimore Jewish Times*, 25 October 1996, p. 24.

Pogrebin, Letty Cottin. *Deborah, Golda, and Me: Being Female and Jewish in America.* New York: Anchor Books, 1991.

————. *Getting Over Getting Older.* New York: Berkley, 1997.

————. *Three Daughters: A Novel.* New York: Farrar, Straus & Giroux, 2002.

Thom, Mary. *Inside Ms.: 24 Years of the Magazine and the Feminist Movement.* New York: Henry Holt, 1997.

Poisonwood Bible, The Barbara Kingsolver (1998)

Barbara KINGSOLVER's anticolonial parable on women's lives resets the commonplaces of rearing four American daughters in the Congolese jungle within a network of peasant women. The universality of wifedom in the struggle of Orleanna Price, a long-suffering spouse to a fanatic Baptist evangelist, unifies her months at Kilanga village on the Kwilu River. The daily tasks of drawing water, collecting firewood, and preparing food portray WOMAN'S WORK from a historical perspective that links Orleanna to the fetchers and carriers of prehistory. In reflecting on her acquiescence to a stern patriarch, she admonishes herself for naiveté: "Maybe I'll even confess the truth, that I rode in with the horsemen and beheld the apocalypse, but still I'll insist I was only a captive witness" (Kingsolver, 9). The primitive conditions, consisting of "a long row of little mud houses set after-one-the-other beside a long red snake of dirt road," alarm her as constant threats to family safety and hygiene and assaults on her sanity (*ibid.*, 30). Without complaint she begins acculturating her daughters to an alien set of manners and establishes homeschooling that includes needlework, an appropriate discipline for women of her former home in Bethlehem, Georgia.

With the grandeur of opera the narrative depicts the evolution of a wife's rebellious spirit. Orleanna's decline from upbeat helpmeet to drudge is the predictable result of combat against monsoons, malnutrition, malaria, hookworm, bats, and snakes. Kingsolver dramatizes Nathan Price's gratuitous assaults on his wife's good nature with one blow on the single dish that she prizes. The emotional breaking point, Ruth May's death from the bite of a green mamba on her shoulder, shifts the gender power struggle and destroys the marriage. Fierce with maternal anger, Orleanna ceases to be Nathan's enabler. She wraps the corpse of her baby girl in mosquito netting at a homemade altar where neighbor women keen and prostrate themselves. No longer a wife, Orleanna leads her twin daughters, Adah and Leah, out of the village and beyond the reach of a demon mate who denigrates the five females who compose his household. An EVE returning to Eden, Orleanna enjoys what peace remains in her life through gardening, grandmothering, and volunteering for African relief, a gesture to the kind peasant women who once offered gifts of oranges and slipped eggs into her henhouse so they would not embarrass her.

Written in Faulknerian circular narrative, Kingsolver's evocative story teems with women's strengths as "messengers of goodwill adrift on a sea of mistaken intentions" (*ibid.*, 323). Adah, the twin who staggers under a neurological handicap, heals her twisted body and tends to Orleanna into her mother's old age. A brilliant researcher into the diseases that lop years from African lives, Adah makes the most of physical wholeness by analyzing the emotional damage of the mission fiasco. For literary and feminist reasons the author contrasts Adah with Rachel, the uncharitable teen queen who inadvertently offers salient observations. Of the Christ-crazed preacher, she smirks, "It's just lucky for Father he never had sons. He might have been forced to respect them" (*ibid.*, 337). Rachel grooms her face, figure, and budding SEXUALITY as bargaining media to barter in exchange for the good life. By successively marrying her way up the social ladder from the mercenary Eeben Axelroot to a diplomat and a hotelier, she insulates herself from Africa's poverty and political turmoil. A far cry from Rachel's sexual opportunism is the pragmatism of Leah, the Earth mother and seeker of redemption who maintains the village lifestyle throughout protracted crisis in Zaire. Her wistful summation of the mission— "We've all ended up giving up body and soul to Africa"—speaks to a number of feminist concerns as well, particularly the Price women's punishment for abetting destructive evangelism (*ibid.*, 474).

Although Kingsolver earns critical rebuke for didacticism, she balances her protest novel with comic relief, suspense, lyricism, and historical background. Allying the four female survivors, the spiritual gravity and pervasive grief for Ruth May, the family's source of joy, undergird a somber tone. Respect for the youngest prohibits the Price women from mourning their father's retreat into the jungle and his bizarre burning death in a colonial watch tower. With a dark pun Orleanna, laden with bitterness and sorrow, becomes the novel's oracle by reflecting on the "price" exacted from each survivor for a catastrophic miscalculation.

In preparation for the writing of *The Poisonwood Bible*, the author relived a childhood experience in the newly liberated Belgian Congo of the late 1960s by journeying to Benin to observe women's marketing and the daily monetary compromises that constrain family nutrition and cleanliness. For background material the author read the Bible and Apocrypha along with missionary journals, the Kikongo-French dictionary, and copies of *Life, Look,* and *Saturday Evening Post* dating from 1958 to 1961. She conducted interviews on life under Belgian overlords and changes after General Joseph Désiré Mobutu's corrupt regime took charge. The novel won a National Book Prize of South Africa, American Booksellers Book of the Year, *Los Angeles Times* Best Book, *New York Times* "Ten Best Books of 1998," Canada's North Forty-Nine Books Most Valuable Picks, *Village Voice* Best Book, New York Public Library "25 Books to Remember," Britain's Orange Prize of £30,000, nomination for the PEN/Faulkner Award, and Oprah Book Club selection.

Bibliography

Bell, Millicent. "Fiction Chronicle: *The Poisonwood Bible,*" *Partisan Review* 66 (1999): 417–430.

Fletcher, Yael Simpson. "History Will One Day Have Its Say: New Perspectives on Colonial and Postcolonial Congo," *Radical History Review* 84 (2002): 195–207.

Kingsolver, Barbara. *The Poisonwood Bible.* New York: HarperCollins, 1998.

Koza, Kimberly. "The Africa of Two Western Women Writers: Barbara Kingsolver and Margaret Laurence," *Critique* 44, no. 3 (Spring 2003): 284–294.

Pollitt, Katha (1949–   )

The feminist poet, political essayist, and witty syndicated columnist Katha Pollitt produces a steady outpouring of commentary on topical issues. A native New Yorker, she grew up in Brooklyn with parents who read classic poetry aloud and who encouraged her gift for verse. Her memories of the McCarthy era involve her father's legal defense of clients accused of being Communists. In her preteens she composed after-school poems in a copybook and penned letters to the editor of the *New York Times*. After earning degrees from Harvard and Columbia Universities, she taught composition as poet in residence at Barnard College.

Incisive writing won Pollitt a growing list of admirers who included critics as well as regular readers of her op-ed pieces. From copy editor and proofreader at *Esquire* and the *New Yorker,* she

moved on to book reviewer. After joining the staff of the *Nation* in 1980, she earned a National Magazine Award and the Whiting Foundation Writing Award for "Why We Read: Canon to the Right of Me" (1992). The thoughtful essay ponders the white male literary canon along with the phenomenon of nonreading students who avoid demanding works. The next year the essay "Why Do We Romanticize the Fetus?" earned Planned Parenthood's Maggie Award for placing the endangered woman at the forefront of ABORTION debate. In this same period Pollitt published popular verse and essays in *Antaeus, Atlantic, Conscience, Glamour, Grand Street, Harper's, Herizons, Mirabella, Mother Jones, MS., New Republic, New York Times, Poetry,* and *Yale Review.* For delicate minimal images in verse anthologized in *Antarctic Traveller* (1982) she earned the National Book Critics Circle Award.

An alliance with the pro-woman writers Barbara EHRENREICH, Eve ENSLER, Susan SONTAG, Gloria STEINEM, and Naomi WOLF places Pollitt among the stars of feminist journalism. In her biweekly "Subject to Debate" column, which debuted in the *Nation* in 1994, Pollitt provokes reader thought and controversy over such problems as the extremism of the Christian Right, reproductive politics and women's health services, and the incarceration of Islamic women in Afghanistan. She speaks knowledgeably of feminist terrain in *Reasonable Creatures: Essays on Women and Feminism* (1994), a title she appropriated from the feminist foremother Mary WOLLSTONECRAFT. Pollitt followed with *Subject to Debate: Sense and Dissents on Women, Politics, and Culture* (2001) and *Nothing Sacred: Women Respond to Religious Fundamentalism and Terror* (2002), coedited by Betsy Reed. In *Subject to Debate* Pollitt moved quickly and cleanly to the heart of world feminism: "Here we are, at the end of the twentieth century, and not only have hundreds of millions of women around the globe yet to obtain even the barest minimum of human rights, but the notion that they are even entitled to such rights is bitterly contested" (Pollitt, 2001, 3–4). Her evidence is grisly—FEMALE GENITAL MUTILATION, bride burning, sexual bondage, jailing of rape victims, and forced abortion and sterilization.

Bibliography

Conniff, Ruth. "Katha Pollitt," *Progressive* 58, no. 12 (December 1994): 34–39.

Pollitt, Katha. *Nothing Sacred: Women Respond to Religious Fundamentalism and Terror.* New York: Nation Books, 2002.

———. *Reasonable Creatures: Essays on Women and Feminism.* New York: Vintage, 1995.

———. *Subject to Debate: Sense and Dissents on Women, Politics, and Culture.* New York: Modern Library, 2001.

Porter, Katherine Anne (1890–1980)

The southern icon Katherine Anne Porter earned critical regard for her precise, sympathetic portraits of the headstrong, autonomous female. Born Callista Russell "Callie" Porter in a humble cabin in Indian Creek, Texas, she grew up in a log home amid a chaotic family she later declared was hexed. She was poorly educated and bereft of female love after the deaths of her mother and her paternal grandmother, Catherine Anne "Aunt Cat" Porter, whose name and STORYTELLING style the author adopted. At age 16 Porter began the first of four disappointing marriages. Without regret she obtained a divorce and changed her name from Callie to Katherine Anne. Living in Chicago, she supported the socialist and suffragist causes espoused by a contemporary, Tillie OLSEN.

Porter initiated a writing career that focused on the shrewd female survivor, suggested, no doubt, by her own beliefs and behavior. Despite tuberculosis and acute respiratory problems that resulted from the 1918 influenza epidemic, she worked as a peripatetic journalist and book reviewer in Denver, Fort Worth, Chicago, New York City, Mexico City, Paris, Rome, and Liège. Her restless wanderings and short-term romances provided insights for psychologically complex stories and novellas. She explained in a letter to the poet Allen Tate, "I have to sweep a track and make a dead run when once I start. . . . I depend . . . on something that is *deeper than knowledge*" (Porter, 1991, 5). As celebrity increased for Porter's intuitive perusal of the human condition, she replaced her laboring-class biography with a fabricated past—the glamorous, but hackneyed Old South

aristocracy. A voyage to Mexico in 1931 inspired a transcultural first novel, which she took three decades to complete. Published in 1962 as *Ship of Fools*, it was a financial and critical disappointment both as fiction and as the subject of Columbia's 1966 film adaptation, starring Vivien Leigh and Simone Signoret. At age 81 the author was still collecting material for an article for *Playboy* on a visit to Cape Kennedy to glimpse a Moon launch.

Female struggles give vigor and texture to Porter's long-lived short fiction. Beginning with the story "María Concepción" (1922), printed in *Century* magazine, Porter's astute glimpses of the female lot enhanced an understanding of agrarian poverty, unfulfilling marriages, loneliness, and sexual VIOLENCE. She starts hard-bargaining María Concepción Manríquez, an 18-year-old pregnant wife, on a barefoot walk down a dusty road of treacherous cacti. Contributing to the suggestion of toil is a burden of 12 trussed hens over her shoulder, a complex image of the lethal challenges and CONFINEMENT of poor farm women. Of the rightness of María's posture and outlook Porter describes her as "the right inevitable proportions of a woman," a trustful mate who quickly ramps into the resolute avenger of her husband's adultery (Porter, 1965, 3). Enriching the overview of Latina womanhood are other resilient self-supporters— Lupe the *curandera* (healer) and María Rosa the beekeeper and husband snatcher. In the story "He" (1930) the author pictures the hardships of raising children and livestock. Mrs. Whipple faces a doomed struggle to give her mentally disabled son a normal childhood. His deterioration forces her to give in and have the nameless child institutionalized. In these stories the author strives for dignity in women who exhibit the on-the-spot decision making that situations require.

Often compared to the writings of Thomas Mann, Porter's Miranda Rhea novellas, "Old Mortality" (1930) and "The Old Order" (1958), develop autobiographical insights. Characters reflect the author's effort to shuck off her own wretched family memories and to develop a unique identity based on dreams and ambitions. In the first example Porter honors women's affinity for lineage and memory. Grandmother's seasonal opening of trunks refreshes memories of photos and events that leave her in tears that are, themselves, a source of comfort. In "Noon Wine" (1936) Porter enhanced narrative with Gothic horrors—an ax murder, insanity, prophetic nightmare, and shotgun suicide. More realistic are the triumph and regret in a stream-of-consciousness deathbed story, "The JILTING OF GRANNY WEATHERALL," originally published in *Hound & Horn* and collected in *Flowering Judas and Other Stories* (1930), one of feminist literature's elevating visions of the elderly matriarch. For Porter's skill at defining human frustration and good intentions *The Collected Stories of Katherine Anne Porter* (1965) earned a Pulitzer Prize and National Book Award. Her woman-centered fiction influenced the style of the Canadian short-story writer Alice MUNRO.

Bibliography

Graham, Don. "Katherine Anne Porter's Journey from Texas to the World," *Southwest Review* 84, no. 1 (Winter 1998): 140.

Porter, Katherine Anne. *The Collected Stories of Katherine Anne Porter.* New York: New American Library, 1965.

———. *Letters of Katherine Anne Porter.* New York: Atlantic Monthly Press, 1991.

———. *Pale Horse, Pale Rider.* New York: Harcourt, 1990.

Powell, Dawn (1896–1965)

An admired wit, ironist, and caricaturist of big-city bohemian life, Dawn Powell succeeded at quirky satire of the social relations of pretentious middle-class and wealthy Americans. Reared in Mount Gilead, an Ohio farm community, at age seven she lost her mother, who died after a botched abortion. Fleeing an unsympathetic stepmother, the author left home with only a quarter and a nickel in her pocket. On her own she read 19th-century European novels by Charles Dickens, Alexandre Dumas, and Victor Hugo and began writing short fiction in her youth. After her graduation from Lake Erie College for Women she married the poet, ad copywriter, and critic Joseph Roebuck Gousha. The couple made a home in Greenwich Village, a sophisticated, exhibitionist artists' enclave, where Powell worked as book critic for *Mademoiselle* and produced feminist views in *The Bride's House* (1929), a poignant examination of a woman's love for two men in a conventional Ohio farm community.

A prolific author, Powell issued mordant short pieces in *Cosmopolitan, Evening Post, Harper's Bazaar, Mademoiselle, Nation, New Yorker, Story,* and *Today's Woman.* For radio, television, screen, and stage she produced dramas—*Big Night* (1933) and *Jig Saw* (1934)—that endorse the confident female survivor who networks with other women for affection and advice. At work in longhand in the children's section of the New York Public Library Powell skewered New York's amorality in *Turn Magic Wheel* (1936), *The Wicked City* (1938), *The Locusts Have No King* (1948), and *The Golden Spur* (1962). In 1942 she turned the rise of the socialite dramatist Clare Booth LUCE into the focus of a roman à clef. Set during World War II, *A Time to Be Born* was the story of the female barracuda Amanda Keller Evans. Of the involvement of female socialites who "had inherited the earth," the author states that on the home front "women were once more armed, and their happy voices of destruction to come. Off to relief offices they rode in their beautiful new cars, off to knit, to sew" (Powell, 1999, 2).

Powell's skill at stripping selfish, willful women of dignity derived from home training. An autobiographical novel, *My Home Is Far Away* (1944), examines the Dickensian second-wife-versus- stepdaughter clash that the author remembers from girlhood, when her stepmother, Sabra Stearns Powell, burned the author's stash of original stories. In retaliation Dawn names the fictional stepmother "She." Of the thanklessness of domestic work for a widowed father the character Bonnie sobs, "A person does the best she knows how but all the good it does! A person could eat her heart out for a kind word" (Powell, 1995, 106). In 1954 she returned to satire of New York bohemians in *The Wicked Pavilion,* a devastating send-up that pictures the egotistic chatter at the Café Julien while "elderly ladies died of starvation in shabby hotels leaving boxes of rags and hundred-dollar bills" (Powell, 1998, 3). She compared the sufferings of elderly, defenseless urbanites to those of Jews under the Gestapo and of peasants during the French Revolution. Of mid-20th-century terrors Powell concluded, "Ask no questions, give no answers, police or be policed, run in fear and silence ahead of the shadow" (*ibid.*, 6). Her picture of the big city out of control and wracked by public apathy, gang VIOLENCE, and street thuggery foresaw a state of affairs that worsened over the next half-century.

Bibliography

Dirda, Michael. "Satyricon in Manhattan," *Washington Post Book World*, 18 March 1990, p. 10.

Page, Tim. *Dawn Powell: A Biography*. New York: Owl Publishing, 1998.

Powell, Dawn. *My Home Is Far Away*. New York: Steerforth Press, 1995.

———. *A Time to Be Born*. New York: Steerforth Press, 1999.

———. *The Wicked Pavilion*. New York: Zoland, 1998.

"Prologue, The" Anne Bradstreet (1650)

The colonial American poet Anne Dudley BRADSTREET's "The Prologue," published in *The Tenth Muse Lately Sprung Up in America* (1650), anticipates feminist literary achievement by writers who remain true to their nature. In the introduction to *The Works of Anne Bradstreet* (1981) the American poet and critic Adrienne RICH described the 17th-century author as "the first non-didactic American poet, the first to give an embodiment to American nature, the first in whom personal intention appears to precede Puritan dogma as an impulse to verse" (Bradstreet, xix). In testimony to Rich's claims, "The Prologue" illustrates Bradstreet's ability to defend the right of women to speak for themselves.

Bradstreet performs for a hostile audience the *quarelle* (argument), an age-old literary mode common to male writers and successfully co-opted by CHRISTINE DE PISAN. In eight stanzas of precise iambic pentameter rhyming ABABCC Bradstreet defends the right of the female writer to use a unique poetic voice. With ironic courtesy she lauds the pomposity of captains, kings, and city founders and admits that her efforts are poor by comparison to the work of the historian Guillaume du Bartas. She states that all authors must accept their faults but upends her logic by describing the labors of Demosthenes, a Greek orator who combated speech defect by placing stones in his mouth. The example attests to weaknesses in the great speechwriter of the ancient world.

Bradstreet recognizes the difficulties of the belittled outsider. Her fifth stave introduces the sexist critic's dismissal of the female poet. She claims her right to the pen by rejecting the gendered role of woman as needleworker. She defends the female place in the literary arts against those who might accuse her of succeeding because of luck or through plagiarism. Bolstering her attack on male critics, she honors the Greek muses, the nine daughters of Mnemosyne (Memory), the female genii whose influence spawned immortal lines. In her frequently cited rallying cry she requests, "Let Greeks be Greeks, and women what they are," a plea for female individuality. After honoring the grand male writers who soar above her lowly station, she accepts as token of her art a simple circlet of parsley and thyme, the humble herbs of the kitchen garden.

Bibliography

Bradstreet, Anne. *The Works of Anne Bradstreet*. Cambridge, Mass.: Belknap Press, 1981.

Harvey, Tamara. " 'Now Sisters . . . Impart Your Usefulness, and Force,' " *Early American Literature* 35, no. 1 (March 2000): 5–28.

Schweitzer, Ivy. "Salutary Decouplings: The Newest New England Studies," *American Literary History* 13, no. 3 (Fall 2001): 578–591.

prostitution

From the diaries of Fanny KEMBLE to the social criticism of Germaine GREER, feminist writing sheds light on the social quandary over the sex trade. During her sojourn in the antebellum American South, the abolitionist actor Fanny Kemble composed a journal that remarked on the cause and effect of miscegenation and class bias on female promiscuity: "In New Orleans, a class of unhappy females exists whose mingled blood does not prevent their being remarkable for their beauty, and with whom no man, no *gentleman*, in that city shrinks from associating" (Kemble, 14). She later adds that racism does not hinder planters "from admitting one or several of his female slaves to the still closer intimacy of his bed" (*ibid.*, 23). Kemble's scandalous commentary on the concubinage of Southern black women earned scorn from her husband, a wealthy Georgia plantation owner who seized her two daughters after the couple's divorce.

Female writers tend to produce well-founded conceptions of sex for sale. Risking condemnation by her peers, the English novelist Elizabeth GASKELL contributed a sympathetic view of the fallen woman turned to prostitution in the social novel *Mary Barton, a Tale of Manchester* (1848). Of the misery of females like the character Esther, who have no way to turn the Industrial Revolution to their personal good, Gaskell asks the reader, "To whom shall the outcast prostitute tell her tale. . . . Hers is the leper-sin, and all stand aloof dreading to be counted unclean" (Gaskell, 185). Retrieving her from the human scrap heap, the author follows Mary to her grave and offers a tender, compassionate view of a fragile, underfed body, "nought but skin and bone . . . a heap of white or lightcolored clothes, . . . the poor crushed Butterfly" (*ibid.*, 461–462). In contrast to Gaskell's pity, the American poet Sara TEASDALE found reason to admire prostitutes in the ode "Union Square," published in *Helen of Troy and Other Poems* (1911). The speaker delivers a monologue about her hesitation to confess her love to a man. She admires prostitutes for avoiding the proprieties of the era and freely grasping sexual pleasure. Teasdale's feminist view ignores value judgments on morality in favor of a womanly regard for honest sensuality.

Another spokeswoman, the feminist journalist Victoria WOODHULL, upset the public disapproval of fallen women that exonerates their clientele. In her newspaper, *Woodhull & Claflin's Weekly*, coedited by her sister, Tennie Claflin, Woodhull proposed a frontal attack on soliciting. In August 1870 in response to the registration of sex workers in Saint Louis, Missouri, she demanded an end to the DOUBLE STANDARD: "The names of the women should not only be registered but published, along with the names of the men who first caused them to become so" (Woodhull and Claflin, 1). Her radical views on WOMEN'S RIGHTS were in-

tended to make both parties share the stigma of social evil. By extension Woodhull charged women who marry for money rather than love with practicing a more insidious form of prostitution, which produces children and lasts a lifetime.

One of Woodhull's contemporaries, the anarchist orator Voltairine DE CLEYRE, spoke directly to the issue of the guilty ruined woman and her guiltless clientele. In "Sex and Slavery" (1890) de Cleyre thundered, "Think of the double social standard the enslavement of our sex has evolved. Women considering themselves very pure and very moral, will sneer at the streetwalker, yet admit to their homes the very men who victimized [her]" (de Cleyre, 1890). The essayist spurned male pity for streetwalkers and charged male clients with the worst perversion of decency. To centuries of male-generated deceit de Cleyre responded, "Pity yourselves, gentlemen—you need it!" (*ibid.*).

Later champions of WOMEN'S RIGHTS to SEXUALITY and motherhood wrote during the socialist era of feminist literature. The South African radical novelist and polemicist Olive SCHREINER described in *Woman and Labour* (1911) the role of economic parasitism that drives women to sell themselves. She believed the issue unsolvable "either from the moral or the scientific standpoint, unless its relation to the general phenomenon of female parasitism be fully recognized. It is the failure to do this which leaves so painful a sense of abortion on the mind" (Schreiner, 1). The anarchist Emma GOLDMAN published feminist essays on labor and sex in her journal *Mother Earth*. In March 1913 she challenged the authoritarian moral standards that men devised to hold women in check. Goldman describes the sex worker as a specter "paying back, in a very small measure, the curse and horrors society has strewn in her path" (Goldman, 1913). The essayist charges that social hypocrisy forces the woman to sell her services as a commodity. For her willingness to exit poverty through carnality "she is hounded, fleeced, outraged, and shunned by the very powers that have made her—the financier, the priest, the moralist, the judge, the jailer, and the detective" (*ibid.*). Goldman's outrage pinpoints the ethical, religious, and legal DOUBLE STANDARD as the origin of prostitution, the degraded twin of marriage. Some 85 years later Germaine Greer's *The Whole Woman* (1999) reminded the squeamish that in Czechoslovakia student prostitutes "earn in an hour what their professionally qualified mothers are paid in a month" (Greer, 10).

Writers from a span of cultural backgrounds muse on the roots of the sex trade. In *All My People* (1942) the poet Margaret WALKER anthologized "Whores," an Elizabeth sonnet honoring the painted women who make their living from youth into old age by satisfying male lust. In the novel *The Adventuress* (1970) the Indian writer Santha Rama RAU exposes the mercenary world of survival for East Asian women in the months preceding the Communist takeover of China. Kay, the title character, recognizes that foreign girls are refugees, "the jetsam of many nations . . . always thinking of themselves as sort of in transit" (Rau, 200). To carve out new lives, these stateless females frequent consulates in search of visas and stake out hotels to lure foreigners with smiles and consensual sex. The women's hope is to find men willing to propose marriage. Rau considers the plight of women bartering their bodies for a ticket out of China as "one of the minor tragedies of Shanghai" (*ibid.*).

The typical unilateral laws that make prostitution a crime base their injustice on classism as well as sexism. In a landmark text, *Hidden from History: Rediscovering Women in History from the 17th Century to the Present* (1976), the feminist historian Sheila ROWBOTHAM remarks that Englishwomen's campaigns against seizure and imprisonment of prostitutes under the 1869 Contagious Diseases Act "[made] the middle-class women aware of the hypocrisy of male-dominated morality toward women of their own class and the evils which . . . bore with murderous cruelty on other women" (Rowbotham, 67). In an undated poem, "Margery" (ca. 1865), Christina ROSSETTI, a volunteer sister at Saint Mary Magdelene Home for Fallen Women at Highgate, expresses sympathy and pity for the girl who grows up too fast. The text describes the lovesickness that deprives Margery of appetite and opens her character to criticism by gossipy neighbors. Using an idealized image of the fallen woman, the narrative acknowledges that society tends to force the compromised woman out of polite society into the demimonde. A more heinous injustice was the sale of lower-class girls to foreign brothels, the subject of Ruthann Lumm McCunn's BIOGRAPHY *Thousand Pieces of Gold* (1981).

The Egyptian journalist and physician Nawal EL SAADAWI took a humanitarian stand against demonizing prostitutes in *Woman at Point Zero* (1973). The novella describes a woman who suffers sexual abuse in childhood, becomes a prostitute to escape an odious arranged marriage, and suffers the death penalty for murdering her pimp. The story evolved from the author's interview with the demented protagonist Firdaus at Qanatir Prison, where neurosis is rampant among inmates. The crux of Firdaus's story is the dilemma of women who turn male manipulation into a source of much-needed income. El Saadawi draws a sad comparison between the life of an unwilling bride and the career of a streetwalker. Through terror, longing, and despair Firdaus experiences a separation of mind and body: "Had I been transported into another woman's body? And where had my own, my real body, gone?" (El Saadawi, 61). The ghoulish question connects Firdaus's confessional to the Gothic scarlet-lady stories popular among Victorian readers.

Anne Rampling, one of the pseudonyms of the pop writer Anne RICE, probed the economic issues of vice. She speaks through the experiences of her title character in *Belinda* (1986), an erotic urban novel about a 44-year-old artist lured by an underage runaway. Belinda is determined to survive on the streets, but she soon must admit that females have a harder time than males. She realizes that "girls went nowhere. They got pregnant, on drugs, maybe even became prostitutes" (Rampling, 318). Even though gay men exploited pretty male teens, the boys gained enough from their looks and availability "to move up and out of the world of the street" (*ibid.*). Belinda is unable to explain the difference in street lifestyles for boys and girls and concludes that male survival derives from a gendered freedom that girls lack.

Bibliography

de Cleyre, Voltairine. "Sex Slavery" (1890). Available online. URL: http://dwardmac.pitzer.edu/Anarchist_Archives/bright/cleyre/sexslavery.html. Accessed on October 16, 2005.

El Saadawi, Nawal. *Woman at Point Zero.* London: Zed Books, 1983.

Gaskell, Elizabeth. *Mary Barton, a Tale of Manchester.* Oxford: Oxford University Press, 1987.

Goldman, Emma. "Victims of Morality" (1913). Available online. URL: http://www.positiveatheism.org/hist/goldmanmor.htm. Accessed on October 14, 2005.

Greer, Germaine. *The Whole Woman.* New York: Anchor, 2000.

Kemble, Fanny. *Journal of a Residence in America* (1863). Available online. URL: http://etext.lib.virginia.edu/toc/modeng/public/KemPlan.html. Accessed on October 16, 2005.

Rampling, Anne. *Belinda.* New York: Berkley, 2000.

Rau, Santha Rama. *The Adventuress.* New York: Dell, 1971.

Rowbotham, Sheila. *Hidden from History: Rediscovering Women in History from the 17th Century to the Present.* New York: Vintage, 1976.

Schreiner, Olive. *Woman and Labour* (1911). Available online. URL: http://etext.library.adelaide.edu.au/s/schreiner_o/woman/woman.html. Accessed on October 13, 2005.

Starr, Elizabeth. " 'A Great Engine for Good': The Industry of Fiction in Elizabeth Gaskell's *Mary Barton* and *North and South,*" *Studies in the Novel* 34, no. 4 (Winter 2002): 386–404.

Woodhull, Victoria, and Tennessee Claflin. *Woodhull & Claflin's Weekly* (1871–1872). Available online. URL: http://www.victoria-woodhull.com/wcarchive.htm. Accessed on October 17, 2005.

Prynne, Hester

Nathaniel Hawthorne, the New World's first great novelist, created an American icon in his fictional saint, Hester Prynne, the disgraced individualist whom sanctimonious Puritans punish and persecute in *The SCARLET LETTER* (1850). In her introduction Hester is "rather a noteworthy personage," an understatement Hawthorne rapidly replaces with allegorical details of her life (Hawthorne, 103). As background he captures in colonial Massachusetts's social codes a Puritan mania for domestic order, the reassuring contrast to the North American wilderness that promises propriety, cohesion, and a social bulwark against dissent. The religious hierarchy determines the choices that affirm female identity, particularly for a lone woman such as the tall, enigmatic Hester. Male ministers have the ultimate power over her. She fears most their right to remove her base-born daughter, Pearl, to a more conventionally Christian household.

Hester is a silenced, disempowered female citizen who becomes for the devout a walking warning, "the figure, the body, the reality of sin" (*ibid.,* 130). Without words the contemplative protagonist indicates her character through posture and symbol, beginning with her departure from prison to stand erect on the scaffold with her three-month-old babe. Amid gesturing, sour-faced matrons, Hester ascends the public platform adjacent to the meeting house to hold her child for all to view. Intended as a model of the fallen woman, her example boomerangs against authoritarian males by revealing a stoic heart given to unheralded acts of goodness and mercy. She maintains her composure despite a pressing need to "shriek out with the full power of her lungs, and cast herself from the scaffold down upon the ground, or else go mad at once" (*ibid.,* 118). Her self-control attests to Hawthorne's character studies of women whom society boxes into inescapable corners.

Hester's SILENCING becomes an impetus to female creativity. Once freed from the cell, Hester expresses through needlecraft of the A on her chest a statement of her crime "in fine red cloth, surrounded with an elaborate embroidery and fantastic flourishes of gold thread" (*ibid.,* 115). The author sanctifies her with his description of beauty and grace that "shone out, and made a halo of the misfortune and ignominy in which she was enveloped" (*ibid.,* 116). Her rebellion is silent, but visually riveting, notably the release of dark tresses from her cap, a symbol of the colonial custom of concealing woman's sensuality. Rather than relegate her to the social scrap heap, the author creates in her a source of fashion for other women, an energetic community member who has "a part to perform in the world" (*ibid.,* 133).

Hawthorne's pro-woman novel retains its value to feminist literature for its depiction of circumscribed female lives. Later demonstrations of Hester's character through neighborliness and circumspect behavior balance beneficence and industry with her refusal to give up personal autonomy within a community bent on hounding her for sexual impropriety. In "the household that was darkened by trouble," Hester attends the bedsides of the dying and provides shrouds for their burial (*ibid.*, 179). She outlines the costumes of upperclass women with embroidered collars, jabots, gloves, and cuffs, all personal adornment that she denies herself. Instead, she chooses the toneless Puritan garments and accessorizes with a scarlet A, the unforgiving mark of the fallen woman that is her burden for life. To the author she is "patient,—a martyr" whose actions override her denunciation for adultery (*ibid.*, 134).

The author walks a thin line in his depiction of sorrow and suffering in his colonial victim. He redeems her from goody-goody sainthood by the fire in her spirit and an emotional depth that extends beyond her lover's ken. After seven years of public humiliation she demands that the Reverend Arthur Dimmesdale cease blaming her for Pearl's conception and birth. In a dramatic posture she flings herself down beside him and asserts, "Let God punish! Thou shalt forgive!" (*ibid.*, 199). The private confrontation concludes with a gesture to her strength: Dimmesdale asks that she think for him and plot a course out of his hypocritical stance as beloved minister and paragon of virtue. By admitting that she is more courageous than he, the minister elevates Hester's stature as fictional heroine.

Hester Prynne's resilience exemplifies the stoicism of the marked woman. As the critic Carolyn G. Heilbrun comments, Hester experiences "social death and social redemption," a purifying process that engenders worth in the Christian martyr and saint (Heilbrun, 64). Hawthorne's marked woman motif infiltrated other feminist works, notably Kate Chopin's *The* Awakening (1899), the controversial story of hidden motivations in the sexually autonomous protagonist, Edna Pontellier. The Caribbean novelist Maryse Condé rewrites Hawthorne's story in *Moi, Tituba, sorcière noire Salem* (*I, Tituba, Black Witch of Salem*, 1986) in which Hester acts on her suicidal urges and hangs herself in prison. Barbara Kingsolver's masterwork *The Poisonwood Bible* (1998) makes a more humorous application. In reference to Leah Price's defiance of African gender codes, her twin, Adah,

sees her sister in Hester's guise marked with a "D for Dramatic, or Diana of the Hunt, or Devil Take Your Social Customs" (Kingsolver, 278).

Bibliography

Hardwick, Elizabeth. *Seduction and Betrayal.* New York: Vintage, 1975.

Hawthorne, Nathaniel. *The Complete Novels and Selected Tales of Nathaniel Hawthorne.* New York: Modern Library, 1937.

Heilbrun, Carolyn G. *Toward a Recognition of Androgyny.* New York: W. W. Norton, 1982.

Kalfopoulou, Adrianne. *A Discussion of the Ideology of the American Dream in the Culture's Female Discourses.* Lewiston, N.Y.: Edwin Mellen Press, 2000.

Kingsolver, Barbara. *The Poisonwood Bible.* New York: HarperCollins, 1998.

Puttermesser Papers, The Cynthia Ozick (1997)

Cynthia Ozick's droll picaresque fable *The Puttermesser Papers* (1997) incorporates nested stories and adventures to examine the frustrations of the creative visionary. In a series of comic-mystic episodes Ozick depicts the 43-year-old attorney Ruth Puttermesser as an outsider, a dowdy Jewish intellectual who mimics Don Quixote on a mission. Living in Brooklyn after her mother settles in Florida, Puttermesser mulls over her self-destructive tendencies, which caused Rappaport, her artist boyfriend, to prefer Plato to lovemaking. City officials further devalue her by booting her from a post in the Department of Disbursements and Receipts. The character's gloomy seriousness becomes a mask through which Ozick comments on the lives of Jews and the corruption of American culture.

As turmoil impels the compulsive neatnik to action, magical realism becomes her ally in the pursuit of reformist ideals. She surveys nepotism in Gotham, a modern-day Babylon that elevates inept male placeholders who are "good at . . . bringing everything to a standstill, like the spindleprick in Sleeping Beauty" (Ozick, 82). With the aid of Xanthippe, a girl robot formed of potting soil and jolted to life by four Hebrew letters, Puttermesser runs for the office of New York City mayor. As a feminist Zorro she pledges her powers to "the PLAN for the

Resuscitation, Reformation, Reinvigoration & Redemption of the City of New York," a feminist platform targeting the underserved (*ibid.*, 123). Ozick exposes the bias and mediocrity of city bureaucracy as well as the disillusion of the idealist, who must slay her dark alter ego, the automaton-daughter Xanthippe. The sacrifice is necessary after the robot morphs into an id figure consumed by carnal passion much as Mary SHELLEY's monster demands companionship and sexual release.

Allegory rules Ozick's slender novel in its unforeseen falling action, "Puttermesser in Paradise," which the author published as a short story in the May 1997 issue of *Atlantic Monthly*. In a puddle of vomit the protagonist anticipates murder, mutilation, and rape by Frankie, a burglar in a ski mask armed with a knife. His slicing her throat and lopping off an earlobe symbolize male brutality and the SILENCING of the city's female citizenry. Through a perverse birthing of the new Puttermesser the author follows her innovative dreamer to paradise, where all desires are fulfilled. The former mayor relishes the liberation of creativity un-encumbered by Jewish fatalism. Paradoxically she encounters a sobering truth that heaven, as yin to yang, cannot exist without hell. By reliving her love for Emil Hauchvogel, she recognizes the male egotist's need for an awestruck female audience and his recoil from an assertive would-be lover. Heaven completes her stunted life by allowing her a postlife marriage to Emil and the birth of a son, but the random wash of relationships and events between past and present leave her miserably resigned to impermanence. Ozick concludes the protagonist's musings with a pun on "butter knife," a rueful memory of the burglar's knife that freed her from Earth to encounter a better life and eternal bitterness.

Bibliography

Gardner, James. "Review: *The Puttermesser Papers*," *National Review*, 1 September 1997, pp. 50–51.

Ozick, Cynthia. *The Puttermesser Papers*. New York: Vintage, 1998.

Pinsker, Sanford. "Review: *The Puttermesser Papers*," *Jewish Exponent*, 1 January 1998, p. 4.

Q

Quindlen, Anna (1953–)

The insightful feminist lecturer, columnist, and novelist Anna Quindlen specializes in gender issues from the point of view of the suburban mother. A native Philadelphian, she was an avid reader in girlhood of Jane AUSTEN, Charlotte and Emily BRONTË, Emily DICKINSON, Daphne DU MAURIER, George ELIOT, and Margaret MITCHELL. Quindlen studied at Barnard College and began publishing fiction in *Seventeen* magazine at age 20. She entered journalism as a part-time reporter and copy clerk for the *New York Post* and joined the full-time staff in 1974 on the city hall beat. She produced a substantive syndicated column, "About New York," for the *New York Times* and a regular column, "The Last Word," for *Newsweek*, alternating biweekly with George F. Will. After child-care leaves, she introduced in 1986 the "Life in the 30s" column, which used her experience with a husband and three children as a springboard. Collected in *Living Out Loud* (1988) and *Thinking Out Loud* (1993), her salient essays describe the impact of historical events and medical and political issues on ordinary families. In a retrospect on her career of commenting on news, she mentions a hate note from a reader who assumed she had been fired for extolling "welfare cheats, boozy vagrants, and perverts," a reactionary's view of her liberal subject matter (Quindlen, *Thinking*, 5).

Quindlen set her sights on commonplace sources of happiness, on unconditional love, and on the everyday samaritans who do good deeds without expecting thanks. At age 47 she increased her exposure with "Public & Private," published on the *Times* op-ed page. For its high-quality essays she became the third woman to win a Pulitzer Prize in commentary. Two years later she published the best-selling novel *One True Thing* (1994), which contrasts a liberated daughter with her stay-at-home mother. Ellen, the protagonist, ponders the uneven needs of her parents and contemplates writing a self-help book called *Women Who Love Men Who Love Themselves* (Quindlen, *One*, 377). In a discussion of Louisa May ALCOTT's *LITTLE WOMEN* (1868–69), Ellen learns from her mother, Kate Gulden, that "women writers of all people should know better than to pigeonhole women, put them in little groups, the smart one, the sweet one" (*ibid.*, 55). Kate detests the dismissive attitude feminists take toward contented homemakers. The film adaptation of the novel starred Meryl Streep as the dying mother of Rene Zellweger, the daughter who reexamines her assumptions about the superiority of career women.

Rather than move up to the editorial staff of the *Times*, Quindlen departed from journalism in December 1994 to devote herself to family and long fiction. She researched *Black and Blue* (1998), a wise and candid novel about a wife's passion for her mate and her loss of identity through 18 years of marital abuse. The author's next novel, *Blessings* (2002), the story of a woman's love for a foundling, was a vehicle for a 2003 CBS-TV film starring Mary Stuart Masterson and Mary Tyler Moore. Quindlen has also taught journalism at Yale and Rutgers Universities and authored children's books,

The Tree That Came to Stay (1992) and *Happily Ever After* (1997).

Quindlen's essays maintain a middle-of-the-road stance on feminism but occasionally erupt with a vengeance. Her divergent thinking makes unusual connections, for example, her views on Lady Liberty: "The Statue of Liberty is meant to be shorthand for a country so unlike its parts that a trip from California to Indiana should require a passport" (Quindlen, 1989, 4). On March 27, 2000, Quindlen exclaimed in her column for *Newsweek*: "I've had it with Women's History Month. . . . A month? We ought to get most of the year" (Quindlen, 2000, 86). The essay differentiates between "women living imitation guys' lives" and those females still relegated to household "scut work" (*ibid.*). She collected relevant columns in *Loud and Clear* (2004), a meditation on women's lives and influence that includes the essays "Stretch Marks," "Putting Up a Good Front," "The Name Is Mine," and "Some Thoughts about Abortion." In "Now It's Time for Generation Next" she anticipates a new wave of bungee jumpers: "Our hearts leap and our adrenaline rises at the sight of them, arms outstretched, poised to do—what? Something wonderful!" (Quindlen, 2004, 41).

Bibliography

Quindlen, Anna. *Living Out Loud.* New York: Ivy, 1989.

———. *Loud and Clear.* New York: Random House, 2004.

———. *One True Thing.* New York: Dell, 1994.

———. "The Reasonable Woman Standard," *Newsweek*, 27 March 2000, p. 86.

———. *Thinking Out Loud.* New York: Ballantine, 1994.

R

Radcliffe, Ann (1764–1823)

A noted refiner of Gothic fiction, Ann Ward Radcliffe helped to emancipate female characters from stereotypes. A native of Bath, England, she was the child of bookish middle-class parents. On her own she read popular works from the town's circulating library. She chose verse by the graveyard poets, fiction by Sophia LEE and Charlotte SMITH, the journals of Lady Mary WALKER, and Abbé Prevost's melodramatic *Manon Lescaut* (1731), a classic study of unbridled passion in the femme fatale. The author wed William Radcliffe, editor of the *English Chronicle*, and paralleled his career with her own composition of prose melodrama. From the romantic novella *The Castles of Athlin and Dunbayne: A Highland Story* (1789) and a female gothic novel, *A Sicilian Romance* (1790), Radcliffe advanced to *The Romance of the Forest* (1791), the first of her writings to appear under her own name. Influencing her feminist style was her familiarity with Smith's *Ethelinde; or, The Recluse of the Lake* (1790) and *Celestina* (1791).

The most read author of her day, Radcliffe redirected terror literature from male titillation at timorous females to realistic portraits of women who rescue themselves. She featured female heroines whose struggles derived from the limited opportunities for women in a patriarchal society. She made her reputation on her next two titles, the suspenseful, psychologically intense novel *The Mysteries of Udolpho* (1794) and *The Italian; or, the Confessional of the Black Penitents* (1797), an atmospheric Gothic work set in a gloomy forest and in urban Rome during the Spanish Inquisition. In *Mysteries of Udolpho* the orphaned protagonist, Emily St. Aubert, suffers disempowerment through a lack of dynastic prestige, patrimony, and choice of husband, the three requisites for women's prosperity in 18th-century England. Homeschooled in Latin and English poetry, she is girlish, yet obedient to her father's admonition that she never let sensitivity overrule self-discipline. Rather, she demonstrates the Victorian principle of purposeful industry, a shield against "the contagion of folly and of vice" (Radcliffe, 1966, 6). To create conflict, the author balances Emily's rationality with repressed hysteria caused by fear of melancholy surroundings and of Signor Montoni, her villainous uncle by marriage. In one instance she faces the unknown: "As the carriage-wheels rolled heavily under the portcullis, Emily's heart sunk, and she seemed as if she was going into a prison" (*ibid.*, 227). Such dread of CONFINEMENT is necessary to elevate the heroine in the novel's resolution for refusing to quail in the face of overwhelming male-controlled odds.

Radcliffe manages to restrain Gothic extremes through stylistic decorum and creation of self-disciplined protagonists. As the result of a gender power struggle against Montoni, Emily draws on logic and nonconfrontational resistance to potential battery, forced marriage, and rape, three subtextual possibilities after she falls into Montoni's hands. Locked in a tower room, a common phallic symbol in Gothic lore, she systematically pinpoints inconsistencies in her captor—"the changing emotions of his soul, and the inexplicable character of his countenance" (*ibid.*, 275). Her recognition of the rule of his intellect over ferocity helps to calm and stabilize her. In the end she triumphs on three levels—she retains her virginity, reclaims inherited property, and marries Valancourt, her beloved. Radcliffe countenances their union with the gift of a grand home, Chateau-le-Blanc, literally "the white castle," a symbolic gesture of regard for chastity where "the bowers of La Vallée became, once more, the retreat of goodness, wisdom and domestic blessedness!" (*ibid.*, 672). The union implies a restoration of order and a reaffirmation of Europe's domestic standards.

Radcliffe's Gothic stories bear a hallmark, the Radcliffean ending, which supplies plausible explanations for enigmas and eerie occurrences that threaten unnamed barbarisms against the heroine. The author's innovative works served imitators. Freelancer Sarah Wilkinson adapted Radcliffe's plots in *The Veiled Picture* (1802) and *The Midnight Assassin; or, the Confessions of the Monk Rinaldi* (1802), two bluebooks or chapbooks, the poorly edited popular fiction aimed at less educated lower-class readers. The novel also suited adaptation into the anonymous stage play *Alexena; or, The Castle of Santa Marco* (1817). In admiration of Radcliffe's high principles Nathan Drake called her "the Shakespeare of romance" (Clery, 1995, 53). After her sudden death of an asthma attack her works continued to influence the feminist authors Jane AUSTEN, the BRONTË sisters, Maria EDGEWORTH, Christina ROSSETTI, Mary Wollstonecraft SHELLEY, Mary WOLLSTONECRAFT, and Anne YEARSLEY.

Bibliography

Clery, E. J. *The Rise of Supernatural Fiction, 1762–1800.* Cambridge: Cambridge University Press, 1995.

———. *Women's Gothic from Clara Reeve to Mary Shelley.* Tavistock, England: Northcote House, 2000.

Mackenzie, Scott. "Ann Radcliffe's Gothic Narrative and the Readers at Home," *Studies in the Novel* 31, no. 4 (Winter 1999): 409.

McIntyre, Clara Frances. *Ann Radcliffe in Relation to Her Time.* New Haven, Conn.: Yale Studies in English, 1970.

Norton, Rictor. *The Mistress of Udolpho.* London: Leicester University Press, 1999.

Poovey, Mary. "Ideology and the Mysteries of Udolpho," *Criticism: A Quarterly for Literature and the Arts* 21 (1979): 307–330.

Radcliffe, Ann. *The Italian.* London: Oxford University Press, 1968.

———. *The Mysteries of Udolpho.* London: Oxford University Press, 1966.

Wilt, Judith. *Ghosts of the Gothic.* Princeton, N.J.: Princeton University Press, 1980.

Raisin in the Sun, A Lorraine Hansberry (1959)

A high point of American stage drama, Lorraine HANSBERRY's realistic domestic play *A Raisin in the Sun* pictures the dilemmas that black urban families faced as they attempted to better their lot in the years before the civil rights movement. In a claustrophobic setting a five-member extended family battles crowded conditions and despair. They choose to invest their financial resources in a home in Clybourne Park, a white residential neighborhood. The clan WISEWOMAN, Lena Eggleston Younger, a widow and mother of two, is a domestic in other people's homes. In the ghetto she becomes the polisher of worn furniture, fighter of roaches, raiser of spirits, and keeper of a drooping house plant on the only windowsill. The plant, like her slum-reared children, gets too little sunshine.

As her names imply, Lena is the one on whom others lean, the nurturer of young, the challenger of disappointments. With dignity and ample grace she revives the moribund dream of Walter Lee, her wayward son, by forgiveness and forbearance. Of his future she ponders, "I'm worried for what can happen to him if something don't happen for him soon. . . . Something that makes him feel like he can beat this world" (Hansberry, 79). His frustration withers his wife, Ruth, who secretly plans to abort their unborn child at eight weeks of gestation. Walter Lee's longing for social and economic advancement contrasts with the familial terrors of a mother about to introduce another child into a discontented family. Threatening her maternity is the absence of support from the infant's sire.

The MOTHER-DAUGHTER RELATIONSHIP between Lena and her only daughter contrasts with her response to Walter Lee's difficulties: She mothers Beneatha "Bennie" Younger with more discipline and head butting. After Beneatha rejects God, Lena orders, "Now—you say after me, in my mother's house there is still God" (ibid., 51). Rather than restore the supreme being to power, the command insists that Beneatha recognize her mother's authority by forgoing blasphemous outbursts. In a later scene Lena reasserts her primacy by scolding her son for shouting: "I don't 'low no yellin' in this house" (ibid., 70). In his mental torment over diminished self-worth Walter Lee denigrates his mother and ignores his wife, who needs to discuss her pregnancy and the problem of housing a sixth family member in their cramped space. Lena recognizes the difference between female and male perspectives. To his search for answers on the street, Lena warns, "It's dangerous, son . . . when a man goes outside his home to look for peace" (ibid., 73). Her patience and wisdom suggest that she has spent years observing imploding families.

The views of an outsider, the West African visitor Joseph Asagai, relieve the family of an ingrown ghetto perspective. He woos Beneatha by calling her Alaiyo, "[meaning] One for Whom Bread—Food—Is Not Enough" (ibid., 65). The pet name acknowledges Beneatha's belonging to the next generation of women, who prefer professional careers to the domestic labors of Lena and Ruth. Nonetheless Beneatha, who prefers her masculine nickname, is not eager to abandon studying medicine to become Asagai's trophy wife and impress a Nigerian village. In the falling action Hansberry shuts out extraneous speakers and returns to the family's instincts and values. Honoring Lena's role as proud head of the family and buyer of their new house, Walter Lee gives her a broad-brimmed garden hat and gardening tools, symbols of her cultivation of family at its roots. Because of its warmth and humor Hansberry's play remains one of the most produced in theater history.

Bibliography

Gourdine, Angeletta K. M. "The Drama of Lynching in Two Blackwomen's Drama, or Relating Grimké's Rachel to Hansberry's A Raisin in the Sun," Modern Drama 41, no. 4 (Winter 1998): 533.

Hansberry, Lorraine. A Raisin in the Sun. New York: Penguin, 1988.

Ratushinskaya, Irina (1954–   )

The Ukrainian dissident poet and human rights activist Irina Georgiyeva Ratushinskaya used free verse as a mental stabilizer and spiritual uplift during a prison term at hard labor. Born in Odessa to professionals—an engineer and a teacher—she began writing poems as soon as she became literate. She earned a physics degree from the University of Odessa and taught primary school for two years before marrying the engineer Igor Geraschenko and settling in Kiev. At age 28, a year after she applied to emigrate, the KGB arrested her for disseminating propaganda and jailed her for 10 days for organizing a peaceful demonstration. Russian courts found her guilty of refusenik acts and anti-Soviet agitation and sentenced her to seven years as a political prisoner in Barashevo, a women's camp in Mordovia. On the train with other inmates she recited verse to give them hope and to build camaraderie.

Ratushinskaya and other female dissidents engineered a prison communication system by which she tapped out the letters of her poems for others to hear. Her works bolstered wavering courage in women who survived on boiled cabbage and whom male jailers routinely strip-searched and marched naked to the showers. After she smuggled these poems to her husband in Moscow, he published two volumes of her prison verse. In one poem, dedicated to a prison sister named Tatyana Mikhailovna, Ratushinskaya promised that freedom was near. "Soon, soon, you will be joining the convoy, / Soon you'll be putting on a warm sweater, / And freedom will be treading on your heels" (ibid., 73).

Handcuffed and beaten, Ratushinskaya continued to refuse orders by starving herself and not answering the interrogator's questions. The staff force-fed her to keep her alive. As her physical condition reached the critical level, the warden refused her a visit with her mother and husband. Emulating her misery in a Soviet punishment cell, an Anglican priest, the Reverend Doctor Richard Rodgers, observed Lent at Saint Martin's Church in Birmingham, England, under privations like those of solitary confinement. Wearing only T-shirt, shorts, and socks, he slept on a board without a blanket. In 1986 the British Broadcasting Corporation (BBC) commissioned Elian Brian to set five of Ratushinskaya's poems to music as "No, I'm Not Afraid" (1981), an orchestral suite.

For four years Ratushinskaya was denied paper. Nonetheless she composed some 300 poems on soap bars with burned matchsticks on subjects of Christianity, love, freedom, human rights, and women's pursuit of the arts. After memorizing the verses, she washed her hands with the soap to remove traces of writing. Because supporters smuggled her verse to publishers in the West, prison authorities tacked on an additional decade to the poet's original sentence. In 1986 President Ronald Reagan's cordial visit with Mikhail Gorbachev at Reykjavik resulted in glasnost and in amnesty for Ratushinskaya, who had joined nine other women in writing to Reagan about their sufferings. After exile to England the poet recapped the hardships of her prison term in verse in *Beyond the Limit* (1987) and *Pencil Letter* (1988). A prison memoir, *Grey Is the Colour of Hope* (1988), describes her compassion for Ukrainian, Latvian, Lithuanian, and Russian inmates whom the state deemed dangerous. She joked, "What a mixed bunch we are: a Catholic, a Pentecostal, several Orthodox, an unbeliever. . . . Later we are to be joined by a Baptist" (Ratushinskaya, 1999, 123). The poet preserves their stories as models of valor, especially the "grannies," elderly women who refuse to abandon religious faith. Of her fond memories of SISTERHOOD the poem "I Will Live and Survive" praises fellow inmates as the Earth's best, most tender people and the ones she will honor for their patience and courage.

Ratushinskaya's exile stripped her of citizenship, but it offered her a chance to receive treatment for heart and kidney disease and to write about the community in a women's prison. A year after her freeing she and her husband arrived in the United States, where she received the Religious Freedom Award of the Institute on Religion and Democracy and assumed a two-year poetry residency at Northwestern University. In 1998 she, her husband, and their twin sons returned to Russia. She completed a novel, *Fiction and Lies* (1999), a depiction of the artist's life in a totalitarian state. The next year she published *Wind of the Journey* (2000), her first new poems since 1992. Her work has influenced the style of the poet Sharon OLDS.

Bibliography

Kuryluk, Ewa. "An Interview with Irina Ratushinskaya." *New York Review of Books*, 7 May 1987, pp. 16–20.

Leigh, S. J., and David J. Leigh. "Hope, Resistance, and Poetry in Two Russian Autobiographies," *Renascence* 56, no. 3 (Spring 2004): 197–207.

Ratushinskaya, Irina. *Fiction and Lies.* London: John Murray, 1999.

———. *Grey Is the Colour of Hope.* London: Trafalgar Square, 1988.

Rau, Santha Rama (1923–)

A noted journalist and travel writer, Vasanthi "Santha" Rama Rau Wattles writes magazine articles, AUTOBIOGRAPHY, fiction, and BIOGRAPHY as means of expressing feminist concerns. She was born to Brahmins in Madras. She followed her mother, Lady Dhanvanthi Handoo Rama Rau, the international president of Planned Parenthood, and her father, Sir Benegal Rama Rau, a governor of the Federal Reserve Bank of India, to embassy postings around the globe. In England she attended Saint Paul's elementary school. When she was 15, her parents settled at the embassy in South Africa. With her mother and sister, Rau sat out World War II in Bombay and then studied English at Wellesley College. After graduation, she became a newspaper and radio reporter and edited *Trend* magazine. She published an autobiography, *Home to India* (1944), an account of her reunion with her paternal grandmother and rebellion against India's gendered social codes, which threatened the author's identity as an emancipated woman.

Rau turned travel into a source of commentary on rituals and social expectations that govern the life of women. She spent time in Tokyo at her father's next post as his embassy hostess and taught English at Mrs. Hani's Freedom School. Rau traveled Afghanistan, Bali, Burma, Cambodia, China, Indonesia, Laos, the Philippines, Sri Lanka, the Suli islands, Thailand, and Vietnam and gathered material for *East of Home: The Discovery of Asia by an Asian Educated in the West* (1950). She reported world events in Africa, Asia, and Russia for *Holiday* magazine while freelancing short sketches in *Eros, Flair, Horizon,* the *New Yorker, New York Times Magazine, Reader's Digest, Reporter,* and *Vogue*. Among eyewitness accounts was her impression of the trial of Jomo Kenyatta, whom the British exiled for abetting a Mau-Mau uprising. She wrote a first novel, *Remember the House* (1956), the story of Baba, an Indian woman who eludes traditional nuptial arrangements to wed a man of her choice. Rau returned to travelogue in 1957 with *View to the Southeast*, in which she describes the influx of American materialism as a source of potential destabilization among Asians. In 1958 Rau summarized more of her observations about Asian life in *Gifts of Passage: An Informal Autobiography*. In the story "Who Cares?" she examines the mind-set of women accustomed to arranged marriages. Speaking through the omniscient narrator, she concludes that Asian women "have inherited, through bitter centuries, a ruthless sense of self-preservation . . . that cool, subtle determination to find her security and hang on to it" (Rau, 1975, 183).

Rau tackled the complex questions of women's lives under colonialism. In January 1962 her adaptation of E. M. Forster's complex novel *A Passage to India* as a three-act stage play opened on Broadway at the Ambassador Theater for a three-month run. One of the sources for the director David Lean's 1984 film version, the play depicts Adela Quested's false accusation of rape against Dr. Aziz, a respected Indian physician. Her courage in admitting the error and in dropping the charge earns the spite of the British Raj, which turns its collective back on her. Additional works by Rau include tandoori recipes of two grandmothers in *The Cooking of India* (1969), an article on Benares for *National Geographic*, and contributions to *Women of the Third World: Twenty Stories Set in Africa, Asia, and Latin America* (1975).

Through fiction Rau contemplated the role of modern women in urban surroundings beset by economic and political turmoil. In *The Adventuress* (1970), she describes Kay, a woman who poses as girl victim in postwar Tokyo, sophisticated club hostess, and intellectual consort amid Shanghai's corrupt bankers. By matching her persona to the demands—and man—of the summer of 1947, Kay, as a mercenary, makes her way in a part of Asia that is rapidly falling to Communism. Only an elderly woman recognizes the cost of bargaining with

American and British authorities: "However all this may turn out, Keiko-san, we will always realize how much you have tried to do for us" (Rau, 1971, 20).

In 1976 Rau ghost-wrote Gayatri Devi's biography, *A Princess Remembers: The Memoirs of the Maharani of Jaipur*, the life of an elegant socialite, feminist, and educator, the daughter of the maharajah of Cooch Behar, the princess of Baroda, and one of the last of Jaipur's queens. The text applauds Devi's violation of purdah, a form of seclusion that forced aristocratic Indian women to remain out of sight of strangers. Devi explained that "strict purdah would have required the women to stay entirely within the [women's] quarters and, if they had any occasion to venture outside, to travel well chaperoned, only in curtained or shaded vehicles" (Rau, 1976, 18). Devi later described the traditional cloistering of women as "a hopelessly dull and claustrophobic existence" (*ibid.*, 195). She earned the world's respect for her membership in the Indian Parliament from 1962 to 1977 and as the founder of the Gayatri Devi Girl's Public School, which initiated EDUCATION for the females of Rajasthan.

Bibliography

Coughlin, Richard J. "Review: *View to the Southeast*," *Journal of Asian Studies* 17, no. 4 (August 1958): 637.

Rau, Santha Rama. *The Adventuress*. New York: Dell, 1971.

———. *A Princess Remembers: The Memoirs of the Maharani of Jaipur*. Philadelphia: J. B. Lippincott, 1976.

———. "Who Cares?" In *Women of the Third World: Twenty Stories Set in Africa, Asia, and Latin America*. London: Victor Gollancz, 1975.

Rawlings, Marjorie Kinnan (1896–1953)

The southern fiction writer, journalist, and feminist Marjorie Kinnan Rawlings lived the independent frontier life she wrote about. Born in Washington, D.C., she earned an award for writing from *McCall's* magazine in 1912. After graduation from the University of Wisconsin with a degree in English she wrote and edited for the *Home Sector, Louisville Courier-Journal,* and *Rochester Journal-American* and produced a feminist column, "Songs of a Housewife," a series of poems syndicated in 50 newspapers. She vacationed in central Florida in 1928 and decided to settle in the Ocala National Forest on Lochloosa Lake near Hawthorne. In a tin-roofed cabin surrounded by a 72-acre orange grove she became an early ecofeminist by developing a love of land and an appreciation for the fragility of living things. She set up an office on her screened-in porch and began a correspondence with the writers Ellen GLASGOW, Zora Neale HURSTON, and Margaret MITCHELL. At the urging of the *Scribner's* editor Max Perkins, Rawlings produced regional treasures for *Atlantic Monthly, Collier's, Harper's,* the *New Yorker,* and *Saturday Evening Post.* Stories such as "Cracker Chidlings" (1931) feature the local dialect, recipes, nature meditations, and humble folk amusements on the marsh.

Solitude at the remote hermitage proved conducive to physical and emotional serenity and offered Rawlings spiritual healing after a divorce. She valued the opportunity to observe and write about the region's mystic timelessness and its sacred harmony with nature. In 1931 she won a prize from *Scribner's* magazine for "Jacob's Ladder," which describes the survival of the squatters Mart and Florry, who live at the barest subsistence level. Two years later "Gal Young 'Un" (1933) won the O. Henry Memorial Short Story Contest for its feminist themes of female coming of age and flight from PATRIARCHY. To a bootlegger named Trax, Mrs. Syles, the lone widow, describes her isolation: "I got no way to go. I kep' up stock for two–three year after Pa died, but 'twa'n't wuth the worry" (Rawlings, 1975, 164). To better herself, she marries the scoundrel and goes into the moonshining business, a southern specialty for mountaineers and rural folk during the Great Depression. She turns the tables on him for blatant adultery by ousting him and keeping his child, the title character, as a friend.

Rawlings achieved a classic treatment of growing up in *The Yearling* (1938), a young adult best seller that won the Lewis Carroll Shelf Award and a Pulitzer Prize. The story of a footloose young man's acceptance of responsiblity depicts the hardships of Ora Baxter, a demanding parent who makes do on the supplies her husband, Penny, can eke out of their farm on the scrubland of the Florida wilderness. Ora's struggle to parcel out berries, cow peas, wild greens, and meat from Penny's hunting worsens with the lack of potable water. She comments briefly, "For twenty years, I been sparin,' " her summation of the family's daily chore of drawing water from a sinkhole, where she also washes their clothes (Rawlings, 1970, 77). Rawlings admires Ora's imaginative make-do spirit amid sparse resources and freakish weather extremes: "Flour sacks went into aprons and dishtowels and chair-backs that she embroidered on winter evenings; and into backs for her packwork quilts" (*ibid.*). A later collection, *When the Whippoorwill* (1940), covers more of the work of women living the hardscrabble existence that accompanies farming and raising livestock.

In 1942 Rawlings turned to autobiography with *Cross Creek* and a sequel, *Cross Creek Cookery,* a collection of recipes, anecdotes, and Florida lore. The two works express her joy in autonomy, cookery, and writing, which, after 30 years of the "spiritual homelessness" of city life, satisfy "a thing that had gone hungry and unfed since childhood" (Rawlings, 1974, 8, 4). In "Hyacinth Drift," the climactic chapter that she published separately in *Scribner's* in 1933, the author and a friend, Dessie Smith, complete a 10-day journey down the Saint Johns River that is an allegory for loss of self through immersion in nature. She realizes, "Like all simple facts, it was necessary to discover for oneself" (*ibid.*, 347). Contributing to Rawlings's contentment are intense privacy and her dependence on 'Geechee, a black woman whose exuberance "seemed always about to burst into a belligerent dance, tearing her garments from her, prancing naked in a savage triumph. The effect from her lioness stride" (*ibid.*, 65). The friendship that Rawlings maintains with her housekeeper and the mature confidence she admires in elderly female neighbors undergird much of her fiction. After numerous writers, including American service personnel, requested specifics of her meals of alligator tail steak, grits and mullet, spoonbread, mango chutney, and carrot soufflé, the author responded with a Florida cookbook.

Rawlings achieved a portion of her renown after her sudden death of a brain hemorrhage at age

57. In addition to two light films, *The Sun Comes Up* (1949) and *Gal Young 'Un* (1979), her works were the source of the multiple-Oscar-nominated *The Yearling* (1946), starring Jane Wyman in the mother's role. A biopic, *Cross Creek* (1983), pairs Mary Steenburgen and Alfre Woodard as Rawlings and her housekeeper 'Geechee. In 1988 fans issued a periodical, the *Marjorie Kinnan Rawlings Journal of Florida Literature*. The University Press of Florida retrieved an unpublished autobiographical novel, *Blood of My Blood* (2002), written in 1928. To account for the struggles of the female artist, the story delineates the author's love-hate relationship with her mother, Ida, and the decision to leave home, marry, and write for a living.

Bibliography

Rawlings, Marjorie Kinnan. *Cross Creek*. Atlanta: Mockingbird Books, 1974.

———. *Cross Creek Cookery*. New York: Fireside Books, 1996.

———. *When the Whippoorwill*. New York: Ballantine, 1975.

———. *The Yearling*. New York: Charles Scribner's Sons, 1970.

Schmidt, Susan. "Finding a Home: Rawlings's *Cross Creek*," *Southern Literary Journal* 26, no. 2 (Spring 1994): 48–57.

Renault, Mary (1905–1983)

The lesbian author Mary Renault introduced to historical fiction of the ancient Mediterranean world a broad view of human sexual choice and fluid gender roles. Born Eileen Mary "Molly" Challans to an upper-middle-class family in London, she ignored the nagging of her mother about attracting males and refused to conceal her intellectual powers. In defiance Renault hid in a stable loft to read without interruption. Like Eurydike in *The Last of the Wine* (1964), Renault "had known as long as she could remember that she should have been a boy" (Renault, *Last*, 118). While attending a boarding school in Bristol, she decided on a career in fiction, through which she could adopt a male perspective. Among the first women admitted to Oxford, she completed an English degree at Saint Hugh's College but hedged her choice with a three-year degree in nursing at Radcliffe Infirmary, Oxford. During World War II she laid aside her writing of short stories and radio plays to work at the Winford Emergency Hospital in Bristol and to treat evacuees from the battle of Dunkirk.

At age 34 Renault published under her pen name a first book, *Purposes of Love* (1939), a novel of manners depicting women's attempt to balance love with their need for INDEPENDENCE. Written in a homophobic society, her fiction turned more openly to homosexual themes, beginning with *The Friendly Young Ladies* (1944), a heavily cloaked autobiographical novel. After publishing *Return to Night* (1947), winner of an MGM award of $150,000, she and her mate, Julie Mullard, a nurse at a tuberculosis clinic, settled first in Durban, then Cape Town, South Africa. The author joined the Black Sash, a women's organization that fought apartheid. A committed activist, she also denounced CENSORSHIP and antigay legislation.

Writing from a lesbian point of view, Renault applied a new perspective to classical gender studies. She stopped masking homosexual desires and consummations in *The Charioteer* (1953), the story of gay soldiers during World War II. For further depictions of gay motifs she retreated to Bronze Age and Classical Greece to write financially successful fictional works on Greek myth and biography: *The King Must Die* (1958), *The Bull from the Sea* (1962), *The Mask of Apollo* (1966), and three on Alexander the Great, *Fire from Heaven* (1969), *The Persian Boy* (1972), and *Funeral Games* (1981). Distancing herself through an impersonal academic pose, she was able to idealize the carnal relationships of men as lyrically as standard romances of her day exalted heterosexual love. To establish the importance of a nonjudgmental milieu, she set the action in a society that placed no shame on homosexuality or bisexuality.

With material she gleaned from the Ashmolean Museum, Renault focused on males who are capable of loving women and men and who find in both types of relationships sources of *arete* (excellence), the Greek ideal. Like the novelist Willa CATHER, who thought of herself as male, Renault identified with the beautiful bodies and active lives of powerful male heroes and tyrants, in part because their lives were more dynamic than those of females. She glimpsed women's roles in religious and cultural enclaves and observed WOMEN'S WORK in an era that discounted or dismissed their activities, intellect, and aims. In *The King Must Die* she describes the labors of laundresses at a stream; in *The Last of the Wine* she expresses sympathy for a concubine who holds on to a sliver of power by perverse and cruel means. In depictions of the rare female authority figure Renault delineates the lives of whole, fulfilled women such as Ariadne, Eurydike, Hippolyta and her Amazons, Medea, Persephone, and Roxane as significant enough to threaten the control of godlike men such as Theseus and Jason. In *The Bull from the Sea* Theseus compliments his consort, Hippolyta, as a warrior and sex partner: "We learned as much of each other in battle as we did in bed" (Renault, *Bull,* 152). In *The King Must Die* Theseus quails at the sight of Ariadne's performing a sacrificial castration during a Dionysian ritual: "[Her hand] had lain closed on her breast. . . . Now when she tried to spread it out, the blood on it had stuck between the fingers, and she could not part them. But she opened her palm, and then I saw what she was holding" (Renault, 1988, 323). The sight of a woman in so controlling a posture devastates Theseus, causing him to lean on an olive tree for support until a wave of nausea subsides. Similarly Roxane, Alexander's wife in *The Persian Boy* (1972), becomes a wielder of influence in the absence of her mate, who returns to combat, leaving an unprotected wife and son in the deadly political aftermath of Alexander's death.

Bibliography

Hoberman, Ruth. "Masquing the Phallus: Genital Ambiguity in Mary Renault's Historical Novels," *Twentieth Century Literature* 42, no. 2 (Summer 1996): 277–293.

Renault, Mary. *The Bull from the Sea.* New York: Vintage, 2001.

———. *The King Must Die.* New York: Vintage, 1988.

———. *The Last of the Wine.* New York: Vintage, 2001.

Sweetman, David. *Mary Renault.* New York: Harvest Books, 1994.

rescue theme

The boy-saves-girl plot is a standard strategem of classic literature and folklore. In a Slavic version of BLUEBEARD lore Clarissa Pinkola ESTÉS, author of *Women Who Run with the Wolves* (1992), pictures family as the appropriate savior of a bride from the famed serial killer. As sisters hover nearby, they spy a whirlwind, "a dust devil in the distance," the upheaval caused by brothers galloping to rescue their sister from beheading (Estés, 1997, 43). The arrival of horsemen in the castle disrupts the domestic scene as brothers challenge a heinous woman killer. The Hungarian tale pictures a grand sword battle on the parapet, where Bluebeard falls dead from slashes and stab wounds that dehumanize him into a heap of human tissue. Symbolically the elevation of conflict from the blood-stained cellar to the castle roof illustrates the evolution of human conflict from dark basement barbarism to a principled battle against evil on the roof under the open sky. In the balance the salvation of a woman suggests that the higher motives of chivalry warrant combat against a bestial predator.

For its faulty depiction of women as helpless the rescue motif became a target of feminist writing, as in E. D. E. N. Southworth's *Capitola's Peril* (1859), the story of a cross-dressing self-rescuer, and in Christina ROSSETTI's girl-save-girl narrative *Goblin Market* (1862). In the words of Margaret ATWOOD, feminist author of the mythic *The Robber Bride* (1993): "FAIRY TALES have sometimes been faulted for the Handsome Prince Syndrome—for showing women as weak and witless and in need of rescue—but only some of them actually display this pattern" (Talese, 14). As Atwood implies, the survival of a tender, untried female naif from modern Gothic tradition boosts her to a new status as achiever and completer of a quest. Unlike shrinking violets of the Gothic bluebook, the new heroine blossoms into a mature adult capable of living in a world where the differences in male and female power and control move closer to a balance.

Two rebels against rescue plots were the Brontë sisters, stouthearted preacher's daughters who grew up on the English moors. Charlotte BRONTË upended familiar gender roles in *JANE EYRE* (1847), a landmark NEW WOMAN novel that allows Jane to mature, initiate a teaching career, and return to Edward Rochester, a lustful man who once offered to make her his mistress. Still in love with him, she saves him from the despair of a ruined estate and disabled body. Brontë caps the scene with Jane's famous summation, "Reader, I married him," a union that allows the wife equality in wedlock (Brontë, 429). For a more stirring pattern of rescue Charlotte's sister, Emily BRONTË, created outsized heroes in *WUTHERING HEIGHTS* (1847). Unlike Jane Eyre and Edward Rochester, neither Catherine EARNSHAW nor Heathcliff, the hero and heroine, has the power to retrieve the other from self-destruction. The novel unites them in limbo, ranging over the windy moors as wraiths bound in an eternal love. Publication of the novel spawned decades of criticism that grapples with the author's intent, which appears to charge passion itself as the villain.

The redemption of women in literature often hinges on the physical beauty and grace of the heroine. In an allegorical drama, *Love's Disguise* (ca. 1910), the playwright Alice DUNBAR-NELSON depicts the importance of beauty to a woman's reception by society and her success at job hunting. Agnes, the main character, astonishes onlookers with a beautiful face marred on one side. In a tableaulike sequence the response of others on first seeing her depends on which side of her face they view, a symbolic commentary on feminine DUALITY. A womanizer, Andy Layfield, offers marriage and taunts that his is the only proposal she will ever receive. To express the nature of true love, the play concludes with Agnes's loving treatment of the elderly mother of Dr. Weaver, who has no visual clue to Agnes's dual face. Because he recognizes inner qualities in Agnes, he restores her face through surgery and embraces her with real affection. Through a reversal of the BEAUTY MYTH the dramatist implies that Agnes deserves rescue and romance.

Feminist authors such as Julia ALVAREZ, Toni Cade BAMBARA, Barbara KINGSOLVER, and Toni MORRISON retain rescue but distribute it even-handedly between the genders. In 1980 Bambara affirmed the woman's role in rescuing other women in *The Salt Eaters*. In describing a low point in the life of the do-gooder Velma Henry, leader of a boy-

cott of city services, the author speaks through a circle of supporters. Palma urges, "Be cool. . . . Don't get overheated, Vee girl" (Bambara, 40). Ruby, the dispenser of situational wisdom, notes, "One monkey don't stop no show. Not one, not six. The struggle continues" (*ibid.*). Bambara's concept of woman-to-woman rescue is not a momentary grandstand but an ongoing process of shoring up sisters in need. Morrison achieves a similar sisterly deliverance in *BELOVED* (1987) through mutual aid to runaway slaves at Grandma Baby Suggs's way station on the north shore of the Ohio River. Kingsolver reprises the Underground Railroad motif in *The Bean Trees* (1988), in which a female tire dealer combs the desert in search of refugees in flight from Central American political upheaval. The repressive regime in Alvarez's historical novel *In the Time of the Butterflies* (1994) describes real sisters who bolster each other's daring as they pluck peasants from life-or-death situations.

Bibliography

Bambara, Toni Cade. *The Salt Eaters*. New York: Vintage, 1980.

Brontë, Charlotte. *Jane Eyre*. New York: Bantam Books, 1981.

Dunbar-Nelson, Alice. *The Works of Alice Dunbar-Nelson*. Oxford: Oxford University Press, 1994.

Estés, Clarissa Pinkola. *Women Who Run with the Wolves: Myths and Stories about the Wild Woman Archetype*. New York: Ballantine, 1997.

Roberts, Sherron Killingsworth. "The Female Rescuer in Newbery Fiction: Exploring the Archetype of Mother," *ALAN Review* 30, no. 1 (Fall 2002): 47–53.

Talese, Nan A. *Book Group Companion to Margaret Atwood's "The Robber Bride."* New York: Doubleday, 1993.

"Revolt of 'Mother,' The"   Mary Wilkins Freeman (1891)

Mary Wilkins FREEMAN's dialect parable "The Revolt of 'Mother' " honors the female anarchist for demolishing tyranny. The story of a feisty homemaker, it first appeared in an 1890 issue of *Harper's Bazaar* before being anthologized in *A New England Nun and Other Stories* (1891). Symbolically the action takes place in spring, a time for regeneration.

The first line opens on a call to "Father," the patriarchal family head. The protagonist, Sarah Penn, disconcerts her husband, Adoniram, with a direct question about his construction project, a guilty secret that causes his jaw to drop. Unshakable as stone entangled in blackberry vines, she challenges his theft of a plot of land intended for a new house. The absence of a parlor in their old house draws meaning from the French root word, *parler* (to talk), and from the implication that Adoniram silences his women by a deliberate and ongoing act of omission.

The narrative links developments in the Penn marriage to the daughter, Nanny's, idealization of her fiancé, George Eastman, a name ominously laden with the region's androcentrism. Sarah, an exemplary homemaker, models the devoted wife by rolling out pie dough for her husband's favorite, mince pie, a suggestion of the minced feelings that lie crusted over in her psyche. She informs Nanny that Adoniram "can't help it, 'cause he don't look at things jest the way we do" (Freeman, 452). While cautioning Nanny about stubborn mates, Sarah envisions the answer to her dilemma. Out of patience with menfolk, Sarah moves her household goods and children into the family's new barn and turns the harness room into a kitchen. After 40 years of marriage Sarah declares her INDEPENDENCE of mind control by ceding the title of "Mother" to embrace wholeness. By declaring the farm's livestock better housed than the family, she shames Adoniram, who is already influencing his son to adapt the same sneakiness and intransigence. In 1917 the author explained the differing gendered beliefs on the prioritizing of animal needs above those of agrarian families.

Freeman poses the immediate consequences of rebellion, a turn of events caused by a possessive male who returns home in his farm wagon like a proud Roman charioteer. Tight-lipped to the point of rudeness, Adoniram mutters, " 'I ain't got nothing' to say about it" and jerks harness on his bay mare, another female under his domination (*ibid.*, 455). Ironically a male rumormonger and an intrusive minister spread the news of Sarah's revolt. Among rural New Englanders the common misconception of willful women is that they must be mad or else criminal, but the author depicts suppressed yearning as Sarah's motivating force. In 1988 Amy Madigan played the role of Sarah Penn in a PBS film version, a segment of the series *The American Short Story Collection* that pictures the empowerment of a dormant female volcano.

Bibliography

Chiwengo, Ngwarsungu. "Renaming the World: Freeman's Revolt of Mother," *Academic Exchange Quarterly* 7, no. 2 (Summer 2003): 262–271.

Freeman, Mary Wilkins. *The New England Nun and Other Stories*. New York: Penguin, 2000.

Rhys, Jean (1890–1979)

The late-blooming Dominican-Scots-Welsh author Jean Rhys contributed a landmark novel to the study of plight and insanity in female characters. The granddaughter of a West Indian slave master, she was named Ella Gwendolen Rees Williams at her birth in Roseau, Dominica. Her observations of the joyous social freedom of black West Indians engendered sympathy with the colonial underdog. She regretted being reared among the white minority, a quality she shared with Antoinette Cosway, protagonist of her masterwork *WIDE SARGASSO SEA* (1966). Also like her heroine, Rhys studied at a convent academy during a period when the Lesser Antilles seethed with discontent and racial strife. In 1906 she entered Perse School, Cambridge, and pursued drama and acting at the Academy of Dramatic Art. After the death of her father, a physician, and the decline of family finances, she modeled, acted, and, during World War I, danced in a touring musical comedy, *Our Miss Gibbs*. After marriage to the Dutch-French journalist and lyricist Jean Lenglet, Rhys lived in Paris, Budapest, and Vienna.

The author Ford Madox Ford, a friend and lover who admired Rhys's subtle island sketches, encouraged her to submit a vignette, "Vienne" (1924), to the *Transatlantic Review* under her pseudonym. She collected short pieces in one volume, *The Left Bank and Other Stories* (1927), which her mentor introduced and edited. At age 39 she began publishing autobiographical novels—*Quartet* (1929), *After Leaving Mr. Mackenzie* (1930), *Voyage in the Dark* (1934), and *Good Morn-*

ing, Midnight (1939), a title she took from a poem by Emily DICKINSON. Aired on British Broadcasting Corporation (BBC) radio in 1957, the latter work is an introverted tale of diminished self-worth focusing on Sasha Jensen, a self-conscious victim of the BEAUTY MYTH. Among the Lost Generation of post–World War II Paris she muses on her plight, "When you've been made very cold and very sane you've also been made very passive (Why worry, why worry?)" (Rhys, 1986, 12). Distrusting the future, she lives out the expatriate insecurity and desperation that the author felt in cafés and on the streets.

In May 1949 Rhys was jailed for five days in the hospital of Holloway Prison for assault. She dropped from public attention until 1958. Until a reporter for the BBC located her Cornwall residence, she made good use of solitude during World War II by composing a major work of female gothic literature. The psychological novella, *WIDE SARGASSO SEA* (1966), is a fearful tale of loving and losing. The story takes place during a tense time after the emancipation of slaves, when blacks "still [waited] for this compensation the English promised when the Emancipation Act was passed" (Rhys, 1982, 17). They retaliate against former white slavers with covert plots and overt vengeance, which erupts into the burning of Coulibri, the Mason family's country home. Symbolically arson incinerates a structural reminder of white superiority at the expense of black slave labor.

Rhys set her revisionary story in Jamaica and based the plot on the colonial underpinnings of Charlotte BRONTË's *JANE EYRE* (1847). Rhys's prequel explains the pathetic madness of Antoinette, renamed Bertha Mason ROCHESTER, a raging monster spurned, drugged, removed from her home at Coulibi, and locked away in the third floor of Thornfield. The author validates the anger of the beautiful 17-year-old heiress, who enters an arranged marriage to Edward Rochester, an impecunious second son. His motives are monetary—the control of an inheritance derived from the cane sugar and rum trade. The willful Englishman feels threatened by the exuberance of Caribbean islanders and the sensuality of his bride. He justifies his honeymoon cruelties by claiming that the MADNESS of Antoinette's mother, Annette Cosway, is an inheritable condition. He returns from Granbois, their getaway cottage on Dominica, to the climate and milieu that he calls home. The bitter English weather, which bears little resemblance to Antoinette's fantasy, robs her of Caribbean hospitality and sunshine. In a marital snarl symbolized by the weedy Sargasso Sea, he thrusts her from sight and blots her from his mind.

The novella netted Rhys the Royal Society of Literature Award, W. H. Smith Award, Arts Council Bursary, Commander of Order of the British Empire, and a fellowship in the Royal Society of Literature. At her death in Exeter at age 89 of injuries caused by a fall, a fragmentary memoir, *Smile, Please: An Unfinished Autobiography* (1979), offered clues to her difficulties with loneliness, depression, insecurity, alcoholism, and suicidal tendencies. Feminists perceived the value of her writings to women's literature, particularly her treatment of PATRIARCHY, female economic dependence, and sexual exploitation. Collections of her stories and novels and *Letters of Jean Rhys, 1931–1966* (1984) increased public familiarity with the author's feminist themes. Ismael Merchant and James Ivory filmed *Quartet* in 1981, featuring a screenplay by Ruth Prawer JHABVALA and starring Isabelle Adjani, Maggie Smith, and Alan Bates. A Dutch film version of *Wide Sargasso Sea* appeared in 1992, featuring Rachel Ward and Michael York as the mismated Rochesters.

Bibliography

Angier, Carole. *Jean Rhys.* New York: Penguin, 1985.

Gregg, Veronica Marie. *Jean Rhys's Historical Imagination: Reading and Writing the Creole.* Chapel Hill: University of North Carolina Press, 1995.

Harrison, Nancy R. *Jean Rhys and the Novel as Women's Text.* Chapel Hill: University of North Carolina Press, 1988.

Kendrik, Robert. "Edward Rochester and the Margins of Masculinity in *Jane Eyre* and *Wide Sargasso Sea*," *Papers on Language and Literature* 30, no. 3 (Summer 1994): 235–256.

Rhys, Jean. *Good Morning, Midnight.* New York: W. W. Norton, 1986.

———. *Wide Sargasso Sea.* New York: W. W. Norton, 1982.

Rice, Anne (1941–)

The controversial Gothic fiction maven Anne O'Brien Rice also composes feminist plots that study vulnerable women at the mercy of exploitive men as well as deadly women who mastermind VIOLENCE. Named Howard Allen O'Brien at birth, she came of age in her native New Orleans and attended a convent school. The appeal of Catholic mysticism and hagiography remained with her into adulthood, when she used religious exoticism as a source for characters and themes. After her mother's death of alcoholism Rice abandoned orthodoxy and cultivated atheism. While enrolled at Texas Women's University, at age 20 she married Stan Rice, her high school sweetheart, who remained a devoted partner and critic until his death in 2001.

With a political science degree from San Francisco State University Rice initiated a phenomenally successful writing career in monster, witch, and vampire tales and erotic novels. She earned instant fame for *Interview with the Vampire* (1976), her foray into a male-dominated literary genre. She followed with the historical detective novel *Cry to Heaven* (1982), a story of young castrati in Renaissance Italy. One of Rice's most successful female characters, Akasha, is the title focus of *The Queen of the Damned* (1988), a mythic tale about the war of evil against good. Off-kilter from anger at abusive males, Akasha adopts their aberrant behavior: She rapes, tortures, and mutilates other women.

Influenced by the Gothic ambiguities in Mary Wollstonecraft SHELLEY's *Frankenstein* (1818) and Henry James's novella *The Turn of the Screw* (1898), Rice continued the intertwining of good and evil in women's lives through a lengthy perusal of conception, ABORTION, and birth. Fictional male-female relations illustrate the free will of women to accept the sexual advances of the villain and dramatize their sufferings from rough sex and betrayal. In 1990 she completed a 1,000-page faustian tale, *The Witching Hour*, the first of the Mayfair trilogy. Beneath the saga of a family of witches and operatic sorcery and sex is an examination of fetal tissue research and the male drive to dominate women and children. In an interview with *Newsweek* Rice acknowledged the layered meanings: "It could be simply about sexuality . . . or it could be about imagination: who's able to use it and who becomes a victim" (Gates, 76).

Under the pen name A. N. Roquelaure Rice branched out to carnal fantasy. She turned to feminist themes in the Sleeping Beauty trilogy, *The Claiming of Sleeping Beauty* (1983), *Beauty's Punishment* (1984), and *Beauty's Release* (1985), a series that draws on the BEAUTY MYTH and FAIRY TALES as well as sadomasochism for its plots. Probing female desire, the erotic fables recreate the mystery of the folk princess through hurtful encounters. The intensity of the episodes precipitated CENSORSHIP in the Lake Lanier Regional Library system in Gwinnett County, Georgia, and the Columbus, Ohio, Metropolitan Library. On April 28, 1996, the Columbus library director labeled the popular trio hard-core pornography and removed all print and audiocassette copies from the system's shelves. Rice intervened to rebut the director's accusations. The author defended the series as elegantly sensual, but harmless to characters and readers.

Battling conservative elements did not distract Rice from writing about female SEXUALITY. In *Belinda* (1986), a rhapsodic novel published under the pseudonym Anne Rampling, the author examines the allure of a modern Goldilocks. The 16-year-old model bewitches Jeremy Walker, a 44-year-old book illustrator who fantasizes about her provocative postures. Rice questions society's demands for safeguards of children's innocence by depicting the young runaway as a predator. The author balances the skewed morals of the story with real concerns for the fate of girls who earn their keep on the street. Her title character muses on the focal question: "How did the streets wear out girls, while boys passed through them? Why did girls lose, while boys won?" (Rampling, 318). From a brief experience on her own in urban settings Belinda wisely concludes that boys "had a kind of freedom that women just never seem to have" (*ibid.*).

Bibliography

Gates, David. "Queen of the Spellbinders," *Newsweek*, 5 November 1990, pp. 76–77.

Keller, James R. *Anne Rice and Sexual Politics: The Early Novels*. Jefferson, N.C.: McFarland, 2000.

Rampling, Anne. *Belinda*. New York: Berkley, 2000.

Rice, Anne. "How I Write," *Writer* 114, no. 2 (February 2001): 66.

Roquelaure, A. N. *Beauty's Punishment*. New York: Plume, 1984.

Smith, Jennifer. *Anne Rice: A Critical Companion*. Westport, Conn.: Greenwood, 1996.

Rich, Adrienne (1929–)

A stellar poet and forthright literary theorist, Adrienne Cecile Rich gives witness to female discontent and gives voice to muted females. A radical awakening to the unfair treatment of the poor, feminists, pacifists, and gays invigorates her prose and poetry. For each marginalized group she demands justice. A native of Baltimore, Maryland, and the elder daughter of a musician, Helen Elizabeth Jones, and a Jewish pathologist at Johns Hopkins University, Arnold Rice Rich, Adrienne studied at home under the control of her demanding father. In "Split at the Root: An Essay on Jewish Identity" (1982) she recalled, "We—my sister, mother, and I—were constantly urged to speak quietly in public, to dress without ostentation, to repress all vividness or spontaneity" to avoid being labeled " 'common' or 'Jewish' " (Rich, 1975, 231). Suppression remained alive in her thoughts for decades as she launched a crusade for female self-definition.

Well read in childhood, Rich claimed Charlotte and Emily BRONTË and Emily DICKINSON as her favorite authors and models. Rich first published at age 10. Her juvenilia include two plays, *Ariadne: A Play in Three Acts and Poems* (1939) and *Not I, Death* (1941). At age 22, she graduated Phi Beta Kappa from Radcliffe and won the Yale Younger Poets Prize for *A Change of World* (1951). The elegant poems bear the influence of Robert Frost, Wallace Stevens, and William Butler Yeats as well as W. H. Auden, who penned the introduction. The flicker of feminism in "Storm Warnings," "Living in Sin," "Aunt Jennifer's Tigers," and "An Unsaid Word" predicts the coming deluge of defiance and self-discovery.

Shortly after a diagnosis of rheumatoid arthritis Rich broke with her domineering father and wed a devout Jew, Alfred Haskell Conrad, a Har-vard economist. By age 30 she was the mother of three sons. After compiling some imitative verse in *The Diamond Cutters and Other Poems* (1955) and translating Dutch poetry while on a Guggenheim Fellowship, she surprised critics with *Snapshots of a Daughter-in-Law: Poems 1954–1962* (1963), which smolders with the rage and terror of losing her core self behind the bars of marriage and motherhood. Bereft of subtle ironies, the title poem uses visual immediacy to destroy misconceptions about women's stagnated lives. By following an Old South debutante as she advances from coy coquetry to individualism, the poem pauses on incidents of patriarchal torment and a slavish emulation of fashion. As the speaker allows her real persona to challenge the poseur, she flees patriarchal tyranny to redirect talents and energies formerly wasted on convention. Rich's next collection, *Necessities of Life* (1966), received a nomination for a National Book Award for detailing her fight against isolation and depression.

Resettled in New York City, Rich taught basic English to minority students at City College and promoted the works of such feminist authors as Tillie OLSEN. Rich aimed an urgent radicalism at feminist and racial issues and denounced the military quagmire in Vietnam with *Selected Poems* (1967), *Leaflets: Poems 1965–1968* (1969), and *The Will to Change: Poems 1969–1970* (1971), which features "The Burning of Paper Instead of Children." Liberated by divorce she published her most anthologized work in *Diving into the Wreck: Poems 1971–1972* (1973), a provocative collection that won a National Book Award. The collection satisfies the poet's pledge to fight militarism and bigotry. She joined her cowinners, Audre LORDE and Alice WALKER, in dedicating the prize money to Sisterhood of Black Single Mothers.

The poet acknowledged the dangers of bucking an androcentric system. The title work, "Diving into the Wreck," perceives feminism as the murky task of the deep-sea diver slipping into the sunken ruins. Steadying herself for serious work, she surveys the damage wreaked by long-lived myth and plunders the hulk for treasure, epitomized by the ship's female figurehead. Grasping at ANDROGYNY, a merger of gender strengths, she pledges herself to a truthful view of the future. The plunge is not without its perils, as Rich recalls from the example of reporter and children's book author Meridel LE SUEUR, whom the Federal Bureau of Investigation (FBI) hounded and employers blacklisted. Despite McCarthy era politics, Le Sueur remained famous for children's FRONTIER LITERATURE, notably *Nancy Hanks of Wilderness Road: A Story of Abraham Lincoln's Mother* (1949), in which Lincoln's grandmother laments that no one treasures the stories of women's lives.

While on staff at City College and later at Rutgers, Rich issued *When We Dead Awaken: Writing as Re-Vision* (1972) and *Of Woman Born: Motherhood as Experience and Institution* (1976), two autobiographical prose works challenging proponents of strict female adherence to traditional marriage. *On Lies, Secrets and Silence: Selected Prose 1966–1978* (1979) shed a harsh light on the truths of women's torments. Recalling the asphyxiation deaths of Sylvia PLATH and Anne SEXTON, Rich lashed out, "We have had enough suicidal women poets, enough suicidal women, enough of self-destructiveness as the sole form of violence permitted to women" (Rich, 1979, 122). As a handhold on survival, she urged women to immunize themselves against self-killing by rechanneling compassion for others to their own needs.

In *Compulsory Heterosexuality and Lesbian Existence* (1980) Rich made a final break with the past by announcing her sexual preference. She outlined the intent of male power to deny women's true SEXUALITY, to confine women and force them to satisfy male lust, to cramp women's creativity and control their productivity, to use them as collateral, to steal their children, and to prohibit female cultural attainment. In *A Wild Patience Has Taken Me This Far: Poems 1978–1981* (1981), *Sources* (1984), and *The Fact of a Doorframe: Poems Selected and New 1950–1984* (1984), she reprises past themes advocating acceptance for society's most marginalized people, including Ethel Rosenberg, an alleged spy whom the federal government electrocuted for treason. After learning that Rosenberg suffered the treachery of her mother and sister and that she sang a prostitute to sleep at the Women's House of Detention, the poet asks if Rosenberg would have taken pity on other females condemned for murder (*ibid.*, 97).

Rich and her partner, the poet and historian Michelle Cliff, settled in western Massachusetts, where the poet edited the pro-woman, pro-lesbian journal *Sinister Wisdom* and cofounded *Bridges: A Journal for Jewish Feminists and Our Friends*. In *Your Native Land, Your Life* (1986), *Time's Power: Poems 1985–1988* (1989), and *An Atlas of the Difficult World: Poems 1988–1991* (1991), winner of the *Los Angeles Times* Book Prize and runner-up for a National Book Critics Circle honorarium, Rich developed a more personal focus through confrontations with her father's spirit and with anti-Semitism. After accepting the Poetry Society of America Frost Silver Medal, she completed *What Is Found There: Notebooks on Poetry and Politics* (1993), which spotlights male-on-female violence. She carried her call for gender freedom to posts at Swarthmore, Bryn Mawr, Columbia, Brandeis, Rutgers, Cornell, San Jose State, Scripps College, and Stanford, a campaign that netted her numerous honorary degrees and the National Gay Task Force's Human Dignity Award. Rich's poetry has influenced a generation of writers, including Olga BROUMAS and Sharon OLDS.

Bibliography

Atwood, Margaret. "Review: *Diving into the Wreck*," *New York Times Book Review,* 30 December 1973, pp. 161–162.

Montenegro, David. "Interview," *American Poetry Review* 20, no. 1 (January–February 1991): 7–14.

Rich, Adrienne. *Adrienne Rich's Poetry and Prose*. New York: W. W. Norton, 1975.

———. *On Lies, Secrets, and Silence: Selected Prose, 1966–1978*. New York: W. W. Norton, 1979.

Roberts, Dmae (ca. 1964–   )

The Asian-American dramatist, actor, educator, and journalist Dmae Roberts promotes awareness of female accomplishments, particularly those of nonwhite women. She was born in Taiwan to a Southern Baptist father and a Taiwanese war bride and mill worker. While growing up in the farm town of Eugene, Oregon, she felt alienated because of her biracial background. After hearing a segment of *All Things Considered*, she began her radio career in 1984 while studying print journalism in college. She freelanced some 400 features, audio collages, and documentaries for National Public Radio and Public Radio International. Eager to entertain and inform, she volunteered to work at KLCC, a public station in Eugene. Her credo accounts for her interest in inclusion and plural culture: "It's important for all voices to be heard. Every culture has something very unique to say, and offering individuals a chance to express their thoughts and feelings in a creative way is an act of empowerment and a contribution to society" (Nelson, 1).

Roberts's enthusiasm translated to teaching at the Northwest Children's Theatre. She flourished as an educator at Young Audiences of Oregon, the Interstate Firehouse Cultural Center's Neighborhood Youth Theatre Project, Tygres Heart Shakespeare Company, Binnsmead Middle School's English as a second language (ESL) Program, Neighborhood Arts Program, and the Gang Resistance Education and Training team. Among her literary achievements are a female rock musical parody, *Janie Bigo* (1997); a 13-part broadcast, *Legacies: Tales from America* (1998); and the Heart of America Award winner *Legacies: Faith, Hope and Peace* (1998). Her promotion of pluralism over radio won her the Robert F. Kennedy Journalism Award, a Casey Medal, a National Lesbian and Gay Journalists Award, and a United Nations Silver Award.

Compared to Maxine Hong KINGSTON's *The Woman Warrior* (1975) and Amy TAN's *The Kitchen God's Wife* (1991), Roberts's masterly play *Mei Mei: A Daughter's Song* (1990), winner of the George Foster Peabody Award, characterizes family turbulence derived from toxic memories. The daughter elicits from her mother the painful account of being sold into slavery by her parents. The candid description of a tenuous mother-daughter relationship appeals to a variety of ethnic groups, including African-American, German, Irish, Italian, Latino, and Polish as well as Asian. Modeled on the author's mother, Chu-Yin Roberts, the proud main character returned in a sequel, *The Journey of Lady Buddha* (1998), a tribute to matriarchal TALK-STORY and to GODDESS LORE about Kuan Yin, the mythic dispenser of compassion and mercy. In 1996 the author won a Portland Drama Critics Circle Award for *Picasso in the Back Seat*. She returned to

her mother's biography with *The Breast Cancer Monologues* (2004), a perusal of the effects of surgery and chemotherapy on American women.

Bibliography

Lai, Tracy A. M. "Janie Bigo," *International Examiner,* 20 May 1997, p. 18.

Ma, Sheng-mei. *Immigrant Subjectivities in Asian American and Asian Diaspora Literature.* Albany: State University of New York Press, 1998.

Nelson, Sean. "Legacies: Faith, Hope and Peace: Radio Documentaries Explore What Moves the Human Spirit," *Asian Reporter,* 14 December 1998, p. 1.

Roberts, Dmae. *The Breast Cancer Monologues.* New York: MediaRites, 2004.

———. *The Journey of Lady Buddha.* New York: Media-Rites, 1998.

———. *Mei Mei: A Daughter's Song.* New York: Media-Rites, 1990.

Robinson, Harriet Jane (1825–1911)

A working-class feminist, Harriet Jane Hanson Robinson wrote and spoke forcefully on the degradation of New England mill girls. A Bostonian, she and her three siblings were left fatherless when she was six. Her mother sold candy and firewood to maintain the family in a one-room flat, where they slept in one bed. Four years later Robinson began working in a mill in Lowell, Massachusetts, to supplement her mother's income as company boarding-house manager. The author received only three months' education each year while she labored in the weaving room for 14 hours a day. At age 23 she married the abolitionist William Stevens Robinson, a news editor, politician, and founder of the *Lowell American.* She developed into an outspoken defender of WOMEN'S RIGHTS and SUFFRAGE and involved herself in the women's club movement. Under the influence of Susan B. ANTHONY and Elizabeth Cady STANTON, Robinson and her daughter, Harriette Robinson Shattuck, founded the Massachusetts branch of the National American Woman Suffrage Association. The author also testified before Congress to the need for gender equity.

Robinson came late to professional writing, beginning with *Warrington: Pen Portraits* (1877), an anthology of her husband's writings. In 1881 she delivered a keynote address to the Boston convention of the National Woman Suffrage Association. Robinson achieved critical significance for a history, *Massachusetts in the Woman Suffrage Movement* (1883), one of the first scholarly chronicles of the women's rights movement. The text lauds Sarah Moore GRIMKÉ for her skill at answering critics and praises Margaret FULLER for her reasoned arguments for making women first-class citizens. Robinson noted the improvement in public and press attitude toward women's rights conventions and credited the publication of a women's journal initiated in the 1840s, the *Lowell Offering*, which was the world's first magazine produced entirely by women. In addition, she penned two feminist plays, *Captain Mary Miller* (1887), which depicts a woman's venture from housekeeping to piloting Mississippi River boats, and *The New Pandora* (1889), a women's rights drama.

At age 73 Robinson composed a labor memoir, *Loom and Spindle; or, Life among the Early Mill Girls* (1898), which describes Lowell as a key manufacturing community where female workers were three times more numerous than males. To keep the mills running, recruiters scoured New England and Canada for bright, industrious girls. The exposé of economic hardship describes how the fee for room and board reduced female loom keepers' wages to about two dollars per week, which was six times the wages of domestics and teachers. She characterized the decline of mill conditions as faster machines required each worker to superintend more production. Contributing to losses were Irish, Italian, and Polish immigrants who competed with local girls for jobs. In October 1836, between 1,200 and 1,500 girls mounted a strike, one of the first in the nation, because mill owners rescinded their one-dollar-per-month stipend for room and board. The workers sang union songs while processing down the street. Although she was only 11 years old at the time, Robinson concluded, "I was more proud than I have ever been since at any success I may have achieved, and more proud than I shall ever be again until my own beloved State gives to its women citizens the right of suffrage" (Robinson, 1976, 85).

Bibliography

Lerner, Gerda. *The Feminist Thought of Sarah Grimké.* Oxford: Oxford University Press, 1998.

Robinson, Harriet. *Loom and Spindle.* Pacifica, Calif.: Press Pacifica, 1976.

———. *Massachusetts in the Woman Suffrage Movement* (1883). Available online. URL: http://www.assumption.edu/whw/old/Massachusetts%20in%20the%20woman.html. Accessed on October 17, 2005.

Robinson, Marilynne (1947–)

The novelist, investigative reporter, and essayist Marilynne Robinson combines scholarship and intuitive feminism in the ongoing debate on humanistic issues. A native of Sandpoint, Idaho, she grew up in northwestern towns within a Bible-reading matriarchal clan. On the advice of a Latin teacher at Coeur d'Alene High School she read Herman Melville's *Moby-Dick* for its intellectual challenge. She earned a degree in religion from Brown University, which formalized her agnosticism and a retreat from godly writings. After teaching in Rennes, France, at the Université de Haute Bretagne, she completed a Ph.D. in English literature at the University of Washington.

In Robinson's feminist novel *Housekeeping* (1981), winner of the P. E. N./Ernest Hemingway Foundation Award and Pulitzer Prize, the protagonist, Ruth Stone, speaks the unsheltered nonwhite's delight in experience that strengthens her, easing the way through a harsh environment and pervasive mother need. In a state of longing Ruth takes as a bulwark Aunt Sylvie, an eccentric migrant worker, who becomes as dear to Ruth as a mother, much as the biblical Ruth finds solace in her mother-in-law, Naomi. Ruth Stone explains, "We are the same, she could as well be my mother. I crouched and slept in her very shape like an unborn child" (Robinson, 1982, 145). When the sheriff of Fingerbone, Idaho, threatens to separate the two, Ruth experiences the security of the womanly bond: "That night . . . we were almost a single person" (*ibid.*, 209). The novel was a vehicle for the actor Christine Lahti, who starred in Columbia Pictures's austere 1988 version of *Housekeeping.*

Robinson's second book, *Mother Country: Britain, the Welfare State and Nuclear Pollution* (1989), a finalist for the National Book Award, created a stir for its pragmatic views on ECOFEMINISM. She raised controversy by denouncing Greenpeace and by charging the British government with mishandling plutonium at the Sellafield plant and dumping nuclear wastes into the sea. As a result her critics suppressed the book in England. Lacking an income after her husband left her, she submitted a flurry of articles and reviews to *Christian Century*, *Harper's*, the *New Yorker*, the *New York Times Book Review*, *Paris Review*, *Social Research*, *Theology Today*, *Wilson Quarterly*, and *Yale Review*. She returned to the classroom at Amherst, Skidmore, and the Universities of Kent and Massachusetts before joining the staff of the University of Iowa Writers' Workshop.

Robinson's interests in humanitarian outreach and public welfare permeate her works. In an article for *Christian Century* she remarks on 19th-century labor's hardships on females and children: "We tend to forget that women of working age were often pregnant or nursing and often obliged to leave infants and small children unattended" (Robinson, "The Way," 826). Her choice of details built a case for compassion: "Sometimes [female workers] gave birth on the factory floor. Children of working age— that is, as young as five—were spared no hardship" (*ibid.*). In an essay for the *Wilson Quarterly* she laments the unaddressed health needs among the poor, "who are malnourished and unsheltered and grossly vulnerable to disease" (Robinson, "Surrendering," 62). Her pro-family, pro-Earth writings, sonorous with biblical morality, have earned a place in American scholarship for their clarity and vision.

In 2005, some 25 years after publication of her first novel, Robinson won the Pulitzer Prize for *Gilead* (2004), a gentle family saga.

Bibliography

Galehouse, Maggie. "Their Own Private Idaho: Transience in Marilynne Robinson's *Housekeeping*," *Contemporary Literature* 41, no. 1 (Spring 2000): 117–137.

Kalfopoulou, Adrianne. *A Discussion of the Ideology of the American Dream in the Culture's Female Discourses.* Lewiston, N.Y.: Edwin Mellen Press, 2000.

Robinson, Marilynne. *Housekeeping.* New York: Bantam, 1982.

———. *Mother Country.* New York: Farrar, Straus & Giroux, 1989.

———. "Surrendering Wilderness," *Wilson Quarterly* 22, no. 4 (Autumn 1998): 60–64.

———. "The Way We Work, the Way We Live," *Christian Century*, 9 September 1998, pp. 823–831.

Schaub, Robert. "An Interview with Marilynne Robinson," *Contemporary Literature* 35, no. 2 (Summer 1994): 230–250.

Robinson, Mary (1758–1800)

A star of the late romantic era, Mary Darby Robinson excelled at Gothic fiction, translation, essay, and feminist verse. Her pro-woman writings earned the praise of Charlotte Dacre, Samuel Taylor Coleridge, and Mary Wollstonecraft SHELLEY. Born to a British teacher and an American whaler, Robinson studied at female academies in Bristol, Chelsea, and Marylebone before marrying Thomas Robinson, a law clerk who wooed her with false claims of inherited wealth. In her late teens, when the couple and their infant daughter were remanded to 10 months' prison time for debt, she wrote a two-volume verse anthology, published by a patron, Georgiana Spencer Cavendish, the duchess of Devonshire. In 1776 Robinson accepted the tutelage of David Garrick and performed in 30 plays at Drury Lane, which included the Shakespearean figures of Cordelia, Juliet, LADY MACBETH, and Perdita, her signature role. During a heady year as mistress of the future George IV she achieved a modicum of financial INDEPENDENCE as well as fame for her beauty, wit, and stagecraft.

Robinson abandoned her stage career after a miscarriage and the onset of rheumatic fever paralyzed her legs. In addition to coediting the *Morning Post*, she supported herself by freelancing verse drama, narrative poems, and historical fiction that championed women's liberation. Her best-selling seduction novel *Vancenza; or, The Dangers of Credulity* (1792) appealed to English, French, and German readers in part because of her notoriety. She reprised the woman's view of seduction and abandonment in *The False Friend, a Domestic Story* (1799). In the spirit of romanticism she championed the underdog with "The Negro Girl" and honored the decapitated French queen Marie Antoinette in 1793 with a verse eulogy and the famed Greek poet with a sonnet sequence, *Sappho and Phaon* (1796). The last of her eight novels, *The*

Natural Daughter: with Portraits of the Leadenhead Family (1799), recalls the ebullience and liberalism of the French Revolution.

Robinson remained faithful to women's concerns. She summarized feminist issues in *Letter to the Women of England, on the Cruelties of Mental Subordination* (1799), a radical polemic decrying gender inequities. A major achievement is the four-volume posthumous AUTOBIOGRAPHY, *Memoirs of the Late Mrs. Robinson* (1801), which enjoyed popularity in English and in translation for its candor about the difficulties of being a female artist. Upon the staging of her little farce *Nobody* (1793) audience response expressed gender prejudice: "Even women of distinguished rank hissed through their fans" (Robinson, 223). However, she was delighted that "the more rational part of the audience seemed inclined to hear before they passed judgment, and, with a firmness that never fails to awe, demanded that the piece should proceed" (*ibid.*).

The author's works continued to flourish after her death. Maria Elizabeth Robinson collected her mother's poems for an anthology, *The Wild Wreath* (1804); Richard Phillips issued a comprehensive three-volume collection in 1806. Two of Robinson's best poems, "January, 1795" and "London's Summer Morning," extend realistic views of upper- and lower-class females mopping, shopping in a boutique, gambling, navigating the tricky subculture of kept women, and trying to make a living as writers. A more poignant image of elderly women earning their keep appeared as "The Poor Singing Dame," which pictures the inmate Mary dying in prison and then returning to haunt the self-important lord who ordered her incarceration.

Bibliography

Bolton, Betsy. "Romancing the Stone: 'Perdita' Robinson in Wordsworth's London," *ELH* 64, no. 3 (Fall 1997): 727–759.

Luther, Susan. "A Stranger Minstrel: Coleridge's Mrs. Robinson," *Studies in Romanticism* 33, no. 3 (Fall 1994): 391–409.

McGann, Jerome. "Mary Robinson and the Myth of Sappho," *Modern Language Quarterly* 56, no. 1 (March 1995): 55–76.

Robinson, Mary. *Memoirs of Mary Robinson* (1895). Available online. URL: http://digital.library.upenn. edu/women/robinson/memoirs/memoirs.html. Accessed on October 17, 2005.

Setzer, Sharon. "Mary Robinson's Sylphid Self: The End of Feminine Self-Fashioning," *Philological Quarterly* 75, no. 4 (Fall 1996): 501–520.

———. "Romancing the Reign of Terror: Sexual Politics in Mary Robinson's 'Natural Daughter,'" *Criticism* 39, no. 4 (Fall 1997): 531–550.

Rochester, Bertha Mason

In *JANE EYRE* (1847) the novelist Charlotte BRONTË establishes ongoing contrasts between her heroine and Edward Rochester's wife, Bertha Antoinetta Mason Rochester, a beautiful Jamaican heiress of a planter. The Creole child of an alcoholic slave owner and his wife, she lives in Spanish Town and awaits an arranged marriage. When Edward meets her, he is unaware that she is tainted by kinship with "a mad family; idiots and maniacs through three generations!" (Brontë, 277). The lacklogic overlap between mental illness and genetic defect illustrates the era's primitive notions of brain and behavior disorders. After Edward courts and marries her in a hurried, loveless nuptial, he transports the bride and her wealth to his estate, Thornfield, the ominous name of his manor on the English moors. In the first four years of their union her mind succumbs to inherited dementia; she shrieks inchoate obscenities that express her hatred. Edward epitomizes the genetic lapse as a female failing—"germs of insanity" passed from Creole mother to daughter (*ibid.*, 334). The onset of MADNESS costs her the role of wife and mistress of the manor and, eventually, her beauty and humanity. As a condemnation of the husband in search of a trophy bride, the author makes no mention of medical diagnosis or treatment to ease Bertha's decline.

The motif of CONFINEMENT manifests the era's lack of sympathy for mentally unbalanced patients, especially women, who wither and lose their charm from too close a tethering to the home scene. For the next 11 years Edward wanders Europe in search of sexual release while restraining Bertha in the third-floor suite under the control of a tippling keeper, Grace Poole. Ironically the lowly job of warder falls to a female employee, who shares the apartment with her charge. Cut off from family and the Caribbean sun and sea breezes, Bertha grows inward, a spider enmeshed in her web. She stokes her anger at Edward, a model of the white slaver. In marital bondage Bertha evolves into the inarticulate, unsexed "maniac upstairs," a hint at the cost to passionate women of Victorian repression and strait-laced propriety (*ibid.*, 301). As a night stalker, she awaits the right moment for vengeance, thus suggesting that her thinking ability is not blunted by psychosis. One of her first victims is Richard Mason, Bertha's half brother, who conspired in the arranged marriage that gave the bride no choice but to comply with the family's wishes.

Brontë uses Bertha as a vehicle for Gothicism and as a moral double of Edward, the sin-ridden libertine and despoiler of women. To build suspense, the author pictures the madwoman outwitting Grace and lurking outside the room of Jane EYRE, Edward's governess and bride-to-be. Brontë dramatizes Bertha's guile in marring only the wedding veil, the symbolic covering that shields Jane from complicity in the fraudulent marriage and prevents her from discerning the truth about Edward's living arrangements and duplicity. The ripped covering also indicates Brontë's intent to shred the hypocrisy of marriage, which ruins one woman's life and sends another fleeing onto the moors to suffer as Christ did in the desert. As the "blackaviced" avenger, Bertha dominates chapter 26, the climactic point, when Richard halts a felonious marriage and forces Edward to admit to attempted bigamy (*ibid.*, 247). Without sympathy for Bertha, Brontë displays a bestial figure: "What it was, whether beast or human being, one could not, at first sight, tell: it grovelled, seemingly, on all fours; it snatched and growled like some strange wild animal" (*ibid.*, 278). The shapeless garb and "a quantity of dark, grizzled hair, wild as a mane, [that] hid its head and face" further demean Bertha while casting ignominy on Edward for tormenting her (*ibid.*).

The theme of sacrifice and redemption demands the fiery death of the mad wife in a fall from the roof to the pavement below, a further devaluation. The flames end the contretemps by extricating Bertha from a living death and by ridding Edward of an obstacle to matrimony. The removal of the madwoman costs him his patrimony and causes "one eye [to be] knocked out, and one hand so crushed" as to require amputation (*ibid.*, 549). At the Rochester Arms Jane learns from a witness that Bertha spread the fire and killed herself "dead as the stones on which her brains and blood were scattered" (*ibid.*, 410). FEMINIST CRITICISM analyzes the thorny issue of the innocent victim as a homesick wretch who chooses her own demise rather than live in misery. Another view of Bertha's death is the symbolic end to female SILENCING and the erasure of colonial crimes in the West Indies through the duping of Edward into marrying a mental defective. From the perspective of women's art Bertha vents the Victorian female's repressed rage at the lack of outlets for her talents. Further explanations of Bertha's pitiable decline derive from the novelist Jean RHYS's woman-centered novel *WIDE SARGASSO SEA* (1966), a prequel that stirred a new era of debate about Brontë's intent.

Bibliography

Beattie, Valerie. "The Mystery at Thornfield: Representations of Madness in *Jane Eyre*," *Studies in the Novel* 28, no. 4 (Winter 1996): 493–505.

Brontë, Charlotte. *Jane Eyre*. New York: Bantam Books, 1981.

Meyer, Susan. "Colonialism and the Figurative Strategy of *Jane Eyre*," *Victorian Studies* 33, no. 2 (1990): 247–268.

Thomas, Sue. "The Tropical Extravagance of Bertha Mason," *Victorian Literature and Culture* 27 (1999): 1–17.

Room of One's Own, A Virginia Woolf (1929)

A seminal work of feminist criticism, Virginia WOOLF's essay *A Room of One's Own* confronts the suppression of women as thinkers and writers. In late October 1928 in a series of heart-to-heart first-person addresses to a female audience at Newnham and Girton Colleges, two female colleges at Cambridge University, Woolf delivered "Women and Fiction," the kernel of *A Room of One's Own*. In the introduction she tosses out a poser: "Are you aware that you are, perhaps, the most discussed animal in the universe?" (Woolf, 1957, 26). To focus on the need for female self-expression, she pictures autonomy as space—rooms free of domestic intrusions in which women can actualize their creative urges. In addition to physical freedom, women require a more difficult aspiration, their monetary liberation from father and husband.

Selecting as models of feminist excellence Aphra BEHN, Charlotte and Emily BRONTË, George ELIOT, Anne FINCH, and George SAND, Woolf honors women who follow their true nature outside the bounds of society and culture. Woolf thanks her aunt, Mary Seton, for willing her £500 per year, enough money to free Woolf "to think of things in themselves" (*ibid.*, 39). Giddy with liberty, she projects her experience on all women and predicts, "Anything may happen when womanhood has ceased to be a protected occupation" (*ibid.*, 41). She proposes a scientific study of the harm of sequestering on women to measure "the effect of discouragement upon the mind of the artist" (*ibid.*, 54). She challenges female authors to practice integrity of thought by shutting out "that persistent voice, now grumbling, now patronising, now domineering, now grieved, now shocked, now angry, now avuncular, that voice which cannot let women alone, but must be at them" (*ibid.*, 78). The sincere annoyance in her words attests to her own experience with male critics.

Central to Woolf's campaign for female creativity is her insistence that women be educated. Instead of training that forces them to write and think as men do, she demands, "Ought not education to bring out and fortify the differences rather than the similarities?" (*ibid.*, 91). She urges women to rid themselves of gender consciousness and to plumb their soul for the depths, strengths, and beauties that make them unique. She exhorts the beginner to prove that women "are very serious, very profound and very humane underneath" (*ibid.*, 95). By focusing on ANDROGYNY in the mind, her ideal writer, whom she identifies as William Shakespeare's sister, can explode obstacles to articulate a panoply of new and intriguing ideas. In 1997 the actor Eileen Atkins dramatized Woolf's famous essay as a one-woman show, *Virginia Woolf: A Room of One's Own*, which Films for the Humanities and Sciences recorded at the original lecture hall at Girton College, Cambridge.

Bibliography

Hussey, Mark. "A Woman Writer for the 1990s—Women and Fiction: The Manuscript Versions of *A Room of One's Own* by Virginia Woolf," *Belles Lettres* 7, no. 4 (Summer 1992): 69.

Woolf, Virginia. *A Room of One's Own*. New York: Harbinger, 1957.

Rose, Wendy (1948–)

The author, artist, teacher, and ethnographer Wendy Rose ventures into the Native American past to re-create scenes and dreamscapes of female tribal traditions. Born Bronwen Elizabeth Edwards in Oakland, California, she claims Hopi-Miwok-Scots-Irish-German heritage but is uncertain of her paternity. After dropping out of high school and briefly attending Cabrillo College and Contra Costa College, she earned cultural anthropology degrees at the University of California at Berkeley, where she later taught ethnic and Indian studies. From her first publication, *Hopi Roadrunner Dancing* (1973), she progressed to collected verse in *Long Division: A Tribal History* (1976), *Academic Squaw: Reports to the World from the Ivory Tower* (1977), *Poetry of the American Indian* (1978), and *Builder Kachina: A Home-Going Cycle* (1979). For *Lost Copper* (1980), a perusal of identity, Rose won a Pulitzer Prize nomination. She supplied original watercolor drawings for her next anthologies, *What Happened When the Hopi Hit New York* (1982) and *The Halfbreed Chronicles and Other Poems* (1985).

At Fresno College Rose edited the *American Indian Quarterly* while she submitted poems to *Contra Costa Advocate*, *Early American*, *Janus*, *Journal of California Anthropology*, *Many Smokes*, and *San Francisco Bay Guardian*. Late in the 20th century she wrote *Going to War with All My Relations: New and Selected Poems* (1993) and *Bone Dance: New and Selected Poems, 1965–1993* (1994), an irate denunciation of the selling of Native arts and skeletons. In the ode "Truganinny" a female Tasmanian has reason to fear that her remains will become a museum exhibit. More poignant is the reduction of a Mexican-Indian woman to a sideshow freak in the dramatic monologue "Julia." The focus is an appeal for help from Julia Pastrana, called "Lion Lady" because of her extreme hairiness. A white manager, whom she marries, fattens his wallet on the proceeds of her suffering. He saves her body and that of her stillborn infant for stuffing as circus attractions.

In *Now Poof She Is Gone* (1994) Rose exhibits uncertainty about her multicultural ancestry. She empathizes with the rootless female in "What Debris-Woman Needs" with suggestions of rape and the Native American's angry backlash against European exploitation: The poem "No One Is as Lost as This Indian Woman" addresses the muting of the female voice. The poet concludes that re-pressed words lead to spiritual emptiness: Referring to androcentric wars that displaced indigenous peoples from their homeland, she charges that the source of VIOLENCE is greed.

Rose accepts the role of the poet as story keeper and dispenser of truths. Her free verse scorns American histories that glaze over the genocide of the Indian Wars. Concerning the value of family STORYTELLING she advised in an in-terview: "If people have some ideas about where they come from, if they go to those places, they can listen for those voices. If there are family heir-looms, they can listen for those voices there" ("In-terview," 30). Of her consciousness of ill treatment she regrets: "With my relations around me, I go into mourning" ("Without," 26). Rose boldly con-fronts her tormentors with a pledge to keep on telling her story to sustain Native American issues dating from colonial times (*ibid.*).

Bibliography

Dame, Enid. "Reclaiming a Culture through Poems," *Belles Lettres* 10, no. 1 (Fall 1994): 87.

"An Interview with Wendy Rose," *News from Native Cal-ifornia* 17, no. 1 (Fall 2003): 30.

Rose, Wendy. *Now Poof She Is Gone.* New York: Fire-brand, 1994.

"Without Discovery: A Native Response to Columbus," *The Circle: News from an American Indian Perspec-tive,* 9 September 1999, p. 26.

Ross, Ishbel (1895–1975)

The biographer, novelist, and newspaper reporter Ishbella Margaret Ross chose worthy women as her subject. A native Scot from the Isle of Skye, she and her five brothers lived in a conservative home and enjoyed affluence after their father invented Drambuie liqueur. While studying at the Tain Royal Academy, she taught herself to write by scouring libraries for reading material composed by female authors. In 1915 she settled in Ontario and joined the staff of the *Toronto Daily News* as a clerk filing clippings. On March 11, 1916, she proved her acumen in a front-page interview with the mil-itant feminist Emmeline PANKHURST entitled "Women Will Win the War." The public statement cost Pankhurst more jailings and spawned hunger strikes among her supporters.

As Ross's career moved into the global arena of war and politics, she became the first Canadian newspaperwoman to travel by plane. She re-ported war news of the Balkan front from Sa-lonika, Serbia. Her valuable diary of events from the period remains on view in London at the Im-perial War Museum. By age 24 she advanced to a demanding job as the first female reporting for the *New York Tribune.* Over a 15-year career her newspaper beats ranged from murders and scan-dals, the White House, and the kidnap of Anne and Charles Lindburgh's baby to the activism of suffragists.

Teamed with her journalist husband, Bruce Rae of the *New York Times,* Ross continued to work in journalism until age 40, when she reared a daughter while writing best-selling fiction and biography. She surveyed women's expertise at media reporting in *Ladies of the Press: The Story of Women in Journalism by an Insider* (1936), the first history of female jour-nalists. Of the rise from jobs as diverse as domestics, dance-hall girls, stenographers, nurses, and shop clerks, the text remarks: "Some have wandered into the profession by accident; others have battered their way in; a few have simply walked in the front door without knocking" (Ross, 1936, 12). Ross characterized the gamut of female lives in *Charmers and Cranks: Twelve Famous American Women Who Defied Conventions* (1965), which incorporates the dances of Isadora Duncan with the suffragism of Victoria WOODHULL, TEMPERANCE demonstrations of Carry Nation, and the investigative reportage of Nelly BLY.

In 20 single-subject biographies Ross again favored notable females—the nurse Clara Barton, the physician and nurse educator Elizabeth BLACKWELL, the Confederate spy "Rebel Rose" O'Neal, the singer Lola Montez, and the first ladies Varina Howell Davis and Mary Todd Lincoln, whom the author honored in *The President's Wife: Mary Todd Lincoln* (1973). In 1975 Ross reported on the life of Edith Wilson in *Power with Grace: The Life Story of Mrs. Woodrow Wilson*, which discusses the first lady's governing position as spokeswoman for her ailing husband. By focusing on presidents' wives, Ross revealed the sacrifice of women who live out periods of personal tragedy and national concern in the eye of the media. The motif pioneered interest in female celebrity that extends to current times.

Bibliography

Merrick, Beverly G. "Reversal of Fortunes, Ishbel Ross Interviews Emmeline Pankhurst: The Cadence of Civilian and Military Career Choices in a Changing Economy," *Global Competitiveness* 10, no. 1 (2002): 400–418.

Ross, Ishbel. *Crusades and Crinolines.* New York: Harper & Row, 1963.

———. *Ladies of the Press.* New York: Harper & Brothers, 1936.

———. *The President's Wife: Mary Todd Lincoln.* New York: G. P. Putnam's Sons, 1973.

———. *Sons of Adam, Daughters of Eve: The Role of Women in American History.* New York: Harper & Row, 1969.

Rossetti, Christina (1830–1894)

The bilingual sonneteer and devotional poet Christina Georgina Rossetti created pictorial verse that extols SISTERHOOD and seraphic femininity while revealing the social and spiritual burdens of misogyny. The London-born sister of the poet and painter Dante Gabriel Rossetti and the essayist Maria Francesca Rossetti, Christina compiled poetry anthologies in English and Italian in girlhood and published under the pseudonym Ellen Alleyne in *Athenaeum* and *Macmillan* magazines and later in *Century* and *Churchman's Shilling Magazine*. One of her early verses, "Song" (1848), professes no expectations of undying love in her instructions "Sing no sad songs for me" (Rossetti, 1993, 36). In her view of a dreamy afterlife she remarks, "Haply I may remember, / And haply may forget" (*ibid.*). The following year she envisioned herself as a corpse in "After Death" (1849), in which she dissociates herself from an earthly love who is capable of only pity for her loss. Looking back on his weeping, she treasures his limited emotion as "very sweet" (*ibid.*, 37). Another poem, "The World" (1854), indicates the struggle the poet had by night in suppressing physical desires.

Rossetti was an energetic, multitalented woman. In addition to posing for her brother's Pre-Raphaelite oil paintings, in 1855 she worked as a governess until frail health curtailed her employment. She published "In an Artist's Studio" (1857), a lyric depiction of Ovid's Pygmalion myth in which the painter falls victim to his IDEAL WOMAN. She examines herself in a mirror in search of a human identity to supplant his romantic vision. The pairing of idealist with dream woman explores the gendered ideals of the period and hints at Dante Rossetti's problematic love for his beautiful chestnut-haired wife, Elizabeth "Lizzie" Siddal Rossetti.

Rather than marry, Christina Rossetti chose a reclusive celibacy, which she allegorized in "An Apple Gathering" (1857). Subject to anxiety attacks and bouts of screaming, she underwent a transformation at the time of her religious conversion to conservative tractarianism. While residing with her ailing mother and elderly aunts, the author devoted herself to domestic duties and lengthy periods of letter writing that included a campaign against vivisection. When she wanted to punish herself for violating orthodoxy with her writings, a scenario illustrated in the book *Maude* (1850), Rossetti denied herself the eucharist. In a poem in the book Maude regrets the fettering of women, who "drag the heavy chain whose every link / Galls to the bone" (Rossetti, 1998, 20). As a nun at Saint Mary Magdelene Home for Fallen Women at Highgate, Rossetti dedicated herself to aiding streetwalkers and unwed mothers and to writing verse on themes of solitude, disappointed love, treachery, mourning, PROSTITUTION, and repentance of carnal sins.

In an era that forbade women's interest in theology and excluded them from ruling bodies of the Church of England, Rossetti applied original biblical interpretations to poems such as "The Convent Threshold" (1858), a meditation on redemption. She also turned prose into allegories of gendered expectations that fell on English females at an early age. In the cautionary fable *Speaking Likenesses* (1874), an imitation of traditional FAIRY TALES, she alerted small girls to hurtful children who masked their torments as friendly games like Hunt the Pincushion. The warning carries a subtextual application to the life of adult women, whose flesh felt the pricks of gossip and disapproval at the slightest deviation from ladylike decorum. In 1881 she championed the female artist in *Monna Innominata,* a Petrarchan sonnet sequence reprising the conventions of COURTLY LOVE. The poems recall the nameless medieval and Renaissance women whom troubadours praised but whom society silenced, leaving them quietly heartsick at the evanescence of their youth and loveliness. Depressed by the deaths of mother, sister, and brother, Rossetti died of Graves's disease and cancer, leaving unpublished a trove of limpid and funereal verse. Her canon, particularly the enigmatic masterwork GOBLIN MARKET (1862), inspired later female writers, including the novelist Barbara KINGSOLVER and the premodernist poet Sara TEASDALE.

Bibliography

Arseneau, Mary, Anthony H. Harrison, and Lorraine Jansen Kooistra, eds. *The Culture of Christina Rossetti: Female Poetics and Victorian Contexts.* Athens: Ohio University Press, 1999.

Rossetti, Christina. *Rossetti: Poems.* New York: Everymans Library, 1993.

———. *Selected Prose by Christina Rossetti.* London: Palgrave Macmillan, 1998.

———. *Sing-Song: A Nursery Rhyme Book* (1893). Available online. URL: http://digital.library.upenn.edu/women/rossetti/singsong/singsong.html. Accessed on October 17, 2005.

Scheinberg, Cynthia, and Gillian Beer, eds. *Women's Poetry and Religion in Victorian England: Jewish Identity and Christian Culture.* Cambridge: Cambridge University Press, 2002.

Rowbotham, Sheila (1943–)

The British historian, biographer, and social critic Sheila Rowbotham concentrates her efforts on women's history of feminism and the impact of economic changes on WOMAN'S WORK. According to her memoir, *The Promise of a Dream: Remembering the Sixties* (2002), she was born in Leeds late in the relationship of a cheerful mother and a controlling Tory engineer, who were never married. Rowbotham and her brother, Peter, grew up in West Riding. At age 16 she attended Hunmanby Hall, a Methodist boarding school in East Yorkshire, and rebelled against regimentation by reading the existential writings of Simone de BEAUVOIR and Jean Paul Sartre. She studied at Saint Hilda's College, Oxford, and at the Sorbonne. Her campus activities ranged from editing the radical socialist newspaper *Black Dwarf* to rallying protesters against nuclear weapons. By her mid-20s she was a sophisticated activist and writer as well as the organizer of the nation's first women's liberation conference. Currently a sociology professor at the University of Manchester, she is a respected orator and polemicist who publishes in *European Journal of Women's Studies, International Feminist Journal of Politics,* and *Socialist History.* She has lectured in Canada, France, Holland, and the United States.

In a period when women's fiction, fashion, and design burgeoned, it was Rowbotham who helped to define economic feminism. She expressed the laboring-class woman's needs in a pamphlet, *Women's Liberation and New Politics* (1971): "We have not even words for ourselves. Thinking is difficult when the words are not your own. Borrowed concepts are like passed down clothes, they fit badly and do not give confidence" (Rowbotham, 1971, 5). Later works display her ability to express stark reality in lyric terms. She asserted her empathy for humanity in *Women's Consciousness, Man's World* (1973): "The oppressed without hope are mysteriously quiet. When the conception of change is beyond the limits of the possible, there are no words to articulate discontent so it is sometimes held not to exist. . . . But the fact that we could not hear does not prove that no pain existed" (Rowbotham, 1973, xi).

Rowbotham's publication of *Hidden from History: 300 Years of Women's Oppression and the Fight against It* (1973) launched a groundswell of women's history scholarship and courses in British colleges. She turned to biographical drama for *The Friends of Alice Wheeldon* (1986), a portrait of a suffragist and pacifist who during World War I welcomed conscientious objectors to her secondhand clothing shop. She was sentenced in 1917 to 10 years in prison on a trumped-up charge of plotting to poison David Lloyd George, who had recently advanced to prime minister. A heroine of the Left, Wheeldon died during the influenza epidemic of 1919. Rowbotham extolled Wheeldon for her rejection of England's class-ridden social code: "What was shocking to the male upper-class establishment was . . . the raucous vulgarity of lower-middle-class women who were not at all socially deferential" (Rowbotham, 1986, 57).

Rowbotham studied the migration from former British colonies to industrial cities in the West and noted that the arrival of ethnic workers produced developing world enclaves within Western urban communities. She warned of the double threat to women, who manage both home and outside jobs. She commented on the duality of women workers who "demand peace sometimes as 'mothers,' sometimes as 'human beings' " (Rowbotham, 1992, 296–297). In 1993 she expanded her writings on women's advancement with *A Century of Women: The History of Women in Britain and the United States*, a popular volume in the British Isles and in North America. The chronicle juxtaposes vignettes of remarkable suffragists, birth control promoters, and union organizers as well as ordinary volunteers who contributed to the war effort during the Blitz. In 2002 she copublished *Women Resist Globalisation: Mobilising for Livelihood and Rights,* which applauds women's global networks in support of environmentalism, reproductive freedom, pluralism, urban safety, and human rights. Her contributions to the compendium include a history of the SUFFRAGE and WOMEN'S RIGHTS movements from the 1700s.

Bibliography

Bahl, Vinay. "Reflections on the Recent Work of Sheila Rowbotham: Women's Movements and Building Bridges," *Monthly Review: An Independent Socialist Magazine* 48, no. 6 (November 1996): 31–42.

Rowbotham, Sheila, ed. *Dignity and Daily Bread: New Forms of Economic Organizing among Poor Women in the Third World and First.* New York: Routledge, 1994.

———. *Friends of Alice Wheeldon.* New York: Monthly Review Press, 1986.

———. *Hidden from History: Rediscovering Women in History from the 17th Century to the Present.* New York: Vintage, 1976.

———. *Promise of a Dream: Remembering the Sixties.* London: Verso, 2001.

———. *Woman's Consciousness, Man's World.* Harmondsworth, England: Penguin, 1973.

———. *Women in Movement: Feminism and Social Action.* New York: Routledge, 1992.

———. *Women Resist Globalisation: Mobilising for Livelihood and Rights.* London: Zed Books, 2002.

———. *Women's Liberation. and New Politics.* London: May Day Manifesto Group, 1971.

Rowlandson, Mary (ca. 1635–1711)

Mary White Rowlandson, a literary success in the American colonial period, produced America's first best seller by a female author and pioneered CAPTIVITY NARRATIVE as a New World genre. A Puritan emigrant from England at age three, she lived with her parents, Joane White and John White, and 10 siblings first in Salem, then in Lancaster, Massachusetts. She took pride in her religious status as an active Christian. At age 21 she married the Reverend Joseph Rowlandson, father of her four children, one of whom died in infancy. On February 10, 1676, midway through the 14-month conflict known as King Philip's War, a turning point in her domestic life occurred at dawn, when the Wampanoag sachem Metacomet and his warriors raided the village, which had once been their homeland. They burned homes and slew, stripped, and mutilated 12 citizens, including Mary's sister, brother-in-law, and nephew. The Indians shot Rowlandson and six-year-old Sarah; seized the wounded mother and two other children, Joseph and Mary; and forced them on a wilderness trek on foot and by raft through forest and swamps northeast into New Hampshire.

Some 30 miles from any white town Rowlandson endured nearly three months among the Wampanoag by knitting and sewing shirts and infant garments, which she traded for bear meat and wheat cakes. In the estimation of the feminist historian Laurel Thatcher ULRICH, Rowlandson "survived because she knew how to use English huswifery in the service of her captors" (Ulrich, 227). On February 18, when Sarah Rowlandson died of hunger and exposure caused by sleeping in the open, her mother took pride in exemplary faith by refusing to give in to suicidal urges. As the slave of Weetamoo, a sunksquaw (female chief) and wife of Chief Quinnapin, Rowlandson ate what the Indians scavenged, including dry corn and peas, spoiled wheat, venison and ground nuts, livestock in thick broth and samp and servings of horse liver and hooves. Upon her ransom on May 2, 1676, for £20, Rowlandson, Mary, and Joseph returned to Boston and then moved to Wethersfield, Connecticut. As punishment for the raid and abductions white retaliators killed Weetamoo and Metacomet, her brother-in-law, and sold his wife and children into slavery in the West Indies for 30 shillings each. Vengeful colonists dismembered both Metacomet and Weetamoo and treasured their body parts as souvenirs.

In 1682 Rowlandson became the first woman to contribute to captivity lore with a prototype, *The Sovereignty and Goodness of God: Being a Narrative of the Captivity and Restauration of Mrs. Mary Rowlandson*, which she published in Cambridge. Rowlandson's memoir takes a Christian point of view by thanking God for a trial that strengthened her faith. Although she at first preferred death to removal from home, she relied on Bible verses for emotional support and exulted, "I chose rather to go along with those (as I may say) ravenous beasts, than that moment to end my days" (Rowlandson, 82). In addition to beatings, she witnessed scalpings and the burning of a living white woman and her baby. Rowlandson expressed gratitude for a network of Indian females who made kidnap and forced labor less painful with gifts of food and a skin to sleep on. On her departure they provided a scarf and hood to protect her from bad weather.

Sold to North American and British readers, Rowlandson's work shaped subsequent accounts of females seized by Indians and went into its 15th edition in 1800. It influenced James Fenimore Cooper's *The Last of the Mohicans* (1826), William Faulkner's *Sanctuary* (1931), Caroline GORDON's feminist survival story "The Captive" (1945), and Janice Holt Giles's *Hannah Fowler* (1956). The latter novel, set in Kentucky, pictures the marriage of Hannah Moore to Tice Fowler, the only taker for a girl suddenly orphaned at Fort Pitt. Upon her capture by Indians in the last weeks of her second pregnancy she applies frontier advice from Daniel Boone to "act as natural as you kin," as though kidnap by Indians is an expected occurrence (Giles, 181).

Bibliography

Giles, Janice Holt. *Hannah Fowler*. Boston: Houghton Mifflin, 1956.

Rowlandson, Mary White. *The Sovereignty and Goodness of God: The True Story of the Captivity of Mrs. Mary Rowlandson among the Indians*. Tucson, Ariz.: American Eagle, 1966.

Ulrich, Laurel Thatcher. *Good Wives: Image and Reality in the Lives of Women in Northern New England, 1650–1750*. New York: Oxford University Press, 1982.

Rowson, Susanna (1762–1824)

One of America's first professional fiction writers, the actor, journalist, and novelist Susanna Haswell Rowson composed realistic seduction lore as instruction to the unwary female reader. An Englishwoman born in Portsmouth, she emigrated to Boston at age four to live on Nantasket Peninsula with her father, a naval officer, and his second wife. The family remained until the American Revolution forced them back to England for an 11-year sojourn. In 1786 she completed an epistolary romance, *Victoria*, followed two years later by *The Inquisitor; or, Invisible Rambler* (1788) and *Mentoria* (1791), a compendium of cautionary anecdotes and verse addressed to women who do not read instructive novels.

That same year Rowson produced her masterwork, a two-volume morality novel, *Charlotte Temple, a Tale of Truth* (1791), which appeared in North America in 1794 and went through over 200 editions. The story of a selfish soldier's abandonment of his teenage lover winds down to her eviction into the streets and beggary until a kind servant woman recognizes that Charlotte is about to give birth. The author sympathizes with the female pariah, who sinks into oblivion: "She has disgraced her friends, forfeited the good opinion of the world, and undone herself; she feels herself a poor solitary being in the surrounding midst of multitudes; shame bows her to the earth, remorse tears her distracted mind, and guilt, poverty, and disease" (Rowson, 67). The narrative describes social mores that praise virtue but that fail to forgive even one transgression.

Rowson's appreciation of women's lot resurged in later work. She wrote about women's EDUCATION in *Rebecca; or, The Fille de Chambre* (1792), in which the title character learns about life through library books. Rowson wrote dramas in which she played central roles. She injected feminist sentiment into her popular abolitionist musical, *Slaves in Algiers: A Struggle for Freedom* (1794), for which she composed lyrics. She revealed more of her past in a four-volume semiautobiographical novel, *Trials of the Human Heart* (1795). After a long career on the stage in England and North America with her husband, the trumpeter William Rowson, the author retired at age 35 from the Federal Street Theater. She edited the *Boston Weekly Magazine* for four years; freelanced for the *Boston Review*, *Monthly Anthology*, and *New England Galaxy*; and published verse, historical fiction, and women's BIOGRAPHY in *A Present for Young Ladies* (1811). Simultaneously she and her sister-in-law, Mary Hasell, managed a boarding school, Mrs. Rowson's Young Ladies' Academy, at Medford until two years before the author's death. She composed both spellers and textbooks on history and geography and mapped out geography curricula before the subject was an established discipline. In addition to campaigning for virtuous, useful female behavior, she advocated a holistic education to salvage girls from wasted lives as decorative, but witless fashion plates.

Bibliography

Rowson, Susanna. *Charlotte Temple*. New York: Modern Library, 2004.

Rust, Marion. "Into the House of an Entire Stranger," *Early American Literature* 37, no. 2 (June 2002): 281–308.

Vining, James W., and Ben A. Smith. "Susanna Rowson: Early American Geography Educator," *Social Studies* 89, no. 6 (November–December 1998): 263–170.

Roy, Gabrielle (1909–1983)

A trendsetting French-Canadian author, autobiographer, and journalist, Gabrielle Roy wrote postcolonial fiction that sympathized with the poor, degraded female Native Americans, immigrants, and farmers. A native of Saint-Boniface, Manitoba, she was the last of 11 children who grew up hearing the French-language stories of Quebec told by their mother, Mélina Roy. After education at a Catholic academy, where she excelled in English and French, Roy attended Winnipeg Normal Institute. During the Great Depression she taught school in Cardinal and Marchand, Manitoba, and in Académie Provencher boy's school in Saint-Boniface. Intrigued by experiences with Le Cercle Molière drama troupe, she studied theater in Britain and France and wrote articles for Canadian and French newspapers—*La Revue Moderne*, *Le Bulletin des Agriculteurs*, and *Le Jour*.

After World War II Roy gave up classroom teaching and, against her mother's urging, turned to fiction, which ironically featured strong maternal figures. According to a posthumous autobiography, *La détresse et l'enchantement* (*Enchantment and Sorrow: The Autobiography of Gabrielle Roy*, 1987), the author withdrew into seclusion to write. In her mid-30s she completed a first novel, *Bonheur d'occasion* (1945), published in English as *The Tin Flute* (1947), a best-selling Québécois novel that sold more than a million copies. The Depression era domestic setting depicts the life of Roseanna Lacasse, the matriarch of a poor family in the Saint-Henri slums of Montreal, an area dominated by church-sanctioned PATRIARCHY. For abandoning the *roman de la terre* (rural novel) in favor of realism, the book earned a first for Canadian writers, the Prix Fémina, plus the first of three Governor General's Awards, and became an American Literary Guild selection. Roy's personal honor was admission to Canada's Royal Society.

The Roy canon encompasses myriad feminist themes, particularly the freedom to travel, to express hidden longings through oral history, and to defy anti-woman Catholic tenets by practicing birth control to ensure personal health and manageable family size. In *Rue deschambault* (*Street of Riches*, 1955) she collected autobiographical stories set in her hometown. With *Windflower* (1970) the author extends her concern for abandoned, emotionally isolated women through the character Elsa Kumachuk, a young Inuit in northern Labrador who epitomizes the author's luminous mother figures. Elsa gives birth to a Caucasian son, Jimmy, fathered by a rapist, an American soldier. Although the Native community accepts the boy, she fears that she will be unable to support his bicultural heritage. In 1977 Roy published *Ces enfants de ma vie* (*Children of My Heart*), an autobiographical novel honoring female creativity, followed the next year by *Fragiles lumières de la Terre* (The fragile lights of Earth, 1978), a collection of journalistic pieces and winner of the Prix Molson. The anthology expresses compassion for Canada's rural black, Chinese, Italian, and Ukrainian immigrants. For her feminist and humanist themes Roy earned the title of the Canadian Willa Cather.

Bibliography

Chapman, Rosemary. "Writing of/from the Fourth World: Gabrielle Roy and Ungava," *Quebec Studies* 35 (Spring–Summer 2003): 45–63.

Clemente, Linda M., and William A. Clement. *Gabrielle Roy: Creation and Memory.* Toronto: ECW Press, 1997.

Green, Mary Jean. "Review: La Voyageuse et la Prisonniere: Gabrielle Roy et la Question des Femmes," *American Review of Canadian Studies* 33, no. 3 (Autumn 2003): 438–440.

Roy, Gabrielle. *Children of My Heart.* Toronto: McClelland & Stewart, 1979.

———. *Enchantment and Sorrow: The Autobiography of Gabrielle Roy.* Toronto: Lester & Orpen Dennys, 1987.

———. *Street of Riches.* Toronto: New Canadian Library, 1991.

———. *Windflower.* Toronto: McClelland & Stewart, 1991.

Rukeyser, Muriel (1913–1980)

A humanist, libertarian, and pacifist poet and educator for a half-century, Muriel Rukeyser exposed the need for social justice for victimized women and minorities. A native New Yorker, she grew up in a nonobservant Jewish household and studied in Manhattan at the School of Ethical Culture. At the height of the Great Depression she completed three years of study at Vassar College and Columbia University while writing articles for the *Masses.* She published *Theory of Flight* (1935), a verse anthology she wrote while receiving instruction at the Roosevelt Aviation School. The collection set the direction of her disavowal of arty, pretty verses in favor of contemporary poetry of witness. As an example of realism, she envisioned how the victim of syphilis dispels the beauty of romantic music. Attuned to global strife, Rukeyser anticipated war in Europe and the Holocaust in *A Turning Wind* (1939), a collection that she paired with a postwar meditation, *Beast in View* (1944). She was jailed for pacifist demonstrations against the Vietnam War and for protests of the imprisonment of the political writer Kim Chi-Ha in Korea.

In midcareer Rukeyser moved from Marxism to feminism. At age 34 she gave birth to a son and embraced the role of single parent, which she described in *Body of Waking* (1958) in moody, intuitive stanzas. While teaching at Sarah Lawrence College, the author mentored the future activist-novelist Alice WALKER. Rukeyser wrote articles on the Alabama trial of the Scottsboro Boys, on black lung among miners, and on domestic upheaval resulting from the Spanish civil war. Her skills extend to children's works, a BIOGRAPHY of the American physicist Willard Gibbs in 1942, the drama *The Color of the Day* (1961), the autobiographical novel *The Orgy: An Irish Journey of Passion and Transformation* (1965), and translations of the Mexican author Octavio Paz's *Early Poems* (1973) and Bertolt Brecht's play *Uncle Eddie's Moustache* (1974). At her death she left incomplete a verse drama, *Houdini: A Musical* (2002), about the contortionist Harry Houdini.

In the essay "Blood, Bread, and Poetry: The Location of the Poet" (1984) Adrienne Rich applauds Muriel Rukeyser's radical works, which spoke so directly to issues of the day that they were "buried by the academic literary canon" during Rich's enrollment at Radcliffe (Rich, 244). Four years after suffering a paralytic stroke Rukeyser issued a verse anthology, *Speed of Darkness* (1968), and *Breaking Open* (1973), a collection that expresses her views on female sensuality and self-determination. Most frequently honored and reprinted is "KÄTHE KOLLWITZ" (1968), a eulogy to a German graphic artist who honored the courage of working women during World War II. A witty dialogue in "Myth" (1973) tweaks the Greek king Oedipus as a symbolic male who underestimates the pervasive corrosion of sexism. Her activism and feminist poems influenced the poets Sharon OLDS, Adrienne RICH, and Anne SEXTON.

Bibliography

Herzog, Anne F., and Janet E. Kaufman. *"How Shall We Tell Other of the Poet": The Life and Writing of Muriel Rukeyser.* New York: Palgrave Macmillan, 1999.

Rich, Adrienne. *Adrienne Rich's Poetry and Prose.* New York: W. W. Norton, 1975.

Rukeyser, Muriel. *Out of Silence: Selected Poems.* Evanston, Ill.: Northwestern University Press, 1994.

Russ, Joanna (1937–)

The radical feminist, science fiction author, and educator Joanna Russ uses speculative fiction to dismantle faulty male-female paradigms and to propose more egalitarian societies. Born in New York City and reared in the Bronx, she displayed an early interest in science and was one of the top 10 students in the Westinghouse Science Talent Search. Opting for an education in the humanities, she completed a degree in English at Cornell University and the Yale School of Drama. While teaching English and women's studies at the University of Washington, she published woman-centered short and long fiction. Her themes parallels the gynocentrism of Margaret ATWOOD, Octavia BUTLER, Charlotte Perkins GILMAN, Ursula LE GUIN, Kathleen NORRIS, and Marge PIERCY

in featuring keen-witted female action figures. Alyx, protagonist of the trilogy *Picnic on Paradise* (1968), *Alyx* (1976), and *The Adventures of Alyx* (1986), prefigures Russ's lesbian utopia in the story "When It Changed" (1972), a winner of Hugo and Nebula citations for gender innovation.

Russ battled sexist barriers in a cult classic, *The Female Man* (1975), which won a *Nebula* Award for Best Novel. In a diatribe against Western sexism the narrative splits one persona into four points of view, the librarian Jeannine Dadier, the wolf stalker and time traveler Janet Evason, the unwed feminist Joanna, and the assassin Jael Reasoner. Each confronts gendered obstacles to personal freedom. The feminist literary historian Carol Farley Kessler, author of *Daring to Dream* (1984), refers to this multipersoned focus as a "cluster protagonist," who presents "a collective self, rather than individual selves, and therefore proposes the values which go with collectivity" (Kessler, 5). Of the worth of MATRIARCHY the author writes, "One cannot fall out of the kinship web and become sexual prey for strangers, for there is no prey and there are no strangers" (Russ, 2000, 81). Through rage at male-on-female VIOLENCE and a beneficial narcissism that defines and directs female powers the characters find sensible ways of becoming whole human beings. In the falling action Joanna, the author's alter ego, summarizes a balanced feminist goal: "I . . . don't . . . want to be a 'feminine' version . . . of the heroes I admire. . . . I want to be the heroes themselves" (*ibid.*, 206). In a subsequent futurist fantasy, *And Chaos Died* (1978), Russ builds an Eden in space where Earthlings retreat to develop extrasensory perception (ESP) and to live in a mutually pleasing bisexual culture.

Russ ridiculed misogynistic publishers in *How to Suppress Women's Writing* (1983). A withering tour de force, the text enumerates the standard put-downs: "She didn't write it. She wrote it but she shouldn't have. She wrote it but look what she wrote about. She wrote it but she isn't really an artist, and it isn't really art. She wrote it but she had help. She wrote it but she's an anomaly. She wrote it BUT . . ." (Russ, 1983, cover). She anthologized pro-woman essays in two sassy collections, *Magic Mommas, Trembling Sisters, Puritans and Perverts*

(1985) and *To Write Like a Woman: Essays in Feminism and Science Fiction* (1995). The latter castigates woman-hating male speculative fiction in the essay "Amor Vincit Foeminam: The Battle of the Sexes in Science Fiction," about the trapping of female personae between the stereotypes of bitch and victim. Another essay, "Recent Feminist Utopias," lauds female sci-fi writers for reviving the family and for furthering the Earth-first goals of ECOFEMINISM.

Bibliography

Freedman, Carl. *Critical Theory and Science Fiction.* Middletown, Conn.: Wesleyan University Press, 2000.

Gardiner, Judith Kegan. "Empathic Ways of Reading: Narcissism, Cultural Politics, and Russ's 'Female Man,'" *Feminist Studies* 20, no. 1 (Spring 1994): 87–111.

Kessler, Carol Farley. *Daring to Dream.* Boston: Pandora Press, 1984.

Russ, Joanna. *The Female Man.* Boston: Beacon Press, 2000.

———. *How to Suppress Women's Writing.* Austin: University of Texas Press, 1983.

———. *To Write Like a Woman: Essays in Feminism and Science Fiction.* Bloomington: Indiana University Press, 1995.

S

Sackville-West, Vita (1892–1962)

The bilingual English poet, biographer, dramatist, and fiction writer Lady Victoria Mary "Vita" Sackville-West was a commercially successful feminist author of many talents. Born to aristocrats in Knole, Kent, she learned in childhood the hard luck of females whom entailment laws prevented from inheriting family properties. She received private tutoring and studied in London at Miss Woolff's academy. By her late teens the author had composed plays and novels in English and French. After marriage at age 21 she lived in a country house, reared two sons, and wrote while her diplomat husband worked largely on the Continent. She wrote verse collections, travelogues, and gardening columns for the *Observer* and the *Sunday Times* and reviewed books for *Athenaeum, Listener,* the *Nation,* and *New Statesman.*

The author pursued lesbian relationships with a number of women, notably the novelist Virginia WOOLF, and wrote about woman-to-woman passions in *The King's Daughter* (1929), which she serialized in *Bookman* the following year. In 1931 Sackville-West produced a feminist novel, *All Passion Spent,* a study of the attempt of 88-year-old Lady Slane to live free of social constraint. The author was better known for feminist BIOGRAPHY; her subjects included a 17th-century feminist playwright in *Aphra Behn: The Incomparable Astrea* (1927), the androgynous warrior-prophet in *Saint Joan of Arc* (1936), Sackville-West's own grandmother in *Pepita* (1937), and Saints Teresa of Avila and Thérèse of Lisieux in *The Eagle and the Dove* (1943). After the publication of *Portrait of a Marriage* (1973) by Sackville-West's son, the publisher Nigel Nicolson, more than a decade after his mother's death of cancer, revelations of private family matters served as the subject of a British Broadcasting Corporation Television (BBC-TV) miniseries in 1990. Public interest in the marriage of two congenial bisexuals overshadowed interest in Sackville-West as a feminist and writer.

Bibliography

Meese, Elizabeth. "When Virginia Looked at Vita, What Did She See: or, Lesbian: Feminist: Woman— What's the Differ(e/a)nce?" *Feminist Studies* 18, no. 1 (Spring 1992): 99–117.

Sackville-West, Vita. *All Passion Spent.* London: Carroll & Graf, 2002.

———. *Saint Joan of Arc.* New York: Grove, 2001.

Sahgal, Nayantara (1927–)

For a half-century the novelist, historian, lecturer, and freelance journalist Nayantara Pandit Sahgal has spoken for civil liberties, especially those that ensure equal rights for women. The daughter of Vijmaya Lakshmi Nehru, India's first legate to Russia, and the attorney Ranjit Sitaram Pandit, the author was born in Allahabad and grew up in a political crucible stirred by her uncle, Prime Minister Jawaharlal Nehru, and by her cousin, Indira Gandhi, also a prime minister. Through the example of both her father and uncle, Sahgal learned in childhood of the honor in serving prison sentences for protesting oppression. After graduation from a missionary academy at Woodstock, Mussoorie, she attended Wellesley College and began her career as a writer.

Sahgal edited Nehru's letters and issued short fiction in the *Guardian*, *Frontline*, the *Times*, and *Journal of Commonwealth Literature*. In 1954 she completed a memoir, *Prison and Chocolate Cake*, and later surveyed social and political modernization in the Indian subcontinent in *The Freedom Movement in India* (1970) and *Indira Gandhi: Her Road to Power* (1982). In *A Voice for Freedom* (1977) the author addresses the issue of CENSORSHIP of women's writings in a climate of crumbling traditions and conservative backlash against change. Chief among her proposals is the establishment of INDEPENDENCE for India's women. In 1962 she completed a second memoir, *From Fear Set Free*, which pictures her struggles as a professional writer and mother of three, a familiar dichotomy in feminist literature.

In addition to favoring the liberalization of Hinduism and redefining of female virtue, Sahgal exposed Indian misogyny. Her narratives reprise the colonial past, when suttee or widow burning was the norm and when male kin battered, killed, and cremated rebellious females in brick kilns. To end the barbarity of Hindu fanaticism, she furthered liberty through membership on media and English language commissions and through representation of her country at the United Nations General Assembly. Her novels *This Time of Morning* (1965), *A Situation in New Delhi* (1977), and *Rich Like Us* (1983) picture the price exacted from female rebels. She dramatized the social restraints on women in a novel, *Mistaken Identity* (1988), set during strikes against the British Raj in 1929. In 1985 she won the Sinclair Prize in fiction; over the next two years she was awarded the Sahitya Akademi Award and the Commonwealth Writers Award. Still involved in the development of civil liberties in India in her 70s, she published *Point of View: A Personal Response to Life, Literature and Politics* (1997), a selection of essays naming liberties still unsecured for women.

Bibliography

Paranjape, Makarand. "The Crisis of Contemporary India and Nayantara Sahgal's Fiction," *World Literature Today* 68, no. 2 (Spring 1994): 291–298.

Sahgal, Nayantara. "Imagining India," *Times Higher Education Supplement*, 21 November 1997, 33.

Salgado, Minoli. "Myths of the Nation and Female (Self) Sacrifice in Nayantara Sahgal's Narratives," *Journal of Commonwealth Literature* 31, no. 2 (Fall 1996): 61.

Sanchez, Sonia (1934–)

The dramatist, scenarist, poet, children's author, and equality advocate Sonia Sanchez redirects rap, European verse forms, haiku, and tanka to the topics and themes of radical verse. Born Wilsonia Benita Driver in Birmingham, Alabama, she grew up motherless from age one and grandmotherless from age six. With her sister, Pat, Sanchez lived with a stepmother and relatives in Harlem. In *Does Your House Have Lions?* (1997), a nominee for a National Book Critics Circle Award, she chants in childish repetition her yearning for her mother. Lacking a blood MATRIARCHY, Sanchez received guidance from a female librarian, Jean Hutson, at the Schomburg Center for Research in Black Culture and read the female authors Margaret WALKER and Gwendolyn BROOKS.

After studying political science at Hunter College, Sanchez enrolled in creative writing classes at New York University and had as her mentor the poet Louise BOGAN. While rearing a daughter and twin sons, Sanchez supported Harlem's black arts movement and taught at Amherst, Rutgers, Spelman, Temple, Tulane, and the University of Pittsburgh. At San Francisco State University curriculum supervisors ejected her from the black studies initiative for disruptive racial ire, a turbulence and vituperation that emerge in her slangy, profane verse and sketches. In 1969 she became the first English professor to create a course on black female writers. She recalled in an interview with Susan Kelly: "I said jokingly [to the English staff], 'What we need'—I was talking to all women, who had settled in my office—'what we need is a course on black women.' And they said, 'Oh! Oh! Oh! Oh! God, yes! Would you teach it?' So I said, 'Uh-huh, yeah, right' " (Kelly, 682).

Sanchez's daring carried over from the classroom to the printed page. In verse for *African American Review*, *Essence*, *Black Issues Book Review*, *Transatlantic Review*, and *Women's Review of Books* she breaches genre bounds by mixing prose with a sharply etched cameo style of poetry that throbs with a doo-wop intensity and visceral immediacy. She published a play, *The Bronx Is Next* (1968); a first verse collection, *Homecoming* (1969); and a feminist monologue, *Sister Son/ji* (1969). Her style in *We a BaddDDD People* (1970) involves innovative spacing, typefaces, and syllabification along with explosive rhythm and fragmented thought. A stellar achievement, "Personal Letter No. 3" (1970), harangues society for its low expectations for black female achievement.

After the gentle *Love Poems* (1973) Sanchez reverted to militancy in *A Blues Book for Blue Black Magical Women* (1974), *I've Been a Woman* (1978), and *homegirls & handgrenades* (1984), winner of an American Book Award from the Before Columbus Foundation. A lyrical women's history in *Under a Soprano Sky* (1987) covers the liberation of black women. In the vignette "Dear Mama" she speaks to the memory of her mother, Lena Jones Driver, who knew from Sanchez's toddlerhood that she would carve out a unique place for herself. The poet blesses her mother for having faith that her child would prosper. In 1995 she published a short story in *Essence* in which she summarizes the self-empowerment of a woman whose adulterous husband has belittled her. At age 70 she released a compact disk (CD) of verbal hip-hop, "Full Moon of Sonia" (2004), which honors such foremothers as the activist Fannie Lou Hamer and the poet Audre LORDE. A biennial, the Sonia Sanchez Literary Review, analyzes her work and that of other black artists of the 1960s.

Bibliography

Kelly, Susan. "Discipline and Craft: An Interview with Sonia Sanchez," *African American Review* 34, no. 4 (Winter 2000): 679–687.

Lewis, Leslie W. Traveling Conversation: India Dennis-Mahmood Interviews Sonia Sanchez," *Feminist Teacher* 12, no. 3 (1999): 198–212.

Sanchez, Sonia. *Does Your House Have Lions?* Boston: Beacon Press, 1997.

———. *Shake Loose My Skin.* Boston: Beacon Press, 2000.

———. *We a BaddDDD People.* New York: Broadside, 1970.

———. "Wounded in the House of a Friend," *Essence* 26, no. 1 (May 1995): 227–230.

Sand, George (1804–1876)

The prolific Parisian novelist and memoirist George Sand demanded for women the freedom to enjoy their SEXUALITY and to assert female creativity. Named Amandine-Aurore Lucille Dupin, Baronne Dudevant, at birth, she was a descendent of French and Polish royalty on her father's side and a working-class prostitute. Sand lived at Nohant, her paternal grandmother's country manor in Berry, and wore men's casual clothes to free her movements during excursions on horseback. She studied under tutors until her teens, when she entered Couvent des Augustines Anglaises. At age 16 she outflanked an unbalanced and controlling mother by marrying a country squire, Casimir Dudevant. The match was disastrous. In a Catholic society that disallowed divorce, she abandoned her husband and took her son, Maurice, and daughter, Solange, to live in Paris on an inheritance from her grandmother.

As a challenge to bourgeois gender STEREOTYPING Sand was unconventional in most aspects of her life. Shocking to the French were her dismissal of Catholic morals and her belief that the sacrament of marriage was an outdated social custom that failed to satisfy the sexual needs of women. She wrote columns and edited for *Le Figaro*, *La République*, *Revue des Deux Mondes*, and *Revue Indépendante*. To enable her to enter male-only clubs, libraries, theaters, and museums, she smoked cigars and dressed as a man. Sexually liberated, she enjoyed a series of love affairs with her choice of mostly male painters, actors, poets, and musicians, including Honoré de Balzac, Frédéric Chopin, Marie Dorval, and Franz Liszt.

Sand's forthright style in INDIANA (1832), *Lélia* (1833), and *Consuelo* (1842–43) set the tone and style emulated by female English novelists, who preferred her translated works to those of any other European author. The first of Sand's three novels applauds Indiana Delmare's choice of freedom over domestic enslavement and her abrupt end to her love-starved existence. In the preface Sand summarizes the difficulties of questing women: "She is

Choice at odds with Necessity; she is Love blindly butting its head against all the obstacles set in its path by civilization" (Sand, 1900, 7). With heroic intent Indiana announces in part 3 that French laws place husbands over their wives, but no bondage can limit or subdue her will. Sand's subtext presses the French government to balance marriage laws to favor neither husband nor wife.

Critics lambasted the author for overturning centuries of European tradition requiring wives to obey husbands. As a result of controversy authorities banned her works from public libraries. Nonetheless Sand survived the critics' disdain and praised the efforts of other female rebels, including Harriet Jane ROBINSON and the Lowell mill girls, who issued the *Lowell Offering*, the world's first magazine produced by women. Sand published *The Castle of Pictures and Other Stories: A Grandmother's Tales* (1859), a compendium of morality narratives that she composed for her granddaughters, Aurore and Gabrielle. In 1876, only months before the author's death, she published *Marianne,* a novel that epitomizes the female rebel in the 25-year-old rural heroine Marianne Chevreuse, who sets her own moral course. Among conservatives of the village of La Faille-sur-Gouvre in 1825, Marianne "was said to be 'difficult' and given to eccentricity, a characteristic which in the eyes of the community was infinitely more dangerous than vice itself" (Sand, 1998, 81). The work provided readers with an autobiographical character study of a writer who had changed little from her rebellious girlhood. Her opinions influenced a contemporary, the feminist philosopher Harriet Taylor MILL, and the South African radical Olive SCHREINER, creator of the NEW WOMAN novel.

Bibliography

Doumic, René. *George Sand: Some Aspects of Her Life and Writings* (1910). Available online. URL: http://etext.lib.virginia.edu/toc/modeng/public/DouSand.html. Accessed on October 17, 2005.

Maurois, André. *Lélia: The Life of George Sand.* New York: Penguin, 1977.

Perkin, J. Russell. "Locking George Sand in the Attic: Female Passion and Domestic Realism in the Victorian Novel," *University of Toronto Quarterly* 63, no. 3 (Spring 1994): 408–428.

Sand, George. *Indiana* (1990). Available online. URL: http://digital.library.upenn.edu/women/sand/indiana/indiana.html. Accessed on October 13, 2005.

———. *Marianne.* New York: Carroll & Graf, 1998.

Schneir, Miriam, ed. *Feminism: The Essential Historical Writings.* New York: Vintage, 1972.

Sanger, Margaret (1879–1966)

The founder of the first women's reproductive health initiative in the United States, Margaret Louise Higgins Sanger wrote essays, speeches, and books on marital sex and family planning that set the tone for the female-controlled birth control movement. Born the middle child of Alice Purcell's brood of 11, Sanger learned early the fragility of women's lives that results cyclical pregnancies. Her parents were socialists who taught her to respect females and to demand WOMEN'S RIGHTS. With a degree in drama from Claverick College and the Hudson River Institute she attempted a stage career, taught school for a year, then returned to her native Corning to nurse her mother during terminal tuberculosis worsened by weakness due to bearing too many babies. At age 21 Sanger graduated with a nursing degree from White Plains Hospital and advanced training at the Manhattan Eye and Ear Clinic.

Married into a wealthy family, Sanger gave up her medical career to rear a son and daughter. In 1910 she joined Lillian Wald's public health mission in the New York slums, where women routinely bled to death or died of infection caused by home deliveries and ABORTIONs or back-street surgeries. To prevent maternal deaths and orphaning of children, she studied population control in Europe and began advising the people at the highest risk: women married to syphilitic men, child brides too undeveloped to bear children, and women threatened with crippling, childbed death, or exhaustion and starvation from growing families. By 1914 she had written her own handouts for women, which skirted laws banning contraceptive information. She published essays on women's rights and population control in *Earth Mother,* the subversive periodical published by the anarchist orator Emma GOLDMAN, one of Sanger's supporters.

Sanger fought mother and infant death as well as hunger and overcrowded homes with counseling, preventive gynecology, and distribution of barrier methods of contraception. On October 16, 1916, among Jews and Italians in the Brownsville section of Brooklyn, New York, she established a discreet woman-operated clinic, the nation's first birth control center. Staffing was limited to three—Fania Mindell, a multilingual volunteer from Chicago; Elizabeth Stuyvesant, a social worker; and Sanger's sister, Ethel Higgins Byrne. Sanger's credo was grim: "I am the partisan of women who have nothing to laugh at" (Chesler, 13). She angered the Catholic hierarchy and broke the law by sending through the United States mail a monthly journal, *The Woman Rebel,* which bore an antipatriarchal slogan, "No Gods, No Masters!" (*ibid.*). Postal officials confiscated her writings as violations of the antiobscenity statutes of the Comstock Act. Because she faced 45 years in prison and public denunciation as a purveyor of immorality, she fled to London and befriended Dr. Marie STOPES, designer of stationary and mobile family planning clinics for Englishwomen.

On return to the United States Sanger enlarged her campaign with more lectures, clinics for poor women, the nation's first tabulation of women's reproductive health data, and the establishment of the National Birth Control League. As she explained in *Margaret Sanger: An Autobiography* (1938), full feminism required that "women should first free themselves from biological slavery" (Sanger, 1999, 166). Her philosophy was sobering: She maintained that the first duty of a mother is to be alive and well. In *The Pivot of Civilization* (1922) she reminded all readers that the physical debilitation of women saps the strength of all humankind. To answer the simplest questions from hundreds of clients, she published *What Every Girl Should Know,* a 10-cent patient pamphlet available in English, Italian, and Yiddish. Her efforts resulted in a police raid and jailing for 30 days in a workhouse.

Sanger toured Asia to survey overpopulation. To do more for poor American women, she smuggled in German diaphragms for free distribution and, in 1921, launched the *Birth Control Review,* which generated 1 million letters from readers. In the face of condemnation by congressmen, male doctors, and Pope Pius XI she compiled women's personal tragedies from 500 letters in *Mothers in Bondage*

(1928), one of 11 books she wrote on contraception. To provide a sound scientific basis for social action, she founded the Clinical Research Bureau of the American Birth Control League, the forerunner of the Planned Parenthood Federation. In 1935, the year before the Supreme Court rescinded the Comstock Act and allowed doctors to advise families on contraception, she began issuing the *Journal of Contraception.* That same year for the 21st anniversary of the birth control movement Charlotte Perkins GILMAN honored Sanger with a poem, "For Birth Control." Meridel LE SUEUR incorporated Sanger's pro-woman style in original treatises and stories.

Bibliography

Chesler, Ellen. *Woman of Valor: Margaret Sanger and the Birth Control Movement in America.* New York: Simon & Schuster, 1992.

Gay, Kathlyn, and Martin K. Gay. *Heroes of Conscience.* Santa Barbara, Calif.: ABC-Clio, 1996.

Sanger, Margaret. *Happiness in Marriage.* New York: Applewood, 1993.

———. *Margaret Sanger: An Autobiography.* New York: Cooper Square, 1999.

Sappho (b. ca. 612 B.C.)

The Greek poet Sappho, whom Plato called the 10th muse, lived independently in an era when Mediterranean women were silenced by lack of education and creative outlets. Born to aristocrats, Cleïs and Scamandronymus, in Eresos, Sappho (or Psappho) was a native of Lesbos, an island west of Asia Minor that served as a center for the Orphic mystery cult. Short and dark haired, she grew up in Mytilene in an atmosphere that encouraged her autonomy, creativity, and study of myth and mysticism. Because she was left fatherless at age six, she took comfort in a trio of brothers—Charaxus, Eurygius, and Larychus—who were both a curse and a blessing. Larychus earned honor as wine bearer to the council chamber. Charaxus joined in the flourishing wine trade south to Naucratis on the Nile delta. He compromised family honor by buying a slave-courtesan, Doricha, who spent all his money. Sappho's verse pictures Doricha lodged among the nobodies in the underworld, a suitable demise for a fortune hunter. The poet herself wed

Cercolas, a trader of her own class from Andros, and bore a beloved fair-haired daughter named Cleïs after her grandmother.

Sappho became an icon of subjective fiction. A devotée of fashion and the arts into middle age, from 604 to 595 B.C. she survived exile to Sicily during a Mediterranean power struggle. She appears to have organized a private academy or women's league who comprised Anactoria, Anagora, Arignota, Atthis, Dika, Eunice, Gongyla, Gyrinno, Hero, Mnasidica, Praxinoa, and Timas, all of whom the poet coddled and adored for their unpretentious grace and good looks. The joy of the assembly gave way to singing and dance, which some literary historians have connected to religious ritual. She wrote precise love poems to pretty girls, paeans to the love goddess Aphrodite, and marriage anthems for former students when they wed. According to a suspect legend, Sappho died for love of Phaon, an egotistic ferryman traveling between Lesbos and the Lydian mainland. After he spurned her, she reportedly jumped to her death from a headland on the isle of Leucas into the Ionian Sea, an event that the English poet Mary ROBINSON reprised in *Sappho and Phaon* (1796) and the novelist Marguerite YOURCE-NAR examined in *Sappho; or, The Suicide* (1952).

To literature Sappho contributed optimistic, flowing stanzas that glimpse young people in the first flush of love. She invented a four-verse bridal hymn, a variant of a traditional ritual prothelamium composed in a strong 11-syllable pattern and sung or recited to the strum of a lyre or small harp. The major writers of Greece and Rome, including Alcaeus, her contemporary, admired her nine volumes of poems for their originality and delightful turns of phrase. Scraps of her verse that survive from antiquity bear epic touches, romantic folklore, and Aeolian diction. The most rhapsodic, her description of a loss of control of her senses through an attack of desire, was a source for the Roman lyricist Catullus, who turned the image into a male suffering in silence for a married woman.

As a touchstone of women's lyrics Sappho's writings have undergone revisions reflecting the attitude toward women artists in the reader's era. When Christianity flourished in the Mediterranean, pursy monks destroyed the works of Sappho, whom they denounced as a libertine. In the

1600s admirers of the frankly erotic plays of Aphra BEHN claimed Behn as the English Sappho. The romantic poet Felicia HEMANS paid homage to Sappho for setting the example of the bold female writer. In the 1900s the poets Louise BOGAN, Anne CARSON, H. D., Amy LOWELL, Edna St. Vincent MILLAY, May SARTON, and Sara TEAS-DALE and the novelist Erica JONG took Sapphic celebratory verse as a model of feminist expression. The mid- and late 20th-century confessional poets Sylvia PLATH, Adrienne RICH, and Anne SEXTON revived the cult of Sappho, who became the feminist writer's foremother, a paragon of lesbian INDE-PENDENCE and lyric self-celebration.

Bibliography

DeJean, Joan. *Fictions of Sappho, 1546–1937.* Chicago: University of Chicago Press, 1989.

Sappho. *The Poems of Sappho.* New York: Prometheus, 1999.

Swiontkowski, Gale. *Imagining Incest: Sexton, Plath, Rich, and Olds on Life with Daddy.* Selinsgrove, Pa.: Susquehanna University Press, 2003.

Sarton, May (1912–1995)

A long-lived contributor to feminist literature, the English-Belgian poet Eleanore Marie "May" Sarton produced diaries, essays, fiction, and verse for some 65 years. A Belgian by birth, she emigrated with her parents from Wondelgem at age two during World War I and grew up in Cambridge, Massachusetts. Unlike her thwarted mother, Mabel Elwes Sarton, who never fulfilled her promise as an art designer, May Sarton began writing verses in girlhood and knew instinctively that poetry would govern her life. Except for her 12th year spent in Belgium, she attended private American schools but rejected further education at Vassar. Instead, she moved to New York City to learn acting from Eva Le Gallienne at the Civic Repertory Theater. At age 21 Sarton established her own troupe, the Associated Actors Theatre, a short-lived effort that concentrated on performing neglected European works.

A reader of Louise BOGAN, Emily DICKINSON, H. D., Amy LOWELL, Christina ROSSETTI, and SAPPHO and a friend of Elizabeth BOWEN, Muriel

RUKEYSER, and Virginia WOOLF, Sarton remained an original in her subtle approach to such provocative themes as femininity, blunted passion, and sexual preference. She developed an idiosyncratic style that stressed structure as well as lyricism and feminist themes regarding the value of SISTER-HOOD, the evanescence of beauty, and the centrality of art as a means of knowing the self. Her admirers, including Bogan, praised her range of mature emotion and her perception of human complexities. During the 1940s she wrote screenplays for the government and translated the French verse of Paul Valéry.

In *Writings on Writing* (1980) the poet expressed the purpose of writing fictional lives: "One is bothered by something one needs to understand and can come to understand only, as the psychiatrists would say, 'by acting out' through the characters in the imagined situation" (Sarton, 1980, 26). In the novel *Mrs. Stevens Hears the Mermaids Singing* (1965) Sarton validates the lesbianism and creativity of Hilary Stevens, whose verse is the fruit of her love for others. Lonely and uncertain, Hilary slips away in mental flight "and so often came to such beautiful understanding and peace with those ghosts who in reality had represented chiefly anguish" (Sarton, 1975, 12). The character's depressive states prefigure a similar barren emotional landscape in Sarton's series of journals, which she tape-recorded in whispers to the end of her troubled, but productive life of breast cancer at Wild Knoll near the Maine coast.

Bibliography

Heilbrun, Carolyn G. *Hamlet's Mother and Other Women.* New York: Ballantine, 1991.

Sarton, May. *Mrs. Stevens Hears the Mermaids Singing.* New York: W. W. Norton, 1975.

———. *Writings on Writing.* Orono, Maine: Puckerbush, 1980.

Wineapple, Brenda. "Licking Her Wounds," *Women's Review of Books* 14, no. 8 (May 1997): 12–13.

Scarlet Letter, The Nathaniel Hawthorne (1850)

An atmospheric allegorical romance, Nathaniel Hawthorne's *The Scarlet Letter* is an indigenous fiction of Puritan New England. With details of misogyny, social ostracism, and prolonged suffering he describes the misery of Hester PRYNNE, one of literature's most compelling fictional pariahs. A moving fable on the issues of religious mania, misogyny, and forgiveness, the story allegedly emerged (according to the introductory section, called "The Custom House") from a yellowed parchment heaped amid rubbish in a Boston customhouse, a symbolic male authoritarian stronghold on the Atlantic coast of colonial Massachusetts Bay. The document attests to the resilience of female victims of misogyny, who refuse to be trashed and forgotten. The text reveals a theocratic cycle—accusations of sin, judgment, and unremitting punishment of an outsider, Hester Prynne, a married, but lone woman whom a Puritan community ousts for adultery and for bearing a child out of wedlock.

Hawthorne contributes to feminist literature with the ruin of a woman whom society depersonalizes and reviles as tangible evidence of carnal sin. As barrels and bales are weighed and charged at the custom house pier, Hester receives an impersonal arraignment, followed by sentencing and imprisonment. During her incarceration she gives birth to Pearl, a symbolic name suggesting the "pearl of great price" that Jesus uses as a teaching model in the Gospel of Matthew 13:45–46. Upon the emergence of mother with babe, the author marks the dreary setting with a single rose, a standard artistic symbol of the VIRGIN MARY, herself an unusual mother. Amid gawkers and gossips Hester lives a daily test of courage suggesting the frontier Indian ordeal of running the gauntlet: "Every gesture, every word, and even the silence of those with whom she came in contact, implied, and often expressed, that she was banished, and as much alone as if she inhabited another sphere" (Hawthorne, 133). With dignity Hester accepts solitude and lives in a hut at the shore far from town, where she enjoys nature in peace and rears her daughter without interference.

The novel gains strength from a power struggle between temporal governing bodies and a forceful woman who refuses to be intimidated. Like the women targeted for persecution, court grilling, and execution during the Salem Witch Trials of 1692 by the author's stodgy ancestor, Judge John Hathorne, the protagonist is friendless and unaided by the law or by the soulless, unhusbandly Roger Chillingworth. Decades before the formation of the republic she is incapable of asserting citizen claims on privacy and free thought, a legal prerogative that 18th-century colonial lawgivers placed first in the Bill of Rights. Over her life span relentless accusers enlarge on the original prison sentence with sneers, rejection, and mockery of mother and child, and threats to remove Pearl from her mother's care. Highly revealing of the community's punitive mind-set is a refusal to allow Hester to embroider a bride's veil, as though the hand of an adulteress could contaminate a virgin and soil her marriage.

As though writing medieval hagiography, Hawthorne elevates Hester from convicted slattern to village saint by developing assets in her character. He extols her humble contributions of worthy motherhood, needlework, counseling of emotionally damaged women, and concern for the sick and dying. Balancing her generosity is a firm defense of principles in Hester's continued refusal to name her child's father. While her husband, Roger Chillingworth, stalks Hester's seducer, the Reverend Arthur Dimmesdale, and plagues his life with torments, Hester creates a safe zone for Pearl in their solitude far from judgmental Puritans and widespread hypocrisy.

At the novel's climax a sylvan setting contrasts the iron-and-wood dungeon, the public scaffold and pillory, and the meetinghouse, where dour ministers expound their unforgiving, un-Christ-like doctrines. In a woodsy respite Hester reunites with her former lover and speaks freely of their quandary. Hawthorne depicts Hester as a firm friend and adviser to Arthur, who lapses into self-pity and terror of unmasking as a fake moral guide and a despoiler of a lone married woman. In a microcosm of human liberty the child frolics near the brook and questions her mother about Satan, the legendary fount of evil. The promise of the moment for the family of three fails upon the discovery of their plan to sail away from colonial New England and its fundamentalist mania. Hawthorne retreats to a single symbol, the scarlet A that gleams from her tombstone with no further information to redeem her humanity.

Hawthorne's fictional re-creation of rigid morality influenced Kate CHOPIN's *The AWAKENING* (1899); Ann PETRY's historical novel *Tituba of Salem Village* (1964); the Caribbean writer Maryse CONDÉ's *Moi, Tituba, sorcière noire Salem* (*I, Tituba, Black Witch of Salem*, 1986); and Margaret ATWOOD's *The HANDMAID'S TALE* (1985), which carries the persecution of colonial females to extreme ends. A number of melodramas attempt to reveal on screen the duress on Hester, beginning in 1926 with MGM's version, featuring Lillian Gish as Hester. In 1950 Westinghouse Studio One cast Mary Sinclair in a live television performance. More successful than an outré subversion of the original in Demi Moore and Gary Oldman's presentation for Cinergi's 1995 film is Meg Foster and Kevin Conway's 1979 enactment of Hester and Arthur in a four-hour miniseries for Boston's WGBH public television.

Bibliography

Hawthorne, Nathaniel. *The Complete Novels and Selected Tales of Nathaniel Hawthorne.* New York: Modern Library, 1937.

Reiss, John, "Hawthorne's 'The Scarlet Letter,' " *Explicator* 53, no. 4 (Summer 1995): 200–201.

Ringe, Donald A., "The Critical Response to Nathaniel Hawthorne's *The Scarlet Letter*" ANQ 7, no. 1 (January 1994): 61–62.

Scenes in the Life of Harriet Tubman
Sarah H. Bradford (1869)

In 1869 Sarah Elizabeth Hopkins Bradford, then 51 years old, published *Scenes in the Life of Harriet Tubman,* the first of two biographies of a legendary conductor on the Underground Railroad. Bradford corroborated her account with a number of letters from dignitaries declaring Tubman's valor. The daughter of the slaves Benjamin Ross and Harriet Greene, Tubman, called Araminta or "Minty" Ross in childhood, was born around 1821 on Brodess plantation near Cambridge on Maryland's eastern shore. She grew strong through chopping wood, plowing, and hoeing the fields of her master. In her teens, she suffered a blow to the forehead when her owner misdirected a two-pound weight aimed at another slave. The trauma left her permanently afflicted with temporal lobe epilepsy or sudden mental blackouts.

Tubman began her odyssey to freedom upon learning that she might be sold to free her master from his debts. After fleeing bondage in 1849 at age 28, she left behind her husband, the freedman John Tubman, whom she had wed three years earlier. When she returned to lead him north two years later, she discovered that a new wife had taken her place. Alone in freedom, Harriet became a respected force for ABOLITIONISM. She earned cash by cooking, washing clothes, and cleaning homes, clubs, and hotel rooms in Philadelphia and Cape May, New Jersey. Additional funds came from a supporter, Quaker Thomas Garrett in Wilmington, Delaware.

Bradford's descriptions of Tubman's ventures south set her journeys typically on a Saturday night over mountains, through the territory of forest Indians, and across streams and rivers. She used her funds to buy food and armed herself with a rifle and revolver. She rescued her sister and two children from Baltimore and then returned for her four brothers and aged parents, whom she transported by wagon. Over another nine journeys south Tubman, disguised in men's clothes, freed 300 slaves without a single loss and earned for herself the compliment of a $40,000 price on her head. Those slaves who jeopardized the missions by lagging behind or turning back she urged onward with her pistol. For her courage the orator Frederick DOUGLASS stated in a letter dated August 29, 1868: "The midnight sky and the silent stars have been the witnesses of your devotion to freedom and of your heroism" (Bradford, 7).

In extolling Tubman's courage, Bradford ranked her alongside the military leader Joan of Arc, the seacoast rescuer Grace Darling, and the wartime nurse Florence Nightingale. The author added that none of the three had more "courage and power of endurance in facing danger and death to relieve human suffering, than has this woman in her heroic and successful endeavors to reach and save all whom she might of her oppressed and suffering race" (ibid., 1). Bradford seems particularly impressed that Tubman used native wit and guile to outfox pursuers. She warned her rescued parties of lurking patrols by singing the spiritual "Go Down,

Moses." Because of increased surveillance that resulted from the passage of the Fugitive Slave Law in 1850, Tubman added hundreds of miles to each journey by pressing north into Saint Catherine's, Ontario, the New World's "land of Canaan" (ibid., 29). After crossing the Canadian border, she knew her passengers were safe.

Before and during the Civil War Tubman had to hustle for funding of her humanitarian deeds. She solicited donations for John Brown's raid on the arsenal at Harpers Ferry, West Virginia, and raised money for his defense by selling homebrewed root beer, pies, and gingerbread. She volunteered as a scout and spy for the Second South Carolina Volunteers and as a nurse for freedmen's hospitals in Virginia. She lectured, collected clothing and books for freedmen's schools, and remodeled her house in Auburn, New York, as the Harriet Tubman Home for Aged and Indigent People. During numerous travels she lived on a pension for war widows and on the returns from Bradford's biographies, *Scenes in the Life of Harriet Tubman* and an expanded version, *Harriet Tubman: The Moses of Her People* (1886).

Tubman progressed from advocacy of abolitionism to support for full citizenship for all women, black and white. She led a campaign for gender equality and encouraged suffragists at the National Association of Colored Women in 1896. For her devotion to human liberty, she earned the friendship and support of the suffragist orator Susan B. ANTHONY and of Queen Victoria, who awarded Tubman a silver medal. Tubman went to her grave with military honors in 1913, some six years before women won the right to vote.

Bibliography

Bradford, Sarah H. *Scenes in the Life of Harriet Tubman.* New York: Beaufort Books, 1971.

Larson, Kate Clifford. *Bound for the Promised Land: Harriet Tubman, Portrait of an American Hero.* New York: Ballantine, 2003.

Schreiner, Olive (1855–1920)

The Anglo-German author of the first NEW WOMAN novel, Olive Emilie Albertina Schreiner wrote from feminist, pacifist, and socialist convictions. Born on a rural farm in Wittebergen, Basutoland, she was the daughter of a strict Lutheran missionary to South Africa, a dreamer and ne'er-do-well. He compensated for failure by superintending and spying on his children. Olive's upbringing among 11 siblings consisted of biblical instruction and discipline but allowed for free choice in self-education. She studied premedical courses at the University of Edinburgh, but asthma pared down her choices from doctor or nurse to governess.

Exasperated by her parents' conservatism, Schreiner broke with them and lived with her brother. Between jobs she composed the novel *Undine* (1874), a character study of a complex young misfit whose intelligence refuses to accept social and religious STEREOTYPING. The choice of first name, from the Latin *unda* (wave), suggests the rising tide of feminism that eventually spread over England and the United States. Schreiner particularizes the source of Undine's unrest as readings in the feminism of the English philosopher John Stuart MILL, who advocated total gender equality. To Undine's male cousin's sneers about girlish romances, she points to Mill's book and retorts, "There lies what I have been reading. There is nothing very sentimental in that, I fancy" (Schreiner, 1928, 70).

Upon migrating to England in 1881 and joining the Fabian Society, Schreiner shed the Calvinist inhibitions forced on her in childhood. She initiated a 36-year correspondence with the English sexologist Havelock Ellis, who agreed with her stand against female dependence on men in a form of financial and sexual parasitism. Among the avant garde she ventured far from her prudish upbringing with a feminist masterpiece, *The STORY OF AN AFRICAN FARM* (1883), an autobiographical settler novel issued under the safely masculine pen name Ralph Iron. She branched into utopian allegory in *Dreams* (1891) and *Dream Life and Real Life: A Little African Story* (1893). In part 2 of the latter work the speaker muses on times when she despairs about sexism and doubts that the future promises anything better. For courage she turns to a little cask of womanly keepsakes and the pressed rose that account for her unshakable ties to ambitions and dreams. The scent of a pressed rose suggests Schreiner's belief in a true femininity that lies locked away, withered but sweetly fragrant in the structured PATRIARCHY of the late Victorian period.

Repatriated to South Africa during a volatile period, Schreiner embroiled herself in colonial controversy that prefigured the clash between anti-imperialists and apartheid. After her marriage to a farmer-politician, Samuel Cronwright, he altered his surname to Cronwright-Schreiner and coauthored their libertarian treatise *The Political Situation in Cape Colony* (1895). That same year she suffered anguish over the death of their baby girl. Like 19th-century Cassandra she campaigned against racism and capitalism in the allegory *Trooper Peter Halket of Mashonaland* (1897) and denounced the dehumanizing of prostitutes in two commentaries, *An English South African Woman's View of the Situation* (1899) and *Closer Union: A Letter on South African Union and the Principles of Government* (1909). After joining the women's movement, she compiled *Woman and Labour* (1911), a prized feminist document that summarizes her thoughts on equal pay, financial INDEPENDENCE, and women's contributions during wartime. She stressed a familiar feminist theme that women's SEXUALITY and motherhood are threatened by war.

At Schreiner's death of a heart attack in Winberg outside Cape Town at age 65 she left unpublished the novel *Undine* (1928); *Stories, Dreams, and Allegories* (1923); *Thoughts on South Africa* (1923); and the unfinished novel *From Man to Man or Perhaps Only*. Circulated posthumously her new woman fiction foretokened late Victorian developments in feminist literature, particularly that of the novelists Doris LESSING and Virginia WOOLF. Schreiner's husband published her letters and composed a BIOGRAPHY, *The Life of Olive Schreiner* (1924). In 2004 the playwright Jessica Goldberg cast Schreiner as the protagonist of *Sex Parasite*, a feminist drama that re-creates the novelist's unprecedented exploration of sexuality and gender differences with a London discussion group.

Bibliography

Burdett, Carolyn. *Olive Schreiner and the Progress of Feminism: Evolution, Gender, Empire*. London: Palgrave Macmillan, 2001.

Horton, Susan R. *Difficult Women, Artful Lives: Olive Schreiner and Isak Dinesen in and out of Africa.* Baltimore: Johns Hopkins University Press, 1995.

Schreiner, Olive. *The Story of an African Farm.* London: Penguin, 1997.

———. *Undine.* Boston: Johnson Reprint, 1928.

Second Sex, The Simone de Beauvoir (1949)

The prominent French philosopher Simone de BEAUVOIR produced an inventive ideology, *Le deuxième sexe* (*The Second Sex*), which Howard Parshley bowdlerized and translated into English in 1953. The treatise draws on concepts from biology, history, literature, philosophy, psychology, and religion to probe the creation of gender norms, the social modeling that produces male and female attitudes and behavior. She introduces the notion that traditional female roles—daughter, wife, mother, lesbian, prostitute—are not biological, not hormonal in nature. Rather, little girls learn these attitudes and behavior from biased familial, religious, and social expectations. At fault are rigid gender roles found in art, pop culture, and FAIRY TALES such as "LITTLE RED RIDING HOOD," "CINDERELLA," and "Sleeping Beauty," which predispose young women to think of themselves as tender, powerless, and doomed to control by male rescuers. In legend the young hero "slays the dragon, he battles giants; she is locked in a tower, a palace, a garden, a cave, she is chained to a rock, a captive, sound asleep: she waits" (Beauvoir, 328). As a result of extensive social conditioning to play a passive, decorative role, pubescent females tend to adopt the BEAUTY MYTH—fashionable hair styles, makeup, and modeled poses—in place of affirmative, self-defining behavior. Thus in an androcentric society the winners of gender struggle are the limpid lovelies born with the attributes that society and the media preselect as desirable.

In lucid, organized fashion Beauvoir looks at the lives of females, young and old, for causes of gender dysfunction. She blames a body of folklore, which she calls male mythologies, that sets women apart from humanity as a whole. In an interview with Margaret A. Simons, professor of philosophy at Southern Illinois University at Edwardsville,

Beauvoir declared: "Better that [woman] identify herself as a human being who happens to be a woman" (Simons, 59). In defense of historical heroines the original French version of *The Second Sex* cites as models Jeanne d'Aragon, Jeanne de Naples, Isabelle d'Este, and the female mercenaries who armed themselves and rode to combat during the Italian Renaissance. In Beauvoir's view genteel morals were a hindrance to self-assertiveness: "A majority of these distinguished women were courtesans who combined a free spirit with their freedom of morals, and assured their economic autonomy by the exercise of their trade" (*ibid.,* 63). She notes that society's response to females who flaunt their emancipation is the body of legends that labeled them criminals and sexual libertines.

Beauvoir remained true to the anti-Christian assumptions of early girlhood. *The Second Sex* launches a diatribe against the punitive Catholicism of her mother and its medieval notions of woman as other, woman as sinner, woman as anything but human. By surveying history, in particular the prejudices promoted by Christianity and Islam, she explains how women, faced with the impossible perfection of the VIRGIN MARY as their role model, have been relegated to a secondary and supportive role in religion, education, and the public sphere. Thus resigned to second best, females create their own survival scenarios. At liberty they devalue outmoded lifestyles that rob the self of its true possibilities. In the summation Beauvoir holds up for examination the independent woman who "ceases to be a parasite" (Beauvoir, 755). By depending on self, the liberated woman rids herself of a "masculine mediator," an unqualified term that implies paternal priests and male deities.

Bibliography

Beauvoir, Simone de. *The Second Sex.* New York: Vintage, 1989.

Caron, Caroline. " 'Le Deuxième Sexe' de Simone de Beauvoir: Une Lecture Susceptible d'Inflechir la Resistance des Jeunnes Femmes Face au Feminisme," *Canadian Woman Studies* 20, no. 4 (Winter–Spring 2001): 36–40.

Simons, Margaret A. *Beauvoir and the Second Sex.* Lanham, Md.: Rowman & Littlefield, 2001.

Vintges, Karen. "Simone de Beauvoir: A Feminist Thinker for Our Times," *Hypatia* 14, no. 4 (Fall 1999): 133.

secrecy

Because of the treatment of women as other, females traditionally chose covert SISTERHOODs and guilds that allowed them self-affirmation without judgmental observation. The cloak of secrecy permeates the mysteries of cultic goddess worship and the myths of EVE, LILITH, LA LLORONA, Pandora, PERSEPHONE, and PHILOMELA. Respect for women's privacy is the core of the savage myth of Artemis/Diana, who sends dogs to rend the flesh of the hunter Actaeon for spying on her in the bath. In FAIRY TALES secrecy threatens the lives of brides in BLUEBEARD tales and the BEAUTY AND THE BEAST story. From the BEAUTY MYTH arises the sequestering of Snow White, a predictable dimension of a story about a young woman so lovely that she stirs jealousy and lust in the outside world. Gothic literature stressed the disguises and CONFINEMENT of characters in Mary SHELLEY's *Frankenstein* (1818) and Mary Elizabeth BRADDON's *Lady Audley's Secret* (1862) and in the novels of Ann RADCLIFFE. Solitude and retreat from scrutiny covered unspeakable crimes and villainous intent. Additional covert actions dominate Marian Engel's *Bear* (1977) and Diane DI PRIMA's eight-part epic cycle *Loba* (1978), two works that merge human and bestial behavior.

The timidity of authors such as the writers of Nushu, a secret Chinese script; and of Gothic pulp fiction and of contributors to early literary journals attests to the courage required to attach a name to an unpopular feminist opinion. Some authors felt compelled to screen their sentiments behind partial identity, as did MARIE DE FRANCE and H. D. Male pseudonyms withheld the feminine identity of authors Louisa May ALCOTT, Gertrude ATHERTON, the BRONTË sisters, Isak DINESEN, George ELIOT, George SAND, Olive SCHREINER, and Anna SEWARD. The shift toward bold public statements of ABOLITIONISM and SUFFRAGE freed Alcott from the need for a pen name. While editing a girl's miscellany, *Merry's Museum,* she issued original short pieces under her own name and identified the sources of poems and stories by Anna Laetitia BARBAULD, Lydia Maria CHILD, Felicia HEMANS, and Sarah Orne JEWETT.

Secrecy is common to the lore of witches, WISEWOMEN, and Wiccans. Practitioners of Old World cults retreated from the harsh critiques of male-dominated culture to practice their gynocentric arts in private, a contributing factor in Ann PETRY's historical novel *Tituba of Salem Village* (1964) and of Maryse CONDÉ's Caribbean novel *I, Tituba, Black Witch of Salem* (1986). The social critics Barbara EHRENREICH and Deirdre English, authors of *Witches, Midwives and Nurses: A History of Women Healers* (1973), add that the forced lurking and hiding caused practitioners to trust nothing to paper. Their reluctance to publicize secret charms and chants cost the world a full appreciation of women's healing and counseling methods, valuable insights that the poet Lucille CLIFTON honors in "If Our Grandchild Be a Girl" (1987), a celebration of Dahomian woman power.

Among the classic feminist works featuring female secrecy are a variety of settings and aims, such as Anne SEXTON's allusive poems suggesting that her father sexually abused her in childhood. Undisclosed locations dominate the feminist scenarios of feminist works, particularly the sequestered utopian society in Charlotte Perkins GILMAN's HERLAND (1915), the protection of Celtic goddess rites against Christian intervention in Marion Zimmer BRADLEY's *The Mists of Avalon* (1982), the plotting of escape in Margaret ATWOOD's dystopic novel *The HANDMAID'S TALE* (1985), and the route from Islamic terrorism followed by the author Betty MAHMOODY in her nonfiction thriller *Not without My Daughter* (1987). Noble acts uplift women under the cloak of secrecy, as in Hester PRYNNE's concealment of the lover who impregnated her in Nathaniel Hawthorne's *The SCARLET LETTER* (1850); the self-emancipation of Harriet JACOBS in *Incidents in the Life of a Slave Girl, Written by Herself* (1861); and the private regrets of a dying matriarch in Katherine Anne PORTER's stream-of-consciousness story "The JILTING OF GRANNY WEATHERALL" (1930). A global shame, the tribal custom of FEMALE GENITAL MUTILATION disclosed in the Egyptian journalist Nawal EL SAADAWI's *The Hidden Face of Eve: Women in the Arab World* (1980) and in

Alice WALKER's *Possessing the Secret of Joy* (1992), has led writers and orators to denounce the desexing of little girls.

The veiling of physical ramifications of womanhood tends to connect with the spilling of blood during the menses and childbirth, a controlling motif of Donna CROSS's medieval fiction in *Pope Joan* (1996) and of Anita DIAMANT's biblical women's club in the historical novel *The Red Tent* (1997). In 1912 the Russian-Jewish lecturer and memoirist Mary ANTIN described in *The Promised Land* the Orthodox Jewish custom of the *mikweh*, a ceremonial ablution required of women after menstrual flow or childbirth. Of the public cleansing among community women, Antin noted that "the name of [*mikweh*] it is indelicate to mention in the hearing of men" (Antin, 97). Although the ritual dates to prehistory, the secrecy suggests an unwholesome condition for which women are responsible. The only way to restore purity is to be pushed under water according to the laws of scripture. Ironically, according to Antin, the obligatory rinsing of impure females takes place in stagnant water that "does not look nor smell fresh" (*ibid.*).

The passage of refugees into new territory precipitates concealment and subterfuge, an issue in Jeanne Wakatsuki HOUSTON and James Houston's *Farewell to Manzanar* (1973) and in the poet Joy HARJO's *Secrets from the Center of the World* (1989). The Amerasian novelist Amy TAN bases her plots on Old World secrets that impact immigrant life in America. In *The Joy Luck Club* (1989) the hidden truth is a mother's abandonment of twin daughters during the Sino-Japanese War. More important to the feminist themes is the secret valuing of self-worth, a hidden strength that emboldens Lindo Jong to flee an unsuitable feudal marriage and emigrate from China. In Tan's semiautobiographical novel *The Kitchen God's Wife* (1991) parallel secrets disrupt a MOTHER-DAUGHTER RELATIONSHIP. Pearl Louie Brandt conceals her multiple sclerosis while her mother, Winnie Louie, hides a more corrosive fear that Pearl was sired by Wen Fu, Winnie's evil first husband. After a catharsis relieves Pearl of pent-up grief for her father, Winnie ends the rift with her daughter through extensive TALK-STORY, Tan's narrative method of unearthing problematic truths from the past.

Bibliography

Antin, Mary. *The Promised Land.* Boston: Houghton Mifflin, 1912.

Francis, Elizabeth. *The Secret Treachery of Words: Feminism and Modernism in America.* Minneapolis: University of Minnesota Press, 2002.

Gilbert, Sandra M. "Jane Eyre and the Secrets of Furious Lovemaking," *Novel: A Forum on Fiction* 31, no. 3 (Summer 1998): 351–372.

Griffin, Susan. *A Chorus of Stones.* New York: Anchor, 1993.

Roiphe, Katie. *The Morning After: Sex, Fear, and Feminism.* New York: Back Bay Books, 1994.

Seward, Anna (1742–1809)

The English religious author, sonneteer, and bluestocking critic and letter writer Anna (or Anne) Seward, dubbed the Swan of Lichfield, ventured into the male-dominated arts and encouraged other female writers to express feminist opinions. A native of Eyam, Derbyshire, she had a pious, learned lineage that included Dr. Samuel Johnson. The only child of four to survive, she flourished under the tutelage of her father, the Reverend Thomas Seward, canon of Lichfield and Salisbury, who taught her French, Italian, and Latin and read her the poems of John Milton. At age three she could recite "L'Allegro." By 1752 she was composing her own devotional poetry.

Trauma dogged Seward's young womanhood. Her mother suppressed evidence of her brilliance by forcing her to abandon poetry for needlework. The marriage of Honora Sneyd, Seward's foster sister, in 1773, and her death of tuberculosis were the sources of an elegy, funereal sonnets, and the soulful "Affection is repaid by causeless hate." An accident handicapped the poet, perhaps contributing to her decision not to marry and to care for her aged parents. She established enduring friendships with Sir Walter Scott and Dr. Erasmus Darwin, to whom she denounced the pollution at Coalbrookdale Gardens. Seward kept up with events leading to the French Revolution, the subject of her poem "To France on her Present Exertions" (1789). She read and critiqued the works of her contemporaries—Anna Laetitia BARBAULD, Hannah More, Charlotte SMITH—and sided with the feminism of

Mary WOLLSTONECRAFT's VINDICATION OF THE RIGHTS OF WOMAN (1792).

At age 38 Seward established her profession by translating Horace's odes and by contributing to Gentleman's Magazine poems and anti-Johnson letters under the pen name Benvolio. She crafted elegies on the executed spy Major John André, Captain James Cook, the actor David Garrick, her sister Sarah, and the author Anne, Lady Miller, Seward's patron in Bath-Easton, Somerset. In 1784 Seward published a four-volume epistolary novel, Louisa, which went into a fifth edition in 1795. In 1796 Seward's poem Llangollen Vale celebrated SISTERHOOD and woman-to-woman love in the elopement of a lesbian couple, Lady Eleanor Butler and Sarah Ponsonby, the controversial "ladies of Llangollen." Seward was an outspoken critic of marriage and maintained covert relationships with a number of women. Her later works consisted of posthumous verse and six volumes of edited correspondence published by Scott and Archibald Constable. Feminists have reclaimed Seward for her defense of the single life for women and for her budding ECOFEMINISM.

Bibliography

Coffey, Donna. "Protecting the Botanic Garden: Seward, Darwin, and Coalbrookdale," Women's Studies 31, no. 2 (March–April 2002): 141–164.

Seward, Anna. Llangollen Vale. Washington, D.C.: Woodstock Books, 1994.

———. The Poetical Works of Anna Seward. Brooklyn, N.Y.: AMS Press, 1974.

sexist language

The identification of discriminatory words in the mid-1970s promoted fairness, accuracy, and inclusiveness. The shift away from sexist language affected advertising and commerce as well as EDUCATION, government, and private discourse. An arbiter of sexist language, the award-winning lexicographer Rosalie Maggio states in Talking about People: A Guide to Fair and Accurate Language (1987) that androcentric language assumes that all people are "male, heterosexual, ablebodied, white, married, between the ages of 25–54, of Western European extraction" (Maggio, 18). Such an erroneous impression perpetuates STEREOTYPING and treats as outsiders or aliens those of other categories. Fortunate insiders sometimes carelessly—or, in some cases, intentionally—use sex-linked expressions that silence or marginalize others, such as the pejorative term doctress tossed at the physician and author Elizabeth BLACKWELL, North America's first female M.D.

Central to the intent to rid language of exclusion and sexism is the removal of gender from terms that can apply to male and female: Actor rather than actress to identify Fanny KEMBLE, for example. In Suzanne Romaine's treatise Communicating Gender (1999) she asserts the damage to women when they and their speech and writings "have been measured against male standards and found to be deficient and deviant" (Romaine, 157). Such discounting of female language leads to SILENCING, disenfranchisement, and bias. In anticipation of gender discrimination, writers such as H. D. and MARIE DE FRANCE shielded their complete identity. In a more vigorous concealment Louisa May ALCOTT, the BRONTË sisters, Mary Ann Evans, Baronne Dudevant, and Olive SCHREINER published their works under the male pseudonyms A. M. Barnard, Acton and Currer Bell, George ELIOT, George SAND, and Ralph Iron. Deceit had a decided effect on critics, who examined their works as though they were written by men.

A skewed education forced generations of girls to avoid the direct and straightforward approach used by men. As though learning a different language and mode of discourse, girls cultivated a coded vocabulary that comprised shallow niceties and ladylike euphemisms. Men replied in kind by adopting the overrefined vocabulary and speech suited to parlor courtships, but devoid of the realities of politics and economics. In GONE WITH THE WIND (1936) the Georgia novelist Margaret MITCHELL satirizes the education of Scarlett O'Hara by governesses and teachers at Fayetteville Female Academy in graceful dancing, smiling and batting the eyelids, and the deceptive practice of "[concealing] from men a sharp intelligence" (Mitchell, 62). Similar scenes of enforced gentility are a source of rancor and parody in the novels of Jane AUSTEN and Carson McCULLERS, the autobiographies of Maya ANGELOU, the works of Margaret ATWOOD, the witty drama of

Eve ENSLER, the women's page humor of Florence KING, and the subversive poems of Sylvia PLATH and Adrienne RICH. In recent decades women's choice of genteel language obscured necessary discourse on SEXUALITY, marital battery, rape, PROSTITUTION, and sexually transmitted diseases, especially gonorrhea, syphilis, and acquired immunodeficiency syndrome (AIDS). Action taken by the National Council of Teachers of English in 1975 and by the American Psychological Association in 1977 helped to legitimize and to advance feminist agendas protesting inappropriate language and promoting gender-neutral discourse.

Bibliography

Lakoff, Robin Tolmach, and Mary Bucholtz. *Language and Woman's Place: Text and Commentaries.* Oxford: Oxford University Press, 2004.

Maggio, Rosalie. *The Nonsexist Wordfinder: A Dictionary of Gender-free Usage.* Boston: Beacon Press, 1988.

———. *Talking about People: A Guide to Fair and Accurate Language.* New York: Oryx, 1997.

Mitchell, Margaret. *Gone with the Wind.* New York: Time Warner, 1964.

Romaine, Suzanne. *Communicating Gender.* Mahwah, N.J.: Lawrence Erlbaum, 1999.

Sexton, Anne (1928–1974)

A groundbreaking confessional poet, Anne Gray Harvey Sexton breached literary taboos in her selection of erotic fantasy, SEXUALITY, menstruation, masturbation, incest, neurosis, sagging flesh, depression, adultery, bastardy, ABORTION, and suicide as suitable topics for feminist verse. Her candid lyrics derive from incisive observations on female choices and the burdens of conventionality and conformity. Exuberant and headstrong with a flair for drama, she concealed doubts about her wealthy family and an alcoholic father. He later dominated incest imagery in her poems "Flee on Your Donkey" (1981) and "All My Pretty Ones" (1981), which extends him a tentative absolution. Reared in Catholicism in Newton, Massachusetts, she cloaked suffering and guilt with pretense. At age 19 she slipped away from Garland Junior College to marry the premed student Alfred Mueller "Kayo" Sexton II. The birth of a daughter during his service in the Korean War

left Sexton depressed and unfulfilled by the stifling female roles of the 1950s.

Sexton, who disdained the writing of female poetasters and their popular poetry clubs, preferred the works of serious crafters of verse. After treatment for suicidal urges, she relieved internal turmoil in confessional writing of finely structured poetry and developed a sisterly fondness for the writers Sylvia PLATH and Maxine KUMIN. In 1961, as poetry scholar at the Radcliffe Institute for Independent Study, Sexton turned inward for her first anthologies, *To Bedlam and Part Way Back* (1960) and *All My Pretty Ones* (1962). Her third collection, *Live or Die* (1966), won a Pulitzer Prize for its honest delving into dark personal hurt. Unresolved gender issues permeated *The Death Notebooks* (1974), her last poems before her suicide at age 46 by inhalation of carbon monoxide gas.

Sexton's monumental contributions to feminist literature range over the heady moments of womanhood and precipitate drops into despair and self-loathing. Bearing the New Englander's consciousness of the female holocaust that followed the Salem witch trials of 1692, the poem "Her Kind" (1960) dramatizes the helplessness of women hunted by pious male predators. She analyzed the DUALITY of practitioners of WITCHCRAFT, who risked torture and public execution by shunning housewifely roles for a wider knowledge of nature and society. An opposing view, "Housewife" (1962), details the humble pose of the female drudge kneeling as she scrubs floors in service to a husband whom the poet describes as a cyclical predator and enslaver.

Sexton won fans for her noble, often painful honesty. She spoke her reverence for her friend Sylvia Plath in "Sylvia's Death" (1966), a eulogy that honors her fellow poet's suicide in a gas oven as an appropriate end to a miserable marriage that diminished her self-esteem. The poem personifies death as the drummer boy who controls life's cadence. Sexton mourns the imprisoning beat as the source of her own misgivings and longing for escape into easeful death. She grasped at a utopian shift in *Transformations* (1971), a collection of story poems adapted from 17 of the Grimms' FAIRY TALES. The saucy stories, replete with lesbianism, cannibalism, and pedophilia, challenge the taboos of children's lore and anticipate a triumph of feminism that never transpired. In "Rumplestiltskin" Sexton characterized the manipulative dwarf as the inner terrors of womanhood and the cause of nightmares. After the maiden defeats him with truth, he splits into two sides, one soft and feminine and the other prickly and narrative (Sexton, 1971, 17). In the introduction to a collection of Sexton's life's work Kumin mused on the irony that "Anne delineated the problematic position of women—the neurotic reality of the [era]" at the same time that she lost a personal battle with stereotyped female roles (Sexton, 1981, xxxiv). In *Beginning with O* (1977) her fellow poet, Olga BROUMAS, honored Sexton's pro-woman verse.

Bibliography

Hall, Caroline King Barnard. *Anne Sexton.* Boston: Twayne, 1989.

Middlebrook, Diane Wood. *Anne Sexton: A Biography.* Boston: Houghton Mifflin, 1991.

Sexton, Anne. *The Complete Poems of Anne Sexton.* Boston: Houghton Mifflin, 1981.

———. *Transformations.* Boston: Houghton Mifflin, 1971.

sexuality

The right of women to express desire and to seek physical pleasure is a central theme in women's literature. As Erica Jong explains in *What Do Women Want?* (1998), sex appeal is a mystic and accessible constant, "out there shimmering for you—slightly out of reach. It is related to beauty, but it has nothing to do with perfect features or a perfect body. It is related to physical passion, but it is in no way hydraulic" (Jong, 145). Examples are legion in the feminist canon—the protagonist Dorothea Casaubon's marriage for love in George ELIOT's *MIDDLEMARCH* (1872), the covert lesbian love verse of the American poets Amy LOWELL and May SARTON, and the pheromonal lust of the hunter Eddie Bondo and forest ranger Deanne Wolfe in Barbara KINGSOLVER's ecofeminist romance *Prodigal Summer* (2000). Acknowledgments of carnality in women earned such authors as the Greek poet SAPPHO and CHRISTINE DE PISAN crit-

ical chastisement for their audacity. The playwright and novelist Aphra BEHN, the first Englishwoman to earn her living by writing, referred openly to mutual carnality in the poem "The Willing Mistress" (1673), which describes the wordless assent of Amyntas's lover to sex in a secluded grove, and of Cloris's dismay at Lysander's impotence in "The Disappointment" (1680). For candid admission of women's need for sexual release Behn suffered the contempt of genteel English society. Another victim, Lady Caroline LAMB, lost her husband and reputation for admitting in print her passion for Lord Byron.

In the early 19th century issues of miscegenation marked fiction that depicted the sexual relations of whites with Native Americans and with African slaves. In 1839 the editor and author Ann Sophia STEPHENS, a Connecticut-born intellectual, composed a classic young adult novel, *Malaeska: Indian Wife of the White Hunter,* which she serialized in the *Ladies' Companion* in three installments. A longer version appeared in 1860 as the first dime novel, the forerunner of the popular paperback. Stephens wrote additional Indian romances based on the human cost of mingled cultures, a motif dating to the legends of Pocahontas. Similarly noble, the widowed heroine of *Malaeska* exudes morality and self-confidence for her refusal to be shamed for loving a white man, the hunter William Danforth.

Feminist literature challenges the male dominator's hypocrisy in rejecting the female persona while embracing the female's body and engaging her breasts and genitals. Any woman who admitted a passion for lovemaking, according to the Danish author Isak DINESEN, risked being labeled a libertine whom any sane bachelor would avoid. In 1890 the anarchist orator Voltairine DE CLEYRE challenged women's complicity in catering to perverted notions of female sexuality by wearing clothing that enhanced the most appealing aspects of their body. She painted an unpleasant picture of the late 19th-century slave to fashion, "her waist surrounded by a high-board fence called a corset, her shoulders and hips angular from the pressure above and below, her feet narrowest where they should be widest, the body fettered by her everlasting prison skirt, her hair fastened tight" (de Cleyre, 1890). In a clever conclusion she contrasts a live female fashion plate to a statue: "Imagine such a thing as that carved in marble!" (*ibid.*). De Cleyre developed her ridicule of perverted sexuality with references to equestrienne outfits and sidesaddles and to baggy swimsuits and bathing hose. She described the typical authoritarian justification of female coercion as a "hollow-log story," a reference to outdated superstitions from myth and legend (*ibid.*).

The motif of visual sexuality recurs in literature about female characters who conform to male fantasy. Jeanne Wakatsuki HOUSTON, coauthor of a World War II memoir *Farewell to Manzanar* (1973), pictured the all-American "Betty co-ed" girlishness of the 1940s. To channel her athleticism, she rejected the stiff Asian femininity of odori dancing in favor of baton, bare legs, and flirty skirt. Because of her Japanese background she failed to grasp why American men admired cheerleaders and majorettes: "I was too young to consciously use my sexuality or to understand how an Oriental female can fascinate Caucasian men, and of course far too young to see that even this is usually just another form of invisibility" (Houston and Houston, 117). Gayl JONES's blues singer Ursa, protagonist of the stream-of-consciousness novel *Corregidora* (1975), complains through lyrics about the negation of self through deliberate sexual enticement. Singing directly to the dominator, she croons: "O Mister who come to my house You do not come to visit You do not come to see me to visit You come to hear me sing with my thighs" (Jones, 67). In Denise LEVERTOV's verse argument "Ancient Airs and Dances" (1992), the speaker, gray-haired and experienced, comprehends the charade. Although she has outgrown coquetry, she acknowledges a persistent DUALITY between her sensual self and the realist that clambers to suppress the vamp. She capitulates to male fantasy by striking the pose of the siren. In the second stave the voice of wisdom identifies the sexual come-on as childish obstinance.

The power of sexuality can terrify a timid female character. Self-muzzling of the pubescent girl colors Carmen Martín Gaite's hypnotic novel *El cuarto de atrás: Apuntes sobre la narración, el amor y la mentira* (*The Back Room*, 1978), winner of Spain's National Prize for Literature. Reviewers note that she restricts her otherwise candid autobiographical fiction by banning the themes of girlhood camaraderie, sexuality, and maternity. The protagonist speaks directly of her fears: "My failures in love have always stemmed from that, from the fear that someone may leave me at a loss for words, reduced to the naked power of my gaze or my body" (Gaite, 182). The phobia implies that a full expression of libido weakens the female by placing her under the control of the lustful male. A more revealing comment occurs a few pages later, when she refers to terrors of losing control: "I preferred to ask questions. Allusions to sex scared me, they were impossible to grasp and of ambiguous gender, like butterflies" (*ibid.*, 192).

In contrast to female inhibition, the manipulation of feminine charms for personal gain is a plus for characters in feminist fiction. In the fictional biography *Dolley* (1994) Rita Mae BROWN places in the mouth of the protagonist Dolley Madison, wife of President James Madison, an astute observation about sexuality and politics. In reference to the slave Sukey's liaisons with André Daschkov, a Russian diplomat, Dolley is philosophical: "You're a beautiful woman. That's a kind of power" (Brown, 160). In sympathy with the black woman's invisibility Dolley muses that "it would be almost impossible to resist that power . . . in your position" (*ibid.*). Sukey, a blunt-spoken individual, retorts that she is no one's chattel: "You can catch me if I run away, but my soul is my own!" (*ibid.*). Dolley later attributes Sukey's joy in sexual release as a temporary shred of freedom.

Bibliography
Brown, Rita Mae. *Dolley.* New York: Bantam Books, 1995.

Charles, Ron, "Mothers of Nature Howling at the Moon," *Christian Science Monitor,* 19 October 2000.

de Cleyre, Voltairine. "Sex Slavery" (1890). Available online. URL: http://dwardmac.pitzer.edu/Anarchist_Archives/bright/cleyre/sexslavery.html. Accessed on October 13, 2005.

Dinesen, Isak. *On Modern Marriage and Other Observations.* New York: St. Martin's, 1977.

Gaite, Carmen Martín. *The Back Room.* San Francisco: City Lights Books, 2000.

Houston, Jeanne Wakatsuki, and James Houston. *Farewell to Manzanar.* New York: Bantam, 1973.

Jones, Gayl. *Corregidora.* New York: Random House, 1975.

Jong, Erica. *What Do Women Want?* New York: Harper-Collins, 1998.

Loy, Mina. *The Lost Lunar Baedeker: Poems of Mina Loy.* New York: Farrar, Straus & Giroux, 1997.

sexual politics

The complex social, ethical, and economic roots of sexual politics invade much of feminist literature as testimony to GENDER BIAS and the DOUBLE STANDARD. Examples dominate Pearl BUCK's agrarian novel *The GOOD EARTH* (1931), Mary Boykin CHESNUT's Civil War diaries, the orations of Emma GOLDMAN and Susan B. ANTHONY, the populist newspaper columns of Molly IVINS, and the gyno-criticism of Sandra M. GILBERT and Susan GUBAR. In the Chicago poet Gwendolyn BROOKS's heroic poem "The ANNIAD" (1949) the focal character struggles to shape her naive idealism to the realities of marriage. Annie, a skillful myth maker and role player, cannot deny the truth of marital relationships in the life of her mother, Maxi Allen, whose life suffers from unstinting personal and monetary restrictions as adamant as the "prim low fencing pinching in the grass" (Brooks, 186). As though expecting her own life to be the one shining exception to the rule, Annie continues to anticipate a happily-ever-after existence in a world governed by males. She eventually finds herself shortchanged of the liberties she daydreamed about in girlish fantasies.

More aggressive feminism refuses to think of sexual politics as inescapable. In a direct challenge of the double standard the poet Marge Piercy issued in the fall 1995 edition of *On the Issues* a humorous six-stanza poem, "The Grey Flannel Sexual Harassment Suit." Beneath the lighthearted quips about real females, the text denounces a legal system based on a self-fulfilling prophecy that complainants against workplace sexism are virginal, dressed buttoned-to-the-throat, and adorned with conservative jewelry. Androcentric authority expects the defendant's character and behavior to conform to a churchgoing, monogamous, and pure-minded ideal. Of the strands of racism and classism that cloud issues of sexual harassment, the poet indicates that the best candidate for redress must be an English speaking blonde caucasian. The poet concludes with a flip remark to those who do not fit the criteria that those who lack the Whites-only stereotype dwell outside the law's protection (Piercy, 60).

Too often, legalities reflect gendered expectations of what women are or are not capable of, a theme of Henrik Ibsen's play *A DOLL'S HOUSE* (1879) and Betty MAHMOODY's *Not without My Daughter* (1987). More suited to developing world feminist concerns are the plays of the Nigerian playwright Tunde Adeyanju. She follows the example of the Ghanian dramatist Ama Ata AIDOO in setting female victimization in a political context common in black African PATRIARCHY. A revealing situation is the unsympathetic response of male tribe members to female abduction and murder in the unpublished work "Democracy on Trial" (1998). In the cynical one-act play *The Ruling Junta* (2002) Adeyanju turns to a repressive regime's brutal acts, the silencing and jailing of Mr. Bamidele's wife. In the ensuing man talk, male politicians consider women such as Mrs. Bamidele too simple-witted to comprehend political issues. They conclude that she brought about her own downfall by publishing an article that criticized the current rule. The subtext is unsettling: that women who venture into the political realm deserve punishment for disagreeing with the status quo.

Bibliography

Adeyanju, Tunde. *Democracy on Trial.* (1998). Available online. URL: http://www.alexanderstreet4.com. Accessed on October 17, 2005.

———. *The Ruling Junta.* Abeokuta, Nigeria: Litany Nigeria, 2002.

Brooks, Gwendolyn. *Blacks.* Chicago: Third World Press, 1987.

Piercy, Marge. "The Grey Flannel Sexual Harassment Suit," *On the Issues* (Fall 1995): 60.

Stanford, Ann Folwell. "An Epic with a Difference: Sexual Politics in Gwendolyn Brooks's 'The Anniad,' " *American Literature* 67, no. 2 (June 1995): 283–301.

Shange, Ntozake (1948–)

The poet, dancer, and dramatist Ntozake Shange merges artistic forms to redeem and honor women.

The oldest of four children of a well-to-do family, she was born in Trenton, New Jersey, and reared in Saint Louis, where racism was more virulent. After completing high school in Trenton, she attended Barnard College, and in her late teens she entered a brief marriage to a law student. She joined an art commune in Los Angeles and changed her birth name, Paulette Linda Williams, to Ntozake Shange, a Zulu phrase meaning "the independent woman who walks like a lion." By enrolling in American studies courses at the University of Southern California, she prepared to teach humanities, black studies, and women's studies on the college level.

While rearing a daughter in New York City, Shange wrote *for colored girls who have considered suicide when the rainbow is enuf* (1975), a choric play reflecting suicidal urges in her youth. The coordinated monologues verbalize women's memories of date rape, physical abuse, ABORTION, and child murder, a horrific moment when Beau Willie Brown drops two of Crystal's children from a five-story building. Emphasizing the author's revolt against sexism and racism is her choice of nonstandard spellings and punctuation. The drama builds to a crisis in a cry from the Lady in Red: "i wanted to jump up outta my bones & be done wit myself leave me alone & go on in the wind it waz too much" (Shange, 1975, 24). A chorus reaches a redemptive epiphany in realizing "*i found god in myself & i loved her*" (ibid.). The play, which debuted at the city's New Federal Theatre, stirred anger in black men who felt stigmatized by Shange's hot-tempered verse. *for colored girls* progressed to the big time late in 1976 as the second work by a black woman after Lorraine HANSBERRY's *A Raisin in the Sun* (1959) to open on Broadway. Shange won an Obie, the Outer Critics Circle Award, and a citation from *Mademoiselle*.

Shange's subsequent works include novels, novellas, essays, and poetry plus edited anthologies of multicultural fiction and dramas. She received a second Obie for her revision of Bertolt Brecht's *Mother Courage and Her Children* (1980). In 1991 Shange surveyed the pangs of lovesickness and heartbreak in a poetry collection, *The Love Space Demands: A Continuing Saga*, an unassuming volume of her famed word pictures. The author re-

turned to her roots for *Betsey Brown: A Novel* (1995), a historical fiction of a teen's conflicted coming of age in Saint Louis in 1957. In an era of dramatic integrations of schools and public buildings, the Browns, Jane and Greer, disagree on their oldest daughter's role in defying segregation. The lyricist Emily MANN and the composer Baikida Carroll adapted the novel in 1998 as a rhythm-and-blues stage opera.

Shange turned domestic for a mock-serious African-American cookbook, *If I Can Cook / You Know God Can* (1998), a kitchen guide to the black diaspora. In the latter she recognizes women's role in preserving the culinary ties to Afro-Caribbean Atlantic foodways from such staples as barbecue, black-eyed peas, collards, couscous, hominy, lamb, okra, pig tails, watermelon, and yams. Of the sources of table riches Shange explained that she and her daughter, Savannah, shared feasts with folk "from different bloodlines, but of the same spirit, reliable, loving, and alone too, except for us" (Shange, 1998, 7). Retreating into her past, the author recalled sharing dill pickles at the pickle barrel "with anyone I jumped double Dutch with" (ibid., 8). The concept of shared food and of communal celebration and play undergirds the generosity of Shange's recipes and their anecdotal descriptions. Her woman-centered works inspired the novelist Gloria NAYLOR.

Bibliography

Lester, Neal A. "Shange's Men: *for colored girls* Revisited, and Movement Beyond," *African American Review* 26, no. 2 (Summer 1992): 319–328.

Shange, Ntozake. *for colored girls who have considered suicide when the rainbow is enuf.* New York: Scribners, 1975.

———. *If I Can Cook / You Know God Can.* Boston: Beacon Press, 1998.

Shelley, Mary (1797–1851)

The London-born diarist and creator of a sci-fi classic, Mary Wollstonecraft Godwin Shelley reversed the unflattering stereotypes of Victorian women by attributing them to a male. Her unusual parentage, the most prominent literary marriage of the era, equipped her with the abstract knowledge to write philosophical speculative fiction. An only child, she came of age hearing the learned discussions of her father, the self-centered philosopher William Godwin, and his second wife, Mary Jane Clairmont, with a host of colleagues, including the impetuous young romantic poet Percy Bysshe Shelley. In girlhood Mary Shelley read sentimental and Gothic novels and verse and began questioning the female STEREOTYPING common in the era's fiction. An analysis of her famed allegory suggests that she felt eclipsed socially and intellectually at home. To her journal she confided, "I seem deserted—alone in the world—cast off—the victim of poverty & neglect—Thus it is—To be poor & so cut off from society—to pass my days in seclusion" (Shelley, 517). She retreated to the grave of her mother, the brilliant protofeminist Mary WOLLSTONECRAFT, who died of puerperal fever when her daughter was 10 days old. Literary historians surmise that Shelley sought parental approval of juvenilia that mimicked her mother's radical feminist writings.

After eloping to France with Shelley, a married man, at age 17, Mary Shelley lived the life of the other woman until Percy's wife, Harriet Westbrook Shelley, drowned herself. Legally wed in a prominent literary union of her own, Mary Shelley spent a summer at Villa Diodati on Lake Geneva among her husband's coterie, including William Hogg, Lord Byron, and his personal physician, John Polidori. The androcentric discussion of medicine and philosophy turned her private thoughts and journal writings toward humanistic questions and personal sorrows about the death of her firstborn and guilt over Harriet's suicide. For diversion Mary Shelley accepted the challenge of a ghost story competition launched by her husband and his three male colleagues. From popular motifs of walking specters, vivisection, grave robbing, and galvanic experiments on living tissue that haunted her dreams she cobbled the plot of a Gothic fable, FRANKENSTEIN; or, the Modern Prometheus (1818), a classic mad scientist novel published when she was 19. The philosophical depth of her novel elevated it above the Gothic shockers of her day and caused critics to wonder whether the story was actually the work of her husband.

A widow at age 25 after Percy Shelley drowned in the Bay of Spezzia off the coast of Livorno, Italy,

Mary Shelley devoted herself to his memory, a foreshadowing of the life-in-death mourning that Queen Victoria modeled for English widows in 1861 at the demise of her beloved consort, Prince Albert. Mary Shelley and her son, William "Mouse" Shelley, bore back to England a memorial box containing the poet's heart, a graphic parallel to Victor Frankenstein's fascination with nonfunctioning human organs. While editing Percy Shelley's unpublished manuscripts, she completed Gothic tales and four more novels, *Valperga* (1823), the apocalyptic tale *The Last Man* (1826), the autobiographical *Lodore* (1835), and *Falkner* (1837), an adventure novel. Feminists such as Anne RICE place Shelley's first novel high on the list of women's accomplishments for its depiction of wrongheadedness in a male intellectual who discounts the value of wife and home. Ironically domestic themes energize the falling action after Victor, the epitome of arrogant masculine science, cheats the unnamed monster of his own made-to-order bride.

Bibliography

Mellor, Anne K. *Mary Shelley: Her Life, Her Fiction, Her Monsters.* New York: Routledge, 1989.

O'Dea, Gregory. "Prophetic History and Textuality in Mary Shelley's *The Last Man,*" *Papers on Language and Literature* 28, no. 3 (Summer 1992): 283–304.

Shelley, Mary. *The Journals of Mary Shelley, 1814–1844.* Baltimore: Johns Hopkins University Press, 1995.

Sheltered Life, The   Ellen Glasgow (1932)

A bold southern ironist, Ellen GLASGOW mocked polite sexism in *The Sheltered Life* (1932), the last of her Queensborough trilogy of manners. As chemical factory fumes assail the Archbald home, conflict takes an indistinct outline in the destabilization of Virginia during a transition in tradition, class stratification, and religious orthodoxy. In early girlhood the protagonist, Jenny Blair Archbald, reads Louisa May ALCOTT's LITTLE WOMEN (1868–69) and murmurs to herself, "I'm different. I'm different" (Glasgow, 3). Heightening Jenny's expression of uniqueness is an open French window, a suggestion of the impulses to emancipation that will tempt her from a repressive atmosphere mirroring Glasgow's hometown of Richmond. The narrative rapidly circumvents Jenny's hopes with a fall from her roller-skates, a suggestion of precipitate urges that stymie her hopes.

To dramatize the onset of modernism, the dark comedy juxtaposes the frivolous with the germane, the fruitful with the sterile. Instead of introduction to society as a proper debutante, Jenny wants smoking privileges, nonstop parties, the vote, a stage career, and a married philanderer, George Birdsong. Contrasted by the brittle asceticism of 75-year-old General David Archbald and the destruction of the city's fine old homes and arbors, Jenny's yearning to live in New York City suggests new life and direction, but it is the profligate charm of Birdsong that anchors her in Queensborough. His childless wife, Eva, a self-absorbed clotheshorse, ignores George's faults while keeping up a front of gracious propriety. The protracted crush on George results in the wife's discovery of her husband in Jenny's arms and the shooting death of George inside their crumbling town home.

Glasgow creates allegory from atmosphere. Like the stultifying relationship of Eva and George, Queensborough sours as the reek of "a glue factory, with a potpourri of acrid train smoke and the horrific odor from smouldering dump heaps" overwhelms "the double-distilled essence of roses, honeysuckle and magnolia," the stereotypical fragrance of the antebellum South (*ibid.*, 7). In agony about his ongoing infidelities to an ailing wife, George confesses, "If she saw me as I am, I might be able to measure up better" (*ibid.*, 185). Images supplant reality in the upright posture of the mulatto Memoria, who cultivates her bearing by balancing laundry baskets on her head as she walks toward her home on Canal Street. Complicit in the domestic posturing of the Birdsongs, Memoria whitens their wash, a cyclical act of rinsing away repeated sins. Similarly Jenny acquires stature and poise by adapting to the demands of southern womanhood, an acquired grace that provides Eva with a mask of her suffering. In the novel's tragic conclusion Jenny experiences a sudden disheartening self-glimpse. Just as George wishes that others could accept him for his faults, Jenny realizes that she has no choice but to live with her failings.

Bibliography

Glasgow, Ellen. *The Sheltered Life.* Charlottesville: University Press of Virginia, 1994.

Goodman, Susan. "Memory and Memoria in *The Sheltered Life*," *Mississippi Quarterly* 49, no. 2 (Spring 1996): 241–254.

Showalter, Elaine (1941–)

An eminent college professor and the founder of FEMINIST CRITICISM, Elaine Cottler Showalter encourages an unbiased reading of women's literature. A native of Cambridge, Massachusetts, she grew up in Boston in a working-class Jewish family and determined in her youth to teach at the university level. In 1962 her parents ended contact with her when she married a gentile. After earning degrees at Bryn Mawr and Brandeis University, in 1970 she completed a doctorate in Victorian and Edwardian literature at the University of California at Davis with the thesis "The Double Critical Standard: Criticism of Women Writers in England, 1845–1880." The following year she published the first textbook on women in literature, *Women's Liberation and Literature* (1971). In subsequent years, she received both a Guggenheim and a Rockefeller Humanities fellowship. She broke a male-only tradition by joining the staff of Rutgers University, where she advanced to full professor. In addition to presiding over the New Jersey chapter of the National Organization of Women and the Modern Language Association Commission on the Status of Women in the Profession, she accepted the prestigious Avalon Foundation humanities and English chair at Princeton University.

In works of feminist criticism, Showalter published provocative critical essays in *American Historical Review, Chronicle of Higher Education,* the *London Times Literary Supplement,* and *New Statesman.* Her first text, *A Literature of Their Own: British Novelists from Brontë to Lessing* (1977), proposed unique critical criteria for judging feminist works. With a collection of female essays, *These Modern Women: Autobiographical Essay of the Twenties* (1979), Showalter enhanced the understanding of such motifs in feminist self-expression as substance abuse, celibacy, and solitude. Through her insightful critiques readers began to reevaluate such writers as the novelist Elizabeth GASKELL and the essayist Susan SONTAG and to discover such modern feminist innovators as the English Gothic fantacist Angela CARTER. In *The Female Malady: Women, Madness, and English Culture (1830–1980)* (1986) Showalter exposed the misdiagnosis of female mental patients under an androcentric psychiatric tyranny. To supply feminist readers with short fiction from the past, she anthologized *Scribbling Women: Short Stories by 19th Century American Women* (1996), which showcases the work of Willa CATHER, Kate CHOPIN, Rebecca Harding DAVIS, Mary E. Wilkins FREEMAN, Frances HARPER, Sarah Orne JEWETT, and Elizabeth Stuart PHELPS.

For *Hystories: Hysterical Epidemics and Modern Culture* (1997) Showalter conducted a decade of research at the Wellcome Institute for the History of Medicine in London. On May 15, 1998, she was the target of a defender of chronic fatigue sufferers who threatened her for labeling the syndrome a modern hysteria. The attack, which her friend, Joyce Carol OATES, had predicted, occurred at a Washington bookshop after an onslaught of hate mail and veiled threats. Showalter was undeterred. In *Inventing Herself: Claiming a Feminist Intellectual Heritage* (2001) she summarized her life's work: "I have not discovered any tidy patterns or plots in the lives of feminist rule-breakers, but I have noticed some common and recurring themes. Above all, these were women who defined themselves, however painfully, as autonomous" (Showalter, 2001, 18).

Bibliography

Showalter, Elaine. *Hystories.* New York: Columbia University Press, 1998.

———. *Inventing Herself: Claiming a Feminist Intellectual Heritage.* New York: Scribner, 2001.

———. *A Literature of Their Own: British Novelists from Brontë to Lessing.* Princeton, N.J.: Princeton University Press, 1998.

———. *Scribbling Women: Short Stories by 19th Century American Women.* Piscataway, N.J.: Rutgers University Press, 1997.

Wineapple, Brenda. "Unparalleled Lives," *Women's Review of Books* 18, no. 10/11 (July 2001): 34–35.

silencing

Silencing is a crucial issue in feminist literature for its potential to obliterate women's needs and desires and to erase their presence from history. The stifling of the female half of society accords to males an outsized importance and authority, as is the case with the mythic King Tereus of Thrace, who raped his sister-in-law, PHILOMELA, and concealed his crime by cutting out her tongue. More heinous is BLUEBEARD, the slayer of wives who pry into his lurid past. In the words of the critic Adrianne Kalfopoulou, Hester PRYNNE, Nathaniel HAWTHORNE's heroine of *THE SCARLET LETTER* (1850), is a victim of the American Victorianism of the author's day. At the hands of a male-run theocracy in Boston she suffers silencing for adultery and illegitimate motherhood and for her refusal to identify her partner. In wordless retort she flourishes in "gendered singularity," an example of selflessness and liberated womanhood she sets for the women of Massachusetts Colony (Kalfopoulou, iii). Living apart at the seashore, she rears her daughter, Pearl, away from village Puritanism and counsels sorrowing female visitors to her cottage. At her death male prerogatives hold sway. Her unlettered tombstone speaks only the community's fanatic misogyny in the scarlet symbol that blazons her shame. Swept from community history are her name, the dates of her life, and her mothering of Pearl. Hawthorne indicates in "The Custom House" that her story survives on the strength of its truths about gendered injustice.

By sanctioning only those subjects that shore up PATRIARCHY, the anti-woman faction seeks to perpetuate the status quo. Suffering a wretched sentence is Precious Auntie, the spurned bride in Amy TAN's *The Bonesetter's Daughter* (2001), who drinks boiling resin that melts one side of her face and mouth and stills her tongue. As in the Chinese metaphor of swallowing sorrows, the ingestion of an ingredient in ink turns a means of communication into a weapon against speech. Tan doubles the tragedy to Precious Auntie by picturing her rage at the news of her daughter, LuLing's, betrothal to the evil Chang family. Unable to speak her terror, Precious Auntie chooses suicide, a death that ends the marriage plans and frees LuLing from the Changs. The motif of silencing and suicide echoes the limited choices of women who faced feudal betrothal in imperial China.

Accounts of females who elect speechlessness form a unique branch of feminist literature for the severity of their self-punishment and isolation. Self-silencing can be the result of both external and internal forces, such as that suffered in patriarchal marriages or in totalitarian states. In part 2 of Jean RHYS's WIDE SARGASSO SEA (1966) Edward Rochester warns his young Jamaican bride, Antoinette Cosway, either to ignore her fears or to tell no one about them. Her prophetic terrors are realized when he installs her at Thornfield, his English manor, where her perverse actions cause him to lock her away from public view. More lethal is the terrorism of the Dominican strongman Rafael Trujillo in Julia ALVAREZ's historicial novel In the Time of the Butterflies (1994). The quelling of female dissidents ends in murder for Dr. Minerva Mirabal de Tavarez and her sisters, Patria Mercedes Mirabal de Gonzalez and Maria Teresa Mirabal de Guzman. Ironically their martyrdom reverses the roadside execution by turning into legend the acts of female freedom fighters.

Another version of self-silencing is the preservation of private thoughts. In Mourning Dove: A Salishan Autobiography, published posthumously in 1990, the author confesses her self-silencing before puberty because she intended to keep secret her resolve to avoid marriage. Because of strong familial influence to follow tribal ways, she asserts, "I had to keep my thoughts to myself because I was afraid of the scolding and rebuke I would get from my parents and native tutor. So I kept my secret in my breast" (Mourning Dove, 54). The choice indicates the dangers of announcing Mourning Dove's yearning for individualism and for a lifestyle that violates the lockstep training of young girls for marriage and family. Her naming for a bird recognized by its plaintive cooing suits the image of the melancholy preteen.

A vivid depiction of girlhood self-silencing is the heart of Maya ANGELOU's AUTOBIOGRAPHY I KNOW WHY THE CAGED BIRD SINGS (1969). She recalls giving up speech at age eight after her mother's lover, Mr. Freeman, raped her and threatened to kill her brother, Bailey, if she reported the assault. Because of her devotion to Bailey and guilt that her uncles kicked the rapist to death, Maya bears her misery in silence. She describes the crime as a palpable enemy in her mouth: "I could feel the evilness flowing through my body and waiting, pent up, to rush off my tongue" (Angelou, 72). To hold in her shame, as though sealing a liquid in a jar, she clamps her jaw shut. Grandmother Baxter compounds the post-rape conspiracy of silence by declaring Mr. Freeman and his unfortunate end two taboo subjects in her house. Maya's moroseness requires a return to Grandmother Henderson in Stamps, Arkansas, where, for a year, the child cocoons, "[sopping] around the house, the Store, the school and the church, like an old biscuit" (ibid., 77). Only through elocution lessons does Maya permit herself to speak.

Bibliography

Angelou, Maya. I Know Why the Caged Bird Sings. New York: Bantam Books, 1970.

Collins, Martha S. "Inscribing the Space of Female Identity in Carmen Martín Gaite's 'Entre Visillos,'" Symposium 51, no. 2 (Summer 1997): 66–78.

Kalfopoulou, Adrianne. A Discussion of the Ideology of the American Dream in the Culture's Female Discourses. Lewiston, N.Y.: Edwin Mellen Press, 2000.

Mourning Dove. Mourning Dove: A Salishan Autobiography. Lincoln: University of Nebraska Press, 1990.

Randall, Margaret, ed. Breaking the Silences: Twentieth-Century Poetry by Cuban Women. Vancouver: Pulp Press, 1982.

Valis, Noël, and Carol Maier, eds. In the Feminine Mode: Essays on Hispanic Women Writers. Lewisburg, Pa.: Bucknell University Press, 1990.

Silko, Leslie Marmon (1948–)

The Laguna-Latina-Caucasian teacher, scenarist, fiction writer, and poet Leslie Marmon Silko speaks for peace, ECOFEMINISM, and the nonwhite American female's bitterness at culture theft. Born in Albuquerque, New Mexico, she grew up in the Laguna tradition at the Pueblo Indian Reservation, which accorded women sexual freedom. She freely traversed the expanse of mesas on horseback. With her sisters, Gigi and Wendy, Silko learned strong womanhood from their maternal great-grandmother and grandmother—Marie Anaya, called Grandma A'mooh, and Lillie Stagner—and from Great-Aunt Susie, all of whom told treasured animal fables, trickster tales, and the GODDESS LORE of Corn Woman and SPIDER WOMAN, the mythic creator. Sessions of family STORYTELLING stressed a memory element requiring even the youngest listener to recall events and names of characters. In *Storyteller* (1981) Silko infuses the text with serious considerations of truth, a divine being, and mystic nature. She recalls, "I grew up at Laguna listening. . . . Most important, I feel the power which the stories still have, to bring us together, especially when there is loss and grief" (Silko, 1981, 7).

From an off-reservation high school, Silko progressed to a degree in English from the University of Mexico along with peripheral study of American Indian law. While teaching literature, she submitted her first story, "The Man to Send Rain Clouds" (1969), to the *New Mexico Quarterly*. After two years of teaching at Navajo Community College she began publishing more short fiction and verse in numerous anthologies and textbooks, including "Lullaby" (1971), published in *Chicago Review*. She earned respect as the youngest author represented in *The Norton Anthology of Women's Literature* and the collection of her best works in *Laguna Woman* (1974), winner of a *Chicago Review* award.

Silko resided for two years in Bethel outside Ketchikan, Alaska, on a National Endowment for the Arts Fellowship. She completed a novel, *Ceremony* (1977), her masterwork, which exhibits the mentorship of the poet James Wright. Its themes reevaluate Native healing through recommitment to nature, myth, and ritual. The combined effects combat the post–World War II malaise in Tayo, a depressed Indian veteran. In *Storyteller* (1980), source of the MacArthur Foundation Prize, the author blends Grandpa Hank's family photos with legend, song, genealogy, and personal essays. Among the short works in the collection is "Yellow Woman," a favorite in feminist courses for its description of a woman's survival of abduction. A decade later Silko turned to creation myth and technical innovation in *Almanac of the Dead* (1991), a jarring Native American epic that moves from prehistory into an era of easy money from the sale of illicit drugs. In the opening paragraphs the author elaborates on the function of Zeta, a Yaqui crone, in preserving proud and empowering stories from pre-Columbian times that counter unanswered questions of the present.

To enlighten non-Indians of the American government's genocidal intent in the 19th century, Silko assembled essays on the Indian point of view in *Yellow Woman and a Beauty of the Spirit* (1996), which refers to ancient Aztec, Inca, Maya, and Mixtec lore and Pueblo mythology. She pays particular attention to the Pueblo tradition of burying family members in collapsed rooms of a multifamily dwelling, where memorabilia and debris are as valuable as the bones of the dead. In a statement of Native ECOFEMINISM she explains that "corncobs and husks, the rinds and stalks and animal bones were not regarded as garbage or filth. The remains were merely resting at a midpoint in their journey back to dust . . . because for the ancient people all these things had spirit and being" (Silko, 1997, 26). She concludes that respect for living things reflects love and devotion to Mother Earth, source of all life. Silko's reverence for myth is a structural element of self: "Through the stories we hear who we are" (ibid., 30). In *Gardens in the Dunes* (1999) she gives flesh to the Indian WISEWOMAN, Grandmother Fleet, who leads her granddaughters, Indigo and Sister Salt, to the joyous ceremonies of Wovoka, the Native evangelist. At the messianic Ghost Dance Indigo foresees an uprooting that takes her far from home but never shakes her faith in her grandmother's Southwest American garden. Silko's writings influenced those of Joy HARJO.

Bibliography

Barnett, Louise, and James Thorson, eds. *Leslie Marmon Silko: A Collection of Critical Essays.* Albuquerque: University of New Mexico Press, 1999.

Donovan, Kathleen M. *Feminist Readings of Native American Literature: Coming to Voice.* Tucson: University of Arizona Press, 1998.

Silko, Leslie Marmon. *Almanac of the Dead.* New York: Simon & Schuster, 1991.

———. *Ceremony.* New York: Penguin, 1977.

———. *Gardens in the Dunes.* New York: Simon & Schuster, 2000.

———. *Storyteller.* New York: Seaver, 1981.

———. *Yellow Woman and a Beauty of the Spirit.* New York: Simon & Schuster, 1997.

single parenting

The subject of mothering fatherless children is a serious motif echoing through feminist literature, especially as it applies to the fallen woman or abandoned wife. The essayist and journalist Margaret OLIPHANT, a polemicist for *Frasier's* and *Blackwood's Edinburgh Magazine,* made the issue of the lone mother's survival the focus of "The Laws Concerning Women" (1856), "The Condition of Women" (1858), and "The Grievances of Women" (1880). She blamed male contempt for women as a cause of illegitimate children's living in poverty. In other works of the feminist canon domestic scenarios generated by the father's absence range from the redoubtable spirit of the NEW WOMAN in Fanny FERN's autobiographical novel, *Ruth Hall: A Domestic Tale of the Present Time* (1854) and Elizabeth PHELPS's melodramatic best seller *Hedged In* (1870) to the departure of father March to the Civil War in Louisa May ALCOTT's LITTLE WOMEN (1868–69). He leaves Marmie March to cope with rearing four daughters on a limited budget further strained by wartime shortages. Rather than limit the girls' experiences, hard times appear to develop character and intense love for the lone mother. To Marmie, Jo declares, "Mothers are the *best* lovers in the world" (Alcott, 409).

The specter of fatherlessness brings out the self-sufficiency of women. Susan B. ANTHONY stated in "Homes of Single Women" (1877) that lone females display satisfaction and economy, proving their abilities to survive without male support. She made clear that women struggled to provide the best of environments and EDUCATION for their children in a sexist job market. In the 1930s Hollywood appeared to agree with Anthony by filming two classic single-parent novels, Fannie HURST's *Back Street* (1932) and *Imitation of Life* (1933). Contributing mid-20th-century views were Ann PETRY's best-selling first novel *The Street* (1946), Lorraine HANSBERRY's classic play *A RAISIN IN THE SUN* (1959), the poet Muriel RUKEYSER's anthology *Body of Waking* (1958), and

a classic short story, "I Stand Here Ironing" (1957), Tillie OLSEN's poignant reminder of the sacrifices that women make for their fatherless young.

In 1987 the novelist Toni MORRISON, herself a single mother, expounded on the heartaches and joys of single parenting in BELOVED, a ghost story built on themes of regret and renewal. Sethe, the former slave who saves two sons and two daughters from field work on a Kentucky plantation, revels in a reunion with her children and their grandmother, Baby Suggs, in the free state of Ohio. Complicating the home scene are the arrival of slave catchers and Sethe's instinctive slicing of her older daughter's throat to spare her the misery of breeding more slaves for the master. After the death of Baby Suggs the emotional and spectral hauntings of the house on Bluestone Road scare away the two boys, leaving Sethe as the single parent of a lonely daughter. Reclamation of the revenant Beloved tilts Sethe toward hysteria. She enacts a manic motherhood of spoiling and pleasing her revived baby girl with ribbons and baubles, a single parent's substitute for missed opportunities for cuddling and love.

Late 20th-century feminist fiction tends to admire single mothers who take pride in managing both children and jobs. The emotional motif of lone parenting undergirds Diane DI PRIMA's autobiographical novel *Memoirs of a Beatnik* (1969), the Nigerian novelist Buchi EMECHETA's *The Joys of Motherhood* (1979) and *Head above Water* (1986), Kaye GIBBONS's self-reliant maternal dynasty in *Charms for the Easy Life* (1993), and Terry McMILLAN's competent lone parenting in *How Stella Got Her Groove Back* (1996). Historical mothers are under scrutiny in Rita Mae BROWN's fictional biography *Dolley* (1994), the story of First Lady Dolley Payne Madison, and in the journalist Jean STAFFORD's survey of the emotional regrets of single motherhood in *A Mother in History* (1966), the life of the widowed mother of the assassin Lee Harvey Oswald. Encouraging more positive works on single motherhood were the donation of the National Book Award purse by the poet Adrienne RICH, Audre LORDE, and Alice WALKER to Sisterhood of Black Single Mothers and the publication of feminist texts by KITCHEN TABLE / WOMEN OF COLOR PRESS, particularly

Barbara Omolade's sociological inquiry in *It's a Family Affair: The Real Lives of Black Single Mothers* (1986).

Barbara KINGSOLVER makes an issue of single motherhood through redemptive fiction that spares no tears for the recalcitrant or worthless father. In *The Bean Trees* (1988) the social and economic extremes faced by the adoptive mother Taylor Greer and the abandoned wife and mother Lou Ann Ruiz generate respect for single parenting. Introducing Taylor to the hardships of earning a living and residing alone, Kingsolver describes a first job, changing motel beds, a reminder of the mind-numbing toil of WOMAN'S WORK and of the empty bed Taylor returns to each night. Kingsolver commented on her choice of a working-class environment as well suited to female poverty—"the down-in-the-heels neighborhoods . . . where there are a lot of working poor and single mothers who know their neighbors because they have to, because in an emergency they'll look after the kids" (Ross, 287). The mutual dependence of the two women involves rotating domestic jobs and cooking and provides support for the mother beset by concerns for child welfare. In Lou Ann's words the shared intimacy results from going "through hell and high water together. We know each other's good and bad sides, stuff nobody else knows" (Kingsolver, 1988, 85).

The choice of rearing a child without help recurs in Kingsolver's fifth novel, *Prodigal Summer* (2000), in which the independent forest ranger Deanna Wolfe chooses not to tell the father of her child of her pregnancy. She rationalizes, "Better for this child, better for everybody, that he not know what he'd left behind—and so he never would" (Kingsolver, 2000, 432). Drawing on the woman-to-woman strength of Nannie Land Rawley, another single mother, Deanna deserts her beloved sylvan cabin to shelter in the mountain community she grew up in and to form a three-person, three-generation MATRIARCHY. A neighbor, Lusa Maluf Landowski, recovers from widowhood by making a home for Crystal Gail and Lowell, the son and daughter of Lois Walker, an abandoned wife who is dying of cancer. Kingsolver's plotting reveals the serendipitous nature of mothering.

Bibliography

Alcott, Louisa May. *Little Women*. New York: Bantam, 1983.

Cross, Donna, and William Woolfolk. *Daddy's Little Girl: The Unspoken Bargain between Fathers and Their Daughters*. Englewood Cliffs, N.J.: Prentice-Hall, 1982.

Kingsolver, Barbara. *The Bean Trees*. New York: Harper & Row, 1988.

———. *Prodigal Summer*. New York: HarperCollins, 2000.

Ross, Jean W., "Interview," *Contemporary Authors*, Vol. 134, pp. 284–290. Detroit: Gale Research, 1992.

sisterhood

In feminist texts sisterhood is a source of validation and spiritual nourishment and a crucial element of women's liberation. The living evidence of sibling love shines through the bonds between writers, particularly the BRONTË sisters, the GRIMKÉ sisters, and the feminist journalists Tennie Claflin and Victoria WOODHULL. The image of sisterly bonding resonates through a variety of titles—Grace AGUILAR's *Woman's Friendship* (1851); Audre LORDE's *I Am Your Sister: Black Women Organizing across Sexualities* (1986); a Harlem memoir, Bessie and Sadie DELANY's *Having Our Say: The Delany Sisters' First 100 Years* (1991); Rebecca WELLS's *Divine Secrets of the Ya-Ya Sisterhood* (1996); and Robin MORGAN's feminist treatises *Sisterhood Is Powerful* (1970) and *Sisterhood Is Forever: The Women's Anthology for a New Millennium* (2003). In Louisa May ALCOTT's two-volume LITTLE WOMEN (1868–69) the protagonist, Jo March, fights the separation of the four sisters who have shared each other's hardships and triumphs. When the teacher John Brooke proposes to Meg, Jo laments, "You can't know how hard it is for me to give up Meg" (Alcott, 219). At a more grievous separation Jo writes an ode to her dying sister Beth. The second stanza begs that Beth bequeath her best qualities to Jo. "Leave me, as a gift, those virtues / Which have beautified your life," a tender plea reminiscent of the poignant Greek myth of Procne and PHILOMELA (*ibid.*, 390).

A mature sisterhood undergirds works about adult women with complex emotions tinged with pride and sorrow. In *Pioneer Work in Opening the*

Medical Profession to Women: Autobiographical Sketches (1895) the physician Elizabeth BLACKWELL displays family pride in the professional collegiality of her sister, the anesthetist Emily Blackwell. The ethnographer Zora Neale HURSTON concludes THEIR EYES WERE WATCHING GOD (1937) on a companionable note that enables Janey to express to her sisterly friend, Pheoby, the worth of winning and losing love. In 1982 Alice WALKER attests to the survival of kinship ties during a long separation of Celie and Nettie in *The COLOR PURPLE*. The author reprises the issue of a lost sibling in *Possessing the Secret of Joy* (1992), which describes one sister's death after FEMALE GENITAL MUTILATION, a womanly trial that an androcentric society inflicts without regard to the pain and loss it causes.

Feminist literature often pictures sisterhood as a makeshift substitute for other positives, particularly social acceptance, freedom, safety, family love, and mothering. The English poet Christina ROSSETTI bases salvation and reclamation on a sister's sacrificial act in "GOBLIN MARKET" (1862), a feminist FAIRY TALE in which the steadfast Lizzie saves Laura from a fatal malaise by risking a confrontation with wicked humanoid fruit peddlers. In 1838 the editor and journalist Lydia CHILD expressed a more daring regard for sisterhood in her concern for her black contemporaries. With an abolitionist's regard for black sisters she published the slogan "Am I Not a Woman, and a Sister?" the preface to *Authentic Anecdotes of American Slavery*. By citing sisterhood as a reason for denouncing SLAVERY, Child reveals a humanity that ingathers all people as members of an earthly family.

Female alliances serve literature as a cause for celebration of womanly kinship. From an American Indian perspective, the Laguna Sioux author Paula Gunn ALLEN's anthology *Spider Woman's Granddaughters: Traditional Tales and Contemporary Writing by Native American Women* (1990) pulls together works by feminist authors who echo her trust in female unity. In the stage play *Wit* (1999) the dramatist Margaret EDSON saves a patient, Vivian Bearing, from total isolation in the critical ward through the tender care and understanding of Nurse Susie. As Allen's compassionate Native women do, Susie and Vivian share the hardest of partings, Vivian's slow death after lethal chemotherapy and her need for a defender from more invasive procedures that might extend her misery. When a crash crew speeds to Vivian's room to revive her withered body with cardiac shock, Susie stands guard over the corpse to halt further indignities to a fellow human being. In a realistic drama lacking in heroism Susie's respect for Vivian contrasts with the barbaric disregard of her doctors, who tend the cancer patient as though she were a laboratory rat.

Other depictions of sisterly love pit emotional ties against deliberate cruelties. The dissolution of sisterly ties in Amy TAN's *The Bonesetter's Daughter* (2001) portrays the power of family SECRECY to oust a beloved daughter from the household. Out of misguided pride in DYNASTY and blood relationships the family rids itself of LuLing after they learn she was illegitimate. More uplifting is the can-do spirit of domestic workers whose sisterhood supports their economic survival in *Nickel and Dimed: On (Not) Getting by in America* (2001), Barbara EHRENREICH's eye-opening treatise on poverty among domestics, cooks, waitresses, retirement home aides, and store clerks. As a housekeeping team the women offer what solace they possess, carrying the load for a disabled cleaning woman, sharing food and supplies, and providing crackers for a pregnant worker who has nausea. Ehrenreich indicates that poverty and despair nurture a mutual benevolence among the lowest-paid female workers in American society.

Feminist views of female bonding often carry a hint of lesbianism or selfishness. Sarah Orne JEWETT expresses a common strand of joy and comfort in the devotion of a pair of old friends in "Martha's Lady," a story published in *Atlantic Monthly* in 1897. Separated after Martha's marriage, the two friends reunite in Martha's widowhood and cherish the loving relationship they had known in girlhood. More poignant is Georgia Douglas JOHNSON's prize-winning folk play *Plumes* (1927), a one-act drama featuring the kindness of Tildy in helping Charity Brown tend her dying 13-year-old daughter, Emmerline. The women pool information about poultices, doctors, and tea leaves while Tildy sews a white dress for the patient. The calm rhythms and gentle voices of the two friends contrast with the stark, unfeeling remarks of Dr. Scott, who charges

Charity with a lack of maternal love because of her misgivings about paying for treatment. Both examples suggest that women gain from each other more personal expressions of concern than they gain from their relationships with men.

The importance of sisterhood to damaged or threatened women permeates feminist literature in scenes of fleeing wives and battered daughters and girlfriends. The Asian-American author Amy TAN stresses the mutual love and networking at a refuge for brutalized women in *The Kitchen God's Wife* (1991), set in Shanghai during the Sino-Japanese War (1937–45). The lethal home environments that women escape send them and their children to the shelter of Peanut, a bold, tough rescuer and former victim of a feudal union. Embracing Communist doctrines, she encourages mutual dependence among previously hopeless women, the ones most likely to grasp at suicide, ABORTION, infanticide, and other drastic solutions to domestic misery. In safety and anonymity the women disgorge the terrors and indignities of the past and find in sisterhood the strength to anticipate the future.

Prison writings, a unique strand of feminist literature, characterize inmate camaraderie and support as the only salve to the hurt and trauma of incarceration and torture. In 1981 the Chilean author Isabel ALLENDE honored the courage of survivors of political prisons in *The HOUSE OF THE SPIRITS,* a powerful novel picturing women locked in cells and joining in a chorus of Beethoven's "Ode to Joy." More somber is the Ukrainian poet Irina RATUSHINSKAYA's prison paean to beloved female inmates in the poem "I Will Live and Survive" (1988). The Dominican-American writer Julia ALVAREZ dramatizes the loving, at times erotic relationship of inmates in a woman's prison in her historical novel *In the Time of the Butterflies* (1994). Like tender mothers, the older women soothe Magdalena, a 14-year-old whose employer abused her, then stole her infant daughter, Amantina. The warmth and caring of cellmates retrieve Magdalena from despair. Of the constant concern for others an older prisoner, María Teresa, remarks, "This has become my home, these girls are like my sisters. I can't imagine the lonely privacy of living without them" (Alvarez, 253).

Bibliography

Alcott, Louisa May. *Little Women.* New York: Bantam, 1983.

Alvarez, Julia. *In the Time of the Butterflies.* Chapel Hill, N.C.: Algonquin, 1994.

Weisser, Susan Ostrov, and Jennifer Fleischner. *Feminist Nightmares: Women at Odds: Feminism and the Problems of Sisterhood.* New York: New York University Press, 1995.

Williams, Deborah Lindsay. *Not in Sisterhood: Edith Wharton, Willa Cather, Zona Gale, and the Politics of Female Authorship.* New York: Palgrave Macmillan, 2001.

Skinner, Cornelia Otis (1901–1979)

The playwright, biographer, essayist, satirist, and actor Cornelia Otis Skinner managed to combine high-spirited prose with themes of female liberation and sexual experimentation from the Victorian era to the Jazz Age. Born to actors, she grew up in her native Chicago and attended Baldwin, a private prep school. She first appeared on stage with her father, Otis Skinner, in *Blood and Sand* (1921), an experience that cooled her enthusiasm for classical drama. At the end of her sophomore year at Bryn Mawr she gave up American schooling for classes at the Sorbonne and an apprenticeship in Paris at the Comédie Française. At age 26 she staged her first original play, *Captain Fury*. She chose royalty as the subjects of three dramatic monologues—*The Wives of Henry VIII* (1931), *The Loves of Charles II* (1933), and *The Empress Eugénie* (1937)—and embedded each with social criticism.

Skinner made a popular splash with a best seller, *Our Hearts Were Young and Gay* (1942), coauthored by Emily Kimbrough, a humorous, subtextually homoerotic take on young women who dare to travel alone in Europe in 1923. During the grim World War II era the book was the source of a lighthearted nostalgia film, starring Gail Russell, Diana Lynn, and Charles Ruggles, for Paramount. In 1954 adapters also reset the book as a television series, *Robert Montgomery Presents,* starring Elizabeth Montgomery. Skinner collected witty sketches she submitted to the *New Yorker* on women's lives in *That's Me All Over* (1948). In 1952 she wrote a one-woman drama, *Paris '90,* on the female models in the portraits of Henri Toulouse-Lautrec; in 1958 her play *The Pleasure of His Company* opened for a 13-month run on Broadway, with Skinner in the lead role opposite Cyril Ritchard.

Skinner's contributions to feminism are unassuming and largely overlaid with self-deprecating comedy. In 1953 she delivered a droll reminder to the male doctors of the American Gynecological Society convention in Lake Placid, New York, in a speech about the terrors women face during pelvic examinations. She enlarged on the DOUBLE STANDARD in *Elegant Wits and Grand Horizontals: Paris—la Belle Epoque* (1962), a witty overview of the European female socialite's use of sexual availability at the end of the 19th century. In 1967 in the early years of the feminist movement Skinner wrote *Madame Sarah*, a BIOGRAPHY of the self-empowered stage diva Sarah Bernhardt. The chronicle reveals eccentricities as well as patriotism in an independent actor beloved for her glamour and audacity. Of interest to Skinner are Bernhardt's reclamation of dignity after being born illegitimate to an unmarried milliner, Bernhardt's rejection of Victorian mores, and her celebration of female SEXUALITY.

Bibliography

Loganbill, G. Bruce. "Cornelia Otis Skinner, Monologist," *Communication* 9, no. 1 (October 1980): 122–128.

Skinner, Cornelia Otis. *Great American Speeches* (1953). Available online. URL: http://www.federalobserver. com/speeches.php?speech=7772. Accessed on October 17, 2005.

———. *Madame Sarah*. Boston: Houghton Mifflin, 1967.

slavery

Feminist literature has had an affinity for antislavery movement, in part because women have been less afraid to show sensitivity to those in bondage. A late 18th-century English poet, Hannah More, expressed the unique position of slaves, whom buyers considered on a par with their investments in livestock. In the dramatic monologue "The Sorrows of Yamba; or, The Negro Woman's Lamentation" (1795) the speaker regrets that "British Laws shall ne'er befriend me; / They protect not Slaves like me!" (More). The situation of the black concu-

bine in England bears a resemblance to the outsider status of white women, who had no power over their property or children. The extension of New World freedoms applied only to white males, while slaves and women continued to be possessions, comparable to land, livestock, and houses. As the novelist Harriet Beecher STOWE bemoans in *UNCLE TOM'S CABIN; or, Life among the Lowly* (1862), masters have no mercy on black families: "Don't dey tear her suckin' baby right off his mother's breast, and sell him, and der little children as is crying and holding on by her clothes?" (Stowe, 57). Female writers moved beyond the surface questions of economics and private ownership to the humanistic issues of one human being's purchasing another. The English actor Fanny KEMBLE, author of *Journal of a Residence on a Georgian Plantation in 1838–1839* (1863), expressed outrage at every stage of human bondage. AGING black slaves had a dirt-floor infirmary thrown together from mud and laths and sheltered by a leaky roof, where she observed the death of a male in his 70s "like a worn-out hound, with no creature to comfort or relieve his last agony, with neither Christian solace or human succor [as] . . . flies buzzed round his lips and nostrils like those of a fallen beast" (Kemble, 359). In 1972 the novelist Margaret WALKER commented on the inhumanity that Kemble's journal denounced. Walker excoriated Southern duplicity for claiming that "slavery was a beneficial system with benign masters" (Walker, 14). She also charged Northerners with complicity in the system.

Through devious methods female slaves exerted what control they could muster over their situations as laborers and concubines. In *Mama Day* (1988) the novelist Gloria NAYLOR introduces the close community of Willow Springs, a Georgia sea island, with the bill of sale of a legendary black matriarch, Sapphira Wade. She takes the surname of her owner, Bascombe Wade, on August 3, 1819, the date of her sale. At age 20 she arrives, stating that she is "half price, inflicted with sullenness and entertains a bilious nature, having resisted under reasonable chastisement the performance of field or domestic labour" (Naylor, 1). The document acknowledges her value as a commodity but warns that she is a "conjure woman" capable of "extreme mischief," the former owner's term for WITCHCRAFT (*ibid.*, 3). Naylor's introduction of Sapphira reflects the win-lose situation that derives from the flesh trade—her valuable skills as nurse and midwife and the purchaser's risk in holding such a female dynamo against her will. Of her smothering of Bascombe Wade in his bed the text states, "It ain't about right or wrong, truth or lies; it's about a slave woman who brought a whole new meaning to both them words" (*ibid.*).

The outcry against bondage intensified in part because of strong individual efforts. Eleven years before Stowe's *Uncle Tom's Cabin* an aristocratic Cuban abolitionist, Gertrudis Gómez de AVELLANEDA, produced *Sab* (1841), a novel describing a white girl's love for her father's mulatto slave. The novel compared the powerlessness of black Africans to the economic enslavement of women in a male-dominated society. Avellaneda's fiction was so shocking that the text, published in Spain, was suppressed in Cuba until 1914. From the 1830s to the 1860s two Massachusetts women, Sarah Moore GRIMKÉ and her younger sister, Angelina Emily GRIMKÉ Weld, braved public ridicule with their forceful ABOLITIONISM. To strengthen their outreach, they wrote speeches, articles, and letters to people of influence and power. In a long letter to Queen Victoria, they stated: "America is awfully guilty; she has professed herself a Republic, while cherishing in her bosom a confederacy of petty tyrants, who are not exceeded in power, nor surpassed in cruelty, by any despots whose bloodstained annals disgrace the pages of history" (Lerner, 51).

At the beginning of the Civil War the editor Lydia Maria CHILD assisted a former slave, Harriet JACOBS, in completing *Incidents in the Life of a Slave Girl, Written by Herself* (1861), a stunning feminist slave narrative. Harriet grew up in a climate of SECRECY, which she described in historical terms: "The secrets of slavery are concealed like those of the Inquisition" (Jacobs, 32). She described the interracial entanglement that made masters the fathers of both their white children and their mulatto slaves, whom the author describes "as marketable as the pigs on the plantation" (*ibid.*, 32). The author gives as an example a black women who bears two of the master's children before being sold to the master's brother. After giving birth two more

times to mulatto children, she again mounts the auction block. Rather than boast of their darker offspring, the white males say nothing. Black breeder slaves were too terrified to acknowledge their children's paternity. Jacobs adds, "Did the other slaves dare to allude to it, except in whispers among themselves? No, indeed! They knew too well the terrible consequences" (*ibid.*). Of her own situation as an enslaved sex toy she lamented that the master "had no scruples whatever about committing a much greater wrong against the helpless young girl placed under his guardianship" (*ibid.*).

Emancipation fills literature from the 1860s with the joy of an oppressed people eager to embrace freedom. In 1869 Sarah Elizabeth Hopkins Bradford wrote a biography, *Scenes in the Life of Harriet Tubman*, in which she describes a mob scene at Beaufort, South Carolina. Despite the whips of overseers and masters, slaves "came down every road, across every field, just as they had left their work and their cabins; women with children clinging around their necks, hanging to their dresses, running behind, all making at full speed for 'Lincoln's gun-boats'" (Bradford, 40). Their convergence on the shores produced a forest of arms aimed at the Union navy. Bradford reports that "eight hundred poor wretches" departed Beaufort by U.S. gunboats (*ibid.*). At the order of Colonel James Montgomery, Tubman sang an impromptu song of reassurance. In the background the victorious Union army torched the masters' farms and outbuildings, the pathetic cabins that served field hands as homes.

According to Bradford's BIOGRAPHY Harriet Tubman cheered hardest for the women with children, who clung to each departing vessel in fear of being left behind. Their fears stemmed from the threat of whipping, which titillated mobs of southern males eager to see the lashing of a female with "a dish of torture" (*ibid.*, 119). Bradford comments that such displays of ownership had to be "peppered very high to please the palates of those epicures in brutality. The helplessness and terror of the victim, the exposure of her person, the opportunity for coarse jests at her expense, all combined to make it a scene of rare enjoyment" (*ibid.*). For these reasons the emancipation of black females was especially joyous.

In the last months preceding the end of American slavery humanitarians made dangerous choices. Jessamyn WEST examined in detail the family and community life of a female pacifist and abettor of runaway slaves. Through Eliza Birdwell, a Quaker minister in rural Indiana in *Except for Me and Thee* (1969), the author characterizes civil disobedience of the Fugitive Slave Laws that involve farm families in potentially life-threatening rescues. After a courier presents Eliza and her husband with a handbill advertising the search for Daffney and Nate Amboy, Eliza reads the casual description of "Brands on inside both legs. Recently cobbed (beaten) for stealing" (West, 148). Eliza's dilemma is the choice between becoming a deceiver and lawbreaker or allowing slave catchers to apprehend the Amboys and return them to bondage. Clarifying her vision is the testimony of John Shelby, who states during Sunday meeting: "If slave catching is what my government requires of me, I will have to turn my back on my government, for I have already turned my back on slavery" (*ibid.*, 157).

In 1981 Ruthanne Lum McCunn, the first biographer of an Asian-American frontier woman, broadened the study of human bondage with *Thousand Pieces of Gold*, a novelized biography of Polly Bemis, the American name of Lalu Nathoy, an 18-year-old slave from northern China whom her impoverished father sold to bandits. Trans-Pacific slavers imported her to serve the Idaho mining camps as cook, servant, and prostitute. Unlike the field hands and slave breeders of the antebellum South, Polly passed from traders to a California warehouse, where she witnessed "the blank faces of women and girls stripped of hope, the splintered boards beneath her feet, the auction block. This was her America" (McCunn, 1981, 14).

The scene introduces Polly to a barbarous merchandising strategy that left to starve those unsalable female goods damaged or maimed during the crossing. At a poker game she passed from the barkeep Hong King to Charlie Bemis, whom she grew to love as her husband. McCunn describes Polly's faith and hard work at innkeeping and her place among Idaho frontier heroines who turned wild country into civilized communities. A similar story of enslavement, Dmae ROBERTS's documentary *Mei Mei: A Daughter's Song* (1990), characterizes a laborer's devotion to hard chores and her eventual sealing off of bad memories of the time when her parents sold her to the highest bidder for 20 yen. Divided into six parts, the radio play describes Roberts's journey to Taiwan with her mother, and who recalls terror and starvation during World War II, her devotion to Lady Buddha, and emigration from Taiwan. She relishes a peaceful stage of her life when she can recollect the demands on a female slave.

Bibliography

Bradford, Sarah H. *Scenes in the Life of Harriet Tubman* (1869). Available online. URL: http://docsouth.unc.edu/neh/bradford/menu.html. Accessed on October 17, 2005.

Jacobs, Harriet A. *Incidents in the Life of a Slave Girl: Written by Herself*. New York: Harvest Books, 1983.

Kemble, Fanny. *Journal of a Residence on a Georgian Plantation in 1838–1839*. Athens: University of Georgia Press, 1984.

Lerner, Gerda. *The Feminist Thought of Sarah Grimké*. Oxford: Oxford University Press, 1998.

McCunn, Ruthanne Lum. "Reclaiming Polly Bemis," *Frontiers: A Journal of Women's Studies* 24, no. 1 (2003): 76–100.

———. *Thousand Pieces of Gold*. San Francisco: Design Enterprises, 1981.

More, Hannah. "The Sorrows of Yamba; or, The Negro Woman's Lamentation" (1795). Available online. URL: http://wyllie.lib.virginia.edu:8086/perl/toccer-new?id=AnoSorr.sgm&images=images/modeng&data=/texts/english/modeng/parsed&tag=public&part=1&division=div1. Accessed on October 17, 2005.

Naylor, Gloria. *Mama Day*. New York: Vintage, 1989.

Roberts, Dmae. *Mei Mei: A Daughter's Song*. New York: MediaRites, 1990.

Stowe, Harriet Beecher. *Uncle Tom's Cabin*. New York: Harper, 1965.

Walker, Margaret. *How I Wrote Jubilee*. Chicago: Third World Press, 1972.

West, Jessamyn. *Except for Me and Thee*. New York: Avon, 1970.

Smiley, Jane (1949–)

The essayist, satirist, biographer, and fiction writer Jane Smiley employs various genres to tell women's stories. Born in Los Angeles, she came of age in Saint Louis, where she first encountered horse racing, a major passion. Specializing in Old Norse and Anglo-Saxon, she completed her education at Vassar College and the University of Iowa, where she joined the English faculty. Her essays have appeared in *Allure, Harper's, Mirabella, Nation,* the *New York Times, Victoria,* and *Vogue.* She authored a variety of fictional works: *Barn Blind* (1980), a pastoral novel about a female obsession with duty, repression, and competition; a mystery, *Duplicate Keys* (1984); and collected short fiction, *The Age of Grief* (1987). While traveling in Iceland on a Fulbright scholarship, Smiley mapped out a 14th-century Norse saga, *The Greenlanders* (1988). Amid skraeling raids, pestilence, and charges of WITCHCRAFT the protagonists, Margret and Birgitta, survive superstition and blood feuds. Margret's daring to seek sexual fulfillment outside marriage prefigures family VIOLENCE and tragedy.

In 1991 Smiley won both the National Book Critics Circle Award and a Pulitzer Prize for *A Thousand Acres,* a best-selling update of William Shakespeare's *King Lear* (ca. 1603) set outside Des Moines, Iowa. The emotional tragedy describes rural adversities, women's economic dependence on males and male-run banks, and the need for self-actualization among rural females. Complicating the story are multiple suspicions and treacheries that weaken the Cook SISTERHOOD at a time when they need it most. Ginny draws on nostalgia for her dead mother as a comfort: "It seemed like Daddy's departure had opened up the possibility of finding my mother . . . now that he was gone, I could look more closely. I could study the attics or the closet, lift things and peer under them, get back into cabinets and the corners of shelves" (Smiley, 2003, 225). By reuniting with memories of her mother and reliving the history of the thousand acres, Ginny ushers family stories into the forefront of her thinking, where they rehabilitate her spirit. The 1997 Buena Vista screen adaptation pits Jason Robards as Larry Cook against Michelle Pfeiffer, Jessica Lange, and Jennifer Jason Leigh as the three daughters, Rose, Ginny, and Caroline.

Smiley retreated to the mid-1800s for historical fiction, *The All-True Travels and Adventures of Lidie Newton: A Novel* (1998), a rambunctious frontier epic set in pre–Civil War Kansas. The plot focuses on the life of the farm wife and widow Lydia Harkness "Lidie" Newton, an abolitionist who is adept at riding bareback, homesteading, and arguing the wisdom of the Missouri Compromise. In familiar family nitpicking over the lone spinster her sisters belabor Lidie's ineptitude at laundry, stoking of a bake oven, and needlework. Lidie herself admits to disdaining female conversation: "Of all the women, it was only I who listened to the men" (Smiley, 1998, 7). In contrast, Smiley depicts Annie, the pampered female, as "too innocent to handle the shock of most topics, though of course not too fragile to be worked to death" (ibid., 9). The author's satiric dig at the domestic DOUBLE STANDARD sets the tone for Lidie's plunge into wifedom.

Smiley emphasizes the rigor of Lidie's domestic work with epigraphs at the beginnings of chapters from Catharine Esther BEECHER's *A Treatise on Domestic Economy for the Use of Young Ladies at Home and at School* (1841). Lidie recalls her childhood, "when my mother and I would keep to her room while my father entertained low company downstairs" (ibid., 312). To free herself from the strictures of womanhood, Lidie chooses short hair and men's clothes for a venture into the countryside in search of her husband's killer. Unlike Huck Finn, whom she emulates with picaresque adventures on an antebellum plantation, Lidie must admit biological limitations after she suffers a miscarriage. The satisfying conclusion to Smiley's novel relieves a national quandary over slavery and Lidie's ambivalence toward matrimony.

Bibliography

Frumkes, Lewis Burke. "A Conversation with Jane Smiley," *Writer* 112, no. 5 (May 1999): 20–22.

McDermott, Sinead. "Memory, Nostalgia, and Gender in *A Thousand Acres,*" *Signs: Journal of Women in Culture and Society* 28, no. 1 (Autumn 2002): 389–407.

Smiley, Jane. *The All-True Travels and Adventures of Lidie Newton: A Novel.* New York: Ballantine, 1998.

———. *A Thousand Acres.* New York: Anchor, 2003.

Smith, Anna Deavere (1950–)

The feminist actor, teacher, and playwright Anna Deavere Smith contributes stellar one-woman performances to realistic theater. Born in Baltimore and educated at Beaver College and the American Conservatory Theatre, she developed her talent for mime into innovative stage documentary. Influenced by the brilliance of the dramatist Lorraine HANSBERRY, Smith taught acting at Carnegie-Mellon University, New York University, Stanford University and Yale University and in 1983 staged an original work, *On the Road*. She directs Harvard's Institute on the Arts and Civic Dialogue and appeared as the U.S. president's press secretary in the film *The American President* (1995). The part led to her regular role in the cast of the hit television series *The West Wing* and a subsequent pivotal appearance in *The Human Stain* (2003) as the mother of a light-skinned man who abandons his black family to marry a white woman.

The dramatist has earned two Obies for her stage works *Fires in the Mirror: Crown Heights, Brooklyn and Other Identities* (1992) and the one-woman show *Twilight Los Angeles, 1992: On the Road: A Search for American Character* (1994), which was successful on Broadway. Both works depict the turmoil of racism and situations that generate anguish at critical moments in American history. The first, drawn from the 1991 Crown Heights riot between blacks and Hasidic Jews living in Brooklyn, New York, earned a Pulitzer Prize nomination. The action features real people—ordinary bystanders as well as the orator and writer Angela DAVIS, the *Ms.* magazine cofounder Letty Cottin POGREBIN, and the dramatist Ntozake SHANGE. In the opening monologue of *Fires in the Mirror* Shange explains identity as "not necessarily what's around me," a clarification that separates her from the cause and effects of urban upheaval (Smith, 1993, 3).

Both one-woman dramas reflect Smith's skills as an observer, impersonator, and storyteller. Narration and mimicry allow her to sink into the personae of women of various ethnic backgrounds and to speak simmering outrage as well as hope for peace and constructive dialogue. She demands of her characters a candid self-definition, which she acquires from interviews with hundreds of participants and eyewitnesses of historic events. The immersion method channels to audiences an immediacy in events with which they may not be familiar. Her talent at crafting interview into stage drama earned her a MacArthur Foundation "Genius Award."

Bibliography

Martin, Carol, ed. *A Sourcebook of Feminist Theatre and Performance.* New York: Routledge, 1996.

Smith, Anna Deavere. *Fires in the Mirror: Crown Heights, Brooklyn and Other Identities.* New York: Anchor, 1993.

———. *Talk to Me: Travels in Media and Politics.* New York: Anchor, 2001.

———. *Twilight Los Angeles, 1992: On the Road: A Search for American Character.* New York: Anchor, 1994.

Smith, Charlotte (1749–1806)

A forerunner of the boom in Gothic literature, Charlotte Turner Smith of London promoted the sensational novel as a valid vehicle for women's literature. She anchored each work to themes of social justice and legal redress. The daughter of the poet Nicholas Turner, she was motherless from age three and attended boarding academies, where she began writing melancholy sonnets. At age 34 Smith reached an impasse in her domestic situation after her husband, the merchant Benjamin Smith, ran through inherited wealth. Both husband and wife received prison sentences for debt. Fleeing a marriage doomed by spousal abuse and want, the author took up residence in France. To support herself and her 12 children, she wrote verse, children's books, and history but made her living from elegant romances and translations of French novels. She converted the Abbé Prévost's classic erotic novel *Manon Lescaut* (1731) into an English version, *Manon L'Escault; or, The Fatal Attachment* (1785). The adaptation transformed the title character from a heartless siren into a believable, multifaceted woman.

Writing at the rate of one novel per year, Smith made full use of her marital misery by depicting women in near enslavement to conniving, abusive males. Her characters tend to suffer penury because of profligate husbands, shifty lawyers, and muddled wills. For *The Romance of*

Real Life (1787) she chose the female Gothic mode and exploited the public's immersion in true crime stories by researching details from French court trials. She profited from the publication of *Emmeline, the Orphan of the Castle* (1788), a best seller that appealed to the gothic novelist Ann RADCLIFFE as well as to ordinary English readers. The story depicts Emmeline's fight for her inheritance, Mowbray manor, a motif that dominates many of the author's plots. Complicating the story are the protagonist's rejection of the womanizer Delamere, who seeks a wealthy wife, and her reliance on other women for succor. The feminist critic Diane Long Hoeveler, author of *Gothic Feminism* (1998), revived interest in Smith's novel and praised its contribution to feminist literature as "the forgotten ur-text for the female Gothic novel tradition" (Hoeveler, 37).

Smith colored her works with autobiographical detail. Her next novels, the five-volume *Ethelinde; or, The Recluse of the Lake* (1790) and *Celestina* (1791), feature home territory, the English castles that the author knew from personal experience. For *Desmond* (1792) the author applies difficulties she encountered overcoming obstacles to finishing her work. After intense labor at a writers' enclave Smith finished the four-volume mystery *The Old Manor House* (1793), her best-received work. Replete with the Gothic conventions of a missing document, convoluted architecture, and Orlando Somerive's controlling love for a naif, Monimia, the novel incorporates smuggling and CONFINEMENT of Monimia in a tower, a common phallic symbol in Gothic thrillers. An anonymous freelancer turned a profit on Smith's suspenseful thriller by condensing the story into *Rayland Hall* (ca. 1810), a pulp potboiler.

In her 50s, Smith progressed in the depiction of women's struggle against PATRIARCHY and tyranny. From her encounters with lawyers she satirized meddlesome attorneys in *The Banished Man* (1794). In her last two Gothic novels, *The Wanderings of Warwick* (1794) and *Montalbert* (1795), she orchestrated multiple upheavals by incorporating an earthquake into a female victimization plot. The novel features bandits who kidnap Rosalie, the artistic young heroine, and imprison her in Sicily. More realistic is *The Young Philosopher* (1798), which denounces English jurisprudence for its reduction of women to the property of their fathers and husbands. Balancing the sober theme of injustice are satiric passages in which Smith contrasts the elegant swoons and nervous prostrations of a wealthy female dignitary and the mimicry of her serving woman. In the five-volume *The Letters of a Solitary Wanderer* (1800–02) Smith features a rebel protagonist, Edouarda, who revolts against Catholic ritual and religious hypocrisy toward women. The choice of a feminized version of "Edward" as her name suits a woman who breaches womanly customs. A cache of the author's letters reveals the tribulations of the female author as well as the importance of patronage to women writers.

Bibliography

Bartolomeo, Joseph F., "Subversion of Romance in 'The Old Manor House,' " *Studies in English Literature, 1500–1900* 33, no. 3 (Summer 1993): 645–657.

Harries, Elizabeth W., " 'Out in Left Field': Charlotte Smith's Prefaces, Bourdieu's Categories, and the Public Sphere," *Modern Language Quarterly* 58, no. 4 (December 1997): 457–473.

Hoeveler, Diane Long. *Gothic Feminism.* University Park: Pennsylvania State University Press, 1998.

Smith, Charlotte. *Montalbert.* Delmar, N.Y.: Scholars Facsimiles & Reprint, 1989.

———. *The Old Manor House* (1794). Available online. URL: http://digital.library.upenn.edu/women/smith/manor/manor.html. Accessed on October 17, 2005.

———. *The Poems of Charlotte Smith.* Oxford: Oxford University Press, 1993.

———. *The Young Philosopher.* Lexington: University Press of Kentucky, 1999.

Smith, Stevie (1902–1971)

The fiction writer, satirist, and quick sketch artist Florence Margaret "Stevie" Smith blended prose and line drawings with a bumpety, singsong versification bristling with anger and despair. Her father, an exporter, deserted her childhood home at Hull, Yorkshire, in 1905, leaving a quartet of women—Stevie and her older sister, Molly; their mother; and their maternal aunt, Margaret Spear. They settled for life in North London at Palmers Green, a refuge that she described in "A House of Mercy"

(1966), a teasing feminist poem dramatizing her father's mercenary treatment of his wife. The writer
suffered an abdominal infection at age six that required seaside recuperation. In 1937 she reflected
in the slyly innocent poem "Papa Love Baby" her
dislike of her father, who chose enlistment in the
North Sea Patrol over residence with a wife and
two daughters. After graduation from the North
London Collegiate School for Girls, Smith joined
the secretarial pool of a publishing house. In her
off-hours she read, produced radio plays for the
British Broadcasting Corporation (BBC), and
wrote breezy, ironic poetry that was eventually
published in *Granta* and the *New Statesman.*

Smith won over dubious critics with her work
of fiction *Novel on Yellow Paper; or, Work It Out for
Yourself* (1936), the first of her sardonic experiments featuring themes of alienation, ambivalence,
and doom. Her view of limitations on female liberty
derives from her work in the publishing industry,
which spewed out WOMEN'S MAGAZINES intended
to ameliorate mounting discontent with women's
choices and their disillusion with marriage and
housewifery. Of Miss Snooks's marriage the author
chortles, "But somehow the gilt is off the gingerbread. It is all washing up and peeling the potatoes,
and there are several *kiddies* and the furniture isn't
paid for. . . . And oh how dim drab and dreary is life
in terms of squawling brats and cash instalments"
(Smith, 1982, 169). On an autobiographical note
the author experiences the protagonist Pompey
Casmilus's emotional immurement: "Forget the
Job-Job-Job with all its paraphernalia of subordination, turning always upon the pivot of littleness,
tunneling, burrowing back, down and through, to
something receding, ever diminishing, suffocating,
close cramping" (*ibid.,* 208). For self-salvation Pompey pleads, "Peel off my wings and pare my claws"
(*ibid.*). Despite critical recognition, Smith's career
sputtered with a series of rejections of verse anthologies and two autobiographical novels, *Over the
Frontier* (1938) and *The Holiday* (1949), which
reprises Pompey in the middle-aged protagonist,
Celia, and her attempt to elude the traditional clo-
sure of romance and courtship.

Smith was adept at deposing female icons. She
disarmed readers with saucy poetic depictions of the
mythic EVE and the VIRGIN MARY, a manifestation

of her rejection of male-dominated Anglicanism.
The author's revisionary FAIRY TALES rescripted traditional female predicaments, such as retreat to the
woods in the Grimm brothers' "Hansel and Gretel,"
to reflect the domestic unrest of her day. In 1966
she won the Chalmondeley Award, followed three
years later by the Queen's Gold Medal for Poetry,
which Smith received within months of her death of
a brain tumor. Her reputation languished until feminist editors at Virago Press restored her neglected
works to circulation.

Bibliography

Civello, Catherine A. "Stevie Smith's 'Ecriture Femi-
    nine': Pre-Oedipal Desires and Wartime Realities,"
    Mosaic 28, no. 2 (June 1995): 109–122.
Severin, Laura. " 'The Gilt Is off the Gingerbread': Ste-
    vie Smith's Revisionary Fairy Tales," *Journal of Gen-
    der Studies* 12, no. 3 (November 2003): 203–214.
Smith, Stevie. *Collected Poems.* New York: New Direc-
    tions, 1972.
———. *Novel on Yellow Paper; or, Work It Out for Your-
    self.* New York: Pinnacle, 1982.

Song, Cathy (1955–)

The Hawaiian poet and educator Cathy Song
weaves Asian lore and Polynesian language into
pictorial verse. Her themes extend wholeness and
welcome to a fragmented social order. Born in
Honolulu of Chinese-Korean lineage, she grew up
in a three-generation setting in Wahiawa in central Oahu. After experimentation with verse in her
teens and mentoring by the critic John Unterecker,
she completed degrees in English and creative
writing at Wellesley College and Boston University.
In 1976 she published her first short fiction in
Hawaii Review, the beginning of a series of works
published in *Asian-Pacific Literature, Bamboo Ridge:
The Hawaii Writers' Quarterly, Dark Brand, Green-
field Review, Kenyon Review,* and *Tendril.*

At age 28 Song published the limpid, woman-
centered poems of *Picture Bride* (1983). The focus
of the text is the marginalization of women, who
must content themselves with minuscule assimilation into society. The suite chronicles the arrival of
her father's Korean mother to the Hawaiian Islands as a mail-order mate. The poet regrets that

her mother married a stranger who was 13 years her senior. Based on the flower portraits of the southwestern painter Georgia O'Keeffe, the collection pictures fragile femininity in "Beauty and Sadness," a poem dedicated to Kitagawa Utamaro, a portrait artist who painted courtesans, geishas, actors, and handmaidens, each uniquely winsome for some aspect of womanly beauty. Scorn of 20th-century hedonism energizes "Sunworshippers," a mother's denunciation of oiled, bikini-clad women. The languor of island life and the passion of a sexual liaison infuse "The White Porch." The poem concludes with an angry mother's reminder that the daughter is too young for carnal pleasures. The collection received a National Book Critics Circle Award nomination and the Yale Younger Poets Award.

After settling in Denver, Song completed *Frameless Windows, Squares of Light* (1988), which presents the title poem as a view of womanly joys gradually eroded by child care, kitchen work, and the loss of marital intimacy. Song depicts the pragmatism of wives in "The Humble Jar," which holds buttons intended "for every need," a treasure chest filled with memories (Song, 2003, 44). The poet delights in conception and pregnancy in a wistful ode, "The Day You Are Born," which marvels at a tactile fetus "no bigger than her thumbnail / burrowing itself into her body" (*ibid.,* 3). The anthology features "The Youngest Daughter," a survey of a MOTHER-DAUGHTER RELATIONSHIP in which parental fingers touch the girl's head to soothe a migraine headache. The speaker honors her mother for her gravelly breathing and affectionately gruff voice. The poem pivots from mother tending daughter to daughter easing her diabetic mother. The speaker soaps her mother's body and feeds her tea, rice, pickled turnip, and gingered fish. The idyll slides into guilt as the daughter admits that her own life outside the curtained window calls her away from fealty to her parent.

In later poems Song reformulates female figures from the mundane to luminescence and nobility. After winning the Hawaii Award for Literature, she published *School Figures* (1994), which received the Shelley Memorial Award for its elegant images of a girl advancing into womanhood. "Points of Reference" looks back in wonder

to prebirth, a time the unborn soul dwells in the stars. She enhanced her verse vignettes of family members in *The Land of Bliss* (2001), a mature meditation on aging and death. In complex views of cultural saturation the poem "Honored Guest" provides a retrospective of the poet's work—the breaking of history into matchsticks that ignite literary fire. Returning to the women in her life, she pictures the corrosion of a female spirit in "Rust," whose subject replaced dreams with despair.

Bibliography

Bloyd, Rebekah. "Cultural Convergences in Cathy Song's Poetry," *Peace Review* 10, no. 3 (September 1998): 393–400.

Song, Cathy. *Frameless Windows, Squares of Light: Poems.* New York: W. W. Norton, 2003.

———. *Picture Bride.* New Haven, Conn.: Yale University Press, 1983.

———. *School Figures.* Pittsburgh, Pa.: University of Pittsburgh Press, 1994.

Sontag, Susan (1933–2004)

A dazzling essayist, social critic, novelist, and screenwriter, Susan Sontag incorporated in a broad canon her idiosyncratic views on feminism and human rights. A native New Yorker, she grew up in her grandparents' home while her father, Jack Rosenblatt, pursued the fur trade in China. After his death of tuberculosis she recuperated at age five from chronic asthma in Arizona with her mother and younger sister. In her teens, Sontag lived in Los Angeles and became a fan of the iconoclastic novelist Djuna BARNES. Sontag graduated from high school at age 16 and studied at the University of California at Berkeley for a semester. By age 18 she had completed a degree in philosophy from the University of Chicago, the preface to dual M.A. degrees in English and philosophy from Harvard University and additional courses at Oxford University and the University of Paris. A brief marriage to a sociologist convinced her that the novelist George ELIOT was right in directing the protagonist Dorothea Casaubon away from a disastrous union in MIDDLEMARCH (1872).

After a stint editing *Commentary* magazine, Sontag began teaching literature, philosophy, and religion at Brown, Columbia, and Harvard Universities. Simultaneously she wrote treatises on aesthetics in European intellectualism and art. Her writings were reliable constants for *Art in America, Atlantic Monthly, Granta,* the *New Yorker, New York Review of Books,* and the *Times Literary Supplement.* She surprised and dismayed feminists in 1969 with the publication of *Styles of Radical Will,* which elevates pornography from base pandering to its own genre. She championed feminism with the essay "The Third World of Women" (1973), published in *Partisan Review.* She challenged the wrongheadedness of standard mores: "Without a change in the very norms of SEXUALITY, the liberation of women is a meaningless goal. Sex as such is not liberating for women. Neither is more sex" (Sontag, 1973, 188). Her renegade status earned the regard of the feminist critic Elaine SHOWALTER, who agreed with Sontag's comparison of colonialism and the enslavement of women.

In reaction to the Arab terrorism that destroyed the World Trade Center and damaged the Pentagon on September 11, 2001, Sontag wrote in her somber essay collection *Regarding the Pain of Others* (2003) about the dulling nature of recurrent images of terror. Her controlling theme, which extends her moral query in an earlier work, *On Photography* (1977), proposes androcentrism as a source of VIOLENCE and war, a long-standing feminist concept. Citing Virginia WOOLF's commentary on war, Sontag states her commitment to peace by lacerating the media for saturating the news with grisly photos. Her conflicted response to modern journalism expresses a global angst: "To suffer is one thing; another thing is living with the photographed images of suffering, which does not necessarily strengthen conscience and the ability to be compassionate. It can also corrupt them" (Sontag, 2004, 20).

Bibliography

Richardson, Marilyn. "Photographing Horror," *Women's Review of Books* 21, no. 1 (October 2003): 12.

Sontag, Susan. *Regarding the Pain of Others.* New York: Picador, 2004.

———. "The Third World of Women," *Partisan Review* 40, no. 2 (1973): 180–206.

Southworth, E. D. E. N. (1819–1899)

The most prolific female author of best sellers in her day, Emma Dorothy Eliza Nevitte Southworth mirrored her own financial self-sufficiency through aggressive heroines who need no rescue. After growing up in Washington, D.C., and completing her education, at age 16 she began teaching school. Upon separating from her husband, she established a home for her son and daughter. She exulted, "I found myself broken in spirit, health, and purse—a widow in fate but not in fact. . . . It was in these darkest days of my *woman's* life, that my *author's* life commenced" (Baym, 111). To support the three of them, she started with domestic fiction and later refined the genre in *The Better Way; or, The Wife's Victory: A Tale of Domestic Trials* and its sequel, *The Married Shrew,* two novellas anthologized in *Old Neighbourhoods and New Settlements; or, Christmas Evening Legends* (1853). At her height she began writing quick-paced novels, often casting female protagonists in Horatio Alger roles of the self-made woman.

For Southworth's skill at entertaining readers with unconventional models of the NEW WOMAN, she became the era's highest-paid author, earning $10,000 a year. Serialized in the *Baltimore Saturday Visitor,* her novel *Retribution; or, The Vale of Shadows* (1849) preceded more works parceled out in the *London Journal, National Era, New York Ledger,* and *Saturday Evening Post. Retribution* introduced Southworth's ABOLITIONISM through the transformation of the heroine, Hester Grey, from slave-owning heiress to defier of slave owners. The author produced a fictional slave narrative in the words of Minny, a Cuban quadroom and friend of Hester. The novel ends tragically with Hester's death before she can free her slaves, even though she leaves a will instructing her husband of her intent. The husband's second wife, Juliette Summers, transforms into a malign demon by retaining the plantation's slave laborers. Southworth attributes the rapid loss of humanity to "the evil principle itself, in its final stage of development" (Southworth, 1856, 19).

In a fiercer abolitionist novel, *India; or, The Pearl of Pearl River* (1853), the novelist batters SLAVERY for its moral and physical effects on women. She protests bondage through the hero, Mark Sutherland, who declares that the owners themselves are "the only one set of persons in the civilized world who are more unhappy than the ne-groes" (Southworth, 1855, 25). The author again transforms a female slave holder into a monster by depicting the decline of India's beauty. Sutherland foresees an afterlife in which India "will see those whom you have left on earth, doomed, with their children and their children's children, to a bondage, from which you no longer have the power and the privilege to free them" (*ibid.*, 364). Southworth's precarious position as Southern fe-male challenging the antebellum status quo earned a rebuke from the *Southern Literary Messenger*, in which a reviewer of *The Mother-in-Law* (1853) op-posed Southworth's vilifying of Virginia plantation culture. An admirer, the novelist Harriet Beecher STOWE, lauded the novel for breaking away from Southern domestic writing by disclosing the vi-cious medievalism of the plantation system.

Southworth's most famous scamp, the French orphan Capitola Le Noir, enlivened two heavily plotted adventure tales, the 23-installment serial *The Hidden Hand; or, Capitola the Madcap* (1859) and the sequel, *Capitola's Peril* (1859). To earn her living, the subversive heroine short-circuits gender discrimination and possible rape by dressing in boy's clothes to apply for a job in New York City, where cross-dressing is a crime. Privately, she chor-tles, "The only thing that made me feel sorry, was to see what a fool I had been, not to turn to a boy before" (Southworth, 1988, 41). For her bravado she later earns the nickname "Napoleon in skirts" (*ibid.*, 274). She preserves her femininity by re-minding herself that although male clothing may be convenient, womanhood is her lot: "Cap, my little man, be a woman! don't you stick at trifles! Think of Jael and Sisera! Think of Judith and Holofernes!" (*ibid.*, 344–345). Louisa May AL-COTT implied that Southworth set a poor example for Jo March, a would-be contributor to the *Weekly Volcano* in LITTLE WOMEN (1868–69). Rather than write her own views, Jo imitates the style and themes of the fictional Mrs. S. L. A. N. G. North-bury, a parody of Southworth's unusual pen name.

Bibliography

Barker, Deborah. *Aesthetics and Gender in American Liter-ature*. Cranbury, N.J.: Associated University Presses, 2000.

Baym, Nina. *Woman's Fiction: A Guide to Novels by and about Women in America, 1820–70*. Chicago: Uni-versity of Illinois Press, 1993.

Levander, Caroline Field. *Voices of the Nation: Women and Public Speech in Nineteenth-Century American Literature and Culture*. Cambridge: Cambridge Uni-versity Press, 1998.

Southworth, E. D. E. N. *The Hidden Hand*. New Brunswick, N.J.: Rutgers University Press, 1988.

———. *India: The Pearl of Pearl River*. Philadelphia: T. B. Peterson, 1855.

———. *Retribution: or The Vale of Shadows*. Philadel-phia: T. B. Peterson, 1856.

Sovereignty and Goodness of God, The
Mary Rowlandson (1682)

Colonial America's first best seller, Mary White Rowlandson's *The Sovereignty and Goodness of God: Being a Narrative of the Captivity and Restauration of Mrs. Mary Rowlandson*, sets the style and tone of subsequent CAPTIVITY NARRATIVE and fiction imi-tations on the subject of white women kidnapped by Indians. Seized from her home in Lancaster, Massachusetts, she and two of her children fall prey to the Wampanoag sachem, Metacomet, and his raiders. On a lengthy forced march northeast at sunrise from the Rowlandsons' hillside house to-ward New Hampshire, she survives for nearly three months while doing needlework for her captors—knitting caps and stockings and sewing shirts—in exchange for bear meat and wheat cakes. Com-posed as a devotional JOURNAL and published six years later, her memoir explains how domestic skills, excerpts from the Psalms, and faith in God keep her safe until her ransom on May 2, 1676. She exhorts her audience with Puritan fervor: "Read, therefore, peruse, ponder, and from hence lay up something from the experience of another, against thine own turn comes: that so thou also through patience and consolation of the Scripture mayest have hope" (Rowlandson, 25). Within a decade her narrative returned to press a dozen times.

Rowlandson's first-person account stresses a number of stoic traits, especially the channeling of outrage to her benefit. She describes the random snatching up of some whites and the slaughter and burning of others after "hell-hounds" set aflame flax and hemp, two staples of woman's fiber work (*ibid.*, 6). After viewing so massive an assault on family and friends, she hardens herself to sorrow: "My heart was many times ready to break, yet could I not shed one tear in their sight" (*ibid.*, 42). By establishing her ability to quote Scripture to the praying Indians and her worth to Weetamoo, her keeper, Rowlandson earns respect from the Wampanoag.

Rowlandson's pragmatism proves her salvation. She makes friends with male murderers, who invite her into their tepee, but she dismisses as the work of Satan the brainwashing and boasts of cannibalizing her son. She actively mediates the ransom process: "If of a great sum, I knew not where it would be procured: yet at a venture, I said Twenty pounds, yet desired them to take less" (*ibid.*, 98). More valuable is her SISTERHOOD with Native women. In one episode a Native woman "gave me a piece of fresh Pork, and a little Salt with it, and lent me her Pan to Fry it in; and I cannot but remember what a sweet, pleasant and delightfull relish that bit had to me, to this day" (*ibid.*, 101). Through the published narrative the author reclaims her humanity and womanhood, the two valuables that kidnap by indigenous peoples threatens.

Bibliography

Newman, Andrew. "Captive on the Literacy Frontier," *Early American Literature* 38, no. 1 (March 2003): 31, 35.

Rowlandson, Mary White. *The Sovereignty and Goodness of God: The True Story of the Captivity of Mrs. Mary Rowlandson among the Indians.* Tucson, Ariz.: American Eagle, Publications, 1966.

Spider Woman

Spider Woman, a mythic parallel to the Greek web spinner Arachne, is a domestic matriarch adept at spinning and weaving, domestic fiber work she taught the Anasazi-Hopi and Navajo of the southwestern United States from the beginning of time. The native myths of Tse-che-nako or Sussistanako (Thinking Woman) describe her layout of the universe and her mating with Tawa, the Sun deity.

The pair produced the first Earthlings, who emerged from a *sipapu*, Earth's birth canal. At their birth the heavenly WISEWOMAN cut the umbilical cords and fed them on corn milk. Her cosmic handiwork accounts for human industry, particularly the womanly arts of basketry and blanket making. Generously Spider Woman relieves Earth's women of male SILENCING by providing outlets for their thoughts and dreams. The feminist author Alice WALKER based her novel *Meridian* (1976) on the dynamism of Spider Woman. The themes refocus the value of woman from bearer of children to sacred thinker and founder of culture.

Born in Canyon de Chelly, Arizona, Grandmother Spider resides at Spider Rock, one of Earth's holiest spots—a stark plane marked by twin sandstone columns, the world's highest free-standing vertical structure. As a model of DUALITY the gracious teacher is both a gobbler of misbehaving children and the motherly provider of survival skills—fire making and pottery, weapons and hunting, herbalism and healing, raising of crops, reverencing of ancestors and Mother Earth, and etching of sacred pictographs on stone walls. Like the Greek Apollo, god of light, creativity, and life, Spider Woman is the initiator of mystic ritual, song and chant, dance, and the womanly arts that undergird the human family. Unlike Apollo, who radiates abstract powers, her myth pictures a physical extrusion of creativity from a female divinity who, as a mother produces breast milk, spins palpable cultural elements from her own body to nourish and enlighten humankind.

According to Native animists Spider Woman stories and poems contribute to a global acknowledgment of Mother Earth. In 1977 the Laguna fiction writer Leslie Marmon SILKO opened her novel *Ceremony* with praise to the female creator who named creatures as they took shape. The goddess's channeling of words into objects, like the FAIRY TALE Rumpelstiltskin's spinning of straw into gold, informs an unbroken line of story keepers, who preserve a mythic world history. Through ECOFEMINISM she activates female powers to protect frail life strands and to bind all nature into a welcoming, interconnected habitat. Through the cohesive element of Silko's introduction the plot honors the Native worldview as a nest to which wanderers such as the soul-damaged protagonist, Tayo, can always return.

The Laguna Sioux author Paula Gunn ALLEN edited *Spider Woman's Granddaughters: Traditional Tales and Contemporary Writing by Native American Women* (1990), a modern retrospect on the mythic creator. The collection features the writings of 24 female authors. In the introduction Allen describes the defiance of tyranny of Native women: "Like our sisters who resist in other ways, we Indian women who write have articulated and rendered the experience of being in a state of war for five hundred years" (Allen, 2). Women's energetic creativity generates the early writings of unnamed story keepers as well as the modern short stories of Ella DELORIA, Louise ERDRICH, Linda HOGAN, Pauline JOHNSON, MOURNING DOVE, and Leslie Marmon Silko. Like a spider web, the net of narrative reaches out to myriad experiences and binds them into a humanistic whole.

Communicating the gynocentric tradition among the Crow, Pretty Shield, a wisewoman and author of "A Woman's Fight," was in her 60s when she described in sign language to Frank B. Linderman her contribution to WOMAN'S WORK. In childhood she helped stack the women's breastwork that surrounded a besieged camp. Pretty Shield witnessed the bravery of Strikes-two, a 60-year-old woman who sang a medicine song and brandished her root digger (dibble) while directing the other women in camp to chant "They are whipped. They are running away" (*ibid.*, 33). As the chant rose, Strikes-two rode into the path of the attacking Lakota. The narrator exults, "I *saw* her, I *heard* her, and my heart swelled, because she was a woman" (*ibid.*). By recharging women's pride in their inborn strengths, Pretty Shield raises an oral monument to foremothers.

The presence of the mythic desert progenitor recurs in feminist literature, notably in Barbara KINGSOLVER's ecofeminist romance *Animal Dreams* (1990), set in the American Southwest. A motherless wanderer, the protagonist, Codi Noline, views daybreak in the multihued canyons of Four Corners in sight of Spider Rock, a locus of native American STORYTELLING. Codi holds her breath and gazes up at canyon walls "ranging from sunset orange to deep rust, mot-

tled with purple. The sandstone had been carved by ice ages and polished by eons of sandpaper winds" (Kingsolver, 210). The shafts of light, like gossamer from Grandmother Spider's spindle, resembled the incarnation of religion. The grandeur of Spider Woman's lair draws the main characters toward the native homeland, the fictional Santa Rosalia Pueblo in the Jemez Mountains of New Mexico, where Loyd Peregrina introduces Codi to his mother and sisters and reveals his intention to marry her. On Christmas Eve amid a gaggle of women cooking holiday dishes and baking bread in an outdoor oven Codi snuggles contentedly in Loyd's bed and, like a baby chick, feels herself well nested in physical passion and female acceptance.

Bibliography

Allen, Paula Gunn. *Spider Woman's Granddaughters: Traditional Tales and Contemporary Writing by Native American Women.* Boston: Beacon, 1989.

Armstrong, Nancy. *Desire and Domestic Fiction: A Political History of the Novel.* Oxford: Oxford University Press, 1995.

Bierhorst, John, ed. *The Way of the Earth: Native America and the Environment.* New York: William Morrow, 1994.

Kingsolver, Barbara. *Animal Dreams.* New York: HarperCollins, 1990.

Newman, Vicky. "Compelling Ties: Landscape, Community, and Sense of Place," *Peabody Journal of Education* 70, no. 4 (Summer 1995): 105–118.

Silko, Leslie Marmon. *Ceremony.* New York: Penguin, 1977.

Turner, Sarah E. " 'Spider Woman's Granddaughter': Autobiographical Writings by Native American Women," *MELUS* 22, no. 4 (Winter 1997): 109–133.

"Spleen, The" Winchilsea, Anne Finch, countess of (1713)

Anne Finch's Pindaric ode "The Spleen" captures the melancholy of the female artist whose temperament suffers in a hostile, androcentric milieu. Published anonymously in 1701 in Charles Gildon's *New Collection of Poems on Several Occasions*, the poem appeared in revised form 12 years later in her collection, *Miscellany Poems on Several Occasions* (1713), one of the first anthologies published by a European female. Through apostrophe she questions spleen, the organ that allegedly harbors negative emotions. Comparing herself to the tragic figures of Brutus and Adam, she regrets a turn of events that encourages the spleen to attack her: "Thy false Suggestions must attend, / Thy whisper'd Griefs, thy fancy'd Sorrows hear, / Breath'd in a Sigh, and witness'd by a Tear" (Finch, 40). She correctly identifies repressed anger as the source of her fits of discontent, outrage, insomnia, suicidal urges, and panic attacks, all symptoms of clinical depression.

Written 250 years before the feminist author Betty FRIEDAN identified "the problem that has no name," Finch's popular narrative vents frustrations with female suppression and forced servility to men. She declares coercion the chief source of female melancholia, which some dismiss as a nebulous ill humor called "the vapors." She chafes at the anti-woman social order that encourages females to expend artistic talents in frivolous painting and needlework. In a soulful outburst the speaker denounces male domination of females (*ibid.*, 41). Internal unrest outpaces the poet's efforts and drowns her artistry in "black Jaundice," a reference to black bile, the most corrosive of the four humors (*ibid.*, 42). Against debilitating sexism Finch offers no panacea, only the temporary remedies of companionship, laughter, and artistic expression.

Bibliography

Finch, Anne. *Anne Finch, Countess of Winchilsea: Selected Poems.* New York: Routledge, 2003.

Messenger, Ann. "Publishing without Perishing: Lady Winchilsea's Miscellany Poems of 1713," *Restoration: Studies in English Literary Culture, 1660–1700* 5 (1981): 28.

Springer, Nancy (1948–)

The Irish-American children's author and lecturer Nancy Connor Springer writes a variety of feminist tales, fantasy, and reengineered myth. Her intent is to extend rather than revise standard folklore by including women in traditionally androcentric narrative. A native of Montclair, New Jersey, she was an only child who grew up adored and coddled in Gettysburg, Pennsylvania, where her family owned and managed a motel. She earned a degree in English literature at Gettysburg College and married a ministerial student. She teaches creative writing at York College and gains insight into children's interests by hiking, riding horses, and rescuing animals.

Springer's purpose in becoming a writer of children's stories was to supply the girl-centered ideals and adventure plots that she wanted to read in childhood. In addition to 30 novels she has published short stories and verse in *Argos, Boys' Life, Cricket, Echoes, Fantasy and Science Fiction, Highlights for Children, Night Voyages Poetry Review, Pirate Writings, Rambler,* and *Weird Tales* and in a variety of anthologies edited by Paul Ganley, Harry Mazer, and Jane Yolen. For her books Springer has won several awards: the Joan Fassler Memorial Book Award, two Edgar Allan Poe Awards, a YALSA Best Book for Young Adults, a YALSA Recommended Book for the Young Adult Reader, a Carolyn W. Field Award Honor Book, and a New York Public Library Book for the Teen Age. Her books have earned starred reviews from *Booklist* and *Publishers Weekly,* a *Parents* Magazine Parents Choice Award, and a *Booklist* Top Ten Fantasy Novel.

To relieve the depression that resulted from dependence on a philandering husband, Springer introduced feminist issues in her psychological plots by showcasing girls in active, positive modes. She examines a mother's mental illness in *The Hex Witch of Seldom* (1989) and commiserates with the children of divorced parents in *Separate Sisters* (2002). In *Sky Rider* (2000) Springer analyzes the effects of a drunken father and the sudden death of his wife on their daughter, Dusty Grove. The author reveals the roots of sorcery in *I Am Morgan Le Fay* (2001), an Arthurian story told from the point of view of Arthur's half sister. The story reinterprets the angst of a complex young father worshiper obsessed with jealousy. After she views the murdered remains of her father, the duke of Cornwall, "a fire dragon" ignites her heart (Springer, 2002, 4). Through sympathetic character development, Springer retrieves Morgan from willfulness and exonerates her for practicing magic, an accomplishment that earned the regard of the feminist fantasy writers Angela CARTER and Marion Zimmer BRADLEY for its extension of innate female perception of nature's powers.

Springer makes the greatest impact on gendered behavior by introducing young readers to the feminist concept of choice. In *Outlaw Princess of Sherwood* (2003), another extension of English folklore, the author presents a female protagonist who combats the misogyny of medieval Europe. Reprising the familiar scenario of the girl child who rejects her father's choice of husband for her, Princess Ettarde, called Etty, faces King Solon's proposal to cage and torment her mother as Etty's punishment for fleeing marriage to the power-mad Lord Basil. Skilled in logic, Etty exits the royal carriage and plots to rescue her mother. Etty survives in the wild by dressing in boy's clothes, a useful ploy that rids her of rigid standards for female behavior.

Springer contributed feminist variations on Robin Hood tales with *Rowan Hood, Outlaw Girl of Sherwood Forest* (2001), the story of 13-year-old Rosemary, child of the wood wife Celandine and Robin, the absent father. The immolation of Celandine in her thatched hut reveals the superstitions and woman hatred of the era. In a harsh world that offers only the lowest work cleaning chimneys and swabbing privies, the orphaned "Ro" fears the power of the lord, *le droit de seigneur* (the lord's right), a familiar motif of medieval lore. In Ro's words he "[exercises] his claim on the maidenhead of every lass who lives in his domain" (Springer, 2001, 5–6). She subsists on the strength of past mothering, symbolized by an invisible cloak that reassures and empowers. In disguise Ro lives as a homeless boy and forms a band composed of the wolf-dog Tykell, Lionel the singing bard, and Etty, the runaway princess. Springer overturns the standard male-initiated rescue plot as Ro's band saves Robin from a death sentence.

Bibliography

Durantine, Peter. "For Pa. Author, Censors Weave Scariest Tales," *Philadelphia Inquirer*, 10 October 1993, p. B1.

Springer, Nancy. *I Am Morgan Le Fay: A Tale from Camelot*. New York: Puffin, 2002.

———. *Rowan Hood, Outlaw Girl of Sherwood Forest*. New York: Philomel, 2001.

———. *Sky Rider*. New York: HarperTrophy, 2000.

Staël, Germaine de (1766–1817)

The Swiss-French scholar, feminist, and political dissident Anne-Louise-Germaine Necker de Staël infused preromantic and libertarian ideals with sympathies for women's secondary role in politics. In *Literary Women: The Great Writers* (1977) the author Ellen MOERS exalts Staël as "the first woman of middle-class origins to impress herself, through her own genius, on all the major public events of her time—events political, literary, in every sense revolutionary" (Moers, 176). The daughter of a Genevan financier, Staël was born in Paris and home schooled in English literature and composition by her mother, Suzanne Curchod Necker, a former governess. Her mother's male-dominated salon educated Germaine in the issues of the day as expounded upon by such men as the encyclopedist Denis Diderot, the American diplomat Thomas Jefferson, the historian Edward Gibbon, the German poets Johann von Goethe and Friedrich von Schiller, and the famed folklorists the Grimm brothers. After a political marriage to a Swedish ambassador to France, Staël became a visible champion of WOMEN'S RIGHTS. She established her own salon and welcomed intellectuals, with whom she debated the issues of the day. Her salient comments were frequently quoted throughout Europe.

In a politically turbulent era Madame de Staël did not conceal her egalitarian principles. Dubbed France's first female ambassador, she conscientiously carried out official embassy duties while privately supporting the full citizenship for women. Because of her disdain for Napoleon and her support for a constitutional monarchy in 1792 she suffered the first of three exiles. She described banishment from her homeland in a memoir, *Dix années d'exile* (*Ten Years' Exile*, 1803–13). After a sojourn in England and Weimar she settled on Lake Geneva and wrote tales and plays for her private theater. With the anonymous essay "Reflections on the Trial of a Queen" (1793) she lauded brave French "women and children, armed with pikes and scythes" who incited the October 1789 Women's March to Versailles (Staël, 1818, 340). The author defended Marie Antoinette after the August 1793 trial and condemnation of the French queen, who stood proudly beside her children on public display as if she were a common criminal. Staël lobbed an emotional challenge to women readers: "If you are sensitive, if you are mothers, she has loved with all of the same power of soul as you" (Staël, 1964, 366).

After Napoleon's defeat at Waterloo Staël lived only three more years. Despite ill health caused by a stroke, she supported French republicanism and the abolition of SLAVERY. In 1821 her son, Auguste, edited a collection, *Oeuvres complètes* (Complete works), which includes the novels *Delphine* (1802) and the semiautobiographical novel *Corinne, ou l'italie* (*Corinne; or, Italy*, 1807), one of the first European works to focus on female artistry. Chief among Staël's themes are the place of women in the arts and society's isolation and barring of females from intellectual ferment, concepts that won the regard of Jane AUSTEN, Elizabeth Barrett BROWNING, George ELIOT, Felicia HEMANS, Madame Récamier, Mary SHELLEY, and Harriet Beecher STOWE. Told through letters, *Delphine* describes the romance of a young widow, Delphine d'Abbémar, which ends because of her liberal notions of women's behavior. After her lover leaves the country to marry a less complicated woman, Delphine swallows a lethal dose of poison. In *Corinne*, the title character's love of poetry and INDEPENDENCE interferes with her affair with Oswald, Lord Nevil, a Scots aristocrat, and causes her to grieve herself to death. Staël's writings on suppression of female passions—*De l'influence des passions sur le bonheur des individus et des nations* (The influence of the passions on the happiness of individuals and nations, 1796)—inspired and heartened women, including the author Lydia Maria CHILD, the essayist Margaret FULLER, the novelists Fanny BURNEY and Maria EDGEWORTH, the regionalist Sarah Orne JEWETT, the memoirist Fanny KEMBLE, and the polemicist Mary WOLLSTONECRAFT.

Bibliography

Marso, Lori J. "Defending the Queen: Wollstonecraft and Staël on the Politics of Sensibility and Feminine Difference," *Eighteenth Century: Theory and Interpretation* 43, no. 1 (Spring 2002): 43–81.

Moers, Ellen. *Literary Women*. New York: Oxford University Press, 1977.

Staël, Germaine de. *Considerations on the Principal Events of the French Revolution*. London: Baldwin, Cradock & Joy, 1818.

———. *Corinne; or, Italy*. Piscataway, N.J.: Rutgers University Press, 1987.

———. *Politics, Literature, and National Character*. London: Sidgwich and Jackson, 1964.

———. *Ten Years of Exile*. Dekalb: Northern Illinois University Press, 2000.

Stafford, Jean (1915–1979)

The impeccable short fiction writer and journalist Jean Wilson Stafford specialized in characterizing lonely, disaffected, and outcast females. Her themes often emphasized the condescension and alienation of snobbish society. Born in Covina, California, she was the daughter of a writer of westerns under the pseudonyms Ben Delight and Jack Wonder. She came of age in Boulder and Colorado Springs and read widely from the feminist works of Willa CATHER and Sarah Orne JEWETT. Stafford completed her education with a B.A. and M.A. in English from the University of Colorado and postgraduate work in philosophy at the University of Heidelberg. After one year in the classroom she found teaching at odds with her interests. With a Royal typewriter purchased in 1937 she retreated to the attic in her Long Island home to write reviews, essays, and short and long fiction in the company of hornets and spiders. She dedicated her work to feminism: "In those olden, golden days, we were already on to the treacheries deriving from Male Chauvinism and this was a little bitty protest" (Stafford, 1972, i).

In 1944 Stafford won *Mademoiselle's* Merit Award for the coming-of-age novel *Boston Adventure*, a keen contrast of women from the upper and immigrant social classes. The feminist themes of mother-daughter love, low-paid domestic work, and the decline of the mother into solitude and MADNESS illuminate the forces that press the protagonist, Sonie Marburg, toward a too-early womanhood. With a Guggenheim Fellowship and an award from the American Acadedmy and National Institute of Arts and Letters Stafford began work on *The Mountain Lion* (1947), a gender study about anorexia and toxic family relations. She remarked in the introduction about being "so deep in my remorse for what I had done to my heroine, Molly Fawcett" that she was unable to concentrate on real conversations (*ibid.*).

Stafford submitted articles and short fiction to *Atlantic, Esquire, Harper's, Kenyon Review, Mademoiselle, New Yorker, Partisan Review,* and *Sewanee Review.* She received the O. Henry award for "In the Zoo" (1955) and participated in the debates of the post-Kennedy era with *A Mother in History* (1966), an objective portrait of Lee Harvey Oswald's mother, Marguerite C. Oswald. The controversial work reflects the iconage of Jackie Kennedy and the demonizing of Oswald and his family, particularly his mother, a working parent in a manless household. In 1970 Stafford won the Pulitzer Prize and the admiration of the writer Joyce Carol OATES for *The Collected Stories of Jean Stafford* (1969), 30 of her best works from 1944 to 1968. One woman-centered story, "The End of a Career," describes an aging woman's adherence to the BEAUTY MYTH.

Bibliography

Baldwin, Kate A. "Between Mother and History: Jean Stafford, Marguerite Oswald, and U. S. Cold War Women's Citizenship," *Differences: A Journal of Feminist Cultural Studies* 13, no. 3 (Fall 2002): 83–120.

Ryan, Maureen. "Green Visors and Ivory Towers: Jean Stafford and the New Journalism," *Kenyon Review* 16, no. 4 (Fall 1994): 104–119.

Stafford, Jean. *Boston Adventure.* Garden City, N.Y.: Sun Dial Press, 1944.

———. *The Collected Stories of Jean Stafford.* Austin: University of Texas Press, 1992.

———. *The Mountain Lion.* Austin: University of Texas Press, 1972.

Stanton, Elizabeth Cady (1815–1902)

The scholar, author, and reformer Elizabeth Cady Stanton was the tactician of a campaign for gender equality in the United States. A native of Johnstown, New York, she was a brilliant graduate of Emma Willard's Troy Female Seminary. She studied law privately under her father, U.S. Representative Daniel Cady, but could not open a practice because women were barred from the profession. Cheerful and spirited, she read widely, in particular, Mary WOLLSTONECRAFT's *A VINDICATION OF THE RIGHTS OF WOMAN* (1792), which echoed her own distress that EDUCATION and the professions were closed to females. From her study of laws that were skewed in favor of white male citizens, Stanton became an outspoken abolitionist in the style of Sarah Moore GRIMKÉ, who composed *Letters on the Equality of the Sexes and the Condition of Women* (1838), the nation's first feminist tract.

Stanton's mounting outrage at the suppression of women caused her to fear she would "die of an intellectual repression, a woman's rights convulsion" (Schneir, 110). She supported the Quaker orator Lucretia MOTT, who, along with Stanton, was ousted from the platform at the World's Anti-Slavery Convention in London, where only male delegates were welcome. Stanton perceived the similarity between slavery and disenfranchisement of women and stated in a speech to the American Anti-Slavery Society that the female "early learns the misfortune of being born an heir to the crown of thorns, to martyrdom, to womanhood. For while the man is born to do whatever he can, to the woman and the negro there is no such privilege" (Stanton, 1860, 2).

In 1848 Stanton began campaigning for WOMEN'S RIGHTS and collecting signatures on petitions that forced New York legislators to grant married women equal property rights. Her speech on September of that year illustrates a straightforward approach to women's right to speak for themselves: "Man cannot speak for us—because he has been educated to believe that we differ from him so materially, that he cannot judge of our thoughts, feelings and opinions by his own. Moral beings can only judge of others by themselves" (Stanton, 1848, 1). The victory encouraged her to unite with Mott in convening delegates to a convention in Seneca Falls, New York, and to additional sessions in nearby Rochester. Stanton presented the planners' rewording of the Declaration of Independence, which she called the "Declaration of Sentiments," a formal presentation of grievances. It characterizes the lowly status of American women in the same literary style and tone as that of Thomas Jefferson lecturing King George III of England on behalf of American colonists.

Stanton stated her resolves with frequent mention of the biblical story of human creation. She charged that male-centered national law barred women from addressing a public audience and from performing political duties. On a second reading the next day delegates accepted her spirited text. She documented this era of women's history in a scrapbook to which her daughter, Harriot Stanton Blatch, later added details and media clippings. In 1854 Stanton's presentation before the New York legislature challenged laws that reduced women in importance while taxing them for "your schools, colleges, churches, your poor-houses, jails, prisons, the army, the navy, the whole machinery of government, and yet we have no voice in your councils" (Schneir, 111). The speech resulted in an unprecedented victory, a law granting women control of their wages and equal rights to their own children.

In addition to composing oratory, Stanton helped Amelia Bloom reshape *The Lily,* a literary journal begun by TEMPERANCE supporters, into a women's rights periodical. Stanton applied a merry pro-woman tone in her first article, a satiric essay on Pilgrims. Stanton also joined Parker Pillsbury in founding *The Revolution,* a newspaper that vented her fury that women were no nearer their goal. In *Eighty Years and More: Reminiscences 1815–1897* Stanton made clear the difference between achievement in women's realm and achievement in the public realm: "A direct power over one's own person and property, an individual opinion to be counted, on all questions of public interest, are better than indirect influence, be that ever so far reaching" (Stanton, 1971, 376).

Into old age Stanton continued crafting lectures and pamphlets, including writing of the Declaration of Rights for Women at the 1876 Centennial Exposition in Philadelphia, publishing *The WOMAN'S BIBLE* (1895–98), and in 1888 at age 73 convening the first International Council of Women, as keynote speaker. Age clarified her philosophies in *The Solitude of Self* (1892), in which she reasoned that gender bias robbed women of education, property rights, political

and economic power, fair wages, and even membership in juries that passed judgment over them. At her home in Tenafly, New Jersey, she helped Susan B. ANTHONY coordinate clippings, letters, and speeches as source material for the first three installments of the six-volume *History of Woman Suffrage,* cowritten by Matilda Joslyn GAGE. The mountain of documents and details swamped the historians, who met often at Stanton's house to tackle the immense editorial task. Ida Husted HARPER, a journalist from Fairfield, Indiana, later supplemented the original three volumes with two more.

The history covers much of the political ferment from 1881 to 1922. The first volume describes women's early struggles for equality; a companion work covers women's contributions to ABOLITIONISM and the winning of the Civil War. Volume 3 surveys changes to local laws, particularly the shift in Wyoming to voting rights for women. The final volumes cover national and international assemblies that preceded the signing of the Nineteenth Amendment into law. The history acknowledges Stanton's carefully worded addition to the Constitution, written in 1878 and resubmitted to each U.S. Congress until women gained suffrage on August 26, 1920. The wording is simple, reasonable, and compelling: "The right of citizens of the United States to vote shall not be denied or abridged by the United States or by any State on account of sex."

Bibliography

Schneir, Miriam, ed. *Feminism: The Essential Historical Writings.* New York: Vintage, 1972.

Stanton, Elizabeth Cady. *Address by Elizabeth Cady Stanton on Women's Rights* (1848). Available online: URL: http://ecssba.rutgers.edu/docs/ecswoman1.html. Accessed on October 17, 2005.

———. *Eighty Years and More: Reminiscences 1815–1897.* New York: Schocken, 1971.

———. "Speech to the American Anti-Slavery Society" (1860). Available online: URL: http://etext.lib.virginia.edu/railton/uncletom/womanmov.html#g. Accessed on October 17, 2005.

———, and Susan B. Anthony. *Elizabeth Cady Stanton/ Susan B. Anthony: Correspondence, Writings, Speeches.* New York: Schocken, 1981.

Starhawk (1952–   )

A California-based ecofeminist, pacifist, and reviver of the goddess cult, Starhawk writes political essays and filmscripts on the subject of spiritual power. She was born Miriam Simos to Jewish parents. Her father, Jack Simos, a Communist and drama therapist, died when she was five. Her mother, psychotherapist and author Bertha Goldfarb Simos, observed traditional religious ritual and homeschooled her in the family's Los Angeles apartment. Starhawk's pious Orthodox Jewish grandparents lived upstairs. While attending a Hebrew high school, she considered becoming a rabbi. During the Vietnam War she organized other teenagers for antiwar protests.

Starhawk prepared for her unusual career with psychology degrees from the University of Southern California and the University of San Francisco. Between wanderings on the Pacific coast she lived in communes. She led antinuclear demonstrations at Diablo Canyon, Livermore Weapons Lab, Vandenberg Air Force Base, and the Nevada Test Site and visited El Salvador, Israel, Nicaragua, and Palestine to support peace and sustainable lifestyles. At the beginning of the Iraq War she coordinated women's peace vigils outside the White House. Her thoughtful pro-Earth, pro-woman essays appear regularly in *Herizons, Michigan Citizen, Creative Woman, Off Our Backs, Peace and Freedom, Sagewoman,* and *Tikkun.*

Starhawk's writings are diverse. She won a Lambda Award for the best gay and lesbian science fiction for *The Spiral Dance: A Rebirth of the Ancient Religion of the Great Goddess* (1979), which reappeared in a quarter-century memorial edition. The neopagan text drew many followers to Wicca. Starhawk holds workshops in Wiccan practice and has produced hymnals, tapes, and compact disks (CDs) of Wiccan chants and songs and instructs beginners in ritual and magic. *Dreaming the Dark: Magic, Sex, and Politics* (1982) expresses the author's concepts on sources of spirituality and group circles and webs. The novel *The Fifth Sacred Thing* (1993) and its sequel, *Walking to Mercury* (1997), feature the rebellion of the priestess Maya Greenwood and her pilgrimage to Nepal in search of her former spiritual wholeness. Seeking "not mindfulness but mindlessness," she carries on her back her mother's ashes, a symbol of the matriarchal past that empowers and strengthens her (Starhawk, 1997, 19). Starhawk cofounded a teaching model for nonviolent action and scripted *Signs Out of Time* (2004), a documentary BIOGRAPHY of the Lithuanian archaeologist Marija Gimbutas, reviver of the goddess movement.

Bibliography

Mirriam-Goldberg, Caryn. "Visionary Activist," *Women's Review of Books* 20, no. 3 (December 2002): 11–12.

Starhawk. *Dreaming the Dark: Magic, Sex, and Politics.* Boston: Beacon Press, 1997.

———. *Walking to Mercury.* New York: Bantam, 1997.

Stein, Gertrude (1874–1946)

An avant-garde novelist, poet, and playwright, Gertrude Stein created a modern narrative style that bridged Victorianism and modern feminism. After her birth in Allegheny, Pennsylvania, to a wealthy Bavarian-Jewish industrialist she grew up in Paris and Passy, France, and in Vienna and Oakland, California. Orphaned in her teens, she followed her brother, Leo, to Baltimore and lived with an aunt. Stein completed her studies in psychology and medicine at Radcliffe and Johns Hopkins but chose writing over a career in obstetrics. In 1903 with the help of her brother, the art critic Leo Stein, she opened a literary salon in Paris and welcomed cubist artists, photographers, writers, and celebrities. Politically she supported SUFFRAGE.

At the beginning of her career Stein published *Three Lives* (1909), a feminist classic that reveals through simple, repetitive sentences her working-class protagonists' ability to feel fulfilled and liberated in unhappy situations and relationships. The protagonist, Melanctha Herbert, a mulatto rebel, uses her body to express womanly experience and yearning in a social milieu that repudiates and squelches the overtly sexual female. Stein based Melanctha's restless complexity on her own sexual experience. After beginning a monogamous liaison with Alice B. Toklas, Stein volunteered them to drive an American Red Cross ambulance during World War I and to visit the sick and wounded in hospitals for the American Friends of the French Wounded. In an era when women concealed lesbian love, Stein published an unabashedly gay love poem, "Love Song of Alice B." (1921). Stein followed with abstract imagery in *Tender Buttons: Objects, Food, Rooms* (1914). In midcareer her works ranged in genre from an experimental saga of three generations in *The Making of Americans: Being a History of a Family's Progress* (1925) to the best-selling memoir *The Autobiography of Alice B. Toklas* (1933) and the opera *Four Saints in Three Acts* (1934) about the life of Saint Teresa of Avila, scored by the composer Virgil Thomson. In addition, the author lectured on modern aesthetics at the universities of Oxford and Cambridge and across the United States. During World War II Stein lived in occupied France and compiled her impressions in two autobiographical works, *Paris, France* (1940) and *Wars I Have Seen* (1945).

The year after Stein's death of a gastric tumor in Neuilly-sur-Seine, France, her insightful opera *The Mother of Us All* (1947) lauded the accomplishments of the suffrage leader and orator Susan B. ANTHONY, both as they actually occurred and as history remembers them. The opera debuted on May 7, 1947, at Columbia University. The unusual scenes and pageantry project the noted campaigner's isolation during the struggle for the vote and her CONFINEMENT in old age, when she depended on the ministrations of her disciple, Anna Howard Shaw, the author of *The Story of a Pioneer* (1915) and the first woman to receive the United States Distinguished Service Medal. A master of feminine dialogue, Stein reconstructed the inner worlds of ordinary women's lives from a revealing alignment of fragments much as a cinematographer makes movies from individual poses or a cubist artist creates a painting from glimpses. Modern feminist critics reclaimed Stein as a challenger of social and religious authority over women, to whom she restored individuality. Among the writers who have named Stein as a foremother are Rita DOVE, Mina LOY, and Grace PALEY.

Bibliography

DeKoven, Marianne. "Introduction: Transformations of Gertrude Stein," *Modern Fiction Studies* 42, no. 3 (Fall 1996): 470–484.

Kalfopoulou, Adrianne. *A Discussion of the Ideology of the American Dream in the Culture's Female Discourses.* Lewiston, N.Y.: Edwin Mellen Press, 2000.

Oestreich, James R. "A Suffragist in Her Den, Bracing for the Circus," *New York Times,* 21 March 2000, p. E1.

Stein, Gertrude. *The Autobiography of Alice B. Toklas.* New York: Vintage, 1990.

———. *Tender Buttons: Objects, Food, Rooms* (1914). Available online. URL: http://www.bartleby.com/140/. Accessed on October 17, 2005.

Steinem, Gloria (1934–)

Gloria Steinem, the most famous feminist spokeswoman, developed her compassion for the poor into a career in oratory and writing in defense of full humanity for women. The younger of two daughters, she grew up in Toledo, Ohio. She described the era of her childhood as a time when "men were valued by what they did, women by how they looked and then by what their husbands did" (Steinem, 1992, 21). After her parents' divorce in 1946 she cared for her mentally ill mother in their basement flat. At age 17 Steinem lived with her sister, Susanne, in Washington, D.C., and enrolled on scholarship at Smith College. While earning a degree in political science, she displayed the keen intellect that marks her canon. She traveled to Calcutta and Delhi, India, on a Chester Bowles Asian Fellowship and lived among the have-nots, her introduction to world poverty and the nonviolent activism of Mohandas Gandhi. From her experiences she wrote a travelogue.

As a journalist in New York City Steinem built a reputation for innovative writing with articles in *Cosmopolitan, Glamour, Ladies Home Journal, Life, McCall's, Parade, Seventeen, Show,* and *Vogue* and with scripts for *That Was the Week That Was* on NBC-TV. She refused assignments on fashion and makeup in favor of celebrity profiling and wrote for *Esquire* the satiric article "The Moral Disarmament of Betty Coed" (1962). Upon cofounding *New York* magazine, she began a column, "The City Politic." While supporting civil rights efforts, she continued investigating the world of women with a witty article on the exploitation of seminude cocktail waitresses in "I Was a Playboy Bunny" (1963). She developed the autobiographical article into a script for the 1985 ABC-TV film *A Bunny's Tale,* starring Kirstie Alley as Steinem in the demeaning rabbit costume that included pointed ears, revealing decolletage, and a fluffy tail.

By the late 1960s the author gravitated toward compassionate causes favoring Hispanic migrant laborers and the Equal Rights Amendment and protesting the Vietnam War and criminalization of ABORTION. Influenced by the feminism of Congresswoman Bella Abzug and the social critic Betty FRIEDAN, Steinem cofounded the National Women's Political Caucus, Voters for Choice, and Ms. magazine. During her years as writer, editor, and consultant for Ms. she collected names of famous women who had undergone abortions and published such popular articles as "Far from the Opposite Shore, or How to Survive Though a Feminist" (1978) and "If Men Could Menstruate" (1978) and coauthored "A Report on the Sex Crisis" (1982). She won a Penney-Missouri Journalism Award for the essay "After Black Power, Women's Liberation" (1969). Her publication of *Outrageous Acts and Everyday Rebellions* (1983), an overview of two decades of feminist progress, displays her polished style and reasoned belief in WOMEN'S RIGHTS. In 1988 she guided Ms. into a new era of nonprofit publication with a groundbreaking article, "Sex, Lies, and Advertising." While demanding inclusion of women in all aspects of life, she won for herself membership in the National Press Club among Washington's elite male political pundits.

While maintaining a public profile of talk shows and interviews, Steinem developed an articulate, humorous style of delivery. She balanced her essays with wit and logic that rejected mythic stereotyping. In "Women's Liberation Aims to Free Men, Too" (1970) for the *Washington Post*, she explained: "We are filled with the popular wisdom of several centuries just past, and we are terrified to give it up. Patriotism means obedience, age means wisdom, woman means submission, black means inferior" (Steinem, 1970). She continues to publish thoughtful polemical works on date rape, acquired immunodeficiency syndrome (AIDS) and toxic shock syndrome, breast cancer, cosmetic surgery, the glass ceiling, the mommy track, displaced homemakers, and reproductive freedom. Because of her own childhood duties as nurse to her disabled mother Steinem frequently reprises issues of primary caregiving, a duty that falls disproportionately on women.

Steinem's writing moved in less polemical spheres in the late 20th century. She redirected public views of the actor Marilyn Monroe with a compassionate biography, *Marilyn: Norma Jeane* (1986). In *Revolution from Within: A Book of Self-Esteem* (1992) she drew on the wisdom of anthropologist Margaret MEAD, the essayist Robin MORGAN, the poets Audre LORDE and Sharon OLDS, the sci-fi writer Marge PIERCY, and the novelist Alice WALKER to discuss the worth of self-discovery. In retrospect of the feminist movement Steinem acknowledges successes and challenges: "We have overcome a lot of hurdles. One of the biggest is that people for the most part now understand that women's position is not immutable; it's not biologically fixed, or fixed by God or Freud. But while we've changed consciousness, we've barely begun to change structure" (Frank, 77). At over 70, she retains hopes for better parenting by both genders and higher-paying opportunities for women in the hierarchy of politics, business, and public life. Her works have influenced the essayist Marcia Gillespie and the ecofeminist Barbara KINGSOLVER.

Bibliography

Frank, Christina. "Life as a Lightning Rod," *Biography* 6, no. 3 (March 2002): 74–78.

Steinem, Gloria. *Moving beyond Words: Age, Race, Sex, Power, Money, Muscles: Breaking the Boundaries of Power*. New York: Touchstone, 1995.

———. *Outrageous Acts and Everyday Rebellions*. New York: Owl, 1995.

———. *Revolution from Within: A Book of Self-Esteem*. Boston: Little, Brown, 1992.

———. "Women's Liberation Aims to Free Men, Too" (7 June 1970). Available online. URL: http://scriptorium.lib.duke.edu/wlm/aims/. Accessed on October 17, 2005.

Thom, Mary. *Inside Ms.: 24 Years of the Magazine and the Feminist Movement*. New York: Henry Holt, 1997.

Stephens, Ann Sophia (1810–1886)

The fiction writer, editor, poet, and journalist Ann Sophia Winterbotham Stephens placed women's needs at the forefront of her publications and writings. A native of Humphreysville, Connecticut, she was reared by her widowed father, a wool manufacturer, and by her maternal aunt. Stephens studied at a dame school and at age 21 married the publisher of the monthly *Portland Magazine*. The journal was an outlet for her early verse and satiric humor as well as a source of regional writings for a chapbook, *The Portland Sketch Book* (1836). She advanced her career as an editor of *Graham's Magazine*, *Ladies' Gazette of Fashion*, and *Peterson's Magazine of Art, Literature, & Fashion*. Simultaneously she submitted articles, short fiction, and vignettes to the *Columbian Lady's and Gentleman's Magazine*, *Ladies' Wreath*, *Sartain's Magazine*, and *Snowden's Ladies' Companion*. At age 33 she published *High Life in New York*, along with articles in *Ladies' World* and *Mrs. Stephens' Illustrated New Monthly*.

Stephens supplied her magazines with original fiction on complex issues involving biracial marriage and miscegenation. Her most significant is an examination of an Indian mother's struggles with a biracial son in a best seller, *Malaeska: The Indian Wife of the White Hunter* (1839), which appeared in *Ladies' Companion* in three installments. Ahead of its time in social consciousness the story is one of the earliest to compare the plight of white women with that of the American Indian. Stephens reissued the novel through Irwin P. Beadle and Company as the first dime novel, followed by *The Wife's Trial* (1856), *King Philip's Daughter* (1858), *Myra, the Child of Adoption* (1860), and *Ahmo's Plot; or, The Governor's Indian Child* (1863). One of the most popular of her historical fictions, *Mary Derwent: A Tale of the Wyoming and Mohawk Valleys in 1778* (1858), presents a disabled woman as the title figure and describes biracial families among the Iroquois of Pennsylvania at the end of the colonial era. Her picture history of the first half of the Civil War, which appeared in 1863, contained first-person reportage and anecdotes from the battlefield.

Stephens followed with a stream of protofeminist themes. She described SISTERHOOD that succors the poor in a masterwork, *Fashion and Famine* (1854), a two-volume domestic melodrama on urban family life. She also surveyed feminist themes

of ruined women, women's prisons and asylums, the plight of widows and orphans in legal battles, and women's property rights and wages. In *The Old Homestead: A Story of New England Farm Life* (1855) her second best-selling novel, the author features the mistreatment of the insane and the role of nurses enlisted from a penitentiary during a fever epidemic to tend the poor and homeless. Additional; views of women's lives appear in *Wives and Widows, or, The Broken Life* (1869). Glimpses of the frontierswoman's privations dominate *Esther: A Story of the Oregon Trail* (1875) and *Sybil Chase; or, The Valley Ranch, a Tale of California Life* (1882). At her death Stephens's editors issued a 23-volume collection of her works written over a period of 52 years.

Bibliography

Baym, Nina. *Woman's Fiction: A Guide to Novels by and about Women in America, 1820–70*. Chicago: University of Illinois Press, 1993.

Stephens, Ann Sophia. *Malaeska: The Indian Wife of the White Hunter* (1839). Available online. URL: http://www.niulib.niu.edu/badndp/dn01.html. Accessed on October 17, 2005.

———. *Mary Derwent: A Tale of the Wyoming and Mohawk Valleys in 1778* (1858). Available online. URL: http://www.letrs.indiana.edu/cgi/t/text/text-idx?c=wright2;idno=wright2-2364. Accessed on October 17, 2005.

———. *The Old Homestead* (1855). Available online. URL: http://www.gutenberg.org/etext/8078. Accessed on October 17, 2005.

———. *Ruby Gray's Strategy* (1869). Available online. URL: http://www.letrs.indiana.edu/cgi/t/text/text-idx?c=wright2;idno=wright2-2372. Accessed on October 17, 2005.

stereotyping

The predetermination of female behavior, needs, and capabilities has hobbled women for centuries. Parallel to androcentric history are the feminist writings that pinpoint unfair and grossly inaccurate gendered set pieces in scripture, mythology, FAIRY TALES, CAPTIVITY NARRATIVE, drama, and film. In the heyday of NEW WOMAN fiction the Union activist, newspaper reporter, and essayist Lizzie May

Holmes, author of *Woman's Future Position in the World* (1898), challenged the bondage that reduced women to limited human roles: "Woman has been considered too much *as* woman, and not enough as a human being. The constant reference to her sex has been neither ennobling, complimentary, nor agreeable" (Holmes, 1898, 343). Holmes listed the gender-specific stereotyping that dehumanized: "Either as slave, toy, pet, or queen, this ceaseless thinking of her sex instead of herself has been degrading. To finally arrive at her best she simply needs consideration as a fellow member of society" (*ibid.*). Holmes's remarks appeared one year before Kate CHOPIN overturned assumptions about wives and mothers in genteel society with the creation of Edna Pontellier, the sexually self-fulfilled protagonist of the classic feminist novella *The* AWAKENING (1899). True to the refined New Orleans milieu, the text generated huffy, out-of-sorts criticisms that pilloried Chopin more for the sexual content than for the story's themes.

Women began fighting back long before Chopin's fictional Edna left her husband and children, moved into her own residence, and took a lover. MARIE DE FRANCE, famed fabulist of the Middle Ages, smashed narrow mental icons with witty stories of clever women capable of holding their own against tricksters. In the Renaissance the Flemish essayist HÉLISENNE DE CRENNE refuted the DOUBLE STANDARD that held women to a higher moral ideal than men. The 18th-century Gothic fiction superstar Ann RADCLIFFE influenced generations of mystery and fantasy writers to abandon the trembling, helpless maidens in favor of gutsy girls capable of thinking their way out of crises. Her thinking females who needed no rescue were forerunners of characters of children's works by Louisa May ALCOTT and Laura Ingalls WILDER, of the feminist mystery and detective fiction by Sue Grafton and Sara PARETSKY, and of the sci-fi stories and speculative novels by Margaret ATWOOD, Octavia BUTLER, Ursula LE GUIN, Marge PIERCY, and Joanna RUSS.

Lizzie Holmes's call for the humanizing of woman was prophetic of the creation of feminist literature as the definitive writing of liberated women. One 19th-century feminist novel, *The House of Ulloa* (1886) by the Spanish novelist Emilia Pardo BAZÁN, combats the relegation of Latinas to servile and reproductive roles. A dominant male character, Don Pedro, a self-important aristocrat, clings to his narrow stereotype of the gentlewoman submissive to male DYNASTY: "The gentleman of ancient lineage . . . believed that the purpose of women was first and foremost the reproduction of the species. Any suggestion to the contrary would have seemed to him criminal" (Bazán, 157). That same line of thinking denies his wife the opportunity to suckle her own infant, who is passed to a peasant wetnurse, who has "an extremely vigorous constitution and a sanguine temperament," both qualities that upper-class ladies reputedly lacked (*ibid.*).

FEMINIST UTOPIAS based their speculation and satire on exploding hackneyed beliefs about females. In 1915 Charlotte Perkins GILMAN applied gentle humor to the perfect world of HERLAND, a fantasy female never-never land where women live comfortably with each other and their children, whom they produce by parthenogenesis. Relieved of the burden of fashion, they wear appealingly unfussy classic garments and hairstyles that suit an active lifestyle. When a male visitor attempts to ingratiate himself with gifts of a multicolored scarf and a rhinestone circlet, the citizens of Herland pass the treasures around without comment because they lack the stereotypical fascination with self-adornment with which the androcentric world charges them.

A more destructive form of stereotyping, the combination of race and gender produced a formidable set of preconceptions about what nonwhite females think and feel. Jessie Redmon FAUSET, author of *There Is Confusion* (1924), met challenges from publishers who expected novels about black Americans to contain VIOLENCE, juke joints, and squalid ghettos rather than portrayals of middle-class females seeking self-actualization. The novelist Terry MCMILLAN's omission of semiliterate dialogue, degraded womanhood, and poverty introduces readers to a different set of females from the hackneyed standards of earlier decades. She further defeats expectations of washerwomen, cheerful mammies, and domestics with her views of the wealth and prestige of rising professional woman in two best sellers, *Waiting to Exhale* (1992) and *How Stella Got Her Groove Back*

(1996), both vehicles of popular films. In the latter novel Stella, a single black parent, succeeds at her job and at motherhood. Despite the stares and gossip of her sisters and friends, she also pairs with a younger black male, Winston Shakespeare, for a satisfying sex life.

After the invigoration of the women's movement in the 1960s, feminist literature moved further afield from the stereotyped individuals of Gothic fiction and from assumptions about women as useless crones, sex-crazed lesbians, and gratifiers of male physical desire. The polemicist Susan BROWNMILLER revised absurd notions about rape and violence against women in *Against Our Will: Men, Women and Rape* (1975), a fundamental feminist social text. The feminist writer and activist Barbara KINGSOLVER noted in her first novel, *The Bean Trees* (1988), the male assumptions of the right to a woman's genitals. In a response to a Tucson porn shop called Fanny Heaven, Lou Ann Ruiz, a deserted wife and single parent, stares at the doorknob located in the groin of the woman that advertises the company's wares. The implication is that "a woman is something you shove on and walk right through" (Kingsolver, 150). Both Lou Ann and the protagonist, Taylor Greer, prove that assumption false. Likewise, the verse of Adrienne RICH and H. D., novels of Louise ERDRICH and Ruth Prawer JHABVALA, satire of Florence KING and Anita LOOS, essays of Letty Cottin POGREBIN and Gloria STEINEM, allegories of Margaret ATWOOD, and memoirs of Rita Mae BROWN redirect thinking from women as helpless victims to females as dreamers and doers.

Bibliography

Bazán, Emilia Pardo. *The House of Ulloa*. London: Penguin, 1990.

Holmes, Lizzie M. "Woman's Future Position in the World" (1898). Available online. URL: http://etext. lib.virginia.edu/toc/modeng/public/HolWoma.html. Accessed on October 17, 2005.

Kingsolver, Barbara. *The Bean Trees*. New York: Harper & Row, 1988.

Stone, Lucy (1818–1893)

The abolitionist writer, orator, and editor Lucy Blackwell Stone joined Elizabeth Cady STANTON and other suffragists in the crusade for WOMEN'S RIGHTS. A feisty scrapper, she was born in West Brookfield, Massachusetts, to stout settlers. In childhood she formed serious opinions about male dominance over women. Despite the second-rate education granted by her family, she taught herself Greek and Hebrew so she could read the Bible in the original languages to look for mistranslations. After teaching at Mount Holyoke Female Seminary, at age 25 she entered Oberlin College, which led the field in admitting female students in 1833. According to her daughter, Alice Stone Blackwell, "At the low wages then paid to women, it took Lucy nine years to save up money enough to enter college. There was no difficulty as to the choice of an alma mater. There was only one college that admitted women" (Blackwell, 42).

Stone earned praise as the first woman at Oberlin to organize a women's debate team and the first female in her state to graduate from college. Aiding in her formation of feminist principles was her reading of Sarah GRIMKÉ's *Letters on the Equality of the Sexes and the Condition of Women* (1838), the nation's first feminist tract. When Stone wed Henry B. Blackwell, the two signed an equitable marital statement that she should maintain her personhood and property, share custody of their offspring, profit from her works, and have ownership of her share of their residence. The document declared that "personal independence and equal human rights can never be forfeited, except for crime; that marriage should be an equal and permanent partnership" (Schneir, 104–105). After marriage Stone ignored ridicule for rejecting her husband's surname in favor of her family name. Wags scorned as "Lucy Stoners" the women who emulated her and used their maiden names. Undeterred, Stone vowed to turn the female's multiple disappointments into strength. Over two decades Stone, her husband, and their followers collected signatures on petitions and amassed campaign funds. For more than four decades Stone faithfully edited and wrote for the *Woman's Journal*, the suffrage news vehicle.

In 1850 Stone convened a national convention in Worcester, Massachusetts. The meeting in the auditorium of Brinley Hall, the first national women's rights convention, attracted more than

1,000 delegates, including the Congregational minister and Bible authority Antoinette L. Brown, the Boston physician and tax protester Harriot K. Hunt, the Quaker suffragist and orator Lucretia Coffin MOTT, and two powerful speakers for the dispossessed, William Lloyd Garrison, editor of *The Liberator*, an antislavery journal, and the former slave Sojourner TRUTH. The purpose of the assembly was to make women's rights a national issue. The gathering drew strong support as well as the condemnation of conservatives who considered it immodest for women to address a sometimes rowdy, catcalling public from a platform. Conservatives also challenged suffragist charges that males had no right to dominate the ministry. The New York *Herald* blasted the convention as insane, sacrilegious, and crack-brained.

Stone's oratory earned a place in feminist literature for its humanistic appeal. One of Stone's harangues defied fashion that doomed women to steel-ribbed corsets, hoop skirts, high heels, heavy panniered skirts, and upswept hairdos that required metal pins to hold them in place. In 1855 she delivered "Disappointment Is the Lot of Women" to a Cincinnati convention. In crisp rhetoric she stated: "We want rights. The flour-merchant, the housebuilder, and the postman charge us no less on account of our sex; but when we endeavor to earn money to pay all these, then, indeed, we find the difference" (Stone, 1855). Her reminder of harsh laws against women as students, heirs, wives, mothers, and widows sparked the interest of the abolitionist and suffragist orator Susan B. ANTHONY.

Only months before her death at age 75, in 1893 Stone delivered "The Progress of Fifty Years," an overview of feminist accomplishments, before the women's pavilion of the World's Columbian Exposition. Her text, as published in the Rochester press, reminded her generation that "the young women of today do not and can never know at what price their right to free speech and to speak at all in public has been earned" (Stone, 1893). Even in death she set records as the first New Englander to be cremated. In *Massachusetts in the Woman Suffrage Movement* (1883) the feminist historian Harriet Jane ROBINSON extolled Stone and her husband's dedication to equity in marriage. In 1930 Stone's daughter, Alice Stone Blackwell, an editor of the *Woman's Journal*, produced a biography of her mother, *Lucy Stone: Pioneer of Women's Rights*.

Bibliography

Blackwell, Alice Stone. *Lucy Stone: Pioneer of Women's Rights*. Richmond: University Press of Virginia, 2001.

Schneir, Miriam, ed. *Feminism: The Essential Historical Writings*. New York: Vintage, 1972.

Stone, Lucy. "Disappointment Is the Lot of Women" (1855). Available online. URL: http://etext.lib.virginia.edu/railton/uncletom/womanmov.html#g. Accessed on October 17, 2005

———. "The Progress of Fifty Years" (1893). Available online. URL: http://womenshistory.about.com/library/etext/bl_1893_lucy_stone.htm. Accessed on October 17, 2005.

———, and Henry B. Blackwell. *Loving Warriors: Selected Letters of Lucy Stone and Henry B. Blackwell, 1853–1893*. New York: Doubleday, 1981.

Stopes, Marie (1880–1950)

A bold voice for women's reproductive health, the scholarly lecturer Marie Carmichael Stopes wrote and circulated handbooks advocating reproductive freedom for women. A Scot from Edinburgh, she grew up in a supportive MATRIARCHY anchored by a feminist mother who home schooled her family. Stopes studied at Saint George's School and earned degrees in botany and chemistry from the University College and a Ph.D. in paleobotany from the Botanical Institute of Munich University. Her brilliance earned her three unprecedented rewards for a female scholar—fellowships from the Linnaean Society and the Royal Society and a staff position at Manchester University.

From learned articles on coal, Stopes progressed to feminist activism. At age 35 she heard Margaret SANGER lecture about her struggle to operate the first birth control clinic in the United States. Sanger shared concepts and writings with her colleague, who published *Married Love: A New Contribution to the Solution of Sex Difficulties* (1918), a classic survey of human desire and conjugal relations. Stopes's book was an early attempt to express males' and females' differing pleasures and expectations in sexual intercourse. She introduced to common parlance the female erogenous zones—"the sensitive interrelation between a woman's breasts and the rest of her sex-life" (Stopes, 1923). For its candor the work received the endorsement of Oxford University, the Welsh Education Board, and the National Birth Rate Commission, which made Stopes a member. Her second work, *Wise Parenthood: Treatises on Birth Control for Married People* (1918), introduced the rubber cervical cap and the quinine pessary or sponge, two barrier methods of contraception. She spoke directly to women's health needs with a pamphlet, "A Letter to Working Mothers on How to Have Healthy Children and Avoid Weakening Pregnancies," which introduced practical family planning to laboring-class families.

In a climate of increasing feminist agitation for redress of laws allowing the arrest and imprisonment of prostitutes, Stopes concentrated on strengthening the nuclear family and encouraged the birth of loved and wanted children. On March 17, 1921, she received the first clients at the Mother's Clinic in Islington, where female nurse-midwives examined women and fitted them with birth control devices. Her staff pioneered the collection of data on marital sex and reproductive health. Those patients who needed medical care received treatment from Dr. Jane Lorrimer Hawthorne, the clinic consultant. Stopes stated her philosophy publicly: "There is nothing that helps so much with the economic emancipation of woman as a knowledge of how to control her maternity" (Rose, xiii). She expanded her outreach with satellite clinics, a horse-drawn mobile unit, and the publication of *Radiant Motherhood* (1921) and the *Birth Control News*. Although married couples expressed their gratitude for her discreet advice and recommended her writings to others, Stopes constantly battled vandals, book banning, and Catholic conservatives. Publication of *Married Love* in the United States resulted in CENSORSHIP and precipitated a demand for underground copies.

By 1923 Stopes's persistent agitation for government sponsorship netted Ministry of Health support for birth control instruction. She demanded of male critics: "Have you, Sir, visualized what it means to be a woman whose every fibre, whose every muscle and blood-capillary is subtly poisoned by the secret, ever-growing horror, more penetrating, more long drawn out than any nightmare, of an unwanted embryo developing beneath her heart?" (*ibid.*, 91). She compared unwanted pregnancies to slavery's fetters, which clamp "on every limb, on every thought, on the very soul of an unwillingly pregnant woman" (*ibid.*). She issued more advisories: *Contraception: Its Theory, History and Practice for the Medical and Legal Professions* (1924), *Roman Catholic Methods of Birth Control* (1933), *Birth Control Today: A Practical Handbook for Those Who Want to Be Their Own Masters in This Vital Matter* (1934), and a monograph, *Your Baby's First Year* (1939). In 1936 she eased concerns about male climacteric and menopause with *Change of Life in Men and Women*, which compares normal aging with birth, adolescence, and procreation. Her clinic remained open during the Blitz, which wrecked her headquarters and a Norbury Park clinic. After her death of breast cancer and brain hemorrhage her work spread globally through the Marie Stopes International Foundation.

Bibliography

Rose, June. *Marie Stopes and the Sexual Revolution.* London: Faber & Faber, 1993.

Rowbotham, Sheila. *Hidden from History: Rediscovering Women in History from the 17th Century to the Present.* New York: Vintage, 1976.

Stopes, Marie. *Married Love* (1923). Available online. URL: http://digital.library.upenn.edu/women/stopes/married/married.html. Accessed on October 17, 2005.

Story of an African Farm, The Olive Schreiner (1883)

The South African radical feminist Olive Schreiner set the course of the NEW WOMAN novel with *The Story of an African Farm*, a landmark contribution to feminist literature. Her portrayal of Lyndall, the independent heroine, breaches taboos against agnosticism, transvestitism, ABORTION, and unmarried sex, topics the author also used in the novel *Undine* (1874). Set on the dry, sandy Karoo plains of Cape Colony, South Africa, *The Story of an African Farm* features bleak terrain, a parallel to the snobbery and hard-heartedness of androcentric patrician society. Waldo reflects on the collapse of outworn beliefs in a dismal confession: "Now we have no God. We have had two: the old God that our fathers handed down to us, that we hated, and never liked; the new one that we made for ourselves" (Schreiner, 149). More painful is Lyndall's depiction of herself as a tortured female, shaped by others "to our cursed end . . . when we are tiny things in shoes and socks. . . . We fit our sphere as a Chinese woman's foot fits her shoe, exactly, as though God had made both—and yet He knows nothing of either" (*ibid.*, 188–189).

Lyndall rejects medieval notions of romance by relying on self-knowledge. Looking into a mirror, she intones a comforting mantra to her reflected self: "Dear eyes! we will never be quite alone till they part us; till then!" (*ibid.*, 242–243). With her longings for liberty only partially fulfilled, she rejects the marriage proposal of her lover, Waldo. She explains that she recognizes his sincerity and generosity, but that she refuses to see herself as a rescued victim. Of the male's wooing, she charges that he chases her as a child follows a butterfly—out of need to master the being that resists capture. She pictures the trapped female as a fragile insect that still struggles to fly even when one wing is broken.

Lyndall clings to her views of marriage as an androcentric trophy hunt. Before she dies within days of her infant, who lives only two hours after childbirth, she searches the reflected image in the mirror that is her only reliable source of affirmation. To herself she promises, "We are not afraid; we will help ourselves!" (*ibid.*, 296). In 1883 the critic Henry Norman, in a book review for the *Fortnightly Review*, offered as a subtitle *The Romance of the New Ethics* (Burdett, 2001, 17). The novel's unconventional themes and feminist actions aroused controversy in London and spurred Anglican authorities to lambaste it as blasphemous.

Bibliography

Burdett, Carolyn. *Olive Schreiner and the Progress of Feminism: Evolution, Gender, Empire.* London: Palgrave Macmillan, 2001.

Horton, Susan R. *Difficult Women, Artful Lives: Olive Schreiner and Isak Dinesen in and out of Africa.* Baltimore: Johns Hopkins University Press, 1995.

Schreiner, Olive. *The Story of an African Farm.* London: Penguin, 1997.

Story of My Life, The Helen Keller (1902)

A treasured American life story dedicated to Alexander Graham Bell, Helen KELLER's *The Story of My Life* (1902) made stellar contributions to AUTOBIOGRAPHY of disabled people and to the history of pedagogy. The story describes the hardships of the life of multiple handicapped Helen Keller up to age 22. Serialized in *Ladies' Home Journal* in late 1902 two years before she graduated cum laude from Radcliffe College, the text pictures a determined, rebellious woman who demands more of herself than others think possible. Written 18 years before women gained the right to vote, the narrative reveals the yearning of women to optimize their humanity. With the gendered outlook of the time, Keller peoples her genealogy with outstanding males. Even her mother, Kate Adams Keller, gains stature by claiming as kin a hero of the Civil War. Nonetheless, it is the patient, resourceful Kate whom Keller honors as a rescuer. Kate is Keller's first nanny and teacher, who "succeeded in making me understand a good deal" (Keller, 5).

Because of her loss of hearing and sight, Keller remains trapped in the arbitrary world of infancy. She depicts early tantrums as visceral outlets for frustration and rage that conclude in exhaustion and tears. After meeting the teacher Annie Sullivan, seven-year-old Keller weeps with joy at learning palm spelling, a source of communication that sets her free of obstacles. From words, she progresses to literature, a source of spiritual release she compares to utopia. During her rapid remedial education she develops a self free of "the valley of twofold solitude," a wasteland devoid of "the tender affections that grow out of endearing words and actions and companionship" (*ibid.*, 11). As a prisoner unlocked from a cage, she reflects, "How isolated, how shrouded in darkness, how cramped by its own impotence is a soul without thought or faith or hope" (*ibid.*, 224). In tribute to wholeness she pledges "to be myself, to live my own life and write my own thoughts" (*ibid.*, 219). It is not surprising that she developed into a suffragist and spokeswoman for peace.

Keller's autobiography illustrates in the extreme the need of early-20th-century women for intellectual stimulus and creative outlets. Early in her training in braille she uses the stiletto to punch words and phrases at random on paper in imitation of narrative. Through letters she draws dignitaries into her dark, silent world. After defending herself of a charge of plagiarism at age 12, she overcomes suicidal urges and months of self-imposed silence to compose a tentative life story for *The Youth's Companion*. The 2002 Centennial-anniversary edition of *The Story of My Life* enhances Keller's reflections with photos, correspondence, background material, and commentaries on her struggle for a normal life. Also in 2002 the American Foundation for the Blind mounted an online edition of Keller's autobiography.

Bibliography

Hurst, Andrea. "Helen and Heidegger: Disabled Dasein, Language and Others," *South African Journal of Philosophy* 22, no. 1 (2003): 97–112.

Keller, Helen. *The Story of My Life*. New York: Bantam, 1991.

storytelling

Storytelling plays a significant role in feminist literature for its evasion of patriarchal suppression and its enhancement of female community and belonging. In the works of the Jungian psychoanalyst Clarissa Pinkola ESTÉS, author of *Women Who Run with the Wolves* (1992), the passing of oral traditions to new listeners benefits both tellers and hearers by reviving faith in archetypal myths of hope and re-creation. The themes of SILENCING and speaking of wisdom dominate the works of the Portuguese-Jewish writer Grace AGUILAR, author of *The Women of Israel: Character Sketches from the Holy Scriptures and Jewish History* (1844) and *Home Influence; a Tale for Mothers and Daughters* (1847). She championed the Jewish mother as transmitter of Jewish oral lore to her children. The value of home schooling for Jews increased after the Inquisition, when Catholic authorities closed synagogues and Jewish schools, thus halting the passing of Midrashic traditions and Jewish law to succeeding generations. Because women flourished outside a structured religious hierarchy, their simple fables and advisories survived.

In many examples significant female narration takes place at the kitchen table, women's domain, where the snapping of beans, the pounding of dough, and the slicing of knives through potatoes accompany a hypnotic voice, a scene that Marion Zimmer BRADLEY presents in *The Mists of Avalon* (1982) and the Chinese-American novelist Amy TAN replicates in mother-and-daughter TALK-STORY, a source of authority in the multivoiced novel *The Joy Luck Club* (1989). The critic Karen Rowe (1986) delineates the value of memories, folklore, and FAIRY TALES as a means for the female teller to relate a good plot on one level. On another the narrator addresses to her SISTERHOOD the secret female meanings worded in a gendered code, a facet of the midwestern immigrant dialect lore in the novels and stories of Willa CATHER and the Scandinavian gothic tales of Isak DINESEN. A familiar children's tale, "LITTLE RED RIDING HOOD," builds up to a suspenseful segment of questions from the wolf about hearing, seeing, feeling, and tasting, which the teller can elongate to stress the cautionary element of Red Riding Hood's encounter with a forest predator. Similarly, the feminist Latina author Gloria ANZALDÚA learned oral narrative method from her grandmother. The elder WISEWOMAN improvised new versions of LA LLORONA, the weeping woman, as insightful verbal mosaics on the punishment awaiting girls, wives, and mothers who violate society's expectations. Concurring with Anzaldúa's respect for warning stories, the short-story writer Toni Cade BAMBARA credited custodians of lore with keeping black women alive by passing on wisdom gained from the consequences of unwise choices.

According to the Egyptian novelist Nawal EL SAADAWI, the Ojibway writer Louise ERDRICH, the Jewish American novelist Edna FERBER, the black ethnographer Zora Neale HURSTON, and the Jewish American dramatist Emily MANN, recalling and spreading ethnic lore are significant touchstones for minority cultures. In the opening scene of *New Anatomies* (1981) the playwright Timberlake WERTENBAKER exalts the storyteller as the central figure of a circle of listeners. The main character, the adventurer Isabelle Eberhardt, shushes her listener. She then remarks on the protocol of Arab sessions: "When I pause, you may praise Allah for having given my tongue such vivid modulations. I shall begin, as is our custom, with a mention of women" (Wertenbaker, 8). In "The Oral Tradition" (1990) the Irish writer Eavan BOLAND pictures two women marveling at a friend's birthing of a son alone in a meadow after twilight. The poet envisions the humanistic significance of such woman-centered tellings. To Boland the exchange, one to another, resonates with feminist truth.

Feminist literature pictures the female in the role of cultural conduit, the trunk line through which pass stories worth hearing and retelling for their universality. A proponent of Native American folksay, the Laguna Sioux author Paula Gunn ALLEN anthologized Native tales and modern vignettes in *Spider Woman's Granddaughters: Traditional Tales and Contemporary Writing by Native American Women* (1990), a collection that reprises SPIDER WOMAN's modeling of female creativity. Another Native teller, Leslie Marmon SILKO, created a function for herself as story keeper in her Laguna Film Project script "Running on the Edge of the Rainbow" (1978). For her preservation of narrative the New Mexico Humanities Council named Silko a Living Cultural Treasure. In her tales of Spider Woman and in two collections set in the American Southwest, *Storyteller* (1981) and the epic cycle *Almanac of the Dead* (1991), she stresses the centrality of memory and MATRIARCHY to ethnic survival. The latter novel elevates Lecha, an elderly female gifted with second sight, by picturing her transcribing ancient notebooks to preserve her people's "truly great legacy" (Silko, 569). Silko recommends a question-and-answer element in narrative sessions as a means of correcting misperceptions and of including the youngest listener in oral give and take. Such interaction trains the next generation of story transmissions.

In matriarchal settings, such as Grandma Baby's kitchen in the slave way station in Toni MORRISON's *Beloved* (1970); in the tribal plays of the Nigerian folklorist Osonye ONWUEME; and in

translations of the Inanna goddess cycle by the mythographer Diane WOLKSTEIN, storytelling binds women of different generations. A feminist salute to storytelling, Velma WALLIS's feminist Gwich'in epic, *Two Old Women: An Alaska Legend of Betrayal, Courage and Survival* (1993), derives from the author's discussions with her mother, Mae Wallis, in the forest north of the Arctic Circle at the mouth of the Yukon. Of female stamina Wallis remarks, "We began to remember how it once was. My grandmother and all those other elders from the past kept themselves busy until they could no longer move or until they died" (Wallis, ix–x). The author recalls the suitability of female oral lore to the situation: "Mom remembered this particular story because it was appropriate to all that we thought and felt at the moment" (*ibid.*, x). In Wallis's estimation such stories are gifts that elders present to the young to strengthen them for hard times.

Bibliography

Boland, Eavan. *Outside History: Selected Poems, 1980–1990.* New York: W. W. Norton, 2001.

Rowe, Karen. "To Spin a Yarn: The Female Voice in Folklore and Fairy Tale." In *Fairy Tales and Society: Illusion, Allusion, and Paradism,* edited by Ruth B. Bottigheimer. Philadelphia: University of Pennsylvania Press, 1986.

Silko, Leslie Marmon. *Almanac of the Dead.* New York: Simon & Schuster, 1991.

Wallis, Velma. *Two Old Women: An Alaska Legend of Betrayal, Courage and Survival.* Fairbanks, Ala.: Epicenter, 1993.

Wertenbaker, Timberlake. *Timberlake Wertenbaker: Plays 1.* Boston: Faber & Faber, 1996.

Stowe, Harriet Beecher (1811–1896)

The American abolitionist author Harriet Elizabeth Beecher Stowe employed melodrama to convince readers that SLAVERY was an abomination. Born to a prestigious family, she came of age in her native Litchfield, Connecticut, in an atmosphere of pious Calvinism. When her mother, Roxana Foote Beecher, died of tuberculosis, five-year-old "Hattie," the seventh of nine children, passed to the care of her older sister, the author Catharine

Esther BEECHER, principal of the Hartford Female Academy and the forerunner of the home economics professional. Their father, Lyman S. Beecher, a Congregationalist minister, insisted on Bible readings and prayer, but Harriet's maternal uncle balanced piety with contemporary romances, which Harriet devoured and put to good use in her career as a novelist. In 1827 she taught at Catharine's school until her father remarried and relocated the family to Lane Theological Seminary in Cincinnati, Ohio. Among eager scholars Harriet heard lively debates on the issues of slavery and states' rights. On her own she taught composition and rhetoric at Catharine's new school, the Western Female Institute. She read eyewitness commentary on slavery in the AUTOBIOGRAPHY of Frederick DOUGLASS and in the abolitionist tracts of Lydia Maria CHILD.

At age 25 Stowe married a theology professor, Calvin Ellis Stowe, who took pride in his wife's writing for *Atlantic*, *Christian Union*, *Godey's Ladies' Book*, the *Independent*, and the *New York Evangelist*. By freelancing Stowe supplied the family with additional income. She won a prize from *Western Monthly Magazine* for a short story on SISTERHOOD, "Isabelle and Her Sister Kate," and published a first collection of tales in *The Mayflower; or, Sketches of Scenes and Characters among the Descendants of the Pilgrims* (1834). Early in her marriage she toured the Old Chopin Plantation in Cloutierville, Louisiana, the source of her recoil from human bondage and cruel slave overseers. At their home across the Ohio River from Kentucky the Stowes witnessed the sufferings of runaways, whom patrollers bludgeoned and returned in shackles to irate masters. After the Stowes and their seven children settled at Bowdoin College in Brunswick, Maine, in 1849 she stood at the First Parish Church cemetery by the grave of her sixth child and experienced a vision of a slave under the master's whip. The loss of her infant to cholera increased her identification with black women, who bore offspring for a slave economy that bred and traded human beings as livestock.

After the passage of the Fugitive Slave Act of 1850 Stowe pitied black slavewomen separated from their young and the return of escaped blacks from the North to more intense punish-ment and labor. An admirer of the antislavery novelist E. D. E. N. SOUTHWORTH, Stowe respected females for their transmissions of social and religious values and their insistence on peaceful, orderly homes. She composed UNCLE TOM'S CABIN; or, Life Among the Lowly (1852), one of the most momentous novels in American history, and serialized it in the *Nation's Era* in 40 installments for $300. Her blend of sentimental and realistic views of women's lives later influenced the New England writer Janet FRAME, the regionalist authors Helen Hunt JACKSON and Sarah Orne JEWETT, the romance writer Mary Wilkins FREEMAN, and the English orator Emmeline PANKHURST.

The author inserted pro-woman epigraphs, such as the introduction to chapter 12 from Matthew 2:18: "In Ramah there was a voice heard,—weeping, and lamentation, and great mourning; Rachel weeping for her children, and would not be comforted" (*ibid.*, 119). The text of Stowe's masterpiece empowers three white females—Mrs. Bird, Mrs. Shelby, and Rachel Halliday—with humane sensibilities and an aggressive stance against PATRIARCHY, the foundation of the plantation slave system. Mrs. Shelby regrets having any part in the flesh market: "It is a sin to hold a slave under laws like ours—I always felt it was,—" (Stowe, 1965, 36). To exonerate her complicity, she adds, "I thought I could gild it over,—I thought, by kindness, and care, I could make the condition of [my slaves] better than freedom—fool that I was!" (*ibid.*, 37). A best seller in North America and Europe, the book caused Southerners to protest the novel as inflammatory propaganda by a Northern meddler. It created such a sensation that Stowe wrote A Key to Uncle Tom's Cabin (1853) to document her charges and justify her abolitionist beliefs. She included the texts of numerous handbills offering slave mothers and their children for sale.

Stowe's later works continued to feature women's hardships. She published a travelogue of her visit to England before authoring her second antislavery novel, *Dred: A Tale of the Great Dismal Swamp* (1856). A romance, *The Pearl of Orr Island* (1862), stressed the strengths of the protagonist, Mara, as a model of women's moral superiority, but the author was forced to kill off Mara as the only means of making an impact on a fictional male-controlled society. Stowe incorporated regional colonial tales in *Oldtown Folks* (1869) and compiled domestic advice in the textbook *An American Woman's Home* (1869), which she wrote with Catharine Beecher as a guide to young homemakers. Stowe poured moral outrage against incest and adultery into the polemical *Lady Byron Vindicated* (1870) and compiled childhood memories of New England in the semiautobiographical *Poganuc People: Their Loves and Lives* (1878). Nothing that she produced in the latter portion of her career, either under her own name or under the pseudonym Christopher Crowfield, equaled in impact her first novel. After a lengthy sojourn in Jacksonville, Florida, to improve her son's health, she spent the last decade of her life in Hartford, Connecticut.

Bibliography

Hedrick, Joan D. *Harriet Beecher Stowe: A Life*. Boston: Little, Brown, 1994.

Romero, Laura. *Home Fronts: Nineteenth-Century Domesticity and Its Critics*. Durham, N.C.: Duke University Press, 1997.

Stowe, Harriet Beecher. *The Key to Uncle Tom's Cabin* (1853). Available online. URL: http://www.iath. virginia.edu/utc/uncletom/key/kyhp.html. Accessed on October 17, 2005.

———. *The Minister's Wooing*. New York: Penguin, 1999.

———. *Old Town Folks* (1869). Available online. URL: http://digital.library.upenn.edu/women/stowe/folks/ folks.html. Accessed on October 17, 2005.

———. *Palmetto Leaves* (1899). Available online. URL: http://etext.lib.virginia.edu/subjects/Women-Writers. html. Accessed on October 17, 2005.

———. *Uncle Tom's Cabin*. New York: Harper, 1965.

suffrage

The demand for full citizenship resonates through 19th- and 20th-century feminist verse and prose. Although female authors differed in their responses to the suffrage movement, few could ignore the explosive impact of the issue on education, social customs, the economy, and government. The first to link WOMEN'S RIGHTS to opinions on ABOLITIONISM were the Scots-American orator and editor Frances WRIGHT and Sarah Moore GRIMKÉ, author of *Letters on the Equality of the Sexes and the Condition of Women* (1838), the nation's first feminist tract. The most renowned sally of the first wave combined the voice of the platform orator and organizer Susan B. ANTHONY with the research and writing talents of Elizabeth Cady STANTON. Stanton described their pairing: "In thought and sympathy we're one, and in the division of labor we exactly complement each other" (Schneir, 117). In 1848 the Quaker orator Lucretia Coffin MOTT added her eloquence by delivering the speech "Progress of Reforms" at the Waterloo Tea Party. Anthony and Stanton joined the orator and historian Matilda Jocelyn GAGE, editor of the *National Citizen and Ballot Box*, in compiling the first three volumes of the six-volume *History of Woman Suffrage* (1881–86).

The roll call of feminist writers who added their commentary stretched over various genres: the journalism and realistic fiction of Rebecca Harding DAVIS, a great admirer of Mott's oratory; the sermons and essays of Elizabeth Brown BLACKWELL, the nation's first female minister; the poetry of Frances HARPER; and the philosophy of Margaret FULLER, who influenced public opinion through the publication of *Woman in the Nineteenth Century* (1845). One of the most important speeches of the mid-19th-century suffrage drive was the message of an illiterate former slave, Sojourner TRUTH. Her delivery of "Ain't I a Woman?" at the Akron, Ohio, women's rights convention of 1851 was a defining moment that swayed hearts and minds and supplied women's history with the keen perceptions of the unlettered. Another powerhouse of the era, the editor and essayist Lydia Maria CHILD, founder of the Massachusetts Woman Suffrage Association, issued a stream of reform tracts, news articles, and a chronicle of women's privations, *History of the Condition of Women, In Various Ages and Nations* (1835).

Overviews of suffrage writing tend to ignore the input of men, including the husbands of Stanton, Lucy STONE, and Harriet Beecher STOWE. William Lloyd Garrison, publisher of the abolitionist paper the *Liberator*, became an avid supporter of suffrage. At a forum in Cleveland in 1853 he interrupted a rude, insinuating male challenger to declare,

"That as man has monopolized for generations all the rights which belong to woman, it has not been accidental, not through ignorance on his part; but I believe that man has done this through calculation" (*ibid.*, 87). The lone black male at the Seneca Falls women's rights convention in New York was the former slave Frederick DOUGLASS, a champion of racial and gender equity who took up the suffrage cause. In his memoirs he saluted women for their devotion to ABOLITIONISM and proclaimed himself a "woman's-rights man": "When the true history of the antislavery cause shall be written, women will occupy a large space in its pages, for the cause of the slave has been peculiarly woman's cause" (*ibid.*, 83). Douglass remained a firm ally and died on February 20, 1895, in action—on a platform at a suffrage rally before the delivery of a speech.

Latecomers supported the leaders of the suffrage movement. Among them were the Paiute mediator Sarah WINNEMUCCA and the orator Harriet Tubman, who led a campaign for suffrage at the National Association of Colored Women in 1896. In 1869 the biographer Sarah Elizabeth Hopkins Bradford reported on Tubman's contributions in *Scenes in the Life of Harriet Tubman.* Another late 19th-century campaigner, Carrie Chapman CATT, author of *The Ballot and the Bullet* (1897), saw the cause attain victory in 1920. Jane Addams, the Nobel Prize–winning creator of Hull House, Chicago's pioneer settlement outreach, wrote "Why Women Should Vote," a prowoman statement, in the January 1910 issue of *Ladies' Home Journal.* From the perspective of ghetto women, she decried the filth of life in a tenement, where a "mother may see her children sicken and die of diseases from which she alone is powerless to shield them" (Addams, 22). In 1923 Catt and Nettie Rogers Shuler coauthored a history of the era, *Woman Suffrage and Politics: The Inner Story of the Suffrage Movement.* Other women writers of the second wave included the Mexican journalist Rosario Castellanos, the dramatist Alice DUNBAR-NELSON, the poet Julia Ward Howe, the London-born satirist Mina LOY, the essayist Rebecca WEST, and the Ohio reformer Victoria WOODHULL. The newswoman Ida Husted HARPER became Susan B. Anthony's official biographer and reported on Elizabeth Cady Stanton's stand for TEMPERANCE as a prominent side issue in the suffrage debate.

In the final decade feminist writers and orators such as Florence KELLEY and the English orator Emmeline PANKHURST influenced the public's perception of change in the voting laws. Kelley supported the fight for the vote as the only way that working women could gain a minimum wage and ensure safety and health standards for themselves and for child laborers. In 1910 the Canadian journalist Nellie MCCLUNG honored her nation's fight for women's rights in *The Second Chance* (1910), a best-selling novel about the suffragist Pearl Watson, and in a sequel, *Purple Springs* (1921). A contemporary, Ishbel ROSS, covered the suffrage issue for the *New York Tribune* with interviews and eyewitness accounts of strategy to win over Congress. The author Charlotte Perkins GILMAN supported the votes-for-women effort with an anthology, *Suffrage Songs and Verses* (1911). One poem, "The Anti-Suffragists," rebukes the fashionable, parasitic socialite for living in comfort in the care of a wealthy man while showing no compassion for the female drudge who supports herself on maid's work or dray labor. Another poem, "The Malingerer," skewers the woman who considers herself above self-support, a view Gilman developed in a verse fable, "Wedded Bliss" (1911). In 1913 the essayist Helen KELLER added fuel to the rising flame by publishing in the *New York Call* "Why Men Need Woman Suffrage."

British suffragists began to merge methods and polemics with those of North American campaigners. In England Emmeline Pankhurst published *Why We Are Militant*, which expressed exasperation at the slow progress toward enfranchisement: "When we were patient, when we believed in argument and persuasion, they said, 'You don't really want it because, if you did, you would do something unmistakable to show you were determined to have it.' And then when we did something unmistakable they said, 'You are behaving so badly that you show you are not fit for it'" (Pankhurst, 1913). The next year the journalist Djuna BARNES informed American women of the struggle for the vote in England with the article "How It Feels to Be Forcibly Fed" (1914). An illustrated account for *New York World Magazine*, the essay describes the subversion of Christabel and Emmeline Pankhurst's hunger strike for WOMEN'S RIGHTS. The forced feedings ended in deaths by choking and pneumonia and led to the Prisoner's Temporary Discharge for Ill-Health Act of 1912. Dubbed the "Cat and Mouse Act," it allowed hunger strikers to return home until they gained weight and then authorized their rearrest and jailing.

In retrospect on the suffrage battle, authors kept before the public past issues that required stamina as well as cooperative effort. The author Susan GLASPELL published the novel *Norma Ashe* (1942) as a reminder to the younger generation that their rights derived from diligent service to the cause. The British social critic Sheila ROWBOTHAM wrote a biography, *The Friends of Alice Wheeldon* (1986), to honor an English suffragist and pacifist falsely imprisoned in 1917. Rowbotham later compiled *A Century of Women: The History of Women in Britain and the United States* (1993), a selection of vignettes recalling American and British freedom fighters who refused to accept second-class citizenship.

Bibliography

Addams, Jane. "Why Women Should Vote," *Ladies' Home Journal*, January 1910, pp. 21–22.

Douglass, Frederick, "An Appeal to Congress for Impartial Suffrage," *Atlantic Monthly* 19, no. 1 (January–June, 1867): 112–117.

Pankhurst, Emmeline. *Why We Are Militant* (1913). Available online. URL: http://www.cooper.edu/humanities/core/hss3/e_pankhurst.html. Accessed on October 17, 2005.

Schneir, Miriam, ed. *Feminism: The Essential Historical Writings*. New York: Vintage, 1972.

"Sylvia's Death" Anne Sexton (1966)

The poet Anne SEXTON's feminist eulogy "Sylvia's Death" (1966) particularizes the emotional torment that caused Sylvia PLATH to end a suffocating marriage by committing suicide. Mournful and immediate, Sexton's poem took shape four days after Plath asphyxiated herself in a gas oven in London on February 11, 1963. Published three years later in the anthology *Live or Die* (1966), the text pictures the silenced mouth and addresses Plath as "Thief!" for retreating into the very escape that Sexton covets (Sexton, 126). Sexton describes a collegiality based on macabre girl talk, a staple of women's confessional writing. In a Boston pub the two poets chat familiarly about psychoanalysis, cures for depression, and the three rounds of dry martinis intended to ease the internal conflicts that stymie them. Through dialogue, one neurotic to another, they explore each other's torments and debate the worth of continuing their unfulfilling lives.

Sexton personifies the women's obsession with death as a boy drummer who follows them home in the cab and taps out a persistent beat like the women's hearts (*ibid.*, 127). The poets contain the unrelenting rhythm in housewifely "cupboards," Sexton's metaphor for the domesticity that cloaks their secret impulses. The intimate throb goads them toward death as an unfeeling tattoo accompanies the last steps of the condemned prisoner to the gallows. Sylvia's sparring with death has a familiar shape and feeling, similar to the hard-edged grave marker that records her birth and death (*ibid.*, 128). Sexton pictures the subversive element of Sylvia's death urge as a mole, an underground digger that claws upward through the turf with wicked nails. In the final elegiac lines the catharsis of sorrow pours out in uninhibited femaleness as Sexton cherishes Plath's maternity, humor, and blonde beauty.

Bibliography

George, Diana Hume. "Anne Sexton's Suicide Poem," *Journal of Popular Culture* 18, no. 1 (Fall 1984): 17.

Schoenberger, Nancy. "Creative Differences: A Portrait of a Star-Crossed Union," *Washington Post*, 14 December 2003, p. T5.

Sexton, Anne. *The Complete Poems of Anne Sexton.* Boston: Houghton Mifflin, 1981.

T

talk-story

An emerging element of feminist narrative, talk-story reclaims a womanly tradition of instructing and warning the young through therapeutic anecdote, confessional, exemplum, fable, folklore, genealogy, legend, and morality tale. More personal is the testimonial, often of consequences of the teller's violation of good sense or her infraction of social or sexual mores. Authors typically set talk-story in a comfortable domestic setting, frequently a kitchen or porch work station where males are unlikely to interrupt or censor free speech. Among the practitioners in modern fiction are Isabel ALLENDE, Laura ESQUIVEL, Maxine Hong KINGSTON, Toni MORRISON, Fae Myenne NG, Leslie Marmon SILKO, and Amy TAN. Their organic narratives tend to follow the rhythm of hands as they chop vegetables, pound dough, launder clothes, or sew. The critic Wendy Ho, author of *In Her Mother's House* (1999), describes the rhythm of female telling as "a complicated vocabulary of rupture—heavy sighs, silences, trembling lips, downcast eyes, weeping, and wringing of hands" (Ho, 19). Nearby the younger generation sits patiently in attendance, hearing accounts of life passages that a skilled author may refine into AUTOBIOGRAPHY or memoir.

The Chinese-American author Maxine Hong Kingston characterizes talk-story as an element of child socialization and cultural knowledge. She popularized with Westerners the Asian concept of talk-story in *The WOMAN WARRIOR: Memoirs of a Girlhood among Ghosts* (1976), a combination of myth, legend, history, and fiction. Kingston opens the second chapter with a salute to women's narration: "When we Chinese girls listened to the adults talk-story, we learned that we failed if we grew up to be but wives or slaves. We could be heroines, swordswomen" (Kingston, 19). At bedtime the girls fall asleep listening to the amazing tales, which develop new episodes in their dreams. Kingston later clarifies the need for conscious listening: "Not when we were afraid, but when we were wide awake and lucid, my mother funneled China into our ears" (*ibid.*, 76). The goal of the mother is to preserve the best of the motherland in a generation who rapidly assimilate American customs and attitudes.

In the life of the Asian-American writer Amy Tan talk-story embodied woman-to-woman cautionary tales and wartime emotional release, sharing of "good times in the past and good times yet to come" (Tan, 1989, 11). After social upheaval personal narratives empowered and affirmed those who had suffered widowhood, homelessness, and the death of children. In the essay "Lost Lives of Women: My Grandmother's Choice" (1991) the author reveres these stories "passed along in our family like heirlooms" as a source of redemption and forgiveness (Tan, 1991, 90). Talk-story vents the repressiveness of feudal marriage and frees wives and mothers of enslavement to SECRECY and SILENCING while affirming the relationship of mother and daughter. The buoyant woman-to-woman communication alleviates despair, spreads hope and cheer, and exonerates the trickster for using deception to achieve self-liberation.

Tan expressed to an interviewer the natural chasms in familial relations: "Every mother and daughter ends up holding a little bit of themselves from one another, and that can widen and widen into a deep gulf" (Doten, 63). As does talk therapy, the author's form of intimate mother-daughter story sessions releases repressed memory and disencumbers women like her own mother, Daisy Du Ching Tan, of the misery of feudal patriarchy and of the nightmares of spousal abuse. Tan affirmed that the writing of *The Joy Luck Club* (1989) and *The Kitchen God's Wife* (1991) benefited Daisy. The author remarked that Daisy needed a female companion to journey back over fearful terrain: "It was a way for her to exorcise her demons, and for me to finally listen and empathize and learn what memory means, and what you can change about the past" ("Bestselling," 22).

Bibliography

"Bestselling Author Amy Tan Is a Wonderful Storyteller," *Chinatown News*, 18 February 1996, pp. 22–23.

Doten, Patti, "Sharing Her Mother's Secrets," *Boston Globe*, 21 June 1991, p. 63.

Ho, Wendy. *In Her Mother's House—The Politics of Asian American Mother-Daughter Writing.* Walnut Creek, Calif.: AltaMira Press, 1999.

Kingston, Maxine Hong. *Woman Warrior.* New York: Vintage, 1989.

Tan, Amy. *The Joy Luck Club,* New York: Putnam, 1989.

———. "Lost Lives of Women: My Grandmother's Choice," *Life* 14 (April 1991): 90–91.

Tan, Amy (1952–   )

Amy Tan is a courageous Amerasian novelist who speaks candidly about the domestic torments and human rights infractions that women have suffered in China and the United States. Born An-mei Ruth "Amy" Tan in Oakland, California, she learned from the example of her maternal grandmother, Gu Jingmei, and her mother, Daisy Du Ching Tan, that strong women need not kowtow to outdated paternalism. Amy's growing up was fraught with rebellion against Chinese mores and against her mother's insistence that she major in medicine. After courses at Linfield College and degrees in English and linguistics from San Jose College and San Jose University Tan married a non-Chinese and began a freelance business writing for major companies. When her job began to pall, she decided to make "her own living, doing what is important to her, which is to tell stories" (Tan, 2003, 103).

By reprising family stories as suspenseful, woman-centered fiction, Tan flourished in Asian-American novels, a trend begun by Jeanne Wakatsuki HOUSTON, Maxine Hong KINGSTON, Joy KOGAWA, Ruthann Lumm McCunn, Nayantara SAHGAL, and Santha Rama RAU. Tan's first book, *The Joy Luck Club* (1989), filled a need in American readers, who identified with the motifs of festering secrets and misaligned MOTHER-DAUGHTER RELATIONSHIPS. Her agent, Sandra Dijkstra, understood the phenomenon of best-selling works by Asian-American writers: "All of a sudden, [readers] could see that this wasn't foreign, this was American" (Nguyen, 48–49). In Tan's rapid climb to the top of ethnic and feminist literature she preceded other successful Asian-American authors, including Gish JEN, Fae Myenne NG, and Yoko Kawashima WATKINS, in relating family history in the form of fiction.

For *The Kitchen God's Wife* (1991) Tan produced a stunning comparison between the Rape of Nanking during the Sino-Japanese War (1937–45) and a psychotic husband's battery of his wife and children. Set during the era when China abandoned feudalism and embraced Communism, the plot pictures the collapse of familiar lifestyles as women give up bound feet and helplessness to free their minds and spirits of male domination. From the overturn of the power structure arises the resilient Peanut, a former pampered darling who opens a women's shelter in Shanghai. For women on the run, she sets the example of no-nonsense feminism through SISTERHOOD, self-reclamation, and networking.

The author's dedication to feminist philosophy is evident throughout her canon. She ameliorates the horrors in the life of the protagonist, Winnie Louie, who suffers cyclical rape, imprisonment, and the death of three children. Tan confers on Winnie a contented widowhood and grandmotherhood that precede communion with Pearl, her estranged daughter. The author banishes the cruel kitchen god and creates a new myth in Lady Sorrowfree, a 20th-century deity who speaks for silenced Asian women. Tan explains, "I believe in self-determination and I believe there are experiences that filter down from generation to generation. It has to do with who we are as women, not who we are married to" (Taylor, F1).

Tan fills her four novels with examples of mother-daughter arguments and separations, a controlling motif in her two novels *The Hundred Secret Senses* (1995) and *The Bonesetter's Daughter* (2001). The cause of much verbal and emotional strife is the creation of new identity in daughters who are more assimilated to American feminism than their mother. In *Asian American Literature: An Introduction to the Writings and Their Social Context* (1982) the feminist critic Elaine H. Kim explains that Chinese-born mothers try to preserve the courtesies they learned in girlhood as social graces intended to feminize their daughters. Simultaneously the mothers project a fierce affection blended with jealousy that their American-born daughters are freer in behavior and choices. At home running the house and raising their children, mothers from the old country maintain their sphere in the old way, without input from their husbands. Confusing the issue of who is in charge is the pidgin English by which mothers manage their daily lives. To their shame and denigration they must turn to Americanized daughters, who are better educated in English and more experienced in the oddities of the white world. As Winnie Louie explains the chasm that grows between her and her American-born daughter Pearl, "Always trying not to bump into each other, just like strangers" (Tan, 1991, 95).

In *The Hundred Secret Senses*, a gynocentric Gothic tale about a ghost seer, Tan moved on to another female gap, the alienation of motherless sisters. A clairvoyant, Kwan Li, looks at the world through "yin eyes," a metaphoric term for female intuition (Tan, 1995, 31). At a poignant moment she grieves for her cruel surrogate mother, Big Ma, who dies on the day that Kwan Li returns to China for a visit. Olivia, Kwan Li's American half sister, asks, "Why do we love the mothers of our lives even if they are lousy caretakers?" (*ibid.*, 236). The puzzle causes Olivia to picture children's hearts as

blank when they are born, a metaphor for the 18th-century philosophers John Locke and Jean Jacques Rousseau's tabula rasa (blank slate) concept. The thought of her own neglectful mother writing her version of maternal affection on an infant's blank heart helps Olivia understand her inability to love her husband, Simon, and her need for a child.

Bibliography

Kim, Elaine H. *Asian American Literature: An Introduction to the Writings and Their Social Context*. Philadelphia: Temple University Press, 1982.

Ma, Sheng-mei. *The Deathly Embrace: Orientalism and Asian American Identity*. Minneapolis: University of Minnesota Press, 2000.

Nguyen, Lan N., "The Next Amy Tan," *A Magazine*, February–March 1997, pp. 46–51, 55.

Tan, Amy. *The Bonesetter's Daughter*. New York: Putnam, 2001.

———. *The Hundred Secret Senses*. New York: Putnam, 1995.

———. *The Kitchen God's Wife*. New York: Putnam, 1991.

———. *The Opposite of Fate: A Book of Musings*. New York: G. P. Putnam, 2003.

Taylor, Noel. "The Luck of Amy Tan," *Ottawa Citizen*, 1 October 1993, p. F1.

Teasdale, Sara (1884–1933)

A beloved lyric poet who anticipated modern feminism, Sara Trevor Teasdale chose to write about the individual woman's response to love, maternity, and loss. She was born in Saint Louis and grew up coddled and treasured in a wealthy Missouri household. She was educated by tutors and in two private academies, the Mary Institute and Hosmer Hall. She read serious poetry, notably that of the Greek poet SAPPHO and the English author Christina ROSSETTI. At age 18 Teasdale self-published her first verse in *Potter's Wheel*, a journal distributed by her teenage friends. After a tour of Europe she submitted "Guenevere" (1907) to *Reedy's Mirror* and published a first anthology, *Sonnets to Duse and Other Poems* (1907), a sheaf of well-crafted poems dedicated to the Italian actor Eleanora Duse, who revolutionized the female stage role of Nora Helmer in Henrik Ibsen's *A DOLL'S HOUSE* (1879). Continuing salutes to famous women, Teasdale published praise of Classical Greece and Rome in *Helen of Troy and Other Poems* (1911), which honored the title figure along with Sappho and Beatrice, the seraphic beloved of Dante Alighieri. Of Helen, Teasdale commiserated with a half-mortal being whom the gods torment: "Yet for me / There is no rest. The gods are not so kind / To her made half immortal like themselves" (Teasdale, 9). In 1912 Teasdale received useful mentoring from the poets Vachel Lindsay and John Hall Wheelock and from two women, Harriet Monroe, editor of the journal *Poetry*, and Jessie Rittenhouse, who established the Poetry Society of America.

During World War I Teasdale worked steadily at her craft, living out her belief that the female artist must choose between writing and domestic duties to husband and children. She suffered self-doubts after a failed marriage and an ABORTION. The anthology *Rivers to the Sea* (1915) sold out in 12 weeks; for *Love Songs* (1917) she earned the Columbia Poetry Prize and the Poetry Society's Award. She also edited *The Answering Voice: One Hundred Love Lyrics by Women* (1917), a cache of amorous and erotic verse written by female poets of the 1800s and early 1900s, including Elizabeth Barrett BROWNING, Willa CATHER, Emily DICKINSON, Amy LOWELL, Christina ROSSETTI, and Edith WHARTON. In 1920 Teasdale spoke directly to the lonely female in *Flame and Shadow*. Of the woman's contemplation of an unlikely love match the poet advises her to enjoy with her heart what her mind condemns. Whatever the cost to her intellectual life, the poet knows that the heart is the wellspring of her verse.

In maturity Teasdale wrote of disillusion and death in *Dark of the Moon* (1926), a collection that expresses the change in female attitudes toward love and sexual expression in the postSUFFRAGE era. Chronically ill with depression and terrified of becoming bedfast and dependent on nurse care, she died of an overdose of sedatives at age 48. A posthumous anthology, *Strange Victory* (1933), earned the regard of the poet Louise BOGAN. Teasdale's collected works remain in print and attest to her belief that women should be autonomous,

even when they fall in love. For strength her poems urge women to avoid financial and emotional dependence on a husband in favor of union with sea and Sun and sky. Her strong feminist ideals influenced the poets Sylvia PLATH, Edna St. Vincent MILLAY, and Elinor WYLIE.

Bibliography
D'Amico, Diane, "Saintly Singer or Tanagra Figurine? Christina Rossetti through the Eyes of Katharine Tynan and Sara Teasdale," *Victorian Poetry* 32, no. 3–4 (Autumn–Winter 1994): 387–407.

Teasdale, Sara. *The Collected Poems of Sara Teasdale.* New York: Buccaneer Books, 1994.

temperance

A potent subissue among suffragists, temperance touched a nerve in women who suffered in silence the misery of absent husbands, misspent wages, and family VIOLENCE. Among the feminist writings that supported moderation in drinking and the banning of saloons were Louisa May ALCOTT's essays for *Woman's Journal* and newspaper articles by the Canadian journalist Nellie McCLUNG and Ishbel ROSS. The suffragists Susan B. ANTHONY, Elizabeth Brown BLACKWELL, Carrie Chapman CATT, Frederick DOUGLASS, Frances HARPER, Lucretia Coffin MOTT, and Elizabeth Cady STANTON made speeches on the subject. In 1902 the journalist and biographer Ida Husted HARPER wrote in the article "Elizabeth Cady Stanton" on the suffragists' differences concerning alcohol: "Stanton was the first to demand that habitual drunkenness should be held as cause for divorce—in that first State Temperance Convention of Women, called by Miss Anthony in Rochester, New York, in 1852" (Harper, 719). Harper is forced to admit that "[Stanton] was not sustained by more than half a dozen of even the most radical reformers, though always by Miss Anthony" (*ibid.*, 719). Another visionary, Charlotte Perkins GILMAN, wrote of peace and ABOLITIONISM as well as sobriety in her social essays and addressed the issue of drunkenness in her orations.

The push for sobriety as a strength of marriage and family snowballed in the 19th century in short and long fiction as well as in political cartoons on corrupt politicians and bootleggers, songbooks and stage melodramas, sermons, youth manuals, and Prohibition Party propaganda. The utopian author Jane Sophia Appleton foresaw an Eden free of alcohol in "Sequel to *The Vision of Bangor in the Twentieth Century*" (1848), which she published in *Voices* magazine. The Victorian-era Gothic writer Ellen WOOD devoted an entire novel, *Danesbury House* (1860), to temperance. With the intent of winning a writing award from the Scottish Temperance League, she wrote on the evils of drink and the terrors of delirium tremens. Less vehement than members of the Women's Christian Temperance Union, Wood produced a best seller that called for moderation and self-control and won her £100. The London-born actor and dramatist Laura Keene produced a temperance melodrama, *The Workmen of America* (1864), and played a lead role in it during a two-year tour. Mary Wheeler wrote a popular ditty, "Charge of the Rum Brigade" (ca. 1890), which parodied the macho militaristic meter and style of Alfred, Lord Tennyson's "Charge of the Light Brigade" (1880). In Canada the journalist Nellie McClung faced the sobriety issue in a novel, *Purple Springs* (1921). In a revelation of female naiveté, she pities the protagonist, Pearl Watson, who is unaware that "liquor interests of the province were the strong supporters of the Government . . . so she was not prepared for it when one of [the governor's] Ministers stoutly defended the bar-room as a social gathering place where men might meet and enjoy an innocent and profitable hour" (McClung, 78–79).

In 1877 the autobiographer, orator, and essayist Frances Elizabeth Willard, who edited the journal *Our Union*, left teaching at Northwestern University to head the Chicago Women's Christian Temperance Union. She wrote editorials about alcohol consumption and solicited more than 100,000 signatories for a petition promoting protection of the home. Vigorously opposed by liquor merchants, who feared a strong female electorate, she presented a formal request to the Illinois legislature to allow women to vote on matters concerning liquor sales. The petition failed in committee in 1879 but influenced other campaigns for partial voting rights on issues that affected the lives of women and their families. Willard's co-campaigner, the publisher Josephine Brawley Hughes, recog-

nized that women must vote on all issues if they were ever to obtain complete freedom. Abandoning temperance in favor of WOMEN'S RIGHTS, she declared woman's suffrage as the gateway to control of the liquor trade.

One of the most notorious names connected to temperance was that of Carry Nation, an innkeeper who developed "hatchetation," a method of combating male drunkenness that combined pious hymn singing with destruction of saloons and terrorizing of barkeeps. In the eighth chapter of her AUTOBIOGRAPHY, *The Use and Need of the Life of Carry A. Nation* (1905), she accounts for the importance of her arrest and jailing for raiding "murder mills" in Wichita, Kansas: "I knew I was right, and God in his own time would come to my help. The more injustice I suffered, the more cause I had to resent the wrongs. I always felt that I was keeping others out of trouble, when I was in it" (Nation, 75). She links the carousing of drunks beneath nude female paintings that adorn barrooms to the degradation of women and the family. Of the outrages committed in male-only gatherings she challenged that bar owners stripped women of dignity: "Her husband is torn from her, she is robbed of her sons, her home, her food and her virtue, and then they strip her clothes off and hang her up bare in these dens of robbery and murder. Well does a saloon make a woman bare of all things!" (*ibid.*, 76).

Bibliography

Frick, John W. *Theatre, Culture, and Temperance Reform in Nineteenth-Century America.* New York: Cambridge University Press, 2003.

Harper, Ida Husted. "Elizabeth Cady Stanton" (1902). Available online. URL: http://etext.lib.virginia.edu/toc/modeng/public/HarStan.html. Accessed on October 16, 2005.

McClung, Nellie. *Purple Springs* (1921). Available online. URL: http://digital.library.upenn.edu/women/mcclung/purple/purple.html. Accessed on October 16, 2005.

Nation, Carry A. *The Use and Need of the Life of Carry A. Nation* (1905). Available online. URL: http://etext.lib.virginia.edu/toc/modeng/public/NatUsea.html. Accessed on October 17, 2005.

Tyrrell, Ian R. *Woman's World / Woman's Empire: The Woman's Christian Temperance Union in International*

Perspective, 1880–1930. Chapel Hill: University of North Carolina Press, 1991.

Willard, Frances. "Address before the Second Biennial Convention of the Women's Christian Temperance Union" (1893). Available online. URL: http://gos. sbc.edu/w/willard.html. Accessed on October 17, 2005.

Their Eyes Were Watching God Zora Neale Hurston (1937)

Zora Neale HURSTON creates a culture-based epic journey in *Their Eyes Were Watching God.* She observes a rural girl, Janie Crawford Woods, through three marriages and into widowhood and self-fulfillment. The plot pictures Janie, an abandoned child, as a recipient of female parables. Her grandmother, Nanny Leafy Washburn, warns, "De white man throw down de load and tell de nigger man tuh pick it up. He pick it up because he have to, but he don't tote it. He hand it to his womenfolks. . . . De nigger woman is de mule uh de world" (Hurston, 14). The bestial imagery depicts the depersonalized toil that black women endured from slave times.

Hurston illustrates the power of a young girl's dreams in Janie's sexual fantasies. Despite Nanny's warnings, Janie naively dreams about universal myths as she contemplates a harmonious coital union: "She saw a dust-bearing bee sink into the sanctum of a bloom; the thousand sister-calyxes arch to meet the love embrace and the ecstatic shiver of the tree from root to tiniest branch creaming in every blossom and frothing with delight. So this was a marriage!" (*ibid.,* 24). An arranged union with Logan Killicks, an elderly husband with dirty feet, deflates her vision of wifely joy until Joe "Jody" Starks lures her away with sweet words and bold courtship. Janie's trust in a skilled seducer attests to a naiveté that leads her out of one bad marriage into another as trophy wife to a self-promoting strutter. Janie survives the putdowns of her second husband through posture and dress. No longer "petal-open," she suffers the epiphany of the just-slapped wife: "She stood there until something fell off the shelf inside her" (*ibid.,* 67).

Still awaiting the right man, at age 37 Janie finds true love in her third marriage, which allies her with 30-year-old Vergible "Tea Cake" Woods.

He woos her with fresh-picked strawberries, an erotic symbol of lush female SEXUALITY. Hurston settles the couple amid the black diaspora, a rough camp of migrant workers on Lake Okechobee. In a grotesque burst of VIOLENCE Janie shoots Tea Cake after he brandishes a gun during a hallucination caused by rabies. The disastrous conclusion to a loving marriage is a double betrayal, by a delusional husband who threatens her life and by blacks who accuse her of murder before a court of law. Exonerated and returned home to grieve, she flaunts her passion and INDEPENDENCE with a cavalier stride, the "great rope of black hair swinging to her waist and unraveling in the wind like a plume" (*ibid.,* 2).

The resolution underscores the SISTERHOOD of Janie and Pheoby, two old friends who validate each other's epiphany. Over a plate of mulatto rice, a flavorful but humble southern specialty, Pheoby listens to Janie's experiences at integrating her inner self. Pheoby declares, "Ah done growed ten feet higher from jus' listenin' tuh you, Janie. Ah ain't satisfied with myself no mo' " (*ibid.,* 284). In private Janie recedes from grief into rapture through memory: "Tea Cake, with the sun for a shawl. Of course he wasn't dead. He could never be dead until she herself had finished feeling and thinking" (*ibid.,* 286). In contentment with her dreams she lets narrative console and uplift her. In 1979 the poet and playwright Mari EVANS adapted the novel as a musical, *Eyes* (1996), which debuted at the Richard Allen Cultural Center in New York City. Oprah Winfrey produced a televised version of the novel in 2005.

Bibliography
Barr, Tina. " 'Queen of the Niggerati' and the Nile: The Isis-Osiris Myth in Zora Neale Hurston's *Their Eyes Were Watching God,*" *Journal of Modern Literature* 25, no. 3–4 (Summer 2002): 101–114.

Hurston, Zora Neale. *Their Eyes Were Watching God.* New York: Harper Perennial, 1990.

Kalfopoulou, Adrianne. *A Discussion of the Ideology of the American Dream in the Culture's Female Discourses.* Lewiston, N.Y.: Edwin Mellen Press, 2000.

Thompson, Dorothy (1894–1961)

The journalist, radio broadcaster, and lecturer Dorothy Thompson, the most influential female of the international press corps in her day, modeled the elan of the era's NEW WOMAN. She championed the right of women to a career and to freedom of sexual expression. The daughter of a Methodist minister in Lancaster, New York, she was motherless from age eight. The arrival of a stepmother forced her to shelter with relatives in Chicago, where she dreamed of world travel. Educated at Syracuse University and enlisted in the New York State Woman Suffrage Party, she worked as publicist, orator, and facilitator of WOMEN'S RIGHTS meetings. After she sailed to Europe at age 26 to gather foreign news for the *Philadelphia Public Ledger*, she injected into media reportage her feminist views of patriarchal regimes and the role of androcentrism in the labor movement and global warfare. Her theory influenced the women's movement to examine the predilection of males for initiating and exacerbating world chaos.

The first female to head a large overseas news bureau and to interview the highest-ranking males of her day, Thompson became the Vienna correspondent for the *Chicago Daily News* and led the Central European news bureau in Berlin for the *Ledger* and the *New York Evening Post*. Her range of contacts included interviews and correspondence with Kemal Ataturk, Winston Churchill, Felix Frankfurter, Sigmund Freud, Charles de Gaulle, Cordell Hull, Clare Booth LUCE, Gamal Abdel Nasser, Eleanor Roosevelt, Franklin Delano Roosevelt, Leon Trotsky, Harry S. Truman, and Rebecca WEST. Thompson remained in the public eye with a syndicated column, "On the Record," for the *New York Herald Tribune*, which reached 8 million readers of 170 newspapers. In 1928 she collected frontline accounts and interviews in *The New Russia* and packed punch into such revealing chapter headings as "The State as a Political Machine," "The War Psychosis," and "The Permanent Crisis." Before *Fuehrer* became a household word, she published *I Saw Hitler!* (1932). Because of her dismissal of Adolf Hitler as an insignificant parvenu and her warnings about the rise of fascism, his regime monitored her news releases. In August 1934 German authorities made her the first correspondent to be forced out of any European country. Russian authorities also refused to honor her passport because of her arguments against Communism.

As Nazi power burgeoned in Central Europe, Thompson gained readership. She took a controversial stand against Neville Chamberlain for capitulating to Hitler's savagery in Czechoslovakia. At the beginning of World War II she published a handbook, *Political Guide: A Study of American Liberalism and Its Relationship to American Totalitarian States* (1938), that urged Americans to rescue the Allies and refugees. Bold warnings of war to come earned her the nickname "the American Cassandra." Her book *Refugees: Anarchy or Organization?* (1938), an extension of an article for *Foreign Affairs Magazine*, revealed a compassion for orphans, war widows, the aged and handicapped, and displaced persons. She expressed rage at the growth of random pilferage and terrorism. Her knowledge of Nazi evil precipitated a vocal stance favoring the release of Jews from labor camps. Admiring Thompson's hardihood in a grueling profession Katharine Hepburn played her in the fictional role of Tess Harding, the central character in the film *Woman of the Year* (1942).

Thompson remained a significant figure in American news reporting into the late 1940s. She extended her outreach with articles for *Ladies' Home Journal, Liberty,* and *Saturday Evening Post* and broadcast coverage of the Democratic and Republican presidential conventions over National Broadcasting Corporation (NBC) radio. In the September 1947 issue of *Ladies' Home Journal* she issued "We Must Find a Radical Solution for the Abolition of War," a passionate essay expressing a feminist view of world order. She gave political speeches at the League for Political Education and read "Women in the United States" and "The State of Democracy" for British Broadcasting Corporation (BBC) radio. In 1940 she migrated from the *Tribune* to the *New York Post*, but she lost her clout in 1948 for siding with the Islamic Palestinians and opposing the establishment of the Jewish state of Israel. In August 1948 she published "The Century of Women's Progress," a celebratory essay on feminist advances. In 1991 publication of more than four decades of correspondence between Thompson and her fellow journalist Rose Wilder Lane, a reporter for the American Red Cross, revealed a literary SISTERHOOD that aided two achievers with the difficulties in melding love and marriage with career.

Bibliography

Kurth, Peter. *American Cassandra: The Life of Dorothy Thompson*. Boston: Little, Brown, 1990.

Thompson, Dorothy. *Dorothy Thompson and Rose Wilder Lane: Forty Years of Friendship Letters, 1920–1961*. Columbia: University of Missouri Press, 1991.

———. *I Saw Hitler!* New York: Farrer & Rinehart, 1932.

———. *Refugees: Anarchy or Organization?* New York: Random House, 1938.

Willis, Lucindy A. *Voices Unbound: The Lives and Works of Twelve Women Intellectuals*. Lanham, Md.: Rowman & Littlefield, 2002.

Three Lives Gertrude Stein (1909)

Gertrude STEIN aired her brash themes, repetitions, and ironic technique in *Three Lives* (1909), a series of psychological portraits depicting the alienation of servant-class women. She developed the experimental concept while translating Auguste Flaubert's *Trois contes* (Three stories, 1877) into English. Stein's narrative breaks into realistic character studies: "The Good Anna," "Melanctha: Each One as She May," and "The Gentle Lena." "Miss Anna" Federner, the thrifty, shrewish housekeeper for Miss Mathilda and the keeper of homeless dogs, reaches age 40 with her humor, generosity, and Old World standards of decency intact (Stein, 5). Obsessed with propriety, she conceals the sexual escapades of her dog, Peter, much as she cloaks her lesbian attachment to Julia Lehntman. After successive breakups and new posts Anna works herself to death without achieving sexual fulfilment.

Stein creates resonance in the second life story, which mirrors Anna's waste of self on drudgery. The middle focus, Melanctha Herbert, a mulatto rebel, suffers alienation after straying from socially correct behavior through bisexuality. Bearing the Greek word for "black earth" as a given name, she is an outcast for being "half made with real white blood" and for jettisoning her virginity to satisfy sexual curiosity—a brief intimacy with Jane Harden, an alcoholic, and overt passion for Dr. Jefferson Campbell, who rejects Melanctha because of her free-loving lifestyle (*ibid.*, 78). Later relationships, with her old friend, Rose Johnson, and the gambler Jem Richards, amount to nothing. As does Anna Federner, Melanctha dies of fever, unloved and unappreciated.

Similarly distanced from sexual choices, Lena Mainz Kreder, the last protagonist of the story cycle, bears a surname meaning "server." She lives on the outskirts of American respectability, works conscientiously, saves her wages, and prefers moral rightness to squalid behavior. Nonetheless, her cousins debase her as a pariah "little better than a nigger" and "as far below them as were Italian or negro workmen" (*ibid.*, 223, 222). Unsociable and glum, she does nothing to reclaim her worth and is dimly aware that the teasing of her friends Nellie and Mary arouses her sexually. After Lena's marriage to Herman her father-in-law dismisses her as a commodity acquired through the marriage contract. Her life ebbs away in domesticity until the birth of a fourth child, when she dies as if she is something that was used up in the process. Stein's intent in depicting three unfulfilled lives was to introduce to modernism the importance of the sexual self to female contentment.

Bibliography

Rowe, John Carlos. "Naming What Is Inside: Gertrude Stein's Use of Names in *Three Lives*," *Novel: A Forum on Fiction* 36, no. 2 (Spring 2003): 219–243.

Stein, Gertrude. *Three Lives and Tender Buttons*. New York: Signet, 2003.

Tituba of Salem Village Ann Petry (1964)

In the first year of the feminist movement Ann PETRY reminded white activists of a neglected black heroine, the protagonist of *Tituba of Salem Village*, a young adult classic. The author studied Barbadian herbalism, STORYTELLING, and second sight to account for an intercultural lynching—the victimization of Tituba Indian, wife of John Indian, during the Salem witch trials of 1692. Through feminist historical fiction the author sets the event against stark chiaroscuro—the biracial female "other" defending herself from a white, male-controlled economic superpower. After gauging her situation in Massachusetts Colony, Tituba begins envisioning herself taunted and menaced by white hysterics. The author ties clairvoyance to a domestic scenario, the farmyard watering trough. The watery vision she views symbolizes impermanence in an amorphous British colony still establishing its place in the world.

To retrieve a black survivor from white myth making, Petry portrays Tituba at the height of conflict—as the marginalized first witness and confessor to a travesty of false accusations based on superstition. She falls victim to Abigail Williams, the troublemaking niece of Tituba's white mistress, the invalid wife of the Reverend Samuel Parris. Petry uses the slave's dilemma as a commentary on sexism, religious fanaticism, and racism. Clouding the issue of guilt is parishioners' consensus that they "don't want a man for a minister who has witches in his house" (Petry, 184). Betrayal turns the West Indian slave into a martyr to Parris's reputation.

The gendering of power reaches a height of hypocrisy during testimony and interrogation by Judge Hathorne. Tituba's word bears no weight with white male colonial officials. Outside her cell mobs focus their complaints and fears on the lone female. At a Boston jail the keeper chuckles, "They're catchin' witches in Salem Village just like they was chickens on a roost" (*ibid.*, 250). One female suspect dies in jail; 19 others die on the gallows. Ironically Tituba survives the cold, leg irons, and fettering by serving the jailer as his cook. Because of her value as a domestic Parris sells her to a new master. In August 2005 an international humanities conference at Cambridge University studied Petry's fiction alongside Arthur Miller's *The Crucible* (1962) and Maryse CONDÉ's *I, Tituba, Black Witch of Salem* (1986).

Bibliography

Petry, Ann. *Tituba of Salem Village*. New York: Thomas Y. Crowell, 1964.

Tucker, Veta Smith. "Purloined Identity: The Racial Metamorphosis of Tituba of Salem Village," *Journal of Black Studies* 30, no. 4 (March 2000): 625.

Truth, Sojourner (1795–1883)

One of the powerful orators of her day, a gaunt former slave who named herself Sojourner Truth crusaded for ABOLITIONISM and SUFFRAGE. Born Isabella Hardenbergh "Belle" Van Wagenen (or Van Wagener) in Hurley, New York, to the slaves James "Bomefree" and Betsey, called "Mau-mau Bett," Sojourner Truth grew up in the Low Dutch–speaking household of Colonel Charles Hardenbergh. She absorbed a unique religion, the Hardenberghs' mystic faith melded with her parents' African animism. After her ownership passed to the colonel's son, Charles, she resided in the dank basement of his hotel with the other slaves and slept on straw. While living in New York City, she was freed at age 22 by state emancipation laws. Aided by a Quaker family, the Van Wagenens, she successfully sued for the return of Peter, one of her five children, whom her owners sold illegally to a Georgia slaver.

Sojourner Truth succeeded in transforming physical strength into the stamina to address difficult audiences. She worked as a domestic and worshiped with pentecostal evangelists. In 1841 she began evangelizing the prostitutes of New York City and traveling to tent revivals and homes to combat slavery through speeches and gospel songs. When a heckler accused her of being a male disguised as a female, she opened her bodice to bare her breasts. Although she never learned to read, she mastered witty aphorisms and STORYTELLING and collected in a scrapbook press clippings, letters, and signatures of supporters, who included the Quaker orator Lucretia Coffin MOTT, the suffrage researcher Elizabeth Cady STANTON, and the novelist Harriet Beecher STOWE.

Sojourner Truth joined the suffragists in 1850, the year she compiled a landmark feminist text, *The Narrative of Sojourner Truth: A Bondswoman of Olden Time*, coauthored by her neighbor, Olive Gilbert. The AUTOBIOGRAPHY was the first of four editions, dated 1850, 1878, 1881, and 1884. At the Akron, Ohio, WOMEN'S RIGHTS convention of 1851 Sojourner Truth delivered one of the era's most quoted speeches, "Ain't I a Woman?" She declared, "I could eat as much as a man (when I could get it), and bear de lash as well—and ain't I a woman?" (Truth, 1850, v–vi). Midway through her brief oration she revealed that almost all of her children had been sold. The delegate Frances D. Gage, who recorded the speech, recalled that others present applauded and wept in response to the vigor and emotion of the speaker's words.

In 1853 at the Broadway Tabernacle Sojourner Truth delivered the speech "The Women

Want Their Rights." She took as an example of female strengths the story of Queen Esther in the Bible. In powerful vernacular the orator shushed the hisses and boos. She lamented, "We have all been thrown down so low that nobody thought we'd ever get up again; but we have been long enough trodden now; we will come up again" (Truth, 1853). She gathered strength as she worked up to a grand challenge to hecklers: "But we'll have our rights, see if we don't; and you can't stop us from them; see if you can. You may hiss as much as you like, but it is coming" (*ibid.*).

In the April 1863 edition of *Atlantic Monthly* Stowe published an eyewitness account of her introduction to the orator in "Sojourner Truth, the Libyan Sibyl." Stowe admired the famed abolitionist's courage and subtlety and dubbed her "mother of myriads": "She had things to say, and was ready to say them at all times, and to any one" (Stowe, 481, 474). Stowe remarked on the misery of female slaves, a subject that Sojourner Truth knew from personal experience with slave breeding and the sale of children. She described to Stowe an instance of separation of mother and child: "She was out of her mind,—a-cryin', an' callin' for her daughter" (*ibid.*, 478). Sojourner Truth's rawboned shape belied the tenderness of her treatment of the childless mother: "I held her poor ole head on my arm, an' watched for her as ef she'd been my babby. An' I watched by her, an' took care on her all through her sickness after that, an' she died in my arms, poor thing!" (*ibid.*).

Sojourner Truth found herself divided in spirit over the Fourteenth Amendment to the Constitution, which in 1866 gave black males the vote. The denial of women's rights enraged Susan B. AN-THONY and Stanton, the leaders of the suffrage movement. The following year Sojourner Truth voiced her quandary: "There is a great stir about colored men getting their rights, but not a word about the colored women" (Schneir, 129). She complained bitterly that black women had no difficulty finding work as domestics and laundresses, but their unemployed husbands, strutting over their new privilege as citizens, seized women's wages and left them with no money to buy food for their dependents. Using simple mathematics she exclaimed, "We do as much, we eat as much, we want

as much" (*ibid.*). Bitterly she accused black males of becoming as possessive of women as slave masters.

In the 20th century Sojourner Truth mutated rapidly from historical figure to mythic icon. In 1935 the dramatist May Miller, a prolific author of the Harlem Renaissance, honored the famed orator with a one-act historical play, *Sojourner Truth*, just as she dramatized female heroism with the dialect play *Harriet Tubman* (1935). The stage version of the imposing evangelist is a bold, upbeat traveler who greets strangers with genuine piety. Standing six feet tall in black skin smoking a pipe, she exudes female pride. To questions about her past she recalls the female version of bondage: " 'Mos' the first thing I kin remember is my Mammy sittin' on her doorstep starin' an' starin' at the stars, then weepin' an' weepin', then starin' some more" (Miller, 15). At the play's climax Sojourner Truth's moral example changes the minds of a gang of boys intent on burning the canvas pavilions at a revival. By her modest demeanor and simple speeches she counters racism, ageism, and sexism and earns the right to address white worshippers.

Other feminist writers based their feminist views on Sojourner Truth's heroic womanhood. Alice WALKER, author of the semiautobiographical novel *Meridian* (1976), portrayed the civil rights movement in the South in the 1960s, which she had experienced through volunteering. In *Living by the Word: Selected Writings 1983–1987* (1988) Walker admitted to reliance on her heroine's image of strength and self-reliance: "And when I walk into a room of strangers who are hostile to the words of women, I do with her/our cloak of authority—as black women and beloved expressions of the universe" (Walker, 98).

Bibliography

Miller, May. *Sojourner Truth* in *Negro History in Thirteen Plays*. Edited by Willis Richardson and May Miller. Washington, D.C.: Associated Publishers, 1935.

Samra, Matthew K. "Shadow and Substance: The Two Narratives of Sojourner Truth," *Midwest Quarterly* 38, no. 2 (Winter 1997): 158–171.

Schneir, Miriam, ed. *Feminism: The Essential Historical Writings*. New York: Vintage, 1972.

Stowe, Harriet Beecher. "Sojourner Truth, the Libyan Sibyl" (1863). Available online. URL: http://wyllie.

lib.virginia.edu:8086/perl/toccer-new?id=StoSojo.
sgm&images=images/modeng&data=/texts/english/
modeng/parsed&tag=public&part=1&division=
div1. Accessed on October 13, 2005.

Truth, Sojourner. *Narrative of Sojourner Truth* (1850).
Available online. URL: http://digital.library.upenn.
edu/women/truth/1850/1850.html. Accessed on October 17, 2005.

————. "The Women Want Their Rights" (1853).
Available online. URL: http://etext.lib.virginia.edu/
railton/uncletom/womanmov.html#g. Accessed on
October 17, 2005.

Walker, Alice. *Living By the Word: Selected Writings
1983–1987.* New York: Harcourt, 1988.

Twilight Los Angeles, 1992 **Anna Deavere Smith** (1994)

The writer-actor Anna Deavere Smith's one-
woman drama *Twilight Los Angeles, 1992: On the
Road: A Search for American Character* (1994) contributes eyewitness immediacy to American documentary theater. Through 50 monologues she
builds an acting feat into a re-creation of class and
race war. In her words, the production "[searches]
for the character of Los Angeles in the wake of the
initial Rodney King verdict" (Smith, xvii). Divided
into a prologue and five acts, the series of solo
pieces lets individuals express their own hostilities
and fears—Michael Zinzun's protest of police brutality, Chung Lee's grievance at the looting and
burning of his store, Judy Tur's estimate of white
rage, and the writer Mike Davis's charge that Los
Angeles "is a city at war with its own children"
(*ibid.,* 29). The result is a cathartic experience that
airs contrasting claims and individual biases.

The gendered responses to an urban war zone
express women's unique concerns. Theresa Allison, founder of Mothers Reclaiming Our Children,
mourns the gang members who end up in prison or
the cemetery. A shooting victim, Elvira Evers, worries that her unborn daughter will not survive the
surgery to remove the bullet that struck the child's
elbow. June Park weeps as she describes the shooting of her husband, Walter, a civic-minded businessman. An anonymous man criticizes a witness,
the realtor Elaine Young, by calling her a "dumb
shit bimbo" for retreating to a safe zone in the Beverly Hills Hotel (*ibid.,* 154). Congresswoman Maxine Waters lambastes President Ronald Reagan for
ignoring the hunger and need of "the unheard"
(*ibid.,* 162). The former Black Panther Elaine
Brown turns from issues of VIOLENCE and injustice
to commitment and "love of your people" (*ibid.,*
230). By threading women's issues among more
militant male demands, Smith implies that females
are more likely to seek peace and moderation during social upheavals. Marc Levin directed a film
version of *Twilight Los Angeles,* which debuted at
the 2000 Sundance Film Festival to a receptive audience.

Bibliography

Klawans, Stuart. "A Riot of Personality." *Nation,* 16 October 2000, pp. 42–43.

Smith, Anna Deavere. *Twilight Los Angeles, 1992: On the
Road: A Search for American Character.* New York:
Anchor, 1994.

U

Ulrich, Laurel Thatcher (1938–)

By reclaiming a professional diary of a frontier nurse-midwife, the historian Laurel Thatcher Ulrich, a Mormon feminist scholar and essayist, contributed to women's journals and to New England community history from preindustrial America. In her native Sugar City, Idaho, Ulrich learned of trappers' wives and Mormon and Shoshone female strengths from family STORYTELLING of pioneers and their Scandinavian roots. By her midteens she was submitting verse to *Seventeen*. Educated in English literature at the University of Utah, Simmons College, and the University of New Hampshire, she married the chemical engineer Gael Ulrich, who shared her ardent Mormonism. The author taught history at the University of New Hampshire before becoming the James Duncan Phillips Professor of Early American History at Harvard. Her purposeful, energetic teaching and writing retrieve from androcentric national history the invisible heroines.

In 1980 Ulrich's *Good Wives: Image and Reality in the Lives of Women in Northern New England, 1650–1750* summarized the uniqueness of ordinary female lives in the American colonies in its emphasis on housekeepers, mothers, and churchgoers rather than witches and outcasts like Tituba and Anne Hutchinson. Of the housewife the historian explained that "her role was defined by a space (a house and its surrounding yards), a set of tasks (cooking, washing, sewing, milking, spinning, cleaning, gardening), and a limited area of authority (the internal economy of a family)" (Ulrich, 1982, 9). In the afterword Ulrich concludes that an understanding of any segment of history requires a full evaluation of the input of women, who educated children for their functions as citizens and patriots.

In 1990 Ulrich earned the Pulitzer Prize for *A Midwife's Tale: The Life of Martha Ballard, Based on Her Diary, 1785–1812*, a volume that frames and explicates the memoirs of a frontier folk healer from Kennebec, Maine. The 9,965 entries in the daybook of Martha Moore Ballard cover 27 years of labor and foot travel with no pause for dark, snow, or high water. In 814 deliveries she recorded 768 live births. During idle moments she made her own salves and potions from home-grown herbs and distilled vinegar for medicinal use. For lint and other supplies she bartered fruit and vegetables. Of the exertion needed for splinting broken legs and treating burns, she notes, "I Laid myself on the bed in the bedroom and was not able to rise from ther. . . . How many times I have been necasatated to rest my self on the bed I am not able to say" (Ulrich, 1990, 226).

Ulrich was pleased to recover a life in Ballard's day-to-day activities. Central to the midwife's authority in the community is her testimony at trials judging paternity and VIOLENCE against females. In a grave criminal matter she spoke in defense of Rebecca Foster, a rape victim. In August 1789 Ballard wrote in her journal that "Colonel North had positively had unlawful concors with a woman which was not his wife" (*ibid.*, 117). An all-male jury dismissed Foster's words to the court of Vassalboro, Maine, and refused to convict a prominent man for his crime solely on the word of a woman. In reference to Ballard's willingness to testify the author summarized the midwife's meticulous record keeping: "[She] not only documented her prayers, her lost sleep, her deeds of charity and compassion, she savored and wrote down the petty struggles and small graces of ordinary life" (ibid., 343). The research project served as the subject of a Public Broadcasting System Television (PBS-TV) documentary on *The American Experience*.

In 2001 Ulrich's scholarly dedication to New England history resulted in *The Age of Homespun: Objects and Stories in the Creation of an American Myth*, based in part on her mother's skill with a needle and on research at the Royal Ontario Museum in Toronto. In explaining cultural differences of the colonies, she describes WOMAN'S WORK as an indicator of skills and the transformation of raw materials into useful objects. She summarizes the gendered division of labor for male and female Indians: "Men worked in stone, metal, and wood, producing impressive tobacco pipes, knot dishes, pendants, and other ornaments. Women netted, twined, sewn, and plaited to cover their houses, dry corn, trap fish, store provisions, carry produce, and line graves" (Ulrich, 2001, 44). The historian's objective view of women's contribution to tribal life indicates a balance of respect that valued females for their knowledge of agricultural and domestic necessities.

Bibliography

Ballard, Martha. *Martha Ballard's Diary Online*. Available online. URL: http://dohistory.org/diary/index.html. Accessed on October 17, 2005.

Ulrich, Laurel Thatcher. *The Age of Homespun: Objects and Stories in the Creation of an American Myth*. New York: Knopf, 2001.

———. *Good Wives: Image and Reality in the Lives of Women in Northern New England, 1650–1750*. New York: Oxford University Press, 1982.

———. *A Midwife's Tale: The Life of Martha Ballard, Based on Her Diary, 1785–1812*. New York: Alfred A. Knopf, 1990.

———. "A Pail of Cream," *Journal of American History* 89, no. 1 (June 2002): 43–47.

Whitcomb, Claire. "Laurel Thatcher Ulrich: A New Spin on Homespun," *Victoria* 16, no. 10 (October 2002): 102–103.

Uncle Tom's Cabin Harriet Beecher Stowe (1852)

The work of a tenderhearted woman and fervid abolitionist, *Uncle Tom's Cabin; or, Life among the Lowly*, a humanitarian masterpiece, was the first book to elevate a black male to hero status. The fact that the novel was the first American fiction to reach sales of more than 1 million attests to the author's skill. The dialect melodrama began as a research project while Harriet Beecher STOWE lived in Brunswick, Maine. Sorrowing over the loss of a child to cholera, she commiserated with slave women whom inhumane masters forced to breed large families of children for enslavement, for sale to other plantations, or for transport to the Caribbean, Europe, or South America. The novel appeared in installments in 1851 and 1852 in the *National Era*, an abolitionist journal published in Washington, D.C. When the work reached bookshops, it sold 10,000 copies in its first week, more than 300,000 by 1853, and a half-million by 1857. Popular in Europe and throughout the Americas, it expanded in outreach from 23 translations and stage adaptations.

The novel stressed the peculiar situation of slave breeders and their attitude toward motherhood. One character lamented, "[The master] tole me that my children were sold, but whether I ever saw their faces again, depended on him. . . . Well, you can do anything with a woman, when you've got her children" (Stowe, 366). Stowe touched the heart of readers, including President Abraham Lincoln, with the poignant story of broken families, the controlling theme of much slave narrative. Because black women were often forced to breed with numerous black males or with the adult white males of the plantation, fatherhood carried less import than motherhood. In chapter 12 Stowe pictures the crux of bondage, the listing of young slaves as property for sale or trade along with cattle, horses, farm equipment, and produce. Aunt Hagar, a 60-year-old domestic, fears separation from her son, Albert, yet she boasts, "I can cook yet, and scrub, and scour,—I'm wuth a buying, if I do come cheap;—tell em dat ar,—you *tell* em" (ibid., 121). Interspersed with commentary on odd lots of slaves tagged for sale on auction blocks and on Hagar's grief at being parted from Albert are the author's Christian views on maternal grief. She declares, "Not one throb of anguish, not one tear of the oppressed is forgotten by the Man of Sorrows, the Lord of Glory" (*ibid.*, 133). She expresses through an unnamed Southern bystander a refusal to denigrate slaves as inhuman: "I was born and brought up among them. I know they *do* feel, just as keenly,—even more so, perhaps,—as we do" (*ibid.*, 125).

The mother's crisis that grips the plot takes place in the fifth chapter, in which Eliza Harris tries to halt the sale of her son, Harry. With a bundle of toys and clothing tied to her waist, she takes the boy past a watchdog, bids farewell to Uncle Tom and Aunt Chloe, and flees to the Ohio River, which she compares to the biblical Jordan River, gateway to Canaan. Using ice chunks as a raft, she makes a miraculous escape on bloodied feet and disappears into the dusk. Against Eliza's heroic maternity Stowe balances the emotional plot with the saintly Little Eva and the lively, mischievous Topsy, a natural challenger of authority. As Eliza moves her family north to Canada, she takes her place as a paid laborer. She promises, "I can do dress-making very well; and I understand fine washing and ironing" (*ibid.*, 188). Stowe creates irony from the fact that the skills that made Eliza a prize domestic slave are useful as the family presses on toward normal roles as citizens and wage earners.

For all its realistic depiction of the conjunction of female bondage with sex and motherhood, *Uncle Tom's Cabin* was still fiction. The former slave Harriet Tubman refused an opportunity to view a stage version of Stowe's novel. According to Sarah H. Bradford's BIOGRAPHY, *Scenes in the Life of Harriet Tubman* (1869), Tubman remarked, "I've heard 'Uncle Tom's Cabin' read, and I tell you Mrs. Stowe's pen hasn't begun to paint what slavery is as I have seen it at the far South. I've seen de *real ting*, and I don't want to see it on no stage or in no teater" (Bradford, 22). In Stowe's defense the essayist Jane SMILEY argues that *Uncle Tom's Cabin* was a greater novel than Mark Twain's *The Adventures of Huckleberry Finn* (1884) because Stowe explicitly denounces the institution of slavery.

Bibliography

Bradford, Sarah H. *Scenes in the Life of Harriet Tubman.* New York: Beaufort Books, 1971.

Frumkes, Lewis Burke. "A Conversation with Jane Smiley," *Writer* 112, no. 5 (May 1999): 18–20.

Stowe, Harriet Beecher. *Uncle Tom's Cabin.* New York: Harper, 1965.

Undset, Sigrid (1882–1949)

The medievalist, novelist, and translator Sigrid Undset adapted the medieval saga into violent, vengeful fiction about female hardships, courage, and redemption. A native of Kalundborg, Denmark, she grew up among tellers of Norwegian history, legend, myth, and folktales. Her father, Ingvald Martin Undset, taught his daughter how to read Old Danish and Old Icelandic and discussed his archaeological digs into the remains of Iron Age Europe. In *Elleve aar* (Eleven years) (1934), she described her girlhood in Christiana (Oslo), where she studied under Frau Ragna Nielsen, a feminist and progressive educator who shocked parents by teaching boys and girls in the same classes. Home life reached a terrible low when Undset's father died of malaria in 1893. At age 17 she studied at Christiana Commercial College because she lacked the funds for a university education. To support the family, she served as secretary to a German electrical contractor. In her spare time she read widely, particularly the novels of Jane AUSTEN and Charlotte and Emily BRONTË.

Undset's empathy with working-class women inspired a sheaf of feminist essays and a series of works dealing with toil and disappointment, beginning with *Fru Marta Oulie* (Mrs. Marta Oulie, 1907), a tale of a wife's infidelity, and *Gunnarsdottir* (*Gunnar's Daughter*, 1909), the story of a woman's refusal to be abased by rape and illegitimate birth. For the quality of her unsentimental glimpses of women's lives she earned a government stipend and devoted her career to writing about women and families. As she matured, she lived her theme of devoted motherhood. After traveling in Denmark, Germany, and Rome, she married the artist Anders Castus Svarstad, bore three children, and reared Svarstad's three children from a previous marriage after their birth mother threatened to place them in an orphanage. The marriage failed, but her commitment to the six children remained firm.

In 1920 Undset initiated a masterwork of historical fiction, the three-volume *Kristin Lavransdatter*, which comprised *Kransen* (*The Bridal Wreath*, 1920), *Husfrue* (*The Wife*, 1921), and *Korset* (*The Cross*, 1922). Set in the 14th century, the trilogy features a tough, self-willed woman whose outlook shifts after her marriage to the feckless Erlend. At the outset the author identifies the violent, self-gratifying PATRIARCHY that controls medieval Scandinavian culture: "Lavrans belonged to a lineage that here in Norway was known as the sons of Lagmand. It originated in Sweden with a certain Laurentius Ösgötelagman, who abducted the Earl of Bjelbo's sister, the maiden Bengta from a Vreta cloister" (Undset, 1997, 3). In *Kristin Lavransdatter: The Wife*, Undset contrasts male and female emotions: "Lodged deep in her soul was that tiny, mute anger toward Erland, who was so free of sorrow" (Undset, 1999, 4). In volume 3, Kristin ponders her desire to climb up to a high pasture, a whim that would cause gossip about her willful running away from a gentlewoman's duty. Through such simple yearnings Undset depicts the daily trials of living in a male-dominated society and the grief of her husband's estrangement and betrayal.

After adopting Roman Catholicism, Undset continued to explore the inner landscape of ordinary people. She pursued historical settings and characters with a tetralogy, *Olav Audunssøn* (*The Master of Hestviken*, 1925–1927), which focuses on religion in two works, *Olav Audunssøon i Hestviken* (*The Axe* and *The Snake Pit*, 1925). She enlarged on spiritual themes in another pair of novels, *Olav Audunssøon og Hans Börn* (*In the Wilderness* and *The Son Avenger*, 1929–30). In 1928 her output earned her the Nobel Prize in literature, in part because of vigorous, dramatic narratives and their objective survey of eroticism and the social and gender differences that hamper male-female relations.

Undset's life changed after the German occupation of Norway during World War II. Because of her fame she set an example in Scandinavia by becoming a civilian volunteer and member of the resistance. After losing a son to combat and her home to German officers, she could describe wartime terrors firsthand in *Tillbake til fremtiden* (*Return to the Future*, 1942). In self-exile she researched information for the U.S. government before fleeing to Siberia, Japan, and San Francisco. In New York City she gained the friendship and support of the feminist author Willa CATHER. Two years before Undset died in Lillehammer, Norway, she received from King Haakon VII the Grand Cross of the Order of Saint Olav both for her patriotism and for her writing of realistic fiction about women.

Bibliography

Grenier, Cynthia. "A Novelist of Moral Power and Passion: A Profile of Sigrid Undset," *World and I* 13, no. 10 (October 1998): 295–299.

Reinert, Otto. "Unfashionable 'Kristen Lavransdatter," *Scandinavian Studies* 71, no. 1 (Spring 1999): 67.

Undset, Sigrid. *Kristin Lavransdatter: The Cross.* New York: Penguin, 2001.

———. *Kristin Lavransdatter: The Wife.* New York: Penguin, 1999.

———. *Kristin Lavransdatter: The Wreath.* New York: Penguin, 1997.

V

Vindication of the Rights of Women, A
Mary Wollstonecraft (1792)

A manifesto of FEMINISM, Mary WOLLSTONE-CRAFT's *A Vindication of the Rights of Women: With Strictures on Political and Moral Subjects* resonates into the present with valid complaints of sexism during the so-called Age of Enlightenment. Published a year after its composition by Joseph Johnson, London's leading liberal publisher, the essay stirred outrage as well as personal attacks on the author's bohemian lifestyle. Her libertarianism emerged during an international backlash against the French Revolution. By demanding female emancipation, Wollstonecraft divests her words of the mask of courtesy that women employed in social discourse. In the introduction she attacks the libeling of assertive women as "masculine" as a sexist means of forcing the female half of the population to act the part of polite second-class citizen. (Wollstonecraft, 80). She chooses to present females as rational rather than graceful or fascinating to men for speaking "pretty feminine phrases," a gibe that vents her anger at the era's faddish small talk (*ibid.*, 82).

Wollstonecraft's arguments challenge obvious fallacies of contemporary philosophy, especially that of Jean Jacques Rousseau. She repudiates home training of little girls in "cunning, softness of temper, *outward* obedience, and a scrupulous attention to a puerile kind of propriety," a gendered curriculum that instills infantilism and deceit (*ibid.*, 100). Her text attacks Rousseau for stressing submission as the core value in female virtue:

"What nonsense! When will a great man arise with sufficient strength of mind to puff away the fumes which pride and sensuality have thus spread?" (*ibid.*, 108). To discredit the view of the female as sex kitten, she describes an ideal marriage as one in which the husband shares family responsibilities with a wife whom he respects for her strength and pragmatism.

The essay batters the trivialization of women as personal adornments of men. By forcing girls to acquire "an artificial character," men mold themselves into tyrants and slave mongers (*ibid.*, 132). Wollstonecraft proposes that equal EDUCATION restores women to a rightful dignity as citizens. She pities the young widow, whom social constraints force into celibacy, and denounces the sex object, whom libertines exploit while "insultingly supporting their own superiority" (*ibid.*, 148). For the sake of civilization she urges that women receive training appropriate to their calling as shapers of the next generation. Employing scriptural gravity, she warns, "It would be as wise to expect corn from tares, or figs from thistles, as that a foolish ignorant woman should be a good mother" (*ibid.*, 324). In conclusion Wollstonecraft foresees a revolution in the female realm more than 260 years before the upsurge of the feminist movement.

Bibliography
Tomalin, Claire. "A Tale of Two Marys," *History Today* 48, no. 2 (February 1998): 29–30.
Wollstonecraft, Mary. *A Vindication of the Rights of Woman.* New York: W. W. Norton, 1988.

violence

The presence of violence in women's writings provides a necessary exposure of wrongs perpetrated against a part of the population kept weak, muted, and financially dependent by males. In the introduction to *Women and Male Violence: The Visions and Struggles of the Battered Women's Movement* (1982) the activist-historian Susan Schechter remarks that battery is not new. Rather, it is the public acknowledgment of male-on-female assault that emerged in the late 20th century that makes the social issue seem recent. The phenomenal growth of Gothic novels and stories gained readership for the decapitations, throttlings, and mad scenes of Grand Guignol melodrama. A majority of works depended on lush, titillating scenes of male-on-female menace and battery, as found in Sophia LEE's *The Recess* (1785) and Charlotte SMITH's *Emmeline, the Orphan of the Castle* (1788). Publishers enhanced sales by hiring the specialist artist George Cruikshank to picture on cover art scantily clad women in extreme terror. In 1797 the Gothic fiction maven Ann RADCLIFFE made a pro-woman departure from threats and gratuitous mayhem by incorporating in her novel *The Italian* a glimpse of a Punch and Judy puppet show, a vicious soap opera that flourished throughout Europe as entertainment for children. Her inclusion of the ongoing spousal abuse in the comic sadomasochistic marriage commented on the nature of vice and its escalation to murder.

Feminist literature indicates that the types of pain and death inflicted on women vary by culture. In Ruth Prawer JHABVALA's bicultural novel *Heat and Dust* (1975) the British women in colonial India muse over the shrines to native women publicly burned to death by suttee, a barbaric practice outlawed in 1829. The intent of self-immolation was a show of devotion to the dead husband as the widow's final duty. Dr. Saunders, spokesman for the British point of view, exclaims, "Plain savagery and barbarism . . . and all, mind you, in the name of religion" (Jhabvala, 59). In *Babette's Feast* (1959), a feminist fable of exile and redemption, the Danish storyteller Isak DINESEN describes the destructive power of war in the bedraggled countenance and trembling body of the title character. An epistle speaks the words her silent lips cannot say: "Madame Hersant's husband and son, both eminent ladies' hairdressers, have been shot. She herself was arrested as [an arsonist]. . . . She has lost all she possesses and dares not remain in France" (Dinesen, 13).

Because children are integral to a study of feminist writing, the violence experienced by the young and helpless becomes all the more intolerable, as in the wartime rape of Japanese girls in Yoko Kawashima WATKINS's autobiography *So Far from the Bamboo Grove* (1986), a father's denial of medical aid to a dying baby girl in Amy TAN's *The Kitchen God's Wife* (1991), and the ritual FEMALE GENITAL MUTILATION of the fictional Olinka girl Tashi in Alice WALKER's novel *Possessing the Secret of Joy* (1992). In *The Signs Reader: Women, Gender and Scholarship* (1983) the feminist critics Judith Herman and Lisa Hirschman explain that "the greater the degree of male supremacy in any culture, the greater the likelihood of father-daughter incest" (Herman and Hirschman, 263). Their commentary elucidates the power struggle in Dorothy ALLISON's *Bastard Out of Carolina* (1992), in which Bone Boatwright struggles to free herself of whippings with her father's belt and of sexual attack. In the essay "Blood, Bread, and Poetry: The Location of the Poet" (1984) Adrienne RICH describes a broader view of male supremacy by pairing "Vietnam and the lovers' bed," a phrase that connects verse with politics. She explains, "I felt driven—for my own sanity—to bring together in my poems the political world 'out there' " (Rich, 248). Her vision transforms into scenes of nightmarish depravity, "the world of children dynamited or napalmed, of the urgan ghetto and militarist violence—and the supposedly private, lyrical world of sex" (*ibid.*). Her verse reflects a pacifist theme in feminist literature that charges male power mongers with fomenting international conflict.

Subtler feminist writings examine the gradual erosion of personal identity when a male lover/husband overpowers and diminishes the beloved/wife, the dominant motif of Elfriede JELINEK's plays *We Are Decoys, Baby* (1970) and *Lust* (1989) and of Faith McNulty's novel *The BURNING BED* (1980). The Irish poet Eavan BOLAND characterizes the controlling male in the poem "In His Own Image" (1980). Gradually the female speaker loses her inner person and becomes the distorted image she sees reflected in a shiny kettle. Lacking proof of identity, she struggles day by day to survive the onslaught of a drunken husband given to slaps and pummels. Her true self gradually shreds as he wounds lip, eye, and neck. The poem drips irony when the speaker marvels as she gradually turns into a "new woman" (Boland, 95).

Ethnic folkways tend to favor unique versions of vicious PATRIARCHY. Gloria ANZALDÚA's *Borderlands/La Frontera: The New Mestiza* (1987) extends the study of spousal abuse to a whole society. She probes the harm of centuries of abuse to the nonwhite female, whom folk custom and androcentric religion have "silenced, gagged, caged, bound into servitude with marriage, bludgeoned for three hundred years" (Anzaldúa, 22). To survive, the resilient woman must learn to protect her own interest while juggling the contradictions and ambiguities that surround her. Less hopeful are the physical and emotional assaults, both historical and personal, that permeate the writings of the Cherokee-Muscogee Creek poet Joy HARJO. She expresses through "Autobiography" the anguish of being a border person, perpetually dispossessed. In a more dramatic vision of social and marital battery to the female spirit Harjo's "The Woman Hanging from the Thirteenth Floor Window" (1983) supplies a palpable image of the outer rim of survival, a slim handhold between life and death.

The courage of women who give eyewitness accounts of violence enhances the drama of feminist genres. Examples range from the slave narratives of Harriet JACOBS and Sojourner TRUTH and descriptions of female prisons and torture chambers such as Julia ALVAREZ's *In the Time of the Butterflies* (1994) and Nawal El Saadawi's *Memoirs from the Women's Prison* (1983), to articles on female asylums by the journalist Nellie BLY, suffrage memoirs like Djuna BARNES's "How It Feels to Be Forcibly Fed" (1914), and rape survival stories like Isabel ALLENDE's historical novel *The HOUSE OF THE SPIRITS* (1982). The essayist and novelist Barbara KINGSOLVER contributed to her canon a personal experience with date rape in 1974 and the aftertaste of sullied virtue. More than a quartercentury after the fact, she expressed the terror of

being overpowered in *Small Wonder* (2002): "My head against a wall, suffocation, hard pushing and flat on my back and screaming for air. Fighting an animal twice my size. My job was to stop him, and I failed" (Kingsolver, 2002, 168). Less vivid is her presentation of pedophilia, kidnap, and child torture in her first novel, *The Bean Trees* (1988), which devotes its major themes to child and family welfare in single-parent homes. A stirring moment in the plot is the physical examination of April Turtle, a Cherokee foundling whose neglect and battery the doctor describes as "failure to thrive" (Kingsolver, 1988, 123), whereas X-rays indicate fractures and irregular motor skills. Staring out at a bird nesting in cactus, Taylor, April's foster mother, muses, "You just couldn't imagine how she'd made a home in there" (*ibid.*).

The author Rita Mae BROWN creates a worldly-wise perspective of spousal abuse in *Dolley* (1994), a fictionalized BIOGRAPHY of First Lady Dolley Madison. In a diary entry for New Year's Day 1814 the protagonist spouts rage at the whoring and wife beating of the French minister, General Louis Marie Turreau. She poses a conundrum of spousal abuse: "Why marry a woman if you're going to betray her, and if you're going to betray her, why beat her? The fault is not hers" (Rita Mae Brown, 24). From private observations of marriages Dolley concludes, "I sometimes think the worst we do, we do behind closed doors" (*ibid.*). After fantasizing union with a brute, unlike women who make no mention of their "blackened eyes and bruises," Dolley declares that her Irish ancestry would overpower her pacifist Quaker upbringing and force her to hit back (*ibid.*). Such spunk suggests why Brown chose Dolley as a focus for historical fiction.

In the 21st century violent anger in feminist theater riveted audiences, sobering them with much to ponder about gendered power structures. The Maryland-born sociopolitical playwright Kia Corthron parallels urban turmoil with the lives of its victims. Like her protagonists she chooses isolated women, such as C Ana, the single parent in *Seeking the Genesis* (1997) and Prix, a girl gang leader in *Breath, Boom* (2001), a drama of suppressed rage and renewal in the Bronx subculture. Molested at age nine by Jerome, her mother's lover/abuser, Prix stores up vengeance and bides her time before assaulting Jerome with a razor blade she hides in her mouth, an ironic symbol for silenced women. Defeating the rapist, however, is surface excision for a deeper spiritual canker that drives Prix relentlessly to gangs, drugs, felonies, juvenile hall, and prison. The redeeming love of Prix's mother hovers in the background and eventually breaks through the emotional logjam that bottles up the daughter's feelings. Corthron celebrates the mother-daughter reunion at the corner of 34th Street and Fifth Avenue in New York City with fireworks from the top of the Empire State Building. About her plays Corthron explained, "It's a very narrow world . . . not an uninviting world, but the whole production—the acting, the directing and the designing—all has to go to support that world" (Reiter, 77).

Bibliography

Anzaldúa, Gloria. *Borderlands/La Frontera: The New Mestiza.* San Francisco: Spinsters/Aunt Lute, 1987.

Boland, Eavan. *An Origin like Water: Collected Poems 1957–1987.* New York: W. W. Norton, 1997.

Brown, Lenora Inez. "The Last Word Is Hope," *American Theatre* 18, no. 9 (November 2001): 54–70.

Brown, Rita Mae. *Dolley.* New York: Bantam Books, 1995.

Corthron, Kia. *Breath, Boom.* New York: Dramatists Play Service, 2002.

———. *Seeking the Genesis.* New York: Dramatists Play Service, 2002.

Dinesen, Isak. *Babette's Feast and Other Anecdotes of Destiny.* New York: Vintage, 1986.

Herman, Judith, and Lisa Hirschmann. "Father-Daughter Incest." In *The Signs Reader: Women, Gender and Scholarship.* Chicago: University of Chicago Press, 1983.

Jhabvala, Ruth Prawer. *Heat and Dust.* New York: Touchstone, 1976.

Kingsolver, Barbara. *The Bean Trees.* New York: Harper & Row, 1988.

———. *Small Wonder* (coauthored by Stephen Hopp). New York: HarperCollins, 2002.

Reiter, Amy. "Kia Corthron: Giving the Voiceless a Voice," *American Theatre* 11, no. 8 (October 1994): 77.

Rich, Adrienne. *Adrienne Rich's Poetry and Prose.* New York: W. W. Norton, 1975.

Viramontes, Helena María (1954–)

The Latina scenarist, essayist, and fiction writer Helena María Viramontes captures the ambivalence of Hispanic women who survive in a patriarchal culture that both treasures and batters them. Born in a barrio of East Los Angeles, she grew up in a working-class family of nine children. The family sheltered a stream of illegal Mexican aliens, who passed through their residence as runaway slaves once entered and exited way stations of the Underground Railroad. In addition to the grueling stoop labor and low-level jobs relegated to her people, she depicts in short fiction the gendered responsibilities of her early life that gave her no time to write.

Educated in creative writing at Immaculate Heart College, the Sundance Workshop, and the University of California at Irvine, Viramontes took as object lessons the writings of Isabel ALLENDE, Sandra CISNEROS, Toni MORRISON, Ntozake SHANGE, and Alice WALKER. Viramontes characterized the ambiguous status of women in an androcentric Chicano culture in the anthology *Paris Rats in E. L. A.* (1993), which she adapted to screen for the American Film Institute. In *The Moth and Other Stories* (1995) the title entry pictures a girl as recipient of a grandmother's love. The sorrowing girl later reciprocates by bathing the body of her dead *abuelita* (grandmother) in preparation for burial. A pair of stories, "The Cariboo Cafe" and "Tears on My Pillow," a version of the LA LLORONA tale about the legendary weeping woman, characterizes the pressures of an unforgiving culture. Most vulnerable are refugee girls and women from Mexico and war-torn El Salvador and Nicaragua, who fled death squads and made their way north through border patrols. Another story, "Growing," describes a father's pontification on women's roles to his daughter, Naomi, a tender young girl who has just entered adolescence.

Viramontes edited *Xhisme Arts Magazine* and wrote impressionistic short fiction on displacement and social injustice for *Maize* and *Statement* magazines. As her prominence increased, she collaborated with María Hererra-Sobek on a commentary on the artistry of Hispanic writers in *Chicana Creativity and Criticism: Creating New Frontiers in American Literature* (1988) and in *Chicana Writers: On*

Word and Film (1993). Viramontes, who experienced in girlhood the short-term work status of grape picker, expressed pity for the female migrant worker, Estrella, and her belabored mother, Petra, in a first novel, *Under the Feet of Jesus* (1995). The importance of mothering to the younger girl takes shape metaphorically in their names, Petra (rock) as the foundation for the next generation, Estrella (star). Looking back to America's multicultural violence of the 1960s, Viramontes depicted gang behavior in a novella, *Their Dogs Came with Them* (1996). Of the plight of the underdog, she commented in an interview on the importance of "[understanding] what a colonized imagination means to a people" (Dulfano, 660). Winner of a National Endowment for the Arts Award in fiction and the John Dos Passos Prize in literature for validating America's immigrant heritage, she manages writing as well as public readings, teaching at Cornell University, and composition workshops for nonwhite female authors.

Bibliography

Carbonell, Ana Maria. "From Llorona to Gritone: Coatlicue in Feminist Tales by Viramontes and Cisneros," *MELUS* 24, no. 2 (Summer 1999): 53.

Dulfano, Isabel. "Some Thoughts Shared with Helena María Viramontes," *Women's Studies* 30, no. 5 (September 2001): 647–662.

Viramontes, Helena María. *The Moth and Other Stories.* Houston, Tex.: Arte Publico, 1985.

———. *Under the Feet of Jesus.* New York: Penguin, 1995.

Virgin Mary

An ambiguous figure in feminist literature, the Virgin Mary of Nazareth embodies the importance of maternity and fully realized womanhood. In earlier times the cult of Marian piety fostered an enforced discipline of women. They struggled and failed at attaining impossible standards of chastity, asexuality, humility, and forebearance, all of which the Virgin exhibits with her customary static pose and downcast eyes. However, historian Barbara Tuchman remarks in *A Distant Mirror* (1978): "The fervid adoration of the Virgin, which developed as a cult . . . left little deposit on the status of women as a whole" (Tuchman, 227). Thus the more people venerated the Madonna, the more distance grew between the unreachable ideal and palpable Earthly women.

Virginity lost out to realism in the 19th century, when writers promoted an acceptance of human females. Leading the effort was the feminist philosopher Mary WOLLSTONECRAFT in *Mary, a Fiction* (1788), a denunciation of saintliness. In *Woman, Church, and State* (1895) the suffrage polemicist Matilda Joslyn GAGE called for a shift to a more approachable female deity. Gage grounds claims of the stability of the matriarchal society on ancient examples of goddesses and priestesses, such as the clairvoyant Pythia of Delphi and the Vestal Virgins of Rome. Gage explains the significance of the Christian variation of goddess worship in the form of Jesus's mother: "In many old religions, the generative principle was regarded as the mother of both gods and men. In the Christian religion we find a tendency to a similar recognition in Catholic worship of the Virgin Mary" (Gage, 23). The link between Mary and ancient goddess mysteries makes Gage's point that only a female deity can claim the reproductive powers of the mother goddess. Thus Gage strips Mary of the handmaiden's passivity and the immobility of the icon on a pedestal to disclose the power within.

The spiritual aura of the mythic Virgin Mary serves writers as a model of the IDEAL WOMAN. Examples include the luminous devotional verse of Christina ROSSETTI and the feminist poem "Our Lady" (1908) by Mary Elizabeth COLERIDGE, who honors the common background and pure song that Mary phrased "To all mankind, in woman's tongue" (Coleridge, *Poems*). In revisionist Arthurian lore the fantasist Marion Zimmer BRADLEY pictures the emergence of Mariology from Celtic lore of WISEWOMEN, the keepers of prehistoric nature lore. According to the feminist critic Marina Warner's *Alone of All Her Sex: The Myth and Cult of the Virgin Mary* (1976), the paradox of Mary's lone pose as God's mother singles her out from humanity and turns her into a sterile being who symbolizes asceticism and subjection. The American romanticist Nathaniel Hawthorne drew on the legendary solitude and maternity of Mary in *The SCARLET LETTER* (1850), an allegory that pictures the public display of the adulteress Hester PRYNNE with her three-month-old daughter, Pearl, as inverted models of the Madonna Dolorosa and the Christ Child. The novel contrasts public ignominy with "Divine Maternity . . . that sacred image of sinless motherhood, whose infant was to redeem the world" (Hawthorne, 117).

English fiction produced its own reengineered madonna in the writings of George ELIOT, an author who published under a male pseudonym to elude misogynist criticism. In the period that followed England's two monumental reform bills, she created a madonnalike glow around Dorothea Brooke, the virtuous, aesthetically pure protagonist of MIDDLEMARCH (1872). Dorothea learns a hard lesson about marrying to satisfy ideals rather than to requite normal human desire. Like Saint Teresa, Dorothea, the neglected wife, bestows concern on social issues that affect the entire community. In honor of her social consciousness, the author rids her heroine of Edward Casaubon, her pompous, unloving husband; releases her from an overburden of virtue; and accords her earthly happiness with Will Ladislaw, a more bed-worthy mate.

To achieve a glimpse of Mary as a nature spirit, the poet Amy LOWELL layered beauty and mysticism in "Madonna of the Evening Flowers" (1919). The poem haloes the mystic figure in shining silver from the evening light. In lines inspired by Lowell's love for Ada Dwyer Russell, the writer allows a visual and verbal search for companionship to introduce the appearance of the resplendent Virgin. Resembling a regal stele, she takes shape as a tall larkspur vivid in pale blue, the symbolic color of loyalty that Mary wears in paintings, tapestries, and stained glass to drape her bosom and conceal her gender. Through imagism, Lowell exalts the silent virgin with bell-shaped flowers that chime in token of womanly beauty and mystery. The austere other-worldliness of the poem suggests the poet's need to elevate her relationship above the titters and judgments of those who scorn woman-to-woman love.

In WIDE SARGASSO SEA (1966) the Caribbean novelist Jean RHYS applies the Virgin's holiness to a scene of failed ideals. Her depiction of the island EDUCATION of Antoinette Cosway pictures the young protagonist at the Mount Calvary convent school "cross-stitching silk roses on a pale background" (Rhys, 53). The human control of needlework combines with otherworldly visions of the rose, a dominant motif in Catholic art, to create a paradox. To Antoinette stitchery is tedious and unfulfilling, yet the finished piece symbolizes the virginity, integrity, and purity of the Virgin Mary. Antoinette manages a nonconfrontational rebellion in her choice of "green, blue and purple . . . my name in fire red," an indication that she rejects the submissive role of the ideal wife and dainty embroiderer (*ibid.*). The signature anticipates her rejection of demure English fashions in favor of bold island garb and fiery Creole passion, an overt defiance of the Virgin's example. Antoinette's adult revolt against PATRIARCHY causes her husband, the staid Englishman Edward Rochester, to accept male-generated allegations that his wild-eyed wife is both crazed and promiscuous. As a result, he treats her as a suspect alien.

Bold feminists such as the painter Frida Kahlo and the authors Gloria ANZALDÚA and Sandra CISNEROS rebelled against the lifeless pose of the ideal woman by translating her myth into a dynamic modern stance. In the main entry in *Woman Hollering Creek and Other Stories* (1991) Cisneros enlarges on a worshiper's reluctance to devote herself to Old World patriarchy: "Virgencita de Guadalupe. For a long time I wouldn't let you in my house. . . . Couldn't look at you without blaming you for all the pain my mother and her mother and all our mothers' mothers have put up with in the name of God" (Cisneros, 127). Moving further from the Virgin's saintliness, Cherríe MORAGA expresses in *The Last Generation: Prose and Poetry* (1993) the hypocrisy of a Chicano Catholic culture that mouths worshipful chants and songs to frozen, blank-eyed statues while subjecting living women to incest, rape, spousal battery, and sexism. The poet prods the victims to assert themselves and seize satisfying, productive lives rather than pray to a plaster goddess for rescue.

Bibliography

Cisneros, Sandra. *Woman Hollering Creek and Other Stories.* New York: Random House, 1991.

Coleridge, Mary Elizabeth. *Poems* (1908). Available online. URL: http://www.poemhunter.com/mary-elizabeth-coleridge/poet-3048/. Accessed on October 17, 2005.

Doyle, Jacqueline. "Assumptions of the Virgin and Recent Chicana Writing," *Women's Studies* 26, no. 2 (April 1997): 171–201.

Gage, Matilda Joslyn. *Woman, Church, and State* (1895). Available online. URL: http://www.sacred-texts.com/wmn/wcs/. Accessed on October 14 2005.

Hawthorne, Nathaniel. *The Complete Novels and Selected Tales of Nathaniel Hawthorne.* New York: Modern Library, 1937.

Rhys, Jean. *Wide Sargasso Sea.* New York: W. W. Norton, 1982.

Tuchman, Barbara. *A Distant Mirror.* New York: Alfred A. Knopf, 1978.

Warner, Marina. *Alone of All Her Sex: The Myth and the Cult of the Virgin Mary.* New York: Alfred A. Knopf, 1976.

Volcano Lover, The Susan Sontag (1992)

A mock-Victorian historical novel, Susan SON-TAG's best seller *The Volcano Lover: A Romance* analyzes complications in the life of an audacious emancipated woman. The plot, an outgrowth of the setting and themes in Sontag's short story "Unguided Tour" (1978), reprises the romantic entanglements of a widower, 56-year-old Sir William "Il Cavaliere" Hamilton, a pedophile and British ambassador to the Court of the Two Sicilies, and Emma, the 20-year-old lover of his nephew, Charles. Set in Sicily in view of Mount Vesuvius during the Age of Enlightenment, the symbolic narrative uses mounting social and political rivalries as a motivating force. At stake is England's monarchy, the target of French republicanism.

Sontag creates in Cavaliere a caricature of the self-indulgent aristocratic voluptuary. A collector of antiques and beautiful women, he identifies with the looming volcano and its ominous phallic presence. Emma, at first glance, is a sexual bauble palmed off as Charles's payment of debts to his uncle. The author explains, "Women like her were supposed to climb as far as they could and be used up, quickly" (Sontag, 122). As Lady Emma Hamilton, a trophy bride shipped from England as if she is a crated treasure, she is an asset to William's career. Entertaining him like Jack, William's pet monkey, does, she sings and poses in tableaux as a living statue. A symbolic Galatea to William's Pygmalion, she receives remedial lessons in art, music, botany and geology, French, and Italian intended to turn a blacksmith's daughter into a gentlewoman. The author comments on Emma's loss of self: "She does not know who she is anymore, but she knows herself to be ascending" (*ibid., 134*).

The novel derives its thrust from explosive energies. In a swirl of revolution and blood lust the narrative focuses on Emma, a vital, but compromised beauty who transforms herself into a man pleaser. She destroys her reputation by falling in love with the era's golden boy, Lord Horatio Nelson, a married man and the star admiral of the British navy. Her social splash begins the round of gossip that turns her into an international curiosity. In Emma's dramatic encounters with Nelson Sontag salutes her for satisfying her passion. The author admires Emma as an Englishwoman who gambles to win but who sells herself too cheaply.

Bibliography

Johnson, Alexandra. "Romance as Metaphor." *Nation,* October 1992, pp. 365–367.

Sontag, Susan. *The Volcano Lover.* New York: Picador, 2004.

Toynton, Evelyn. "Review: *The Volcano Lover,*" *Commentary* 94, no. 5 (November 1992): 62–64.

W

Walker, Alice (1944–)

The American novelist, poet, and scenarist Alice Malsenior Walker voices the resistance of downtrodden females to abuse, FEMALE GENITAL MUTILATION, and CONFINEMENT. The daughter of sharecroppers, she was born in poverty in Eatonton, Georgia, but blossomed under the encouragement of a loving mother who grew flowers and told stories as a respite from unending toil. Despite the loss of vision in one eye at age eight through the discharge of her brother's BB gun, Walker showed promise in her teens by graduating first in her class. While studying literature at Spelman College and Sarah Lawrence College, she escaped depression by composing verse, which caught the attention of the poet Muriel RUKEYSER. Walker's first novel, *The Third Life of Grange Copeland* (1970), reflects her memories of growing up at the least profitable end of southern agribusiness. Three years later she received a National Book Award nomination for *Revolutionary Petunias and Other Poems* (1973) and an American Academy and Institute of Arts and Letters Award for an anthology, *In Love and Trouble: Stories of Black Women* (1973). With the encouragement of Gloria STEINEM Walker began contributing essays to MS. magazine and in 1974 published a children's biography, *Langston Hughes: American Poet.*

At the high point of her career Walker earned critical acclaim for the themes of SISTERHOOD and community in the Pulitzer Prize–winning epistolary novel *The COLOR PURPLE* (1982), a controversial portrayal of sex crimes, bisexuality, deception, and marital abuse. It is the encouragement of Shug Avery that enables the protagonist, Celie, to leave her ogre husband Mr. _____ and to blossom into a clothing designer. Through self-empowerment Celie overcomes both domestic abuse and the institutional power of the white male. A parallel dominance that renders Sofia helpless under the control of the mayor's wife, Miz Millie, illustrates the complicity of women in subjugation and bigotry. At a telling moment in Sofia's gradual rehabilitation during a Christmas visit with her children Millie's interruption provokes an observation on the dominant race: "White folks is a miracle of affliction" (Walker, 1983, 103). In a subsequent droll observation on cowardice Sofia proclaims, "Some colored people so scared of whitefolks they claim to love the cotton gin" (*ibid.*, 233). Although Walker faced accusations of demeaning black males, her uplifting novel won a National Book Award and a revered place in American, multicultural, and feminist literature. In 1985 Warner Studios filmed the novel with an all-star cast who included Whoopi Goldberg, Oprah Winfrey, and Danny Glover.

Walker's subsequent outpouring of works retained a feminist thrust. She introduced readers to matriarchal myth in the New Age novel *The Temple of My Familiar* (1989). The tribal custom of genital mutilation dominates *Possessing the Secret of Joy* (1992) and the screenplay *Warrior Marks* (1993). In the former work the focal character, Tashi, an Olinka virgin, suffers irreversible scarring from the excision of her clitoris and inner and outer labia and the stitching that narrows her vaginal opening.

Before introducing the story with an animal fable, Walker braces the reader for Tashi's spiritual trauma with the opening sentence, "I did not realize for a long time that I was dead" (Walker, 1993, 3). She later realizes that M'Lissa, the circumcisor of woman, killed Tashi's sister, Dura, who bled to death. Tashi begins to fear all blood loss, a human element drawn from the FAIRY TALE of Sleeping Beauty. A more personal view of repressed sexual desire in *By the Light of My Father's Smile* (1998) resets the PERSEPHONE myth by picturing a deceased father's spirit trying to atone for beating his daughter for falling in love with a Mexican native. *Now Is the Time to Open Your Heart* (2004) casts as protagonist Kate Talkingtree, an aging female who readies her spirit for change through river pilgrimages and a psychotropic drug experience in the Amazon jungle.

Bibliography

Walker, Alice. *The Color Purple.* New York: Washington Square Press, 1983.

———. *Possessing the Secret of Joy.* New York: Pocket Books, 1993.

Weisser, Susan Ostrov, and Jennifer Fleischner. *Feminist Nightmares: Women at Odds: Feminism and the Problems of Sisterhood.* New York: New York University Press, 1995.

Walker, Lady Mary (1739–1816)

A bold feminist letter writer and novelist, Lady Mary Walker Hamilton wrote pro-woman texts in English and French. Born Mary Leslie to civic-minded parents, she grew up in Edinburgh's privileged class. At age 23 she married a Scots physician, James Walker of Innerdovat, who superintended the prison infirmary in Edinburgh. Over a 20-year period she bore 10 children and survived infant illnesses and deaths before rebelling against the bonds of matrimony. Under the influence of the Scottish Enlightenment she fled to France with a lover, George Robinson Hamilton, and adopted the name Lady Mary Hamilton. The couple enjoyed a salon of cosmopolitan friends and developed progressive ideas on social welfare. After his death she lived in Amiens from 1797 to her death in 1816. She wrote in the veins of epistolary novel, journal, and speculative fiction, beginning with *Letters from*

the *Duchess de Crui: On Subjects Moral and Entertaining* (1776) and *Memoirs of the Marchioness de Louvoi* (1777).

An influence on Ann RADCLIFFE's *The Mysteries of Udolpho* (1794) and on Jane AUSTEN's *Pride and Prejudice* (1813), Walker's popular two-volume utopian fiction, *Munster Village* (1778), is her masterwork. It depicts the life of an elderly idealist and philanthropist, Lady Frances Munster-Darnley, daughter of the selfish, antisocial Lord Munster, who commits suicide. The heiress postpones marriage to live out her fantasy of the perfect world. In place of domesticity, she designs and builds a made-from-scratch village. As though manipulating toys on a board, she experiments with new agricultural crops and methods and bankrolls a university for women. Her philosophy is simple, but effective: "Society is manifestly maintained by a circulation of kindness" (Walker, 4). Populating Munster Village are fallen women and wives escaping oppressive marriages and intolerable divorce laws.

Walker displayed the idealism of the late 18th-century educated European. The utilitarian philosophy undergirding her planned community anticipates the feminist writings of Harriet MILL and John Stuart MILL and the emergence of the FEMINIST UTOPIAS of Charlotte Perkins GILMAN. Freed of domestic drudgery, Walker produced *The Life of Mrs. Justman* (1782) and *Duc de Popoli* (The People's Duke, 1810). In addition, Walker's letters to family and friends establish her interest in female EDUCATION, women's INDEPENDENCE from male financial support, and the comforts of a mother-child relationship with her daughter, Betsey Walker Thiebault, nicknamed "Kanker" for her birth under the zodiac sign Cancer.

Bibliography

Paradise, Nathaniel. "Interpolated Poetry, the Novel, and Female Accomplishment," *Philological Quarterly* 74, no. 1 (Winter 1995): 57–76.

Walker, Lady Mary. *Munster Village.* London: Pandora, 1987.

Walker, Margaret (1915–1998)

Numbered among the Leftist writers of the 1940s, the poet, teacher, critic, and fiction writer Margaret

Abigail Walker depicted the staying power of black women during war and community upheaval. Born in Birmingham, Alabama, and reared in New Orleans, she was the child of educated parents who encouraged her scholarship. From a grandmother she heard stories of Georgia slave times. When her parents complained that STORYTELLING kept the child up too late, the teller replied, "I'm not telling her tales; I'm telling her the naked truth" (Walker, 1972, 12). After studying at a New Orleans church school, Walker completed an undergraduate degree in English at Northwestern University. She came under the influence of poems by Gwendolyn BROOKS and Langston Hughes, the novels of Richard Wright, and the philosophy of W. E. B. DuBois. The association readied Walker for the hard task of retelling the stories of female sufferings in slave times, in a folk novel that she began outlining in 1934.

After publishing verse in *Crisis*, Walker found work at the Chicago Writers' Project. The completion of graduate work in creative writing at the University of Iowa resulted in the publication of an anthology, *All My People* (1942), for which she became the first black author to win the Yale Younger Poets Series Award. Her most famous poem, "For My People" (1942), honors centuries of toil and endurance, especially the hardships of domestic work and the grace of blues songs. A later poem, "Lineage," pictures a tough grandmother who plows and sows seeds and who exudes the smells of laundry soap and onions. A ballad, "Molly Means," dramatizes the emergence of WITCHCRAFT gossip about a widow targeted by superstition. Her legend plagues a community that fears her ghost long after Molly's death. A more poignant view of abuse of females permeates "Kissie Lee," a rhythmic ballad that denounces gender bias and mistreatment as the cause of a girl's delinquency.

Walker taught English for 35 years in colleges in North Carolina, West Virginia, and Mississippi, where she proposed the first collegiate black studies department. After completion of a doctorate at the University of Iowa, she received a Rosenwald Fellowship and began researching data at the Schomburg Collection of Negro History in Harlem. With authentic details about her family's lineage she wrote *Jubilee* (1966), a dialect saga of black family life during and after the Civil War. For source material she researched history and reprised the experiences of her great-grandmother, Margaret Duggans, the model for Vyry, the protagonist. For Minna, Walker used her maternal grandmother, Elvira Ware Dozier, an immigrant from the West Indies. The chronicle features the terrors and restrictions of black women, including Big Missy's doctoring of black females with ergot, ipecac, and saltpeter to control their sexual passions. Contrasting the folk pharmacist are the attempts of the midwife, Granny Ticey, to save Hetta, a parturient patient who dies after years of childbearing for her owner. Walker exposes raw VIOLENCE toward black women in Marse John's savage beating of Vyry for her attempt to escape on the Underground Railroad. Lucy, another runaway, flees from dogs to no avail. After her capture and staking to the ground, she receives a branding that leaves the letter *R* for "runaway" on her face. In a swoon Vyry hears "the terrible bellowing sound like a young bull or calf crying out in pain" (Walker, 1967, 95).

A starker scene derives from the Fourth of July hanging of two slave women for murdering their owner. At the execution a racist white minister exhorts onlookers to honor the "natural and righteous state" of bondage: "God meant for you to be humble, obedient, honest, truthful and God-fearing servants of your earthly masters" (*ibid.*, 102). The double hanging begins with the throttling and mutilation of the eyes and tongue of the first victim. The second screams hysterically, "Ain't done nothing to be sorry for. Ain't, I tells you. Ain't" (*ibid.*, 103). Walker notes the gendered response to public execution: Female onlookers swooned, but males took on a "look, neither human nor sane, a look of pleasurable excitement, a naked look of thrills born from cruel terror" (*ibid.*, 104).

Significant to Walker's novel is the SISTERHOOD of black and white women. Vyry grows up in the household of her white half sister, Lillian, and remains loyal to her despite the racial and class divide that separates them. While Vyry makes a living for the family, her friendship with white customers for her fresh turnip greens and eggs leads to a deeper commitment to her midwifery services. As a result of the community's need for a birthing coach Vyry earns for her family a new house constructed by grateful white males. Women contribute their traditional offering, hand-patched quilts in the Rose of Sharon, Star of California, and Star of Texas patterns. A year before her death Walker anthologized a variety of feminist commentary in *On Being Female, Black, and Free: Essays by Margaret Walker, 1932–1992* (1997), which captures the tone and intent of her Christian humanism. Her writing inspired the radical poet Sonia SANCHEZ.

Bibliography

Berke, Nancy. *Women Poets on the Left: Lola Ridge, Genevieve Taggard, Margaret Walker*. Gainesville: University Press of Florida, 2001.

Graham, Maryemma, ed. *Conversations with Margaret Walker*. Jackson: University Press of Mississippi, 2002.

Walker, Margaret. *How I Wrote Jubilee*. Chicago: Third World Press, 1972.

———. *Jubilee*. New York: Bantam, 1967.

———. *On Being Female, Black, and Free: Essays by Margaret Walker, 1932–1992*. Nashville: University of Tennessee Press, 1997.

Wallis, Velma (1960–)

The Gwich'in ethnographer Velma Wallis contributed a first to feminist literature—a Native American epic written by a woman about women. Born the sixth of 13 children in Fort Yukon, a town of 500 in the Alaskan interior north of the Arctic Circle, she quit school at age 13 to aid her widowed mother, Mae Wallis. The author moved 12 miles away to live alone in a cabin, to learn traditional methods of hunting and trapping marten, and to work in her free time toward a high school equivalency diploma. From a pre-Columbian oral story that Mae passed on, Velma produced *Two Old Women: An Alaska Legend of Betrayal, Courage and Survival* (1993), which her brother, Barry, helped her publish. In an era that saw the adoption of English as the dominant language, she intended to preserve the wisdom and experience of elders. She put on paper the oral legend of two Athapascan women, Ch'idzigyaak and Sa', aged 80 and 75, respectively, who battle near-starvation and Arctic weather extremes. The dignity and authenticity of the story won Wallis a Pacific Northwest Booksellers Association Award and a Western States Book Award and garnished a film option for a major movie.

Set in prehistory shortly before the onset of winter on the confluence of the Porcupine River with the upper Yukon River, the parable is a crone story, a subgenre reflecting a form of misogyny against the aged that permeates human history. The text combines themes of rejection and martyrdom with the validation of elderly females whom a wasteful clan jettisons. Even the daughter and grandson of one of the elderly women say nothing about the devaluation of two healthy tribe members because of their advanced age. The reason for exiling the pair is feral, bordering on savagery: "Like the younger, more able wolves who shun the old leader of the pack, these people would leave the old behind so they could move faster without the extra burden" (Wallis, 1993, 5).

As warriors against anti-female and anti-aged traditions the protagonists resolve to die "trying" (ibid., 16). They reestablish competence and dignity by refusing to die as a convenience for the tribe. Sa' looks back at her betrayers with disbelief: "She and the other old woman were not close to dying! Had they not sewed and tanned for what the people gave them? They did not have to be carried from camp to camp. They were neither helpless nor hopeless" (ibid., 14). To lift their spirits, the two do more than survive the winter: They trap and preserve enough moose flesh and hides to rescue the heartless tribe who willed them to starve or freeze in the wild. The epic struggle ennobles the hardships of other aged women and allows them to empower themselves and to maintain self-esteem in a society that is quick to strip them of worth. Sa' summarizes the tribe's transgression in a simple epigram: "The body needs food, but the mind needs people" (ibid., 65). The moral of the fable is enough to expunge an atavistic tribal custom that denigrated the aged.

Wallis continued to record survival lore that her mother treasured. In 1996 the author published *Bird Girl and the Man Who Followed the Sun: An Athabascan Indian Legend from Alaska*, an amalgam of two legends. Like Ayla in Jean AUEL's *The Clan of the Cave Bear* (1980), Wallis's protagonist, Jutthunvaa' or Bird Girl, is a nontraditional woman who seeks tribal sanction to hunt like a man, just as her father, Zhoh, taught her. Paired with the story of Daagoo, a young male dreamer who tries to corroborate tales of the "Land of the Sun," Bird Girl finds a way to heal division and return to her people and their culture. Wallis followed with *Raising Ourselves: A Gwich'in Coming of Age Story from the Yukon River* (2002), an AUTOBIOGRAPHY about life in a crowded two-room cabin with a father who abused his wife and died young of addiction to home brew and with a mother who frittered away monthly government checks on 14-day binges. The disclosures of tribal secrets generated first disapproval, then gratitude from Native people who welcomed the impetus to stop self-destructive behavior.

Bibliography

Ruppert, James. "Review: *Two Old Women*," *Ethnohistory* 42, no. 4 (Fall 1995): 670–671.

Wallis, Velma. *Bird Girl and the Man Who Followed the Sun*. New York: Perennial, 1997.

———. *Raising Ourselves: A Gwich'in Coming of Age Story from the Yukon River*. New York: Graphic Arts Center, 2003.

———. *Two Old Women: An Alaska Legend of Betrayal, Courage and Survival*. Fairbanks, Alaska: Epicenter, 1993.

Warren, Mercy Otis (1728–1814)

The historian, propagandist, journalist, and satiric dramatist Mercy Otis Warren supported WOMEN'S RIGHTS and equal citizenship with men. Born at Barnstable on Cape Cod, Massachusetts, she counted among her forebears a signer of the Mayflower Compact and an attorney-politician. Home schooling by her uncle introduced Mercy and her brothers to Classical authors, William Shakespeare, John Milton, and Molière. At age 26 she married James Warren, a member of the high command on George Washington's staff. While rearing five sons at their home in Plymouth, she held a regular salon in her parlor, supported the essays and poems of Judith Sargent MURRAY, and involved her-

self in the revolt against English colonialism. Among her contemporaries she contended that a republican form of government was the only choice likely to validate domesticity as a significant contribution to society.

After her husband died at the hands of a gang of Tory thugs, Warren began writing fiery closet dramas, beginning with *The Adulateur: A Tragedy* (1772). She styled it in the mode of medieval morality plays and serialized it anonymously in two installments for the *Massachusetts Spy*. The play and its sequel, *The Defeat* (1773), ridiculed Governor Thomas Hutchinson in the knavish, tendentious character Rapatio. In 1774 she stirred more controversy by publishing *The Blockheads; or, The Affrighted Officers, A Farce*, in which she mocks male leadership by naming Disneyesque characters Dapper, Dupe, Meagre, Paunch, Puff, Shallow, Simple, and Surly. Tabitha, a young patriot, insists that marriage to an old and crotchety male for title and money is foolish. In the months leading up to the Battle of Lexington, fought on April 19, 1775, Warren completed *The Group*, another satire of Tory politics and a celebration of the Boston Tea Party.

Warren turned to pamphleteering in 1788 with a demand for human rights in *Observations on the New Constitution, and on the Federal and State Conventions*, the first work she published under her own name. When accused of unladylike behavior, she retorted that female patriots are endowed with the same wit as men. Her works attest to her political consciousness and patriotism and to her feminism. To President Washington she dedicated *Poems, Dramatic and Miscellaneous* (1790). That same year at the urging of her collaborator Abigail ADAMS, Warren wrote *The Ladies of Castile* (1790), a depiction of women's methods of surviving national crises: To beef up the rebel war chest, the women heist church relics. She featured Roman heroines in the Classical verse tragedy *The Sack of Rome* (1787). In 1805 she contributed to colonial American chronicles the three-volume *History of the Rise, Progress, and Termination of the American Revolution*, a radical chronicle that she compiled over three decades. In relation to women's role in the rebellion against England Warren assures the reader in the preface, "Every domestic enjoyment depends on the unimpaired possession of civil and religious liberty" (Warren, 1988, iv). The text demands women's enfranchisement, a political view that annoyed John Adams, who believed women were too trivial-minded to compile a scholarly history.

Bibliography

Baym, Nina. "Between Enlightenment and Victorian: Toward a Narrative of American Women Writers Writing History," *Critical Inquiry* 18, no. 1 (Autumn 1991): 22–41.

Warren, Mercy Otis. *History of the Rise, Progress, and Termination of the American Revolution.* Indianapolis, Ind.: Liberty Fund, 1988.

———. *Plays and Poems of Mercy Otis Warren.* Delmar, N.Y.: Scholars Facsimiles & Reprint, 1980.

Wasserstein, Wendy (1950–2006)

A provocative Jewish-American actor, playwright, film and television scenarist, and editor, Wendy Wasserstein turned out thought-provoking essays and dramas in which women seek identity and validation of the ideals that make them feminists. Reared in Flatbush in her native Brooklyn, New York, she was directed toward the stage at birth; because her parents gave her the same first name as Wendy Darling, the heroine of *Peter Pan.* Wasserstein, who became a Yiddish quipster in childhood, later commented on her Jewish upbringing: "I came to accept that when my work was described as 'too New York' it was really a euphemism for something else" (Wasserstein, 2002, 4). She spent her teens in Manhattan, where her mother introduced her to stage plays, musicals, and ballets. Educated in history and playwriting at Mount Holyoke College and Smith College and in creative writing at the City College of New York, she began writing drama before graduation. The farce *Any Woman Can't* (1973) opened off Broadway to a feminist audience with scenes of a hasty marriage and droll commentary on women's attempts to pierce the glass ceiling. Before completing an M.F.A. at the Yale University School of Drama, she teamed with Christopher Durang to write *When Dinah Shore Ruled the Earth* (1975), a send-up of the beauty contest industry.

Following the example of Clare Booth LUCE's all-woman satiric comedy of manners *The Women*

(1936), Wasserstein produced an articulate social critique in the feminist comedy *Uncommon Women and Others* (1977), winner of an Obie. Set at the playwright's alma mater Mount Holyoke in South Hadley, Massachusetts, the plot gathers alumnae approaching the age of 30 who relive their undergraduate silliness and idealism. One alumna, Muffet, describes course work for marriage and the family as readings in "*The Feminine Mystique, Sexual Politics,* [and] Mabel Dodge's diary," a reference to the gossipy autobiographer Mabel Dodge Luhan, who joined an artists' colony in Taos, New Mexico (Wasserstein, 1991, 24). Muffet ponders: "Do you think women will lose their relevancy in five years? Like 'Car 54, Where Are You?' " (*ibid.*). For the Public Broadcasting Television (PBS-TV) version in 1978 the director cast Meryl Streep, Swoosie Kurtz, and Jill Eikenberry in the lead parts in a live performance at the Phoenix Theater in New York. Wasserstein's next play, *Isn't It Romantic* (1981), dropped the white affluent class to feature urban working-class women and their unique difficulties with romantic involvements and the biological urge to reproduce while there is still time. In an interview the playwright commented on the evasive character of Janie Blumberg, who avoids reality by hiding behind nonthreatening humor.

In 1989 Wasserstein's *The Heidi Chronicles* made the dramatist the first woman to win a Tony for best play and the first playwright to receive both a Tony and a Pulitzer Prize for the same work. The poignant story of Dr. Heidi Holland, an art history expert, describes the angst of middle age for single women through a recap of historical events from the 1960s to the 1980s. The final curtain descends on Heidi, her newly adopted baby, and a backdrop of the artworks of the feminist painter George O'Keeffe. Wasserstein produced additional comic takes on women's lives in *Bachelor Girls* (1991), *The Sisters Rosensweig* (1992), and *An American Daughter* (1997). The latter play pictures a media feeding frenzy over the revelation that Lyssa Dent Hughes, a nominee for surgeon general, once skipped jury duty. Christine Lahti played the role of Hughes in the 2000 Lifetime-TV performance. Wasserstein's comic screenplay *The Object of My Affection* (1998) starred Jennifer Anniston as the ingenue who falls for a gay man.

Wasserstein's irreverent wit moved into new territory in the 21st century. In 2004 she mocked the health and fitness mania in *Sloth: The Seven Deadly Sins*, a parody of frenetic Atkins dieters and self-help guides to the fast lane. At the core of the satire are the driven multitasking weight watchers, for whom she invents the sloth plan and Lethargiosis—the process of eliminating energy and drive. In addition to comic essays for *Advocate* and *American Theatre*, Wasserstein has edited the *New York Woman*, *Harper's Bazaar*, and *New Woman* magazines. For the anthology *Shiksa Goddess (or How I Spent My Forties)* (2001) she collected breezy autobiographical essays previously published in *Allure*, *Harper's Bazaar*, *New York Times*, *New Yorker*, *Slate*, *Stagebill*, *Vogue*, and the *Washington Post*. In the time-traveling play *Old Money* (2002) she contrasts the Gilded Age with contemporary manners among the oh-so-fashionable.

Bibliography

Ciociola, Gail. *Wendy Wasserstein: Dramatizing Women, Their Choices and Their Boundaries.* Jefferson, N.C.: McFarland, 1998.

Cohen, Esther. "Uncommon Woman: An Interview with Wendy Wasserstein," *Women's Studies* 15, no. 1–3 (1998): 257–270.

Wasserstein, Wendy. *American Daughter.* New York: Harvest, 1999.

———. *The Heidi Chronicles and Other Plays.* New York: Vintage, 1991.

———. *Shiksa Goddess (or How I Spent My Forties).* New York: Vintage, 2002.

———. *Sloth: The Seven Deadly Sins.* Oxford: Oxford University Press, 2004.

Watkins, Yoko Kawashima (1933–   )

The children's author and speaker Yoko Kawashima Watkins describes the survival techniques of lone Asian women during World War II. The daughter of a Japanese diplomat, she was born in Harbin, Manchuria, and grew up in comfort in Nanam, North Korea, where her father was an ambassador. After the outbreak of war the home situation rapidly depleted. Still answering to the name "Little One" at age 11, she sustained a shrapnel injury to the chest while she; her 16-year-old sister, Ko; and their mother fled the Communist takeover of Korea. Scenes of VIOLENCE against young girls filled their days. To spare the sisters possible rape and torture, the mother used a ceremonial sword to shave their heads. Dressed in Korean soldiers' uniforms, they survived the journey from northeastern Korea across the Sea of Japan to refugee facilities in Fukuoko, Japan. The girls formed a two-member family after their mother died in a Kyoto train station and their father was imprisoned in Siberia until 1950.

Because the family home was destroyed by bombs, the girls attended to their mother's cremation and then found a space to sleep in a clog factory. Under Ko's supervision they washed in a stream and ate scraps that Ko carefully selected from trash cans behind high-class hotels and restaurants. The two girls were surprised to find $100 in their mother's clothing but still had to make and sell bean bags and aprons and shine shoes to earn their living. While Ko studied home economics at Seian University, Yoko, a strong believer in education, attended the Sagano Girls' School, where wealthy pupils made her feel like an outsider. Yoko used her writing skills to win an essay contest that paid 10,000 yen for first place. In 1944 her brother, Hideyo, reunited with his sisters, ending the need to conceal that the two girls had survived on their own without a parent or male relative caring for them.

After studying English at Kyoto University, Watkins worked as a bilingual typist and translator at Misawa Air Force Base in Aomori. In 1953 she married an American flier and settled in Brewster, Massachusetts, where she reared their four children and two Chinese orphans. Ko's tenuous health, compromised by injuries sustained in a warehouse fire, placed additional responsibility on Watkins. In 1976 she began a decade-long process of compiling their family's experiences in a children's war story, *So Far from the Bamboo Grove* (1986), an American Library Association (ALA) Notable Book. She lectured on her war experiences in England, Guam, and Japan. Her memories focus on the lives of female refugees and the rules that prevent virgins from going into hotels and banquet halls unaccompanied. While the Kawashima women hurry toward Japan, a nurse and medic care for destitute women and children in their rail car. After tossing a dead infant from the hospital train, the medical team is unable to prevent the mother from leaping after her baby. The delivery of another infant gives the nurse a placenta to use as a ruse to disguise the Kawashima girls and their mother from the Korean authorities as injured patients and possible plague victims.

Watkins's subsequent works laud the pragmatism of female choices in difficult situations. She added to her autobiography with *My Brother, My Sister, and I* (1994), an ALA, *Publisher's Weekly,* and *Parenting* Magazine Best Book and *New York Times* Notable Book. At the core of the family's value system is deep respect for their mother, whose ashes occupy a place of honor on their only table, an apple box. In need of matriarchal solace, Yoko prays to her mother's spirit for protection in a world turned vicious by World War II. Yoko remarks, "Ever since we had become refugees, I had had a fear of strange men. We had stayed in places were girls were raped and often killed in the dark. I had seen brutality many times" (Watkins, 1996, 10–11). In *Tales from the Bamboo Grove* (1992), she compiled one Ainu and five Japanese entries on morals and ethics, including "Dragon Princess, Tatsuko," the story of a vain girl blinded by dreams of eternal beauty. The collection illustrates the value of mother-to-daughter STORYTELLING as cautionary and cultural instruction.

Bibliography

Roback, Diane, and Richard Donahue. "*Tales from the Bamboo Grove* by Yoko Kawashima Watkins," *Publishers Weekly,* 6 July 1992, p. 6.

Watkins, Yoko Kawashima. *My Brother, My Sister, and I.* New York: Simon Pulse, 1996.

———. *So Far from the Bamboo Grove.* New York: 1986.

Weil, Simone (1909–1943)

The Parisian writer, philosopher, theologian, and social activist Simone Adolphine Weil was a lifelong pacifist and protofeminist who denounced VIOLENCE and the virtual enslavement of women to the needs of the family. She was the brilliant child of Russian-Alsatian Jews, Selma Weil and Dr. Bernard Weil, a physician. She memorized French verse in kindergarten and read Homer's works, from which she learned that the controlling metaphor of masculine epic is force. She studied at Lycée Henri IV and completed a philosophy degree at age 15 with honors from the École Normale Supérieure, where students ridiculed her as the Red Virgin. After graduating at the head of her class, she taught for seven years at girls' academies in Auxerre, Bourges, Le Puy, Roanne, and Saint-Quentin and donated her time to tutoring miners and railroad and field laborers. While writing for liberal journals, she lived among the poor, dressed in burlap, and slept in a sleeping bag. On behalf of workers and political prisoners she involved herself in picketing, fasting, and activism. In 1934 she studied the apathy and obedience that stultified heavy factory labor at a Renault plant by joining forces with unskilled female workers. A year later she moved to Zaragoza, Spain, to aid the International Brigade against Francisco Franco during the Spanish civil war. A severe burn from boiling oil required rehabilitation in Portugal.

Weil's passion and writing altered after the onset of anorexia, asceticism, and a series of mystical encounters. Because anti-Jewish laws prohibited her employment as a teacher, she fled Nazi-occupied Paris to work on a farm outside Marseille. As Nazism gained control, she expatriated to New York. At the height of the Blitz she joined a London cell of the Free French Forces and volunteered to parachute into France. In what doctors called suicide, she limited her intake of food to that rationed to French citizens during Nazi occupation. She died in Ashford, Kent, of a weak heart, pulmonary tuberculosis, and pleurisy worsened by stress, exhaustion, migraines, and malnutrition. A 20-volume posthumous collection of Weil's writings includes "L'iliade ou le poème de la force" ("The Iliad, or the Poem of Force," 1940), *La pesanteur et la grâce* (*Gravity and Grace,* 1947), *L'enracinement* (*The Need for Roots,* 1949), *Attente de Dieu* (*Waiting for God,* 1950), *Oppression et liberté* (*Oppression and Liberty,* 1955), and *Cahiers* (*The Notebooks of Simone Weil,* 1951, 1955, 1956). Her feminism influenced a demand for WOMEN'S RIGHTS by the journalist Rosario Castellanos.

Bibliography

Heilbrun, Carolyn G. *Toward a Recognition of Androgyny.* New York: W. W. Norton, 1982.

Ignatieff, Michael. "The Limits of Sainthood," *New Republic*, 18 June 1990, pp. 40–46.

Meltzer, Francoise. "The Hands of Simone Weil," *Critical Inquiry* 27, no. 4 (Summer 2001): 611–628.

Weldon, Fay (1931–)

The dramatist, novelist, and screenwriter Fay Weldon balances crisp feminist drollery, black humor, and extravagant plotting against a relentless parade of picaresque skirt chasers, womanizers, bullies, and lusty old goats. Born Franklin Birkinshaw in Alvechurch, Worcestershire, she claimed a lineage that included two writers, her grandfather, Edgar Weldon, and her uncle, Selwyn Jepson. She was reared in London and Christchurch, New Zealand, and completed a master's degree at Saint Andrew's University in Fife, Scotland. By age 24 she was a single parent. After composing ad copy in London, in her 30s she began a writing career in plays and fiction marked by understated irony and staccato repartee, a feature of her episodes for the British Broadcasting Corporation Television (BBC-TV) series *Upstairs, Downstairs*. In her first success, the teleplay *The Fat Woman's Tale* (1966) developed into *The Fat Woman's Joke* (1967). In obeisance to the BEAUTY MYTH, the protagonist, Esther Sussman, ventures into the female quest for the ideal body.

Weldon continued depicting the struggles of contemporary women through aggressive feminism in the novels *Down among the Women* (1971), *Female Friends* (1974), and *Remember Me* (1976). In *Praxis* (1978) the title character charges, "Nature does not know best, or if it does, it is on the man's side" (Weldon, 1978, 133). The author blends the supernatural and pregnancy in *Puffball* (1980), in which a disgruntled narrator fumes, "Auntie Evolution, Mother Nature—bitches both!" (Weldon, 1985, 110). Weldon's most successful Gothic novel, *The Life and Loves of a She-Devil* (1983), a witty, high-energy survey of the beauty myth, is an anti–FAIRY TALE—the story of fat, ugly Ruth Patchett, resident of Eden Grove. Weldon establishes her theme early on: "Better to hate than to grieve"

(Weldon, 1983, 3). The revenge anthem thrived on film as *She-Devil* (1989), starring Meryl Streep as the other woman and Roseanne Barr as Ruth.

In 1995 Weldon examined divorce in *Splitting*, a satire about a woman's self-reclamation as she cleanses her mind of extraneous masks she has adapted to make marriage work. In an interview the playwright explained a shift from little white lies of marriage to honesty: "What happens now is that people have got very bad at telling lies and deceit. . . . It's how the world used to get by, and marriages stayed together by everyone telling a few lies" ("Fay's Way"). Weldon advanced from themes of DUALITY and motifs of shredded wedlock to major revenge with *Big Girls Don't Cry* (1997), a wry survey of the feminist heyday in which five disgruntled wives form Medusa Press, a book publisher.

Bibliography

Brown, Craig. "Fay Weldon: A Short Story," *Vogue*, January 1989, pp. 182–185.

"Fay's Way Is Learning to Give the Lie to Truth," *Europe Intelligence Wire*, 2 October 2003.

Martin, Sara. "The Power of Monstrous Women: Fay Weldon's *The Life and Loves of a She-Devil* (1983), Angela Carter's *Nights at the Circus* (1984), and Jeanette Winterson's *Sexing the Cherry* (1989)," *Journal of Gender Studies* 8, no. 2 (July 1999): 193–210.

Weldon, Fay. *Life and Loves of a She-Devil.* New York: Ballantine, 1983.

———. *Praxis.* New York: Summit Books, 1978.

———. *Puffball.* New York: Pocket Books, 1985.

Well of Loneliness, The Radclyffe Hall (1928)

Radclyffe HALL shocked society with the publication of her semiautobiographical *The Well of Loneliness* (1928), the first truly explicit lesbian novel. Hall focuses on the identity crisis of a woman born with a man's name, Stephen. The characterization furthers the stereotype of the sexually inverted female, whose parents call her Stephen Mary Olivia Gertrude Gordon. Her birth on Christmas Eve and the choice of a first name link her to the first Christian martyr, Saint Stephen, whom pagans stoned to death. The Gordons countenance her boyish ways as solace for their longing for a son. After puberty

Stephen wanders unmarked terrain in search of affirmation for a fragmented self: "I'm nothing—yes I am, I'm Stephen—but that's being nothing" (Hall, 1950, 70). A neighbor's free-floating qualms about the Gordons register the antigay spirit of genteel society: "What [Mrs. Antrim] called Stephen's 'queerness' aroused her suspicion—she was never quite clear as to what she suspected, but felt sure that it must be something outlandish" (*ibid.*, 91). Community hostility forces Stephen to enfold herself in the nonjudgmental environs of Morton, the Gordons' ancestral home, a masculine retreat reflecting her father's tastes and needs.

Through suicide, jealous confrontations, emotional collapse, and a deathbed farewell Hall speaks knowledgeably on the ostracism of homosexuals in a purportedly Christian environment. Severance from home and family ends Stephen's ability to escape social approbation. Trapped in otherness and banished from Morton, Stephen resorts to male attire and gentlemanly behavior as she pursues a fulfilling relationship with a female beloved. Public recoil at lesbian couples excludes Stephen from the spiritual haven of religious services and from patriotic expressions of love for England. The melodramatic conclusion, in which Stephen begs God to acknowledge gay people, reflects a life of internal torment and personal nullification. Vilified in the *Sunday Express*, the candid novel precipitated an obscenity trial and suppression of Hall's work in England, but not in France and North America.

Bibliography

Green, Laura. "Hall of Mirrors: Radclyffe Hall's *The Well of Loneliness* and Modern Fictions of Identity," *Twentieth Century Literature* 49, no. 3 (Fall 2003): 277–297.

Hall, Radclyffe. *The Well of Loneliness*. New York: Pocket Books, 1950.

Taylor, Melanie A. " 'The Masculine Soul Heaving in the Female Bosom': Theories of Inversion and *The Well of Loneliness*," *Journal of Gender Studies* 7, no. 3 (November 1998): 287–296.

Wells, Rebecca (ca. 1950–   )

The novelist, dramatist, and actor Rebecca Wells uses humor to reveal the damage wreaked by mother-daughter conflicts and SECRECY. Reared as a traditional southerner and Catholic with her four siblings, she grew up in Alexandria, Rapides Parish, in rural central Louisiana. She kept a diary of her earliest impressions of outrageous misconduct and the accompanying guilt for misbehaving. She learned the value of STORYTELLING as a form of belonging to the community. Her self-training in stagecraft began with juvenilia acted out at home and with participation in community theater. While studying at Louisiana State University, she learned playwriting by composing a series of original scenarios. To master human attitudes and poses, she made an extensive train tour of the United States and developed speech control at the Naropa Institute in Boulder, Colorado.

Wells's flexible writing features a variety of genres. With a background in the Stanislavski method gained in New York City, she created roles for herself in the critically acclaimed plays *Splittin' Hairs* (1995) and *Gloria Duplex* (1987), for which she acted the lead. From autobiographical episodes of growing up in the 1960s published in *Crab Creek Review, Ergo!, Mississippi Review, Seattle Week,* and *Writers Arts* grew longer works. Reconnecting with the patois and humor of her childhood was her first novel, *Little Altars Everywhere* (1992), winner of the Western States Book Award. She began outlining the plot in 1987 while sidelined from the stage with a broken foot. The text is the source of a one-actor show enriched by dialect and typical female fun. She became famous for the best-selling sequel, *Divine Secrets of the Ya-Ya Sisterhood* (1996), a girl club saga set in fictional Thornton, Louisiana. Warner filmed the novel in 2002 as a raucous "chick flick" starring Ellen Burstyn and Sandra Bullock as warring mother and daughter, Vivi and Siddalee Walker. Both book and film plus the sequel, *Ya-Ya's in Bloom* (2004), brought to light friendship clubs and spawned national Ya-Ya clubs in the North and South.

Wells's fiction builds drama from the complex relationships of female friends and from loving-but-hating mother and daughter traditions. The cult of SISTERHOOD reveals women's reliance on each other to make sense of human foibles. The plot gains seriousness as it expands from girlish rebellions and exhibitionism to betrayal, child abuse, mental illness, and alcoholism. Drawing on the outré feminism of Catholic saints, Shirley Temple look-alikes, and voodoo priestesses, the characterization shifts in tone from the revelation of secrets dating back over half a century to betrayal of woman-to-woman disclosures never meant for the public. Wells explains that Siddalee's "relationship with her mother had never been smooth, but this latest episode was disastrous" (Wells, 2004, 2).

Wells navigates the mother-daughter clash into dangerous waters. Vivi's excesses of outrage develop a lethal edge as she declares to Sidda, "You are dead to me. You have killed me. Now I am killing you" (ibid.). Sidda's mental picture calls up an image as visceral as the yawning mouth of Medusa in Greek myth: "You bitch . . . you devouring, melodramatic bitch" (ibid., 3). Sidda's remedy is a contrite letter requesting talk therapy, a filial request intended to undo a parent's emotional divorce from her grown daughter. Wells supplies a psychological panacea: In place of healing conversation Vivi offers the club scrapbook, the bits and pieces of women's lives.

Bibliography
Van Boven, Sarah. "Getting Their Ya-Yas Out," *Newsweek*, 6 July 1998, p. 71.

Wells, Rebecca. *Divine Secrets of the Ya-Ya Sisterhood.* New York: Perennial, 2004.

———. *Little Altars Everywhere.* New York: Perennial, 1996.

Wells-Barnett, Ida B. (1862–1931)

The social activist, pamphleteer, lecturer, diarist, and journalist Ida Bell Wells-Barnett fought sexual and racial STEREOTYPING of blacks. Born to slaves in Holly Springs, Mississippi, she grew up among seven siblings, whom she mothered after yellow fever killed their parents in 1878. After studying at a Methodist preparatory school and at Shaw University, she taught school until age 21 while taking graduate course in summer at Fisk University. While working in Memphis, Tennessee, she made an issue of riding among white passengers on a train and suffered expulsion to the smoking car. She successfully sued the Chesapeake, Ohio and Southwestern Railroad but lost her case on appeal. At the beginning of her career as an investigative

journalist she wrote under the pen name Iola for *Living Way.* Her articles covered important topics—racial issues, convict leasing, equal EDUCATION for black children, and the rise of the women's club movement.

At age 30 Wells-Barnett suffered a terrifying loss after vicious whites lynched her friends Thomas Moss, Calvin McDonald, and Will Stewart. She crusaded for an end to violence against blacks through her weekly newspaper, the *Free Speech and Headlight,* and through articles and columns for the *Chicago Conservator, Chicago Inter-Ocean, Detroit Plaindealer, Gate City Press, Indianapolis World, Little Rock Sun,* and *New York Age.* She exposed the social, gender, and economic roots of race envy and bias in a treatise, *Southern Horror* (1892), which destroys the myth that black men deserved lynching for their lust for white women. Wells-Barnett challenged, "If assaulting white women is a threadbare lie, then what might the truth be?" (Wells-Barnett, 1996, 2). She followed with *A Red Record: Tabulated Statistics and Alleged Causes of Lynching in the United States, 1892–1893–1894* (1895), which encouraged blacks to abandon the South and move west.

The writer was successful at bridging the cultural divide, in part by informing white and black women of nationwide injustices. She established Chicago's first black women's political pressure group, the Alpha Suffrage Club. In 1909 she co-founded the National Association for the Advancement of Colored People. At her death she left incomplete her life story, *Crusade for Justice: The Autobiography of Ida B. Wells* (1970), edited by her daughter, Alfreda Duster. The text expresses Wells-Barnett's gratitude to her mother and her dedication to SUFFRAGE and to the leadership of the orator Susan B. ANTHONY. In 1950 the city of Chicago named Wells-Barnett one of its 25 outstanding female citizens.

Bibliography
Schechter, Patricia A. *Ida B. Wells-Barnett and American Reform, 1880–1930.* Chapel Hill: University of North Carolina Press, 2001.

Wells-Barnett, Ida B. *Crusade for Justice: The Autobiography of Ida B. Wells.* Chicago: University of Chicago Press, 1991.

———. *Lynch Law in Georgia* (1899). Available online. URL: http://memory.loc.gov/cgi-bin/query/r?ammem/ murray:@field(DOCID+@lit(lcrbmrpt1612)): @@@REF. Accessed on October 17, 2005.

———. *Southern Horrors and Other Writings: The Anti-Lynching Campaign of Ida B. Wells, 1892–1900.* New York: Bedford/St. Martin's, 1996.

Welty, Eudora (1909–2001)

The Mississippi fiction writer and humorist Eudora Welty presented energetic female individuals who battered the gendered limitations on women's freedom. She spent most of her life in the Delta region around Jackson, her hometown. In *One Writer's Beginnings* (1984) she describes how extensive reading during recuperation from a heart condition introduced her to literature. Her mother, the schoolteacher Chestine Welty, entertained Eudora with STORYTELLING and folk songs. Welty completed her education at Mississippi State College for Women and the University of Wisconsin and in postgraduate work in advertising at Columbia University. Her first jobs involved composition for radio and for the society page of a newspaper, an introit to her folksy scenarios at weddings, funerals, and family reunions. Through a camera lens she observed survivors of the Great Depression on assignment as a publicist for the Works Progress Administration. She began producing stories of quirky Gothic characters for *Atlantic, Harper's, Hudson Review, Manuscript, New Yorker, Prairie Schooner,* and *Sewanee Review.* Her unique handling of absurd humor drew on mythic allusions and human idiosyncrasies to enliven dialogue and engaging plots. Her cast of characters ranged from rascals, curmudgeons, and grotesques to home folks speaking the rural vernacular wisdom common to black and white residents of the region.

Welty demonstrated compassion toward women in acute crises. One of her most anthologized short works, the escapist story "WHY I LIVE AT THE P.O.," appeared in her first anthology, *A Curtain of Green and Other Stories* (1941). The story focuses on an alienated girl called "Sister," amid a wrangle of family disagreements. She chooses July 4, Independence Day, as the right moment to leave home and move into the post office. More unsettling is "Lily Daw and

the Three Ladies" (1941), a tale of the incarceration of a local woman at the "Ellisville Institution for the Feeble-Minded of Mississippi" (Welty, 3). In "Livvie Is Back" (1943), a winner of an O. Henry Memorial Contest Award anthologized in *The Wide Net and Other Stories* (1943), the author described a miserable marriage; for "The Golden Apples" (1949) she created Miss Eckhart, an unhappy outsider. More complex views of women's life choices energize *Delta Wedding* (1946), a novel rich in the hurtful gossip that punishes the female rebel and risk taker.

One of Welty's most poignant views of womanhood is a rural black grandmother, Phoenix Jackson, who is the sole caregiver for a small boy in the quest story "A Worn Path" (1941). Set on the Old Natchez Trace, the text follows a painful trek to town for medication to ease his throat pain, caused by ingestion of lye. Phoenix suffers the humiliations of rude white hunters, menacing dogs, and superior townspeople who patronize and annoy her. The final descent from the second-floor doctor's office implies that she is on a declining path fraught with responsibilities and hazards too numerous for an elderly woman to manage. For honest, loving representations of women's lives, Welty earned a Pulitzer Prize, the Presidential Medal of Freedom and the respect of the playwright Beth HENLEY, the ecofeminist Barbara KINGSOLVER, the southern novelists Carson MCCULLERS and Flannery O'CONNOR, and the Canadian short story writer Alice MUNRO.

Bibliography

Champion, Laurie. *The Critical Response to Eudora Welty's Fiction.* Westport, Conn.: Greenwood, 1994.

Marrs, Suzanne. *One Writer's Imagination: The Fiction of Eudora Welty.* Baton Rouge: Louisiana State University Press, 2002.

Welty, Eudora. *The Collected Stories of Eudora Welty.* New York: Harcourt Brace Jovanovich, 1980.

Wertenbaker, Timberlake (1946–)

Timberlake Wertenbaker is a prolific Anglo-American journalist, translator, scenarist, and playwright who specializes in reenacting the sexual ravishment of women. At her best she stresses women's ability to accept challenge. Born in the United States, she grew up in southwestern France among the Basques of the Pyrenees Mountains and later studied at Saint John's College in Annapolis, Maryland. While living in Greece, she taught French. In her 30s she composed *This Is No Place for Tallulah Bankhead* (1978), *Breaking Through* (1980), and the humorous *Case to Answer* (1980). In London she served one year as the writer in residence at the Royal Court Theatre. Her translations of the plays of Sophocles and Euripides were performed on British Broadcasting Corporation (BBC) radio.

Wertenbaker's developing talents turned more pointedly to feminist themes of identity and male-on-female VIOLENCE. She wrote historical drama about the Welsh explorer and Islamic mystic Isabelle Eberhardt in *New Anatomies* (1981), which pictures the independent woman demanding her right to sexual fulfillment. In answer to a question about her deceased mother, Isabelle recalls a delicate, unassuming women. Isabelle's explanation of her mother's courage in running away is lyric, yet fundamentally feminist: "Even the violet resists domestication" (Wertenbaker, 1996, 8).

The dramatist overturned gender in the Japanese legend *Inside Out* (1982) and similarly subverted male and female roles in *Abel's Sister* (1984), which recasts the biblical narration of the first siblings, Cain and Abel. More hostile is *The Grace of Mary Traverse* (1985), which accounts for violent outbursts against disempowerment. The play debuted at the Royal Court Theatre in 1985 with Janet McTeer in the title role. The author reprises the myth of Procne and PHILOMELA in the parody *The Love of the Nightingale* (1988), which fuses versions by Ovid and Sophocles to expose male-on-female violence and permanent SILENCING. The action takes place in Athens, Greece, where the sisters fall under rigid gendered laws that tolerate no input from females. For avant-garde drama that forces viewers to rethink stereotypes, the playwright won two Olivier Awards for *Our Country's Good* (1989), winner of the New York Drama Critics Circle Award for Best New Foreign Play, and for *Three Birds Alighting on a Field* (1992). In 2004 she adapted to stage Dava Sobel's historical novel *Galileo's Daughter*, a winsome father-daughter story that depicts the astronomer's love for his child, Sister Maria Celeste.

Bibliography

Komporály, Jozefina. "Maternal Longing as Addiction: Feminism Revisited in Timberlake Wertenbaker's *The Break of Day,*" *Journal of Gender Studies* 13, no. 2 (July 2004): 129–138.

Wertenbaker, Timberlake. *The Love of the Nightingale and the Grace of Mary Traverse.* Boston: Faber & Faber, 1991.

———. *Timberlake Wertenbaker: Plays 1.* Boston: Faber & Faber, 1996.

———. *Timberlake Wertenbaker: Plays 2.* Boston: Faber & Faber, 2002.

West, Jessamyn (1902–1984)

A gentle, but insistent feminist fiction writer, screenwriter, and essayist, Jessamyn West reprised the era of the Underground Railroad, Fugitive Slave Laws, and Civil War through the eyes of a Quaker clergywoman. Born to a Plains Indian father and Quaker mother in North Vernon, Indiana, she had a matrilineal heritage of determined females. She grew up in California and studied at Fullerton Junior College and Whittier College. After four years in the classroom in Hemet, California, she began work on a Ph.D. at the University of California but halted at the onset of bilateral tuberculosis, which appeared to be terminal. While recuperating at her childhood home, she absorbed her mother's settler tales, which supplied a stock of characters and situations for West's novels, screenplays, and short fiction. She published frontier fiction and a string of Cress Delahanty stories about teenage angst in *Atlantic*, *Good Housekeeping*, *Harper's*, *Kenyon Review*, *Ladies' Home Journal*, *Mademoiselle*, *McCall's*, *New Mexico Quarterly*, *New Yorker*, *Reader's Digest*, *Saturday Evening Post*, *Redbook*, and *Woman's Day*.

West gained fame for a pair of romantic novels, *The Friendly Persuasion* (1945) and the sequel, *Except for Me and Thee* (1969), the story of Eliza and Jess Birdwell, who farm and tend an orchard in the Indiana heartland. The pairing interlaces powerful themes of domestic arguments and the wife's disquieting choice between personal morals and the demands of housewifery. When Eliza, a Quaker minister, faces the Underground Railroad conductor who is bearing the runaways Burk and Lily, a pair of starving slaves, her decision to help rises from a deep humanity: "I'm not against the hungry and hunted" (West, 1970, 174). More feminist themes influence *The Massacre at Fall Creek* (1975), historical fiction that discloses women's place in Plains Indian culture. During the filming of *The Friendly Persuasion* in 1956, West served William Wyler as scenarist and technical director. The film earned five Oscar nominations. A personal commentary on her sister's decision about living and dying with cancer infuses with love and duty *The Woman Said Yes: Encounters with Life and Death* (1976).

Bibliography

Bacon, Margaret Hope. *Mothers of Feminism: The Story of Quaker Women in America*. San Francisco: Harper, 1986.

West, Jessamyn. *Except for Me and Thee*. New York: Avon, 1970.

———. *The Friendly Persuasion*. New York: Harvest Books, 2003.

West, Rebecca (1892–1983)

A distinguished novelist and freelance writer, Dame Rebecca West, called the elder stateswoman of English literature, wrote cogent depictions of the feminist and socialist issues of her day. A native Londoner, she was born Cicily Isabel Fairfield to Scotch-Irish parents, the journalist Charles Fairfield and Isabel Campbell Mackenzie, a working mother who gave piano lessons. When West's father died, she received a scholarship to George Watson's Ladies' College in Edinburgh. Moved by a speech by the suffragist Emmeline PANKHURST, at age 13 West hawked copies of *Votes for Women*, a publication of the Women's Social & Political Union. After seeing a performance by Sarah Bernhardt, West learned acting at the Royal Academy of Dramatic Art. While playing in Henrik Ibsen's *Rosmersholm* (1886), she adopted the pen name Rebecca West, a pseudonym more suited to a willful, independent female.

In writing West allowed her intellect to roam freely. At age 19 she began reviewing for a feminist journal, *Freewoman*, and a socialist paper, *Clarion*. She published intense articles on suffragists and the sins of PATRIARCHY. She denounced conservative divorce laws and testified before Parliament to WOMEN'S RIGHTS to gainful employment. In "A New Woman's Movement: The Need for Riotous Living" (1913) and "The Sheltered Sex: 'Lotus Eating' on Seven-and-Six a Week" (1913) she addressed the issue of the need for a living wage for female workers to allow them a contented lifestyle equal to that enjoyed by men. After she critiqued *Marriage* (1912), a novel by H. G. Wells, he became her lover and the father of their son, Anthony West. She assumed the role of single parent and advanced her reputation with increasingly difficult literary modes and subjects, including the hardships faced by unwed mothers.

West rapidly blossomed into an accomplished feminist writer. At age 24 she published a critical volume, *Henry James* (1916), that accuses the novelist of limiting the range of female characterization to sexual roles. For its pro-woman stance the overview has been called the first feminist criticism. For a half-century, she worked at her own fiction, beginning with a short story, "Indissoluble Matrimony" (1914), a grotesque tale of a husband's extreme hatred of his wife. She produced a feminist view of World War I in the novel *The Return of the Soldier* (1918), a masterwork in which she identifies combat trauma and women's separation anxiety as the results of rigid social roles for male and female. Twitchy with worry, the protagonist, Jenny, quails at the uncertainty of secondhand information: "On the war-films I have seen men slip down as softly from the trench-parapet, and none but the grimmer philosophers could say that they had reached safety by their fall. And when I escaped into wakefulness it was only to lie stiff and think of stories I had heard" (West, 1918, 9). In the story "Elegy" (1930) West examines how society squelches women's laughter, a form of SILENCING that protects patriarchy from criticism. During the Spanish civil war, she joined Emma GOLDMAN in a feminist project, the Committee to Aid Homeless Spanish Women and Children.

World War II placed West in a supervisory role for the British Broadcasting Corporation (BBC). In

1942 she published *Black Lamb and Grey Falcon: The Record of a Journey through Yugoslavia*, an incisive two-volume survey of Balkan culture and politics. Her feminist perspective typifies obsessive macho posturing as a cause of violent territoriality and war. Three years later on assignment for the *New Yorker* she covered the Nuremberg Trials of Nazi war criminals. Her notes were the source of *A Train of Powder* (1955) and an impetus to *The Phoenix: Meaning of Treason* (1949), which earned her a Women's Press Club Award and a Commander of the British Empire citation.

Bibliography

Kavka, Misha. "Men in (Shell-) Shock: Masculinity, Trauma, and Psychoanalysis in Rebecca West's 'The Return of the Soldier,'" *Studies in Twentieth Century Literature* 22, no. 1 (Winter 1998): 151–171.

Stetz, Margaret Diane. "Rebecca West's 'Elegy': Women's Laughter and Loss," *Journal of Modern Literature* 18, no. 4 (Spring 1994): 369–380.

Thomas, Sue. "Rebecca West's Second Thoughts on Feminism," *Genders* 13, no. 90 (Spring 1992): 90–107.

West, Rebecca. *The Return of the Soldier* (1918). Available online. URL: http://digital.library.upenn.edu/women/west/soldier/soldier.html. Accessed on October 17, 2005.

Wharton, Edith (1862–1937)

The author of classic American social novels and polished short ficton, Edith Newbold Jones Wharton directed stouthearted female characters on quests for meaningful lives and contentment. Born of Dutch-French Huguenot ancestry, she grew up in wealth and privilege in New York City, where she was privately tutored in "needlework, music, drawing, and the 'languages,'" a reference to the modern foreign languages that the wealthy spoke during their sojourns in Europe (Wharton, 1998, 16). At social gatherings she observed the false values and mannered confrontations that she used for the face-off between the beautiful social belle, Lily Bart, and Gus Trenor, a rapacious womanizer, in *The House of Mirth* (1905). Early on Lily sighs, "What a miserable thing it is to be a woman," her response to the stuffy gendered codes of femininity limiting the behavior of marriageable gentlewomen, who must remain above suspicion of unladylike conduct (Wharton, 2000, 5). Wharton extends pity to Lily for demeaning herself in the search for a husband and for killing herself with an overdose of chloral. In a suffocating, morally corrupt society Lily would rather die than struggle on against gendered roles that keep her poor and single.

Wharton's fiction found immediate favor with readers of *Harper's*, *Quarterly Review*, *Scribner's*, and *Youth's Companion*. She is revered for a finely crafted novella, *Ethan Frome* (1911), a New England story of cold landscapes and colder hearts. At the climax the title character surrenders hope for abandoning his cruel wife, Zenobia "Zeena" Pierce Frome, a whining hypochondriac. His passion for Mattie Silver develops after he rescues her from the ignominious toil of shopgirl and gives her a home at his farm as Zeena's companion. From her own unhappy wedlock to a mentally unstable husband the author understood the claustrophobic misery and understated cruelties of a loveless marriage. The gothic scenario concludes with the unexpected end of a suicidal sled ride down a hill into an elm tree. The crash cripples Ethan and leaves him with two foul-tempered invalids, Zeena and Mattie. The former ingenue, Mattie, retreats into a "witch-like stare," a gaze that curses Ethan with more misery (Wharton, 1970, 85).

Wharton spoke more openly of the complexities of female SEXUALITY and moral dilemmas in *The Reef* (1912) and *The Custom of the Country* (1914), in which Undine Spragg tests the emerging climate of liberation. One of the early victims who venture too far for her family's tastes, she hovers on the threshold of social change. Restricted among less daring women, she "beheld her future laid out for her, not directly and in blunt words, but obliquely and affably, in the allusions, the assumptions, the insinuations of the amiable women among whom her days were spent" (Wharton, 1981, 333). In *The Mother's Recompense* (1925) Wharton looks inward to more corrosive emotions. Her protagonist, Kate Clephane, ponders a lapsed relationship with her daughter, Anne: "Jealous? Was she jealous of her daughter? Was she physically jealous? Was that the real secret of her repugnance, her instinctive revulsion . . . as if some incestuous horror hung between them?" (Wharton, 1996, x). Because Kate violates the rules of propriety favoring latitude in male sexual adventuring but limiting females to home, husband, and family, she loses her values and her self-respect.

Wharton's steady gaze at society's flawed values changed during World War I, when she lived in France as an expatriate. To aid the war effort, she established the American Hostel for Refugees and the Children of Flanders Rescue Committee. In her autobiography, *A Backward Glance* (1934), she recalled that combat "abruptly tore down the old frame-work, and what had seemed unalterable rules of conduct became of a sudden observances as quaintly arbitrary as the domestic rites of the Pharaohs" (Wharton, 1998, 7). In 1918 she reported on noncombatant survival in *Fighting France*. Her survey honors steady, keen-eyed Parisian women who live in a female enclave during World War I, who make do by window shopping "to distinguish between the dull purchase of necessities and the voluptuousness of acquiring things one might do without" (Wharton, 1918, 37). The lengthy conflict forces a series of leveling experiences that drive some women further from their economic class to near-beggary. Near war's end Wharton lauds the resilient female spirit: "The habitual cheerfulness of the Parisian workwoman rises, in moments of sorrow, to the finest fortitude. . . . If an order has to be rushed through for a hospital they give up that one afternoon as gaily as if they were doing it for their pleasure" (*ibid.*, 228). For the author's greatheartedness she received the French Legion of Honor.

Wharton's career in feminist fiction had multiple rewards. In 1920 she won the Pulitzer Prize for *The Age of Innocence*, an account of an unhappy marriage that results in fantasies of adultery. The novel was thrice filmed, the last time in 1993 featuring Winona Ryder and Daniel Day-Lewis as a mismated couple devoted to keeping up appearances for the sake of their social position. In *Old New York* (1924) she collected four novellas commenting on the social price of adultery, illegitimacy, envy, solitary females, and women's struggle for autonomy. At her death of stroke in St.-Brice-sous-Forêt, France, she left unfinished *The Buccaneers* (1938), a female quest novel de-

picting the perils of the MARRIAGE MARKET for American women seeking husbands among European aristocrats. The author spiked the irony of their intent by naming the protagonist Nan St. George, a surname recalling the English patron saint and his combat with a dragon, a symbol of Old World perils to untried American youth. Wharton was the first female to earn a gold medal from the National Institute of Arts and Letters and the first to receive an honorary degree from Yale University.

Bibliography

Fedorko, Kathy Anne. *Gender and Gothic in the Fiction of Edith Wharton*. Tuscaloosa: Alabama Universitiy Press, 1995.

Inness, Sherry. " 'Loyal Saints or Devious Rascals': Domestic Servants in Edith Wharton's Stories 'The Lady's Maid's Bell' and 'All Souls,' " *Studies in Short Fiction* 36, no. 4 (Fall 1999): 337–350.

Singley, Carol J. *Edith Wharton: Matters of Mind and Spirit*. Cambridge: Cambridge University Press, 1998.

Wharton, Edith. *A Backward Glance*. New York: Scribner, 1998.

———. *The Custom of the Country*. New York: Berkley, 1981.

———. *Ethan Frome*. New York: Charles Scribner, 1970.

———. *Fighting France* (1918). Available online. URL: http://digital.library.upenn.edu/women/wharton/france/france.html. Accessed on October 17, 2005.

———. *The House of Mirth*. New York: New American Library, 2000.

———. *A Mother's Recompense*. New York: Scribner, 1996.

Wheatley, Phillis (ca. 1753–1784)

The poet and letter writer Phillis Wheatley Peters voiced her impressions of life as a black woman amid distinguished white males in the American colonies. A slave transported to America over the Middle Passage from Senegal in West Africa, she left behind a grieving father and arrived in Boston at age eight. The businessman and tailor John Wheatley purchased her at auction to serve his wife, Susannah. The family made a pet of the child, who resided as a member of the family in a private bedroom. She studied English and Classical authors, Latin, and the Bible with the Wheatleys' teenaged daughter. By age 14 the poet expressed evangelical piety in verse, which she published in the *Philadelphia Magazine*. In 1770 Bostonians learned of her virtuosity with the publication of "An Elegiac Poem, on the Death of That Celebrated, Divine, and Eminent Servant of Jesus Christ, the Reverend and Learned George Whitefield."

At age 20 Wheatley completed *Poems on Various Subjects, Religious and Moral* (1773), the first book published by an American black author. The volume earned her admiration in England and manumission from bondage. Her marriage to a freedman, John Peters, experienced the hardships of poverty and the death of their three children at their home in Wilmington, Massachusetts. In addition to stress and overwork as a domestic at an inn, she contended with single parenthood during her husband's sentencing to debtors' prison. After more than two decades of treatment for respiratory ailments she died of hunger and cold at age 31, leaving her poems as a testimony to a spirited colonial author. Her remarks on the disgrace of slavery and the value of morals, friendship, and EDUCATION reveal a logical mind that creates vivid imagery. Feminists embrace her heartfelt descriptions of motherhood and the sorrows of children's deaths.

Bibliography

Gates, Henry Louis. *The Trials of Phillis Wheatley: America's First Black Poet and Encounters with the Founding Fathers*. New York: BasicCivitas Books, 2003.

Wheatley, Phillis. *Complete Writings*. New York: Penguin, 2001.

"Where Are You Going, Where Have You Been?" Joyce Carol Oates (1970)

Joyce Carol OATES's gothic story "Where Are You Going, Where Have You Been?" in *The Wheel of Love and Other Stories* (1970) surveys the teen scenario of the 1960s. In the eyes of 15-year-old Connie, liberation from home prefaces endless possibilities. While she dries freshly shampooed hair in the summer sun, she fantasizes stereotypes of male-female relations—"how sweet it always was . . . the way it was in movies and promised in songs" (Oates, 39). Her pubescent outlook establishes an inexperience with the evil implied by shrieking pop tunes on XYZ *Sunday Jamboree* and the cajolery of Arnold Friend, who coaxes her out the screen door toward his jalopy. His exhibitionist paint job, makeup, and dyed hair bear out Connie's mother's assertion that her daughter's mind is filled with trash.

Critical wrangling over interpretations of the story attest to Oates's ability to tease the mind with Connie's "possibilities." First published in the fall 1966 issue of *Epoch*, the story appears to mimic media coverage of a Tucson murder case, 23-year-old Charles Schmid and 18-year-old John Saunders's rape and fatal beating of 15-year-old Alleen Rowe on May 31, 1964. Oates draws on news images of shocking random VIOLENCE by lurking males who share Arnold's crass philosophy: "What else is there for a girl like you but to be sweet and pretty and give in . . . ?" (*ibid.*, 53). Oates foreshadows a sexual violation in which Arnold, a demon lover, is "stabbing her again and again with no tenderness" (*ibid.*, 52), an ambiguous image of thrusts by either a penis or knife. The implications of rape and a lethal assault account for the power of the story to convey vulnerability in a pubescent girl who foresees that she can never return to the safety of childhood.

Oates's allegory captures the child's hovering on the threshold of adulthood under the influence of erotic reveries. Connie reassures herself with promises that Daddy will return and rescue her or that she will summon the police. Luring her into a sexual tryst are the Presleyesque posturing and satanic wheedling of Arnold, who appears to know the details of Connie's life right down to her sexual innocence and helplessness in an empty house. As the wolf sizes up LITTLE RED RIDING HOOD, he advances from flirtation and charming mockery to verbal coercion and threats against the family. The narrative focuses on Connie's boredom and the titillation she receives through toying with danger—a driving date with Arnold in the company of his 40-year-old psychopathic friend Ellie Oscar. Left to the reader's imagination is whether the encounter is a dream or a real event.

Bibliography

Hurley, D. F. "Impure Realism: Joyce Carol Oates's 'Where Are You Going, Where Have You Been?'" *Studies in Short Fiction* 28, no. 3 (Summer 1991): 371–375.

Oates, Joyce Carol. *The Wheel of Love and Other Stories.* New York: Vanguard, 1970.

"Why I Live at the P.O." Eudora Welty
(1941)

Popular in anthologies of American short fiction, Eudora WELTY's comic family debacle in "Why I Live at the P.O." exemplifies the author's skill at irony and domestic humor. Introduced in the *Atlantic* in 1940, the story appeared in her first collection, *A Curtain of Green and Other Stories* (1941). The narrative dramatizes the life of Sister, the peevish, backbiting postmistress of China Grove, Mississippi, who empowers herself over family members through self-ennobling STORY-TELLING. At the crux of the first-person account is Sister's need to triumph in her rivalry with her younger sibling, Stella-Rondo. To bolster self-esteem, Sister fights imaginary slights while concealing from herself jealousy that Mr. Whitaker abandoned her in favor of Stella-Rondo. Feminist critics read into Sister's seething disgruntlement a need to salve a spirit wounded by male rejection.

The burden of spinsterhood generates confrontations and manipulation in Sister, who must juggle the balance of female power back into her own favor. To diminish her rival's womanhood, Sister implies that Stella-Rondo's daughter is retarded. As with other forays into enemy territory, this venture backfires on Sister after Shirley T. begins singing the theme song from a Popeye cartoon. To the storyteller's detriment Sister flies into a snit, abandons her family and takes up residence at the tiny post office, hauling along oddments from home that suggest a pathetic contribution to the household. Without an audience of family she lives in CONFINEMENT like green tomatoes pickled in a jar and feeds her flair for melodrama on other people's comings and goings. At the heart of her self-alienation lie stunted maturity and a need to dramatize personal devaluation through outbursts and tantrums. Symbolically she sets up her new

quarters "cater-cornered," a deliberate perversity suited to her contrary personality (Welty, 85). In part because of Welty's intriguing portrait of Sister, Harcourt issued a 50th-anniversary edition of *A Curtain of Green* (1991).

Bibliography

Bouton, Reine Dugas. "The Struggle for Agency in Eudora Welty's 'Why I Live at the P.O.,'" *Arkansas Review: A Journal of Delta Studies* 32, no. 3 (December 2001): 201–206.

Welty, Eudora. *A Curtain of Green and Other Stories.* New York: Harcourt Brace Jovanovich, 1941.

Wide Sargasso Sea Jean Rhys (1966)

In the novel *Wide Sargasso Sea* the Caribbean fiction writer Jean RHYS uses MADNESS to elucidate Charlotte BRONTË's characterization of Bertha Mason ROCHESTER, the female monster in *JANE EYRE* (1847). Antoinette Cosway, the bartered bride of Edward Rochester, accepts a stuffy suitor seeking a union with a teenaged girl who offers £30,000 in dowry. Fearful scenes of voodoo and DREAMSCAPES of unnamed perils precipitate rebellion against the betrothal until Rochester wins Antoinette's trust with promises of loving care. Their marriage begins with physical attraction between the sexually appealing Rochester and his Jamaican wife, who releases a vibrant SEXUALITY that both delights and unsettles Rochester. Although Antoinette looks forward to a FAIRY TALE life in a new land, she experiences a series of dreams that predict a cold cell in an unfeeling English household far from the island warmth and natural grandeur she has known.

Rhys stresses the importance of surrogate motherhood to Antoinette after her own mother's lapse into insanity. Christophine, the steely-eyed family housekeeper and obeah priestess, is a wedding gift to Annette Cosway, Antoinette's mother. The elderly servant knows about the tensions that assail Annette in her memories of a riot of black islanders who burned the family home and caused the death of Annette's baby brother, Pierre, and of Coco the parrot. Separated from Christophine at Mount Calvary Convent school, Antoinette endures taunts from black students. She survives 18 months of convent prayers and enforced modesty and rebels against false gentility by embroidering pious samplers with brightly colored silk roses, a subversion of the white rose, the traditional symbol of the VIRGIN MARY. The feeling of displacement carries over to Antoinette's marriage and her need for a love philtre to restore Rochester's passion for her. The damning evidence of the name *Bertha*, which he renames her, attests to his distaste for her island ways. As the marriage falls apart, Antoinette has two defenders—Christophine and Aunt Cora, who rages at the theft of her niece's inheritance. Neither woman can deflect the menace that threatens to unleash the girl's inherited mental instability.

Rhys introduces a new identity in Antoinette in part 3, in which the new Mrs. Rochester loses possession of mind, husband, and position. She falls under the care of Grace Poole, a keeper who demands double wages to tend an insane wife. The story characterizes the splintered personality in memories of the red dress that Antoinette wore in Jamaica. As though inflamed by its swirling skirts, she plots retreat from Rochester's estate. In dreams Antoinette relives the long voyage to the British Isles. She sees herself escaping the locked chamber and setting the house afire. On the battlements as Rochester observes her manic behavior, she reenters her island self and leaps to the pavement below. Her death frees Rochester of an oversexed island sybarite, the pariah he hides from polite society. Rhys empathizes with the outsider for her naive romanticism and her failure as a trophy bride.

Bibliography

Rhys, Jean. *Wide Sargasso Sea.* New York: W. W. Norton, 1982.

Su, John J. " 'Once I Would Have Gone Back . . . but Not Any Longer': Nostalgia and Narrative Ethics in 'Wide Sargasso Sea,' " *CRITIQUE: Studies in Contemporary Fiction* 44, no. 2 (Winter 2003): 157–174.

Uraizee, Joy. " 'She Walked Away without Looking Back': Christophine and the Enigma of History in Jean Rhy's 'Wide Sargasso Sea,' " *CLIO* 38, no. 3 (Spring 1999): 261.

Wife of Bath

An ebullient, life-loving female traveler in Geoffrey Chaucer's *Canterbury Tales* (1387), Alys, the coarse, bumptious Wife of Bath, adds spice to a medieval travel tapestry. Among the 29 people who set out on a pilgrimage from the Tabard Inn in Southwark, England, on April 17, she contributes liberal sprinklings of her feminist point of view and chatty reminiscences of her five husbands and "oother compaignye in youthe" (Chaucer, 21). Her justification of women's overt SEXUALITY is remarkable for the 14th century. She stands apart from the male-dominant company by relating a woman's idiosyncratic STORYTELLING with a tale drawn from Jean de Meung's version of *Le roman de la rose* (The Romance of the Rose, 1277). After an 856-line discourse she relates in half that length, the quest episode of an Arthurian knight. He eludes a death sentence by accepting the wisdom of an elderly WISEWOMAN about the thing that women most love. He follows the chivalric code by keeping his promise to marry the old sage, whom he transforms into a beautiful bride with a single kiss, a metamorphosis that parallels the FAIRY TALE of Snow White. The exemplum supports Alys's belief that men who respect women's intellect reap rewards in sexual satisfaction and a contented marriage.

Dame Alys is familiar with marital woes. From her hobby of collecting husbands she speaks freely of flirtation, split maidenheads, lechery, extramarital dalliance, and bedtime frolics initiated by women. In a swipe at biblical PATRIARCHY she asks, "Where comanded [God] virginitee?" (*ibid.*, 76). She denounces the apostle Paul as a lawgiver with no experience of women: "Whan he speketh of maydenhede, / He seyde that precept therof hadde he noon," a point that feminists make against the misogynistic letters of the founder of Christianity (*ibid.*, 76). In Alys's logic perpetual virginity would cancel God's intent that humankind should mate and multiply to populate the Earth. She concludes, "If ther were no seed ysowe, / Virginitee, thanne wherof sholde it growe?" (*ibid.*). As in the Chinese concept of yin and yang, Alys justifies human coition as the necessary sequel to idealistic sexual purity.

Alys's insistence on freedom for married women sets her apart from the example of the IDEAL WOMAN, Griselda, a literary foil in the Clerk's Tale, whose submission to her husband uplifts her from reality to near-sainthood. In humorous episodes Alys describes the sufferings of her wandering fourth husband, whom she assures her listeners went to heaven as a reward for tolerating the purgatory of marriage. She charges Jankyn, her fifth husband, with the delusion of Oxford intellectuals that the most valuable women are the saints depicted in medieval hagiography. To annoy Alys, Jankyn reads aloud each night from a "book of wikked wyves" (*ibid.*, p. 82). The couple's opposing views of noble womanhood end with mutual battery and Jankyn's apology. The uproar clears the air of private griefs. Alys declares, "I was to hym as kynde / As any wyf . . . / And also trewe, and so was he to me" (*ibid.*, 84). Her story concludes similarly with the knight's wife in new form—rejuvenated, agreeable, and obedient to a man of honor. True to her snippy tone, Alys ends with a curse calling down a plague from Christ to shorten the lives of husbands who are "olde and angry nygardes of dispence," a precursor of Nathaniel Hawthorne's Roger Chillingworth in *The SCARLET LETTER* (1850) (*ibid.*, 88). Chaucer's feminist stance appears to have influenced the pro-woman philosophy of the author CHRISTINE DE PISAN, author of *Livre de la cité des dames* (*Book of the City of Ladies*, ca. 1405).

Bibliography

Chaucer, Geoffrey. *The Works of Geoffrey Chaucer.* Boston: Houghton Mifflin, 1961.

Chute, Marchette. *Geoffrey Chaucer of England.* New York: E. P. Dutton, 1946.

Rigby, S. H. "The Wife of Bath, Christine de Pizan, and the Medieval Case for Women," *Chaucer Review* 32, no. 2 (Fall 2000): 133–165.

Wilder, Laura Ingalls (1867–1957)

One of the spokeswomen who first touch the minds of children, the diarist and author Laura Elizabeth Ingalls Wilder produced a feminist saga that expresses the courage and autonomy of women and disrupts the myth of staunch males of the American frontier. The daughter of pioneers seeking new opportunities in the Midwest, she grew up in rural farm country in a series of homes in six states. Choosing new land and building a home are the work of her father, Charles Ingalls; the rest of the homemaking falls to her mother, Caroline Quiner Ingalls, who manages family life in a covered wagon, log cabin, and sod house. The matriarchal underpinnings of Wilder's family parallel those of Louisa May ALCOTT's children's classic *LITTLE WOMEN* (1868–69), in which a family of girls learn early to emulate their life-affirming mother and her traits in the next generation. In lieu of schooling Laura's mother reads aloud and teaches the girls to read and write. By dancing a jig in old age, Laura's French-Canadian grandmother sets the tone of female strength and the endurance of frequent moves deeper into the wilderness.

While the Ingalls family lived in Wisconsin and later on the Kansas prairie and in Walnut Grove, Minnesota, and De Smet, South Dakota, Laura and her sisters, Mary and Carrie, learned the domestic responsibilities of making cheese, salting fish, and stoking a smokehouse fire, tasks Wilder describes in *Little House in the Big Woods* (1932), *Little House on the Prairie* (1935), *On the Banks of Plum Creek* (1937), and *By the Shores of Silver Lake* (1939). The saga continues in the diary *On the Way Home: The Diary of a Trip from South Dakota to Mansfield, Missouri, in 1874* (1962), a glimpse of Laura's rearing of her daughter, Rose. In their father's absence Laura, her sisters, and their mother, Caroline, keep the homestead functioning while they watch out for attacks by Osage, wolves, panthers, and bears. In Pa's absence to trade furs in town Ma and Laura ready the table for dinner and complete barn chores. Wilder characterizes motherly education as Laura helps with dairy work by superintending the lantern: "Laura was proud to be helping Ma with the milking, and she carried the lantern very carefully" (Wilder, *Little House in the Big Woods*, 103). Wilder does not belabor the fact that the lantern illuminates the barn but also threatens equipment and livestock if it is dropped into the straw. Likewise, the author understates the danger from a marauding bear, which Ma and Laura elude with swift, but unpanicked actions.

Wilder's women flourish because work receives appreciation. Rewards appear the next morning, when Pa gives his daughters candy and calico for dresses. Examples of femininity from Aunt Docia and Aunt Ruty impress on Laura and her sister how to braid and coil their hair in neat circlets out of the way of domestic duties and how to use plain sealing wax and a darning needle to make a rose for hair decoration. The paired lessons create in Wilder's young women a balance between domestic drudgery and the moments of relaxation when women dress up for a feast and dancing. Completing the scene is the square dance to "The Irish Washerwoman," a song of toil and marital abuse that the fiddle transforms into a cheerful jig to add sparkle to the evening (ibid., 146).

Wilder's self-sufficiency bolstered her family after her husband, Almanzo "Manly" Wilder, suffered a stroke. In her 40s while the family lived on a farm in Mansfield, Missouri, she edited the *Missouri Ruralist*. She began publishing essays in the *Christian Science Monitor, Country Gentleman, McCall's, Missouri State Farmer,* and Saint Louis newspapers. She organized local farm women and, with the aid of her daughter, the journalist Rose Wilder Lane, uplifted her neighbors during the Great Depression with optimistic articles on community and thrift. As did the frontier authors Willa CATHER, Mary Hunter AUSTIN, and Jessamyn WEST, Wilder affirmed women's autonomy and self-reliance during the settlement of the American West by defeating the helpless female stereotype. Humanistic lessons in these works cover local cooperation, responsibility, and generosity as well as national patriotism, racial tolerance, and stoicism. A cultural icon, Wilder won a Newbery-Caldecott Award and the first American Library Association Laura Ingalls Wilder Award for her images of female self-reliance. Her works inspired the ecofeminist Barbara KINGSOLVER and the novelist Sena NASLUND.

Bibliography

Fellman, Anita Clair. " 'Don't Expect to Depend on Anybody Else': The Frontier as Portrayed in the Little House Books," *Children's Literature* 24 (1996): 101–116.

Miller, John. *Laura Ingalls Wilder's Little Town: Where History and Literature Meet.* Lawrence: University Press of Kansas, 1994.

Romines, Ann. *Constructing the Little House: Gender, Culture, and Laura Ingalls Wilder.* Amherst: University of Massachusetts Press, 1997.

Wilder, Laura Ingalls. *Little House in the Big Woods.* New York: HarperTrophy, 1953.

———. *Little House on the Prairie.* New York: HarperTrophy, 1953.

———. *On the Way Home: The Diary of a Trip from South Dakota to Mansfield, Missouri, in 1874.* New York: HarperTrophy, 1976.

Williams, Patricia (1951–)

The teacher, social critic, and columnist Patricia Joyce Williams takes a sane, studied approach to feminist quandaries that worsen 21st-century culture wars. She is the great-great granddaughter of Sophie Miller, a Tennessee slave woman and mother to Williams's great-grandmother, Mary, sired by a white attorney. Williams's grandfather overcame slavery and miscegenation by graduating from Meharry Medical College in 1907. A native of Boston and the only black child in her neighborhood, the author was readying herself for elementary school after desegregation demanded by the *Brown v. Board of Education* decision. White flight emptied the environs of familiar faces as blacks altered the racial dynamics of the community. Williams, who became one of the first black female graduates of Wellesley College, took up her great-grandfather's profession by earning a degree from Harvard Law School. She taught contract law at the City University of New York, Dartmouth College, University of Wisconsin Law School, and Columbia University Law School.

Williams's intellectual development in the late 20th century nudged her toward an understanding of domestic quandaries. In "Diary of a Mad Law Professor," a regular column for the *Nation,* she creates thoughtful essays and humanistic parables on inequities of race, class, and gender. She collected her scholarly thoughts in *The Alchemy of Race and Rights* (1991). The introduction lists one view of her writings as "the exclusive interdisciplinary property of constitutional law, contract, African-American history, feminist jurisprudence, political science, and rhetoric" (Williams, 1991, 6). She accepts the estimation as a compliment for being a trendy black female intellectual.

To satisfy her family's desire for grandchildren, at age 41 Williams became a single working mother after adopting a son, Peter Williams, whose presence in her life generated new insights on racial bias and female depression. Williams published *The Rooster's Egg: On the Persistence of Prejudice* (1995) and *Seeing a Colorblind Future: The Paradox of Race* (1997), a collection of five lectures on social topics. In 2000 she received a MacArthur Fellowship of $500,000 for academic excellence in examining American law and championing consumer rights. In 2004 she mused on the harsh criticism of far Right conservatives in *Open House: Of Family, Friends, Food, Piano Lessons, and the Search for a Room of My Own*. In the first essay she jokes about her Leftist tendencies in a self-appraisal: "I have no regrets. I like the independence. My life is good. When not consumed by official duties as a politically correct feminazi black single mother, I read poetry" (Williams, 2004, 6). Her sane and unexaggerated examination of women's problems wins her a steady readership and vocal give and take from letters to the editor.

Bibliography

Lee, Felicia R. "Having Her Say," *Essence* 35, no. 7 (November 2004): 136.

Williams, Patricia J. *The Alchemy of Race and Rights.* Cambridge, Mass.: Harvard University Press, 1991.

———. *Open House: Of Family, Friends, Food, Piano Lessons, and the Search for a Room of My Own.* New York: Farrar, Straus & Giroux, 2004.

———. *Seeing a Colorblind Future: The Paradox of Race.* New York: Noonday Press, 1997.

Winchilsea, Anne Finch, countess of
(1661–1720)

The English poet and playwright Anne Kingsmill Finch, countess of Winchilsea, led writers of her day in expressing feminist sentiment. Orphaned early at her birthplace, Sydmonton outside Newbury, Berkshire, she and her sister, Bridget, passed to the custody of their paternal grandmother, Bridget, Lady Kingsmill, until her death in 1672, and then to that of their maternal uncle, William Haslewood. Both girls studied history, French and Italian, classical literature, poetry, drama, and the Bible. By 1681 the restoration of Charles II altered family fortunes with the selection of Anne as a maid of honor to Mary of Modena, duchess of York. Married at age 23, Finch settled at Eastwell Park, Kent, where she wrote feminist verse and cultivated friendships with the poets Alexander Pope and Jonathan Swift. She furthered a lively competition by mailing both writers her poems.

Finch was one of the first Englishwomen to publish poetry. In 1701 the anthologist Charles Gildon collected her poems and a play, *Aristomenes; or, The Royal Shepherd*, in *New Collection of Poems on Several Occasions*. She published one volume, *Miscellany Poems on Several Occasions* (1713), at first anonymously, then in a second edition bearing her name. Among the poems is "A Letter to Daphnis, April 2, 1685" (1713), a verse epistle on happiness in wedlock. She admits, "My hopes and joys are bounded all in you," a reference to her beloved husband, the soldier and courtier Heneage Finch (Finch, 20). As her health declined in 1715, she gave up satire, humor, and parody and began writing religious works, some published posthumously.

Finch longed for a thorough EDUCATION in women's history, which was unavailable in the Restoration era. In the poems "The Circuit of Apollo" (1702) and "The Introduction" (1737), she expresses hero worship of the biblical judge Deborah and the English playwright Aphra BEHN. The poet lamented the DOUBLE STANDARD that applied a singular set of rules to women's behavior and interests. She saw the powerlessness of women as immutable: "All in vain are prayers, ecstatic thoughts, / Recovered moments and retracted faults" (*ibid.*). Nonetheless, she responded to denigration of women in Pope's mock epic *The Rape of the Lock* with the poem "The Answer" (1717), a fine-edged, but polite retort to his depiction of the antiheroic Belinda, a vain, silly social butterfly.

Often pilloried in print and snubbed in person by anti-intellectuals, Finch suffered depression. She expressed the strife in her career in "Fragment" (1713), a poem that identifies her with the pastoral name Ardelia and speaks of her intellect as "female clay" (*ibid.*, 17). She is most admired for a Pindaric ode, "The Spleen" (1713), a vehicle for her bitterness against a society that denied women a place in literature. In "To the Nightingale" (1713), she worded her praise with careful subtextual commentary on her own songs: "This Moment is thy Time to sing, / This Moment I attend to Praise, / And set my Numbers to thy Layes. / Free as shine shall be my Song; / As thy Musick, short, or long. / Muse, thy Promise now fulfill!" (*ibid.*, 67). Her feminist verse maintains that women writers must persevere in their art as a personal outlet, a concept much favored by Simone de BEAUVOIR and Virginia WOOLF.

Bibliography

Finch, Anne. *Anne Finch, Countess of Winchilsea: Selected Poems.* New York: Routledge, 2003.

Hinnant, C. H. "Song and Speech in Anne Finch's 'To the Nightingale,'" *Studies in English Literature* 31, no. 3 (Summer 1991): 499–513.

Winnemucca, Sarah (1844–1891)

The Native American scholar, teacher, and trilingual orator Sarah Winnemucca championed Native American families and campaigned for their rights. Born in Humboldt Lake, Nevada, to Tuboitony and Old Winnemucca, a shaman and headman of the Northern Paiute, she bore the name Thocmetony (Shellflower). At age 13 she received her Christian name, that of the biblical wife of Abraham. Tuboitony and other women set the pattern of defiant feminism by rejecting male plans to move from the desert homeland closer to white settlements because the MATRIARCHY who influenced Paiute life feared that the move would court the danger of sexual predators. As did other female Paiutes, Sarah became a formidable debater and horsewoman. She earned her family's respect by rescuing them from an enemy camp.

At age 20 Winnemucca journeyed to Virginia City, Nevada, to beg for food and donations for her starving people. Four years later she scouted and interpreted for the U.S. Cavalry. In April 1870 she composed letters to supervisors of Indians in her state and in Washington, D.C., requesting farmland and training in agriculture. She denounced the duplicity of racists posing as Christians and supported full citizenship for women as a means of injecting the female point of view into U.S. legislation. As the wife of Lt. Edward C. Bartlett, an abusive alcoholic, she supported the family and

continued lecturing and writing treatises on the plight of the Paiute. When her people resettled on Malheur Reservation, Oregon, in April 1875, she taught bilingual classes and worked as reservation mediator until her defiance of a cruel sexist Indian agent caused her expulsion from government land.

In her 30s Winnemucca gained repatriation during a rebellion of the Bannock, when the cavalry needed her services as a charismatic negotiator. She spoke to large audiences on the hardships of Paiute women, who traveled long distances to gather firewood, roots, bird eggs, and healing plants. In 1880 she conferred with Secretary of the Interior Carl Schurz and President Rutherford B. Hayes on behalf of women and children confined to the Yakima Reservation. While she visited Boston the following year, she networked with Elizabeth Palmer Peabody and Mary Mann, philanthropists who supported her demand for government aid to Paiute families and who funded Winnemucca's tour of six states. Winnemucca published *Life among the Piutes: Their Wrongs and Claims* (1883), the first AUTOBIOGRAPHY of a Native American woman. Before her death of tuberculosis she established a bicultural school at Lovelock, Nevada, and extended her campaign for Indian rights to a demand for citizenship and SUFFRAGE.

Bibliography

McClure, Andrew S. "Sarah Winnemucca: [Post]Indian Princess and Voice of the Paiutes," *MELUS* 24, no. 2 (Summer 1999): 29–51.

Winnemucca, Sarah. *Life among the Piutes: Their Wrongs and Claims.* Lincoln: University of Nevada Press, 1994.

Zanjani, Sally. *Sarah Winnemucca.* Lincoln: University of Nebraska Press, 2001.

wisewomen

The gemlike advice of wisewomen is a constant in feminist literature. In the description of the Jungian psychoanalyst Clarissa Pinkola ESTÉS, author of *Women Who Run with the Wolves* (1992), the bearer of wisdom is *La Que Sabe* (the One Who Knows), an intuitive female icon who knows humanity from the outside in (Estés, 76). Authors link the old ones with aphorism and STORYTELLING, myths of PHILOMELA and EVE, LA LLORONA's haunting songs, legends of LILITH and SPIDER WOMAN, and TALK-STORY, all manifestations of the global phenomenon of woman-to-woman oral education of the young. The faith of the old ones in their instinctive knowing sets them apart from ordinary humanity and allies them with GODDESS LORE. In Estés's introduction to the Slavic wisewoman tale "Vasalisa" the narrative refers to an in-between cognitive state, "the world between worlds where nothing is as it first seems" (*ibid.*, 77). The story describes the knowledge passed from a dying mother to her untried daughter, a CINDERELLA figure, and the quest that takes the girl into the forest. Her willingness to undergo a trial of courage sets her apart from her stepmother and sisters. In the conclusion the bright light of wisdom "burnt the wicked trio to cinders" (*ibid.*, 82).

Folklore tends to charge crones with two extremes, MADNESS and prophecy. The Roman epicist Virgil scripted the DUALITY in the erratic actions of the Cumaean Sybil, a deranged visionary. The ethnographer Paula Gunn ALLEN reshaped the double-stranded gift into a blessing in *Spider Woman's Granddaughters: Traditional Tales and Contemporary Writing by Native American Women* (1990). A list of feminist titles—Isabel ALLENDE's *The* HOUSE OF THE SPIRITS (1981), Marion Zimmer BRADLEY's *The Mists of Avalon* (1982), Terry McMILLAN's *Mama* (1987), Laurel Thatcher ULRICH's *A Midwife's Tale: The Life of Martha Ballard, Based on Her Diary, 1785–1812* (1990), and Velma WALLIS's *Two Old Women: An Alaska Legend of Betrayal, Courage and Survival* (1993)— honor the shared experiences of elderly women. Repeated motifs of persecution and a female holocaust warn of the world's hesitation to accept the philosophy and insights of aging females. Suffering social ostracism are the least refined and least empowered, such as the orator and evangelist Sojourner TRUTH, Phoenix Jackson, the heroic grandmother in Eudora WELTY's story "A Worn Path" (1941), and Nancha, the maternal cook in Laura ESQUIVEL's kitchen-centered novel *Like Water for Chocolate* (1989). In 1981 Erica JONG's book *Witches* identified the pervasive ambivalence toward female sages as a time-honored male preju-

dice: "That the female principle is dark, unruly, anarchic, while the male is orderly, rational, wise" (Jong, 15). Typically it is women who seek counsel from wisewomen and who profit from matriarchal survival of earthly pain and gendered sufferings, the dominant themes in Ann PETRY's *Tituba of Salem Village* (1964), historical fiction that gives ear to the woman whom history accuses of importing Caribbean voodoo to Massachusetts Colony.

Social turmoil increases the need for the wisewoman's consolation for losses and pitiless fate. In Elizabeth Stuart PHELPS's popular utopian novel *The Gates Ajar* (1868) Aunt Winifred possesses insight into historic shifts, including the after-conflict turmoil besetting U.S. war widows in the late 1860s. Another wise viewer of the Reconstruction era is Mammy, Margaret MITCHELL's redoubtable maid of all work and surrogate mother in GONE WITH THE WIND (1936). The characterization of a female majordomo confers on Mammy an understanding of white women and their need of black servants. She helps to maintain the illusion of white fragility and propriety, an old-guard notion destroyed by the fall of the plantation South. When Uncle Peter arrives at Tara, she scolds him for leaving unguarded Pittypat Hamilton, a child-woman accustomed to protection: "Huccome you leave Miss Pitty by herseff lak dis w'en she so scary lak? You know well's Ah do Miss Pitty ain' never live by herself an' she been shakin' in her lil shoes ever since she come back frum Macom" (Mitchell, 496). In the novel's melodramatic conclusion Mammy accounts for the source of her wisdom in racial insight: "Niggers knows a heap of things quicker dan w'ite folks" (*ibid.*, 984). She follows her instinct after the separation of Rhett Butler and Scarlett Butler by returning to Tara as though obeying the hovering spirit of Ellen Robillard O'Hara, her former mistress. Mammy's departure from Atlanta implies the doom of the heroine to loneliness and social ostracism for her repeated rebellions against Atlanta's gendered code of conduct.

Mothering and counsel are parallel motifs in literature about improvident choices. In Jean RHYS's slim novella WIDE SARGASSO SEA (1966) the wisdom accrued along with gray hair offers a frail backup to the motherless Antoinette Cosway, fiancée of the grasping English suitor, Edward

Rochester. Aunt Cora views the patriarchal betrothal arranged between father and future husband as a damnable infringement on woman's freedom. She considers the man-to-man deal an outright theft of her niece's inheritance. Christophine, a forbidding nanny and obeah practitioner whom Annette received as a wedding present, warns the inexperienced daughter Antoinette to escape the MARRIAGE MARKET and flee an unpromising union with an outsider bent on quick riches through matrimony. In island patois Christophine sings, "The children leave us, will they come back?" (Rhys, 20). In contrast to the womanly self-confidence of her two protectors, Antoinette admits that her prayers "fell to the ground meaning nothing" (*ibid.*, 61). As the time for departure from Jamaica nears, Antoinette climbs the hill to Christophine's hut and inhales the clean odor of starched and ironed cottons. The restoration of domestic order causes the young woman to think, "This is my place and this is where I belong" (*ibid.*, 108). The older woman gives good advice—escape from the unsuitable husband while there is still an opportunity.

Less aggressive than Christophine is Toni MORRISON's stalwart Grandma Baby Suggs, holy, the folk therapist for former slaves in BELOVED (1987). Called Jenny Whitlow at birth, she extends an all-inclusive grandmotherhood to shamed, hurting, emotionally wracked blacks. To Sethe, her daughter-in-law, Grandma Baby extends gentle words and healing touch to soothe away the terrors of giving birth on the run from Sweet Home Plantation. To exorcise hauntings from slave times, the wise elder gathers a congregation at a clearing near her safe house and leads a vocal exercise in self-love. Conferring grace as Christ does in the Beatitudes, Grandma Baby delivers her own Sermon on the Mount, a spiritual caress that begins with a welcome, "Let the children come!" (Morrison, 87). From hospitality and acceptance she builds on positive images of laughter, dance, cries, and joy in the flesh. The climax of her sermon is an inner cleansing: "More than your life-holding womb and your life-giving private parts, hear me now, love your heart. For this is the prize" (*ibid.*, 89). For all the heartache of her own life Grandma Baby departs as easy as cream, Sethe's description of a well-earned calm demise that ends a wise and tender ministry.

Bibliography

Estés, Clarissa Pinkola. *Women Who Run with the Wolves: Myths and Stories about the Wild Woman Archetype.* New York: Ballantine, 1997.

Jong, Erica. *Witches.* New York: Harry N. Abrams, 1999.

Mitchell, Margaret. *Gone with the Wind.* New York: Time Warner, 1964.

Morrison, Toni. *Beloved.* New York: Plume, 1987.

Rhys, Jean. *Wide Sargasso Sea.* New York: W. W. Norton, 1982.

Wit **Margaret Edson** (1999)

Margaret EDSON gained recognition for her play *Wit*, which moved slowly into the mainstream. It migrated from the Long Wharf Theatre in New Haven, Connecticut, to Winnepeg to Broadway's Union Square Theatre in 1999. The drama reached a larger audience in 2001, when Emma Thompson played the role of 50-year-old Dr. Vivian Bearing in the HBO-TV adaptation.

In an austere setting Bearing, a knowledge-driven academic, survives the initial eight-month treatment for ovarian cancer in an isolation ward by reciting supportive lines from 17th-century verse and by analyzing word etymology. The onslaught of impersonal treatment, medical indignities, and experimentation by Dr. Harvey Kelekian, a brusque academic, reduces the patient to a frail, bedfast form clinging to life. During grand rounds he barely acknowledges her presence with a chipper remark: "Dr. Bearing. Full dose. Excellent. Keep pushing the fluids" (Edson, 40). As the cancer metastasizes to her pelvis and femurs and pain erodes her courage, she curses Kelekian for failing to see what full-course chemotherapy does to her body and mind.

Edson introduces SISTERHOOD as a source of Vivian's redemption. Contributing to the misery of vomiting, wakefulness, and groaning are the visits of Dr. Jason Posner, an oncology fellow and Kelekian's assistant, who treats a disease rather than a human being: "Professor Bearing. How are you feeling today? Three p.m. IV hydration totals. Two thousand in. Thirty out. Uh-oh. That's it. Kidneys gone" (*ibid.*, 81). The dialogue counters the hubris of the mad scientist stereotype with the woman-to-woman respect and kindness of the primary nurse,

Susie Monahan, who dispenses hand lotion and conveys her concern for Vivian's last moments. With only days left to live Vivian swims through morphine-dimmed pain to register the thought that oncology drugs are more predatory than a malignant tumor at wiping out her self-esteem and will to live. Susie's remedy for middle-of-the-night terrors are a shared Popsicle and a promise to remain close until the patient's death. In the final scene Susie faces down the crash team, who ignore Vivian's wish not to be resuscitated. The play is often included in curricula of women's studies, pretheology, and premedical courses.

Bibliography

Eads, Martha Greene, "Unwitting Redemption in Margaret Edson's 'Wit,'" *Christianity and Literature* 51, no. 2 (Winter 2002): 241–255.

Edson, Margaret. *Wit.* New York: Faber & Faber, 1999.

witchcraft

The subject of sorcery and the persecution of alleged witches forms a singular strand of the WISE-WOMEN branch of feminist literature. Compilers of medieval examples of the black arts skewed facts by injecting issues of class, gender, and EDUCATION in accounts of the accused satanists Sibillia and Pierina de' Bugatis of Milan; the prostitute Margot de la Barre of Paris; the graverobber Catherine Delort; the madwoman Angèle de la Barthe of Toulouse, France; and martyred heretics Jehenna de Brigue of Meaux, France, and Alice Kyteler of Ireland. In *The WOMAN'S BIBLE* (1895–1898) the commentator Elizabeth Cady STANTON expressed her outrage at the use of witchcraft as an excuse to torture and murder such women, often for the delight of onlookers. She charged clergymen with dragging innocent females before corrupt judges: "While women were tortured, drowned, and burned by the thousands, scarce one wizard to a hundred was ever condemned. . . . The same distinction of sex appears in our own day. One code of morals for men, another for women" (Stanton, 93–94). The social critics Barbara EHRENREICH and Deirdre English, authors of *Witches, Midwives, and Nurses: A History of Women Healers* (1973), explain the lack of credible firsthand testimony: "Un-

fortunately, the witch herself—poor and illiterate—did not leave us her story. It was recorded, like all history, by the educated elite, so that today we know the witch only through the eyes of her persecutors" (Ehrenreich and English, 8). The text blames church and state for organizing witch hunts, fanning hysteria, and carrying the campaign through to a feminist holocaust concluding in the display of burned and mutilated female corpses.

Late in the American SUFFRAGE crusade the feminist historian and polemicist Matilda Joslyn GAGE compiled a chronicle on diabolism in chapter 5 of *Women, Church, and State* (1895), a controversial diatribe against Christianity's subjugation of women to male control. Of the cruelties to alleged sorcerers, she explained that Charlemagne's creation of the Holy Roman Empire resulted in aggrandizing of an earthly king to rival the pope. The great Gallic king wielded powers over the church and its priests: "He forced Christianity upon the Saxons at immense sacrifice of life, added to the wealth and power of the clergy by tithe lands, recognized their judicial and canonical authority, made marriage illegal without priestly sanction and still further degraded womanhood through his own polygamy" (Gage, 221). His sanctioning of torture of evil women reached fearful extremes: "At first, young children and women expecting motherhood, were exempted, but afterwards neither age nor condition freed them from accusation and torture, and women even in the pangs of maternity were burned at the stake" (ibid., 223). In a footnote Gage cites a case from the isle of Guernsey: "A married woman with child, was delivered in the midst of her torments, and the infant, just rescued, was tossed back into the flames by a priest with the cry, 'One heretic the less'" (ibid.). Gage blames the androcentric church for self-corruption through its love of power and treachery.

The issue of collective hysteria against the unknown emerges in numerous feminist texts, particularly imputations against the dramatic character Mistress Hibbins, "the bitter-tempered widow of the magistrate" in Nathaniel Hawthorne's allegorical romance *The SCARLET LETTER* (1850) (Hawthorne, 113). In his typical ambiguous fashion, he pictures the "reputed witch-lady" confronting the Reverend Arthur Dimmesdale, an unrepentant hypocrite and father of an illegitimate daughter (*ibid.*, 215). Mistress Hibbins promises to escort him into the forest to gain him "a fair reception from yonder potentate you wot of!," a sly reference to camaraderie with Satan (*ibid.*). As the meeting time and place she chooses the deserted woods at midnight, a romantic touch linking Mistress Hibbins to such women as Ann Turner, a victim falsely charged and hanged for murdering Sir Thomas Overbury, and Tituba, a historical Barbadian slave jailed in Massachusetts Colony for instructing white girls in witchery and fortune telling. Hawthorne pictures Mistress Hibbins as an outsider viewing the otherness of Hester PRYNNE and acknowledging the threat of religious hypocrisy in a male-dominated theocracy. A less subversive interpretation of Mistress Hibbins as an herbalist and teacher of colonial women is Joan Plowright's creative role in the 1995 Cinergi film *The Scarlet Letter*, starring Demi Moore and Gary Oldman as Hester Prynne and Arthur Dimmesdale.

More thoroughly than Hawthorne, the historical novelist Ann PETRY, author of *Tituba of Salem Village* (1964), gave serious thought to the male perversion of STORYTELLING and of female knowledge of nature as sorcery. In detailing the hanging of Witch Glover, Petry refers to the victim as "an old woman, dirty, crazy," a testimony to the mounting misogyny against the aged, disabled, penniless, and hungry females of Salem and its environs (Petry, 27). An eyewitness reports on the sport of executing witches as an occasion calling for a group tipple at the local tavern, "so many they couldn't even sit down. And they drank rum and laughed and said, 'A hanging is thirsty work'" (*ibid.*). The lightheartedness of male persecutors signifies the insignificance of female sufferings and the absence of social and legal deterrents to lawlessness and lynching.

Petry lambastes local fury as mob violence. As hysteria mounts and religious mania seizes the community, Tituba retreats from beatings and implications of bewitching by dreaming of Barbados, picturing herself free at the edge of its blue water and shady palm clusters. For her ability to fantasize better times, John Parris accuses her of being a night flier capable of "[being] in two places at once" (*ibid.*, 198). Under the stern eyes of the judges Corin and Hathorne, Tituba fares poorly.

Transported to Boston, locked in a cold cell, and chained by the leg, she and her hapless companions quail at the news: "They're catchin' witches in Salem Village just like they was chickens on a roost" (*ibid.*, 250). By May 1693, when the hysteria dies down, 20 women have died, one in her cell and 19 others on the gallows.

After the mid-20th-century women's liberation movement began, feminist literature returned to unsettled issues of woman baiting and the hounding of lone and eccentric female elders. The black poet Lucille CLIFTON welcomed supernatural powers in the young as symbols of matrilineal connection to Earth's powers. In the poem "If Our Grandchild Be a Girl" (1987) the speaker hopes for six-fingered hands as symbols of tribal powers that date to Dahomean ancestors. In 1981 Erica JONG surveyed the history of sorcery in *Witches*, a text that characterizes practitioners of Wicca as "merely women who were not afraid to fly" (Jong, 2). Of the gendered prejudice surrounding witchery Jong intones a capsule history: "Her father is man. Her midwife, his fears. Her torturer, his fears. Her executioner, his fears. Her malignant power, his fears. Her healing power, her own" (*ibid.*, 12).

Bibliography

Dukats, Mara L. "The Hybrid Terrain of Literary Imagination: Maryse Conde's Black Witch of Salem, Nathaniel Hawthorne's Hester Prynne, and Aime Cesaire's Heroic Poetic Voice," *College Literature* 22, no. 1 (February 1995): 51–61.

Ehrenreich, Barbara, and Deirdre English. *Witches, Midwives and Nurses: A History of Women Healers*. New York: Feminist Press, 1973.

Gage, Matilda Joslyn. *Woman, Church, and State* (1895). Available online. URL: http://www.sacred-texts.com/wmn/wcs/. Accessed on October 14, 2005.

Hawthorne, Nathaniel. *The Complete Novels and Selected Tales of Nathaniel Hawthorne*. New York: Modern Library, 1937.

Jong, Erica. *Witches*. New York: Harry N. Abrams, 1999.

Petry, Ann. *Tituba of Salem Village*. New York: Thomas Y. Crowell, 1964.

Stanton, Elizabeth Cady. *The Woman's Bible* (1895–1898). Available online. URL: http://www.sacred-texts.com/wmn/wb/. Accessed on October 17, 2005.

Williams, Anne. *Art of Darkness: A Poetics of Gothic.* Chicago: University of Chicago Press, 1995.

Wolf, Christa (1929–)

The leading literary voice of Germany, Christa Ihlenfeld Wolf is an outspoken pacifist who protests typically male obsessions with heroism, militarism, and PATRIARCHY. A native of Gorzów Wielkopolski, Poland, she came of age during Hitler's rise to power. She survived the European nightmare of World War II as well as a severe lung infection and studied philology in Jena and Leipzig before establishing a career in editing. When Communism crumbled, she protested the reunification of Germany, which she felt demonized the German Democratic Republic and obliterated its heroic recovery from Nazism.

In feminist revisions of Greek mythology Wolf resets iconic figures as contemporaries. She revisits the scorned Trojan woman in *Cassandra* (1987), a doom-laden survey of her life as royal princess in the house of Priam and as priestess of Apollo. A magical reverse of the silenced female, Cassandra is the truth sayer who wields the gift of prophecy to a people prohibited from believing or trusting her. After accepting her dehumanization and death, which she foresees at the hand of Agamemnon's wife, Clytemnestra, Cassandra withdraws from speech and leaves history to its irrevocable course. In *Medea* (1996), a similar feminist take on the much-maligned wife of the mythic hero Jason, Wolf creates a powerful, yet vulnerable woman abandoned by her husband, ridiculed as a hysteric, and left at the mercy of the public as a scapegoat for Jason's destructive ambitions. The depiction of the famed witch from the Black Sea suggests the author's autobiographical presentation of her own experience with horror during the rise of Nazism and the protracted cold war. By exonerating Cassandra and Medea, the author defends all females whose perspectives carry no weight with a rapacious male hierarchy.

Bibliography

Bridge, Helen. "Christa Wolf's *Kassandra* and *Medea*: Continuity and Change," *German Life and Letters* 57, no. 1 (January 2004): 33–43.

Cormican, Muriel. "Woman's Heterosexual Experience in Christa Wolf's *Kassandra*: A Critique of GDR Feminism," *Philological Quarterly* 81, no. 1 (Winter 2002): 109–128.

Pickle, Linda Schelbitzki. "Christa Wolf's *Cassandra*: Parallels to Feminism in the West," *CRITIQUE: Studies in Contemporary Fiction* 28, no. 3 (Spring 1987): 149–157.

Wolf, Naomi (1962–)

The essayist and lecturer Naomi Wolf provided feminism one of its most powerful slogans, the BEAUTY MYTH. A native of San Francisco, she studied at Yale University and at New College, Oxford University, on a Rhodes Scholarship. She began publishing social criticism in *Esquire, Glamour,* MS., *New Republic, New York Times, Wall Street Journal,* and the *Washington Post.* In one of her most beneficial roles as pro-woman polemicist she exposed the assault on women's egos with her first book, *The Beauty Myth: How Images of Beauty Are Used against Women* (1991), an immediate best seller. The insecurities that emerge in viewers of pop culture predispose women to dependence on fasting, purging, destructive exercise regimens, drugs, and plastic surgery. At the far end of cyclic body abuse lies the mirage of the ideal woman, an impossible standard of loveliness out of reach of all but those born to facial beauty and a pencil-thin body. A parallel to the medieval stereotype of the mother-*hausfrau,* the beauty myth imprisons mind and spirit with an insidious self-abuse that gives no rest to the follower. Self-punishing mythology raises the ante as the 20s give place to middle age and ease into the elder nightmare of wrinkles, bifocals, and paunch. Wolf notes that as women's liberation frees females from economic and legal restrictions, a backlash of the worship of decorative women replaces former hindrances with cruel cynicism. She chooses as an example the Iron Maiden, a German torture device: "The modern hallucination in which women are trapped or trap themselves is similarly rigid, cruel, and euphemistically painted" (Wolf, 2002, 17).

In a subsequent work, *Fire with Fire: The New Female Power and How to Use It* (1993), Wolf bolsters emerging feminists with new role models and strategies and "[offers] a mighty yes to all women's individual wishes to forge their own definition" (Wolf, 1994, 62). She holds up for admiration such women as the author Marilyn FRENCH, the attorney Anita Hill, and the women occupying cabinet positions under President Bill Clinton. In lieu of the polite, receding female, Wolf proposes an elevated image of the female citizen and consumer who grasps an equal place in the social order. A third volume, *Promiscuities: The Secret Struggle for Womanhood* (1997), uses memories of the author's coming of age to interpret and dispel taboos that limit the female's access to a pleasurable sex life. Venturing further into destructive mythology, Wolf produced the feminist take on the isolated mother in *Misconceptions: Truth, Lies, and the Unexpected on the Journey to Motherhood* (2003). The work exposes unnecessary stresses and gendered preconceptions that limit the full integration of the family.

Bibliography

Bendis, Debra. "Intruder in My Arms," *Christian Century*, 19 April 2003, pp. 30–33.

Wolf, Naomi. *The Beauty Myth: How Images of Beauty Are Used against Women*. New York: Perennial, 2002.

———. *Fire with Fire: The New Female Power and How to Use It*. New York: Ballantine Books, 1994.

———. *Misconceptions: Truth, Lies, and the Unexpected on the Journey to Motherhood*. New York: Anchor Books, 2003.

———. *Promiscuities: The Secret Struggle for Womanhood*. New York: Ballantine Books, 1998.

Wolkstein, Diane (1942–)

The Jewish American storyteller, teacher, translator, and mythographer Diane S. Wolkstein preserves the female love stories, parables, and cautionary tales from the original Sanskrit. Born in Maplewood, New Jersey, she learned the gestures and pauses of oral narrative in childhood from her mother and the town rabbi. Drawn to humanistic tales, in her late teens she joined the STORYTELLING renaissance that developed concurrently with the women's movement. With degrees in drama and music education from Smith College and Bank State College, she sought to improve her platform skill through study-

ing mime in Paris and telling Bible stories to English-speaking children in Europe.

At age 23 Wolkstein settled on feminist ethnography as her life's work. She concentrated on familiar Esther lore from Hebrew literature, which she debuted in Paris during children's classes at Temple Copernic. Two years later she moved to Greenwich Village and began a three-decade tradition of telling stories in Central Park. She was enamored of the myth of Inanna, also called Astarte or Ishtar, the Sumerian queen of heaven and Earth and consort of the shepherd-king Dumuzi. Dating two millennia before the Torah, the story teased Wolkstein's mind, causing her to work out details by translating the cuneiform text from bits of 4,000-year-old tablets. When she completed the interpretation, she began performing the Cycle of Inanna for a goddess conference.

With her mentor, Samuel Noah Kramer, Wolkstein published *Inanna: Queen of Heaven and Earth, Her Stories and Hymns from Sumer* (1983), a suite of rhapsodic stories of female maturation, love, sex, fertility, separation, loss, and regeneration. Inanna, the only female accorded her own epic, speaks openly of her wonder at her vulva, the magic entrance to passion and the exit of future children. The author captures the pensive nature of the goddess in direct questions: "How long will it be until I have a shining throne to sit upon? / How long will it be until I have a shining bed to lie upon?" (Wolkstein and Kramer, 5). Inanna looks forward to attaining full womanhood and perceives in the future the net of narratives that will keep her cycle alive. While teaching mythology at Sarah Lawrence College, Wolkstein pursued her understanding of Inanna's longing and its impact on Sanskrit lore and herself became the goddess's conduit.

In 1991 Wolkstein set Inanna's lore in global perspective in *The First Love Stories: From Isis and Osiris to Tristan and Iseult*. By contrasting the loves of Psyche with Eros in Greek mythology, Shiva with Sati in Hindu mythology, the Celtic Iseult with Tristan, and Layla with Majnun in Arabic-Persian romance, the author gives fuller representation to the female side of world myth. She reveals the universal nature of women's sexual longings and their willingness to suffer for a love match of their choosing. She performed the stories orally in Australia, Egypt, England, France, Greece, Ireland, Israel, and Turkey and returned to the United States to give readings at Lincoln Center and at the Smithsonian Institution. She made an audiocassette and video of the Inanna cycle and taught narrative method at Bank State College of Education and at the New School for Social Research. Still immersed in ancient love tales, she compiled *Esther's Story* in 1996, in a fictional diary drawn from strands in the Old Testament and the Midrash.

Bibliography

Schnur, Susan. "The Once and Future Womantasch: Celebrating Purim's Full Moon as 'Holy Body Day,' " *Lilith*, 31 March 1998, p. 28.

Smith, Karen. "Inanna: Queen of Heaven and Earth," *Whole Earth Review* no. 75 (Summer 1992): 74.

Wolkstein, Diane. *The First Love Stories: From Isis and Osiris to Tristan and Iseult.* New York: HarperCollins, 1991.

————, and Samuel Noah Kramer. *Inanna: Queen of Heaven and Earth, Her Stories and Hymns from Sumer.* New York: HarperCollins, 1983.

Wollstonecraft, Mary (1759–1797)

Mary Wollstonecraft Godwin, a radical feminist, novelist, translator, and philosopher, overthrew the frivolous female images in romantic fiction to examine the pitfalls of women's real lives. An Anglo-Irish Londoner from the Spitalfields district she was born to semiliterate working-class parents. Her girlhood bore the strains of spousal abuse and alcoholism and the self-doubt that arose from parental favoritism toward her brother. She prepared herself for the future by reading philosophy and history and by teaching herself French and German. After working as a widow's companion in Bath, a governess for an Irish family, and a teacher in her own girls' academy at Islington, she began writing and editing for the *New Analytical Review.* The proceeds paid tuition for her sisters and bought a commission in the English navy for her brother. To aid classroom teachers, she compiled *Original Stories from Real Life with Conversations, Calculated to Regulate the Affections, and Form the Mind to Truth and Goodness* (1788). A collection of parables and historical

anecdotes illustrated by William Blake, the textbook lauds the ideal mother-nurturer for her influence on the next generation. Ironically the author cites as examples of misguided young women two motherless girls like the two Wollstonecraft daughters, Fanny Imlay and Mary, left at her tragic death.

In a professional treatise, *Thoughts on the Education of Daughters, with Reflections on Female Conduct in the More Important Duties of Life* (1786), she justified training equal to that of men for women to teach them to think for themselves. Her intent was to end young girls' need to flirt and adorn themselves to ensnare a likely suitor. To halt the degrading practice of marrying for money, she proposed careers by which women could excel and support themselves. In defiance of church extremes of Mariology, she turned to fiction in *Mary, a Fiction* (1788), a fantasy that denounces the sanctification of female virginity. The author introduces the novel as a deviation from the female stereotypes that fail to capture real women. Instead Wollstonecraft presents women who "wish to speak for themselves, and not to be an echo. . . . The paradise they ramble in must be of their own creating" (Wollstonecraft, 1993, 3). The title figure, trapped in wedlock to a repulsive husband, longs to die and pass on to a haven where women choose their own lifestyles.

Wollstonecraft defied the Victorian notion of the IDEAL WOMAN by discarding domestic training in favor of a liberal EDUCATION for women. Her revolt against female homebodies was the impetus for the textbook *The Female Reader* (1789), an anthology of instructive prose and poetry. Feminism was also the controlling theme of her passionate essay *A Vindication of the Rights of Women* (1792), a philosophy classic. In her arguments against male supremacy she cites the tendency of males toward "vile intrigues, unnatural crimes, and every vice that degrades" (Wollstonecraft, 1988, 16). She denounces society's exoneration of male scoundrels and villains and charges that androcentrism allows "such rapacious prowlers to rest quietly on their ensanguined thrones" (*ibid.*). In 1794 she discovered firsthand the social ostracism of the single mother after giving birth to Fanny Imlay. The author's efforts to maintain a family affirmed her beliefs that women deserve a chance at autonomy.

Influenced by Germaine De STAËL, Wollstonecraft wrote with gravity and knowledge of women's history. At age 38 she was completing a psychological novel, *MARIA; OR, THE WRONGS OF WOMEN* (1798), at the time of her first pregnancy, delivery, and death 10 days later from puerperal fever. She left her husband a baby girl, Mary Wollstonecraft SHELLEY, and an unfinished manuscript that became a cornerstone of feminist literature. The suite of nested stories dramatizes the treachery of George Venables against his wife, Maria. Her sufferings range from trauma and sorrow at the alleged death of her child, her trial for adultery, abandonment by her lover, and a suicide attempt through an overdose of laudanum.

Wollstonecraft remains a force for women's rights. In the essay "Blood, Bread, and Poetry: The Location of the Poet" (1984) Adrienne Rich refers to Wollstonecraft as a witness to "eighteenth-century middle-class Englishwomen brain-starved and emotionally malnourished through denial of education" (Rich, 245). According to "Women's Progress: A Comparison of Centuries," a feminist essay by Mary K. Ford, Wollstonecraft was "one of the first Englishwomen to resent the inferior position of her sex" (Ford, 621). Ford dramatizes women's situation in the late 18th century: "[Wollstonecraft] pleaded earnestly, not for political equality—such a thing was undreamed of—but for an education for women which should develop their minds and elevate their understanding" (*ibid.*). Wollstonecraft's influence surfaces in the lives of a host of feminist thinkers and writers, including the novelists George SAND and the BRONTË sisters, the poets Elizabeth Barrett BROWNING and Anna SEWARD, the mythographer Marion Zimmer BRADLEY, the historical fiction writer Donna CROSS, the orators Emma GOLDMAN and Voltairine DE CLEYRE, the biographer and playwright Lorraine HANSBERRY, the suffragist Elizabeth Cady STANTON, the gynocritic Elaine SHOWALTER, the essayist Virginia WOOLF, and the feminist philosophers Margaret FULLER and Harriet MARTINEAU.

Bibliography

Ford, Mary K. "Woman's Progress: A Comparison of Centuries" (1909). Available online. URL: http://etext.lib.virginia.edu/toc/modeng/public/ForWoma.html. Accessed on October 13, 2005.

Hoeveler, Diane Long. "Reading the Wound: Wollstonecraft's 'Wrongs of Women; or, Maria' and Trauma Theory," *Studies in the Novel* 31, no. 4 (Winter 1999): 387.

Rich, Adrienne. *Adrienne Rich's Poetry and Prose.* New York: W. W. Norton, 1975.

Showalter, Elaine. *Inventing Herself: Claiming a Feminist Intellectual Heritage.* New York: Scribner, 2001.

Wollstonecraft, Mary. *Mary/Maria/Matilda.* New York: Penguin, 1993.

———. *A Vindication of the Rights of Woman.* New York: W. W. Norton, 1988.

Woman on the Edge of Time Marge Piercy (1976)

Significant to feminist speculative literature is the dystopic *Woman on the Edge of Time,* a best seller on female coercion and MADNESS that critics compare to Margaret ATWOOD's *The HANDMAID'S TALE* (1985). In Marge Piercy's fictional setting the draconian male-controlled medical profession accepts the lies of male witnesses claiming crazy female behavior. Male doctors torture female patients on the violent ward of an asylum and overmedicate them with thorazine to subdue and silence them. As a focus Piercy created one of the landmark figures in feminist literature. The heroine, 35-year-old Consuelo "Connie" Camacho Ramos, a Latina inmate at Bellevue Hospital in Brooklyn, New York, and later at the New York University trauma center, recalls her admission without a physical examination for bruises, burns on her back, and broken ribs: "They had pushed her into restraint, shot her up immediately" (Piercy, 9). Over time Connie begins to worry that incarceration spells doom: "They had forgotten her, locked her away in this broom closet to starve. . . . She was a body checked into the morgue; meat registered for the scales" (*ibid.,* 9, 11). Without legal recourse she is labeled a child batterer. She serves a seemingly endless sentence as a hallucinating schizophrenic and alcohol and drug addict. Because of her troubled past no one believes her claims of assault by the man who committed her to the mental ward.

In lieu of physical liberties Piercy chooses as Connie's release imagination, a feminist staple that fuels journals, letters, and the arts. Through fantasy Connie eludes sadistic warders by time tripping to the pastoral commune of the unisex geneticist Luciente, a rescuer in Mattapoisett, Massachusetts, in the year A.D. 2137. Before Connie can make peace with herself and her coercive brother, Luis, she is yanked back into treatment at Rockover State Psychiatric Hospital. Like a laboratory rat, she undergoes perverse technological tinkering in her brain—the implantation of wires in her cerebrum that staff activate by remote control. Piercy extends the horror of robotism to decry the loss of identity and volition in a modern female Frankenstein's monster. At Connie's lowest point emotionally she rationalizes a murderous revenge: "I have nothing. Why shouldn't I strike back?" (*ibid.*, 372). After poisoning the institution's physicians, she muses: "I murdered them dead. Because they are the violence-prone. Theirs is the money and the power, theirs the poisons that slow the mind and dull the heart. Theirs are the powers of life and death" (*ibid.*, 375).

Bibliography

Chesler, Phyllis. *Women and Madness.* New York: Doubleday, 1972.

Piercy, Marge. *Woman on the Edge of Time.* New York: Fawcett, 1976.

Rudy, Kathy. "Ethics, Reproduction, Utopia: Gender and Childbearing in *Woman on the Edge of Time* and *The Left Hand of Darkness*," *NWSA Journal* 9, no. 1 (Spring 1997): 22–38.

Seabury, Marcia Bundy. "The Monsters We Create: *Woman on the Edge of Time* and *Frankenstein*," *CRITIQUE: Studies in Contemporary Fiction* 42, no. 3 (Winter 2001): 131–143.

The Woman's Bible Elizabeth Cady Stanton (1895–1898)

The most radical feminist attempt at reconciling Judeo-Christian tradition with WOMEN'S RIGHTS, *The Woman's Bible* waved a red flag before the eyes of conservative and patriarchal religious leaders. Because Stanton charged that patriarchal scripture degraded women and blamed them for introducing sin into the world, she and a committee of 24 contributors—including Lillie Devereux Blake, Harriot Stanton Blatch, Frances Ellen Burr, Clara Bewick Colby, Ellen Batelle Dietrick, Matilda Joslyn GAGE, Ursula N. Gestefeld, the Reverend Phoebe Ann Coffin Hanaford, Frances Lord, and Louisa Southworth—set about righting the antifemale text. They began by purchasing two copies of the Bible, which they dissected for passages referring to women. They pasted each passage into a scrapbook and left room for commentary, which each contributor initialed.

Stanton introduced volume 1 with comments on the Pentateuch—Genesis, Exodus, Leviticus, Numbers, and Deuteronomy. She states in the preface the group's intent: "The object is to revise only those texts and chapters directly referring to women, and those also in which women are made prominent by exclusion" (Stanton, 6). She stoutly rejects biblical traditions that a male god created the Earth and inspired the laws of Moses. Of the two versions of EVE's creation her exegesis attests that the second "was manipulated by some Jew, in an endeavor to give 'heavenly authority' for requiring a woman to obey the man she married" (*ibid.*, 19). Stanton dismisses Adam's charges against his wife as the self-serving cowardice of a whiny tattletale. At the end of the Eden episode Stanton questions why God would saddle women with painful parturition and motherhood as a curse for questioning authority.

Subsequent commentary on female characters, particularly the matriarchs Sarah, Rebecca, and Rachel, reshapes their personalities and behavior to a more realistic view of women's lives. Stanton makes a swipe at lazy males by describing Rebecca drawing water from her father's well while men lounged about and did nothing to help. In the book of Ruth the feminist version pictures two women, Ruth and her mother-in-law, Naomi, as poor, but contented females living alone on their own industry. Of Esther and Vashti the feminist revision makes one of its strongest cases for women's centrality in God's plan: "It is the seed of woman which is to bruise the head of the serpent. It is not man's boasted superiority of intellect through which the eternally working Divine power will perfect the race, but the receptiveness and the love of woman" (*ibid.*, 93). More daring is the second volume, which challenges the New Testament book of John for saying so little about the VIRGIN MARY. The revisionists denounced medieval mariology, which *The Woman's Bible* calls "a slur on all the natural motherhood of the world" (*ibid.*, 115). Stanton's committee labeled Paul's jaded remarks on women's subservience to men outright forgeries inserted by impious bishops seeking the permanent SILENCING of women.

At the core of Stanton's diatribe against the Bible was her belief that misogynistic elements of world scriptures evidenced the immorality and arrogance of male writers rather than the inspiration of God. With a generous application of humor, sarcasm, and outrage she refuted notions that had from ancient times subjugated women to male contempt and sexual whims. She reserved most sympathy for the no-names of Bible lore such as Samson's mother and the woman at the well, the faceless females whom male writers reduced to a mere presence. Stanton sought to end women's support of and dependence on organized religion by characterizing piety and dogma as alternate forms of pagan superstition. She stated, "All history shows that there have been more outrages committed by the Church, through its ecclesiastics, in the name of religion, on the sacred rights of humanity and the best interests of society, than by all other organizations together" (*ibid.*, 42).

The most conservative of suffragists and TEMPERANCE leaders rebuffed Stanton's reframing of far-reaching and culturally ingrained traditions. In January 1896, two years before the project was complete, the National American Woman Suffrage Association, led by Carrie Chapman CATT and Anna Howard Shaw, distanced itself from Stanton and from her committee's dissent from orthodoxy. Members disavowed any part in the rewriting of scripture; instead, they recommitted the association to traditional visions of home and family. Under serious pressure from the Right, Susan B. ANTHONY maintained her support of Stanton and the liberal suffrage wing. When the second volume was published only two weeks after Stanton's death, she was once again praised and reviled for attempting so huge a task. Detractors charged her

with diverting the public's attention from temporal consideration of women's political and economic liberation. Outbursts from pulpits dominated headlines in the *Denver Post*, *State Journal of Ohio*, *Washington Post*, and *West Virginia Echo*. Despite calumny from disparate quarters, *The Woman's Bible* became a best seller in English and in translation into six languages.

Bibliography

Kern, Kathi. *Mrs. Stanton's Bible*. Ithaca, N.Y.: Cornell University Press, 2001.

Stanton, Elizabeth Cady. *The Woman's Bible* (1895–1898). Available online. URL: http://www.sacred-texts.com/wmn/wb/. Accessed on October 17, 2005.

Strange, Lisa S. "Elizabeth Cady Stanton's *Woman's Bible* and the Roots of Feminist Theology," *Gender Issues* 17, no. 4 (Fall 1999): 15.

woman's work

Women shoulder the least glamorous of labors, which they transform into traditional strengths. As Igraine, King Arthur's mother, explains in the fantasist Marion Zimmer BRADLEY's *The Mists of Avalon* (1982), the traditional view of women's tasks was of a form of self-ennobling martyrdom. She instructs her daughter, 13-year-old Morgause: "Every lady must learn to spin. . . . Your fingers will lose their weariness as you accustom them to work. Aching fingers are a sign that you've been lazy, since they are not hardened to the task" (Bradley, 5). The work itself is crucial to human survival, a fact explained by Barbara EHRENREICH and Deidre English's social commentary in *For Her Own Good: 150 Years of the Experts' Advice to Women* (1978). In colonial times American women controlled fiber work, livestock care, gardening, and herbal skills. Nonetheless, the authors note, "within the patriarchal order, all decisions of consequence would be made *for* her by father or husband, if they were not already determined by tradition" (Ehrenreich and English, 9).

In 1895 the feminist historian and polemicist Matilda Joslyn GAGE commented in *Woman, Church, and State* on the introduction of Christianity to Europe, when historic cruelties against German women turned them into beasts of burden.

Gage describes the images of brute strength: "Women and dogs harnessed together are found drawing milk carts in the streets; women and cows yoked draw the plough in the fields; the German peasant wife works on the roads or carries mortar to the top of the highest buildings, while her husband smokes his pipe at the foot of the ladder until she descends" (Gage, 447). The dehumanization of women fostered multiple assaults on body and spirit. Because men could objectify wives as servants, the hunting and execution of accused witches seemed less religious sport and than due punishment of women who forget their place.

During the struggle for the vote suffragists, like the feminists who followed them, received constant warnings from conservative citizens that the vote would cost women the traditional power they enjoyed over their home and housework. In *Eighty Years and More, 1815–1897*, Elizabeth Cady STANTON rebutted such claims: "In seeking political power, are we abdicating that social throne where they tell us our influence is unbounded? No, No!" (Stanton, 63). Alice Ruth DUNBAR-NELSON, a feminist columnist for the *Pittsburgh Courier* and fiction writer of the Harlem Renaissance, refuted notions that domestic toil ennobled or empowered women. She pictured the waste of female skills and insights in the short story "Sister Josepha" (1899) and in the poem "I Sit and Sew" (1920). The dramatic monologue describes the speaker's frustration about sewing a neat seam, "My hands grown tired, my head weighted down with dreams" (Dunbar-Nelson, 84); meanwhile outside her window she sees "The Panoply of war, the martial tread of Men" (*ibid.*). The depiction of the woman's frail weapon—a sewing needle—at work making order in her narrow world generates a wearying endlessness.

Similarly sensitive to woman's labor are works by Harlem Renaissance dramatists: Mary Powell Burrill's dialect play *They That Sit in Darkness* (1919), a mild satire on the unending work of mothers of large families, and Georgia Douglas JOHNSON's one-act folk play *Plumes* (1927), a tragic view of futile female labors. The latter pictures old friends at the bedside of Emmerline Brown, a dying 13-year-old girl. As her mother, Charity, formulates a poultice with red pepper, her

friend, Tildy, sits nearby hemming a white dress that becomes Emmerline's shroud. Symbolizing the rhythms of female dialogue is the rocking chair, a soothing resting place for women in emotional distress.

Published in the same year is *Her* (1927), a one-act ghost play by Eulalie Spence of Nevis, another contributor to the Harlem Renaissance. The plot parallels the endless chores and low pay of the laundress, Martha, with the disappointment of the unnamed "Her," the ghost who haunts John Kinney, Martha's skinflint employer, for cheating and lying. Spence introduces the drama from the perspective of a laundress—"old, black Martha who takes in washing for some 'very old families,' who is, herself, always immaculate in her grey dress and white apron" (Spence, 1). Spence commiserates with Martha, "who takes care of Pete, her husband—crippled and an idler for more than fifteen years—Martha, who irons in the living room" (*ibid.*, 1). In the conclusion Martha, still loyal to her sour, ungrateful employer, cowers from the ghost, who delivered John's comeuppance for taking women for granted.

The tradition of women as household drudges faults a life of mental and emotional misery. The women's historian Sheila ROWBOTHAM summarizes in *Woman's Consciousness, Man's World* (1973): "Housework devours itself, there is a kind of cyclical rhythm of endeavour and collapse— into exhaustion" (Rowbotham, 72). The repetition of petty tasks, like that of O-lan, the slave wife in Pearl BUCK's domestic parable *The GOOD EARTH* (1931), and of Olivia Rivers in Ruth Prawer JHABVALA's novella *HEAT AND DUST* (1975), is the all-consuming consciousness of work to finish and more work to start, a round-after-round obsession of "keep things going, patch and cover up, settle everyone down" that grays out the mind and forces bored, wearied workers into a hollow somnambulance (*ibid.*, 73). In *Mrs. Stevens Hears the Mermaids Singing* (1965) May SARTON describes the stultifying, crazy-making nature of domesticity: "It consisted chiefly . . . in being able to stand constant interruption and keep your temper" (Sarton, 18). For the writer the task of saving a part of self for creativity is a constant combat: "Each single day [the poet Hilary Stevens] fought a war to get to her desk before her little bundle of energy had been dissipated, to push aside or cut through an intricate web of slight threads pulling her in a thousand directions" (*ibid.*).

Feminism uplifts common domestic labors in glimpses of women's rewards for perseverance. The poet Elizabeth BISHOP honored the womanly skill of her grandmother in "Gwendolyn" (1953), a character study that rewards the artistry of common things. Piecing together cloth donations from friends, the seamstress shapes irregular slips of silk and velvet into a crazy quilt. Between the feather stitches that bind the contrasting colors are dates, names, and greetings from the donor that the grandmother outlines in chain stitch. The quilt becomes a binder of matriarchal love as the grandmother wraps the ailing Elizabeth in the folds and rocks her to sleep. The poet observes that her grandmother enjoyed the soothing sessions as much as Elizabeth did. A more realistic view of women's work and longings colors the half-light of Eavan BOLAND's poem "The Women" (1987), a hymn to the twilight hour and to the dual thoughts of a worker conscious of two minds. Her outward thoughts tend to the everydayness of knitting and freshly ironed laundry while her subconscious broods over the victimization of vulnerable females in masculine myth.

The control of housework is accompanied by a jaded philosophy based on centuries of more of the same that only death or widowhood can relieve. As the novelist Barbara KINGSOLVER notes in *The Bean Trees* (1988), "A woman knows she can walk away from a pot to tend something else and the pot will go on boiling; if she couldn't this world would end at once" (Kingsolver, 1988, 185). Kingsolver witnessed the down-and-dirty response of men to women's demand for workplace equality in the documentary *Holding the Line: Women in the Great Arizona Mine Strike of 1983* (1989), a chronicle of an 18-month strike at the Phelps Dodge Copper Corporation. The clash between management and labor pitted a coalition of white, Hispanic, and Indian women of the Morenci Mine Women's Auxiliary against mine owners, the media, police, and the National Guard. At stake were cost-of-living raises for women who lifted heavy loads over month-long stretches of work without a day of rest.

Kingsolver abandoned objectivity on page 1 to declare that "the women who walked to work every morning in their coveralls, hairnets, and hard hats, telling jokes and swinging their lunch buckets, were tugging at the moorings of the status quo" (Kingsolver, *Holding,* 1). Reset as fiction in "Why I Am a Danger to the Public" (1989), collected in *Homeland and Other Stories* (1989), the miners' strike focused on the face-off between women and an intimidating male hierarchy that "don't like cunts or coloreds" (Kingsolver, *Homeland,* 235). The author pictures a Chicana crane operator, Vicki Morales, as a defiant, independent employee. Against the male-controlled job market, she vows not "to support my kids in no little short skirt down at the Frosty King" (*ibid.,* 227).

The Dominican-American writer Julia AL-VAREZ broached a more sobering view of gendered domestic work in *In the Time of the Butterflies* (1994), which exposes the VIOLENCE against women during the reign of the dictator Rafael Trujillo. Magdalena, one of the inmates of a women's prison, loses her virginity and innocence at age 13 while working as the maid of the prominent de la Torres family. At night after the completion of her day's work, "she was 'used' by the young man of the house" (Alvarez, 248). She conceals the cycle of rape from her mistress, "since she thought it was part of her job" (*ibid.*). As a result of an unconcealable pregnancy, Magdalena suffers accusations of whoring and lands on the street. No longer employable, she, with her infant daughter, Amantina, survives at an abandoned shed near the airport tarmac. The snobbish de la Torres family further degrades her by claiming the child because it resembles their son. The intrusion of classism into Magdalena's toil further demotes her from the house staff to a dehumanizing enslavement to the idle rich.

Bibliography

Alvarez, Julia. *In the Time of the Butterflies.* Chapel Hill, N.C.: Algonquin, 1994.

Bradley, Marion Zimmer. *The Mists of Avalon.* New York: Del Rey, 1987.

Burrill, Mary Powell. *They That Sit in Darkness.* In *Zora Neale Hurston, Eulalie Spence, Marita Bonner, and Others: The Prize Plays and Other One-Acts Published in Periodicals.* Edited by Jennifer Burton and Henry Louis Gates Jr. New York: G. K. Hall, 1996.

Dunbar-Nelson, Alice. *The Works of Alice Dunbar-Nelson.* Oxford: Oxford University Press, 1994.

Ehrenreich, Barbara, and Deidre English. *For Her Own Good: 150 Years of the Experts' Advice to Women.* Garden City, N.Y.: Anchor Books, 1978.

Gage, Matilda Joslyn. *Woman, Church, and State* (1895). Available online. URL: http://www.sacred-texts.com/wmn/wcs/. Accessed on October 14, 2005.

Kingsolver, Barbara. *The Bean Trees.* New York: Harper & Row, 1988.

———. *Holding the Line: Women in the Great Arizona Mine Strike of 1983.* Ithaca, N.Y.: Cornell University Press, 1989.

———. *Homeland and Other Stories.* New York: HarperCollins, 1989.

Ross, Ishbel. *Crusades and Crinolines.* New York: Harper & Row, 1963.

Rowbotham, Sheila. *Woman's Consciousness, Man's World.* Harmondsworth, England: Penguin, 1973.

Sarton, May. *Mrs. Stevens Hears the Mermaids Singing.* New York: W. W. Norton, 1975.

Spence, Eulalie. *Her.* In *Black Female Playwrights: An Anthology of Plays Before 1950.* Edited by Kathy A. Perkins. Bloomington: Indiana University Press, 1989.

Stanton, Elizabeth Cady. *Eighty Years and More: Reminiscences 1815–1897.* New York: Shocken, 1971.

Woman Warrior, The Maxine Hong Kingston (1976)

A classic autobiographical novel, *The Woman Warrior: Memoirs of a Girlhood among Ghosts* (1976) appeared in print at the height of the Women's Movement. It won a National Book Critics Circle Award for reconciling feminism with ethnic and national constraints. Maxine Hong KINGSTON's textured style allies TALK-STORY, legend, epic, memoir, ghost tales, and anecdote to contrast the lives of two women, Brave Orchid and her sister, Moon Orchid. Layers of feminist oral tradition epitomize patriarchal culture in imperial China, where women learned cooking, spinning of wool, and care of children, gardens, and livestock. Disobedience, sexual impropriety, adultery, and the birth of illegitimate children could end a woman's marriageability and cost her acceptance and forgiveness by other family members. The pariahs became wanderers, prostitutes, beggars, and suicides or developed into heroes of their self-directed scripts. Among the women whom Kingston extols as self-defining are the legendary female swordswoman Fa Mu Lan, the second-century poet and singer Ts'ai Yen, and a nameless woman of the Han people in the early 1600s who invented white crane boxing and mastered pole fighting at a Shao-lin temple.

Kingston characterizes the assimilation of Chinese women in American society as disconcerting, even for the stalwart. She describes Brave Orchid's medical training at the Te Keung School of Midwifery in Kwangtung [Guangdong] City (Canton). A determined NEW WOMAN, Brave Orchid demonstrates her prowess by dispelling ghosts, a symbol of disapproving males, and by refusing to smother baby girls, a grisly practice of families building DYNASTY through male bloodlines. After reuniting with Moon Orchid, Brave Orchid revives a SISTERHOOD that has lapsed over three decades. She forces Moon Orchid to locate her husband, who intends to abandon her and marry a pretty young American. The text notes that Moon Orchid originally chose him as "the ideal in masculine beauty, the thin scholar with the hollow cheeks and the long fingers" (*ibid.,* 119). The import of her views when she arrives in Los Angeles bodes ill for her survival, especially in the company of a bossy sister more in touch with reality.

Kingston uses the sisters' contrasting personalities to emphasize the strengths that set women free of male control. Unlike Brave Orchid, who asserts herself and refuses to be bullied, the weaker sister maintains a victim mentality and plays with paper dolls of Fa Mu Lan. Because Moon Orchid lacks the drive to support herself, she rejects the idea of working as a hotel maid. To Brave Orchid's accusations that the husband deserves a comeuppance, Moon Orchid makes a feeble case in his defense: "He didn't abandon me. He's given me so much money. . . . And he's supported our daughter too, even though she's only a girl" (*ibid.,* 125). Rather than fight for spousal and child support, Moon Orchid retreats into MADNESS at the California state mental asylum and imagines a female utopia: "No one ever leaves.

Isn't that wonderful? We are all women here" (*ibid.*, 160). Her fantasy world, a common theme in feminist literature, recurs in the subsequent episode of Crazy Mary, an unassimilated girl reared in China and disoriented by her family's departure for America.

The speaker, Brave Orchid's daughter, suffers the fragmented identity of the Asian offspring raised American style. The unnamed girl internalizes "a great power, my mother talking-story," a valuable source of socialization (Kingston, 1). The daughter later recognizes, "They would not tell us children because we had been born among ghosts, were taught by ghosts, and were ourselves ghost-like. They called us a kind of ghosts" (*ibid.*, 183). The daughter honors the authority of Brave Orchid, an emblem of the motherland, and of her stories of China experiences that instruct and discipline at the same time that they polarize MOTHER-DAUGHTER RELATIONSHIPS. The mother's intent is to restrict the younger generation to cultured norms, but the results are the daughter's alienation from both societies and free-floating aura of belonging nowhere.

Kingston uses her alter ego as justification for the author's choice to write women's stories. Because the daughter feels excluded from her mother's memories of the homeland, she opts for liberated American womanhood. She muses, "The swordswoman and I are not so dissimilar. May my people understand the resemblance soon so that I can return to them" (*ibid.*, 62). She rejects an arranged marriage and prefers to study journalism and become a newspaper reporter. During the academic ferment of the late 1970s Kingston's matriarchal and feminist themes of the novel contributed to the establishment of women's studies and ethnic studies departments.

Bibliography

Kingston, Maxine Hong. *The Woman Warrior.* New York: Vintage, 1989.

Nishime, LeiLani. "Engendering Genre: Gender and Nationalism in *China Men* and *The Woman Warrior,*" *MELUS* 20, no. 1 (Spring 1995): 67–82.

Yuan Shu. "Cultural Politics and Chinese-American Female Subjectivity: Rethinking Kingston's 'Woman Warrior,'" *MELUS* 26, no. 2 (Summer 2001): 199–224.

women's magazines

From their inception women's magazines have mirrored society's assumptions about feminine concerns. Contributing to women's reading material after centuries of etiquette and cosmetic manuals and recipe anthologies, the book dealer John Dunton issued *The Ladies' Mercury* (1693), containing the prototype of the question-and-answer column. In 1727 Irish readers could look forward to updates on styles and manners in the *Ladies' Journal* and *The Female Tatler* (1709–11) and to Eliza Haywood's *The Female Spectator* (1744–46), a woman's miscellany published three times a week and featuring Mrs. Crackenthrope, a fictional guru on women's issues. The popular *Lady's Magazine* (1770–1832) and *New Lady's Magazine* (1786–1895) offered Englishwomen a wealth of home and personal advice. In the United States from 1792 educated women found light and amusing reading in *Lady's Magazine, and Repository of Entertaining Knowledge*, which offered readers relief from male-centered publications. From 1814 the Philadelphia publisher Mary Clarke Carr provided more stimulating essays and book reviews in *Intellectual Female; or, Ladies Tea Tray*; in Baltimore in 1830 Mary Chase Barney compiled similar material in *National Magazine*; the writer Fanny FERN stocked the *Mother's Assistant* with dialect vignettes. An unidentified female correspondent declared in the January 1829 issue of *Ladies' Magazine* the crucial role that women played in the creation of a democratic nation: "There is no country where the right direction of female influence is so necessary as in America because here the popular breath guides, as it were, the bark of state" (Everton, 3).

The midcentury shift from lighter reading to polemics presaged the feminist groundswell that fueled the SUFFRAGE movement. In 1838 the Bostonian Caroline Gilman initiated *Lady's Annual Register and Housewife's Memorandum Book*; in contrast by midcentury the *Women's Suffrage Journal* influenced young Emmeline PANKHURST with articles by the editor, Lydia Becker, on WOMEN'S RIGHTS to the vote. A New Englander, Ann Sophia STEPHENS, the author of the first dime novel, serialized *Malaeska: Indian Wife of the White Hunter*, in the *Ladies' Companion* (1839), a source of adventure reading for women on the subject of a biracial marriage and miscegenation.

In this same period women became bolder about revealing authorship and writing about women's issues. The *Lady's Magazine and Museum of Belles Lettres* boasted on the cover the female writers of its contents; the Gothicist Ellen WOOD treated readers to *East Lynne; or, The Earl's Daughter* (1861), a bold melodrama on sexual scandal serialized in *New Monthly Magazine*. Louisa May ALCOTT, editor of *Merry's Museum*, a girl's miscellany, published her own writings as well as the signed works of Anna Laetitia BARBAULD, Lydia Maria CHILD, Felicia HEMANS, and Sarah Orne JEWETT. Simultaneously Alcott supplied to *Woman's Journal* an essay on TEMPERANCE, a subject that paralleled the demand for the ballot. In a salute to careers for women *Hours at Home* featured Elizabeth Stuart PHELPS's NEW WOMAN fiction "Jane Gurley's Story" (1866). By 1890 the *Girl's Own Paper* published feminist articles for young readers, including "Young Women as Journalists." In the late 1890s the importance of women's careers was reflected in "How Women May Earn a Living," an article in a 1896 issue of *Woman's Life*, and in "What It Means to Be a Lady Journalist" and "Interviewing as Women's Work" (1899) in *Young Woman*, which enticed girls to the journalistic trade with profiles of such feminist writers as Sarah GRAND. The practice of honoring female authors increased in Isabella Tod's *Leisure Hour* and in Charlotte O'Connor Eccles's *Windsor Magazine*. Eccles expounded on feminist issues regarding the BEAUTY MYTH in "Are Pretty Women Popular?" To aid women's finances, the magazine published a practical article, "How Women Can Easily Make Provision for Their Old Age."

A realistic periodical, *English Woman's Journal* was the brainchild of the activists Barbara Leigh Smith Bodichon and Bessie Rayner Parkes, who was one of the first women to sign a petition to the English Parliament favoring married women's property rights. Featuring articles written by women of the caliber of Elizabeth BLACKWELL, the periodical introduced meatier social topics with features on asylums, immigrant life, and child health. Submissions posed suggestions about female EDUCATION and careers, which at that time limited gentlewomen to child care, teaching, portrait painting, lady's companion, hat making, and sewing. The

forerunner of the modern women's magazine was the creation of Isabella Beeton, who issued the monthly *Englishwoman's Domestic Magazine* in 1852 and sold each issue for tuppence. The inexpensive periodical compiled domestic and child care columns, advice to the lovelorn, and essay contests. The tone of articles bolstered women's self-esteem by treating the domestic realm with dignity. Within seven years Beeton had assessed the popularity of her work at 60,000 copies annually. She extended the company's reach to the United States, Canada, and Australia with a domestic manual, *The Book of Household Management* (1859). By 1860 she could upgrade the quality of women's reading material with heavier paper stock and the first color engravings in the business. She followed with *Young Englishwoman*, a forerunner of modern teen magazines. In 1893 a competitor, the Scots romantic novelist Annie S. Swan of Edinburgh, edited *Woman at Home*, which acknowledged activism on behalf of homemakers and single women. The journal featured stories by Sarah Grand and Swan's "Elizabeth Glen M. B.: The Experiences of a Lady Doctor" (1894), a nod to the professional woman.

In the Western Hemisphere female ferment was no less demanding of reading material by, about, and for women. In 1840 Harriet Jane Hanson Robinson and some 60 mill laborers at Merrimack Manufacturing in Lowell, Massachusetts, founded *The Lowell Offering: A Repository of Original Articles Written by Factory Girls*, which for five years spoke the thoughts of the female factory employee. When Charles Dickens visited the publication, he was pleased to find literary outlets for employees at the public library and the intellectual outlets of religious and social debates and letter-writing circles. Other women's papers in Cincinnati, Philadelphia, Providence, and New York outlasted the *Lowell Offering* but did not survive national upheaval during the Civil War. One that did, *Demorest's Illustrated Monthly Magazine and Mme. Demorest's Mirror of Fashions*, got its start in September 1864 and maintained its appeal by supplying a dress pattern in each issue. Four years later Harriet Beecher STOWE, perhaps the most powerful female writer of the era, joined the editorial board of *Hearth and Home*, one of the Demorest family's rivals.

Contemporaneously with the efforts of the "Lowell Mill girls," Sarah Josepha HALE founded a moralistic periodical, *The Good Housekeeper,* a fount of housewifely suggestions, travel and reading updates, verse, and short stories. A competitor, *Godey's Ladies Book,* which Hale began editing, thrived until 1877. It cut into the market with fashion advice and high-toned essays and stories, including the writings of Harriet Beecher Stowe. *Women's Journal* published the essays of Elizabeth Stuart Phelps and in 1877 featured Julia Ward Howe's call to support full citizenship for women by demanding the vote. A variety magazine, *Frank Leslie's Popular Monthly,* introduced in 1876, ranged from homey topics to features on the arts and sciences, satire, and more fiction, both short stories and serialized novellas. The poet Louise BOGAN comments in *Achievement in American Poetry* (1951) on the light offerings of an early "little magazine," the fortnightly *M'lle New York,* established in 1895 to provide "a surface and witty" survey of social happenings (Bogan, 29). Consumer interest in *Good Housekeeping, Homes and Gardens,* and *Ideal Home* acknowledged women's value to the national economy and to the reception of innovative products. Feeding women's demand for readable fiction were *Harper's Bazaar,* with the short stories of Mary Wilkins FREEMAN and Susan GLASPELL; *Atlantic,* which carried short fiction by Antoinette Brown BLACKWELL; *Crisis,* purveyor of Harlem Renaissance writings by Jessie Redmond FAUSET and Zora Neale HURSTON; *Mother's Magazine and Family Journal,* publisher of Pauline JOHNSON's poems; *Everybody's,* which issued Edna FERBER's first story, "The Homely Heroine" (1911); and *McClure's,* which serialized Willa CATHER's first novel, *Alexander's Bridge* (1912).

Women's magazines in the early 20th century attempted to appease women and soften the unease that surfaced between the two world wars. Frances Low, a contributor to *Girl's Realm,* published a series of articles on journalism for young women, which she collected in a career manual, *Press Work for Women: A Textbook for the Young Woman Journalist* (1903). In London the bimonthly *New Freewoman* courted feminist writers, particularly Rebecca WEST. The title of *Today's Woman,* a vehicle for the stories of Dawn POWELL, implied a

shift from passé sentimentality and a grasp of modernity. The conservative English magazine *Woman,* which boasted a circulation of 750,000 in 1939, propagandized the role of women as professional housekeepers and suppliers of the nation's children. The English poet Stevie SMITH worked for a publishing house and spoke from an insider's perspective about the standard proportion of articles on given topics in her experimental novel *Novel on Yellow Paper; or, Work It Out for Yourself* (1936): "It is awfully funny I think the way their allowance of fiction is doled out to these little sweeties" (Smith, 169). She develops her meditation on didactic layout with observations about articles that link married sex with feminine appeal, thus implying that the life of a relationship is the woman's duty. In conclusion she remarks, "That I fear is where they get their funny thoughts on matrimony," a reflection on her disdain for the limited choices open to women (*ibid.*). Herself unmarried by choice, she knew from experience the anti-woman pressures generated by the media.

In North America *The Delineator, McCall's, Pictorial Review,* and *Woman's Day* entered the crowded field with mass circulation appeal through such serials as Jessamyn WEST's frontier tales. *McCall's* made its mark on female publications in 1956 with the unsigned article "The Mother Who Ran Away," which drew the highest readership in the magazine's history and alerted staff to the unhappiness of homemakers. In 1965 Jean STAFFORD's first-person reportage, "The Strange World of Marguerite Oswald," offered *McCall's* readers a preview of a forthcoming book, *A Mother in History* (1966), a glimpse of the mother of Lee Harvey Oswald and her philosophy of single parenting. The standard of the women's media industry, *Ladies' Home Journal,* edited by Louisa Knapp Curtis, upgraded women's fiction with poems and essays by Ella Wheeler Wilcox, a column by Dorothy THOMPSON, and stories by Louisa May ALCOTT, Isak DINESEN, Kate Greenaway, Elizabeth JANEWAY, and Kate Douglass Wiggins. Timely articles met the demand for information on house plans, sanitation and disease, sex education, temperance and urban ills, and woman suffrage, which the social worker Jane Addams supported in the essay "Why Women Should Vote" (1910). Emerging writers—the ecofeminist Rachel

CARSON, Shirley JACKSON, Kathleen NORRIS, and Ann PETRY—turned to such journals as *Charm, Cosmopolitan, Hesperian, Overland Monthly, Prairie Schooner, Redbook, Saturday Evening Post,* and *Woman's Home Companion.* Many of these accepted stories from the feminist writer Willa Cather, an editor and writer for *Home Monthly* and a spokesperson for the underappreciated prairie settler and farm wife.

As feminism stirred in American women, readers began to see their needs answered in popular magazines. Periodicals offered employment to female writers, editors, and copywriters, whom marketers preferred for their ability to speak intimately and knowledgeably to women. In *Woman's Journal* the author Ada Bowles declared women's intent to organize the voting rights campaign and remain in their ranks until they won. The turning point for women's periodicals began in the mid-1960s, after Betty FRIEDAN published *The FEMININE MYSTIQUE* (1963), a touchstone that challenged women to develop all their talents by curtailing their enslavement to the home. She derided the least imaginative women's magazines for perpetuating the notion that female readers are man-hungry, beauty and weight conscious, and limited in their ability to grasp public and world affairs. In the hope of introducing feminism to the mainstream the journalist Pat Carbine began editing *McCall's* in 1970 as a model journalist "who cared about whatever this was that was happening to women" (Thom, 9). By 1973 more than 560 feminist journals and newsletters had begun publication.

Throughout the 1970s the outpouring of women's magazines offered new markets for photos, art, graphics, articles, humor, verse, and short fiction. During a cultural renaissance the longest lived of the media originated all over North America: *Bloodroot, Broomstick, Bust, Calyx, Creative Woman, Earth's Daughters, Everywoman, Feminist Review, Frontiers, Heresies, Herizons, Iowa Woman, Iris, Kalliope, Lilith, Moving Out, Ms., On the Issues, Plainswoman, Second Shift, Sing Heavenly Muse, Shameless Hussy, 13th Moon,* and *Thirteenth Woman.* The *Black Maria,* an outgrowth of the Chicago Women's Liberation Union, took its name from the police paddy wagon that hauled suffrag-

ists to jail. The periodical counteracted the SILENCING of women and encouraged networking by offering such gems as Ntozake SHANGE's *for colored girls who have considered suicide/when the rainbow is enuf* (1975). In this same period the poetry of Louise ERDRICH appeared in *Primavera,* a publication of feminists at the University of Chicago to encourage writers. From 1969 to 1976 the high standards of *Aphra,* named for the 17th-century playwright and novelist Aphra BEHN and edited by dramatist and novelist Elizabeth Fisher, suited the first feminist literary journal. The makeup served an audience eager for creative writing as well as critical articles on the arts and society. Among the contributors were the playwright Myrna Lamb, author of the satiric *Mod Donna* (1970) and *Apple Pie* (1976); the novelists Marge PIERCY and Rita Mae BROWN; the theorist Kate MILLET; and the poets Audre LORDE and Adrienne RICH. The magazine serialized the playwright Dacia Maraini's *Manifesto* from 1972 to 1973 and, in summer 1974, Daphne Patai's essay "Utopia for Whom?"

Bibliography

Everton, Michael J. "The Courtesies of Authorship: Hannah Adams and Authorial Ethics in the Early Republic," *Legacy: A Journal of American Women Writers* 20, no. 1–2 (January–June 2003): 1–21.

Fraser, Hilary, Stephanie Green, and Judith Johnston. *Gender and the Victorian Periodical.* Cambridge: Cambridge University Press, 2003.

Heller, Janet Ruth. "*Primavera* and *Black Maria*: Two Chicago Women's Literary Magazines," *Women's Studies* 23, no. 2 (March 1994): 175–190.

Mather, Anne. "A History of Feminist Periodicals, Part I," *Journalism History* 1, no. 3 (Autumn 1974): 82–85.

———. "A History of Feminist Periodicals, Part II," *Journalism History* 2, no. 1 (Winter 1974): 19–23.

———. "A History of Feminist Periodicals, Part III," *Journalism History* 2, no. 1 (Spring 1975): 19–23, 31.

Naether, Carl A. *Advertising to Women.* New York: Prentice Hall, 1928.

Smith, Stevie. *Novel on Yellow Paper; or, Work It Out for Yourself.* New York: Pinnacle, 1982.

Tebbel, John, and Mary Ellen Zuckerman. *The Magazine in America, 1741–1990.* New York: Oxford University Press, 1991.

Thom, Mary. *Inside Ms.: 24 Years of the Magazine and the Feminist Movement.* New York: Henry Holt, 1997.

White, Cynthia L. *Women's Magazines 1693–1968.* London: Michael Joseph, 1970.

Zuckerman, Mary Ellen. *A History of Popular Women's Magazines in the United States, 1792–1995.* Westport, Conn.: Greenwood Press, 1998.

women's movements

An ongoing vehicle for dissent by women of different races, classes, and cultures, women's movements interlace the tapestry of Western history from beginning to end. As the feminist critic Carolyn G. Heilbrun explains in *Writing a Woman's Life* (1989), the movement produced an essential ferment that allows "women to see themselves collectively, not individually, not caught in some individual erotic and familial plot and, inevitably, found wanting" (Heilbrun, 46). The antebellum groundswell, which began in 1830 with ABOLITIONISM and concluded with the American Civil War, allied colonial and republican efforts to extend liberty and happiness to males and females of all races. The strongest voices range over a variety of genres, from the colonial closet dramas of Mercy Otis WARREN and the wife-to-husband letters of Abigail ADAMS in the government-shaping year of 1776 to the stringent pamphlets of Mary WOLLSTONECRAFT, the Anglo-Irish author of *A Vindication of the Rights of Women* (1792). In England, the novelist Maria EDGEWORTH demanded higher standards of education for women in *Letters for Literary Ladies* (1795). The philosopher Harriet Taylor MILL made demands on Parliament with a feminist suffrage manifesto, "The Enfranchisement of Women" (1851). The first American feminist tract, Sarah GRIMKÉ's *Letters on the Equality of the Sexes and the Condition of Women* (1838), organized a logical defense of WOMEN'S RIGHTS. Her demands for equal citizenship inspired the first formal wave of feminism by the suffrage organizers Susan B. ANTHONY, Matilda Joslyn GAGE, Lucretia Coffin MOTT, and Lucy STONE. One of their company, Elizabeth Cady STANTON, lobbed a stinging rebuke to organized religion with *The Woman's Bible* (1895–98). Another, the pamphleer Carrie Chapman CATT, challenged misconceptions about SUFFRAGE with the tract "Do You Know?" (1918). Female journalists added punch to the movement with the pro-woman articles of Nellie BLY for the *Pittsburgh Dispatch* and Annie Laurie's sob sister journalism for the *San Francisco Examiner.* More scholarly was Margaret FULLER's revolutionary treatise *Woman in the Nineteenth Century* (1845), the first feminist work of philosophy in North America, which drew on the rhetoric of the British polemicist and sociologist Harriet MARTINEAU, author of the 25-volume *Illustrations of Political Economy* (1832–33).

In the period from 1900 to World War I feminists took to print and the podium to shape a campaign for the enfranchisement of American women. In addition to the essays and editorials of TEMPERANCE leaders and unionists and of the house journal of the American Woman Suffrage Association, the era spawned the first concerted effort at universal birth control. The campaign was advanced through the essays and journalism of Scots-American lecturer and editor Frances WRIGHT, the American health clinic manager Margaret SANGER, and the English physician Marie STOPES and from the radical orations of Voltairine DE CLEYRE and Emma GOLDMAN, who also channeled dissent into the subversive prolabor periodical *Mother Earth.* Additional ammunition came from the pens of the dramatist Alice DUNBAR-NELSON, the poet Julia Ward Howe, the essayist Rebecca WEST, the Mexican journalist Rosario Castellanos, the Ohio reformer and editor Victoria WOODHULL, and her sister and partner Tennie Claflin, and the London-born satiric poet Mina LOY. Charlotte Perkins GILMAN constructed feasible alternatives to domestic drudgery in *Women and Economics* (1898) and added visions of a feminist haven in *Herland* (1915), the cornerstone of feminist utopianism.

The era crystallized past efforts through the writings of women privileged by EDUCATION and freedom from repressive home environments. The kickoff was Betty FRIEDAN's *The Feminine Mystique* (1963), a morale booster for disgruntled, dissatisfied women. Of its place in the women's liberation movement Adrienne RICH stated in "Split at the Root: An Essay on Jewish Identity" (1982), "It was an astonishing time to be a woman of my age" (Rich, 237). An impressive array of women's journals, fiction, drama, verse, essay, and AUTOBIOGRAPHY allied unlike participants, from the editorials of Gloria STEINEM, a cofounder of Ms. magazine, to the incisive writings of Shulamith FIRESTONE, Marilyn FRENCH, and Robin MORGAN. High points of the second wave ranged from Toni MORRISON's receipt of the Nobel Prize in literature to the poet Maya ANGELOU's reading of original occasional verse honoring the election of President Bill Clinton. Strands of political pressure fleshed out the late 20th-century campaign with Marge PIERCY's description of maligned mental patients in the dystopic fantasy novel WOMAN ON THE EDGE OF TIME (1976), Faith McNulty's exposé on domestic VIOLENCE in the novel The BURNING BED (1980), Naomi WOLF's denunciation of fantasies of the ideal woman in The Beauty Myth (1991), and Alice WALKER's protest of FEMALE GENITAL MUTILATION in the novel Possessing the Secret of Joy (1992) and the screenplay Warrior Marks (1993). At the beginning of a new millennium Barbara EHRENREICH reminded readers of the bottom level of female labors in Nickel and Dimed: On (Not) Getting By in America (2001), a sympathetic view of pink collar jobs. Memoirist Sheila ROWBOTHAM added her nostalgic overview in The Promise of a Dream: Remembering the Sixties (2002). Tweaking the stodginess of anti-female readers are the continuing efforts of columnists Susan BROWNMILLER, Ellen GOODMAN, Mollie IVINS, Elizabeth JANEWAY, Katha POLLITT, Anna QUINDLEN, and Patricia J. WILLIAMS.

Bibliography

Heilbrun, Carolyn G. Writing a Woman's Life. New York: W. W. Norton, 1989.

Naples, Nancy A. Community Activism and Feminist Politics: Organizing across Race, Class, and Gender. New York: Routledge, 1997.

Orleck, Annelise. Common Sense and a Little Fire: Women and Working-Class Politics in the United States, 1900–1965. Chapel Hill: University of North Carolina Press, 1995.

Rich, Adrienne. Adrienne Rich's Poetry and Prose. New York: W. W. Norton, 1975.

women's rights

The attainment of liberation and full citizenship for women recurs as a two-stage goal in feminist literature from the past into the 21st century, today especially among developing-world writers. A preliminary salvo on behalf of liberation arose from the works of two American playwrights, Mercy Otis WARREN's colonial closet dramas and Judith Sargent MURRAY's satiric play The Medium; or, Virtue Triumphant (1795), performed at the Federal Street Theatre as Boston's first American stage play. By 1832 the issue of gaining full citizenship rights absorbed strong feminist proponents in England, both male and female. In 1839 the beginnings of a formal women's rights movement accompanied England's Custody of Infants Act, which guaranteed separated and divorced women the guardianship of their young children. Despite advances Florence Nightingale mourned in 1852, "Look at the poor lives we lead. It is a wonder that we are so good as we are" (Gilbert and Gubar, 805). Trying to improve that dismal lot in the United States were the speeches of the abolitionists and suffragists Frederick DOUGLASS and Sojourner TRUTH. In 1885 the novelist Mary Theresa Shelhamer quipped at the expense of male voters in Life and Labor in the Spirit World about the furor over women's SUFFRAGE: "For the fuss made . . . one would think it took a week to put a small slip of paper into a medium-sized box. Why, we have known of men who could put in half a dozen in less than half that time, and no one suspects women to be less clever than men" (Kessler, 12).

Parallel to the suffrage drive were women's writings about substantive improvement to female lives, issues that took strength from the essays of Louisa May ALCOTT, Mary ANTIN, and COLETTE. The poet Emily DICKINSON chose lyric verse to denounce female SILENCING in "Tell All the Truth But Tell It Slant" (ca. 1868). In a scholarly treatise, The Sexes throughout Nature (1875), Antoinette BLACKWELL railed against traditions and customs ossified into repressive laws against women's freedom to establish careers. The Londoner Grace AGUILAR demanded an end to Jewish PATRIARCHY and limited EDUCATION for girls in The Spirit of Judaism (1842). The journalist Fanny FERN injected a new slant in the essay collection Fern Leaves from Fanny's Portfolio (1852), which promotes children's rights in an anti-woman climate that suppressed both mothers and their offspring. In the post–Civil

War malaise Elizabeth Stuart PHELPS proposed a dreamy all-woman haven in *The Gates Ajar* (1868), the first of a trilogy on utopian feminism. Helen Hunt JACKSON disclosed in nonfiction, *A Century of Dishonor: The Early Crusade for Indian Reforms* (1881), and in a best-selling novel, *Ramona* (1894), the genocidal tendencies of frontier politics, which deprived Indian women of dignity and means of survival. The editor and memoirist Harriet Jane ROBINSON focused on the coercion of working women in *Loom and Spindle; or, Life among the Early Mill Girls* (1898), which denounces male industrialists who treated young white girls as slave laborers.

The 20th century saw the proliferation of articulate, logical position papers on female liberties, including the pyrotechnic outbursts of the suffragist Emmeline PANKHURST, the pro-woman journalism of the Canadian writer Nellie MCCLUNG and the American foreign correspondent Dorothy THOMPSON, and the antiparasitism views of the economically independent woman in the South African polemicist Olive SCHREINER's *Woman and Labour* (1911). Zona GALE lobbied for better workplace conditions for women in *Daughter of the Morning* (1917). The poet Edna St. Vincent MILLAY pressed for sexual equality and self-determination in *A Few Figs from Thistles* (1920); her Chilean contemporary, Gabriela MISTRAL, issued verse calling for women's rights as an essential basis for nationalism. Susan BROWNMILLER expressed views on the roots of male-on-female violence in the essay "Let's Put Pornography Back in the Closet" (1969). The poet Nikki GIOVANNI stressed in *Racism 101* (1994) the importance of female authorship to the battle against racism and sexism. The playwright Eve ENSLER stressed women's rights to explore and understand their own genitals in the humorous hit play *The Vagina Monologues* (1996).

The fruit of the suffragists' labors continued to nourish waves of feminists globally. The fabulist Isak DINESEN extolled the life of the NEW WOMAN in *Out of Africa* (1937) and *Shadows on the Grass* (1961), memoirs of her establishment of a coffee farm in Kenya. A fellow expatriate, the pilot and autobiographer Beryl MARKHAM, delighted in the freedom of owning her own business in *West with the Night* (1942). Farther south Na-

dine GORDIMER produced a half-century of short and long fiction protesting the gendered hardships under South Africa's apartheid policies; the poets Joy HARJO and Linda HOGAN had similar charges to lodge against the white world for denigration of Native American women. At the 50th anniversary march and celebration of the vote the exuberance of women infected the Mexican writer, poet, and journalist Rosario Castellanos, prizewinning author of *Balun-Canan* (*The Nine Guardians*, 1957) and *The Book of Lamentations* (1968). A champion of women, particularly poor Mayan women, she was already influenced by the writings of Simone de BEAUVOIR, Simone WEIL, and Virginia WOOLF when the American spirit of liberty and equality seized her imagination. In addition to being the minister of culture for Chiapas and a lecturer to feminist groups, she spread her enthusiasm for women's literature in Central and North American universities, including Colorado, Indiana, and Wisconsin as well as Hebrew University in Jerusalem. A fellow libertarian, Angela DAVIS, spoke for nonwhite women, female prisoners, and ghetto dwellers in *If They Come in the Morning* (1971). In Egypt the freedom fighter and physician Nawal EL SAADAWI encouraged the demand for women's rights with two autobiographies: *Daughter of Isis* (1999) and *Walking through Fire* (2002).

Bibliography

Castellanos, Rosario. *A Rosario Castellanos Reader.* Austin: University o f Texas, 1988.

Gilbert, Sandra M., and Susan Gubar. *The Madwoman in the Attic.* 2nd ed. New Haven, Conn.: Yale University Press, 2000.

Kessler, Carol Farley. *Daring to Dream.* Boston: Pandora Press, 1984.

Wood, Ellen (1814–1887)

A powerhouse of the Gothic era, Ellen Price Wood exploited occult themes, sensational ghost lore, bigamy and marital intrigue, a murder trial, and SECRECY and the disguise motif, all promising vehicles for women freelancers during the Victorian age. The daughter of the glovemaker Thomas Price and his wife, Elizabeth, of Worcester, England, she was confined by scoliosis to a chair, where she turned out juvenilia about Catherine de' Medici and Lady Jane Grey. After marrying the entrepreneur and ambassador Henry Wood in 1836, she enjoyed the perquisites of a privileged wife. Twenty years later, at the end of their term at the French embassy, she supported the family by publishing some 100 short pieces in *Bentley's Miscellany, Colburn's New Monthly Magazine, Good Words, The Leisure Hour,* and *New Monthly Magazine.* Feminist themes fueled her most popular tales, notably the themes of CONFINEMENT and murder in "The Punishment of Gina Montani" (1852), the story of live burial of the title character, whose angry spirit bedevils the lord of Visinara.

After winning a prize for a TEMPERANCE novel, *Danesbury House* (1860), Wood produced a three-volume best seller, *East Lynne; or, The Earl's Daughter* (1861), a melodrama originally serialized in *New Monthly Magazine.* Over five printings in the first year it sold a half-million copies by piquing Victorian interests in sexual misconduct, illegitimate birth, and resulting scandal. A breakthrough in women's fiction is the insistence of Lady Isabel Vane Carlyle, the protagonist, on abandoning an unsatisfying home life with an attorney, Archibald Carlyle, and eloping with the roué Captain Francis Levison. Under an assumed name she reclaims her home and child, two ties to the past that errant women typically lost in domestic proceedings. The groundbreaking action preceded two changes to female status in English law, the Married Women's Property Act of 1870 and the Infant Custody Law of 1873. Vying with Mary Elizabeth BRADDON's much seamier *Lady Audley's Secret* (1892) for popularity, Wood's classic enjoyed additional success as popular three-act drama, stage musical, radio, and film adaptations as well as in translation into Hindustani and Welsh and into French as *Les châtelaines d'East Lynne* (The mistresses of East Lynne). Of the dominance of female writers in William Lane's circulating library system, the novelist Charles Reade complained, "They will only take in ladies' novels. Mrs. Henry Wood, 'Ouida,' Miss Braddon—these are their gods" (Carnell, 169).

Readers in England and North America generated a demand for Wood's published works. In a single year she turned out two detective thrillers, *Mrs. Halliburton's Troubles* (1862) and *The Chan-*nings* (1862), and a supernatural novel, *Shadow of Ahslydyat* (1862), as well as sketches for *Argosy* on the themes of necromancy, confinement, curses, and insanity. In 1874 she initiated her most popular crime and mystery series, the Johnny Ludlow stories. Although her productivity slowed after she contracted diphtheria, she gained critical and popular regard as well as a fortune in royalties for producing sensationalism devoid of lewdness. At her death of heart failure her son and biographer, Charles William Wood, reissued her works, which reached sales of 2.5 million by 1900.

Bibliography

Carnell, Jennifer. *The Literary Lives of Mary Elizabeth Braddon.* Hastings, England: Sensation Press, 2000.

Rosenman, Ellen Bayuk. " 'Mimic Sorrows': Masochism and the Gendering of Pain in Victorian Melodrama," *Studies in the Novel* 35, no. 1 (Spring 2003): 22–43.

Wood, Charles W. "Mrs. Henry Wood: In Memoriam," *Argosy* 43 (1887): 251–270.

Woodhull, Victoria (1838–1927)

The reformer and pamphleteer Victoria Claflin Woodhull used journalism as a means of securing woman SUFFRAGE. Born in Homer, Ohio, to a barkeep and an itinerant domestic worker, she and her sister, Tennessee Celeste "Tennie C." Claflin, traveled the Midwest with their parents' medicine show. The duo performed acts of clairvoyance and channeling of the voices of the dead. When the sisters moved to New York City, Cornelius Vanderbilt, one of their clients for regular seances, gave them work as the nation's first female stockbrokers in the office of Woodhull, Claflin, & Company. The location put them in the ferment of WOMEN'S RIGHTS and campaigns favoring birth control and women's labor issues. In 1870 Woodhull composed utopian essays for the *New York Herald* and published the series as *Origin, Tendencies and Principles of Government* (1871).

A born grandstander, Woodhull took unconventional measures to denounce the DOUBLE STANDARD. She and Tennie published a reformist journal, *Woodhull & Claflin's Weekly,* under the motto "Upward & Onward" (Woodhull and Claflin, 1). The

16-page forum surveys economic and social issues affecting women's lives, including the male thugs of the Tammany ring who corrupted government, the one-sided punishment of prostitutes but not their clients, and the adulteries of a prominent husband, the Reverend Henry Ward Beecher. For the latter article the editors went to prison for obscenity and libel. On September 16, 1871, the article "The Social Volcano" demanded sympathy for Alice Bowlsby, the victim of an abortionist: "Ladies and gentlemen, you cannot carry out your social system; you have taught it in your schools, at your firesides, in your churches; you have made it a tool of respectability; you visit the deepest, the blackest, the direst of punishment upon all who transgress your rule, and yet you fail" (*ibid.*). Despite the publisher's notoriety for such taboo topics, her paper reached a circulation of 20,000.

Woodhull's progressive stance kept her in the headlines. She made history with her *Lecture on Constitutional Equality*. In 1871 she caused a stir by publishing an English translation of Karl Marx and Friedrich Engels's *Communist Manifesto*. In 1872, a year after becoming the first female to address a congressional judiciary committee, Woodhull campaigned as the Equal Rights Party candidate for the U.S. presidency, the first woman to run for the highest office. She breached decorum for genteel women by justifying her right to divorce an alcoholic husband, Canning Woodhull, whom she married when she was 14. After defending the right to sexual liberty and privacy, she earned scurrilous nicknames and political cartoons calling her a queen of free love.

In part because of Woodhull's peculiarities the original body of the National Woman Suffrage Association (NWSA) split in 1872 after conservative delegates abandoned their membership and formed the American Woman Suffrage Association (AWSA), led by Lucy STONE, cofounder of the American Equal Rights Association, chair of the New Jersey Woman Suffrage Association, and cofounder of the New England Woman Suffrage Association and the Woman's International Peace Association. Although the tide of rumor and slander turned women against Woodhull, she maintained friendly ties with Susan B. ANTHONY, Lucretia Coffin MOTT, and Elizabeth Cady STAN-

TON. In defense of a fellow suffragist, Stanton wrote: "Women have crucified the Mary Wollstonecrafts, the Fanny Wrights, the George Sands, the Fanny Kembles of all ages, and now men mock us with the fact, and say we are ever cruel to each other. Let us end this ignoble record and henceforth stand by womanhood" (Underhill, 120). Woodhull concluded with a self-ennobling fillip: "If Victoria Woodhull must be crucified, let men drive the spikes and plait the crown of thorns" (*ibid.*).

Until her marriage to a staid Englishman, Woodhull continued in her flamboyant career. In 1875 she shocked hearers at the Cooper Institute in New York City with the speech "The Garden of Eden; or, Paradise Lost and Found." At age 52 she outraged conservative readers by publishing *The Human Body: The Temple of God* (1890), an attack on Victorian prissiness. In 1892 she and her daughter, Zula Maud Woodhull, founded a new magazine, the *Humanitarian*, on the subject of eugenics.

Bibliography

Frisken, Amanda. "Sex in Politics: Victoria Woodhull as an American Public Woman, 1870–1876," *Journal of Women's History* 12, no. 1 (Spring 2000): 89–111.

Underhill, Beachy. *The Woman Who Ran for President: The Many Lives of Victoria Woodhull.* Bridgehampton, N.Y.: Bridge Works, 1995.

Woodhull, Victoria, and Tennessee Claflin. *Woodhull & Claflin's Weekly* (1871–1872). Available online. URL: http://www.victoria-woodhull.com/wcwarchive.htm. Accessed on October 17, 2005.

Woolf, Virginia (1882–1941)

A touchstone of feminist writing and artistic INDEPENDENCE, the diarist, critic, and novelist Adeline Virginia Stephen Woolf engaged feminist themes with modernist techniques to express the urgency and value of women's writing. Homeschooled by her learned father in their home at Hyde Park Gate, London, she resented family favoritism of her brothers, Adrian and Thoby, who received a university education. After study at King's College she joined her sister, Vanessa Bell, and other female thinkers and artists in the Bloomsbury Group, a coterie who met in the

Bloomsbury section of London near the British Museum. They dedicated their collaboration to guiding English arts into the modernist era. She remained under the shadow of educated men after marrying the publisher Leonard Woolf, with whom she initiated Hogarth Press.

While teaching at Morley College, Woolf began her career with stories written with her husband and composed book reviews for London weeklies. She advanced to preliminary novels. The first, *The Voyage Out* (1915), a description of women's search for an artistic niche, reaches beyond conversations and acts to inner complexities. As one character states the author's intent, "I want to write a novel about Silence . . . the things people don't say" (Woolf, 1915, 216). The second, *Night and Day* (1919), is a satire on courtship. She achieved critical fame with the publication of her literary principles in "Mr. Bennett and Mrs. Brown" (1923), an essay for the *Nation and Athenaeum.* Increasing her repute for innovation were two experimental stream-of-consciousness novels, *Mrs. Dalloway* (1925) and the elegaic *To the Lighthouse* (1927), both of which probe the secret coded relations of men and women. *Mrs. Dalloway* characterizes a seemingly unimportant turning point in a day in the life of Clarissa Dalloway. The closing sentiment summarizes her problems with the past: "What does the brain matter . . . compared with the heart?" (Woolf, 1953, 296). In *To the Lighthouse* Woolf expresses her pervasive gloom in doubts about God's wisdom: "How could any Lord have made this world? she asked. . . . There is no reason, order, justice: but suffering, death, the poor. . . . No happiness lasted" (Woolf, 1955, 98). Woolf expanded her metafictional experiments in the late phase of her career. For *Orlando* (1928), a novel dedicated to her lover, Vita SACKVILLE-WEST, Woolf unleashed her imagination to picture time tripping and ANDROGYNY, the liberation of characters from the constraints of time and gender.

Woolf is revered for *A Room of One's Own* (1929), a meditative lecture series delivered at Girton College. Her thesis questions why males retain power, wealth, and influence while women remain relegated to home and children. On behalf of most females of modest means she complains that "to

have a room of her own, let alone a quiet room or a sound-proof room, was out of the question" (Woolf, 1957, 54). She extols the change in literature in the 1700s, when middle-class women—Fanny BURNEY, Elizabeth GASKELL, Ann RADCLIFFE, and Charlotte SMITH—began violating codes of female SILENCING by publishing original, thought-provoking fiction. In Woolf's opinion generations of frustrated women packed the world with untapped energy: "Women have sat indoors all these millions of years, so that by this time the very walls are permeated by their created force, which has, indeed, so overcharged the capacity of bricks and mortar that it must needs harness itself to pens and brushes and business and politics" (*ibid.*, 91). The expression of such lives and thoughts as those of SAPPHO, Lady MURASAKI, George ELIOT, and Emily BRONTË outranked the Crusades and the Wars of the Roses in importance. Woolf thanks two wars for liberating women: the Crimean War for "[letting] Florence Nightingale out of her drawing-room" and World War I for "[opening] the door to the average woman" (*ibid.*, 112).

Woolf was both clever and versatile. After penning the most significant work of her career, she reverted to conventional fiction for *Flush* (1933), the playful parody of serious BIOGRAPHY with the life story of the poet Elizabeth Barrett BROWNING's red cocker spaniel. The perceptive picture of the dog's introduction to the invalid poet's bedroom and his observation of busts of 10 poets and a window shade made from "painted fabric with a design of castles and gateways and groves of trees" expresses to the reader Browning's unique character, which immediately won the heart of her new pet (Woolf, 1933). The daily itinerary of "Flushie" reveals the limits of Browning's world to carriage rides, the sniffing of nasturtiums in the window box, and curious looks at a cloaked man who exchanged letters with Flushie's mistress. The secret marriage of the two poets results in Flush's long journey to Italy and his cautious welcome to a tiny human brother. Woolf concludes the biography with Elizabeth Barrett Browning's immersion in her work and her pet's lapse into eternal sleep at her feet.

The value of Woolf's divergent thought continues to resonate in new possibilities for a fairer world. In the essay "Blood, Bread, and Poetry: The Location of the Poet" (1984) the American poet Adrienne RICH admires the feminism and antifascism in Woolf's *Three Guineas* (1938), which pictures women as citizens of the world. Rich explains, "Woolf was attacking—as a feminist—patriotism, nationalism, the values of the British patriarchal establishment for which so many wars have been fought all over the world" (Rich, 249). Woolf's life and works have inspired three films—*Orlando* (1992), which casts Elizabeth I in a time warp and a gender swap; Vanessa Redgrave's dramatization of *Mrs. Dalloway* (1998); and *The Hours* (2002), which pictures Nicole Kidman as the depressive Woolf who puts stones into her pockets to press her body under the flow of the Ouse River to drown her. Woolf's enlightened feminism influenced the writers Olga BROUMAS, Rosario Castellanos, Louise DESALVO, Anita DIAMANT, H. D., Margaret DRABBLE, and Grace PALEY.

Bibliography

Armstrong, Nancy. *Desire and Domestic Fiction: A Political History of the Novel.* Oxford: Oxford University Press, 1995.

Rich, Adrienne. *Adrienne Rich's Poetry and Prose.* New York: W. W. Norton, 1975.

Woolf, Virginia. *Flush: A Biography* (1933). Available online. URL: http://etext.library.adelaide.edu.au/w/woolf/virginia/w91f/. Accessed on October 17, 2005.

———. *Monday or Tuesday: Eight Stories* (1921). Available online. URL: http://digital.library.upenn.edu/women/woolf/monday/monday.html. Accessed on October 17, 2005.

———. *Mrs. Dalloway.* New York: Harvest Books, 1953.

———. *Orlando: A Biography.* New York: Harvest Books, 1956.

———. *A Room of One's Own.* New York: Harbinger, 1957.

———. *To the Lighthouse.* New York: Harvest Books, 1955.

———. *The Voyage Out.* London: Duckworth, 1915.

Wright, Frances (1795–1852)

A Scots-American playwright, letter writer, lecturer, and radical social critic, Frances "Fanny" Wright D'Arusmont adopted American citizenship and the freedom to voice her feminism and ABOLITIONISM. After the death of her parents in Dundee, Scotland, she inherited at age two a comfortable legacy and passed to the guardianship of an aunt in London. At age 11 Wright lived in Devon, where she became self-educated by reading history, politics, and philosophy of the European Enlightenment era. At age 23 she traveled to North America with her sister, Camilla, to radicalize women to the SUFFRAGE cause. Upon her arrival in the United States she published a tragedy, *Altorf* (1818), a historical drama on the fight for Swiss liberties, which she produced on stages in New York City and Philadelphia.

Wright discovered that American women enjoyed less patriarchal control than British women, but that two issues, suffrage and the abolition of slavery, required immediate address. Her dismay at human bondage resulted in inflammatory abolitionist orations, the first by a female in North America. Dressed in white linen tunic and trousers, she strode to the dais to demand an accounting of American actions: "Who speaks of liberty while the human mind is in chains? Who of equality while the thousands are in squalid wretchedness, the millions harassed with health-destroying labour?" (Wright, 2004, 205). Among her solutions to the slavery question were immediate emancipation and miscegenation, a proposal that drove conservative Christians and slave holders into a frenzy. Her authoritarian tone and condescending air provoked some of her hearers to refer to her style of delivery as "Fanny Wrightism." She published a collection of letters to a Scots friend in a scathing travelogue, *Views of Society and Manners in America* (1821), a source of contention for shaming male citizens for denying women their right to equality. Her next work, the novel *A Few Days in Athens* (1822), was similarly controversial.

Wright devoted much of her energy to utopianism. When she traveled to Robert Dale Owen's New Harmony colony in Indiana and to New Orleans in 1824, her observations about Americans became more negative. She issued progressive lectures in print in the colony newspaper, the widely distributed *New Harmony Gazette.* From 1825 to 1830 she superintended Nashoba, a 640-acre freedman's colony she plotted outside Memphis,

Tennessee. A severe bout of malaria ended the experiment. In 1828 she delivered a renowned address on Independence Day, which she calls "a day, which calls to memory the conquest achieved by knowledge over ignorance, willing cooperation over blind obedience, opinion over prejudice, new ways over old ways" (Wright, 1972, 117). After medical treatment in France she escorted her black colonists to Haiti. She anthologized incendiary orations in *Course of Popular Lectures* (1836) and published the New York *Free Enquirer*, a feminist journal of fables, book reviews, and historical essays that championed liberal education for women, less stringent marriage and divorce laws, and free access to birth control. Her divorce in Ohio from William S. Phiquepal D'Arusmont set a precedent for generous court settlements to wives. Wright's polished oratory outraged the homemaking maven Catharine BEECHER, but it influenced the liberal activism of Susan B. ANTHONY, Matilda Joslyn GAGE, and Elizabeth Cady STANTON. Two decades after Wright's death in Cincinnati of complications to a broken hip, the National Woman Suffrage Association marked her passing with a tribute.

Bibliography

Morris, Celia. *Fanny Wright: Rebel in America.* Urbana: University of Illinois Press, 1992.

Travis, Molly Abel. "Frances Wright: The Other Woman of Early American Feminism," *Women's Studies* 22, no. 3 (June 1993): 389–396.

Voss, Cary R. W., and Robert C. Rowland. "Pre-Inception Rhetoric in the Creation of a Social Movement: The Case of Frances Wright," *Communication Studies* 51, no. 1 (Spring 2000): 1.

Wright, Frances. *Life, Letters, and Lectures: 1834/1844.* New York: Arno Press, 1972.

———. *Reason, Religion, and Morals.* New York: Humanity Books, 2004.

Wuthering Heights Emily Brontë (1847)

A riveting model of sensational female Gothic, Emily BRONTË's only novel advanced compelling images of sexist restraints imposed by social traditions and cloying marital expectations. Brontë sets the romance at Wuthering Heights, a raw stone-and-timber Tudor manse on the windswept Yorkshire plateau in north central England, a site that she adapted from the setting of an article in *Blackwood's Literary Magazine*. Her narrative channels through memory, letters, and diary entries the contrasting accounts of Catherine EARNSHAW and Heathcliff's affair from the point of view of the stranded visitor, Lockwood, and the housekeepers, Ellen "Nelly" Dean and Zillah. A tension develops from the day Cathy's father rescues a brooding foundling. The boy develops into a smoldering, dark-skinned lad enlivened by sexual energy and a potential for evil.

The author triangulates the main players by depicting Cathy as the failed negotiator of peace. Cathy's brother, Hindley, the heir to Wuthering Heights, ramps up ill feeling that she negates through camaraderie with the Gypsy boy. Hindley fights back with chants of "beggarly interloper" and "imp of Satan" (Brontë, 43). To escape the high-handedness and spite of her brother, the heroine flees the male turf war. Her retreat to the blighted vegetation of the moors as a refuge and a stimulus to her romantic imagination endears her to an unsuitable mate, her foster brother, whose ardor inflicts a hint of forbidden, quasi-incestual love. The heightening of their waywardness and of their destructive passions for wild countryside and for each other bodes ill for the Earnshaw DYNASTY and for individual happiness.

The shift in male-to-male ownership precipitates disaster. When Hindley takes possession of his patrimony, the author illustrates the unfairness of standard arrangements that award property to sons rather than to all the family's children. With no hope for equality Cathy, like a bondswoman, changes hands from father to brother. Building suspense are the idyllic romps on the moors that liberate Cathy from the glum, foul-tempered Hindley. The unmonitored intimacy between Cathy and Heathcliff encounters rivalry from a benign homeplace, Thrushcross Grange, a splendid manse that lures Cathy toward domestic order and risk-free ease as the wife of Edgar Linton. Brontë provides a subtextual warning in the latticed windows, metaphoric bars that foreshadow the fetters of genteel marriage.

Brontë built a huge fan base for her mystical story of pride, monstrous obsessions, and an unobtainable consummation that shocked staid

Victorians. The psychological impact of jealousy and unresolved childhood conflicts precipitates overt clashes that reveal Hindley's snobbery and Heathcliff's SEXUALITY, addictive love, and blunted passion. Heathcliff develops into the irredeemable villain, a calculating stalker who manages to debauch Hindley through two male vices, carousing and gambling. The victory gains Heathcliff no joy. His grief at losing his beloved Cathy results in bizarre expressions of sorrow, including insomnia and his removal of her husband's light-colored hair from her locket to give place to his own dark tress. Heathcliff's raging physical ache compels him to imitate Cathy's self-starvation, invalidism after childbirth, and the scratching of her name on a windowsill overlooking the moors.

Brontë's depiction of gendered pressures accounts for a far-reaching tragedy. Enhancing suspense is the mounting stress on Cathy from the warring halves of her personality—the free-roaming nature lover and the refined wife. As catastrophe looms, the author depicts female and male escape valves—Cathy's loyalty to a suitable, but dull husband and Heathcliff's rage to bring both families to heel and to usurp their estates. An outsized fixation gives neither party respite, even after Cathy accepts Edgar's settled lifestyle. In place of carnal scenarios, Brontë compensates with glimpses of nature's tumult, a parallel to internal landscapes of betrayal and unrequited yearnings.

Brontë stresses the inability of the main characters to lie to each other. After Cathy lapses into delirium, her anguish pours out in telltale mutters like the sleepwalking texts of LADY MACBETH. Heathcliff treasures the limp form of his beloved and exclaims, "You know you lie to say I have killed you, and, Catherine, you know that I could as soon forget you as my existence" (*ibid.*, 156). The outcry laments their entrapment in a doomed attraction. The story closes on the terror of Lockwood, an outsider, at unquiet souls that find no peace in death. His recoil from the sobbing ghost's icy hand precedes his slicing of its wrist on glass shards: "Terror made me cruel; and finding it useless to attempt shaking the creature off, I pulled its wrist on to the broken pane, and rubbed it to and fro till the blood ran down and soaked the bedclothes" (*ibid.*, 30).

The sadistic act echoes Brontë's controlling theme, the susceptibility of males to barbaric extremes of lust and anger.

Bibliography

Brontë, Emily. *Wuthering Heights*. New York: New American Library, 1959.

Goodlett, Debra, "Love and Addiction in 'Wuthering Heights,' " *Midwest Quarterly* 37, no. 3 (Spring 1996): 316–327.

Levy, Eric P. "The Psychology of Loneliness in 'Wuthering Heights,' " *Studies in the Novel* 28, no. 2 (Summer 1996): 158–177.

Thormahlen, Marianne, "The Lunatic and the Devil's Disciple: The 'Lovers' in 'Wuthering Heights,' " *Review of English Studies* 48, no. 190 (May 1997): 183–197.

Wylie, Elinor (1885–1928)

The lyricist and sonneteer Elinor Morton Hoyt Wylie expressed through passionate contradictions and ironies the fragility of human relations. Born in Somerville, New Jersey, she enjoyed a privileged childhood that afforded her fashionable dress for European travel and a nursemaid who sang English ballads. The emotional entanglements of Wylie's prestigious family precipitated a lifelong sickliness caused by depression, migraine headaches, and high blood pressure. The malaise later precipitated premature labor and miscarriage. After studying at Miss Baldwin's School, she progressed to Bryn Mawr and Miss Flint's Academy in Washington, D.C., where she chafed under the constraints of ladylike city life. In rebellion against an unfulfilling marriage, she abandoned her three-year-old son and her mentally unstable husband to elope with a married man, the attorney Horace Wylie, a scandalous series of choices in her day.

In 1912 Wylie published admirably crafted verse in *Incidental Numbers* and submitted poems to *Poetry* magazine. She edited and reviewed for *Vanity Fair* and earned a Julia Ellsworth Ford Prize in 1921 for *Nets to Catch the Wind*, an anthology. She dramatized her poems with fable and dialect and experimented with scenes of gendered VIOLENCE and Gothic haunting. The poem "From the Wall" (1922) warns women to reserve some of their inner selves from love relationships. She pictures profligate males spending their sweethearts as they would pennies from a purse. Her tone urges females to remain steely-eyed and coldly distant from possessive lovers. Cinching her literary reputation were the poems in *Black Armour* (1923), which depict the terrors of mortality and the importance of artistic expression to female authors. The most existential is "LET NO CHARITABLE HOPE," a lyric statement of female solitude.

Wylie channeled more feminist commentary into fiction. She warns of idealistic expectations in the romantic novel *Jennifer Lorn: A Sedate Extravaganza* (1923), an account of husbandly obsession that ruins a marriage. She followed with a fantasy, *The Venetian Glass Nephew* (1925), which describes the discounting of a trophy wife whom her husband values as a mere bauble for public display. The author's infatuation with Percy Bysshe Shelley's works suffuses the novels *The Orphan Angel* (1926) and *Mr. Hodge and Mr. Hazard* (1928) and the verse anthology *Trivial Breath* (1928). A sonnet collection, *Angels and Earthly Creatures* (1929), published the year after Wylie's death of stroke in New York City at age 43, casts doubt on the stability of love relationships. The poet Edna St. Vincent MILLAY honored her contemporary with a suite of six elegies comparing Wylie to a bright but short-lived comet. Louise BOGAN praised Wylie for adding maturity and richness to feminist verse.

Bibliography

Hoagwood, Terence Allan. "Wylie's 'The Crooked Stick,'" *Explicator* 44, no. 3 (Spring 1986): 54–57.

Wineapple, Brenda. "The Transformations," *Parnassus: Poetry in Review* 24, no. 2 (2000): 224–242.

Wylie, Elinor. *Nets to Catch the Wind* (1921). Available online. URL: http://www.gutenberg.org/etext/. Accessed on October 17, 2005.

Yamada, Mitsuye (1923–)

The Japanese-American poet Mitsuye May Yasu-take Yamada builds themes of female liberation in her pro-woman verse. Born in Fukuoka in Kyushu, Japan, she moved to Seattle's Beacon Hill with her mother in 1926 while her father, the interpreter Jack Kaichiro Yasutake, worked for the U.S. Department of Immigration. He encouraged Mitsuye to keep a journal as an outlet for thoughts and feelings. After his arrest in 1942 under President Franklin D. Roosevelt's Executive Order 9066, the family interned with other alienated Japanese Americans at Camp Minidoka, Idaho, where Yamada worked in the infirmary as a nurse's aide. The poet kept her experiences secret from her own daughter, Jeni, until the girl was a teenager. Although first denied admission because of her birth in Japan, Yamada eventually studied art and English at the University of Cincinnati and New York University and earned postgraduate degrees in English literature and research from the University of Chicago and the Graduate School of Linguistics at Columbia University. Her teaching career in the English Department at Cypress College lasted 21 years and spanned courses in ethnic and children's literature and in creative writing. A second career as visiting professor of English and Asian-American studies at the University of California at Irvine kept her in touch with the multi-cultural movement.

Like the memoirist Jeanne Wakatsuki HOUS-TON and the short-story writer Hisaye YAMAMOTO, Yamada draws on memories of internment and the invisibility of female Asian outsiders for poetic themes and for an impetus to human rights and WOMEN'S RIGHTS activism. In addition to submissions to *Café Solo*, *Calyx*, and *Feminist Studies*, she published prison camp impressions in *Camp Notes and Other Poems* (1976) and in *Camp Notes and Other Writings* (1998). Her imagery calls up family MATRIARCHY and vast changes to domestic rhythms in the prisonlike atmosphere of a desert barracks, where sounds of a pregnant wife's sobs echo through thin walls. Yamada stresses a mother's attempt at normality by darning tattered clothes and by disciplining a child in the dining hall for wasting mushy beans.

A more feminist text, *Desert Run: Poems and Stories* (1988), dramatizes through metaphor and character conflict the identity crisis of Asian women within a white majority. Particularly troubling to the newcomer is the violation of Asian codes of silence for women. In the dialect poem "Marriage Was a Foreign Country," the speaker ponders the Asian stereotype of the compliant wife who follows her husband to America like a picture bride. In addition to publishing her own works, Yamada assisted other nonwhite female authors by founding Multicultural Women Writers of Orange County and by coediting two anthologies—*The Webs We Weave* (1986) and *Sowing Ti Leaves: Writings by Multi-cultural Women* (1990). A subsequent textbook, *Teaching Human Rights Awareness through Poetry* in 1999, expresses her views of women's functions as teachers and artists. In 2003 she joined Nellie Wong and Merle Woo in compiling *Three*

Asian American Writers Speak Out on Feminism. Supporting Yamada is KITCHEN TABLE / WOMEN OF COLOR PRESS, which publishes out-of-print works by feminist and lesbian authors.

Bibliography

Woolley, Lisa. "Racial and Ethnic Semiosis in Mitsuye Yamada's 'Mrs. Higashi Is Dead,'" *MELUS* 24, no. 4 (1999): 77–91.

Yamada, Mitsuye. *Camp Notes and Other Writings.* Piscataway, N.J.: Rutgers University Press, 1998.

Yamamoto, Hisaye (1921–   )

The short stories of Hisaye Yamamoto examine the SILENCING of women, whose patriarchal marriages become a lesson in oppression for their daughters. The child of immigrants from Kumamoto, Japan, she was born in Redondo Beach, California. She became a compulsive reader and writer in her youth. After graduating from Excelsior Union High and completing supplemental courses from Japanese schools, she majored in Latin and Romance languages at Compton Junior College. Her education ended in 1942 with the internment of her family at a camp in Poston, Arizona, where she wrote news articles and composed "Death Rides the Rails to Poston" and "Surely I Must Be Dreaming" for the camp newspaper, the *Poston Chronicle.*

At the end of World War II, while Yamamoto worked as a columnist and proofreader for the *Los Angeles Tribune,* she contributed to the *Partisan Review* a feminist short story, "The High-Heeled Shoes, a Memoir" (1948), which describes sexual harassment. As a single mother of her adopted son, Paul, she earned a living and won a John Hay Whitney Foundation Opportunity Fellowship by submitting minimalist fiction to the *Arizona Quarterly, Carleton Miscellany, Furioso, Harper's Bazaar,* and *Kenyon Review.* At age 32 she moved to Staten Island to take a job at the *Catholic Worker* commune. After marrying Anthony DeSoto, she reared their four children and Paul in Los Angeles while producing high-quality short fiction, including four listed among America's best short stories: "Seventeen Syllables" (1949), "The Brown House" (1951), "Yoneko's Earthquake" (1952), and "Epithalamium" (1960).

Over a half-century career the author developed themes of dislocation and assimilation, insanity, female dispair, and Asian PATRIARCHY and gender bias. She is best known for "Seventeen Syllables," a mother-daughter story about a Nisei (second-generation Japanese American) who learns from her mother's submission to a volatile father that marriage destroys women's creativity. To the mother's dismay, as a manly show of control, her traditional husband burns a valuable Japanese art print, her prize for writing haiku. In 1988 KITCHEN TABLE / WOMEN OF COLOR PRESS published a Yamamoto collection, *Seventeen Syllables and Other Stories,* which won a citation from the Association for Asian American Studies.

Bibliography

Cheng, Ming L. "The Unrepentant Fire: Tragic Limitations in Hisaye Yamamoto's 'Seventeen Syllables,'" *MELUS* 19, no. 4 (Winter 1994): 91–107.

Kalfopoulou, Adrianne. *A Discussion of the Ideology of the American Dream in the Culture's Female Discourses.* Lewiston, N.Y.: Edwin Mellen Press, 2000.

Sugiyama, Naoko. "Issei Mothers' Silence, Nisei Daughters' Stories: The Short Fiction of Hisaye Yamamoto," *Comparative Literature Studies* 33, no. 1 (1996): 1–14.

Yamamoto, Hisaye. *Seventeen Syllables and Other Stories.* Piscataway, N.J.: Rutgers University Press, 1998.

Yearsley, Ann (1753–1806)

The British peasant poet and dramatist Ann Cromartie Yearsley redirected French revolutionary fervor toward women's liberation. Born at Clifton Hill near Bristol, England, to a working-class family, she taught herself reading and grammar and read classic English poets. While working in a dairy and peddling milk on the streets of Bristol, she wrote poems. Under the pen name Lactilla at age 32 she began publishing her protofeminist work with the help of the retired playwright Hannah More and the socialite Elizabeth Montagu, whose 1,000 bluestocking followers subscribed to a first collection, *Poems on Several Occasions* (1785). More invested the £600 proceeds for Yearsley, who took offense at her patron's meddling. The poet became the first female writer to reject patronage and to publish independently.

She gained attention for an abolitionist work, "A Poem on the Inhumanity of the Slave Trade" (1788), which promises a sadder story than that of the mythic victims Procne and PHILOMELA. The poet stresses the motif of fragmented black families, the focus of the novelist Harriet Beecher STOWE's UNCLE TOM'S CABIN (1852).

Yearsley excelled at motifs of female INDEPENDENCE and self-sufficiency. Her history play *Earl Goodwin* (1791), a verse tragedy about an 11th-century rebel against King Edward the Confessor, debuted at Bristol's Theatre Royal. A melodramatic scene dramatizes the torture of Edward's mother, Queen Emma, a stalwart heroine whom the evil Lodowicke falsely accuses of fornication with priests. He maintains, "Thro' every age it has been our chief care / to rule the thought of Woman" (Yearsley, 1791, 14). The misogynistic archbishop of Canterbury adds that men must never allow the female "mind to stretch beyond our bound. . . . It must not be! custom and law are ours" (*ibid.*, 21). Emma's trial by ordeal requires her to walk barefoot across burning plowshares.

Yearsley earned enough money to support her six children from royalties and on the profits from a circulating library that the poet managed at Bristol Hot Wells. From readings in Gothic fiction she ventured into stage melodrama with *The Royal Captives: A Fragment of Secret History: Copied from an Old Manuscript* (1795). Set in France, the suspenseful tale reprises the legend of the Man in the Iron Mask, whom a political cabal allegedly imprisoned in the Bastille in 1698. To support feminist issues, the themes focus on political dissenters and WOMEN'S RIGHTS. In 1846 Alexandre Dumas produced the play. Although Yearsley withdrew from society and died of despair, her works maintained their popularity, particularly for their motifs of female friendship. She influenced other writers to enlarge on maternity and the influence of mothers on children's character. One of her most radical feminist poems, a salute to the martyred French queen, Marie Antoinette, appeared in Yearsley's last volume, *The Rural Lyre* (1796).

Bibliography

Kucich, Greg. "Women's Historiography and the (Dis)embodiment of Law: Ann Yearsley, Mary Hays, Eliza-beth Benger," *Wordsworth Circle* 33, no. 1 (Winter 2002): 3–7.

Markley, Robert. "Lactilla, Milkwoman of Clifton: The Life and Writings of Ann Yearsley, 1753–1806," *Studies in English Literature, 1500–1900* 37, no. 3 (Summer 1997): 637–672.

Yearsley, Ann. *Earl Goodwin*. London: G. G. J. and J. Robinson, 1791.

———. "A Poem on the Inhumanity of the Slave Trade" (1788). Available online. URL: http://www.brycchancarey.com/slavery/yearsley1.htm. Accessed on October 17, 2005.

———. *The Royal Captives*. New York: Garland, 1974.

"Yellow Wallpaper, The" Charlotte Perkins Gilman (1892)

One of the prize reclamations of the feminist canon, Charlotte Perkins GILMAN's impressionist short fiction "The Yellow Wallpaper" is a Gothic drama about gendered medical treatment. After CONFINEMENT and SILENCING the hypersensitive protagonist goes insane. Composed as a secret journal and published in January 1892 in *New England Magazine*, the domestic horror tale depicts the hapless unnamed wife/patient victimized by John, an all-knowing husband/doctor who deliberately isolates her from her baby and friends. The subtext protests male-created rest cures that deprive women of autonomy and creative outlets. In opposition to John's dicta she exclaims, "I *must* say what I feel and think in some way—it is such a relief!" (Gilman, 9). Gilman's accurate depiction of treatment in female asylums earned the respect of a Kansas physician, who validated the author's observations on claustrophobia and loss of self.

Submission spells the doom of Gilman's protagonist. To placate John, his "blessed little goose" tries to subdue the need for mental engagement and to quell a lively imagination (*ibid.*, 5). The setting becomes villainous after she has nothing to occupy her senses but an expanse of arabesque paper and a permeating odor that the biographer Ann Lane identifies as the smell of coitus. Instead of confronting John for his inhumanity, the patient channels anger at the monstrous wallpaper, which is the color of wilting plants. The haunting stimuli cause her to consider arson, the recourse of the madwoman Bertha Mason ROCHESTER, locked away at Thornfield Hall in Charlotte BRONTË's *JANE EYRE* (1847).

Gilman's perspective on torture echoes prisoner-of-war memoirs. As relentless as patriarchal oppression, the four walls glare at her, offering no respite from shattered nerves. She anticipates no escape from the room's emotional VIOLENCE. As does psychological noise enlarged to visual menace, the serpentine figures entrap and torment with two-dimensional elements that "suddenly commit suicide—plunge off at outrageous angles, destroy themselves in unheard of contradictions" (*ibid.*, 4). Nightmarish to the point of battery, the images writhe and engage her whole being in a fight to preserve her sanity. The protagonist must decline to a bestial state before John realizes that he has stripped his wife of her humanity.

Unlike overt spousal abuse, John's mistreatment of his wife is insidious, but peculiarly praiseworthy for his intention to heal her skittishness. Like Offred, the human breeder immured in her keeper's bedroom in Margaret ATWOOD's dystopic best seller *The HANDMAID'S TALE* (1985), Gilman's protagonist faces a male diagnosis of too much imagination, too active a fancy. Rendered powerless, she battles psychic shock until it forces her into paranoia and hallucination. Delusion convinces her that the "awful paper began to laugh at me" (*ibid.*, 17). A doppelgänger motif pairs the female patient with a submerged phantasm that appears to spring to life to crush an overly ambitious female. On her hands and knees the patient crawls about the room, stripping paper and muttering ominously at "all those strangled heads and bulbous eyes and waddling fungus growths" (*ibid.*, 19). The result of weeks of captivity is psychic disintegration.

Gilman wrote from her personal experience with the Philadelphia neurologist Silas Weir Mitchell's treatment for neurasthenia, a psychological decline often linked to postpartum depression that causes melancholia and nervous hysteria. After she "had been as far as one could go and get back," she contrived her own rescue by abandoning doctor-prescribed torpor and by returning to writing (Lane, 131). In October 1913 Gilman published "Why I Wrote 'The Yellow Wallpaper'" in *The Forerunner*, offering as a simple antidote to female depression "work, the normal life of every human being; work, in which is joy and growth and service, without which one is a pauper and a parasite" (*ibid.*, xv). Her understanding of female malaise foretokens recognition of the "problem that has no name" in Betty FRIEDAN's feminist treatise *The Feminine Mystique* (1963).

In addition to its contribution to feminist literature Gilman's feverish tale wrought an alteration in the way Mitchell treated depression in women. William Dean Howells labeled "The Yellow Wallpaper" as a horror story in his compendium *Great Modern American Stories* (1920), giving "recognition to the supreme awfulness of your thing" (*ibid.*, 146). Ronald Perera's pseudobiographic two-act opera *The Yellow Wallpaper,* which premiered at Smith College in Northampton, Massachusetts, on May 17, 1989, featured a women's chorus and showcased Charlotte Gilman as the main character.

Bibliography

Bak, John S. "Escaping the Jaundiced Eye: Foucauldian Panopticism in Charlotte Perkins Gilman's 'The Yellow Wallpaper,'" *Studies in Short Fiction* 31, no. 1 (Winter 1994): 39–46.

Gilman, Charlotte Perkins. *The Yellow Wallpaper and Other Writings.* New York: Bantam, 1989.

Hume, Beverly A. "Managing Madness in Gilman's 'The Yellow Wall-Paper,'" *Studies in American Fiction* 30, no. 1 (Spring 2002): 3–30.

Lane, Ann J. *To Herland and Beyond.* New York: Penguin, 1991.

Roth, Marty. "Gilman's Arabesque Wallpaper," *Mosaic* 34, no. 4 (December 2001): 145–162.

Weales, Gerald. "Perera: The Yellow Wallpaper." *Commonweal,* 12 February 1993, pp. 16–17.

Yezierska, Anzia (ca. 1880–1970)

The teacher, reviewer, and fiction writer Anzia Yezierska spoke of the misgivings and SILENCING of Jewish-American immigrant females, whose lives seldom emerged from drudgery and shame. To survive, they salve their hurt with wry humor. The youngest of nine children and the fourth daughter of poor Jews scratching out a living in a mud shack on the Polish-Russian border, she lived in a Plinsk shtetl until 1890, when her parents immigrated to New York City's Lower East Side. Her father, Baruch, dedicated himself to the Torah while her mother, Pearl, supported the family with domestic labor. As is common under PATRIARCHY, only the Yezierska sons were privileged to go to school.

Under the more amenable name of Harriet "Hattie" Mayer that she received at Ellis Island, Yezierska learned English in night classes while spending her days at a sweatshop sewing machine. In 1903 with only two years of formal schooling she left the Clara de Hirsch settlement house and entered Columbia University to study home economics on a scholarship supplemented by her earnings from doing laundry. After 10 years of English teaching and two failed marriages she gave up her daughter, Louise Henriksen, to her second husband and began publishing essays and short stories in *Century*, *Cosmopolitan*, *Forum*, *Harper's*, and *Scribner's*. In splintered Yiddish-English her writings enlarged on the immigrant's dehumanizing labors and homelessness. More destructive was the assimilated Jews' distancing from ethnic roots.

Yezierska published "The Fat of the Land," issued as number one in *The Best Short Stories of 1919*. In *Hungry Hearts and Other Stories* (1920) she collected semiautobiographical dialogue tales about powerless, spiritually desiccated Jewish American women. In the story "How I Found America," a seamstress, the widow Balah Rifkin, reacts to the news that their wages will be cut by a third: "Oi weh!" (Yezierska, 1920, 115). Balah rakes at her neck and shrieks, "The blood-sucker—the thief! How will I give them to eat—my babies—my hungry little lambs! . . . Can we help ourselves? Our life lies in his hands" (*ibid.*). The anthology served as the basis of a silent movie by Samuel Goldwyn, who published advertisements naming the author an immigrant CINDERELLA and the Queen of the Ghetto. Her radical feminist novel, *Salome of the Tenements* (1923), a melodramatic satire of American materialism and superficiality, also found favor in Hollywood. Through the heroine Sonya Vrunsky's verbal jousting with her first husband, John Manning, she confronts a male-dominated household and social stratum given to affectation, which women displayed in stiff, braided clothing that concealed the curves of the female figure.

The author earned a place in feminist literature for a modern feminist work, *Bread Givers* (1925), a dialect novel about a first-generation American daughter's revolt against a tyrannic Jewish father as self-absorbed and sexist as Baruch Yezierska. The protagonist, Sara Smolinsky, struggles from the Jewish ghetto to become a middle-class NEW WOMAN who rejects the traditional Jewish matchmaking. Speaking of her father's dominance she compares him to David, Isaiah, Jeremiah, and Solomon, all monolithic males of the Bible. As she blossoms into her own person, she proclaims, "I'm smart enough to look out for myself. It is a new life now. In America, women don't need men to boss them" (Yezierska, 2003, 137). The self-affirmation of her statement suggests the courage required to escape both a domineering father and a symbol of Old World Jewish misogyny. In the last view of Sara she proceeds under a shadow: "It wasn't just my father, but the generations who made my father whose weight was still upon me" (*ibid.*, 297). Her somber vision indicates the author's awareness of how slowly women are liberated.

At first literary success weighed heavily on Yezierska. Resettled in Hollywood for the filming of *Hungry Hearts* and *Salome of the Tenements*, she felt out of her element. She abandoned scriptwriting and returned to New York to work in a familiar milieu without the intrusions of directors and producers. She served as writer in residence at the University of Wisconsin and wrote for the Works Progress Administration Writer's Project and for the *New York Times Book Review*. Her feminist works disappeared until their reclamation in the 1970s by the women's movement.

Bibliography

Ebest, Ron. "Anzia Yezierska and the Popular Debate over the Jews," *MELUS* 25, no. 1 (Spring 2000): 105–127.

Okonkwo, Christopher N. "Of Repression, Assertion, and the Speakerly Dress: Anzia Yezierska's *Salome of the Tenements*," *MELUS* 25, no. 1 (Spring 2000): 129–145.

Yezierska, Anzia. *Bread Givers*. New York: Persea Books, 2003.

———. *Hungry Hearts*. Boston: Houghton Mifflin, 1920.

Yourcenar, Marguerite (1903–1987)

The Belgian-born novelist, essayist, translator, dramatist, and poet Marguerite Antoinette Ghislaine Cleenewerck de Crayencour (later changed to Yourcenar, an anagram of *Crayencour*) described the price of aberrant SEXUALITY. As did Mary WOLLSTONECRAFT, Yourcenar lost her mother to puerperal fever soon after the author's birth in Brussels. She lived with an aunt while her father traveled. At age 15 she took up residence in Paris and studied under a tutor. During World War I she lived in England, where she polished her English and mastered Latin. In Paris she learned Greek and Italian, but the loss of her inheritance in 1929 limited her travels. In 1939 the novel *Coup de Grâce* became a best seller. When World War II began, she and a lifelong companion and translator, Grace Frick, settled in Bar Harbor, Maine. Yourcenar earned a salary teaching French literature at Sarah Lawrence College. As an expatriate, Yourcenar seemed to enhance her European qualities with a measured lyricism and eroticism balanced by classical elements.

In every case except *Sappho; or, The Suicide* (1952), Yourcenar chose to examine aberrant behavior in men rather than in women. At age 48 she published her most memorable work, the historical novel *Memoirs of Hadrian* (1951). The elegantly paced epistolary work won the Prix Femina for the psychological depth in her probings into the psyche of a conflicted world leader. The novel received popular and critical acclaim for its aphoristic sentiments and reflective narrative. She produced another work on scholarship, *The Abyss* (1968), a fictional study of alchemy that won a second Prix Femina and the author's election to the Royal Belgian Academy. She published two volumes of poetic dramas revered for their lyricism. In 1980 she became the first female elected to the Académie Française in its 346 years. She approached issues of lesbianism through the suicidal writer Yukio Mishima in *Mishima; ou, La vision du vide* (*Mishima: A Vision of the Void*, 1981). As in Yourcenar's earlier works, without direct dissection of bisexual, homosexual, and incestuous experiences, she balances characters' secret passions and repressed yearnings with consequences. The writing reveals her admiration for Lady MURASAKI, an 11th-century predecessor.

Bibliography

Savigneau, Josyane. *Marguerite Yourcenar: Inventing a Life.* Chicago: University of Chicago Press, 1993.

Yourcenar, Marguerite. *Memoirs of Hadrian.* New York: Farrar, Straus & Giroux, 1963.

———. *Mishima: A Vision of the Void.* New York: Farrar, Straus & Giroux, 1986.

Authors by Genre

Allegory

Gertrude Atherton
Margaret Atwood
Marita Bonner
Charlotte Brontë
Nawal El Saadawi
Janet Frame
Nathaniel Hawthorne
Hélisenne de Crenne
Henriette-Julie de Murat (*see* FAIRY
    TALES)
Doris Lessing
Audre Lorde
Clare Boothe Luce
Gloria Naylor
Joyce Carol Oates
Flannery O'Connor
Grace Paley
Katherine Anne Porter
Marjorie Kinnan Rawlings
Christina Rossetti
Olive Schreiner
Mary Shelley

Autobiography

Jane Addams (*see* AUTOBIOGRAPHY)
Dorothy Allison
Maya Angelou
Mary Hunter Austin
Elizabeth Blackwell
Winifred Bonfils (*see* JOURNALISM)
Calamity Jane (*see* FRONTIER
    LITERATURE)
Maria Campbell (*see*
    AUTOBIOGRAPHY)
Marie Cardinal
Beatrice Culleton (*see*
    AUTOBIOGRAPHY)

Angela Davis
A. Elizabeth Delany
Sarah L. Delany
Louise DeSalvo
Diane Di Prima
Frederick Douglass
Nawal El Saadawi
Janet Frame
Emma Goldman
Germaine Greer
Lorraine Hansberry
Josephine Herbst
bell hooks
Zora Neale Hurston
Harriet Jacobs
Florence Kelley
Fanny Kemble
Adrienne Kennedy
Florence King
Joy Kogawa
Doris Lessing
Audre Lorde
Betty Mahmoody
Beryl Markham
Harriet Martineau
Margaret Mead
Rigoberta Menchú
Kate Millett
Mourning Dove
Carry Nation (*see* TEMPERANCE)
Kathleen Norris
Margaret Oliphant
Emmeline Pankhurst
Irina Ratushinskaya
Santha Rama Rau
Marjorie Kinnan Rawlings
Adrienne Rich
Gabrielle Roy

Gertrude Stein
Gloria Steinem
Sojourner Truth
Sigrid Undset
Velma Wallis
Ide B. Wells-Barnett
Jessamyn West
Edith Wharton
Laura Ingalls Wilder
Frances Willard (*see* TEMPERANCE)
Sarah Winnemucca

Biography

Paula Gunn Allen
Mary Catherine Bateson (*see*
    MARGARET MEAD)
Alice Stone Blackwell (*see* LUCY
    STONE)
Sarah H. Bradford (*see* SCENES IN
    THE LIFE OF HARRIET
    TUBMAN)
Rita Mae Brown
Louise DeSalvo
Elizabeth Gaskell
Olive Gilbert (*see* SOJOURNER
    TRUTH)
Angelina Weld Grimké
Elizabeth Hardwick
Ida Husted Harper
Nathaniel Hawthorne
Pauline Johnson
Helen Keller
Amy Lowell
Ruthanne Lum McCunn (*see*
    SLAVERY)
Judith Sargent Murray
Diana Norman
Margaret Oliphant

Sylvia Pankhurst (*see* EMMELINE
    PANKHURST)
Santha Rama Rau
Mary Renault
Ishbel Ross
Sheila Rowbotham
Muriel Rukeyser
Vita Sackville-West
Cornelia Otis Skinner
Jane Smiley
Starhawk
Gloria Steinem
Margaret Walker

CAPTIVITY NARRATIVE
Minnie Bruce Carrigan (*see*
    CAPTIVITY LORE)
Janet Holt Giles (*see* MARY
    ROWLANDSON)
Caroline Gordon
Elizabeth Hanson (*see* CAPTIVITY
    LORE)
Mary Jemison (*see* CAPTIVITY LORE)
Susannah Johnson (*see* CAPTIVITY
    LORE)
Mary Ann and Olive Ann Oatman
    (*see* CAPTIVITY LORE)
Rachel Plummer (*see* CAPTIVITY
    LORE)
Mary Rowlandson

CHILDREN'S LITERATURE
Gloria Anzaldúa
Margaret Atwood
Judy Blume
Susan Brownmiller
Lucille Clifton
Karen Cushman
Anita Desai
Maria Edgeworth
Buchi Emecheta
Mari Evans
Fanny Fern
Dorothy Canfield Fisher
Janet Frame
Nikki Giovanni
Jennifer L. Holm
Elizabeth Janeway
Adrienne Kennedy
Maxine Kumin
Tanith Lee
Ursula Le Guin

Meridel LeSueur
Bette Bao Lord
Patricia MacLachlan (*see* FRONTIER
    LITERATURE)
Harriet Martineau
Robin McKinley (*see* BEAUTY AND
    THE BEAST)
Toni Morrison
Anna Quindlen
Christina Rossetti
Muriel Rukeyser
Sonia Sanchez
George Sand
Anne Sexton
Ntozake Shange
Charlotte Smith
Carol Sobieski (*see* FRONTIER
    LITERATURE)
Nancy Springer
Marlo Thomas (*see* FEMINIST
    THEMES)
Alice Walker
Yoko Kawashima Watkins
Eudora Welty
Timberlake Wertenbaker
Laura Ingalls Wilder

COLUMNIST
Isabel Allende
Nellie Bly
Louise Bryant
Carrie Chapman Catt
Colette
Anita Diamant
Alice Dunbar-Nelson
Barbara Ehrenreich
Fanny Fern
Ellen Gilchrist
Ellen Goodman
Germaine Greer
Ida Husted Harper
Bessie Head
bell hooks
Molly Ivins
Jamaica Kincaid
Florence King
Nellie McClung
Margaret Mead
Judith Murray
Diana Norman
Dorothy Parker
Letty Cottin Pogrebin

Katha Pollitt
Anna Quindlen
Marjorie Kinnan Rawlings
Vita Sackville-West
George Sand
Gloria Steinem
Dorothy Thompson
Laura Ingalls Wilder
Patricia Williams
Hisaye Yamamoto

COOKBOOK
Maya Angelou
Louise DeSalvo
Laura Esquivel
Santha Rama Rau
Marjorie Kinnan Rawlings
Ntozake Shange
Ida Wells-Barnett

DETECTIVE FICTION/MYSTERY
Mary Elizabeth Braddon
Rita Mae Brown
Daphne du Maurier
Sue Grafton (*see* FEMALE DETECTIVE
    NOVELS)
Tanith Lee
Adrienne Kennedy
Sara Paretsky
Mary Roberts Rinehart (*see* FEMALE
    DETECTIVE NOVELS, the NEW
    WOMAN)
Ellen Wood

DIARY/JOURNAL
Grace Aguilar
Eliza Andrews (*see* DIARIES AND
    JOURNALS)
Martha Ballard (*see* LAUREL
    THATCHER ULRICH)
Fanny Burney
Mary Boykin Chesnut
Ellen Gilchrist
Etty Hillesum (*see* DIARIES AND
    JOURNALS)
Fanny Kemble
Katherine Mansfield
Bharati Mukherjee
Murasaki Shikibu
Anaïs Nin
Sylvia Plath
Ishbel Ross

May Sarton
Mary Shelley
Catherine Parr Traill (*see* DIARIES
　　AND JOURNALS)
Simone Weil
Ida Wells-Barnett
Laura Ingalls Wilder
Virginia Woolf

DICTIONARY/GRAMMAR

Donna Cross
Ella Deloria
Rosalie Maggio (*see* SEXIST
　　LANGUAGE)

DRAMA

Tunde Adeyanju (*see* SEXUAL
　　POLITICS)
Ama Ata Aidoo
Gertrudis Gómez de Avellaneda
Maxine Bailey (*see* FEMINIST
　　THEATER)
Joanna Baillie
Aphra Behn
Marita Bonner (*see* FEMINIST
　　THEATER)
Jane Bowles
Mary Elizabeth Braddon
Elizabeth Brown-Guillory (*see*
　　FEMINIST THEATER)
Louise Bryant
Fanny Burney
Mary Powell Burrill (*see* WOMEN'S
　　WORK)
Caryl Churchill
Hélène Cixous
Maryse Condé
Kia Corthron (*see* VIOLENCE)
Rachel Crothers (*see* FEMINIST
　　THEATER)
Rita Dove
Alice Dunbar-Nelson
Eve Ensler
Anne Finch
Zona Gale
Susan Glaspell
Jessica Goldberg (*see* OLIVE
　　SCHREINER)
Angelina Weld Grimké
Jessica Hagedorn
Lorraine Hansberry
Valerie Harper (*see* PEARL BUCK)

Lillian Hellman
Felicia Hemans
Beth Henley
Henrietta Maria (*see* FEMINIST
　　THEATER)
Linda Hogan
Hroswitha von Gandersheim (*see*
　　FEMINIST THEATER)
Zora Neale Hurston
Elfriede Jelinek
Georgia Douglas Johnson
Laura Keene (*see* TEMPERANCE)
Fanny Kemble
Adrienne Kennedy
Myrna Lamb (*see* WOMEN'S
　　MAGAZINES)
Harriet Lee
Sophia Lee
Doris Lessing
Sharon M. Lewis (*see* FEMINIST
　　THEATER)
Olive Logan (*see* FEMINIST THEATER)
Anita Loos
Clare Boothe Luce
Emily Mann
Dacia Maraini (*see* WOMEN'S
　　MAGAZINES)
Carson McCullers
Edna St. Vincent Millay
May Miller (*see* SOJOURNER TRUTH)
Susan M. Miller (*see* FEMINIST
　　THEATER)
Anna Cora Mowatt
Judith Sargent Murray
Gloria Naylor
Marsha Norman
Joyce Carol Oates
Osonye Tess Onwueme
Cynthia Ozick
Ann Petry
Marge Piercy
Sylvia Plath
Adrienne Rich
Dmae Roberts
Susanna Rowson
Muriel Rukeyser
Vita Sackville-West
Sonia Sanchez
Ntozake Shange
Cornelia Otis Skinner
Anna Deavere Smith

Eulalie Spence (*see* WOMEN'S WORK)
Germaine de Staël
Gertrude Stein
Katherine Tillman (*see* AGING)
Mercy Otis Warren
Wendy Wasserstein
Chris Weatherhead (*see* MARY
　　BOYKIN CHESNUT)
Fay Weldon
Rebecca Wells
Timberlake Wertenbaker
Frances Wright
Ann Yearsley
Marguerite Yourcenar

ECOFEMINISM

Paula Gunn Allen
Isabel Allende
Mary Hunter Austin
Rachel Carson
Willa Cather
Mary Crow Dog (*see* ECOFEMINISM)
Marjorie Stoneman Douglas (*see*
　　ECOFEMINISM)
Joy Harjo
Linda Hogan
Zora Neale Hurston
Sarah Orne Jewett
Barbara Kingsolver
Maxine Kumin
Rigoberto Menchú
Brenda Peterson (*see* ECOFEMINISM)
Marge Piercy
Marjorie Kinnan Rawlings
Alice Walker
Kate Wilhelm (*see* ECOFEMINISM)

EDITING

Susan B. Anthony
Gertrudis Gómez de Avellaneda
Mary Chase Barney (*see* WOMEN'S
　　MAGAZINES)
Emilia Pardo Bazán
Lydia Becker (*see* WOMEN'S
　　MAGAZINES)
Isabella Beeton (*see* WOMEN'S
　　MAGAZINES)
Barbara Leigh Smith Bodichon (*see*
　　WOMEN'S MAGAZINES)
Mary Elizabeth Braddon
Pat Carbine (*see* WOMEN'S
　　MAGAZINES)

Lydia Maria Child
Hélène Cixous
Louisa Knapp Curtis (*see* WOMEN'S
    MAGAZINES)
Karen Cushman
Louise DeSalvo
Hilda Doolittle (H. D.)
Rita Dove
Charlotte O'Connor Eccles (*see*
    WOMEN'S MAGAZINES)
Mari Evans
Jessie Redmon Fauset
Elizabeth Fisher (*see* WOMEN'S
    MAGAZINES)
Carolyn Forché
Betty Friedan
Margaret Fuller
Matilda Joslyn Gage
Ellen Gilchrist
Caroline Gilman (*see* WOMEN'S
    MAGAZINES)
Emma Goldman
Jessica Hagedorn
Sarah Josepha Hale
Lorraine Hansberry
Joy Harjo
Ida Husted Harper
Eliza Haywood (*see* WOMEN'S
    MAGAZINES)
Molly Ivins
Erica Jong
Melanie Kaye/Kantrowitz
Sahar Khalifeh
Carolyn Kizer
Suzanne LaFollette
Denise Levertov
Amy Lowell
Clare Boothe Luce
Tatyana Mamonova (*see* GENDER
    BIAS)
Harriet Monroe (*see* SARA
    TEASDALE)
Cherríe Moraga
Robin Morgan
Sena Naslund
Joyce Carol Oates
Margaret Oliphant
Emmeline Pankhurst
Sylvia Pankhurst (*see* MARXIST
    FEMINISM)
Bessie Rayner Parkes (*see* WOMEN'S
    MAGAZINES)

Ann Petry
Letty Cottin Pogrebin
Katha Pollitt
Harriet Jane Robinson
Susanna Rowson
Elizabeth Cady Stanton
Gloria Steinem
Ann Sophia Stephens
Lucy Stone
Annie S. Swan (*see* WOMEN'S
    MAGAZINES)
Isabella Tod (*see* WOMEN'S
    MAGAZINES)
Ida B. Wells-Barnett
Eudora Welty
Ella Wheeler Wilcox (*see* WOMEN'S
    MAGAZINES)
Laura Ingalls Wilder
Mary Wollstonecraft
Frances Wright
Elinor Wylie
Mitsuye Yamada

EPIC

Marion Zimmer Bradley
Gwendolyn Brooks
Diane Di Prima
Hilda Doolittle (H. D.)
Joy Kogawa
Bette Bao Lord
Osonye Tess Onwueme
Anne Provoost (*see* AGING)
Karen Rowe (*see* STORYTELLING)
Leslie Marmon Silko
Velma Wallis
Wendy Wasserstein
Frances Willard (*see* TEMPERANCE)

EPISTOLARY NOVEL

Mariama Bâ
Aphra Behn
Christine de Pisan
Maria Edgeworth
Hannah Foster (*see* GENDER BIAS)
Cristina García (*see* MATRIARCHY)
Hélisenne de Crenne
Ruth Prawer Jhabvala
Sophia Lee
Anita Loos
Susanna Rowson
Anna Seward
Germaine de Staël

Alice Walker
Lady Mary Walker
Marguerite Yourcenar

ESSAY/REVIEW

Jane Addams (*see* SUFFRAGE)
Paula Gunn Allen
Susan B. Anthony
Gloria Evangelina Anzaldúa
Gertrude Atherton
Margaret Atwood
Anna Laetitia Barbauld
Djuna Barnes
Antoinette Brown Blackwell
Elizabeth Blackwell
Marita Bonner
Susan Brownmiller
Louise Bryant
Mary Clarke Carr (*see* WOMEN'S
    MAGAZINES)
Carrie Chapman Catt
Anne Carson
Caroline Clive
Mary Elizabeth Coleridge
Anna Julia Cooper
Mary Crow Dog (*see* ECOFEMINISM)
Angela Davis
Voltairine de Cleyre
Anita Diamant
Marjory Stoneman Douglas (*see*
    ECOFEMINISM)
Andrea Dworkin
Julie Olsen Edwards (*see* TILLIE
    OLSEN)
Barbara Ehrenreich
Clarissa Pinkola Estés
Mari Evans
Fanny Fern
Dorothy Canfield Fisher
Mary K. Ford (*see* EDUCATION)
Betty Friedan
Zona Gale
Ellen Gilchrist
Nikki Giovanni
Emma Goldman
Ellen Goodman
Caroline Gordon
Lizzie May Holmes (*see*
    STEREOTYPES)
Molly Ivins
Sarah Orne Jewett
June Jordan

Melanie Kaye/Kantrowitz
Helen Keller
Fanny Kemble
Sahar Khalifeh
Jamaica Kincaid
Florence King
Maxine Hong Kingston
Maxine Kumin
Emma Lazarus
Ursula Le Guin
Doris Lessing
Meridel Le Sueur
Denise Levertov
Audre Lorde
Amy Lowell
Alison Lurie
Natasha Maltseva (see GENDER BIAS)
Katherine Mansfield
Beryl Markham
Harriet Martineau
Rigoberto Menchú (see
    ECOFEMINISM)
Harriet Taylor Mill
John Stuart Mill
Edna St. Vincent Millay
Ekaterina Miranova (see GENDER
    BIAS)
Gabriela Mistral
Ellen Moers
Judith Sargent Murray
Joyce Carol Oates
Flannery O'Connor
Tillie Olsen
Susan Orlean (see ECOFEMINISM)
Cynthia Ozick
Grace Paley
Daphne Patai (see WOMEN'S
    MAGAZINES)
Ann Petry
Elizabeth Stuart Phelps
Letty Cottin Pogrebin
Katha Pollitt
Katherine Anne Porter
Dawn Powell
Santha Rama Rau
Adrienne Rich
Marilynne Robinson
Sheila Rowbotham
Muriel Rukeyser
Joanna Russ
Nayantara Sahgal
Margaret Sanger

May Sarton
Olive Schreiner
Ntozake Shange
Elaine Showalter
Leslie Marmon Silko
Cornelia Otis Skinner
Jane Smiley
Susan Sontag
Starhawk
Lucy Stone
Laurel Thatcher Ulrich
Helena María Viramontes
Margaret Walker
Mercy Otis Warren
Wendy Wasserstein
Jessamyn West
Rebecca West
Laura Ingalls Wilder
Frances Willard (see TEMPERANCE)
Naomi Wolf
Mary Wollstonecraft
Virginia Woolf
Anzia Yezierska
Marguerite Yourcenar

FABLE
Marie de France
Joyce Carol Oates
Mary Shelley

FAIRY TALE
Olga Broumas
Angela Carter
Jane Campion (see FAIRY TALES)
Marie-Catherine le Jumelle de
    Barneville, comtesse d'Aulnoy
    (see EVE, FAIRY TALES)
Henriette-Julie de Murat (see EVE,
    FAIRY TALES)
Marie-Jeanne L'Héritier de
    Villandon (see FAIRY TALES)
Eve Ensler
Louise Erdrich
Margaret Peterson Haddix (see
    CINDERELLA)
Madonna Kolbenschlag (see
    CINDERELLA)
Maxine Kumin
Rosemary Lake (see LITTLE RED
    RIDING HOOD)
Tanith Lee (see ALISON LURIE,
    PERSEPHONE)

Ursula Le Guin
Robin McKinley (see BEAUTY AND
    THE BEAST)
George Sand
Anne Sexton
Anne Sharpe (see LITTLE RED
    RIDING HOOD)
Stevie Smith
Jane Yolen (see LITTLE RED RIDING
    HOOD)

FEMINIST/SOCIAL CRITICISM
Margaret Atwood
Deborah Barker (see KATE CHOPIN)
Nina Baym (see FEMINIST CRITICISM)
Simone de Beauvoir
Susan Brownmiller
Phyllis Chesler (see SYLVIA PLATH)
Christine de Pisan
Hélène Cixous
Maryse Condé
Donna Cross
Margaret Anne Doody (see GOTHIC
    FICTION)
Margaret Drabble
Andrea Dworkin
Betty Friedan
Sandra Gilbert
Susan Gubar
Carol Gilligan (see INDEPENDENCE)
Germaine Greer
Judith Halberstam (see GOTHIC
    FICTION)
Carolyn G. Heilbrun (see GOTHIC
    FICTION)
Judith Herman (see VIOLENCE)
María Hererra-Sobek (see HELENA
    MARÍA VIRAMONTES)
Lisa Hirschman (see VIOLENCE)
Diane Long Hoeveler (see
    CHARLOTTE SMITH)
bell hooks
Luce Irigaray
Helen Hunt Jackson
Elizabeth Janeway
June Jordan
Adrianne Kalfopoulou (see
    SILENCING)
Florence Kelley
Carol Farley Kessler (see FEMINIST
    UTOPIAS)
Elaine H. Kim (see AMY TAN)

Bobbie Ann Mason
Kate Millett
Ellen Moers
Nancy Morejón
Margaret Oliphant
Catherine Orenstein (*see* FAIRY
    TALES)
Alicia Suskin Ostriker
Emilie Hawkes Peacocke (*see*
    JOURNALISM)
Katha Pollitt
Adrienne Rich
Sheila Rowbotham
Karen Rowe (*see* STORYTELLING)
Elaine Showalter
Jane Smiley
Fannie Stenhouse (*see* FRONTIER
    LITERATURE)
Helena María Viramontes
Alice Walker
Marina Warner (*see* BEAUTY MYTH,
    EVE, FAIRY TALES, VIRGIN MARY)
Naomi Wolf
Francis Wright

FEMINIST PHILOSOPHY
Mary Antin
Simone de Beauvoir
Susan Brownmiller
Christine de Pisan
Voltairine de Cleyre
Clarissa Pinkola Estés
Shulamith Firestone
Marilyn French
Margaret Fuller
Charlotte Perkins Gilman
bell hooks
Luce Irigaray
Harriet Taylor Mill
John Stuart Mill
Letty Cottin Pogrebin
Adrienne Rich
Sheila Rowbotham
Elaine Showalter
Germaine de Staël
Gertrude Stein
Simone Weil
Naomi Wolf
Mary Wollstonecraft

FOLKLORE
Maryse Condé

Ella Deloria
Zora Neale Hurston
Elizabeth Janeway
Mourning Dove
Osonye Tess Onwueme
Ethel Johnston Phelps (*see* FAIRY
    TALES)

GOTHIC LITERATURE
Louisa May Alcott
Isabel Allende
Gertrude Atherton
Margaret Atwood
Jane Austen
Anna Laetitia Barbauld
Djuna Barnes
Emilia Bazán
Elizabeth Bowen
Mary Elizabeth Braddon
Charlotte Brontë
Emily Brontë
Octavia Butler
Angela Carter
Caroline Clive
Marie Corelli
Edwidge Danticat
Isak Dinesen
Margaret Drabble
Mary Wilkins Freeman
Charlotte Perkins Gilman
Beth Henley
Zora Neale Hurston
Shirley Jackson
Emma Lazarus
Mary McCarthy
Carson McCullers
Robin McKinley (*see* BEAUTY AND
    THE BEAST)
Toni Morrison
Marsha Norman
Joyce Carol Oates
Flannery O'Connor
Jean Rhys
Mary Robinson
Mary Shelley
Fay Weldon
Eudora Welty
Ellen Wood

HISTORICAL FICTION/DRAMA
Grace Aguilar
Isabel Allende

Julia Alvarez
Lydia Maria Child
Mary Elizabeth Coleridge
Maryse Condé
Marie Corelli
Donna Cross
Karen Cushman
Edwidge Danticat
Anita Diamant
Maria Edgeworth
Helen Webb Harris
Felicia Hemans
Jennifer L. Holm
Elizabeth Janeway
Erica Jong
Harriet Lee
Sophia Lee
Meridel Le Sueur
Nellie McClung
Faith McNulty (*see* THE BURNING
    BED)
May Miller
Margaret Mitchell
Sena Naslund
Diana Norman
Margaret Oliphant
Ann Petry
Elizabeth Stuart Phelps
Marge Piercy
Anne Provoost (*see* AGING)
Mary Renault
Anne Rice
Susanna Rowson
Ntozake Shange
Jane Smiley
Dava Sobel (*see* TIMBERLAKE
    WERTENBAKER)
Ann Sophia Stephens
Helena María Viramontes
Margaret Walker
Timberlake Wertenbaker
Jessamyn West
Frances Wright
Ann Yearsley
Marguerite Yourcenar

HISTORY
Grace Aguilar
Susan B. Anthony
Elizabeth Bowen
Susan Brownmiller
Louise Bryant

Carrie Chapman Catt
Mary Boykin Chesnut
Angela Davis
Annie Elizabeth Delany
Sarah Louise Delany
Ella Deloria
Matilda Joslyn Gage
Sarah Josepha Hale
Ida Husted Harper
Jennifer Holm
Elizabeth Janeway
Harriet Martineau
Anne Mather (*see* Ms.)
Judith Sargent Murray
Margaret Oliphant
Emmeline Pankhurst
Sylvia Pankhurst (*see* EMMELINE
    PANKHURST)
Cokie Roberts (*see* ABIGAIL
    ADAMS)
Harriet Jane Robinson
Sheila Rowbotham
Nayantara Sahgal
Susan Schechter (*see* VIOLENCE)
Lillian Schlissel (*see* DIARIES AND
    JOURNALS)
Elizabeth Cady Stanton
Ann Sophia Stephens
Barbara Tuchman (*see* COURTLY
    LOVE)
Laurel Thatcher Ulrich
Mercy Otis Warren

HUMOR
Aristophanes
Annie Elizabeth Delany
Sarah Louise Delany
Maria Edgeworth
Eve Ensler
Fanny Fern
Elizabeth Gaskell
Ellen Gilchrist
Zora Neale Hurston
Molly Ivins
Erica Jong
Florence King
Carolyn Kizer
Rosemary Lake (*see* LITTLE RED
    RIDING HOOD)
Anita Loos
Alison Lurie
Carson McCullers

Lynn Nottage (*see* DOMESTIC
    ABUSE)
Flora Nwapa (*see* INDEPENDENCE)
Flannery O'Connor
Cynthia Ozick
Grace Paley
Dorothy Parker
Elizabeth Stuart Phelps
Joanna Russ
Mary Theresa Shelhamer (*see*
    WOMEN'S RIGHTS)
Cornelia Otis Skinner
Jane Smiley
E. D. E. N. Southworth
Ann Sophia Stephens
Mercy Otis Warren
Wendy Wasserstein
Rebecca Wells
Eudora Welty
Timberlake Wertenbaker

JOURNALISM
Mariama Bâ
Isabella Bird (*see* FRONTIER
    LITERATURE)
Nellie Bly
Therese Bonney (*see* JOURNALISM)
Susan Brownmiller
Louise Bryant
Tennessee Claflin (*see* VICTORIA
    WOODHULL)
Colette
Rebecca Harding Davis
Voltairine de Cleyre
Anita Diamant
Alice Dunbar-Nelson
Barbara Ehrenreich
Oriana Fallaci
Susan Faludi
Jill Barrett Fein (*see* BARBARA
    KINGSOLVER)
Fanny Fern
Carolyn Forché
Betty Friedan
Matilda Joslyn Gage
Zona Gale
Ellen Goodman
Caroline Gordon
Germaine Greer
Frances Harper
Ida Husted Harper
Bessie Head

Amy Hill Hearth (*see* A. ELIZABETH
    DELANY AND SARAH L. DELANY)
Josephine Herbst
Molly Ivins
Florence King
Barbara Kingsolver
Suzanne LaFollette
Annie Laurie (*see* JOURNALISM)
Meridel LeSueur
Anita Loos
Clare Boothe Luce
Paule Marshall
Harriet Martineau
Mary McCarthy
Harriet Taylor Mill
John Stuart Mill
Margaret Mitchell
Judith Sargent Murray
Diana Norman
Marsha Norman
Emmeline Pankhurst
Dorothy Parker
Ann Petry
Letty Cottin Pogrebin
Katherine Anne Porter
Anna Quindlen
Santha Rama Rau
Marjorie Kinnan Rawlings
Dmae Roberts
Marilynne Robinson
Ishbel Ross
Gabrielle Roy
Muriel Rukeyser
Nayantara Sahgal
George Sand
Gloria Steinem
Ann Sophia Stephens
Harriet Beecher Stowe
Dorothy Thompson
Mercy Otis Warren
Ida B. Wells-Barnett
Eudora Welty
Timberlake Wertenbaker
Rebecca West
Laura Ingalls Wilder
Ellen Wood
Victoria Woodhull

LEGEND
Gloria Anzaldúa
Joanna Baillie
Jeanne Wakatsuki Houston

Pauline Johnson
Joy Kogawa
Elizabeth Stuart Phelps
Alina Reyes (*see* LILITH)
Leslie Marmon Silko
Jane Smiley
Velma Wallis

LESBIAN FICTION/NONFICTION
Paula Gunn Allen
Dorothy Allison
Gloria Anzaldúa
June Arnold (*see* LESBIAN AUTHORS)
Djuna Barnes
Aphra Behn
Elizabeth Bishop
Marie-Claire Blais
Elizabeth Bowen
Jane Bowles
Marion Zimmer Bradley
Dionne Brand
Olga Broumas
Rita Mae Brown
Willa Cather
Margaret Cavendish (*see* LESBIAN AUTHORS)
Hélène Cixous
Colette
Marie Corelli
Clemence Dane (*see* LESBIAN AUTHORS)
Hilda Doolittle (H. D.)
Andrea Dworkin
Mary Wilkins Freeman
Angelina Weld Grimké
Radclyffe Hall
Lorraine Hansberry
Sarah Orne Jewett
Melanie Kaye/Kantrowitz
Florence King
Tanith Lee
Audre Lorde
Amy Lowell
Katherine Mansfield
Carson McCullers
Edna St. Vincent Millay
Cherríe Moraga
Margaret Newcastle (*see* FEMINIST UTOPIAS)
Anaïs Nin
Mary Renault
Adrienne Rich

Christina Rossetti
Muriel Rukeyser
Joanna Russ
Vita Sackville-West
Sappho
Mary Sarton
Anna Seward
Starhawk
Gertrude Stein
Winchilsea, Anne Finch, countess of
Virginia Woolf
Marguerite Yourcenar

LETTERS
Abigail Adams
Susan B. Anthony
Mary Antin
Louise Bogan
Fanny Burney
Alice Kirk Grierson (*see* FRONTIER LITERATURE)
Angelina Grimké
Sarah Grimké
Radclyffe Hall
Lorraine Hansberry
Hélisenne de Crenne
Helen Keller
Fanny Kemble
Caroline Lamb
Emma Lazarus
Katherine Mansfield
Anaïs Nin
Flannery O'Connor
Elizabeth Stuart Phelps
Katherine Anne Porter
Frances M. A. Roe (*see* LETTER WRITING)
Olive Schreiner
Anna Seward
Germaine de Staël
Elizabeth Cady Stanton
Elinore Pruitt Stewart (*see* LETTER WRITING)
Dorothy Thompson
Lady Mary Walker
Phillis Wheatley
Frances Wright

LIBRETTO/LYRICS/HYMNS
Mari Evans
Felicia Hemans
Georgia Douglas Johnson

June Jordan
Edna St. Vincent Millay
Susanna Rowson
Gertrude Stein
Mary Wheeler (*see* TEMPERANCE)

MEMOIR
Isabel Allende
Mary Antin
Isabella Bird (*see* FRONTIER LITERATURE)
Louise Bogan
Rita Mae Brown
Nien Cheng (*see* FEMINIST THEMES)
Isak Dinesen
Nawal El Saadawi
Louise Erdrich
Oriana Fallaci
Janet Frame
Marilyn French
Margaret Fuller
Ellen Glasgow
Lillian Hellman
Josephine Herbst
James Houston
Jeanne Wakatsuki Houston
Shirley Jackson
Erica Jong
June Jordan
Fanny Kemble
Susan Magoffin (*see* FRONTIER LITERATURE)
Bobbie Ann Mason
Mary McCarthy
Nellie McClung
Kate Millett
Robin Morgan
Malike Oufkir (*see* FEMINIST THEMES)
Marjorie Kinnan Rawlings
Harriet Jane Robinson
Sheila Rowbotham
Mary Canaga Rowland (*see* FRONTIER LITERATURE)
Nayantara Sahgal
George Sand
Germaine de Staël
Gertrude Stein
Sophie Trupin (*see* FRONTIER LITERATURE)
Yoko Kawashima Watkins
Jessamyn West

MYTH

Gloria Anzaldúa
Eavan Boland
Marion Zimmer Bradley
Olga Broumas
Hilda Doolittle (H. D.)
Louise Glück
Joy Harjo
Maxine Hong Kingston
Tanith Lee (*see* PERSEPHONE)
Denise Levertov
Audre Lorde
Yxta Maya Murray (*see* LA
    LLORONA)
Pretty Shield (*see* SPIDER WOMAN)
Anne Rice
Dmae Roberts
Leslie Marmon Silko
Nancy Springer
Christa Wolf
Diane Wolkstein

NONFICTION

Isabel Allende
Mary Antin
Mary Hunter Austin
Catharine Beecher
Nellie Bly
Rachel Carson
Lydia Maria Child
Hélène Cixous
Louise DeSalvo
Maria Edgeworth
Charlotte Perkins Gilman
Zora Neale Hurston
Helen Keller
Bette Bao Lord
Betty Mahmoody
Robin Morgan
Patricia O'Brien (*see* ELLEN
    GOODMAN)
Margaret Sanger
Germaine de Staël
Gloria Steinem
Marie Stopes
Rebecca West

NOVEL

Grace Aguilar
Ama Ata Aidoo
Louisa May Alcott
Paula Gunn Allen

Isabel Allende
Dorothy Allison
Julia Alvarez
Harriette Arnow
Gertrude Atherton
Margaret Atwood
Jean Auel
Jane Austen
Mary Hunter Austin
Djuna Barnes
Emilia Pardo Bazán
Aphra Behn
Antoinette Brown Blackwell
Marie-Claire Blais
Elizabeth Bowen
Jane Bowles
Mary Elizabeth Braddon
Dionne Brand
Charlotte Brontë
Emily Brontë
Gwendolyn Brooks
Rita Mae Brown
Susan Brownmiller
Pearl Buck
Fanny Burney
Octavia Butler
Marie Cardinal
Angela Carter
Rosario Castellanos (*see* WOMEN'S
    RIGHTS)
Willa Cather
Kate Chopin
Sandra Cisneros
Caroline Clive
Mary Elizabeth Coleridge
Colette
Maryse Condé
Marie Corelli
Donna Cross
Helena Parente Cunha (*see* LETTER
    WRITING)
Edwidge Danticat
Rebecca Harding Davis
Anita Desai
Anita Diamant
Diane Di Prima
Margaret Drabble
Daphne du Maurier
Marguerite Duras
Andrea Dworkin
Maria Edgeworth
George Eliot

Buchi Emecheta
Marian Engel (*see* BEAUTY AND THE
    BEAST)
Laura Esquivel
Oriana Fallaci
Jessie Redmon Fauset
Edna Ferber
Fanny Fern
Dorothy Canfield Fisher
Hannah Webster Foster (*see* GENDER
    BIAS)
Janet Frame
Marilyn French
Carmen Martín Gaite (*see*
    SILENCING)
Zona Gale
Cristina García (*see* MATRIARCHY)
Elizabeth Gaskell
Kaye Gibbons
Ellen Gilchrist
Susan Glaspell
Nadine Gordimer
Caroline Gordon
Sarah Grand
Jessica Hagedorn
Elizabeth Forsythe Hailey (*see*
    LETTER WRITING)
Sarah Josepha Hale
Radclyffe Hall
Frances Harper
Nathaniel Hawthorne
Bessie Head
Hélisenne de Crenne
Fannie Hurst
Zora Neale Hurston
Helen Hunt Jackson
Shirley Jackson
Elizabeth Janeway
Elfriede Jelinek
Gish Jen
Sarah Orne Jewett
Ruth Prawer Jhabvala
Elizabeth Jolley (*see* LETTER
    WRITING)
Gayl Jones
Erica Jong
Sahar Khalifeh
Jamaica Kincaid
Barbara Kingsolver
Maxine Hong Kingston
Joy Kogawa
Maxine Kumin

Caroline Lamb
Nella Larsen
Emma Lazarus
Harper Lee
Ursula Le Guin
Doris Lessing
Meridel Le Sueur
Anita Loos
Bette Bao Lord
Alison Lurie
Harriet Martineau
Bobbie Ann Mason
Mary McCarthy
Nellie McClung
Carson McCullers
Terry McMillan
Margaret Mitchell
Sylvia Molloy (*see* LETTER WRITING)
Toni Morrison
Mourning Dove
Bharati Mukherjee
Alice Munro
Murasaki Shikibu
Judith Sargent Murray
Sena Naslund
Gloria Naylor
Fae Myenne Ng
Anaïs Nin
Diana Norman
Marsha Norman
Kathleen Norris
Elizabeth Nuñez
Joyce Carol Oates
Margaret Oliphant
Cynthia Ozick
Teresa de la Parra (*see* MARRIAGE
    MARKET)
Elizabeth Stuart Phelps
Sylvia Plath
Letty Cotten Pogrebin
Katherine Anne Porter
Dawn Powell
Anne Provoost (*see* AGING)
Anna Quindlen
Ann Radcliffe
Santha Rama Rau
Marjorie Kinnan Rawlings
Mary Renault
Jean Rhys
Alexandra Ripley (*see* MARGARET
    MITCHELL)
Dmae Roberts

Marilynne Robinson
Mary Robinson
Gabrielle Roy
Vita Sackville-West
Nayantara Sahgal
May Sarton
Olive Schreiner
Ntozake Shange
Mary Shelley
Leslie Marmon Silko
Jane Smiley
Charlotte Smith
Stevie Smith
Susan Sontag
E. D. E. N. Southworth
Germaine de Staël
Jean Stafford
Gertrude Stein
Ann Sophia Stephens
Harriet Beecher Stowe
Amy Tan
Sigrid Undset
Alice Walker
Margaret Walker
Fay Weldon
Rebecca Wells
Eudora Welty
Jessamyn West
Rebecca West
Edith Wharton
Christa Wolf
Mary Wollstonecraft
Ellen Wood
Virginia Woolf
Frances Wright
Elinor Wylie
Marguerite Yourcenar

NOVELLA

Grace Aguilar
Mariama Bâ
Emilia Pardo Bazán
Kate Chopin
Rebecca Harding Davis
Maria Edgeworth
Nawal El Saadawi
Zona Gale
Kaye Gibbons
Nadine Gordimer
Jessica Hagedorn
Sarah Josepha Hale
Paule Marshall

Carson McCullers
Sena Naslund
Flannery O'Connor
Cynthia Ozick
Ann Petry
Katherine Anne Porter
Ann Radcliffe
Marjorie Kinnan Rawlings
Susanna Rowson
George Sand
Ntozake Shange
Jane Smiley
E. D. E. N. Southworth
Helena María Viramontes
Edith Wharton

ORATION/LECTURE

Susan B. Anthony
Antoinette Brown Blackwell
Dionne Brand
Carri Chapman Catt
Angela Davis
Voltairine de Cleyre
Frederick Douglass
Andrea Dworkin
Barbara Ehrenreich
Clarissa Pinkola Estés
Susan Faludi
Marilyn French
Betty Friedan
Matilda Joslyn Gage
William Lloyd Garrison (*see*
    SUFFRAGE)
Emma Goldman
Germaine Greer
Angelina Grimké
Sarah Grimké
Anne Hutchinson
Molly Ivins
Elizabeth Janeway
Pauline Johnson
Helen Keller
Florence Kelley
Audre Lorde
Nellie McClung
Lucretia Mott
Tillie Olsen
Osonye Tess Onwueme
Emmeline Pankhurst
Elizabeth Stuart Phelps
Letty Cottin Pogrebin
Anna Quindlen

Harriet Jane Robinson
Sheila Rowbotham
Margaret Sanger
Starhawk
Lucy Stone
Marie Stopes
Dorothy Thompson
Sojourner Truth
Yoko Kawashima Watkins
Angelina Grimké Weld
Ida B. Wells-Barnett
Frances Willard (*see* TEMPERANCE)
Patricia Williams
Sarah Winnemucca
Frances Wright

PARODY
Louisa May Alcott
Aristophanes (*see* LYSISTRATA)
Margaret Atwood
Jane Austen
Angela Carter
Elizabeth T. Corbett (*see* FEMINIST
    UTOPIAS)
Laura Esquivel
Elizabeth Gaskell
Alice Randall (*see* MARGARET
    MITCHELL)
Dmae Roberts
Timberlake Wertenbaker
Winchilsea, Anne Finch, countess of
Naomi Wolf
Virginia Woolf

POLEMICS
Susan B. Anthony
Simone de Beauvoir
Ada Bowles (*see* WOMEN'S
    MAGAZINES)
Lydia Maria Child
Christine de Pisan
Juana Inés de la Cruz
Frederick Douglass
Matilda Joslyn Gage
Emma Goldman
Sarah Grand
Josephine Herbst
Julia Ward Howe (*see* FEMINIST
    THEMES, WOMEN'S MAGAZINES)
Helen Hunt Jackson
Helen Keller
Barbara Kingsolver

Meridel Le Sueur
Robin Morgan
Emmeline Pankhurst
Mary Robinson
Sheila Rowbotham
Nayantara Sahgal
Elizabeth Cady Stanton
Lois Nichols Waisbrooker (*see*
    FEMINIST UTOPIAS)

SATIRE
Aristophanes (*see* LYSISTRATA)
Margaret Atwood
Fanny Burney
Angela Carter
Caroline Clive
Annie Denton Cridge (*see* FEMINIST
    UTOPIAS)
Anita Desai
Maria Edgeworth
Eve Ensler
Fanny Fern
Mary Wilkins Freeman
Elizabeth Gaskell
Ellen Glasgow
Susan Glaspell
Lorraine Hansberry
Molly Ivins
Shirley Jackson
Elfriede Jelinek
Fanny Kemble
Adrienne Kennedy
Florence King
Carolyn Kizer
Caroline Lamb
Myrna Lamb (*see* WOMEN'S
    MAGAZINES)
Tanith Lee (*see* PERSEPHONE)
Anita Loos
Mina Loy
Clare Boothe Luce
Alison Lurie
Katherine Mansfield
Mary McCarthy
Edna St. Vincent Millay
Marianne Moore
Judith Sargent Murray
Kathleen Norris
Joyce Carol Oates
Flannery O'Connor
Margaret Oliphant
Osonye Tess Onwueme

Cynthia Ozick
Dorothy Parker
Dawn Powell
Cornelia Otis Skinner
Jane Smiley
Charlotte Smith
Stevie Smith
E. D. E. N. Southworth
Gloria Steinem
Mercy Otis Warren
Fay Weldon (*see* BEAUTY MYTH)
Rebecca Wells
Winchilsea, Anne Finch, countess of
Virginia Woolf

SCHOLARLY TREATISE
Grace Aguilar
Antoinette Blackwell
Elizabeth Blackwell
Susan Brownmiller
Maria Edgeworth
Margaret Fuller
Matilda Gage
Charlotte Perkins Gilman
Zora Neale Hurston
Harriet Martineau
Margaret Mead
Harriet Taylor Mill
Sheila Rowbotham
Margaret Sanger
Germaine de Staël
Marie Stopes
Dorothy Thompson
Mary Wollstonecraft
Virginia Woolf

SCIENCE FICTION/FANTASY
Margaret Atwood
Margaret Ball (*see* ANNE
    McCAFFREY)
Marion Zimmer Bradley
Octavia Butler
Angela Carter
Marie Corelli
Charlotte Perkins Gilman
Shirley Jackson
Tanith Lee
Ursula Le Guin
Doris Lessing
Anne McCaffrey
Marge Piercy
Joanna Russ

Mary Shelley
Nancy Springer
Starhawk
Elinor Wylie

SCREENPLAY/RADIO PLAY/
  TELEPLAY

Susan Brownmiller
Marguerite Duras
Eve Ensler
Mari Evans
Nadine Gordimer
Lillian Hellman
Ruth Prawer Jhabvala
Adrienne Kennedy
Tanith Lee
Patricia MacLachlan (*see* FRONTIER
  LITERATURE)
Terry McMillan
Kate Millett
Marsha Norman
Kathleen Norris
Dorothy Parker
Dawn Powell
Santha Rama Rau
Sonia Sanchez
May Sarton
Leslie Marmon Silko
Stevie Smith
Carol Sobieski (*see* FRONTIER
  LITERATURE)
Susan Sontag
Starhawk
Gloria Steinem
Helena María Viramontes
Alice Walker
Wendy Wasserstein
Fay Weldon
Rebecca Wells
Timberlake Wertenbaker
Anzia Yezierska

SCRIPTURE

Matilda Joslyn Gage
Elizabeth Cady Stanton

SHORT FICTION

Jane Addams (*see* WOMEN'S
  MAGAZINES)
Grace Aguilar
Ama Ata Aidoo
Isabel Allende

Dorothy Allison
Gertrude Atherton
Margaret Atwood
Toni Cade Bambara
Emilia Pardo Bazán
Antoinette Blackwell
Judy Blume
Marita Bonner
Elizabeth Bowen
Jane Bowles
Dionne Brand
Octavia Butler
Angela Carter
Willa Cather
Lydia Maria Child
Kate Chopin
Mary Elizabeth Coleridge
Marie Corelli
Edwidge Danticat
Anita Desai
Daphne du Maurier
Alice Dunbar-Nelson
Andrea Dworkin
Buchi Emecheta
Louise Erdrich
Jessie Redmon Fauset
Edna Ferber
Dorothy Canfield Fisher
Janet Frame
Mary Wilkins Freeman
Zona Gale
Elizabeth Gaskell
Ellen Gilchrist
Charlotte Perkins Gilman
Ellen Glasgow
Nadine Gordimer
Caroline Gordon
Kate Greenaway (*see* WOMEN'S
  MAGAZINES)
Radclyffe Hall
Bessie Head
Felicia Hemans
Josephine Herbst
Fannie Hurst
Shirley Jackson
Elizabeth Janeway (*see* WOMEN'S
  MAGAZINES)
Gish Jen
Sarah Orne Jewett
Ruth Prawer Jhabvala
Pauline Johnson
Melanie Kaye/Kantrowitz

Adrienne Kennedy
Jamaica Kincaid
Barbara Kingsolver
Maxine Kumin
Nella Larsen
Harriet Lee
Sophia Lee
Tanith Lee
Ursula Le Guin
Doris Lessing
Meridel Le Sueur
Katherine Mansfield
Beryl Markham
Bobbie Ann Mason
Anne McCaffrey
Edna St. Vincent Millay
Bharati Mukherjee
Alice Munro
Sena Naslund
Kathleen Norris
Joyce Carol Oates
Flannery O'Connor
Margaret Oliphant
Tillie Olsen
Cynthia Ozick
Grace Paley
Sara Paretsky
Dorothy Parker
Ann Petry
Elizabeth Stuart Phelps
Katherine Anne Porter
Marjorie Kinnan Rawlings
Jean Rhys
Christina Rossetti
Joanna Russ
Sonia Sanchez
George Sand
May Sarton
Leslie Marmon Silko
Cathy Song
Susan Sontag
Jean Stafford
Ann Sophia Stephens
Harriet Beecher Stowe
Helena María Viramontes
Eudora Welty
Rebecca West
Edith Wharton
Kate Wiggins (*see* WOMEN'S
  MAGAZINES)
Hisaye Yamamoto
Anzia Yezierska

TALES
Isak Dinesen
Elizabeth Gaskell
Mary Griffith (*see* FEMINIST
     UTOPIAS)
Anne Sexton
Germaine de Staël
Ellen Wood

TEXTBOOKS
Gloria Anzaldúa
Mary Hunter Austin
Catharine Beecher
Antoinette Brown Blackwell
Elizabeth Blackwell
Ella Deloria
Maria Edgeworth
Sandra Gilbert
Caroline Gordon
Susan Gubar
Cherríe Moraga
Susanna Rowson
Elaine Showalter
Marie Stopes
Harriet Beecher Stowe
Mary Wollstonecraft
Mitsuye Yamada

TRANSLATION
Grace Aguilar
Elizabeth Bishop
Elizabeth Barrett Browning
Anne Carson
Mary Boykin Chesnut
Ella Deloria
Maria Edgeworth
Dorothy Canfield Fisher
Carolyn Forché
Felicia Hemans
Florence Kelley
Fanny Kemble
Carolyn Kizer
Emma Lazarus
Harriet Lee
Sophia Lee
Ursula Le Guin
Amy Lowell
Emily Mann
Marie de France
Harriet Martineau
Edna St. Vincent Millay
Marianne Moore

Nancy Morejón
Mourning Dove
Cynthia Ozick
Adrienne Rich
Mary Robinson
Muriel Rukeyser
May Sarton
Charlotte Smith
Sigrid Undset
Timberlake Wertenbaker
Diane Wolkstein
Mary Wollstonecraft
Marguerite Yourcenar

TRAVELOGUE
Grace Aguilar
Susan Brownmiller
Margaret Fuller
Helen Hunt Jackson
Fanny Kemble
Beryl Markham
Harriet Martineau
Mary McCarthy
Margaret Oliphant
Vita Sackville-West
Mary Shelley
Gloria Steinem
Harriet Beecher Stowe
Frances Wright

UTOPIAN/DYSTOPIAN LITERATURE
Louisa May Alcott
Jane Sophia Appleton (*see* FEMINIST
     UTOPIAS)
Margaret Atwood
Marion Zimmer Bradley
Martha S. Bensley Bruère (*see*
     FEMINIST UTOPIAS)
Octavia Butler
Angela Carter
Winnifred Harper Cooley (*see*
     FEMINIST UTOPIAS)
Marie Corelli
Annie Denton Cridge (*see* FEMINIST
     UTOPIAS)
Mary H. Ford (*see* FEMINIST
     UTOPIAS)
Charlotte Perkins Gilman
Marie Stevens Case Howland (*see*
     FEMINIST UTOPIAS)
Alice Ilgenfritz Jones (*see* FEMINIST
     UTOPIAS)

Mary E. Bradley Lane (*see* FEMINIST
     UTOPIAS)
Ursula Le Guin
Eveleen Laura Knaggs Mason (*see*
     FEMINIST UTOPIAS)
Anne McCaffrey
Ella Merchant (*see* FEMINIST
     UTOPIAS)
Kathleen Norris
Elizabeth Stuart Phelps
Marge Piercy
Joanna Russ
Olive Schreiner
Mary Teresa Shelhamer (*see*
     FEMINIST UTOPIAS)
Mary Shelley
Caroline Dale Parke Snedeker (*see*
     FEMINIST UTOPIAS)
Starhawk
Lois Nichols Waisbrooker (*see*
     FEMINIST UTOPIAS)
Lady Mary Walker
Kate Wilhelm (*see* ECOFEMINISM)
Victoria Woodhull
Frances Wright

VERSE
Kareen Fleur Adcock
Grace Aguilar
Claribel Alegría (*see* CAROLYN
     FORCHÉ)
Paula Gunn Allen
Dorothy Allison
Maya Angelou
Gloria Anzaldúa
Margaret Atwood
Mary Hunter Austin
Joanna Baillie
Anna Laetitia Barbauld
Djuna Barnes
Gwendolyn Bennetta Bennett (*see*
     ABOLITIONISM)
Mei-Mei Berssenbrugge (*see*
     FEMINIST THEMES)
Elizabeth Bishop
Antoinette Brown Blackwell
Louise Bogan
Eavan Boland
Anne Bradstreet
Dionne Brand
Gwendolyn Brooks
Olga Broumas

Rita Mae Brown
Elizabeth Barrett Browning
Anne Carson
Marilyn Chin
Christine de Pisan
Sandra Cisneros
Lucille Clifton
Caroline Clive
Mary Elizabeth Coleridge
Enid Dame (see LILITH)
Voltairine de Clayre
Toi Derricotte (see MARRIAGE
    MARKET)
Emily Dickinson
Hilda Doolittle (H. D.)
Rita Dove
Alice Dunbar-Nelson (see WOMEN'S
    WORK)
Barbara Elovic (see FEMINIST
    THEMES)
Clarissa Pinkola Estés
Mari Evans
Carolyn Forché
Janet Frame
Elizabeth Gaskell
Nikki Giovanni
Louise Glück
Judy Grahn (see FEMINIST THEMES)
Angelina Weld Grimké
Jessica Hagedorn
Radclyffe Hall
Joy Harjo
Frances Harper
Ida Husted Harper
Felicia Hemans
Linda Hogan
Cynthia Huntington (see FEMINIST
    THEMES)
Georgia Douglas Johnson
Pauline Johnson
Erica Jong
June Jordan
Fanny Kemble
Carolyn Kizer
Joy Kogawa
Maxine Kumin
Suzanne LaFollette

Caroline Lamb
Emma Lazarus
Meridel Le Sueur
Denise Levertov
Audre Lorde
Amy Lowell
Mina Loy
Marie de France
Mary McArthur (see LA LLORONA)
Edna St. Vincent Millay
Gabriela Mistral
Marianne Moore
Cherríe Moraga
Hannah More (see SLAVERY)
Nancy Morejón
Kathleen Norris (see MARRIAGE
    MARKET)
Sharon Olds
Tillie Olsen
Grace Paley
Dorothy Parker
Elizabeth Stuart Phelps
Antonia Quintan Pigno (see LA
    LLORONA)
Sylvia Plath
Katha Pollitt
Irina Ratushinskaya
Marjorie Kinnan Rawlings
Adrienne Rich
Mary Robinson
Wendy Rose
Christina Rossetti
Susanna Rowson
Muriel Rukeyser
Vita Sackville-West
Sonia Sanchez
Sappho
May Sarton
Susan Fromberg Schaeffer (see
    MARRIAGE MARKET)
Anna Seward
Anne Sexton
Ntozake Shange
Leslie Marmon Silko
Charlotte Smith
Stevie Smith
Cathy Song

Nancy Springer
Gertrude Stein
Ann Sophia Stephens
Alice Walker
Jeanne Murray Walker (see
    MATRIARCHY)
Margaret Walker
Mercy Otis Warren
Phillis Wheatley
Ella Wheeler Wilcox (see WOMEN'S
    MAGAZINES)
Elinor Wilner (see CHARLOTTE
    BRONTË)
Winchilsea, Anne Finch, countess of
Elinor Wylie
Mitsuye Yamada
Ann Yearsley
Marguerite Yourcenar

YOUNG ADULT LITERATURE
Mary Hunter Austin
Margaret Ball (see ANNE
    MCCAFFREY)
Judy Blume
Marion Zimmer Bradley
Sandra Cisneros
Kaye Gibbons
Gish Jen
Joy Kogawa
Ursula Le Guin
Lois Lowry (see LITTLE RED RIDING
    HOOD)
Sarah MacLachlan (see LETTER
    WRITING)
Bobbie Ann Mason
Anne McCaffrey
Joyce Carol Oates
Ann Petry
Elizabeth Stuart Phelps
Marjorie Kinnan Rawlings
Ntozake Shange
Ann Sophia Stephens (see
    SEXUALITY)
Jane Yolen (see LITTLE RED RIDING
    HOOD)

Major Authors of Feminist Literature and Their Works

ADCOCK, FLEUR
The Faber Book of Twentieth Century Women's Poetry (1988)
High Tide in the Garden (1971)

ADDAMS, JANE
Twenty Years at Hull-House (1910)
"Why Women Should Vote" (1910)

ADEYANJU, TUNDE
Democracy on Trial (1998)
The Ruling Junta (2002)

AGUILAR, GRACE
"The Festival of Purim" (1845)
Home Influence (1847)
The Mother's Recompense (1851)
The Spirit of Judaism (1842)
Woman's Friendship (1851)
Women of Israel (1844)

AIDOO, AMA ATA
Anowa (1970)
Changes: A Love Story (1991)
Dilemma of a Ghost (1965)
No Sweetness Here (1970)
Our Sister Killjoy (1977)

AKHMATOVA, ANNA
Anno Domini MCMXXI (1921)
Evening (1912)
The Rosary (1914)
White Flock (1917)

ALCOTT, LOUISA MAY
Hospital Sketches (1863)
Little Women (1868–1869)
Moods (1865)

"A Whisper in the Dark" (1863)
Work: A Story of Experience (1871)

ALDERSON, NANNIE
A Bride Goes West (1942)

ALLEN, PAULA GUNN
"Beloved Women" (1982)
Grandmother of the Light (1991)
The Heavenly Twins (1893)
Ideala (1888)
Pocahontas: Medicine Woman, Spy, Entrepreneur, Diplomat (2003)
Shadow Country (1982)
Spider Woman's Granddaughters (1990)
"Who Is Your Mother" (1984)
The Woman Who Owned the Shadows (1983)

ALLENDE, ISABEL
Aphrodite, a Memoir of the Senses (1998)
Daughter of Fortune (1999)
Eva Luna (1987)
The House of the Spirits (1982)
My Invented Country (2003)
Of Love and Shadows (1984)
Paula (1991)
The Stories of Eva Luna (1990)

ALLISON, DOROTHY
Bastard Out of Carolina (1992)

ALVAREZ, JULIA
How the García Girls Lost Their Accent (1991)
In the Name of Salomé (2002)
In the Time of the Butterflies (1994)

ANDREWS, FANNY
The Wartime Journal of a Georgia Girl (1908)

ANGELOU, MAYA
Halleluia! The Welcome Table (2004)
I Know Why the Caged Bird Sings (1969)
Now Sheba Sings the Song (1994)

ANNE OF SWANSEA
The Conviction; or, She Is Innocent! (1814)
Lovers and Friends (1821)

ANTHONY, SUSAN B.
"The Homes of Single Women" (1877)
The Trial of Susan B. Anthony (1872)
"Woman: The Great Unpaid Laborer" (1848)

————, AND **MATILDA GAGE**
"Declaration of Rights of Women" (1876)

————, **MATILDA GAGE, IDA HUSTED HARPER,**
 AND **ELIZABETH CADY STANTON**
History of Woman Suffrage (1881–86)

ANTIN, MARY
From Plotz to Boston (1899)
The Promised Land (1912)
They Who Knock at Our Gates (1914)

ANZALDÚA, GLORIA
Borderlands/La Frontera (1987)
Making Face, Making Soul (1989)

————, AND **ANALOUISE KEATING**
Interviews/Entrevistas (2000)
This Bridge We Call Home (2002)

————, AND **CHERRÍE MORAGA, EDS.**
This Bridge Called My Back (1981)

APPLETON, JANE SOPHIA
"*Vision of Bangor in the Twentieth Century*" (1848)

ARISTOPHANES
Lysistrata (411 B.C.)

ARNOW, HARRIETTE
The Dollmaker (1954)

ATHERTON, GERTRUDE
"The Bell in the Fog" (1905)
Black Oxen (1923)
Can Women Be Gentlemen? (1938)
The Christmas Witch (1893)
The Foghorn (1934)
The House of Lee (1940)

Julia France and Her Times (1912)
What Dreams May Come (1888)

ATWOOD, MARGARET
The Blind Assassin (2001)
Cat's Eye (1988)
Double Persephone (1961)
The Handmaid's Tale (1985)
Lady Oracle (1976)
The Robber Bride (1993)
"The Woman Who Could Not Live with Her Faulty
 Heart" (1976)

AUEL, JEAN
The Clan of the Cave Bear (1980)
The Mammoth Hunters (1985)
The Plains of Passage (1990)
Shelters of Stone (2002)
The Valley of Horses (1982)

AUSTEN, JANE
Emma (1815)
Mansfield Park (1814)
Northanger Abbey (1818)
Persuasion (1818)
Pride and Prejudice (1813)
Sense and Sensibility (1811)

AUSTIN, MARY HUNTER
The Arrow-Maker (1910)
The Basket Woman (1904)
Children Sing in the Far West (1928)
Earth Horizon (1932)
The Land of Little Rain (1903)
The Starry Adventure (1931)
Stories from the Country of Lost Borders (1909)
"Walking Woman" (1907)

AVELLANEDA, GERTRUDIS DE
Sab (1841)

BÂ, MARIAMA
The Scarlet Song (1981)
So Long a Letter (1979)

BAILEY, MAXINE, AND SHARON MAREEKA LEWIS
Sistahs (1998)

BAILLIE, JOANNA
Ahalya Baee (1849)
De Montfort (1800)
The Legend of Lady Griseld Baillie (1821)
A Series of Plays on the Passions (1798)

BAMBARA, TONI CADE
"Blues Ain't No Mockin Bird" (1971)
Gorilla, My Love (1972)
The Salt Eaters (1980)
"Salvation Is the Issue" (1984)
The Sea Birds Are Still Alive (1977)

BARBAULD, ANNA LAETITIA
British Novelists (1810–20)
"Epistle to William Wilberforce" (1790)
Evenings at Home (1794)
"The Rights of Woman"
    (ca. 1792)
"To a Little Invisible Being Who Is Expected Soon to
    Become Visible" (ca. 1795)
"Washing-Day" (1797)

BARKER, DEBORAH
Aesthetics and Gender in American Literature (2000)

BARNES, DJUNA
The Book of Repulsive Women (1915)
"How It Feels to Be Forcibly Fed" (1914)
The Ladies Almanack (1928)
Nightwood (1930)
Ryder (1928)

BAYM, NINA
Woman's Fiction (1978)

BAZÁN, EMILIA PARDO
The House of Ulloa (1886)
The Woman (1895)

BEAUVOIR, SIMONE DE
Hard Times (1963)
Memoirs of a Dutiful Young Girl (1958)
Old Age (1970)
The Second Sex (1949)
She Came to Stay (1943)
A Very Easy Death (1964)
Woman Destroyed (1968)

BEECHER, CATHARINE
The American Woman's Home (1869)
Letters to Persons Engaged in Domestic Service (1842)
Treatise on Domestic Economy (1841)

BEHN, APHRA
Abdelazar, or Moor's Revenge (1676)
The City Heiress, or, Sir Timothy Treat-all (1682)
"Disappointment" (1680)
The Forc'd Marriage, or The Jealous Bridegroom (1670)

Love Letters between a Nobleman and His Sister (1684–87)
The Luckey Chance; or, An Alderman's Bargain (1687)
Oroonoko (1688)
The Rover, or The Banish't Cavaliers (1677)
"The Willing Mistress" (1673)

BENNETT, GWENDOLYN BENNETTA
"To a Dark Girl" (1927)

BERSSENBRUGGE, MEI-MEI
"Chronicle" (1988)

BIRD, ISABELLA
A Lady's Life in the Rocky Mountains (1888)

BISHOP, ELIZABETH
A Cold Spring (1955)
Geography III (1976)
"Gwendolyn" (1953)
North and South (1946)
Questions of Travel (1965)
"Vague Poem" (2000)

BLACKWELL, ALICE STONE
Lucy Stone: Pioneer of Women's Rights (1930)

BLACKWELL, ANTOINETTE BROWN
"A Plea for the Afternoon" (1868)
Sexes Throughout Nature (1875)
Shadows of Our Social System (1856)

BLACKWELL, ELIZABETH
Essays on Medical Sociology (1902)
*Laws of Life with Special Reference to the Physical
    Education of Girls* (1852)
"Letter to Young Ladies Desirous of Studying Medicine"
    (1859)
Pioneer Work in Opening the Medical Profession to Women
    (1895)

BLAIS, MARIE-CLAIRE
The Angel of Loneliness (1989)
Anna's World (1982)
Deaf to the City (1979)
The Mad Shadows (1959)
Nights in the Underground (1978)
A Season in the Life of Emmanuel (1965)
Thirsts (1995)

BLUME, JUDY
Are You There God? It's Me, Margaret (1970)
Blubber (1974)
Deenie (1973)

Forever: A Novel of Good and Evil, Love and Hope (1975)
Places I Never Meant to Be (1999)
Tiger Eyes (1981)

BLY, NELLIE
Nelly Bly's Book: Around the World in 72 Days (1890)
Six Months in Mexico (1888)
Ten Days in a Mad-House (1887)
"Trying to Be a Servant" (1890)

BOGAN, LOUISE
Body of This Death (1923)
Dark Summer (1929)
Journey Around My Room (1980)
What the Woman Lived (1973)
"Women" (1923)

BOLAND, EAVAN
"Anorexic" (1980)
Domestic Interior (1982)
In a Time of Violence (1994)
In Her Own Image (1980)
Journey (1986)
"The Making of an Irish Goddess" (1990)
New Territory (1967)
Object Lesson (1995)
"The Oral Tradition" (1990)
War Horse (1975)

BONFILS, WINIFRED
The Life and Personality of Phoebe Apperson Hearst (1928)

BONNER, MARITA
Exit (1923)
"Light in Dark Places" (1941)
"On Being Young—A Woman—and Colored" (1925)
"One True Love" (1941)
The Purple Flower (1928)

BOWEN, ELIZABETH
Friends and Relations (1930)
The Heat of the Day (1949)
Last September (1929)

BOWLES, JANE
The Heat of the Day (1949)
"A Stick of Green Candy" (1957)
Two Serious Ladies (1943)

BRADDON, MARY ELIZABETH
Aurora Floyd (1862)
The Doctor's Wife (1864)

Eleanor's Victory (1863)
"Good Lady Ducayne" (1896)
Henry Dunbar (1864)
John Marchmont's Legacy (1863)
Lady Audley's Secret (1862)
Thou Art the Man (1864)

BRADFORD, SARAH ELIZABETH
Scenes in the Life of Harriet Tubman (1869)

BRADLEY, MARION ZIMMER
The Firebrand (1987)
The Forest House (1994)
The Lady of Avalon (1997)
The Mists of Avalon (1982)
The Priestess of Avalon (2002)
Return to Avalon (1996)
The Ruins of Isis (1978)
The Shattered Chain (1976)
Thendara House (1983)

BRADSTREET, ANNE
Severall Poems (1678)
The Tenth Muse Lately Sprung up in America (1650)

BRAND, DIONNE
At the Full and Change of the Moon (1999)

BRODIE, FAWN
Thomas Jefferson (1974)

BRONTË, CHARLOTTE
Jane Eyre (1847)
Shirley (1849)
Villette (1853)

BRONTË, EMILY
Wuthering Heights (1847)

BROOKS, GWENDOLYN
Annie Allen (1949)
Maud Martha (1953)
Report from Part One (1972)
"A Song in the Front Yard" (1971)
A Street in Bronzeville (1945)
"When Mrs. Martin's Booker T" (1947)
Winnie (1991)

BROUMAS, OLGA
Beginning with O (1977)
Black Holes, Black Stockings (1985)
Pastoral Jazz (1983)

BROWN, RITA MAE
Dolley (1994)
Full Cry (2003)
The Hand That Cradles the Rock (1971)
A Plain Brown Rapper (1973)
Rita Will (1997)
The Rubyfruit Jungle (1973)
Songs to a Handsome Women (1973)
Venus Envy (1996)

BROWN-GUILLORY, ELIZABETH
Mam Phyllis (1990)

BROWNING, ELIZABETH BARRETT
Aurora Leigh (1847)
The Cry of the Children (1843)
"Lord Walter's Wife" (1861)
"Mother and Poet" (1861)
"The Runaway Slave at Pilgrim's Point" (1846)
Sonnets from the Portuguese (1850)

BROWNMILLER, SUSAN
Against Our Will (1975)
In Our Time (1999)
"Let's Put Pornography Back in the Closet" (1969)
"Making Female Bodies the Battlefield" (1993)

BRUÈRE, MARTHA
Mildred Carver, U.S.A. (1919)

BRYANT, LOUISE
"Fables for Proletarian Children" (1919)
Mirrors of Moscow (1923)
Six Months in Red Russia (1918)

BUCK, PEARL
The Good Earth (1931)
The Mother (1934)

BURNEY, FANNY
A Busy Day (1801)
Camilla, or Female Difficulties (1796)
Cecilia; or, Memoirs of an Heiress (1782)
The Diary and Letters of Madame d'Arblay (1889)
Evelina (1778)
Love and Fashion (1799)
Witlings (1779)
The Woman-Hater (1801)

BURRILL, MARY POWELL
They That Sit in Darkness (1919)

BUTLER, OLIVIA
Kindred (1979)
The Parable of the Sower (1993)
The Parable of the Talents (1998)

CAMONA, MARIANA ROMO, AND ALMA GÓMEZ
Cuentos: Stories by Latinas (1983)

CAMPBELL, MARIA
Halfbreed (1973)

CANNARY, MARTHA JANE
Autobiography (1896)

CARDINAL, MARIE
Disorderly Conduct (1987)
The Key in the Door (1972)
A Life for Two (1979)
The Past Encroached (1983)
Words to Say It (1975)

CAROLYN, KIZER
"Bitch" (1971)
"Fearful Women" (1996)
"For Jan, in Bar Maria" (1964)
"Gerda" (1996)
Mermaids in the Basement (1984)
"Pro Femina" (1965)
"Valley of the Fallen" (1984)
Yin: New Poems (1984)

CARRIGAN, MINNIE BRUCE
Captured by the Indians (1862)

CARSON, ANNE
The Beauty of the Husband (2001)
Eros the Bittersweet (1986)
Glass, Irony, and God (1995)
If Not, Winter: Fragments of Sappho (2002)

CARSON, RACHEL
The Edge of the Sea (1955)
The Sea Around Us (1951)
Silent Spring (1962)
Under the Sea-Wind (1941)

CARTER, ANGELA
The Bloody Chamber (1979)
Burning Your Boats (1995)
The Magic Toyshop (1967)
Nights at the Circus (1984)

The Passion of New Eve (1977)
The Sadeian Woman (1979)
The Shadow Dance (1966)
"Werewolf" (1995)

CATHER, WILLA
A Lost Lady (1923)
My Ántonia (1918)
One of Ours (1922)
O Pioneers! (1913)
Sapphira and the Slave Girl (1940)
The Song of the Lark (1915)

CATT, CARRIE CHAPMAN
The Ballot and the Bullet (1897)
"Do You Know" (1918)

————, AND NETTIE ROGERS
Woman Suffrage and Politics (1923)

CHAUCER, GEOFFREY
"The Wife of Bath's Tale" (1387)

CHENG, NIEN
Life and Death in Shanghai (1986)

CHESLER, PHYLLIS
Women and Madness (1972)

CHESNUT, MARY
A Diary from Dixie (1905)
Mary Chestnut's Civil War (1981)
The Private Mary Chesnut (1984)

CHEVALIER, TRACY
The Girl with a Pearl Earring (1999)

CHILD, LYDIA
An Appeal for the Indians (1868)
An Appeal in Favor of That Class of Americans Called Africans (1833)
Authentic Anecdotes of American Slavery (1838)
The Family Nurse (1838)
The Frugal Housewife (1829)
The History of the Condition of Women (1835)
Hobomok (1824)
The Mother's Book (1831)
"Over the river and thro' the woods" (1844)
"Quadroons" (1843)

CHIN, MARILYN
"Floral Apron" (1987)

Phoenix Gone Terrace Empty (1994)
Rhapsody in Plain Yellow (2002)

CHOPIN, KATE
The Awakening (1899)
"Désirée's Baby" (1893)
Night in Acadie (1897)
"A Pair of Silk Stockings" (1897)
"A Respectable Woman" (1894)
The Storm and Other Stories (1897)

CHRISTINE DE PISAN
Book of the City of Ladies (ca. 1405)
"Hymn to Joan of Arc" (1429)
Letter on the Three Virtues (1406)
Letter to the God of Love (1399)
Letters on the Debate of "The Romance of the Rose" (1402)

CHURCHILL, CARYL
Cloud Nine (1979)
The Judge's Wife (1972)
Objections to Sex and Violence (1975)
Owners (1972)
Top Girls (1982)
Vinegar Tom (1976)

CISNEROS, SANDRA
Caramelo (2003)
The House on Mango Street (1983)
The Loose Woman (1994)
Woman Hollering Creek (1991)

CIXOUS, HÉLÈNE
The Book of Promethea (1983)
Coming to Writing (1986)
The Laugh of the Medusa (1975)
The Newly Born Woman (1975)
The Portrait of Dora (1976)

CLIFTON, LUCILLE
Blessing the Boats (2000)
The Book of Light (1993)
"Daughters" (1993)
Generations: A Memoir (1976)
Good Times (1969)
Quilting (1991)
Two Headed Woman (1980)

CLIVE, CAROLINE
Essays of the Human Intellect (1828)
Paul Ferroll (1855)
Why Paul Ferroll Killed His Wife (1860)

COLERIDGE, MARY ELIZABETH
"A Clever Woman" (1907)
"Marriage" (1908)
"The Other Side of the Mirror" (1908)
"Our Lady" (1908)
"Witch" (1907)

COLETTE
Claudine at School (1900)
Gigi (1944)

CONDÉ, MARYSE
Célanire Cou-coupé (2001)
Désirada (2000)
Hérémakhonon (1976)
I, Tituba, Black Witch of Salem (1986)
A Season in Rihata (1981)
Segu: The Children of Segu (1984)
Segu: The Earth in Pieces (1985)
Windward Heights (1995)

COOLEY, WINNIFRED HARPER
A Dream of the 21st Century (1902)

COOPER, ANNA JULIA
A Voice from the South by a Black Woman of the South
    (1892)

CORBETT, ELIZABETH T.
"My Visit to Utopia" (1869)

CORELLI, MARIE
Ardath: The Story of a Dead Self (1889)
Free Opinions Freely Expressed (1905)
The Murder of Delicia (1896)
Sorrows of Satan (1895)
The Soul of Lilith (1892)
The Treasures of Heaven (1906)
The Vendetta! (1886)

CORTHRON, KIA
Breath, Boom (2001)
Seeking the Genesis (1997)

CROSS, DONNA
Pope Joan (1996)

CROTHERS, RACHEL
Let Us Be Gay (1929)
A Man's World (1910)
39 East (1925)

CRUZ, JUANA DE LA
The Reply to Sister Filotea (1691)

CULLETON, BEATRICE
In Search of April Raintree (1983)

CUNHA, HELENA PARENTE
The Woman Between Mirrors (1983)

CUSHMAN, KAREN
Catherine, Called Birdy (1994)
The Midwife's Apprentice (1995)

DANTICAT, EDWIDGE
Breath, Eyes, Memory (1994)
The Farming of Bones (1998)
Krik? Krak! (1995)

D'AULNOY, COMTESSE
Tales of the Fairies (1699)
The White Cat (1698)

DAVIS, ANGELA
Angela Davis: An Autobiography (1974)
Blues Legacy and Black Feminism (1998)
If They Come in the Morning (1971)
Women, Race and Class (1981)

DAVIS, REBECCA HARDING
Bits of Gossip (1906)
Earthen Pitchers (1873–74)
Life in the Iron Mills (1861)
Margret Howth: A Story of Today (1861)
"The Wife's Story" (1864)

DE CLEYRE, VOLTAIRINE
Anarchism and American Traditions (1914)
"The Case of Woman vs. Orthodoxy" (1896)
"The Gates of Freedom" (1891)
"In Defense of Emma Goldman and Free Speech"
    (1893)
"The Making of an Anarchist" (1914)
"Sex Slavery" (1890)
"Those Who Marry Do Ill" (1908)
"The Woman Question" (1913)

DELANY, BESSIE, AND SARAH DELANY
Having Our Say (1991)

DE LA PARRA, TERESA
Iphigenia (1924)

DELORIA, ELLA
Waterlily (1947)

DERRICOTTI, TOI
"Doll Poem" (1989)

DESAI, ANITA
Cry Peacock (1963)
Diamond Dust (1999)
Fire on the Mountain (1977)
Games at Twilight (1978)
Journey to Ithaca (1996)
Voices in the City (1965)

DESALVO, LOUISE
Adultery (1999)
Breathless: An Asthma Journal (1998)
Crazy in the Kitchen (2004)
Melymbrosia (2002)
Vertigo: A Memoir (1996)
Virginia Woolf (1989)
Writing As a Way of Healing (2000)

DIAMANT, ANITA
Good Harbor (2002)
Pitching My Tent (2003)
The Red Tent (1997)

DICKINSON, EMILY
"Forbidden Fruit" (1876)
"Her Breast Is Fit for Pearls" (ca. 1859)
"Her sweet Weight on my Heart" (ca. 1862)
"Hope Is the Thing with Feathers" (ca. 1861)
"My Life had stood—a Loaded Gun" (1863)
"Tell All the Truth but Tell It Slant" (ca. 1868)
"They put me in the Closet" (ca. 1862)
"We lose—because we win" (ca. 1858)
"What Is Paradise" (ca. 1860)
"Where Thou art—that—is Home" (ca. 1863)
"Who Is It Seeks My Pillow Nights" (ca. 1884)
"Why—do they shut Me out of Heaven?"
    (ca. 1861)
"Wild Night" (ca. 1861)
"Within that little Hive/Such Hints of Honey lay"
    (ca. 1884)

DINESEN, ISAK
Babette's Feast (1959)
Out of Africa (1937)
Seven Gothic Tales (1934)
Shadows on the Grass (1961)

DI PRIMA, DIANE
Loba (1978)
Recollections of My Life as a Woman (2001)

DOODY, MARGARET ANNE
The True Story of the Novel (1996)

DOOLITTLE, HILDA (H. D.)
The Flowering of the Rod (1946)
Helen in Egypt (1961)
Heliodora and Other Poems (1924)
HERmione (1927)
Hymen (1921)
Sea Garden (1916)
Tribute to the Angels (1945)
The Walls Do Not Fall (1944)

DOUGLASS, FREDERICK
Narrative of the Life of Frederick Douglass (1845)

DOVE, RITA
The Darker Face of the Earth (1994)
Mother Love (1995)
On the Bus with Rosa Parks (1999)
Thomas and Beulah (1986)
The Yellow House on the Corner (1980)

DRABBLE, MARGARET
The Ice Age (1977)
The Millstone (1965)
The Needle's Eye (1972)
The Realms of Gold (1975)
The Red Queen (2004)
Seven Sisters (2002)
The Waterfall (1967)
The Witch of Exmoor (1996)

DU MAURIER, DAPHNE
Rebecca (1938)
The Rebecca Notebook (1980)

DUNBAR-NELSON, ALICE
The Author's Evening at Home (1900)
The Goodness of St. Rocque (1899)
"I Sit and Sew" (1920)
Mine Eyes Have Seen (1919)
"Sister Josepha" (1899)

DURAS, MARGUERITE
Hiroshima, Mon Amour (1959)
The Lover (1984)
The North China Lover (1990)

DWORKIN, ANDREA
Heartbreak (2002)
Ice and Fire (1988)
Intercourse (1987)
Letters from a War Zone, 1976–1987 (1988)
Mercy (1991)
Pornography: Men Possessing Women (1981)
Right-Wing Women (1983)
Woman Hating (1974)

EDGEWORTH, MARIA
The Absentee (1812)
Belinda (1801)
Early Lessons (1801)
Essays on Professional Education (1809)
Letters for Literary Ladies (1795)
The Parent's Assistant (1795)
Practical Education (1798)

EDSON, MARGARET
Wit (1999)

EHRENREICH, BARBARA
Nickel and Dimed (2001)

———, AND DEIRDRE ENGLISH
For Her Own Good (1978)
Witches, Midwives and Nurses (1973)

ELIOT, GEORGE
Adam Bede (1859)
Daniel Deronda (1876)
Middlemarch (1872)
The Mill on the Floss (1860)
Scenes of Clerical Life (1857)
Silas Marner (1861)

ELLIS, KATE FERGUSON
The Contested Castle (1989)

ELOVIC, BARBARA
"Light Years" (1985)

EL SAADAWI, NAWAL
The Daughter of Isis (1999)
The Fall of the Imam (1987)
God Dies by the Nile (1974)
The Hidden Face of Eve (1980)
Memoirs from the Women's Prison (1983)
"The Rite and the Right" (1996)
Walking through Fire (2002)
Woman at Point Zero (1973)

EMECHETA, BUCHI
Head above Water (1986)
In the Ditch (1972)
The Joys of Motherhood (1979)
The Second-Class Citizen (1974)

ENGEL, MARIAN
Bear (1977)

ENSLER, EVE
The Good Body (2003)
Necessary Targets (2001)
The Vagina Monologues (1996)

ERDRICH, LOUISE
The Blue Jay's Dance (1996)
The Last Report on the Miracles at Little No Horse (2001)
Love Medicine (1984)
Tales of Burning Love (1997)
Tracks (1988)

ESQUIVEL, LAURA
Like Water for Chocolate (1989)

ESTÉS, CLARISSA PINKOLA
The Faithful Gardener (1995)
The Gift of Story (1993)
Warming the Stone Child (1992)
Women Who Run with the Wolves (1992)

EVANS, MARI
Boochie (1979)
Eyes (1979)
"I Am a Black Woman" (1970)
"Where Have You Gone?" (1970)

FALLACI, ORIANA
Letter to a Child Never Born (1975)
Penelope at War (1962)
The Rage and the Pride (2002)
The Useless Sex (1964)

FALUDI, SUSAN
Backlash (1991)
"Don't Get the Wrong Message" (2001)

FAUSET, JESSIE REDMON
The Chinaberry Tree (1931)
"Emmy" (1912)
Plum Bun (1929)
"The Sleeper Wakes" (1920)
Redmon *There Is Confusion* (1924)

FERBER, EDNA
Cimarron (1929)
Emma McChesney & Co. (1915)
Giant (1952)
Personality Plus: Some Experiences of Emma McChesney and Her Son Jock (1914)
Roast Beef Medium: The Business Adventures of Emma McChesney (1913)
Show Boat (1926)
So Big (1924)

FERN, FANNY
Leaves from Fanny's Portfolio (1852)
Ruth Hall (1854)

FIRESTONE, SHULAMITH
The Dialectics of Sex (1970)
The Women's Rights Movement in the U.S. (1968)

FISHER, DOROTHY CANFIELD
The Bedquilt and Other Stories (1906)
The Squirrel Cage (1912)
Understood Betsy (1915)

FLANDERS, LAURA
W Effect: Bush's War on Women (2004)

FORCHÉ, CAROLYN
Gathering the Tribes (1976)

FORD, MARY H.
"The Feminine Iconoclast" (1889)

FORD, MARY K.
"Women's Progress: A Comparison of Centuries" (1909)

FOSTER, HANNAH WEBSTSER
The Coquette: or History of Eliza Wharton (1797)

FRAME, JANET
Faces in the Water (1961)
Janet Frame: An Autobiography (1991)
Owls Do Cry (1957)

FREEMAN, MARY WILKINS
"A Church Mouse" (1891)
"The Long Arm" (1895)
"A Moral Exigency" (1891)
"A New England Nun" (1891)
"The Revolt of 'Mother' " (1891)
"Two Friends" (1887)

FRENCH, MARILYN
Beyond Power: On Women, Men, and Morals (1985)
The Bleeding Heart (1980)
Her Mother's Daughter (1987)
Shakespeare's Division of Experience (1981)
The War Against Women (1992)
The Women's Room (1966)

FRIEDAN, BETTY
Beyond Gender (1997)
The Feminine Mystique (1963)
The Fountain of Age (1994)
"It Changed My Life" (1976)
The Second Stage (1981)

FULLER, MARGARET
"The Great Lawsuit" (1843)
Summer on the Lakes in 1843 (1843)
Woman in the Nineteenth Century (1845)

GAGE, MATILDA
Woman, Church, and State (1893)

BAILLIE, LADY GRISELL
The Household Book of Lady Griselle Baillie (1692–1733)

GAITE, CARMEN MARTÍN
The Back Room (1978)

GALE, ZONA
Birth (1918)
Daughter of the Morning (1917)
The Heart's Kindred (1915)
Miss Lulu Bett (1920)
Romance Island (1906)

GARCÍA, CRISTINA
Dreaming in Cuban (1992)

GASKELL, ELIZABETH
Cranford (1855)
The Life of Charlotte Brontë (1857)
Mary Barton (1848)
North and South (1855)
"Old Woman Magoun" (1909)
Ruth (1853)
"Sex and Slavery" (1890)
Wives and Daughters (1866)

GIBBONS, KAYE
Charms for the Easy Life (1993)

Divining Women (2004)
Ellen Foster (1987)

GILBERT, SANDRA AND SUSAN GUBAR

The Madwoman in the Attic (1981)
Mothersongs (1995)
No Man's Land (1989)
Shakespeare's Sisters (1979)
The War of the Words (1987)

GILBERT, SANDRA, SUSAN GUBAR, AND DIANA O'HEHIR

Mothersongs (1995)

GILCHRIST, ELLEN

The Anna Papers (1988)
Flights of Angels (1998)
In the Land of Dreamy Dreams (1981)
Rhoda (1995)
Victory Over Japan (1984)

GILLIGAN, CAROL

In a Different Voice (1982)

GILMAN, CHARLOTTE PERKINS

Concerning Children (1900)
The Crux (1910)
The Dress of Women (1886)
Herland (1915)
Home: Its Work and Influence (1903)
The Man-Made World (1911)
"Martha's Mother" (1910)
Moving the Mountain (1911)
"Three Thanksgivings" (1909)
"The Waste of Private Housekeeping" (1913)
What Diantha Did (1910)
With Her in Ourland (1916)

GIOVANNI, NIKKI

Cotton Candy on a Rainy Day (1978)
Gemini (1971)
"Griots" (1994)
"Light the Candles" (1995)
Those Who Ride the Night Wind (1983)
The Women and the Men (1975)

GLASGOW, ELLEN

Barren Ground (1925)
The Battle-Ground (1925)
Deliverance (1904)
"Jordan's End" (1923)
Life and Gabriella (1916)

"A Point of Morals" (1899)
The Sheltered Life (1932)
Virginia (1913)
The Woman Within (1954)

GLASPELL, SUSAN

Alison's House (1930)
Fidelity (1915)
The Inheritors (1921)
Norma Ashe (1942)
Suppressed Desires (1915)
Trifles (1916)
The Verge (1921)

GLÜCK, LOUISE

The Descending Figure (1980)
Firstborn (1968)
The Garden (1976)
The House on Marshland (1975)
Meadowlands (1996)
The Seven Ages (2002)
Wild Iris (1992)

GOLDBERG, JESSICA

Sex Parasite (2003)

GOLDMAN, EMMA

Anarchism and Other Essays (1911)
Living My Life (1931)
Social Significance of the Modern Drama (1914)

GOODMAN, ELLEN

The Paper Trail (2004)
Turning Points (1979)

————, AND PATRICIA O'BRIEN

I Know Just What You Mean (2000)

GORDIMER, NADINE

The Burger's Daughter (1979)
My Son's Story (1990)

GORDON, CAROLINE

"The Captive" (1945)
The Forest of the South (1945)
The Malefactors (1956)
Women on the Porch (1944)

GRAFTON, SUE

"A" Is for Alibi (1983)
"D" Is for Deadbeat (1987)
"K" Is for Killer (1994)

GRAND, SARAH
The Beth Book (1897)
A Domestic Experiment (1891)

GRAUL, ROSA
"Hilda's Home" (1897)

GREER, GERMAINE
Daddy We Hardly Knew You (1989)
The Female Eunuch (1970)
The Madwoman's Underclothes (1986)
The Obstacle Race (1979)
Sex and Destiny: The Politics of Human Fertility (1984)
The Whole Woman (1999)

GRIERSON, ALICE KIRK
A Colonel's Lady on the Western Frontier (1989)

GRIFFITH, MARY
Three Hundred Years Hence (1826)

GRIMKÉ, ANGELINA
An Appeal to the Christian Women of the South (1836)
An Appeal to the Women of the Nominally Free States (1837)
Letters on the Equality of the Sexes and the Condition of Women (1838)
"The Rights of Women and Negroes" (1863)

GRIMKÉ, ANGELINA WELD
Rachel (1916)

GRIMKÉ, SARAH
Epistle to the Clergy of the Southern States (1836)

HADDIX, MARGARET PETERSON
Just Ella (2001)

HAGEDORN, JESSICA
The Dogeaters (1990)
Four Young Women (1973)

HAILEY, ELIZABETH FORSYTHE
A Woman of Independent Means (1978)

HALBERTAM, JUDITH
The Skin Shows (1995)

HALE, SARAH JOSEPHA
The Lecturess; or, Woman's Sphere (1839)
Liberia: or Mr. Peyton's Experiment (1852)
Traits of American Life (1835)
Woman's Record (1853, 1855, 1872)

HALL, RADCLYFFE
Adam's Breed (1926)
Miss Ogilvy Finds Herself (1934)
The Sixth Beatitude (1936)
Twixt Earth and Stars (1906)
The Unlit Lamp (1925)
The Well of Loneliness (1928)

HANSBERRY, LORRAINE
A Raisin in the Sun (1959)
To Be Young, Gifted, and Black (1969)

HANSON, ELIZABETH
An Account of the Captivity of Elizabeth Hanson (1796)
God's Mercy Surmounting Man's Cruelty (1728)

HARDWICK, ELIZABETH
Herman Melville (2000)

HARJO, JOY
"Eagle Poem" (1990)
In Mad Love and War (1990)
Last Song (1975)
She Had Some Horses (1983)
That's What She Said (1984)
The Third Woman (1980)
What Moon Drove Me to This? (1980)
"The Woman Hanging from the Thirteenth Floor Window" (1983)
The Woman Who Fell from the Sky (1996)

HARPER, FRANCES ELLEN
"Bury Me in a Free Land" (1858)
"A Double Standard" (1895)
Iola Leroy; or, Shadows Uplifted (1892)
Sketches of Southern Life (1872)
"The Slave Mother" (1854)
"The Two Offers" (1859)

HARPER, IDA HUSTED
The Life and Work of Susan B. Anthony (1898, 1908)

HARPER, VALERIE
All under Heaven (1988)

HARRIS, HELEN WEBB
Ganifrede (1935)

HAWTHORNE, NATHANIEL
"Mrs. Hutchinson" (1830)
The Scarlet Letter (1850)

HEAD, BESSIE
Collector of Treasures and Other Botswana Village Tales
(1977)
Maru (1971)
"Notes from a Quiet Backwater I" (1982)
A Question of Power (1973)
When Rain Clouds Gather (1969)
A Woman Alone (1990)

HÉLISENNE DE CRENNE
The Dream of Madame Hélisenne (1540)
Painful Torments That Procede from Love (1538)
Personal and Invective Letters (1539)

HELLMAN, LILLIAN
Children's Hour (1934)
The Little Foxes (1939)
Pentimento: A Book of Portraits (1973)
An Unfinished Woman (1969)

HEMANS, FELICIA
Forget Me Not (1826)
"The Indian Woman's Death-Song" (1828)
Records of Woman and Other Poems (1828)
"Stanzas on the Death of the Princess Charlotte"
(1818)
The Widow of Crescentius (1819)
The Wife of Asdrubal (1819)

HENLEY, BETH
Abundance (1990)
Crimes of the Heart (1979)
Debutante Ball (1985)
Family Week (2000)
The Impossible Marriage (1998)
Miss Firecracker Contest (1980)
The Wake of Jamey Foster (1982)

HERBST, JOSEPHINE
The Executioner Waits (1934)
Money for Love (1929)
Pity Is Not Enough (1933)
The Rope of Gold (1939)

HERMAN, JUDITH, AND LISA HIRSCHMAN
The Signs Reader (1983)

HO, WENDY
In Her Mother's House (1999)

HOEVELER, DIANE
Gothic Feminism (1998)

HOGAN, LINDA
Book of Medicines (1993)
Daughters, I Love You (1981)
Dwellings (1996)
Power (1999)
Savings (1988)
Seeing through the Sun (1985)
Solar Storms (1995)
The Sweet Breathing of Plants (2002)

HOLM, JENNIFER L.
Boston Jane: An Adventure (2001)
Boston Jane: The Claim (2004)
Boston Jane: Wilderness Days (2002)
Our Only Amelia May (1999)

HOLMES, LIZZIE MAY
Woman's Future Position in the World (1898)

HOOKS, BELL
Ain't I a Woman (1981)
Bone Black (1996)
Feminist Theory (1984)
Teaching to Transgress (1994)

HOUSTON, JEANNE WAKATSUKI, AND JAMES HOUSTON
A Farewell to Manzanar (1973)

HOWE, JULIA WARD
"The Mother's Day Proclamation" (1870)

HOWLAND, MARIE
"Papa's Own Girl" (1874)

HUNTINGTON, CYNTHIA
"Patchwork" (1989)

HURST, FANNIE
Back Street (1932)
"Don't Get the Wrong Message" 2001
"Hattie Turner versus Hattie Turner" (1935)
The Imitation of Life (1933)
The Lummox (1923)
Star-Dust: The Story of an American Girl (1921)
The Stories of Fannie Hurst (2005)

HURSTON, ZORA NEALE
Color Struck (1926)
"Drenched in Light" (1924)
Dust Tracks on a Road (1942)
Jonah's Gourd Vine (1934)

"Mother Catherine" (1934)
"Sweat" (1926)
Their Eyes Were Watching God (1937)

IBSEN, HENRIK
A Doll's House (1879)

IRIGARAY, LUCE
"And One Doesn't Stir without the Other" (1977)
Je, Tu, Nous: Toward a Culture of Difference (1990)
Sexes and Genres through Languages (2003)
Speculum of the Other Woman (1985)
This Sex Which Is Not One (1977)
To Be Two (1994)

IVINS, MOLLY
Molly Ivins Can't Say That, Can She? (1991)
Nothin' but Good Times Ahead (1993)
Shrub (2000)
You Got to Dance with Them What Brung You (1998)

IZUMI SHIKIBU AND MURASAKI SHIKIBU
Diaries of Court Ladies of Old Japan (1920)

JACKSON, HELEN HUNT
A Century of Dishonor (1881)
Ramona (1884)

JACKSON, SHIRLEY
Hangsaman (1951)
The Haunting of Hill House (1959)
Just an Ordinary Day (1996)
Life Among the Savages (1953)
"The Lottery" (1948)
We Have Always Lived in the Castle (1962)

JACOBS, HARRIET
Incidents in the Life of a Slave Girl (1861)

JANEWAY, ELIZABETH
Between Myth and Morning (1974)
Cross Sections from a Decade of Change (1982)
Daisy Kenyon (1945)
Improper Behavior (1987)
Leaving Home (1953)
Man's World, Woman's Place (1971)
Powers of the Weak (1980)
The Third Choice (1959)
Women on Campus (1975)
Women: Their Changing Roles, the Great Contemporary (1973)

JELINEK, ELFRIEDE
Lust (1989)
The Piano Teacher (1983)
We Are Decoys, Baby (1970)
What Happened after Nora Left Her Husband or Pillars of Societies (1979)
Wonderful, Wonderful Times (1980)

JEMISON, MARY
Life and Times of Mrs. Mary Jemison (1827)

JEN, GISH
Mona in the Promised Land (1996)
Typical American (1991)
Who's Irish? (1999)

JEWETT, SARAH ORNE
A Country Doctor (1884)
The Country of the Pointed Firs (1896)
Deephaven (1877)
"The Fly" (1922)
"In Dark New England Days" (1890)
Old Friends and New (1879)
"Tom's Husband" (1882)
A White Heron (1886)

JHABVALA, RUTH PRAWER
Heat and Dust (1975)
My Nine Lives: Chapters of a Possible Past (2004)

JOHNSON, GEORGIA DOUGLAS
And Yet They Paused (1999)
An Autumn Love Cycle (1928)
A Bill to Be Passed (1999)
Blue Blood (1926)
Blue-Eyed Black Boy (ca. 1930)
Frederick Douglass (1935)
Plumes (1927)
The Starting Point (1931)
Sunday Morning in the South (ca. 1925)
William and Ellen Craft (1935)

JOHNSON, PAULINE
Flint and Feather (1912)
"The Legend of Au'Appelle Valley" (1903)
The Moccasin Maker (1913)
"Two Sisters" (1911)

JOHNSON, SUSANNAH WILLARD
A Narrative of the Captivity of Mrs. Johnson (1796)

JOLLEY, ELIZABETH
Miss Peabody's Inheritance (1983)

JONES, ALICE ILGENFRITZ, AND ELLA MERCHANT
Unveiling a Parallel (1893)

JONES, GAYL
Corregidora (1975)
Eva's Man (1976)
The Healing (1998)
Song for Anninho (1981)

JONG, ERICA
Fear of Flying (1973)
How to Save Your Own Life (1977)
Parachutes and Kisses (1984)
Witches (1981)

JORDAN, JUNE
"A New Politics of Sexuality" (1991)
Soldier: A Poet's Childhood (1999)
"Where Is the Love?" (2002)

KASSARJIAN, MARY CATHERINE
With a Daughter's Eye (1984)

KAYE/KANTROWITZ, MELANIE
The Color of Jews (2004)
The Issue Is Power (1992)
My Jewish Face (1990)

KEENE, LAURA
Workmen of America (1864)

KELLER, HELEN
"Why Men Need Woman Suffrage" (1913)

KELLEY, FLORENCE
The Labor of Women and Children in Tenements (1912)
Modern Industry in Relation to the Family (1914)

KEMBLE, FANNY
Journal of a Residence in America (1835)
Journal of a Residence on a Georgian Plantation (1863)

KEMPE, MARGERY
The Book of Margery Kempe (1436)

KENNEDY, ADRIENNE
The Funnyhouse of a Negro (1962)
A Lesson in Dead Language (1964)
A Movie Star Has to Star in Black and White (1976)
The Owl Answers (1963)
People Who Led to My Plays (1987)
The Sleep Deprivation Chamber (1996)

KESSLER, CAROL FARLEY
Daring to Dream (1984)

KHALIFEH, SAHAR
Memoirs of an Unrealistic Woman (1986)
The Sunflower (1980)
We Are Not Your Slave Girls Anymore (1974)
Wild Thorns (1976)

KIM, ELAINE H.
*Asian American Literature: An Introduction to the Writings
    and Their Social Context* (1982)

KIMBROUGH, EMILY, AND CORNELIA OTIS SKINNER
Our Hearts Were Young and Gay (1942)

KINCAID, JAMAICA
Annie John (1985)
At the Bottom of the River (1983)
The Autobiography of My Mother (1996)
Lucy (1990)
"Sowers and Reapers" (2001)

KING, FLORENCE
Confessions of a Failed Southern Lady (1985)
Southern Ladies and Gentlemen (1975)

KINGSOLVER, BARBARA
Animal Dreams (1990)
The Bean Trees (1988)
Holding the Line (1989)
"Homeland" (1989)
I've Always Meant to Tell You (1997)
Last Stand: America's Virgin Lands (2002)
Pigs in Heaven (1993)
The Poisonwood Bible (1998)
Prodigal Summer (2000)
"Rose-Johnny" (1988)
Small Wonder (2002)
"Why I Am a Danger to the Public" (1989)

KINGSTON, MAXINE HONG
The Woman Warrior (1976)

KIZER, CAROLYN
"An American Beauty" (1996)
Mermaids in the Basement: Poems for Women (1984)
"Pro Femina" (1965)

KOGAWA, JOY
Obasan (1981)
A Song of Lilith (2003)

KOLBENSCHLAG, MADONNA
Kiss Sleeping Beauty Good-bye (1979)

KUMIN, MAXINE
"Envelope" (1978)
Halfway (1961)
"Making the Jam without You" (1970)
Our Ground Time Here Will Be Brief (1982)
The Retrieval System (1978)
Up Country: Poems of New England (1972)

LaFOLLETTE, SUZANNE
Concerning Women (1926)

LAKE, ROSEMARY
Once Upon a Time When the Princess Rescued the Prince
   (2003)

LAMB, CAROLINE
Ada Reis (1823)
Glenarvon (1816)

LANE, MARY E. BRADLEY
Mizora: A Prophecy (1880–81)

LARSEN, NELLA
Passing (1929)
Quicksand (1928)

LAZARUS, EMMA
"Echoes" (ca. 1880)
"The New Colossus" (1883)
The Spagnoletto (1876)

LEE, HARPER
To Kill a Mockingbird (1960)

LEE, SOPHIA
The Recess (1783–85)

LEE, TANITH
Faces under Water (1998)
Fatal Women (1998)
Piratica (2001)
The Silver Metal Lover (1985)
White As Snow (2001)

LE GUIN, URSULA
Dancing at the Edge of the World (1990)
"The Eye of the Heron" (1983)
The Farthest Shore (1972)
The Left Hand of Darkness (1969)

"Sur" (1982)
Tehanu (1990)
The Word for World Is Forest (1976)

LESSING, DORIS
The Diaries of Jane Somers (1984)
The Golden Notebook (1962)
The Grass Is Singing (1950)
Marriages Between Zones Three, Four, and Five (1994)

LE SUEUR, MERIDEL
Crusaders (1955)
The Girl (1978)
Nancy Hanks of Wilderness Road (1949)
"Persephone" (1927)
The Ripening (1982)
The Rites of Ancient Ripening (1975)
Winter Prairie Woman (1990)
Women Are Hungry (1934)
Women on the Breadlines (1932)

LEVERTOV, DENISE
"Abel's Bride" (1967)
"The Ache of Marriage" (1964)
"Canción" (1975)
"Death in Mexico" (1978)
"Dragonfly-Mother" (1982)
"Goddess" (1959)
"Hypocrite Women" (1964)
"Mutes" (1967)
"Pig Dreams" (1982)
"Song for Ishtar" (1964)
"Stepping Westward" (1967)
The Stream & the Sapphire (1997)
"A Woman Alone" (1978)

LEWES, GEORGE HENRY
Lady Novelists (1852)

LOGAN, OLIVE
Apropos of Women and Theatre (1869)
Eveleen (1864)
The Mimic World and Public Exhibitions (1871)
The Voice as a Source of Income (1874)

LOOS, ANITA
But Gentlemen Marry Brunettes (1929)
Gentlemen Prefer Blondes (1925)

LORD, BETTE BAO
The Eighth Moon (1964)
Middle Heart (1996)
Spring Moon (1981)

LORDE, AUDRE
The Black Unicorn (1978)
From a Land Where Other People Live (1973)
I Am Your Sister (1986)
Need (1990)
Sister Outsider (1984)
Zami (1982)

LOWELL, AMY
"The Letter" (1919)
"Madonna of the Evening Flowers" (1919)
"Opal" (1919)
"Patterns" (1916)
"Sisters" (1925)
"Summer Rain" (1919)
"Venus Transiens" (1919)
"The Weather-Cock Points South" (1919)

LOWRY, LOIS
Number the Stars (1989)

LOY, MINA
Futurism X Feminism (1920)
"Gertrude Stein" (1914)
"Songge Byrd" (1982)
Songs to Joannes (1917)
"Widow's Jazz" (1931)

LUCE, CLARE BOOTH
Slam the Door Softly (1971)
The Women (1936)

LURIE, ALISON
Boys and Girls Forever (2004)
"Fairy Tale Liberation" (1970)
The Language of Clothes (1981)
Only Children (1979)
The War Between the Tates (1974)
Women and Ghosts (1994)

MACLACHLAN, PATRICIA, AND CAROL SOBIESKI
Sarah, Plain and Tall (1985)
Skylark (1994)

MAGGIO, ROSALIE
Talking about People (1987)

MAGOFFIN, SUSAN
Down the Santa Fe Trail and into Mexico (1926)

MAHMOODY, BETTY
For Love of a Child (1992)
Not Without My Daughter (1987)

MALLOY, SYLVIA
Certificate of Absence (1981)

MAMONOVA, TATYANA
Women and Russia (1979)

MANN, EMILY
Annulla Allen: The Autobiography of a Survivor (1977)
Still Life (1980)

MANSFIELD, KATHERINE
The Garden Party (1922)
In a German Pension (1911)

MARACLE, LEE
Bobbi Lee, Indian Rebel (1975)

MARIE DE FRANCE
L'Ysopet (ca. 1189)

MARIE DE VILLANDON
"Donkeyskin" (1694)

MARKHAM, BERYL
"Splendid Outcast" (1944)
West with the Night (1942)

MARSHALL, PAULE
Brown Girl, Brownstones (1959)
Daughters (1991)
Praisesong for the Widow (1983)
Soul Clap Hands and Sing (1961)

MARTINEAU, HARRIET
Autobiography (1855)
Biographical Sketches (1877)
"Female Writers of Practical Divinity" (1821)
Illustrations of Political Economy (1832–33)
"On Female Education" (1823)
Society in America (1837)

MASON, BOBBIE ANN
Clear Springs (1999)
Feather Crowns (1993)
Girl Sleuth (1975)
In Country (1989)
Shiloh and Other Stories (1982)
Zigzagging Down a Wild Trail (2001)

MASON, EVELEEN
Hiero-Salem: The Vision of Peace (1889)

McARTHUR, MARY
"La Llorona" (2000)

McCAFFREY, ANNE
Acorna's Quest (1998)
Dragonsong (1977)
The Girl Who Heard Dragons (1994)
Restoree (1967)

McCARTHY, MARY
The Company She Keeps (1942)
The Group (1963)

McCAULEY, ROBBIE
Sally's Rape (1992)

McCLUNG, NELLIE
"Can a Woman Raise a Family and Have a Career?" (1928)
The Clearing in the West (1935)
In Times Like These (1915)
Painted Fires (1925)
Purple Springs (1921)
The Second Chance (1910)
Sowing Seeds in Danny (1908)
The Streams Run Fast (1945)

McCULLERS, CARSON
The Ballad of the Sad Café (1951)
The Heart Is a Lonely Hunter (1940)
The Member of the Wedding (1946)

McCUNN, RUTHANNE LUMM
Thousand Pieces of Gold (1981)

McKINLEY, ROBIN
Beauty (1978)

McMILLAN, TERRY
A Day Late and a Dollar Short (2001)
How Stella Got Her Groove Back (1996)
Mama (1987)
Waiting to Exhale (1992)

McNULTY, FAITH
The Burning Bed (1980)

MEAD, MARGARET
Blackberry Winter (1972)
Coming of Age in Samoa (1928)
Male and Female (1949)

MENCHÚ, RIGOBERTA
I, Rigoberta Menchú (1983)

MILL, HARRIET TAYLOR
"The Enfranchisement of Women" (1851)
Principles of Political Economy (1848)

MILL, JOHN STUART
"On Liberty" (1859)
The Subjection of Women (1869)

MILLAY, EDNA ST. VINCENT
A Few Figs from Thistles (1920)
Huntsman, What Quarry? (1939)
"Renascence" (1912)
"To Inez Milholland" (1928)

MILLER, MAY
Sojourner Truth (1935)

MILLER, SUSAN
My Left Breast (1995)

MILLETT, KATE
The Basement (1979)
The Cavedweller (1998)
Mother Millett (2001)
The Politics of Cruelty (1994)
The Prostitution Papers (1971)
Sexual Politics (1970)
Token Learning (1967)
Trash (1988)
Two or Three Things I Know for Sure (1995)
The Women Who Hate Me (1983)

MISTRAL, GABRIELA
"Profile of Sor Juana Inés de la Cruz" (1952)
Readings for Women (1923)
Tenderness (1925)

MITCHELL, MARGARET
Gone with the Wind (1936)

MOERS, ELLEN
"Angry Young Women" (1963)
Harriet Beecher Stowe and American Literature (1978)
Literary Women (1977)

MOORE, MARIANNE
"Marriage" (1923)
"Roses Only" (1924)
"Sojourn in the Whale" (1915)

MORAGA, CHERRÍE
The Circle in the Dirt (1995)
The Last Generation (1993)

Loving in the War Years (1983)
Waiting in the Wings (1997)
Watsonville: Some Place Not Here (1996)

MORE, HANNAH
"The Sorrows of Yamba" (1795)

MOREJÓN, NANCY
Black Woman and Other Poems (2004)
"Praise for Debate" (1982)
Where the Island Sleeps Like a Wing (1985)
With Eyes and Soul: Images of Cuba (2004)

MORGAN, ROBIN
The Anatomy of Freedom (1982)
The Demon Lover (1989)
Going Too Far (1977)
New Women (1970)
Sisterhood Is Forever (2003)
Sisterhood Is Powerful (1970)

MORRISON, TONI
Beloved (1987)
The Bluest Eye (1970)
Love (2003)
Song of Solomon (1977)
Sula (1973)

MOTT, LUCRETIA
"Discourse on Woman" (1849)
"The Progress of Reforms" (1848)

MOURNING DOVE
Cogewea Half-Blood (1927)
Mourning Dove: A Salishan Autobiography (1990)

MUKHERJEE, BHARATI
Desirable Daughters (2002)
The Holder of the World (1993)
Jasmine (1989)
Leave It to Me (1997)
Tiger's Daughter (1972)
The Wife (1975)

MUNRO, ALICE
Hateship, Friendship, Courtship, Loveship, Marriage (2001)
The Lives of Girls and Women (1971)
Runaway (2004)

MURASAKI SHIKIBU
Diary (1003)
The Tale of Genji (1019)

MURAT, COMTESSE DE
Histoires Sublimes et Alléoriques (1699)

MURRAY, JUDITH SARGENT
"Encouraging a Degree of Self-Complacency in the Female Bosom" (1784)
The Medium, or Virtue Triumphant (1795)
"On the Equality of the Sexes" (1779)
"Some Deduction from . . . Divine Revelation" (1782)
The Story of Margaretta (1798)

MURRAY, YXTA MAYA
"La Llorona" (1996)

NASLUND, SENA
Ahab's Wife (1999)
Sherlock in Love (1993)

NATION, CARRY
The Use and Need of the Life of Carry A. Nation (1905)

NAYLOR, GLORIA
Mama Day (1988)
Women of Brewster Place (1982)

NEWCASTLE, MARGARET CAVENDISH
The Convent of Pleasure (1668)

NG, FAE MYENNE
Bone (1993)

NIN, ANAÏS
Delta of Venus (1969)
The Diary of Anaïs Nin (1966–78)
The House of Incest (1936)
Little Birds (1979)
A Woman Speaks (1975)

NORMAN, DIANA
A Catch of Consequence (2003)
Taking Liberties (2004)
Terrible Beauty (1987)
The Vizard Mask (1994)

NORMAN, MARSHA
Circus Valentine (1979)
The Fortune Teller (1987)
Getting Out (1978)
'night Mother (1983)

NORRIS, KATHLEEN
Beauty's Daughter (1935)
"The Bride" (1989)
Mother (1911)

The Rich Mrs. Burgoyne (1913)
Saturday's Child (1914)
Through a Glass Darkly (1957)
What Price Peace? (1928)

NOTTAGE, LYNN
Poof (1993)

NUÑEZ, ELIZABETH
Beyond the Limbo Silence (1998)
Bruised Hibiscus (2000)
Discretion (2002)
Grace (2003)

NWAPA, FLORA
Two Women in Conversation (1993)

OATES, JOYCE CAROL
Big Mouth and Ugly Girl (2003)
Foxfire: Confessions of a Girl Gang (1993)
Marriages and Infidelities (1972)
We Were the Mulvaneys (1995)
"Where Are You Going, Where Have You Been"
   (1970)

**OATMAN, MARY ANN, AND OLIVE ANN
   OATMAN**
Captivity of the Oatman Girls (1859)

O'CONNOR, FLANNERY
"Good Country People" (1955)
"A Good Man Is Hard to Find" (1955)
"The Revelation" (1965)

OLDS, SHARON
The Gold Cell (1987)
"The Language of the Brag" (1980)
Wellspring (1996)

OLIPHANT, MARGARET
"Condition of Women" (1858)
"The Grievances of Women" (1880)
Jeanne d'Arc (1896)
"Laws Concerning Women" (1856)
Miss Marjoribanks (1866)

OLSEN, TILLIE
"I Stand Here Ironing" (1957)
"One Out of Twelve" (1971)
Silences (1978)
"Tell Me a Riddle" (1961)
Yonnondio: From the Thirties (1974)

OMOLADE, BARBARA
It's a Family Affair (1986)

ONWUEME, OSONYE TESS
The Broken Calabash (1993)
The Missing Face (1997)
Parables for a Season (1993)
The Reign of Wazobia (1993)
Shakara: Dance Hall Queen (2002)
Tell It to Women (1997)
Then She Said It (2002)

ORENSTEIN, CATHERINE
Little Red Riding Hood Uncloaked (2002)

OUFKIR, MALIKE
Stolen Lives (1999)

OZICK, CYNTHIA
Heir to the Glimmering World (2004)
"Literature and the Politics of Sex" (1996)
The Puttermesser Papers (1997)

PALEY, GRACE
Begin Again (2001)
Enormous Changes at the Last Minute (1974)
Little Disturbances of Man (1959)

PANKHURST, EMMELINE
The Importance of the Vote (1912)
My Own Story (1914)
Suffrage Speeches from the Dock (1913)
The Suffragette (1911)
Why We Are Militant (1913)

PANKHURST, SYLVIA
The Life of Emmeline Pankhurst (1935)

PARETSKY, SARA
Blacklist (2003)
Blood Shot (1988)
Hard Time (1999)
Indemnity Only (1982)

PARKER, DOROTHY
"Big Blonde" (1929)
Enough Rope (1926)
Ladies of the Corridor (1953)
"Waltz" (1933)

PEACOCKE, EMILIE HAWKES
Writing for Women (1936)

PETRY, ANN
Harriet Tubman (1955)
The Narrows (1953)
The Street (1946)
Tituba of Salem Village (1964)

PHELPS, ELIZABETH STUART
Doctor Zay (1882)
Friends: A Duet (1881)
Hedged In (1870)
"Jane Gurley's Story" (1866)
Old Maids (1879)
The Silent Partner (1871)
The Story of Avis (1877)
"The Tenth of January" (1868)
"Victurae Salutamus" (1880)

PHELPS, ETHEL JOHNSTON
The Maid of the North (1981)

PIERCY, MARGE
The Art of Blessing the Day (2000)
Dance the Eagle to Sleep (1971)
"The Grey Flannel Sexual Harassment Suit" (1995)
The Moon Is Always Female (1980)
My Mother's Body (1985)
Small Changes (1973)
Three Women (2001)
Woman on the Edge of Time (1976)

PIRKIS, CATHERINE LOUISA
Experiences of Loveday Brooke, Lady Detective (1893)

PLATH, SYLVIA
The Bell Jar (1963)
"Bluebeard" (1981)
"Daddy" (1962)
"Electra on Azalea Path" (1981)
"Lady Lazarus" (1963)
Letters Home (1975)
Three Women (1962)

PLUMMER, RACHEL
Narrative of the Capture and Subsequent Sufferings of Mrs. Rachel Plummer (1839)

POGREBIN, LETTY COTTIN
Deborah, Golda and Me (1992)
Getting Over Getting Older (1997)
How to Make It in a Man's World (1970)
Three Daughters (2002)

POLLITT, KATHA
Reasonable Creatures (1994)
Subject to Debate (2001)
"Why Do We Romanticize the Fetus?" (1993)

————, AND BETSY REED
Nothing Sacred (2002)

PORTER, KATHERINE ANNE
"He" (1930)
"The Jilting of Granny Weatherall" (1930)
"María Concepción" (1922)
"Noon Wine" (1936)
"Old Mortality" (1930)
"The Old Order" (1958)

POWELL, DAWN
The Bride's House (1929)
My Home Is Far Away (1944)
A Time to Be Born (1942)
The Wicked Pavilion (1954)

PRETTY SHIELD
"Woman's Fight" (1990)

PROVOOST, ANNE
In the Shadow of the Ark (2004)

QUINDLEN, ANNA
Black and Blue (1998)
Loud and Clear (2004)
One True Thing (1994)

RADCLIFFE, ANN
The Italian (1797)
The Mysteries of Udolpho (1794)
A Sicilian Romance (1790)

RANDALL, ALICE
The Wind Done Gone (2001)

RATUSHINSKAYA, IRINA
Beyond the Limit (1987)
Fiction and Lies (1999)
Grey Is the Colour of Hope (1988)
The Pencil Letter (1988)

RAU, SANTHA RAMA
The Adventuress (1970)
Home to India (1944)
A Princess Remembers (1976)
Remember the House (1956)

RAWLINGS, MARJORIE KINNAN
Blood of My Blood (2002)
Cross Creek (1942)
Cross Creek Cookery (1942)
"Gal Young 'Un" (1933)
When the Whippoorwill (1940)

RENAULT, MARY
The Friendly Young Ladies (1944)
Purposes of Love (1939)

REYES, ALINA
Lilith (1999)

RHYS, JEAN
Wide Sargasso Sea (1966)

RICE, ANNE
Beauty's Punishment (1984)
Beauty's Release (1985)
Belinda (1986)
The Claiming of Sleeping Beauty (1983)
The Queen of the Damned (1988)
The Witching Hour (1990)

RICH, ADRIENNE
"Blood, Bread, and Poetry" (1984)
Compulsory Heterosexuality and Lesbian Existence
    (1980)
Diving into the Wreck (1973)
Of Woman Born (1976)
On Lies, Secrets and Silence (1979)
Snapshots of a Daughter-in-Law (1963)
"Vesuvius at Home: The Power of Emily Dickinson"
    (1975)
What Is Found There (1993)
When We Dead Awaken (1972)

RICHARDS, MARY HASKIN
Winter Quarters (1996)

RINEHART, MARY ROBERTS
The Circular Staircase (1907–8)

ROBERTS, COKIE
Founding Mothers (2004)

ROBERTS, DMAE
The Breast Cancer Monologues (2004)
Janie Bigo (1997)
The Journey of Lady Buddha (1998)
Legacies: Faith, Hope and Peace (1998)

Legacies: Tales from America (1998)
Mei Mei: A Daughter's Song (1990)

ROBINSON, HARRIET JANE
Captain Mary Miller (1887)
Loom and Spindle (1898)
Massachusetts in the Woman Suffrage Movement (1881)
The New Pandora (1889)

ROBINSON, MARILYNNE
Housekeeping (1981)
Mother Country (1989)

ROBINSON, MARY
False Friend (1799)
Letter to the Women of England (1799)
Memoirs of the Late Mrs. Robinson (1801)
The Natural Daughter (1799)
Nobody (1793)
Sappho and Phaon (1796)
Vancenza; or, The Dangers of Credulity (1792)

ROE, FRANCES
Army Letters of an Officer's Wife (1909)

ROMAINE, SUZANNE
Communicating Gender (1999)

ROSE, WENDY
Now Poof She Is Gone (1994)

ROSS, ISHBEL
Charmers and Cranks (1965)
Ladies of the Press (1936)
Power with Grace: The Life Story of Mrs. Woodrow Wilson
    (1975)
The President's Wife (1973)

ROSSETTI, CHRISTINA
The Goblin Market (1862)
"In an Artist's Studio" (1857)
Speaking Likenesses (1874)
"The World" (1854)

ROWBOTHAM, SHEILA
The Friends of Alice Wheeldon (1986)
Hidden from History (1973)
Women Resist Globalisation (2002)
Women's Liberation and New Politics (1971)

ROWLAND, MARY ELLEN
As Long as Life (1995)

ROWLANDSON, MARY
The Sovereignty and Goodness of God (1682)

ROWSON, SUSANNA
Charlotte Temple (1791)
Mentoria (1791)
A Present for Young Ladies (1811)
Rebecca, or The Fille de Chambre (1792)
Slaves in Algiers (1794)

ROY, GABRIELLE
Children of My Heart (1977)
The Tin Flute (1947)
Windflower (1970)

RUKEYSER, MURIEL
Body of Waking (1958)
Breaking Open (1973)
"Käthe Kollwitz" (1968)
"Myth" (1973)
The Speed of Darkness (1968)

RUSS, JOANNA
The Adventures of Alyx (1986)
Alyx (1976)
And Chaos Died (1978)
The Female Man (1975)
How to Suppress Women's Writing (1983)
Magic Mommas, Trembling Sisters, Puritans and Perverts (1985)
Picnic on Paradise (1968)
To Write Like a Woman (1995)
"When It Changed" (1972)

SACKVILLE-WEST, VITA
All Passion Spent (1931)
Aphra Behn: The Incomparable Astrea (1927)
The Eagle and the Dove (1943)
The King's Daughter (1929)
Saint Joan of Arc (1936)

SAHGAL, NAYANTARA
From Fear Set Free (1962)
Mistaken Identity (1988)
Point of View (1997)
Rich Like Us (1983)
A Situation in New Delhi (1977)
This Time of Morning (1965)
A Voice for Freedom (1977)

SANCHEZ, SONIA
A Blues Book for Blue Black Magical Women (1974)

Does Your House Have Lions? (1997)
homegirls & handgrenades (1984)
I've Been a Woman (1978)
"Personal Letter No. 3" (1970)
Sister Son/ji (1969)
Under a Soprano Sky (1987)

SAND, GEORGE
The Castle of Pictures (1859)
Consuelo (1842–43)
Indiana (1832)
Lélia (1833)
Marianne (1876)

SANFORD, MOLLIE DORSEY
Mollie (1959)

SANGER, MARGARET
Margaret Sanger: An Autobiography (1938)
Mothers in Bondage (1928)

SAPPHO
Poems (ca. 590 B.C.)

SARTON, MAY
The Education of Harriet Hatfield (1965)
Mrs. Stevens Hears the Mermaids Singing (1965)

SCHAEFFER, SUSAN FROMBERG
"The Wedding Ring Poem" (1984)

SCHECHTER, SUSAN
Women and Male Violence (1982)

SCHLISSELL, LILLIAN
Women's Diaries of the Westward Journey (1982)

SCHREINER, OLIVE
Closer Union (1909)
Dream Life and Real Life (1893)
Dreams (1891)
An English South African Woman's View of the Situation (1899)
The Story of an African Farm (1883)
Undine (1874)
Woman and Labour (1911)

SEWARD, ANNA
Llangollen Vale (1796)
Louisa (1784)

SEXTON, ANNE
"All My Pretty Ones" (1981)

"Briar Rose" (1981)
"Flee on Your Donkey" (1981)
"Her Kind" (1960)
"Housewife" (1962)
"Red Riding Hood" (1971)
"Sylvia's Death" (1966)
Transformations (1971)

SHANGE, NTOZAKE
Betsey Brown (1995)
*for colored girls who have considered suicide when the
        rainbow is enuf* (1975)
If I Can Cook/You Know God Can (1998)
Love Space Demands (1991)

SHELHAMER, MARY THERESA
Life and Labor in the Spirit World (1885)

SHELLEY, MARY
Frankenstein (1818)

SHOWALTER, ELAINE
The Female Malady (1986)
Hystories (1997)
Inventing Herself (2001)
A Literature of Their Own (1977)
Scribbling Women (1996)
These Modern Women (1979)
Women's Liberation and Literature (1971)

SILKO, LESLIE MARMON
Almanac of the Dead (1991)
Ceremony (1977)
"The First Rain of Spring" (1961)
Gardens in the Dunes (1999)
"Hark, Hark" (2001)
Laguna Woman (1974)
"Yellow Woman" (1981)
Yellow Woman and a Beauty of the Spirit (1996)

SKINNER, CORNELIA OTIS
Elegant Wits and Grand Horizontals (1962)
Madame Sarah (1967)
Paris '90 (1952)

SMILEY, JANE
The All-True Travels and Adventures of Lidie Newton
        (1998)
Barn Blind (1980)
Greenlanders (1988)
A Thousand Acres (1991)

SMITH, ANNA DEAVERE
Fires in the Mirror (1992)
Twilight Los Angeles, 1992 (1994)

SMITH, BARABARA
Home Girls (1983)

SMITH, CHARLOTTE
Emmeline Orphan of the Castle (1788)
The Letters of a Solitary Wanderer (1800–02)
Manon L'Escault; or Fatal Attachment (1785)
Montalbert (1795)
Old Manor House (1793)
The Romance of Real Life (1787)
The Wanderings of Warwick (1794)
The Young Philosopher (1798)

SMITH, STEVIE
"A Dream of Comparison" (1957)
Holiday (1949)
"A House of Mercy" (1966)
"How Cruel Is the Story of Eve" (1996)
Novel on Yellow Paper (1936)
"Papa Love Baby" (1937)

SNEDEKER, CAROLINE
The Beckoning Road (1929)
Seth Way (1917)

SONG, CATHY
Frameless Windows, Squares of Light (1988)
The Land of Bliss (2001)
The Picture Bride (1983)
School Figures (1994)

SONTAG, SUSAN
On Photography (1977)
"The Third World of Women" (1973)

SOUTHWORTH, E. D. E. N.
The Deserted Wife (1850)
The Hidden Hand; or, Capitola the Mad-Cap (1859)
Old Neighbourhoods and New Settlements (1853)
The Retribution (1849)

SPRINGER, NANCY
The Hex Witch of Seldom (1989)
I Am Morgan Le Fay (2001)
The Outlaw Princess of Sherwood (2003)
Rowan Hood, Outlaw Girl of Sherwood Forest (2001)
Separate Sisters (2002)
Sky Rider (2000)

STAËL, GERMAINE DE
"Reflections on the Trial of a Queen" (1793)

STAFFORD, JEAN
Boston Adventure (1944)
A Mother in History (1966)

STANTON, ELIZABETH CADY
Eighty Years and More (1897)
The Solitude of Self (1892)
The Woman's Bible (1895–98)

STARHAWK
Dreaming the Dark (1982)
The Fifth Sacred Thing (1993)
Spiral Dance (1979)
Walking to Mercury (1997)

STEIN, GERTRUDE
The Autobiography of Alice B. Toklas (1933)
"I Am Rose" (1939)
"The Love Song of Alice B." (1921)
The Mother of Us All (1947)
Tender Buttons (1914)
Three Lives (1909)

STEINEM, GLORIA
"After Black Power, Women's Liberation" (1969)
"Far from the Opposite Shore" (1978)
"If Men Could Menstruate" (1978)
"I Was a Playboy Bunny" (1963)
Marilyn: Norma Jeane (1986)
"The Moral Disarmament of Betty Coed" (1962)
Outrageous Acts and Everyday Rebellions (1983)
Revolution from Within (1992)
"Women's Liberation Aims to Free Men, Too" (1970)

STENHOUSE, FANNIE
Tell It All (1874)

STEPHENS, ANN SOPHIA
Ahmo's Plot (1863)
Esther (1875)
Fashion and Famine (1854)
King Philip's Daughter (1858)
Malaeska (1839)
Mary Derwent (1858)
Myra Child of Adoption (1860)
Sybil Chase (1882)
The Wife's Trial (1856)
Wives and Widows (1869)

STEWART, ELINORE PRUITT
Letters of a Woman Homesteader (1914)

STONE, LUCY
"Disappointment Is the Lot of Women" (1855)
"The Progress of Fifty Years" (1893)

STOPES, MARIE
Birth Control Today (1934)
Change of Life in Men and Women (1936)
Contraception (1924)
Married Love (1918)
Radiant Motherhood (1921)
Roman Catholic Methods of Birth Control (1933)
Wise Parenthood (1918)

STOWE, HARRIET BEECHER
Lady Byron Vindicated (1870)
The Pearl of Orr Island (1862)
"Sojourner Truth, the Libyan Sibyl" (1863)
Uncle Tom's Cabin (1852)

TAGGART, GENEVIEVE
The Life and Mind of Emily Dickinson (1930)

TAN, AMY
The Bonesetter's Daughter (2001)
The Hundred Secret Senses (1995)
The Joy Luck Club (1989)
The Kitchen God's Wife (1991)
"Lost Lives of Women: My Grandmother's Choice"
   (1991)

TEASDALE, SARA
The Answering Voice (1917)
Dark of the Moon (1926)
Flame and Shadow (1920)
"Guenevere" (1907)
Helen of Troy and Other Poems (1911)

THOMAS, MARLO
Free to Be, You and Me (1974)

THOMAS, MARTHA CAREY
"Should Higher Education for Women Differ?"
   (1899)

THOMPSON, DOROTHY
Refugees: Anarchy or Organization? (1938)
"We Must Find a Radical Solution for the Abolition of
   War" (1947)

TILLMAN, KATHERINE
Aunt Betsy's Thanksgiving (1914)

TRAILL, CATHERINE PARR
The Backwoods of Canada (1871)

TRUTH, SOJOURNER
"Ain't I a Woman?" (1851)
The Narrative of Sojourner Truth (1850)
"Women Want Their Rights" (1853)

TUCHMAN, BARBARA
A Distant Mirror (1978)

ULRICH, LAUREL THATCHER
The Age of Homespun (2001)
Good Wives (1980)
A Midwife's Tale (1990)

UNDSET, SIGRID
The Bridal Wreath (1920)
The Cross (1922)
Gunnar's Daughter (1909)
Mistress of Husaby (1921)
Mrs. Marta Oulie (1907)

VILLANDON, MARIE DE
"Subtle Princess" (1694)

VILLENEUVE, MADAME GABRIELLE-SUZANNE BARBOT DE GALLON DE
The Young American and the Sea Stories (1740)

VIRAMONTES, HELEN
The Moth and Other Stories (1995)
Paris Rats in E.L.A. (1993)
Under the Feet of Jesus (1995)

————, AND MARÍA HERERRA-SOBEK
Chicana Creativity and Criticism (1988)
Chicana Writers (1993)

WAISBROOKER, LOIS
A Sex Revolution (1894)

WALKER, ALICE
By the Light of My Father's Smile (1998)
The Color Purple (1982)
Meridian (1976)
Now Is the Time to Open Your Heart (2004)
Possessing the Secret of Joy (1992)
Temple of My Familiar (1989)

WALKER, JEANNE MURRAY
"The Shawl" (1985)

WALKER, LADY MARY
Munster Village (1778)

WALKER, MARGARET
Jubilee (1966)
On Being Female, Black, and Free (1997)
"Whores" (1942)

WALLIS, VELMA
Bird Girl and the Man Who Followed the Sun (1996)
Raising Ourselves (2002)
Two Old Women (1993)

WANDOR, MICHELINE
The Belle of Amherst (1987)

WARNER, MARINA
Alone of All Her Sex (1976)
From the Beast to the Blonde (1994)

WARREN, MERCY OTIS
The Blockheads (1774)
The Ladies of Castile (1790)
Observations on the New Constitution (1788)
The Sack of Rome (1787)

WASSERSTEIN, WENDY
An American Daughter (1997)
Any Woman Can't (1973)
Bachelor Girls (1991)
The Heidi Chronicles (1989)
Isn't It Romantic (1981)
The Sisters Rosensweig (1992)
Uncommon Women and Others (1977)
When Dinah Shore Ruled the Earth (1975)

WATKINS, YOKO KAWASHIMA
My Brother, My Sister and I (1994)
So Far from the Bamboo Grove (1986)
Tales from the Bamboo Grove (1992)

WEATHERHEAD, CHRIS
Mary Chesnut's War for Independence! (1997)

WEIL, SIMONE
Gravity and Grace (1947)
The Need for Roots (1949)
Oppression and Liberty (1955)

WELDON, FAY
Big Girls Don't Cry (1997)
Down among the Women (1971)
The Fat Woman's Joke (1967)
Female Friends (1974)
The Life and Loves of a She-Devil (1983)
Praxis (1978)
Puffball (1980)
Remember Me (1976)
Splitting (1995)

WELLS, REBECCA
Divine Secrets of the Ya-Ya Sisterhood (1996)
Little Altars Everywhere (1992)
Ya-Ya's in Bloom (2004)

WELLS-BARNETT, IDA
The Crusade for Justice (1970)
Southern Horror (1892)

WELTY, EUDORA
Delta Wedding (1946)
"The Golden Apples" (1949)
"Lily Daw and the Three Ladies" (1941)
"Livvie Is Back" (1943)
"Why I Live at the P.O." (1941)
"A Worn Path" (1941)

WERTENBAKER, TIMBERLAKE
Abel's Sister (1984)
Galileo's Daughter (2004)
The Grace of Mary Traverse (1985)
Inside Out (1982)
Love of the Nightingale (1988)
New Anatomies (1981)

WEST, JESSAMYN
Except for Me and Thee (1969)
The Friendly Persuasion (1945)
The Massacre at Fall Creek (1975)
The Woman Said Yes (1976)

WEST, REBECCA
Black Lamb and Grey Falcon (1942)
"Elegy" (1930)
Henry James (1916)
"Indissoluble Matrimony" (1914)
"A New Woman's Movement" (1913)
The Return of the Soldier (1918)
"The Sheltered Sex" (1913)

WHARTON, EDITH
The Age of Innocence (1920)

A Backward Glance (1934)
The Buccaneers (1938)
Ethan Frome (1911)
Fighting France (1918)
The House of Mirth (1905)
The Mother's Recompense (1925)
Old New York (1924)
The Reef (1912)

WHEATLEY, PHILLIS
Poems on Various Subjects, Religious and Moral (1773)

WILDER, LAURA INGALLS
By the Shores of Silver Lake (1939)
Little House in the Big Woods (1932)
Little House on the Prairie (1935)
On the Banks of Plum Creek (1937)
On the Way Home (1962)

WILHELM, KATE
Where Late the Sweet Birds Sang (1977)

WILLIAMS, PATRICIA
The Alchemy of Race and Rights (1991)
Open House (2004)
The Rooster's Egg (1995)

WILNER, ELEANOR
"Emigration" (1980)

WILSON, JANE
The Thrilling Narrative of the Sufferings of Mrs. Jane Adeline Wilson (1853)

WINCHILSEA, ANNE FINCH, COUNTESS OF
"Circuit of Apollo" (1702)
"Fragment" (1713)
"Introduction" (1737)
"A Letter to Daphnis, April 2, 1685" (1713)
"Spleen" (1713)
"To the Nightingale" (1713)

WINNEMUCCA, SARAH
Life among the Piutes (1883)

WOLF, CHRISTA
Cassandra (1987)
Medea (1996)

WOLF, NAOMI
The Beauty Myth (1991)
Fire with Fire (1996)

Misconceptions (2003)
Promiscuities (1997)

WOLKSTEIN, DIANE
Esther's Story (1996)
First Love Stories (1991)
Inanna (1983)

WOLLSTONECRAFT, MARY
The Female Reader (1789)
Mary (1788)
Thoughts on the Education of Daughters (1786)
A Vindication of the Rights of Women (1792)

WOOD, ELLEN
Danesbury House (1860)
East Lynne (1861)

WOODHULL, VICTORIA
The Human Body (1890)
Origin, Tendencies and Principles of Government (1871)
"The Social Volcano" (1871)

WOOLF, VIRGINIA
Course of Popular Lectures (1936)
Flush (1933)
Mrs. Dalloway (1925)
Night and Day (1919)
Orlando (1928)
A Room of One's Own (1929)
Three Guineas (1938)
To the Lighthouse (1927)
The Voyage Out (1915)

WRIGHT, FRANCES
A Plan for the Gradual Abolition of Slavery in the United States (1825)
Views of Society and Manners in America (1821)

WYLIE, ELINOR
Angels and Earthly Creatures (1929)
Black Armour (1923)
Jennifer Lorn (1923)
The Venetian Glass Nephew (1925)

YAMADA, MITSUYE
Camp Notes and Other Poems (1976)
Camp Notes and Other Writings (1998)
Desert Run (1988)
Teaching Human Rights Awareness Through Poetry (1999)

YAMAMOTO, HISAYE
"High-Heeled Shoes, a Memoir" (1948)
"Seventeen Syllables" (1949)

YEARSLEY, ANN
Earl Goodwin (1791)
"A Poem on the Inhumanity of the Slave Trade" (1788)
The Royal Captives (1795)
The Rural Lyre (1796)

YEZIERSKA, ANZIA
Bread Givers (1925)
Hungry Hearts and Other Stories (1920)
Salome of the Tenements (1923)

YOLEN, JANE
Briar Rose (1993)

YOURCENAR, MARGUERITE
The Abyss (1968)
Memoirs of Hadrian (1951)
Mishima: A Vision of the Void (1981)

A Time Line of Major Works of Feminist Literature

Note: Recovered texts reflect the times in which they first appeared in print, as is the case with versions of Mary Chesnut's Civil War diary, Georgia Douglas Johnson's *A Bill to Be Passed* and *And Yet They Paused*, Lillian Schlissel's *Women's Diaries of the Westward Journey*, Laurel Thatcher Ulrich's *A Midwife's Tale*, and *Diaries of Court Ladies of Old Japan* (1920), by Izumi Shikibu and Murasaki Shikibu.

590 B.C.
Poems, Sappho

411 B.C.
Lysistrata, Aristophanes

1003
Diary, Murasaki Shikibu

1019
The Tale of Genji, Murasaki Shikibu

1189
L'Ysopet, Marie de France

1387
"The Wife of Bath's Tale," Geoffrey Chaucer

1399
Letter to the God of Love, Christine de Pisan

1402
Letters on the Debate of "The Romance of the Rose," Christine de Pisan

1405
Book of the City of Ladies, Christine de Pisan

1406
Letter on the Three Virtues, Christine de Pisan

1429
"Hymn to Joan of Arc," Christine de Pisan

1436
The Book of Margery Kempe, Margery Kempe

1538
Painful Torments That Procede from Love, Hélisenne de Crenne

1539
Personal and Invective Letters, Hélisenne de Crenne

1540
The Dream of Madame Hélisenne, Hélisenne de Crenne

1650
The Tenth Muse Lately Sprung Up in America, Anne Bradstreet

1668
The Convent of Pleasure, Margaret Cavendish Newcastle

1670
The Forc'd Marriage, or The Jealous Bridegroom, Aphra Behn

1673
"The Willing Mistress," Aphra Behn

1676
Abdelazar, or Moor's Revenge, Aphra Behn

1677
The Rover, or The Banish't Cavaliers, Aphra Behn

1678
Severall Poems, Anne Bradstreet

1680
"Disappointment," Aphra Behn

1682
The City Heiress, or, Sir Timothy Treat-all, Aphra Behn
The Sovereignty and Goodness of God, Mary Rowlandson

1687
Love Letters between a Nobleman and His Sister, Aphra Behn
The Luckey Chance; or, An Alderman's Bargain, Aphra Behn

1688
Oroonoko, Aphra Behn

1691
The Reply to Sister Filotea, Sor Juana de la Cruz

1694
"Donkeyskin," Marie de Villandon
"Subtle Princess," Marie de Villandon

1698
The White Cat, Comtesse d'Aulnoy

1699
Histoires Sublimes et Allégoriques, Comtesse de Murat
Tales of the Fairies, Comtesse d'Aulnoy

1702
"Circuit of Apollo," Anne Finch

1713
"Fragment," Anne Finch, countess of Winchilsea
"A Letter to Daphnis, April 2, 1685," Anne Finch, countess of Winchilsea
"Spleen," Anne Finch, countess of Winchilsea
"To the Nightingale," Anne Finch, countess of Winchilsea

1728
God's Mercy Surmounting Man's Cruelty, Elizabeth Hanson

1733
The Household Book of Lady Griselle Baillie, Lady Grisell Baillie

1737
"Introduction," Anne Finch

1740
The Young American and the Sea Stories, Madame Gabrielle-Suzanne de Villeneuve

1773
Poems on Various Subjects, Religious and Moral, Phillis Wheatley

1774
The Blockheads, Mercy Otis Warren

1778
Evelina, Fanny Burney
Munster Village, Lady Mary Walker

1779
"On the Equality of the Sexes," Judith Sargent Murray
Witlings, Fanny Burney

1782
Cecilia; or, Memoirs of an Heiress, Fanny Burney
"Some Deduction from . . . Divine Revelation," Judith Sargent Murray

1784
"Encouraging a Degree of Self-Complacency in the Female Bosom," Judith Sargent Murray
Louisa, Anna Seward

1785
Manon L'Escault; or Fatal Attachment, Charlotte Smith
The Recess, Sophia Lee

1786
Thoughts on the Education of Daughters, Mary Wollstonecraft

1787
The Romance of Real Life, Charlotte Smith
The Sack of Rome, Mercy Otis Warren

1788
Emmeline Orphan of the Castle, Charlotte Smith
Mary, Mary Wollstonecraft
Observations on the New Constitution, Mercy Otis Warren
"A Poem on the Inhumanity of the Slave Trade," Ann Yearsley

1789
The Female Reader, Mary Wollstonecraft

1790
"Epistle to William Wilberforce," Anna Laetitia
  Barbauld
The Ladies of Castile, Mercy Otis Warren
A Sicilian Romance, Ann Radcliffe

1791
Charlotte Temple, Susanna Rowson
Earl Goodwin, Ann Yearsley
Mentoria, Susanna Rowson

1792
Rebecca, or The Fille de Chambre, Susanna Rowson
"The Rights of Woman," Anna Laetitia Barbauld
Vancenza; or, The Dangers of Credulity, Mary Robinson
A Vindication of the Rights of Women, Mary
  Wollstonecraft

1793
Nobody, Mary Robinson
Old Manor House, Charlotte Smith
"Reflections on the Trial of a Queen," Germaine de
  Staël

1794
Evenings at Home, Anna Laetitia Barbauld
The Mysteries of Udolpho, Ann Radcliffe
Slaves in Algiers, Susanna Rowson
The Wanderings of Warwick, Charlotte Smith

1795
Letters for Literary Ladies, Maria Edgeworth
The Medium, or Virtue Triumphant, Judith Sargent
  Murray
Montalbert, Charlotte Smith
The Parent's Assistant, Maria Edgeworth
The Royal Captives, Ann Yearsley
"The Sorrows of Yamba," Hannah More
"To a Little Invisible Being Who Is Expected Soon to
  Become Visible," Anna Laetitia Barbauld

1796
An Account of the Captivity of Elizabeth Hanson, Elizabeth
  Hanson
Camilla, or Female Difficulties, Fanny Burney
Llangollen Vale, Anna Seward
A Narrative of the Captivity of Mrs. Johnson, Susannah
  Willard Johnson

The Rural Lyre, Ann Yearsley
Sappho and Phaon, Mary Robinson

1797
The Coquette: or History of Eliza Wharton, Hannah
  Webster Foster
The Italian, Ann Radcliffe
"Washing-Day," Anna Laetitia Barbauld

1798
Practical Education, Maria Edgeworth
A Series of Plays on the Passions, Joanna Baillie
The Story of Margaretta, Judith Sargent Murray
The Young Philosopher, Charlotte Smith

1799
False Friend, Mary Robinson
Letter to the Women of England, Mary Robinson
Love and Fashion, Fanny Burney
The Natural Daughter, Mary Robinson

1800
De Montfort, Joanna Baillie

1801
Belinda, Maria Edgeworth
A Busy Day, Fanny Burney
Early Lessons, Maria Edgeworth
The Woman-Hater, Fanny Burney

1802
The Letters of a Solitary Wanderer, Charlotte Smith

1803
Memoirs of the Late Mrs. Robinson, Mary Robinson

1809
Essays on Professional Education, Maria Edgeworth

1811
A Present for Young Ladies, Susanna Rowson
Sense and Sensibility, Jane Austen

1812
The Absentee, Maria Edgeworth

1813
Pride and Prejudice, Jane Austen

1814
The Conviction; or, She Is Innocent!, Anne of Swansea
Mansfield Park, Jane Austen

1815
Emma, Jane Austen

1816
Glenarvon, Caroline Lamb

1818
Frankenstein, Mary Shelley
Northanger Abbey, Jane Austen
Persuasion, Jane Austen
"Stanzas on the Death of the Princess Charlotte," Felicia
　　Hemans

1819
The Widow of Crescentius, Felicia Hemans
The Wife of Asdrubal, Felicia Hemans

1820
British Novelists, Anna Laetitia Barbauld

1821
"Female Writers of Practical Divinity," Harriet
　　Martineau
Lovers and Friends, Anne of Swansea

1823
"On Female Education," Harriet Martineau

1824
Hobomok, Lydia Child

1825
*A Plan for the Gradual Abolition of Slavery in the United
　　States*, Frances Wright

1826
Forget Me Not, Felicia Hemans
Three Hundred Years Hence, Mary Griffith

1827
The Life and Times of Mrs. Mary Jemison, Mary Jemison

1828
Essays of the Human Intellect, Caroline Clive
"The Indian Woman's Death-Song," Felicia Hemans
Records of Woman and Other Poems, Felicia Hemans

1829
The Frugal Housewife, Lydia Child

1830
"Mrs. Hutchinson," Nathaniel Hawthorne

1831
Mother's Book, Lydia Child

1832
Ada Reis, Caroline Lamb
Indiana, George Sand
The Legend of Lady Griseld Baillie, Joanna Baillie

1833
*An Appeal in Favor of That Class of Americans Called
　　Africans*, Lydia Child
Illustrations of Political Economy, Harriet Martineau
Lélia, George Sand

1835
The History of the Condition of Women, Lydia Child
Journal of a Residence in America, Fanny Kemble
Traits of American Life, Sarah Josepha Hale

1836
An Appeal to the Christian Women of the South, Angelina
　　Grimké

1837
An Appeal to the Women of the Nominally Free States,
　　Angelina Grimké
Society in America, Harriet Martineau

1838
Authentic Anecdotes of American Slavery, Lydia Child
The Family Nurse, Lydia Child
*Letters on the Equality of the Sexes and the Condition of
　　Women*, Angelina Grimké

1839
The Lecturess; or, Woman's Sphere, Sarah Josepha Hale
Malaeska, Ann Sophia Stephens
*Narrative of the Capture and Subsequent Sufferings of Mrs.
　　Rachel Plummer*, Rachel Plummer

1841
Sab, Gertrudis de Avellaneda
Treatise on Domestic Economy, Catharine Beecher

1842
Letters to Persons Engaged in Domestic Service, Catharine
　　Beecher
The Spirit of Judaism, Grace Aguilar

1843
Consuelo, George Sand
Cry of the Children, Elizabeth Barrett Browning

"The Great Lawsuit," Margaret Fuller
"Quadroons," Lydia Child
Summer on the Lakes in 1843, Margaret Fuller

1844
"Over the river and thro' the woods," Lydia Child
Women of Israel, Grace Aguilar

1845
"The Festival of Purim," Grace Aguilar
Narrative of the Life of Frederick Douglass, Frederick
   Douglass
Woman in the Nineteenth Century, Margaret Fuller

1846
"The Runaway Slave at Pilgrim's Point," Elizabeth
   Barrett Browning

1847
Aurora Leigh, Elizabeth Barrett Browning
Home Influence, Grace Aguilar
Jane Eyre, Charlotte Brontë
Wuthering Heights, Emily Brontë

1848
Mary Barton, Elizabeth Gaskell
Principles of Political Economy, Harriet Taylor Mill
"The Progress of Reforms," Lucretia Mott
"Sequel to *Vision of Bangor in the Twentieth Century*,"
   Jane Sophia Appleton
"Woman: The Great Unpaid Laborer," Susan B. Anthony

1849
Ahalya Baee, Joanna Baillie
"Discourse on Woman," Lucretia Mott
The Retribution, E. D. E. N. Southworth
Shirley, Charlotte Brontë

1850
The Deserted Wife, E. D. E. N. Southworth
The Narrative of Sojourner Truth, Sojourner Truth
The Scarlet Letter, Nathaniel Hawthorne
Sonnets from the Portuguese, Elizabeth Barrett Browning

1851
"Ain't I a Woman?," Sojourner Truth
"The Enfranchisement of Women," Harriet Taylor Mill
The Mother's Recompense, Grace Aguilar
Woman's Friendship, Grace Aguilar

1852
Fern Leaves from Fanny's Portfolio, Fanny Fern
Lady Novelists, George Henry Lewes

*Laws of Life with Special Reference to the Physical
   Education of Girls*, Elizabeth Blackwell
Liberia: or Mr. Peyton's Experiment, Sarah Josepha Hale
Uncle Tom's Cabin, Harriet Beecher Stowe

1853
Maud Martha, Gwendolyn Brooks
Old Neighbourhoods and New Settlements, E. D. E. N.
   Southworth
Ruth, Elizabeth Gaskell
*The Thrilling Narrative of the Sufferings of Mrs. Jane
   Adeline Wilson*, Jane Wilson
Villette, Charlotte Brontë
"Women Want Their Rights," Sojourner Truth

1854
Fashion and Famine, Ann Sophia Stephens
Ruth Hall, Fanny Fern
"The Slave Mother," Frances Ellen Harper
The Wicked Pavilion, Dawn Powell
"The World," Christina Rossetti

1855
Autobiography, Harriet Martineau
Cranford, Elizabeth Gaskell
"Disappointment Is the Lot of Women," Lucy Stone
North and South, Elizabeth Gaskell
Paul Ferroll, Caroline Clive

1856
"Laws Concerning Women," Margaret Oliphant
Shadows of Our Social System, Antoinette Brown Blackwell
The Wife's Trial, Ann Sophia Stephens

1857
"In an Artist's Studio," Christina Rossetti
The Life of Charlotte Brontë, Elizabeth Gaskell
Scenes of Clerical Life, George Eliot

1858
"Bury Me in a Free Land," Frances Ellen Harper
"The Condition of Women," Margaret Oliphant
King Philip's Daughter, Ann Sophia Stephens
Mary Derwent, Ann Sophia Stephens
"We lose—because we win," Emily Dickinson

1859
Adam Bede, George Eliot
Captivity of the Oatman Girls, Mary Ann Oatman and
   Olive Ann Oatman
The Castle of Pictures, George Sand
"Her Breast Is Fit for Pearls," Emily Dickinson

The Hidden Hand; or, Capitola the Mad-Cap, E. D. E. N. Southworth
"Letter to Young Ladies Desirous of Studying Medicine," Elizabeth Blackwell
"On Liberty," John Stuart Mill
"The Two Offers," Frances Ellen Harper

1860

Danesbury House, Ellen Wood
The Mill on the Floss, George Eliot
Myra Child of Adoption, Ann Sophia Stephens
"What Is Paradise," Emily Dickinson
Why Paul Ferroll Killed His Wife, Caroline Clive

1861

East Lynne, Ellen Wood
"Hope Is the Thing with Feathers," Emily Dickinson
Incidents in the Life of a Slave Girl, Harriet Jacobs
Life in the Iron Mills, Rebecca Harding Davis
"Lord Walter's Wife," Elizabeth Barrett Browning
Margret Howth: A Story of Today, Rebecca Harding Davis
"Mother and Poet," Elizabeth Barrett Browning
Silas Marner, George Eliot
"Why—do they shut Me out of Heaven?," Emily Dickinson
"Wild Night," Emily Dickinson

1862

Aurora Floyd, Mary Elizabeth Braddon
The Goblin Market, Christina Rossetti
"Her sweet Weight on my Heart," Emily Dickinson
Lady Audley's Secret, Mary Elizabeth Braddon
The Pearl of Orr Island, Harriet Beecher Stowe
"They put me in the Closet," Emily Dickinson

1863

Ahmo's Plot, Ann Sophia Stephens
Eleanor's Victory, Mary Elizabeth Braddon
Hospital Sketches, Louisa May Alcott
John Marchmont's Legacy, Mary Elizabeth Braddon
Journal of a Residence on a Georgian Plantation, Fanny Kemble
"My Life had stood—a Loaded Gun," Emily Dickinson
"The Rights of Women and Negroes," Angelina Grimké
"Sojourner Truth, the Libyan Sibyl," Harriet Beecher Stowe
"Where Thou art—that—is Home," Emily Dickinson
"A Whisper in the Dark," Louisa May Alcott

1864

The Doctor's Wife, Mary Elizabeth Braddon
Eveleen, Olive Logan
Henry Dunbar, Mary Elizabeth Braddon

Thou Art the Man, Mary Elizabeth Braddon
"The Wife's Story," Rebecca Harding Davis
Workmen of America, Laura Keene

1865

Moods, Louisa May Alcott

1866

"Jane Gurley's Story," Elizabeth Stuart Phelps
Miss Marjoribanks, Margaret Oliphant
Wives and Daughters, Elizabeth Gaskell

1868

An Appeal for the Indians, Lydia Child
"A Plea for the Afternoon," Antoinette Brown Blackwell
"Tell All the Truth but Tell It Slant," Emily Dickinson
"The Tenth of January," Elizabeth Stuart Phelps

1869

The American Woman's Home, Catharine Beecher
Apropos of Women and Theatre, Olive Logan
Little Women, Louisa May Alcott
"My Visit to Utopia," Elizabeth T. Corbett
Scenes in the Life of Harriet Tubman, Sarah Elizabeth Bradford
The Subjection of Women, John Stuart Mill
Wives and Widows, Ann Sophia Stephens

1870

Hedged In, Elizabeth Stuart Phelps
Lady Byron Vindicated, Harriet Beecher Stowe
"The Mother's Day Proclamation," Julia Ward Howe

1871

The Backwoods of Canada, Catherine Parr Traill
The Mimic World and Public Exhibitions, Olive Logan
Origin, Tendencies and Principles of Government, Victoria Woodhull
The Silent Partner, Elizabeth Stuart Phelps
"The Social Volcano," Victoria Woodhull
Work: A Story of Experience, Louisa May Alcott

1872

Middlemarch, George Eliot
Sketches of Southern Life, Frances Ellen Harper
The Trial of Susan B. Anthony, Susan B. Anthony
Woman's Record, Sarah Josepha Hale

1874

Earthen Pitchers, Rebecca Harding Davis
"Papa's Own Girl," Marie Howland
Speaking Likenesses, Christina Rossetti

Tell It All, Fannie Stenhouse
Undine, Olive Schreiner
The Voice as a Source of Income, Olive Logan

1875
Esther, Ann Sophia Stephens
Sexes Throughout Nature, Antoinette Brown Blackwell

1876
Daniel Deronda, George Eliot
"Declaration of Rights of Women," Susan B. Anthony
   and Matilda Gage
"Forbidden Fruit," Emily Dickinson
Marianne, George Sand
The Spagnoletto, Emma Lazarus

1877
Biographical Sketches, Harriet Martineau
Deephaven, Sarah Orne Jewett
"The Homes of Single Women," Susan B. Anthony
The Story of Avis, Elizabeth Stuart Phelps

1879
A Doll's House, Henrik Ibsen
Old Friends and New, Sarah Orne Jewett
Old Maids, Elizabeth Stuart Phelps

1880
"Echoes," Emma Lazarus
"The Grievances of Women," Margaret Oliphant
"Victurae Salutamus," Elizabeth Stuart Phelps

1881
A Century of Dishonor, Helen Hunt Jackson
Friends: A Duet, Elizabeth Stuart Phelps
Massachusetts in the Woman Suffrage Movement, Harriet
   Jane Robinson
Mizora: A Prophecy, Mary E. Bradley Lane

1882
Doctor Zay, Elizabeth Stuart Phelps
Sybil Chase, Ann Sophia Stephens
"Tom's Husband," Sarah Orne Jewett

1883
Life among the Piutes, Sarah Winnemucca
"The New Colossus," Emma Lazarus
The Story of an African Farm, Olive Schreiner

1884
A Country Doctor, Sarah Orne Jewett
Ramona, Helen Hunt Jackson

"Who Is It Seeks My Pillow Nights," Emily Dickinson
"Within that little Hive/Such Hints of Honey lay," Emily
   Dickinson

1885
Life and Labor in the Spirit World, Mary Theresa
   Shelhamer

1886
The Dress of Women, Charlotte Perkins Gilman
History of Woman Suffrage, Susan B. Anthony, Matilda
   Gage, Ida Husted Harper, and Elizabeth Cady
   Stanton
The House of Ulloa, Emilia Pardo Bazán
The Vendetta!; or Story of One Forgotten, Marie Corelli
A White Heron, Sarah Orne Jewett

1887
Captain Mary Miller, Harriet Jane Robinson
Ten Days in a Mad-House, Nellie Bly
"Two Friends," Mary Wilkins Freeman

1888
Ideala, Sarah Grand
A Lady's Life in the Rocky Mountains, Isabella Bird
Six Months in Mexico, Nellie Bly
What Dreams May Come, Gertrude Atherton

1889
Ardath: The Story of a Dead Self, Marie Corelli
The Diary and Letters of Madame d'Arblay, Fanny Burney
"The Feminine Iconoclast," Mary H. Ford
Hiero-Salem: The Vision of Peace, Eveleen Mason
The New Pandora, Harriet Jane Robinson

1890
The Human Body, Victoria Woodhull
"In Dark New England Days," Sarah Orne Jewett
Nelly Bly's Book: Around the World in 72 Days, Nellie
   Bly
"Sex and Slavery," Elizabeth Gaskell
"Sex Slavery," Voltairine de Cleyre
"Trying to Be a Servant," Nellie Bly

1891
"A Church Mouse," Mary Wilkins Freeman
A Domestic Experiment, Sarah Grand
Dreams, Olive Schreiner
"The Gates of Freedom," Voltairine de Cleyre
"A Moral Exigency," Mary Wilkins Freeman
"A New England Nun," Mary Wilkins Freeman
"The Revolt of 'Mother,'" Mary Wilkins Freeman

1892

Iola Leroy; or, Shadows Uplifted, Frances Ellen Harper
The Solitude of Self, Elizabeth Cady Stanton
The Soul of Lilith, Marie Corelli
Southern Horror, Ida Wells-Barnett
A Voice from the South by a Black Woman of the South,
    Anna Julia Cooper

1893

The Christmas Witch, Gertrude Atherton
"Désirée's Baby," Kate Chopin
Dream Life and Real Life, Olive Schreiner
Experiences of Loveday Brooke, Lady Detective, Catherine
    Louisa Pirkis
The Heavenly Twins, Sarah Grand
"In Defense of Emma Goldman and Free Speech,"
    Voltairine de Cleyre
"The Progress of Fifty Years," Lucy Stone
Unveiling a Parallel, Alice Ilgenfritz Jones and Ella
    Merchant
Woman, Church, and State, Matilda Gage

1894

"A Respectable Woman," Kate Chopin
A Sex Revolution, Lois Waisbrooker

1895

"A Double Standard," Frances Ellen Harper
"The Long Arm," Mary Wilkins Freeman
Pioneer Work in Opening the Medical Profession to Women,
    Elizabeth Blackwell
Sorrows of Satan, Marie Corelli
The Woman, Emilia Pardo Bazán

1896

Autobiography, Martha Jane Cannary
The Country of the Pointed Firs, Sarah Orne Jewett
"The Case of Woman vs. Orthodoxy," Voltairine de
    Cleyre
"Good Lady Ducayne," Mary Elizabeth Braddon
Jeanne d'Arc, Margaret Oliphant
The Murder of Delicia, Marie Corelli

1897

The Ballot and the Bullet, Carrie Chapman Catt
The Beth Book, Sarah Grand
Eighty Years and More, Elizabeth Cady Stanton
"Hilda's Home," Rosa Graul
Night in Acadie, Kate Chopin
"A Pair of Silk Stockings," Kate Chopin
The Storm and Other Stories, Kate Chopin

1898

Loom and Spindle, Harriet Jane Robinson
The Woman's Bible, ed. Elizabeth Cady Stanton
Woman's Future Position in the World, Lizzie May Holmes

1899

The Awakening, Kate Chopin
An English South African Woman's View of the Situation,
    Olive Schreiner
From Plotz to Boston, Mary Antin
The Goodness of St. Rocque, Alice Dunbar-Nelson
"A Point of Morals," Ellen Glasgow
"Should Higher Education for Women Differ?," Martha
    Carey Thomas
"Sister Josepha," Alice Dunbar-Nelson

1900

The Author's Evening at Home, Alice Dunbar-Nelson
Claudine at School, Colette
Concerning Children, Charlotte Perkins Gilman

1902

A Dream of the 21st Century, Winnifred Harper Cooley
Essays on Medical Sociology, Elizabeth Blackwell

1903

Home: Its Work and Influence, Charlotte Perkins Gilman
The Land of Little Rain, Mary Hunter Austin
"The Legend of Au'Appelle Valley," Pauline Johnson

1904

The Basket Woman, Mary Hunter Austin
Deliverance, Ellen Glasgow

1905

"The Bell in the Fog," Gertrude Atherton
A Diary from Dixie, Mary Chesnut
Free Opinions Freely Expressed, Marie Corelli
The House of Mirth, Edith Wharton
The Use and Need of the Life of Carry A. Nation, Carry
    Nation

1906

The Bedquilt, Dorothy Canfield Fisher
Bits of Gossip, Rebecca Harding Davis
Romance Island, Zona Gale
The Treasures of Heaven, Marie Corelli
Twixt Earth and Stars, Radclyffe Hall

1907

"A Clever Woman," Mary Elizabeth Coleridge
"Guenevere," Sara Teasdale

Mrs. Marta Oulie, Sigrid Undset
"Walking Woman," Mary Hunter Austin
"Witch," Mary Elizabeth Coleridge

1908

The Circular Staircase, Mary Roberts Rinehart
The Life and Work of Susan B. Anthony, Ida Husted Harper
"Marriage," Mary Elizabeth Coleridge
"The Other Side of the Mirror," Mary Elizabeth Coleridge
"Our Lady," Mary Elizabeth Coleridge
"Those Who Marry Do Ill," Voltairine de Cleyre
Sowing Seeds in Danny, Nellie McClung
The Wartime Journal of a Georgia Girl, Fanny Andrews

1909

Army Letters of an Officer's Wife, Frances Roe
Closer Union, Olive Schreiner
Gunnar's Daughter, Sigrid Undset
"Old Woman Magoun," Elizabeth Gaskell
Stories from the Country of Lost Borders, Mary Hunter Austin
Three Lives, Gertrude Stein
"Three Thanksgivings," Charlotte Perkins Gilman
"Women's Progress: A Comparison of Centuries," Mary K. Ford

1910

The Arrow-Maker, Mary Hunter Austin
The Crux, Charlotte Perkins Gilman
A Man's World, Rachel Crothers
"Martha's Mother," Charlotte Perkins Gilman
The Second Chance, Nellie McClung
Twenty Years at Hull-House, Jane Addams
What Diantha Did, Charlotte Perkins Gilman
"Why Women Should Vote," Jane Addams

1911

Anarchism and Other Essays, Emma Goldman
Ethan Frome, Edith Wharton
Helen of Troy and Other Poems, Sara Teasdale
In a German Pension, Katherine Mansfield
The Man-Made World, Charlotte Perkins Gilman
Mother, Kathleen Norris
Moving the Mountain, Charlotte Perkins Gilman
The Suffragette, Emmeline Pankhurst
"Two Sisters," Pauline Johnson
Woman and Labour, Olive Schreiner

1912

"Emmy," Jessie Redmon Fauset
Evening, Anna Akhmatova
Flint and Feather, Pauline Johnson

The Importance of the Vote, Emmeline Pankhurst
Julia France and Her Times, Gertrude Atherton
The Labor of Women and Children in Tenements, Florence Kelley
The Promised Land, Mary Antin
The Reef, Edith Wharton
"Renascence," Edna St. Vincent Millay
The Squirrel Cage, Dorothy Canfield Fisher

1913

The Moccasin Maker, Pauline Johnson
"A New Woman's Movement," Rebecca West
O Pioneers!, Willa Cather
The Rich Mrs. Burgoyne, Kathleen Norris
Roast Beef Medium, Edna Ferber
"The Sheltered Sex," Rebecca West
Suffrage Speeches from the Dock, Emmeline Pankhurst
Virginia, Ellen Glasgow
"The Waste of Private Housekeeping," Charlotte Perkins Gilman
"Why Men Need Woman Suffrage," Helen Keller
Why We Are Militant, Emmeline Pankhurst
"The Woman Question," Voltairine de Cleyre

1914

Anarchism and American Traditions, Voltairine de Cleyre
Aunt Betsy's Thanksgiving, Katherine Tillman
"Gertrude Stein," Mina Loy
"How It Feels to Be Forcibly Fed," Djuna Barnes
"Indissoluble Matrimony," Rebecca West
Letters of a Woman Homesteader, Elinore Pruitt Stewart
"The Making of an Anarchist," Voltairine de Cleyre
Modern Industry in Relation to the Family, Florence Kelley
My Own Story, Emmeline Pankhurst
Personality Plus, Edna Ferber
The Rosary, Anna Akhmatova
Saturday's Child, Kathleen Norris
Social Significance of the Modern Drama, Emma Goldman
Tender Buttons, Gertrude Stein
They Who Knock at Our Gates, Mary Antin

1915

The Book of Repulsive Women, Djuna Barnes
Emma McChesney & Co., Edna Ferber
Fidelity, Susan Glaspell
The Heart's Kindred, Zona Gale
Herland, Charlotte Perkins Gilman
In Times Like These, Nellie McClung
"Sojourn in the Whale," Marianne Moore
The Song of the Lark, Willa Cather
The Story of a Pioneer, Anna Howard Shaw

Suppressed Desires, Susan Glaspell
The Voyage Out, Virginia Woolf

1916

Henry James, Rebecca West
Life and Gabriella, Ellen Glasgow
"Patterns," Amy Lowell
Rachel, Angelina Weld Grimké
Sea Garden, H. D.
Trifles, Susan Glaspell
Understood Betsy, Dorothy Canfield Fisher
With Her in Ourland, Charlotte Perkins Gilman

1917

The Answering Voice, Sara Teasdale
Daughter of the Morning, Zona Gale
Seth Way, Caroline Snedeker
Songs to Joannes, Mina Loy
White Flock, Anna Akhmatova

1918

Birth, Zona Gale
"Do You Know," Carrie Chapman Catt
Fighting France, Edith Wharton
Married Love, Marie Stopes
My Ántonia, Willa Cather
The Return of the Soldier, Rebecca West
Six Months in Red Russia, Louise Bryant
Wise Parenthood, Marie Stopes

1919

"Fables for Proletarian Children," Louise Bryant
"The Letter," Amy Lowell
"Madonna of the Evening Flowers," Amy Lowell
Mildred Carver, U.S.A., Martha Bruère
Mine Eyes Have Seen, Alice Dunbar-Nelson
Night and Day, Virginia Woolf
"Opal," Amy Lowell
"Summer Rain," Amy Lowell
They That Sit in Darkness, Mary Powell Burrill
"Venus Transiens," Amy Lowell
"The Weather-Cock Points South," Amy Lowell

1920

The Age of Innocence, Edith Wharton
The Bridal Wreath, Sigrid Undset
Diaries of Court Ladies of Old Japan, Izumi Shikibu and
    Murasaki Shikibu
A Few Figs from Thistles, Edna St. Vincent Millay
Flame and Shadow, Sara Teasdale
Futurism X Feminism, Mina Loy
Hungry Hearts and Other Stories, Anzia Yezierska
"I Sit and Sew," Alice Dunbar-Nelson

Miss Lulu Bett, Zona Gale
"The Sleeper Wakes," Jessie Redmon Fauset

1921

Anno Domini MCMXXI, Anna Akhmatova
Hymen, H. D.
The Inheritors, Susan Glaspell
Mistress of Husaby, Sigrid Undset
Purple Springs, Nellie McClung
Radiant Motherhood, Marie Stopes
Star-Dust: The Story of an American Girl, Fannie Hurst
The Verge, Susan Glaspell
Views of Society and Manners in America, Frances Wright

1922

The Cross, Sigrid Undset
"The Fly," Katherine Mansfield
The Garden Party, Katherine Mansfield
"María Concepción," Katherine Anne Porter
One of Ours, Willa Cather

1923

Black Armour, Elinor Wylie
Black Oxen, Gertrude Atherton
Body of This Death, Louise Bogan
Exit, Marita Bonner
Jennifer Lorn, Elinor Wylie
"Jordan's End," Ellen Glasgow
A Lost Lady, Willa Cather
The Lummox, Fannie Hurst
"Marriage," Marianne Moore
Mirrors of Moscow, Louise Bryant
Readings for Women, Gabriela Mistral
Salome of the Tenements, Anzia Yezierska
Woman Suffrage and Politics, Carrie Chapman Catt and
    Nettie Rogers Shuler
"Women," Louise Bogan

1924

Barren Ground, Ellen Glasgow
Contraception, Marie Stopes
"Drenched in Light," Zora Neale Hurston
Heliodora and Other Poems, H. D.
Iphigenia, Teresa de la Parra
The Life of Olive Schreiner, S. C. Cronwright-Schreiner
Old New York, Edith Wharton
"Roses Only," Marianne Moore
So Big, Edna Ferber
There Is Confusion, Jessie Redmon Fauset

1925

The Battle-Ground, Ellen Glasgow
Bread Givers, Anzia Yezierska

Gentlemen Prefer Blondes, Anita Loos
The Mother's Recompense, Edith Wharton
Mrs. Dalloway, Virginia Woolf
"On Being Young—A Woman—and Colored," Marita Bonner
Painted Fires, Nellie McClung
"Sisters," Amy Lowell
39 East, Rachel Crothers
Sunday Morning in the South, Georgia Douglas Johnson
Tenderness, Gabriela Mistral
The Unlit Lamp, Radclyffe Hall
The Venetian Glass Nephew, Elinor Wylie

1926

Adam's Breed, Radclyffe Hall
Blue Blood, Georgia Douglas Johnson
Color Struck, Zora Neale Hurston
Concerning Women, Suzanne LaFollette
Dark of the Moon, Sara Teasdale
Down the Santa Fe Trail and into Mexico, Susan Magoffin
Enough Rope, Dorothy Parker
Show Boat, Edna Ferber
"Sweat," Zora Neale Hurston

1927

Aphra Behn: The Incomparable Astrea, Vita Sackville-West
Cogewea Half-Blood, Mourning Dove
HERmione, H. D.
"Persephone," Meridel Le Sueur
Plumes, Georgia Douglas Johnson
"To a Dark Girl," Gwendolyn Bennetta Bennett
To the Lighthouse, Virginia Woolf

1928

An Autumn Love Cycle, Georgia Douglas Johnson
"Can a Woman Raise a Family and Have a Career?," Nellie McClung
Children Sing in the Far West, Mary Hunter Austin
Coming of Age in Samoa, Margaret Mead
The Ladies Almanack, Djuna Barnes
The Life and Personality of Phoebe Apperson Hearst, Winifred Bonfils
Mothers in Bondage, Margaret Sanger
Orlando, Virginia Woolf
The Purple Flower, Marita Bonner
Quicksand, Nella Larsen
Ryder, Djuna Barnes
"To Inez Milholland," Edna St. Vincent Millay
The Well of Loneliness, Radclyffe Hall
What Price Peace?, Kathleen Norris

1929

Angels and Earthly Creatures, Elinor Wylie
The Beckoning Road, Caroline Snedeker
"Big Blonde," Dorothy Parker
The Bride's House, Dawn Powell
But Gentlemen Marry Brunettes, Anita Loos
Cimarron, Edna Ferber
Dark Summer, Louise Bogan
The King's Daughter, Vita Sackville-West
Last September, Elizabeth Bowen
Let Us Be Gay, Rachel Crothers
Money for Love, Josephine Herbst
Plum Bun, Jessie Redmon Fauset
A Room of One's Own, Virginia Woolf

1930

Alison's House, Susan Glaspell
Blue-Eyed Black Boy, Georgia Douglas Johnson
"Elegy," Rebecca West
Friends and Relations, Elizabeth Bowen
"He," Katherine Anne Porter
"The Jilting of Granny Weatherall," Katherine Anne Porter
The Life and Mind of Emily Dickinson, Genevieve Taggart
Lucy Stone: Pioneer of Women's Rights, Alice Stone Blackwell
Nightwood, Djuna Barnes
"Old Mortality," Katherine Anne Porter

1931

All Passion Spent, Vita Sackville-West
The Chinaberry Tree, Jessie Redmon Fauset
The Good Earth, Pearl Buck
Living My Life, Emma Goldman
The Starry Adventure, Mary Hunter Austin
The Starting Point, Georgia Douglas Johnson
"Widow's Jazz," Mina Loy

1932

Back Street, Fannie Hurst
Earth Horizon, Mary Hunter Austin
Little House in the Big Woods, Laura Ingalls Wilder
"The Love Song of Alice B.," Gertrude Stein
The Sheltered Life, Ellen Glasgow
Women on the Breadlines, Meridel Le Sueur

1933

The Autobiography of Alice B. Toklas, Gertrude Stein
Flush, Virginia Woolf
"Gal Young 'Un," Marjorie Kinnan Rawlings
The Imitation of Life, Fannie Hurst
Pity Is Not Enough, Josephine Herbst

Roman Catholic Methods of Birth Control, Marie Stopes
"Waltz," Dorothy Parker

1934

A Backward Glance, Edith Wharton
Birth Control Today, Marie Stopes
The Children's Hour, Lillian Hellman
The Executioner Waits, Josephine Herbst
The Foghorn, Gertrude Atherton
Jonah's Gourd Vine, Zora Neale Hurston
Miss Ogilvy Finds Herself, Radclyffe Hall
The Mother, Pearl Buck
"Mother Catherine," Zora Neale Hurston
Seven Gothic Tales, Isak Dinesen
Women Are Hungry, Meridel Le Sueur

1935

Beauty's Daughter, Kathleen Norris
The Clearing in the West, Nellie McClung
Frederick Douglass, Georgia Douglass Johnson
Ganifrede, Helen Webb Harris
"Hattie Turner versus Hattie Turner," Fannie Hurst
The Life of Emmeline Pankhurst, Sylvia Pankhurst
Little House on the Prairie, Laura Ingalls Wilder
Sojourner Truth, May Miller
William and Ellen Craft, Georgia Douglas Johnson

1936

Change of Life in Men and Women, Marie Stopes
Course of Popular Lectures, Virginia Woolf
Gone with the Wind, Margaret Mitchell
The House of Incest, Anaïs Nin
Ladies of the Press, Ishbel Ross
"Noon Wine," Katherine Anne Porter
Novel on Yellow Paper, Stevie Smith
Saint Joan of Arc, Vita Sackville-West
The Sixth Beatitude, Radclyffe Hall
The Women, Clare Booth Luce
Writing for Women, Emilie Hawkes Peacocke

1937

On the Banks of Plum Creek, Laura Ingalls Wilder
Out of Africa, Isak Dinesen
"Papa Love Baby," Stevie Smith
Their Eyes Were Watching God, Zora Neale Hurston

1938

The Buccaneers, Edith Wharton
Can Women Be Gentlemen?, Gertrude Atherton
Margaret Sanger: An Autobiography, Margaret Sanger
Rebecca, Daphne du Maurier

Refugees: Anarchy or Organization?, Dorothy Thompson
Three Guineas, Virginia Woolf

1939

By the Shores of Silver Lake, Laura Ingalls Wilder
Huntsman, What Quarry?, Edna St. Vincent Millay
"I Am Rose," Gertrude Stein
The Little Foxes, Lillian Hellman
Purposes of Love, Mary Renault
The Rope of Gold, Josephine Herbst

1940

The Heart Is a Lonely Hunter, Carson McCullers
The House of Lee, Gertrude Atherton
Sapphira and the Slave Girl, Willa Cather
When the Whippoorwill, Marjorie Kinnan Rawlings

1941

"Light in Dark Places," Marita Bonner
"Lily Daw and the Three Ladies," Eudora Welty
"One True Love," Marita Bonner
Under the Sea-Wind, Rachel Carson
"Why I Live at the P. O.," Eudora Welty
"A Worn Path," Eudora Welty

1942

Black Lamb and Grey Falcon, Rebecca West
A Bride Goes West Nannie Alderson
The Company She Keeps, Mary McCarthy
Cross Creek, Marjorie Kinnan Rawlings
Cross Creek Cookery, Marjorie Kinnan Rawlings
Dust Tracks on a Road, Zora Neale Hurston
Norma Ashe, Susan Glaspell
Our Hearts Were Young and Gay, Emily Kimbrough and
    Cornelia Otis Skinner
A Time to Be Born, Dawn Powell
West with the Night, Beryl Markham
"Whores," Margaret Walker

1943

The Eagle and the Dove, Vita Sackville-West
"Livvie Is Back," Eudora Welty
She Came to Stay, Simone de Beauvoir
Two Serious Ladies, Jane Bowles

1944

Boston Adventure, Jean Stafford
The Friendly Young Ladies, Mary Renault
Gigi, Colette
Home to India, Santha Rama Rau
My Home Is Far Away, Dawn Powell

"Splendid Outcast," Beryl Markham
The Walls Do Not Fall, H. D.
Women on the Porch, Caroline Gordon

1945
"The Captive," Caroline Gordon
Daisy Kenyon, Elizabeth Janeway
The Forest of the South, Caroline Gordon
The Friendly Persuasion, Jessamyn West
The Streams Run Fast, Nellie McClung
A Street in Bronzeville, Gwendolyn Brooks
Tribute to the Angels, H. D.

1946
Delta Wedding, Eudora Welty
The Flowering of the Rod, H. D.
The Member of the Wedding, Carson McCullers
North and South, Elizabeth Bishop
The Street, Ann Petry

1947
Gravity and Grace, Simone Weil
The Mother of Us All, Gertrude Stein
The Tin Flute, Gabrielle Roy
Waterlily, Ella Deloria
"We Must Find a Radical Solution for the Abolition of War," Dorothy Thompson
"When Mrs. Martin's Booker T," Gwendolyn Brooks

1948
"High-Heeled Shoes, a Memoir," Hisaye Yamamoto
"The Lottery," Shirley Jackson

1949
Annie Allen, Gwendolyn Brooks
"The Golden Apples," Eudora Welty
The Heat of the Day, Elizabeth Bowen
Holiday, Stevie Smith
Male and Female, Margaret Mead
Nancy Hanks of Wilderness Road, Meridel Le Sueur
The Need for Roots, Simone Weil
The Second Sex, Simone de Beauvoir
"Seventeen Syllables," Hisaye Yamamoto

1950
The Grass Is Singing, Doris Lessing

1951
The Ballad of the Sad Café, Carson McCullers
Hangsaman, Shirley Jackson

Memoirs of Hadrian, Marguerite Yourcenar
The Sea Around Us, Rachel Carson

1952
Giant, Edna Ferber
Paris '90, Cornelia Otis Skinner
"Profile of Sor Juana Inés de la Cruz," Gabriela Mistral

1953
"Gwendolyn," Elizabeth Bishop
Ladies of the Corridor, Dorothy Parker
Leaving Home, Elizabeth Janeway
Life Among the Savages, Shirley Jackson
Maud Martha, Gwendolyn Brooks
The Narrows, Ann Petry

1954
The Dollmaker, Harriette Arnow
The Woman Within, Ellen Glasgow

1955
A Cold Spring, Elizabeth Bishop
Crusaders, Meridel Le Sueur
The Edge of the Sea, Rachel Carson
"Good Country People," Flannery O'Connor
"A Good Man Is Hard to Find," Flannery O'Connor
Harriet Tubman, Ann Petry
Oppression and Liberty, Simone Weil

1956
The Malefactors, Caroline Gordon
Remember the House, Santha Rama Rau

1957
"A Dream of Comparison," Stevie Smith
"I Stand Here Ironing," Tillie Olsen
Owls Do Cry, Janet Frame
"A Stick of Green Candy," Jane Bowles
Through a Glass Darkly, Kathleen Norris

1958
Body of Waking, Muriel Rukeyser
Memoirs of a Dutiful Young Girl, Simone de Beauvoir
"The Old Order," Katherine Anne Porter

1959
Babette's Feast, Isak Dinesen
Brown Girl, Brownstones, Paule Marshall
"Goddess," Denise Levertov
The Haunting of Hill House, Shirley Jackson
Hiroshima, Mon Amour, Marguerite Duras

Little Disturbances of Man, Grace Paley
The Mad Shadows, Marie-Claire Blais
Mollie, Mollie Dorsey Sanford
A Raisin in the Sun, Lorraine Hansberry
The Third Choice, Elizabeth Janeway

1960

"Her Kind," Anne Sexton
To Kill a Mockingbird, Harper Lee

1961

Double Persephone, Margaret Atwood
Faces in the Water, Janet Frame
"The First Rain of Spring," Leslie Marmon Silko
Halfway, Maxine Kumin
Helen in Egypt, H. D.
Shadows on the Grass, Isak Dinesen
Soul Clap Hands and Sing, Paule Marshall
"Tell Me a Riddle," Tillie Olsen

1962

Captured by the Indians, Minnie Bruce Carrigan
"Daddy," Sylvia Plath
Elegant Wits and Grand Horizontals, Cornelia Otis
    Skinner
From Fear Set Free, Nayantara Sahgal
The Funnyhouse of a Negro, Adrienne Kennedy
The Golden Notebook, Doris Lessing
"Housewife," Anne Sexton
"The Moral Disarmament of Betty Coed," Gloria Steinem
On the Way Home, Laura Ingalls Wilder
Penelope at War, Oriana Fallaci
Silent Spring, Rachel Carson
Three Women, Sylvia Plath
We Have Always Lived in the Castle, Shirley Jackson

1963

"Angry Young Women," Ellen Moers
The Bell Jar, Sylvia Plath
Cry Peacock, Anita Desai
The Feminine Mystique, Betty Friedan
The Group, Mary McCarthy
Hard Times: Forces of Circumstances, Simone de Beauvoir
"I Was a Playboy Bunny," Gloria Steinem
"Lady Lazarus," Sylvia Plath
The Owl Answers, Adrienne Kennedy
Snapshots of a Daughter-in-Law, Adrienne Rich

1964

"The Ache of Marriage," Denise Levertov
The Eighth Moon, Bette Bao Lord

"For Jan, in Bar Maria," Carolyn Kizer
"Hypocrite Women," Denise Levertov
A Lesson in Dead Language, Adrienne Kennedy
"Song for Ishtar," Denise Levertov
Tituba of Salem Village, Ann Petry
The Useless Sex, Oriana Fallaci
A Very Easy Death, Simone de Beauvoir

1965

Charmers and Cranks, Ishbel Ross
Dilemma of a Ghost, Ama Ata Aidoo
The Education of Harriet Hatfield, May Sarton
The Millstone, Margaret Drabble
Mrs. Stevens Hears the Mermaids Singing, May Sarton
"Pro Femina," Carolyn Kizer
Questions of Travel, Elizabeth Bishop
"The Revelation," Flannery O'Connor
A Season in the Life of Emmanuel, Marie-Claire Blais
This Time of Morning, Nayantara Sahgal
Voices in the City, Anita Desai

1966

"A House of Mercy," Stevie Smith
Jubilee, Margaret Walker
A Mother in History, Jean Stafford
The Shadow Dance, Angela Carter
"Sylvia's Death," Anne Sexton
Wide Sargasso Sea, Jean Rhys
The Women's Room, Marilyn French

1967

"Abel's Bride," Denise Levertov
The Fat Woman's Joke, Fay Weldon
Madame Sarah, Cornelia Otis Skinner
The Magic Toyshop, Angela Carter
"Mutes," Denise Levertov
New Territory, Eavan Boland
Restoree, Anne McCaffrey
"Stepping Westward," Denise Levertov
Token Learning, Kate Millett
The Waterfall, Margaret Drabble

1968

The Abyss, Marguerite Yourcenar
Firstborn, Louise Glück
"Käthe Kollwitz," Muriel Rukeyser
Picnic on Paradise, Joanna Russ
The Speed of Darkness, Muriel Rukeyser
Woman Destroyed, Simone de Beauvoir
Women's Rights Movement in the U.S., Shulamith
    Firestone

1969

"After Black Power, Women's Liberation," Gloria Steinem
Delta of Venus, Anaïs Nin
Except for Me and Thee, Jessamyn West
Good Times, Lucille Clifton
I Know Why the Caged Bird Sings, Maya Angelou
The Left Hand of Darkness, Ursula Le Guin
"Let's Put Pornography Back in the Closet," Susan Brownmiller
Sister Son/ji, Sonia Sanchez
To Be Young, Gifted, and Black, Lorraine Hansberry
An Unfinished Woman, Lillian Hellman
When Rain Clouds Gather, Bessie Head

1970

The Adventuress, Santha Rama Rau
Anowa, Ama Ata Aidoo
Are You There God? It's Me, Margaret, Judy Blume
The Bluest Eye, Toni Morrison
The Crusade for Justice, Ida Wells-Barnett
The Dialectics of Sex, Shulamith Firestone
"Fairy Tale Liberation," Alison Lurie
The Female Eunuch, Germaine Greer
How to Make It in a Man's World, Letty Cottin Pogrebin
"I Am a Black Woman," Mari Evans
"Making the Jam without You," Maxine Kumin
New Women, Robin Morgan
No Sweetness Here, Ama Ata Aidoo
Old Age, Simone de Beauvoir
"Personal Letter No. 3," Sonia Sanchez
Sexual Politics, Kate Millett
Sisterhood Is Powerful, Robin Morgan
We Are Decoys, Baby, Elfriede Jelinek
"Where Are You Going, Where Have You Been," Joyce Carol Oates
"Where Have You Gone?," Mari Evans
Windflower, Gabrielle Roy
"Women's Liberation Aims to Free Men, Too," Gloria Steinem

1971

"Bitch," Carolyn Kizer
"Blues Ain't No Mockin Bird," Toni Cade Bambara
Dance the Eagle to Sleep, Marge Piercy
Down among the Women, Fay Weldon
Gemini, Nikki Giovanni
The Hand That Cradles the Rock, Rita Mae Brown
High Tide in the Garden, Fleur Adcock
If They Come in the Morning, Angela Davis
The Lives of Girls and Women, Alice Munro

Man's World, Woman's Place, Elizabeth Janeway
Maru, Bessie Head
"One Out of Twelve," Tillie Olsen
The Prostitution Papers, Kate Millett
"Red Riding Hood," Anne Sexton
Slam the Door Softly, Clare Booth Luce
"A Song in the Front Yard," Gwendolyn Brooks
Transformations, Anne Sexton
Women's Liberation and Literature, Elaine Showalter
Women's Liberation and New Politics, Sheila Rowbotham

1972

Blackberry Winter, Margaret Mead
The Farthest Shore, Ursula Le Guin
Gorilla, My Love, Toni Cade Bambara
In the Ditch, Buchi Emecheta
The Judge's Wife, Caryl Churchill
The Key in the Door, Marie Cardinal
Marriages and Infidelities, Joyce Carol Oates
The Needle's Eye, Margaret Drabble
Owners, Caryl Churchill
Report from Part One, Gwendolyn Brooks
Tiger's Daughter, Bharati Mukherjee
Up Country: Poems of New England, Maxine Kumin
"When It Changed," Joanna Russ
When We Dead Awaken, Adrienne Rich
Women and Madness, Phyllis Chesler

1973

Any Woman Can't, Wendy Wasserstein
Breaking Open, Muriel Rukeyser
Deenie, Judy Blume
Diving into the Wreck: Poems 1971–1972, Adrienne Rich
A Farewell to Manzanar, Jeanne Wakatsuki Houston and James Houston
Fear of Flying, Erica Jong
Four Young Women, Jessica Hagedorn
From a Land Where Other People Live, Audre Lorde
Halfbreed, Maria Campbell
Hidden from History, Sheila Rowbotham
"Myth," Muriel Rukeyser
Pentimento: A Book of Portraits, Lillian Hellman
A Plain Brown Rapper, Rita Mae Brown
The President's Wife, Ishbel Ross
A Question of Power, Bessie Head
The Rubyfruit Jungle, Rita Mae Brown
Small Changes, Marge Piercy
Songs to a Handsome Women, Rita Mae Brown
Sula, Toni Morrison
"The Third World of Women," Susan Sontag
What the Woman Lived, Louise Bogan

Witches, Midwives and Nurses, Barbara Ehrenreich and
   Deirdre English
Woman at Point Zero, Nawal El Saadawi
Women: Their Changing Roles, the Great Contemporary,
   Elizabeth Janeway

1974

Angela Davis: An Autobiography, Angela Davis
Between Myth and Morning, Elizabeth Janeway
A Blues Book for Blue Black Magical Women, Sonia
   Sanchez
Blubber, Judy Blume
Enormous Changes at the Last Minute, Grace Paley
Female Friends, Fay Weldon
Free to Be, You and Me, Marlo Thomas
God Dies by the Nile, Nawal El Saadawi
Laguna Woman, Leslie Marmon Silko
The Second-Class Citizen, Buchi Emecheta
Thomas Jefferson, Fawn Brodie
The War Between the Tates, Alison Lurie
We Are Not Your Slave Girls Anymore, Sahar Khalifeh
Woman Hating, Andrea Dworkin
Yonnondio, Tillie Olsen

1975

Against Our Will, Susan Brownmiller
Bobbi Lee, Indian Rebel, Lee Maracle
"Canción," Denise Levertov
Corregidora, Gayl Jones
The Female Man, Joanna Russ
*for colored girls who have considered suicide when the
   rainbow is enuf*, Ntozake Shange
Forever: A Novel of Good and Evil, Love and Hope, Judy
   Blume
Girl Sleuth, Bobbie Ann Mason
Heat and Dust, Ruth Prawer Jhabvala
The House on Marshland, Louise Glück
Last Song, Joy Harjo
The Laugh of the Medusa, Hélène Cixous
Letters Home, Sylvia Plath
Letter to a Child Never Born, Oriana Fallaci
The Massacre at Fall Creek, Jessamyn West
The Newly Born Woman, Hélène Cixous
Objections to Sex and Violence, Caryl Churchill
Power with Grace: The Life Story of Mrs. Woodrow Wilson,
   Ishbel Ross
The Realms of Gold, Margaret Drabble
The Rites of Ancient Ripening, Meridel Le Sueur
Southern Ladies and Gentlemen, Florence King
"Vesuvius at Home," Adrienne Rich
War Horse, Eavan Boland
When Dinah Shore Ruled the Earth, Wendy Wasserstein

The Wife, Bharati Mukherjee
A Woman Speaks, Anaïs Nin
The Women and the Men, Nikki Giovanni
Women on Campus, Elizabeth Janeway
Words to Say It, Marie Cardinal

1976

Alone of All Her Sex, Marina Warner
Alyx, Joanna Russ
Camp Notes and Other Poems, Mitsuye Yamada
Eva's Man, Gayl Jones
The Garden, Louise Glück
The Gathering the Tribes, Carolyn Forché
Generations: A Memoir, Lucille Clifton
Geography III, Elizabeth Bishop
Hérémakhonon, Maryse Condé
"It Changed My Life," Betty Friedan
Lady Oracle, Margaret Atwood
Meridian, Alice Walker
A Movie Star Has to Star in Black and White, Adrienne
   Kennedy
Of Woman Born, Adrienne Rich
The Portrait of Dora, Hélène Cixous
A Princess Remembers, Santha Rama Rau
Remember Me, Fay Weldon
The Shattered Chain, Marion Zimmer Bradley
Vinegar Tom, Caryl Churchill
Wild Thorns, Sahar Khalifeh
Woman on the Edge of Time, Marge Piercy
The Woman Said Yes, Jessamyn West
The Woman Warrior, Maxine Hong Kingston
"The Woman Who Could Not Live with Her Faulty
   Heart," Margaret Atwood
The Word for World Is Forest, Ursula Le Guin

1977

"And One Doesn't Stir without the Other," Luce Irigaray
Annulla Allen: The Autobiography of a Survivor, Emily
   Mann
Bear, Marian Engel
Beginning with O, Olga Broumas
Ceremony, Leslie Marmon Silko
Children of My Heart, Gabrielle Roy
Collector of Treasures and Other Botswana Village Tales,
   Bessie Head
Dragonsong, Anne McCaffrey
Fire on the Mountain, Anita Desai
Going Too Far, Robin Morgan
How to Save Your Own Life, Erica Jong
The Ice Age, Margaret Drabble
Literary Women, Ellen Moers
A Literature of Their Own, Elaine Showalter

On Photography, Susan Sontag
Our Sister Killjoy, Ama Ata Aidoo
The Passion of New Eve, Angela Carter
The Sea Birds Are Still Alive, Toni Cade Bambara
A Situation in New Delhi, Nayantara Sahgal
Song of Solomon, Toni Morrison
This Sex Which Is Not One, Luce Irigaray
Uncommon Women and Others, Wendy Wasserstein
A Voice for Freedom, Nayantara Sahgal
Where Late the Sweet Birds Sang, Kate Wilhelm

1978

And Chaos Died, Joanna Russ
The Back Room, Carmen Martín Gaite
Beauty, Robin McKinley
The Black Unicorn, Audre Lorde
Cotton Candy on a Rainy Day, Nikki Giovanni
"Death in Mexico," Denise Levertov
The Diary of Anaïs Nin, Anaïs Nin
A Distant Mirror, Barbara Tuchman
"Envelope," Maxine Kumin
"Far from the Opposite Shore," Gloria Steinem
For Her Own Good, Barbara Ehrenreich and Deirdre
    English
Games at Twilight, Anita Desai
Getting Out, Marsha Norman
The Girl, Meridel Le Sueur
Harriet Beecher Stowe and American Literature, Ellen
    Moers
"If Men Could Menstruate," Gloria Steinem
I've Been a Woman, Sonia Sanchez
Loba, Diane Di Prima
Nights in the Underground, Marie-Claire Blais
Praxis, Fay Weldon
The Retrieval System, Maxine Kumin
The Ruins of Isis, Marion Zimmer Bradley
Silences, Tillie Olsen
"A Woman Alone," Denise Levertov
A Woman of Independent Means, Elizabeth Forsythe
    Hailey
Woman's Fiction, Nina Baym

1979

The Basement, Kate Millett
The Bloody Chamber, Angela Carter
Boochie, Mari Evans
Burger's Daughter, Nadine Gordimer
Circus Valentine, Marsha Norman
Cloud Nine, Caryl Churchill
Crimes of the Heart, Beth Henley
Deaf to the City, Marie-Claire Blais
Eyes, Mari Evans

Joys of Motherhood, Buchi Emecheta
Kindred, Olivia Butler
Kiss Sleeping Beauty Good-bye, Madonna Kolbenschlag
A Life for Two, Marie Cardinal
Little Birds, Anaïs Nin
The Obstacle Race, Germaine Greer
On Lies, Secrets and Silence, Adrienne Rich
Only Children, Alison Lurie
The Sadeian Woman, Angela Carter
Shakespeare's Sisters, Sandra Gilbert and Susan Gubar
So Long a Letter, Mariama Bâ
Spiral Dance, Starhawk
These Modern Women, Elaine Showalter
Turning Points, Ellen Goodman
*What Happened after Nora Left Her Husband or Pillars of
    Societies*, Elfriede Jelinek
Women and Russia, ed. Tatyana Mamonova

1980

"Anorexic," Eavan Boland
Barn Blind, Jane Smiley
The Bleeding Heart, Marilyn French
The Burning Bed, Faith McNulty
The Clan of the Cave Bear, Jean Auel
Compulsory Heterosexuality and Lesbian Existence,
    Adrienne Rich
The Descending Figure, Louise Glück
"Emigration," Eleanor Wilner
Good Wives, Laurel Thatcher Ulrich
The Hidden Face of Eve, Nawal El Saadawi
In Her Own Image, Eavan Boland
Journey Around My Room, Louise Bogan
"The Language of the Brag," Sharon Olds
Miss Firecracker Contest, Beth Henley
The Moon Is Always Female, Marge Piercy
Powers of the Weak, Elizabeth Janeway
Puffball, Fay Weldon
The Rebecca Notebook, Daphne du Maurier
The Salt Eaters, Toni Cade Bambara
Still Life, Emily Mann
The Sunflower, Sahar Khalifeh
The Third Woman, Joy Harjo
Two Headed Woman, Lucille Clifton
What Moon Drove Me to This?, Joy Harjo
Wonderful, Wonderful Times, Elfriede Jelinek
The Yellow House on the Corner, Rita Dove

1981

Ain't I a Woman, bell hooks
"All My Pretty Ones," Anne Sexton
"Bluebeard," Sylvia Plath
"Briar Rose," Anne Sexton

Certificate of Absence, Sylvia Molloy
Daughters, I Love You, Linda Hogan
"Electra on Azalea Path," Sylvia Plath
"Flee on Your Donkey," Anne Sexton
Housekeeping, Marilynne Robinson
In the Land of Dreamy Dreams, Ellen Gilchrist
Isn't It Romantic, Wendy Wasserstein
The Language of Clothes, Alison Lurie
The Madwoman in the Attic, Sandra Gilbert and Susan
    Gubar
The Maid of the North, Ethel Johnston Phelps
Mary Chesnut's Civil War, Mary Chesnut
Mishima: A Vision of the Void, Marguerite Yourcenar
New Anatomies, Timberlake Wertenbaker
Obasan, Joy Kogawa
Pornography: Men Possessing Women, Andrea Dworkin
The Scarlet Song, Mariama Bâ
A Season in Rihata, Maryse Condé
The Second Stage, Betty Friedan
Shakespeare's Division of Experience, Marilyn French
Song for Anninho, Gayl Jones
Spring Moon, Bette Bao Lord
This Bridge Called My Back, ed. Gloria Anzaldúa and
    Cherríe Moraga
Thousand Pieces of Gold, Ruthanne Lumm McCunn
Tiger Eyes, Judy Blume
Witches, Erica Jong
Women, Race and Class, Angela Davis
"Yellow Woman," Leslie Marmon Silko

1982

Anatomy of Freedom, Robin Morgan
Anna's World, Marie-Claire Blais
*Asian American Literature: An Introduction to the Writings
    and Their Social Context*, Elaine H. Kim
"Beloved Women," Paula Gunn Allen
The Color Purple, Alice Walker
Cross Sections from a Decade of Changes, Elizabeth
    Janeway
Cuentos: Stories by Latinas, Mariana Romo Camona and
    Alma Gómez
Domestic Interior, Eavan Boland
"Dragonfly-Mother," Denise Levertov
Dreaming the Dark, Starhawk
The House of the Spirits, Isabel Allende
In a Different Voice, Carol Gilligan
Indemnity Only, Sara Paretsky
Inside Out, Timberlake Wertenbaker
The Mists of Avalon, Marion Zimmer Bradley
"Notes from a Quiet Backwater I," Bessie Head
Our Ground Time Here Will Be Brief, Maxine Kumin
"Pig Dreams," Denise Levertov

"Praise for Debate," Nancy Morejón
The Ripening, Meridel Le Sueur
Shadow Country, Paula Gunn Allen
Shiloh and Other Stories, Bobbie Ann Mason
"Songge Byrd," Mina Loy
"Sur," Ursula Le Guin
Top Girls, Caryl Churchill
The Valley of Horses, Jean Auel
The Wake of Jamey Foster, Beth Henley
Women and Male Violence, Susan Schechter
Women of Brewster Place, Gloria Naylor
Women's Diaries of the Westward Journey, Lillian Schlissel
Zami, Audre Lorde

1983

"A" Is for Alibi, Sue Grafton
At the Bottom of the River, Jamaica Kincaid
Book of Promethea, Hélène Cixous
The Claiming of Sleeping Beauty, Anne Rice
"The Eye of the Heron," Ursula Le Guin
Home Girls, Barbara Smith
The House on Mango Street, Sandra Cisneros
How to Suppress Women's Writing, Joanna Russ
I, Rigoberta Menchú, Rigoberta Menchú
Inanna, Diane Wolkstein
In Search of April Raintree, Beatrice Culleton
The Life and Loves of a She-Devil, Fay Weldon
Loving in the War Years, Cherríe Moraga
Memoirs from the Women's Prison, Nawal El Saadawi
Miss Peabody's Inheritance, Elizabeth Jolley
'night Mother, Marsha Norman
Outrageous Acts and Everyday Rebellions, Gloria Steinem
The Past Encroached, Marie Cardinal
Pastoral Jazz, Olga Broumas
The Piano Teacher, Elfriede Jelinek
The Picture Bride, Cathy Song
Praisesong for the Widow, Paule Marshall
Rich Like Us, Nayantara Sahgal
Right-Wing Women, Andrea Dworkin
She Had Some Horses, Joy Harjo
Signs Reader, Judith Herman and Lisa Hirschman
Thendara House, Marion Zimmer Bradley
Those Who Ride the Night Wind, Nikki Giovanni
The Woman Between Mirrors, Helena Parente Cunha
"The Woman Hanging from the Thirteenth Floor
    Window," Joy Harjo
The Woman Who Owned the Shadows, Paula Gunn Allen
The Women Who Hate Me, Dorothy Allison

1984

Abel's Sister, Timberlake Wertenbaker
Beauty's Punishment, Anne Rice

"Blood, Bread, and Poetry," Adrienne Rich
Daring to Dream, Carol Farley Kessler
The Diaries of Jane Somers, Doris Lessing
Feminist Theory, bell hooks
homegirls & handgrenades, Sonia Sanchez
Love Medicine, Louise Erdrich
The Lover, Marguerite Duras
Mermaids in the Basement, Carolyn Kizer
Nights at the Circus, Angela Carter
Of Love and Shadows, Isabel Allende
Parachutes and Kisses, Erica Jong
The Private Mary Chesnut, Mary Chesnut
"Salvation Is the Issue," Toni Cade Bambara
Segu: The Children of Segu, Maryse Condé
Sex and Destiny: The Politics of Human Fertility, Germaine Greer
Sister Outsider, Audre Lorde
Speculum of the Other Woman, Luce Irigaray
That's What She Said, Joy Harjo
"Valley of the Fallen," Carolyn Kizer
Victory Over Japan, Ellen Gilchrist
"The Wedding Ring Poem," Susan Fromberg Schaeffer
"Who Is Your Mother," Paula Gunn Allen
With a Daughter's Eye, Mary Catherine Kassarjian
Yin: New Poems, Carolyn Kizer

1985

Annie John, Jamaica Kincaid
Beauty's Release, Anne Rice
Beyond Power: On Women, Men, and Morals, Marilyn French
Black Holes, Black Stockings, Olga Broumas
Confessions of a Failed Southern Lady, Florence King
Debutante Ball, Beth Henley
The Grace of Mary Traverse, Timberlake Wertenbaker
The Handmaid's Tale, Margaret Atwood
"Light Years," Barbara Elovic
Magic Mommas, Trembling Sisters, Puritans and Perverts, Joanna Russ
The Mammoth Hunters, Jean Auel
My Mother's Body, Marge Piercy
Sarah, Plain and Tall, Patricia MacLachlan and Carol Sobieski
Seeing Through the Sun, Linda Hogan
Segu: The Earth in Pieces, Maryse Condé
"The Shawl," Jeanne Murray Walker
The Silver Metal Lover, Tanith Lee
Where the Island Sleeps Like a Wing, Nancy Morejón

1986

The Adventures of Alyx, Joanna Russ
Belinda, Anne Rice

Coming to Writing, Hélène Cixous
Eros the Bittersweet, Anne Carson
The Female Malady, Elaine Showalter
The Friends of Alice Wheeldon, Sheila Rowbotham
Head Above Water, Buchi Emecheta
I Am Your Sister, Audre Lorde
I, Tituba, Black Witch of Salem, Maryse Condé
It's a Family Affair, Barbara Omolade
Journey, Eavan Boland
Life and Death in Shanghai, Nien Cheng
The Madwoman's Underclothes, Germaine Greer
Marilyn: Norma Jeane, Gloria Steinem
Memoirs of an Unrealistic Woman, Sahar Khalifeh
So Far from the Bamboo Grove, Yoko Kawashima Watkins
Thomas and Beulah, Rita Dove

1987

The Belle of Amherst, Micheline Wandor
Beloved, Toni Morrison
Beyond the Limit, Irina Ratushinskaya
Borderlands/La Frontera, Gloria Anzaldúa
Cassandra, Christa Wolf
"D" Is for Deadbeat, Sue Grafton
Disorderly Conduct, Marie Cardinal
Ellen Foster, Kaye Gibbons
Eva Luna, Isabel Allende
The Fall of the Imam, Nawal El Saadawi
The Firebrand, Marion Zimmer Bradley
"Floral Apron," Marilyn Chin
The Fortune Teller, Marsha Norman
The Gold Cell, Sharon Olds
Her Mother's Daughter, Marilyn French
Improper Behavior, Elizabeth Janeway
Intercourse, Andrea Dworkin
Mama, Terry McMillan
Not Without My Daughter, Betty Mahmoody
People Who Led to My Plays, Adrienne Kennedy
Talking About People, Rosalie Maggio
Terrible Beauty, Diana Norman
Under a Soprano Sky, Sonia Sanchez
The War of the Words, Sandra Gilbert and Susan Gubar

1988

All under Heaven, Valerie Harper
The Anna Papers, Ellen Gilchrist
The Bean Trees, Barbara Kingsolver
Blood Shot, Sara Paretsky
Cat's Eye, Margaret Atwood
Chicana Creativity and Criticism, Helen Viramontes and María Hererra-Sobek
"Chronicle," Mei-Mei Berssenbrugge
Desert Run, Mitsuye Yamada

The Faber Book of Twentieth Century Women's Poetry, ed. Fleur Adcock
Frameless Windows, Squares of Light, Cathy Song
Greenlanders, Jane Smiley
Grey Is the Colour of Hope, Irina Ratushinskaya
Ice and Fire, Andrea Dworkin
Letters from a War Zone, Andrea Dworkin
Love of the Nightingale, Timberlake Wertenbaker
Mama Day, Gloria Naylor
Mistaken Identity, Nayantara Sahgal
The Pencil Letter, Irina Ratushinskaya
The Queen of the Damned, Anne Rice
"Rose-Johnny," Barbara Kingsolver
Savings, Linda Hogan
The Splendid Outcast, Beryl Markham
Tracks, Louise Erdrich
Trash, Dorothy Allison

1989

The Angel of Loneliness, Marie-Claire Blais
"The Bride," Kathleen Norris
The Colonel's Lady on the Western Frontier, Alice Kirk Grierson
The Contested Castle, Kate Ferguson Ellis
Daddy We Hardly Knew You, Germaine Greer
The Demon Lover, Robin Morgan
"Doll Poem," Toi Derricotte
The Heidi Chronicles, Wendy Wasserstein
The Hex Witch of Seldom, Nancy Springer
Holding the Line, Barbara Kingsolver
"Homeland," Barbara Kingsolver
In Country, Bobbie Ann Mason
Jasmine, Bharati Mukherjee
The Joy Luck Club, Amy Tan
Like Water for Chocolate, Laura Esquivel
Lust, Elfriede Jelinek
Making Face, Making Soul, Gloria Anzaldúa
Mother Country, Marilynne Robinson
No Man's Land, Sandra Gilbert and Susan Gubar
Number the Stars, Lois Lowry
"Patchwork," Cynthia Huntington
Temple of My Familiar, Alice Walker
Virginia Woolf, Louise DeSalvo
"Why I Am a Danger to the Public," Barbara Kingsolver
Writing a Woman's Life, Carolyn G. Heilbrun

1990

Abundance, Beth Henley
Animal Dreams, Barbara Kingsolver
Dancing at the Edge of the World, Ursula Le Guin
The Dogeaters, Jessica Hagedorn

"Eagle Poem," Joy Harjo
In Mad Love and War, Joy Harjo
Je, Tu, Nous: Toward a Culture of Difference, Luce Irigaray
Lucy, Jamaica Kincaid
"The Making of an Irish Goddess," Eavan Boland
Mam Phyllis, Elizabeth Brown-Guillory
Mei Mei: A Daughter's Song, Dmae Roberts
A Midwife's Tale, Laurel Thatcher Ulrich
Mourning Dove: A Salishan Autobiography, Mourning Dove
My Jewish Face & Other Stories, Melanie Kaye/Kantrowitz
My Son's Story, Nadine Gordimer
Need, Audre Lorde
The North China Lover, Marguerite Duras
"The Oral Tradition," Eavan Boland
The Plains of Passage, Jean Auel
Spider Woman's Granddaughters, ed. Paul Gunn Allen
The Stories of Eva Luna, Isabel Allende
Tehanu, Ursula Le Guin
Winter Prairie Woman, Meridel Le Sueur
The Witching Hour, Anne Rice
A Woman Alone, Bessie Head
"Woman's Fight," Pretty Shield

1991

The Alchemy of Race and Rights, Patricia Williams
Almanac of the Dead, Leslie Marmon Silko
Bachelor Girls, Wendy Wasserstein
Backlash, Susan Faludi
The Beauty Myth, Naomi Wolf
Changes: A Love Story, Ama Ata Aidoo
Daughters, Paule Marshall
First Love Stories, Diane Wolkstein
Grandmother of the Light, Paula Gunn Allen
Having Our Say, Bessie Delany and Sarah Delany
How the García Girls Lost Their Accent, Julia Alvarez
Janet Frame: An Autobiography, Janet Frame
The Kitchen God's Wife, Amy Tan
"Lost Lives of Women: My Grandmother's Choice," Amy Tan
Love Space Demands, Ntozake Shange
Mercy, Andrea Dworkin
Molly Ivins Can't Say That, Can She?, Molly Ivins
"A New Politics of Sexuality," June Jordan
Paula, Isabel Allende
Quilting, Lucille Clifton
A Thousand Acres, Jane Smiley
Typical American, Gish Jen
Winnie, Gwendolyn Brooks
Woman Hollering Creek, Sandra Cisneros

1992

Bastard Out of Carolina, Dorothy Allison
Deborah, Golda and Me, Letty Cottin Pogrebin
Dreaming in Cuban, Cristina García
Fires in the Mirror, Anna Deavere Smith
For Love of a Child, Betty Mahmoody
The Issue Is Power, Melanie Kaye/Kantrowitz
Little Altars Everywhere, Rebecca Wells
Passing, Nella Larsen
Possessing the Secret of Joy, Alice Walker
Revolution from Within, Gloria Steinem
Sally's Rape, Robbie McCauley
The Sisters Rosensweig, Wendy Wasserstein
Tales from the Bamboo Grove, Yoko Kawashima Watkins
Waiting to Exhale, Terry McMillan
The War against Women, Marilyn French
Warming the Stone Child, Clarissa Pinkola Estés
Wild Iris, Louise Glück
Women Who Run with the Wolves, Clarissa Pinkola Estés

1993

Bone, Fae Myenne Ng
The Book of Light, Lucille Clifton
Book of Medicines, Linda Hogan
Briar Rose, Jane Yolen
The Broken Calabash, Osonye Tess Onwueme
Charms for the Easy Life, Kaye Gibbons
Chicana Writers, Helen Viramontes and María Hererra-Sobek
"Daughters," Lucille Clifton
Feather Crowns, Bobbie Ann Mason
The Fifth Sacred Thing, Starhawk
Foxfire: Confessions of a Girl Gang, Joyce Carol Oates
The Gift of Story, Clarissa Pinkola Estés
The Holder of the World, Bharati Mukherjee
The Last Generation, Cherríe Moraga
"Making Female Bodies the Battlefield," Susan Brownmiller
Nothin' but Good Times Ahead, Molly Ivins
The Parable of the Sower, Olivia Butler
Parables for a Season, Osonye Tess Onwueme
Paris Rats in E.L.A., Helen Viramontes
Pigs in Heaven, Barbara Kingsolver
Poof, Lynn Nottage
The Reign of Wazobia, Osonye Tess Onwueme
The Robber Bride, Margaret Atwood
Sherlock in Love, Sena Naslund
Two Old Women, Velma Wallis
Two Women in Conversation, Flora Nwapa
What Is Found There, Adrienne Rich
"Why Do We Romanticize the Fetus?" Katha Pollitt

1994

Breath, Eyes, Memory, Edwidge Danticat
Catherine, Called Birdy, Karen Cushman
The Darker Face of the Earth, Rita Dove
Dolley, Rita Mae Brown
The Forest House, Marion Zimmer Bradley
The Fountain of Age, Betty Friedan
From the Beast to the Blonde, Marina Warner
The Girl Who Heard Dragons, Anne McCaffrey
"Griots," Nikki Giovanni
In a Time of Violence, Eavan Boland
In the Time of the Butterflies, Julia Alvarez
"*K*" *Is for Killer*, Sue Grafton
The Loose Woman, Sandra Cisneros
Marriages Between Zones Three, Four, and Five, Doris Lessing
My Brother, My Sister and I, Yoko Kawashima Watkins
Now Poof She Is Gone, Wendy Rose
Now Sheba Sings the Song, Maya Angelou
One True Thing, Anna Quindlen
Phoenix Gone Terrace Empty, Marilyn Chin
The Politics of Cruelty, Kate Millett
Reasonable Creatures, Katha Pollitt
School Figures, Cathy Song
Skylark, Patricia MacLachlan and Carol Sobieski
Teaching to Transgress, bell hooks
To Be Two, Luce Irigaray
Twilight Los Angeles, 1992, Anna Deavere Smith
The Vizard Mask, Diana Norman
Women and Ghosts, Alison Lurie

1995

As Long as Life, Mary Ellen Rowland
Betsey Brown, Ntozake Shange
Burning Your Boats, Angela Carter
The Circle in the Dirt, Cherríe Moraga
The Faithful Gardener, Clarissa Pinkola Estés
Glass, Irony, and God, Anne Carson
"The Grey Flannel Sexual Harassment Suit," Marge Piercy
The Hundred Secret Senses, Amy Tan
Krik? Krak!, Edwidge Danticat
"Light the Candles," Nikki Giovanni
The Midwife's Apprentice, Karen Cushman
The Moth and Other Stories, Helen Viramontes
Mother Love, Rita Dove
Mothersongs, Sandra Gilbert, Susan Gubar, and Diana O'Hehir
My Left Breast, Susan Miller
Object Lesson, Eavan Boland
Rhoda, Ellen Gilchrist
Solar Storms, Linda Hogan
Splitting, Fay Weldon

The Rooster's Egg, Patricia Williams
The Skin Shows, Judith Halberstam
Thirsts, Marie-Claire Blais
To Write Like a Woman, Joanna Russ
Two or Three Things I Know for Sure, Dorothy Allison
Under the Feet of Jesus, Helen Viramontes
"Werewolf," Angela Carter
We Were the Mulvaneys, Joyce Carol Oates
Windward Heights, Maryse Condé

1996

"An American Beauty," Carolyn Kizer
The Autobiography of My Mother, Jamaica Kincaid
Bird Girl and the Man Who Followed the Sun, Velma
    Wallis
The Blue Jay's Dance, Louise Erdrich
Bone Black, bell hooks
Divine Secrets of the Ya-Ya Sisterhood, Rebecca Wells
Dwellings, Linda Hogan
Esther's Story, Diane Wolkstein
"Fearful Women," Carolyn Kizer
Fire with Fire, Naomi Wolf
"Gerda," Carolyn Kizer
"How Cruel Is the Story of Eve," Stevie Smith
How Stella Got Her Groove Back, Terry McMillan
Journey to Ithaca, Anita Desai
Just an Ordinary Day, Shirley Jackson
"La Llorona," Yxta Maya Murray
"Literature and the Politics of Sex," Cynthia Ozick
Meadowlands, Louise Glück
Medea, Christa Wolf
Middle Heart, Bette Bao Lord
Mona in the Promised Land, Gish Jen
Pope Joan, Donna Cross
Return to Avalon, Marion Zimmer Bradley
"The Rite and the Right," Nawal El Saadawi
Scribbling Women, Elaine Showalter
The Sleep Deprivation Chamber, Adrienne Kennedy
The True Story of the Novel, Margaret Anne Doody
The Vagina Monologues, Eve Ensler
Venus Envy, Rita Mae Brown
Vertigo: A Memoir, Louise DeSalvo
Watsonville: Some Place Not Here, Cherríe Moraga
Wellspring, Sharon Olds
Winter Quarters, Mary Haskin Richards
The Witch of Exmoor, Margaret Drabble
The Woman Who Fell from the Sky, Joy Harjo
Yellow Woman and a Beauty of the Spirit, Leslie Marmon
    Silko

1997

An American Daughter, Wendy Wasserstein
Beyond Gender, Betty Friedan

Big Girls Don't Cry, Fay Weldon
Does Your House Have Lions?, Sonia Sanchez
Getting Over Getting Older, Letty Cottin Pogrebin
Hystories, Elaine Showalter
I've Always Meant to Tell You, ed. Barbara Kingsolver
Janie Bigo, Dmae Roberts
The Lady of Avalon, Marion Zimmer Bradley
Leave It to Me, Bharati Mukherjee
Mary Chesnut's War for Independence!, Chris
    Weatherhead
The Missing Face, Osonye Tess Onwueme
On Being Female, Black, and Free, Margaret Walker
Point of View, Nayantara Sahgal
Promiscuities, Naomi Wolf
The Puttermesser Papers, Cynthia Ozick
The Red Tent, Anita Diamant
Rita Will, Rita Mae Brown
Seeking the Genesis, Kia Corthron
The Stream & the Sapphire, Denise Levertov
Tales of Burning Love, Louise Erdrich
Tell It to Women, Osonye Tess Onwueme
Waiting in the Wings, Cherríe Moraga
Walking to Mercury, Starhawk

1998

Acorna's Quest, Anne McCaffrey
The All-True Travels and Adventures of Lidie Newton, Jane
    Smiley
Aphrodite, a Memoir of the Senses, Isabel Allende
Beyond the Limbo Silence, Elizabeth Nuñez
Black and Blue, Anna Quindlen
Blues Legacy and Black Feminism, Angela Davis
Breathless: An Asthma Journal, Louise DeSalvo
By the Light of My Father's Smile, Alice Walker
Camp Notes and Other Writings, Mitsuye Yamada
The Cavedweller, Dorothy Allison
Democracy on Trial, Tunde Adeyanju
Faces under Water, Tanith Lee
The Farming of Bones, Edwidge Danticat
Fatal Women, Tanith Lee
Flights of Angels, Ellen Gilchrist
Gothic Feminism, Diane Hoeveler
The Healing, Gayl Jones
If I Can Cook/You Know God Can, Ntozake Shange
The Impossible Marriage, Beth Henley
The Journey of Lady Buddha, Dmae Roberts
Legacies: Faith, Hope and Peace, Dmae Roberts
Legacies: Tales from America, Dmae Roberts
The Parable of the Talents, Olivia Butler
The Poisonwood Bible, Barbara Kingsolver
Sistahs, Maxine Bailey and Sharon Mareeka Lewis
You Got to Dance with Them What Brung You, Molly
    Ivins

1999

Adultery, Louise DeSalvo
Ahab's Wife, Sena Naslund
And Yet They Paused, Georgia Douglas Johnson
At the Full and Change of the Moon, Dionne Brand
A Bill to Be Passed, Georgia Douglas Johnson
Clear Springs, Bobbie Ann Mason
Communicating Gender, Suzanne Romaine
Daughter of Fortune, Isabel Allende
The Daughter of Isis, Nawal El Saadawi
Diamond Dust, Anita Desai
Fiction and Lies, Irina Ratushinskaya
Gardens in the Dunes, Leslie Marmon Silko
The Girl with a Pearl Earring, Tracy Chevalier
Hard Time, Sara Paretsky
In Her Mother's House, Wendy Ho
In Our Time, Susan Brownmiller
Lilith, Alina Reyes
On the Bus with Rosa Parks, Rita Dove
Our Only Amelia May, Jennifer Holm
Places I Never Meant to Be, Judy Blume
Power, Linda Hogan
Soldier: A Poet's Childhood, June Jordan
Stolen Lives, Malike Oufkir
Teaching Human Rights Awareness through Poetry, Mitsuye
      Yamada
The Whole Woman, Germaine Greer
Who's Irish?, Gish Jen
Wit, Margaret Edson

2000

Aesthetics and Gender in American Literature, Deborah
      Barker
The Art of Blessing the Day, Marge Piercy
Blessing the Boats, Lucille Clifton
Bruised Hibiscus, Elizabeth Nuñez
Family Week, Beth Henley
Herman Melville, Elizabeth Hardwick
If Not, Winter: Fragments of Sappho, Anne Carson
I Know Just What You Mean, Ellen Goodman and Patricia
      O'Brien
Interviews/Entrevistas, Gloria Anzaldúa and AnaLouise
      Keating
"La Llorona," Mary McArthur
Prodigal Summer, Barbara Kingsolver
Shrub, Molly Ivins
Sky Rider, Nancy Springer
"Vague Poem," Elizabeth Bishop
Writing As a Way of Healing, Louise DeSalvo

2001

The Age of Homespun, Laurel Thatcher Ulrich
The Beauty of the Husband, Anne Carson

Begin Again, Grace Paley
The Blind Assassin, Margaret Atwood
The Bonesetter's Daughter, Amy Tan
Boston Jane: An Adventure, Jennifer Holm
Breath, Boom, Kia Corthron
Célanire Cou-coupé, Maryse Condé
A Day Late and a Dollar Short, Terry McMillan
"Don't Get the Wrong Message," Susan Faludi
"Hark, Hark," Leslie Marmon Silko
Hateship, Friendship, Courtship, Loveship, Marriage, Alice
      Munro
I Am Morgan Le Fay, Nancy Springer
Inventing Herself, Elaine Showalter
Just Ella, Margaret Peterson Haddix
The Land of Bliss, Cathy Song
The Last Report on the Miracles at Little No Horse, Louise
      Erdrich
Mother Millett, Kate Millett
Necessary Targets, Eve Ensler
Nickel and Dimed: On (Not) Getting by in America,
      Barbara Ehrenreich
Piratica, Tanith Lee
Recollections of My Life as a Woman, Diane Di Prima
Rowan Hood, Outlaw Girl of Sherwood Forest, Nancy
      Springer
"Sowers and Reapers," Jamaica Kincaid
Subject to Debate, Katha Pollitt
Three Women, Marge Piercy
White As Snow, Tanith Lee
The Wind Done Gone, Alice Randall
Zigzagging Down a Wild Trail, Bobbie Ann Mason

2002

Blood of My Blood, Marjorie Kinnan Rawlings
Boston Jane: Wilderness Days, Jennifer Holm
Desirable Daughters, Bharati Mukherjee
Désirada, Maryse Condé
Discretion, Elizabeth Nuñez
Good Harbor, Anita Diamant
Heartbreak, Andrea Dworkin
In the Name of Salomé, Julia Alvarez
Last Stand: America's Virgin Lands, Barbara Kingsolver
Little Red Riding Hood Uncloaked, Catherine Orenstein
Melymbrosia, Louise DeSalvo
Nothing Sacred, Katha Pollitt and Betsy Reed
The Priestess of Avalon, Marion Zimmer Bradley
The Rage and the Pride, Oriana Fallaci
Raising Ourselves, Velma Wallis
Rhapsody in Plain Yellow, Marilyn Chin
The Ruling Junta, Tunde Adeyanju
Separate Sisters, Nancy Springer
The Seven Ages, Louise Glück
Seven Sisters, Margaret Drabble

Shakara: Dance Hall Queen, Osonye Tess Onwueme
Shelters of Stone, Jean Auel
Small Wonder, Barbara Kingsolver
The Sweet Breathing of Plants, Linda Hogan
Then She Said It, Osonye Tess Onwueme
This Bridge We Call Home, ed. Gloria Anzaldúa and
    AnaLouise Keating
Three Daughters, Letty Cottin Pogrebin
Walking Through Fire, Nawal El Saadawi
"Where Is the Love?," June Jordan
Women Resist Globalisation, Sheila Rowbotham

2003

Big Mouth and Ugly Girl, Joyce Carol Oates
Blacklist, Sara Paretsky
Caramelo, Sandra Cisneros
A Catch of Consequence, Diana Norman
Full Cry, Rita Mae Brown
The Good Body, Eve Ensler
Grace, Elizabeth Nuñez
Legends and Lyrics, Adelaide Ann Proctor
Love, Toni Morrison
Misconceptions, Naomi Wolf
My Invented Country, Isabel Allende
Once Upon a Time When the Princess Rescued the Prince,
    Rosemary Lake
The Outlaw Princess of Sherwood, Nancy Springer
Pitching My Tent, Anita Diamant
Pocahontas: Medicine Woman, Spy, Entrepreneur, Diplomat,
    Paula Gunn Allen
Sex Parasite, Jessica Goldberg

Sexes and Genres through Languages, Luce Irigaray
Sisterhood Is Forever, ed. Robin Morgan

2004

Black Woman and Other Poems, Nancy Morejón
Boston Jane: The Claim, Jennifer Holm
Boys and Girls Forever, Alison Lurie
The Breast Cancer Monologues, Dmae Roberts
The Color of Jews, Melanie Kaye/Kantrowitz
Crazy in the Kitchen, Louise DeSalvo
Divining Women, Kaye Gibbons
Founding Mothers, Cokie Roberts
Galileo's Daughter, Timberlake Wertenbaker
Halleluia! The Welcome Table, Maya Angelou
Heir to the Glimmering World, Cynthia Ozick
In the Shadow of the Ark, Anne Provoost
Loud and Clear, Anna Quindlen
My Nine Lives: Chapters of a Possible Past, Ruth Prawer
    Jhabvala
Now Is the Time to Open Your Heart, Alice Walker
Open House, Patricia Williams
The Paper Trail, Ellen Goodman
The Red Queen, Margaret Drabble
Runaway, Alice Munro
Taking Liberties, Diana Norman
W Effect: Bush's War on Women, Laura Flanders
With Eyes and Soul: Images of Cuba, Nancy Morejón
Ya-Ya's in Bloom, Rebecca Wells

2005

The Stories of Fannie Hurst, Fannie Hurst

PRIMARY SOURCE BIBLIOGRAPHY

Many works of women's literature are available in print because organizations like the Feminist Press have retrieved valuable texts and offered them for sale in inexpensive editions. Many more works are still not available except on loan from rare book collections or on microfische. Nonetheless free access on the Internet has allowed teachers, students, researchers, literary historians, and feminist readers the run of a collection of precious writings that have earned their place in world literature.

PRINT

Adcock, Fleur. *High Tide in the Garden*. Oxford: Oxford University Press, 1971.

Addams, Jane. *Twenty Years at Hull House*. New York: Signet, 1999.

———. "Why Women Should Vote." *Ladies' Home Journal*, January 1910, pp. 21–22.

Adeyanju, Tunde. *The Ruling Junta*. Abeokuta, Nigeria: Litany Nigeria, 2002.

Aguilar, Grace. *Grace Aguilar: Selected Writings*. New York: Broadview, 2003.

Aidoo, Ama Ata. *The Dilemma of a Ghost and Anowa: Two Plays*. Harlow, England: Longman, 1987.

———. "The Message," in *Women of the Third World: Twenty Stories Set in Africa, Asia, and Latin America*. London: Victor Gollancz, 1975.

———. *No Sweetness Here and Other Stories*. New York: Feminist Press, 1995.

Akhmatova, Anna. *The Complete Poems of Anna Akhmatova*. Brookline, Mass.: Zephyr Press, 1998.

———. *Selected Poems of Anna Akhmatova*. Brookline, Mass.: Zephyr Press, 2000.

Alcott, Louisa May. *The Inheritance*. New York: E. P. Dutton, 1997.

———. *Little Women*. New York: Bantam, 1983.

———. *Moods*. Piscataway, N.J.: Rutgers University Press, 1991.

———. *The Portable Louisa May Alcott*. New York: Penguin, 2000.

Alderson, Nannie T. *A Bride Goes West*. Lincoln: University of Nebraska Press, 1942.

Allen, Paula Gunn. *Pocahontas: Medicine Woman, Spy, Entrepreneur, Diplomat*. New York: HarperCollins, 2003.

———. *The Sacred Hoop: Recovering the Feminine in American Indian Traditions*. Boston: Beacon, 1986.

———. *Spider Woman's Granddaughters: Traditional Tales and Contemporary Writing by Native American Women*. Boston: Beacon, 1989.

———. *The Woman Who Owned the Shadows*. San Francisco: Spinsters/Aunt Lute, 1983.

Allende, Isabel. *Daughter of Fortune*. New York: HarperTorch, 2001.

———. *Eva Luna*. New York: Bantam, 1989.

———. *The House of the Spirits*. New York: Bantam, 1986.

———. *The Infinite Plan*. London: Flamingo, 1994.

———. *My Invented Country*. New York: HarperCollins, 2003.

———. *Of Love and Shadows*. New York: Bantam, 1987.

Allison, Dorothy. *Bastard Out of Carolina*. New York: Plume Books, 1993.

———. *Cavedweller*. New York: Plume Books, 1999.

———. *Two or Three Things I Know for Sure*. New York: Plume Books, 1996.

Alvarez, Julia. *Before We Were Free*. New York: Laurel-Leaf, 2004.

———. *How the Garcia Girls Lost Their Accents*. New York: Plume, 1992.

———. *In the Name of Salomé: A Novel*. Chapel Hill, N.C.: Algonquin, 2000.

———. *In the Time of the Butterflies*. Chapel Hill, N.C.: Algonquin, 1994.

Angelou, Maya. *I Know Why the Caged Bird Sings*. New York: Bantam Books, 1970.

———. *Maya Angelou: Poems.* New York: Bantam Books, 1986.

———. *Now Sheba Sings the Song.* New York: Plume Books, 1994.

Anthony, Susan B. *The Selected Papers of Elizabeth Cady Stanton and Susan B. Anthony: Against an Aristocracy of Sex, 1866–1873.* Piscataway, N.J.: Rutgers University Press, 2000.

———. *The Trial of Susan B. Anthony.* New York: Humanity Books, 2003.

Antin, Mary. *From Plotzk to Boston.* Boston: W. B. Clarke, 1899.

———. *Selected Letters of Mary Antin.* New York: Syracuse University Press, 2000.

Anzaldúa, Gloria. *Borderlands/La Frontera: The New Mestiza.* San Francisco: Spinsters/Aunt Lute, 1987.

———. *Interviews/Entrevistas.* New York: Routledge, 2000.

———, ed. *Making Face, Making Soul/Haciendo Caras: Creative and Critical Perspectives by Feminists of Color.* San Francisco: Spinsters/Aunt Lute, 1989.

———. *Prietita and the Ghost Woman/Prietita y La Llorona.* New York: Children's Book Press, 2001.

———, and AnaLouise Keating, eds. *This Bridge We Call Home: Radical Visions for Transformation.* New York: Routledge, 2002.

Appleton, Jane Sophia. "Sequel to *The Vision of Bangor in the Twentieth Century.*" In *Daring to Dream.* Boston: Pandora Press, 1984.

Aristophanes. *The Birds, Lysistrata, Assembly-Women, Wealth.* Oxford: Oxford University Press, 1997.

Arnow, Harriette. *The Dollmaker.* New York: Avon, 1954.

Atherton, Gertrude. *Black Oxen.* New York: Boni & Liveright, 1923.

Atwood, Margaret. *The Blind Assassin.* New York: Anchor Books, 2001.

———. *The Handmaid's Tale.* New York: Anchor Books, 1998.

———. *Lady Oracle.* New York: Anchor Books, 1998.

———. *The Robber Bride.* New York: Anchor Books, 1998.

———. *Selected Poems. Vol. 2. 1976–1986.* New York: Mariner, 1987.

Auel, Jean. *The Clan of the Cave Bear.* New York: Bantam, 1984.

———. *The Shelters of Stone.* New York: Bantam, 2003.

Austen, Jane. *Emma.* New York: Signet Classic, 1964.

———. *Persuasion.* Ware, England: Wordsworth Editions, 1995.

———. *Pride and Prejudice.* New York: Signet Classic, 1980.

Austin, Mary Hunter. *Children Sing in the Far West.* Boston: Houghton Mifflin, 1928.

———. *Stories from the Country of Lost Borders.* New York: Harper & Brothers, 1909.

Avellaneda, Gertrudis Gómez de. *Sab and the Autobiography.* Austin: University of Texas Press, 1993.

Bâ, Mariama. *The Scarlet Song.* London: Longman, 1995.

———. *So Long a Letter.* Portsmouth, N.H.: Heinemann, 1989.

Bailey, Maxine, and Sharon M. Lewis. *Sistahs.* Toronto: Playwrights Canada Press, 1998.

Baillie, Joanna. *Ahalya Baee: A Poem.* London: Spottiswoodes & Shaw, 1849.

———. *Metrical Legends of Exalted Characters.* London: Longman, 1821.

Bambara, Toni Cade. *Deep Sightings and Rescue Missions: Fiction, Essays, and Conversations.* New York: Pantheon, 1996.

———. *The Salt Eaters.* New York: Vintage, 1980.

———. "Salvation Is the Issue." In *Black Women Writers (1950–1980), A Critical Evaluation.* Edited by Mari Evans. New York: Doubleday, 1984.

Barbauld, Anna Laetitia. *Hymns in Prose for Children.* New York: Garland, 1977.

———. *A Legacy for Young Ladies.* Boston: David Reed, 1826.

———. *The Poems of Anna Letitia Barbauld.* Athens: University of Georgia Press, 1994.

Barnes, Djuna. *The Book of Repulsive Women.* Los Angeles: Sun & Moon, 1994.

———. "How It Feels to Be Forcibly Fed," *New York World Magazine,* 4 September 1914, pp. 3, 17.

———. *Nightwood.* New York: Harcourt, 1937.

———. *Ryder.* Elmwood Park, Ill.: Dalkey Archive, 1990.

Bazán, Emilia Pardo. *The House of Ulloa.* London: Penguin, 1990.

Beauvoir, Simone de. *All Men Are Mortal.* New York: W. W. Norton, 1992.

———. *The Second Sex.* New York: Vintage, 1989.

———. *A Very Easy Death.* New York: Pantheon, 1985.

———. *Woman Destroyed.* New York: Pantheon, 1987.

Beecher, Catharine E. *The New Housekeeper's Manual.* New York: J. B. Pond, 1873.

———, and Harriet Beecher Stowe. *American Woman's Home.* Hartford, Conn.: Stowe-Day Foundation, 1994.

Berssenbrugge, Mei-Mei. *Four-Year-Old Girl.* New York: Kelsey St. Press, 1998.

Bishop, Elizabeth. *The Collected Prose of Elizabeth Bishop.* New York: Farrar, Straus & Giroux, 1984.

———. *The Complete Poems of Elizabeth Bishop, 1927–1979.* New York: Farrar, Straus & Giroux, 1979.

————. *The Diary of Helena Morley.* New York: Ecco Press, 1957.

Blackwell, Alice Stone. *Lucy Stone: Pioneer of Women's Rights.* Richmond, Va.: University of Richmond Press, 2001.

Blackwell, Antoinette. *The Sexes throughout Nature.* New York: Hyperion, 1976.

Blackwell, Elizabeth. *Essays on Medical Sociology.* London: Ernest Bell, 1902.

————. *The Laws of Life with Special Reference to the Physical Education of Girls.* Colville, Wash.: Reprint Service, 1989.

————. *Pioneer Work in Opening the Medical Profession to Women.* Delanco, N.J.: privately printed, 2000.

Blais, Marie-Claire. *Anna's World.* Toronto: Lester & Orpen Dennys, 1985.

————. *Deaf to the City,* Woodstock, N.Y.: Overlook, 1987.

————. *Nights in the Underground: An Exploration of Love.* Toronto: Musson, 1979.

————. *A Season in the Life of Emmanuel.* New York: Farrar, Straus, & Giroux, 1966.

————. *Thirsts.* Toronto: Anansi, 1997.

Block, Francesca Lia. *The Rose and the Beast: Fairy Tales Retold.* New York: Joanna Cotler, 2000.

Blume, Judy. *Are You There God? It's Me, Margaret.* New York: Dell, 1970.

Bly, Nellie. *Around the World in 72 Days.* Brookfield, Conn.: Twenty-First Century Books, 1998.

————. *Six Months in Mexico.* New York: American Publishers, 1888.

————. *Ten Days in a Mad-House and Miscellaneous Sketches: "Trying to Be a Servant," and "Nellie Bly as a White Slave."* New York: Ian L. Munro, 1890.

Bogan, Louise. *Achievement in American Poetry.* Los Angeles: Gateway, 1951.

————. *The Blue Estuaries: Poems 1923–1968.* New York: Farrar, Straus & Giroux, 1995.

Boland, Eavan. *In a Time of Violence.* New York: W. W. Norton, 1995.

————. *Object Lesson: The Life of the Woman and the Poet in Our Time.* New York: W. W. Norton, 1996.

————. *An Origin Like Water: Collected Poems 1957–1987.* New York: W. W. Norton, 1997.

————. *Outside History: Selected Poems, 1980–1990.* New York: W. W. Norton, 2001.

Bonner, Marita. *Frye Street and Environs: A Collection of Works of Marita Bonner.* Boston: Beacon, 1987.

Bowen, Elizabeth. *The Death of the Heart.* New York: Anchor Books, 2000.

————. *The House in Paris.* New York: Anchor Books, 2002.

————. *Eva Trout; or, Changing Scenes.* New York: Anchor Books, 2003.

Bowles, Jane. *The Collected Works of Jane Bowles.* New York: Noonday Press, 1966.

Braddon, Mary Elizabeth. *Eleanor's Victory.* London: Alan Sutton, 1997.

————. *Henry Dunbar.* New York: IndyPublish, 2004.

Bradford, Sarah H. *Scenes in the Life of Harriet Tubman.* New York: Beaufort Books, 1971.

Bradley, Marion Zimmer. *The Forest House.* New York: Roc, 1995.

————. *The Mists of Avalon.* New York: Del Rey, 1987.

————. *Priestess of Avalon.* New York: Roc, 2002.

Bradstreet, Anne. *The Works of Anne Bradstreet.* Cambridge, Mass.: Belknap Press, 1981.

Brand, Dionne. *At the Full and Change of the Moon.* New York: Grove, 1999.

————. *In Another Place, Not Here.* New York: Grove, 1996.

Brontë, Charlotte. *Jane Eyre.* New York: Bantam Books, 1981.

————. *The Letters of Charlotte Brontë: With a Selection of Letters by Family and Friends.* Vol. 2. *1848–1851.* New York: Oxford University Press, 2000.

————. *The Professor and Emma.* London: J. M. Dent, 1985.

————. *Villette.* New York: Modern Library, 1997.

Brontë, Emily. *Wuthering Heights.* New York: New American Library, 1959.

Brooks, Gwendolyn. *Blacks.* Chicago: Third World Press, 1987.

————. "An Old Black Woman, Homeless and Indistinct," *Drum Voices Revue* (Fall–Winter 1992–1993): 120.

————. *Selected Poems.* New York: HarperPerennial, 1999.

————. *Winnie.* Chicago: Third World Press, 1991.

————. *The World of Gwendolyn Brooks.* New York: Harper, 1971.

Broumas, Olga. *Beginning with O.* New Haven, Conn.: Yale University Press, 1977.

————. *Rave: Poems 1975–1999.* Townsend, Wash.: Copper Canyon Press, 1999.

Brown, Rita Mae. *Dolley.* New York: Bantam Books, 1995.

————. *Full Cry.* New York: Ballantine, 2003.

————. *Rita Will: Memoir of a Literary Rabble-Rouser.* New York: Bantam, 1999.

————. *Rubyfruit Jungle.* New York: Bantam, 1983.

Brown-Guillory, Elizabeth. *Mam Phyllis.* In *Wines in the Wilderness: Plays by African American Women from the Harlem Renaissance to the Present,* edited by Elizabeth Brown-Guillory. New York: Greenwood Press, 1990.

Browning, Elizabeth Barrett. *Aurora Leigh.* New York: W. W. Norton, 1996.

————. *Elizabeth Barrett Browning: Selected Poems.* London: Gramercy, 2000.

Brownmiller, Susan. *Against Our Will: Men, Women and Rape.* New York: Bantam Books, 1975.

————. *In Our Time: Memoir of a Revolution.* New York: Delta, 2000.

————. "Making Female Bodies the Battlefield," *Newsweek,* 4 January 1993, p. 37.

Buck, Pearl. *The Good Earth.* New York: Pocket Books, 1975.

————. *The Mother.* New York: HarperCollins, 1971.

Burney, Fanny. *Camilla.* Oxford: Oxford University Press, 1983.

————. *Evelina; or, A Young Lady's Entrance into the World.* New York: Modern Library, 2001.

————. *The Witlings and the Woman-Hater.* New York: Broadview, 2002.

Burrill, Mary Powell. *They That Sit in Darkness.* In *Zora Neale Hurston, Eulalie Spence, Marita Bonner, and Others: The Prize Plays and Other One-Acts Published in Periodicals.* Edited by Jennifer Burton and Henry Louis Gates Jr. New York: G. K. Hall, 1996.

Campbell, Maria. *Halfbreed.* Lincoln: University of Nebraska Press, 1973.

Cardinal, Marie. *The Past Encroached.* New York: French & European Publications, 1984.

————. *The Words to Say It.* Cambridge: Van Vactor & Goodheart, 1983.

Carson, Anne. *Autobiography of Red.* New York: Vintage, 1999.

————. *The Beauty of the Husband: A Fictional Essay in 29 Tangos.* New York: Vintage, 2002.

————. *Eros the Bittersweet.* Normal, Ill.: Dalkey Archive, 1998.

————. *Glass, Irony and God.* New York: New Directions, 1995.

————. *If Not, Winter: Fragments of Sappho.* New York: Vintage, 2003.

Carson, Rachel. *Silent Spring.* Boston: Houghton Mifflin, 1962.

Carter, Angela. *The Bloody Chamber and Other Stories.* London: Penguin, 1987.

————. *Burning Your Boats: Collected Stories.* London: Penguin, 1997.

————. *Nights at the Circus.* London: Penguin, 1986.

————. *The Passion of New Eve.* New York: Gollancz, 1977.

————. *The Sadeian Woman and the Ideology of Pornography.* New York: Pantheon, 1979.

Castellanos, Rosario. *The Book of Lamentations.* New York: Marsilio, 1996.

————. *The Nine Guardians.* London: Readers International, 1993.

————. *A Rosario Castellanos Reader.* Austin: University of Texas Press, 1988.

Cather, Willa. *My Ántonia.* Boston: Houghton Mifflin, 1977.

————. *O Pioneers!* New York: New American Library, 1989.

————. *Willa Cather: Later Novels.* New York: Library of America, 1990.

————. *Willa Cather's Collected Short fiction, 1892–1912.* Lincoln: University of Nebraska Press, 1970.

Catt, Carrie Chapman, and Nettie Rogers Shuler. *Woman Suffrage and Politics: The Inner Story of the Suffrage Movement.* New York: William S. Hein, 2004.

Chaucer, Geoffrey. *The Works of Geoffrey Chaucer.* Boston: Houghton Mifflin, 1961.

Chesnut, Mary Boykin. *Mary Chesnut's Civil War.* New Haven, Conn.: Yale University Press, 1981.

————. *The Private Mary Chesnut: The Unpublished Civil War Diaries.* Oxford: Oxford University Press, 1984.

Chevalier, Tracy. *The Girl with a Pearl Earring.* New York: Plume Books, 2001.

Child, Lydia Maria. *An Appeal in Favor of That Class of Americans Called Africans.* Boston: Allen & Ticknor, 1833.

————. *Authentic Anecdotes of American Slavery.* Newburyport, Mass.: Charles Whipple, 1838.

————. *The Frugal Housewife: Dedicted to Those Who Are Not Ashamed of Economy.* Boston: Applewood, 1989.

————. *The Liberty Bell.* Boston: Anti-Slavery Fair, 1843.

————. *A Lydia Child Reader.* Durham, N.C.: Duke University Press, 1997.

————. *The Mother's Book.* Boston: Applewood, 1989.

Chin, Marilyn. *The Phoenix Gone, the Terrace Empty.* New York: Milkweed Editions, 1994.

————. *Rhapsody in Plain Yellow.* New York: W. W. Norton, 2002.

Chopin, Kate. *The Awakening and Selected Stories.* New York: Penguin, 1983.

Christine de Pizan. *Christine's Vision.* New York: Garland, 1993.

————. *The Selected Writings of Christine de Pizan.* New York: W. W. Norton, 1997.

Churchill, Caryl. *Cloud Nine.* New York: Theatre Communications Group, 1995.

————. *Far Away.* New York: Theatre Communications Group, 2001.

————. *Top Girls.* London: Methuen, 1982.

Cisneros, Sandra. *Caramelo.* New York: Vintage, 2003.

————. *The House on Mango Street.* Houston: Arte Público, 1983.

————. *Loose Woman.* New York: Vintage, 1995.

————. *Woman Hollering Creek and Other Stories.* New York: Random House, 1991.

Cixous, Hélène. *The Book of Promethea*. Lincoln: University of Nebraska Press, 1991.

———. *Coming to Writing and Other Essays*. Cambridge, Mass.: Harvard University Press, 1992.

———. *The Hélène Cixous Reader*. New York: Routledge, 1994.

———. "We Who Are Free, Are We Truly Free?" *Cultural Critique* 24 (Spring 1993): 201–219.

———, and Catherine Clément. *The Newly Born Woman*. Minneapolis: University of Minnesota Press, 1986.

Clifton, Lucille. *Blessing the Boats: New and Selected Poems, 1988–2000*. New York: Boa, 2000.

———. *The Book of Light*. Townsend, Wash.: Copper Canyon Press, 1993.

———. *Good Woman: Poems and a Memoir, 1969–1980*. New York: Boa, 1989.

Colette. *The Colette Omnibus*. Garden City, N.Y.: Nelson Doubleday, 1974.

———. *Gigi, Julie de Corneilha, and Chance Acquaintances: Three Short Novels*. New York: Farrar, Straus & Giroux, 1952.

Condé, Maryse. *I, Tituba, Black Witch of Salem*. New York: Ballantine, 1994.

———. *Ségu*. New York: Penguin, 1998.

———. *Windward Heights*. New York: Soho, 1998.

Cooper, Anna Julia Haywood. *Slavery and the French Revolutionists*. Lewiston, N.Y.: Edwin Mellen Press, 1988.

———. *A Voice from the South*. Xenia, Ohio: Aldine Printing House, 1892.

———. *The Voice of Anna Julia Cooper*. Lanham, Md.: Rowman & Littlefield, 1998.

Corbett, Elizabeth T. "My Visit to Utopia." In *Daring to Dream*. Boston: Pandora Press, 1984.

Corelli, Maria. *The Murder of Delicia*. Whitefish, Mont.: Kessinger, 1997.

Corthron, Kia. *Breath, Boom*. New York: Dramatists Play Service, 2002.

———. *Seeking the Genesis*. New York: Dramatists Play Service, 2002.

Cross, Donna. *Pope Joan*. New York: Ballantine, 1997.

———, and William Woolfolk. *Daddy's Little Girl: The Unspoken Bargain between Fathers and Their Daughters*. Englewood Cliffs, N.J.: Prentice-Hall, 1982.

Cruz, Sor Juana Inés de la. *Poems, Protest and a Dream*. London: Penguin, 1997.

Culleton, Beatrice. *In Search of April Raintree*. Winnipeg, Canada: Pemmican, 1983.

Cunha, Helena Parente. *Woman between Mirrors*. Austin: University of Texas Press, 1989.

Cushman, Karen. *Catherine, Called Birdy*. New York: HarperTrophy, 1994.

———. *The Midwife's Apprentice*. New York: HarperTrophy, 1995.

Danticat, Edwidge. *Breath, Eyes, Memory*. New York: Soho Press, 1994.

———. *The Farming of Bones*. New York: Soho Press, 1999.

Davis, Angela Y. *The Angela Y. Davis Reader*. Malden, Mass.: Blackwell, 1998.

———. *Blues Legacy and Black Feminism: Gertrude "Ma" Rainey, Bessie Smith, and Billie Holiday*. New York: Vintage, 1999.

———. "Women in Prison," *Essence* 31, no. 5 (September 2000): 150–151.

———. *Women, Race and Class*. New York: Random House, 1981.

Davis, Rebecca Harding. *Life in the Iron Mills*. Houndmills, England: Palgrave Macmillan, 1997.

de Cleyre, Voltairine. *The Selected Works of Voltairine de Cleyre, Pioneer of Women's Liberation*. New York: Revisionist Press, 1972.

Delany, Sarah L. *On My Own at 107: Reflections on Life without Bessie*. San Francisco: HarperSanFrancisco, 1998.

———. *Having Our Say: The Delany Sisters' First 100 Years*. New York: Dell, 1993.

———, and A. Elizabeth Delany. *The Delany Sisters' Book of Everyday Wisdom*. New York: Kodansha America, 1996.

Deloria, Ella. *Waterlily*. Lincoln: University of Nebraska Press, 1988.

Desai, Anita. *Diamond Dust: Stories*. New York: Mariner, 2000.

———. *Fasting, Feasting*. New York: Mariner, 2000.

———. *Journey to Ithaca*. New York: Penguin, 1996.

———. *Voices in the City*. New Delhi: Orient Paperbacks, 1965.

DeSalvo, Louise. *Adultery*. Boston: Beacon, 2000.

———. *Vertigo: A Memoir*. New York: Plume, 1997.

———. *Writing As a Way of Healing: How Telling Our Stories Transforms Our Lives*. Boston: Beacon, 2000.

Diamant, Anita. *Good Harbor*. New York: Scribner, 2002.

———. *Pitching My Tent: On Marriage, Motherhood, and Other Leaps of Faith*. New York: Scribner, 2003.

———. *The Red Tent*. New York: Picador, 1998.

Dickinson, Emily. *The Complete Poems of Emily Dickinson*. Boston: Little, Brown, 1957.

Dinesen, Isak. *Babette's Feast and Other Anecdotes of Destiny*. New York: Vintage, 1986.

———. *On Modern Marriage and Other Observations*. New York: St. Martin's, 1986.

———. *Winter's Tales*. New York: Vintage Books, 1970.

Di Prima, Diane. *Loba*. New York: Penguin, 1998.

———. *Memoirs of a Beatnik*. New York: Penguin, 1998.

————. *Recollections of My Life as a Woman: The New York Years.* New York: Viking, 2001.

Doolittle, Hilda. *Helen in Egypt.* New York: New Directions, 1974.

Douglass, Frederick. "An Appeal to Congress for Impartial Suffrage," *Atlantic Monthly,* January–June 1867, pp. 112–117.

————. *Frederick Douglass on Women's Rights.* Westport, Conn.: Greenwood, 1976.

————. *The Frederick Douglass Papers.* Edited by John W. Blassingame. New Haven. Conn.: Yale University Press, 1979.

————. "Speech," *Boston Cultivator,* April 15, 1865.

————. *Speech at the Unveiling of the Freedman's Monument.* Washington, D.C.: Gibson Brothers Printers, 1876.

Dove, Rita. *The Darker Face of the Earth.* Ashland, Ore.: Story Line Press, 1994.

————. *Mother Love.* New York: W. W. Norton, 1995.

————. *On the Bus with Rosa Parks.* New York: W. W. Norton, 1999.

————. *Selected Poems.* New York: Vintage, 1993.

————. *Through the Ivory Gate.* New York: Pantheon, 1992.

————. *The Yellow House on the Corner.* Pittsburgh: Carnegie Mellon University Press, 1980.

Drabble, Margaret. *The Red Queen.* New York: Viking, 2004.

————. *The Seven Sisters.* Orlando, Fla.: HarcourtBooks, 2002.

————. *The Witch of Exmoor.* Orlando, Fla.: Harcourt Brace, 1996.

du Maurier, Daphne. *Rebecca.* New York: Avon Books, 1971.

————. *The Rebecca Notebook and Other Memories.* Garden City, N.Y.: Doubleday, 1980.

Dunbar-Nelson, Alice. "The Author's Evening at Home," *Smart Set,* September 1900, pp. 105–106.

————. "Mine Eyes Have Seen," *Crisis,* April 1919, pp. 271–275.

————. *The Works of Alice Dunbar-Nelson.* Oxford: Oxford University Press, 1994.

Duras, Marguerite. *Hiroshima, Mon Amour.* New York: Grove, 1987.

————. *The Lover.* New York: Pantheon, 1998.

————. *The North China Lover.* New York: New Press, 1992.

Dworkin, Andrea. *Heartbreak: The Political Memoir of a Feminist Militant.* New York: Basic Books, 2002.

————. *Letters from a War Zone.* Brooklyn, N.Y.: Lawrence Hill Books, 1993.

————. *Mercy: A Novel.* New York: Four Walls Eight Windows, 1992.

————. *Woman Hating.* New York: Dutton, 1974.

Edgeworth, Maria. *Castle Rackrent and Ennui.* New York: Penguin, 1992.

Edson, Margaret. *Wit.* New York: Faber & Faber, 1999.

Ehrenreich, Barbara. *Nickel and Dimed: On (Not) Getting By in America.* New York: Owl Books, 2002.

————. *Witches, Midwives and Nurses: A History of Women Healers.* New York: Feminist Press, 1973.

————, and Deidre English. *For Her Own Good: 150 Years of the Experts' Advice to Women.* Garden City, N.Y.: Anchor Books, 1978.

Eliot, George. *Daniel Deronda.* New York: Penguin, 1996.

————. *Middlemarch.* New York: Bantam, 1985.

————. *Silas Marner.* New York: New American Library, 1960.

El Saadawi, Nawal. *The Fall of the Imam.* London: Saqi Books, 2002.

————. *God Dies by the Nile.* London: Zed Books, 1985.

————. *The Hidden Face of Eve: Women in the Arab World.* London: Zed Books, 1980.

————. *Memoirs from the Women's Prison.* Berkeley: University of California Press, 1994.

————. "The Rite and the Right," *Feminist Voices,* 30 September 1996, p. 1.

————. *Walking Through Fire: A Life of Nawal El Saadawi.* London: Zed Books, 2002.

————. *Woman at Point Zero.* London: Zed Books, 1983.

Emecheta, Buchi. *The Joys of Motherhood.* New York: George Braziller, 1980.

————. *Second-Class Citizen.* New York: George Braziller, 1983.

Engel, Marian. *Bear.* New York: Atheneum, 1976.

Ensler, Eve. *Necessary Targets: A Story of Women and War.* New York: Villard, 2001.

————. *The Vagina Monologues.* New York: Villard, 1998.

Erdrich, Louise. *The Blue Jay's Dance.* New York: Perennial, 1996.

————. *The Last Report on the Miracles at Little No Horse.* New York: HarperCollins, 2001.

————. *Tales of Burning Love.* New York: Perennial, 1997.

————. *Tracks.* New York: Harper and Row, 1988.

Esquivel, Laura. *Like Water for Chocolate.* New York: Bantam, 1992.

Estés, Clarissa Pinkola. *The Faithful Gardener: A Wise Tale about That Which Can Never Die.* San Francisco: HarperCollins, 1995.

————. "The Rose Warrior," *National Catholic Reporter,* 17 October 2003, p. 16.

————. *Women Who Run with the Wolves: Myths and Stories about the Wild Woman Archetype.* New York: Ballantine, 1997.

Evans, Mari. *Black Women Writers, 1950–1980: A Critical Evaluation.* New York: Anchor Books, 1984.

———. *I Am a Black Woman.* New York: Writers and Readers, 1993.

Fallaci, Oriana. *The Rage and the Pride.* New York: Rizzoli, 2002.

Faludi, Susan. *Backlash: The Undeclared War against American Women.* New York: Anchor Books, 1992.

———. "Don't Get the Wrong Message," *Newsweek,* 8 January 2001, p. 56.

———. "The Moms' Secret Weapon," *Newsweek,* 15 May 2000, p. 30.

———. *Stiffed: The Betrayal of the American Male.* New York: Perennial, 2000.

Fauset, Jessie Redmon. *The Chinaberry Tree and Selected Writings.* Boston: Northeastern University Press, 1995.

———. *Plum Bun.* Boston: Beacon, 1990.

———. *There Is Confusion.* Boston: Northeastern University Press, 1989.

Ferber, Edna. *Cimarron.* New York: Amereon Limited, 1998.

———. *Giant.* New York: Perennial Classics, 2000.

———. *Show Boat.* New York: Lightyear Press, 1992.

———. *So Big.* New York: Perennial Classics, 2000.

Fern, Fanny. *Ruth Hall: A Domestic Tale of the Present Time.* New York: Penguin, 1997.

Finch, Anne. *Anne Finch, Countess of Winchilsea: Selected Poems.* New York: Routledge, 2003.

Firestone, Shulamith. *The Dialectics of Sex.* New York: Women's Press, 1979.

Fisher, Dorothy Canfield. *The Bedquilt and Other Stories.* Columbia: University of Missouri Press, 1997.

———. *Understood Betsy.* New York: Henry Holt, 1999.

Forché, Carolyn. *Against Forgetting: Twentieth Century Poetry of Witness.* New York: W. W. Norton, 1993.

———. *The Country between Us.* New York: Perennial, 1982.

———. *Gathering the Tribes.* New Haven, Conn.: Yale University Press, 1976.

Ford, Mary H. "A Feminine Iconoclast." In *Daring to Dream.* Boston: Pandora, 1984.

Foster, Hannah Webster. *The Coquette.* Oxford: Oxford University Press, 1987.

Frame, Janet. *Janet Frame: An Autobiography.* New York: George Braziller, 1991.

———. *Owls Do Cry.* New York: George Braziller, 1960.

Freeman, Mary Wilkins. *The New England Nun and Other Stories.* New York: Penguin, 2000.

French, Marilyn. *A Season in Hell: A Memoir.* New York: Ballantine, 2000.

———. *The War against Women.* New York: Ballantine, 1993.

———. *The Women's Room.* New York: Ballantine, 1988.

Friedan, Betty. *The Feminine Mystique.* New York: W. W. Norton, 2001.

———. *The Fountain of Age.* New York: Simon & Schuster, 1994.

Fuller, Margaret. *My Heart Is a Large Kingdom: Selected Letters of Margaret Fuller.* Ithaca, N.Y.: Cornell University Press, 2001.

———. *Summer on the Lakes in 1843.* Urbana: University of Illinois Press, 1991.

———. *Woman in the Nineteenth Century.* New York: Norton, 1971.

Gage, Matilda Joslyn. *Woman, Church and State.* Watertown, Mass.: Persephone, 1980.

Gaite, Carmen Martín. *The Back Room.* San Francisco: City Lights Books, 2000.

Gale, Zona. *Miss Lulu Bett: Birth.* Oregon, Wis.: Badger Books, 1994.

García, Cristina. *Dreaming in Cuban.* New York: Knopf, 1992.

Gaskell, Elizabeth. *Cranford.* Oxford: Oxford University Press, 1998.

———. *Mary Barton, a Tale of Manchester.* Oxford: Oxford University Press, 1987.

———. *Ruth.* London: Penguin, 1998.

———. *Wives and Daughters.* London: Penguin, 2001.

Gibbons, Kaye. *Charms for the Easy Life.* New York: Avon, 1994.

———. *Divining Women.* New York: Grosset & Dunlap, 2004.

———. *Ellen Foster.* New York: Vintage Books, 1990.

Gilbert, Sandra M., and Susan Gubar. *The Madwoman in the Attic.* 2nd ed. New Haven, Conn.: Yale University Press, 2000.

———. *No Man's Land: Sexchanges: The Place of the Woman Writer in the Twentieth Century: The War of the Words.* New Haven, Conn.: Yale University Press, 1989.

———, and Diana O'Hehir, eds. *Mothersongs: Poems for, by, and about Mothers.* New York: W. W. Norton, 1995.

Gilchrist, Ellen. *Falling through Space.* Boston: Little, Brown, 1987.

———. *Flights of Angels.* Boston: Little, Brown, 1998.

———. *Rhoda: A Life in Stories.* New York: Back Bay Books, 1995.

Giles, Janice Holt. *Hannah Fowler.* Boston: Houghton Mifflin, 1956.

Gilman, Charlotte Perkins. *Herland and Selected Stories.* New York: Signet Classics, 1992.

———. *The Living of Charlotte Perkins Gilman: An Autobiography.* Madison: University of Wisconsin Press, 1991.

———. *The Man-Made World; or, Our Androcentric Culture.* Rochester, N.Y.: Source Book Press, 1970.

———. *With Her in Ourland.* Westport, Conn.: Praeger, 1997.

———. *Women and Economics.* New York: Dover, 1998.

———. *The Yellow Wallpaper and Other Writings.* New York: Bantam, 1989.

Giovanni, Nikki. "Light the Candles," *Essence* 26, no. 1 (May 1995): 109–111.

———. *Racism 101.* New York: HarperCollins, 1994.

Glasgow, Ellen. *The Battle-Ground.* Garden City, N.Y.: Doubleday, 1929.

———. *The Sheltered Life.* Charlottesville: University Press of Virginia, 1994.

———. *A Woman Within.* New York: Hill & Wang, 1980.

Glaspell, Susan. *Every Week.* New York: Crowell, 1918.

———. *Plays by Susan Glaspell.* New Haven, Conn.: Cambridge University Press, 1987.

Glück, Louise. *First Four Books of Poems.* New York: Ecco, 1990.

———. *The Wild Iris.* New York: Ecco, 1994.

Goldman, Emma. *Anarchism and Other Essays.* New York: Dover, 1969.

———. *Living My Life.* New York: Dover, 1930.

Gómez de Avellaneda, Gertrudis. *Sab and Autobiography.* Austin: University of Texas Press, 1993.

Goodman, Ellen. *At Large.* New York: Fawcett Crest, 1981.

———. "The Life of a Political Wife: Who Wants It?" *Charlotte Observer,* 25 July 2004, p. 3P.

———. "Women Still Fight for Rights," *Charlotte Observer,* 26 June 2004, p. A.

Gordimer, Nadine. *Burger's Daughter.* London: Penguin, 1980.

———. *My Son's Story.* London: Penguin, 1990.

Gordon, Caroline. *The Collected Stories of Caroline Gordon.* Nashville, Tenn.: J. S. Sanders, 2000.

———. *The Women on the Porch.* Nashville, Tenn.: J. S. Sanders, 2000.

Grafton, Sue. *"A" Is for Alibi.* New York: Bantam, 1987.

———. *"D" Is for Deadbeat.* New York: Bantam, 1988.

Grahn, Judy. *The Work of a Common Woman.* Freedom, Calif.: Crossing Press, 1978.

Grand, Sarah. *The Beth Book.* New York: Dial Press, 1980.

Greer, Germaine. *The Female Eunuch.* New York: Farrar, Straus & Giroux, 2002.

———. *The Madwoman's Underclothes: Essays and Occasional Writings.* London: Picador, 1986.

———. *The Obstacle Race: The Fortunes of Women Painters and Their Works.* New York: Farrar, Straus & Giroux, 1982.

———. *The Whole Woman.* New York: Anchor, 2000.

Griffith, Mary. *Three Hundred Years Hence.* Boston: Gregg Press, 1975.

Grimké, Angelina Emily Weld. *Rachel: A Play in Three Acts.* Boston: Cornhill, 1920.

———. *Selected Works of Angelina Weld Grimké.* New York: Oxford University Press, 1991.

Haddix, Margaret Peterson. *Just Ella.* New York: Aladdin, 2001.

Hagedorn, Jessica. *Dogeaters.* New York: Penguin, 1991.

———. *The Gangster of Love.* New York: Penguin, 1997.

Hailey, Elizabeth Forsythe. *A Woman of Independent Means.* New York: Penguin, 1998.

Hale, Sarah Josepha. "Editor's Table." *Godey's Lady's Book,* July 1857, p. 82.

———. *Liberia; or, Mr. Peyton's Experiments.* New York: Harper & Brothers, 1853.

Hall, Radclyffe. *The Well of Loneliness.* New York: Pocket Books, 1950.

———. *Your John: The Love Letters of Radclyffe Hall.* Albany: New York University Press, 1997.

Hansberry, Lorraine. *A Raisin in the Sun.* New York: Penguin, 1988.

———. *To Be Young, Gifted, and Black.* New York: Vintage, 1995.

Hardwick, Elizabeth. *Herman Melville.* New York: Penguin, 2000.

———. *Seduction and Betrayal.* New York: Vintage, 1975.

Harjo, Joy. *In Mad Love and War.* Middletown, Conn.: Wesleyan University Press, 1990.

———. *She Had Some Horses.* New York: Thunder's Mouth, 1983.

———. *The Woman Who Fell from the Sky.* New York: W. W. Norton, 1994.

———, and Stephen Strom. *Secrets from the Center of the World.* Tucson: University of Arizona Press, 1989.

Harper, Frances. *Iola Leroy or Shadows Uplifted.* Boston: Beacon, 1999.

Harris, Helen Webb. *Genifrede.* In *Negro History in Thirteen Plays.* Edited by Willis Richardson and May Miller. Washington, D.C.: Associated Publishers, 1935.

Hawthorne, Nathaniel. *The Complete Novels and Selected Tales of Nathaniel Hawthorne.* New York: Modern Library, 1937.

Head, Bessie. *The Collector of Treasures and Other Botswana Village Tales.* London: Heinemann, 1977.

———. *Maru.* London: Heinemann, 1997.

———. *A Woman Alone.* London: Heinemann, 1990.

Hélisenne de Crenne. *A Renaissance Woman: Hélisenne's Personal and Invective Letters.* Syracuse, N.Y.: Syracuse University Press, 1986.

———. *The Torments of Love.* Minneapolis: University of Minnesota Press, 1996.

Hellman, Lillian. *The Collected Plays of Lillian Hellman.* Boston: Little, Brown, 1971.

———. *Pentimento.* Boston: Little, Brown, 1973.

———. *Scoundrel Time.* New York: Bantam, 1976.

———. *An Unfinished Woman.* Boston: Little, Brown, 1969.

Henley, Beth. *Crimes of the Heart.* New York: Dramatists Play Service, 1981.

———. *The Miss Firecracker Contest.* New York: Dramatists Play Service, 1985.

Herbst, Josephine. *Pity Is Not Enough.* Urbana: University of Illinois Press, 1998.

———. *The Starched Blue Sky of Spain and Other Memoirs.* Boston: Northeastern University Press, 1999.

Hogan, Linda. *Dwellings: A Spiritual History of the Living World.* New York: Touchstone, 1996.

———. *Mean Spirit.* New York: Ivy Books, 1991.

———. *Power.* New York: W. W. Norton, 1999.

———. *Solar Storms.* New York: Scribner, 1997.

———. *The Woman Who Watches Over the World: A Native Memoir.* New York: W. W. Norton, 2002.

———, and Brenda Peterson, eds. *The Sweet Breathing of Plants: Women Writing on the Green World.* New York: Farrar, Straus & Giroux, 2002.

Holm, Jennifer. *Boston Jane: The Claim.* New York: HarperCollins, 2004.

———. *Boston Jane: Wilderness Days.* New York: HarperCollins, 2002.

———. *Our Only Amelia May.* New York: HarperCollins, 1999.

hooks, bell. *Bone Black: Memories of Girlhood.* New York: Henry Holt, 1996.

———. *Feminist Theory: From Margin to Center.* Cambridge, Mass.: South End Press, 2000.

———. *Killing Rage-Ending Racism.* New York: Henry Holt, 1995.

———. *Teaching to Transgress.* New York: Routledge, 1994.

Houston, Jeanne Wakatsuki. *The Legend of Fire Horse Woman.* New York: Kensington, 2003.

———, and James Houston. *Farewell to Manzanar.* New York: Bantam, 1973.

Hurst, Fannie. *Anatomy of Me.* New York: Arno Press, 1958.

———. *Gaslight Sonatas.* New York: Harper's, 1918.

———. *Imitation of Life.* Durham, N.C.: Duke University Press, 2004.

———. *Lummox.* London: Howard Baker, 1970.

Hurston, Zora Neale. "Color Struck." In *Black Female Playwrights: An Anthology of Plays Before 1950.* Edited by Kathy A. Perkins. Bloomington: Indiana University Press, 1989.

———. *The Complete Stories.* New York: HarperCollins, 1995.

———. *Dust Tracks on a Road.* New York: Harper Perennial, 1996.

———. *Jonah's Gourd Vine.* New York: Harper Perennial, 1990.

———. *Mules and Men.* New York: Harper Perennial, 1990.

———. *Their Eyes Were Watching God.* New York: Harper Perennial, 1990.

Ibsen, Henrik. *A Doll's House.* In *Four Great Plays by Ibsen.* New York: Bantam, 1984.

Irigaray, Luce. *This Sex Which Is Not One.* Ithaca, N.Y.: Cornell University Press, 1985.

Jackson, Helen Hunt. *A Century of Dishonor.* New York: Harper Torchbook, 1965.

———. *Ramona: A Story.* New York: Signet Classics, 2002.

Jackson, Shirley. *The Haunting of Hill House.* New York: Penguin, 1984.

———. *Just an Ordinary Day: The Uncollected Stories of Shirley Jackson.* New York: Bantam, 1997.

———. *Life among the Savages.* New York: Penguin, 1997.

———. *The Lottery; or, The Adventures of James Harris.* New York: Farrar, Straus, & Giroux, 1949.

———. *We Have Always Lived in the Castle.* New York: Penguin, 1984.

Jacobs, Harriet A. *Incidents in the Life of a Slave Girl: Written by Herself.* New York: Harvest Books, 1983.

Janeway, Elizabeth. *Improper Behavior: When and How Misconduct Can Be Healthy for Society.* New York: William Morrow, 1987.

Jelinek, Elfriede. *Lust.* London: Serpent's Tale, 1993.

———. *The Piano Teacher.* London: Serpent's Tale, 1989.

———. *Wonderful, Wonderful Times.* London: Serpent's Tale, 1990.

Jen, Gish. *Typical American.* New York: Plume, 1992.

———. *Who's Irish.* New York: Vintage, 2000.

Jewett, Sarah Orne. *A Country Doctor.* New York: Bantam, 1999.

———. "Tom's Husband," *Atlantic Monthly* 49, no. 292 (February 1882): 205–213.

Jhabvala, Ruth Prawer. *Heat and Dust.* New York: Touchstone, 1976.

———. *My Nine Lives: Chapters of a Possible Past.* Washington, D.C.: Shoemaker & Hoard, 2004.

Johnson, Georgia Douglas. *Blue Blood.* In *Wines in the Wilderness: Plays by African American Women from the Harlem Renaissance to the Present.* Edited by Elizabeth Brown-Guillory. New York: Greenwood, 1990.

———. *Blue-Eyed Black Boy.* In *Wines in the Wilderness: Plays by African American Women from the Harlem*

Renaissance to the Present. Edited by Elizabeth Brown-Guillory. New York: Greenwood, 1990.

———. *Frederick Douglass.* In *Negro History in Thirteen Plays.* Edited by May Miller and Willis Richardson. Washington, D.C.: Associated Publishers, 1935.

———. *Plumes.* In *Plays by American Women, 1900–1930.* Edited by Judith E. Barlow. New York: Applause, 2001.

———. *Safe.* In *Wines in the Wilderness: Plays by African American Women from the Harlem Renaissance to the Present.* Edited by Elizabeth Brown-Guillory. New York: Greenwood, 1990.

———. *The Selected Works of Georgia Douglas Johnson.* New York: G. K. Hall, 1997.

———. "A Sunday Morning in the South." In *Black Theatre, U. S. A.: Plays By African Americans: The Early Period, 1847–1938.* Edited by James V. Hatch and Ted Shine. New York: Free Press, 1996.

———. "William and Ellen Craft." In *Negro History in Thirteen Plays.* Edited by May Miller and Willis Richardson. Washington, D.C.: Associated Publishers, 1935.

Johnson, Pauline. *Flint and Feathers.* Toronto: Musson Books, 1913.

Jolley, Elizabeth. *Miss Peabody's Inheritance.* New York: Penguin, 1984.

Jones, Alice Ilgenfritz, and Ella Merchant. *Unveiling a Parallel: A Romance* in *Daring to Dream.* Boston: Pandora, 1984.

Jones, Gayl. *Corregidora.* New York: Random House, 1975.

———. *Eva's Man.* Boston: Beacon, 1987.

———. *The Healing.* Boston: Beacon, 1998.

———. *Song for Anninho.* Boston: Beacon, 1999.

Jong, Erica. *Fear of Flying.* New York: Signet, 2003.

———. "Introduction." In *The Colette Omnibus.* Garden City, N.Y.: Nelson Doubleday, 1974.

———. *What Do Women Want?* New York: HarperCollins, 1998.

———. *Witches.* New York: Harry N. Abrams, 1999.

Jordan, June. "A New Politics of Sexuality," *Progressive* 55, no. 7 (July 1991): 12.

———. *Soldier: A Poet's Childhood.* New York: BasicCivitas Books, 2001.

———. *Some of Us Did Not Die: New and Selected Essays.* New York: BasicCivitas Books, 2003.

Kaye/Kantrowitz, Melanie. "How Did 'Correct' Become a Dirty Word? Theory and Practice for a Social Justice," *Transformations,* 30 September 1999, p. 42.

———. "Liberation Studies Now," *Women's Review of Books* 16, no. 5 (February 1999): 15–16.

———, and Esther F. Hyneman, eds. *The Tribe of Dina: A Jewish Women's Anthology.* Boston: Beacon, 1989.

Keller, Helen. *Light in My Darkness.* New York: Chrysalis, 2000.

———. *The Story of My Life.* New York: Bantam, 1991.

Kelley, Florence. *The Autobiography of Florence Kelley.* Chicago: Charles Kerr, 1986.

Kemble, Fanny. *Journal of a Residence on a Georgian Plantation in 1838–1839.* Athens: University of Georgia Press, 1984.

Kennedy, Adam P., and Adrienne Kennedy. *Sleep Deprivation Chamber.* New York: Theater Communications Group, 1996.

Kennedy, Adrienne. *Adrienne Kennedy in One Act.* Minneapolis: University of Minnesota Press, 1988.

———. *People Who Led to My Plays.* New York: Theatre Communications Group, 1996.

Khalifeh, Sahar. "My Life, Myself, and the World," *Aljadid* 8, no. 39 (Spring 2002): 1.

———. *Wild Thorns.* London: Al Saqi, 1984.

Kincaid, Jamaica. *Annie John.* New York: Farrar, Straus & Giroux, 1997.

———. *The Autobiography of My Mother.* New York: Plume, 1997.

———. *A Small Place.* New York: Farrar, Straus & Giroux, 2000.

King, Florence. *Confessions of a Failed Southern Lady.* New York: St. Martin's, 1990.

———. *Reflections in a Jaundiced Eye.* New York: St. Martin's, 1989.

———. *Southern Ladies and Gentlemen.* New York: St. Martin's, 1993.

Kingsolver, Barbara. "And Our Flag Was Still There," *San Francisco Chronicle,* September 25, 2001.

———. *Animal Dreams.* New York: HarperCollins, 1990.

———. *Another America: Otra America* (verse). Seattle: Seal Press, 1992.

———. *The Bean Trees.* New York: Harper & Row, 1988.

———. *High Tide in Tucson: Essays from Now or Never.* New York: HarperCollins, 1995.

———. *Holding the Line: Women in the Great Arizona Mine Strike of 1983.* Ithaca, N.Y.: Cornell University Press, 1989.

———. *Homeland and Other Stories.* New York: HarperCollins, 1989.

———. *I've Always Meant to Tell You: Letters to Our Mothers: An Anthology of Contemporary Women Writers.* New York: Pocket Star, 1997.

———. *Last Stand: America's Virgin Lands.* Washington, D.C.: National Geographic Society, 2002.

———. *Pigs in Heaven.* New York: HarperCollins, 1993.

———. *The Poisonwood Bible.* New York: HarperCollins, 1998.

———. *Prodigal Summer.* New York: HarperCollins, 2000.

———, and Stephen Hopp. *Small Wonder.* New York: HarperCollins, 2002.

Kingston, Maxine Hong. *China Men.* New York: Vintage, 1989.

———. *Woman Warrior.* New York: Vintage, 1989.

Kizer, Carolyn. *Calm, Cool and Collected: Poems 1960–2000.* Townsend, Wash.: Copper Canyon, 2002.

———. *Carrying Over: Poems from the Chinese, Urdu, Macedonian, Yiddish, and French-African.* Port Townsend, Wash.: Copper Canyon, 1989.

———. *Harping On.* Port Townsend, Wash.: Copper Canyon, 1996.

———. *The Nearness of You: Poems.* New York: Consortium, 1986.

Kogawa, Joy. *Obasan.* New York: Anchor, 1993.

———. *A Song of Lilith.* New York: Laurel Glen, 2001.

Kumin, Maxine. *Always Beginning.* Port Townsend, Wash.: Copper Canyon, 2000.

———. *The Long Marriage: Poems.* New York: W. W. Norton, 2001.

———. *Our Ground Time Here Will Be Brief.* New York: Viking, 1982.

———. *Selected Poems 1960–1990.* New York: W. W. Norton, 1998.

LaFollette, Suzanne. *Concerning Women.* New York: Arno, 1972.

Lake, Rosemary. *Once Upon a Time When the Princess Rescued the Prince.* Guerneville, Calif.: Dragon Tree Press, 2002.

Lamb, Caroline. *Glenarvon.* London: Everymans Library, 1995.

Lane, Mary E. Bradley. *Mizora: A Prophecy.* Syracuse, N.Y.: Syracuse University Press, 2000.

Larsen, Nella. *Passing.* New York: Collier, 1971.

———. *Quicksand.* New York: Collier, 1971.

Lazarus, Emma. *Emma Lazarus: Selected Poems and Other Writings.* Peterborough, Canada: Broadview, 2002.

Lee, Harper. *To Kill a Mockingbird.* New York: Warner, 1982.

Lee, Sophia. *The Recess; or, A Tale of Other Times.* Lexington: University Press of Kentucky, 2000.

Lee, Tanith. *Piratica, Being a Tale of a Singular Girl's Adventure upon the High Seas.* New York: E. P. Dutton, 2004.

———. "The Reason for Not Going to the Ball," *Fantasy and Science Fiction* (October–November 1996): 83–91.

———. *The Silver Metal Lover.* New York: Random House, 1985.

———. *White as Snow.* New York: Tor, 2001.

Le Guin, Ursula. *The Compass Rose.* New York: Bantam, 1983.

———. *Dancing at the Edge of the World: Thoughts on Words, Women and Places.* New York: Grove, 1997.

———. *The Left Hand of Darkness.* New York: Ace, 1969.

Lessing, Doris. *The Diaries of Jane Sommers.* New York: Vintage, 1984.

———. *The Golden Notebook.* London: Michael Joseph, 1972.

———. *The Marriages between Zones Three, Four, and Five.* London: Acacia, 1994.

Le Sueur, Meridel. *Ripening: Selected Work, 1927–1980.* New York: Feminist Press, 1982.

———. *Winter Prairie Woman.* Minneapolis: Minnesota Center for Book Arts, 1990.

Levertov, Denise. *The Stream and the Sapphire: Selected Poems on Religious Themes.* New York: New Directions, 1997.

Logan, Olive. *The Mimic World and Public Exhibitions; Their History, Their Morals, and Effects.* Philadelphia: New-World, 1871.

Loos, Anita. *Gentlemen Prefer Blondes.* New York: Liveright, 1998.

———. *No Mother to Guide Her.* New York: Prion, 2000.

Lord, Bette Bao. *Spring Moon: A Novel of China.* New York: HarperTorch, 1994.

Lorde, Audre. *The Cancer Journals.* New York: Aunt Lute, 1980.

———. *The Collected Poems of Audre Lorde.* New York: W. W. Norton, 2000.

———. *Sister Outsider: Essays and Speeches.* New York: Crossing, 1984.

———. *Zami: A New Spelling of My Name: A Biomythography.* New York: Crossing, 1983.

Lowry, Lois. *Number the Stars.* New York: Laurel-Leaf, 1998.

Loy, Mina. *The Lost Lunar Baedeker: Poems of Mina Loy.* New York: Farrar, Straus & Giroux, 1997.

Luce, Clare Boothe, ed. *Saints for Now.* Fort Collins, Colo.: Ignatius, 1993.

———. *Slam the Door Softly.* New York: Dramatists Play Service, 1971.

———. *The Women.* New York: Dramatists Play Service, 1998.

Lurie, Alison. *Foreign Affairs.* New York: Quill, 1995.

———. *The Oxford Book of Modern Fairy Tales.* Oxford: Oxford University Press, 2003.

MacLachlan, Patricia. *Sarah, Plain and Tall.* New York: HarperTrophy, 2004.

———. *Skylark.* New York: HarperTrophy, 1997.

Mahmoody, Betty. *Not without My Daughter.* New York: St. Martin's, 1993.

Mamonova, Tatyana, ed. *Women and Russia: Feminist Writings from the Soviet Union.* Boston: Beacon, 1984.

Mann, Emily. *Having Our Say: The Delany Sisters' First 100 Years*. New York: Dramatists Play Service, 1998.

———. *Testimonies: Four Plays*. New York: Theatre Communications Group, 1997.

———, trans. *The House of Bernarda Alba* by Federico García Lorca. New York: Dramatist's Play Service, 1998.

Mansfield, Katherine. *The Short Stories of Katherine Mansfield*. New York: Knopf, 1941.

Maracle, Lee. *Bobbi Lee, Indian Rebel: Struggles of a Native Canadian Woman*. Richmond, Canada: LSM, 1975.

Marie de France. *Fables*. Toronto: University of Toronto Press, 1994.

———. *The Lais of Marie de France*. London: Penguin, 1986.

Markham, Beryl. *The Splendid Outcast: Beryl Markham's African Stories*. San Francisco: North Point, 1987.

———. *West with the Night*. San Francisco: North Point, 1983.

Marshall, Paule. *Brown Girl, Brownstones*. New York: Feminist Press, 1981.

———. *Daughters*. New York: Athenaeum, 1991.

———. *Praisesong for the Widow*. New York: E. P. Dutton, 1983.

Martineau, Harriet. *Retrospect of Western Travel*. Armonk, N.Y.: M. E. Sharpe, 2000.

Mason, Bobbie Mason. *Clear Springs: A Family Story*. New York: Perennial, 2000.

———. *Feather Crowns*. New York: Perennial, 1994.

———. *The Girl Sleuth: A Feminist Guide to the Bobbsey Twins, Nancy Drew, and Their Sisters*. Athens: University of Georgia Press, 1975.

———. *Zigzagging down a Wild Trail: Stories*. New York: Modern Library, 2002.

McCaffrey, Anne. *Acorna's Quest*. New York: Eos, 1998.

———. *Acorna's Triumph*. New York: HarperTorch, 2004.

———. *Dragonsong*. New York: Aladdin, 2003.

McCarthy, Mary. *The Company She Keeps*. New York: Harvest, 2003.

———. *The Group*. New York: Harvest, 1991.

———. *How I Grew*. New York: Harvest, 2004.

———. *Memories of a Catholic Girlhood*. New York: Harvest, 1972.

McCauley, Robbie. *Sally's Rape*. In *Black Theatre, U.S.A.: Plays by African Americans: The Recent Period, 1935–Today*. Edited by James V. Hatch and Ted Shine. New York: Free Press, 1996.

McClung, Nellie. "Can a Woman Raise a Family and Have a Career?" *Maclean's*, 12 December 1995, p. 64.

———. *The Complete Autobiography: Clearing in the West and The Stream Runs Fast*. Peterborough, Canada: Broadview, 2003.

McCullers, Carson. *The Ballad of the Sad Café and Other Stories*. New York: Bantam, 1951.

———. *Collected Stories of Carson McCullers*. New York: Mariner, 1998.

———. *The Heart Is a Lonely Hunter*. New York: Bantam, 1967.

———. *The Member of the Wedding*. New York: Bantam, 1973.

McCunn, Ruthanne Lum. "Reclaiming Polly Bemis," *Frontiers: A Journal of Women's Studies* 24, no. 1 (2003): 76–100.

———. *Thousand Pieces of Gold*. San Francisco: Design Enterprises, 1981.

McMillan, Terry. *A Day Late and a Dollar Short*. New York: Signet, 2002.

———. *How Stella Got Her Groove Back*. New York: Signet, 1997.

———. *Mama*. New York: Pocket, 1994.

———. *Waiting to Exhale*. New York: Pocket, 1995.

McNulty, Faith. *The Burning Bed*. New York: Harcourt, Brace Jovanovich, 1980.

Menchú, Rigoberta. *I, Rigoberta Menchú, an Indian Woman in Guatemala*. London: Verso, 1987.

Mill, John Stuart. *Autobiography*. London: Penguin, 1990.

———. *On Liberty*. New York: Penguin, 1983.

———. *The Subjection of Women*. New York: Dover, 1997.

Millay, Edna St. Vincent. *Selected Poems*. New York: Perennial, 1999.

Miller, May. *Sojourner Truth*. In *Negro History in Thirteen Plays*. Edited by Willis Richardson and May Miller. Washington, D.C.: Associated Publishers, 1935.

Miller, Susan M. *My Left Breast*. In *The Breast: An Anthology*. Edited by Susan Thames and Marin Gazzanniga. New York: Global City Press, 1995.

Millett, Kate. *The Loony-Bin Trip*. Urbana: University of Illinois Press, 2000.

———. *Sexual Politics*. Urbana: University of Illinois Press, 2000.

Mistral, Gabriela. *Poemas de las Madres: The Mothers' Poems*. Spokane: Eastern Washington University Press, 1996.

———. *Selected Poems of Gabriela Mistral*. Albuquerque: University of New Mexico Press, 2003.

Mitchell, Margaret. *Gone with the Wind*. New York: Time Warner, 1964.

Molloy, Sylvia. *Certificate of Absence*. Austin: University of Texas Press, 1989.

Moore, Marianne. *The Complete Poems of Marianne Moore*. New York: Viking, 1981.

———. *The Complete Prose of Marianne Moore*. New York: Viking, 1986.

Moraga, Cherríe. *Heroes and Saints and Other Plays.* Albuquerque: University of New Mexico Press, 2001.

———. *The Last Generation: Prose and Poetry.* Boston: South End, 1993.

———. *Waiting in the Wings.* Ann Arbor, Mich.: Firebrand, 1997.

———, and Gloria Anzaldúa, eds. *This Bridge Called My Back: Writings by Radical Women of Color.* New York: Kitchen Table / Women of Color Press, 1981.

Morejón, Nancy. *Black Woman and Other Poems.* London: Mango, 2004.

———. "Persona," *Black Renaissance* 3, no. 3 (Summer–Fall 2001–2002), 171–172.

Morgan, Robin. *The Anatomy of Freedom: Feminism, Physics, and Global Politics.* New York: Anchor, 1982.

———. *The Demon Lover: The Roots of Terrorism.* New York: Washington Square, 2001.

———. *A Hot January: Poems 1996–1999.* New York: W. W. Norton, 2001.

———. *Saturday's Child: A Memoir.* New York: W. W. Norton, 2000.

———. *Sisterhood Is Forever: The Women's Anthology for a New Millennium.* New York: Washington Square, 2003.

———. *Upstairs in the Garden: Poems Selected Old and New, 1968–1988.* New York: W. W. Norton, 1991.

Morrison, Toni. *Beloved.* New York: Plume, 1987.

———. *The Bluest Eye.* New York: Plume, 1993.

———. *Song of Solomon.* New York: Plume, 1987.

Mott, Lucretia. *Selected Letters of Lucretia Coffin Mott.* Chicago: University of Illinois Press, 2002.

Mourning Dove. *Cogewea, The Half-Blood: A Depiction of the Great Montana Cattle Range.* Lincoln: University of Nebraska Press, 1981.

———. *Mourning Dove: A Salishan Autobiography.* Lincoln: University of Nebraska Press, 1990.

Mukherjee, Bharati. *Desirable Daughters.* New York: Hyperion, 2003.

———. *Leave It to Me.* New York: Ballantine, 1998.

Munro, Alice. *Hateship, Friendship, Courtship, Loveship, Marriage: Stories.* New York: Vintage, 2002.

Murasaki Shikibu. *The Diary of Lady Murasaki.* New York: Penguin, 1999.

———. *The Tale of Genji.* New York: Penguin, 2002.

Murray, Judith Sargent. *The Gleaner.* Schenectady, N.Y.: Union College Press, 1992.

———. *Selected Writings of Judith Sargent Murray.* Oxford: Oxford University Press, 1995.

———. *The Traveller Returned.* In *Plays by Early American Women, 1775–1850.* Edited by Amelia Kritzer. Ann Arbor: University of Michigan Press, 1995.

Murray, Yxta Maya, "La Llorona," *North American Review* 281, no. 6 (November–December 1996): 24–27.

Naslund, Sena. *Ahab's Wife; or, The Star-Gazer.* New York: Perennial, 2000.

Naylor, Gloria. *Bailey's Cafe.* New York: Vintage, 1993.

———. *Linden Hills.* New York: Vintage, 1995.

———. *Mama Day.* New York: Vintage, 1989.

———. *The Women of Brewster Place.* New York: Penguin, 1983.

Newcastle, Margaret Cavendish. *The Convent of Pleasure and Other Plays.* Baltimore, Md.: Johns Hopkins University Press, 1999.

Ng, Fae Myenne. *Bone.* New York: Perennial, 1994.

Nin, Anaïs. *Delta of Venus.* New York: Harvest, 2004.

———. *The Diary of Anaïs Nin: 1931–1934.* New York: Harvest, 1969.

———. *Incest: From "A Journal of Love," The Unexpurgated Diary of Anaïs Nin, 1932–1934.* New York: Harcourt Brace Jovanovich, 1992.

———. *Little Birds.* New York: Harvest, 2004.

Norman, Diana. *A Catch of Consequence.* London: Berkley, 2003.

———. *Taking Liberties.* London: Berkley, 2004.

———. *Terrible Beauty: A Life of Constance Markievicz (1868–1927).* London: Hodder & Stoughton, 1987.

———. *The Vizard Mask.* London: Penguin, 1995.

Norman, Marsha. *'night, Mother.* New York: Hill & Wang, 1983.

Norris, Kathleen. *Mother.* San Antonio, Tex.: Vision Forum, 2001.

———. *Through a Glass Darkly.* Garden City, N.Y.: Doubleday, 1957.

Nottage, Lynn. *Poof!* In *Plays for Actresses.* Edited by Eric Lane and Nina Shengold. New York: Vintage, 1997.

Nuñez, Elizabeth. *Beyond the Limbo Silence.* New York: Seal, 1998.

———. *Bruised Hibiscus.* New York: Seal, 2000.

———. *Discretion.* New York: One World, 2002.

Nwapa, Flora. *Plays: Conversations.* Enugu, Nigeria: Tana Press, 1993.

Oates, Joyce Carol. *Big Mouth and Ugly Girl.* New York: HarperTempest, 2003.

———. *Blonde.* New York: HarperCollins, 2002.

———. *Foxfire: Confessions of a Girl Gang.* New York: Plume, 1994.

———. *We Were the Mulvaneys.* New York: Plume, 1996.

O'Connor, Flannery. *A Good Man Is Hard to Find and Other Stories.* New York: Harvest Books, 1977.

———. *The Habit of Being: Letters of Flannery O'Connor.* New York: Farrar, Straus & Giroux, 1988.

———. *Mystery and Manners: Occasional Prose.* New York: Farrar, Straus & Giroux, 1969.

Olds, Sharon. *Blood, Tin, Straw.* New York: Alfred A. Knopf, 1999.

———. *The Dead and the Living.* New York: Alfred A. Knopf, 1984.

———. *The Gold Cell.* New York: Alfred A. Knopf, 1987.

———. "The Language of the Brag," *Calyx* 10, no. 2–3 (1987): 8–9.

———. *The Wellspring.* New York: Alfred Knopf, 1996.

Oliphant, Margaret. *Hester.* Oxford: Oxford University Press, 2000.

———. *Miss Marjoribanks.* London: Penguin, 1999.

Olsen, Tillie. *Mothers and Daughters: An Exploration in Photographs.* New York: Aperture, 1987.

———. *Mother to Daughter, Daughter to Mother.* Old Westbury, N.Y.: Feminist Press, 1984.

———. *Silences.* New York: Dell, 1978.

———. *Yonnondio: From the Thirties.* New York: Delta, 1979.

Onwueme, Osonye Tess. *Tell It to Women: An Epic Drama for Women.* Detroit, Mich.: Wayne State University Press, 1997.

———. *Three Plays: An Anthology of Three Plays.* Detroit, Mich.: Wayne State University Press, 1993.

Ozick, Cynthia. *Heir to the Glimmering World: A Novel.* Boston: Houghton Mifflin, 2004.

———. *The Puttermesser Papers.* New York: Vintage, 1998.

———. *The Shawl.* New York: Vintage, 1990.

Paglia, Camille. *Sex, Art, and American Culture.* New York: Vintage, 1992.

———. *Sexual Personae: Art and Decadence from Nefertiti to Emily Dickinson.* New York: Vintage, 1991.

———. *Vamps and Tramps: New Essays.* New York: Vintage, 1994.

Pankhurst, Emmeline. *The Importance of the Vote.* London: Women's Press, 1912.

Paretsky, Sara. *Bitter Medicine.* New York: Dell, 1999.

———. *Blood Shot.* New York: Dell, 1989.

Parker, Dorothy. *Not Much Fun: The Lost Poems of Dorothy Parker.* New York: Scribner, 1996.

———. *The Poetry and Short Stories of Dorothy Parker.* New York: Modern Library, 1994.

———. *The Portable Dorothy Parker.* New York: Penguin, 1991.

Parra, Teresa de la. *Iphigenia.* Austin: University of Texas Press, 1993.

Petry, Ann. *Harriet Tubman: Conductor on the Underground Railroad.* New York: HarperTrophy, 1996.

———. *The Street.* New York: Pyramid, 1961.

———. *Tituba of Salem Village.* New York: Thomas Y. Crowell, 1964.

Phelps, Elizabeth Stuart. *Doctor Zay.* New York: Consortium, 1987.

———. *Hedged In.* Boston: Fields & Osgood, 1870.

———. *The Silent Partner.* New York: Feminist Press, 1983.

———. *Songs of the Silent World.* Boston: Houghton Mifflin, 1885.

———. *The Story of Avis.* Piscataway, N.J.: Rutgers University Press, 1985.

———. *Three Spiritual Novels: The Gates Ajar, Beyond the Gates, The Gates Between.* Chicago: University of Illinois Press, 2000.

Phelps, Ethel Johnston. *The Maid of the North: Feminist Folk Tales from around the World.* New York: Holt, Rinehart & Winston, 1981.

Piercy, Marge. *The Art of Blessing the Day.* New York: Knopf, 2000.

———. *Circles on the Water.* New York: Knopf, 1982.

———. *City of Darkness City of Light.* New York: Ballantine, 1997.

———. *Gone to Soldiers.* New York: Fawcett, 1988.

———. "The Grey Flannel Sexual Harassment Suit," *On the Issues* (Fall 1995): 60.

———. *The Moon Is Always Female.* New York: Random House, 1980.

———. *Small Changes.* New York: Ballantine, 1996.

———. *Woman on the Edge of Time.* New York: Fawcett, 1976.

Pirkis, Catherine Louisa. *The Experiences of Loveday Brooke, Lady Detective.* Whitefish, Mont.: Kessinger, 2004.

Plath, Sylvia. *The Bell Jar.* New York: Bantam, 1972.

———. *The Collected Poems of Sylvia Plath.* New York: HarperCollins, 1981.

———. *Johnny Panic and the Bible of Dreams: Short Stories, Prose, and Diary Extracts.* New York: Harper & Row, 1979.

———. *The Unabridged Journal of Sylvia Plath, 1950–1963.* New York: Anchor, 2000.

Pogrebin, Letty Cottin. *Deborah, Golda and Me: Being Female and Jewish in America.* New York: Anchor, 1991.

———. *Family Politics: Love and Power on an Intimate Frontier.* New York: McGraw-Hill, 1983.

———. *Getting Over Getting Older.* New York: Berkley, 1997.

———. *Three Daughters: A Novel.* New York: Farrar, Straus & Giroux, 2002.

Pollitt, Katha. *Nothing Sacred: Women Respond to Religious Fundamentalism and Terror.* New York: Nation, 2002.

———. *Reasonable Creatures: Essays on Women and Feminism.* New York: Vintage, 1995.

————. *Subject to Debate: Sense and Dissents on Women, Politics, and Culture.* New York: Modern Library, 2001.

Porter, Katherine Anne. *The Collected Stories of Katherine Anne Porter.* New York: New American Library, 1965.

————. *Letters of Katherine Anne Porter.* New York: Atlantic Monthly Press, 1991.

————. *Pale Horse, Pale Rider.* New York: Harcourt, 1990.

Powell, Dawn. *My Home Is Far Away.* New York: Steerforth, 1995.

————. *A Time to Be Born.* New York: Steerforth, 1999.

————. *The Wicked Pavilion.* New York: Zoland, 1998.

Provoost, Anne. *In the Shadow of the Ark.* New York: Arthur A. Levine, 2004.

Quindlen, Anna. *Living Out Loud.* New York: Ivy, 1989.

————. *Loud and Clear.* New York: Random House, 2004.

————. *One True Thing.* New York: Dell, 1994.

————. "The Reasonable Woman Standard," *Newsweek* 27 March 2000, p. 86.

————. "Still Needing the F Word," *Newsweek,* 20 December 2003, p. 74.

————. *Thinking Out Loud.* New York: Ballantine, 1994.

————. "What Damage Has Barbie Wrought? Barbie at 35: She Isn't Just a Toy," *Greensboro News Record,* 18 September 1994, p. F4.

Radcliffe, Ann. *The Italian.* London: Oxford University Press, 1968.

————. *The Mysteries of Udolpho.* London: Oxford University Press, 1966.

Rampling, Anne. *Belinda.* New York: Berkley, 2000.

Randall, Alice. *The Wind Done Gone.* Boston: Houghton Mifflin, 2001.

Ratushinskaya, Irina. *Fiction and Lies.* London: John Murray, 1999.

————. *Grey Is the Colour of Hope.* London: Trafalgar Square, 1988.

Rau, Santha Rama. *The Adventuress.* New York: Dell, 1971.

————. *A Princess Remembers: The Memoirs of the Maharani of Jaipur.* Philadelphia: J. B. Lippincott, 1976.

————. "Who Cares?" In *Women of the Third World: Twenty Stories Set in Africa, Asia, and Latin America.* London: Victor Gollancz, 1975.

Rawlings, Marjorie Kinnan. *Cross Creek.* Atlanta, Ga.: Mockingbird, 1974.

————. *Cross Creek Cookery.* New York: Fireside, 1996.

————. *When the Whippoorwill.* New York: Ballantine, 1975.

————. *The Yearling.* New York: Scribner, 1970.

Renault, Mary. *The Bull from the Sea.* New York: Vintage, 2001.

————. *The King Must Die.* New York: Vintage, 1988.

————. *The Last of the Wine.* New York: Vintage, 2001.

Rhys, Jean. *Good Morning, Midnight.* New York: W. W. Norton, 1986.

————. *Wide Sargasso Sea.* New York: W. W. Norton, 1982.

Rich, Adrienne. *Adrienne Rich's Poetry and Prose.* New York: W. W. Norton, 1975.

————. *Blood, Bread, and Poetry: Selected Prose, 1979–1985.* New York: W. W. Norton, 1986.

————. *On Lies, Secrets, and Silence: Selected Prose, 1966–1978.* New York: W. W. Norton, 1979.

————. "When We Dead Awaken: Writing as Re-Vision," *College English* 34, 1 (October 1972): 18–25.

Richards, Mary Haskin. *Winter Quarters: The 1846–1848 Life Writings of Mary Haskin Parker Richards.* Logan: Utah State University Press, 1996.

Rinehart, Mary Roberts. *The Case of Jennie Brice.* London: Kensington, 1997.

————. *The Circular Staircase.* New York: Dover, 1997.

————, "The Young Visitor," *Saturday Evening Post* 261, no. 4 (May–June 1989): 32–36.

Roberts, Dmae. *The Breast Cancer Monologues.* New York: MediaRites, 2004.

————. *The Journey of Lady Buddha.* New York: MediaRites, 1998.

————. *Mei Mei: A Daughter's Song.* New York: MediaRites, 1990.

Robinson, Harriet. *Loom and Spindle.* Pacifica, Calif.: Press Pacifica, 1976.

Robinson, Marilynne. *Housekeeping.* New York: Bantam, 1982.

————. *Mother Country.* New York: Farrar, Straus & Giroux, 1989.

————. "The Way We Work, the Way We Live," *Christian Century,* 9 September 1998, pp. 823–831.

Roquelaure, A. N. *Beauty's Punishment.* New York: Plume, 1984.

Rose, Wendy. *Now Poof She Is Gone.* New York: Firebrand, 1994.

Ross, Ishbel. *Crusades and Crinolines.* New York: Harper & Row, 1963.

————. *Ladies of the Press.* New York: Harper & Brothers, 1936.

————. *The President's Wife: Mary Todd Lincoln.* New York: G. P. Putnam's Sons, 1973.

————. *Sons of Adam, Daughters of Eve: The Role of Women in American History.* New York: Harper & Row, 1969.

Rossetti, Christina, *The Goblin Market.* New York: Dover, 1994.

————. *Rossetti: Poems.* New York: Everymans Library, 1993.

————. *Selected Prose by Christina Rossetti.* London: Palgrave Macmillan, 1998.

————. *Speaking Likenesses.* London: Macmillan, 1874.

Rowbotham, Sheila. *A Century of Women.* New York: Penguin, 1997.

————. *Dignity and Daily Bread: New Forms of Economic Organizing among Poor Women in the Third World and First.* New York: Routledge, 1994.

————. *Friends of Alice Wheeldon.* New York: Monthly Review, 1986.

————. *Hidden from History: Rediscovering Women in History from the 17th Century to the Present.* New York: Vintage, 1976.

————. *Promise of a Dream: Remembering the Sixties.* London: Verso, 2001.

————. *Woman's Consciousness, Man's World.* Harmondsworth, England: Penguin, 1973.

————. *Women in Movement: Feminism and Social Action.* New York: Routledge, 1992.

————. *Women Resist Globalisation: Mobilising for Livelihood and Rights.* London: Zed Books, 2002.

————. *Women's Liberation and New Politics.* London: May Day Manifesto Group, 1971.

Rowlandson, Mary White. *The Sovereignty and Goodness of God: The True Story of the Captivity of Mrs. Mary Rowlandson among the Indians.* Tucson, Ariz.: American Eagle, 1966.

Rowson, Susanna. *Charlotte Temple.* New York: Modern Library, 2004.

Roy, Gabrielle. *Children of My Heart.* Toronto: McClelland & Stewart, 1979.

————. *Enchantment and Sorrow: The Autobiography of Gabrielle Roy.* Toronto: Lester & Orpen Dennys, 1987.

————. *Street of Riches.* Toronto: New Canadian Library, 1991.

————. *Windflower.* Toronto: McClelland & Stewart, 1991.

Rukeyser, Muriel. *Out of Silence: Selected Poems.* Evanston, Ill.: Northwestern University Press, 1994.

Russ, Joanna. *The Female Man.* Boston: Beacon, 2000.

————. *How to Suppress Women's Writing.* Austin: University of Texas Press, 1983.

————. *To Write like a Woman: Essays in Feminism and Science Fiction.* Bloomington: Indiana University Press, 1995.

Sahgal, Nayantara. "Imagining India," *Times Higher Education Supplement,* 21 November 1997, 33.

Sanchez, Sonia. *Does Your House Have Lions?* Boston: Beacon, 1997.

————. *Shake Loose My Skin.* Boston: Beacon, 2000.

————. *We a BaddDDD People.* New York: Broadside, 1970.

————. "Wounded in the House of a Friend," *Essence* 26, no. 1 (May 1995): 227–230.

Sand, George. *Marianne.* New York: Carroll & Graf, 1998.

Sanford, Mollie. *Mollie: The Journal of Mollie Dorsey Sanford in Nebraska and Colorado Territories, 1857–1866.* Lincoln: University of Nebraska Press, 1959.

Sanger, Margaret. *Happiness in Marriage.* New York: Applewood, 1993.

————. *Margaret Sanger: An Autobiography.* New York: Cooper Square, 1999.

Sappho. *The Poems of Sappho.* New York: Prometheus, 1999.

Sarton, May. *The Education of Harriet Hatfield.* New York: W. W. Norton, 1993.

————. *Mrs. Stevens Hears the Mermaids Singing.* New York: W. W. Norton, 1975.

————. *Writings on Writing.* Orono, Maine: Puckerbush, 1980.

Schaeffer, Susan Fromberg. *Granite Lady.* New York: Collier Books, 1984.

Schlissel, Lillian. *Women's Diaries of the Westward Journey.* New York: Schocken, 1982.

Schreiner, Olive. *The Story of an African Farm.* London: Penguin, 1997.

————. *Undine.* Boston: Johnson Reprint, 1928.

Seward, Anna. *Llangollen Vale.* Washington, D.C.: Woodstock Books, 1994.

————. *The Poetical Works of Anna Seward.* Brooklyn, N.Y.: AMS Press, 1974.

Sexton, Anne. *The Complete Poems of Anne Sexton.* Boston: Houghton Mifflin, 1981.

————. *Transformations.* Boston: Houghton Mifflin, 1971.

Shakespeare, William. *Macbeth.* New York: Folger Library, 1959.

Shange, Ntozake. *for colored girls who have considered suicide when the rainbow is enuf.* New York: Scribner, 1975.

————. *If I Can Cook/You Know God Can.* Boston: Beacon, 1998.

Shelley, Mary. *Frankenstein.* New York: Bantam, 1984.

————. *The Journals of Mary Shelley, 1814–1844.* Baltimore: Johns Hopkins University Press, 1995.

Silko, Leslie Marmon. *Almanac of the Dead.* New York: Simon & Schuster, 1991.

————. *Ceremony.* New York: Penguin, 1977.

————. *Gardens in the Dunes.* New York: Simon & Schuster, 2000.

————. *Storyteller.* New York: Seaver, 1981.

————. *Yellow Woman and a Beauty of the Spirit.* Simon & Schuster, 1997.

Skinner, Cornelia Otis. *Madame Sarah*. Boston: Houghton Mifflin, 1967.

Smith, Anna Deavere. *Fires in the Mirror: Crown Heights, Brooklyn and Other Identities*. New York: Anchor, 1993.

———. *Talk to Me: Travels in Media and Politics*. New York: Anchor, 2001.

———. *Twilight Los Angeles, 1992: On the Road: A Search for American Character*. New York: Anchor, 1994.

Smith, Charlotte. *Montalbert*. Delmar, N.Y.: Scholars Facsimiles & Reprint, 1989.

———. *The Poems of Charlotte Smith*. New York: Oxford University Press, 1993.

———. *The Young Philosopher*. Lexington: University Press of Kentucky, 1999.

Smith, Stevie. *Collected Poems*. New York: New Directions, 1972.

———. *Novel on Yellow Paper; or, Work It Out for Yourself*. New York: Pinnacle, 1982.

Song, Cathy. *Frameless Windows, Squares of Light: Poems*. New York: W. W. Norton, 2003.

———. *Picture Bride*. New Haven, Conn.: Yale University Press, 1983.

———. *School Figures*. Pittsburgh: University of Pittsburgh Press, 1994.

Sontag, Susan. *Regarding the Pain of Others*. New York: Picador, 2004.

———. "The Third World of Women," *Partisan Review* 40, no. 2 (1973): 180–206.

Southworth, E. D. E. N. *The Deserted Wife*. Philadelphia: T. B. Peterson, 1875.

———. *The Hidden Hand*. New Brunswick, N.J.: Rutgers University Press, 1988.

———. *India: The Pearl of Pearl River*. Philadelphia: T. B. Peterson, 1855.

———. *Retribution; or, The Vale of Shadows*. Philadelphia: T. B. Peterson, 1856.

Spence, Eulalie. *Her*. In *Black Female Playwrights: An Anthology of Plays before 1950*. Edited by Kathy A. Perkins. Bloomington: Indiana University Press, 1989.

Springer, Nancy. *I Am Morgan Le Fay: A Tale from Camelot*. New York: Puffin, 2002.

———. *Rowan Hood, Outlaw Girl of Sherwood Forest*. New York: Philomel, 2001.

———. *Sky Rider*. New York: HarperTrophy, 2000.

Staël, Germaine de. *Considerations on the Principal Events of the French Revolution*. London: Baldwin, Cradock & Joy, 1818.

———. *Corinne; or, Italy*. Piscataway, N.J.: Rutgers University Press, 1987.

———. *Politics, Literature, and National Character*. London: Sidgwich and Jackson, 1964.

———. *Ten Years of Exile*. Dekalb: Northern Illinois University Press, 2000.

Stafford, Jean. *Boston Adventure*. Garden City, N.Y.: Sun Dial, 1944.

———. *The Collected Stories of Jean Stafford*. Austin: University of Texas Press, 1992.

———. *The Mountain Lion*. Austin: University of Texas Press, 1972.

Stanton, Elizabeth Cady. *Eighty Years and More: Reminiscences 1815–1897*. New York: Schocken, 1971.

———, and Susan B. Anthony. *Elizabeth Cady Stanton / Susan B. Anthony: Correspondence, Writings, Speeches*. New York: Schocken, 1981.

Starhawk. *Dreaming the Dark: Magic, Sex, and Politics*. Boston: Beacon, 1997.

———. *Walking to Mercury*. New York: Bantam, 1997.

Stein, Gertrude. *The Autobiography of Alice B. Toklas*. New York: Vintage, 1990.

———. *The Making of Americans*. Estate of Gertrude Stein, 1995.

———. *Paris France*. New York: W. W. Norton, 1996.

———. *Three Lives*. New York: Penguin, 1990.

Steinem, Gloria. *Marilyn: Norma Jeane*. New York: New American Library, 1986.

———. *Moving beyond Words: Age, Race, Sex, Power, Money, Muscles: Breaking the Boundaries of Power*. New York: Touchstone, 1995.

———. *Outrageous Acts and Everyday Rebellions*. New York: Owl, 1995.

———. *Revolution from Within: A Book of Self-Esteem*. Boston: Little, Brown, 1992.

Stewart, Elinore Pruitt. *Letters of a Woman Homesteader*. New York: Mariner Books, 1998.

Stone, Lucy, and Henry B. Blackwell. *Loving Warriors: Selected Letters of Lucy Stone and Henry B. Blackwell, 1853–1893*. New York: Doubleday, 1981.

Stowe, Harriet Beecher. *The Minister's Wooing*. New York: Penguin, 1959.

———. *Uncle Tom's Cabin*. New York: Harper, 1965.

Stratton, R. B. *Captivity of the Oatman Girls: Being an Interesting Narrative of Life among the Apache and Mohave Indians*. Lincoln: University of Nebraska Press, 1983.

Tan, Amy. *The Bonesetter's Daughter*. New York: Putnam, 2001.

———. *The Hundred Secret Senses*. New York: Putnam, 1995.

———. *The Joy Luck Club*. New York: Putnam, 1989.

———. *The Kitchen God's Wife*. New York: Putnam, 1991.

————. "Lost Lives of Women: My Grandmother's Choice," *Life* 14 (April 1991): 90–91.

————. *The Moon Lady*. New York: Macmillan, 1992.

————. *The Opposite of Fate: A Book of Musings*. New York: G. P. Putnam, 2003.

Teasdale, Sara. *The Collected Poems of Sara Teasdale*. New York: Buccaneer, 1994.

Thames, Susan, and Marin Gazzaniga. *The Breast: An Anthology*. New York: Global City, 1995.

Thomas, Marlo. *Free to Be, You and Me*. New York: Mcgraw-Hill, 1974.

Thompson, Dorothy. *Dorothy Thompson and Rose Wilder Lane: Forty Years of Friendship Letters, 1920–1961*. Columbia: University of Missouri Press, 1991.

————. *I Saw Hitler!* New York: Farrer & Rinehart, 1932.

————. *Refugees: Anarchy or Organization?* New York: Random House, 1938.

Tillman, Katherine. *Works of Katherine Davis Chapman Tillman*. New York: Oxford University Press, 1991.

Tuchman, Barbara. *A Distant Mirror*. New York: Alfred A. Knopf, 1978.

Ulrich, Laurel Thatcher. *The Age of Homespun: Objects and Stories in the Creation of an American Myth*. New York: Knopf, 2001.

————. *Good Wives: Image and Reality in the Lives of Women in Northern New England, 1650–1750*. New York: Oxford University Press, 1982.

————. *A Midwife's Tale: The Life of Martha Ballard, Based on Her Diary, 1785–1812*. New York: Alfred A. Knopf, 1990.

————. "A Pail of Cream," *Journal of American History* 89, no. 1 (June 2002): 43–47.

Undset, Sigrid. *The Axe*. New York: Vintage, 1994.

————. *Gunnar's Daughter*. New York: Penguin, 1998.

————. *Kristin Lavransdatter: The Cross*. New York: Penguin, 2001.

————. *Kristin Lavransdatter: The Wife*. New York: Penguin, 1999.

————. *Kristin Lavransdatter: The Wreath*. New York: Penguin, 1997.

Viramontes, Helena María. *The Moth and Other Stories*. Houston, Tex.: Arte Publico, 1985.

————. *Under the Feet of Jesus*. New York: Penguin, 1995.

Waisbrooker, Lois. *A Sexual Revolution*. New York: New Society Publishers, 1984.

Walker, Alice. *The Color Purple*. New York: Washington Square, 1983.

————. *Living by the Word: Selected Writings 1983–1987*. New York: Harcourt, 1988.

————. *Possessing the Secret of Joy*. New York: Pocket, 1993.

Walker, Jeanne Murray. "The Shawl," *Poetry* 147 (November 1985): 76–77.

Walker, Lady Mary. *Munster Village*. London: Pandora, 1987.

Walker, Margaret. *How I Wrote* Jubilee. Chicago: Third World Press, 1972.

————. *Jubilee*. New York: Bantam, 1967.

————. *On Being Female, Black, and Free: Essays by Margaret Walker, 1932–1992*. Nashville: University of Tennessee Press, 1997.

Wallis, Velma. *Bird Girl and the Man Who Followed the Sun*. New York: Perennial, 1997.

————. *Raising Ourselves: A Gwich'in Coming of Age Story from the Yukon River*. New York: Graphic Arts Center, 2003.

————. *Two Old Women: An Alaska Legend of Betrayal, Courage, and Survival*. Fairbanks, Alaska: Epicenter, 1993.

Warren, Mercy Otis. *History of the Rise, Progress, and Termination of the American Revolution*. Indianapolis, Ind.: Liberty Fund, 1988.

————. *Plays and Poems of Mercy Otis Warren*. Delmar, N.Y.: Scholars Facsimiles & Reprint, 1980.

Wasserstein, Wendy. *American Daughter*. New York: Harvest, 1999.

————. *The Heidi Chronicles and Other Plays*. New York: Vintage, 1991.

————. *Shiksa Goddess (or How I Spent My Forties)*. New York: Vintage, 2002.

————. *Sloth: The Seven Deadly Sins*. Oxford: Oxford University Press, 2004.

Watkins, Yoko Kawashima. *My Brother, My Sister and I*. New York: Simon Pulse, 1996.

————. *So Far from the Bamboo Grove*. New York: 1986.

Weil, Simone. *Gravity and Grace*. Lincoln: University of Nebraska Press, 1997.

————. *The Need for Roots: Prelude to a Declaration of Duties toward Mankind*. New York: Routledge, 1997.

————. *Simone Weil: An Anthology*. New York: Grove, 2000.

Weld, Angelina Grimké. *An Appeal to the Christian Women of the South*. Whitefish, Mont.: Kessinger, 2004.

Weldon, Fay. *Big Girls Don't Cry*. New York: Grove/Atlantic, 1997.

————. *The Bulgari Connection*. New York: Grove, 2000.

————. *Letters to Alice on First Reading Jane Austen*. New York: Carroll & Graf, 1999.

————. *Life and Loves of a She-Devil*. New York: Ballantine, 1983.

————. *Praxis*. New York: Summit, 1978.

————. *Puffball*. New York: Pocket, 1985.

————. *Splitting*. New York: Atlantic Monthly Press, 1996.

————, "Where Women Are Women and So Are Men," *Harper's* 296, 1,776 (May 1998): 65–69.

————. *Wicked Women*. New York: Atlantic Monthly Press, 1999.

Wells, Rebecca. *Divine Secrets of the Ya-Ya Sisterhood*. New York: Perennial, 2004.

————. *Little Altars Everywhere*. New York: Perennial, 1996.

Wells-Barnett, Ida B. *Crusade for Justice: The Autobiography of Ida B. Wells*. Chicago: University of Chicago Press, 1991.

————. *Southern Horrors and Other Writings: The Anti-Lynching Campaign of Ida B. Wells, 1892–1900*. New York: Bedford/St. Martin's, 1996.

Welty, Eudora. *The Collected Stories of Eudora Welty*. New York: Harcourt Brace Jovanovich, 1980.

Wertenbaker, Timberlake. *The Love of the Nightingale and The Grace of Mary Traverse*. Boston: Faber & Faber, 1991.

————. *Timberlake Wertenbaker: Plays 1*. Boston: Faber & Faber, 1996.

————. *Timberlake Wertenbaker: Plays 2*. Boston: Faber & Faber, 2002.

West, Jessamyn. *Except for Me and Thee*. New York: Avon, 1970.

————. *The Friendly Persuasion*. New York: Harvest, 2003.

West, Rebecca. *Black Lamb and Grey Falcon: The Record of a Journey through Yugoslavia*. New York: Penguin, 1995.

————. *Henry James*. London: Nesbit, 1916.

————. *The Return of the Soldier*. London: Virago, 1980.

Wharton, Edith. *A Backward Glance*. New York: Scribner, 1998.

————. *The Custom of the Country*. New York: Berkley, 1981.

————. *Ethan Frome*. New York: Scribner, 1970.

————. *The House of Mirth*. New York: New American Library, 2000.

————. *A Mother's Recompense*. New York: Scribner, 1996.

Wheatley, Phillis. *Complete Writings*. New York: Penguin, 2001.

Wilder, Laura Ingalls. *Little House in the Big Woods*. New York: HarperTrophy, 1953.

————. *Little House on the Prairie*. New York: HarperTrophy, 1953.

————. *On the Way Home: The Diary of a Trip from South Dakota to Mansfield, Missouri, in 1874*. New York: HarperTrophy, 1976.

Williams, Patricia J. *The Alchemy of Race and Rights*. Cambridge, Mass.: Harvard University Press, 1991.

————. *Open House: Of Family, Friends, Food, Piano Lessons, and the Search for a Room of My Own*. New York: Farrar, Straus & Giroux, 2004.

————. *Seeing a Colorblind Future: The Paradox of Race*. New York: Noonday, 1997.

Winnemucca, Sarah. *Life among the Piutes: Their Wrongs and Claims*. Lincoln: University of Nevada Press, 1994.

Wolf, Christa. *Cassandra*. New York: Noonday, 1988.

————. *Medea*. New York: Solaris, 1998.

Wolf, Naomi. *The Beauty Myth: How Images of Beauty Are Used against Women*. New York: Perennial, 2002.

————. *Fire with Fire: The New Female Power and How to Use It*. New York: Ballantine, 1994.

————. *Misconceptions: Truth, Lies, and the Unexpected on the Journey to Motherhood*. New York: Anchor, 2003.

————. *Promiscuities: The Secret Struggle for Womanhood*. New York: Ballantine, 1998.

Wolkstein, Diane, and Samuel Noah Kramer. *Inanna: Queen of Heaven and Earth, Her Stories and Hymns from Sumer*. New York: HarperCollins, 1983.

Wollstonecraft, Mary. *Mary/Maria/Matilda*. New York: Penguin, 1993.

————. *A Vindication of the Rights of Woman*. New York: W. W. Norton, 1988.

Wood, Ellen. *East Lynne; or, The Earl's Daughter*. Richmond, England: West & Johnston, 1864.

————. "The Punishment of Gina Montani," *Colburn's New Monthly Magazine* 5, no. 2 (February 1852): 189–196.

Woolf, Virginia. *Mrs. Dalloway*. New York: Harvest, 1953.

————. *Orlando: A Biography*. New York: Harvest, 1956.

————. *A Room of One's Own*. New York: Harbinger, 1957.

————. *Three Guineas*. New York: Harcourt Brace, 1966.

————. *To the Lighthouse*. New York: Harvest Books, 1955.

————. *The Voyage Out*. London: Duckworth, 1915.

Wright, Frances. *Life, Letters, and Lectures: 1834/1844*. New York: Arno Press, 1972.

————. *Reason, Religion, and Morals*. New York: Humanity Books, 2004.

Yamada, Mitsuye. *Camp Notes and Other Writings*. Piscataway, N.J.: Rutgers University Press, 1998.

Yamamoto, Hisaye. *Seventeen Syllables and Other Stories*. Piscataway, N.J.: Rutgers University Press, 1998.

Yearsley, Ann. *Earl Goodwin*. London: G. G. J. and J. Robinson, 1791.

————. *The Royal Captives*. 4 vols. New York: Garland, 1974.

Yezierska, Anzia. *Bread Givers*. New York: Persea Books, 2003.

————. *How I Found America: Collected Stories of Anzia Yezierska*. New York: Persea Books, 1991.

————. *Hungry Hearts*. Boston: Houghton Mifflin, 1920.

————. *Salome of the Tenements*. Chicago: University of Illinois Press, 1995.

Yolen, Jane. *Briar Rose*. New York: Perfection Learning, 1993.

Yourcenar, Marguerite. *Memoirs of Hadrian*. New York: Farrar, Straus & Giroux, 1963.

————. *Mishima: A Vision of the Void*. New York: Farrar, Straus & Giroux, 1986.

Etext

Adeyanju, Tunde. *Democracy on Trial*. Available online. URL: http://www.alexanderstreet4.com. Accessed on October 17, 2005.

Aguilar, Grace. "Festival of Purim" (1845). Available online. URL: http://www.jewish-history.com/Occident/volume3/aug1845/stanzas.html. Accessed on October 13, 2005.

————. *The Frankfurt Journal of Grace Aguilar* (1847). Available online. URL: http://www.familyhistory.fsnet.co.uk/aguilar/The%20Frankfurt%20Jornal%20of%20Grace%20Aguilar.htm. Accessed on October 13, 2005.

————. *The Vale of Cedars* (1874). Available online. URL: http://www.abacci.com/books/book.asp?bookID=4233. Accessed on October 13, 2005.

————. *Women of Israel* (1844). Available online. URL: http://aleph.haifa.ac.il/F/?func=find-b&find_code=SYS&request=1015236. Accessed on October 13, 2005.

Alcott, Louisa May. *Hospital Sketches* (1863). Available online. URL: http://digital.library.upenn.edu/women/alcott/sketches/sketches.html. Accessed on October 13, 2005.

————. "Transcendental Wild Oats" (1873). Available online. URL: http://www.vcu.edu/engweb/transcendentalism/ideas/wildoats.html. Accessed on October 13, 2005.

Anne of Swansea. *Lovers and Friends* (1821). Available online. URL: http://www.chawton.org/novels/Lovers/Lovers1.html. Accessed on October 13, 2005.

"Ann Julia Hatton." *Sheffield Hallam University: Corvey Women Writers* (2000). Available online. URL: http://www.2.shu.ac.uk/corvey/CW3/AuthorPage.cfm?Author=AJKH. Accessed on October 13, 2005.

Anthony, Susan B. *Letter Written by Susan B. Anthony to Ida Husted Harper the Day before Elizabeth Cady Stanton's Funeral* (1902). Available online. URL: http://ecssba.rutgers.edu/docs/sbatoharp.html. Accessed on October 13, 2005.

————. *Remarks by Susan B. Anthony at Her Trial for Illegal Voting* (1873). Available online. URL: http://ecssba.rutgers.edu/docs/sbatrial.html. Accessed on October 13, 2005.

————. *Woman's Half Century of Evolution* (1902). Available online. URL: http://etext.lib.virginia.edu/toc/modeng/public/AntWoma.html. Accessed on October 13, 2005.

————. "Woman: The Great Unpaid Laborer" (1848). Available online. URL: http://etext.lib.virginia.edu/railton/uncletom/womanmov.html#g. Accessed on October 13, 2005.

————, and Ida Husted Harper, eds. *History of Woman Suffrage*, vol. 4 (1902). Available online. URL: http://www.alexanderstreet6.com/wasm/wasmrestricted/doctext/S10010057-D0076.001.htm. Accessed on October 13, 2005.

Antin, Mary. *The Promised Land* (1912). Available online. URL: http://digital.library.upenn.edu/women/antin/land/land.html. Accessed on October 18, 2005.

Atherton, Gertrude. *What Dreams May Come* (1888). Available online. URL: http://www.gutenberg.org/etext/12833. Accessed on October 13, 2005.

Austin, Mary Hunter. *The Land of Little Rain* (1903). Available online. URL: http://etext.lib.virginia.edu/toc/modeng/public/AusRain.html. Accessed on October 13, 2005.

————. *Walking Woman* (1907). Available online. URL: http://etext.lib.virginia.edu/toc/modeng/public/AusWalk.html. Accessed on October 13, 2005.

Ballard, Martha. *Martha Ballard's Diary Online*. Available online. URL: http://dohistory.org/diary/index.html. Accessed on October 17, 2005.

Barbauld, Anna Laetitia. *The Works of Anna Laetitia Barbauld: With a Memoir* (1825). Available online. URL: http://etext.lib.virginia.edu/toc/modeng/public/BarWork.html. Accessed on October 18, 2005.

Beecher, Catharine E. *Essay on Slavery and Abolitionism, with Reference to the Duty of American Females* (1837). Available online. URL: http://etext.lib.virginia.edu/toc/modeng/public/BeeEssa.html. Accessed on October 17, 2005.

Behn, Aphra. *The City Heiress* (1862). Available online. URL:http://etext.lib.virginia.edu/toc/modeng/public/BehCity.html. Accessed on October 13, 2005.

————. *Love Letters between a Nobleman and His Sister* (1687). Available online. URL: http://www.gutenberg.org/dirs/etext05/8lvlr10h.htm. Accessed on October 13, 2005.

————. *The Rover; or, The Banish't Cavaliers* (1677). Available online. URL: http://etext.library.adelaide.edu.au/b/behn/aphra/b42r/. Accessed on October 13, 2005.

Blackwell, Antoinette. "A Plea for the Afternoon" (1868). Available online. URL: http://cdl.library. cornell.edu/cgi-bin/moa/sgml/moa-idx?notisid= ABK2934-0021–61. Accessed on October 13, 2005.

Bly, Nellie. *Around the World in 72 Days* (1890). Available online. URL: http://digital.library.upenn.edu/ women/bly/world/world.html. Accessed on October 18, 2005.

———. *Ten Days in a Mad-House* (undated). URL: http://digital.library.upenn.edu/women/bly/madhouse/ madhouse.html. Accessed on October 18, 2005.

Bradford, Sarah H. *Scenes in the Life of Harriet Tubman* (1869). Available online. URL: http://docsouth. unc.edu/neh/bradford/menu.html. Accessed on October 17, 2005.

Bryant, Louise. "Fables for Proletarian Children" (1919). Available online. URL: http://www.marxists.org/ archive/bryant/works/fables.htm. Accessed on October 13, 2005.

———. *Mirrors of Moscow* (1923). Available online. URL: http://www.marxists.org/archive/bryant/works/1923- mom/index.htm. Accessed on October 13, 2005.

———. *Six Months in Red Russia* (1918). Available online. URL: http://digital.library.upenn.edu/women/bryant/ russia/russia.html. Accessed on October 13, 2005.

Calamity Jane. *The Life and Adventures of Calamity Jane* (1896). Available online. URL: http://etext.lib. virginia.edu/toc/modeng/public/CalLife.html. Accessed on October 14, 2005.

Carrigan, Minnie Bruce. *Captured by the Indians* (1862). Available online. URL: http://womenshistory. about.com/library/weekly/aa020920c.htm. Accessed on October 13, 2005.

Catt, Carrie Chapman. *The Ballot and the Bullet* (1897). Available online. URL: http://www.catt.org/ccread3. html. Accessed on October 13, 2005.

———. "Do You Know" (1918). Available online. URL: http://memory.loc.gov/cgi-bin/query/S?ammem/ nawbib:@field(TITLE+@od1(Do+you+know? ++)). Accessed on October 13, 2005.

———. "Speech before Congress" (1917). Available online. URL: http://womenshistory.about.com/library/ etext/bl_1917_catt_congress.htm. Accessed on October 13, 2005.

———. *Woman Suffrage by Federal Constitutional Amendment* (1917). Available online. URL: http:// www.catt.org/ccread3.html. Accessed on October 13, 2005.

Child, Lydia Maria. *The Mother's Book* (1831). Available online. URL: http://digital.library.upenn.edu/women/ child/book/book.html. Accessed on October 18, 2005.

Chopin, Kate. "A Pair of Silk Stockings" (1897). Available online. URL: http://etext.lib.virginia.edu/ toc/modeng/public/ChoSilk.html. Accessed on October 13, 2005.

———. "A Respectable Woman" (1894). Available online. URL: http://wyllie.lib.virginia.edu:8086/ perl/toccer-new?id=ChoResp.sgm&images= images/modeng&data=/texts/english/modeng/ parsed&tag=public&part=1&division=div1. Accessed on October 13, 2005.

Clive, Caroline. *Paul Ferroll* (1855). Available online. URL: http://www.indiana.edu/~letrs/vwwp/clive/ ferroll.html. Accessed on October 13, 2005.

———. *Why Paul Ferrol Killed His Wife* (1860). Available online. URL: http://www.indiana.edu/~letrs/vwwp/ clive/why.html. Accessed on October 13, 2005.

Coleridge, Mary Elizabeth. *Poems.* Available online. URL: http://www.poemhunter.com/mary-elizabeth- coleridge/poet-3048/. Accessed on October 17, 2005.

Corelli, Maria. *Ardath* (1889). Available online. URL: http://www.gutenberg.org/etext/5114. Accessed on October 13, 2005.

———. *Vendetta* (1886). Available online. URL: http:// www.gutenberg.org/dirs/etext03/vndtt10.txt. Accessed on October 13, 2005.

"Correspondence between John and Abigail Adams" (1762–1801). Available online. URL: http://www. masshist.org/digitaladams/aea/letter/. Accessed on June 20, 2004. Accessed on October 13, 2005.

Davis, Rebecca Harding. *Margaret Howth: A Story of To- Day* (1862). Available online. URL: http://etext. lib.virginia.edu/toc/modeng/public/DavMarg.html. Accessed on October 13, 2005.

de Cleyre, Voltairine. *Anarchism and American Traditions* (1914). Available online. URL: http://www.infoshop. org/texts/voltairine_traditions.html. Accessed on October 13, 2005.

———. "Sex Slavery" (1890). Available online. URL: http://dwardmac.pitzer.edu/Anarchist_Archives/ bright/cleyre/sexslavery.html. Accessed on October 13, 2005.

———. "Those Who Marry Do Ill" (1908). Available online. URL: http://praxeology.net/VC-MDI.htm. Accessed on October 13, 2005.

Diaries of Court Ladies of Old Japan (1920). Available online. URL: http://digital.library.upenn.edu/women/ omori/court/court.html. Accessed on October 13, 2005.

Dickinson, Emily. *The Single Hound: Poems of a Lifetime* (1924). Available online. URL: http://digital.library. upenn.edu/women/dickinson/hound/hound.html. Accessed on October 18, 2005.

Doolittle, Hilda. *Hymen* (1914). Available online. URL: http://digital.library.upenn.edu/women/doolittle/hymen/hymen.html. Accessed on October 13, 2005.

Doumic, René. *George Sand: Some Aspects of Her Life and Writings* (1910). Available online. URL: http://etext.lib.virginia.edu/toc/modeng/public/DouSand.html.

Edgeworth, Maria. *The Absentee* (1812). Available online. URL: http://emotional-literacy-education.com/classic-books-online-a/bsnte10.htm. Accessed on October 13, 2005.

———. *Belinda* (1811). Available online. URL: http://digital.library.upenn.edu/women/edgeworth/belinda/belinda.html. Accessed on October 13, 2005.

———. *Letters for Literary Ladies* (1798). Available online. URL: http://digital.library.upenn.edu/women/edgeworth/ladies/ladies.html. Accessed on October 13, 2005.

Fern, Fanny. *Fern Leaves from Fanny's Portfolio* (1853). Available online. URL: http://www.merrycoz.org/voices/leaves/LEAVES00.HTM. Accessed on October 14, 2005.

Firestone, Shulamith. *The Women's Rights Movement in the U.S.: A New View* (1968). Available online. URL: http://scriptorium.lib.duke.edu/wlm/notes/#newview. Accessed on October 14, 2005.

Ford, Mary K. "Woman's Progress: A Comparison of Centuries" (1909). Available online. URL: http://etext.lib.virginia.edu/toc/modeng/public/ForWoma.html. Accessed on October 13, 2005.

Gage, Matilda Joslyn. *Woman, Church & State* (1895). Available online. URL: http://www.sacred-texts.com/wmn/wcs/. Accessed on October 14, 2005.

Gale, Zona. *Miss Lulu Bett* (1920). Available online. URL: http://www.bookrags.com/ebooks/10429/2.html. Accessed on October 14, 2005.

———. *Romance Island* (1906). Available online. URL: http://www.gutenberg.org/newsletter/gutenbergglobe/newsletters/PGWeekly_2004_10_13_Part_2.txt. Accessed on October 14, 2005.

Gaskell, Elizabeth. *Cousin Phillis* (1864). Available online. URL: http://www.gutenberg.org/etext/4268. Accessed on October 18, 2005.

———. *Lizzie Leigh and Other Tales* (1896). Available online. URL: http://www.bookrags.com/ebooks/2547/1.html#1. Accessed on October 14, 2005.

Gilman, Charlotte Perkins. *Suffrage Songs and Verses* (1911). Available online. URL: http://digital.library.upenn.edu/women/gilman/suffrage/suffrage.html. Accessed on October 18, 2005.

———. "The Woman's Congress of 1899" (1899). Available online. URL: http://wyllie.lib.virginia.edu:8086/perl/toccer-new?id=SteWoma.sgm&images=images&data=/texts/english/modeng/parsed&tag=public&part=1&division=div1. Accessed on October 13, 2005.

———. *Women and Economics* (1898). Available online. URL: http://digital.library.upenn.edu/women/gilman/economics/economics.html. Accessed on October 18, 2005.

Glasgow, Ellen. *The Deliverance: A Romance of the Virginia Tobacco Fields* (1904). Available online. URL: http://www.readbookonline.net/title/238/. Accessed on October 14, 2005.

———. "A Point of Morals" (1899). Available online. URL: http://etext.lib.virginia.edu/subjects/Women-Writers.html. Accessed on October 14, 2005.

Glaspell, Susan. "A Jury of Her Peers" (1917). Available online. URL: http://etext.lib.virginia.edu/toc/modeng/public/GlaJury.html. Accessed on October 14, 2005.

Goldman, Emma. *Anarchism and Other Essays* (1911). Available online. URL: http://arthursclassicnovels.com/arthurs/women/nrcsm10.html. Accessed on October 14, 2005.

———. "Victims of Morality" (1913). Available online. URL: http://www.positiveatheism.org/hist/goldmanmor.htm. Accessed on October 14, 2005.

———. "Voltairine de Cleyre" (1932). Available online. URL: http://sunsite.berkeley.edu/Goldman/Writings/Essays/voltairine.html. Accessed on October 13, 2005.

Grand, Sarah. *The Heavenly Twins* (1893). Available online. URL: http://www.gutenberg.org/dirs/etext05/8htwn10.txt. Accessed on October 14, 2005.

Harper, Ida Husted. "Elizabeth Cady Stanton." (1902). Available online. URL: http://etext.lib.virginia.edu/toc/modeng/public/HarStan.html. Accessed on October 14, 2005.

Hawthorne, Nathaniel. "Mrs. Hutchinson" (1830). Available online. URL: http://www.eldritchpress.org/nh/mrsh.html. Accessed on October 13, 2005.

Hemans, Felicia. *Records of Women: With Other Poems* (1828). Available online. URL: http://digital.library.upenn.edu/women/hemans/records/records.html. Accessed on October 14, 2005.

Holmes, Lizzie M. "Woman's Future Position in the World" (1898). Available online. URL: http://etext.lib.virginia.edu/toc/modeng/public/HolWoma.html. Accessed on October 17, 2005.

hooks, bell. "Postmodern Blackness" (1990). Available online. URL: http://jefferson.village.virginia.edu/pmc/text-only/issue.990/hooks.990. Accessed on October 14, 2005.

Ivins, Molly. "Class Warfare and the Decline of Feminism" (2 January 2004). Available online. URL: http://progressivetrail.org/articles/040101Ivins.shtml.

Accessed on November 17, 2004. Accessed on October 14, 2005.

———. "One Million Women Strong" (April 27, 2004). Available online. URL: http://www.funnytimes.com/notfunny/20040427MI.html. Accessed on October 14, 2004.

Johnson, Pauline. *Legends of Vancouver* (1911). Available online. URL: http://digital.library.upenn.edu/women/johnson/vancouver/vancouver.html. Accessed on October 18, 2005.

Johnson, Susannah. *A Narrative of the Captivity of Mrs. Johnson* (1796). Available online. URL: http://womenshistory.about.com/library/weekly/aa020920c.htm. Accessed on October 13, 2005.

Keller, Helen. *The Story of My Life* (1903–5). Available online. URL: http://digital.library.upenn.edu/women/keller/life/life.html. Accessed on October 18, 2005.

Kelly, Fanny Wiggins. *Narrative of My Captivity among the Sioux Indians, 1845* (1871). Available online. URL: http://womenshistory.about.com/library/weekly/aa020920c.htm. Accessed on October 13, 2005.

Kemble, Fanny. *Journal of a Residence in America* (1863). Available online. URL: http://etext.lib.virginia.edu/toc/modeng/public/KemPlan.html. Accessed on October 16, 2005.

Mansfield, Katherine. *Bliss and Other Stories* (1920). Available online. URL: http://digital.library.upenn.edu/women/mansfield/bliss/bliss.html. Accessed on October 16, 2005.

———. *The Garden Party and Other Stories* (1922). Available online. URL: http://digital.library.upenn.edu/women/mansfield/garden/garden.html. Accessed on October 13, 2005.

Martineau, Harriet. *Harriet Martineau's Autobiography* (1877). Available online. URL: http://www.indiana.edu/~letrs/vwwp/martineau/martineau1.html. Accessed on October 13, 2005.

———. *Society in America: Observations Made during a Stay in 1837* (1837). Available online. URL: http://xroads.virginia.edu/~HYPER/DETOC/fem/martineau.htm. Accessed on October 16, 2005.

McClung, Nellie. *Purple Springs* (1921). Available online. URL: http://digital.library.upenn.edu/women/mcclung/purple/purple.html. Accessed on October 16, 2005.

———. *Sowing Seeds in Danny* (1908). Available online. URL: http://digital.library.upenn.edu/women/mcclung/danny/danny.html. Accessed on October 18, 2005.

Mill, Harriet Taylor. "The Claim of Englishwomen to the Suffrage Constitutionally Considered" (1867). Available online. URL: http://www.indiana.edu/~letrs/vwwp/taylor/suffrage.html. Accessed on October 16, 2005.

———. "The Enfranchisement of Women" (1851). Available online. URL: http://www.pinn.net/~sunshine/book-sum/ht_mill3.html. Accessed on October 16, 2005.

Millay, Edna St. Vincent. *The Ballad of the Harp Weaver* (1922). Available online. URL: http://digital.library.upenn.edu/women/millay/ballad/ballad.html. Accessed on October 18, 2005.

———. *A Few Figs from Thistles* (1922). Available online. URL: http://digital.library.upenn.edu/women/millay/figs/figs.html. Accessed on October 18, 2005.

———. *Renascence and Other Poems* (1917). Available online. URL: http://etext.lib.virginia.edu/subjects/Women-Writers.html. Accessed on October 16, 2005.

———. *Second April* (1921). Available online. URL: http://digital.library.upenn.edu/women/millay/april/second-april.html. Accessed on October 18, 2005.

Moodie, Susannah. *Roughing It in the Bush* (1852). Available online. URL: http://digital.library.upenn.edu/women/wr-mine.html. Accessed on October 14, 2005.

More, Hannah. "The Sorrows of Yamba; or, The Negro Woman's Lamentation" (1795). Available online. URL: http://wyllie.lib.virginia.edu:8086/perl/toccer-new?id=AnoSorr.sgm&images=images/mod eng&data=/texts/english/modeng/parsed&tag=public&part= 1&division=div1. Accessed on October 17, 2005.

Mott, Lucretia. "Discourse on Women" (1849). Available online. URL: http://memory.loc.gov/cgi-bin/query/D?nawbib:1:./temp/~ammem_YWLe::. Accessed on October 16, 2005.

Murphy, Emily. *Janey Canuck in the West* (1910). Available online. URL: http://digital.library.upenn.edu/women/murphy/west/west.html. Accessed on October 14, 2005.

Nation, Carry A. *The Use and Need of the Life of Carry A. Nation* (1905). Available online. URL: http://etext.lib.virginia.edu/toc/modeng/public/NatUsea.html. Accessed on October 17, 2005.

Norton, Caroline. *English Laws for Women* (1854). Available online. URL: http://digital.library.upenn.edu/women/norton/elfw/elfw.html. Accessed on October 14, 2005.

Pankhurst, Emmeline. *My Own Story* (1914). Available online. URL: http://www.fordham.edu/halsall/mod/1914Pankhurst.htm. Accessed on October 13, 2005.

———. *Why We Are Militant* (1913). Available online. URL: http://www.cooper.edu/humanities/core/hss3/e_pankhurst.html. Accessed on October 17, 2005.

Parker, Dorothy. "On the Siege of Madrid" (1937). Available online. URL: http://archive.8m.net/parker.htm. Accessed on October 18, 2005.

Plummer, Rachel. *Narrative of the Capture and Subsequent Sufferings of Mrs. Rachel Plummer* (1839). Available online. URL: http://womenshistory.about.com/library/weekly/aa020920c.htm. Accessed on October 13, 2005.

Robinson, Harriet. *Massachusetts in the Woman Suffrage Movement* (1883). Available online. URL: http://www.assumption.edu/whw/old/Massachusetts%20in%20the%20woman.html. Accessed on October 18, 2005.

Robinson, Mary. *Memoirs of Mary Robinson* (1895). Available online. URL: http://digital.library.upenn.edu/women/robinson/memoirs/memoirs.html. Accessed on October 17, 2005.

Rossetti, Christina. *Selected Poetry of Christina Rossetti* (1862–93). Available online. URL: http://celtic.benderweb.net/ cr/. Accessed on October 18, 2005.

———. *Sing-Song: A Nursery Rhyme Book* (1893). Available online. URL: http://digital.library.upenn.edu/women/rossetti/singsong/singsong.html. Accessed on October 18, 2005.

Sand, George. *Indiana* (1900). Available online. URL: http://digital.library.upenn.edu/women/sand/indiana/indiana.html. Accessed on October 13, 2005.

Sanger, Margaret. *The Pivot of Civilization* (1922). Available online. URL: http://onlinebooks.library.upenn.edu/webbin/gutbook/lookup?num=1689. Accessed on October 18, 2005.

———. *Woman and the New Race* (1920). Available online. URL: http://www.gutenberg.net/dirs/etext05/8wmnr10.txt. Accessed October 18, 2005.

Schreiner, Olive. *Dream Life and Real Life* (1893). Available online. URL: http://etext.library.adelaide.eduau/aut/schreiner_olive.html. Accessed on October 13, 2005.

———. *Woman and Labour* (1911). Available online. URL: http://etext.library.adelaide.edu.au/s/schreiner_o/woman/woman.html. Accessed on October 13, 2005.

Seaver, James. *The Life and Times of Mrs. Mary Jemison* (1824). Available online. URL: http://womenshistory.about.com/library/etext/bl_nlmj00.htm. Accessed on October 13, 2005.

Shelley, Mary. *The Last Man* (1826). Available online. URL: http://etext.lib.virginia.edu/toc/modeng/ public/SheLast.html. Accessed on October 18, 2005.

Skinner, Cornelia Otis. *Great American Speeches* (1953). Available online. URL: http://www.federalobserver.com/speeches.php?speech=7772. Accessed on October 18, 2005.

Smith, Charlotte. *The Old Manor House* (1794). Available online. URL: http://digital.library.upenn.

edu/women/smith/manor/manor.html. Accessed on October 17, 2005.

Stanton, Elizabeth Cady. *Address by Elizabeth Cady Stanton on Women's Rights* (1848). Available online. URL: http://ecssba.rutgers.edu/docs/ecswoman1.html. Accessed on October 17, 2005.

———. "Speech to the American Anti-Slavery Society" (1860). Available online. URL: http://etext.lib.virginia.edu/railton/uncletom/womanmov.html#g. Accessed on October 17, 2005.

———. *The Woman's Bible* (1895–98). Available online. URL:http://www.sacred-texts.com/wmn/wb/. Accessed on October 17, 2005.

Stein, Gertrude. *Tender Buttons: Objects, Food, Rooms* (1914). Available online. URL: http://www.bartleby.com/140/. Accessed on October 17, 2005.

Steinem, Gloria. "Women's Liberation Aims to Free Men, Too." (June 7, 1970). Available online. URL: http://scriptorium.lib.duke.edu/wlm/aims/. Accessed on October 17, 2005.

Stenhouse, Fannie. *Tell It All, the Story of a Life's Experience in Mormonism* (1874). Available online. URL: http://www.antimormon.8m.com/fstenhouseindex.html. Accessed on October 14, 2005.

Stephens, Ann Sophia. *Malaeska: The Indian Wife of the White Hunter* (1839). Available online. URL: http://www.niulib.niu.edu/badndp/dn01.html. Accessed on October 17, 2005.

———. *Mary Derwent: A Tale of the Wyoming and Mohawk Valleys in 1778* (1858). Available online. URL: http://www.letrs.indiana.edu/cgi/t/text/text-idx?c=wright2;idno=wright2-2364. Accessed on October 17, 2005.

———. *The Old Homestead* (1855). Available online. URL: http://www.gutenberg.org/etext/8078. Accessed on October 17, 2005.

Ruby Gray's Strategy (1869). Available online. URL: http://www.letrs.indiana.edu/cgi/t/text/text-idx?c=wright2;idno=wright2-2372. Accessed on October 17, 2005.

Stone, Lucy. "Disappointment Is the Lot of Women" (1855). Available online. URL: http://etext.lib.virginia.edu/railton/uncletom/womanmov.html#g. Accessed on October 17, 2005.

———. "The Progress of Fifty Years" (1893). Available online. URL: http://womenshistory.about.com/library/etext/bl_1893_lucy_stone.htm. Accessed on October 13, 2005.

Stopes, Marie. *Married Love* (1923). Available online. URL: http://digital.library.upenn.edu/women/stopes/married/married.html. Accessed on October 17, 2005.

Stowe, Harriet Beecher. *The Key to Uncle Tom's Cabin* (1853). Available online. URL: http://www.iath.

virginia.edu/utc/uncletom/key/kyhp.html. Accessed on October 17, 2005.

———. *Old Town Folks* (1869). Available online. URL: http://digital.library.upenn.edu/women/stowe/folks/folks.html. Accessed on October 17, 2005.

———. *Palmetto Leaves* (1899). Available online. URL: http://etext.lib.virginia.edu/subjects/Women-Writers.html. Accessed on October 17, 2005.

———. "Sojourner Truth, the Libyan Sibyl" (1863). Available online. URL: http://wyllie.lib.virginia.edu:8086/perl/toccer-new?id=StoSojo.sgm&images=images/modeng&data=/texts/english/modeng/parsed&tag=public&part=1&division=div1. Accessed on October 13, 2005.

Truth, Sojourner. *Narrative of Sojourner Truth* (1850). Available online. URL: http://digital.library.upenn.edu/women/truth/1850/1850.html. Accessed on October 17, 2005.

———. "The Women Want Their Rights" (1853). Available online. URL: http://etext.lib.virginia.edu/railton/uncletom/womanmov.html#g,1853. Accessed on October 17, 2005.

Weld, Angelina Grimké. "The Rights of Women and Negroes" (1863). Available online. URL: http://etext.lib.virginia.edu/railton/uncletom/womanmov.html#g. Accessed on October 14, 2005.

Wells-Barnett, Ida B. *Lynch Law in Georgia* (1899). Available online. URL: http://memory.loc.gov/cgibin/query/r?ammem/murray:@field(DOCID+@lit(lcrbmrpt1612)):@@@REF. Accessed on October 17, 2005.

West, Rebecca. *The Return of the Soldier* (1918). Available online. URL: http://digital.library.upenn.edu/women/west/soldier/soldier.html. Accessed on October 17, 2005.

Wharton, Edith. *Fighting France*. Available online. URL: http://digital.library.upenn.edu/women/wharton/france/france.html. Accessed on October 17, 2005.

Willard, Frances. "Address before the Second Biennial Convention of the Women's Christian Temperance Union" (1893). Available online. URL: http://gos.sbc.edu/w/willard.html. Accessed on October 17, 2005.

Wollstonecraft, Mary. *Maria, or, The Wrongs of Woman* (1797). Available online. URL: http://etext.lib.virginia.edu/etcbin/browse-mixed-new?id=WolMari&images=images/modeng&data=/lv1/Archive/eng-parsed&tag=public. Accessed on October 16, 2005.

Woodhull, Victoria, and Tennessee Claflin. *Woodhull & Claflin's Weekly* (1871–72). Available online. URL: http://www.victoria-woodhull.com/wcwarchive.htm. Accessed on October 17, 2005.

Woolf, Virginia. *Flush: A Biography* (1933). Available online. URL: http://etext.library.adelaide.edu.au/w/woolf/virginia/w91f/. Accessed on October 17, 2005.

———. *Monday or Tuesday: Eight Stories* (1921). Available online. URL: http://digital.library.upenn.edu/women/woolf/monday/monday.html. Accessed on October 17, 2005.

Wylie, Elinor. *Nets to Catch the Wind* (1921). Available online. URL: http://www.gutenberg.org/etext/6682. Accessed on October 17, 2005.

Yearsley, Ann. "A Poem on the Inhumanity of the Slave Trade" (1788) Available online. URL: http://www.brycchancarey.com/slavery/yearsley1.htm. Accessed on October 17, 2005.

Yezierska, Anzia. *Hungry Hearts* (1920). Available online. URL: http://digital.library.upenn.edu/women/yezierska/hearts/hearts.html. Accessed on October 18, 2005.

SECONDARY SOURCE BIBLIOGRAPHY

Aay, Henry. "Environmental Themes in Ecofiction: *In the Center of the Nation* and *Animal Dreams*," *Journal of Cultural Geography* 14, no. 2 (Spring–Summer 1994): 65–85.

Abbe, Elfrieda. "Risky Business," *Writer* 116, no. 10 (October 2003): 22–26.

Abrahams, Cecil. *The Tragic Life: Bessie Head and Literature in South Africa.* Trenton, N.J.: African World, 1990.

Acocella, Joan. "Cather and the Academy," *New Yorker,* 27 November 1995, pp. 56–70.

———. *Willa Cather and the Politics of Criticism.* New York: Vintage, 2002.

Afshar, Haleh, ed. *Women in the Middle East: Perceptions, Realities, and Struggles for Liberation.* London: Macmillan, 1993.

Ahearn, Edward J. "The Modern English Visionary: Peter Ackroyd's *Hawksmoor* and Angela Carter's *The Passion of New Eve*," *Twentieth Century Literature* 46, no. 4 (Winter 2000): 453–469.

Aidoo, Ama Ata. "Feminist Furore," *New Internationalist,* 336 (July 2001): 5.

Alaimo, Stacy. "The Undomesticated Nature of Feminism: Mary Austin and the Progressive Women Conservationists," *Studies in American Fiction* 26, no. 1 (Spring 1998): 73–96.

Alexie, Sherman. "She Had Some Horses: The Education of a Poet," *Teachers and Writers* (March–April 1995): 1–3.

Allen, Carolyn. *Following Djuna: Women Lovers and the Erotics of Loss.* Bloomington: Indiana University Press, 1996.

Allende, Isabel. "Pinochet's Ghost," *New Perspectives Quarterly* 16, no. 3 (Spring 1999): 22–26.

Allison, Dorothy. "The Future of Females: Octavia Butler's Mother Lode." In *Reading Black, Reading Feminist.* Edited by Henry Louis Gates, Jr. New York: Meridian, 1990.

Altaba-Artal, Dolors. *Aphra Behn's English Feminism: Wit and Satire.* Selingsgrove, Pa.: Susquehanna University Press, 1999.

Altman, Meryl. "Beyond Trashiness: The Sexual Language of 1970s Feminist Fiction," *Journal of International Women's Studies* 4, no. 2 (April 2003): 1–25.

———. "Lives on the Line," *Women's Review of Books* 19, no. 7 (April 2002): 6–7.

———. "Looking for Sappho," *Women's Review of Books* 21, no. 4 (January 2004): 8–10.

Amago, Samuel. "The Form and Function of Homosocial Desire in *La Madre Naturaleza*," *Romance Quarterly* 48, no. 1 (Winter 2001): 54–63.

Anderlini-D'Onofrio, Serena. *The "Weak" Subject: Modernity, Eros, and Women's Playwriting.* Cranbury, N.J.: Associated University Press, 1998.

Angier, Carole. *Jean Rhys.* New York: Penguin, 1985.

Arcana, Judith. *Grace Paley's Life Stories: A Literary Biography.* Chicago: University of Illinois Press, 1993.

Ardis, Ann L., and Leslie W. Lewis. *Women's Experience of Modernity 1875–1945.* Baltimore: Johns Hopkins University Press, 2003.

Aresty, Esther B. *The Delectable Past.* New York: Simon & Schuster, 1964.

Arias, Arturo. *The Rigoberta Menchú Controversy.* Minneapolis: University of Minnesota Press, 2001.

Aricò, Santo L. *Oriana Fallaci: The Woman and the Myth.* Carbondale: Southern Illinois University Press, 1998.

Armstrong, Nancy. *Desire and Domestic Fiction: A Political History of the Novel.* Oxford: Oxford University Press, 1995.

Arseneau, Mary, Anthony H. Harrison, and Lorraine Jansen Kooistra, eds. *The Culture of Christina Rossetti: Female Poetics and Victorian Contexts.* Athens: Ohio University Press, 1999.

Ashbery, John. "Tradition and Talent," *New York Herald Tribune Book Week,* September 4 1966.

Astrachan, Anthony. "Rebellion and the Rules We Live By," *Washington Post,* 12 July 1987, p. O3.

Atwood, Margaret. "Review: *Diving into the Wreck,*" *New York Times Book Review,* 30 December 1973, pp. 161–162.

———. *Strange Things: The Malevolent North in Canadian Literature.* Oxford: Clarendon Press, 1995.

———. *Survival: A Thematic Guide to Canadian Literature.* Toronto: Anansi, 1972.

Auchincloss, Louis. *Pioneers and Caretakers: A Study of Nine American Women Novelists.* Minneapolis: University of Minnesota Press, 1965.

Auerbach, Nina. *Daphne du Maurier: Haunted Heiress.* Philadelphia: University of Pennsylvania Press, 1999.

———. *Our Vampires, Ourselves.* Chicago: University of Chicago Press, 1995.

Avrich, Paul. *An American Anarchist: The Life of Voltairine de Cleyre.* Princeton, N.J.: Princeton University Press, 1978.

Babb, Genie. "Paula Gunn Allen's Grandmothers: Toward a Responsive Feminist-Tribal Reading of *Two Old Women,*" *American Indian Quarterly* 21, no. 2 (Spring 1997): 299–320.

Bacon, Margaret Hope. *Mothers of Feminism: The Story of Quaker Women in America.* San Francisco: Harper, 1986.

Bahl, Vinay. "Reflections on the Recent Work of Sheila Rowbotham: Women's Movements and Building Bridges," *Monthly Review: An Independent Socialist Magazine* 48, no. 6 (November 1996): 31–42.

Bak, John S., "Escaping the Jaundiced Eye: Foucauldian Panopticism in Charlotte Perkins Gilman's 'The Yellow Wallpaper,' " *Studies in Short Fiction* 31, no. 1 (Winter 1994): 39–46.

Baker, Dorothy Z. " 'Detested Be the Epithet!': Definition, Maxim, and the Language of Social Dicta in Hannah Webster Foster's 'The Coquette,' " *Essays in Literature* 23, no. 1 (Spring 1996): 58–68.

Baker, Houston A. *Modernism and the Harlem Renaissance.* Chicago: University of Chicago Press, 1989.

Baker, Ray Palmer. *The History of English-Canadian Literature to the Confederation.* New York: Russell & Russell, 1968.

Baldwin, Kate A. "Between Mother and History: Jean Stafford, Marguerite Oswald, and U.S. Cold War Women's Citizenship," *Differences: A Journal of Feminist Cultural Studies* 13, no. 3 (Fall 2002): 83–120.

Barban, Judith. "Lai Ester: Acceptance of the Status Quo in the Fables of Marie de France," *Romance Quarterly* 49, no. 1 (Winter 2002): 3–11.

Barker, Deborah. *Aesthetics and Gender in American Literature.* Cranbury, N.J.: Associated University Presses, 2000.

Barnes, Steven. "Octavia E. Butler," *American Visions* 15, no. 5 (October–November 2000): 24–28.

Barnett, Louise, and James Thorson, eds. *Leslie Marmon Silko: A Collection of Critical Essays.* Albuquerque: University of New Mexico Press, 1999.

Barr, Tina. " 'Queen of the Niggerati' and the Nile: The Isis-Osiris Myth in Zora Neale Hurston's *Their Eyes Were Watching God,*" *Journal of Modern Literature* 25, no. 3–4 (Summer 2002): 101–114.

Bartkowski, Frances. *Feminist Utopias.* Lincoln: University of Nebraska Press, 1991.

Bartlet, Alison. "A Passionate Subject: Representations of Desire in Feminist Pedagogy," *Gender and Education* 10, no. 1 (March 1998): 85–92.

Bartlett, Karen. "When Caprice and Meera Get Together," *New Statesman,* 15 March 2004, pp. 26–27.

Bartley, Paula. *Emmeline Pankhurst.* New York: Routledge, 2003.

Bartolomeo, Joseph F. "Subversion of Romance in 'The Old Manor House,' " *Studies in English Literature, 1500–1900* 33, no. 3 (Summer 1993): 645–657.

Bashir, Samiya A. "Who Do You Love?" *Lambda Book Report* 11, no. 3 (October 2002): 28–30.

Bassett, Mark T. "Imagination, Control, and Betrayal in Jane Bowles' 'A Stick of Green Candy,' " *Studies in Short Fiction* 24, no. 1 (Winter 1987): 25–29.

Bauer, Margaret Donovan. *The Fiction of Ellen Gilchrist.* Gainesville: University Press of Florida, 1999.

Baum, Geraldine. "An Activist in Control of Her Outrage: Diplomacy: Bette Bao Lord Brings a Cool Civility to Her Cause," *Los Angeles Times,* 31 October 1997, p. 1.

Baym, Nina. "Between Enlightenment and Victorian: Toward a Narrative of American Women Writers Writing History," *Critical Inquiry* 18, no. 1 (Autumn 1991): 22–41.

———. *Woman's Fiction: A Guide to Novels by and about Women in America, 1820–70.* Chicago: University of Illinois Press, 1993.

Beasley, Maurine Hoffman, and Sheila Jean Gibbons. *Taking Their Place: A Documentary History of Women and Journalism.* State College, Pa.: Strata, 2002.

Beattie, Valerie. "The Mystery at Thornfield: Representations of Madness in *Jane Eyre,*" *Studies in the Novel* 28, no. 4 (Winter 1996): 493–505.

Becker, Jillian. *Giving Up: The Last Days of Sylvia Plath.* New York: St. Martin's, 2003.

Bellanca, Mary Ellen. "Science, Animal Sympathy, and Anna Barbauld's 'The Mouse's Petition,' "

Eighteenth-Century Studies 37, no. 1 (2003): 47–67.

Bellman, Samuel Irving. "Shirley Jackson: A Study of the Short Fiction," *Studies in Short Fiction* 31, no. 2 (Spring 1994): 282–293.

Bendis, Debra. "Intruder in My Arms," *Christian Century,* 19 April 2003, pp. 30–33.

Bennett, Paula. "Critical Clitoridectomy: Female Sexual Imagery and Feminist Psychoanalytic Theory," *Signs: Journal of Women in Culture and Society* 18, no. 2 (Winter 1993): 235–259.

Berg, Allison, and Meridith Taylor. "Enacting Difference: Marita Bonner's 'Purple Flower' and the Ambiguities of Race," *African American Review* 32, no. 3 (Fall 1998): 469–480.

Bergland, Renee L. *The National Uncanny: Indian Ghosts and American Subjects.* Hanover, N.H.: Dartmouth College/University Press of New England, 2000.

Berke, Nancy. *Women Poets on the Left: Lola Ridge, Genevieve Taggard, Margaret Walker.* Gainesville: University Press of Florida, 2001.

Bernstein, Susan Naomi. "Writing and *Little Women:* Alcott's Rhetoric of Subversion," *ATQ* 7, no. 1 (March 1993): 25–43.

"Bestselling Author Amy Tan Is a Wonderful Storyteller," *Chinatown News,* 18 February 1996, pp. 22–23.

"Betty Friedan," *Workforce* 81, no. 1 (January 2002): 29.

Bierhorst, John, ed. *The Way of the Earth: Native America and the Environment.* New York: William Morrow, 1994.

Bilger, Audrey. *Laughing Feminism: Subversive Comedy in Frances Burney, Maria Edgeworth, and Jane Austen.* Detroit, Mich.: Wayne State University Press, 1998.

Blackford, Holly. "Figures of Orality: The Master, the Mistress, the Slave Mother in Harriet Jacobs's *Incidents in the Life of a Slave Girl: Written by Herself,*" *Papers on Language and Literature* 37, no. 3 (Summer 2001): 314–336.

Blakey, Dorothy. *The Minerva Press, 1790–1820.* London: Oxford University Press, 1939.

Bloyd, Rebekah. "Cultural Convergences in Cathy Song's Poetry," *Peace Review* 10, no. 3 (September 1998): 393–400.

Blumenfeld-Kosinski, Renate. " 'Femme de Corps et Femme par Sens': Christine de Pizan's Saintly Women," *Romanic Review* 87, no. 2 (March 1996): 157–175.

Blyth, Ian. "An Interview with Hélène Cixous," *Paragraph* 23, no. 3 (November 2000): 338–343.

Boehm, Beth A. "Feminist Metafiction and Androcentric Reading Strategies: Angela Carter's Reconstructed Reader in *Nights at the Circus,*" *Critique* 37, no. 1 (Fall 1995): 35–49.

Bogiatzis, Demetris. "Sexuality and Gender: 'The Interlude' of Sarah Grand's 'The Heavenly Twins,' " *English Literature in Transition 1880–1920* 44, no. 1 (Winter 2001): 46–63.

Bolton, Betsy. "Romancing the Stone: 'Perdita' Robinson in Wordsworth's London," *ELH* 64, no. 3 (Fall 1997): 727–759.

Booth, Alison. "The Mother of All Cultures: Camille Paglia and Feminist Mythologies," *Kenyon Review* 21, no. 1 (Winter 1999): 27–45.

Bottum, J. "Flannery O'Connor Banned," *Crisis* 18, no. 9 (October 2000): 48–49.

Bouson, J. Brooks. " 'You Nothing but Trash': White Trash Shame in Dorothy Allison's *Bastard Out of Carolina,*" *Southern Literary Journal* 34, no. 1 (Fall 2001): 101–123.

Boyd, Melba Joyce. *Discarded Legacy: Politics and Poetics in the Life of Frances E. W. Harper, 1825–1911.* Detroit, Mich.: Wayne State University Press, 1994.

Bradford, Helen. "Olive Schreiner's Hidden Agony: Fact, Fiction and Teenage Abortion," *Journal of South African Studies* 21, no. 4 (1995): 623–641.

Bradley, Jennifer. "Woman at the Golden Gate: The Last Works of Gertrude Atherton," *Women's Studies* 12, no. 1 (1986): 17–30.

Brammer, Leila R. *Excluded from Suffrage History: Matilda Joslyn Gage, Nineteenth-Century American Feminist.* Westport, Conn.: Greenwood, 2000.

Brant, Beth, ed. *A Gathering of Spirit: A Collection by North American Indian Women.* Ithaca, N.Y.: Firebrand, 1989.

———. *Writing as Witness: Essays and Talk.* Toronto: Women's Press, 1994.

Brewer, Derek. *English Gothic Literature.* New York: Schocken Books, 1983.

Brice, Jennifer. "Earth as Mother, Earth as Other in Novels by Silko and Hogan," *Critique* 39, no. 2 (Winter 1998): 127–138.

Bridge, Helen. "Christa Wolf's *Kassandra* and *Medea:* Continuity and Change," *German Life and Letters* 57, no. 1 (January 2004): 33–43.

Brody, Ervin C. "The Poet in the Trenches: *The Complete Poems of Anna Akhmatova,*" *Literary Review* 37, no. 4 (Summer 1994): 689–704.

Bromberg, P. S. "Margaret Drabble's *The Radiant Way:* Feminist Metafiction," *Novel: A Forum on Fiction* 24, no. 1 (Fall 1990): 5–25.

Brontë, Charlotte. *The Letters of Charlotte Brontë: With a Selection of Letters by Family and Friends.* Vol. 2. *1848–1851.* New York: Oxford University Press, 2000.

Brooks, Kristina. "Alice Dunbar-Nelson's Local Colors of Ethnicity, Class, and Place," *MELUS* 23, no. 2 (Summer 1998): 3–26.

Brown, Anne E., and Marjanne E. Gooze. *International Women's Writing: New Landscapes of Identity.* Westport, Conn.: Greenwood, 1995.

Brown, Craig. "Fay Weldon: A Short Story," *Vogue,* January 1989, pp. 182–185.

Brown, E. Barnsley. "Passover Over: The Tragic Mulatta and (Dis)Integration of Identity in Adrienne Kennedy's Plays," *African American Review* 35, no. 2 (Summer 2001): 281–295.

Brown, Jordan. *Elizabeth Blackwell.* New York: Chelsea House, 1989.

Brownworth, Victoria A. "Who Will Publish Our Books? Lesbian and Feminist Presses Imperiled by Industry Crunch," *Lambda Book Report* 5, no. 11 (May 1997): 10.

Brunazzi, Elizabeth. "The Question of Colette and Collaboration," *Tulsa Studies in Women's Literature* 13, no. 2 (Fall 1994): 281–291.

Brustein, Robert. "Women in the Theater," *New Republic,* 15 May 2000, pp. 32–34.

Bryson, Valerie. "Marxism and Feminism: Can the 'Unhappy Marriage' Be Saved," *Journal of Political Ideologies* 9, no. 1 (February 2004): 13–30.

Buckley, William F. "Suzanne La Follette, RIP." *National Review,* 13 May 1983, p. 541.

Burdett, Carolyn. *Olive Schreiner and the Progress of Feminism: Evolution, Gender, Empire.* London: Palgrave Macmillan, 2001.

Burgess, Miranda J. "Courting Ruin: The Economic Romances of Frances Burney," *Novel: A Forum on Fiction* 28, no. 2 (Winter 1995): 131–153.

Burke, Carolyn. *Becoming Modern: The Life of Mina Loy.* Berkeley: University of California Press, 1997.

Burns, Christy. "Beautiful Labors: Lyricism and Feminist Revisions in Eavan Boland's Poetry," *Tulsa Studies in Women's Literature* 20, no. 2 (Fall 2001): 217–236.

Burns, E. Jane. *Bodytalk: When Women Speak in Old French Literature.* Philadelphia: University of Pennsylvania Press, 1993.

Burr, Zofia. *Of Women, Poetry, and Power: Strategies of Address in Dickinson, Miles, Brooks, Lorde, and Angelou.* Chicago: University of Illinois Press, 2002.

Burroughs, Catherine B. "A Reasonable Woman's Desire": The Private Theatrical and Joanna Baillie's 'The Tryal,' " *Texas Studies in Literature and Language* 38, no. 3/4 (Fall–Winter 1996): 265–284.

Burton-Hardee, C. "Red Dirt Girl as Hero: Dorothy Allison's *Cavedweller* as Southern White Trash Hero," *Journal of American and Comparative Cultures* 25, no. 3/4 (Fall 2002): 243–245.

Campbell, Elizabeth. "Re-visions, Re-flections, Re-creations: Epistolarity in Novels by Contemporary Women," *Twentieth Century Literature* 41, no. 3 (Fall 1995): 332–348.

Campbell, Kim. "It's 'Best' Lists Time: Here's *Ms.* Magazine's," *Christian Science Monitor,* 13 December 2001, p. 17.

Capaldi, Nicholas. *John Stuart Mill: A Biography.* Cambridge: Cambridge University Press, 2004.

Capozzella, Michele. "Anne McCaffrey: Science Fiction Storyteller," *School Library Journal* 47, no. 9 (September 2001): 257.

Carbonell, Ana Maria. "From Llorona to Gritone: Coatlicue in Feminist Tales by Viramontes and Cisneros," *MELUS* 24, no. 2 (Summer 1999): 53.

Carlson, Kathie. *Life's Daughter/Death's Bride.* Boston: Shambhala, 1997.

Carnell, Jennifer. *The Literary Lives of Mary Elizabeth Braddon.* Hastings, England: Sensation, 2000.

Carney, Sean. "The Passion of Joanna Baillie: Playwright as Martyr," *Theatre Journal* 52, no. 2 (May 2000): 227–252.

Caron, Caroline. " 'Le Deuxième Sexe' de Simone de Beauvoir: Une Lecture Susceptible d'Inflechir la Resistance des Jeunnes Femmes Face au Feminisme," *Canadian Woman Studies* 20, no. 4 (Winter–Spring 2001): 36–40.

Carr, Brenda. " 'A Woman Speaks . . . I Am Woman and Not White': Politics of Voice, Tactical Essentialism, and Cultural Intervention in Audre Lorde's Activist Poetics and Practice," *College Literature* 20, no. 2 (June 1993): 133–153.

Carroll, Denolyn. "Grace," *Black Issues Book Review* 5, no. 2 (March–April 2003): 34–35.

Carter, Cynthia, Gill Branston, and Stuart Allan, eds. *News, Gender and Power.* New York: Routledge, 1998.

Case, Sue-Ellen, ed. *Performing Feminisms: Feminist Critical Theory and Theatre.* Baltimore: Johns Hopkins University Press, 1990.

Cavalcanti, Ildney. "Utopias of/f Language in Contemporary Feminist Literary Dystopias," *Utopian Studies* 11, no. 2 (Spring 2000): 152.

Chalberg, John. *Emma Goldman: American Individualist.* Harlow, England: Pearson Education, 1997.

Champion, Laurie. *The Critical Response to Eudora Welty's Fiction.* Westport, Conn.: Greenwood, 1994.

———. " 'I Keep Looking Back to See Where I've Been': Bobbie Ann Mason's *Clear Springs* and Henry David Thoreau's *Walden*," *Southern Literary Journal* 36, no. 2 (Spring 2004): 47–58.

Chang, Joan Chiung-Heiu. *Transforming Chinese American Literature: A Study of History, Sexuality, and Ethnicity.* New York: Peter Lang, 2000.

Chapman, Rosemary. "Writing of/from the Fourth World: Gabrielle Roy and Ungava," *Quebec Studies* 35 [cq] (Spring–Summer 2003): 45–63.

Charles, Ron, "Mothers of Nature Howling at the Moon," *Christian Science Monitor,* 19 October 2000, p. 20.

Chase, Karen, and J. P. Stern, eds. *Eliot: Middlemarch.* Cambridge: Cambridge University Press, 1991.

Chaucer, Geoffrey. *The Canterbury Tales.* Translated by Nevill Coghill. London: Cressed, 1992.

Cheng, Ming L. "The Unrepentant Fire: Tragic Limitations in Hisaye Yamamoto's 'Seventeen Syllables,' " *MELUS* 19, no. 4 (Winter 1994): 91–107.

Chesler, Ellen. *Woman of Valor: Margaret Sanger and the Birth Control Movement in America.* New York: Simon & Schuster, 1992.

Chesler, Phyllis. *Women and Madness.* New York: Doubleday, 1972.

Cheung, King-Kok. *An Interethnic Companion to Asian American Literature.* New York: Cambridge University Press, 1997.

Chinoy, Helen Krich, and Linda Walsh Jenkins, eds. *Women in American Theatre.* New York: Theatre Communications Group, 1987.

Christ, Carol P. *Diving Deep and Surfacing: Women Writers on Spiritual Quest.* Boston: Beacon, 1980.

Chung, Haeja K. "Harriette Simpson Arnow's Authorial Testimony: Toward a Reading of *The Dollmaker,*" *Critique* 36, no. 2 (Spring 1995): 211–223.

Chute, Marchette. *Geoffrey Chaucer of England.* New York: E. P. Dutton, 1946.

Ciociola, Gail. *Wendy Wasserstein: Dramatizing Women, Their Choices and Their Boundaries.* Jefferson, N.C.: McFarland, 1998.

Civello, Catherine A. "Stevie Smith's 'Ecriture Feminine': Pre-Oedipal Desires and Wartime Realities," *Mosaic* 28, no. 2 (June 1995): 109–122.

Clark, Keith. "A Distaff Dream Deferred? Ann Petry and the Art of Subversion," *African American Review* 26, no. 3 (Fall 1992): 495–505.

Clayton, Cherry. "Interview with Joy Kogawa," *Canadian Ethnic Studies* 34, no. 2 (2002): 106–116.

Clemente, Linda M., and William A. Clement. *Gabrielle Roy: Creation and Memory.* Toronto: ECW, 1997.

Clery, E. J. *The Rise of Supernatural Fiction, 1762–1800.* Cambridge: Cambridge University Press, 1995.

———. *Women's Gothic from Clara Reeve to Mary Shelley.* Tavistock, England: Northcote House, 2000.

Clinton, Catherine. *Fanny Kemble's Civil Wars.* Oxford: Oxford University Press, 2001.

Clough, Patricia Ticineto. "The Hybrid Criticism of Patriarchy: Rereading Kate Millett's 'Sexual Politics,' " *Sociological Quarterly* 35, no. 3 (August 1994): 473–486.

Coelsch-Foisner, Sabine, "Rossetti's 'Goblin Market,' " *Explicator* 61, no. 1 (Fall 2002): 28–30.

Coen, Stephanie. "Marsha Norman's Triple Play," *American Theatre* 8, no. 12 (March 1992): 22–26.

Coffey, Donna. "Protecting the Botanic Garden: Seward, Darwin, and Coalbrookdale," *Women's Studies* 31, no. 2 (March–April 2002): 141–164.

Cohen, Esther. "Uncommon Woman: An Interview with Wendy Wasserstein," *Women's Studies* 15, no. 1–3 (1998): 257–270.

Cohen, Jeffrey Jerome, ed. *Monster Theory.* Minneapolis: University of Minnesota Press, 1996.

Coiner, Constance. *Better Red: The Writing and Resistance of Tillie Olsen and Meridel Le Sueur.* Chicago: University of Illinois Press, 1998.

Collecott, Diana. "Remembering Oneself: The Reputation and Later Poetry of H. D.," *Critical Quarterly* 27, no. 1 (Spring 1985): 7–22.

Collins, Martha S. "Inscribing the Space of Female Identity in Carmen Martín Gaite's 'Entre Visillos,' " *Symposium* 51, no. 2 (Summer 1997): 66–78.

Conn, Peter. *Pearl S. Buck: A Cultural Biography.* Cambridge: Cambridge University Press, 1996.

Conniff, Ruth. "Katha Pollitt," *Progressive* 58, no. 12 (December 1994): 34–39.

"A Conversation with Gloria Naylor," *Essence* 29, no. 2 (June 1998): 70.

Conway, Alison. "The Protestant Cause and a Protestant Whore: Aphra Behn's Love-letters," *Eighteenth-Century Life* 25, no. 3 (Fall 2001): 1–19.

Cook, B. W. "Books: The Womanly Art of Biography." *Ms.,* January–February 1991, pp. 60–62.

Cook, Richard M. *Carson McCullers.* New York: Frederick Unger, 1975.

Coontz, Stephanie. *The Way We Weren't: American Families and the Nostalgia Trap.* New York: Basic, 2000.

Copeland, Edward. *Women Writing about Money: Women's Fiction in England, 1790–1820.* Cambridge: Cambridge University Press, 1995.

Cooper, Jane Roberta, ed. *Reading Adrienne Rich: Reviews and Re-visions, 1951–1981.* Ann Arbor: University of Michigan Press, 1984.

Cooperman, Jeannette Batz. *The Broom Closet: Secret Meanings of Domesticity in Postfeminist Novels by Louise Erdrich, Mary Gordon, Toni Morrison, Marge Piercy, Jane Smiley, and Amy Tan.* New York: Peter Lang, 1999.

Cormican, Muriel. "Woman's Heterosexual Experience in Christa Wolf's *Kassandra*: A Critique of GDR

Feminism," *Philological Quarterly* 81, no. 1 (Winter 2002): 109–128.

Cormier-Hamilton, Patrice. "Black Naturalism and Toni Morrison: The Journey away from Self-Love in *The Bluest Eye*," *MELUS* 19, no. 4 (Winter 1994): 109–127.

Cornfield, Jill. " 'A Prism of Personal Experience': Letty Cottin Pogrebin Will Speak about Being Jewish and a Feminist," *Baltimore Jewish Times*, 25 October 1996, p. 24.

Cosslett, Tess, "Maria, or the Wrongs of Woman," *Notes and Queries* 42, no. 4 (December 1995): 502.

Coughlin, Richard J. "Review: *View to the Southeast*," *Journal of Asian Studies (pre–1986)* 17, no. 4 (August 1958): 637.

Cowan, Ruth Schwartz. *More Work for Mother*. New York: Basic, 1983.

Cowell, Andrew. "Deadly Letters: 'Deus Amanz,' Marie's 'Prologue' to the Lais and the Dangerous Nature of the Gloss," *Romanic Review* 88, no. 3 (May 1997): 337–363.

Craig, Amanda. "A Jane for Our Age," *New Statesman*, 22 May 1998, pp. 56–57.

Creighton, Joanne V. *Joyce Carol Oates: Novels of the Middle Years*. New York: Twayne, 1992.

Cujec, Carol, "Excavating Memory, Reconstructing Legacy," *World and I* 16, no. 7 (July 2001): 215–223.

Cutter, Martha J. "Beyond Stereotypes: Mary Wilkins Freeman's Radical Critique of Nineteenth-Century Cults of Femininity," *Women's Studies* 21, no. 4, (September 1992): 383–395.

———. "Philomela Speaks: Alice Walker's Revisioning of Rape Archetypes in *The Color Purple*," *MELUS* 25, no. 3–4 (Fall–Winter 2000): 161–180.

D'Albertis, Deirdre, "The Domestic Drone: Margaret Oliphant and a Political History of the Novel," *Studies in English Literature, 1500–1900* 37, no. 4 (Autumn 1997): 805–830.

Daly, Brenda. "Sexual Politics in Two Collections of Joyce Carol Oates's Short Fiction," *Studies in Short Fiction* 32, no. 1 (Winter 1995): 83–93.

Dame, Enid. "Reclaiming a Culture through Poems," *Belles Lettres* 10, no. 1 (Fall 1994): 87.

———, Lilly Rivlin, and Henny Wenkart, eds. *Which Lilith? Feminist Writers Recreate the World's First Woman*. Lanham, Md.: Jason Aronson, 1998.

D'Amico, Diane, "Saintly Singer or Tanagra Figurine? Christina Rossetti through the Eyes of Katharine Tynan and Sara Teasdale," *Victorian Poetry* 32, no. 3–4 (Autumn–Winter 1994): 387–407.

Danford, Natalie. "Feminist Publishing for Fun and Profit," *Publishers Weekly*, 6 October 2003, p. 18.

Daniel, Janice Barnes. "Function or Frill: The Quilt as Storyteller in Toni Morrison's *Beloved*," *Midwest Quarterly* 41, no. 3 (Spring 2000): 321–329.

Dart, William. "Something to Sing About in 2003," *New Zealand Herald*, 17 December 2003.

David, Kathy S. "Beauty and the Beast: The 'Feminization' of Weyland in the Vampire Tapestry," *Extrapolation* 43, no. 1 (Spring 2002): 62–80.

Davies, Catherine. "Founding-Fathers and Domestic Genealogies: Situating Gertrudis Gómez de Avellaneda," *Bulletin of Latin American Research* 22, no. 4 (October 2003): 423–444.

Davies, Kathleen. "Spinster's Revenge: Creating a Child of One's Own," *Mississippi Quarterly* 49, no. 2 (Spring 1996): 227–239.

Davis, Allen F. *American Heroine: The Life and Legend of Jane Addams*. Chicago: Ivan R. Dee, 1973.

Davis, Rocio G., and Sami Ludwig. *Asian American Literature in the International Context: Readings on Fiction, Poetry and Performance*. London: Lit Verlag, 2002.

Davy, Jennifer Anne. "The Trace of Desires: Sexuality, Gender and Power," *Journal of Women's History* 12, no. 2 (Summer 2000): 227.

Dearborn, Mary V. *Queen of Bohemia: The Life of Louise Bryant*. Boston: Houghton Mifflin, 1995.

DeCosta-Willis, Miriam. "Afra-Hispanic Writers and Feminist Discourse," *NWSA Journal* 5, no. 2 (Summer 1993): 204–217.

DeCoster, Cyrus. "Pardo Bazán and Ideological Literature," *Romance Quarterly* 40, no. 4 (Fall 1993): 226–234.

Dederer, Claire. "She's Gotta Have It," *Nation*, 6 October 2003, p. 23.

Deegan, Mary Jo, and Christopher W. Podeschi. "The Ecofeminist Pragmatism of Charlotte Perkins Gilman," *Environmental Ethics* 23, no. 1 (Spring 2001): 19–36.

Deiter, Kristen. "Cultural Expressions of the Victorian Age: The New Woman, *Jane Eyre*, and Interior Design," *Lamar Journal of the Humanities* 25, no. 2 (2000): 27–42.

DeJean, Joan. *Fictions of Sappho, 1546–1937*. Chicago: University of Chicago Press, 1989.

DeKoven, Marianne. "Introduction: Transformations of Gertrude Stein," *Modern Fiction Studies* 42, no. 3 (Fall 1996): 470–484.

De La Motte, Eugenia. "Refashioning the Mind: The Revolutionary Rhetoric of Voltairine de Cleyre," *Legacy*, 30 April 2003, p. 153.

Dellamora, Richard. "Apocalyptic Irigaray," *Twentieth Century Literature* 46, no. 4 (Winter 2000): 492–512.

DelRosso, Jeanna. "The Convent as Colonist: Catholicism in the Works of Contemporary Women Writers of the Americas," *MELUS* 26, no. 3 (Fall 2001): 183–201.

Demastes, William W. "Jessie and Thelma Revisited: Marsha Norman's Conceptual Challenge in *'night, Mother*," *Modern Drama* 36, no. 1 (March 1993): 109–119.

"Denise Levertov," *Chicago Review* 45, no. 2 (1999): 107–110.

D'Eramso, Stacey. "Just an Ordinary Day," *Nation*, 23 December 1996, pp. 25–26.

DeRose, David J. "Cherríe Moraga," *American Theatre* 13, no. 8 (October 1996): 76–78.

Deshazer, Mary K. "Fractured Borders: Women's Cancer and Feminist Theatre," *NWSA Journal* 15, no. 2 (Summer 2003): 1–26.

Des Pres, Terrence. *Praises and Dispraises: Poetry and Politics, the 20th Century.* New York: Viking, 1988.

Diamond, Elin. *Performance and Cultural Politics.* New York: Routledge, 1996.

———. *Unmaking Mimesis: Essays on Feminism and Theater.* New York: Routledge, 1997.

DiCicco, Lorraine. "The Dis-Ease of Katherine Anne Porter's Greensick Girls in 'Old Mortality,' " *Southern Literary Journal* 33, no. 2 (Spring 2001): 80–98.

Dickson, E. Jane. "Somerset Mourn: What's Eating Novelist Margaret Drabble," *The Australian*, 21 September 2002, p. B1.

Didicher, Nicole E. "Adolescence, Imperialism, and Identity in Kim and Pegasus in Flight," *Mosaic* 34, no. 2 (June 2001): 149.

Diehl, Joanne Feit. *Women Poets and the American Sublime.* Bloomington: Indiana University Press, 1990.

Dillon, Brian. " 'Never Having Had You, I Cannot Let You Go': Sharon Olds's Poems of a Father-Daughter Relationship," *Literary Review* 1, no. 108 (Fall 1993): 108–118.

Dingledine, Donald. "Woman Can Walk on Water: Island, Myth, and Community in Kate Chopin's *The Awakening* and Paule Marshall's *Praisesong for the Widow*," *Women's Studies* 22, no. 2 (March 1993): 197–216.

Dirda, Michael. "Satyricon in Manhattan," *Washington Post Book World*, 18 March 1990, p. 10.

Dodd, Elizabeth. *The Veiled Mirror and the Woman Poet: H. D., Louise Bogan, Elizabeth Bishop, and Louise Glück.* Columbia: University of Missouri Press, 1992.

Dole, Pat. "Review: *Priestess of Avalon*," *Kliatt* 36, no. 1 (January 2002): 46.

Domecq, Alcina Lubitch. "La Llorona," *Literary Review* 43, no. 1 (Fall 1999): 17.

Donaldson, Elizabeth J. "The Corpus of the Madwoman: Toward a Feminist Disability Studies Theory of Embodiment and Mental Illness," *NWSA Journal* 14, no. 3 (Fall 2002): 99–119.

Donovan, Kathleen M. *Feminist Readings of Native American Literature: Coming to Voice.* Tucson: University of Arizona Press, 1998.

Doten, Patti, "Sharing Her Mother's Secrets," *Boston Globe*, 21 June 1991, p. 63.

Douglas, Foster. "Love, Death, and the Written Word: The Lonely Passion of Oriana Fallaci," *Los Angeles Times*, 10 January 1993, p. 20.

Douglass, Paul. *Lady Caroline Lamb, a Biography.* London: Palgrave Macmillan, 2004.

"Down and Out in America," *Women's Review of Books* 18, no. 10/11 (July 2001): 6–7.

Doyle, Jacqueline. "Assumptions of the Virgin and Recent Chicana Writing," *Women's Studies* 26, no. 2 (April 1997): 171–201.

Dubek, Laura. "Lessons in Solidarity: Buchi Emecheta and Mariama Bâ on Female Victim(izer)s," *Women's Studies* 30, no. 3 (June 2001): 199–223.

Dublin, Thomas, and Kathryn Kish Sklar. *Women and Power in American History.* Vol. 1. New York: Prentice-Hall, 2001.

Dukats, Mara L. "The Hybrid Terrain of Literary Imagination: Maryse Conde's Black Witch of Salem, Nathaniel Hawthorne's Hester Prynne, and Aime Cesaire's Heroic Poetic Voice," *College Literature* 22, no. 1 (February 1995): 51–61.

Dulfano, Isabel. "Some Thoughts Shared with Helena María Viramontes," *Women's Studies* 30, no. 5 (September 2001): 647–662.

Durantine, Peter. "For Pa. Author, Censors Weave Scariest Tales," *Philadelphia Inquirer*, 10 October 1993, p. B1.

Eads, Martha Greene, "Unwitting Redemption in Margaret Edson's 'Wit,' " *Christianity and Literature* 51, no. 2 (Winter 2002): 241–255.

Ebest, Ron. "Anzia Yezierska and the Popular Debate over the Jews," *MELUS* 25, no. 1 (Spring 2000): 105–127.

Echols, Alice. *Daring to Be Bad: Radical Feminism in America, 1967–1975.* Minneapolis: University of Minnesota Press, 1990.

Edgar, Blake. "Chronicler of Ice Age Life," *Archaeology* 55, no. 6 (November 2002): 36–41.

Ehat, Carla, and Anne Kent. "Interview with Helen Thompson Dreyfus," *Oral History Project of the Marin County Free Library*, San Rafael, California (20 February 1979).

Elia, Nada. " 'To Be an African Working Woman': Levels of Feminist Consciousness in Ama Ata Aidoo's *Changes*," *Research in African Literatures* 30, no. 2 (Summer 1999): 136–147.

"*Ellen Foster* and *A Virtuous Woman*," *Wilson Quarterly* 14, no. 1 (Winter 1990): 95.

Elliot, Ian. "Karen Cushman: Pursuing the Past," *Teaching PreK-8* 28, no. 5 (February 1998): 42–44.

Ellis, Kate Ferguson. *The Contested Castle: Gothic Novels and the Subversion of Domestic Ideology*. Urbana: University of Illinois Press, 1989.

Elz, A. Elizabeth. "*The Awakening* and *A Lost Lady*: Flying with Broken Wings and Raked Feathers," *Southern Literary Journal* 35, no. 2 (Spring 2003): 13–27.

Epstein, Daniel Mark. *What Lips My Lips Have Kissed: The Loves and Love Poems of Edna St. Vincent Millay*. New York: John MacRae Books, 2001.

Evangelista, Susan. "Jessica Hagedorn and Manila Magic," *MELUS* 18, no. 4 (Winter 1993–1994): 41–52.

Everton, Michael J. "The Courtesies of Authorship: Hannah Adams and Authorial Ethics in the Early Republic," *Legacy: A Journal of American Women Writers* 20, no. 1–2 (January–June 2003): 1–21.

Faderman, Lillian. *Scotch Verdict: Miss Pirie and Miss Woods v. Dame Cumming Gordon*. New York: Columbia University Press, 1994.

Farr, Judith. *The Passion of Emily Dickinson*. Cambridge, Mass.: Harvard University Press, 1994.

"Fay's Way Is Learning to Give the Lie to Truth," *Europe Intelligence Wire*, 2 October 2003.

Fedorko, Kathy Anne. *Gender and Gothic in the Fiction of Edith Wharton*. Tuscaloosa: Alabama University Press, 1995.

Feldman, Gayle. "Laboring for a Living Classic," *Publishers Weekly*, 20 August 2001, pp. 49–50.

Fellman, Anita Clair. " 'Don't Expect to Depend on Anybody Else': The Frontier as Portrayed in the Little House Books," *Children's Literature* 24 (1996): 101–116.

Ferguson, Moira. *Jamaica Kincaid: Where the Land Meets the Body*. Charlottesville: University of Virginia Press, 1994.

———. "Of Bears and Bearings: Paule Marshall's Diverse Daughters," *MELUS* 24, no. 1 (Spring 1999): 177–195.

Ferguson, Robert. *Henrik Ibsen: A New Biography*. London: Cohen, 1996.

Fiedler, Leslie. *Love and Death in the American Novel*. Cleveland, Ohio: Meridian, 1962.

Finseth, Ian. " 'A Melancholy Tale': Rhetoric, Fiction, and Passion in *The Coquette*," *Studies in the Novel* 33, no. 2 (Summer 2001): 125–159.

Fischer, Avery R. "Bradstreet's 'On My Dear Grandchild Simon Bradstreet' and 'Before the Birth of One of Her Children,' " *Explicator* 59, no. 1 (Fall 2000): 11–14.

Fleenor, Juliann E., ed. *The Female Gothic*. Montreal: Eden, 1983.

Fletcher, Andrew. "Top Girls or Iron Ladies?" *English Review* 12, no. 2 (November 2001): 32–33.

Foreman, Gabrielle. "Past-On Stories: History and the Magically Real, Morrison and Allende on Call," *Feminist Studies* 18, no. 2 (Summer 1992): 369–388.

Forrest, W. G. "Aristophanes *Lysistrata* 231," *Classical Quarterly* 45, no. 1 (January–June 1995): 240–241.

Forster, Margaret. *Daphne du Maurier*. New York: Doubleday, 1993.

Forsyth, Beverly, "The Two Faces of Lucy Snowe: A Study in Deviant Behavior," *Studies in the Novel* 29, no. 1 (Spring 1997): 17–25.

Forward, Stephanie, "Idol of Suburbia: Marie Corelli and Late-Victorian Culture," *Critical Survey* 13, no. 2 (May 2001): 141–144.

Foy, R. R. "Chopin's 'Désirée's Baby,' " *Explicator* 49, no. 4 (Summer 1991): 222–223.

Francis, Donette A. " 'Silences Too Horrific to Disturb': Writing Sexual Histories in Edwidge Danticat's *Breath, Eyes, Memory*," *Research in African Literatures* 35, no. 2 (Summer 2004): 75–90.

Francis, Elizabeth. *The Secret Treachery of Words: Feminism and Modernism in America*. Minneapolis: University of Minnesota Press, 2002.

Frank, Christina. "Life as a Lightning Rod," *Biography* 6, no. 3 (March 2002): 74–78.

Franklin, J. Jeffrey. "The Merging of Spiritualities: Jane Eyre as Missionary of Love," *Nineteenth-Century Literature* 49, no. 4 (March 1995): 456–482.

Franklin, Rosemary. "Louisa May Alcott's Father(s) and 'The Marble Woman,' " *American Transcendental Quarterly* 13, no. 4 (December 1999): 253.

Fraser, Hilary, Stephanie Green, and Judith Johnston. *Gender and the Victorian Periodical*. Cambridge: Cambridge University Press, 2003.

Fraser, Rebecca. *The Brontës: Charlotte Brontë and Her Family*. New York: Crown, 1988.

Freedman, Carl. *Critical Theory and Science Fiction*. Middletown, Conn.: Wesleyan University Press, 2000.

Freeman, Jo, ed. *Women: A Feminist Perspective*. New York: McGraw-Hill, 1994.

———, and Victoria Johnson, eds. *Waves of Protest: Social Movements since the Sixties*. Lanham, Md.: Rowman & Littlefield, 1999.

Frick, John W. *Theatre, Culture, and Temperance Reform in Nineteenth-Century America*. New York: Cambridge University Press, 2003.

Friedman, Susan Stanford. *Mappings: Feminism and the Cultural Geographies of Encounter.* Cambridge, Mass.: Princeton University Press, 1998.

———. *Penelope's Web: Gender, Modernity, H. D.'s Fiction.* Cambridge: Cambridge University Press, 1991.

Frisken, Amanda. "Sex in Politics: Victoria Woodhull as an American Public Woman, 1870–1876," *Journal of Women's History* 12, no. 1 (Spring 2000): 89–111.

Frost, Robert, "The Fable of the Poor Orphan Child," *English Review* 10, no. 2 (November 1999): 10.

Frumkes, Lewis Burke. "A Conversation with Cynthia Ozick," *Writer* 111, no. 3 (March 1998): 18–20.

———. "A Conversation with Jane Smiley," *Writer* 112, no. 5 (May 1999): 20–22.

Fuss, Diana. "Interior Chambers: The Emily Dickinson Homestead," *Differences: A Journal of Feminist Cultural Studies* 20, no. 3 (Fall 1998): 1–46.

Galehouse, Maggie. "Their Own Private Idaho: Transience in Marilynne Robinson's *Housekeeping*," *Contemporary Literature* 41, no. 1 (Spring 2000): 117–137.

Galtz, Liz. "Stories into Words, Words into Attention, Voices into Hearing: The Creative and Political Process of Melanie Kaye/Kantrowitz," *Gay Community News,* 20 January 1991, p. 8.

Ganz, Robin. "Sandra Cisneros: Border Crossings and Beyond," *MELUS* 19, no. 1 (Spring 1994): 19–29.

Gardiner, Judith Kegan. "Empathic Ways of Reading: Narcissism, Cultural Politics, and Russ's Female Man,'" *Feminist Studies* 20, no. 1 (Spring 1994): 87–111.

Gardner, Kate. "The Subversion of Genre in the Short Stories of Mary Wilkins Freeman," *New England Quarterly* 65, no. 3 (September 1992): 447–468.

Gardner, Susan. "Speaking of Ella Deloria," *American Indian Quarterly* 24, no. 3 (Summer 2000): 456–481.

———. "'Though It Broke My Heart to Cut Some Bits I Fancied': Ella Deloria's Original Design for *Waterlily*," *American Indian Quarterly* 27, no. 3/4 (Summer 2003): 667–696.

Gates, Barbara T., and Ann B. Shteir, eds. *Natural Eloquence: Women Reinscribe Science.* Madison: University of Wisconsin Press, 1997.

Gates, David. "Queen of the Spellbinders," *Newsweek,* 5 November 1990, pp. 76–77.

Gates, Henry Louis, ed. *Reading Black, Reading Feminist: A Critical Anthology.* New York: Meridian, 1990.

———. *The Trials of Phillis Wheatley: America's First Black Poet and Encounters with the Founding Fathers.* New York: BasicCivitas, 2003.

Gaul, Theresa Strouth. "'Equal Communion': Racial Hierarchy and Gender Identity in Ann Stephens's *Malaeska*," *Prospects* 27 (2002): 121–135.

Gayles, Gloria Wade. *Conversations with Gwendolyn Brooks.* Jackson: University Press of Mississippi, 2003.

Gazarian-Gautier, Marie-Lise. "Teacher from the Valley of Elqui," *World and I* 14, no. 10 (October 1999): 286.

Gee, Allen. "Deconstructing a Narrative Hierarchy: Leila Leong's 'I' in Fae Myenne Ng's *Bone*," *MELUS* 29, no. 2 (Summer 2004): 129–140.

Gelderman, Carol. *Conversations with Mary McCarthy.* Jackson: University Press of Mississippi, 1991.

Gelpi, Barbara Charlesworth, and Albert Gelpi, eds. *Adrienne Rich's Poetry.* New York: W. W. Norton, 1975.

Gemme, Paola. "Rewriting the Indian Tale: Science, Politics, and the Evolution of Ann S. Stephens's Indian Romances," *Prospects* 19 (1994): 375–388.

George, Olakunle. "Alice Walker's Africa: Globalization and the Province of Fiction," *Comparative Literature* 53, no. 4 (Fall 2001): 354–372.

Gery, John. "'Mocking My Own Ripeness': Authenticity, Heritage, and Self-Erasure in the Poetry of Marilyn Chin," *LIT: Literature Interpretation Theory* 12, no. 1 (2001): 25–45.

Giddings, Paula. "Book Marks," *Essence* 19, no. 11 (March 1989): 26.

Giffen, Allison. "Savage Daughters: Emma Lazarus, Ralph Waldo Emerson, and *The Spagnoletto*," *ATQ* 15, no. 2 (June 2001): 89–107.

Gilbert, Sandra M. "Jane Eyre and the Secrets of Furious Lovemaking," *Novel: A Forum on Fiction* 31, no. 3 (Summer 1998): 351–372.

———. *No Man's Land: Sexchanges: The Place of the Woman Writer in the Twentieth Century: The War of the Words.* New Haven, Conn.: Yale University Press, 1989.

———, and Susan Gubar. *The Madwoman in the Attic.* 2nd ed. New Haven, Conn.: Yale University Press, 2000.

Giles, Ron. "Brooks's 'A Song in the Front Yard,'" *Explicator* 57, no. 3 (Spring 1999): 169–171.

Gilligan, Carol. *In a Different Voice: Psychological Theory and Women's Development.* Cambridge, Mass.: Harvard University Press, 1982.

Glasberg, Elena. "Refusing History at the End of the Earth: Ursula Le Guin's 'Sur,'" *Tulsa Studies in Women's Literature* 21, no. 1 (Spring 2002): 99–121.

Gleeson-White, Sarah. "A Peculiarly Southern Form of Ugliness: Eudora Welty, Carson McCullers, and Flannery O'Connor," *Southern Literary Journal* 36, no. 1 (Fall 2003): 46–57.

Goffman, Ethan. "Grace Paley's Faith: The Journey Homeward, the Journey Forward," *MELUS* 25, no. 1 (Spring 2000): 197–208.

Goodlett, Debra, "Love and Addiction in 'Wuthering Heights,' " *Midwest Quarterly* 37, no. 3 (Spring 1996): 316–327.

Goodman, Susan. *Ellen Glasgow: A Biography.* Baltimore: Johns Hopkins University Press, 1998.

Gooneratne, Yasmine. *Silence, Exile, and Cunning: The Fiction of Ruth Prawer Jhabvala.* New Delhi: Orient Longman, 1983.

Gordon, Lyndall. *Charlotte Brontë: A Passionate Life.* New York: W. W. Norton, 1994.

Goto, Hiromi. "Manzanar as Metaphor," *Women's Review of Books* 21, no. 10/11 (July 2004): 22.

Gourdine, Angeletta K. M. "The Drama of Lynching in Two Blackwomen's Drama, or Relating Grimké's *Rachel* to Hansberry's *A Raisin in the Sun,*" *Modern Drama* 41, no. 4 (Winter 1998): 533.

Govan, Sovan Y. "Homage to Tradition: Octavia Butler Renovates the Historical Novel," *MELUS* 13, no. 1–2 (1986): 79–96.

Graham, Don. "Katherine Anne Porter's Journey from Texas to the World," *Southwest Review* 84, no. 1 (Winter 1998): 140.

Graham, Maryemma, ed. *Conversations with Margaret Walker.* Jackson: University Press of Mississippi, 2002.

Grass, Sean C. "Nature's Perilous Variety in Rossetti's 'Goblin Market,' " *Nineteenth-Century Literature* 51, no. 3 (December 1996): 356–376.

Gray, Paul. "Call of the Eco-Feminist," *Time,* 24 September 1990, p. 87.

Green, Barbara. "Spectacular Confessions: 'How It Feels to Be Forcibly Fed,' " *Review of Contemporary Fiction* 13, no. 3 (Fall 1993): 70–88.

Green, Laura. "Hall of Mirrors: Radclyffe Hall's *The Well of Loneliness* and Modern Fictions of Identity," *Twentieth Century Literature* 49, no. 3 (Fall 2003): 277–297.

Green, Mary Jean. "Review: La Voyageuse et la Prisonniere: Gabrielle Roy et la Question des Femmes," *American Review of Canadian Studies* 33, no. 3 (Autumn 2003): 438–440.

Green, Michelle. "Sara Paretsky's Cult Heroine Is a Woman's Woman—V. I. Warshawski, the Funky Feminist Private Eye," *People Weekly,* 14 May 1990, pp. 132–134.

Greene, Carol Hurd, "This Land Is Her Land," *Nation,* 11 February 1991, pp. 172–174.

Greenland, Cyril. "Dangerous Women—Dangerous Ideas," *Canadian Journal of Human Sexuality* 11, no. 3/4 (2002): 179–186.

Greeson, Jennifer Rae. "The 'Mysteries and Miseries' of North Carolina: New York City, Urban Gothic Fiction, and *Incidents in the Life of a Slave Girl,*" *American Literature* 73, no. 2 (2001): 277–309.

Gregg, Veronica Marie. *Jean Rhys's Historical Imagination: Reading and Writing the Creole.* Chapel Hill: University of North Carolina Press, 1995.

Grenier, Cynthia. "A Novelist of Moral Power and Passion: A Profile of Sigrid Undset," *World and I* 13, no. 10 (October 1998): 295–299.

Grice, Helena. "Reading the Nonverbal: The Indices of Space, Time, Tactility, and Taciturnity in Joy Kogawa's 'Obasan,' " *MELUS* 24, no. 4 (Winter 1999): 93–105.

Griffin, Amy A. "Jackson's 'The Lottery,' " *Explicator* 58, 1 (Fall 1999): 44.

Griffin, Susan. *A Chorus of Stones.* New York: Anchor, 1993.

———. " 'The Dark Stranger': Sensationalism and Anti-Catholicism in Sarah Josepha Hale's *Traits of American Life,*" *Legacy* 14, no. 1 (1997): 13–24.

Guest, Barbara. *Herself Defined: The Poet H. D. and Her World.* Garden City, N.Y.: Doubleday, 1984.

Ha, Marie-Paule. "The (M)otherland in Marie Cardinal," *Romance Quarterly* 43, no. 4 (Fall 1996): 206–216.

Hackett, Joyce. "The Reawakening," *Harper's* 307, no. 1,841 (October 2003): 82–86.

Haining, Peter, ed. *Gothic Tales of Terror.* New York: Taplinger, 1972.

Halberstam, Judith. *Skin Shows: Gothic Horror and the Technology of Monsters.* Durham, N.C.: Duke University Press, 1995.

Hall, Joan Wylie. *Shirley Jackson: A Study of the Short Fiction.* New York: Twayne, 1993.

Hamilton, Cynthia S. "Revisions, Rememories, and Exorcisms: Toni Morrison and the Slave Narrative," *Journal of American Studies* 30, no. 3 (1996): 30–32.

Hamilton, Patricia L. "Feng Shui, Astrology, and the Five Elements: Traditional Chinese Belief in Amy Tan's *The Joy Luck Club,*" *MELUS* 24, no. 2 (Summer 1999): 125–145.

Hanssen, Beatrice. "Elfriede Jelinek's Language of Violence," *New German Critique* 96, no. 68 (Spring–Summer 1996): 79–112.

Hard, Wendy. "Medieval Women's Unwritten Discourse on Motherhood: A Reading of Two Fifteenth-Century Texts," *Women's Studies* 21, no. 2 (May 1992): 197–209.

Hargrove, Nancy D. "The Tragicomic Vision of Beth Henley's Drama," *Southern Quarterly* 22, no. 4 (Summer 1984): 54–70.

Harries, Elizabeth W. "'Out in Left Field': Charlotte Smith's Prefaces, Bourdieu's Categories, and the Public Sphere," *Modern Language Quarterly* 58, no. 4 (December 1997): 457–473.

Harrison, Elizabeth. "Intolerable Human Suffering and the Role of the Ancestor: Literary Criticism as a Means of Analysis," *Journal of Advanced Nursing* 32, no. 3 (September 2000): 689–694.

Harrison, Nancy R. *Jean Rhys and the Novel as Women's Text*. Chapel Hill: University of North Carolina Press, 1988.

Hartman, James D. "Providence Tales and the Indian Captivity Narrative: Some Transatlantic Influence on Colonial Puritan Discourse," *Early American Literature* 32, no. 1 (January 1997): 66–81.

Harvey, Tamara. "'Now Sisters . . . Impart Your Usefulnesse, and Force,'" *Early American Literature* 35, no. 1 (March 2000): 5–28.

Hawley, John C. "Assimilation and Resistance in Female Fiction of Immigration: Bharati Mukherjee, Amy Tan, and Christine Bell." In *Rediscovering America 1492–1992: National, Cultural and Disciplinary Boundaries Re-examined*. Edited by Arnulfo G. Ramirez. Baton Rouge: Louisiana State University Press, 1992: 226–234.

Head, Dominic. *Nadine Gordimer*. Cambridge: Cambridge University Press, 1991.

Hearth, Amy Hill. "The American Century of Bessie and Sadie Delany," *American Heritage* 44, no. 6 (October 1993): 68–79.

Hedrick, Joan D. *Harriet Beecher Stowe: A Life*. Boston: Little, Brown, 1994.

Heilbrun, Carolyn G. *Hamlet's Mother and Other Women*. New York: Ballantine, 1991.

———. *Reinventing Womanhood*. New York: W. W. Norton, 1979.

———. *Toward a Recognition of Androgyny*. New York: W. W. Norton, 1982.

———. *Writing a Woman's Life*. New York: W. W. Norton, 1989.

Heller, Janet Ruth. "*Primavera* and *Black Maria*: Two Chicago Women's Literary Magazines," *Women's Studies* 23, no. 2 (March 1994): 175–190.

———. "Toni Cade Bambara's Use of African American Vernacular English in 'The Lesson,'" *Style* 37, no. 3 (Fall 2003): 279–293.

Heller, Scott. "The Book That Created a Canon: 'Madwoman in the Attic' Turns 20," *Chronicle of Higher Education*, 17 December 1999, pp. 20–21.

Heller, Terry. *The Delights of Terror: An Aesthetics of the Tale of Terror*. Urbana: University of Illinois Press, 1987.

Hemenway, Robert. *Zora Neale Hurston: A Literary Biography*. Champaign: University of Illinois Press, 1977.

Hendershot, Cyndy. *The Animal Within: Masculinity and the Gothic*. Ann Arbor: University of Michigan Press, 1998.

Hennessy, Brendan. *The Gothic Novel*. London: Longman, 1978.

Hennessy, Rosemary. *Materialist Feminism and the Politics of Discourse*. New York: Routledge, 1993.

Henstra, Sarah. "Looking the Part: Performative Narration in Djuna Barnes's *Nightwood* and Katherine Mansfield's 'Je Ne Parle Pas Francais,'" *Twentieth Century Literature* 46, no. 12 (Summer 2000): 125–149.

Henwood, Dawn. "Slaveries 'in the Borders': Rebecca Harding Davis's 'Life in the Iron Mills' in Its Southern Context," *Mississippi Quarterly* 52, no. 4 (Fall 1999): 567–592.

Herman, Judith, and Lisa Hirschmann. "Father-Daughter Incest." In *The Signs Reader: Women, Gender, and Scholarship*. Edited by Elizabeth Abel and Emily K. Abel. Chicago: University of Chicago Press, 1983.

Herrmann, Dorothy. *Helen Keller: A Life*. New York: Alfred A. Knopf, 1998.

Herzog, Anne F., and Janet E. Kaufman. *"How Shall We Tell Other of the Poet": The Life and Writing of Muriel Rukeyser*. New York: Palgrave MacMillan, 1999.

Hester, Michelle. "An Examination of the Relationship between Race and Gender in an Early Twentieth Century Drama: A Study of Angelina Weld Grimké's Play *Rachel*," *Journal of Negro History* 79, no. 2 (Spring 1994): 248–256.

Hetter, Katia, and Dorian Friedman. "The Animating Role of Women's Pundits." *U.S. News & World Report*, 7 August 1995, pp. 33–34.

Heung, Marina. "Daughter-Text/Mother-Text: Matrilineage in Amy Tan's Joy Luck Club," *Feminist Studies* 19, no. 3 (Fall 1993): 597–616.

Heuving, Jeanne. *Omissions Are Not Accidents: Gender in the Art of Marianne Moore*. Detroit: Wayne State University Press, 1992.

Higonnet, Margaret R. *Borderwork: Feminist Engagements with Comparative Literature*. Ithaca, N.Y.: Cornell University Press, 1994.

Hill, Michael R., Susan Hoecker-Drysdale, and Helena Z. Lopata. *Harriet Martineau: Theoretical and Methodological Perspectives*. New York: Routledge, 2001.

Himmelfarb, Gertrude. "George Eliot for Grown-ups," *American Scholar* 63, no. 4 (Autumn 1994): 577–581.

Hinnant, C. H. "Song and Speech in Anne Finch's 'To the Nightingale,'" *Studies in English Literature* 31, no. 3 (Summer 1991): 499–513.

Hirsch, Marianne. *The Mother/Daughter Plot: Narrative, Psychoanalysis, Feminism.* Bloomington: Indiana University Press, 1989.

Ho, Wendy. *In Her Mother's House—The Politics of Asian American Mother-Daughter Writing.* Walnut Creek, Calif.: AltaMira, 1999.

Hoagwood, Terence Allan. "Wylie's 'The Crooked Stick,'" *Explicator* 44, no. 3 (Spring 1986): 54–57.

Hobbs, Michael. "World beyond the Ice: Narrative Structure in *The Country of the Pointed Firs*," *Studies in Short Fiction* 29, no. 1 (Winter 1992): 27–34.

Hoberman, Ruth. "Masquing the Phallus: Genital Ambiguity in Mary Renault's Historical Novels," *Twentieth Century Literature* 42, no. 2 (Summer 1996): 277–293.

Hoefel, Roseanne L. "The Jilting of (Hetero)sexist Criticism: Porter's Ellen Weatherall and Hapsy," *Studies in Short Fiction* 28, no. 1 (Winter 1991): 9–20.

Hoeller, Hildegard. "A Quilt for Life: Lydia Maria Child's *The American Frugal Housewife*," *ATQ* 13, no. 2 (June 1999): 89.

Hoeveler, Diane Long. *Gothic Feminism.* University Park: Pennsylvania State University Press, 1998.

———. "Postgothic Fiction: Joyce Carol Oates Turns the Screw on Henry James," *Studies in Short Fiction* 35, no. 4 (Fall 1998): 355–372.

———. "Reading the Wound: Wollstonecraft's 'Wrongs of Women; or, Maria' and Trauma Theory," *Studies in the Novel* 31, no. 4 (Winter 1999): 387.

Hogsette, David S. "Margaret Atwood's Rhetorical Epilogue in 'The Handmaid's Tale': The Reader's Role in Empowering Offred's Speech Act," *CRITIQUE: Studies in Contemporary Fiction* 38, no. 4 (Summer 1997): 262.

Hogue, Cynthia. "Poetry, Politics and Postmodernism," *Women's Review of Books* 17, no. 9 (June 2000): 20–21.

Holladay, Hilary. *Wild Blessings: The Poetry of Lucille Clifton.* Baton Rouge: Louisiana State University Press, 2004.

Hood, Richard A. "Framing a 'Life in the Iron Mills,'" *Studies in American Fiction* 23, no. 1 (Spring 1995): 73–84.

Hoogland, Rene C. *Elizabeth Bowen: A Reputation in Writing.* New York: New York University Press, 1994.

hooks, bell. "Uniquely Toni Cade Bambara," *Black Issues Book Review* 2, no. 1 (January–February 2000): 14–16.

Hopkins, Chris. "Elizabeth Bowen," *Review of Contemporary Fiction* 21, no. 2 (Summer 2001): 114–151.

Horner, Avril, ed. *European Gothic: A Spirited Exchange 1760–1960.* Manchester: Manchester University Press, 2002.

Horrigan, Bonnie J. *Red Moon Passage: The Power and Wisdom of Menopause.* New York: Harmony Books, 1996.

Horton, Susan R. *Difficult Women, Artful Lives: Olive Schreiner and Isak Dinesen in and out of Africa.* Baltimore: Johns Hopkins University Press, 1995.

Horvitz, Deborah. "'Sadism Demands a Story': Oedipus, Feminism, and Sexuality in Gayl Jones's 'Corregidora' and Dorothy Allison's *Bastard Out of Carolina*," *Contemporary Literature* 39, no. 2 (Summer 1998): 238–261.

Howe, Florence. "From Race and Class to the Feminist Press," *Massachusetts Review* 44, no. 1/2 (Spring–Summer 2003): 117–135.

Howells, Carol Ann. *Margaret Atwood.* London: Macmillan, 1996.

Hoy, Suellen. *Chasing Dirt: The American Pursuit of Cleanliness.* New York: Oxford University Press, 1995.

Hubler, Angela E. "Josephine Herbst's 'The Starched Blue Sky of Spain and Other Memoirs': Literary History 'In the Wide Margin of the Century,'" *Papers on Language and Literature* 33, no. 1 (Winter 1997): 71–98.

Hudak, Jennifer. "The Social Inventor: Charlotte Perkins Gilman and the (Re) Production of Perfection," *Women's Studies* 32, no. 4 (June 2003): 455–477.

Hull, Gloria T. *Color, Sex, and Poetry: Three Women Writers of the Harlem Renaissance.* Bloomington: Indiana University Press, 1987.

———. Patricia Bell Scott, and Barbara Smith, eds. *But Some of Us Are Brave: Black Women's Studies.* New York: Feminist Press, 1982.

Hume, Beverly A. "Managing Madness in Gilman's 'The Yellow Wall-Paper,'" *Studies in American Fiction* 30, no. 1 (Spring 2002): 3–30.

Hume, Robert. "Gothic versus Romantic: A Revaluation of the Gothic Novel," *Publication of the Modern Language Association* 84 (1969): 282–290.

Hunt, Linda. "Charlotte Brontë and the Suffering Sisterhood," *Colby Library Quarterly* 19, no. 1 (1983): 7–17.

Hurtig, Dolliann Margaret. "'I Do, I Do': Medieval Models of Marriage and Choice of Partners in Marie de France's 'Le Fraisne,'" *Romanic Review* 92, no. 4 (November 2001): 363–379.

Hyman, Paula E., and Deborah Dash Moore, eds. *Jewish Women in America: An Historical Encyclopedia*. New York: Routledge, 1997.

Hymowitz, Carol, and Michael E. Weissman. *A History of Women in America*. New York: Bantam, 1978.

Ibsen, Kristine. *The Other Mirror: Women's Narrative in Mexico, 1980–1995*. Westport, Conn.: Greenwood, 1997.

Ignatieff, Michael. "The Limits of Sainthood," *New Republic*, 18 June 1990, pp. 40–46.

Inness, Sherry. " 'Loyal Saints or Devious Rascals': Domestic Servants in Edith Wharton's Stories 'The Lady's Maid's Bell' and 'All Souls,' " *Studies in Short Fiction* 36, no. 4 (Fall 1999): 337–350.

"An Interview with Wendy Rose," *News from Native California* 17, no. 1 (Fall 2003): 30.

Irigaray, Luce. *Sexes and Genres through Languages: Elements of Sexual Communication*. New York: Routledge, 2003.

———. *This Sex Which Is Not One*. Ithaca, N.Y.: Cornell University Press, 1985.

Isaac, Megan Lynn. "Sophia Lee and the Gothic of Female Community," *Studies in the Novel* 28, no. 2 (Summer 1996): 200–217.

Istel, John. "Emily Mann," *American Theatre* 13, no. 2 (February 1996): 44–45.

———. "Say It, Sisters," *American Theatre* 12, no. 5 (May–June 1995): 6–7.

Jacobs, Jo Ellen. *The Voice of Harriet Taylor Mill*. Bloomington: Indiana University Press, 2002.

Jaffe, Janice. "Hispanic American Women Writers' Novel Recipes and Laura Esquivel's *Como Agua para Chocolate*," *Women's Studies* 22, no. 2 (March 1993): 217–230.

Jay, Elisabeth. *Mrs. Oliphant, "A Fiction to Herself": A Literary Life*. Oxford: Clarendon, 1995.

Jay, Karla. "What Ever Happened to Baby Robin?" *Lambda Book Report* 9, no. 11 (June 2001): 8–11.

Jellinek, Estelle. "Anaïs Reconsidered," *Off Our Backs*, 31 December, 1974, p. 18.

Jimoh, A. Yemisi. "Double Consciousness, Modernism, and Womanist Themes in Gwendolyn Brooks's 'The Anniad,' " *MELUS* 23, no. 3 (Fall 1998): 167–186.

Johns, Alessa. *Women's Utopias of the Eighteenth Century*. Chicago: University of Illinois Press, 2003.

Johnson, Claudia L. " 'Let Me Make the Novels of a Country': Barbauld's *The British Novelists (1810–1820)*," *Novel: A Forum on Fiction* 34, no. 2 (Spring 2001): 163.

Johnson, Greg. "Blonde Ambition: An Interview with Joyce Carol Oates," *Prairie Schooner* 75, no. 3 (Fall 2001): 15.

Johnson, Patricia E. "Sex and Betrayal in the Detective Fiction of Sue Grafton and Sara Paretsky," *Journal of Popular Culture* 27, no. 4 (Spring 1994): 97–106.

Johnson, Sarah Anne. "Women of Substance: Author Sena Jeter Naslund Found Few Heroes in Classic Literature, So She Created Some," *Writer* 115, no. 11 (November 2002): 26–32.

Jones, Ann Goodwyn. *Tomorrow Is Another Day: The Woman Writer in the South, 1859–1936*. Baton Rouge: Louisiana State University Press, 1981.

Jones, Paul Christian. " 'This Dainty Woman's Hand . . . Red with Blood': E. D. E. N. Southworth's *The Hidden Hand* as Abolitionist Narrative," *ATQ* 15, no. 1 (March 2001): 59.

Jones, Susan. " 'Creatures of Our Light Literature': The Problem of Genre in *The Inheritors* and Marie Corelli's *A Romance of Two Worlds*," *Conradiana* (Spring–Summer 2002): 107–122.

Jones, Vivien, ed. *Women and Literature in Britain, 1700–1800*. Cambridge: Cambridge University Press, 2000.

Jonza, Nancylee Novell. *The Underground Stream: The Life and Art of Caroline Gordon*. Athens: University of Georgia Press, 1995.

Juhasz, Suzanne, and Christanne Miller, eds. *Emily Dickinson: A Celebration for Readers*. New York: Gordon & Breach, 1989.

Jusova, Iveta. "Imperialist Feminism: Colonial Issues in Sarah Grand's 'The Heavenly Twins' and 'The Beth Book,' " *English Literature in Transition 1880–1920* 43, no. 3 (Summer 2000): 298–315.

Kalfopoulou, Adrianne. *A Discussion of the Ideology of the American Dream in the Culture's Female Discourses*. Lewiston, N.Y.: Edwin Mellen, 2000.

Kanaganayakam, Chelva. "Isak Dinesen and Narrativity: Reassessments for the 1990s," *University of Toronto Quarterly* 66, no. 1 (Winter 1996–1997): 7.

Kanfer, Stefan. "Odd Couples," *New Leader*, 9 August 1993, pp. 22–23.

Kaplan, Amy. "Manifest Domesticity," *American Literature* 70, no. 3 (September 1998): 581–606.

Kaplan, Carla. *Zora Neale Hurston: A Life in Letters*. New York: Anchor, 2003.

Kavka, Misha. "Men in (Shell-) Shock: Masculinity, Trauma, and Psychoanalysis in Rebecca West's 'The Return of the Soldier,' " *Studies in Twentieth Century Literature* 22, no. 1 (Winter 1998): 151–171.

Keeling, Bret L. "H. D. and 'The Contest': Archaeology of a Sapphic Gaze," *Twentieth Century Literature* 44, no. 2 (Summer 1998): 176–203.

Keller, James R. *Anne Rice and Sexual Politics: The Early Novels*. Jefferson, N.C.: McFarland, 2000.

Kelley, Klara Bonsack, and Harris Francis. *Navajo Sacred Places*. Bloomington: Indiana University Press, 1994.

Kelley, Mary. *Private Woman, Public State: Literary Domesticity in Nineteenth-Century America*. Oxford: Oxford University Press, 1985.

Kelly, Susan. "Discipline and Craft: An Interview with Sonia Sanchez," *African American Review* 34, no. 4 (Winter 2000): 679–687.

Kendrik, Robert, "Edward Rochester and the Margins of Masculinity in *Jane Eyre* and *Wide Sargasso Sea*," *Papers on Language and Literature* 30, no. 3 (Summer 1994): 235–256.

Kensey, Barbara. "Mari Evans' Musical, *Eyes*, Debuts in Chicago on ETA's Mainstage," *Chicago Defender*, 24 June 2004, p. 19.

Kent, Alicia. "Mourning Dove's *Cogewea*: Writing Her Way into Modernity," *MELUS* 24, no. 3 (Fall 1999): 39–66.

Kerker, Milton. "Grace Aguilar, a Woman of Israel," *Midstream* 47, no. 1 (February 2001): 35.

Kern, Kathi. *Mrs. Stanton's Bible*. Ithaca, N.Y.: Cornell University Press, 2001.

Kerr, Frances. " 'Nearer the Bone': Louise Bogan, Anorexia, and the Political Unconscious of Modernism," *Literature Interpretation Theory* 8, no. 3/4 (June 1998): 305–330.

Kessler, Carol Farley. *Daring to Dream*. Boston: Pandora, 1984.

———. *Elizabeth Stuart Phelps*. Boston: Twayne, 1982.

Keyser, Elizabeth Lennox. *Whispers in the Dark: The Fiction of Louisa May Alcott*. Knoxville: University of Tennessee Press, 1993.

Kim, Elaine H. *Asian American Literature: An Introduction to the Writings and Their Social Context*. Philadelphia: Temple University Press, 1982.

Kim, Thomas W. " 'For a Paper Son, Paper Is Blood': Subjectivation and Authenticity in Fae Myenne Ng's *Bone*," *MELUS* 24, no. 4 (Winter 1999): 41–56.

Kimmel, Michael S. "Men Supporting Women," *UNESCO Courier* 48, no. 9 (September 1995): 30–31.

King, Patricia. "The Call of the Wild Woman," *Newsweek*, 21 December 1992, p. 59.

Kingston, Maxine Hong. *Conversations with Maxine Hong Kingston*. New York: Jackson, University Press of Mississippi, 1998.

Kinnahan, Linda A. *Poetics of the Feminine*. Cambridge: Cambridge University Press, 1994.

Kirk, Pamela. *Sor Juana Inés de la Cruz: Religion, Art, and Feminism*. New York: Continuum, 1999.

Kirsch, Jonathan. "Westwords: The Woman behind 'Ramona,' " *Los Angeles Times*, 30 March 2003, p. R2.

Kitch, Sally L. *Higher Ground: From Utopianism to Realism in American Feminist Thought and Theory*. Chicago: University of Chicago Press, 2000.

Klein, Carole. *Doris Lessing, a Biography*. New York: Carroll & Graf, 2000.

Knapp, Bettina. "Lady Murasaki Shikibu's *The Tale of Genji*: Search for the Mother," *Symposium* 46, no. 1 (Spring 1992): 34–48.

Knox, Alice. "No Place like Utopia: Cross-Racial Couples in Nadine Gordimer's Later Novels," *Ariel* 27, no. 1 (January 1996): 63–80.

Kolbenschlag, Madonna. *Kiss Sleeping Beauty Good-Bye: Breaking the Spell of Feminine Myths and Models*. Toronto: Bantam, 1981.

Komporály, Jozefina. "Maternal Longing as Addiction: Feminism Revisited in Timberlake Wertenbaker's *The Break of Day*," *Journal of Gender Studies* 13, no. 2 (July 2004): 129–138.

Koppelman, Susan. "Fannie: The Talent for Success of Writer Fannie Hurst," *Women's Review of Books* 17, no. 1 (October 1999): 20.

Kornfeld, Eve. *Margaret Fuller: A Brief Biography with Documents*. New York: Bedford/St. Martin's, 1997.

Kovac, Ita. "Marguerite Duras: From Silent Writing to a Film without Pictures," *Bread and Roses* 12 (Fall 1999).

Krasner, David. "Migration, Fragmentation, and Identity: Zora Neale Hurston's *Color Struck* and the Geography of the Harlem Renaissance," *Theatre Journal* 53, no. 4 (December 2001): 533–550.

Kristeva, Julia. *Powers of Horror: An Essay on Abjection*. New York: Columbia University Press, 1982.

Kritzer, Amelia Howe. "Playing with Republican Motherhood," *Early American Literature* 31, no. 2 (September 1996): 150–166.

Kroeger, Brooke. "Nellie Bly: She Did It All," *Quarterly of the National Archives* 28, no. 1 (Spring 1996): 7–15.

Kucich, Greg, "Women's Historiography and the (Dis)embodiment of Law: Ann Yearsley, Mary Hays, Elizabeth Benger," *Wordsworth Circle* 33, no. 1 (Winter 2002): 3–7.

Kurth, Peter. *American Cassandra: The Life of Dorothy Thompson*. Boston: Little, Brown, 1990.

Kuryluk, Ewa. "An Interview with Irina Ratushinskaya," *New York Review of Books*, 7 May 1987, pp. 16–20.

Lacey, Candida Ann, ed. *Barbara Leigh Smith and the Langham Place Group*. New York: Routledge & Kegan Paul, 1987.

Lackey, Michael. "Larsen's *Quicksand*," *Explicator* 59, no. 2 (Winter 2001): 103–106.

Lai, Tracy A. M. "Janie Bigo," *International Examiner*, 20 May 1997, p. 18.

Lakoff, Robin Tolmach, and Mary Bucholtz. *Language and Woman's Place: Text and Commentaries.* Oxford: Oxford University Press, 2004.

Lamonaca, Maria. "Jane's Crown of Thorns: Feminism and Christianity in *Jane Eyre,*" *Studies in the Novel* 34, no. 3 (Fall 2002): 245–263.

Lane, Ann J. *To Herland and Beyond.* New York: Penguin, 1991.

Larkin, Joan, and Elly Bulkin, eds. *Amazon Poetry.* New York: Out & Out Books, 1975.

Larson, Kate Clifford. *Bound for the Promised Land: Harriet Tubman, Portrait of an American Hero.* New York: Ballantine, 2003.

Lathers, Marie. " 'L'Eve Future' and the Hypnotic Feminine," *Romantic Review* 84, no. 1 (January 1993): 43–54.

Latta, Alan D. "Spinell and Connie: Joyce Carol Oates Re-imagining Thomas Mann?" *Connotations* 9, no. 3 (1999–2000): 316–329.

Laughlin, Karen L. "Criminality, Desire, and Community: A Feminist Approach to Beth Henley's *Crimes of the Heart,*" *Women and Performance* (1986): 35–51.

Lauter, Devorah. "Out-of-Print Victorian Feminist Worth a Second Read," *Jewish Bulletin of Northern California,* 5 September 2003, p. 34.

Lawrence, Kelli-an, David Taylor, and E. Sandra Byers. "Differences in Men's and Women's Global, Sexual, and Ideal-Sexual Expressiveness and Instrumentality," *Sex Roles: A Journal of Research* 34, no. 5–6 (March 1996): 337–357.

Lear, Linda. *Rachel Carson: Witness for Nature.* New York: Henry Holt, 1997.

Lee, Felicia R. "Having Her Say," *Essence* 35, no. 7 (November 2004): 136.

Lee, Rachel. "Who's Chinese?" *Women's Review of Books* 19, no. 5 (February 2002): 13–14.

Leen, Mary. "An Art of Saying: Joy Harjo's Poetry and the Survival of Storytelling," *American Indian Quarterly* 19, no. 1 (Winter 1995): 1–16.

Lehman, David. "Colossal Ode," *Smithsonian* 35, no. 1 (Apil 2004): 120–122.

Leigh, S. J., and David J. Leigh. "Hope, Resistance, and Poetry in Two Russian Autobiographies," *Renascence* 56, no. 3 (Spring 2004): 197–207.

Leithauser, Brad. "The Hard Life of the Lyric," *New Republic,* 23 May 1988, pp. 30–34.

Lennon, Peter. "The Brutal Realist of Romance," *Manchester Guardian,* 13 June 1992, p. 28.

Lenz, Brooke. "Postcolonial Fiction and the Outsider Within: Toward a Literary Practice of Feminist Standpoint Theory," *NWSA Journal* 16, no. 2 (Summer 2004): 98–110.

Lenz, Carolyn Ruth Swift. *The Woman's Part: Feminist Criticism of Shakespeare.* Chicago: University of Illinois Press, 1983.

Leonard, George, ed. *The Asian Pacific American Heritage: A Companion to Literature and Arts.* New York: Garland, 1998.

Lerner, Gerda. *The Feminist Thought of Sarah Grimké.* Oxford: Oxford University Press, 1998.

Lester, Neal A. "Shange's Men: *for colored girls* Revisited, and Movement Beyond," *African American Review* 26, no. 2 (Summer 1992): 319–328.

Levander, Caroline Field. *Voices of the Nation: Women and Public Speech in Nineteenth-Century American Literature and Culture.* Cambridge: Cambridge University Press, 1998.

Levine, George, and U. C. Knoepflmacher, eds. *The Endurance of Frankenstein: Essays on Mary Shelley's Novel.* Berkeley: University of California Press, 1979.

Levy, Barbara. "Southern Rebel," *Women's Review of Books* 15, no. 10/11 (July 1998): 36–37.

Levy, Bronwen. "Agony and Ecstasy: Feminists among Feminists," *Hecate* 26, no. 1 (May 2000): 107.

Levy, Eric P. "The Psychology of Loneliness in *Wuthering Heights,*" *Studies in the Novel* 28, no. 2 (Summer 1996): 158–177.

Lewis, Leslie W. "Traveling Conversation: India Dennis-Mahmood Interviews Sonia Sanchez," *Feminist Teacher* 12, no. 3 (1999): 198–212.

Lewis, R. W. B. *Edith Wharton: A Biography.* New York: Fromm International, 985.

Lichtenstein, Grace. "In the Presence of Mystery," *Washington Post,* 12 July 1998, p, X3.

Ling, Amy. *Between Worlds: Women Writers of Chinese Ancestry.* New York: Pergamon, 1990.

Lin-Liu, Jen. "In China, a Scholar, a Once-Forbidden Script, and Tourism," *Chronicle of Higher Education,* 5 November 2004, p. A56.

Lockett, Andrea. "Sister Difference: An Audre Lorde Memorial Conversation," *Belles Lettres* 8, no. 4 (Summer 1993): 39.

Loganbill, G. Bruce. "Cornelia Otis Skinner, Monologist," *Communication* 9, no. 1 (October 1980): 122–128.

Lootens, Tricia. "Women Who Kill: The Burning Bed," *Off Our Backs,* 31 December 1983, p. 16.

Louis, Margot K. "Proserpine and Pessimism: Goddesses of Death, Life, and Language from Swinburne to Wharton," *Modern Philology* 96, no. 3 (February 1999): 312–346.

Love, Heather. "The Second Time Around," *Women's Review of Books* 20, no. 4 (January 2003): 1–2.

Lovell-Smith, Rose, "Anti-Housewives and Ogres' Housekeepers: The Roles of Bluebeard's Female Helper," *Folklore* 113, no. 2 (October 2002): 197–214.

Lucenti, Lisa Marie. "Willa Cather's *My Antonia*: Haunting the Houses of Memory," *Twentieth Century Literature* 46, no. 2 (Summer 2000): 193–213.

Lund, Elizabeth. "Poet's Challenge: Speaking in a Distinctive Voice That Elevates," *Christian Science Monitor*, 20 March 1996, p. 13.

Lundeen, Kathleen. "Who Has the Right to Feel?: The Ethics of Literary Empathy," *Style* 32, no. 2 (Summer 1998): 261–271.

Lupton, Mary Jane. *Maya Angelou*. Westport, Conn.: Greenwood, 1998.

Luther, Susan. "A Stranger Minstrel: Coleridge's Mrs. Robinson," *Studies in Romanticism* 33, no. 3 (Fall 1994): 391–409.

Lyall, Sarah. "Termites Are Interesting but Books Sell Better," *New York Times*, 1 September 1993, p. C1.

Ma, Sheng-mei. *The Deathly Embrace: Orientalism and Asian American Identity*. Minneapolis: University of Minnesota Press, 2000.

———. *Immigrant Subjectivities in Asian American and Asian Diaspora Literature*. Albany: State University of New York Press, 1998.

Mackenzie, Craig. *Bessie Head*. New York: Twayne, 1999.

MacKenzie, Midge. *Shoulder to Shoulder*. New York: Alfred A. Knopf, 1975.

Mackenzie, Scott. "Ann Radcliffe's Gothic Narrative and the Readers at Home," *Studies in the Novel* 31, no. 4 (Winter 1999): 409.

MacNeil, Robert. *Eudora Welty: Seeing Black and White*. Jackson: University Press of Mississippi, 1990.

Madigan, Mark J. "Willa Cather's Commentary on Three Novels by Dorothy Canfield Fish," *ANQ* 3, no. 1 (January 1990): 13–15.

"The Madwoman in the Attic: The Woman Writer and the 19th Century Literary Imagination," *Women and Language* 24, no. 1 (Spring 2001): 39.

Maggio, Rosalie. *The Nonsexist Wordfinder: A Dictionary of Gender-Free Usage*. Boston: Beacon, 1988.

———. *Talking about People: A Guide to Fair and Accurate Language*. New York: Oryx, 1997.

Maguire, Sarah. "Dilemmas and Developments: Eavan Boland Re-examined," *Feminist Review* 62 (Summer 1999): 58–66.

Makowsky, Veronica. *Susan Glaspell's Century of American Women: A Critical Interpretation of Her Work*. Oxford: Oxford University Press, 1993.

Malmgren, Carl D. "Texts, Primers, and Voices in Toni Morrison's *The Bluest Eye*," *Critique* 41, no. 3 (Spring 2000): 251–262.

Marcus, Steven. "*Frankenstein*: Myths of Scientific and Medical Knowledge and Stories of Human Relations," *Southern Review* 38, no. 1 (Winter 2002): 188–202.

Markels, Julian. "Coda: Imagining History in *The Poisonwood Bible*," *Monthly Review Press* (September 2003): 1.

Markley, Robert. "Lactilla, Milkwoman of Clifton: The Life and Writings of Ann Yearsley, 1753–1806," *Studies in English Literature, 1500–1900* 37, no. 3 (Summer 1997): 637–672.

Markus, Julia. *Dared and Done: The Marriage of Elizabeth Barrett and Robert Browning*. Athens: Ohio University Press, 1998.

Marom, Daniel. "Who Is the 'Mother of Exiles'? Jewish Aspects of Emma Lazarus's 'The New Colossus,' " *Prooftexts: A Journal of Jewish Literary History* 20, no. 3 (Autumn 2000): 231–261.

Marquis, Margaret. "The Female Body, Work, and Reproduction in Deland, Cather, and Dreiser," *Women's Studies* 32, no. 8 (December 2003): 979–1000.

Marrs, Suzanne. *One Writer's Imagination: The Fiction of Eudora Welty*. Baton Rouge: Louisiana State University Press, 2002.

Marshall, Paule. "Paule Marshall," *Writer* 115, no. 9 (September 2002): 66.

Marso, Lori J. "Defending the Queen: Wollstonecraft and Staël on the Politics of Sensibility and Feminine Difference," *Eighteenth Century: Theory and Interpretation* 43, no. 1 (Spring 2002): 43–81.

Martens, Catherine. "Mother-Figures in *Surfacing* and *Lady Oracle*: An Interview with Margaret Atwood," *American Studies in Scandinavia* 16, no. 1 (1984): 45–54.

Martin, Carol, ed. *A Sourcebook of Feminist Theatre and Performance*. New York: Routledge, 1996.

Martin, Robert K. "*The Children's Hour*: A Postcolonial Turn of the Screw," *Canadian Review of American Studies* 31, no. 1 (2001): 101–107.

Martin, Sara. "The Power of Monstrous Women: Fay Weldon's *The Life and Loves of a She-Devil* (1983), Angela Carter's *Nights at the Circus* (1984), and Jeanette Winterston's *Sexing the Cherry* (1989)," *Journal of Gender Studies* 8, no. 2 (July 1999): 193–210.

Martin, Taffy. *Marianne Moore: Subversive Modernist*. Austin: University of Texas Press, 1986.

Martini, Adrienne. "The Playwright in Spite of Herself," *American Theatre* 16, no. 8 (October 1999): 22–25.

Martyniuk, Irene. "Troubling the 'Master's Voice': Djuna Barnes's Pictorial Strategies," *Mosaic* 31, no. 3 (September 1998): 61–81.

Marvin, Thomas F. " 'Preachin' the Blues': Bessie Smith's Secular Religion and Alice Walker's *The Color Purple*," *African American Review* 28, no. 3 (Fall 1994): 411–421.

Mason, Mary G. *Autobiography: Essays Theoretical and Critical.* Princeton, N.J.: Princeton University Press, 1980.

Matchie, Tom. "*Ahab's Wife, or the Star-Gazer*: A Wider/Deeper View of Melville's Tragic Hero and His Times," *Journal of American and Comparative Cultures* (Spring–Summer 2001): 85–91.

Mather, Anne. "A History of Feminist Periodicals, Part I," *Journalism History* 1, no. 3 (Autumn 1974): 82–85.

———. "A History of Feminist Periodicals, Part II," *Journalism History* 2, no. 1 (Winter 1974): 19–23.

———. "A History of Feminist Periodicals, Part III," *Journalism History* 2, no. 1 (Spring 1975): 19–23, 31.

Maurois, André. *Lélia: The Life of George Sand.* New York: Penguin, 1977.

Mazer, Norma Fox, and Marjorie Lewis, eds. *Waltzing on Water.* New York: Dell, 1989.

McArthur, Mary. "La Llorona," *Midwest Quarterly* 42, no. 1 (Autumn 2000): 42.

McCash, June Hall. "La Vie Seinte Audrée: A Fourth Text by Marie de France?" *Speculum* 77, no. 3 (July 2002): 744–777.

McClure, Andrew S. "Sarah Winnemucca: [Post]Indian Princess and Voice of the Paiutes," *MELUS* 24, no. 2 (Summer 1999): 29–51.

McDermott, Sinead. "Memory, Nostalgia, and Gender in *A Thousand Acres*," *Signs: Journal of Women in Culture and Society* 28, no. 1 (Autumn 2002): 389–407.

McDonough, C. J. "Hugh Primas and the Archpoet," *Review of English Studies* 48, no. 189 (February 1997): 80–81.

McElroy, Wendy. *Sexual Correctness: The Gender-Feminist Attack on Women.* Jefferson, N.C.: McFarland, 2001.

McGann, Jerome. "Mary Robinson and the Myth of Sappho," *Modern Language Quarterly* 56, no. 1 (March 1995): 55–76.

McGinity, Keren R. "The Real Mary Antin: Woman on a Mission in the Promised Land," *American Jewish History* 86, no. 3 (September 1998): 285.

McIntyre, Clara Frances. *Ann Radcliffe in Relation to Her Time.* New Haven, Conn.: Yale Studies in English, 1970.

McNair, Wesley. "Taking the World for Granite: Four Poets in New Hampshire," *Sewanee Review* 104, no. 1 (Winter 1996): 70–81.

McPherson, Robert S. *Sacred Land, Sacred View: Navajo Perceptions of the Four Corners.* Salt Lake City, Utah: Signature, 1992.

McRae, Laura Kathryn. "Interpretation and the Acts of Reading and Writing in Christine de Pisan's 'Livre de la Cité des Dames,' " *Romanic Review* 82, no. 4 (November 1991): 412–433.

Meade, Marion. *Dorothy Parker: What Fresh Hell Is This?* New York: Penguin, 1989.

Meese, Elizabeth. "When Virginia Looked at Vita, What Did She See: or, Lesbian: Feminist: Woman—What's the Differ(e/a)nce?" *Feminist Studies* 18, no. 1 (Spring 1992): 99–117.

Mellor, Anne K. *Mary Shelley: Her Life, Her Fiction, Her Monsters.* New York: Routledge, 1989.

———, ed. *Romanticism and Feminism.* Bloomington: Indiana University Press, 1988.

Meltzer, Francoise. "The Hands of Simone Weil," *Critical Inquiry* 27, no. 4 (Summer 2001): 611–628.

Mendible, Myra. "Desiring Images: Representation and Spectacle in Dogeaters," *CRITIQUE: Studies in Contemporary Fiction* 43, no. 3 (Spring 2002): 289–305.

Merchant, Ismail. "Ismail Merchant, Britain's Foremost Maker of Indian Films, Reflects on a Subcontinent's Change as Seen through His Lens," *New Statesman*, 15 August 1997, p. 29.

Mermin, Dorothy. *Elizabeth Barrett Browning: The Origin of a New Poetry.* Chicago: University of Chicago Press, 1989.

Merriam, Eve, and Morris U. Schappes. *Emma Lazarus Rediscovered.* New York: Holmes & Meier, 1999.

Merrick, Beverly G. "Reversal of Fortunes, Ishbel Ross Interviews Emmeline Pankhurst: The Cadence of Civilian and Military Career Choices in a Changing Economy," *Global Competitiveness* 10, no. 1 (2002): 400–418.

Meyer, Susan. "Colonialism and the Figurative Strategy of *Jane Eyre*," *Victorian Studies* 33, no. 2 (1990): 247–268.

Mezei, Kathy, ed. *Ambiguous Discourse: Feminist Narratology and British Women Writers.* Chapel Hill: University of North Carolina Press, 1996.

Michie, Elsie B. "Buying Brains: Trollope, Oliphant, and Vulgar Victorian Commerce," *Victorian Studies* 44, no. 1 (Autumn 2001): 77–99.

Mighall, Robert. *A Geography of Victorian Gothic Fiction: Mapping History's Nightmares.* Oxford: Oxford University Press, 1999.

Miller, Christanne. *Marianne Moore: Questions of Authority.* Cambridge, Mass.: Harvard University Press, 1995.

Miller, John. *Laura Ingalls Wilder's Little Town: Where History and Literature Meet.* Lawrence: University Press of Kansas, 1994.

Miller, Nina. "Femininity, Publicity, and the Class Division of Cultural Labor: Jessie Redmon Fauset's

'There Is Confusion,' " *African American Review* 30, no. 2 (Summer 1996): 205–220.

———. *Making Love Modern: The Intimate Public Worlds of New York's Literary Women.* New York: Oxford University Press, 1998.

Milne, Courtney. *Sacred Places in North America: A Journey into the Medicine Wheel.* New York: Stewart, Tabori & Chang, 1995.

Mirriam-Goldberg, Caryn. "Visionary Activist," *Women's Review of Books* 20, no. 3 (December 2002): 11–12.

Mitchell, Hayley R., ed. *Readings on* A Doll's House. Westport, Conn: Greenhaven, 1999.

Mitchell, Marea. "Ambitious Women and Strange Monsters: Simone de Beauvoir and Germaine Greer," *Hecate* 26, no. 1 (2000) 98–106.

Mitchell, Penni. "Pope Joan," *Herizons* 12, no. 1 (Spring 1998): 39.

Moers, Ellen. "Female Gothic: Monsters, Goblins, Freaks," *New York Review of Books,* 4 April 1974, pp. 30–42.

———. *Literary Women.* New York: Oxford University Press, 1977.

———. "The Monster's Mother," *New York Review of Books,* 21 March 1974, pp. 24–33.

Moi, Toril. *Sexual, Textual Politics: Feminist Literary Theory.* New York: Routledge, 1984.

Monteith, Sharon. *Advancing Sisterhood?: Interracial Friendships in Contemporary Southern Fiction.* Athens: University of Georgia Press, 2001.

Montenegro, David. "Interview," *American Poetry Review* 20, no. 1 (January–February 1991): 7–14.

Moran, Patricia. "Unholy Meanings: Maternity, Creativity, and Orality in Katherine Mansfield," *Feminist Studies* 17, no. 1 (Spring 1991): 105–125.

Morantz-Sanchez, Regina. "Feminist Theory and Historical Practice: Rereading Elizabeth Blackwell," *History and Theory* 31, no. 4 (December 1992): 51–69.

Morgan, Janice, and Colette T. Hall, eds. *Redefining Autobiography in Twentieth-Century Women's Fiction.* New York: Garland, 1991.

Morris, Celia. *Fanny Wright: Rebel in America.* Urbana: University of Illinois Press, 1992.

Morris, Sylvia Jukes. *Rage for Fame: The Ascent of Clare Boothe Luce.* New York: Modern Library, 1997.

Morrison, Sarah R. "Of Woman Borne: Male Experience and Feminine Truth in Jane Austen's Novels," *Studies in the Novel* 26, no. 4 (Winter 1994): 337–349.

Motley, Warren. "The Unfinished Self: Willa Cather's *O Pioneers!* and the Psychic Cost of a Woman's Success," *Women's Studies* 12, no. 2 (1986): 149–165.

Mullins, Maire. "Home, Community, and the Gift That Gives in Isak Dinesen's 'Babette's Feast,' " *Women's Studies* 23, no. 3 (July 1994): 217–228.

Munich, Adrienne, and Melissa Bradshaw. *Amy Lowell, an American Modern.* Piscataway, N.J.: Rutgers University Press, 2004.

Munt, Sally. *Murder by the Book?: Feminism and the Crime Novel.* New York: Routledge, 1994.

Murray, Victoria Christopher. "Everybody Wants to Be Terry McMillan," *Black Issues Book Review* 4, no. 1 (January–February 2002): 36–40.

Murrey, Loretta Martin. "The Loner and the Matriarchal Community in Barbara Kingsolver's *The Bean Trees* and *Pigs in Heaven,*" *Southern Studies* 5, no. 1–2 (Spring–Summer 1994): 155–164.

Musser, Judith. "African American Women and Education: Marita Bonner's Response to the 'Talented Tenth,' " *Studies in Short Fiction* 23, no. 1 (Winter 1997): 73–85.

Muther, Elizabeth. "Bambara's Feisty Girls: Resistance Narratives in *Gorilla, My Love,*" *African American Review* 36, no. 3 (Fall 2002): 447–459.

Naether, Carl A. *Advertising to Women.* New York: Prentice-Hall, 1928.

Napier, Elizabeth R. *The Failure of the Gothic.* Oxford: Oxford University Press, 1987.

Napieralski, Edmund A. "Morrison's *The Bluest Eye,*" *Explicator* 53, no. 1 (Fall 1994): 59–62.

Naples, Nancy A. *Community Activism and Feminist Politics: Organizing across Race, Class, and Gender.* New York: Routledge, 1997.

Nash, Jerry C. "Renaissance Misogyny, Biblical Feminism, and Hélisenne de Crenne's 'Epistres Familieres et Invectives,' " *Renaissance Quarterly* 50, no. 2 (Summer 1997): 379–410.

Needham, Anuradha Dingwa. "An Interview with Ama Ata Aidoo," *Massachusetts Review* 36, no. 1 (Spring 1995): 123–133.

Nelson, Sean. "Legacies: Faith, Hope and Peace: Radio Documentaries Explore What Moves the Human Spirit," *Asian Reporter,* 14 December 1998, p. 1.

Nemesvari, Richard. "Robert Audley's Secret: Male Homosocial Desire in *Lady Audley's Secret,*" *Studies in the Novel* 27, no. 4 (Winter 1995): 515–528.

Newcomb, Timberman. "The Woman as Political Poet: Edna St. Vincent Millay and the Mid-Century Canon," *Criticism* 37, no. 2 (Spring 1995): 261–279.

Newman, Louise M. "Coming of Age, but Not in Samoa: Reflections on Margaret Mead's Legacy for Western Liberal Feminism," *American Quarterly* 48, no. 2 (June 1996): 233–272.

Newman, Vicky. "Compelling Ties: Landscape, Community, and Sense of Place," *Peabody Journal of Education* 70, no. 4 (Summer 1995): 105–118.

Newton, Judith, and Deborah Rosenfelt. *Feminist Criticism and Social Change*. New York: Methuen, 1985.

Nguyen, Lan N. "The Next Amy Tan," *A Magazine* (February–March 1997): 46–51, 55.

Nidal, Nazih Abu. "The Novels of Sahar Khalifeh," *Palestine—Israel Journal of Politics, Economics and Culture* 10, no. 2 (2003): 113–114.

Nishime, LeiLani. "Engendering Genre: Gender and Nationalism in *China Men* and *The Woman Warrior*," *MELUS* 20, no. 1 (Spring 1995): 67–82.

Nixon, Nicola. "*Wide Sargasso Sea* and Jean Rhys's Interrogation of the 'Nature Wholly Alien' in *Jane Eyre*," *Essays in Literature* 21, no. 2 (Fall 1994): 267–284.

Nord, Deborah Epstein. "Commemorating Literary Women: Ellen Moers and Feminist Criticism after Twenty Years," *Signs: Journal of Women in Culture and Society* 24, no. 3 (Spring 1999): 733–737.

Nordius, Janina. "A Tale of Other Places: Sophia Lee's 'The Recess' and Colonial Gothic," *Studies in the Novel* 34, no. 2 (Summer 2002): 162–176.

Northey, Margot. *The Haunted Wilderness: The Gothic and Grotesque in Canadian Fiction*. Toronto: University of Toronto Press, 1976.

Norton, Rictor, ed. *Gothic Readings: The First Wave 1764–1840*. London: Leicester University Press, 2000.

———. *The Mistress of Udolpho*. London: Leicester University Press, 1999.

Nuñez, Elizabeth. "Talking to Maryse Condé: Grand Dame of Caribbean Literature," *UNESCO Courier* 53, no. 11 (November 2000): 46–51.

Oates, Joyce Carol. "Romance and Anti-Romance: From Brontë's *Jane Eyre* to Rhys's *Wide Sargasso Sea*," *Virginia Quarterly Review* 61, no. 6 (Winter 1985): 44–58.

O'Brien, John. "Vox Faucibus Haesit," *Symposium* 49, no. 4 (Winter 1996): 297–306.

O'Brien, Sharon. *Willa Cather: The Emerging Voice*. Cambridge, Mass.: Harvard University Press, 1997.

O'Dea, Gregory. "Prophetic History and Textuality in Mary Shelley's *The Last Man*," *Papers on Language and Literature* 28, no. 3 (Summer 1992): 283–304.

Odessky, Marjory H. "The Feminist as Humanist," *Humanist* 55, no. 1 (January–February 1995): 34–35.

Oestreich, James R. "A Suffragist in Her Den, Bracing for the Circus," *New York Times*, 21 March 2000, p. E1.

Okonkwo, Christopher N. "Of Repression, Assertion, and the Speakerly Dress: Anzia Yezierska's *Salome of the Tenements*," *MELUS* 25, no. 1 (Spring 2000): 129–145.

Oldfield, Sybil. "The News from the Confessional— Some Reflections on Recent Autobiographical Writing by Women and Its Areas of Taboo," *Critical Survey* 8, no. 3 (September 1996): 296–285.

Orenstein, Catherine. *Little Red Riding Hood Uncloaked: Sex, Morality and the Evolution of a Fairy Tale*. New York: Basic, 2002.

Orleck, Annelise. *Common Sense and A Little Fire: Women and Working-Class Politics in the United States, 1900–1965*. Chapel Hill: University of North Carolina Press 1995.

Ostriker, Alicia. "Beyond Confession: The Poetics of Postmodern Witness," *American Poetry Review* 30, no. 2 (March–April 2001): 35–39.

———. *Stealing the Language: The Emergence of Women's Poetry in America*. Boston: Beacon, 1987.

"The Other Side of a Mirror," *Victorian Poetry* 35, no. 4 (Winter 1997): 508.

Ozolins, Aija. "Dreams and Doctrines: Dual Strands in Frankenstein," *Science-Fiction Studies* 2, no. 2 (1975): 103–110.

Page, Tim. *Dawn Powell: A Biography*. New York: Owl, 1998.

Palumbo-Liu, David, ed. *The Ethnic Canon: Histories, Institutions, and Interventions*. Minneapolis: University of Minnesota Press, 1995.

Paradise, Nathaniel. "Interpolated Poetry, the Novel, and Female Accomplishment," *Philological Quarterly* 74, no. 1 (Winter 1995): 57–76.

Paranjape, Makarand. "The Crisis of Contemporary India and Nayantara Sahgal's Fiction," *World Literature Today* 68, no. 2 (Spring 1994): 291–298.

Parsell, D. L. "New Photo Book an Homage to Last U.S. Wildlands," *National Geographic News*, 29 October 2002.

Pascale, De Souza. "Demystifying Female Marooning: Oppositional Strategies and the Writing of Testimonios in the French Caribbean," *International Journal of Francophone Studies* 3, no. 3 (2000): 141–150.

Pastor, Brigida. "Cuba's Covert Cultural Critics: The Feminist Writings of Gertrudis Gómez de Avellaneda," *Romance Quarterly* 42, no. 3 (Summer 1995): 178–189.

Paton, Elizabeth M. "Landscape and Female Desire: Elizabeth Bishop's 'Closet' Tactics," *Mosaic* 31, no. 3 (September 1998): 133–151.

Payant, Katherine B. "From Alienation to Reconciliation in the Novels of Cristina García," *MELUS* 26, no. 3 (Fall 2001): 163–182.

Pearce, R. "To the Light," *Novel: A Forum on Fiction* 24, no. 2 (Winter 1991): 222–225.

Pearl, Nancy. "Gaslight Thrillers: The Original Victorians," *Library Journal*, 15 February 2001, p. 228.

Pearlman, Mickey, and Katherine Usher Henderson. *Inter/view: Talks with America's Writing Women.* Lexington: University Press of Kentucky, 1990.

Pela, Robert L. "Our Lesbian Roots," *Advocate*, 15 August 2000, pp. 94–95.

Pereira, Malin. "An Interview with Rita Dove," *Contemporary Literature* 40, no. 2 (Summer 1999): 182–213.

Perkin, J. Russell. "Locking George Sand in the Attic: Female Passion and Domestic Realism in the Victorian Novel," *University of Toronto Quarterly* 63, no. 3 (Spring 1994): 408–428.

Perry, Donna. *Backtalk: Women Writers Speak Out.* New Brunswick, N.J.: Rutgers University Press, 1993.

Peters, John G. "Inside and Outside *Jane Eyre* and Marginalization through Labeling," *Studies in the Novel* 28, no. 1 (Spring 1996): 57–75.

Pettingell, Phoebe. "Anna of All Rus," *New Leader,* 19 December 1995, pp. 26–27.

———. "Mourners and Harpies," *New Leader,* 24 January 1997, pp. 14–15.

Pickle, Linda Schelbitzki. "Christa Wolf's *Cassandra:* Parallels to Feminism in the West," *CRITIQUE: Studies in Contemporary Fiction* 28, no. 3 (Spring 1987): 149–157.

Pitono, Stephen P. "Susan Brownmiller and the History of Rape," *Women's Studies* 14, no. 3 (1988): 265–276.

Plasa, Carl. *Toni Morrison:* Beloved. New York: Columbia University Press, 1998.

Poovey, Mary. "Ideology and the Mysteries of Udolpho," *Criticism: A Quarterly for Literature and the Arts* 21 (1979): 307–330.

Powell, Raymond A. "Margery Kempe: An Exemplar of Late Medieval Piety," *Catholic Historical Review* 89, no. 1 (January 2003): 1–23.

Prebel, Julie. "Engineering Womanhood: The Politics of Rejuvenation in Gertrude Atherton's *Black Oxen,*" *American Literature* 76, no. 2 (June 2004): 307–337.

Proefriedt, William A. "The Immigrant or 'Outsider' Experience as Metaphor for Becoming an Educated Person in the Modern World: Mary Antin, Richard Wright, and Eva Hoffman," *MELUS* 16, no. 2 (Spring 1989/1990): 77–89.

Prown, Katherine Hemple. *Revising Flannery O'Connor: Southern Literary Culture and the Problem of Female Authorship.* Charlottesville: University of Virginia Press, 2001.

Pulio, Gus. "Remembering and Reconstructing the Mirabal Sisters in Julia Alvarez's *In the Time of the Butterflies,*" *Bilingual Review* 23, no. 1 (January–April 1998): 11–20.

Punter, David. *The Literature of Terror.* London: Longman, 1996.

Purnell, Kim L. "Blues Legacies and Black Feminism: Gertrude 'Ma' Rainey, Bessie Smith, and Billie Holiday," *Women's Studies in Communication* 24, no. 2 (Fall 2001): 262–265.

Purvis, June. *Emmeline Pankhurst: A Biography.* New York: Routledge, 2002.

Pyron, Darden Ashbury. *Recasting:* Gone with the Wind *in American Culture.* Miami: Florida International University, 1983.

Rae, Ian. "Reconsidering Lilith," *Canadian Literature* no. 174 (Autumn 2002): 162–163.

Rainey, Lawrence S. "Canon, Gender, and Text: The Case of H. D.," *College Literature* 18, no. 3 (October 1991): 106–125.

Rajkowska, Barbara Ozieblo. *Susan Glaspell: A Critical Biography.* Chapel Hill: University of North Carolina Press, 2000.

Randall, Margaret, ed. *Breaking the Silences: Twentieth-Century Poetry by Cuban Women.* Vancouver: Pulp Press, 1982.

Randle, Gloria T. "Between the Rock and the Hard Place: Mediating Spaces in Harriet Jacobs's *Incidents in the Life of a Slave Girl,*" *African American Review* 33, no. 1 (Spring 1999): 43–56.

Reddy, Maureen T. *Sisters in Crime: Feminism and the Crime Novel.* New York: Continuum, 1988.

Reed, Brian K. "Behold the Woman: The Imaginary Wife in Octavia Butler's *Kindred,*" *CLA Journal* 47, no. 1 (September 2003): 66–74.

Rege, Josna. "Codes in Conflict: Post-independence Alienation in Anita Desai's Early Novels," *Journal of Gender Studies* 5, no. 3 (November 1996): 317–328.

Reichard, Gladys A. *Spider Woman.* Tucson: University of New Mexico Press, 1997.

Reid, Jo-Ann. "Inside Our Secrets," *Lesbian Review of Books* 7, no. 1 (Fall 2000): 24

Reinert, Otto. "Unfashionable Kristen Lavransdatter," *Scandinavian Studies* 71, no. 1 (Spring 1999): 67.

Reiter, Amy. "Kia Corthron: Giving the Voiceless a Voice," *American Theatre* 11, no. 8 (October 1994): 77.

Renner, Pamela. "The Mellowing of Miss Firecracker," *American Theatre* 15, no. 9 (November 1998): 18–19.

Reuman, Ann. "Coming into Play: An Interview with Gloria Anzaldúa," *MELUS* 25, no. 2 (Summer 2000): 3–45.

"Review: Caroline Lamb, This Infernal Woman," *Contemporary Review* 279, no. 1,627 (August 2001): 126.

"Review: *Piratica: Being a Daring Tale of a Singular Girl's Adventure upon the High Seas.*" *Kirkus Reviews,* 1 September 2004, p. 869.

"Review: Sarah Orne Jewett," Available online. URL: http://etext.lib.virginia.edu/toc/modeng/public/AnoJewe.html, 1894. Accessed on October 14, 2005.

Rice, Anne. "How I Write," *Writer* 114, no. 2 (February 2001): 66.

Richardson, Angelique. "The Eugenization of Love: Sarah Grand and the Morality of Genealogy," *Victorian Studies* 42, no. 2 (Winter 1999): 227–255.

———, and Chris Willis, eds. *The New Woman in Fiction and in Fact: Fin-de-Siècle Feminisms.* London: Palgrave Macmillan, 2002.

Richardson, Marilyn. "Photographing Horror," *Women's Review of Books* 21, no. 1 (October 2003): 12.

Rigby, S. H. "The Wife of Bath, Christine de Pizan, and the Medieval Case for Women," *Chaucer Review* 32, no. 2 (Fall 2000): 133–165.

Roback, Diane, and Richard Donahue. "*Tales from the Bamboo Grove* by Yoko Kawashima Watkins," *Publishers Weekly,* 6 July 1992, p. 6.

Roberts, Cokie. *Founding Mother: The Women Who Raised Our Nation.* New York: William Morrow, 2004.

Roberts, Nora. *Three Radical Women Writers: Class and Gender in Meridel Le Sueur, Tillie Olsen, and Josephine Herbst.* New York: Taylor & Francis, 1996.

Roberts, Sherron Killingsworth. "The Female Rescuer in Newbery Fiction: Exploring the Archetype of Mother," *ALAN Review* 30, no.1 (Fall 2002): 47–53.

Robinson, Harriet Jane Hanson. *History of Woman Suffrage.* Rochester, N. Y., privately published, 1886.

Rodden, John. "The Responsibility to Tell You: An Interview with Isabel Allende," *Kenyon Review* 13, no. 1 (Winter 1991): 113–123.

Roiphe, Katie. *The Morning After: Sex, Fear, and Feminism.* New York: Back Bay Books, 1994.

Romaine, Suzanne. *Communicating Gender.* Mahwah, N.J.: Lawrence Erlbaum, 1999.

Romero, Laura. *Home Fronts: Nineteenth-Century Domesticity and Its Critics.* Durham, N.C.: Duke University Press, 1997.

Romines, Ann. *Constructing the Little House: Gender, Culture, and Laura Ingalls Wilder.* Amherst: University of Massachusetts Press, 1997.

Roof, Maria. "Maryse Condé and Isabel Allende: Family Saga Novels," *World Literature Today* 70, no. 2 (Spring 1996): 283–288.

Roper, Ingrid. "Jennifer Holm," *Publishers Weekly,* 28 June 1999, pp. 28–29.

Rose, Ellen Cronan. "Through the Looking Glass: When Women Tell Fairy Tales." In *The Voyage In: Fiction of Female Development.* Eds. Elizabeth Abel, Marianne Hirsch, and Elizabeth Langland. Hanover, N.H.: University Press of New England, 1983.

Rose, June. *Marie Stopes and the Sexual Revolution.* London: Faber & Faber, 1993.

Rosen, Judith. "Anita Diamant's *Red Tent* Turns to Gold," *Writer* 114, no. 4 (April 2001): 30–33.

Rosenman, Ellen Bayuk. " 'Mimic Sorrows': Masochism and the Gendering of Pain in Victorian Melodrama," *Studies in the Novel* 35, no. 1 (Spring 2003): 22–43.

———. "Spectacular Women: The Mysteries of London and the Female Body," *Victorian Studies* 40, no. 1 (Autumn 1996): 31–64.

Ross, Jean W. "Interview." In *Contemporary Authors.* Vol. 134, pp. 284–290. Detroit: Gale Research, 1992.

Rossi, Alice, ed. *Essays on Sexual Equality.* Chicago: University of Chicago Press, 1970.

Roth, Marty. "Gilman's Arabesque Wallpaper," *Mosaic* 34, no. 4 (December 2001): 145–162.

Rowe, Karen. "To Spin a Yarn: The Female Voice in Folklore and Fairy Tale." In *Fairy Tales and Society: Illusion, Allusion, and Paradism.* Edited by Ruth B. Bottigheimer. Philadelphia: University of Pennsylvania Press, 1986.

Rubinstein, Roberta. "The Mark of Africa," *World and I* 14, no. 4 (April 1999): 254.

Rudnitzsky, Lesi. "Darkness Visible," *Nation,* 31 May 2004, pp. 29–30.

Rudy, Kathy. "Ethics, Reproduction, Utopia: Gender and Childbearing in *Woman on the Edge of Time* and *The Left Hand of Darkness,*" *NWSA Journal* 9, no. 1 (Spring 1997): 22–38.

Ruland, Richard, and Malcolm Bradbury. *From Puritanism to Postmodernism: A History of American Literature.* New York: Penguin, 1991.

Rundstrom, Beth. "Harvesting Willa Cather's Literary Fields," *Geographical Review* 85, no. 2 (April 1995): 217–228.

Ruppert, James. "Review: *Two Old Women,*" *Ethnohistory* 42, no. 4 (Fall 1995): 670–671.

Ruppert, Jim. "Paula Gunn Allen and Joy Harjo: Closing the Distance between Personal and Mythic Space," *American Indian Quarterly* 7, no. 1 (1983): 27–40.

Rusk, Lauren. *The Life Writing of Otherness: Woolf, Baldwin, Kingston, and Winterson.* New York: Routledge, 2002.

Rust, Marion. "Into the House of an Entire Stranger," *Early American Literature* 37, no. 2 (June 2002): 281–308.

Ruta, Suzanne. "Decoding the Language," *Women's Review of Books* 19, no. 10/11 (July 2002): 13.

Ruttenberg, Danya. *Yentl's Revenge: The Next Wave of Jewish Feminism*. Seattle: Seal, 2001.

Ryan, Kay. "Falling in Public: Larsen's *Passing*, McCarthy's *The Group*, and Baldwin's *Another Country*," *Studies in the Novel* 36, no. 1 (Spring 2004): 95–119.

Ryan, Maureen. "Green Visors and Ivory Towers: Jean Stafford and the New Journalism," *Kenyon Review* 16, no. 4 (Fall 1994): 104–119.

Rye, Gill. "Agony or Ecstasy? Reading Cixous's Recent Fiction," *Paragraph* 23, no. 3 (November 2000): 298–312.

Saldivar-Hull, Sonia. "Women Hollering Transfronteriza Feminisms," *Cultural Studies* 13, no. 2 (April 1999): 251–262.

Salgado, Minoli. "Myths of the Nation and Female (Self) Sacrifice in Nayantara Sahgal's Narratives," *Journal of Commonwealth Literature* 31, no. 2 (Fall 1996): 61.

Samra, Matthew K. "Shadow and Substance: The Two Narratives of Sojourner Truth," *Midwest Quarterly* 38, no. 2 (Winter 1997): 158–171.

Santana, Mario. "An Essay in Feminist Rhetoric: Emilia Pardo Bazán's 'El Indulto,' " *MLN* 116, no. 2 (March 2001): 250.

Saul, Joanna. "In the Middle of Becoming: Dionne Brand's Historical Vision," *Canadian Woman Studies* 23, no. 2 (Winter 2004): 59–63.

Savigneau, Josyane. *Marguerite Yourcenar: Inventing a Life*. Chicago: University of Chicago Press, 1993.

Savona, Jeanelle Laillou. "Hélène Cixous and Utopian Thought: From 'Tancredi Continues' to 'The Book of Promethea,' " *University of Toronto Quarterly* 72, no. 2 (Spring 2003): 615–630.

Schatz, Sueann. "*Aurora Leigh* as Paradigm of Domestic-Professional Fiction," *Philological Quarterly* 79, no. 1 (Winter 2000): 91.

Schaub, Robert. "An Interview with Marilynne Robinson," *Contemporary Literature* 35, no. 2 (Summer 1994): 230–250.

Schechter, Patricia A. *Ida B. Wells-Barnett and American Reform, 1880–1930*. Chapel Hill: University of North Carolina Press, 2001.

Schechter, Susan. *Women and Male Violence: The Visions and Struggles of the Battered Women's Movement*. Chicago: South End, 1983.

Scheinberg, Cynthia, and Gillian Beer, eds. *Women's Poetry and Religion in Victorian England: Jewish Identity and Christian Culture*. Cambridge: Cambridge University Press, 2002.

Schiwy, Marlene A. *Voice of Her Own: Women and the Journal Writing Journey*. New York: Fireside, 1996.

Schmidt, Susan. "Finding a Home: Rawlings's *Cross Creek*," *Southern Literary Journal* 26, no. 2 (Spring 1994): 48–57.

Schneir, Miriam, ed. *Feminism: The Essential Historical Writings*. New York: Vintage, 1972.

Schnur, Susan. "The Once and Future Womantasch: Celebrating Purim's Full Moon as 'Holy Body Day,' " *Lilith*, 31 March 1998, p. 28.

Scott, Ellen K. "Creating Partnerships for Change: Alliances and Betrayal in the Racial Politics of Two Feminist Organizations," *Gender and Society* 12, no. 4 (August 1998): 400–423.

Scrafford, Barbara. "Nature's Silent Scream: A Commentary on Cynthia Ozick's 'The Shawl,' " *Critique* 31, no. 1 (Fall 1989): 11–15.

Scroggins, Mark. "Truth, Beauty, and the Remote Control," *Parnassus: Poetry in Review* 26, no. 2 (2002): 127–147.

Seabury, Marcia Bundy. "The Monsters We Create: *Woman on the Edge of Time* and *Frankenstein*," *CRITIQUE: Studies in Contemporary Fiction* 42, no. 3 (Winter 2001): 131–143.

Seager, Joni. "Rachel Carson Died of Breast Cancer: The Coming Age of Feminist Environmentalism," *Signs: Journal of Women in Culture and Society* 28, no. 3 (Spring 2003): 945–973.

Sedgwick, Eve Kosofsky. *Epistemology of the Closet*. Berkeley: University of California Press, 1990.

Selzer, Linda. "Race and Domesticity in *The Color Purple*," *African American Review* 29, no. 1 (Spring 1995): 67–82.

Setzer, Sharon. "Mary Robinson's Sylphid Self: The End of Feminine Self-Fashioning," *Philological Quarterly* 75, no. 4 (Fall 1996): 501–520.

———. "Romancing the Reign of Terror: Sexual Politics in Mary Robinson's 'Natural Daughter,' " *Criticism* 39, no. 4 (Fall 1997): 531–550.

Severin, Laura. " 'The Gilt Is off the Gingerbread': Stevie Smith's Revisionary Fairy Tales," *Journal of Gender Studies* 12, no. 3 (November 2003): 203–214.

Shavelson, Susanne A. "Anxieties of Authorship in the Autobiographies of Mary Antin and Aliza Greenblatt," *Prooftexts* 18, no. 2 (May 1998): 161–186.

Shaw, Robert B., ed. *American Poetry since 1960*. Cheadle, England: Carcanet, 1973.

Shaw, S. Bradley. "New England Gothic by the Light of Common Day: Lizzie Bordon and Mary E. Wilkins Freeman's 'The Long Arm,' " *New England Quarterly* 70, no. 2 (1997): 211–236.

Shawn, St. John. "An Updated Publication History of 'The Yellow Wall-Paper,' " *Studies in Short Fiction* 34, no. 2 (Spring 1997): 237.

Shepard, Alan Clarke. "Aborted Rage in Beth Henley's *Women*," *Modern Drama* 36, no. 1 (March 1993): 96–108.

Sherr, Lynn, and Jurate Kazickas. *Susan B. Anthony Slept Here: A Guide to American Women's Landmarks.* New York: Times, 1976.

Showalter, Elaine. "Feminist Foremother," *Wilson Quarterly* 25, no. 1 (Winter 2001): 129–131.

———. *Hystories.* New York: Columbia University Press, 1998.

———. *Inventing Herself: Claiming a Feminist Intellectual Heritage.* New York: Scribner, 2001.

———. "Killing the Angel in the House: The Autonomy of Women Writers," *Antioch Review* 50, no. 1–2 (Winter–Spring 1992): 207–220.

———. *A Literature of Their Own: British Novelist from Brontë to Lessing.* Princeton, N.J.: Princeton University Press, 1998.

———. *The New Feminist Criticism: Essays on Women, Literature, and Theory.* New York: Pantheon, 1985.

———. "Responsibilities and Realities: Curriculum for the Eighties," *ADE Bulletin* no. 70 (Winter 1981): 17–21.

———. *Scribbling Women: Short Stories by 19th Century American Women.* Piscataway, N.J.: Rutgers University Press, 1997.

———. *Sister's Choice: Tradition and Change in American Women's Writing.* Oxford: Clarendon, 1991.

Siegel, Kristi. *Women's Autobiographies, Culture, Feminism.* New York: Peter Lang, 2001.

Siegel, Lee. "De Sade's Daughters," *Atlantic Monthly* 279, no. 2 (February 1997): 97–101.

Simons, Margaret A. *Beauvoir and the Second Sex.* Lanham, Md.: Rowman & Littlefield, 2001.

Simonson, Harold P. *Zona Gale.* New York: Twayne, 1962.

Singh, Christine. "Review: Windward Heights," *Canadian Woman Studies* 20, no. 1 (Spring 2000): 110.

Singley, Carol J. *Edith Wharton: Matters of Mind and Spirit.* Cambridge: Cambridge University Press, 1998.

Slowik, Mary. "Beyond Lot's Wife: The Immigration Poems of Marilyn Chin, Garrett Hongo, Li-Young Lee, and David Mura," *MELUS* 25, no. 3/4 (Fall–Winter 2000): 221–242.

Smiley, Jane. "In the Fields of the Lord," *Washington Post,* 11 October 1998.

Smith, Angela. *Katherine Mansfield: A Literary Life.* London: Macmillan, 2000.

Smith, Jennifer. *Anne Rice: A Critical Companion.* Westport, Conn.: Greenwood, 1996.

Smith, Karen. "Inanna: Queen of Heaven and Earth," *Whole Earth Review* no. 75 (Summer 1992): 74.

Smith, Margaret Supplee, and Emily Herring Wilson. *North Carolina Women Making History.* Chapel Hill: University of North Carolina Press, 1999.

Snodgrass, Mary Ellen. *Amy Tan: A Literary Companion.* Jefferson, N.C.: McFarland, 2004.

———. *Barbara Kingsolver: A Literary Companion.* Jefferson, N.C.: McFarland, 2004.

Southworth, Helen. "Rooms of Their Own: How Colette Uses Physical and Textual Space to Question a Gendered Literary Tradition," *Tulsa Studies in Women's Literature* 20, no. 2 (Fall 2001): 253–278.

Spencer, Jane. *Aphra Behn's Afterlife.* Oxford: Oxford University Press, 2001.

Spiegelman, Willard. *The Didactic Muse.* Princeton, N.J.: Princeton University Press, 1989.

Stambaugh, Sara. "Isak Dinesen in America." Available online. URL: http://www.ualberta.ca/%7Ecins/lectures/isak_dinesen.htm. Accessed on April 28, 2004.

Stanford, Ann Folwell. "An Epic with a Difference: Sexual Politics in Gwendolyn Brooks's 'The Anniad,' " *American Literature* 67, no. 2 (June 1995): 283–301.

Starr, Elizabeth. " 'A Great Engine for Good': The Industry of Fiction in Elizabeth Gaskell's *Mary Barton* and *North and South*," *Studies in the Novel* 34, no. 4 (Winter 2002): 386–404.

Steindorf, Sara. "Betty and Mahtob Mahmoody," *Christian Science Monitor,* 6 June 2000, p. 23.

Stephens, Judith. " 'And Yet they Paused' and 'A Bill to Be Passsed': Newly Recovered Lynching Dramas by Georgia Douglas Johnson," *African American Review* 33, no. 3 (Fall 1999): 519–522.

Stetz, Margaret Diane. "Rebecca West's 'Elegy': Women's Laughter and Loss," *Journal of Modern Literature* 18, no. 4 (Spring 1994): 369–380.

Stevens, David. *The Gothic Tradition.* Cambridge: Cambridge University Press, 2000.

Stone, Carole. "Elegy As Political Expression in Women's Poetry: Akhmatova, Levertov, Forché," *College Literature* 18, no. 1 (February 1991): 84–91.

Stoneman, Patsy. *Brontë Transformations: The Cultural Dissemination of* Wuthering Heights *and* Jane Eyre. Upper Saddle River, N.J.: Prentice Hall, 1996.

———. "Catherine Earnshaw's Journey to Her Home among the Dead: Fresh Thoughts on *Wuthering Heights* and *Epipsychidion*," *Review of English Studies* 47, no. 188 (November 1996): 521–533.

Stout, Janis P. "Mary Austin's Feminism: A Reassessment," *Studies in the Novel* 30, no. 1 (Spring 1998): 77–101.

Strange, Lisa S. "Elizabeth Cady Stanton's *Woman's Bible* and the Roots of Feminist Theology," *Gender Issues* 17, no. 4 (Fall 1999): 15.

Strout, Cushing. "Border Crossing: History, Fiction, and Dead Certainties," *History and Theory* 31, no. 2 (May 1992): 153–162.

Su, John J. " 'Once I Would Have Gone Back . . . but Not Any Longer': Nostalgia and Narrative Ethics in *Wide*

Sargasso Sea," *CRITIQUE: Studies in Contemporary Fiction* 44, no. 2 (Winter 2003): 157–174.

Sugiyama, Naoko. "Issei Mothers' Silence, Nisei Daughters' Stories: The Short Fiction of Hisaye Yamamoto," *Comparative Literature Studies* 33, no. 1 (1996): 1–14.

Sullivan, Rosemary. *The Red Shoes: Margaret Atwood Starting Out.* New York: HarperCollins, 1998.

Summers, Montague. *The Gothic Quest: A History of the Gothic Novel.* London: Fortune, 1969.

Sutton, Roger. "An Interview with Judy Blume Forever . . . Yours," *School Library Journal* 42, no. 6 (June 1996): 24–27.

Sweet, Nanora, and Julie Melnyk. *Felicia Hemans: Reimagining Poetry in the Nineteenth Century.* New York: St. Martin's, 2001.

Sweetman, David. *Mary Renault.* New York: Harvest, 1994.

Swindell, Larry. "There's Nothing Funny about Fannie Hurst's Literary Legacy," *Fort Worth Star-Telegram,* 19 January 2000, p. K3.

Swiontkowski, Gale. *Imagining Incest: Sexton, Plath, Rich, and Olds on Life with Daddy.* Selinsgrove, Pa.: Susquehanna University Press, 2003.

Sypher, Eileen. "Resisting Gwendolen's 'Subjection': Daniel Deronda's Proto-feminism," *Studies in the Novel* 28, no. 4 (Winter 1996): 506–518.

Talese, Nan A. *Book Group Companion to Margaret Atwood's The Robber Bride.* New York: Doubleday, 1993.

Tatar, Maria, ed. *The Annotated Classic Fairy Tales.* New York: W. W. Norton, 2002.

———. "It's Time for Fairy Tales with the Bite of Reality," *New York Times,* 29 November 1998, p. 2.1

Tate, Claudia, ed. *Black Women Writers at Work.* New York: Continuum, 1986.

Tayko, Gail. "Teaching Isabel Allende's *La Casa de los Espiritus,*" *College Literature* 19, no. 3 (October–February 1992): 228–232.

Taylor, Melanie A. " 'The Masculine Soul Heaving in the Female Bosom': Theories of Inversion and *The Well of Loneliness,*" *Journal of Gender Studies* 7, no. 3 (November 1998): 287–296.

Taylor, Noel. "The Luck of Amy Tan," *Ottawa Citizen,* 1 October 1993, p. F1.

Taylor-Guthrie, Danille Kathleen, ed. *Conversations with Toni Morrison.* Jackson: University Press of Mississippi, 1994.

Tebbel, John, and Mary Ellen Zuckerman. *The Magazine in America, 1741–1990.* New York: Oxford University Press, 1991.

Teleky, Richard. "Entering the Silence: Voice, Ethnicity, and the Pedagogy of Creative Writing," *MELUS* 26, no. 1 (Spring 2001): 205–219.

Temple-Thurston, Barbara. *Nadine Gordimer Revisited.* New York: Twayne, 1999.

Terry, Reginald. *Victorian Popular Fiction, 1860–80.* London: Macmillan, 1983.

Terwilliger, Thomas. *Root of Evil.* New York: Herald Tribune Books, 1929.

"That's Obasan's Home," *Maclean's,* 22 December 2003, p. 16.

Theiss, Nola. "Review: A *Catch of Consequence,*" *Kliatt* 37, no. 5 (September 2003): 20.

Thom, Mary. *Inside Ms.: 24 Years of the Magazine and the Feminist Movement.* New York: Henry Holt, 1997.

Thomas, Jeanie G. "An Inconvenient Indefiniteness: George Eliot, Middlemarch, and Feminism," *University of Toronto Quarterly* 56, no. 3 (March 1987): 392–415.

Thomas, Sue. "Rebecca West's Second Thoughts on Feminism," *Genders* 13, no. 90 (Spring 1992): 90–107.

———. "The Tropical Extravagance of Bertha Mason," *Victorian Literature and Culture* 27 (1999): 1–17.

Thormahlen, Marianne. "The Lunatic and the Devil's Disciple: The 'Lovers' in *Wuthering Heights,*" *Review of English Studies* 48, no. 190 (May 1997): 183–197.

Thurman, Judith. *Isak Dinesen: The Life of a Storyteller.* New York: St. Martin's, 1982.

———. *Secrets of the Flesh: A Life of Colette.* New York: Ballantine, 1999.

Timleck, Sarah Lorraine. "Volumes of Silence: The Non-Narratability of Middle-Class Wife-Assault in the Victorian Novel," *University of Guelph* (1998): 113.

Tinkler, Alan. "Janet Frame," *Review of Contemporary Fiction* 24, no. 2 (Summer 2004): 89–122.

Tischler, Barbara L. "Holding the Line: Women in the Great Arizona Mine Strike of 1983," *Labor Studies Journal* 17, no. 1 (Spring 1992): 82–83.

Todd, Janet M. *The Secret Life of Aphra Behn.* Piscataway, N.J.: Rutgers University Press, 1997.

Tolin, Lisa. " 'Monologues' Author Expands Scope," *Charlotte Observer,* 28 November 2004, p. 8H.

Tomlinson, Susan. "Vision to Visionary: The New Negro Woman as Cultural Worker in Jessie Redmon Fauset's 'Plum Bun,' " *Legacy: A Journal of American Women Writers* 19, no. 1 (January 2002): 90–97.

Travis, Molly Abel. "Frances Wright: The Other Woman of Early American Feminism," *Women's Studies* 22, no. 3 (June 1993): 389–396.

Tremblay, Victor-Laurent. "L'Inversion Mythique dans 'La Belle Bete' de Marie-Claire Blais," *Studies in Canadian Literature* 25, no. 2 (Summer 2000): 74–95.

Trotman, Nat. "The Burning Between: Androgyny/Photography/Desire," *Women's Studies* 28, no. 4 (September 1999): 379–402.

Trousdale, Rachel. "Self-Invention in Isak Dinesen's "The Deluge at Norderney," *Scandinavian Studies* 74, no. 2 (Summer 2002): 205–222.

Trzebinski, Errol. *The Lives of Beryl Markham.* New York: W. W. Norton, 1993.

Tuan, Yi-Fu. *Landscapes of Fear.* New York: Pantheon, 1979.

Turner, Sarah E. " 'Spider Woman's Granddaughter': Autobiographical Writings by Native American Women," *MELUS* 22, no. 4 (Winter 1997): 109–133.

Tyrrell, Ian R. *Woman's World/Woman's Empire: The Woman's Christian Temperance Union in International Perspective, 1880–1930.* Chapel Hill: University of North Carolina Press, 1991.

Underhill, Beachy. *The Woman Who Ran for President: The Many Lives of Victoria Woodhull.* Bridgehampton, N.Y.: Bridge Works, 1995.

Uraizee, Joy. " 'She Walked Away without Looking Back': Christophine and the Enigma of History in Jean Rhy's *Wide Sargasso Sea*," *CLIO* 38, no. 3 (Spring 1999): 261.

Valis, Noël, and Carol Maier, eds. *In the Feminine Mode: Essays on Hispanic Women Writers.* Lewisburg, Pa.: Bucknell University Press, 1990.

Van Boven, Sarah. "Getting Their Ya-Yas Out," *Newsweek,* 6 July 1998, p. 71.

Varma, Devendra P. *The Gothic Flame.* New York: Russell & Russell, 1966.

Veltman, Laura J. " 'The Bible Lies the One Way, but the Night-Gown the Other': Dr. Matthew O'Connor, Confession, and Gender in Djuna Barnes's *Nightwood*," *Modern Fiction Studies* 49, no. 2 (Summer 2003): 204–227.

Vendler, Helen. "Ghostlier Demarcations, Keener Sounds," *Parnassus* 2, no. 1 (Fall–Winter 1973): 5–10, 15–16, 18–24.

Vining, James W., and Ben A. Smith. "Susanna Rowson: Early American Geography Educator," *Social Studies* 89, no. 6 (November–December 1998): 263–270.

Vintges, Karen. "Simone de Beauvoir: A Feminist Thinker for Our Times," *Hypatia* 14, no. 4 (Fall 1999): 133.

Voss, Cary R. W., and Robert C. Rowland. "Pre-Inception Rhetoric in the Creation of a Social Movement: The Case of Frances Wright," *Communication Studies* 51, no. 1 (Spring 2000): 1.

Wagner, Lilya. *Women War Correspondents of World War II.* Westport, Conn.: Greenwood, 1989.

Wagner, Linda W. "Plath's *The Bell Jar* as Female Bildungsroman," *Women's Studies* 12, no. 1 (1986): 55–68.

Wagner-Lawlor, Jennifer A. "From Irony to Affiliation in Margaret Atwood's *The Handmaid's Tale*," *Critique* 45, no. 1 (Fall 2003): 83–96.

Waldron, Mary. "Ann Yearsley: The Bristol Manuscript Revisited," *Triangle Journals* 3, no. 1 (1996).

Walker, Gina Luria. "Learning History's Lessons," *Women's Review of Books* 14, no. 8 (May 1997): 22–23.

Walker, Pierre A. "Radical Protest, Identity, Words, and Form in Maya Angelou's *I Know Why the Caged Bird Sings*," *College Literature* 22, no. 3 (October 1995): 91–108.

Walker, Steven F. "James's *The Turn of the Screw*," *Explicator* 61, no. 2 (Winter 2003): 94–96.

Walker, Sue, and Eugenie Hamner, eds. *Ways of Knowing: Critical Essays on Marge Piercy.* Mobile, Ala.: Negative Capability Press, 1984.

Wallace, Miriam L. "Laughing Feminism," *Women's Studies* 29, no. 5 (September 2000): 695–698.

Warhol, Robyn A. "The Look, the Body, and the Heroine: A Feminist-Narratological Reading of *Persuasion*," *Novel: A Forum on Fiction* 26, no. 1 (Fall 1992): 5–19.

Warner, Marina. *Alone of All Her Sex: The Myth and the Cult of the Virgin Mary.* New York: Alfred A. Knopf, 1976.

———. *From the Beast to the Blonde: On Fairy Tales and Their Tellers.* New York: Noonday, 1994.

———. *Monuments and Maidens: The Allegory of the Female Form.* Berkeley: University of California Press, 2001.

Warren, James Perrin. *Culture of Eloquence: Oratory and Reform in Antebellum America.* University Park: Pennsylvania State University Press, 1999.

Warshall, Peter. "The Tapestry of Possibility," *Whole Earth* 98 (Fall 1999): 20–22.

Waters, Harold A. "Tell It to Women: An Epic Drama for Women," *World Literature Today* 72, no. 3 (Summer 1998): 672–673.

Watkins-Goffman, Linda. *Lives in Two Languages: An Exploration of Identity and Culture.* Detroit: University of Michigan Press, 2003.

Watson, Mary Sidney. "When Flattery Kills: The Silencing of Anna Laetitia Barbauld," *Women's Studies* 28, no. 6 (December 1999): 617–643.

Watson, William Lynn. " 'The Facts Which Go to Form This Fiction': Elizabeth Stuart Phelps's *The Silent Partner* and the Massachusetts Bureau of Labor Statistics Reports," *College Literature* 29, no. 4 (Fall 2002): 6–25.

Weales, Gerald. "Perera: The Yellow Wallpaper." *Commonweal,* 12 February 1993, pp. 16–17.

Weinert, Laura. "Angela Carter's *The Bloody Chamber* at the Metal Shed at the Toy Factory," *Back Stage West,* 23 January 2003, p. 19.

———."The Love of the Nightingale." *Back Stage West*, 31 January 2002, p. 18.

Weinhouse, Linda. "Alice Munro: Hard-Luck Stories or There Is No Sexual Tension," *Critique* 36, no. 2 (Winter 1995): 121–129.

Weir, John. "The 10 Most Hated Books," *Advocate*, 24 June 1997, pp. 91–96.

Weir, Robert E. "Betty Friedan and the Making of the Feminine Mystique: The American Left, the Cold War, and Modern Feminism," *Journal of American and Comparative Cultures* 23, no. 3 (Fall 2000): 133–134.

Weisman, Leslie Kanes. *Discrimination by Design: A Feminist Critique of the Man-Made Environment.* Urbana: University of Illinois Press, 1994.

Weisser, Susan Ostrov, and Jennifer Fleischner. *Feminist Nightmares: Women at Odds: Feminism and the Problems of Sisterhood.* New York: New York University Press, 1995.

Wesley, Marilyn C. *Refusal and Transgression in Joyce Carol Oates' Fiction.* Westport, Conn.: Greenwood, 1993.

———. "Reverence, Rape, Resistance: Joyce Carol Oates and Feminist Film Theory," *Mosaic* 32, no. 3 (September 1999): 75.

West, Genevieve. "Feminist Subversion in Zora Neale Hurston's 'Jonah Gourd Vine,' " *Women's Studies* 31, no. 4 (July–August 2002): 499–515.

Wheatwind, Marie-Elise. "Breaking Boundaries," *Women's Review of Books* 15, no. 12 (September 1998): 18–20.

Whitcomb, Claire. "Laurel Thatcher Ulrich: A New Spin on Homespun," *Victoria* 16, no. 10 (October 2002): 102–103.

White, Cynthia L. *Women's Magazines 1693–1968.* London: Michael Joseph, 1970.

White, Lesley. "Feminism with No Ad-ditives," *London Sunday Times*, 22 November 1992, pp. 5.1–5.2.

Wiesenthal, Christine. "Regarding Christina Rossetti's 'Reflection,' " *Victorian Poetry* 39, no. 3 (Fall 2001): 389–407.

Wilcox, Clyde. "The Not-So-Failed Feminism of Jean Auel," *Journal of Popular Culture* 28, no. 3 (Winter 1994): 63–70.

Wilcox, Janelle. "Resistant Silence, Resistant Subject: (Re)reading Gayl Jones's 'Eva's Man,' " *Genders* 23 (Spring 1996): 72–96.

Wilde, Alan. "Bold, but Not Too Bold: Fay Weldon and the Limits of Poststructuralist Criticism," *Contemporary Literature* 29, no. 3 (Fall 1988): 403–419.

Wilentz, Gay. *Emerging Perspective on Ama Ata Aidoo.* Lawrenceville, N.J.: Africa World, 2003.

Willard, Charity Cannon. *Christine de Pizan: Her Life and Works.* New York: Persea, 1984.

Williams, A. Susan, ed. *The Lifted Veil: The Book of Fantastic Literature by Women, 1800–World War II.* New York: Carroll & Graf, 1992.

Williams, Anne. *Art of Darkness: A Poetics of Gothic.* Chicago: University of Chicago Press, 1995.

Williams, Bettye J. "Nella Larsen: Early Twentieth-Century Novelist of Afrocentric Feminist Thought," *CLA Journal* 39, no. 2 (December 1995): 165–178.

Williams, Deborah Lindsay. *Not in Sisterhood: Edith Wharton, Willa Cather, Zona Gale, and the Politics of Female Authorship.* New York: Palgrave Macmillan, 2001.

Williams, Gary. "Resurrecting Carthage: *Housekeeping* and Cultural History," *English Language Notes* 29, no. 2 (December 1991): 70–78.

Williams, Merryn. *Margaret Oliphant: A Critical Biography.* London: Macmillan, 1986.

Willis, Chris. "The Female Sherlock: 'Lady Detectives' in Victorian and Edwardian Fiction" (December 1999). Available online. URL: http://www.chriswillis.freeserve.co.uk/femsherlock.htm. Accessed on October 13, 2005.

———. "Mary Elizabeth Braddon and the Literary Marketplace: A Study in Commercial Authorship" (1998). Available online. URL: http://www.chriswillis.freeserve.co.uk/meb2.html. Accessed on October 13, 2005.

Willis, Lucindy A. *Voices Unbound: The Lives and Works of Twelve Women Intellectuals.* Lanham, Md.: Rowman & Littlefield, 2002.

Wilson, Carol Shiner, and Joel Haefner, eds. *Re-Visioning Romanticism: British Women Writers, 1776–1831.* Philadelphia: University of Pennsylvania Press, 1994.

Wilson, Christopher P. "Charlotte Perkins Gilman's Steady Burghers: The Terrain of Herland," *Women's Studies* 12, no. 3 (1986): 271–292.

Wilson, Deborah S. "Dora, Nora and Their Professor: The 'Talking Cure,' 'Nightwood,' and Feminist Pedagogy," *Literature and Psychology* 42, no. 3 (Summer 1996): 48–71.

Wilson, Sharon Rose. *Margaret Atwood's Fairy-Tale Sexual Politics.* Jackson: University Press of Mississippi, 1993.

Wilt, Judith. *Ghosts of the Gothic.* Princeton, N.J.: Princeton University Press, 1980.

Wineapple, Brenda. "Licking Her Wounds," *Women's Review of Books* 14, no. 8 (May 1997): 12–13.

———. "The Transformations," *Parnassus: Poetry in Review* 24, no. 2 (2000): 224–242.

———. "Unparalleled Lives," *Women's Review of Books* 18, no. 10/11 (July 2001): 34–35.

Winer, Laurie. "Mother and Child Reunion," *Los Angeles Times*, 3 March 1996, p. 7.

Winston, Jane. "Marguerite Duras: Marxism, Feminism, Writing," *Theatre Journal* 47, no. 3 (October 1995): 345–365.

Winter, Kari. "Sexual/Textual Politics of Terror." In *Misogyny in Literature: An Essay Collection.* Edited by Katherine Anne Ackley, 89–101. New York: Garland, 1992.

"Without Discovery: A Native Response to Columbus," *The Circle: News from an American Indian Perspective,* 9 September 1999, p. 26.

Wolf, Leonard. *Bluebeard: The Life and Crimes of Gilles de Rais.* New York: Clarkson N. Potter, 1980.

Wolff, Cynthia. "The Radcliffean Gothic Model." In *The Female Gothic.* Edited by Juliann Fleenor, 207–223. Montreal: Eden, 1983.

Wong, Sau-ling Cynthia. *Reading Asian American Literature: From Necessity to Extravagance.* Princeton, N.J.: Princeton University Press, 1993.

Wood, Charles W. "Mrs. Henry Wood: In Memoriam," *Argosy* 43 (1887): 251–270.

Wood, Rebecca S. " 'Two Warring Ideals in One Dark Body': Universalism and Nationalism in Gloria Naylor's *Bailey's Cafe,*" *African American Review* 30, no. 3 (Fall 1996): 381–395.

Woodward, Kathleen. "In Sickness and Health," *Women's Review of Books* 16, no. 4 (January 1999): 1–3.

Woolley, Lisa. "Racial and Ethnic Semiosis in Mitsuye Yamada's Mrs. Higashi Is Dead," *MELUS* 24, no. 4 (1999): 77–91.

Wucker, Michele. "Edwidge Danticat: A Voice for the Voiceless," *Americas* 52, no. 3 (May–June 2000): 40–48.

Wurtzel, Elizabeth. *Bitch: In Praise of Difficult Women.* New York: Anchor Books/Doubleday, 1998.

Wussow, Helen. "Language, Gender, and Ethnicity in Three Fictions by Willa Cather," *Women and Language* 18, no. 1 (Spring 1995): 52–55.

Wylie, Joan. *Shirley Jackson: A Study of the Short Fiction.* New York: Twayne, 1994.

Yardley, Jonathan. "Anita Loos and the Spell of Lorelei Lee," *Washington Post,* 23 October 1988, p. 3.

Yaszek, Lisa. "A Grim Fantasy: Remaking American History in Butler's *Kindred,*" *Signs: Journal of Women in Culture and Society* 28, no. 4 (Summer 2003): 1,053–1,066.

Yiannopoulou, Effie. "Autistic Adventures: Love, Auto-Portraiture, and White Women's Colonial Disease," *European Journal of English Studies* 2, no. 3 (December 1998): 324–342.

Youngman, Nicole. "Molly Ivins Spoke in Honor of Women's History Month in Pensacola." Available online. URL: http://www.theharbinger.org/xvii/990330/youngman.html, 1999. Accessed on October 14, 2005.

Yousef, Nancy. "The Monster in a Dark Room: Frankenstein, Feminism, and Philosophy," *Modern Language Quarterly* 63, no. 2 (June 2002): 197–226.

Yuan Shu. "Cultural Politics and Chinese-American Female Subjectivity: Rethinking Kingston's 'Woman Warrior,' " *MELUS* 26, no. 2 (Summer 2001): 199–224.

Zabus, Chantal. "Review: Soifs," *World Literature Today* 71, no. 4 (Autumn 1997): 745–746.

Zanjani, Sally. *Sarah Winnemucca.* Lincoln: University of Nevada Press, 2001.

Zoglin, Richard. "The Burning Bed," *Time,* 8 October 1984, p. 85.

Zona, Kirstin Hotelling. *Marianne Moore, Elizabeth Bishop, and May Swenson: The Feminist Poetics of Self-Restraint.* Chicago: University of Michigan Press, 2002.

Zuckerman, Mary Ellen. *A History of Popular Women's Magazines in the United States, 1792–1995.* Westport, Conn.: Greenwood Press, 1998.

The Age of Innocence, RKO, 1934
The Age of Innocence, Judson/Willoughby, 1977
The Age of Innocence, Columbia 1993
An American Daughter, Lifetime-TV, 2000
An Angel at My Table, New Line, 1990
Babette's Feast, Orion, 1987
Back Street, Universal, 1932
Back Street, Universal, 1941
Back Street, Universal, 1961
The Ballad of the Sad Café, Merchant-Ivory, 1990
Bastard Out of Carolina, Showtime, 1996
Beauty and the Beast, Jean Cocteau, 1946
The Bell Jar, Avco, 1979
Beloved, Buena Vista, 1998
Blessings, CBS-TV, 2003
The Bombing of Osage Avenue, Scribe Video Center, 1985
The Bostonians, Merchant-Ivory, 1983
The Buccaneers, BBC-TV, 1995
A Bunny's Tale, ABC-TV, 1985
The Burning Bed, NBC-TV, 1984
But Gentlemen Marry Brunettes, Richard Sale, 1928
Charms for the Easy Life, Showtime, 2002
The Children's Hour, Universal, 1961
Chisholm '72: Unbought and Unbossed, Shola Lynch, 2004
Cimarron, RKO, 1931
Cimarron, MGM, 1960
Clan of the Cave Bear, Warner, 1986
The Color Purple, Warner, 1985
The Company of Wolves, Neil Jordan, 1984
Crimes of the Heart, de Laurentis, 1986
Cross Creek, EMI, 1983
Daisy Kenyon, Fox, 1947
Daughters of the Dust, Kino, 1991
Days and Nights in Calcutta, 1991
Disappearing Acts, HBO-TV, 2000
Divine Secrets of the Ya-Ya Sisterhood, Warner, 2002
The Dollmaker, Fox, 1984

Ellen Foster, Hallmark, 1997
Emma, BBC-TV, 1997
Enslavement: The True Story of Fanny Kemble, CBS-TV, 2000
Ethan Frome, BBC, 1993
Ever After, TCF, 1988
Except for Me and Thee, Allied Artists, 1956
Except for Me and Thee, ABC-TV, 1975
Faint Perfume, Paramount, 1925
Farewell to Manzanar, John Korty, 1976
Foreign Affairs, Turner, 1993
Freeway, Republic Studios, 1996
The Friendly Persuasion, Allied Artists, 1956
The Friendly Persuasion, ABC-TV, 1975
Gentlemen Prefer Blondes, TCF, 1953
Giant, Warner, 1956
Gigi, Codo Cinema, 1948
Gigi, MGM, 1958
The Girl with a Pearl Earring, Lionsgate/Fox, 2004
God's Good Man, Stoll, 1919
Gone with the Wind, MGM, 1939
The Good Earth, MGM, 1937
The Group, United Artists, 1966
The Haunting, MGM, 1963
The Haunting, DreamWorks, 1999
Having Our Say, CBS-TV, 1999
The Heart Is a Lonely Hunter, Warner-Seven Arts, 1968
Heat and Dust, Merchant-Ivory, 1983
Holy Orders, Davidson, 1917
The Hours, Paramount, 2002
Housekeeping, Columbia, 1988
The House of Mirth, Granada, 2000
Howard's End, Merchant-Ivory, 1992
How Stella Got Her Groove Back, TCF, 1998
How to Make an American Quilt, Universal, 1995
Hungry Hearts, Samuel Goldwyn, 1922
I Know Why the Caged Bird Sings, Artisan Entertainment, 1979

Imitation of Life, Universal, 1934
Imitation of Life, Universal-International, 1959
In Country, Warner, 1989
The Inheritance, CBS, 1997
Innocent, Stoll, 1921
In the Time of the Butterflies, Showtime, 2001
I Stand Here Ironing, Midge MacKenzie, 1980
Jane Eyre, Monogram, 1934
Jane Eyre, TCF, 1943
Jane Eyre, Lion/Omnibus/Sagittarius, 1970
Jane Eyre, Miramax, 1996
Julia, TCF, 1977
Kristin Lavransdatter, Public Media, 1995
Like Water for Chocolate, Arau, 1992
*Listening for Something—Adrienne Rich and Dionne Brand
    in Conversation*, National Film Board of Canada,
    1996
The Little Foxes, MGM, 1941
Little Women, Lasky, 1919
Little Women, RKO, 1933
Little Women, MGM, 1949
Little Women, Columbia, 1995
Long Time Comin', National Film Board of Canada, 1999
The Lottery, Encyclopedia Britannica, 1950
Madame Sousatzka, Merchant-Ivory, 1988
The Magic Donkey, Jacques Demy, 1971
Maid in Manhattan, Sony, 2002
Mansfield Park, BBXC-TV, 1986
The Member of the Wedding, Columbia, 1952
The Member of the Wedding, Hallmark, 1997
The Miss Firecracker Contest, HBO, 1989
The Mists of Avalon, Warner, 2001
A Modern Thelma, Fox, 1916
Mrs. Dalloway, Fox, 1998
Mrs. Parker and the Vicious Circle, Miramax, 1991
My Ántonia, USA, 1995
'night, Mother, Universal, 1986
Not Without My Daughter, Universal International, 1991
The Object of My Affection, TCF, 1998
Older, Stronger, Wiser, National Film Board of Canada,
    1989
One True Thing, Universal, 1998
O Pioneers!, Hallmark, 1992
The Opposite Sex, MGM, 1956
Orlando, Sony, 1992
Our Hearts Were Young and Gay, Paramount, 1944
Out of Africa, Universal, 1985
Paris Rats in E.L.A., American Film Institute, 1994
Persuasion, BBC-TV, 1971
Persuasion, Roger Michell, 1995
The Piano, CIBY, 1993
The Piano Teacher, Michael Haneke, 2000

Portrait of a Marriage, BBC-TV, 1990
Pretty Woman, Buena Vista, 1990
Pride and Prejudice, MGM, 1940
Pride and Prejudice, BBC-TV, 1980
Pride and Prejudice, Arts & Entertainment, 1995
Pride and Prejudice, Working Title Films, 2005
Quartet, Merchant-Ivory, 1981
A Raisin in the Sun, Columbia, 1961
Ramona, TCF, 1936
Rebecca, Selznick, 1940
Reds, Paramount, 1981
The Return of the Soldier, Brent Walker/Barry R. Cooper,
    1982
A Room with a View, Merchant-Ivory, 1986
The Right to Love, Paramount, 1930
Salome of the Tenements, Sidney Alcott, 1925
Sarah, Plain and Tall, Hallmark, 1991
The Scarlet Letter, MGM, 1926
The Scarlet Letter, WGBH-TV, 1979
The Scarlet Letter, Cinergi, 1995
Scarlett, RHI Entertainment, 1994
The Search, MGM, 1948
Sense and Sensibility, BBC-TV, 1985
Shadow on the Sun, ETV, 1988
She-Devil, Orion, 1989
Ship of Fools, Columbia, 1965
Showboat, Universal, 1936
Showboat, MGM, 1951
Sisters in the Struggle, National Film Board of Canada,
    2000
The Skylark, Hallmark, 1993
Smash-up: The Story of a Woman, Universal-
    International, 1947
The Sorrows of Satan, Samuelson, 1917
The Sorrows of Satan, Dreadnaught, 1926
The Sorrows of Satan, Lasky, 1926
A Star Is Born, David O. Selznick, 1937
A Star Is Born, Warner, 1954
A Star Is Born, Warner, 1976
Tell Me a Riddle, Filmways, 1980
Their Eyes Were Watching God, ABC-TV, 2005
Thelma, Davidson, 1918
Thelma, Chester Bennett, 1922
A Thousand Acres, Buena Vista, 1997
Three Lives, Women's Liberation Cinema Production,
    1971
To Kill a Mockingbird, Universal-International, 1962
A Touch of Love, Amicus/Palomar, 1969
Two or Three Things I Know for Sure, PBS, 1998
Uncommon Women and Others, PBS-TV, 1978
Until the Violence Stops, Lifetime, 2004
The Vagina Monologues, HBO, 2002

V. I. Warshawski, Warner, 1991
Waiting to Exhale, TCF, 1995
The War Between the Tates. NBC-TV, 1976
Warrior Marks, Women Make Movies, 1995
We Were the Mulvaneys, Lifetime TV, 2002
When the Mountains Tremble, Newton Sigel, 1984
Wide Sargasso Sea, Rank, 1992
Wit, HBO, 2001
The Witching Hour, NBC-TV, 2005
A Woman of Independent Means, NBC-TV, 1995
Woman of the Year, MGM, 1942
The Women of Brewster Place, Harpo, 1989

The Women's Room, ABC Theatre, 1980
Working Girl, 20th Century Fox, 1988
World without Walls: Beryl Markham's African Memoir,
    PBS-TV, 1986
Wormwood, Fox, 1915
Wuthering Heights, Samuel Goldwyn, 1939
Wuthering Heights, AIP, 1970
Wuthering Heights, Paramount, 1992
The Yearling, MGM, 1946
The Young Diana, Cosmopolitan, 1922
Zora Is My Name, PBS-TV, 1990

INDEX

Note: **Boldface** page numbers indicate main entries.